MW01115986

~ THE MOST COMPLETE ~
150-BOOK
APOCRYPHA

Featuring 1-3 Enoch, the Book of Giants, Jasher, Pseudepigrapha, Deuterocanonical Texts, Apocalypses, Gnostic Gospels, Sibylline Oracles, and More...

The author dedicates this book to the pursuit of love and understanding, thanking the divine for inspiration and acknowledging the help from other translations. This work is a heartfelt act of devotion.

Book Title: The Most Complete 150-Book Apocrypha: Featuring 1-3 Enoch, Giants, Jasher, Pseudepigrapha, Deuterocanonical Texts, Apocalypses, Gnostic Gospels, Sibylline Oracles, and More...
Book Author: Ethan J. Whitlock (@biblebookstore.org)
Book Genre / Category: Christian Bible; Spiritual, Religious Books;

First Edition.
Cover Design by SM.

Table of Contents

The New Apocrypha

Introduction

Apocrypha refers to a collection of ancient religious writings that are not part of the canonical Bible. These texts are often similar in style and content to the books in the Bible but were not included in the official canon.

Importance of Apocrypha:
- **Historical Insight**: Apocryphal books provide valuable historical information about the periods in which they were written. They offer context and background that help us understand the social, cultural, and religious environment of those times.
- **Cultural Influence**: These texts have influenced literature, art, and theology throughout history. They reflect the beliefs, traditions, and values of various communities.
- **Theological Perspectives**: Apocrypha offers diverse theological viewpoints that can deepen our understanding of religious beliefs and practices. They show how different groups interpreted spiritual concepts and stories.
- **Literary Value**: Many apocryphal books are beautifully written and have significant literary merit. They include compelling narratives, poetry, wisdom literature, and prophetic visions.
- **Spiritual Enrichment**: For many, these writings provide spiritual inspiration and moral guidance. They explore themes of faith, ethics, and the human condition.

By studying apocryphal books, readers can gain a broader and richer understanding of religious history and thought.

Purpose of the Collection:

The purpose of this collection is to bring together the most comprehensive and complete anthology of apocryphal books ever assembled. Apocryphal texts hold a unique place in religious literature, often existing in the shadows of canonical scriptures. By compiling these 150 apocryphal writings, our goal is to shine a light on these fascinating and diverse works, making them accessible to both scholars and casual readers alike. We believe that these texts deserve to be read, studied, and appreciated for their historical, theological, and literary value. This collection aims to bridge the gap between the familiar and the obscure, providing readers with an opportunity to explore the richness and depth of apocryphal literature. Whether you are a student of religion, a lover of ancient texts, or someone seeking spiritual enrichment, this anthology offers a treasure trove of insights and inspirations. Our hope is that by bringing these texts together in one volume, we can foster a greater appreciation for the breadth of religious thought and tradition that has shaped human history.

Scope of the Collection:

The scope of this collection is truly expansive, encompassing a wide array of texts that span different genres, themes, and historical periods. Here's what you can expect:
- **Diverse Genres**: The apocryphal books included in this collection cover a range of literary genres. You will find captivating narratives, profound poetry, wise sayings, visionary prophecies, and apocalyptic revelations. Each genre offers its own unique perspective and insights, contributing to the rich tapestry of religious literature.
- **Wide-Ranging Themes**: The themes explored in these texts are as varied as the human experience itself. You will encounter stories of heroism and morality, reflections on divine justice and human suffering, explorations of the afterlife, and teachings on wisdom and virtue. These themes resonate across time and culture, offering timeless lessons and reflections.
- **Historical Breadth**: The apocryphal books span several centuries and originate from various cultural and geographical contexts. This collection includes writings from the intertestamental period, early Christian centuries, and beyond. By presenting these texts together, we offer a panoramic view of the evolving religious landscape and the diverse voices that contributed to it.
- **Complementary Perspectives**: While these texts are not part of the canonical Bible, they often provide complementary perspectives that enrich our understanding of biblical themes and characters. They fill in gaps, offer alternative viewpoints, and sometimes present stories and teachings that were influential in early religious communities but did not make it into the official canon.
- **Additional Resources**: To enhance your reading experience, we have included a range of additional resources. These tools are designed to help you navigate and appreciate the apocryphal books more fully.

In bringing together this collection, our aim is to create a resource that is both comprehensive and accessible. We invite you to explore these texts with an open mind and heart, ready to discover the wisdom and beauty that lie within. Whether you read them for academic study, personal growth, or spiritual reflection, we hope that these apocryphal books will inspire and enrich your journey.

Historical Context:

The apocryphal books, a fascinating and diverse collection of ancient writings, have an intriguing historical context that enriches their significance. These texts, written over many centuries and across different regions, offer a unique glimpse into the religious, cultural, and social landscapes of their times. To fully appreciate these writings, it's essential to understand the backdrop against which they emerged and were preserved.

Origins and Authorship:

The origins of apocryphal books are as varied as the texts themselves. These writings were produced in a range of historical periods, from the centuries before the Common Era (BCE) to the early centuries of the Common Era (CE). Many of these texts were written during times of significant social and political change, which often influenced their themes and content. The authors of apocryphal books were equally diverse. Some were attributed to well-known religious figures, while others remain anonymous. These authors wrote in various languages, including Hebrew, Aramaic, Greek, and Latin, reflecting the multicultural environments in which they lived. The diversity in authorship and language highlights the widespread nature of these writings and their broad appeal across different communities.

Historical and Cultural Significance:

The apocryphal books were composed in a world where oral and written traditions were deeply intertwined. These texts often sought to fill gaps in the canonical scriptures, offering additional stories, teachings, and insights that were highly valued by certain religious groups. For example, books like the Book of Enoch and the Gospel of Thomas provided expanded narratives and teachings that complemented existing scriptural accounts. Culturally, these writings were influenced by the prevailing philosophies, religious beliefs, and political conditions of their time. For instance, the apocalyptic literature found in texts like 2 Esdras and Apocalypse of Peter reflects the anxieties and hopes of communities living under foreign domination or experiencing social upheaval. Similarly, wisdom literature such as Sirach and Wisdom of Solomon offers moral and ethical guidance shaped by the philosophical currents of the Hellenistic period.

Transmission and Preservation:
The journey of apocryphal books from their origins to modern times is a testament to their enduring value and appeal. These texts were often preserved through meticulous copying by scribes and were passed down through generations. Many were included in collections alongside canonical scriptures, particularly in early Christian communities and certain Jewish sects. Significant discoveries in the 20th century, such as the Dead Sea Scrolls and the Nag Hammadi library, have shed new light on the transmission and preservation of apocryphal writings.

These discoveries have provided scholars with original manuscripts and fragments that offer invaluable insights into the textual history and development of these works. In some cases, apocryphal books were preserved within the liturgical and devotional practices of specific religious traditions. For example, the Ethiopian Orthodox Church includes several apocryphal texts in its biblical canon, maintaining their use and reverence over centuries. This highlights the regional variations in how these writings were valued and transmitted.

Influence and Legacy:
The historical context of apocryphal books is also marked by their influence on later religious thought and literature. These texts have inspired countless religious thinkers, writers, and artists throughout history. Their themes and stories have found echoes in the works of early Church Fathers, medieval theologians, and even modern scholars and authors. Moreover, the debates and discussions surrounding the inclusion of certain apocryphal books in canonical scriptures have played a significant role in shaping the development of religious canons. The criteria for canonicity, the authority of texts, and the boundaries of sacred scripture were all influenced by the existence and popularity of these apocryphal writings.

Understanding the historical context of apocryphal books allows us to appreciate their richness and depth. These writings, born out of diverse historical periods and cultural settings, offer a window into the spiritual and intellectual world of their time. They have been cherished, debated, and transmitted through centuries, leaving a lasting legacy that continues to intrigue and inspire. As we delve into this comprehensive collection, we embark on a journey through history, exploring the faith, wisdom, and creativity of the ancient authors who brought these remarkable texts to life.

Literary and Theological Significance:
The apocryphal books are a treasure trove of literary artistry, showcasing the diverse and rich storytelling traditions of their time. These texts, often written with a profound sense of beauty and purpose, offer a window into the literary culture that flourished alongside the canonical scriptures. One of the most striking features of the apocryphal writings is their variety. From vivid narratives that recount the lives of saints and heroes to poetic hymns that sing of divine mysteries, the apocryphal books are a testament to the creative and expressive capacities of their authors. These texts often employ a range of literary techniques, including allegory, parable, and metaphor, to convey their messages in a manner that is both engaging and thought-provoking. Take, for example, the Book of Tobit, a charming narrative that weaves themes of piety, family loyalty, and divine providence into a captivating story. Or the Wisdom of Solomon, which employs eloquent and philosophical prose to explore profound themes of wisdom, justice, and the nature of God. These texts, among many others, are not only religious documents but also literary masterpieces that have inspired readers for generations.

Theological Insights:
Beyond their literary beauty, the apocryphal books offer a wealth of theological insights that deepen our understanding of the religious landscape of antiquity. These writings provide alternative perspectives and elaborate on themes that are sometimes only touched upon in the canonical texts, enriching our grasp of theological concepts and debates. Theologically, the apocryphal books explore a wide range of topics, from the nature of God and the afterlife to ethical living and the pursuit of wisdom. For instance, the Book of Enoch presents a vivid and imaginative account of the heavenly realm and the fall of the angels, offering insights into early Jewish eschatological beliefs. Similarly, the Prayer of Manasseh, a brief but poignant text, delves into themes of repentance and divine mercy, illustrating the profound belief in God's boundless compassion and forgiveness. These texts also reflect the spiritual struggles and hopes of their communities. In the 2 Maccabees, we see the valor and faith of the Jewish martyrs, who face persecution with unwavering trust in God's justice. This narrative not only highlights the resilience of faith but also underscores the theological conviction that God is actively involved in human history, guiding and protecting His people.

Bridging Gaps and Building Connections:
One of the remarkable aspects of the apocryphal books is their ability to bridge gaps between different traditions and communities. They often incorporate elements from various cultural and religious backgrounds, creating a rich tapestry of shared stories and beliefs. This inclusivity makes the apocryphal texts a valuable resource for understanding the interconnectedness of ancient religious traditions. For example, the Wisdom of Sirach, draws upon both Jewish and Hellenistic philosophical traditions, offering practical and spiritual guidance that resonates with a broad audience. Its teachings on ethical conduct, family relationships, and the pursuit of wisdom reflect a synthesis of cultural influences that enriches its theological depth and universal appeal.

Personal and Communal Enrichment:
For modern readers, engaging with the apocryphal books can be a deeply enriching experience. These texts invite us to reflect on timeless questions about the human condition, our relationship with the divine, and the moral principles that guide our lives. They challenge us to think critically and compassionately, fostering a deeper appreciation for the spiritual heritage they represent. In a world that often feels fragmented and uncertain, the

apocryphal books offer a sense of continuity and connection. They remind us that the quest for meaning, justice, and transcendence is a universal and enduring human endeavor. By exploring these ancient writings, we can find inspiration and guidance for our own spiritual journeys, drawing strength from the faith and wisdom of those who came before us.

Scholarly Perspectives:
The study of apocryphal texts has long been a fascinating and rich field of academic inquiry. Scholars from various disciplines, including theology, history, literature, and religious studies, have dedicated countless hours to uncovering, interpreting, and preserving these writings. Their meticulous work has enabled us to understand the depth and breadth of religious thought outside the traditional biblical canon.

Academic Interest:
Apocryphal texts have captured the attention of scholars due to their unique insights into early religious communities and their beliefs. These writings provide valuable perspectives on how different groups understood and practiced their faith. By studying these texts, scholars have been able to piece together a more comprehensive picture of religious history, highlighting the diversity of beliefs and practices that existed alongside the canonical scriptures. One of the key areas of scholarly interest is the exploration of how these texts reflect the socio-political contexts in which they were written. For instance, certain apocryphal books offer glimpses into the lives of marginalized groups, their struggles, and their spiritual responses to the challenges they faced. This has allowed historians and theologians to gain a deeper understanding of the lived experiences of communities.

Key Studies and Contributors:
Over the years, numerous scholars have made significant contributions to the study of apocryphal literature. Their research has often involved painstaking efforts to locate, translate, and interpret ancient manuscripts. Notable figures in this field include:
- **R. H. Charles**, renowned for his comprehensive work on the Apocrypha and Pseudepigrapha, which remains a seminal reference for scholars and students alike.
- **James H. Charlesworth**, whose work on the Old Testament Pseudepigrapha has been instrumental in bringing these texts to a wider audience.
- **Geza Vermes**, known for his translations and interpretations of the Dead Sea Scrolls, many of which include apocryphal writings.
- **M.R. James**, a pioneering scholar whose cataloging and analysis of apocryphal texts set the foundation for much of the modern study in this field.

These and many other dedicated scholars have opened windows into the past, allowing contemporary readers to access the spiritual and intellectual richness of apocryphal literature.

Debates and Controversies:
The study of apocryphal texts is not without its debates and controversies. Scholars often engage in lively discussions about the authenticity, dating, and authorship of these writings. Some texts have multiple versions, leading to debates over which is the original or most authoritative. Additionally, the very definition of what constitutes an "apocryphal" text can vary, adding another layer of complexity to scholarly discourse. These debates, however, are a testament to the vibrant and dynamic nature of this field of study. They reflect the ongoing efforts to refine our understanding and interpretation of these ancient texts. Through rigorous analysis and open dialogue, scholars continue to enhance our knowledge, ensuring that these writings are studied with the depth and respect they deserve.

Acknowledgment and Gratitude:
It is essential to acknowledge and express our profound gratitude to the countless scholars whose work has made this collection possible. Without their tireless dedication, this book would not exist. Their contributions span centuries, involving meticulous research, careful preservation, and insightful interpretation. It is through their collective efforts that the knowledge contained within these pages has been preserved and passed down through generations. We owe a debt of gratitude to the early scribes who painstakingly copied these texts by hand, to the medieval scholars who safeguarded them, and to the modern academics who have brought them to light in contemporary times. This book is a testament to hundreds and thousands of years of knowledge transfer and scholarly dedication.

In conclusion, the scholarly perspectives on apocryphal texts enrich our understanding and appreciation of these writings. By delving into their historical contexts, exploring their themes, and engaging with ongoing academic debates, we can fully appreciate the significance of this collection. We extend our heartfelt thanks to all the scholars whose invaluable contributions have made this collection possible, ensuring that the wisdom and insights of these ancient texts continue to inspire and enlighten readers today.

Notes From the Author:
We are thrilled to welcome you to this comprehensive collection of 150 apocryphal books. We've put together these notes to help you navigate and fully appreciate the richness of these texts. Here are some tips and insights for a better reading experience:

How to Approach the Text:
The book is thoughtfully divided into two parts for optimal usage: the Old Apocrypha and the New Apocrypha.

This division is based on the type of writings, the period they were written in, and their importance. Think of it as a categorization similar to the Old and New Testaments. For a deeper understanding of their sub-categorization, please refer to the apocrypha classification table included in the book.

Reading Tips:
- **Ellipses ("...")**: If you encounter "..." within a text, it indicates that a verse or line was not found.

- **Missing Chapters or Verses**: If you notice that a chapter does not start with "chapter 1" or "verse 1" or that certain verses are missing, it means those parts were not found during the creation of this translation.
- **Flexible Reading Order**: Feel free to start reading from any chapter. The introductions are written to stand alone, even if they are part of a specific collection, so you might encounter some repetition.
- **Fragmentary Texts**: Some books are only available as fragments. These can be short and quick reads but still offer valuable insights. For better readability, we have even created pointers for some texts.
- **Reconstructed Texts**: Some of the books are not even fragments but have been mentioned in ancient texts. We have made efforts to recreate these works by gathering all the available data from the internet. These are hypothetical texts, and this has been clearly stated in the introduction section of those books.

Significance for Modern Readers:
Each book in this collection has been meticulously studied and translated into modern English to ensure that today's English-speaking audience can understand and appreciate the texts. This effort aims to bridge the gap between ancient writings and contemporary readers, making the wisdom and teachings of these apocryphal books accessible and relevant.

Additional Free Resources:
To support your journey through these ancient texts, we have created multiple free resources. Your learning doesn't have to stop here. We've made modern translations of the Ethiopian Bible, the Geneva Bible, and many more available for free. You can easily access these resources by scanning the QR code on the last page of this book.

Thank you for embarking on this journey with us. we hope this collection enriches your understanding and appreciation of these fascinating texts. Happy reading!

Classification	Writings
Apocryphal Books	1 Esdras, 2 Esdras, 1 Maccabees, 2 Maccabees, 3 Maccabees, 4 Maccabees, 5 Maccabees, Tobit, Judith, Wisdom of Solomon, Wisdom of Sirach, 1 Baruch, 2 Baruch, 3 Baruch, 4 Baruch, Prayer of Azariah, Prayer of Manasseh, Bel and the Dragon, Susanna, Letter of Jeremiah, Additional Esther, Additional Psalms
Pseudepigrapha	1 Enoch, 2 Enoch, 3 Enoch, 1 Adam and Eve, 2 Adam and Eve, 3 Adam and Eve, Vita Adae et Evae, Slavonic Vita Adae et Evae, Giants, Story of Ahikar, Jubilees, Testaments of the Twelve Patriarchs, Testament of Reuben, Testament of Simeon, Testament of Levi, Testament of Judah, Testament of Issachar, Testament of Zebulun, Testament of Dan, Testament of Naphtali, Testament of Gad, Testament of Asher, Testament of Joseph, Testament of Benjamin, 1 Meqabyan, 2 Meqabyan, 3 Meqabyan, Jasher, Sibylline Oracles (Books I-XIV), Fragments of Zadokite Work
Apocalypses	Apocalypse of Adam, Apocalypse of Abraham, Apocalypse of Paul, Apocalypse of Moses, Apocalypse of Zephaniah, Ascension of Isaiah
Letters/Epistles	Epistle of Jesus Christ and King Abgarus, Epistle of Barnabas, Epistle of Paul and Seneca, Epistle of Paul to the Laodiceans, Epistle of Ignatius (to the Ephesians, Magnesians, Trallians, Romans, Philadelphians, Smyrnaeans, Polycarp), Epistle of Polycarp to the Philippians, Epistle of Mathetes to Diognetus, Epistle of Peter to Philip, Epistle of Ptolemy, Epistle of Pontius Pilate (to Herod, to Tiberius Caesar, to Augustus Caesar), Epistle of Herod to Pontius Pilate, Report of Pontius Pilate (to Tiberius Caesar, to Augustus Caesar)
Creeds	Apostles' Creed, Nicene Creed, Athanasian Creed
Gospels	Gospel of Thomas, Gospel of Philip, Secret Gospel of Mark, Gospel of Bartholomew, Gospel of Nicodemus, Lost Gospel of Peter, Fragments of Greek Gospel of Thomas, Oxyrhynchus 1224 Gospel, Egerton Gospel, Gospel of the Egyptians, Gospel of the Nazoreans, Oxyrhynchus 840 Gospel, Gospel of the Nativity of Mary, Protevangelium, Arabic Gospel of the Infancy of the Saviour, Infancy Gospel of Thomas, Gospel of Pseudo-Matthew, Gospel of Truth, Lost Sayings Gospel Q
Acts and Martyrdoms	Acts of Peter and the Twelve Apostles, Passion of the Scillitan Martyrs, Martyrdom of Ignatius, Martyrdom of Polycarp, Martyrdom of Isaiah
Testaments	Testament of Abraham, Testament of Moses, Testament of Solomon
Writings of Early Church Fathers	1 Clement, 2 Clement, Tertullian (on Spectacles, on Prayer, on Patience, on Martyrs, on Apparel of Women I-II, on Exhortation to Chastity), Epistle of Pliny and King Trajan
Other Early Christian Writings	Preaching of Peter, Epistula Apostolorum, Pre-Markan Passion Narrative, Dialogue of the Savior, Avenging of the Saviour, Shepherd of Hermas, Didache, Traditions of Matthias, Sinodos, Prayer of Thanksgiving
Other	Jannes and Jambres, Eldad and Modad, Fragments of Zadokite Work, Melchizedek, Fragments of Sibylline Oracles, Tertullian on Martyrs, Report of Pontius Pilate to Tiberius Caesar, Death of Pilate, Trial and Condemnation of Pilate, Basilides, Epiphanes on Righteousness, Marcion

(© Apocrypha Classification Table)

THE OLD
APOCRYPHA

1 Esdras

The book of 1 Esdras, an ancient Jewish text, holds a unique position within the corpus of biblical literature. It is a Greek version of parts of the canonical books of Chronicles, Ezra, and Nehemiah, with some variations and additional material, reflecting its complex textual history. Its origins can be traced back to the Hellenistic period, a time when Jewish communities were dispersed across the Mediterranean and deeply influenced by Greek culture. This book is included in the Septuagint, the Greek translation of the Hebrew Bible, but is not part of the Hebrew Masoretic Text, which has led to its exclusion from the Jewish canon and its varied acceptance among Christian traditions. Despite its exclusion from the Jewish canon, 1 Esdras was highly regarded in early Christianity and remains canonical in the Eastern Orthodox Church. The book begins with the legendary account of Josiah's Passover and spans significant events such as the fall of Jerusalem, the Babylonian exile, and the return of the exiles under the Persian king Cyrus, culminating in the reforms of Ezra. Notably, 1 Esdras features the story of the three bodyguards and their debate on the strongest force, which is unique to this text and highlights its didactic and rhetorical character. This narrative serves as a profound exploration of themes such as truth, power, and governance, reflecting the philosophical currents of its time. The book's emphasis on temple worship, covenant fidelity, and religious reform underscores its theological significance, offering insights into the post-exilic community's struggles and aspirations. It blends historical annals with theological reflection, offering insight into Jewish identity and faith during a key historical period. Scholars often study its textual differences from the Hebrew canon, its theological themes, and its role in shaping Jewish and Christian scriptural traditions.

{1:1} Josiah celebrated the Passover to the Lord in Jerusalem, slaughtering the Passover lamb on the fourteenth day of the first month. {1:2} He organized the priests according to their divisions, dressed in their ceremonial garments, in the temple of the Lord. {1:3} Josiah instructed the Levites, who served in the temple, to sanctify themselves to the Lord and place the holy ark in the temple that King Solomon, son of David, had built. {1:4} He told them they no longer needed to carry it on their shoulders, but to worship the Lord and serve His people Israel. They were to prepare themselves by their families and kindred. {1:5} According to the instructions of King David and the grandeur of his son Solomon, they were to stand in order in the temple by their family groupings and serve their fellow Israelites. {1:6} They were to slaughter the Passover lamb and prepare the sacrifices for their brethren, keeping the Passover as commanded by the Lord through Moses. {1:7} Josiah provided the people present with thirty thousand lambs and kids, and three thousand calves, all from the king's possessions, for the people, priests, and Levites. {1:8} Hilkiah, Zechariah, and Jehiel, the chief officers of the temple, gave the priests two thousand six hundred sheep and three hundred calves for the Passover. {1:9} Jeconiah, Shemaiah, Nethanel, Hashabiah, Ochiel, and Joram, captains over thousands, gave the Levites five thousand sheep and seven hundred calves for the Passover. {1:10} This is what happened: the priests and Levites, properly dressed and with the unleavened bread, stood by their family groupings before the people to make the offering to the Lord as written in the book of Moses. They did this in the morning. {1:11} They roasted the Passover lamb with fire as required and boiled the sacrifices in brass pots and cauldrons, creating a pleasing aroma. {1:12} They distributed these to all the people. They then prepared the Passover for themselves and their fellow priests, the sons of Aaron. {1:13} Because the priests were busy offering the fat until night, the Levites prepared the Passover for themselves and the priests, the sons of Aaron. {1:14} The temple singers, the sons of Asaph, were in their places according to the arrangement made by David, Asaph, Zechariah, and Eddinus, representing the king. {1:15} The gatekeepers were at each gate, and no one had to leave their duties because their fellow Levites prepared the Passover for them. {1:16} That day, all the sacrifices to the Lord were completed, and the Passover was observed. {1:17} The sacrifices were offered on the altar of the Lord as commanded by King Josiah. {1:18} The Israelites present kept the Passover and the Feast of Unleavened Bread for seven days. {1:19} Such a Passover had not been observed in Israel since the time of Samuel the prophet. {1:20} None of the kings of Israel had observed a Passover like Josiah did with the priests, Levites, men of Judah, and all Israel in Jerusalem. {1:21} This Passover was kept in the eighteenth year of Josiah's reign. {1:22} Josiah's deeds were righteous in the sight of the Lord, for he had a heart full of godliness. {1:23} The events of his reign have been recorded, including how the sinful and wicked actions of others deeply grieved the Lord, causing Him to rise up against Israel. {1:24} After Josiah's acts, Pharaoh, king of Egypt, went to fight at Carchemish on the Euphrates, and Josiah went out against him. {1:25} The king of Egypt sent a message to Josiah, saying, "What have we to do with each other, king of Judah? I was not sent against you by the Lord God; my war is at the Euphrates. The Lord is with me, urging me on. Stand aside and do not oppose the Lord." {1:26} But Josiah did not turn back but tried to fight him, ignoring the words of Jeremiah the prophet from the mouth of the Lord. {1:27} Josiah engaged in battle at the plain of Megiddo, and the commanders attacked him. {1:28} Josiah told his servants, "Take me away from the battle, for I am very weak." His servants took him out of the line of battle. {1:29} Josiah was brought back to Jerusalem in his second chariot, where he died and was buried in the tomb of his ancestors. {1:30} All of Judah mourned for Josiah. Jeremiah the prophet lamented for him, and it was decreed that this lamentation be observed by the nation of Israel. {1:31} These events are written in the book of the histories of the kings of Judah, detailing all Josiah's acts, his splendor, understanding of the law of the Lord, and everything he did before and after. {1:32} The people took Jeconiah, Josiah's son, who was twenty-three years old, and made him king in his father's place. {1:33} Jeconiah reigned for three months in Judah and Jerusalem before the king of Egypt deposed him and fined the nation a hundred talents of silver and a talent of gold. {1:34} The king of Egypt made Jehoiakim, Jeconiah's brother, king of Judah and Jerusalem. {1:35} Jehoiakim imprisoned the nobles and brought his brother Zarius out of Egypt. {1:36} Jehoiakim was twenty-five years old when he began his reign and did evil in the sight of the Lord. {1:37} Nebuchadnezzar, king of Babylon, came against him, bound him in brass chains, and took him to Babylon. {1:38} Nebuchadnezzar also took holy vessels from the Lord's temple and stored them in his temple in Babylon. {1:39} Reports of Jehoiakim's uncleanness and impiety are recorded in the chronicles of the kings. {1:40} Jehoiachin, Jehoiakim's son, became king at eighteen and reigned for three months and ten days in Jerusalem, doing evil in the sight of the Lord. {1:41} After a year, Nebuchadnezzar sent for Jehoiachin and took him to Babylon along with the holy vessels of the Lord, making Zedekiah king of Judah and Jerusalem. {1:42} Zedekiah was twenty-one years old when he began his eleven-year reign. {1:43} He also did evil in the sight of the Lord, ignoring the words spoken by Jeremiah the prophet. {1:44} Though King Nebuchadnezzar had made him swear by the name of the Lord, Zedekiah broke his oath and rebelled, hardening his heart against the Lord's laws. {1:45} The leaders and priests committed many acts of sacrilege and lawlessness, surpassing the unclean deeds of other nations, and polluted the temple in Jerusalem. {1:46} The God of their ancestors sent messengers to call them back, but they mocked and scoffed at the prophets. {1:47} In His anger, the Lord commanded the kings of the Chaldeans to come against them. {1:48} They killed their young men with the sword around the temple, sparing no one, and took the survivors to Babylon. {1:49} They carried away all the holy vessels and treasures of the Lord and the royal stores. {1:50} They burned the house of the Lord, broke down the walls of Jerusalem, and destroyed its towers and glorious things. {1:51} The survivors were taken to Babylon, serving the king and his sons until the Persians began to reign, fulfilling the Lord's word by Jeremiah: {1:52} "Until the land enjoys its sabbaths, it shall rest all the time of its desolation until seventy years are completed."

{2:1} In the first year of Cyrus, king of the Persians, to fulfill the word of the Lord spoken by Jeremiah, {2:2} the Lord stirred the spirit of Cyrus, who made a proclamation throughout his kingdom and put it in writing: {2:3} "This is what Cyrus, king of the Persians, says: The Lord Most High of Israel has made me king of the world, {2:4} and he has commanded me to build him a house in Jerusalem, which is in Judea. {2:5} Therefore, any of his people among you may go to Jerusalem in Judea and build the house of the Lord, the God of Israel, who dwells in Jerusalem. {2:6} Let each person be assisted by their neighbors with silver, gold, goods, and livestock, along with voluntary offerings for the house of God in Jerusalem." {2:7} Then the family heads of Judah and Benjamin, the priests and Levites, and everyone whose spirit God had stirred, prepared to go up and build the house of the Lord in Jerusalem. {2:8} All their neighbors assisted them with silver, gold, goods, livestock, and valuable gifts, in addition to all the freewill offerings. {2:9} King Cyrus also brought out the articles belonging to the temple of the Lord, which Nebuchadnezzar had carried away from Jerusalem and placed in the temple of his gods. {2:10} Cyrus, king of the Persians, brought these out and entrusted them to Mithridates the treasurer, who counted them out to Sheshbazzar, the prince of Judah. {2:11} The inventory included a thousand gold dishes, a thousand silver dishes, twenty-nine silver pans, thirty gold bowls, two thousand four hundred and ten silver bowls, and a thousand other articles. {2:12} In total, there were five thousand four hundred and sixty-nine gold and silver articles. Sheshbazzar brought all these along when the exiles came up from Babylon to Jerusalem. {2:13} During the reign of Artaxerxes, king of the Persians, Bishlam, Mithridates, Tabeel, Rehum, Beltethmus, Shimshai the scribe, and their associates in Samaria and other places wrote a letter against the inhabitants of Judah and Jerusalem. {2:14} They wrote to King Artaxerxes: "To King Artaxerxes, your servants, Rehum the recorder and Shimshai the scribe, and the other judges of their council in Coelesyria and Phoenicia: {2:15} Let it be known to the king that the Jews who came up from you to us have gone to Jerusalem and are rebuilding that rebellious and wicked city. They are restoring the marketplaces and repairing the walls and laying the foundations for a temple. {2:16} If this city is rebuilt and its walls are finished, they will refuse to pay tribute and will resist kings. {2:17} Since the temple construction is ongoing, we suggest that you investigate this matter. {2:18} Search the records of your ancestors; you will find that this city has been rebellious, troubling kings and other cities. {2:19} The Jews were rebels, often setting up blockades. This is why the city was destroyed. {2:20} We now inform you, O king, that if this city is rebuilt and its walls finished, you will lose control of Coelesyria and Phoenicia." {2:21} King Artaxerxes responded to Rehum, Beltethmus, Shimshai the scribe, and their associates in Samaria, Syria, and Phoenicia: {2:22} "I have read the letter you sent. I ordered a search, and it was found that this city has a history of rebellion and war. {2:23} Powerful and cruel kings ruled in Jerusalem, extracting tribute from Coelesyria and Phoenicia. {2:24} I have now ordered that these men be stopped from rebuilding the city to prevent further annoyance to kings." {2:25} When the letter from King Artaxerxes was read, Rehum, Shimshai the scribe, and their associates hurried to Jerusalem with horsemen and a large force, hindering the builders. {2:26} The construction of the temple in Jerusalem ceased until the second year of the reign of Darius, king of the Persians.

{3:1} King Darius held a grand banquet for everyone under his rule, including those born in his household and all the nobles of Media and Persia. {3:2} He invited all the satraps, generals, and governors from the one hundred and twenty-seven provinces stretching from India to Ethiopia. {3:3} After they ate and drank their fill, they departed, and Darius went to his bedroom, slept, and then awoke. {3:4} The three young men of the bodyguard, who guarded the king, said to each other, {3:5} "Let's each state what we believe is the strongest thing. The one whose statement is judged the wisest by King Darius will receive rich gifts and great honors. {3:6} He will be dressed in purple, drink from gold cups, sleep on a gold bed, have a chariot with gold bridles, wear a fine linen turban, and have a necklace around his neck. {3:7} Because of his wisdom, he will sit next to Darius and be called a kinsman of Darius." {3:8} Each man wrote his statement, sealed it, and placed it under King Darius's pillow. {3:9} They decided that when the king awoke, they would present the writings to him, and the one whose statement the king and three Persian nobles judged the wisest would receive the victory and rewards. {3:10} The first wrote, "Wine is the strongest." {3:11} The second wrote, "The king is the strongest." {3:12} The third wrote, "Women are the strongest, but truth conquers all things." {3:13} When the king awoke, they handed him the writings, and he read them. {3:14} He then summoned all the nobles of Persia and Media, along with the satraps, generals, governors, and prefects. {3:15} Seated in the council chamber, he had the writings read aloud. {3:16} He said, "Call the young men and have them explain their statements." So they were summoned and brought in. {3:17} He asked them, "Explain what you have written." The first, who spoke of the strength of wine, began: {3:18} "Gentlemen, how is wine the strongest? It confuses the minds of all who drink it. {3:19} It makes the king and the orphan, the slave and the free, the poor and the rich all feel equal. {3:20} It turns every thought to feasting and joy, making everyone forget their sorrow and debt. {3:21} It makes all hearts feel wealthy, forgets kings and satraps, and makes everyone speak in exaggerated terms. {3:22} When people drink, they forget to be friendly with their friends and brothers, and soon they draw their swords. {3:23} When they sober up, they don't remember what they did. {3:24} Gentlemen, isn't wine the strongest, since it forces people to do these things?" Having said this, he stopped speaking.

{4:1} Then the second, who spoke of the strength of the king, began to speak: {4:2} "Gentlemen, aren't men powerful, ruling over land and sea and all that is in them? {4:3} But the king is even stronger; he is their lord and master, and they obey his every word. {4:4} If he commands them to make war, they do it; if he sends them against an enemy, they go and conquer mountains, walls, and towers. {4:5} They kill and are killed, never disobeying the king's orders; if they win, they bring all the spoils and everything else to the king. {4:6} Similarly, those who don't serve in the army but work the land, whenever they sow and reap, they bring some of the harvest to the king, and they make each other pay taxes to him. {4:7} And yet he is just one man! If he commands them to kill, they kill; if he commands them to release, they release; {4:8} if he commands them to attack, they attack; if he commands them to destroy, they destroy; if he commands them to build, they build; {4:9} if he commands them to cut down, they cut down; if he commands them to plant, they plant. {4:10} All his people and armies obey him. Moreover, he reclines, eats, drinks, and sleeps, {4:11} while they watch over him and cannot attend to their own affairs, nor do they disobey him. {4:12} Gentlemen, why is not the king the strongest, given that he is obeyed in this way?" And he stopped speaking. {4:13} Then the third, Zerubbabel, who spoke of women and truth, began to speak: {4:14} "Gentlemen, is not the king great, and are not men many, and is not wine strong? Who then is their master, or who is their lord? Is it not women? {4:15} Women gave birth to the king and to every person who rules over sea and land. {4:16} From women, they came; and women raised the very men who plant the vineyards that produce wine. {4:17} Women make men's clothes; they bring men honor; men cannot exist without women. {4:18} If men gather gold and silver or any other beautiful thing and then see a woman lovely in appearance and beauty, {4:19} they let all those things go and stare at her with open mouths, preferring her over gold or silver or any other beautiful thing. {4:20} A man leaves his own father, who raised him, and his own country, and clings to his wife. {4:21} With his wife, he spends the rest of his days, forgetting his father, mother, and country. {4:22} Thus, you must realize that women rule over you! "Do you not work and toil and bring everything to women? {4:23} A man takes his sword and goes out to travel, rob, steal, and sail the sea and rivers; {4:24} he faces lions and walks in darkness, and when he steals and robs and plunders, he brings it back to the woman he loves. {4:25} A man loves his wife more than his father or mother. {4:26} Many men have lost their minds because of women and have become slaves because of them. {4:27} Many have perished, stumbled, or sinned because of women. {4:28} And now, do you not believe me? "Is not the king powerful? Do not all lands fear to touch him? {4:29} Yet I have seen him with Apame, the king's concubine, the daughter of the illustrious Bartacus; she would sit at the king's right hand, {4:30} take the crown from his head, put it on her own, and slap the king with her left hand. {4:31} At this, the king would gaze at her with open mouth. If she smiled at him, he laughed; if she got angry with him, he would flatter her to calm her down. {4:32} Gentlemen, why aren't women the strongest, given that they can do such things?" {4:33} Then the king and the nobles looked at one another, and he began to speak about truth: {4:34} "Gentlemen, aren't women strong? The earth is vast, and heaven is high, and the sun is swift in its course, making the circuit of the heavens and returning to its place in one day. {4:35} Is he not great who does these things? But truth is greater and stronger than all things. {4:36} The whole earth calls upon truth, and heaven blesses her. All God's works quake and tremble, and there is nothing unrighteous in Him. {4:37} Wine is unrighteous, the king is unrighteous, women are unrighteous, all the sons of men are unrighteous, all their works are unrighteous, and all such things. There is no truth in them, and in their unrighteousness, they will perish. {4:38} But truth endures and is strong forever, living and prevailing for eternity. {4:39} With her, there is no partiality or preference; she does what is righteous instead of anything unrighteous or wicked. All men approve of her deeds, {4:40} and there is nothing unrighteous in her judgment. To her belongs strength, kingship, power, and majesty through all ages. Blessed be the God of truth!" {4:41} He stopped speaking; then all the people shouted, "Great is truth, and strongest of all!" {4:42} Then the king said to him, "Ask what you wish, even beyond what is written, and we will give it to you, for you have been found the wisest. You shall sit next to me and be called my kinsman." {4:43} Then he said to the king, "Remember the vow you made to rebuild Jerusalem on the day you became king, {4:44} and to return all the vessels taken from Jerusalem, which Cyrus set aside when he began to destroy Babylon, and vowed to send them back there. {4:45} You also vowed to rebuild the temple, which the Edomites burned when Judea was laid waste by the Chaldeans. {4:46} Now, O lord the king, this is what I ask and request of you, and this befits your greatness. I pray, therefore, that you fulfill the vow you made to the King of heaven with your own lips." {4:47} Then King Darius rose, kissed him, and wrote letters to all the treasurers, governors, generals, and satraps, commanding them to provide an escort for him and all who were going up with him to rebuild Jerusalem. {4:48} He wrote letters to all the governors in Coelesyria and Phoenicia and those in Lebanon, instructing them to bring cedar timber from Lebanon to Jerusalem to help build the city. {4:49} He also wrote to all the Jews going up from his kingdom to Judea, ensuring their freedom and stating that no officer, satrap, governor, or treasurer should forcefully enter their homes; {4:50} that the land they would occupy would be theirs without tribute; that the Idumeans should return the villages of the Jews they held; {4:51} that twenty talents a year should be given for the building of the temple until it was completed, {4:52} and an additional ten talents a year for burnt offerings on the altar every day, according to the commandment to make seventeen offerings; {4:53} and that all who came from Babylonia to build the city would have their freedom, along with their children and all the priests who came. {4:54} He wrote concerning their support and the priests' garments for their ministry. {4:55} He wrote that support for the Levites should be provided until the temple was finished and Jerusalem was built. {4:56} He ordered land and wages for all who guarded the city. {4:57} He sent back from Babylon all the vessels that Cyrus had set apart; everything that Cyrus had ordered was to be done and sent to Jerusalem. {4:58} When the young man left, he lifted his face to heaven toward Jerusalem and praised the King of heaven, saying, {4:59} "From You is the victory; from You is wisdom, and Yours is the glory. I am Your servant. {4:60} Blessed are You, who have given me wisdom; I give You thanks, O Lord of our fathers." {4:61} So he took the letters and went to Babylon, telling his brethren about all this. {4:62} They praised the God of their fathers, because He had granted them release and permission {4:63} to go up and rebuild Jerusalem and the temple called by His name; and they feasted with music and rejoicing for seven days.

{5:1} After this, the heads of the families were chosen to return, according to their tribes, along with their wives, sons, daughters, servants, and livestock. {5:2} Darius sent a thousand horsemen with them to ensure their safe return to Jerusalem, accompanied by music from drums and flutes; {5:3} and their relatives celebrated. He made them proceed together. {5:4} These are the names of the men who went up, according to their family heads in the tribes: {5:5} The priests, sons of Phinehas, son of Aaron; Jeshua, son of Jozadak, son of Seraiah, and Joakim, son of Zerubbabel, son of Shealtiel, of the house of David, from the lineage of Phares, tribe of Judah, {5:6} who spoke wisely before Darius, king of the Persians, in the second year of his reign, in the month of Nisan, the first month. {5:7} These are the men of Judea who returned from captivity, whom Nebuchadnezzar, king of Babylon, had taken to Babylon, {5:8} and who came back to Jerusalem and the rest of Judea, each to their own town, with Zerubbabel, Jeshua, Nehemiah, Seraiah, Resaiah, Bigvai, Mordecai, Bilshan, Mispar, Reeliah, Rehum, and Baanah as their leaders. {5:9} The number of men and their leaders: the sons of Parosh, two thousand one hundred seventy-two; the sons of Shephatiah, four hundred seventy-two. {5:10} The sons of Arah, seven hundred fifty-six. {5:11} The sons of Pahath-Moab, of Jeshua and Joab, two thousand eight hundred twelve. {5:12} The sons of Elam, one thousand two hundred fifty-four; the sons of Zattu, nine hundred forty-five; the sons of Chorbe, seven hundred five; the sons of Bani, six hundred forty-eight. {5:13} The sons of Bebai, six hundred twenty-three; the sons of Azgad, one thousand three hundred twenty-two. {5:14} The sons of Adonikam, six hundred sixty-seven; the sons of Bigvai, two thousand sixty-six; the sons of Adin, four hundred fifty-four. {5:15} The sons of Ater, namely of Hezekiah, ninety-two; the sons of Kilan and Azetas, sixty-seven; the sons of Azaru, four hundred thirty-two. {5:16} The sons of Annias, one hundred one; the sons of Arom; the sons of Bezai, three hundred twenty-three; the sons of Jorah, one hundred twelve. {5:17} The sons of Baiterus, three thousand five; the sons of Bethlehem, one hundred twenty-three. {5:18} The men of Netophah, fifty-five; the men of Anathoth, one hundred fifty-eight; the men of Bethasmoth, forty-two. {5:19} The men of Kiriatharim, twenty-five; the men of Chephirah and Beeroth, seven hundred forty-three. {5:20} The Chadiasans and Ammidians, four hundred twenty-two; the men of Ramah and Geba, six hundred twenty-one. {5:21} The men of Michmas, one hundred twenty-two; the men of Bethel, fifty-two; the sons of Magbish, one hundred fifty-six. {5:22} The sons of the other Elam and Ono, seven hundred twenty-five; the sons of Jericho, three hundred forty-five. {5:23} The sons of Senaah, three thousand three hundred thirty. {5:24} The priests: the sons of Jedaiah, son of Jeshua, of the sons of Anasib, nine hundred seventy-two; the sons of Immer, one thousand fifty-two. {5:25} The sons of Pashhur, one thousand two hundred forty-seven; the sons of Harim, one thousand seventeen. {5:26} The Levites: the sons of Jeshua and Kadmiel and Bannas and Sudias, seventy-four. {5:27} The temple singers: the sons of Asaph, one hundred twenty-eight. {5:28} The gatekeepers: the sons of Shallum, the sons of Ater, the sons of Talmon, the sons of Akkub, the sons of Hatita, the sons of Shobai, totaling one hundred thirty-nine. {5:29} The temple servants: the sons of Ziha, the sons of Hasupha, the sons of Tabbaoth, the sons of Keros, the sons of Siaha, the sons of Padon, the sons of Lebanah, the sons of Hagabah, {5:30} the sons of Akkub, the sons of Uthai, the sons of Ketab, the sons of Hagab, the sons of Shamlai, the sons of Hana, the sons of Cathua, the sons of Gahar, {5:31} The sons of Reaiah, the sons of Rezin, the sons of Nekoda, the sons of Chezib, the sons of Gazzam, the sons of Uzza, the sons of Paseah, the sons of Hasrah, the sons of Besai, the sons of Asnah, the sons of the Meunites, the sons of Nephisim, the sons of Bakbuk, the sons of Hakupha, the sons of Asur, the sons of Pharakim, the sons of Bazluth, {5:32} the sons of Mehida, the sons of Cutha, the sons of Charea, the sons of Barkos, the sons of Sisera, the sons of Temah, the sons of Neziah, the sons of Hatipha. {5:33} The sons of Solomon's servants: the sons of Hassophereth, the sons of Peruda, the sons of Jaalah, the sons of Lozon, the sons of Giddel, the sons of Shephatiah, {5:34} the sons of Hattil, the sons of Pochereth-hazzebaim, the sons of Sarothie, the sons of Masiah, the sons of Gas, the sons of Addus, the sons of Subas, the sons of Apherra, the sons of Barodis, the sons of Shaphat, the sons of Ami. {5:35} All the temple servants and the sons of Solomon's servants numbered three hundred seventy-two. {5:36} These are the ones who came up from Telmelah and Telharsha, under the leadership of Cherub, Addan, and Immer, {5:37} although they couldn't prove their lineage or descent from Israel: the sons of Delaiah, son of Tobiah, the sons of Nekoda, totaling six hundred fifty-two. {5:38} Among the priests, those who assumed the priesthood but weren't found in the register: the sons of Habaiah, the sons of Hakkoz, the sons of Jaddus, who married Agia, one of the daughters of Barzillai, and took his name. {5:39} When they sought their genealogy in the register and couldn't find it, they were excluded from serving as priests. {5:40} Nehemiah and Attharias told them not to partake in holy things until a high priest should appear wearing Urim and Thummim. {5:41} All those of Israel, twelve years or older, besides servants, numbered forty-two thousand three hundred sixty; {5:42} their servants were seven thousand three hundred thirty-seven; there were two hundred forty-five musicians and singers. {5:43} They had four hundred thirty-five camels, seven thousand thirty-six horses, two hundred forty-five mules, and five thousand five hundred twenty-five donkeys. {5:44} Some family heads, upon arriving at the temple in Jerusalem, vowed to rebuild it to the best of their ability, {5:45} contributing a thousand minas of gold, five thousand minas of silver, and one hundred priestly garments to the treasury for the work. {5:46} The priests, Levites, and some of the people settled in Jerusalem and its vicinity; the temple singers, gatekeepers, and all Israel in their towns. {5:47} When the seventh month arrived and the Israelites were in their homes, they gathered as one in the square before the first gate toward the east. {5:48} Jeshua, son of Jozadak, with his fellow priests, and Zerubbabel, son of Shealtiel, with his kinsmen, took their places and prepared the altar of the God of Israel, {5:49} to offer burnt offerings as instructed in the book of Moses, the man of God. {5:50} Some joined them from the other peoples of the land. They erected the altar in its place, despite opposition, and offered sacrifices morning and evening. {5:51} They kept the Feast of Booths as commanded and offered the prescribed sacrifices daily, {5:52} and continued with regular offerings, sabbath sacrifices, new moon offerings, and all the appointed feasts. {5:53} Those who had made vows to God began offering sacrifices from the new moon of the seventh month, though the temple was not yet built. {5:54} They provided money for masons and carpenters, and food and drink {5:55} and carts to the Sidonians and Tyrians to bring cedar logs from Lebanon to Joppa, as decreed by Cyrus, king of Persia. {5:56} In the second year after their arrival at the temple of God in Jerusalem, in the second month, Zerubbabel, son of Shealtiel, and Jeshua, son of Jozadak, began the work with their fellow priests, Levites, and all who had returned from captivity; {5:57} they laid the foundation of the temple on the new moon of the second month, two years after returning to Judea and Jerusalem. {5:58} They appointed Levites aged twenty and above to oversee the work of the Lord. Jeshua and his sons and brothers, Kadmiel his brother, and the sons of Jeshua Emadabun and the sons of Joda, son of Iliadun, with their sons and brothers, all Levites, united to advance the work on the house of God. So the builders constructed the temple of the Lord. {5:59} The priests, arrayed in their garments, with musical instruments and trumpets, and the Levites, sons of Asaph, with cymbals, {5:60} praised and blessed the Lord according to the instructions of David, king of Israel; {5:61} they sang hymns, giving thanks to the Lord, for His goodness and glory are everlasting upon all Israel. {5:62} All the people sounded trumpets and shouted loudly, praising the Lord for the construction of His house. {5:63} Some Levitical priests and family heads, old men who had seen the former temple, wept loudly, {5:64} while many others rejoiced with trumpets and joyful noise, {5:65} so that the people could not distinguish the sound of the trumpets from the weeping of the people. The multitude sounded trumpets so loudly that the sound was heard far away; {5:66} when the enemies of the tribes of Judah and Benjamin heard it, they came to investigate the noise. {5:67} They learned that those who had returned from captivity were building the temple for the Lord God of Israel. {5:68} They approached Zerubbabel, Jeshua, and the family heads and said, "We want to build with you. {5:69} For we worship your God just as you do, and we have been sacrificing to Him since the days of Esarhaddon, king of the Assyrians, who brought us here." {5:70} But Zerubbabel, Jeshua, and the family heads of Israel replied, "You have no part in building the house of our God. {5:71} We alone will build it for the Lord of Israel, as commanded by Cyrus, king of Persia." {5:72} The local peoples then tried to discourage and intimidate the builders, cutting off their supplies and hindering their work; {5:73} by schemes, demagoguery, and uprisings, they prevented the completion of the building during King Cyrus's life. The work was halted for two years until the reign of Darius.

{6:1} During the second year of King Darius's reign, the prophets Haggai and Zechariah, son of Iddo, prophesied to the Jews in Judea and Jerusalem in the name of the Lord God of Israel. {6:2} Inspired by these prophecies, Zerubbabel, son of Shealtiel, and Jeshua, son of Jozadak, began rebuilding the house of the Lord in Jerusalem, with the prophets of the Lord supporting them. {6:3} At that time, Sisinnes, the governor of Syria and Phoenicia, along with Sathrabuzanes and their colleagues, approached them and asked, {6:4} "Who gave you the authority to build this house and its roof and to complete all these other things? And who are the builders responsible for this work?" {6:5} Despite their inquiry, the elders of the Jews were treated kindly because the providence of the Lord was upon them, and they were allowed to continue building while a report was sent to Darius. {6:6} The following is a copy of the letter that Sisinnes, governor of Syria and Phoenicia, Sathrabuzanes, and their associates, local rulers in Syria and Phoenicia, sent to Darius: {6:7} "To King Darius, greetings. We want to inform our lord the king that when we visited Judea and entered Jerusalem, we found the elders of the Jews who had been in captivity {6:8} constructing a grand new house for the Lord in Jerusalem using hewn stone and expensive timber laid in the walls. {6:9} The work is progressing swiftly, and it is being carried out with great care and excellence. {6:10} We asked the elders, 'Who authorized you to build this house and lay the foundations for this structure?' {6:11} In order to provide you with a written account of the leaders, we requested the names of those in charge. {6:12} They replied, 'We are the servants of the Lord who created heaven and earth. {6:13} This house was originally built many years ago by a great and strong king of Israel and was completed. {6:14} However, when our ancestors sinned against the Lord of Israel in heaven, He handed them over to Nebuchadnezzar, king of Babylon, who destroyed the house, burned it, and took the people captive to Babylon. {6:15} In the first year of King Cyrus's reign over Babylon, he issued a decree for this house to be rebuilt. {6:16} Cyrus also returned the holy vessels of gold and silver that Nebuchadnezzar had taken from the temple in Jerusalem and placed in the Babylonian temple. These Cyrus returned to Zerubbabel and Sheshbazzar the governor {6:17} with instructions to bring them back to the temple in Jerusalem and to rebuild the temple on its original site. {6:18} Sheshbazzar laid the foundations of the Lord's house in Jerusalem, and although it has been under construction from then until now, it has not yet been completed.' {6:19} Therefore, if it pleases the king, let a search be made in the royal archives of Babylon to verify if King Cyrus did indeed issue such a decree, and let the king send us his decision regarding this matter." {6:20} Upon receiving this request, King Darius ordered a search of the royal archives in Babylon. In Ecbatana, the fortress in Media, a scroll was found that recorded: {6:21} "In the first year of King Cyrus's reign, he decreed that the house of the Lord in Jerusalem should be rebuilt where sacrifices are made with perpetual fire. {6:22} Its dimensions are to be sixty cubits high and sixty cubits wide, with three layers of hewn stone and one layer of new timber, funded from the royal treasury. {6:23} Furthermore, the holy vessels of gold and silver that Nebuchadnezzar took from the temple in Jerusalem and carried to Babylon are to be restored to their place in the Jerusalem temple." {6:24} Darius then commanded Sisinnes, the governor of Syria and Phoenicia, Sathrabuzanes, and their associates, and all local rulers in Syria and Phoenicia, to stay away from the construction site and to allow Zerubbabel, the servant of the Lord and governor of Judea, and the elders of the Jews to rebuild the house of the Lord on its site. {6:25} Darius decreed that the house must be completed without interference, and that full support should be provided to those who returned from captivity in Judea until the temple is finished. {6:26} He also ordered that a portion of the tribute from Coelesyria and Phoenicia be allocated to these men, specifically to Zerubbabel the governor, for sacrifices to the Lord, including bulls, rams, and lambs, along with wheat, salt, wine, and oil, to be provided regularly each year as indicated by the priests in Jerusalem, {6:27} so that libations might be made to the Most High God for the king and his children, and prayers offered for their lives. {6:28} He further commanded that anyone who violated or nullified any of these provisions would have a beam taken from their house and be hanged upon it, with their property confiscated by the king. {6:29} "May the Lord, whose name is called upon there, destroy any king or nation that tries to hinder or damage the house of the Lord in Jerusalem. {6:30} I, King Darius, have decreed that this be carried out with all diligence as prescribed here."

{7:1} Sisinnes, the governor of Coelesyria and Phoenicia, along with Sathrabuzanes and their associates, followed King Darius's orders. {7:2} They carefully supervised the holy work, assisting the Jewish elders and the chief officers of the temple. {7:3} The holy work prospered while the prophets Haggai and Zechariah continued to prophesy. {7:4} The work was completed by the command of the Lord God of Israel, with the approval of the Persian kings Cyrus, Darius, and Artaxerxes. {7:5} The holy house was finished on the twenty-third day of the month of Adar, in the sixth year of King Darius's reign. {7:6} The people of Israel, including the priests, the Levites, and the rest of those who had returned from captivity, followed what was written in the book of Moses. {7:7} They dedicated the temple of the Lord with offerings of one hundred bulls, two hundred rams, four hundred lambs, {7:8} and twelve goats for the sin of all Israel, according to the twelve tribes of Israel. {7:9} The priests and Levites, dressed in their garments, were organized by families for the service of the Lord God of Israel, as prescribed in the book of Moses, with gatekeepers stationed at each gate. {7:10} The returned exiles celebrated the Passover on the fourteenth day of the first month, after the priests and Levites had purified themselves together. {7:11} Not all of the returned captives were purified, but all the Levites were purified together. {7:12} They sacrificed the Passover lamb for all the returned captives, for their fellow priests, and for themselves. {7:13} The Israelites who had returned from captivity ate it, along with those who had separated themselves from the abominations of the land's peoples to seek the Lord. {7:14} They celebrated the Feast of Unleavened Bread for seven days, rejoicing before the Lord, {7:15} because He had changed the will of the king of Assyria to support their service to the Lord God of Israel.

{8:1} After these events, during the reign of King Artaxerxes of Persia, Ezra arrived. He was the son of Seraiah, who was the son of Azariah, son of Hilkiah, son of Shallum, descendant of Zadok, son of Ahitub, son of Amariah, son of Uzzi, son of Bukki, son of Abishua, son of Phinehas, son of Eleazar, son of Aaron the chief priest. {8:2} Ezra, skilled in the law of Moses given by the God of Israel, came up from Babylon. The king honored him greatly, granting all his requests. {8:3} Accompanying Ezra to Jerusalem were some Israelites, priests, Levites, temple singers, gatekeepers, and temple servants. {8:4} They departed Babylon in the seventh year of Artaxerxes's reign, arriving in Jerusalem safely, blessed by the Lord. {8:5} Ezra was known for his deep knowledge of the law; he taught all Israel the statutes and ordinances of the Lord. {8:6} Here is the copy of the decree King Artaxerxes gave to Ezra the priest and scholar of the law of the Lord: {8:7} "King Artaxerxes sends greetings to Ezra the priest and scholar of the law of the Lord. {8:8} By my decree, I allow Jews, priests, Levites, and others in our kingdom who wish to go with you to Jerusalem. {8:9} Let those who are willing accompany you, appointed by myself and my seven counselors, to assess Judea and Jerusalem in accordance with the law of the Lord. {8:10} Take with you the gifts for the Lord of Israel that I and my counselors have pledged, and gather all the gold and silver found in Babylonia for the Lord in Jerusalem. {8:11} Also, collect donations from the people for the temple of their Lord in Jerusalem—gold, silver, and offerings for the sacrifices on the altar. {8:12} Use the gold and silver according to the will of your God. {8:13} Deliver the holy vessels for the temple of your God in Jerusalem. {8:14} Use royal funds for whatever else is needed for the temple of your God. {8:15} I command the treasurers of Syria and Phoenicia to provide Ezra the priest and scholar of the Most High God with up to a hundred talents of silver, a hundred cors of wheat, a hundred baths of wine, and salt in abundance. {8:16} Fulfill all that is prescribed in the law of God for the Most High God, so that no wrath may come upon the kingdom of the king and his sons. {8:17} No tribute or tax shall be imposed on priests, Levites, temple singers, gatekeepers, or temple servants, as they serve in the temple of their God. {8:18} Ezra, according to the wisdom of your God, appoint judges and justices to administer justice to all who know the law of your God throughout Syria and Phoenicia. {8:19} Teach those who do not know the law. {8:20} Punish severely anyone who violates the law of your God or the law of the kingdom, whether by death, fine, or imprisonment." {8:21} Blessed be the Lord, who inspired King Artaxerxes to honor His temple in Jerusalem. {8:22} Ezra received support from the Lord his God and gathered Israelites to accompany him. {8:23} These are the leaders of the priests who came with Ezra from Babylon in the reign of King Artaxerxes: {8:24} Gershom, of the sons of Phinehas; Gamael, of the sons of Ithamar; and Hattush, son of Shecaniah, of the sons of David. {8:25} Also with Ezra were Zechariah of the sons of Parosh and a hundred and fifty men; Eliehoenai, son of Zerahiah, of the sons of Pahath-moab, with two hundred men; {8:26} Shecaniah, son of Jahaziel, of the sons of Zattu, with three hundred men; Obed, son of Jonathan, of the sons of Adin, with two hundred and fifty men; {8:27} Jeshaiah, son of Gotholiah, of the sons of Elam, with seventy men; Zeraiah, son of Michael, of the sons of Shephatiah, with seventy men; {8:28} Obadiah, son of Jehiel, of the sons of Joab, with two hundred and twelve men; Shelomith, son of Josiphiah, of the sons of Bani, with a hundred and sixty men; {8:29} Zechariah, son of Bebai, of the sons of Bebai, with twenty-eight men; Johanan, son of Hakkatan, of the sons of Azgad, with a hundred and ten men; {8:30} Eliphelet, Jeuel, and Shemaiah, of the sons of Adonikam, with seventy men; Uthai, son of Istalcurus, of the sons of Bigvai, with seventy men. {8:31} Ezra gathered them by the river called Theras and camped there for three days, inspecting them. {8:32} Finding no sons of priests or Levites among them, Ezra sent for leaders and men of understanding. {8:33} He instructed them to bring priests for the house of the Lord from Iddo and the treasury officials. {8:34} By God's mighty hand, they brought competent men from Mahli's descendants, sons of Levi, including Sherebiah and eighteen kinsmen. {8:35} They also brought Hashabiah, Annunus, Jeshaiah, and twenty men from Hananiah's descendants. {8:36} Additionally, they brought two hundred and twenty temple servants who were designated by David and the leaders for the service of the Levites. {8:37} Ezra proclaimed a fast by the river before the Lord, seeking a safe journey for themselves, their children, and their cattle. {8:38} Ezra was reluctant to ask the king for a military escort, trusting in the Lord's protection. {8:39} Through prayer, they found the Lord to be merciful and supportive. {8:40} Ezra set apart twelve leaders of the priests—Sherebiah, Hashabiah, and ten of their kinsmen. {8:41} He entrusted them with silver, gold, and holy vessels for the house of the Lord, donated by the king, his counselors, nobles, and all Israel. {8:42} He weighed out six hundred and fifty talents of silver, one hundred talents of gold, and a hundred silver vessels. {8:43} He also gave them twenty golden bowls and twelve bronze vessels as fine as gold. {8:44} Addressing them, Ezra said, "You are consecrated to the Lord, and so are these vessels, silver, and gold, dedicated to the Lord, the God of our ancestors. {8:45} Guard them carefully until you deliver them to the leaders of the priests, Levites, and heads of Israelite families in Jerusalem, to be stored in the chambers of the house of the Lord." {8:46} The priests and Levites received the silver, gold, and vessels for the temple of the Lord in Jerusalem. {8:47} By the mighty hand of the Lord, we were provided with capable men from the descendants of Mahli, son of Levi, son of Israel. Sherebiah and his eighteen sons and relatives came, along with Hashabiah, Annunus, Jeshaiah, and twenty men from the sons of Hananiah. {8:48} Additionally, there were two hundred and twenty temple servants, as appointed by David and the leaders for the service of the Levites, all listed by name. {8:49} At that time, I proclaimed a fast before the Lord for the young men among us, seeking His guidance for a safe journey for ourselves, our children, and our livestock. {8:50} I refrained from asking the king for soldiers and cavalry to protect us from our adversaries. Instead, we relied on the power of our Lord, confident that He would support all who seek Him. {8:51} We continued to pray earnestly to the Lord, finding Him exceedingly merciful. {8:52} Afterward, I appointed twelve leaders among the priests—Sherebiah, Hashabiah, and ten of their kinsmen. {8:53} I entrusted them with the silver, gold, and holy vessels donated by the king, his counselors, nobles, and all Israel. {8:54} I carefully weighed out six hundred and fifty talents of silver, one hundred talents of gold, twenty golden bowls, twelve vessels of fine bronze, and other items. {8:55} Addressing them, I emphasized their holiness to the Lord and the sanctity of the vessels, silver, and gold dedicated to the Lord, the God of our ancestors. {8:56} I instructed them to guard these treasures until they could deliver them to the leaders of the priests, Levites, and heads of Israelite families in Jerusalem, to be stored in the temple of the Lord. {8:57} The priests and Levites who received the silver, gold, and vessels transported them to the temple of the Lord in Jerusalem. {8:58} We departed from the river Theras on the twelfth day of the first month, reaching Jerusalem safely by the mighty hand of the Lord that protected us from every enemy along the way. {8:59} After three days in Jerusalem, the silver, gold, and vessels were weighed and delivered to Meremoth the priest, son of Uriah, along with Eleazar son of Phinehas, Jozabad son of Jeshua, and Moeth son of Binnui, the Levites. {8:60} Everything was counted and weighed, and the total recorded meticulously at that time. {8:61} Those who returned from captivity offered sacrifices to the Lord, the God of Israel: twelve bulls for all Israel, ninety-six rams, seventy-two lambs, and twelve male goats as a sin offering. {8:62} The king's decrees were delivered to the royal stewards and governors of Coelesyria and Phoenicia, who honored the people and the temple of the Lord. {8:63} Following these events, the leaders approached me and said, {8:64} "The people of Israel, leaders, priests, and Levites have not separated themselves from the peoples of the land and their abominations—the Canaanites, Hittites, Perizzites, Jebusites, Moabites, Egyptians, and Edomites. {8:65} They have taken their daughters as wives for themselves and their sons, mixing the holy race with the peoples of the land. From the leaders and nobles, this violation of the law has spread." {8:66} Upon hearing this, I tore my garments and mantle, plucked hair from my head and beard, and sat down in deep distress and sorrow. {8:67} Those who feared the word of the Lord of Israel gathered around me as I mourned this transgression, sitting in anguish until the evening sacrifice. {8:68} After my fast, with my garments and mantle torn, I knelt down and stretched out my hands to the Lord, {8:69} saying, "O Lord, I am ashamed and embarrassed before Your face. {8:70} Our sins are piled high above our heads, and our wrongdoings have reached up to heaven, from the days of our fathers until now, and we are deep in sin to this day. {8:71} Because of our sins and those of our fathers, we, our kings, and our priests have been handed over to foreign kings, to the sword, captivity, and plundering, in shame to this day. {8:72} Yet now, in some measure, You have shown us mercy, O Lord, allowing us a remnant and a name in Your holy place, {8:73} and providing a light for us in the house of the Lord our God, giving us food even in our servitude. {8:74} Even in our bondage, You have not abandoned us; instead, You have made us favorable to the kings of Persia, who have provided us with sustenance and restored Zion from desolation, giving us a stronghold in Judea and Jerusalem. {8:75} "And now, O Lord, what can we say after these things? For we have violated Your commandments, given through Your servants the prophets, saying, {8:76} 'The land you are entering to possess is a land polluted by the impurity of the peoples of the land, who have filled it with their uncleanness. {8:77} Therefore, do not give your daughters in marriage to their sons, nor take their daughters for your sons. {8:78} Never seek their peace or prosperity, so that you may be strong and enjoy the good things of the land, leaving it as an inheritance to your children forever.' {8:79} All that has happened to us is due to our evil deeds and great sins. O Lord, You pardoned our sins to leave us this remnant, but we have returned to transgress Your law by mingling with the impurity of the peoples of the land. {8:80} Were You not angry enough to destroy us completely, leaving no remnant, root, or name? {8:81} O Lord of Israel, You are righteous; we are left only as a remnant to this day. {8:82} Here we are, standing before You in our sins, unable to stand in Your presence because of these things." {8:83} As Ezra prayed and confessed, weeping and prostrated before the temple, a large crowd gathered around him from Jerusalem—men, women, and children—weeping bitterly. {8:84} Shecaniah son of Jehiel, a member of the community, stood up and said to Ezra, "We have sinned against the Lord by marrying foreign women from the peoples of the land, but there is still hope for Israel. {8:85} Let us make a covenant with the Lord to put away all these foreign wives and their children, as you and those who tremble at the commandment of the Lord advise. {8:86} Arise, for it is your task, and we are with you. Be strong and take action." {8:87} So Ezra arose and made the leaders of the priests and Levites and all Israel take an oath to do as had been said. And they swore to it.

{9:1} Ezra then stood up and left the temple courtyard, going to the chamber of Jehohanan son of Eliashib, where he spent the night. During this time, he abstained from food and drink, deeply troubled by the widespread sins of the people. {9:2} A proclamation was issued throughout Judea and Jerusalem, summoning all those who had returned from exile to gather in Jerusalem. {9:3} It was decreed that those who did not assemble within two or three days would forfeit their livestock, which would be dedicated for sacrifice, and they themselves would be expelled from the community of those who had returned from captivity. {9:4} In response, men from the tribes of Judah and Benjamin gathered in Jerusalem within the specified timeframe, which was the ninth month on the twentieth day. {9:5} The assembly convened in the open square before the temple, enduring the harsh winter conditions. {9:6} Ezra addressed the multitude, declaring, "You have violated God's law by marrying foreign women, thereby multiplying Israel's sin. {9:7} Now, confess your wrongdoing and give glory to the Lord, the God of our ancestors. {9:8} Commit to doing His will by separating yourselves from the peoples of the land and from your foreign wives." {9:9} The entire assembly responded loudly, pledging to obey Ezra's instructions. {9:10} However, they acknowledged the enormity of their task, considering the large number of people and the winter season, realizing it could not be accomplished hastily. {9:11} They proposed that the leaders stay in Jerusalem while those in the settlements with foreign wives gathered at the appointed time, accompanied by the elders and judges of each place, to resolve the matter in stages. {9:12} Jonathan son of Asahel and Jahzeiah son of Tikvah, along with Meshullam, Levi, and Shabbethai, agreed to oversee this process as judges. {9:13} All those who had returned from exile followed through with these arrangements. {9:14} Ezra, the priest, selected prominent men from each ancestral clan, registering them by name. On the new moon of the tenth month, they began their deliberations to address the issue. {9:15} By the new moon of the first month, they had resolved the cases of men who had married foreign women. {9:16} The priests found among those guilty of having foreign wives were the descendants of Jeshua son of Jozadak, Maaseiah, Eliezar, Jarib, and Jodan. {9:17} They committed to divorcing their wives and offering rams as a penalty for their offense. {9:18} Among the sons of Immer were Hanani, Zebadiah, Maaseiah, Shemaiah, Jehiel, and Azariah. {9:19} From the sons of Pashhur were Elioenai, Maaseiah, Ishmael, Nathanael, Gedaliah, and Elasah. {9:20} The Levites involved were Jozabad, Shimei, Kelaiah (also known as Kelita), Pethahiah, Judah, and

Jonah. {9:21} Among the temple singers were Eliashib and Zaccur, while among the gatekeepers were Shallum and Telem. {9:22} Those from Israel who were guilty included Ramiah, Izziah, Malchijah, Mijamin, Eleazar, Asibias, and Benaiah. {9:23} The descendants of Elam found with foreign wives included Mattaniah, Zechariah, Jehiel, Abdi, Jeremoth, and Elijah. {9:24} From the sons of Zattu were Elioenai, Eliashib, Othoniah, Jeremoth, Zabad, and Zerdaiah. {9:25} Among the sons of Bebai were Jehohanan, Hananiah, Zabbai, and Emathis. {9:26} The sons of Bani who had foreign wives were Meshullam, Malluch, Adaiah, Jashub, Sheal, and Jeremoth. {9:27} The sons of Addi found in similar circumstances were Naathus, Moossias, Laccunus, Naidus, Bescaspasmys, Sesthel, Belnuus, and Manasseas. {9:28} The descendants of Annan involved were Elionas, Asaias, Melchias, Sabbaias, and Simon Chosamaeus. {9:29} From the sons of Hashum were Mattenai, Mattattah, Zabad, Eliphelet, Manasseh, and Shimei. {9:30} Among the sons of Bani, Jeremai, Maadai, Amram, Joel, Mamdai, Bedeiah, Vaniah, Carabasion, Eliashib, Machnadebai, Eliasis, Binnui, Elialis, Shimei, and Shelemiah had married foreign women. {9:31} The sons of Ezora who were guilty included Shashai, Azarel, Azael, Shemaiah, Amariah, and Joseph. {9:32} Among the sons of Nebo, those found with foreign wives were Mattithiah, Zabad, Iddo, Joel, Benaiah, and all the others listed. {9:33} All these men had married foreign women, and they divorced them along with their children. {9:34} Afterward, the priests, Levites, and Israelites settled in Jerusalem and in the towns throughout Judea. On the new moon of the seventh month, when the Israelites were in their towns, {9:35} the entire assembly gathered as one in the open square before the east gate of the temple. {9:36} They asked Ezra the chief priest and scribe to bring the Book of the Law of Moses, which the Lord had given to Israel. {9:37} On the new moon of the seventh month, Ezra the chief priest brought the Law before the assembly—men, women, and all who could understand. {9:38} He read it aloud from early morning until midday in the open square before the Water Gate, in the presence of the men and women and those who could understand. All the people listened attentively to the Book of the Law. {9:39} Ezra stood on the elevated wooden platform constructed for the occasion, flanked by Mattathiah, Shema, Anaiah, Azariah, Uriah, Hezekiah, and Baalsamus on his right, and Pedaiah, Mishael, Malchijah, Lothasubus, Nabariah, and Zechariah on his left. {9:40} As Ezra opened the Book of the Law in full view of all the people, they all stood up. {9:41} Ezra praised the Lord, the great God, and all the people lifted their hands and responded, "Amen! Amen!" Then they bowed down and worshiped the Lord with their faces to the ground. {9:42} Jeshua, Bani, Sherebiah, Jamin, Akkub, Shabbethai, Hodiah, Maaseiah, Kelita, Azariah, Jozabad, Hanan, Pelaiah, and the Levites explained the Law to the people, while they remained in their places. {9:43} They read from the Book of the Law of God, making it clear and giving meaning so that the people understood what was being read. {9:44} Then Nehemiah the governor, Ezra the priest and scribe, and the Levites who were instructing the people said to them all, "This day is holy to the Lord your God. Do not mourn or weep." For all the people had been weeping as they listened to the words of the Law. {9:45} Nehemiah continued, "Go and enjoy choice food and sweet drinks, and send some to those who have nothing prepared. This day is holy to our Lord. Do not grieve, for the joy of the Lord is your strength." {9:46} The Levites calmed all the people, saying, "Be still, for this is a holy day. Do not grieve." {9:47} So all the people went away to eat and drink, to send portions of food, and to celebrate with great joy, because they now understood the words that had been made known to them.

2 Esdras

The book of 2 Esdras, also known as 4 Ezra in the Vulgate and sometimes referred to as the Apocalypse of Ezra, is a significant text in the Apocrypha and Pseudepigrapha of the Old Testament. Its composition is generally dated to the late first century CE, in the aftermath of the destruction of the Second Temple in 70 CE, a context that profoundly influences its themes and messages. This work is attributed to Ezra, a scribe and priest, although it is widely recognized that the attribution is pseudonymous, a common practice for apocalyptic literature of this period. The book is primarily concerned with theodicy, eschatology, and the exploration of divine justice, particularly in the face of catastrophic events. The narrative is structured around a series of visions and angelic dialogues, which address the profound questions of why the righteous suffer and the wicked prosper, and how the faithful can find hope amidst apparent divine abandonment. Notable sections include the depiction of the Eagle Vision, which is often interpreted as a critique of Roman imperial power, and the Woman in Mourning vision, symbolizing the plight of Jerusalem. 2 Esdras is distinguished by its intense emotional tone and its raw grappling with issues of faith, doubt, and despair. The text is part of the biblical canon for certain Christian traditions, including the Ethiopian Orthodox Church, while it holds a more ambiguous status in others, often studied more for its literary and theological insights rather than its canonical authority. The influence of 2 Esdras extends beyond religious boundaries, impacting later apocalyptic literature and even secular thought, as it reflects the universal human struggle to understand suffering and maintain hope in times of trial.

{1:1} This is the second book of the prophet Ezra, son of Seraiah, descendant of Azariah, Hilkiah, Shallum, Zadok, Ahitub, Ahijah, Phinehas, Eli, Amariah, Azariah, Meraioth, Arna, Uzzi, Borith, Abishua, Phinehas, and Eleazar, tracing his lineage back to Aaron of the tribe of Levi. Ezra wrote this during the captivity in Media, in the reign of King Artaxerxes of Persia. {1:2} The word of the Lord came to Ezra, saying, {1:3} "Go and proclaim to my people their evil deeds, and to their children the sins they have committed against me, so that they may pass on the legacy of their ancestors' sins. For they have forgotten me and worshipped foreign gods. {1:4} "Was it not I who brought them out of Egypt, out of slavery? Yet they have provoked me and rejected my guidance. {1:5} "Tear out your hair in despair and pronounce all manner of woes upon them, for they have not obeyed my law; they are a rebellious people. {1:6} "How long must I endure them, after all the blessings I have bestowed upon them? {1:7} "For their sake, I have defeated many kings. I struck down Pharaoh and his servants, and decimated his army. {1:8} "I have annihilated nations before them and scattered the peoples of Tyre and Sidon to the east. {1:9} "But speak to them and say, 'Thus says the Lord: {1:10} "'It was I who led you through the sea, carving safe paths where there was no road. I appointed Moses as your leader and Aaron as your priest. {1:11} "'I provided light for you with a pillar of fire and performed great miracles among you. Yet you have forgotten me,' says the Lord. {1:12} "'Thus says the Lord Almighty: The quails were a sign for you, I provided camps for your protection, yet you grumbled in them. {1:13} "'You did not exult in my name when your enemies were defeated. To this day, you continue to complain. {1:14} "'Where are the benefits I bestowed upon you? When you were hungry and thirsty in the wilderness, did you not cry out to me? {1:15} "'I pitied your cries and gave you manna to eat, the bread of angels. {1:16} "'When you were thirsty, did I not split the rock so that water gushed out? I shaded you with tree leaves from the scorching heat. {1:17} "'I allotted fertile lands to you; I drove out the Canaanites, Perizzites, and Philistines before you. What more could I have done for you?' says the Lord Almighty. {1:18} "'Thus says the Lord Almighty: When you were at the bitter stream in the wilderness, thirsty and blaspheming my name, {1:19} "'I did not send fire upon you for your blasphemies; instead, I threw a tree into the water and made it sweet.' {1:20} "'What shall I do with you, O Jacob? You have not obeyed me, O Judah. {1:21} "'I will turn to other nations and give them my name, that they may keep my statutes. {1:22} "'Because you have forsaken me, I will also forsake you. When you cry out for mercy, I will show you none. {1:23} "'When you call upon me, I will not listen, for your hands are stained with blood, and your feet rush to commit murder. {1:24} "'It is not that you have forsaken me; you have forsaken yourselves,' says the Lord. {1:25} "'Thus says the Lord Almighty: Have I not treated you as a father treats his sons, a mother her daughters, or a nurse her children, {1:26} "'that you should be my people and I should be your God? Yet now, what shall I do with you? I will cast you out from my presence. {1:27} "When you offer sacrifices to me, I will turn my face away; I have rejected your festivals, new moons, and circumcisions. {1:28} "'I sent my servants the prophets to you, but you seized and killed them, tearing their bodies apart. Their blood will be on you,' says the Lord. {1:29} "'Thus says the Lord Almighty: Your house is desolate; I will scatter you like straw in the wind. {1:30} "'Your descendants will be childless because you have abandoned my commandments and done evil in my sight. {1:31} "'I will give your houses to a people who will come, who have not heard my words but will believe. {1:32} "'They have not seen prophets, yet they will remember their former state. {1:33} "'I call upon the future generations to witness their gratitude, whose children will rejoice in gladness. {1:34} "'Though they do not see me with physical eyes, they will believe in the spirit the things I have spoken. {1:35} "'And now, look with pride, O father, as the people come from the east. {1:36} "'To them, I will give leaders like Abraham, Isaac, Jacob, Hosea, Amos, Micah, Joel, Obadiah, Jonah, Nahum, Habakkuk, Zephaniah, Haggai, Zechariah, and Malachi, who is known as the messenger of the Lord.'"

{2:1} The Lord declares: I led this people out of bondage and gave them commandments through my prophets, but they refused to listen and nullified my counsel. {2:2} The mother of these people says to them, "Go, my children, for I am a widow and abandoned. {2:3} "I raised you with joy, but now I have lost you to mourning and sorrow because you have sinned before the Lord and done evil in my sight. {2:4} "But what can I do for you now? I am a widow and abandoned. Go, my children, and seek mercy from the Lord." {2:5} Father, I call upon you as a witness beside the mother of these children because they did not keep my covenant. {2:6} May you bring confusion upon them and bring ruin to their mother, so that they may have no descendants. {2:7} Let them be scattered among the nations; let their names be wiped out from the earth because they have despised my covenant. {2:8} "Woe to you, Assyria, who harbor the unrighteous! O wicked nation, remember what I did to Sodom and Gomorrah, {2:9} whose land remains as pitch and heaps of ashes. So I will deal with those who have not listened to me, says the Lord Almighty." {2:10} The Lord spoke to Ezra, saying, "Tell my people that I will give them the kingdom of Jerusalem, which I had intended for Israel. {2:11} "Moreover, I will take their glory back to myself and give these others the everlasting dwellings that I had prepared for Israel. {2:12} "The tree of life will emit a sweet fragrance for them; they will neither toil nor grow weary. {2:13} "Ask, and you will receive; pray that your days may be few, shortened. The kingdom is already prepared for you; be vigilant! {2:14} "Heaven and earth, bear witness that I excluded evil and created good because I live, says the Lord. {2:15} "Mother, embrace your sons; raise them with joy, like a dove does; establish their feet, for I have chosen you, says the Lord. {2:16} "I will raise the dead from their places, bringing them out from their tombs because I acknowledge my name in them. {2:17} "Do not fear, mother of sons, for I have chosen you, says the Lord. {2:18} "I will send you help, my servants Isaiah and Jeremiah. According to their advice, I have consecrated and prepared twelve trees laden with various fruits for you. {2:19} "Likewise, the same number of springs flowing with milk and honey, and seven mighty mountains where roses and lilies bloom; by these, I will fill your children with joy. {2:20} "Protect the rights of widows, ensure justice for orphans, give to the needy, defend the orphan, clothe the naked, {2:21} "care for the wounded and the weak, do not mock the lame, protect the maimed, and grant sight to the blind to witness my glory. {2:22} "Guard the old and the young within your walls; {2:23} "When you find anyone deceased, bury them and mark the grave, and I will give you a place of honor in my resurrection. {2:24} "Pause and be still, my people, for your rest will come. {2:25} "Good caregiver, nourish your sons and strengthen their feet. {2:26} "None of the servants I have given you will perish, for I will gather them from among your midst. {2:27} "Do not worry, for when the day of tribulation and distress arrives, others will weep and mourn, but you will rejoice and have plenty. {2:28} "Nations will envy you, but they will be unable to harm you, says the Lord. {2:29} "My hands will cover you so that your sons do not see Gehenna. {2:30} "Rejoice, O mother, with your sons, for I will deliver you, says the Lord. {2:31} "Remember your sleeping sons, for I will bring them out from the depths of the earth and show them mercy; for I am merciful, says the Lord Almighty. {2:32} "Embrace your children until my arrival and proclaim mercy to them; for my springs overflow, and my grace will never fail." {2:33} I, Ezra, received a command from the Lord on Mount Horeb to go to Israel. But when I came to them, they rejected me and disregarded the Lord's commandment. {2:34} Therefore, I say to you, O nations who hear and understand, "Wait for your shepherd; he will give you eternal rest, for he who comes at the end of the age is near at hand. {2:35} "Prepare for the rewards of the kingdom, for the eternal light will shine upon you forevermore. {2:36} "Flee from the shadow of this age; receive the joy of your glory. I call on my Savior publicly as witness. {2:37} "Receive what the Lord has entrusted to you and rejoice, giving thanks to him who has called you to heavenly kingdoms. {2:38} "Rise and stand, and see at the feast of the Lord the number of those who have been sealed. {2:39} "Those who have departed from the shadow of this age have received glorious garments from the Lord. {2:40} "Gather your full number again, O Zion, and complete the count of your people clothed in white, who have fulfilled the law of the Lord. {2:41} "The count of your children, whom you desired, is complete; implore the power of the Lord that your people, called from the beginning, may be sanctified." {2:42} I, Ezra, saw on Mount Zion a vast multitude, which I could not count, all praising the Lord with songs. {2:43} Among them was a young man of great stature, taller than any others, and he placed a crown on the head of each of them, yet he was more exalted than they. And I was mesmerized. {2:44} So I asked an angel, "Who are these, my lord?" {2:45} He replied, "These are the ones who have shed their mortal garments and put on immortality, confessing the name of God; now they are being crowned and receiving palms." {2:46} Then I asked the angel, "Who is that young man placing crowns on them and giving them palms?" {2:47} He answered, "He is the Son of God, whom they confessed in the world." So I began to praise those who had stood bravely for the name of the Lord. {2:48} Then the angel said to me, "Go, tell my people about the great and numerous wonders of the Lord God that you have seen."

{3:1} Thirty years after our city was destroyed, I, Salathiel also known as Ezra, was in Babylon. Troubled, I lay on my bed, my thoughts swirling within me, {3:2} as I beheld the desolation of Zion and the prosperity of those in Babylon. {3:3} My spirit was greatly troubled, and I began to speak anxiously to the Most High, {3:4} saying, "O sovereign Lord, didn't you speak in the beginning when you created the earth without assistance? {3:5} You commanded the dust and it formed Adam, a lifeless body. Yet he was your handiwork; you breathed into him the breath of life, and he became alive in your presence. {3:6} You led him into the garden that your right hand had planted before the earth was formed. {3:7} You laid upon him one commandment, but he disobeyed, and immediately you appointed death for him and his descendants. From him arose countless nations, tribes, peoples, and clans. {3:8} Every nation followed its own will, committing ungodly acts before you, scorning you, and you did not stop them. {3:9} But in due time, you brought the flood upon the world's inhabitants and destroyed them. {3:10} They met the same fate as Adam, death. {3:11} But you left Noah and his household, along with all the righteous who descended from him. {3:12} "When the earth's inhabitants began to multiply, they gave birth to children, peoples, and many nations. They became even more ungodly than their ancestors. {3:13} And while they were sinning before you, you chose one of them, Abraham, {3:14} whom you loved and to whom you revealed the end of times in secret, by night. {3:15} You made with him an everlasting covenant and promised never to forsake his descendants. You gave him Isaac, and to Isaac, you gave Jacob and Esau. {3:16} You chose Jacob for yourself, but rejected Esau, and Jacob became a great multitude. {3:17} When you led his descendants out of Egypt, you brought them to Mount Sinai. {3:18} You bent the heavens, shook the earth, moved the world, made the depths tremble, and troubled the times. {3:19} Your glory passed through fire, earthquake, wind, and ice, to give the law to Jacob's descendants and your commandment to Israel's posterity. {3:20} "Yet you did not remove their evil hearts so that your law might bear fruit in them. {3:21} The first Adam, burdened with an evil heart, transgressed and was overcome, as did all who descended from him. {3:22} Thus, the disease became permanent; the law resided in the people's hearts along with the evil root, but what was good departed, and evil remained. {3:23} So the ages passed, the years completed, and you raised up for yourself a servant named David. {3:24} You commanded him to build a city for your name and offer you offerings from what is yours. {3:25} This continued for many years, but the city's inhabitants transgressed, {3:26} doing everything Adam and all his descendants had done, for they too had evil hearts. {3:27} So you delivered the city into the hands of its enemies. {3:28} "Then I pondered in my heart, are the deeds of those who dwell in Babylon any better? Is that why she has dominion over Zion? {3:29} For when I came here, I saw countless ungodly deeds, and my soul has witnessed many sinners over these thirty years. My heart was dismayed, {3:30} for I have seen how you endure those who sin, spare the wicked, destroy your people, and preserve your enemies, {3:31} without revealing how your way can be understood by anyone. Are Babylon's deeds better than Zion's? {3:32} Has any other nation known you besides Israel? What tribes have believed your covenants like these tribes of Jacob? {3:33} Yet their reward has not appeared, and their labor has borne no fruit. I have traveled extensively among nations and found them wealthy but forgetful of your commandments. {3:34} Therefore, weigh our iniquities against those of the world's inhabitants; thus, it will be determined which way the scale will tip. {3:35} When have the inhabitants of the earth not sinned before you? What nation has kept your commandments faithfully? {3:36} You may find individual men who have kept your commandments, but entire nations you will not find."

{4:1} Then the angel sent to me, whose name was Uriel, answered and said, "Your understanding has completely failed regarding this world. Do you think you can comprehend the ways of the Most High?" {4:2} I replied, "Yes, my lord." And he continued, "I have been sent to show you three paths and present three challenges to you. {4:3} If you can solve one of them for me, I will show you the path you desire and teach you why the human heart is evil." {4:4} "Speak," I said, "my lord." And he said, "Go, weigh for me the weight of fire, or measure for me a portion of wind, or call back for me the day that has passed." {4:5} I replied, "Who among those born of women can do this? You ask me about such things." {4:6} He said to me, "If I had asked you how many dwellings are in the heart of the sea, or how many rivers flow at the source of the deep, or how many streams are above the sky, or where the exits of Hades are, or where the entrances to paradise are, {4:7} perhaps you would have said, 'I have never gone down into the deep, nor into Hades, nor ascended into heaven.' {4:8} But now I have asked you about fire, wind, and the passing day—things through which you have passed and without which you cannot exist—and you have given me no answer." {4:9} He continued, "You cannot understand the things you grew up with; how then can your mind grasp the ways of the Most High? How can one worn out by the corrupt world understand incorruption?" When I heard this, I fell face down {4:10} and said to him, "It would be better for us not to be here than to come here and live in ungodliness, to suffer and not understand why." {4:11} He answered me, "I went into a forest of plain trees, and they made a plan {4:12} saying, 'Come, let us go and make war against the sea, so it retreats before us, and we can expand our territory with more forests.' {4:13} In a similar way, the waves of the sea also devised a plan, saying, 'Come, let us rise up and conquer the forest of the plain, so we can gain more land there.' {4:14} But the plan of the forest failed, for fire came and consumed it; {4:15} likewise, the plan of the sea's waves failed, for the sand stood firm and halted them. {4:16} If you were to judge between them, which would you justify, and which would you condemn?" {4:17} I replied, "Both made foolish plans, for the land belongs to the forest, and the sea has its designated place to carry its waves." {4:18} He said, "You have judged rightly. But why have you not judged the same in your own case? {4:19} Just as the land is allotted to the forest and the sea to its waves, those who dwell on earth can only comprehend what is on earth. He who is above the heavens understands what is beyond the heights of heaven." {4:20} I asked, "My lord, why then was I given the gift of understanding? {4:21} For I did not seek knowledge of the heavens, but rather about things we experience daily: why Israel has been handed over to the Gentiles in shame, why the people you loved have been given to godless tribes, why our fathers' law has become ineffective, and why written covenants no longer hold. {4:22} And why do we pass through the world like locusts, our lives like a fleeting mist, unworthy of mercy? {4:23} But what will you do for your name by which we are called? These are the things I ask." {4:24} He answered, "If you are alive, you will see; if you live long, you will marvel often, for the age hastens swiftly to its end. {4:25} It will not bring the promised things to the righteous at their appointed times, for this age is full of sorrow and weaknesses. {4:26} The evil you inquire about has been sown, but its harvest has not yet come. {4:27} If what has been sown is not reaped and the place where evil was sown does not pass away, the field where good was sown will not come forth. {4:28} A grain of evil seed was sown in Adam's heart from the beginning, and look at how much ungodliness it has produced until now and will produce until the time of threshing arrives! {4:29} Consider for yourself how much fruit of ungodliness a grain of evil seed has borne. {4:30} When countless grains are sown, how vast a threshing floor they will fill!" {4:31} I asked, "How long will these things be? Why are our years few and evil?" {4:32} He replied, "You do not hasten faster than the Most High, for your haste is for yourself, but the Highest hurries on behalf of many. {4:33} Did not the souls of the righteous in their chambers inquire about these matters, saying, 'How long must we remain here? When will the harvest of our reward come? {4:34} And the archangel Jeremiel answered them, saying, 'When the number of those like you is complete, for he has weighed the age on the balance, {4:35} measured the times by measure, and numbered the times by number. He will not move or wake them until that measure is fulfilled.'" {4:36} I replied, "O sovereign Lord, we are all filled with ungodliness. {4:37} Perhaps it is because of us that the time of threshing is delayed for the righteous—because of the sins of those who dwell on earth." {4:38} He answered, "Go and ask a woman who is pregnant if, when her nine months are completed, her womb can contain the child any longer." {4:39} I said, "No, lord, it cannot." {4:40} He said to me, "In Hades, the chambers of souls are like the womb. {4:41} Just as a woman in labor hurries to escape the birth pangs, so these places hasten to return what was entrusted to them from the beginning. {4:42} Then the things you desire to see will be revealed to you." {4:43} I asked, "If I have found favor in your sight and if it is possible and I am worthy, {4:44} show me this: Is there more time to come than has passed, or has the greater part already gone by? {4:45} I know what has passed, but I do not know what is to come." {4:46} He said to me, "Stand at my right side, and I will show you the interpretation of a parable." {4:47} So I stood and watched as a blazing furnace passed by before me; after the flames passed, I saw that smoke remained. {4:48} Then a cloud full of water passed before me and poured down a heavy, violent rain. After the storm passed, drops remained in the cloud. {4:49} He said to me, "Consider this for yourself: Just as the rain is more than the drops and the fire is greater than the smoke, so much more passed by, but drops and smoke remained." {4:50} I prayed, "Do you think I will live until those days? Who will be alive in those times?" {4:51} He answered, "I can partly tell you about the signs you ask, but I was not sent to tell you about your life, for I do not know."

{5:1} "Regarding the signs: behold, the days will come when those on earth will be seized with great fear, and the path of truth will be obscured, and faith will wither away. {5:2} Unrighteousness will exceed anything seen before, surpassing all previous reports. {5:3} The land that now rules will become desolate and uninhabited, laid waste before men's eyes. {5:4} Yet if the Most High permits you to live, you will witness its confusion after the third period. The sun will shine suddenly at night, and the moon during the day. {5:5} Wood will drip blood, stones will speak, and peoples will be troubled; stars will fall from the sky. {5:6} An unexpected ruler will emerge, and birds will flock together; the Sea of Sodom will yield fish, and an unknown voice will be heard in the night, audible to all. {5:7} Chaos will reign in many places, fires will break out frequently, wild beasts will wander from their domains, and monstrous births will occur from menstruating women. {5:8} Salt waters will be found in sweet, and friends will turn against each other. Reason will hide, and wisdom will retreat to its chamber. {5:9} Many will seek wisdom in vain; unrighteousness and lawlessness will proliferate on earth. {5:10} One nation will question another, 'Has righteousness or anyone who does right passed through you?' And the answer will be, 'No.' {5:11} At that time, people will hope but not receive; they will labor but find no success. {5:12} These are the signs I am allowed to reveal. If you pray again, weep as you do now, and fast for seven days, you will hear even greater things." {5:13} I awoke trembling violently, my soul deeply troubled to the point of fainting. {5:14} "But the angel who came and spoke with me held me, strengthened me, and stood me on my feet. {5:15} On the second night, Phaltiel, a leader of the people, approached me, asking, 'Where have you been? Why is your face troubled? {5:16} Do you not know that Israel has been entrusted to you in their exile land? {5:17} Rise, eat bread, lest you abandon us like a shepherd who leaves his flock to cruel wolves.' {5:18} I replied, 'Leave me for seven days, then you may come.' He listened and departed. {5:19} So I fasted seven days, mourning and weeping, as Uriel the angel had instructed. {5:20} After seven days, my heart's distress weighed heavily upon me once more. {5:21} Then my soul regained its understanding, and I began to speak again in the presence of the Most High. {5:22} I said, 'O Lord, from every forest and tree on earth, you chose one vine. {5:23} From all lands, you selected one region; from every flower, one lily. {5:24} From the depths of the sea, one river fills your purpose; from all cities built, Zion is consecrated to you. {5:25} From every bird created, one dove is named for you; from all flocks, one sheep is provided for you. {5:26} From the multitude of peoples, you have taken one people. To them, whom you loved, you gave the law approved by all. {5:27} Now, O Lord, why have you given up the one to the many? Why have you dishonored the root above others and scattered your chosen one among many? {5:28} Those who opposed your promises have trampled those who believed your covenants. {5:29} If you truly despise your people, they should face your punishment.' {5:30} When I finished speaking, the angel who had come to me before returned. {5:31} He said, 'Listen to me, and I will instruct you; pay attention, and I will tell you more.' {5:32} I said, 'Speak, my lord.' And he asked, 'Are you greatly troubled over Israel? Do you love them more than their Maker does?' {5:33} I answered, 'No, my lord, but my grief compels me to speak. Each hour brings me heartache as I seek to understand the ways of the Most High and uncover a fraction of his judgment.' {5:34} He replied, 'You cannot.' {5:35} I asked, 'Why not, my lord? Why was I born? Why did my mother's womb not become my grave, sparing me from witnessing Jacob's struggle and Israel's weariness?' {5:36} He said, 'Count those yet to come for me, gather scattered raindrops, make withered flowers bloom again. {5:37} Open closed chambers, release the winds confined within them, or show me the image of a voice. Then I will explain the turmoil you wish to understand.' {5:38} I said, 'O sovereign Lord, who can comprehend these things except the one who does not dwell among men? {5:39} I lack wisdom; how can I speak on what you ask of me?' {5:40} He said, 'Just as you cannot perform those tasks, you cannot fathom my judgment or the purpose of my love for my people.' {5:41} I said, 'Yet you oversee those who live until the end. What of those before us, or we, or those who come after us?' {5:42} He answered, 'My judgment is like a circle; for the last, there is no delay, and for the first, no haste.' {5:43} I responded, 'Could you not have created those who were, are, and will be together, hastening your judgment?' {5:44} He replied, 'The creation cannot hasten more than the Creator; the world cannot contain all created beings simultaneously.' {5:45} I asked, 'How can you promise to give life to all creation at once? If all creatures live simultaneously and the world supports them, could it not sustain them all now?' {5:46} He said, 'Ask a woman's womb: if she bears ten children, why not all at once?' {5:47} I said, 'She cannot; only each in its time.' {5:48} He said, 'Similarly, I have ordained the earth's womb for those sown in it. Just as an infant does not bear offspring, and an aged woman no longer gives birth, so have I ordered the world I created.' {5:49} I asked, 'Is our mother, of whom you spoke, still young or nearing old age?' {5:50} He answered, 'Ask a woman who gives birth; she will tell you.' {5:51} I inquired, 'Why are those born now smaller than those born earlier?' {5:52} He replied, 'Those born in youth differ from those born in old age, when the womb weakens.' {5:53} Understand that you and your contemporaries are smaller than those before you, {5:54} and those after you will be smaller than you, born into a creation aging and losing its youth.' {5:55} I said, 'O Lord, if I have found favor, reveal to me through whom you visit your creation.'

{6:1} He said to me, "In the beginning, before the earth's cycles began, before the gates of the world were set, before the winds gathered, before thunder roared, before lightning flashed, before paradise's foundations were laid, {6:2} before flowers bloomed, before movement's powers stirred, before countless angels assembled, {6:3} before the sky's heights rose, before firmaments were named, before Zion's footstool was established, {6:4} before years were counted, before sinful thoughts arose, before faithful treasures were sealed away — {6:5} I planned these things. They were made through me, and I alone will bring their end." {6:6} I asked, "When will time divide? When does the first era end and the next begin?" {6:7} He replied, "From Abraham to Isaac, for Jacob and Esau were born of Isaac. Jacob grasped Esau's heel from the start. {6:8} Esau marks the end of this era, and Jacob heralds the next. {6:9} A man's beginning is in his hand, his end in his heel. Between the two, seek no other, Ezra." {6:10} I said, "O Lord, if I have your favor, {6:11} show me the conclusion of the signs you revealed partially before." {6:12} He answered, "Rise and listen to a powerful voice. {6:13} If the ground shakes while it speaks, fear not; its words concern the end, and the earth's foundations will comprehend {6:14} that it speaks of them. They will tremble, knowing their end will be altered." {6:15} I stood and listened; the voice sounded like rushing waters. {6:16} It said, "Behold, the days approach when I will visit the earth's inhabitants, {6:17} judge the wicked, complete Zion's humiliation, {6:18} and seal the ending age. Then these signs will appear: the books will open before the firmament, seen by all. {6:19} Infants of a year will speak; women with child will bear premature children at three or four months, who will live and dance. {6:20} Sown places will suddenly appear unsown, full storehouses will abruptly empty; {6:21} the trumpet will sound loudly, terrifying all who hear it. {6:22} Then friends will make war as enemies, the earth and its people will tremble, fountains will stop flowing for three hours. {6:23} Whoever remains after these events will be saved, witnessing my salvation and the world's end. {6:24} Those taken up without death since birth will be seen; the hearts of the earth's inhabitants will change, {6:25} evil will be eradicated, deceit quenched, {6:26} faithfulness will thrive, corruption defeated, and truth, long dormant, will be revealed." {6:27} As he spoke, the ground beneath me began to sway. {6:28} He said, "I reveal these things to you tonight. {6:29} Pray and fast another seven days; I will reveal even greater things, {6:30} for your voice has reached the Most High; he has seen your integrity and your purity from youth. {6:31} Thus he sent me to show you all this, saying, 'Believe and do not fear! {6:32} Do not hastily judge the former times, lest you misjudge the last times.'" {6:33} After this, I wept and fasted another seven days to complete the three weeks as instructed. {6:34} On the eighth night, my heart was troubled again, and I spoke before the Most High. {6:35} My spirit was stirred, and my soul distressed. {6:36} I said, "O Lord, you spoke at creation's dawn, 'Let heaven and earth be,' and your word accomplished it. {6:37} Then the Spirit hovered, darkness and silence enveloped all; man's voice had not yet sounded. {6:38} You commanded light to emerge from your treasuries; thus your works appeared. {6:39} "On the second day, you created the firmament's spirit, ordering it to divide waters: some above, some below. {6:40} On the third day, you gathered waters to a seventh of the earth; six parts dried up for planting and service. {6:41} Your word went forth; the work was done immediately. {6:42} Fruits and flowers in abundance, colors and fragrances beyond compare, emerged on the third day. {6:43} "On the fourth day, you commanded sun's brilliance, moon's light, stars' arrangement, {6:44} to serve man soon to be formed. {6:45} "On the fifth day, you commanded the seventh part, where waters gathered, to bring forth life: birds and fish. {6:46} And so it was. {6:47} The lifeless water bore living creatures, as commanded, that nations might declare your wondrous works. {6:48} "You preserved two creatures: Behemoth and Leviathan. {6:49} Behemoth received a part dried on the third day to live among thousand mountains; {6:50} Leviathan received the watery seventh part; you keep them for whom and when you will. {6:51} "On the sixth day, you commanded earth to bring forth cattle, beasts, creeping things; {6:52} Adam, whom you placed over all your works, and from whom we descend, the people you chose. {6:53} "I speak before you, O Lord, because you created this world for us. {6:54} Other nations from Adam, you said, are nothing, like spittle; their abundance a drop in a bucket. {6:55} Yet these nations, deemed nothing, rule over and consume us, your first-born, your beloved. {6:56} If indeed this world is for us, why do we not possess it as our inheritance? How long will this endure?"

{7:1} After I finished speaking, the angel sent to me on previous nights appeared again and said, "Rise, Ezra, and hear the words I have come to speak." {7:2} I replied, "Speak, my lord." And he began, "Imagine a sea in a vast expanse, wide and expansive, {7:3} yet with an entrance in a narrow place, like a river. {7:4} How can one reach the expansive part of the sea to explore or sail unless passing through the narrow entrance? {7:5} Another analogy: Picture a city built on a plain, filled with every good thing, {7:6} yet its entrance is narrow, set in a perilous place between fire on one side and deep water on the other, {7:7} with only one narrow path between them where only one person can walk. {7:8} If this city is given as inheritance, how will the heir receive it without facing the dangers ahead?" {7:9} I responded, "He cannot, my lord." He continued, "So it is with Israel's destiny. {7:10} I created the world for them, but when Adam disobeyed my laws, judgment came upon creation. {7:11} Thus, the entrances to this world became narrow, filled with sorrow, toil, few and fraught with danger. {7:12} However, the entrances to the greater world are broad, safe, and yield the fruit of immortality. {7:13} Therefore, only by passing through difficult and vain experiences can one receive what awaits them. {7:14} Why then are you troubled, knowing you will perish? Why are you moved, knowing you are mortal? {7:15} Have you not considered what is to come rather than the present?" {7:16} I replied, "O sovereign Lord, your law decrees that the righteous inherit these things, while the ungodly perish. {7:17} The righteous endure hardships, hoping for easier times, but the wicked suffer and will not see ease." {7:18} He admonished, "You are not wiser than the Most High! {7:19} Many may perish, but God's law must not be disregarded. {7:20} God strictly commanded what people should do to live and avoid punishment upon entering the world. {7:21} Yet they were disobedient, speaking against him, entertaining vain thoughts, {7:22} plotting wicked schemes, denying God's existence, and ignoring his ways. {7:23} They scorned his law, denied his covenants, were unfaithful to his statutes, and neglected his works. {7:24} Therefore, Ezra, empty things await the empty, and fullness awaits the full. {7:25} The time will come when the signs I foretold will come to pass, when the unseen city will appear and hidden lands will be revealed. {7:26} All who are delivered from the foretold evils will witness my wonders. {7:27} My son the Messiah will be revealed with his followers, and those who remain will rejoice for four hundred years. {7:28} After these years, my son the Messiah will die, and all who breathe human breath. {7:29} The world will return to primordial silence for seven days, as at the beginning, with none left. {7:30} After seven days, the world, still dormant, will awaken; corruption will perish. {7:31} The earth will yield its sleeping ones and the dust its silent dwellers; tombs will release the souls within. {7:32} The Most High will preside over judgment; compassion and patience will cease. {7:33} Only judgment will remain, truth will stand, and faithfulness will prevail. {7:34} Recompense will follow, rewards will be revealed; righteous deeds will awaken, and unrighteous deeds will not sleep. {7:35} The pit of torment will appear, and opposite it the place of rest; hell's furnace will be exposed, and opposite it the paradise of delight. {7:36} The Most High will address the resurrected nations, saying, 'See whom you denied, whom you did not serve, whose commandments you despised! {7:37} Look here for delight and rest, there for fire and torment!' Thus he will speak on judgment day, {7:38} a day without sun, moon, stars, cloud, thunder, lightning, wind, water, air, darkness, evening, morning, {7:39} summer, spring, heat, winter, frost, cold, hail, rain, dew, noon, night, dawn, shining, brightness, or light. {7:40} Only the splendor of the Most High's glory will be visible, revealing each one's fate. {7:41} This will endure for about a week of years. {7:42} This is my judgment and its order; I have revealed this to you alone." {7:43} I replied, "O sovereign Lord, I declared then and now: Blessed are those alive who keep your commandments! {7:44} But what of those for whom I prayed? For who among the living has not sinned or transgressed your covenant? {7:45} Now I see the coming world will bring joy to few but torment to many. {7:46} An evil heart has separated us from God, leading to corruption, death's ways, and perdition, affecting nearly all of us, not just a few." {7:47} He answered, "Listen, Ezra, and I will instruct and admonish you again. {7:48} The Most High did not make one world but two. {7:49} You said the righteous are few and the ungodly many; let me explain. {7:50} If you have precious stones, would you mix them with lead and clay?" {7:51} I asked, "How could that be, Lord?" {7:52} He replied, "Ask the earth; she will tell you. Consult her, and she will declare it. {7:53} Tell her, 'You produce gold, silver, brass, iron, lead, and clay. {7:54} Silver is more abundant than gold, brass than silver, iron than brass, lead than iron, and clay than lead.' {7:55} Judge which are more precious and desirable, the abundant or the rare." {7:56} I said, "O sovereign Lord, what is abundant is of lesser value; what is rare is more precious." {7:57} He said, "Reflect on what you have thought. One rejoices more in what is hard to obtain than what is abundant. {7:58} Such will be my judgment; I will rejoice in the few saved, who have glorified my name. {7:59} I will not grieve for the multitude that perish; they are like mist, flame, smoke — ignited, blazing hot, then extinguished." {7:60} I responded, "O earth, what have you brought forth, if the mind, like other creations, arises from dust? {7:61} Better that dust never gave birth, so the mind would not exist. {7:62} Yet the mind grows with us, causing torment as we perish, aware of our fate. {7:63} Let humanity lament; let beasts and flocks rejoice. {7:64} Beasts do not expect judgment or know of torments or salvation after death. {7:65} What gain is it to preserve us in life, only to torment us cruelly? {7:66} All who are born are burdened with iniquities, sins, and transgressions. {7:67} If there were no judgment after death, perhaps it would be better for us." {7:68} He answered, "When the Most High made the world, Adam, and all from him, he prepared judgment and its matters first. {7:69} Consider your words: the mind grows with us. {7:70} Thus, those on earth will suffer, having understanding but committing iniquity. {7:71} Though they received commandments, they did not keep them, and though they had the law, they were unfaithful. {7:72} What will they say in judgment, how will they answer in the end times? {7:73} How long has the Most High patiently endured the world's inhabitants, not for their sake, but as foretold!" {7:74} I asked, "If I find favor, Lord, tell me: after death, when each yields their soul, {7:75} do we rest until your renewal of creation or face immediate torment?" {7:76}, He replied to me, saying, "I will reveal this to you, but do not associate with those who scorn, nor count yourself among the tormented. {7:77} You have a store of good deeds with the Most High, but it will not be shown until the end times. {7:78} Concerning death: when the final decree comes from the Most High for a person to die, as the spirit leaves the body to return to its Creator, it first worships the glory of the Most High. {7:79} But if it's someone who scorned, disobeyed His law, and hated those who fear God— {7:80} their spirits won't find rest in dwellings; instead, they'll wander in torment, grieving in seven ways. {7:81} First, because they scorned the law of the Most High. {7:82} Second, because they cannot repent now to live rightly. {7:83} Third, they'll see the rewards promised to those who trusted the covenants of the Most High. {7:84} Fourth, they'll contemplate the torments awaiting them in the last days. {7:85} Fifth, they'll witness how the dwellings of others are peacefully guarded by angels. {7:86} Sixth, they'll see some entering into torment. {7:87} Seventh, worst of all, they'll waste away in shame and fear before the glory of the Most High, whom they sinned against in life and face in judgment. {7:88} Now for those who kept the ways of the Most High, when they depart their mortal bodies— {7:89} during life, they diligently served the Most High, facing constant danger to uphold His law perfectly. {7:90} So this is their fate: {7:91} First, they'll joyously see the glory of the one who receives them, finding rest in seven orders. {7:92} First, they overcame evil thoughts that could lead them astray from life to death. {7:93} Second, they'll witness the anguish of ungodly souls and the punishment awaiting them. {7:94} Third, they'll see the testimony that their Creator bears, confirming their faithful life under His entrusted law. {7:95} Fourth, they'll enjoy the peace and angel-guarded quiet of their chambers, anticipating future glory. {7:96} Fifth, they'll rejoice in escaping corruption and inheriting what's to come, embracing the freedom and immortality they've earned. {7:97} Sixth, they'll see how their faces will shine like the sun, made incorruptible forever. {7:98} Seventh, the greatest order of all, they'll rejoice boldly, confident and without fear, eager to see the face of the One they served and from whom they'll receive their glorified reward. {7:99} This is the destiny of the righteous, as proclaimed henceforth; and these are the torments awaiting those who refused to heed. {7:100} I asked, 'Will souls have time after death to witness what you've described?' {7:101} He answered, 'They'll have seven days of freedom to see these things, then they'll be gathered to their dwellings.' {7:102} I asked further, 'On judgment day, can the righteous plead for the ungodly or appeal to the Most High?' {7:103} He replied, 'On that decisive day, {7:104} no one can intercede or burden another; {7:105} each will bear their own righteousness and unrighteousness.' {7:106} I asked, 'But didn't Abraham, Moses, Joshua, Samuel, David, Solomon, Elijah, Hezekiah, and many others pray for others?' {7:107} If the righteous pray for the ungodly now amidst rising corruption, why not then?' {7:108} He said, 'This world isn't the end; true glory isn't here. The strong pray for the weak now, but on judgment day, corruption will end, righteousness will reign, and no one can show mercy to the condemned or harm the victorious.' {36:109} I replied, 'Wouldn't it have been better if Adam hadn't sinned, or if his descendants hadn't failed so miserably? {7:110} What good is it to live in sorrow now and face punishment after death? {7:118} Adam's sin affected us all; our deeds bring death despite promises of an eternal age. {7:111} We've lived wickedly, missing out on safe havens and the defense of the Most High's glory. {7:112} Paradise awaits, but our unseemly lives keep us out. {7:113} Those who practiced self-control will shine, but we'll be in darkness. {7:114} While we lived in sin, we never thought of the suffering after death. {7:115} He replied, 'This is the struggle every person on earth faces: {7:116} If defeated, they suffer as you've said; if victorious, they receive what I've promised. {7:117} As Moses urged, 'Choose life, that you may live!' {7:118} But they didn't listen to Moses, the prophets, or even me. {7:119} So there'll be more joy over those saved than sorrow over those lost. {7:120} I know the Most High is called merciful for having mercy on those yet to come; gracious to those who repent; patient with sinners, His own creations; generous, giving more than taking; full of compassion, showing abundant mercy to those living, gone, and yet to come; {7:121} judged not for our iniquities; and spared for the most part of humanity. {7:122} If not for His goodness, few would survive."

{8:1} He responded, "The Most High created this world for the sake of many, but the world to come for the sake of few. {8:2} Let me tell you a parable, Ezra. Just as the earth yields much clay for pottery but only a little gold dust, so goes the course of the present world. {8:3} Many are born, but few will be saved." {8:4} I replied, "Therefore, my soul, drink deeply of understanding; my heart, imbibe wisdom! {8:5} You did not come into this world by your own choice, and against your will, you depart, given only a short time to live. {8:6} O Lord who reigns above, grant your servant the ability to pray before you. Give us fertile hearts and cultivate our understanding, that fruitful lives may result for all who bear the human likeness. {8:7} You alone exist, and we are your handiwork, as you have declared. {8:8} You give life to the body formed in the womb, furnishing it with limbs. What you create is preserved through fire and water, and for nine months, the womb endures your creation. {8:9} Both what is kept and what keeps shall be under your care. When the womb releases its creation, {8:10} you decree that from the breasts milk should nourish what has been formed, {8:11} sustaining it for a time, guided afterwards by your mercy. {8:12} You've raised us in righteousness, instructed us in your law, and corrected us with wisdom. {8:13} You take life away, for we are your creation; you make us live, for we are your work. {8:14} If you were to suddenly destroy the one you've meticulously fashioned by your command, what would be the purpose of his making? {8:15} Now I will speak: You know best about all humanity, but I speak of your people, for whom I grieve, {8:16} your inheritance, for whom I lament, Israel, for whom I am saddened, and the seed of Jacob, for whom I am troubled. {8:17} So I pray for myself and them, seeing our faults in this land {8:18} and hearing of the swift judgment to come. {8:19} Therefore, hear my voice, understand my words, and I will speak before you." The beginning of Ezra's prayer before he was taken up: {8:20} "O Lord, who dwells in eternity, whose eyes are exalted, whose upper chambers are in the air, {8:21} whose throne is immeasurable, whose glory is beyond understanding, before whom angels stand trembling, {8:22} at whose command they change to wind and fire, whose word is steadfast, whose decrees are certain, whose ordinances are strong, and whose commands are dreadful, {8:23} whose gaze dries up the abyss and melts mountains in anger, whose truth endures forever— {8:24} hear, O Lord, the prayer of your servant; listen to the plea of your creation; pay attention to my words. {8:25} As long as I live, I will speak; as long as I have understanding, I will answer. {8:26} Do not look upon the sins of your people, but on those who have served you faithfully. {8:27} Do not regard the actions of the wicked, but the efforts of those who kept your covenants despite afflictions. {8:28} Do not think of those who lived wickedly before your eyes; remember those who willingly acknowledged you with fear. {8:29} Do not desire to destroy those who behaved like cattle; but honor those who gloriously taught your law. {8:30} Do not be angry with those who are considered worse than animals; but love those who always trusted in your glory. {8:31} We and our ancestors have lived lives leading to death, yet you, in your mercy, are called compassionate because of us sinners. {8:32} If you desire to show mercy to us who lack righteous deeds, then indeed you are called merciful. {8:33} The righteous, with many works stored up with you, will receive their reward according to their deeds. {8:34} But what is man, that you are angry with him? What is a mortal race, that you are so bitter against it? {8:35} Indeed, no one born has been without sin, and no one who has existed has been without transgression. {8:36} Thus, O Lord, your righteousness and goodness are displayed when you show mercy to those lacking good works." {8:37} He replied, "You have spoken rightly about some things, and they will happen as you have said. {8:38} For I will not concern myself with those who have sinned, their fashioning, death, judgment, or destruction. {8:39} Instead, I will rejoice in the creation of the righteous, their journey, salvation, and reward. {8:40} As I have spoken, so it will be. {8:41} Just as a farmer sows many seeds in the ground and plants numerous seedlings, not all sown will sprout in due time, nor will all planted take root. Likewise, not all sown into the world will be saved." {8:42} I replied, "If I have found favor with you, let me speak. {8:43} If the farmer's seed fails to sprout because it lacked your timely rain or if it perishes from too much rain, {8:44} man, whom you formed with your hands, made in your image, for whom you created all things—did you also make him like the farmer's seed? {8:45} No, O Lord who reigns over us! Spare your people and have mercy on your inheritance, for you are merciful to your own creation." {8:46} He answered, "Present things are for those who live now, but future things are for those who will live afterward. {8:47} You fall short of loving my creation as much as I do. Yet you have often compared yourself to the unrighteous. Cease doing so! {8:48} Yet even in this matter, you will be praised before the Most High, {8:49} for you have humbled yourself fittingly and not considered yourself among the righteous to receive the greatest glory. {8:50} Many misfortunes will befall those who inhabit the world in the last times, due to their great pride. {8:51} Consider your own situation and inquire about the glory of those like you, {8:52} for paradise is opened for you, the tree of life planted, the age to come prepared, abundance provided, a city built, rest appointed, goodness established, and wisdom perfected beforehand. {8:53} Evil's root is sealed away from you, illness banished, death hidden, hell fled, and corruption forgotten; sorrows have passed, and finally, the treasure of immortality is revealed. {8:54} Therefore, do not inquire further about the multitude who perish. {8:55} They too received freedom but despised the Most High, scoffed at his law, and abandoned his ways. {8:56} They trampled on his righteous ones, {8:57} claiming in their hearts there is no God, knowing full well their impending death. {8:58} Just as what I have foretold awaits you, thirst and torment await those prepared. The Most High did not intend for men to be destroyed, {8:59} but those created have defiled the name of their Maker and been ungrateful to the one who prepared life for them. {8:60} So my judgment approaches; {8:61} I have not shown this to all men, but only to you and a few like you." Then I replied, {8:62} "Behold, O Lord, you have shown me many signs that you will perform in the last times, but you have not revealed when you will do them."

{9:1}, he replied to me, saying, "Pay close attention in your mind. When you observe that a portion of the predicted signs has come to pass, {9:2} then you will recognize that it is the precise moment when the Most High is preparing to visit the world He has created. {9:3} When earthquakes shake the earth, nations are in turmoil, leaders are uncertain, and princes are confused, {9:4} you will know that these were the things the Most High spoke of from ancient times, from the beginning. {9:5} Just as the beginning of everything in the world is evident and the end is clear, {9:6} so too are the times of the Most High: beginnings are marked by wonders and mighty works, and endings by retribution and signs. {9:7} Those who are saved, through their works or faith, will escape the foretold dangers and witness my salvation in the land I have sanctified since the beginning. {9:8} Those who have misused my ways will be astonished, and those who have scorned and rejected them will dwell in torment. {9:9} For those who did not acknowledge me in life, despite receiving my blessings, {9:10} and those who despised my law when they had freedom and opportunity for repentance, {9:11} will acknowledge their wrongdoing in torment after death. {9:12} Therefore, do not inquire further about how the ungodly will be punished, but focus on how the righteous will be saved—the ones for whom this age was made and to whom it belongs." {9:13} I responded, {9:14} "I've said before and will say again: more will perish than will be saved, as a wave is greater than a drop of water." {9:15} He answered me, {9:16} "As is the field, so is the seed; as are the flowers, so are the colors; as is the work, so is the product; as is the farmer, so is the threshing floor. {9:17} In this age, I prepared for those who now exist before the world was made for them to dwell in. No one opposed me then, for none existed. {9:18} But now, those created in this world, provided with an unfailing table and inexhaustible pasture, have become corrupted. {9:19} I observed my world and found it lost, my earth endangered by those who entered it. {9:20} I saw and with great difficulty spared some, saving one grape from a cluster and one plant from a vast forest. {9:21} Let the multitude born in vain perish, but let my chosen grape and plant be saved, perfected through much labor. {9:22} Yet if you wait another seven days—do not fast, but go to a field of flowers where no house stands, eat only the flowers, refrain from meat and wine, and pray continuously to the Most High—then I will come and speak with you." {9:23} So I followed his instructions, going to the field named Ardat, where I sat among the flowers and ate from the plants, finding sustenance in them. {9:24} After seven days, lying on the grass, my heart troubled me as before. {9:25} My mouth opened, and I began to speak before the Most High, {9:26} saying, "O Lord, you revealed yourself to our fathers in the wilderness, after they left Egypt and entered the untrodden, barren wilderness. {9:27} You said, 'Listen, O Israel, heed my words, descendants of Jacob. {9:28} I sow my law in you; it shall bear fruit and bring you everlasting glory.' {9:29} Our fathers received the law but did not obey or keep the statutes. {9:30} Yet the fruit of the law did not perish; it couldn't, for it was yours. {9:31} Those who received it perished for not keeping what was sown in them. {9:32} It's like when seed falls on ground, a ship sets sail, or food and drink are placed in a vessel—if destroyed, they perish, but the vessel remains. {9:33} Yet with us, it's different: we received the law, sinned, and will perish, including our hearts that received it, but the law endures in its glory." {9:34} Contemplating this in my heart, I looked up and saw a woman on my right, mourning and weeping loudly, deeply troubled and dressed in torn clothes with ashes on her head. {9:35} I set aside my thoughts and turned to her, {9:36} asking, "Why are you weeping? What troubles you so deeply?" {9:37} She replied, {9:38} "Leave me be, my lord, so I may weep for myself and continue to mourn. I am bitterly distressed in spirit and deeply afflicted." {9:39} I asked her, {9:40} "What has happened to you? Please, tell me." {9:41} She said to me, {9:42} "Your servant was barren, childless for thirty years with my husband. {9:43} Day and night throughout those years, I prayed earnestly to the Most High. {9:44} After thirty years, God heard my plea, saw my distress, and blessed me with a son. {9:45} I rejoiced greatly, as did my husband and neighbors; we gave great glory to the Mighty One. {9:46} I raised him with great care. {9:47} When he grew up and I prepared to find him a wife, I set a date for the wedding feast."

{10:1} my son entered his wedding chamber, he suddenly collapsed and died. {10:2} We extinguished the lamps, and neighbors tried to console me. I remained silent until the evening of the second day. {10:3} When their consoling ceased, I fled in the night to this field where you find me now. {10:4} I've decided not to return to the city; I'll stay here, neither eating nor drinking, mourning and fasting until my end." {10:5} I interrupted my thoughts and angrily replied to her, {10:6} "You foolish woman, do you not see our mourning and what has befallen us? {10:7} Zion, our mother, is deeply grieved and afflicted. {10:8} It's fitting to mourn now; we all mourn and sorrow. You grieve for one son, but we mourn for our entire world, our mother. {10:9} Ask the earth itself; it should mourn for the many born upon it. {10:10} From the beginning, all have been born from her, and more will come. Yet almost all face perdition, destined for destruction. {10:11} Who should mourn more—she who lost a multitude or you grieving for one? {10:12} If you say, 'My grief is unlike the earth's; I lost the fruit of my womb, born in pain,' {10:13} yet it's the same for the earth: the multitude it holds goes as it came. {10:14} As you bore in sorrow, the earth has from the start produced its fruit—man, for the Maker. {10:15} So bear your sorrow and bravely endure the trials. {10:16} If you accept God's justice, you will see your son again in due time and be honored among women. {10:17} Go back to the city to your husband." {10:18} She replied, "I will not. I'll die here." {10:19} I persisted, {10:20} "Do not say that. Be persuaded by Zion's troubles and comforted by Jerusalem's sorrow. {10:21} Our sanctuary lies desolate, the altar demolished, the temple destroyed. {10:22} Our harp lies silent, our song is stilled, our joy extinguished. The lamp's light is gone, the covenant ark plundered, our holy things defiled, our name dishonored. {10:23} Free men are abused, priests burned, Levites captive, virgins defiled, wives ravished. Righteous men are taken, little ones cast out, youth enslaved, strong men powerless. {10:24} Above all, Zion's seal—its glory—is lost to those who hate us. {10:25} So cast off your sadness and sorrows; let the Mighty One show mercy again and grant you relief." {10:26} While I spoke, her face suddenly shone brightly, her countenance flashing like lightning, terrifying me. Wondering what this meant, {10:27} she let out a loud, fearful cry that shook the earth. {10:28} I looked, but she was gone, replaced by a established city with vast foundations. Afraid, I cried out, {10:29} "Where is the angel Uriel who first came to me? He caused this overwhelming confusion; my end seems corrupted, my prayers a reproach." {10:30} As I spoke, the angel returned, {10:31} looking at me, lifting me up when I lay like a corpse, devoid of understanding. {10:32} He grasped my right hand, strengthened me, stood me on my feet, asking, {10:33} "What troubles you? Why is your understanding troubled?" {10:34} I said, "You left me! I followed your instructions, went to the field, and saw what I cannot explain." {10:35} He said, "Stand firm, and I will instruct you." {10:36} I said, "Speak, my lord, do not abandon me lest I die before my time. {10:37} I've seen the unknown, heard the incomprehensible. {10:38} Is my mind deceived, my soul dreaming? {10:39} Explain this bewildering vision to your servant." {10:40} He answered, {10:41} "Listen, I will inform you. The Most High revealed many secrets because he saw your righteousness, sorrowing continually for your people, mourning for Zion. {10:42} The woman who appeared, seen mourning, now an established city you saw— {10:43} she told of her son's misfortune, interpreted thus: {10:44} She you saw, now the city, is Zion. {10:45} Her barren years echo the world's three thousand before any offering. {10:46} After, Solomon's city rose, offerings made, the once-barren woman bore a son. {10:47} Her careful upbringing? Jerusalem's residence. {10:48} 'Son dies in the wedding chamber,' her misfortune, Jerusalem's destruction. {10:49} You consoled her for it. {10:50} The Most High, seeing your deep grief, revealed Zion's brilliance and beauty. {10:51} Stay in the field without buildings, {10:52} where the city of the Most High would show. {10:53} Fear not; see the grandeur where your eyes reach, {10:54} hear what your ears can. {10:55} You are blessed, called to the Most High, as few. {10:56} Remain here tomorrow night, {10:57} for the Most High will show what awaits earth's dwellers in the last days." {10:58} I slept, as commanded, that night and the next.

{11:1} In my dream on the second night, {11:2} I saw an eagle rising from the sea, with twelve feathered wings and three heads. {11:3} This eagle stretched its wings over the entire earth, caught in the winds of heaven with clouds gathering around it. {11:4} From its wings emerged opposing wings, though they were smaller and weaker. {11:5} The heads were at rest; the middle head larger but tranquil like the others. {11:6} I watched as the eagle flew, asserting dominion over the earth and its inhabitants. {11:7} All things under heaven bowed to its power; no creature challenged it. {11:8} Then the eagle raised on its talons, commanding its wings, {11:9} "Watch in turns; do not all be vigilant together." {11:10} The command did not come from the heads but from its body's midst. {11:11} I counted eight opposing wings. {11:12} One wing on the right rose and ruled over the earth, then vanished. {11:13} Another followed, reigning long before disappearing like the first. {11:14} A voice declared, {11:15} "You who ruled for so long, {11:16} know your reign is ending; none will rule as long again." {11:17} The third wing ruled briefly then vanished. {11:18} Thus all wings wielded power, then disappeared one by one. {11:19} Eventually, {11:20} only the eagle's three heads {11:21} and six small wings remained. {11:22} Two small wings moved under the right-side head, {11:23} while four stayed in place. {11:24} These small wings sought to rule. {11:25} One rose and vanished suddenly, {11:26} followed faster by another. {11:27} The remaining two planned to reign together. {11:28} Then the middle head, {11:29} greater than the others, awoke, allied with the two heads, {11:30} devouring the two small wings planning to rule. {11:31} This head then gained control over the earth, oppressing its inhabitants severely, surpassing the previous wings in power. {11:32} Soon, the middle head also vanished like the wings. {11:33} Only the two heads remained, ruling over the earth and its people. {11:34} The right-side head devoured the left. {11:35} Then I heard a voice saying, {11:36} "Look and understand." {11:36} I saw a lion-like creature rise from the forest, roaring with a human voice to the eagle, {11:37} saying, {11:38} "Listen to the Most High's message: {11:39} Are you the last of the four beasts I created to reign, bringing about the end of my times? {11:39} You, the fourth beast, conquered all before you, terrorizing the world with oppression and deceit. {11:40} You judged unjustly, afflicting the meek, harming the peaceful, hating truth and loving lies. {11:41} You destroyed the homes of the fruitful innocents. {11:42} Your arrogance and pride have reached the Most High and the Mighty One. {11:43} The Most High has seen the end of your time; your era is over. {11:44} Therefore, you, eagle, with your terrifying wings, malicious heads, and worthless body, will disappear. {11:45} The earth, freed from your violence, will find relief and await judgment and mercy from its Creator."

{12:1} As the lion spoke to the eagle, I observed and suddenly, the remaining head vanished. The two wings that had aligned with it rose up to rule but their reign was brief and tumultuous {12:2}. Soon, they too disappeared, and the entire eagle's body was consumed by fire, terrifying the earth greatly {12:3}. I woke in deep perplexity and fear, addressing my spirit {12:4}, "You have brought this upon me by seeking the ways of the Most High. My mind is weary and my spirit weak; I am left without strength due to the fear of this night. {12:5} Therefore, I pray to the Most High for strength until the end." {12:6} I pleaded, "O Lord, if I have found favor and righteousness before you, and if my prayers have reached you, {12:7} strengthen me and reveal the interpretation of this terrifying vision to comfort my soul completely. {12:8} You have deemed me worthy to see the end times and their events." {12:9} He answered, "This is the interpretation of the vision: {12:10} The eagle rising from the sea represents the fourth kingdom seen by Daniel, {12:11} though not as fully explained then as now to you. {12:12} In days to come, a kingdom more terrifying than any before will arise, {12:13} with twelve successive kings. {12:14} The second king will reign longest among the twelve. {12:15} The twelve wings symbolize these kings. {12:16} The voice heard from the eagle's body amidst its wings signifies great turmoil in the kingdom's midst times, almost falling but recovering. {12:17} The eight small wings {12:18} clinging to its wings represent eight short-reigning kings. {12:19} Two will perish near the midpoint, {12:20} four will remain until the end times, and two will persist until the very end. {12:21} The three heads at rest signify the Most High's raising of three kings in its final days, {12:22} who will rule oppressively and renew much upon the earth {12:23}. They are known as the heads of the eagle, {12:24} culminating its wickedness and actions. {12:25} The large head's disappearance indicates a king's death in bed, agonizingly {12:26}, while the remaining two heads will fall by the sword in the last days {12:27}. The two small wings passing to the right-side head signify their brief tumultuous reign, {12:28} leading to the eagle's end {12:29}. As for the lion seen rebuking the eagle, {12:30} speaking of its unrighteousness, {12:31} this is the Messiah, kept by the Most High until the end days, descended from David's lineage. {12:32} He will come, condemn their ungodliness and wickedness, reproving them before judgment, {12:33} saving the remnant of his people, bringing them joy until the final judgment, as foretold. {12:34} This is the dream and its interpretation. {12:35} Only you were worthy to learn this secret of the Most High. {12:36} Therefore, write all you've seen in a book, keep it hidden, and teach the wise among your people who can comprehend these secrets. {12:37} Wait here seven more days for further revelations." {12:38} After the people waited and I did not return to the city, {12:39} they gathered in concern, {12:40} asking why I had left them. They acknowledged my role as the last prophet among them {12:41}, a beacon of hope despite the ongoing tribulations. {12:42} They pleaded for my return, lamenting their plight. {12:43} I reassured them, {12:44} "Be strong, {12:45} O Israel & House of Jacob. {12:46} The Most High remembers you; He has not forgotten in your struggles. {12:47} I have not forsaken you but come here to pray for Zion's desolation and seek mercy for our sanctuary's humiliation. {12:48} Return to your homes now; I will come to you after these days." {12:49} The people obeyed and returned to the city, {12:50} while I remained in the field for 7 days as commanded, sustaining myself on wildflowers & plants.

{13:1} After seven days, I had a dream one night: {13:2} I saw a strong wind arise from the sea, stirring up its waves. {13:3} As I watched, a figure resembling a man emerged from the heart of the sea. He flew with the clouds of heaven, and wherever he looked, everything trembled. {13:4} When he spoke, his voice melted those who heard it, like wax before fire. {13:5} Then I saw an immense multitude gathered from the four winds of heaven, preparing to wage war against the man from the sea. {13:6} He carved out a great mountain for himself and ascended it. {13:7} I tried to discern where the mountain was carved from, but couldn't. {13:8} Those gathered against him were terrified, yet still dared to fight. {13:9} When he saw the approaching multitude, he did not raise a hand or wield any weapon. {13:10} Instead, he sent forth fire from his mouth, flaming breath, and a storm of sparks from his tongue. {13:11} This fiery onslaught consumed the multitude, reducing them to dust and ashes in an instant, leaving only the smell of smoke. I was astonished by what I saw. {13:12} Afterwards, the man descended from the mountain and called forth another peaceful multitude. {13:13} Some approached joyfully, others sorrowful, some bound, and others bringing offerings. Filled with fear, I awoke and prayed earnestly to the Most High, saying, {13:14} "You have shown me these wonders from the beginning, and deemed me worthy to have my prayers heard. {13:15} Now, reveal to me the interpretation of this dream. {13:16} As I ponder it, woe to those who will live in those days! Even greater woe to those who will not! {13:17} Those who are left will suffer sorrow, {13:18} understanding what awaits in the last days but unable to attain it. {13:19} Alas for those who remain, for they will face great danger and distress, as these dreams foretell. {13:20} Yet it is better to endure these perils and witness the events of the last days than to pass away like a cloud without knowing what is to come." {13:21} The Most High answered me, {13:22} "I will explain the vision and interpret what you have seen. {13:23} Regarding those who are left, know that they are blessed, protected by the One who brings peril in those times, those who have works and faith in the Almighty. {13:24} Understand that those who survive are more blessed than those who have died. {13:25} As for the man emerging from the sea, he is the one the Most High has preserved through ages, who will deliver his creation and guide those who remain. {13:26} The wind, fire, and storm from his mouth signify the tumultuous events to come. {13:27} He will not wield weapons but will destroy those who come to conquer him. {13:28} These are the days when the Most High will rescue the inhabitants of the earth. {13:29} Confusion will grip those who dwell on the earth, {13:30} planning wars among themselves—city against city, nation against nation—until my Son is revealed. {13:31} All nations will hear his voice, abandoning their lands and warfare to gather against him. {13:32} He will stand upon Mount Zion. {13:33} Zion will be revealed to all, as you saw the mountain carved without hands. {13:34} My Son will rebuke the nations for their ungodliness and torment them with fire and judgment. {13:35} He will effortlessly destroy them by the law. {13:36} The peaceful multitude you saw represents the ten tribes led away into captivity, now returning in peace. {13:37} Those left within my holy borders will be saved when he destroys the gathered nations. {13:38} He will reveal many wonders to them." {13:39} I asked, "Why did I see the man emerging from the sea?" {13:40} The Lord replied, {13:41} "Just as the depths of the sea are unfathomable, so are my Son and those with him, unseen except in their appointed time. {13:42} You alone have been enlightened because you have forsaken your ways for mine, sought my law, and devoted your life to wisdom and understanding." {13:43} The Most High revealed these things, promising to explain more weighty matters in three days.

{13:44} I rose and praised the Most High, marveling at his wonders and sovereignty over time & seasons. I stayed there for 3 days.

{14:1} On the third day, while sitting under an oak tree, I heard a voice calling from a bush nearby, saying, "Ezra, Ezra." {14:2} I answered, "Here I am, Lord," and I stood up. {14:3} The voice spoke to me, saying, "I revealed myself in a burning bush to Moses when my people were enslaved in Egypt. {14:4} I sent him to lead them out and took him up on Mount Sinai, where I kept him for many days. {14:5} I revealed to him many marvelous things and showed him the secrets of the times, declaring the end of days to him. I commanded him, saying, {14:6} 'Some of these words you shall proclaim openly, and some you shall keep secret.' {14:7} Now I say to you, {14:8} Remember and treasure the signs, dreams, and interpretations I have shown you. {14:9} For you will be taken away from among men and will dwell with my Son and those like you until the end of times. {14:10} The age has passed its prime, and the times grow old. {14:11} Divided into twelve parts, nine of them have already passed, along with half of the tenth part; two parts remain, plus half of the tenth. {14:12} Therefore, prepare yourself, set your house in order, reprove your people, comfort the humble, and instruct the wise. Renounce corruptible life, {14:13} abandon mortal thoughts, cast off the burdens of humanity, and shed your weak nature. {14:14} Turn away from your most grievous thoughts and hasten to escape these times. {14:15} Worse evils than you have seen will come. {14:16} As the world weakens with age, evils will multiply among its inhabitants. {14:17} Truth will recede, and falsehood will advance. The eagle you saw in the vision is swiftly approaching." {14:18} I replied, "Let me speak before you, Lord. {14:19} I will go as you have commanded and reprove the current generation, but who will warn those yet to be born? The world is in darkness, lacking light. {14:20} Your law has been neglected, and no one knows what has been done or will be done by you. {14:21} If I have found favor with you, send the Holy Spirit to me, that I may write down everything from the beginning of the world, as recorded in your law. {14:22} This will guide men on the path, enabling those in the last days to live." {14:23} He answered, "Gather the people and tell them not to seek you for forty days. {14:24} Prepare many writing tablets and take Sarea, Dabria, Selemia, Ethanus, and Asiel with you—they are skilled in swift writing. {14:25} Come back here, and I will illuminate your heart with understanding, which will endure until you finish writing. {14:26} Afterward, make some writings public and entrust others to the wise in secret. Start writing tomorrow at this hour." {14:27} I obeyed and gathered the people, proclaiming, {14:28} "Listen, O Israel! Our ancestors were strangers in Egypt and were delivered from there. {14:29} They received the law of life but did not keep it, just as you have also transgressed. {14:30} You were given land in Zion, but you and your forefathers committed iniquity and disobeyed the Most High's commands. {14:31} Therefore, he took back what he had given, for he is a just judge. {14:32} Now you are here, and your brothers are farther away. {14:33} If you govern your minds and discipline your hearts, you will live and find mercy after death. {14:34} Judgment follows death, and then the names of the righteous will be revealed while the deeds of the ungodly will be exposed. {14:35} Do not approach me now; do not seek me for forty days." {14:36} So I took the five men as commanded and went to the field, where we stayed. {14:37} The next day, a voice instructed me, saying, "Ezra, open your mouth and drink what I give you." {14:38} I opened my mouth, and a full cup was offered to me, containing something like fiery water. {14:39} I drank it, and my heart overflowed with understanding; wisdom grew within me, and my mouth was opened. {14:40} The Most High granted understanding to the five men, who wrote down what was dictated in unfamiliar characters. {14:41} They wrote during the day, and we ate bread at night, continuing this for forty days. {14:42} During this time, I spoke in the day and did not keep silent at night. {14:43} Ninety-four books were written in these forty days. {14:44} When the forty days ended, the Most High said to me, "Publish the twenty-four books you wrote first; let both the worthy and the unworthy read them. {14:45} Keep the seventy books written last, for they contain the spring of understanding, the fountain of wisdom, and the river of knowledge, to be given to the wise among your people." {14:46} I did as commanded.

{15:1} The Lord declares, "Listen as I speak to my people the words of prophecy that I will place in your mouth. {15:2} Have them written down, for they are trustworthy and true. {15:3} Do not fear the schemes devised against you, nor be troubled by the disbelief of those who oppose you. {15:4} Every unbeliever will perish in their unbelief." {15:5} "Behold," says the Lord, "I bring upon the world evils: sword, famine, death, and destruction. {15:6} Iniquity has spread throughout every land, and their harmful deeds have reached their limit. {15:7} Therefore," says the Lord, {15:8} "I will no longer remain silent about their ungodly deeds, nor tolerate their wicked practices. Innocent blood and righteous souls cry out to me continually. {15:9} I will surely avenge them," says the Lord, "and will gather to myself all the innocent blood shed among them. {15:10} My people are led like sheep to the slaughter; I will no longer allow them to remain in the land of Egypt. {15:11} With a mighty hand and an outstretched arm, I will bring them out and strike Egypt with plagues as before, and lay waste to its entire land." {15:12} Let Egypt mourn, along with its foundations, for the punishment and chastisement the Lord will bring upon it. {15:13} Let the farmers who till the ground mourn, for their seeds will fail and their trees will be ruined by blight, hail, and terrible storms. {15:14} Alas for the world and its inhabitants! {15:15} Sword and misery draw near, and nation will rise against nation with swords in hand. {15:16} There will be unrest among men; they will grow strong against each other, showing no respect for their king or leaders. {15:17} A man will desire to enter a city but will not be able. {15:18} Because of their pride, cities will be in turmoil, houses destroyed, and people filled with fear. {15:19} Men will show no mercy to their neighbors, assaulting their houses with swords and plundering their goods due to hunger and great tribulation. {15:20} "Behold," declares God, "I summon all the kings of the earth to fear me, from the rising of the sun, from the south, from the east, and from Lebanon. They will turn and repay what they have been given. {15:21} Just as they have treated my chosen ones until now, so I will act and repay into their bosom," declares the Lord God. {15:22} "My right hand will not spare the sinners, and my sword will not cease from those who shed innocent blood on the earth." {15:23} His wrath will send forth fire, consuming the foundations of the earth and sinners like kindling straw. {15:24} "Woe to those who sin and do not obey my commandments," says the Lord. {15:25} "I will not spare them. Depart, you faithless children! Do not defile my sanctuary." {15:26} The Lord knows all who transgress against him; he will hand them over to death and slaughter. {15:27} Calamities have now come upon the entire earth, and you will endure them; for God will not deliver you, because you have sinned against him. {15:28} Behold, a terrifying vision appears from the east! {15:29} The nations of the dragons of Arabia will come out with many chariots, and from the day they set out, their hissing will spread over the earth, causing fear and trembling in all who hear them. {15:30} Also, the Carmonians, raging with wrath, will go forth like wild boars from the forest. With great power, they will come and engage in battle, devastating a portion of the Assyrian land with their teeth. {15:31} Then the dragons, recalling their origin, will become even stronger; if they unite in great power and turn to pursue them, {15:32} these adversaries will be disorganized and silenced by their might, fleeing in confusion. {15:33} From the land of Assyria, an enemy lying in wait will besiege them, striking down one of them with destruction, causing fear and trembling in their army, and indecision among their kings. {15:34} Behold, clouds come from the east, and from the north to the south, their appearance threatening, full of wrath and storm. {15:35} They will clash against each other, unleashing a severe tempest upon the earth, and their own tempest. There will be blood from the sword up to a horse's belly and a man's thigh and a camel's hock. {15:36} Fear and great trembling will come upon the earth; those who witness this wrath will be horrified and seized with trembling. {15:37} Afterward, heavy storm clouds will be stirred up from the south, north, and another part from the west. {15:38} The winds from the east will prevail over the wrathful cloud, dispelling it; the tempest intended for destruction by the east wind will violently drive toward the south and west. {15:39} Great and mighty clouds, full of wrath and tempest, will rise to destroy the entire earth and its inhabitants, pouring out a terrible tempest upon every high and lofty place, {15:40} fire, hail, flying swords, and floods of water, filling all fields and streams with their abundance. {15:41} They will destroy cities, walls, mountains, hills, forests' trees, meadows' grass, and crops. {15:42} They will proceed relentlessly to Babylon and lay it waste. {15:43} They will surround Babylon, unleashing the tempest and all its wrath upon it. Dust and smoke will rise to the heavens, and those around will lament. {15:44} Those who survive will serve those who destroyed Babylon. {15:45} Asia, sharing Babylon's glamour and her pride's glory—woe to you! {15:46} You have made yourself like her, adorning your daughters in harlotry to please and revel in your lovers, always lusting after you. {15:47} You have imitated that detestable harlot in all her deeds and devices. Therefore, God declares, {15:48} "I will send evils upon you: widowhood, poverty, famine, sword, and pestilence, laying waste your homes and bringing you to ruin and death. {15:49} The splendor of your power will wither like a flower when the heat rises against you. {15:50} You will be weakened like a beaten, wounded woman, unable to receive your mighty lovers. {15:51} Would I have dealt so harshly," says the Lord, {15:52} "if you had not continually killed my chosen people, rejoicing and clapping at their deaths while drunk? {15:53} Adorn your face's beauty! {15:54} A harlot's reward is in your bosom; therefore, you will receive your retribution. {15:55} As you have done to my chosen people," says the Lord, "so God will do to you, delivering you to adversity. {15:56} Your children will die of hunger, you will fall by the sword, your cities will be razed, and all your people in the open country will perish by the sword. {15:57} Those in the mountains and highlands will perish from hunger, eating their own flesh in bread's hunger and drinking their blood in water's thirst. {15:58} You will be more miserable than others, coming to suffer new afflictions. {15:59} They will wreck the detested city, destroying part of your land and removing some of your glory, returning from Babylon's devastation. {15:60} They will break you down like stubble, becoming fire to you. {15:61} They will consume you and your cities, your land and your mountains, burning all your forests and fruitful trees with fire. {15:62} They will take your children captive, plunder your wealth, and remove the splendor from your face."

{16:1} Woe to Babylon and Asia, woe to Egypt and Syria! {16:2} Prepare yourselves with mourning garments, lament for your children, for your destruction is imminent. {16:3} The sword is sent against you; who can turn it back? {16:4} Fire is unleashed upon you; who can extinguish it? {16:5} Calamities are upon you; who can drive them away? {16:6} Can a hungry lion be chased away in the forest, or a fire quenched once it starts to burn? {16:7} Can an arrow shot by a strong archer be turned back? {16:8} The Lord God sends calamities; who can prevent them? {16:9} Fire will go forth from his wrath; who can quench it? {16:10} He will flash lightning; who will not be afraid? He will thunder; who will not be terrified? {16:11} The Lord's presence will shatter all before him; the earth and sea will tremble. {16:12} His mighty arrows will strike to the ends of the earth, sharp and unerring. {16:13} Once unleashed, these calamities will not retreat from the earth. {16:14} Fire is kindled that will consume the foundations of the earth. {16:15} Just as an arrow shot by a skilled archer does not return, so these calamities will not relent. {16:16} Alas for me! Alas for me! Who will deliver me in those days? {16:17} These are the beginnings of sorrows: lamentations, famine, wars, and calamities that will cause all to tremble. {16:18} These scourges are sent to correct humanity, yet many will not turn from their iniquities. {16:19} Famine, plague, tribulation, and anguish will afflict the earth. {16:20} Despite this, people will not repent or heed the warnings. {16:21} False peace will deceive many before sudden calamities—sword, famine, and confusion—overwhelm the earth. {16:22} Many will perish by famine, and those surviving will perish by the sword. {16:23} The dead will lie unburied, and desolation will reign. {16:24} There will be no one left to cultivate the earth or sow it. {16:25} Trees will bear fruit in vain; who will harvest it? {16:26} Grapes will ripen unharvested; who will tread them? {16:27} Solitude will spread across the land; people will long for companionship but find none. {16:28} From a city, ten will be left; from the field, two hiding in groves and caves. {16:29} Like olives left on the tree after harvest or grapes overlooked in the vineyard, so few will remain. {16:30} In those days, few will survive the sword as they search for refuge. {16:31} The earth will be desolate, overrun with thorns, its roads deserted. {16:32} Virgins will mourn without bridegrooms; women without husbands; daughters without protectors. {16:33} Their men will perish in war or famine. {16:34} Listen, servants of the Lord, and understand these words. {16:35} Embrace the word of the Lord; do not doubt what he says. {16:36} Calamity approaches swiftly, without delay. {16:37} As a woman in labor knows her time has come, so will these calamities swiftly come forth upon the earth, causing it to groan in pain. {16:38} Prepare yourselves, O people; be vigilant amidst calamity, living as strangers in your own land. {16:39} Those who sell should do so as if fleeing; those who buy, as if losing; those who engage in commerce, as if gaining nothing; those who build, as if not dwelling in their homes; {16:41} those who plant, as if not reaping; those who prune, as if not gathering grapes; {16:42} those who marry, as if having no children; those who abstain, as if widowed. {16:43} Labor will be in vain; strangers will plunder and ravage. {16:44} Business ventures will end in plunder; cities and homes will be adorned only to provoke divine anger. {16:45} God will judge the righteous and the wicked, separating righteousness from iniquity. {16:46} Let no one claim innocence before God, for all will be judged. {16:47} The Lord knows every deed, thought, and intention of the heart. {16:48} He commands creation with a word, knows the stars' number, and searches the depths of the earth. {16:49} He knows your thoughts and intentions. Woe to those who sin and seek to hide it! {16:50} The Lord will expose every sin and judge it publicly. {16:51} When your sins are laid bare, shame will be your companion. {16:52} Do not hide your sins from God; repent and turn from iniquity. {16:53} God is the righteous judge; fear him and forsake your sins, for he will deliver you from tribulation. {16:54} A multitude's fiery wrath is kindled against the wicked; they will suffer indignity and oppression. {16:55} Those who persist in sin will face revolt and destruction from those who fear the Lord. {16:56} The tested quality of the elect will shine like gold purified by fire. {16:57} "Listen, my chosen ones," declares the Lord. "The days of tribulation are near, but I will deliver you. {16:58} Fear not, for God guides you. {16:59} Keep my commandments and precepts," says the Lord God. "Do not let sin drag you down or iniquity overwhelm you. {16:60} Woe to those choked by their sins and overwhelmed by iniquity, destined for destruction."

1 Maccabees

The book of 1 Maccabees, a significant historical text within the Apocrypha, offers a detailed account of the Jewish struggle for independence during the 2nd century BCE. Set against the backdrop of the Hellenistic period, it chronicles the events from the rise of Antiochus IV Epiphanes to the establishment of the Hasmonean dynasty, emphasizing the revolt led by Judas Maccabeus and his brothers. This text, originally written in Hebrew but surviving in Greek through the Septuagint, is crucial for understanding the socio-political and religious upheavals of the era. It provides a narrative that intertwines the military, religious, and political aspects of the Jewish resistance against the Seleucid Empire's imposition of Hellenistic culture and practices. The book's historical narrative is marked by detailed descriptions of battles, strategies, and alliances, reflecting a keen interest in the military history of the period. Furthermore, 1 Maccabees highlights themes of piety, loyalty, and divine intervention, presenting the Maccabean leaders as devout figures chosen by God to deliver Israel. The work's historiographical style combines annalistic and episodic elements, offering both a chronological framework and detailed accounts of specific events. Its portrayal of the Maccabean revolt has been pivotal in Jewish historiography and collective memory, influencing subsequent Jewish literature and thought.

{1:1} After Alexander, son of Philip the Macedonian from the land of Greece, defeated Darius, the king of Persia and Media, he succeeded him as king. {1:2} Alexander waged numerous battles, captured fortified cities, and executed kings across the known world. {1:3} His conquests extended to distant lands, plundering many nations. As the earth quieted before him, his pride soared. {1:4} Amassing a formidable army, he ruled over lands, nations, and princes, exacting tribute from all. {1:5} Later, falling gravely ill, he realized his end was near. {1:6} Summoning his trusted officers, who had been with him since youth, he divided his kingdom among them while still alive. {1:7} After reigning twelve years, Alexander passed away. {1:8} His officers then assumed their respective rulerships. {1:9} Each took the throne, passing it down through their descendants, causing great turmoil in the land. {1:10} From this line arose a sinful ruler, Antiochus Epiphanes, son of King Antiochus, who had been a hostage in Rome. He seized power in the one hundred and thirty-seventh year of Greek rule. {1:11} During his reign, lawless men from Israel emerged, persuading many to form alliances with neighboring Gentiles, claiming it would bring prosperity. {1:12} This proposal found favor among some, {1:13} and they approached the king, who sanctioned their adoption of Gentile customs. {1:14} They erected a gymnasium in Jerusalem, following Gentile practices, {1:15} abandoned circumcision, and renounced the sacred covenant, joining in evil practices. {1:16} Antiochus, secure in his kingdom, aimed to conquer Egypt, aspiring to rule both kingdoms. {1:17} Leading a mighty force including chariots, elephants, cavalry, and a large fleet, he invaded Egypt. {1:18} He clashed with Ptolemy, the Egyptian king, who fled in defeat, leaving many wounded. {1:19} Antiochus seized fortified cities and plundered Egypt before returning triumphant. {1:20} Subsequently, in the one hundred and forty-third year, he turned his attention to Israel, marching on Jerusalem with a powerful army. {1:21} Brazenly entering the sanctuary, he seized the golden altar, lampstand, and all its sacred vessels. {1:22} He looted the temple's treasures, including silver, gold, and costly artifacts. {1:23} Departing with his spoils, he committed acts of murder and boasted in his arrogance. {1:24} Israel mourned deeply; {1:25} rulers, elders, maidens, and young men lamented as the land trembled in shame. {1:26} Every wedding became a mourning; joy turned to sorrow. {1:27} The land shook under its inhabitants; all of Jacob's house was clothed in shame. {1:28} Two years later, the king dispatched a tax collector to Judah's cities, who arrived in Jerusalem with a formidable force. {1:29} Deceptively speaking peace, he deceived them; then suddenly attacked, inflicting great harm and death upon Israel. {1:30} He plundered and burned Jerusalem, destroying homes and walls. {1:31} Capturing women, children, and livestock, he fortified the city of David with a strong wall and towers. {1:32} He stationed lawless people there, amassing weapons and provisions from Jerusalem's spoils, creating a formidable threat to the sanctuary. {1:33} The sanctuary became a place of ambush, an adversary of Israel, shedding innocent blood on all sides. {1:34} Because of this, Jerusalem's inhabitants fled, becoming a stranger in their own land; their offspring abandoned them. {1:35} The sanctuary lay desolate as a desert; feasts turned to mourning, and sabbaths to shame. {1:36} Dishonor overshadowed former glory, and exaltation turned to mourning. {1:37} The king then decreed across his kingdom that all should unite under one people, forsaking their customs. {1:38} Many Gentiles and even some from Israel embraced his decree, sacrificing to idols and desecrating sabbaths. {1:39} The king sent decrees to Jerusalem and Judah, commanding foreign customs be followed, banning burnt offerings, sacrifices, and sabbath observances in the sanctuary. {1:40} He defiled the sanctuary, its priests, and established altars and shrines for idols, sacrificing unclean animals. {1:41} Sons were left uncircumcised, defiling themselves with every abomination, forsaking the law and changing ordinances. {1:42} Anyone who disobeyed faced death, as the king's decree was enforced throughout the cities of Judah. {1:43} Many people, forsaking the law, joined them, perpetrating evil in the land, driving Israel into hiding. {1:44} On the fifteenth day of Chislev, in the one hundred and forty-fifth year, they desecrated the altar with an abomination. {1:45} They erected altars in Judah's cities, burning incense at house doors and in streets. {1:46} They tore and burned the law wherever found; those found with the covenant faced death by the king's decree. {1:47} They oppressed Israel month after month in the cities. {1:48} On the twenty-fifth day of the month, sacrifices were offered on the altar of burnt offering. {1:49} Women who circumcised their children were put to death, along with their families. {1:50} Israel's devout resisted, refusing to eat unclean food or defile the holy covenant, even unto death. {1:51} Israel endured great wrath.

{2:1} During that time, Mattathias, son of John and descendant of Simeon, a priest of the Joarib lineage, left Jerusalem and settled in Modein. {2:2} He had five sons: John, known as Gaddi, {2:3} Simon, called Thassi, {2:4} Judas, known as Maccabeus, {2:5} Eleazar, called Avaran, and Jonathan, known as Apphus. {2:6} Seeing the blasphemies in Judah and Jerusalem, {2:7} he lamented, "Why was I born to witness the destruction of my people and our holy city? To live here as it falls to enemies, our sanctuary desecrated by foreigners? {2:8} Our temple, once honored, now dishonored; {2:9} its sacred vessels taken captive. Our children slaughtered in the streets, our youth slain by enemy swords. {2:10} Every nation has plundered her palaces and seized her treasures. {2:11} Stripped of all its splendor, she is enslaved, no longer free. {2:12} Our holy place, once so beautiful and glorious, now lies in ruins, defiled by Gentiles. {2:13} What reason do we have to continue living?" {2:14} Mattathias and his sons tore their clothes, donned sackcloth, and mourned deeply. {2:15} Then the king's officers enforcing apostasy came to Modein to compel them to offer sacrifice. {2:16} Many from Israel complied, but Mattathias and his sons assembled together. {2:17} The king's officers addressed Mattathias, "You are a respected leader in this city, supported by sons and brothers. {2:18} Be the first to obey the king's command, as all Gentiles and the remaining men of Judah and Jerusalem have done. Then you and your sons will be honored with silver, gold, and many gifts as friends of the king." {2:19} Mattathias replied loudly, "Even if all nations under the king's rule obey and forsake their ancestral faith, {2:20} I, my sons, and my brothers will uphold the covenant of our fathers. {2:21} We will not stray from our religion to the right or left to obey the king's words." {2:22} When he finished speaking, a Jew stepped forward in sight of all to offer sacrifice on the altar in Modein, as the king commanded. {2:23} Mattathias, filled with zeal, was stirred to action. He slew him on the altar in righteous anger. {2:24} Simultaneously, he killed the king's officer forcing them to sacrifice and tore down the altar. {2:25} Thus, he burned with zeal for the law, reminiscent of Phinehas against Zimri son of Salu. {2:26} Mattathias then cried out in the city, "Let all who are zealous for the law and uphold the covenant come with me!" {2:27} He and his sons fled to the hills, leaving all they had in the city. {2:28} Many seeking righteousness and justice joined them in the wilderness, {2:29} along with their families and livestock, oppressed by evils. {2:30} The king's officers and troops in Jerusalem were informed that those who defied the king's command had taken refuge in wilderness hideouts. {2:31} They pursued and encamped against them, preparing to battle on the Sabbath. {2:32} They demanded, "Enough! Come out and obey the king's command to live!" {2:33} They replied, "We will not come out or disobey the king's command to desecrate the Sabbath." {2:34} The enemy attacked swiftly. {2:35} Yet they did not resist or defend themselves, declaring, "Let us die in innocence. Heaven and earth testify against you, unjustly killing us." {2:36} They were attacked on the Sabbath, and a thousand perished, including their wives, children, and livestock. {2:37} Mattathias and his friends deeply mourned upon learning of this. {2:38} Each said to the other, "If we refuse to fight for our lives and laws like our brethren, the Gentiles will destroy us swiftly." {2:39} That day, they decided, "Let us fight anyone attacking us on the Sabbath. Let us not perish like our brethren in hiding." {2:40} They were joined by a company of Hasideans, brave warriors who volunteered for the law. {2:41} All who fled troubles to join them strengthened their ranks. {2:42} They formed an army, striking sinners in anger and lawbreakers in wrath; survivors sought refuge among the Gentiles. {2:43} Mattathias and his allies demolished altars; {2:44} they forcibly circumcised uncircumcised boys in Israel's borders. {2:45} They pursued arrogant men, their work prospering. {2:46} They preserved the law from Gentiles and kings, never allowing sinners to prevail. {2:47} As Mattathias neared death, he told his sons, "Arrogance and reproach are strong; it is a time of ruin and fury. {2:48} My children, be courageous and uphold the law. By it, you will gain honor. {2:49} Remember the deeds of our forefathers, who were honored and remembered. {2:50} Show zeal for the law and give your lives for our ancestors' covenant. {2:51} Abraham's faith was counted as righteousness in his test. {2:52} Joseph obeyed in distress and became lord of Egypt. {2:53} Phinehas, zealous, received an everlasting priesthood covenant. {2:54} Joshua judged Israel for fulfilling the command. {2:55} Caleb, witnessing in assembly, inherited land. {2:56} David's mercy won him an eternal throne. {2:57} Elijah, zealous for the law, ascended to heaven. {2:58} Hananiah, Azariah, and Mishael, believing, were saved from fire. {2:59} Daniel's innocence saved him from lions' mouths. {2:60} Trust in God gives strength from generation to generation. {2:61} Fear not sinners' words; their splendor turns to waste. {2:62} They are exalted today, but tomorrow are dust; their plans perish. {2:63} Be strong in the law, my children, gaining honor by it. {2:64} Simeon, your wise brother, shall be your father, always listen to him. {2:65} Judas Maccabeus, a mighty warrior, shall lead the army and fight against peoples. {2:66} Gather those who uphold the law; avenge your people's wrongs. {2:67} Repay Gentiles in full, obeying the law's commands." {2:68} Mattathias blessed them and joined his fathers in death. {2:69} He died at one hundred and forty-six, buried in his fathers' tomb at Modein. All Israel mourned him greatly.

{3:1} Then Judas, known as Maccabeus, took command after his father. {3:2} Supported by his brothers and those loyal to his father, they fought willingly for Israel. {3:3} Judas adorned himself like a giant, putting on his armor and waging war, defending his people with his sword. {3:4} His deeds were fierce like a lion's, roaring against his prey. {3:5} He sought out and punished the lawless, burning those who troubled his people. {3:6} His reputation made lawless men tremble; all evildoers were confused, and deliverance thrived by his hand. {3:7} He frustrated many kings, bringing joy to Jacob through his deeds; his memory is blessed forever. {3:8} He traveled through Judah's cities, purging the land of the ungodly, turning away wrath from Israel. {3:9} His fame spread to distant lands; he gathered the perishing. {3:10} Apollonius gathered Gentiles and a large force from Samaria to fight Israel. {3:11} Hearing this, Judas confronted and defeated him, causing many casualties; the rest fled. {3:12} They seized spoils, and Judas wielded Apollonius's sword for the remainder of his life. {3:13} Seron, Syrian army commander, heard of Judas's growing force and set out to battle. {3:14} Seeking personal glory and the king's favor, he aimed to wage war on Judas and his followers, who defied the king's commands. {3:15} With a strong army, he marched to aid in avenging Israel's sons. {3:16} Approaching Beth-horon's ascent, Judas met him with a small band. {3:17} Seeing the approaching army, Judas's men hesitated, overwhelmed by their size and their hunger. {3:18} Judas reassured them, "Heaven doesn't judge victory by numbers; many can be overwhelmed by a few." {3:19} Victory doesn't hinge on army size; strength comes from Heaven. {3:20} The enemy's pride and lawlessness threaten to destroy us, our families, and our possessions, but we fight for our lives and our laws. {3:21} He will crush them; do not fear them." {3:22} With these words, he charged against Seron and his army, crushing them. {3:23} Pursuing them to Beth-horon's descent, eight hundred fell, and the rest fled to Philistine lands. {3:24} Judas and his brothers became feared, spreading terror among Gentiles. {3:25} His fame reached the king, and Gentiles spoke of Judas's battles. {3:26} King Antiochus, angered by these reports, assembled a strong army from across his kingdom. {3:27} He funded them generously for immediate readiness and future expenses. {3:28} When he saw treasury funds dwindling due to turmoil from his law changes, {3:29} he feared future financial shortages and sought additional revenues from Persia. {3:30} Distressed, he left Lysias in charge from the Euphrates to Egypt, with half his army and elephants. {3:31} Lysias was tasked with managing Antiochus's affairs and his son's welfare until his return. {3:32} Antiochus commanded Lysias to eradicate Judea's strength and Jerusalem's remnants, resettling foreigners and confiscating land. {3:33} Taking the remaining troops, Antiochus departed from Antioch in his 147th year, crossing the Euphrates to upper provinces. {3:34} Lysias, aided by Ptolemy, Nicanor, and Gorgias, marched with forty thousand infantry and seven thousand cavalry into Judah as commanded by the king. {3:35} They encamped near Emmaus in the plain, where local traders came with immense wealth of silver, gold, and chains to trade for Israelites as slaves. {3:36} Judas and his brothers saw the escalating threats and the army encamped on their land. They learned of the king's plan to destroy them and their people. {3:37} They resolved, "Let us repair our people's ruin, fight for our people and our sanctuary." {3:38} The assembly readied for battle, fasting, donning sackcloth, and sprinkling ashes. {3:39} They consulted the Law about matters Gentiles sought from their idols. {3:40} They brought priestly garments, first fruits, tithes, and rallied Nazirites who had completed their vows, crying to Heaven, "Our sanctuary is trampled and desecrated; our priests mourn in shame. {3:41} Gentiles unite to destroy us; you know their plots against us. {3:42} Without your help, how can we withstand them?" {3:43} They sounded trumpets and shouted loudly. {3:44} Judas appointed leaders over thousands, hundreds, fifties, and tens. {3:45} He instructed those building, betrothed, planting, or fearful to return home as the law prescribed. {3:46} The army camped south of Emmaus. {3:47} Judas urged, "Prepare yourselves; be courageous. Tomorrow morning, we fight these assembled Gentiles who seek our destruction and that of our sanctuary. {3:48} It's better to die in battle than witness our nation's ruin and our sanctuary's desecration. {3:49} May Heaven's will prevail."

{4:1} Gorgias led five thousand infantry and a thousand elite cavalry, moving under cover of night to ambush the Jewish camp. {4:2} Guided by locals from the citadel, he aimed to strike the Jews by surprise. {4:3} However, Judas learned of the plan and marched with his formidable men to confront the king's forces at Emmaus, while Gorgias's division was away. {4:4} Finding Judas's camp empty upon arrival, Gorgias assumed the Jews had fled to the hills. {4:5} At daybreak, Judas and three thousand men appeared on the plain, lacking the desired armor and swords. {4:6} They faced a fortified Gentile camp with skilled cavalry surrounding it. {4:7} But Judas encouraged his men, saying, "Do not fear their numbers or their charge. {4:8} Remember how our ancestors were saved at the Red Sea when Pharaoh pursued them. {4:9} Let us cry out to Heaven to favor us today, remembering his covenant with our fathers, and crush this army before us. {4:10} Then all the Gentiles will know that there is one who redeems and saves Israel." {4:11} When the Gentiles saw Judas's approach, they left their camp to battle. {4:12} Judas's men blew their trumpets and engaged in combat. The Gentiles were defeated and fled into the plain; {4:13} those in the rear fell by the sword. Pursuing them to Gazara, Idumea's plains, Azotus, and Jamnia, three thousand were slain. {4:14} Judas and his men turned back from pursuit, {4:15} and he warned against greed for plunder, as Gorgias and his forces remained in the hills. {4:16} Suddenly, a detachment emerged from the hills, seeing their army routed and the Jews burning the camp, the smoke signaling the outcome. {4:17} Terrified, they fled to Philistine lands upon sighting Judas's army assembled for battle on the plain. {4:18} Judas then plundered the camp, seizing much gold, silver, dyed cloth, purple, and other riches. {4:19} On their return, they praised Heaven with hymns and thanks, acknowledging his enduring mercy. {4:20} Thus Israel celebrated a great deliverance that day. {4:21} Survivors among the Gentiles reported all to Lysias, who was dismayed as events unfolded differently than intended. {4:22} The next year, he amassed sixty thousand infantry and five thousand cavalry to subdue them. {4:23} They encamped at Beth-zur in Idumea, where Judas met them with ten thousand men. {4:24} Seeing the formidable army, Judas prayed, "Blessed are you, O Savior of Israel, who crushed the mighty warrior through your servant David's hand. {4:25} May you confound this army through your people Israel, humbling their troops and cavalry. {4:26} Fill them with fear, weakening their boldness; let them tremble in their defeat. {4:27} Strike them down by the sword of those who love you, that all who know your name may sing your praises." {4:28} Both sides clashed, and Lysias's army lost five thousand men in battle. {4:29} Observing the boldness and courage of Judas's forces, Lysias withdrew to Antioch, recruiting mercenaries for another assault on Judea with a larger force. {4:30} Judas and his brothers declared, "Our enemies are vanquished; let us cleanse and rededicate the sanctuary." {4:31} The entire army gathered, ascending Mount Zion. {4:32} They found the sanctuary desolate, the altar defiled, and the gates burnt. {4:33} The priestly chambers lay in ruins, overgrown like a thicket. {4:34} They tore their clothes, mourning and sprinkling themselves with ashes. {4:35} Prostrating themselves, they sounded trumpets and cried out to Heaven. {4:36} Judas assigned men to fight those in the citadel until the sanctuary was cleansed. {4:37} Choosing blameless priests devoted to the law, they cleansed the sanctuary, removing defiled stones to an unclean place. {4:38} They deliberated on the defiled altar of burnt offering, deciding to dismantle it to avoid reproach, storing the stones on the temple hill for a prophet's guidance. {4:39} Following the law, they built a new altar with unhewn stones, {4:40} rebuilding and consecrating the sanctuary and its courts. {4:41} They crafted new holy vessels, reinstated the lampstand, altar of incense, and table in the temple. {4:42} Incense burned on the altar, and the lampstand's light illumined the temple. {4:43} They set out the bread and hung curtains, completing all they had set out to do. {4:44} On the twenty-fifth day of the ninth month, Chislev, in the 148th year, {4:45} they offered sacrifices on the new altar of burnt offering, exactly when it had been profaned by the Gentiles. {4:46} The dedication was celebrated with songs, harps, lutes, and cymbals, {4:47} as all bowed in worship and blessed Heaven for prospering them. {4:48} For eight days they rejoiced in the altar's dedication, offering burnt offerings with joy, a sacrifice of deliverance and praise. {4:49} They adorned the temple with golden crowns and small shields, restoring gates and priestly chambers with new doors. {4:50} There was great joy among the people, removing the Gentiles' reproach. {4:51} Judas and his brothers, with all Israel, decreed that each year they would observe the altar's dedication with joy and gladness for eight days, beginning on the 25th of Chislev. {4:52} They fortified Mount Zion with strong walls and towers, preventing the Gentiles from trampling them again. {4:53} They stationed a garrison there and fortified Beth-zur, facing Idumea.

{5:1} When the surrounding Gentiles heard that the altar had been rebuilt and the sanctuary rededicated to its former state, they grew furious. {5:2} They resolved to annihilate the descendants of Jacob who lived among them, initiating a campaign of killing and destruction among the people. {5:3} Judas, however, waged war against the Edomites in Idumea at Akrabattene, where they lay in ambush against Israel. He struck them fiercely, humbling and plundering them. {5:4} He also remembered the treachery of the sons of Baean, who laid traps and ambushed Israelites on the highways. {5:5} Judas besieged them in their towers, vowing their complete destruction, burning their towers and all inside with fire. {5:6} Crossing over, he attacked the Ammonites, finding a strong force led by Timothy. {5:7} They engaged in multiple battles, and Judas decisively defeated them. {5:8} He seized Jazer and its villages before returning to Judea. {5:9} Meanwhile, Gentiles in Gilead gathered against the Israelites, who fled to the stronghold of Dathema. {5:10} They sent a plea to Judas and his brothers, informing them of the Gentiles' intent to destroy them. {5:11} Timothy led the charge, aiming to capture their refuge. {5:12} Urged by the dire situation, they called for rescue, having suffered heavy losses and devastation. {5:13} As they read the letter, messengers arrived from Galilee with torn garments, reporting a similar threat from men of Ptolemais, Tyre, Sidon, and all Galilee. {5:14} They too sought annihilation. {5:15} Judas convened a great assembly upon hearing these reports, {5:16} deciding with his brothers: Simon would lead men to rescue Galilee, while he and Jonathan would face the crisis in Gilead. {5:17} Leaving Joseph and Azariah to guard Judea, {5:18} Judas instructed them not to engage until their return. {5:19} Simon led three thousand men to Galilee, while Judas took eight thousand to Gilead. {5:20} Simon fought and crushed the Gentiles, pursuing them to Ptolemais, where many fell and were plundered. {5:21} He brought the Jews of Galilee and Arbatta back to Judea amid great rejoicing. {5:22} Meanwhile, Judas and Jonathan crossed the Jordan into the wilderness, meeting the Nabateans who recounted the plight of their brethren in Gilead. {5:23} Learning of imminent attacks on the strongholds, Judas swiftly returned via the wilderness road to Bozrah, taking the city, slaying all males, seizing their spoils, and burning it. {5:24} Continuing to Dathema, they found a massive enemy force with ladders and war engines attacking the stronghold at dawn. {5:25} Judas rallied his men, sounding trumpets and praying loudly. {5:26} They defeated the army of Timothy, causing a severe blow with the loss of eight thousand men. {5:27} Judas proceeded to Alema, Maked, Chaspho, and Bosor, conquering all Gilead's cities. {5:28} Timothy regrouped and camped against Raphon, where Judas sent spies who reported a vast force, including Arab mercenaries, preparing to fight. {5:29} Judas met them boldly, approaching the stream where Timothy strategized. {5:30} Timothy planned to cross first if Judas hesitated, but Judas ordered immediate battle preparation upon reaching the stream. {5:31} Crossing first, Judas and his army overcame all Gentiles who fled to the sacred precincts at Carnaim. {5:32} Judas took Carnaim, burning the sacred precincts and all inside, establishing dominance. {5:33} He gathered all Israelites from Gilead, with their families and belongings, to return to Judah. {5:34} They rejoiced on Mount Zion, offering burnt offerings for their safe return. {5:35} While Judas was in Gilead and Simon in Galilee before Ptolemais, {5:36} Joseph and Azariah, hearing of their exploits, sought to make a name for themselves by attacking Jamnia. {5:37} They clashed with Gorgias and were defeated, losing two thousand men. {5:38} The people suffered a great defeat for not heeding Judas and his brothers, {5:39} who were honored throughout Israel and among the Gentiles for their valor. {5:40} Judas turned to battle the Edomites in the southern land, conquering Hebron, its villages, strongholds, and towers. {5:41} He proceeded through the land of the Philistines, passing Marisa. {5:42} That day, some priests fell in battle, venturing out unwisely. {5:43} Judas redirected to Azotus in Philistine territory, destroying their altars, burning idols, plundering cities, and returning to Judah.

{6:1} King Antiochus was traveling through the upper provinces when he heard about the city of Elymais in Persia, known for its immense wealth in silver and gold. {6:2} The city housed a temple with great riches, including golden shields, breastplates, and weapons left there by Alexander, the Macedonian king who first ruled over the Greeks. {6:3} Antiochus attempted to seize the city and plunder it, but his plans were exposed to the city's inhabitants. {6:4} They resisted him in battle, causing him to flee in great sorrow, returning to Babylon. {6:5} In Persia, news reached him that the armies sent into Judea had been defeated; {6:6} Lysias had led a strong force but was routed by the Jews, who grew stronger from the arms, supplies, and spoils they seized. {6:7} They had removed the abomination Antiochus had set up on the altar in Jerusalem, fortified the sanctuary and Beth-zur, his city. {6:8} Hearing this, Antiochus was shocked and deeply troubled. He fell ill from grief as his plans had failed. {6:9} He lay sick for many days, overwhelmed by profound sorrow, believing he was dying. {6:10} Summoning his friends, he lamented his troubled sleep and heavy heart, reflecting on his former power and kindness. {6:11} Now, in distress and facing overwhelming adversity, he regretted the evils he had done in Jerusalem: seizing their precious vessels and unjustly attacking the people of Judah. {6:12} Convinced these misfortunes befell him for these acts, he felt his end approaching in a foreign land. {6:13} Antiochus appointed Philip, a trusted friend, to govern his kingdom. {6:14} He entrusted him with the crown, robe, and signet to guide his son Antiochus into kingship. {6:15} Thus, Antiochus died in the 149th year of his reign. {6:16} Upon learning of the king's death, Lysias installed Antiochus' son, whom he had raised and named Eupator, as king. {6:17} Meanwhile, the citadel's inhabitants in Jerusalem continued to oppress Israel, aiding the Gentiles against them. {6:18} Judas resolved to destroy them, gathering the people for a siege. {6:19} They besieged the citadel in the 150th year, building siege towers and war machines. {6:20} Despite some garrison and unfaithful Israelites escaping, they persisted. {6:21} These rebels sought the king's support, accusing the Jews of injustice and seeking vengeance for their losses. {6:22} They highlighted their loyalty to Antiochus' father and the hostilities they faced from the Jews. {6:23} Urged to act swiftly, the king assembled his advisors and received mercenary reinforcements. {6:24} His forces included 100,000 foot soldiers, 20,000 horsemen, and 32 war elephants. {6:25} Advancing through Idumea, they camped against Beth-zur, engaging in prolonged battles with the Jews. {6:26} The Jews sallied out, burning enemy engines of war and fighting valiantly. {6:27} Judas moved his forces to Beth-zechariah opposite the king's camp. {6:28} Early one morning, the king marched toward Beth-zechariah, preparing his army for battle with trumpet blasts. {6:29} They readied the war elephants, showing them the juices of grapes and mulberries to incite them. {6:30} Deploying the elephants with a thousand men each, and 500 horsemen, they formed a formidable front. {6:31} Wooden towers atop the elephants held armed men and their Indian drivers, protected by phalanxes and flanked by cavalry. {6:32} They advanced with their gleaming shields, marching in disciplined order. {6:33} Judas and his forces met them courageously, causing 600 men from the king's army to fall. {6:34} Eleazar Avaran noticed one elephant adorned with royal armor, assuming the king was aboard. {6:35} Sacrificing himself to save his people, he charged into the phalanx, killing many before falling under the elephant he managed to kill. {6:36} Witnessing the king's might, the Jews momentarily retreated. {6:37} The king's soldiers pursued them toward Jerusalem, encamping in Judea and Mount Zion. {6:38} Making peace with the men of Beth-zur due to lack of provisions during the sabbatical year, the king took control of the city. {6:39} He laid siege to the sanctuary for many days, using siege towers, fire-throwing engines, arrows, and catapults. {6:40} The Jews retaliated with their own war machines, but faced food shortages during the seventh year. {6:41} The sanctuary's few defenders were scattered by famine, and many perished. {6:42} Hearing Philip's return with reinforcements, the king sought peace with the Jews, breaking his oath upon entering Mount Zion by ordering the dismantling of its walls. {6:43} Hastening back to Antioch, he clashed with Philip for control of the city and prevailed.

{7:1} In the year 151, Demetrius, son of Seleucus, returned from Rome and assumed kingship after arriving at a coastal city with a small retinue. {7:2} Upon entering his ancestral palace, he ordered the arrest of Antiochus and Lysias by his troops. {7:3} When informed of their capture, he refused to see them and commanded their execution. {7:4} Thus, Demetrius ascended the throne of his kingdom. {7:5} Meanwhile, Alcimus, supported by lawless men from Israel, sought to become high priest. {7:6} They accused Judas and his brothers of causing widespread destruction and driving them from their land. {7:7} Urged by them, Demetrius sent Bacchides, a trusted friend and governor, to assess the situation and punish Judas and his supporters. {7:8} Bacchides, accompanied by the ungodly Alcimus whom he appointed high priest, marched with a large force into Judah. {7:9} He sent deceptive messages of peace to Judas and his brothers. {7:10} Ignoring these, Judas saw through the treachery as Bacchides' forces arrived. {7:11} A group of scribes approached Alcimus and Bacchides seeking fair terms, but the trust was betrayed. {7:12} Despite initial peace talks, tensions escalated when Bacchides seized and executed sixty Hasideans. {7:13} Fear spread as they violated agreements, spreading chaos and bloodshed. {7:14} Bacchides then camped at Beth-zaith and executed deserters, consolidating his power with Alcimus. {7:15} Alcimus, backed by troublemakers, undermined Judah, inflicting severe damage. {7:16} Witnessing the injustice, Judas retaliated against deserters and fortified the city against further breaches. {7:17} When Alcimus realized Judas' strength, he returned to Demetrius, falsely accusing Judas and his allies. {7:18} Demetrius then dispatched Nicanor, a fierce enemy of Israel, commanding him to crush Judas and his people. {7:19} Nicanor arrived with a formidable army and deceitfully proposed peace to Judas. {7:20} Judas, wary of the trap, avoided further negotiations. {7:21} Learning of the plot's exposure, Nicanor prepared for battle near Caphar-salama. {7:22} Five hundred of Nicanor's soldiers fell, and the rest fled to David's city. {7:23} Nicanor then moved to Mount Zion, mocking and defiling the priests and elders. {7:24} Enraged, the priests appealed for divine justice against Nicanor and his blasphemous army. {7:25} Nicanor regrouped at Beth-horon with Syrian reinforcements while Judas gathered his forces at Adasa. {7:26} Judas prayed for victory against Nicanor's wicked intentions. {7:27} Battle ensued on the thirteenth day of Adar, resulting in Nicanor's defeat and death. {7:28} The Jews pursued and routed the enemy, celebrating their victory with great rejoicing. {7:29} They established the day as a festival of remembrance, rejoicing in the deliverance of their people. {7:30} Thus, Judah enjoyed a brief period of peace after these events.

{8:1} Judas heard about the mighty Romans, renowned for their strength and goodwill toward allies. {8:2} People spoke of their conquests among the Gauls, their control over mines in Spain for silver and gold, and their strategic dominion over distant lands. {8:3} They subdued kings from the ends of the earth and exacted tribute, including from formidable foes like Antiochus the Great. {8:4} Even when faced with armies and elephants, the Romans triumphed and imposed heavy tributes and territorial concessions. {8:5} They vanquished foes like Philip and Perseus, and any who opposed them were either defeated or paid homage. {8:6} Antiochus the Great himself was no match for them in battle. {8:7} Captured alive, he and his successors were compelled to pay tribute and yield territories to Rome. {8:8} These conquests extended from India to Media and Lydia, which were entrusted to Rome's allies like Eumenes. {8:9} The Greeks once planned to challenge them, but their designs were swiftly thwarted. {8:10} The Romans decisively defeated the Greeks, capturing many and subjugating their lands. {8:11} They continued to conquer kingdoms and islands, enslaving those who resisted but fostering alliances with their supporters. {8:12} Though mighty, they avoided kingship and instead governed through a senate of 320 senators, ensuring fair rule without envy or discord. {8:13} They appointed and deposed kings at will, earning great respect and influence. {8:14} Yet despite their power, they wore no crowns nor flaunted their authority. {8:15} Instead, they built a senate chamber where governance was deliberated daily for the welfare of the people. {8:16} Each year, they entrusted leadership to one individual, fostering unity and stability. {8:17} Judas, seeing the Romans' might and wisdom, sent Eupolemus and Jason to Rome to seek alliance and liberation from Greek oppression. {8:18} They undertook the arduous journey to Rome, entering the senate chamber to propose an alliance. {8:19} There, they spoke on behalf of Judas Maccabeus and the Jewish people, seeking to be recognized as allies of Rome. {8:20} Their plea resonated with the senators, who drafted a bronze tablet letter affirming peace and alliance with Jerusalem. {8:21} The Romans' response pleased them greatly. {8:22} The letter promised mutual support in times of war and peace between Rome and the Jewish nation, ensuring solidarity against common enemies. {8:23} It declared that if war threatened Rome or its allies, the Jews would support them wholeheartedly, and vice versa. {8:24} Conversely, neither side would aid enemies of the other. {8:25} The treaty solidified a bond of trust and mutual defense. {8:26} In response to King Demetrius' oppression of the Jews, Rome warned him against further mistreatment.

{9:1} Upon learning of Nicanor's defeat, Demetrius dispatched Bacchides and Alcimus once more into Judah, accompanied by a significant contingent of their army. {9:2} They advanced through Gilgal towards Mesaloth in Arbela, seizing the city and causing great casualties. {9:3} In the first month of the hundred and fifty-second year, they laid siege to Jerusalem. {9:4} Moving on to Berea with a formidable force of twenty thousand infantry and two thousand cavalry, they positioned themselves for battle. {9:5} Meanwhile, Judas camped at Elasa with three thousand elite soldiers. {9:6} Fear gripped them as they observed the overwhelming enemy numbers, leading many to desert until only eight hundred remained. {9:7} Judas, seeing his dwindling army and imminent battle, was deeply troubled but urged those remaining to stand firm. {9:8} Though weakened, he encouraged them to face their foes bravely. {9:9} Some advised retreat to save themselves, but Judas rebuked the idea, resolved to fight valiantly or perish honorably. {9:10} As Bacchides' army prepared for battle, Judas and his men also readied themselves, sounding trumpets in defiance. {9:11} The clash began with Bacchides' forces deploying strategically, supported by cavalry, slingers, archers, and seasoned warriors. {9:12} Bacchides led from the right flank as both sides advanced amid thunderous trumpets. {9:13} The battlefield shook as fierce combat raged from dawn till dusk. {9:14} Judas observed Bacchides' strength on the right flank and rallied his bravest men to counter them, pursuing them vigorously. {9:15} Sensing victory, they chased the enemy as far as Mount Azotus. {9:16} Seeing their right flank collapse, Bacchides' left wing turned to flee, pursued closely by Judas and his forces. {9:17} The battle intensified, resulting in heavy casualties on both sides. {9:18} Tragically, Judas fell in battle, and the remaining forces scattered. {9:19} Jonathan and Simon retrieved Judas' body and laid him to rest in Modein amid deep mourning throughout Israel. {9:20} They lamented the loss of their mighty leader, the defender of Israel. {9:21} Many heroic deeds of Judas remain unrecorded due to their multitude. {9:22} After Judas' death, lawlessness spread across Israel, with injustice rampant. {9:23} A severe famine struck, driving many to side with the enemy. {9:24} Bacchides capitalized on the chaos, appointing ungodly men to oversee Judah. {9:25} They hunted down Judas' supporters, exacting revenge and mocking them. {9:26} Israel faced unprecedented distress, reminiscent of times when prophets were absent. {9:27} Judas' loyalists gathered under Jonathan's leadership, acknowledging the dire need for a new champion against Bacchides and their adversaries. {9:28} They chose Jonathan to succeed Judas as their leader in the ongoing struggle. {9:29} Learning of Jonathan's rise, Bacchides attempted to eliminate him. {9:30} Jonathan, Simon, and their allies fled to the wilderness of Tekoa, encamping near the pool of Asphar. {9:31} On a Sabbath day, Bacchides pursued them, crossing the Jordan with his army. {9:32} Jonathan sought refuge with the Nabateans, while Bacchides' forces seized John and his belongings in Medeba. {9:33} News reached Jonathan and Simon about a grand wedding celebration of the sons of Jambri. {9:34} Remembering their slain brother John, they ambushed the wedding party near Nadabath, causing havoc and reclaiming their goods. {9:35} The festive occasion turned into mourning as they avenged their brother's death. {9:36} After exacting justice, they withdrew to the marshes of the Jordan. {9:37} Bacchides, upon learning of the ambush, marshaled his forces to the banks of the Jordan. {9:38} Jonathan and his men prepared for battle, facing imminent danger with the Jordan at their backs and enemies on all sides. {9:39} They prayed for deliverance and engaged Bacchides' army. {9:40} In the ensuing chaos, Jonathan attempted to strike Bacchides, who narrowly escaped. {9:41} Jonathan and his men then plunged into the Jordan and reached safety on the opposite shore, while Bacchides' army did not pursue them across the river. {9:42} On that day, about one thousand of Bacchides' soldiers perished. {9:43} Bacchides returned to Jerusalem and fortified several cities in Judea, including Jericho, Emmaus, Beth-horon, Bethel, Timnath, and Pharathon, with strong defenses to oppress Israel. {9:44} He stationed garrisons in these cities to enforce his rule. {9:45} Bacchides also fortified Beth-zur, Gazara, and the citadel, placing troops and supplies there. {9:46} Taking prominent men's sons as hostages, he confined them in Jerusalem's citadel. {9:47} In the hundred and fifty-third year, Alcimus ordered the destruction of the sanctuary's inner court wall, defying the prophets' work. {9:48} His attempt was halted when he was struck down, paralyzed and unable to speak or command. {9:49} Alcimus died in agony, and Bacchides, upon hearing of his death, departed to report to the king. {9:50} For two years, Judah enjoyed peace. {9:51} But lawless factions conspired to bring back Bacchides, seeking to capture Jonathan and his followers in a single night. {9:52} They approached Bacchides with their plan, who mobilized a large force and covertly contacted his Judean allies. {9:53} Jonathan's supporters, however, discovered the plot, capturing and executing about fifty conspirators. {9:54} Jonathan and Simon retreated to Bethbasi in the wilderness, where they fortified the town. {9:55} Bacchides pursued them, besieging Bethbasi with siege engines and waging a prolonged assault. {9:56} Jonathan left Simon to defend the city while he launched a surprise attack on Odomera and his allies, inflicting heavy losses. {9:57} Engaging Bacchides' forces directly, Jonathan and Simon's men set fire to the siege engines, causing great distress to their enemy. {9:58} Bacchides' plans faltered, and he faced defeat and humiliation. {9:59} Enraged at his failed campaign, Bacchides executed many of his treacherous allies. {9:60} He then retreated to his homeland, acknowledging Jonathan's resilience. {9:61} Jonathan sought peace with Bacchides, securing the release of Judean captives and ensuring a period of calm. {9:62} Bacchides honored his agreement, returned the captives, and refrained from further aggression against Jonathan. {9:63} Thus, the sword ceased to threaten Israel, and Jonathan began his leadership in Michmash, purging ungodliness from the land.

{10:1} In the year 160 BCE, Alexander Epiphanes, the son of Antiochus, arrived and took control of Ptolemais. The city welcomed him, and there he established his reign. {10:2} When King Demetrius heard about this, he gathered a large army and marched out to confront Alexander in battle. {10:3} Demetrius then sent Jonathan a letter filled with peaceful words, seeking to honor him. {10:4} He reasoned, "Let us make peace with Jonathan before he joins forces with Alexander against us. {10:5} Alexander will remember the injustices we committed against him, his brothers, and his people." {10:6} Thus, Demetrius granted Jonathan authority to raise troops, arm them, and form an alliance. He also ordered the release of hostages from the citadel to Jonathan. {10:7} Jonathan returned to Jerusalem and read Demetrius's letter aloud to the people and those in the citadel. {10:8} Hearing that Jonathan was authorized to raise an army, they were alarmed. {10:9} Nonetheless, the men in the citadel released the hostages to Jonathan, who then reunited them with their families. {10:10} Jonathan remained in Jerusalem and began to rebuild and fortify the city. {10:11} He directed the workers to strengthen the walls and fortify Mount Zion with squared stones for added defense, which they did diligently. {10:12} The foreigners who had taken refuge in the strongholds Bacchides built fled, each to their own lands. {10:13} Only in Beth-zur did some remain who had forsaken the law, using it as a refuge. {10:14} Meanwhile, King Alexander learned of the promises Demetrius made to Jonathan. {10:15} Reports of Jonathan and his brothers' battles, their bravery, and the hardships they endured reached Alexander. {10:16} Impressed, Alexander declared, "Can we find another like him? Let us make him our ally and friend." {10:17} Alexander then sent a letter to Jonathan, addressing him as follows: {10:18} "King Alexander sends greetings to his brother Jonathan. {10:19} We have heard of your valor and deem you worthy of friendship. {10:20} Today, we appoint you as the high priest of your people. You shall be known as the king's friend." Along with the letter, Alexander sent Jonathan a purple robe and a golden crown, urging him to align with them. {10:21} Thus, Jonathan donned the holy garments in the seventh month of the 160th year, during the Feast of Tabernacles. He recruited and armed troops extensively. {10:22} Upon hearing this, Demetrius was troubled and said, {10:23} "What have we done? Alexander has outmaneuvered us by befriending the Jews to strengthen himself." {10:24} He then resolved to write to Jonathan, offering encouragement, honor, and gifts, seeking his support. {10:25} Demetrius sent a message to Jonathan, stating: {10:26} "King Demetrius greets the Jewish nation. {10:27} We have heard of your loyalty and friendship towards us, which has brought us joy. {10:28} Continue to stand by us, and we will reward you generously. {10:29} I exempt all Jews from tribute, salt tax, and crown levies, and release them from grain and fruit taxes. This exemption extends to Judea, Samaria, and Galilee. {10:30} Let Jerusalem and its surroundings, along with its tithes and revenues, be exempt from taxes. {10:31} I relinquish control of the citadel in Jerusalem to the high priest, who may station his own guards there. {10:32} Every Jewish captive in my kingdom is to be freed without ransom, and their cattle taxes are canceled. {10:33} Let all feasts, Sabbaths, new moons, and appointed days be days of exemption and release for Jews in my kingdom. {10:34} No one shall impose taxes or trouble them in any way. {10:35} Enroll thirty thousand Jews in the king's forces, providing them with the necessary provisions. {10:36} Station them in strategic strongholds and appoint their own leaders according to their laws in Judea. {10:37} Let Judea and the added districts from Samaria be under one ruler, subject only to the high priest. {10:38} Ptolemais and its territory are given as a gift to the Jerusalem sanctuary for its upkeep. {10:39} Additionally, I grant fifteen thousand shekels of silver annually from the royal revenues. {10:40} Government officials must contribute for the temple's service as needed. {10:41} Cancel the annual five thousand shekels collected from temple service income, which rightfully belongs to the priests. {10:42} Any debtor taking refuge in Jerusalem or its precincts shall be released, recovering all properties in my kingdom. {10:43} The cost of rebuilding and restoring the sanctuary shall be funded from royal revenues, as well as the walls of Jerusalem and Judea. {10:44} When Jonathan and the people heard these promises, they hesitated, recalling Demetrius's past injustices and oppression in Israel. {10:45} They favored Alexander, who had initially spoken peaceably to them, remaining his allies throughout his reign. {10:46} Alexander assembled a large army and confronted Demetrius in battle. {10:47} Demetrius's forces fled, and Alexander pursued, defeating them soundly. {10:48} After the battle, Alexander sent messengers to King Ptolemy of Egypt, proposing an alliance. {10:49} He boasted of his victory over Demetrius and his ascension to the throne of his kingdom. {10:50} Alexander recounted how he vanquished Demetrius and his army, seizing control of his kingdom. {10:51} Ptolemy responded, expressing joy at Alexander's return and agreeing to his proposal. {10:52} Ptolemy journeyed from Egypt with his daughter Cleopatra, arriving at Ptolemais in the 162nd year. {10:53} There, Alexander welcomed them, and Ptolemy gave Cleopatra to Alexander in marriage, celebrating the union with grandeur fitting for kings. {10:54} Alexander then summoned Jonathan to meet him. {10:55} Jonathan arrived at Ptolemais, bringing gifts of silver, gold, and other valuables for the kings and their allies, gaining their favor. {10:56} However, a group of troublemakers from Israel plotted against him, but the kings paid them no heed. {10:57} They honored Jonathan by clothing him in purple and seating him beside Alexander. {10:58} Alexander commanded his officers to proclaim throughout the city that Jonathan was not to be accused or harassed. {10:59} Witnessing the honor bestowed upon Jonathan, his accusers fled in fear. {10:60} The king elevated Jonathan among his closest advisors, appointing him as governor and leader of the region. {10:61} Jonathan returned to Jerusalem, rejoicing in peace. {10:62} In the year 165 BCE, Demetrius's son arrived from Crete to reclaim his father's kingdom. {10:63} When Alexander heard this news, he returned to Antioch, leaving Apollonius as governor of Coelesyria with a formidable army. {10:64} Apollonius sent a challenging message to Jonathan, taunting him for his opposition. {10:65} Roused, Jonathan gathered ten thousand men and marched toward Joppa, where his brother Simon joined him. {10:66} They besieged Joppa, whose inhabitants initially resisted but eventually surrendered to Jonathan. {10:67} Apollonius, hearing of this, mobilized three thousand cavalry and a large infantry, advancing toward Azotus. {10:68} Jonathan pursued Apollonius to Azotus, engaging his forces in battle. {10:69} Apollonius had secretly stationed a thousand cavalry as reinforcements, attacking Jonathan's army from behind with arrows. {10:70} Jonathan's troops endured the assault, standing firm until Simon's forces arrived and overwhelmed the enemy, forcing them to flee to safety. {10:71} Jonathan then set Azotus and its surrounding towns ablaze, including the temple of Dagon where many had sought refuge. {10:72} The spoils of war were abundant, and Jonathan marched triumphantly back to Jerusalem. {10:73} Upon hearing of Jonathan's exploits, Alexander esteemed him even more highly, sending him a golden buckle and granting him Ekron and its surroundings as his possession.

{11:1} The king of Egypt amassed a vast army, likened to the sands along the seashore, and a formidable fleet, plotting to seize Alexander's kingdom through deceit and annex it to his own. {11:2} He journeyed to Syria under the guise of peace, and the cities welcomed him, obeying Alexander's command since he was the father-in-law of the king. {11:3} But once Ptolemy entered the cities, he stationed garrisons in each one. {11:4} Upon reaching Azotus, they showed him the burned temple of Dagon, the devastation of Azotus and its surroundings, and the bodies strewn about—victims of Jonathan's war. {11:5} They accused Jonathan before the king, seeking to cast blame on him, but the king remained silent. {11:6} Jonathan met the king at Joppa with great ceremony, and they exchanged greetings and spent the night there. {11:7} Then Jonathan escorted the king to the River Eleutherus, after which he returned to Jerusalem. {11:8} King Ptolemy gained control of the coastal cities up to Seleucia by the sea and plotted against Alexander. {11:9} He sent messengers to King Demetrius, proposing a pact and offering his daughter, who was Alexander's wife, in marriage, suggesting Demetrius should rule his father's kingdom. {11:10} Regretting his earlier decision due to Alexander's attempts on his life, he sought to blame Alexander. {11:11} Consequently, he took back his daughter and gave her to Demetrius, further souring relations with Alexander. {11:12} Ptolemy entered Antioch and crowned himself ruler of Asia, wearing both the crowns of Egypt and Asia. {11:13} Meanwhile, Alexander was in Cilicia dealing with local revolts. {11:14} Hearing of this, Alexander marched against Ptolemy, and they clashed in battle. {11:15} Ptolemy met him with a strong force and routed Alexander, who fled to Arabia seeking refuge. {11:16} In Arabia, Zabdiel the Arab slew Alexander and sent his head to Ptolemy. {11:17} Ptolemy, however, died three days later, and his forces in the strongholds were slaughtered by the inhabitants. {11:18} Thus, Demetrius ascended the throne in the one hundred and sixty-seventh year. {11:19} During this time, Jonathan gathered Judea's men to besiege the citadel in Jerusalem, constructing war machines for the task. {11:20} But some lawless men, hating their nation, informed the king that Jonathan was besieging the citadel. {11:21} Angered, the king summoned Jonathan to Ptolemais, instructing him to cease the siege and meet for talks promptly. {11:22} Despite this, Jonathan ordered the siege to continue, risking himself by sending elders and priests to the king. {11:23} He went to Ptolemais with silver, gold, clothing, and other gifts, winning the king's favor. {11:24} Though lawless men continued to slander him, the king treated Jonathan with respect, confirming him as high priest and granting him honors. {11:25} Jonathan requested the king to exempt Judea and its districts from tribute, promising three hundred talents in return. {11:26} The king agreed and wrote a letter detailing these concessions to Jonathan. {11:27} With the land pacified, Demetrius disbanded his troops, keeping only foreign units from island nations, alienating those who had served his predecessors. {11:28} Trypho, once Alexander's supporter, saw the troops' discontent and allied with Imalkue to install Antiochus, Alexander's young son, as king. {11:29} He persuaded Imalkue by revealing Demetrius's misdeeds and the soldiers' animosity toward him. {11:30} Jonathan appealed to Demetrius to remove the citadel and stronghold garrisons in Jerusalem, as they opposed Israel. {11:31} Demetrius responded promising not only this but also great honors if opportunity allowed. {11:32} Jonathan sent three thousand men to Antioch to assist, greatly pleasing the king. {11:33} Antioch's citizens, numbering a hundred and twenty thousand, sought to kill the king, forcing him into the palace. {11:34} The Jews aided the king, fighting through the city and killing a hundred thousand men, burning the city and claiming much plunder. {11:35} Witnessing Jewish prowess, the city's people begged for peace, which was granted, bringing honor to the Jews in the king's eyes as they returned to Jerusalem with spoils. {11:36} Demetrius secured his reign on the throne, facing no opposition. {11:37} However, he broke his promises to Jonathan, neglecting the kindness Jonathan had shown him and oppressing him greatly. {11:38} Trypho returned with Antiochus, who ascended the throne and wore the crown. {11:39} Demetrius's abandoned troops joined Trypho, battling Demetrius who fled and was defeated. {11:40} Trypho seized the elephants and Antioch, writing to Jonathan to confirm him as high priest, governor over four districts, and a royal friend. {11:41} He sent Jonathan gold plates, tableware, gold cups, and a golden buckle, appointing Simon, Jonathan's brother, as governor from Tyre's ascent to Egypt's border. {11:42} Jonathan traveled to various cities beyond the river, amassing allies from Syria's army. {11:43} At Askalon, he was received with honor, and then proceeded to Gaza where he was initially rebuffed but later made peace, taking hostages and journeying to Damascus. {11:44} Learning of Demetrius's officers amassing in Kadesh in Galilee to remove him, Jonathan met them while Simon besieged Beth-zur. {11:45} After negotiations, he captured Beth-zur, stationed garrisons there, and camped by Gennesaret's waters. {11:46} In the morning, they moved to Hazor's plain where foreign forces ambushed them in the mountains but were defeated in battle. {11:47} Pursuing them to Kadesh, 3000 foreigners fell that day as Jonathan returned triumphant to Jerusalem.

{12:1} When Jonathan saw the opportune moment, he selected men to send to Rome to reaffirm and strengthen their alliance. {12:2} He also dispatched letters to the Spartans and other places for the same purpose. {12:3} Arriving in Rome, they entered the senate and declared, "Jonathan the high priest and the Jewish nation have sent us to renew our former friendship and alliance." {12:4} The Romans responded by providing them with letters to ensure safe passage throughout the regions on their journey back to Judah. {12:5} Here is the copy of the letter Jonathan wrote to the Spartans: {12:6} "Jonathan the high priest, the senate of the Jewish nation, the priests, and all the people send greetings to our brethren, the Spartans. {12:7} Long ago, a letter was sent to Onias the high priest from Arius, your king, acknowledging our brotherhood, as the enclosed copy shows. {12:8} Onias received this envoy with honor and accepted the letter, affirming a clear alliance and friendship. {12:9} Though we have the encouragement of the holy scriptures in our possession and have no urgent need, {12:10} we have undertaken to renew our brotherhood and friendship with you, mindful not to grow distant over the years since your last letter to us. {12:11} We remember you regularly in our feasts, prayers, and sacrifices, as is fitting for brethren. {12:12} We rejoice in your prosperity. {12:13} As for us, we have faced numerous afflictions and wars; surrounding kings have waged war against us. {12:14} We chose Numenius son of Antiochus and Antipater son of Jason to go to Rome and renew our alliance. {12:15} They are also instructed to visit you, conveying this letter concerning the renewal of our brotherhood. {12:16} We await your reply." {12:17} They also sent a letter to Onias: {12:18} "Arius, king of the Spartans, sends greetings to Onias the high priest. {12:19} It is documented that the Spartans and Jews are brethren, descendants of Abraham's family. {12:20} Having learned this, we request an update on your well-being. {12:21} We inform you that our possessions are yours, and yours are ours. Our envoys will report accordingly." {12:22} Jonathan learned that Demetrius's commanders had returned with a larger force, preparing to wage war against him. {12:23} He marched to meet them near Hamath, preventing them from invading Judah. {12:24} Jonathan sent spies to their camp, who reported that the enemy planned a night attack against the Jews. {12:25} At sunset, Jonathan ordered his men to remain vigilant, armed and ready for battle throughout the night, with outposts surrounding their camp. {12:26} When the enemy heard of Jonathan's preparedness, they became fearful and kindled fires in their camp before withdrawing. {12:27} Unaware of their retreat until morning, Jonathan pursued them but they had crossed the Eleutherus river. {12:28} Jonathan turned his attention to the Zabadeans, known as Arabs, defeating and plundering them. {12:29} He then moved to Damascus, traversing the region. {12:30} Simon also ventured out, journeying to Askalon and neighboring strongholds, surprising Joppa, which was ready to surrender to Demetrius's men. {12:31} He stationed a garrison there to protect it. {12:32} Jonathan convened the elders to plan building strongholds in Judea, reinforcing Jerusalem's walls, and erecting a barrier to isolate the citadel from the city, preventing trade. {12:33} They gathered to rebuild, focusing on the fallen section called Chaphenatha in the eastern valley. {12:34} Simon fortified Adida in the Shephelah, installing gates with bolts. {12:35} Meanwhile, Trypho sought kingship in Asia and moved against Antiochus. {12:36} Fearing Jonathan's opposition, Trypho plotted his capture and death, marching to Beth-shan. {12:37} Jonathan met him with forty thousand troops, engaging at Beth-shan. {12:38} Seeing Jonathan's formidable army, Trypho welcomed him with honor, giving gifts and commanding his allies and troops to obey him. {12:39} Trypho proposed peace, suggesting Jonathan dismiss his forces, keep a few men, and accompany him to Ptolemais, offering him control of the strongholds, remaining troops, and officials. {12:40} Jonathan trusted Trypho, disbanded his troops, and returned to Judah. {12:41} He retained three thousand men, leaving two thousand in Galilee and taking a thousand with him. {12:42} Upon entering Ptolemais, its inhabitants closed the gates, seizing and killing Jonathan's companions. {12:43} Trypho then dispatched troops and cavalry to Galilee and the Great Plain, aiming to eliminate Jonathan's remaining soldiers. {12:44} Learning of Jonathan's capture and presumed demise, his troops rallied, preparing for battle. {12:45} When their pursuers saw their determination, they retreated. {12:46} Safely returning to Judah, they mourned deeply for Jonathan and his companions, fearing destruction from neighboring nations who saw them leaderless.

{13:1} Simon received news that Trypho had gathered a formidable army to invade Judah and annihilate it. {13:2} Observing the fear and anxiety among the people, Simon traveled to Jerusalem and gathered them together. {13:3} He encouraged them, saying, "You know well the great deeds my brothers and our family have accomplished for the laws and the sanctuary, and the wars and hardships we have endured. {13:4} Because of these struggles, all my brothers have perished in defense of Israel, and I alone remain. {13:5} I will not seek to preserve my own life in times of trouble, for I am no better than my brothers. {13:6} Instead, I will seek vengeance for our nation, our sanctuary, and the safety of your families. All the nations have united in hatred to destroy us." {13:7} The people were greatly encouraged by these words. {13:8} They responded loudly, "You are our leader in place of Judas and your brother Jonathan. {13:9} Lead us in battle, and we will do all that you command." {13:10} Simon gathered all the warriors and hurried to complete the fortification of Jerusalem, strengthening its defenses on every side. {13:11} He sent Jonathan son of Absalom to Joppa with a sizable force, expelled its inhabitants, and took control of the city. {13:12} Meanwhile, Trypho left Ptolemais with a large army to invade Judah, keeping Jonathan under guard. {13:13} Simon encamped at Adida, facing the plain. {13:14} Learning that Simon had replaced Jonathan, Trypho prepared to confront him in battle. He sent envoys to Simon, saying, {13:15} "We are detaining Jonathan due to debts owed to the royal treasury from his official duties. {13:16} Send us a hundred talents of silver and two of his sons as hostages. Upon receipt, we will release him to prevent any rebellion against us." {13:17} Simon knew they spoke deceitfully but sent the silver and sons to avoid public backlash. {13:18} He feared people might say, "Simon's failure to send payment led to Jonathan's death." {13:19} Despite sending the payment, Trypho broke his promise and did not release Jonathan. {13:20} Trypho then advanced to invade Judah, circling by way of Adora. Simon and his army pursued him wherever he went. {13:21} Meanwhile, the men in the citadel sent messengers to Trypho, urging him to approach through the wilderness and send them supplies. {13:22} Trypho prepared his cavalry for this but heavy snowfall that night prevented his advance, forcing him to march into the land of Gilead. {13:23} Near Baskama, he executed Jonathan, burying him there. {13:24} Trypho then returned to his own land. {13:25} Simon retrieved Jonathan's remains and buried him in Modein, their ancestral city. {13:26} All Israel mourned Jonathan deeply for many days. {13:27} Simon erected a monument over the tombs of his father and brothers, a tall structure visible with polished stones at the front and back. {13:28} He also built seven pyramids facing each other for his father, mother, and four brothers. {13:29} Each pyramid was adorned with columns supporting suits of armor as a lasting memorial, with carved ships beside them, visible to all who sailed the seas. {13:30} This tomb in Modein remains to this day. {13:31} Trypho betrayed young King Antiochus, assassinating him and seizing the crown of Asia, plunging the land into great calamity. {13:32} Simon fortified Judea's strongholds with high towers, mighty walls, gates, and bolts, storing provisions within. {13:33} He selected emissaries to plead with King Demetrius for aid, as Trypho continued plundering the land. {13:34} King Demetrius responded favorably, writing Simon a letter, {13:35} "King Demetrius to Simon, the high priest and friend of kings, and to the elders and people of the Jews, greetings. {13:36} We have received your gifts and are ready to make a lasting peace with you. I order our officials to exempt you from tribute and uphold the strongholds you have built. {13:37} Any past debts and offenses are forgiven, including the crown tax owed. Taxes from Jerusalem are no longer collected. {13:38} Those qualified may join our bodyguard, and let there be peace between us." {13:39} In the one hundred and seventieth year, the Gentile yoke was lifted from Israel. {13:40} People began marking their documents, "In the first year of Simon, the great high priest, commander, and leader of the Jews." {13:41} Simon besieged and captured Gazara, surrounding it with troops and using siege engines to breach its walls. {13:42} The defenders of the city made a tumult, but they negotiated peace with Simon. {13:43} They requested mercy, pleading, "Do not punish us for our sins but act with your usual kindness." {13:44} Simon agreed to terms, expelling them from the city and purifying it from idolatry. {13:45} With hymns and praises, he entered Gazara, cleansing it of all impurities and resettling it with law-abiding men. {13:46} Simon fortified Gazara's defenses and built a residence for himself there. {13:47} In Jerusalem, the citadel inhabitants were unable to leave for provisions and were starving. {13:48} They begged Simon for mercy, and he expelled them from the citadel, cleansing it from defilement. {13:49} On the twenty-third day of the second month in the one hundred and seventy-first year, Jews entered the citadel with joy, celebrating their victory over a great enemy. {13:50} Simon agreed to peace with them, then expelled them from the citadel, purging it of impurities. {13:51} Simon appointed his son John as commander of all forces, and he settled in Gazara.

{14:1} In the year 172, King Demetrius gathered his forces and marched into Media seeking assistance to wage war against Trypho. {14:2} When Arsaces, the king of Persia and Media, heard of Demetrius' invasion, he dispatched a commander to capture Demetrius alive. {14:3} The commander engaged Demetrius' army, defeated them, and seized Demetrius himself, delivering him to Arsaces who imprisoned him. {14:4} Throughout Simon's reign, the land enjoyed peace. He diligently pursued the welfare of his nation, and his leadership was greatly appreciated. {14:5} To enhance his accomplishments, Simon acquired Joppa as a port, opening trade routes to distant islands. {14:6} He expanded the borders of his nation and gained full control over the land. {14:7} Simon took numerous captives, ruled over Gazara, Beth-zur, and the citadel, purging them of impurities without opposition. {14:8} The people cultivated their lands in peace, yielding abundant harvests, and the trees bore plentiful fruit. {14:9} Elders conversed peacefully in the streets, while youths adorned themselves with glory and prepared for battle. {14:10} Simon ensured cities were well-supplied and fortified, spreading his renown far and wide. {14:11} He established lasting peace throughout the land, bringing great joy to Israel. {14:12} Each person enjoyed security under their own vine and fig tree, free from fear. {14:13} No adversaries remained to challenge them, and the kings were subdued during his time. {14:14} Simon supported the humble among his people, upheld the law, and eliminated lawless individuals. {14:15} He glorified the sanctuary and added to its sacred vessels. {14:16} News of Jonathan's death reached Rome and Sparta, causing deep sorrow. {14:17} Upon hearing Simon succeeded his brother as high priest and ruler over the land and its cities, they sent him bronze tablets renewing their friendship and alliance with Judas and Jonathan. {14:18} These tablets were read publicly in Jerusalem. {14:19} The Spartans' letter to Simon read: "To Simon the high priest, elders, priests, and all Jews, our brothers, greetings. {14:20} Envoys informed us of your glory and honor, which brought us joy. {14:21} We have recorded their words in our public decrees, preserving our friendship with you." {14:22} Simon later sent Numenius to Rome with a large gold shield to solidify their alliance. {14:23} People marveled at Simon and his family's steadfastness in defending Israel's freedom against their enemies. {14:24} They engraved their gratitude on bronze tablets and erected pillars on Mount Zion. {14:25} These tablets documented their appreciation: "On the 18th day of Elul in the year 172, Simon, the great high priest, and his brothers risked their lives to defend their nation's sanctuary and law, bringing great honor to Israel. {14:26} Jonathan led the nation as high priest before being gathered to his ancestors. {14:27} When enemies sought to invade and defile their sanctuary, Simon rose to defend his nation. He financed his army, fortified Judean cities, and established Jewish garrisons. {14:28} He strengthened cities like Joppa and Gazara, settling Jews and providing for their restoration. {14:29} The people recognized Simon's devotion and sought him as their leader and high priest forever, until a trustworthy prophet emerged. {14:30} Simon governed them, managed the sanctuary, appointed officials, fortified the land, and maintained order. {14:31} In his time, prosperity flourished, driving out Gentiles and those who defiled Jerusalem's sacred spaces. {14:32} They decreed that King Demetrius confirm Simon in the high priesthood, honor him, and recognize him as a friend. {14:33} They ensured no one opposed Simon's decrees or convened assemblies without his consent, and only he could wear purple and gold. {14:34} Anyone who defied these decrees faced severe punishment." {14:35} The people agreed unanimously to grant Simon authority according to these decrees. {14:36} Simon accepted the roles of high priest, commander, ethnarch of the Jews, and protector of his people. {14:37} They inscribed these decrees on bronze tablets and prominently displayed them at the sanctuary. {14:38} Copies were kept in the treasury for Simon and his sons.

{15:1} Antiochus, the son of King Demetrius, sent a letter from the islands of the sea to Simon, the high priest and leader of the Jews, and to the entire nation. {15:2} The letter read: "King Antiochus to Simon the high priest, leader, and the Jewish nation, greetings. {15:3} Certain troublesome individuals have taken control of our ancestral kingdom. I intend to reclaim it and restore it to its former glory. I have gathered a host of mercenaries and equipped warships for this purpose. {15:4} I plan to land in the country and confront those who have ravaged our land and destroyed many cities within my realm. {15:5} Therefore, I confirm to you all the tax exemptions granted by my predecessors, and I release you from other financial obligations imposed upon you. {15:6} You are permitted to mint your own coins for your country's currency. {15:7} I grant freedom to Jerusalem and its sanctuary. All weapons you have prepared, the strongholds you have built and now possess, shall remain under your control. {15:8} Any debts you owe to the royal treasury, now or in the future, are canceled permanently. {15:9} Upon reclaiming our kingdom, I will bestow great honor upon you, your nation, and the temple, so that your glory will be renowned throughout the earth." {15:10} In the year 174, Antiochus set out and invaded his ancestral land. Troops rallied to him, greatly reducing Trypho's forces. {15:11} Antiochus pursued Trypho, who fled to Dor by the sea, recognizing the grave situation he faced and deserted by his troops. {15:12} Antiochus laid siege to Dor with 120,000 infantry and 8,000 cavalry. {15:13} He surrounded the city and engaged its defenders from both land and sea, blocking all ingress and egress. {15:14} Meanwhile, Numenius and his companions arrived from Rome with letters for various kings and nations. {15:15} The letter read: "Lucius, consul of Rome, to King Ptolemy, greetings. {15:16} The Jewish envoys have visited us as friends and allies, sent by Simon the high priest and the Jewish people. {15:17} They brought a thousand mina gold shield as a gift." {15:18} We decree that no harm should befall them or their cities, country, or anyone making alliances against them. {15:19} We accept the gift from them. {15:20} If any troublesome individuals flee to your lands, hand them over to Simon the high priest for punishment under their laws." {15:21} The consul sent similar messages to Demetrius the king, Attalus, Ariarathes, Arsaces, and various other nations and cities. {15:22} Copies of these letters were also sent to Simon the high priest. {15:23} Antiochus resumed the siege of Dor, relentlessly assaulting it with war machines, and kept Trypho trapped inside, preventing his escape. {15:24} Simon sent 2,000 elite soldiers to aid Antiochus, along with silver, gold, and military supplies. {15:25} However, Antiochus rejected these offerings and violated previous agreements with Simon, growing estranged from him. {15:26} He sent Athenobius as his emissary to negotiate, pointing out Simon's wealth and splendor. {15:27} Athenobius reported to Antiochus, "You control Joppa, Gazara, and the citadel in Jerusalem, all part of your kingdom. {15:28} Simon has devastated these territories, causing great harm. {15:29} He has taken over many places within your kingdom. {15:30} Therefore, demand the return of these cities and tribute from outside Judea, or receive 500 talents of silver for each." {15:31} Athenobius traveled to Jerusalem, astonished by Simon's magnificence and riches, relaying the king's demands. {15:32} Simon responded, "We have not seized foreign land or property, only our ancestral inheritance unjustly taken by our enemies. {15:33} We reclaim what rightfully belongs to us. {15:34} As for Joppa and Gazara, which you request, they were causing harm to our people and our land. We offer 100 talents for them." {15:35} Athenobius, enraged, returned to the king and reported Simon's response and his grandeur. {15:36} King Trypho fled by ship to Orthosia. {15:37} Antiochus appointed Cendebeus as commander-in-chief of the coastal region, providing infantry and cavalry. {15:38} Cendebeus was ordered to camp against Judea, fortify Kedron, and wage war on the people, while the king pursued Trypho. {15:39} Cendebeus arrived at Jamnia, inciting conflict, capturing people, and initiating raids on Judea, as commanded by the king.

{16:1} John returned from Gazara and informed his father Simon about Cendebeus' actions. {16:2} Simon called his two elder sons, Judas and John, and spoke to them: "From our youth until now, I and my brothers and our family have fought for Israel. By the grace of God, we have achieved many victories. {16:3} But now I am old, and you are mature. Take my place and your brother's, go out, and continue to fight for our nation. May Heaven's help be with you." {16:4} John gathered twenty thousand soldiers and cavalry from the countryside and marched against Cendebeus. They camped in Modein that night. {16:5} Early the next morning, they moved into the plain and saw a large enemy force of infantry and cavalry approaching, with a stream between them. {16:6} John noticed that the soldiers hesitated to cross the stream, so he crossed first. Seeing him, his men followed suit. {16:7} He divided his army, placing cavalry in the midst of the infantry to counter the enemy's numerous cavalry. {16:8} They sounded the trumpets, and Cendebeus' forces were routed; many were wounded and fell, and the rest fled to their stronghold. {16:9} During the battle, Judas, John's brother, was wounded. John pursued Cendebeus to Kedron, which Cendebeus had fortified. {16:10} Some enemies fled to towers in the fields of Azotus, which John burned, causing about two thousand deaths. He returned safely to Judea. {16:11} Meanwhile, Ptolemy, son-in-law of the high priest, had been appointed governor of the plain of Jericho. {16:12} He amassed wealth in silver and gold and harbored ambitions to seize control of the country, devising treacherous plans against Simon and his sons. {16:13} Simon, attending to the needs of the cities, visited Jericho with his sons Mattathias and Judas in the 177th year, during the month of Shebat. {16:14} Ptolemy betrayed them at the fortress of Dok, where he had arranged a banquet and hidden men. {16:15} When Simon and his sons were intoxicated, Ptolemy's men seized their weapons and attacked them in the banquet hall, killing Simon, his two sons, and some of their servants. {16:16} This was a grievous act of treachery and ingratitude. {16:17} Ptolemy reported these events to the king, seeking military aid and control over the cities and the country. {16:18} He dispatched men to Gazara to eliminate John, and sent letters inviting captains to join him with promises of silver, gold, and gifts. {16:19} Additional men were sent to seize Jerusalem and the Temple Mount. {16:20} Meanwhile, someone hastened to Gazara to inform John that his father and brothers had been slain, and that men were coming to kill him as well. {16:21} Shocked by the news, John apprehended those sent to assassinate him and executed them upon learning of their intentions. {16:22} The chronicles of John's high priesthood recount his deeds, including his military campaigns, courageous acts, the construction of city walls, and his achievements. {16:23} These are documented from the time he assumed the high priesthood after his father.

2 Maccabees

The book of 2 Maccabees, a significant work within the Apocrypha and Deuterocanonical literature, is a historical account that complements the narrative found in 1 Maccabees. Written in Greek, it focuses on the events of the Jewish revolt against the Seleucid Empire during the second century BCE, specifically covering the period from the high priest Onias III to the defeat of Nicanor in 161 BCE. Unlike 1 Maccabees, which presents a straightforward historical chronicle, 2 Maccabees offers a theological interpretation of the events, emphasizing themes of divine intervention, martyrdom, and the struggle for religious identity and purity. The book begins with two letters addressed to the Jews in Egypt, encouraging them to observe the festival of Hanukkah, which commemorates the purification of the Temple. The narrative proper, attributed to the historian Jason of Cyrene and abridged by an anonymous editor, highlights the heroism of Judas Maccabeus and his brothers, the miraculous occurrences that signaled God's support for the Jewish cause, and the severe trials faced by the Jewish people under the oppressive rule of Antiochus IV Epiphanes. This work is also notable for its vivid descriptions of the sufferings endured by the Jewish martyrs, such as the elderly scribe Eleazar and the seven brothers who, along with their mother, chose death over transgressing the Jewish laws. These accounts serve to inspire piety and endurance among the faithful. Furthermore, 2 Maccabees provides valuable insight into Jewish beliefs during the Hellenistic period, including the concepts of the afterlife, resurrection, and intercessory prayer. The text's rich blend of historical events, theological reflection, and didactic purpose makes it a unique and invaluable resource for understanding the complex interplay between faith, politics, and culture in the Hellenistic Jewish world.

{1:1} The Jewish community in Jerusalem and throughout Judea sends greetings and wishes of peace to their Jewish brethren in Egypt. {1:2} May God bless you and remember His covenant with Abraham, Isaac, and Jacob, His faithful servants. {1:3} May He give all of you a heart to worship Him and to follow His will with courage and willingness. {1:4} May He open your hearts to His law and commandments, bringing peace into your lives. {1:5} May He hear your prayers, reconcile with you, and never abandon you in times of trouble. {1:6} We are praying earnestly for you here. {1:7} During the reign of Demetrius in the 169th year, we, the Jews, wrote to you amidst great distress following the revolt led by Jason and his supporters against the holy land and the kingdom. {1:8} We prayed to the Lord and He heard us. We offered sacrifices, set out the loaves, and lit the lamps, celebrating His deliverance. {1:9} Now, observe the Feast of Booths in the month of Chislev, in the 188th year. {1:10} To Aristobulus, of the family of the anointed priests, teacher of King Ptolemy, and to the Jews in Egypt, greetings and good health from those in Jerusalem, Judea, the senate, and Judas. {1:11} Having been saved by God from grave dangers, we thank Him greatly for siding with us against the king. {1:12} He expelled those who fought against the holy city. {1:13} When the leader advanced with a seemingly invincible force toward Persia, he and his troops were defeated in the temple of Nanea by a cunning plan devised by the priests of Nanea. {1:14} Antiochus, under the pretext of marrying her, entered the temple with his friends to seize its treasures as a dowry. {1:15} The priests of the temple of Nanea laid out the treasures and, once Antiochus entered, shut the temple doors. {1:16} Opening a secret door in the ceiling, they hurled stones at him and his men, dismembering them and tossing their heads to the crowd outside. {1:17} Blessed be our God, who has brought judgment upon the wicked. {1:18} On the 25th day of Chislev, we celebrate the purification of the temple. We inform you so that you may also celebrate the Feast of Booths and the Feast of Fire, as Nehemiah did when he rebuilt the temple and altar. {1:19} During the exile to Persia, the pious priests concealed altar fire in a dry cistern, hidden so well it remained unknown for years. {1:20} Many years later, Nehemiah, commissioned by the king of Persia, sent descendants of those priests to retrieve it. {1:21} They found not fire, but thick liquid, which Nehemiah ordered them to draw out. {1:22} When Nehemiah instructed the priests to sprinkle this liquid on the wood and offerings, a great fire suddenly blazed forth after the sun had been clouded over. {1:23} During the sacrifice, priests offered prayers, led by Jonathan with Nehemiah and others responding. {1:24} Their prayer: "O Lord, Creator of all, mighty and just, merciful and eternal, accept this sacrifice for Your people Israel. Preserve Your chosen ones and sanctify them. {1:25} Gather our scattered people, release those enslaved among the nations, and show the Gentiles that You are our God. {1:26} Punish the oppressors and the proud. {1:27} Plant Your people in Your holy place, as Moses proclaimed." {1:28} The priests then sang hymns. {1:29} When the sacrifice was consumed, Nehemiah ordered the remaining liquid poured onto large stones. {1:30} As they did, flames burst forth, but when the light from the altar reflected back, the fire extinguished. {1:31} This event became known, and the king of Persia investigated the spot where the exiled priests had hidden the fire, discovering the liquid used by Nehemiah for sacrifices. {1:32} The king sanctified the place and exchanged many valuable gifts with those he favored. {1:33} Nehemiah and his companions called this substance "nephthar," meaning purification, though most knew it as naphtha.

{2:1} According to historical records, Jeremiah the prophet instructed those being deported to take some of the fire, as previously mentioned. {2:2} He also warned them not to forget the commandments of the Lord amidst the allure of gold, silver statues, and their adornments. {2:3} Jeremiah exhorted them to keep the law steadfastly in their hearts with similar words of wisdom. {2:4} It was recorded that Jeremiah, receiving a divine oracle, ordered the tent, the ark, and the altar of incense to be taken along with him. {2:5} Jeremiah found a cave and brought the sacred items there, sealing the entrance. Some who followed him attempted to mark the way but failed to find it. {2:6} Upon learning this, Jeremiah rebuked them, declaring that the location would remain unknown until God gathers His people again in mercy. {2:7} He prophesied that God would then reveal these things, accompanied by the glory and cloud, akin to Moses' experiences and Solomon's consecration request. {2:8} Solomon, renowned for his wisdom, performed sacrifices for the temple's dedication and completion, seeking divine favor. {2:9} Just as Moses prayed and fire descended from heaven to consume sacrifices, Solomon's prayers were similarly answered. {2:10} Moses had noted that the sacrifices were fully consumed because the sin offering had not been eaten. {2:11} Solomon observed the eight days, in accordance with the sacred customs. {2:12} These accounts are found in the records and Nehemiah's memoirs, including his founding of a library containing books on kings, prophets, David's writings, and royal correspondence on offerings. {2:13} Judas Maccabeus also gathered lost books due to war, now in their possession, offering them to those in need. {2:14} As they prepared for the purification celebration, they invited others to join them in observing the days. {2:15} God, who saved His people, restored their inheritance, kingship, priesthood, and sanctification, fulfilling promises made in the law. {2:16} They hoped for God's mercy, believing He would gather them from every corner of the earth to His holy place, purifying it after rescuing them from great evils. {2:17} The narrative includes Judas Maccabeus' story, the temple's purification, altar dedication, wars against Antiochus Epiphanes and Eupator, and heavenly interventions aiding Jewish zealots who regained control of the land. {2:18} They reclaimed and freed the renowned temple, restoring nearly abolished laws, as the Lord showed great kindness to them. {2:19} Jason of Cyrene chronicled these events in five volumes, which they aimed to condense into a single book. {2:20} Acknowledging the complexity of historical accounts, they sought to please readers, aid memorization, and benefit all who engage with their condensed history. {2:21} While summarizing requires effort and sleepless nights, they accepted the challenge to offer a streamlined narrative, leaving detailed compilation to others. {2:22} Their focus was on outlining key events for clarity, akin to a builder completing a structure before considering its adornment. {2:23} They recognized the original historian's exhaustive approach while striving for brevity and clarity in their retelling. {2:24} Thus, they began their narrative, ensuring to maintain a balance between introduction and detailed history.

{3:1} In a time of enduring peace in the holy city, the laws were meticulously upheld due to the piety of High Priest Onias and his steadfast abhorrence of evil. {3:2} The city's reverence grew as even kings honored and adorned the temple with magnificent gifts. {3:3} Seleucus, king of Asia, generously funded the temple's sacrifices from his own treasury. {3:4} However, Simon of the tribe of Benjamin, appointed as temple overseer, clashed with Onias over city market affairs. {3:5} Failing to sway Onias, Simon sought aid from Apollonius of Tarsus, governor of Coelesyria and Phoenicia. {3:6} He falsely reported that Jerusalem's treasury overflowed with wealth, hinting it could benefit the king. {3:7} Apollonius, informing the king, dispatched Heliodorus to seize these funds. {3:8} Heliodorus, ostensibly touring Coelesyria and Phoenicia, was tasked with executing the king's order. {3:9} Welcomed by Jerusalem's high priest, Heliodorus disclosed the king's command and sought verification. {3:10} The high priest explained the funds included deposits for widows, orphans, and Hyrcanus' assets—400 talents of silver and 200 of gold—exposing Simon's deceit. {3:11} Emphasizing the sanctity of the temple, he opposed any misuse. {3:12} Despite this, Heliodorus insisted on confiscation per royal decree. {3:13} Setting a date, he proceeded with the treasury inspection, causing distress in the city. {3:14} Priests, in despair, prayed for divine protection of entrusted deposits. {3:15} The high priest's anguish was evident, as the city's people gathered in supplication. {3:16} Amid prayers, Heliodorus proceeded with his task. {3:17} However, upon reaching the treasury, a divine manifestation struck terror among all present, revealing God's power. {3:18} A majestic horse and its fearsome rider appeared, attacking Heliodorus with divine force. {3:19} Two glorious young men, striking in appearance, scourged him, causing deep darkness and dread. {3:20} Heliodorus, incapacitated, was carried away, his entourage witnessing God's sovereignty. {3:21} Speechless and hopeless, he lay prostrate, while the temple rejoiced at God's intervention. {3:22} As prayers continued, Heliodorus' fate hung in the balance. {3:23} Miraculously spared, he praised the Lord and vowed solemnly. {3:24} Having bid farewell to Onias, Heliodorus departed, testifying widely of God's supremacy. {3:25} He recounted his ordeal to the king, urging caution in dealings with Jerusalem. {3:26} Reflecting on divine justice, he advised sending enemies there, where God's power was evident. {3:27} Thus, the episode of Heliodorus & the temple's protection underscored God's intervention and divine justice.

{4:1} Simon, who had previously accused Onias to secure his own interests, now slandered him further, blaming Onias for instigating Heliodorus and causing the troubles. {4:2} He audaciously labeled the benefactor of the city, protector of his people, and staunch defender of the law as a traitor to the government. {4:3} Simon's animosity grew to the point where his agents even resorted to murder. {4:4} Onias realized the severity of the rivalry and understood that Apollonius, governor under Seleucus' son Antiochus Epiphanes, was exacerbating the situation at Simon's behest. {4:5} Seeking justice and peace for all, Onias approached the king, not to accuse his fellow citizens, but to safeguard the welfare of the people. {4:6} With Seleucus' death and Antiochus Epiphanes assuming the throne, Jason, Onias' brother, secured the high priesthood through bribery. {4:7} Promising Antiochus substantial silver and other revenues, Jason sought to Hellenize Jerusalem, introducing Greek customs and institutions. {4:8} With royal approval, Jason implemented these changes swiftly upon assuming office. {4:9} He undermined Jewish traditions and laws, replacing them with foreign customs, including the establishment of a gymnasium. {4:10} This shift towards Hellenization caused great distress among the priests and the people who cherished their ancestral ways. {4:11} The sacrificial rituals were neglected, and many priests abandoned their duties at the altar to pursue Greek athletic competitions. {4:12} The admiration for Greek culture and prestige led to disastrous consequences as those they emulated turned against them. {4:13} The blatant disregard for divine laws and the ensuing consequences serve as a warning in later events. {4:14} During the Tyrian games, Jason sent delegates with money intended for Hercules' sacrifice, which they diverted for naval construction. {4:15} Antiochus, hearing of unrest in Egypt, traveled to Jerusalem, where Jason welcomed him with great pomp. {4:16} Three years later, Jason was replaced by Menelaus, Simon's brother, who bribed his way to the high priesthood. {4:17} Menelaus, lacking any qualifications, exploited his position for personal gain, neglecting payments to the king. {4:18} Tensions escalated when Sostratus, demanding payment, confronted Menelaus, leading to a royal summons. {4:19} Menelaus and Sostratus left deputies in Jerusalem, but unrest continued, exacerbated by foreign rule and corruption. {4:20} Meanwhile, unrest spread to Tarsus and Mallus due to Antiochis' actions, prompting the king's intervention. {4:21} Upon returning, the king addressed the Jews' grievances and the Greeks' discontent over Menelaus' misdeeds. {4:22} The unjust murder of Onias by Menelaus and Andronicus stirred widespread sorrow and condemnation. {4:23} In a swift act of justice, Antiochus publicly executed Andronicus where he had committed the crime against Onias. {4:24} Menelaus' sacrilege and corruption incited further unrest, leading to clashes with the populace. {4:25} Despite Menelaus' attempts to evade justice through bribery, public sentiment turned against him as more injustices came to light. {4:26} The city mourned the unjust deaths caused by Menelaus' greed and abuse of power.

{5:1} Around this time, Antiochus launched his second campaign into Egypt. {5:2} During this period, an eerie phenomenon gripped the city for nearly forty days: golden-clad horsemen appeared in the sky, fully armed with lances and swords. {5:3} Spectators witnessed intense aerial battles, with troops maneuvering, shields clashing, spears thrusting, and missiles flying amidst flashes of golden armor. {5:4} The people prayed fervently, hoping this apparition signaled good fortune. {5:5} Amidst rumors of Antiochus' death, Jason led a surprise attack on Jerusalem with a thousand men. Breaching the city walls, they caused chaos until Menelaus sought refuge in the citadel. {5:6} Jason, blinded by ambition, ruthlessly slaughtered his own people, believing he was achieving victory over enemies rather than his fellow citizens. {5:7} His conspiracy failed to gain lasting control, and he fled in disgrace to the Ammonite territory. {5:8} Pursued and reviled as a traitor and murderer, Jason met a miserable end in Egypt, far from home. {5:9} Seeking refuge among the Spartans due to kinship ties, he died in exile, unmourned and without a proper burial. {5:10} The man who had caused many to be exiled and left unburied now faced a fate devoid of dignity or familial honor. {5:11} Learning of these events, Antiochus perceived a revolt in Judea, prompting him to leave Egypt and seize the city violently. {5:12} His soldiers were ordered to mercilessly cut down anyone they encountered and slay those seeking shelter in their homes. {5:13} The massacre spared no one: young or old, men, women, children, virgins, or infants. {5:14} In three days, eighty thousand were killed, with forty thousand perishing in close combat, while many others were sold into slavery. {5:15} Antiochus, emboldened, even desecrated the holiest temple, guided by Menelaus, who had betrayed his own laws and people. {5:16} He defiled sacred vessels and plundered offerings made by previous kings to enhance the temple's honor. {5:17} In his arrogance, Antiochus failed to see that divine anger had been stirred by the city's sins, leading to disregard for its sanctity. {5:18} Had it not been for their transgressions, Antiochus would have been thwarted like Heliodorus before him. {5:19} The nation was chosen for the sake of the temple, not the other way around, and endured the consequences of their actions. {5:20} Despite suffering, the temple eventually regained its glory when reconciliation came from the Almighty. {5:21} Antiochus seized eighteen hundred talents from the temple and departed for Antioch, deluded by his own pride and arrogance. {5:22} He appointed ruthless governors: Philip in Jerusalem, Andronicus at Gerizim, and Menelaus, who oppressed his own people with malice. {5:23} Antiochus dispatched Apollonius with twenty-two thousand troops to slaughter men, sell women and children into slavery, and enforce his tyranny. {5:24} Apollonius waited until the Sabbath, then attacked Jerusalem, massacring those who came out unarmed. {5:25} Judas Maccabeus and his small band fled to the wilderness, surviving like wild animals in the mountains to avoid defilement.

{6:1} Shortly thereafter, the king dispatched an Athenian envoy to enforce Hellenization among the Jews, compelling them to forsake their ancestral laws and abandon the ways of God. {6:2} The envoy's mandate was to desecrate the Jerusalem temple, renaming it after Olympian Zeus, and similarly defile the temple at Gerizim as the sanctuary of Zeus the Hospitable, as practiced by the local populace. {6:3} The onslaught of evil was severe and grievous. {6:4} The temple became a den of debauchery and revelry, with Gentiles engaging in immoral acts, including sacrilegious offerings and illicit practices within its sacred precincts. {6:5} The altar was desecrated with forbidden offerings, violating the laws of God. {6:6} Jews were prohibited from observing the Sabbath, celebrating their traditional feasts, or even openly identifying as Jews. {6:7} On the king's birthday and during the Dionysian feasts, Jews were forcibly coerced to participate in sacrificial rituals and processionals, wearing ivy wreaths in honor of Dionysus. {6:8} At Ptolemy's urging, neighboring Greek cities were instructed to adopt similar policies, forcing Jews to conform under threat of death for non-compliance. The misery inflicted upon them was evident. {6:9} For instance, two women were publicly punished for circumcising their children, paraded with their babies before being thrown to their deaths from the city walls. {6:10} Others who secretly observed the Sabbath in caves were betrayed and burned alive by Philip's forces. {6:11} Despite these calamities, the author encourages readers not to despair, but to understand these trials as disciplinary measures rather than total destruction. {6:12} Prompt punishment of the impious reflects divine kindness, sparing the nation from greater wrath when sins reach their peak. {6:13} Unlike other nations, which face delayed punishment, God's mercy ensures that His people are disciplined for their ultimate good. {6:14} The Lord disciplines with calamity but never abandons His people. {6:15} These reminders are crucial as the narrative continues. {6:16} Eleazar, a respected elder, faced the ordeal of being compelled to eat swine's flesh under penalty of death. {6:17} He chose death with honor rather than defilement, refusing to compromise his principles. {6:18} Even when offered a deceptive way out by friends, he courageously rejected it, embracing death in accordance with God's law and his own dignity. {6:19} Eleazar declared that pretending to eat the forbidden meat would set a dangerous precedent and dishonor his old age. {6:20} He emphasized the importance of refusing what is wrong, even at the cost of life itself. {6:21} Knowing that even if he escaped immediate death, he could not escape God's judgment, he resolved to face martyrdom bravely. {6:22} He chose to leave a noble example for the young and future generations, showing how to die with dignity for the sake of revered laws. {6:23} Thus resolved, Eleazar willingly faced the torture device. {6:24} Those who once showed him kindness now turned against him, unable to comprehend his steadfastness. {6:25} As he endured excruciating pain, Eleazar's soul found solace in his commitment to God, despite the physical suffering. {6:26} He died with the conviction that enduring suffering for righteousness' sake was better than compromising for a brief extension of life. {6:27} His courageous death became a testament to nobility and a legacy of bravery, inspiring both the youth and the entire nation.

{7:1} It so happened that seven brothers and their mother were arrested and forcibly compelled by the king, under torture with whips and cords, to eat unlawful swine's flesh. {7:2} One of the brothers, speaking on behalf of them all, boldly declared, "What do you intend to ask and learn from us? We are prepared to die rather than violate the laws of our fathers." {7:3} Enraged, the king ordered pans and cauldrons to be heated immediately. {7:4} He commanded that the tongue of the spokesman be cut out, his scalp peeled off, and his hands and feet amputated, while his brothers and mother were made to watch. {7:5} Helpless, the spokesman was then taken to the fire, still breathing, and fried in a pan. The smoke spread far, but the brothers and their mother encouraged each other to die nobly, saying, {7:6} "The Lord God is watching over us and has true compassion for us, as Moses declared in his song, testifying against the people when he said, 'And he will have compassion on his servants.'" {7:7} After the first brother died in this manner, they brought forward the second to be tortured for their amusement. They stripped the skin from his head with the hair and asked him, "Will you eat rather than endure your body being tortured limb by limb?" {7:8} He answered in his native tongue, "No." Thus he endured the same tortures as his brother. {7:9} When he was near death, he defiantly proclaimed, "You accursed tyrant, you dismiss us from this life, but the King of the universe will raise us up to an everlasting renewal of life, because we have died for his laws." {7:10} Following him, the third brother suffered the same fate. When demanded to comply, he quickly extended his hands and said boldly, {7:11} "These I received from Heaven, and for his laws I scorn them, and from him I hope to receive them again." {7:12} The king and his entourage were astonished at the young man's courage; he endured his sufferings as though they were nothing. {7:13} After his death, they subjected the fourth brother to the same torment. {7:14} As he approached death, he said, "It is inevitable to die at the hands of men and cherish the hope that God provides of being raised again by him. But for you, there will be no resurrection to life!" {7:15} They then brought forward the fifth brother and subjected him to maltreatment. {7:16} He looked at the king and said, "You wield authority among men, though mortal. You do as you please, but do not think that God has abandoned our people. {7:17} Continue, and witness how his mighty power will afflict you and your descendants!" {7:18} Next, they brought forward the sixth brother. As he faced death, he declared, {7:19} "Do not delude yourself in vain. We suffer these things because of our own sins against our God. Therefore, extraordinary things have occurred. {7:20} But do not think that you will escape punishment for attempting to fight against God!" {7:21} The mother was particularly remarkable and deserving of honorable remembrance. Despite witnessing her seven sons perish in one day, she endured with courage because of her trust in the Lord. {7:22} Encouraging each son in their native language, she spoke with a noble spirit, blending feminine wisdom with masculine courage, saying to them, {7:23} "I do not know how you came into being in my womb. It was not I who gave you life and breath, nor I who set in order the elements within each of you. {7:24} Therefore, the Creator of the world, who formed the beginning of mankind and devised the origin of all things, will in his mercy restore life and breath to you again, since you now disregard yourselves for the sake of his laws." {7:25} Antiochus perceived that he was being treated with disdain and became suspicious of her reproachful tone. Since the youngest brother was still alive, Antiochus not only appealed to him with words but also promised with oaths that he would make him wealthy and honored if he would abandon the ways of his fathers and become his friend, entrusted with public affairs. {7:26} When the young man refused to listen at all, the king summoned the mother and urged her to persuade her son to save himself. {7:27} After much pleading from him, she attempted to persuade her son. {7:28} Drawing close to him, she spoke to him in their native tongue, ridiculing the cruel tyrant, saying, "My son, have pity on me. I carried you for nine months in my womb, nursed you for three years, raised and cared for you until this moment in your life. {7:29} I beg you, my child, look at the heavens and the earth and all that is in them, and recognize that God did not create them out of pre-existing materials. This is also how humanity came into being. {7:30} Do not fear this butcher, but prove yourself worthy of your brothers. Accept death, so that in God's mercy, I may be reunited with you and your brothers." {7:31} While she was still speaking, the young man said, "What are you waiting for? I will not obey the king's command, but I obey the command of the law given to our fathers through Moses. {7:32} But you, who have devised all sorts of evil against the Hebrews, will certainly not escape God's hands. {7:33} We are suffering because of our own sins. {7:34} If our living Lord is briefly angry to rebuke and discipline us, he will again be reconciled with his servants. {7:35} But you, unholy tyrant, most defiled of all men, do not be vainly elated and puffed up by uncertain hopes, when you raise your hand against the children of heaven. {7:36} You have not yet escaped the judgment of the almighty, all-seeing God. {7:37} Like my brothers, I surrender my body and life for the laws of our fathers, appealing to God to soon show mercy to our nation and through afflictions and plagues make you acknowledge that he alone is God. {7:38} By me and my brothers, may the wrath of the Almighty, justly fallen upon our entire nation, come to an end." {7:39} The king, enraged, treated him worse than the others, infuriated by his defiance. {7:40} So he died with integrity, placing his full trust in the Lord. {7:41} Lastly, the mother died after her sons. {7:42} This concludes the account of the sacrifices and the extreme tortures endured.

{8:1} Judas, also known as Maccabeus, along with his companions, entered villages secretly and gathered about six thousand men, rallying those who remained faithful to the Jewish faith. {8:2} They prayed earnestly to the Lord to look upon the oppressed people, to have mercy on the desecrated temple, {8:3} and to spare the city on the brink of destruction, listening to the cries of those whose blood was shed unjustly. {8:4} They also pleaded for justice against the unlawful killing of innocent children and blasphemies against God's name, asking for God's hatred of evil to be shown. {8:5} As soon as Maccabeus organized his army, the Gentiles could not withstand them, for the wrath of the Lord had turned into mercy. {8:6} They launched surprise attacks, setting fire to towns and villages, seizing strategic positions, and putting many enemies to flight. {8:7} Nighttime raids proved advantageous, and tales of their bravery spread widely. {8:8} Seeing Judas gaining ground, Philip wrote urgently to Ptolemy, governor of Coelesyria and Phoenicia, seeking aid for the king's cause. {8:9} Ptolemy sent Nicanor, a close friend of the king, with twenty thousand troops of diverse nations, alongside experienced general Gorgias, to annihilate the Jews. {8:10} Nicanor aimed to pay the Romans the tribute owed by selling captured Jews into slavery. {8:11} He sent messengers to coastal cities to sell Jewish slaves at a price, unaware of the divine judgment that awaited him. {8:12} When Judas learned of Nicanor's invasion, some of his fearful companions fled, while others sold their possessions, praying to the Lord to rescue those enslaved by Nicanor before they were harmed. {8:13} Maccabeus rallied six thousand men and encouraged them not to fear the wicked Gentiles amassing against them but to fight courageously. {8:14} He reminded them of the Gentiles' sacrilege against the holy place, the torment of their city, and the destruction of their ancestral way of life. {8:15} "They trust in their weapons and boldness," he declared, "but we trust in Almighty God, who can with a mere nod strike down our enemies and even the entire world." {8:16} He recounted past instances of divine intervention for their ancestors, such as against Sennacherib and the Galatians, to bolster their resolve to die for their laws and country. {8:17} Judas divided his army into four parts, appointing his brothers to lead three and preparing Eleazar to read from the holy book. {8:18} Leading the first division himself, they engaged Nicanor's forces in battle, supported by the Almighty, who enabled them to slay over nine thousand enemies and scatter the rest. {8:19} They seized the enemy's wealth intended for buying Jewish slaves and pursued them until late, returning due to the approaching Sabbath. {8:20} They kept the Sabbath, giving thanks to the Lord for preserving them and marking it as a day of mercy. {8:21} After the Sabbath, they shared spoils with the tortured, widows, and orphans, and prayed for God's full reconciliation. {8:22} In subsequent battles against Timothy and Bacchides, they killed over twenty thousand enemies, seized strongholds, and distributed plunder generously. {8:23} They collected enemy arms and stored them strategically, bringing the spoils to Jerusalem. {8:24} They also executed Callisthenes and others who had desecrated the sacred gates, celebrating their victory in their ancestral city. {8:25} Nicanor, humbled by opponents he underestimated, fled disgracefully, stripped of his glory, until he reached Antioch, having ruined his own army. {8:26} Thus, the one who sought Roman tribute by enslaving Jerusalem's people acknowledged the Jews' Divine Protector, affirming their invincibility in following God's ordained laws.

{9:1} Around that time, Antiochus found himself in disarray after retreating from Persia. {9:2} He had entered Persepolis with intentions to plunder temples and assert control, but the people rose up in defense, armed themselves, and defeated Antiochus and his men. He was forced to flee in disgraceful defeat. {9:3} While in Ecbatana, news reached him of Nicanor's and Timothy's defeats. {9:4} Filled with rage, he decided to avenge his humiliation by turning against the Jews. He ordered his charioteer to rush without pause towards Jerusalem, boasting arrogantly, "I will turn Jerusalem into a graveyard for Jews." {9:5} But the all-seeing Lord, the God of Israel, struck him with an incurable and invisible affliction. As soon as he spoke those words, he was seized with excruciating pain in his bowels, with no relief and intense internal agony — a just punishment for his cruelty towards others. {9:6} Despite this suffering, Antiochus did not repent but became even more arrogant, burning with rage against the Jews and hastening his journey. {9:7} As he rushed in his chariot, he fell out violently, injuring every limb of his body. {9:8} Thus, the one who thought he could command the seas and measure mountains with arrogance was humbled, carried away in a litter, demonstrating God's power to all. {9:9} His body became infested with worms while he still lived in agony, his flesh rotting away and spreading a foul stench that repulsed his entire army. {9:10} His unbearable odor prevented anyone from carrying him, a stark contrast to his earlier pride of touching the stars. {9:11} Broken in spirit, he began to realize his arrogance under God's punishment, tortured by constant pain. {9:12} Unable to bear his own stench, he acknowledged, "It is right to submit to God; no mortal should think himself equal to God." {9:13} In his desperation, he vowed to the Lord, but mercy was no longer with him. {9:14} He declared Jerusalem free from his intended destruction, {9:15} promised to treat the Jews as citizens equal to those of Athens, whom he had planned to throw to beasts and birds. {9:16} He pledged to adorn the holy sanctuary and return its vessels many times over, funding sacrifices from his own treasury. {9:17} Moreover, he proclaimed his intention to convert to Judaism and travel widely to proclaim God's power. {9:18} However, his suffering continued unabated, the rightful judgment of God upon him, leading him to despair for himself. He then wrote a supplication to the Jews, as follows: {9:19} "To my esteemed Jewish citizens, greetings from Antiochus, your king and general. I wish you health and prosperity. {9:20} If you and your children are well and all is as you wish, I am glad. {9:21} I remember fondly your goodwill towards me. On my return from Persia, I fell ill, prompting me to consider the security of all. {9:22} Though I have hope for recovery, I recall how my father appointed a successor during his expeditions, ensuring stability in the realm. {9:23} I have appointed my son Antiochus as king, entrusting him to many of you during my absence in the upper provinces. I have written to him as well. {9:24} I urge you to remember the services I rendered, both publicly and privately, and to maintain your goodwill towards me and my son. {9:25} I trust he will continue my policies and treat you with fairness and kindness." {9:26} Thus, the murderer and blasphemer, suffering the intense agony he had inflicted on others, met a pitiful end in a foreign land among the mountains. {9:27} His body was taken by Philip, one of his courtiers, who then fled to Ptolemy Philometor in Egypt, fearing Antiochus's son.

{10:1} At this time, Maccabeus and his followers, guided by the Lord, reclaimed the temple and the city. {10:2} They demolished the altars erected by foreigners in the public square and destroyed the idolatrous shrines. {10:3} After purifying the sanctuary, they constructed a new altar for sacrifices. Using flint, they kindled fire for offerings after a lapse of two years. They burned incense, lit lamps, and presented the Bread of the Presence. {10:4} Upon completing these rituals, they humbly prostrated themselves, entreating the Lord never to allow such calamities to befall them again. If they were to sin, they prayed for God's merciful discipline instead of being delivered into the hands of blasphemous nations. {10:5} It so happened that the day the sanctuary was profaned by foreigners coincided with its purification — the twenty-fifth day of the month of Chislev. {10:6} They celebrated this purification for eight days with joy, similar to the Feast of Booths, recalling their recent hardships when they had wandered like wild animals in mountains and caves during the Feast of Booths. {10:7} Carrying ivy-wrapped wands, beautiful branches, and palm fronds, they offered hymns of gratitude to God, who had enabled the cleansing of His holy place. {10:8} By public decree and unanimous vote, they ordained that all Jews should observe these days annually. {10:9} This marked the end of Antiochus Epiphanes. {10:10} Now, let us recount the events under Antiochus Eupator, son of that wicked man, and summarize the main calamities of the wars. {10:11} Upon assuming the throne, he appointed Lysias as governor over Coelesyria and Phoenicia. {10:12} Ptolemy Macron, who had shown justice to the Jews due to the injustices they suffered, attempted to maintain peace with them. {10:13} However, he was accused before Eupator by the king's supporters. Constantly called a traitor for abandoning Cyprus entrusted to him by Philometor to join Antiochus Epiphanes, he, unable to maintain his dignity, took his own life by poison. {10:14} When Gorgias became governor, he maintained a mercenary force and persistently waged war against the Jews. {10:15} Additionally, the Idumeans controlled key strongholds, welcomed exiles from Jerusalem, and continued the conflict. {10:16} Maccabeus and his men prayed earnestly, asking God to fight alongside them, then attacked the Idumean strongholds. {10:17} They vigorously assaulted and seized the fortresses, defeating all defenders and killing more than twenty thousand enemies. {10:18} When nine thousand sought refuge in two well-fortified towers, Maccabeus left Simon, Joseph, and Zacchaeus to besiege them while he dealt with other urgent matters. {10:19} However, the men with Simon were bribed and allowed some enemies to escape by accepting seventy thousand drachmas. {10:20} Learning of this betrayal, Maccabeus assembled the leaders and accused those who had sold out their brethren for money, executed them, and captured the two towers. {10:21} Successful in all his military endeavors, he slew more than twenty thousand defenders in the two strongholds. {10:22} Timothy, previously defeated by the Jews, gathered a large force of mercenaries and cavalry from Asia to attack Judea. {10:23} As he approached, Maccabeus and his men prayed, sprinkling dust on their heads and wearing sackcloth, appealing to God. {10:24} They prayed fervently before the altar, asking God to favor them, oppose their enemies, and fulfill the Law. {10:25} Rising from prayer, they armed themselves and advanced toward the enemy, stopping near them. {10:26} At dawn, the two armies clashed; the Jews relied on their valor and faith in the Lord for victory, while their enemies fought in blind rage. {10:27} In the midst of fierce battle, five radiant men on horses with golden bridles appeared from heaven to lead the Jews, surrounding Maccabeus and shielding him with their armor and weapons. {10:28} They launched arrows and thunderbolts at the enemy, causing confusion and disorder, leading to their defeat and slaughter. {10:29} Twenty thousand five hundred were killed, including six hundred cavalrymen. {10:30} Timothy fled to the well-fortified Gazara, defended by Chaereas. {10:31} Maccabeus besieged the fortress for four days, and on the fifth day, twenty young men, incensed by blasphemies, stormed the walls and slaughtered the defenders. {10:32} They set fire to the towers, burned the blasphemers alive, and captured the city. {10:33} They killed Timothy, hiding in a cistern, along with his brother Chaereas and Apollophanes. {10:34} With hymns and thanksgivings, they praised the Lord, who had shown great kindness to Israel and granted them victory.

{11:1} Shortly after these events, Lysias, the guardian and relative of the king who was overseeing the government, became greatly troubled by what had transpired. {11:2} He assembled around eighty thousand soldiers and all his cavalry, marching against the Jews with the intention to Hellenize Jerusalem, impose taxes on the temple like other sacred sites, and auction off the high priesthood annually. {11:3} Disregarding the power of God, he relied on his vast infantry, cavalry, and eighty elephants. {11:4} Approaching Judea, he besieged the fortified city of Beth-zur, located about twenty-five miles from Jerusalem. {11:5} When Maccabeus and his men heard that Lysias was laying siege to their strongholds, they and the people beseeched the Lord with tears and lamentations to send a divine messenger to rescue Israel. {11:6} Maccabeus took up arms first, urging others to join him in risking their lives to aid their brethren. Together, they hurried off in determination. {11:7} While still near Jerusalem, a horseman appeared leading them, dressed in white and wielding golden weapons. {11:8} Unified in praising God, they were emboldened, ready to confront any enemy or obstacle. {11:9} They marched into battle formation, accompanied by their celestial ally, as the Lord showed them mercy. {11:10} Like lions, they charged against the enemy, slaying eleven thousand infantry and sixteen hundred cavalry, causing the rest to flee in disarray. {11:11} Most of them escaped stripped and wounded, while Lysias himself fled in shameful retreat. {11:12} Reflecting on his defeat, Lysias realized the invincibility of the Hebrews, aided by the mighty God. {11:13} He sent envoys to negotiate peace terms, promising to persuade the king to befriend the Jews. {11:14} Maccabeus, concerned for the common good, agreed to Lysias' terms. The king granted all requests Maccabeus presented in writing. {11:15} Lysias' letter to the Jews declared the king's approval: Lysias to the Jewish people, greetings. {11:16} John and Absalom have delivered your message and inquired about your requests. {11:17} I have informed the king and he has agreed to what is feasible. {11:18} If you maintain loyalty to the government, I will strive for your welfare. {11:19} I have dispatched representatives to discuss these matters with you. Farewell. {11:20} King Antiochus' letter to Lysias affirmed the king's intentions: Antiochus to his brother Lysias, greetings. {11:21} We wish the kingdom's subjects to manage their own affairs without disturbance. {11:22} We have learned the Jews prefer their own customs to Greek ways and request their traditions be respected. {11:23} Therefore, we decree their temple be restored and they live according to their ancestral customs. {11:24} Encourage them with assurances of friendship, so they may prosper and govern their affairs joyfully. {11:25} The king's message to the Jewish assembly read: Antiochus to the Jewish senate and people, greetings. {11:26} If you are well, we are pleased. {11:27} Menelaus reports your desire to return home and manage your affairs. {11:28} Those who return by the thirtieth day of Xanthicus will have our friendship and permission to observe your customs freely, without fear of reprisal for past misunderstandings. {11:29} Menelaus is dispatched to offer further encouragement. Farewell. {11:30} The Romans also sent a letter of approval: Quintus Memmius and Titus Manius, Roman envoys, to the Jewish people, greetings. {11:31} We consent to the terms granted by Lysias. {11:32} Regarding matters to be referred to the king, send representatives promptly for our discussions in Antioch. {11:33} Hurry and send your delegates so we can proceed accordingly. Farewell.

{12:1} After reaching an agreement, Lysias returned to the king, and the Jews resumed their agricultural pursuits. {12:2} However, certain governors in different regions—Timothy, Apollonius (son of Gennaeus), Hieronymus, Demophon, and Nicanor (governor of Cyprus)—refused to let the Jews live in peace. {12:3} In Joppa, some men committed a heinous act: they deceitfully invited Jews to board boats with their families, feigning friendship, but then drowned over two hundred of them at sea, sanctioned by a public vote. {12:4} Hearing of this cruelty, Judas Maccabeus, invoking God as the righteous Judge, launched a retaliatory attack. Under cover of night, he set fire to the harbor, burned the boats, and massacred those seeking refuge. {12:5} Facing closed city gates, he withdrew with plans to return and eradicate the entire community of Joppa. {12:6} Learning that the people of Jamnia also intended harm against the Jews living there, he launched a surprise night attack, setting their harbor and fleet ablaze, visible from Jerusalem, thirty miles away. {12:7} While marching towards Timothy, they encountered five thousand Arabs and five hundred cavalry. {12:8} After a fierce battle, Judas emerged victorious with God's help, and the defeated Arabs offered pledges of friendship and support. {12:9} Judas accepted peace with them, recognizing their potential assistance. {12:10} He then besieged Caspin, a strongly fortified city of Gentiles, known for their insolence and blasphemy against God. {12:11} Calling upon the Almighty, Judas stormed the walls and captured the city, slaughtering countless enemies, staining the nearby lake with blood. {12:12} Moving on, they reached Charax, among the Toubiani Jews, where they found no trace of Timothy but destroyed his garrison elsewhere, eliminating over ten thousand men. {12:13} Organizing his forces, Judas pursued Timothy, who had a large army of infantry and cavalry. {12:14} Learning of Judas' approach, Timothy sent away women, children, and baggage to Carnaim, a hard-to-reach place. {12:15} When Judas' forces arrived, fear spread among the enemy, and in the ensuing chaos, thirty thousand were slain as Judas relentlessly pursued them. {12:16} Capturing Timothy, Dositheus and Sosipater spared him due to his hostages, although they released him under solemn promise. {12:17} Judas then attacked Carnaim and the temple of Atargatis, massacring twenty-five thousand people. {12:18} He proceeded to Ephron, where Lysias resided with a well-defended population of various nationalities. {12:19} Calling upon God's power, the Jews overcame the city, killing twenty-five thousand within. {12:20} Continuing to Scythopolis, seventy-five miles from Jerusalem, they were received warmly by the residents, who had previously shown kindness to Jewish refugees. {12:21} Thanking them, Judas urged continued goodwill towards their people. {12:22} They returned to Jerusalem just before the Feast of Weeks. {12:23} Following Pentecost, they confronted Gorgias, governor of Idumea, with three thousand infantry and four hundred cavalry. {12:24} Though a few Jews fell, Dositheus managed to capture Gorgias briefly, until a Thracian horseman severed his arm, allowing Gorgias to escape. {12:25} Encouraged by God, Judas rallied his men against Gorgias' forces, surprising them and forcing their retreat. {12:26} Judas then led his army to Adullam, where they purified themselves and observed the Sabbath. {12:27} The next day, they retrieved and buried their fallen comrades, discovering idols under their garments, revealing why they had perished. {12:28} Acknowledging God's righteous judgment, they prayed for forgiveness and exhorted one another to avoid sin. {12:29} Judas collected two thousand drachmas for a sin offering to Jerusalem, acting with great honor and foresight concerning resurrection. {12:30} For if he did not believe in resurrection, praying for the dead would have been pointless. {12:31} However, expecting the reward for the godly, he performed a holy and devout act, making atonement for the fallen.

{13:1} In the one hundred and forty-ninth year, Judas and his men received word that Antiochus Eupator was coming against Judea with a massive army. {13:2} Accompanied by his guardian Lysias, they had a Greek force consisting of one hundred and ten thousand infantry, five thousand three hundred cavalry, twenty-two elephants, and three hundred scythe-equipped chariots. {13:3} Menelaus also joined them, hypocritically urging Antiochus forward, not for his country's benefit, but to secure his own position. {13:4} However, the King of kings stirred Antiochus' anger against Menelaus, and Lysias informed the king that Menelaus was the cause of their troubles. Antiochus ordered Menelaus to be executed in Beroea according to their custom. {13:5} In Beroea, there is a fifty-cubit tower filled with ashes, with a rim around it sloping steeply into the ashes. {13:6} They push any man guilty of sacrilege or other notorious crimes into the ashes to their death. {13:7} Thus, Menelaus the lawbreaker met his end without burial. {13:8} This was fitting, as he had sinned against the holy altar's fire and ashes and died in ashes. {13:9} The king, with barbarous arrogance, intended to inflict worse atrocities on the Jews than his father had. {13:10} When Judas heard this, he urged the people to call upon the Lord day and night for help, as they were on the verge of losing their law, country, and holy temple. {13:11} He did not want the recently revived people to fall into the hands of blasphemous Gentiles. {13:12} After three days of continuous weeping, fasting, and praying, Judas encouraged the people and ordered them to prepare for battle. {13:13} Consulting privately with the elders, he decided to confront the king's army before they could enter Judea. {13:14} Trusting the outcome to the Creator, he exhorted his men to fight bravely for their laws, temple, city, country, and community, and camped near Modein. {13:15} He gave his men the watchword, "God's victory," and with a select force of brave young men, he attacked the king's camp at night, killing two thousand men and the leading elephant with its rider. {13:16} They caused terror and confusion in the camp and withdrew triumphantly. {13:17} This occurred at dawn, with the Lord's help protecting them. {13:18} Having experienced the Jews' daring, the king tried a strategic approach to attack their positions. {13:19} He advanced against Beth-zur, a Jewish stronghold, but was repelled and defeated again. {13:20} Judas ensured the garrison had all necessary supplies. {13:21} However, Rhodocus, a Jew, secretly informed the enemy; he was caught and imprisoned. {13:22} The king negotiated again with the people in Beth-zur, exchanged pledges, withdrew, and then attacked Judas and his men but was defeated. {13:23} He received news that Philip, left in charge of the government, had revolted in Antioch. Distressed, he made peace with the Jews, swore to honor their rights, and offered sacrifices, showing respect and generosity to the holy place. {13:24} He received Maccabeus, appointed Hegemonides as governor from Ptolemais to Gerar, {13:25} and went to Ptolemais, where the people were angry over the treaty and wanted to annul it. {13:26} Lysias addressed them publicly, made a strong defense, appeased their anger, gained their goodwill, and then set out for Antioch. Thus, the king's attack and subsequent withdrawal concluded.

{14:1} Three years later, Judas and his men learned that Demetrius, the son of Seleucus, had arrived in the harbor of Tripolis with a strong army and fleet, taking over the country after killing Antiochus and his guardian Lysias. {14:2} He had seized control of the region. {14:3} Alcimus, who had been the high priest but had defiled himself during the separation, realized he had no way to return safely to the holy altar. {14:4} He went to King Demetrius in the one hundred and fifty-first year, presenting him with a gold crown, a palm, and olive branches from the temple. He remained silent that day. {14:5} Finding an opportunity to further his plans, he spoke when invited by Demetrius to a council meeting, where he was asked about the Jews' intentions. {14:6} He said, "The Hasideans, led by Judas Maccabeus, are stirring up rebellion and preventing the kingdom from finding peace. {14:7} I have laid aside my ancestral glory, the high priesthood, and come here {14:8} out of genuine concern for the king and my fellow citizens. Our nation suffers greatly due to the folly of these men. {14:9} Knowing the details, O king, please consider our country's plight with your usual kindness. {14:10} As long as Judas lives, peace is impossible for the government." {14:11} This speech inflamed Demetrius further, supported by the king's friends who were hostile to Judas. {14:12} He immediately appointed Nicanor, formerly in charge of the elephants, as governor of Judea, with orders to kill Judas, scatter his men, and install Alcimus as high priest. {14:13} Gentiles throughout Judea, who had fled from Judas, joined Nicanor, hoping the Jews' misfortunes would bring them prosperity. {14:14} Hearing of Nicanor's approach, the Jews sprinkled dust on their heads and prayed to God, who protects his people and heritage. {14:15} At Judas' command, they set out and engaged in battle at a village called Dessau. {14:16} Simon, Judas' brother, faced Nicanor but was initially checked by the enemy's sudden attack. {14:17} Nonetheless, Nicanor, aware of Judas' valor and courage, hesitated to resolve the issue with bloodshed. {14:18} He sent Posidonius, Theodotus, and Mattathias to negotiate peace. {14:19} After considering the terms and informing the people, who were united, they agreed to a covenant. {14:20} The leaders set a meeting date, with honor seats prepared and armed men posted by Judas to prevent treachery. {14:21} The conference was held without incident. {14:22} Nicanor remained in Jerusalem, dismissed the gathered crowds, and maintained a friendly relationship with Judas. {14:23} He urged Judas to marry and have children, which Judas did, settling down to a normal life. {14:24} When Alcimus saw their goodwill, he took the covenant to Demetrius, accusing Nicanor of disloyalty for supporting Judas. {14:25} Provoked by these false accusations, the king wrote to Nicanor, expressing displeasure with the covenant and commanding him to send Judas to Antioch as a prisoner. {14:26} Nicanor, troubled by this order, sought a way to comply without opposing the king. {14:27} Noticing Nicanor's changed behavior, Judas suspected ill intentions and went into hiding with his men. {14:28} Realizing he had been outwitted, Nicanor went to the temple, where priests were offering sacrifices, and demanded they hand over Judas. {14:29} When they swore they did not know his whereabouts, {14:30} Nicanor threatened to destroy the temple and build one for Dionysus if they did not comply. {14:31} Leaving after his threat, the priests prayed to God for protection of the holy temple. {14:32} Razis, a respected elder known as the father of the Jews for his goodwill, was accused of supporting Judaism and had zealously defended it. {14:33} Nicanor, wishing to demonstrate his enmity, sent over five hundred soldiers to arrest Razis, thinking this would harm the Jews. {14:34} Surrounded and with doors being burned, Razis chose to die nobly and fell on his sword. {14:35} Missing his vital organs, he ran to the wall and threw himself into the crowd. {14:36} Falling into an open space, {14:37} he rose despite severe wounds, ran through the crowd, and standing on a rock, tore out his entrails, throwing them at the crowd while calling on the Lord to restore his spirit. This was how he died.

{15:1} When Nicanor heard that Judas and his men were in the region of Samaria, he planned to attack them on the Sabbath, thinking it would be safe. {15:2} The Jews following him begged him not to be so savage and to respect the holy day. {15:3} Nicanor arrogantly asked if there was a heavenly ruler who commanded the observance of the Sabbath. {15:4} They affirmed that it was the living Lord in heaven who ordered them to keep the seventh day holy. {15:5} Nicanor replied, "I am a ruler on earth, and I command you to take up arms and finish the king's business." However, he failed in his plan. {15:6} In his arrogance, Nicanor had planned to build a monument celebrating his victory over Judas and his men. {15:7} But Judas, trusting completely in the Lord, encouraged his men to remember past times when they had received help from heaven and to trust that the Almighty would give them victory again. {15:8} He reminded them of the law and the prophets and the battles they had won, making them more eager to fight. {15:9} He aroused their courage, pointing out the treachery of the Gentiles and their broken oaths. {15:10} He armed them more with brave words than with weapons, inspiring them with a vision he had. {15:11} In his vision, he saw Onias, a former high priest, praying for the Jews. {15:12} Another man appeared, distinguished and majestic. {15:13} Onias identified him as Jeremiah, the prophet of God, who loved and prayed for the people and the holy city. {15:14} Jeremiah gave Judas a golden sword, telling him it was a gift from God to strike down his enemies. {15:15} Inspired by Judas' words and the vision, his men resolved to fight bravely to protect the city and the sanctuary. {15:16} Their concern for their families was secondary; their primary fear was for the consecrated sanctuary. {15:17} Those left in the city were deeply distressed, anxious about the battle. {15:18} As the enemy approached, with elephants strategically placed and cavalry on the flanks, {15:19} Judas saw the vast forces and the array of weapons. He stretched out his hands to heaven, calling on the Lord who works wonders, knowing that victory comes from God. {15:20} He prayed, "O Lord, you sent an angel in Hezekiah's time to slay 185,000 in Sennacherib's camp. {15:21} Now, send a good angel to spread terror before us, and by your mighty arm, strike down these blasphemers." {15:22} With this prayer, he ended. {15:23} Nicanor and his men advanced with trumpets and battle songs, {15:24} while Judas and his men met them with prayers and invocations to God. {15:25} Fighting with their hands and praying in their hearts, they killed 35,000 men and rejoiced in God's help. {15:26} After the battle, they found Nicanor dead in his armor. {15:27} They praised the Sovereign Lord in their native language. {15:28} Judas, the defender of his people, ordered Nicanor's head and arm to be cut off and taken to Jerusalem. {15:29} When he arrived, he called his countrymen and the priests to the altar, summoning those in the citadel. {15:30} He showed them Nicanor's head and the arm that had boasted against God's holy house. {15:31} He cut out Nicanor's tongue and said he would give it to the birds, then hung the head opposite the sanctuary. {15:32} Everyone blessed the Lord, saying, "Blessed is he who has kept his place undefiled." {15:33} They hung Nicanor's head on the citadel as a clear sign of the Lord's help. {15:34} They decreed to celebrate the thirteenth day of the twelfth month, called Adar, the day before Mordecai's day, as a perpetual holiday. {15:35} This is how Nicanor was defeated, and the city remained in Hebrew hands. {15:36} Thus, I conclude my story. If it is well told and effective, that is what I desired; if it is poorly done, it was the best I could do. {15:37} Just as wine mixed with water is sweet and enhances enjoyment, so too does a well-told story delight its readers. And here will be the end.

3 Maccabees

The Book of 3 Maccabees, a part of the Apocrypha, is a fascinating text that offers rich insights into Jewish history and culture during the Hellenistic period. Despite its name, it is not directly related to the first two books of Maccabees but shares the common theme of Jewish perseverance under foreign oppression. Composed in Greek, it likely originated in the first century BCE or early first century CE, during the time when the Jewish diaspora community in Alexandria faced significant challenges. The narrative centers around the persecution of Jews in Egypt under Ptolemy IV Philopator and details their miraculous deliverance. The book opens with a description of Ptolemy IV's victory over Antiochus III at the Battle of Raphia and his subsequent visit to Jerusalem, where he attempts to enter the Holy of Holies in the Temple, an act prevented by divine intervention. Enraged by this, Ptolemy returns to Egypt and initiates severe repressive measures against the Jews, including an attempt to register them as slaves. The climax of the book features a dramatic account of the Jews being confined in the hippodrome of Alexandria and threatened with mass execution by intoxicated elephants, only to be saved by a series of divine interventions. This miraculous rescue leads to a decree of favor towards the Jews and a period of peace and prosperity. Through its vivid storytelling and theological themes, 3 Maccabees emphasizes the power of faith and divine protection, serving as both a historical account and a piece of inspirational literature. The book also reflects broader issues of identity, assimilation, and resistance within the Jewish diaspora, making it a valuable text for understanding the complex dynamics of Jewish life under Hellenistic rule.

{1:1} When Philopator learned from his returning forces that Antiochus had taken control of his territories, he ordered all his troops, both infantry and cavalry, to assemble. He took his sister Arsinoe with him and marched to the area near Raphia, where Antiochus's supporters were camped. {1:2} A man named Theodotus, intent on executing a plan he had devised, took the best Ptolemaic weapons he had been given and sneaked into Ptolemy's tent at night, intending to kill him and end the war. {1:3} However, Dositheus, son of Drimylus, a Jew who had abandoned his faith, had secretly moved the king and placed a low-ranking man in his tent. Theodotus ended up killing this decoy instead. {1:4} During a fierce battle that favored Antiochus, Arsinoe, with disheveled hair and tears streaming down her face, urged her troops to fight bravely for their families, promising each of them two minas of gold if they won. {1:5} As a result, the enemy was defeated, and many were captured. {1:6} After foiling the plot, Ptolemy decided to visit nearby cities to encourage the people. {1:7} By doing this and donating gifts to their sacred places, he boosted the morale of his subjects. {1:8} When the Jews sent some of their council and elders to greet him, bringing gifts and congratulations, Ptolemy became eager to visit them. {1:9} Upon arriving in Jerusalem, he offered sacrifices to the supreme God, made thank-offerings, and performed other rituals appropriate for the holy place. Impressed by the temple's beauty and order, {1:10} he developed a desire to enter the holy of holies. {1:11} When he was told this was forbidden, as not even all the priests could enter—only the high priest, and only once a year—he was not persuaded. {1:12} Even after hearing the law, he insisted that he should be allowed to enter, arguing that he was not subject to the same restrictions. {1:13} He questioned why no other temple had restricted his entry. {1:14} Someone carelessly remarked that this shouldn't be taken as a sign. {1:15} The king replied, "Since this has happened, why shouldn't I enter, regardless of their wishes?" {1:16} The priests, in their full vestments, prostrated themselves and prayed to the supreme God to prevent this evil act, filling the temple with cries and tears. {1:17} Those in the city, sensing something serious was happening, rushed out in agitation. {1:18} Virgins left their chambers, sprinkling dust on their hair, and filled the streets with lamentations. {1:19} Brides abandoned their bridal chambers and modesty, joining the chaotic rush in the city. {1:20} Mothers and nurses left newborns behind, some in houses and some in the streets, and crowded around the temple. {1:21} Diverse were the prayers of those gathered, fearful of the king's sacrilegious intentions. {1:22} The bolder citizens refused to allow his plans to proceed, calling on others to take up arms and die for their ancestral laws, causing a significant disturbance in the holy place. {1:23} Barely restrained by the elders, they too joined in supplication. {1:24} Meanwhile, the crowd continued praying fervently. {1:25} Elders near the king tried various methods to dissuade him from his arrogant plan. {1:26} But in his arrogance, he ignored them and moved forward, determined to carry out his plan. {1:27} Observing this, those around him, along with the people, called upon the all-powerful God to defend them and stop this unlawful act. {1:28} The continuous, fervent cries of the crowd created a massive uproar. {1:29} It seemed as if not only the people but also the walls and the ground echoed their cries, as everyone preferred death over the desecration of their sacred place.

{2:1} The high priest Simon, kneeling before the sanctuary with extended hands, prayed with calm dignity: {2:2} "Lord, King of the heavens, ruler of all creation, holy among the holy ones, give attention to us who suffer under an impious and arrogant man, inflated by his power. {2:3} You, creator and governor of all, are a just Ruler and judge those who act with insolence and arrogance. {2:4} You destroyed the giants of old who trusted in their strength and boldness by sending a great flood. {2:5} You consumed the arrogant men of Sodom with fire and sulfur, making them an example for future generations. {2:6} You demonstrated your mighty power by inflicting various punishments on the audacious Pharaoh who enslaved your holy people Israel. {2:7} When he pursued them with chariots and a massive army, you overwhelmed him in the sea while safely guiding those who trusted in you. {2:8} Seeing your works, they praised you, the Almighty. {2:9} O King, you created the boundless earth and chose this city, sanctifying this place for your name, glorifying it as a foundation for the glory of your great and honored name. {2:10} You promised to listen to our prayers if we faced tribulation and came to this place to pray. {2:11} You are faithful and true. {2:12} You have often helped our oppressed ancestors, rescuing them from great evils. {2:13} Now, O holy King, we are crushed by suffering due to our many sins, oppressed by enemies, and helpless. {2:14} This arrogant man seeks to violate the holy place dedicated to your name on earth. {2:15} Your heavenly dwelling is unapproachable by man, but you graciously bestowed your glory upon Israel, sanctifying this place. {2:16} Do not punish us for their defilement or hold us accountable for this profanation, lest the transgressors boast in their wrath, saying, {2:17} 'We have trampled down the sanctuary as if it were nothing.' {2:18} Wipe away our sins, reveal your mercy, and let it overtake us quickly, putting praises in the mouths of the downcast and giving us peace." {2:19} God, overseeing all, heard the lawful supplication and struck down the arrogant man. {2:20} He was shaken like a reed in the wind, left paralyzed and speechless by righteous judgment. {2:21} His friends and bodyguards, seeing his severe punishment, feared for his life and quickly dragged him out in great panic. {2:22} After a while, he recovered but did not repent, leaving with bitter threats. {2:23} When he returned to Egypt, his malice increased, aided by his corrupt companions. {2:24} Unsatisfied with his licentious deeds, he spread evil reports in various places, with his friends following his lead. {2:25} He sought to disgrace the Jewish community publicly, setting up a stone inscription on the tower stating: {2:26} "No one who does not sacrifice shall enter their sanctuaries. All Jews will be registered, taxed, and enslaved. Those who refuse will be taken by force and killed; {2:27} those who register will be branded with the ivy-leaf symbol of Dionysus and reduced to a lower status." {2:28} To appear less hostile, he added, "Those who join the initiated will have equal citizenship with the Alexandrians." {2:29} Some, hoping to improve their reputation, readily gave in, seeking future association with the king. {2:30} However, the majority stood firm, not abandoning their religion, paying money to avoid registration. {2:31} They remained hopeful for help and considered those who separated themselves as enemies, depriving them of fellowship and mutual support.

{3:1} When the wicked king realized this situation, he became so enraged that he targeted not only the Jews in Alexandria but also those in the countryside. He ordered that they all be gathered into one place and executed by the most cruel means. {3:2} During these arrangements, a hostile rumor was spread by those conspiring against the Jews, claiming that they hindered others from following their customs. {3:3} However, the Jews continued to show good will and unwavering loyalty to the dynasty. {3:4} Because they worshiped God and adhered to His laws, especially regarding food, they were viewed with hostility by some. {3:5} Despite this, their upright conduct earned them a good reputation among all people. {3:6} Nevertheless, people of other races ignored their good service to the nation, which was well-known. {3:7} Instead, they focused on the Jews' different worship and food practices, accusing them of disloyalty to the king and his authorities and of opposing his government, which brought them significant reproach. {3:8} The Greeks in the city, though not harmed, were powerless to help the Jews due to living under tyranny. They tried to console them and hoped for a change in their situation. {3:9} Such a large community, having committed no offense, should not be abandoned. {3:10} Some neighbors, friends, and business associates privately pledged to protect and assist them more earnestly. {3:11} The king, boasting of his current fortune and disregarding the might of the supreme God, assumed his plans would succeed and wrote this letter against the Jews: {3:12} "King Ptolemy Philopator to his generals and soldiers in Egypt and all its districts, greetings and good health. {3:13} I and our government are faring well. {3:14} During our expedition in Asia, as you know, the gods aided us in battle, and we concluded it successfully. {3:15} We decided not to rule Coele-Syria and Phoenicia by force but with clemency and benevolence, treating the inhabitants well. {3:16} We granted great revenues to the temples in these cities and went to Jerusalem to honor the temple of these ungrateful people. {3:17} They accepted our presence in words but not in deeds. When we proposed to enter their inner temple with magnificent offerings, {3:18} they, driven by their traditional arrogance, barred our entry. Despite this, we spared them out of benevolence. {3:19} Their manifest ill-will shows they are the only people who defy kings and benefactors, refusing to see any action as sincere. {3:20} On returning to Egypt victorious, we tolerated their folly and acted appropriately, treating all nations with benevolence. {3:21} We announced our amnesty toward their compatriots here because of their past alliance and entrusted affairs. We even offered them Alexandrian citizenship and participation in our religious rites. {3:22} But in their malice, they spurned this, disdaining our good intentions and suspecting us of future changes. {3:23} Their constant inclination to evil led them to reject our priceless citizenship and abhor those few among them who are sincerely disposed toward us. {3:24} Convinced of their ill-will, we have taken precautions to prevent them from becoming traitors and enemies in case of sudden disorder. {3:25} Therefore, upon receiving this letter, you are to send all Jews living among you, with their families, under harsh treatment and iron fetters, to suffer a shameful death. {3:26} Once they are punished, we believe the government will be stable and orderly. {3:27} Anyone sheltering a Jew, old or young, will be tortured to death with their family. {3:28} Informants will receive the punished person's property, two thousand drachmas from the royal treasury, and their freedom. {3:29} Any place found sheltering a Jew will be burned and rendered unusable forever." {3:30} The letter was written in this manner.

{4:1} In every place where this decree arrived, the Gentiles celebrated with feasts paid for by the public, shouting and rejoicing, as their long-standing hatred for the Jews became openly expressed. {4:2} But the Jews were in constant mourning, crying and lamenting, their hearts burning with grief over the unexpected decree of destruction. {4:3} Every district, city, habitable place, and street was filled with mourning and wailing for them. {4:4} The generals in each city sent them off with such harshness that even some of their enemies, witnessing their suffering, reflected on the uncertainty of life and shed tears for their miserable expulsion. {4:5} Many elderly men, gray-haired and bent with age, were forced to march quickly, driven violently in such a shameful manner. {4:6} Young women who had just entered their bridal chambers exchanged joy for wailing, their perfumed hair sprinkled with ashes, carried away unveiled, raising a lament instead of a wedding song as they were harshly treated by the heathen. {4:7} In public view and in bonds, they were violently dragged to the place of embarkation. {4:8} Husbands, in their youth, had ropes around their necks instead of garlands, spending the days of their marriage festivals in lamentations instead of joy, seeing death before them. {4:9} They were loaded onto ships like wild animals, constrained by iron bonds; some were fastened by the neck to the benches, others had their feet secured by unbreakable fetters. {4:10} Additionally, they were confined under a solid deck, kept in total darkness, enduring treatment fitting for traitors throughout the voyage. {4:11} When they reached Schedia, and the voyage ended as the king ordered, he commanded that they be enclosed in the hippodrome, which had a monstrous perimeter wall and was perfect for making them an obvious spectacle to all who entered or left the city. {4:12} Hearing that the Jews' compatriots often went out in secret to lament their brothers' misfortune, the king, in a rage, ordered these men to be punished in the same way. {4:13} The entire Jewish race was to be registered individually, not for hard labor but to be tortured and eventually destroyed in a single day. {4:14} The registration was conducted with bitter haste from sunrise to sunset, but after forty days, it remained incomplete. {4:15} The king, filled with joy, organized feasts for his idols, his mind alienated from truth, and his mouth profaning the supreme God. {4:16} After this interval, the scribes informed the king that they could no longer take the census of the Jews due to their overwhelming numbers. {4:17} Many were still in the countryside, some in their homes, and some at the place, making the task impossible for all the generals in Egypt. {4:18} After severe threats and accusations of bribery, the king was convinced of their honesty when they showed that they had exhausted their paper and pens. {4:19} This was an act of the invincible providence of God, who was aiding the Jews from heaven.

{5:1} The king, unwavering and filled with uncontrollable anger, summoned Hermon, the keeper of the elephants. {5:2} He ordered Hermon to drug all five hundred elephants with large amounts of frankincense and unmixed wine the following day, then drive them in a frenzy to destroy the Jews. {5:3} After giving these orders, he returned to his feasting with his friends and army officers who were especially hostile towards the Jews. {5:4} Hermon diligently followed the orders. {5:5} That evening, the guards bound the Jews and kept them in custody overnight, certain that the entire nation would be annihilated. {5:6} The Gentiles believed the Jews had no hope, {5:7} as they were bound and surrounded. But the Jews, with tearful and fervent prayers, called upon the Almighty Lord for mercy and rescue. {5:8} They prayed for God to thwart the evil plot against them and save them gloriously. {5:9} Their prayers fervently ascended to heaven. {5:10} Meanwhile, Hermon drugged the elephants with wine and frankincense, and early in the morning, he reported to the king that everything was ready. {5:11} However, the Lord sent the king into a deep, pleasant sleep, making him forget his cruel intentions. {5:12} Overcome by this sleep, the king failed to carry out his plan. {5:13} The Jews, having escaped their doom, praised their holy God and prayed for Him to show His power to the arrogant Gentiles. {5:14} Near the middle of the tenth hour, the person in charge of invitations nudged the king awake, reminding him that the banquet hour was slipping away. {5:15} With difficulty, the king was roused and informed of the situation. {5:16} After considering this, the king returned to drinking and ordered the banquet guests to continue their revelry. {5:17} He urged them to make the banquet joyful by celebrating even more. {5:18} As the party continued, the king summoned Hermon and angrily demanded to know why the Jews were still alive. {5:19} Hermon and his friends confirmed that they had carried out the orders during the night. {5:20} The king, filled with greater savagery, declared that the Jews had been spared by his sleep but ordered Hermon to prepare the elephants again for their destruction the next day. {5:21} The guests approved of the king's order and each departed to their homes, devising insults for the Jews they believed were doomed. {5:22} As soon as the rooster crowed, Hermon began preparing the elephants and moving them along the colonnade. {5:23} Crowds eagerly gathered to witness the pitiful spectacle. {5:24} The Jews, at their last gasp, stretched their hands toward heaven, tearfully imploring God for help. {5:25} Before dawn, while the king received his friends, Hermon arrived, inviting him to witness the preparations. {5:26} The king, struck by the unusual invitation, asked what was so urgently prepared. {5:27} God had implanted forgetfulness in the king's mind about his previous plans. {5:28} Hermon and the king's friends pointed out that everything was ready for action. {5:29} The king, filled with wrath, responded with threats, stating that if Hermon's parents or children were present, they would be prepared for the beasts instead of the Jews. {5:30} The king declared that the Jews had shown extraordinary loyalty and should not be punished. {5:31} Hermon, terrified, saw his eyes waver and face fall. {5:32} The king's friends sullenly departed, dismissing the crowds. {5:33} Hearing the king's words, the Jews praised their God for His aid. {5:34} The king resumed the banquet, urging guests to continue celebrating. {5:35} He summoned Hermon again, demanding the elephants be prepared to destroy the Jews the next day. {5:36} The officials, bewildered by the king's instability, questioned how many times he would change his orders. {5:37} They noted the city was in turmoil, crowded with people and in danger of being plundered. {5:38} Ignoring the changes of mind, the king swore an irrevocable oath to send the Jews to their deaths, and to march against Judea, leveling it with fire and spear, and burning the temple. {5:39} The friends and officers, joyful and confident, posted armed forces to keep guard. {5:40} When the elephants were driven to madness with wine and frankincense and equipped with frightful devices, Hermon entered the courtyard at dawn. {5:41} The city was filled with crowds, eagerly awaiting the spectacle. {5:42} The Jews, seeing the elephants and armed forces, thought their end had come. They lamented, embracing relatives, and falling into each other's arms. {5:43} They prostrated themselves, removing babies from their breasts, and cried out loudly, imploring God to save them from death.

{6:1} Eleazar, a renowned and elderly priest known for his virtue, instructed the elders to stop calling upon God and prayed, {6:2} Almighty God Most High, ruler of all creation, {6:3} look upon the descendants of Abraham and Jacob, who are perishing in a foreign land. {6:4} Just as you destroyed Pharaoh and his arrogant army in the sea, showing mercy to Israel, {6:5} and broke Sennacherib's oppressive forces, show your power again. {6:6} You saved the three companions in Babylon from the fiery furnace, {6:7} rescued Daniel from the lions, {6:8} and restored Jonah from the belly of the sea monster. {6:9} Now, merciful protector, reveal yourself to Israel, who are suffering at the hands of the Gentiles. {6:10} Even if we have sinned, rescue us from the enemy and deal with us as you will. {6:11} Do not let the arrogant mock us, saying our God did not save us. {6:12} Watch over us and have mercy as we are unjustly killed. {6:13} Let the Gentiles fear your power, O Lord, who can save the nation of Jacob. {6:14} The whole throng of infants and their parents cry out to you. {6:15} Show the Gentiles that you are with us and have not abandoned us, as you promised even in our enemies' land." {6:16} Just as Eleazar finished his prayer, the king arrived at the hippodrome with the elephants and his forces. {6:17} The Jews cried out to heaven, causing the valleys to echo and instilling terror in the army. {6:18} God revealed His presence by sending two glorious angels, visible to all but the Jews, {6:19} who opposed the enemy forces and filled them with fear and confusion. {6:20} The king began to tremble and forgot his arrogance. {6:21} The elephants turned on the armed forces, trampling and destroying them. {6:22} The king's anger turned to pity and tears as he saw his plans fail. {6:23} Hearing the cries and seeing the destruction, he blamed his friends, {6:24} accusing them of treason and cruelty. {6:25} He questioned who had senselessly gathered the Jews, {6:26} and mistreated those who had shown goodwill. {6:27} He ordered their bonds to be loosed and sent them home in peace, apologizing for past actions. {6:28} He commanded the release of the Jews, acknowledging their God who had protected his kingdom. {6:29} The Jews, immediately freed, praised their holy God for their escape from death. {6:30} The king returned to the city, ordered the official in charge of revenues to provide the Jews with everything needed for a seven-day festival, {6:31} turning their expected death into a celebration. {6:32} They ceased mourning, praised God with joyful songs, and formed choruses as a sign of peace. {6:33} The king, hosting a great banquet, continuously thanked heaven for their unexpected rescue. {6:34} Those who had anticipated the Jews' destruction groaned in disgrace, their arrogance quenched. {6:35} The Jews, now celebrating, arranged joyful feasts and psalms. {6:36} They instituted a public festival to commemorate their deliverance by God, not for excess but for gratitude. {6:37} They petitioned the king to return home. {6:38} Their registration had taken place over forty days, and their destruction was planned for three days when God revealed His mercy. {6:39} They feasted until the fourteenth day and then requested to leave. {6:40} The king granted their request, writing a letter to the city generals.

{7:1} King Ptolemy Philopator to the generals in Egypt and all in authority in his government, greetings and good health. {7:2} My family and I are well, thanks to the guidance of the great God. {7:3} Some of our advisors, with malicious intent, persuaded us to gather the Jews in the kingdom and punish them severely as traitors. {7:4} They claimed our government wouldn't be stable until this was done, citing the Jews' ill-will toward all nations. {7:5} They treated the Jews harshly, like slaves or traitors, and tried to kill them without proper investigation. {7:6} We severely reprimanded these advisors and spared their lives out of our clemency. Recognizing that the God of heaven protects the Jews like a father does his children, {7:7} and acknowledging their goodwill toward us and our ancestors, we have acquitted them of all charges. {7:8} We have ordered everyone to return home without harm or reproach. {7:9} If we harm them, we will face the wrath of the Most High God, who will avenge such acts. Farewell." {7:10} Upon receiving this letter, the Jews did not rush to leave but requested that those among them who had willingly transgressed against God and His laws be punished by their own hands. {7:11} They argued that those who broke divine commandments would never be loyal to the king's government. {7:12} The king agreed and allowed them to punish those who had violated God's law without royal oversight. {7:13} After praising the king, the priests and the whole multitude shouted Hallelujah and departed joyfully. {7:14} On their way, they publicly executed any fellow Jews who had defiled themselves. {7:15} That day, they put over three hundred men to death and celebrated, having destroyed the profaners. {7:16} Those who remained faithful to God, now saved, left the city adorned with fragrant flowers, joyfully thanking God with songs of praise. {7:17} When they reached Ptolemais, known as "rose-bearing," they waited for a fleet for seven days, as was commonly desired. {7:18} They celebrated their deliverance there, with the king providing generously for their journey home. {7:19} Upon landing safely, they decided to observe these days as a joyous festival. {7:20} They inscribed these events on a pillar, dedicated a place of prayer, and left unharmed, free, and overjoyed, safely brought to their homes by the king's command. {7:21} They gained greater respect among their enemies, who honored and feared them. They were not subject to property confiscation. {7:22} They recovered all their property, as recorded, with those holding it returning it in fear. Thus, the supreme God performed great deeds for their deliverance. {7:23} Blessed be the Deliverer of Israel through all times! Amen.

4 Maccabees

The Book of 4 Maccabees, an intriguing text within the corpus of Hellenistic Jewish literature, offers a unique blend of philosophical discourse and historical narrative, reflecting the intersection of Jewish theology and Greek philosophy. Traditionally attributed to an unknown Jewish author of the 1st or 2nd century CE, 4 Maccabees is preserved primarily in Greek and is situated within the broader context of Jewish writings that engage with Hellenistic culture. The central theme of the book is the supremacy of reason over passion, a concept deeply rooted in Stoic philosophy. The author employs the narrative of the martyrdom of Eleazar, a ninety-year-old priest, and the seven brothers and their mother, which is also recounted in 2 Maccabees, to illustrate the power of piety and rational faithfulness to God's law in the face of persecution. Through detailed rhetorical arguments and vivid descriptions of the martyrs' steadfastness, the text seeks to demonstrate that reason, guided by religious piety, can triumph over bodily desires and suffering. This philosophical treatise not only reinforces the Jewish commitment to the Torah but also dialogues with contemporary Hellenistic thought, showcasing the adaptability and resilience of Jewish religious identity in a multicultural environment. The book's emphasis on the moral and ethical dimensions of human behavior, framed within the context of divine law, provides profound insights into the Jewish understanding of virtue, suffering, and the ultimate triumph of faith. As such, 4 Maccabees occupies a distinctive place in the landscape of ancient Jewish literature, reflecting a synthesis of Jewish religious tradition and Hellenistic philosophical ideals.

{1:1} The topic I'm about to discuss is deeply philosophical: whether reason can govern our emotions effectively. Therefore, it's important for me to urge you to pay close attention to this philosophical inquiry. {1:2} This subject is crucial for anyone seeking knowledge, as it involves praising the highest virtue—rational judgment itself. {1:3} If it's clear that reason can control emotions like gluttony and lust, which undermine self-control, {1:4} then it logically follows that reason can also master emotions that obstruct justice, such as malice, and those that hinder courage, like anger, fear, and pain. {1:5} Some may ask why reason doesn't dominate forgetfulness and ignorance. This argument, however, is nonsensical. {1:6} Reason doesn't govern its own emotions but those contrary to justice, courage, and self-control, aiming not to eradicate them but to prevent yielding to them. {1:7} I could provide many examples showing reason's dominion over emotions. {1:8} The best demonstration is seen in the courageous deaths of Eleazar, the seven brothers, and their mother, who chose martyrdom for virtue's sake. {1:9} By facing death with disdain for suffering, they exemplified reason's control over emotions. {1:10} On this occasion, it's fitting to honor their virtues and bless them for the honor they've received. {1:11} Even their tormentors admired their bravery and endurance, leading to the downfall of tyranny over their people. Through their endurance, they conquered the tyrant, purifying their homeland. {1:12} I will soon delve into their story, but first, as is my custom, I'll lay out my main principle and then recount their tale, giving glory to the all-wise God. {1:13} So, our inquiry revolves around whether reason indeed reigns over emotions. {1:14} We'll define reason and emotion, discuss the types of emotions, and determine if reason governs them all. {1:15} Reason is the faculty that, through sound logic, prefers a life of wisdom. {1:16} Wisdom itself encompasses knowledge of divine and human matters and their causes. {1:17} This includes education in the law, which teaches reverence for divine matters and practical wisdom in human affairs. {1:18} The types of wisdom are rational judgment, justice, courage, and self-control. {1:19} Rational judgment stands supreme over these, allowing reason to rule over emotions. {1:20} The two broadest emotions are pleasure and pain, each affecting both body and soul. {1:21} These emotions have numerous consequences and implications. {1:22} Desire precedes pleasure, and satisfaction follows it. {1:23} Fear precedes pain, and sorrow follows. {1:24} Anger, as anyone reflecting on experience can attest, combines elements of both pleasure and pain. {1:25} Pleasure itself can lead to harmful inclinations, the most intricate of emotions. {1:26} In the soul, it manifests as arrogance, greed, thirst for recognition, rivalry, and malice; {1:27} in the body, as excessive eating, gluttony, and indulgence. {1:28} Just as pleasure and pain stem from both body and soul, they sprout many ramifications. {1:29} Reason, like a skilled gardener, prunes, tends, waters, and cultivates these emotional habits, bringing them under control. {1:30} Reason guides virtues, but it governs emotions absolutely. Notice first that rational judgment reigns over emotions through the restraining power of self-control. {1:31} Self-control is mastery over desires. {1:32} Some desires are mental, others physical, yet reason governs both. {1:33} When we abstain from forbidden foods despite craving them, it's because reason can control appetites. {1:34} So, when we desire seafood, poultry, or other forbidden foods, reason restrains us. {1:35} Reason moderates appetites, tempering the impulses of the body with a disciplined mind.

{2:1} Why should we find it surprising that the mind's desires for enjoying beauty can be subdued? {2:2} Indeed, Joseph's temperance is celebrated precisely for this reason — he overcame sexual desire through mental discipline. {2:3} In his youth, when he was at the peak of physical desire, he used reason to quell the frenzy of passions. {2:4} It's not just sexual desire that reason governs; it extends its mastery over all desires. {2:5} This is evident in the commandment: "You shall not covet your neighbor's wife...or anything that belongs to your neighbor." {2:6} The law's prohibition against coveting demonstrates how reason can control desires. Similarly, reason governs emotions that obstruct justice. {2:7} How else could a habitual glutton, drunkard, or excessive eater reform without reason reigning over emotions? {2:8} When someone, despite being fond of wealth, adheres to the law by lending without interest and forgiving debts in the seventh year, reason directs their actions against their natural inclinations. {2:9} The law, guided by reason, curbs greed, ensuring one doesn't glean every last harvest or gather the final grapes. {2:10} In all aspects, reason asserts its authority over emotions. {2:11} It prevails over affection for parents, ensuring virtue isn't forsaken for their sake. {2:12} It overrides love for a spouse, prompting rebuke when they transgress the law. {2:13} It takes precedence over parental love, leading to discipline for their children's misdeeds. {2:14} Reason even governs friendships, allowing rebuke when friends behave wickedly, and it can reconcile even enmity through adherence to the law. {2:15} Reason controls even the most intense emotions — the desire for power, vanity, boasting, arrogance, and malice. {2:16} A disciplined mind rejects these harmful emotions, including anger, for reason is sovereign over them all. {2:17} When Moses was angered by Dathan and Abiram, reason prevented him from acting rashly. {2:18} As stated, a temperate mind can triumph over emotions, correcting some and neutralizing others. {2:19} Why else would Jacob rebuke Simeon and Levi for their rash massacre of the Shechemites, saying, "Cursed be their anger," if not to show reason's control over anger? {2:20} When God created humanity, he implanted emotions and inclinations within them, yet he also placed reason as a sacred governor among their senses. {2:21} To reason, he imparted the law, allowing those who follow it to govern a kingdom marked by temperance, justice, goodness, and courage. {2:22} One might ask, if reason governs emotions, why does it not control forgetfulness and ignorance?

{3:1} This idea is quite absurd; it's clear that reason doesn't govern its own emotions but those of the body. {3:2} None of us can eliminate such desires entirely, but reason can show us how not to be enslaved by them. {3:3} Similarly, none of us can eradicate anger from our minds, but reason can teach us how to manage it. {3:4} We can't rid ourselves of malice, but reason can aid us in resisting and not succumbing to it. {3:5} Reason doesn't eradicate emotions but acts as their counterforce. {3:6} This can be illustrated through the story of King David's thirst. {3:7} After a day of battling the Philistines, David, exhausted, returned to camp where his troops were dining. {3:8} Despite abundant springs nearby, he couldn't quench his thirst. {3:9}

Irrationally, he desired water from enemy territory, consumed by this craving. {3:10} His guards, understanding his desire, fetched it risking their lives. {3:11} They located the spring in the enemy camp and brought him the water. {3:12} But David, fearing the moral implications, poured it out as an offering to God. {3:13} This demonstrates how reason can oppose desire. {3:14} A temperate mind can conquer emotional impulses and extinguish frenzied desires, even in extreme situations, rejecting emotional dominance with nobility of reason. {3:15} The current narrative exemplifies the power of reasoned temperance. {3:16} During a time of peace and prosperity under observance of the law, disturbances arose.

{4:1} In the time when Onias, a noble and righteous high priest, held office for life, there arose a political adversary named Simon who, failing to discredit Onias through slander, fled the country with a treacherous plan. {4:2} He sought out Apollonius, the governor of Syria, Phoenicia, and Cilicia, and fabricated a story about vast sums of private funds in Jerusalem that belonged to King Seleucus, not the temple treasury. {4:3} Pleased with Simon's deceitful report, Apollonius informed Seleucus and received authorization to seize these supposed funds. {4:4} With Simon at his side and a formidable army, Apollonius swiftly marched to Jerusalem, claiming royal authority to confiscate the funds. {4:5} Outraged by this intrusion, the people protested vehemently, defending the sanctity of the temple treasury. {4:6} Undeterred by their resistance, Apollonius proceeded arrogantly toward the temple, issuing threats. {4:7} Inside, priests, women, and children prayed desperately for divine protection as Apollonius and his troops approached the treasury. {4:8} Suddenly, angelic beings on horseback appeared from heaven, terrifying Apollonius and his soldiers with flashes of lightning. {4:9} Overcome by fear, Apollonius collapsed in the temple courtyard, pleading tearfully for the Hebrews to intercede on his behalf with God. {4:10} Moved by his repentance, Onias the high priest prayed for him despite his reservations, fearing divine retribution. {4:11} Apollonius, spared from death, returned to report these miraculous events to King Seleucus. {4:12} After Seleucus's death, his son Antiochus Epiphanes ascended the throne, a tyrant who removed Onias from the priesthood and appointed Jason, Onias's brother, as high priest. {4:13} Jason agreed to pay a hefty annual tribute to the king, gaining the high priesthood and authority over the nation. {4:14} Jason then implemented sweeping changes, defying the ancestral laws and introducing Greek customs, including constructing a gymnasium within the citadel and abolishing traditional temple rituals. {4:15} Infuriated by these sacrileges, divine justice incited Antiochus to wage war against the Jews. {4:16} Hearing rumors of his death while battling Ptolemy in Egypt, Antiochus swiftly marched against Jerusalem, seeking vengeance.

{5:1} During a council session atop a high place, the tyrant Antiochus, surrounded by his advisors and armed soldiers, commanded his guards to arrest every Hebrew present and force them to eat pork and food sacrificed to idols. {5:2} Anyone who refused to comply was to be subjected to torture and death. {5:3} Among those apprehended was Eleazar, an elderly leader from a priestly family known for his wisdom and adherence to Jewish law. {5:4} When Antiochus saw Eleazar, he addressed him, attempting to persuade him to eat pork to save himself from torture. {5:5} "Old man," Antiochus began, "before I proceed with your punishment, consider saving yourself by eating this meat. {5:6} I respect your age, but I cannot comprehend how a wise man like you adheres to the Jewish faith. {5:7} Why reject such fine food that nature itself offers? {5:8} It is senseless to deny oneself such pleasures and wrong to refuse nature's gifts. {5:9} You'll act even more foolishly if you persist in defying me and your own well-being due to your stubborn beliefs. {5:10} Consider this: if your God truly protects you, he will forgive you for this forced transgression." {5:11} Antiochus pressed Eleazar to eat the forbidden meat, but Eleazar requested permission to speak. {5:12} When granted, he addressed the assembly. {5:13} "O Antiochus, we who live by divine law believe obedience to it outweighs any compulsion. {5:14} Therefore, we cannot violate it under any circumstances. {5:15} Even if our law were not divine, we would still maintain our reputation for piety. {5:16} Do not underestimate the seriousness of breaking the law, whether in small matters or large. {5:17} You mock our faith, but it teaches us self-control over desires and courage to endure suffering. {5:18} It guides us in justice and piety toward the true God. {5:19} We cannot eat defiling food because we believe God ordained our law for our well-being. {5:20} He permits what is suitable and forbids what is harmful. {5:21} It is tyrannical for you to force us to break the law and mock us for it. {5:22} But you will not ridicule me, nor will I betray the sacred oath of my ancestors. {5:23} Not even if you torture me severely will I forsake the law. {5:24} I will not dishonor the teachings that shaped me, nor abandon self-control. {5:25} I will not disgrace reason nor forsake the honored priesthood and knowledge of the law. {5:26} O king, your tyranny cannot tarnish the dignity of my old age and my lifelong adherence to the law. {5:27} The ancestors will receive me as pure, unyielding to your violence even unto death. {5:28} You may rule over the godless, but you will not sway my religious convictions by word or deed."

{6:1} After Eleazar eloquently responded to the tyrant's exhortations, the guards forcibly dragged him towards the instruments of torture. {6:2} They stripped the old man, whose demeanor still radiated piety and grace. {6:3} They bound his arms and scourged him while a herald shouted, "Obey the king's commands!" {6:4} Yet Eleazar, courageous and noble, endured the torment as if in a dream, his eyes fixed on heaven while his flesh was torn and blood flowed from his wounds. {6:5} Though he collapsed from the pain, his spirit remained steadfast and resolute. {6:6} A cruel guard kicked him to force him up, but Eleazar endured, scorned the punishment, and bore the agonies. {6:7} Like a valiant athlete, he triumphed over his tormentors even in the midst of his suffering. {6:8} Sweat drenched his face, and he amazed even his torturers with his unwavering spirit. {6:9} Moved by pity and admiration, some in the king's retinue approached him. {6:10} "Eleazar, why destroy yourself needlessly with these torments? {6:11} We can offer you cooked meat; pretend to eat pork and save yourself." {6:12} But Eleazar, deeply distressed by their suggestion, cried out, {6:13} "May we, descendants of Abraham, never stoop so low as to feign compliance out of fear! {6:14} It would be irrational to abandon our lifelong commitment to truth and law to set a shameful example of impiety. {6:15} It would bring disgrace to survive momentarily as cowards, mocked by all. {6:16} Let us die nobly for our faith, O children of Abraham! {6:17} Guards of the tyrant, why hesitate?" {6:18} Seeing his unwavering courage and refusal to yield, the guards subjected him to fire. {6:19} They burned him with cruel devices, poured foul liquids into his nostrils, and brought him to the brink of death. {6:20} In his final moments, burned to the bone, he lifted his eyes to God and prayed, {6:21} "You know, O God, that I die in burning torment for the sake of your law. {6:22} Have mercy on your people; let my suffering suffice for them. {6:23} Let my blood be their purification." {6:24} With these words, the holy man nobly embraced death for the sake of the law. {6:25} Thus, reason proved sovereign over emotions. {6:26} If emotions had prevailed, they would have shown dominance, but reason conquered, rightly asserting its authority. {6:27} Reason's mastery over external agony is undeniable and deserves recognition. {6:28} Indeed, reason not only conquers agony but also masters pleasures without yielding to them.

{7:1} Like a skilled pilot, the reason of our forefather Eleazar guided the ship of faith through the turbulent sea of emotions. {7:2} Despite the tyrant's fierce onslaughts and the overwhelming waves of torture, he steadfastly held to the course of his religious convictions. {7:3} He did not waver in his commitment to faith until he reached the haven of immortal victory. {7:4} No besieged city, no matter how fortified, has endured as Eleazar did. Though his sacred life was consumed by torment, he defended his beliefs with the shield of devout reason. {7:5} Setting his mind firm as a steadfast cliff, Eleazar defied the raging emotions. {7:6} O worthy priest, you preserved your sacred integrity, refusing to defile yourself with forbidden foods. {7:7} O man in harmony with divine law, philosopher of a righteous life! {7:8} This is the example for those who uphold the law, shielding it with their blood and enduring suffering unto death. {7:9} Father Eleazar, through your glorious endurance, you strengthened our commitment to the law and proved the credibility of divine philosophy by your deeds. {7:10} O aged man, stronger than tortures, elder fiercer than fire, supreme ruler over passions! {7:11} Just as Aaron confronted the fiery angel with his censer, so did Eleazar, enduring the flames with steadfast reason. {7:12} Remarkably, though aged and physically weakened, he was rejuvenated in spirit through reason, rendering the torturous rack ineffective. {7:13} O blessed elder with venerable gray hair and a life of righteousness, perfected by faithful devotion unto death! {7:14} Therefore, if an aged man, for the sake of piety, defied tortures unto death, devout reason indeed governs emotions. {7:15} Some may argue that not everyone commands their emotions due to lack of prudent reason. {7:16} Yet those who wholeheartedly follow faith alone can control their passions, believing like Abraham, Isaac, and Jacob that they live eternally in God. {7:17} Thus, it's not contradictory if some seem overcome by emotions due to weak reason. {7:18} Who, living as a true philosopher by the rule of faith, trusting in God's blessings, wouldn't overcome emotions through piety? {7:19} Only the wise and courageous can master their emotions.

{8:1} Even the youngest among them, guided by a philosophy grounded in devout reason, triumphed over the most brutal instruments of torture. {8:2} When the tyrant's initial attempt failed to coerce an elderly man into eating forbidden food, he became enraged and ordered more Hebrew captives to be brought forth. {8:3} Among them were seven brothers, handsome, modest, noble in bearing, and accomplished in every way, accompanied by their aged mother. {8:4} Struck by their appearance and dignity as they stood together with their mother, the tyrant smiled and summoned them closer. {8:5} "Young men," he began, "I admire each of you and respect your unity as brothers. I urge you not to follow the same path as the old man who was recently tortured. {8:6} Yield to me, and I will show favor to you. {8:7} Trust me, and you will hold high positions in my government if you forsake your ancestral traditions. {8:8} Embrace the Greek way of life and adopt a new manner of living, enjoying your youth." {8:9} He warned them, "Disobey me, and I will punish you with severe tortures that will lead to your deaths. {8:10} Have pity on yourselves, even your enemy has compassion for your youth and beauty." {8:11} He then ordered the instruments of torture to be brought forward to compel them through fear to eat defiled food. {8:12} As the guards presented wheels, joint-dislocators, racks, hooks, catapults, caldrons, braziers, thumbscrews, iron claws, wedges, and bellows, the tyrant continued his threats. {8:13} "Fear these devices, young men. Justice will be lenient if you transgress under duress." {8:14} Yet, instead of fear, they countered the tyrant with their own philosophy and sound reasoning, nullifying his tyranny. {8:15} Reflecting on what arguments might have swayed the cowardly, {8:16} "Why risk death by defying the king's kindness? {8:17} Shouldn't we fear torture, heed the threats, abandon arrogance, and consider divine justice?" {8:18} They remained resolute, despising fear and mastering agony, {8:19} so when the tyrant ceased his counsel to eat forbidden food, they collectively declared without hesitation:

{9:1} "Why do you hesitate, tyrant? We are prepared to die rather than violate our ancestral commandments. {9:2} It would bring shame upon our forefathers if we were to forsake obedience to the law and to Moses, our guide. {9:3} Tyrant, in your hostility toward us, do not show us more pity than we show ourselves. {9:4} We consider your compassion, which promises safety through disobedience to the law, more dreadful than death itself. {9:5} You try to frighten us with threats of torture, as if you have not learned from the example of Eleazar. {9:6} If aged Hebrew men endured torture for their faith, how much more fitting is it for us young men to face death while defying your coercive tortures, which even our aged mentor overcame? {9:7} So test us, tyrant. Even if you take our lives for our faith, know that you cannot harm us by torturing us. {9:8} Through these severe sufferings and endurance, we will earn the reward of virtue and be with God, for whom we endure. {9:9} But your bloodthirsty actions toward us will rightfully bring upon you eternal torment by divine justice." {9:10} Enraged not only by their disobedience but also by their ingratitude, the tyrant commanded the guards to bring forth the eldest brother. {9:11} They stripped him, bound his hands and arms, and relentlessly beat him with scourges to no avail before placing him on the wheel. {9:12} As they stretched him out, his limbs were dislocated. {9:13} Despite excruciating pain, he condemned the tyrant, {9:14} declaring, "Most vile tyrant, enemy of divine justice, you torture me not for murder or impiety, but for upholding the law of God." {9:15} When urged to eat to end his torment, {9:16} he retorted, "You despicable lackeys, your torture cannot break my resolve. Cut me, burn me, twist my joints—I will show you Hebrews are invincible in virtue." {9:17} They then set fire beneath him, fanned the flames, and tightened the wheel. {9:18} Despite severed ligaments and the wheel drenched in blood, the courageous youth, worthy of Abraham, did not waver but nobly endured. {9:19} "Follow my example, brothers," he urged. "Do not falter in our struggle or forsake our brotherhood. {9:20} Fight this noble battle for our faith, so that our ancestors' providence may show mercy to our nation and punish the tyrant." {9:21} With these words, the youth breathed his last. {9:22} As all marveled at his bravery, the guards brought forth the next eldest brother. {9:23} They bound him with sharp iron gauntlets, affixed him to the torture machine, and prepared to inflict agony. {9:24} Asked if he would eat to avoid torture, {9:25} he proclaimed, "Any death is sweet for the sake of our fathers' faith." {9:26} Addressing the tyrant, he said, "You suffer more than I, as your tyrannical designs are thwarted by our endurance for our faith." {9:27} "My pain is eased by the joy of virtue," he continued, {9:28} "while your torment stems from your impiety. Most vile tyrant, you will not escape divine judgment."

{10:1} After the third brother had also bravely faced death, the fourth was brought forward amidst many urging him to save himself by eating the meat. {10:2} He cried out defiantly, "Do you not realize that the same father begot me and my deceased brothers, and the same mother bore me? We were raised on the same teachings. {10:3} I will not forsake the noble bond that unites me with my brothers." {10:4} Enraged by his boldness, they used their instruments to disjoint his hands and feet, {10:5} dismembering him by wrenching his limbs from their sockets, breaking his fingers, arms, legs, and elbows. {10:6} Unable to break his spirit, they resorted to scalping him with their nails in a barbaric manner. {10:7} They then brought him to the wheel, where his vertebrae were dislocated, his flesh torn, and blood flowed from his wounds. {10:8} {10:9} As he faced death, he declared, "We suffer, most abominable tyrant, {10:9} because of our godly upbringing and virtue. {10:10} But you, due to your impiety and cruelty, will endure unending torments." {10:11} After his honorable death, they brought in the fourth brother, {10:12} urging him not to follow his brothers' path but to obey the king and save himself. {10:13} He retorted, "Your fire cannot scorch me into cowardice. {10:14} No, by the blessed deaths of my brothers, the eternal destruction of the tyrant, and the everlasting life of the righteous, I will not forsake our noble brotherhood. {10:15} Bring forth your tortures, tyrant, and learn that I am a brother to those who were tortured before me." {10:16} Hearing this, the bloodthirsty Antiochus ordered his tongue to be cut out. {10:17} But he replied, "Even if you silence me, God hears the mute. {10:18} Here is my tongue; cut it off. Yet you cannot silence our reason." {10:19} "Gladly," he continued, "for God's sake, {10:20} we endure mutilation of our bodies. {10:21} Swiftly shall God judge you, for you cut out a tongue that sang divine hymns."

{11:1} When the fifth brother died after enduring cruel torture, the sixth one stepped forward defiantly, declaring, {11:2} "I will not refuse, tyrant, to suffe r for the sake of virtue. {11:3} I have come willingly, and by killing me, you will only increase your punishment from heavenly justice for your many crimes. {11:4} O hater of virtue, enemy of mankind, for what reason do you destroy us in this manner? {11:5} Is it because we honor the Creator of all things and live according to His virtuous law? {11:6} But such deeds deserve honor, not torture." {11:7} {11:9} As he spoke, {11:8} the guards bound him and dragged him to the catapult; {11:9} they tied him on his knees, secured iron clamps around them, {11:10} and twisted his back around the wheel's wedge, contorting him like a scorpion until all his limbs were disjointed. {11:11} In this agonizing state, struggling to breathe, he said, {11:12} "Tyrant, unwittingly you grant us great favors, for through these noble sufferings, you provide us an opportunity to demonstrate our endurance for the law." {11:13} After his death, the sixth, a young boy, was brought in. When the tyrant asked if he would eat and be spared, {11:14} he replied, "I am younger than my brothers in age, but equal to them in mind. {11:15} We were born and raised for this purpose—to die for these principles. {11:16} So if you intend to torture me for refusing defiling foods, proceed!" {11:17} They then led him to the wheel, {11:18} stretched him tightly upon it, broke his back, and roasted him from underneath. {11:19} They applied sharp spits heated in fire to his back, piercing his ribs and burning through his entrails. {11:20} Amidst his torment, he proclaimed, "O struggle worthy of holiness, where so many of us brothers are called to suffer for our faith, and where we remain undefeated! {11:21} For religious conviction, O tyrant, is unconquerable. {11:22} Equipped with valor, I too will die with my brothers, {11:23} and I will bring a great avenger upon you, inventor of tortures and foe of the devout. {11:24} We six boys have defied your tyranny! {11:25} Since you could not persuade us to change our minds or compel us to eat defiling foods, is this not your defeat? {11:26} Your fire does not intimidate us, your catapults do not pain us, and your violence does not overpower us. {11:27} For it is not the guards of the tyrant but those of divine law who watch over us; therefore, undefeated, we hold fast to reason."

{12:1} When the sixth brother had also died in the blessed manner, thrown into the cauldron, the seventh and youngest of them all stepped forward. {12:2} Despite being reproached by the brothers, the tyrant felt a surge of compassion for this child as he saw him already in chains. He called him closer and tried to comfort him, saying, {12:3} "You see what happened to your brothers because of their foolishness—they died in agony due to their disobedience. {12:4} If you do not obey, you too will suffer miserable torture and die prematurely. {12:5} But if you listen to reason, you can be my friend and a leader in the kingdom." {12:6} After making this plea, he sent for the boy's mother, hoping her influence would persuade the surviving son to comply and save himself. {12:7} But when his mother spoke to him in Hebrew, as we will explain shortly, {12:8} he responded, "Release me so I can speak to the king and all his companions." {12:9} Delighted by the boy's boldness, they immediately set him free. {12:10} Hurrying to the nearest brazier, {12:11} he addressed the tyrant, "You profane tyrant, most impious of all evildoers! Though you received good things and your kingdom from God, were you not ashamed to murder His servants and torture those who uphold religion on the wheel? {12:12} Because of this, justice has prepared intense and eternal fire and torment for you, which will never release you throughout all eternity. {12:13} Were you not ashamed as a man, you savage beast, to cut out the tongues of men who share your feelings and are made of the same elements as you, and to treat and torture them in such a manner? {12:14} They died nobly fulfilling their duty to God, but you will lament bitterly for unjustly slaying those who contend for virtue." {12:15} As he faced his imminent death, {12:16} he declared, "I do not abandon the noble example set by my brothers, {12:17} and I call upon the God of our fathers to show mercy to our nation; {12:18} but upon you, He will exact vengeance in this life and beyond." {12:19} After uttering these curses, he threw himself into the brazier, thus ending his life.

{13:1} Therefore, since the seven brothers endured suffering even unto death, it must be acknowledged that devout reason reigns supreme over emotions. {13:2} Had they been slaves to their emotions and eaten defiling food, we would say they were overcome by their passions. {13:3} But it was not so; rather, it was by reason, which is esteemed before God, that they triumphed over their emotions. {13:4} The dominance of the mind over these cannot be overlooked, as the brothers mastered both their emotions and their pains. {13:5} How can one deny the sovereignty of right reason over emotion in those who were not deterred by fiery agonies? {13:6} Just as towers projecting over harbors repel threatening waves and bring calm to those entering the inner basin, {13:7} so the seven-towered fortress of right reason in these youths, fortifying the harbor of religion, conquered the storm of emotions. {13:8} They formed a holy chorus of faith and encouraged one another, saying, {13:9} "Brothers, let us die united for the sake of our faith; let us emulate the three youths in Assyria who defied the furnace. {13:10} Let us not falter in demonstrating our piety." {13:11} While one said, "Be courageous, brother," another urged, "Endure nobly," {13:12} and another reminded them, "Remember your origins and the faith of our father who was ready to sacrifice Isaac for the sake of religion." {13:13} Each and all, looking at one another with cheer and steadfastness, declared, "Let us dedicate ourselves wholeheartedly to God, who gave us life, and let us use our bodies as a stronghold for His law. {13:14} Let us not fear those who think they are killing us, {13:15} for the struggle of the soul is great and eternal torment awaits those who transgress God's commandments. {13:16} Therefore, let us wear the full armor of self-control, which is divine reason. {13:17} For if we die thus, Abraham, Isaac, and Jacob will welcome us, and all our ancestors will praise us." {13:18} Those left behind said to each of the brothers being dragged away, "Do not dishonor us, brother, or betray those who have gone before us." {13:19} You are not unaware of the brotherly love bestowed by divine and all-wise Providence through our ancestors to their descendants, nurtured in the womb. {13:20} Each brother dwelt for the same span, shaped in the same period, born from the same blood and life, brought into the light together. {13:21} After equal gestation, they nursed from the same source. Such embraces nurture loving souls. {13:22} Their bond grew stronger through shared upbringing, daily companionship, and education in God's law. {13:23} Thus, established in sympathy and brotherly affection, they supported each other even more. {13:24} Educated in the same law, trained in the same virtues, and raised in righteousness, their love for each other deepened. {13:25} A shared zeal for righteousness expanded their mutual goodwill and harmony. {13:26} Through their faith, they intensified their brotherly love. {13:27} Though nature, companionship, and virtuous habits strengthened their bond, those who remained endured for their faith, witnessing their brothers' suffering and martyrdom.

{14:1} Moreover, they encouraged each other to face torture, not only enduring their agonies but also mastering the emotions born of brotherly love. {14:2} O reason, more majestic than kings and freer than the free! {14:3} O sacred and harmonious unity of the seven brothers for the sake of their faith! {14:4} None of these youths proved cowardly or shrank from death; {14:5} rather, they hastened toward it as if running a race toward immortality through torture. {14:6} Just as hands and feet move in harmony guided by the mind, these holy youths, moved by an immortal spirit of devotion, willingly embraced death for the sake of their faith. {14:7} O most holy seven, united in brotherhood! Like the seven days of creation dancing in harmony around religion, {14:8} these youths formed a chorus, encircling and dispelling the fear of tortures sevenfold. {14:9} Even now, we shudder as we hear of the trials of these young men; they not only witnessed and heard threats directly but also endured agonizing sufferings with patience, even in the midst of fiery torment. {14:10} What could be more intensely agonizing? The power of fire is swift and consuming, quickly reducing their bodies. {14:11} It's not surprising that reason held full sway over these men in their torments, just as the mother of these seven young men endured the tortures inflicted on each of her children. {14:12} Consider the complexity of a mother's love for her children, drawing from the depths of her being. {14:13} Even irrational animals, like humans, exhibit sympathy and parental love for their offspring. {14:14} Birds, for instance, tame ones nesting on rooftops, and wild ones in cliffs, holes, and treetops, protect their nestlings, warding off intruders with circling flights and warning calls in their anguish of love. {14:15} It's unnecessary to illustrate sympathy for children through the examples of irrational animals, {14:16} for even bees, in their time for making honeycombs, defend their hives with a sting like an iron dart against intruders, defending them to the death. {14:17} Yet the mother of these young men was not swayed by sympathy for her children; she shared the resolve of Abraham.

{15:1} O reason prevailing over the emotions of children! O religion, more precious to this mother than her own children! {15:2} This mother faced two choices: to preserve her seven sons temporarily as the tyrant had promised, or to uphold their faith. {15:3} She loved their faith more, knowing it promised them eternal life according to God's word. {15:4} How can I express the emotions of parents who love their children? From the earliest years, they imprint upon their character a remarkable likeness in mind and form, especially mothers, whose deep sympathy springs from the pains of childbirth. {15:5} Mothers, though physically weaker and bearing many children, are often more devoted to them. {15:6} This mother of the seven boys loved her children more than any other. Through seven pregnancies, she nurtured tender love for them, {15:7} suffering with them through many pains, and {15:8} yet, out of reverence for God, she scorned their temporary safety. {15:9} Moreover, because of their noble character, obedience to the law, and love for each other and their mother, she felt even greater tenderness toward them. {15:10} They were righteous, self-controlled, brave, and magnanimous, obeying her unto death in keeping the commandments. {15:11} Despite these influences, the mother did not waver in reason, even as each faced unimaginable tortures. {15:12} Instead, she urged them individually and together to embrace death for the sake of their faith. {15:13} O sacred nature and affection of parental love, the yearning of parents for their offspring, nurturing and enduring suffering by mothers! {15:14} This mother, witnessing each son tortured and burned, did not relent because of their faith. {15:15} She watched as their flesh was consumed by fire, their limbs scattered, and their faces exposed like masks. {15:16} O mother, enduring now more bitter pains than even the childbirth you endured for them! {15:17} O woman, who alone bore such complete devotion! {15:18} The death of the first, the piteous looks of the second, and the passing of the third did not sway you. {15:19} Nor did you weep as each bravely faced their agonies, nearing death. {15:20} Seeing children's flesh burned together, hands severed, heads scalped, and corpses piled among spectators, you did not shed tears. {15:21} Neither the melodies of sirens nor the songs of swans could distract as did the voices of your tortured children calling to you. {15:22} How great and numerous were the torments you endured as your sons suffered on the wheel and with hot irons! {15:23} Yet devout reason gave you a courage akin to a man's amid your emotions, strengthening you to prioritize faith over temporal love for your children. {15:24} Witnessing the destruction of all seven and their various tortures, this noble mother remained steadfast in her faith in God. {15:25} In her own soul's council chamber, she weighed mighty advocates: nature, family, parental love, and her children's sufferings. {15:26} Holding two choices, one of death and the other of deliverance for her children, {15:27} she did not choose the temporary deliverance offered by the tyrant. {15:28} Rather, like the daughter of God-fearing Abraham, she remembered his fortitude. {15:29} O mother of the nation, defender of the law and champion of religion, you won the contest in your heart! {15:30} More steadfast than men and enduring beyond males in endurance! {15:31} Just as Noah's ark bore the world through the universal flood, enduring the waves, {15:32} so you, guardian of the law, surrounded by the flood of emotions and violent winds, endured nobly and withstood the storms assailing religion.

{16:1} If a woman advanced in years, mother of seven sons, endured watching her children tortured to death, it must be acknowledged that devout reason triumphs over emotions. {16:2} Thus, I've shown not only that men can master their emotions, but also that a woman can withstand the fiercest tortures. {16:3} The lions around Daniel were not as savage, nor was the fiery furnace of Mishael as intensely hot, as the innate parental love inflamed when she saw her seven sons tortured in such diverse ways. {16:4} Yet the mother extinguished many and great emotions through devout reason. {16:5} Consider this as well: If this woman, though a mother, had been weak-hearted, she might have mourned and perhaps said: {16:6} "Oh, how wretched I am, so often unhappy! After bearing seven children, I am now left with none! {16:7} Oh, seven pregnancies in vain, seven fruitless labors, nurturing and nursing all in vain! {16:8} I endured countless birth pangs for you, my sons, and the anxieties of raising you were even more burdensome. {16:9} Alas for my children, some unmarried, some married without offspring. I won't see your children or know the joy of being called grandmother. {16:10} Alas, I, who had many beautiful children, am now a widow, alone with my sorrows. {16:11} And when I die, I won't have any of my sons to bury me." {16:12} Yet this sacred, God-fearing mother did not lament in this manner for any of them, nor did she dissuade them from dying, nor did she grieve as they died. {16:13} Instead, with a steadfast resolve and granting rebirth to her sons for immortality, she encouraged and urged them to embrace death for the sake of their faith. {16:14} O mother, soldier of God for the cause of religion, elder and woman! Your steadfastness conquered even a tyrant, and in word and deed, you proved more powerful than many men. {16:15} When you and your sons were arrested together, you witnessed Eleazar's torture and spoke to your sons in Hebrew, {16:16} "My sons, the contest you are called to witness is noble for our nation. Fight zealously for our ancestral law. {16:17} It would be shameful if, while an aged man endures such agonies for religion, you young men were to be frightened by torture. {16:18} Remember, it is through God that you have shared in this world and enjoyed life, {16:19} and therefore, you must endure any suffering for God's sake. {16:20} For the sake of God, our father Abraham was zealous to sacrifice his son Isaac, the ancestor of our nation. When Isaac saw his father's hand with the sword descending upon him, he did not falter. {16:21} Righteous Daniel faced the lions, and Hananiah, Azariah, and Mishael endured the fiery furnace for God's sake. {16:22} You too must have the same faith in God and not be dismayed. {16:23} It's unreasonable for those who have religious knowledge not to endure pain." {16:24} With these words, the mother of the seven sons encouraged and persuaded each of her sons to die rather than violate God's commandment. {16:25} They also knew that those who die for God's sake live in God, like Abraham, Isaac, Jacob, and all the patriarchs.

{17:1} Some of the guards reported that when she also was about to be seized and put to death, she threw herself into the flames so that no one could touch her body. {17:2} O mother, who with your seven sons nullified the violence of the tyrant, frustrated his evil plans, and demonstrated the courage of your faith! {17:3} Firmly established like a roof atop the pillars of your sons, you stood resolute and unwavering against the earthquake of tortures. {17:4} Therefore, take courage, O holy-minded mother, maintaining a steadfast hope in God. {17:5} The moon in the sky, along with the stars, does not shine as splendidly as you, who, after guiding your star-like seven sons to piety, now stand honored before God and are firmly established in heaven with them. {17:6} For your children were true descendants of Father Abraham. {17:7} If it were possible for us to paint the story of your piety as an artist might, wouldn't those who first beheld it have shuddered as they saw the mother enduring the varied tortures of her seven children to death for the sake of religion? {17:8} Indeed, it would be fitting to inscribe on their tomb these words as a reminder to the people of our nation: {17:9} "Here lie buried an aged priest and an aged woman and seven sons, because of the violence of the tyrant who sought to destroy the Hebrew way of life. {17:10} They defended their nation, trusted in God, and endured torture even to death." {17:11} Truly, the contest in which they engaged was divine, {17:12} for on that day virtue awarded them and tested their endurance. The prize was immortality in eternal life. {17:13} Eleazar was the first contestant, the mother of the seven sons entered the fray, and the brothers competed. {17:14} The tyrant was the adversary, and the world and humanity were the spectators. {17:15} Reverence for God emerged victorious and crowned its own champions. {17:16} Who would not admire the champions of divine law? Who would not be amazed? {17:17} Even the tyrant himself and all his council marveled at their endurance, {17:18} because of which they now stand before the divine throne and live in blessed eternity. {17:19} For Moses says, "All who are consecrated are under your hands." {17:20} These, then, who were consecrated for the sake of God, are honored not only with this distinction but also because through them our enemies did not prevail over our nation, {17:21} the tyrant was punished, and the homeland purified -- they became a kind of ransom for the sins of our nation. {17:22} And through the blood of those devout individuals and their deaths as an offering, divine Providence preserved Israel, which had previously been afflicted. {17:23} When the tyrant Antiochus saw the courage of their virtue and their endurance under torture, he held them up as an example to his soldiers for their own endurance. {17:24} This inspired them with bravery and fortitude for infantry battles and sieges, and he overcame and conquered all his enemies.

{18:1} O children of Israel, descendants of Abraham's lineage, heed this law and practice piety in every aspect of your lives. {18:2} Understand that devout reason governs all emotions, whether internal sufferings or those inflicted from outside. {18:3} Therefore, those who sacrificed their bodies in suffering for the sake of religion were not only admired by people but also deemed worthy to share in a divine inheritance. {18:4} Through them, the nation found peace, and by restoring adherence to the law in their homeland, they devastated their enemies. {18:5} The tyrant Antiochus was punished in his lifetime and continues to be chastised after death. Unable to compel the Israelites to forsake their ancestral customs and adopt paganism, he departed Jerusalem and waged war against the Persians. {18:6} The mother of seven sons imparted these principles to her children: {18:7} "I was a pure virgin and never left my father's house. I preserved the rib from which woman was made. {18:8} No seducer defiled me on the open plain, nor did the deceitful serpent corrupt my virginity. {18:9} In my prime, I remained faithful to my husband, and after my sons grew up, their father passed away content, having lived a good life with virtuous children and without the sorrow of bereavement. {18:10} While he was with you, he taught you the law and the prophets. {18:11} He recounted stories of Abel slain by Cain, Isaac offered as a burnt offering, and Joseph in prison. {18:12} He spoke of the zeal of Phineas and taught you about Hananiah, Azariah, and Mishael in the fiery furnace. {18:13} He praised Daniel in the den of lions and blessed him. {18:14} He reminded you of Isaiah's prophecy, 'Though you pass through the fire, it shall not consume you.' {18:15} He sang to you the psalms of David, who said, 'Many are the afflictions of the righteous.' {18:16} He shared Solomon's proverb with you, 'There is a tree of life for those who do his will.' {18:17} He affirmed Ezekiel's words, 'Can these dry bones live?' {18:18} He did not forget to teach you the song Moses taught, saying, {18:19} 'I kill and I make alive; this is your life and the length of your days.'" {18:20} Bitter indeed was that day -- yet strangely not bitter -- when the cruel tyrant of the Greeks extinguished fire with fire in his savage cauldrons, subjecting the seven sons of Abraham's daughter to catapults and further tortures in his burning wrath. {18:21} He pierced their eyes, cut out their tongues, and executed them with various tortures. {18:22} For these crimes, divine justice pursued and will continue to pursue the accursed tyrant. {18:23} But the sons of Abraham, together with their victorious mother, are gathered into the company of the patriarchs, having received pure and immortal souls from God. {18:24} To whom be glory forever and ever. Amen.

5 Maccabees

The hypothetical Book of 5 Maccabees represents an extension of the Maccabean tradition, reflecting themes of persecution, martyrdom, divine justice, and the ultimate triumph of faith. Rooted in the historical context of the Jewish struggle against Hellenistic oppression, this imagined text seeks to capture the spirit of resilience and devotion that characterized the Maccabean revolt, while also expanding on the theological reflections common to later interpretations of these events. The narrative structure, presented in seven chapters, explores the steadfastness of the faithful remnant, the severe trials they endure, and the eventual restoration and blessings promised by God. The text delves into the eschatological hope of a new heaven and earth, emphasizing the eternal reward for those who remain true to their faith. In creating this work, the intention is to provide a cohesive, reflective, and spiritually enriching narrative that honors the legacy of the Maccabean literature. However, it is essential to note that the content of this Book of 5 Maccabees is entirely hypothetical. It is not based on any historical or canonical source but rather serves as a creative exercise to explore themes consistent with the Maccabean tradition within a fictional framework.

This hypothetical nature is highlighted by the fact that no original or historical text exists under the name 5 Maccabees, and the verses presented here are a product of imaginative construction rather than an authentic religious or historical document.

{1:1} In the days of oppression, when the rulers of the land sought to extinguish the light of the faithful, a decree was issued throughout the kingdom. {1:2} The rulers, filled with pride and wickedness, commanded that all people should forsake their ancient customs and bow before the idols of the empire. {1:3} Many among the people, fearing the sword, turned away from the God of their fathers and embraced the false gods of the land. {1:4} But a remnant, steadfast and unwavering, refused to submit to the tyrants' demands, for they trusted in the Lord of Hosts. {1:5} These faithful ones hid in caves and secret places, continuing to worship the one true God in spirit and truth. {1:6} The rulers, enraged by their defiance, sent soldiers to seek out and destroy all who would not bow to their idols. {1:7} Many were captured, and the trials began. {1:8} The faithful were brought before the rulers and were commanded to renounce their God, but they stood firm in their resolve. {1:9} The leaders mocked them, saying, "Where is your God now? Will He save you from our hands?" {1:10} But the faithful replied, "The Lord is our strength and our shield; even if we perish, we will not forsake Him." {1:11} And so the rulers, in their cruelty, ordered that they be put to death in the most horrific ways. {1:12} Yet, in their suffering, the faithful glorified God, singing hymns of praise as they were led to their deaths. {1:13} The blood of the martyrs flowed like a river, and their cries reached the heavens. {1:14} The earth trembled, and the sun was darkened, as if in mourning for the righteous. {1:15} And the rulers, though they had silenced the voices of the faithful, could not extinguish the fire of their faith. {1:16} For the memory of the martyrs inspired many others to stand firm in their devotion to the Lord. {1:17} In every corner of the land, the faithful gathered in secret, encouraging one another to remain true to their God. {1:18} They recalled the words of the prophets and the promises of the covenant, finding strength in the knowledge that the Lord was with them. {1:19} And they prayed earnestly, asking the Lord to deliver them from the hand of their enemies. {1:20} But the persecution did not cease; it grew more severe with each passing day. {1:21} The rulers, in their madness, sought to destroy not only the people but also the very memory of their God. {1:22} They tore down the altars and desecrated the holy places, thinking that they could erase the name of the Lord from the earth. {1:23} But the faithful knew that the Lord was greater than any earthly power, and they trusted in His ultimate justice. {1:24} They believed that, though they suffered now, the day of the Lord's vengeance would come, and their enemies would be brought low. {1:25} And so they continued to resist, even in the face of death, for their hope was in the Lord. {1:26} The rulers, in their arrogance, did not understand the strength of the faithful, nor did they comprehend the power of the God they sought to destroy. {1:27} But the faithful knew that the Lord was their refuge, and they took comfort in His promises. {1:28} Though the night was long and dark, they believed that the dawn of deliverance would surely come. {1:29} And so they waited, enduring their trials with patience and hope. {1:30} The rulers, growing ever more desperate, intensified their efforts to root out the faithful. {1:31} They sent spies into every town and village, offering rewards for those who would betray their neighbors. {1:32} But the faithful would not be moved; they refused to turn against one another, even under the threat of death. {1:33} Instead, they strengthened their bonds of fellowship, supporting each other in every way they could. {1:34} They shared their food, their homes, and their prayers, trusting that the Lord would provide for their needs. {1:35} The rulers, seeing that their efforts were in vain, became even more ruthless. {1:36} They decreed that all who were found worshiping the Lord would be put to death without trial. {1:37} The faithful, hearing this, were filled with fear, but they did not waver in their faith. {1:38} They continued to gather in secret, praying for courage and strength. {1:39} And the Lord heard their prayers, sending His Spirit to comfort and sustain them. {1:40} Though they were surrounded by enemies, they knew that they were not alone, for the Lord was with them.

{2:1} The first among the martyrs was a man of great faith and courage, named Eleazar. {2:2} He was brought before the rulers and commanded to eat the flesh of unclean animals, in violation of the law of his God. {2:3} But Eleazar refused, saying, "I will not defile myself with such food, for I serve the living God, who has commanded me to keep His statutes." {2:4} The rulers, angered by his defiance, ordered that he be tortured until he complied. {2:5} But Eleazar, even in his suffering, remained steadfast, refusing to abandon his faith. {2:6} As the pain grew unbearable, he cried out to the Lord, saying, "O Lord, you know my heart and my desire to remain faithful to you. Give me the strength to endure this trial for your sake." {2:7} And the Lord heard his prayer, granting him the strength to endure his suffering without complaint. {2:8} Finally, the rulers, seeing that they could not break his spirit, ordered that he be put to death. {2:9} And so Eleazar, with his last breath, praised the Lord, saying, "Blessed be the name of the Lord, who gives me the strength to remain faithful to Him, even unto death." {2:10} And with these words, he passed into the presence of the Lord, where he was welcomed as a faithful servant. {2:11} The testimony of Eleazar inspired many others to stand firm in their faith, even in the face of death. {2:12} Among them were seven brothers and their mother, who were brought before the rulers and commanded to bow to the idols. {2:13} The brothers, filled with courage, refused, saying, "We will not bow to these lifeless statues, for we serve the living God, who created the heavens and the earth." {2:14} The rulers, enraged by their defiance, ordered that they be tortured one by one, in the presence of their mother. {2:15} But the brothers, encouraged by each other's faith, endured the tortures without wavering. {2:16} The first brother, after being severely beaten, was asked once more to bow to the idols, but he replied, "I will never forsake my God for the sake of this fleeting life." {2:17} And so he was put to death. {2:18} The second brother was then brought forward, and after enduring similar torments, was given the same choice. {2:19} He too refused, saying, "The Lord will reward me for my faithfulness, even if I lose my life." {2:20} And so he was also put to death. {2:21} The third brother was then brought forward, and though he saw the fate of his brothers, he remained resolute in his faith. {2:22} After enduring great suffering, he too refused to bow to the idols and was put to death. {2:23} The fourth brother, seeing the courage of his brothers, was filled with even greater faith. {2:24} He endured his tortures with a joyful heart, knowing that he would soon be with the Lord. {2:25} When the rulers offered him his life in exchange for bowing to the idols, he replied, "My life belongs to the Lord, and I will not give it to anyone else." {2:26} And so he was put to death. {2:27} The fifth brother was then brought forward, and though he was the youngest, he showed the greatest courage of all. {2:28} He endured his tortures with a smile on his face, saying, "I rejoice that I am counted worthy to suffer for the name of the Lord." {2:29} When the rulers offered him his life, he replied, "I do not fear death, for I know that the Lord will raise me up on the last day." {2:30} And so he was put to death. {2:31} The sixth brother was then brought forward, and though his body was weak from the torments he had already endured, his spirit was strong. {2:32} He refused to bow to the idols, saying, "My body may be broken, but my faith remains whole." {2:33} And so he was put to death. {2:34} Finally, the seventh brother, who was the oldest, was brought forward. {2:35} He had seen the death of all his brothers, but his faith had not been shaken. {2:36} He endured his tortures with patience, trusting in the Lord's promises. {2:37} When the rulers offered him his life, he replied, "I will not trade my eternal reward for a few more days on this earth." {2:38} And so he was put to death. {2:39} Their mother, who had watched the death of all her sons, was then brought before the rulers. {2:40} They offered her mercy if she would renounce her faith, but she refused, saying, "I have given my sons to the Lord, and I will not take them back." {2:41} And so she was also put to death, joining her sons in the presence of the Lord.

{3:1} The blood of the martyrs cried out to the Lord, and He heard their cries. {3:2} The Lord, in His righteous anger, prepared to pour out His wrath upon the wicked rulers who had persecuted His people. {3:3} The earth trembled, and the heavens were darkened, as the Lord's judgment drew near. {3:4} The rulers, confident in their power, continued in their wickedness, unaware of the doom that awaited them. {3:5} But the Lord, who sees all things, was not blind to their evil deeds. {3:6} He sent forth His angels to strike down the wicked, and they were consumed by fire from heaven. {3:7} The rulers, who had once mocked the Lord, were now filled with terror, for they realized that their end had come. {3:8} They cried out for mercy, but it was too late, for the Lord's judgment was upon them. {3:9} The people, seeing the destruction of the wicked, were filled with awe and fear. {3:10} They realized that the Lord is a God of justice, who does not tolerate evil. {3:11} The faithful, who had endured so much suffering, were comforted by the knowledge that the Lord had avenged them. {3:12} They praised the Lord, saying, "Great and mighty are your works, O Lord, and just are all your judgments." {3:13} The survivors of the persecution, seeing the fate of their enemies, were filled with hope, for they knew that the Lord was with them. {3:14} They gathered together to rebuild the altars that had been torn down, and they offered sacrifices to the Lord in thanksgiving. {3:15} The land, which had been desolate and barren, began to flourish once more, as the Lord blessed His people. {3:16} The faithful, who had been scattered, returned to their homes, and peace was restored to the land. {3:17} The rulers who had survived the Lord's wrath were filled with fear, and they no longer dared to persecute the faithful. {3:18} They realized that the Lord was the true ruler of the earth, and they submitted to His authority. {3:19} The people, seeing the repentance of the rulers, prayed for their salvation, asking the Lord to show them mercy. {3:20} The Lord, who is compassionate and merciful, heard their prayers and forgave the rulers for their sins. {3:21} The rulers, now humbled, sought to make amends for their wickedness by protecting the faithful and restoring the holy places. {3:22} The faithful, seeing the rulers' repentance, forgave them and accepted their protection. {3:23} They continued to worship the Lord in peace, thanking Him for His mercy and justice. {3:24} The land, once filled with violence and bloodshed, was now a place of peace and prosperity, as the Lord blessed His people. {3:25} The faithful, who had suffered so much, were now rewarded for their perseverance and faith. {3:26} The Lord, who is faithful and true, fulfilled His promises to His people, and they were filled with joy. {3:27} They sang praises to the Lord, saying, "Great are your works, O Lord, and your mercy endures forever."

{4:1} In those days, there arose a group of men and women who were known as the faithful remnant. {4:2} They were the descendants of those who had suffered persecution, and they were determined to remain true to the Lord. {4:3} They gathered together in secret, worshiping the Lord in spirit and truth, even when it was dangerous to do so. {4:4} The rulers of the land, though they had repented of their past wickedness, still sought to maintain control over the people. {4:5} They passed laws that made it difficult for the faithful to practice their religion openly, but the remnant did not waver in their faith. {4:6} They continued to worship the Lord in secret, trusting that He would protect them. {4:7} The remnant, though small in number, were mighty in spirit, for they knew that the Lord was with them. {4:8} They encouraged one another with the words of the prophets, reminding each other of the promises of the Lord. {4:9} They prayed for strength and courage, asking the Lord to help them remain faithful in the face of opposition. {4:10} The Lord, who hears the prayers of His people, sent His Spirit to comfort and strengthen the remnant. {4:11} They were filled with courage and determination, knowing that the Lord was with them. {4:12} The rulers, seeing that the remnant would not be moved, sought to intimidate them with threats and persecution. {4:13} But the remnant did not fear, for they trusted in the Lord, who had delivered their ancestors from the hands of their enemies. {4:14} They continued to gather in secret, worshiping the Lord with all their hearts. {4:15} The rulers, frustrated by their inability to break the remnant's spirit, intensified their efforts to root them out. {4:16} They sent spies into the homes of the faithful, seeking to uncover their secret gatherings. {4:17} But the remnant, aware of the danger, took great care to protect themselves, and the rulers' efforts were in vain. {4:18} The remnant continued to worship the Lord, knowing that their true safety lay in His hands. {4:19} They prayed for the rulers, asking the Lord to open their eyes to the truth. {4:20} The Lord, who is gracious and merciful, heard their prayers, and He began to soften the hearts of the rulers. {4:21} The rulers, seeing the faithfulness of the remnant, began to question their own beliefs. {4:22} They realized that the remnant, though few in number, had something that they did not: a deep and abiding faith in the Lord. {4:23} The rulers, moved by the remnant's example, began to seek the Lord for themselves. {4:24} They gathered together in secret, studying the scriptures and praying for guidance. {4:25} The remnant, seeing the change in the rulers, welcomed them with open arms, sharing with them the truths of the faith. {4:26} The rulers, humbled by the remnant's love and acceptance, confessed their sins and turned to the Lord. {4:27} The remnant, filled with joy, praised the Lord for His mercy and grace. {4:28} They continued to worship the Lord together, both remnant and rulers, united in their faith. {4:29} The land, once divided by fear and mistrust, was now united in worship of the one true God. {4:30} The remnant, who had remained faithful through so many trials, were now honored by all the people. {4:31} The rulers, who had once persecuted the faithful, were now their protectors, defending their right to worship the Lord. {4:32} The people, seeing the unity and faith of the remnant and the rulers, were inspired to turn to the Lord themselves. {4:33} The land was filled with the knowledge of the Lord, and His name was praised in every corner. {4:34} The remnant, who had once been few in number, now saw their faith spread throughout the land. {4:35} They rejoiced in the Lord's goodness, giving thanks for His faithfulness and love. {4:36} The rulers, now servants of the Lord, sought to govern the land according to His will. {4:37} The people, seeing the rulers' devotion to the Lord, were filled with confidence and hope. {4:38} They knew that as long as the Lord was with them, they would be safe and prosperous. {4:39} The remnant, who had endured so much, were now blessed beyond measure, for they had remained true to the Lord. {4:40} They continued to worship Him with all their hearts, trusting in His promises and rejoicing in His love.

{5:1} In the days following the great deliverance, the people of the land gathered together to renew their covenant with the Lord. {5:2} The rulers, who had turned to the Lord, led the assembly, calling the people to repentance and faith. {5:3} The people, moved by the Spirit of the Lord, confessed their sins and turned from their wicked ways. {5:4} They vowed to serve the Lord with all their hearts, to keep His commandments, and to teach their children His ways. {5:5} The rulers, seeing the sincerity of the people, praised the Lord, saying, "Great and mighty is the Lord our God, who has delivered us from our enemies and brought us back to Himself." {5:6} The people, filled with joy, offered sacrifices to the Lord, giving thanks for His mercy and grace. {5:7} They sang songs of praise, lifting their voices to the heavens, for the Lord had done great things for them. {5:8} The remnant, who had remained faithful through all the trials, were honored by the people, for they had led the way in faith and courage. {5:9} The rulers, who had once persecuted the faithful, now sought their counsel and guidance, for they knew that the Lord was with them. {5:10} The people, seeing the unity and faith of the remnant and the rulers, were inspired to turn to the Lord themselves.

{6:1} The Lord, who is faithful and just, blessed His people for their obedience. {6:2} The land, once barren and desolate, now flowed with milk and honey, for the Lord had restored it to its former glory. {6:3} The people, who had suffered so much, were now prosperous and at peace, for the Lord had blessed them with abundance. {6:4} The rulers, who had turned to the Lord, governed the land with wisdom and justice, and the people were content. {6:5} The faithful, who had remained true to the Lord, were honored and respected by all, for they had shown great courage and faith. {6:6} The remnant, who had endured so many trials, were now blessed beyond measure, for the Lord had rewarded them for their faithfulness. {6:7} The people, seeing the blessings of the Lord, were filled with gratitude and joy. {6:8} They continued to worship the Lord with all their hearts, giving thanks for His mercy and grace. {6:9} The rulers, who had once been enemies of the Lord, now served Him with all their hearts, seeking to do His will. {6:10} The people, seeing the rulers' devotion to the Lord, were filled with confidence and hope, for they knew that the Lord was with them. {6:11} The land, once filled with violence and bloodshed, was now a place of peace and prosperity, for the Lord had blessed His people. {6:12} The faithful, who had suffered so much, were now rewarded for their perseverance and faith, for the Lord had fulfilled His promises to them.

{7:1} The Lord, who is faithful and true, revealed to His people the promise of future glory. {7:2} He spoke through His prophets, saying, "Behold, the days are coming when I will make all things new. {7:3} I will create a new heaven and a new earth, and my people will dwell with me forever. {7:4} There will be no more pain, no more sorrow, for the former things will have passed away. {7:5} I will wipe away every tear from their eyes, and they will see my face, and my name will be on their foreheads." {7:6} The people, hearing these words, were filled with hope and joy, for they knew that the Lord had great things in store for them. {7:7} They continued to worship the Lord with all their hearts, trusting in His promises and looking forward to the day of His coming. {7:8} The rulers, who had turned to the Lord, encouraged the people to remain faithful, saying, "Let us hold fast to the hope we have, for He who promised is faithful." {7:9} The people, inspired by these words, continued to serve the Lord with all their hearts, looking forward to the day when they would see Him face to face. {7:10} The remnant, who had remained faithful through so many trials, were now filled with joy, for they knew that their reward was great in heaven. {7:11} They encouraged one another, saying, "Let us press on toward the goal, for the prize that awaits us is beyond our imagination." {7:12} The people, hearing these words, were filled with determination, for they knew that the Lord was with them. {7:13} They continued to worship the Lord with all their hearts, trusting in His promises and looking forward to the day of His coming. {7:14} The Lord, who is gracious and compassionate, blessed His people with peace and prosperity, as they awaited the fulfillment of His promises. {7:15} The land, once filled with violence and bloodshed, was now a place of peace and prosperity, for the Lord had blessed His people. {7:16} The faithful, who had suffered so much, were now rewarded for their perseverance and faith, for the Lord had fulfilled His promises to them. {7:17} The people, seeing the blessings of the Lord, were filled with gratitude and joy. {7:18} They continued to worship the Lord with all their hearts, giving thanks for His mercy and grace. {7:19} The rulers, who had once been enemies of the Lord, now served Him with all their hearts, seeking to do His will. {7:20} The people, seeing the rulers' devotion to the Lord, were filled with confidence and hope, for they knew that the Lord was with them.

1 Baruch

The Book of 1 Baruch, also known as the Prophecy of Baruch, is an ancient Jewish text traditionally attributed to Baruch ben Neriah, the scribe and disciple of the prophet Jeremiah. Although not part of the Hebrew Bible, it is included in the Septuagint and recognized as canonical by the Catholic and Orthodox Christian traditions. The text is believed to have been composed in the second century BCE, reflecting the socio-political realities of Jewish life during the Hellenistic period. 1 Baruch is structured into a series of prayers, confessions, and exhortations, beginning with an introduction that situates the work within the context of the Babylonian Exile. It presents a profound theological reflection on themes of sin, repentance, and divine justice, underscoring the belief that the suffering of the Jewish people was a direct consequence of their disobedience to God. The book calls for a return to righteousness and faithfulness to the covenant, emphasizing the hope for divine mercy and restoration. This hope is articulated through Baruch's role as a prophet and scribe, conveying messages of consolation and future redemption. The text also includes a letter attributed to Jeremiah, which serves to reinforce its themes and historical context. Scholars note that 1 Baruch offers a rich tapestry of theological ideas, interweaving elements from Deuteronomistic theology, wisdom literature, and apocalyptic thought. It stands as a testament to the enduring faith and resilience of the Jewish community in the face of adversity, providing valuable insights into the religious and cultural milieu of the time.

{1:1} These are the words recorded by Baruch, son of Neraiah, descendant of Mahseiah, Zedekiah, Hasadiah, and Hilkiah, written in Babylon. {1:2} It was the fifth year, on the seventh day of the month, when the Chaldeans captured Jerusalem and set it ablaze. {1:3} Baruch read aloud from this book before Jeconiah, son of Jehoiakim, the king of Judah, and all the people who gathered to hear it. {1:4} The audience included mighty men, princes, elders, and all who lived in Babylon by the river Sud. {1:5} Deeply moved, they wept, fasted, and prayed to the Lord. {1:6} They gathered money, each contributing what they could. {1:7} They sent these offerings to Jerusalem for Jehoiakim the high priest, son of Hilkiah, along with the priests and the people present in Jerusalem. {1:8} Baruch, on the tenth day of Sivan, returned the vessels of the Lord's house taken from the temple to Judah—the silver vessels made by Zedekiah, son of Josiah, king of Judah. {1:9} This happened after Nebuchadnezzar, king of Babylon, carried away Jeconiah, princes, prisoners, mighty men, and the people to Babylon. {1:10} They wrote, "We send money to buy burnt offerings, sin offerings, incense, and grain offerings to offer on the altar of our God, and pray for the lives of Nebuchadnezzar, king of Babylon, and his son Belshazzar, that their days may be blessed like the days of heaven. {1:11} The Lord will strengthen us, enlighten our eyes, and under the protection of Nebuchadnezzar and Belshazzar, we will serve them and find favor in their sight. {1:12} Pray for us to the Lord our God, for we have sinned against him, and his anger has not turned away from us. {1:13} Read this book we send you, confessing in the house of the Lord during feasts and appointed times. {1:14} Say, 'Righteousness belongs to our God, but we are ashamed, as we are today, we, the men of Judah, and the inhabitants of Jerusalem. {1:15} Our kings, princes, priests, prophets, and fathers have sinned against the Lord. {1:16} We have disobeyed him, and ignored the voice of the Lord our God, not following the statutes he gave us. {1:17} From the day the Lord brought our fathers out of Egypt to this day, we have been disobedient and negligent in listening to his voice. {1:18} Until today, the disasters and curses declared by the Lord through Moses his servant, when he brought our fathers out of Egypt to give us the land flowing with milk and honey, have clung to us. {1:19} We have not listened to the voice of the Lord our God in all the words of the prophets he sent us, but each followed the desires of our own wicked hearts, serving other gods and doing evil in the sight of the Lord our God."

{2:1} The Lord fulfilled his word against us and our leaders who governed Israel, as well as against our kings, princes, and all the people of Israel and Judah. {2:2} Never before has such devastation been seen under heaven as what happened in Jerusalem, in accordance with the law of Moses, where people resorted to unimaginable acts in desperation. {2:3} They resorted to unthinkable measures, even eating the flesh of their own children. {2:4} The Lord subjected them to surrounding kingdoms, making them a byword and a desolation among all peoples where he scattered them. {2:5} They were brought low and not raised up, all because we disobeyed the Lord our God and did not listen to his voice. {2:6} "Righteousness belongs to the Lord our God, but shame covers us and our fathers to this day. {2:7} The calamities the Lord warned us about have come upon us. {2:8} Yet we have not sought the favor of the Lord by turning from our wicked ways and thoughts. {2:9} The Lord has kept his word and brought calamity upon us because he is righteous in all his actions, fulfilling what he commanded us to do. {2:10} But we have not obeyed his voice or walked in his statutes set before us. {2:11} "Now, O Lord God of Israel, who brought your people out of Egypt with great power, signs, wonders, and a mighty hand, you have made a name for yourself to this day. {2:12} We have sinned, acted wickedly, and rebelled against your commandments, O Lord our God. {2:13} Turn away your anger from us, for we are few among the nations where you have scattered us. {2:14} Hear, O Lord, our prayer and supplication. Save us for your own sake and grant us favor in the eyes of those who have exiled us. {2:15} Let all the earth know that you are the Lord our God, for Israel and his descendants are called by your name. {2:16} O Lord, look down from your holy dwelling place and consider us. Incline your ear, O Lord, and hear; open your eyes, O Lord, and see. {2:17} The dead in Hades cannot praise you or acknowledge your righteousness. {2:18} But we, the living, with bowed heads and weakened spirits, hunger for your glory and righteousness, O Lord. {2:19} We do not bring our prayers before you because of any righteous deeds of our ancestors or kings. {2:20} You have poured out your anger and wrath upon us, fulfilling what your prophets foretold. {2:21} "Thus says the Lord: Submit to the king of Babylon and remain in the land I gave your ancestors. {2:22} If you do not obey the Lord's voice and serve the king of Babylon, {2:23} I will silence joy and gladness in Judah and Jerusalem, and the land will become desolate without inhabitants." {2:24} "Yet we did not obey your voice to serve the king of Babylon. You have confirmed your words spoken through your prophets that the bones of our kings and ancestors would be brought out of their graves. {2:25} They have been exposed to heat and cold, perishing in great suffering from famine, sword, and pestilence. {2:26} The house called by your name now stands as it does because of the wickedness of Israel and Judah. {2:27} Yet, O Lord our God, you have treated us with kindness and great compassion. {2:28} As you commanded through your servant Moses, when you instructed him to write your law before the people of Israel, {2:29} saying, 'If you do not obey my voice, this great multitude will become a small number among the nations where I scatter them. {2:30} For I know they will not obey me, for they are a stiff-necked people. But in their exile, they will come to their senses {2:31} and acknowledge that I am the Lord their God. I will give them obedient hearts and listening ears. {2:32} In the land of their exile, they will praise me and remember my name. {2:33} They will turn from their stubbornness and wicked deeds, recalling the sins of their ancestors who sinned against the Lord. {2:34} I will bring them back to the land I promised their ancestors—Abraham, Isaac, and Jacob. They will rule over it, and I will increase their numbers, and they will not decrease. {2:35} I will make an everlasting covenant with them to be their God, and they will be my people. Never again will I remove them from the land I have given them.'"

{3:1} "O Lord Almighty, God of Israel, the troubled soul and weary spirit cry out to you. {3:2} Hear, O Lord, and have mercy, for we have sinned against you. {3:3} You are enthroned forever, while we are perishing. {3:4} O Lord Almighty, God of Israel, hear the prayer of those who are now dead, descendants of those who sinned against you and did not obey your voice. Thus calamities have befallen us. {3:5} Do not remember the sins of our ancestors; in this time of crisis, remember your power and your name. {3:6} For you, O Lord, are our God, and we will praise you. {3:7} You have instilled fear of you in our hearts so that we may call upon your name. Even in exile, we praise you, having turned away from the iniquities of our ancestors who abandoned you. {3:8} Here we are today in exile, where you have scattered us, reproached, cursed, and punished for the sins of our ancestors who deserted the Lord our God." {3:9} Hear, O Israel, the commandments of life; listen and gain wisdom! {3:10} Why, O Israel, are you in the land of your enemies, growing old in a foreign land, defiled among the dead? {3:11} You are counted among those in Hades because you have forsaken the fountain of wisdom. {3:12} If you had walked in the ways of God, you would dwell in eternal peace. {3:13} Learn where wisdom resides, where strength and understanding are found, where there is long life, light for the eyes, and peace. {3:14} Who has discovered her dwelling place? Who has entered her storehouses? {3:15} Where are the leaders of the nations, those who rule over beasts and birds, who amass silver and gold without end, who scheme endlessly? {3:16} They have vanished into Hades, replaced by others. {3:17} Young men born into light and dwelling on earth have not found the path to knowledge or understood its ways. {3:18} Their descendants have strayed far from wisdom. {3:19} Wisdom is not found in Canaan or Teman; those who seek understanding have not grasped her paths. {3:20} O Israel, how magnificent is the house of God and the vast territory he possesses! {3:21} It is immense, boundless, and lofty. {3:22} Giants of old were born there, renowned for their stature and skill in war. {3:23} Yet God did not choose them or give them knowledge; they perished due to their foolishness. {3:24} Who has ascended to heaven, taken wisdom, and brought her down from the clouds? {3:25} Who has crossed the sea, found wisdom, and purchased her with pure gold? {3:26} No one knows her path except the one who knows all things, who found her through understanding. {3:27} He created the earth for all time, filling it with creatures. {3:28} He sends forth light and it obeys; he calls the stars and they shine joyfully. {3:29} This is our God; there is no other like him! {3:30} He discovered the entire path to wisdom and gave her to Jacob his servant and to Israel whom he loved. {3:31} Wisdom appeared on earth and lived among humanity thereafter.

{4:1} "She is the book of God's commandments, an enduring law. Those who hold onto her will live, but those who forsake her will perish. {4:2} Turn back, O Jacob, and embrace her; walk towards the light she shines. {4:3} Do not give your honor to another or your advantages to foreign nations. {4:4} Happy are we, O Israel, for we know what pleases God. {4:5} Take courage, my people, O memorial of Israel! {4:6} You were not sold to the nations for destruction, but handed over to your enemies because you angered God. {4:7} You provoked the God who created you by worshiping demons instead of God. {4:8} You forgot the everlasting God who brought you up, and you brought grief upon Jerusalem who nurtured you. {4:9} Jerusalem saw the wrath that God brought upon you and lamented, saying: 'Listen, neighbors of Zion, great sorrow has come upon me; {4:10} for I have seen my sons and daughters taken captive, as the Everlasting One ordained. {4:11} I nurtured them with joy but sent them away with weeping and sorrow. {4:12} Let no one rejoice over me, a widow bereft of many; I am desolate because my children turned away from God's law. {4:13} They disregarded his statutes, did not walk in God's commandments, and neglected the paths of righteousness. {4:14} Let the neighbors of Zion remember the captivity of my sons and daughters, as the Everlasting One ordained. {4:15} For a nation from afar, ruthless and speaking a foreign language, brought them into captivity without regard for the old or pity for the young. {4:16} They took away the beloved sons of widows and left lonely women without their daughters. {4:17} 'But how can I help you? {4:18} The one who brought these calamities upon you will deliver you from the hand of your enemies. {4:19} Go, my children, for I am left desolate. {4:20} I have exchanged the garment of peace for the sackcloth of my supplication; I will cry to the Everlasting all my days. {4:21} 'Take courage, my children, cry out to God, and he will deliver you from the power of your enemies. {4:22} For I have placed my hope in the Everlasting to save you, and joy has come to me from the Holy One, because of the mercy that will soon come to you from your eternal Savior. {4:23} For I sent you away with sorrow and weeping, but God will restore you to me with joy and gladness forever. {4:24} Just as the neighbors of Zion have witnessed your capture, they will soon witness your salvation from God, which will come to you with great glory and splendor from the Everlasting. {4:25} My children, endure patiently the wrath that has come upon you from God. Though your enemy has overtaken you, you will soon witness their destruction and tread upon their necks. {4:26} My tender sons have endured rough paths, taken away like a flock by the enemy. {4:27} 'Take courage, my children, and cry out to God, for he remembers those whom he brought this upon. {4:28} Return with tenfold zeal to seek God, for the one who brought these calamities upon you will bring you everlasting joy and salvation.' {4:29} Take courage, O Jerusalem, for the one who named you will comfort you. {4:30} Wretched will be those who afflicted you and rejoiced at your downfall. {4:31} Wretched will be the cities where your children served as slaves; wretched will be the city that received your sons. {4:32} Just as she rejoiced at your downfall and gloated over your ruin, she will mourn her own desolation. {4:33} I will strip her of her pride in her numerous population; her insolence will turn to mourning. {4:34} Fire will come upon her from the Everlasting for many days, and she will be inhabited by demons for a long time. {4:35} Look eastward, O Jerusalem, and see the joy that God is bringing to you! {4:36} Behold, your sons are returning, gathered from east and west at the command of the Holy One, rejoicing in the glory of God."

{5:1} "Remove the garments of sorrow and affliction, O Jerusalem, and wear forever the beautiful glory given by God. {5:2} Clothe yourself with the robe of God's righteousness; place on your head the crown of the glory of the Everlasting. {5:3} For God will display your splendor everywhere under heaven. {5:4} Your name will forever be called by God, 'Peace of righteousness and glory of godliness.' {5:5} Rise up, O Jerusalem, stand tall on the heights, and look eastward. See your children gathered from west and east, at the command of the Holy One, rejoicing that God has remembered them. {5:6} They departed from you on foot, led away by their enemies, but God will bring them back to you in glory, as if on a royal throne. {5:7} For God has ordained that every high mountain and everlasting hill be leveled, and the valleys filled, to create smooth ground so that Israel may walk securely in God's glory. {5:8} The forests and every fragrant tree have provided shade for Israel at God's command. {5:9} For God will lead Israel with joy in the light of his glory, with mercy and righteousness that flow from him."

2 Baruch

The book of 2 Baruch, also known as the Syriac Apocalypse of Baruch, is a significant pseudepigraphal text that is part of the Jewish apocalyptic literature. Attributed to Baruch, the scribe and disciple of the prophet Jeremiah, the book is set during the period immediately following the destruction of Jerusalem by the Babylonians in 586 BCE. Composed in the late first century CE, it reflects the socio-political and religious turmoil of the Jewish community in the aftermath of the Second Temple's destruction in 70 CE. Written in Syriac, it survives in several manuscripts, indicating its widespread influence among early Jewish and Christian communities. The narrative unfolds through a series of divine visions and dialogues between Baruch and God, emphasizing themes of divine justice, theodicy, and eschatological hope. Baruch laments the devastation of Jerusalem and questions God's allowance of such suffering, only to receive reassurance of future restoration and the ultimate triumph of divine justice. The text is characterized by its vivid imagery, elaborate symbolism, and profound theological reflections. It addresses issues of communal identity, faith, and perseverance amidst adversity, providing insights into Jewish thought during a critical historical juncture.

{1:1} In the twenty-fifth year of Jeconiah, king of Judah, the word of the Lord came to Baruch, son of Neriah, saying: {1:2} "Have you seen all that this people are doing to Me? The evils committed by these two remaining tribes are greater than those of the ten tribes that were taken captive. {1:3} For the earlier tribes were compelled by their kings to sin, but these two tribes have been compelling their kings to sin by their own will. {1:4} Therefore, I will bring disaster upon this city and its inhabitants. It shall be removed from My presence for a time, and I will scatter this people among the Gentiles so that they may benefit the Gentiles. My people will be disciplined, and a time will come when they will seek the prosperity they once had."

{2:1} "I have said these things to you so that you may instruct Jeremiah and all those like you to leave this city. {2:2} For your actions are like a firm pillar to this city, and your prayers are like a strong wall."

{3:1} And I said, "O Lord, my God, have I come into the world to witness the suffering of my people? Not so, my Lord. {3:2} If I have found favor in Your eyes, take my spirit first, so that I may join my ancestors and not witness the destruction of my people. For two things weigh heavily on me: I cannot oppose You, and my soul cannot endure seeing the suffering of my people. {3:3} But I will say one thing in Your presence, O Lord. {3:4} What will happen after these events? If You destroy Your city and deliver up Your land to those who hate us, how will the name of Israel be remembered again? {3:5} Who will speak of Your praises, or to whom will Your law be explained? Will the world return to its former state, and will the age revert to primeval silence? Will the multitude of souls be taken away, and the nature of humanity be forgotten? Where is all that You have promised us?"

{4:1} And the Lord said to me: "This city will be delivered up for a time, and the people will be disciplined for a time, but the world will not be forgotten. {4:2} Do you think this is the city of which I said, 'I have engraved you on the palms of My hands'? This building now standing among you is not the one revealed to Me, the one prepared beforehand since the time I decided to create Paradise and showed it to Adam before he sinned. But when he disobeyed My commandment, it was taken away from him, as was Paradise. {4:3} After these things, I showed it to My servant Abraham by night among the portions of the sacrifices. {4:4} And again, I showed it to Moses on Mount Sinai when I revealed the likeness of the tabernacle and all its vessels. {4:5} And now, behold, it is kept with Me, as Paradise is. {4:6} Go, therefore, and do as I command you."

{5:1} And I answered and said: "So, am I destined to grieve for Zion? For Your enemies will come to this place, defile Your sanctuary, lead Your people into captivity, and take control of those You love. They will return to their idols and boast before them. What will You do for Your great name?" {5:2} And the Lord said to me: "My name and My glory endure for all eternity; My judgment will uphold its justice in its own time. {5:3} You will see with your own eyes that the enemy will not overthrow Zion, nor will they burn Jerusalem. Instead, they will serve as agents of the Judge for a time. {5:4} But you, go and do everything I have commanded you." {5:5} So I went and gathered Jeremiah, Adu, Seriah, Jabish, Gedaliah, and all the honorable men of the people, and I led them to the valley of Kidron. I told them everything that had been said to me. {5:6} They raised their voices and wept, and we sat there and fasted until evening.

{6:1} The next day, the Chaldean army surrounded the city, and in the evening, I, Baruch, left the people and went to stand by the oak tree. {6:2} I was mourning over Zion and lamenting the captivity that had befallen the people. {6:3} Suddenly, a strong spirit lifted me and carried me over the wall of Jerusalem. {6:4} I saw four angels standing at the four corners of the city, each holding a torch of fire. {6:5} Another angel descended from heaven and said to them, "Hold your lamps, and do not light them until I give the command. {6:6} For I am sent first to speak a word to the earth and to place in it what the Lord Most High has commanded me." {6:7} I saw him descend into the Holy of Holies and take the veil, the holy ark, the mercy-seat, the two tablets, the holy garments of the priests, the altar of incense, the forty-eight precious stones that adorned the priest, and all the holy vessels of the tabernacle. {6:8} He spoke to the earth in a loud voice: "Earth, earth, earth, hear the word of the mighty God, Receive what I commit to you, Guard them until the last times, So that when commanded, you may restore them, So that strangers may not possess them. {6:9} For the time will come when Jerusalem will be delivered for a period, Until it is restored forever." {6:10} The earth opened its mouth and swallowed them up.

{7:1} After these events, I heard the angel instructing those holding the lamps, "Destroy and demolish its wall to the foundation, so the enemy cannot boast and say: 'We have overthrown the wall of Zion, And burned the place of the mighty God.'" {7:2} They then seized the place where I had been standing before.

{8:1} The angels followed his command, and when they broke the corners of the walls, a voice from inside the temple was heard after the wall fell, saying: {8:2} "Enter, you enemies, And come, you adversaries; For the guardian of the house has abandoned it." {8:3} I, Baruch, then departed. {8:4} After these events, the Chaldean army entered and seized the temple and everything around it. They took the people captive, killed some, and bound King Zedekiah, sending him to the king of Babylon.

{9:1} I, Baruch, along with Jeremiah, whose heart was pure from sins and who had not been captured during the city's fall, tore our garments, wept, mourned, and fasted for seven days.

{10:1} After seven days, the word of God came to me, saying: {10:2} "Tell Jeremiah to go and support the people in their captivity to Babylon. {10:3} But you remain here in the desolation of Zion, and I will show you what will happen at the end of days." {10:4} I conveyed this to Jeremiah as the Lord commanded. {10:5} He departed with the people, while I, Baruch, returned and sat before the temple gates, lamenting over Zion with these words: {10:6} "Blessed is he who was not born, or who, having been born, has died. {10:7} But for us who live, woe unto us, because we witness the afflictions of Zion and what has befallen Jerusalem. {10:8} I will call the Sirens from the sea, and you Lilin from the desert, and you Shedim and dragons from the forests: Awake and gird up your loins for mourning, take up dirges with me, and make lamentation with me. {10:9} Farmers, sow not again; and, O earth, why give your harvest fruits? Keep within you the sweets of your sustenance. {10:10} And you, vine, why further give your wine; for offerings will no longer be made in Zion, nor will first-fruits be offered again. {10:11} And you, O heavens, withhold your dew, and do not open the treasuries of rain. {10:12} And you, O sun, withhold the light of your rays. And you, O moon, extinguish your multitude of light; for why should light rise again where the light of Zion is darkened? {10:13} And you, bridegrooms, do not enter, and let brides not adorn themselves with garlands; and you women, do not pray to bear children. {10:14} For the barren shall rejoice above all, and those without sons shall be glad, while those with sons shall have anguish. {10:15} For why should they bear in pain only to bury in grief? {10:16} Or why should mankind have sons? Why should their kind be named again, where this mother is desolate, and her sons are led into captivity? {10:17} From now on, speak not of beauty, and do not discuss gracefulness. {10:18} Moreover, you priests, take the keys of the sanctuary and cast them into the height of heaven, giving them to the Lord and saying, 'Guard Your house Yourself, for we are found to be false stewards.' {10:19} And you, virgins, who weave fine linen and silk with gold from Ophir, hastily take all these things and cast them into the fire, that it may carry them to Him who made them, and the flame send them to Him who created them, lest the enemy gain possession of them."

{11:1} Furthermore, I, Baruch, declare this against you, Babylon: "If you had prospered, And Zion had remained in her glory, Yet the sorrow to us would have been great That you could be compared to Zion. {11:2} But now, behold, the sorrow is immeasurable, And the mourning without end, For indeed, you have prospered While Zion lies desolate. {11:3} Who will judge concerning these matters? Or to whom shall we complain about what has happened to us? O Lord, how have you endured it? {11:4} Our ancestors departed without this grief, And lo, the righteous sleep in the earth in peace; For they did not know this anguish, Nor had they heard of what has happened to us. {11:5} Would that you had ears, O earth, And a heart, O dust, That you might go and announce in Sheol, And say to the dead: {11:6} 'You are more blessed than we who live.'"

{12:1} But I will say what I think, And I will speak against you, O prosperous land. {12:2} The midday sun does not always scorch, Nor do the rays of the sun constantly shine. {12:3} Do not expect and hope that you will always be prosperous and joyful, And do not be greatly uplifted and boastful. {12:4} For surely, in its own time, divine wrath will awaken against you, Which for now is restrained as if by reins of patience. {12:5} And after I had spoken these words, I fasted for seven days.

{13:1} And after these events, I, Baruch, stood upon Mount Zion, and behold, a voice came from above and said to me: {13:2} "Stand on your feet, Baruch, and listen to the word of the mighty God. {13:3} Because you have been astonished at what has happened to Zion, you shall be preserved until the end of times, that you may bear witness. {13:4} So when those prosperous cities ask, 'Why has the mighty God brought this retribution upon us?' You and those like you who have seen this calamity shall say to them: {13:5} 'This is the retribution that is coming upon you and your people at its appointed time, so that the nations may be thoroughly punished. {13:6} And then they will be in anguish. {13:7} And if they ask at that time: {13:8} 'How long?' You shall say to them: "You who have drunk the finest wine, Drink also its dregs; It is the judgment of the Most High, Who shows no partiality." {13:9} Because of this, he showed no mercy to his own sons in the past, But treated them harshly as enemies because they sinned. {13:10} Thus they were disciplined So that they might be sanctified. {13:11} But now, you peoples and nations, you are guilty Because you have always trampled upon the earth And exploited the creation unjustly. {13:12} For I have always blessed you abundantly, Yet you have always been ungrateful for my blessings.

{14:1} And I replied, saying: "You have shown me the course of time and what will happen after these events. You have also told me that the retribution spoken of will come upon the nations. {14:2} Now I understand that many who have sinned have lived in prosperity and departed from the world, while only a few nations will remain in those times to whom your words will be spoken. {14:3} What advantage is there in this? What worse evil than what we have already seen should we expect to witness? {14:4} Yet again I will speak in Your presence: {14:5} What have those gained who knew your ways before me, who did not walk in vanity like the rest of the nations, who did not seek to revive the dead, but always feared you and remained faithful to Your ways? {14:6} Yet they were taken away, and for their sake, you did not have mercy on Zion. {14:7} If others did evil, should Zion suffer because of those who did good works, that she should not be spared due to the works of the unrighteous? {14:8} But who, O LORD my Lord, can understand Your judgment, Or fathom the depth of Your ways? Or comprehend the weight of Your path? {14:9} Who can understand Your unfathomable counsel, Or among those born has ever discovered The beginning or end of Your wisdom? {14:10} For we are all like a breath. {14:11} Just as breath rises involuntarily and then fades away, so it is with humanity, who do not depart according to their own will and do not know what will happen to them in the end. {14:12} The righteous hope rightly for the end, and without fear they leave this earthly dwelling, for they have stored up their works with You in treasuries. {14:13} Therefore, they depart this world without fear, trusting with joy that they will receive the world You have promised them. {14:14} But woe to us who are now treated shamefully and look forward only to evils in that time. {14:15} You know exactly what You have done through Your servants, for we cannot understand what is good as You do, our Creator. {14:16} Yet again I will speak in Your presence, O LORD my Lord. {14:17} When there was no world with its inhabitants, You devised and spoke a word, and immediately the works of creation stood before You. {14:18} You said that You would create man as the steward of Your works, not because of the world, but the world for his sake. {14:19} Now I see that while the world made for our sake endures, we who were made for its sake depart."

{15:1} The Lord responded to me, saying, "You are rightly perplexed by the departure of humanity, but you have not judged well concerning the afflictions that befall those who sin. {15:2} As for what you have said about the righteous being taken away and the wicked prospering, {15:3} and your statement 'Man does not understand Your judgment'—listen now, and I will speak to you; pay attention, and I will make My words known to you. {15:4} Man would not rightly comprehend My judgment unless he accepted the law and I instructed him in understanding. {15:5} But now, because he knowingly transgressed, {15:6} precisely because he knows better, he will face torment. {15:7} Regarding what you said about the righteous, that this world has come for their sake, so too will the future world come on their account. {15:8} For this present world is full of struggle and hardship, but the world to come will be a crown of great glory."

{16:1} I said, "O Lord, the years are few and troubled. Who can acquire the immeasurable in such a brief life?"

{17:1} The Lord answered and said to me, "With the Most High, time and a few years do not matter. {17:2} For what did Adam gain by living nine hundred and thirty years and yet disobeying what he was commanded? The many years he lived did not benefit him; instead, they brought death and shortened the lives of those born from him. {17:3} How did Moses suffer by living only 120 years, despite his submission to God, delivering the law to Jacob's descendants, and guiding Israel?

{18:1} I replied, "The one who lit the lamp has taken from the light, but few have followed his example. {18:2} Instead, many whom he enlightened have remained in the darkness of Adam and have not rejoiced in the light of the lamp."

{19:1} And He replied, saying to me, "Therefore, at that time, He established a covenant for them and said: 'Behold, I have set before you life and death,' and He called heaven and earth as witnesses against them. {19:2} For He knew that their time was short, but that heaven and earth endure forever. {19:3} Yet after his death, they sinned and transgressed, although they knew they were reproved by the law, guided by unfailing light, and witnessed by the celestial spheres and Me. {19:4} Now concerning all things, I am the judge, so do not counsel within your soul concerning these matters, nor distress yourself over what has passed. {19:5} For now is the culmination of time to be considered, whether of success, prosperity, or shame—not merely its beginning. {19:6} For if a person prospers in their youth but faces disgrace in old age, they will forget all the prosperity they once enjoyed. {19:7} Conversely, if someone suffers shame in their youth but prospers in the end, they will no longer remember their early hardships. {19:8} Furthermore, listen: even if someone were to prosper throughout their entire life—from the day when death was decreed for transgressors—and then be destroyed in the end, everything would have been in vain."

{20:1} "Therefore, look! The days are coming when time shall hasten more than before, seasons shall speed by faster than those of the past, and years shall pass swiftly compared to the present. {20:2} Thus, I have taken away Zion now, so that I may more quickly visit the world in its appointed time. {20:3} Therefore, hold firmly in your heart all that I command you, and seal it in the depths of your mind. {20:4} Then I will reveal to you the judgment of My might and My ways that are beyond understanding. {20:5} "So go now, sanctify yourself for seven days: eat no bread, drink no water, and speak to no one. {20:6} Afterward, come to that place where I will reveal Myself to you, speak true words with you, and give you instructions about the unfolding of time, for it approaches without delay."

{21:1} I went and sat in the valley of Kidron, inside a cave in the earth, where I sanctified my soul. I ate no bread, yet hunger did not afflict me; I drank no water, yet thirst did not trouble me. I remained there until the seventh day as commanded. {21:2} Afterward, I went to the place where He had spoken to me. {21:3} At sunset, my soul was deeply troubled, and I began to speak in the presence of the Mighty One, saying: {21:4} "O Creator of the earth, hear me, who established the firmament by Your word, and secured the height of heaven by Your spirit. You called forth from the beginning of the world things that did not yet exist, and they obeyed You. {21:5} You command the air with Your nod, and see all that is to come as if it were already done. {21:6} You govern with great wisdom the hosts before You—countless holy beings made of flame and fire, who stand around Your throne. {21:7} To You alone belongs the power to do whatever You wish instantly. {21:8} You cause the drops of rain to fall in number upon the earth, and You alone know the end of times before they arrive. Listen to my prayer. {21:9} Only You can sustain all who are, those who have passed away, and those who are to come—both sinners and the righteous—because You alone are immortal and beyond comprehension, knowing the number of mankind. {21:12} You know where the end of sinners is kept, and the final state of the righteous. {21:10} For what benefit is strength that turns to sickness, or fullness of food that turns to famine, or beauty that turns to ugliness? {21:11} The nature of man is ever-changing. {21:12} What we once were, we are no longer, and what we are now, we will not remain forever. {21:13} How long will corruption endure, and how long will the wicked prosper in the world? {21:14} Act in mercy and fulfill all that You have promised, so Your power may be known to those who mistake Your patience for weakness. {21:15} Show those who do not know that everything that has befallen us and our city is due to Your enduring power, for the sake of Your name by which You called us Your beloved people. {21:16} Therefore, put an end to mortality. {21:17} Rebuke the angel of death, reveal Your glory, make Your beauty known, and seal Sheol so it may no longer receive the dead. Let the souls held in its treasuries be restored. {21:18} Many years have passed since the days of Abraham, Isaac, and Jacob—years of desolation as You foretold when You created the world. {21:19} Now, show Your glory swiftly and fulfill Your promises without delay." {21:20} When I finished this prayer, I was greatly weakened.

{22:1} After these events, the heavens opened, and I saw a vision. Power was given to me, and a voice from above said, "Baruch, Baruch, why are you troubled? {22:2} Just as one who travels a road but does not finish it, or sails a sea but does not reach the port, can they find comfort? {22:3} Or one who promises a gift but does not deliver, is that not deception? {22:4} Or someone who sows a field but does not harvest its fruit in due season, do they not lose everything? {22:5} Or a planter who does not see his plant bear fruit at the expected time, can he expect a yield? {22:6} Likewise, a woman who gives birth prematurely, does she not tragically lose her child? {22:7} And one who builds a house but does not finish it, can it rightly be called a house? Tell me about these things first."

{23:1} I replied, "Not so, O LORD my Lord." {23:2} He answered me, "Then why are you troubled by what you do not know, and why are you distressed about things beyond your understanding? {23:3} Just as you have not forgotten the present people and those who have passed away, so I remember those appointed to come. {23:4} When Adam sinned and death was decreed for his descendants, the number of those to be born was determined, and a place was prepared where the living would dwell and the dead would be guarded. {23:5} Until this predetermined number is fulfilled, no one will live again, for My spirit is the creator of life, and Sheol will receive the dead. {23:6} I will now reveal to you what will happen after these times. {23:7} Truly, My redemption is near and not far off as before."

{24:1} "For behold, the days are coming when the books shall be opened, containing the sins of all those who have sinned, and also the treasuries where the righteousness of all those who have been righteous in creation is gathered. {24:2} At that time, you shall see—and many others with you—the long-suffering of the Most High, which has extended through all generations, showing patience toward all who are born, whether they be sinners or righteous." {24:3} I responded, "But behold, O Lord, no one knows the number of past events or those yet to come. {24:4} I know what has happened to us, but I do not know what will happen to our enemies, or when you will fulfill your works."

{25:1} He replied, "You too shall be preserved until that time when the sign which the Most High will perform for the inhabitants of the earth at the end of days comes to pass. {25:2} This shall be the sign: {25:3} When a stupor seizes the inhabitants of the earth and they fall into many tribulations, and when they endure great torments. {25:4} And when, due to their severe tribulations, they think in their hearts, 'The Mighty One no longer remembers the earth,' then it will be that hope will return."

{26:1} I asked, "Will that tribulation which is to come last a long time? Will that necessity endure for many years?"

{27:1} He replied to me, "That time is divided into twelve parts, and each part has its appointed events. {27:2} In the first part, there will be beginnings of commotions. {27:3} In the second part, the slaying of the great ones. {27:4} In the third part, many will fall by death. {27:5} In the fourth part, the sword will be sent forth. {27:6} In the fifth part, there will be famine and withholding of rain. {27:7} In the sixth part, earthquakes and terrors. {27:8} [Missing.] {27:9} In the eighth part, a multitude of specters and attacks by demons. {27:10} In the ninth part, the fall of fire. {27:11} In the tenth part, rapine and much oppression. {27:12} In the eleventh part, wickedness and unchastity. {27:13} In the twelfth part, confusion from the mingling of all these events. {27:14} These divisions of that time are set and will intermingle and serve one another. {27:15} Some events will be left by some and taken up by others, so that those living in those days on earth may not fully understand that this is the end of times.

{28:1} "Nevertheless, whoever understands will be wise. {28:2} The measure and reckoning of that time are two parts of a week of seven weeks." {28:3} I responded, "It is good for a person to come and see, but it is better that they do not come lest they fall. {28:4} [But I will also say this: {28:5} Will the incorruptible one despise those things that are corruptible, and whatever happens to those corruptible things, will they only look to those that are not corruptible?] {28:6} But if, O Lord, those things you have foretold to me will surely come to pass, then show me this also if I have found favor in Your sight. {28:7} Will these events happen in one place or in parts of the earth, or will the whole earth experience them?"

{29:1} He answered and said to me, "Whatever will happen will happen to the whole earth; therefore, all who live will experience them. {29:2} For at that time, I will protect only those found in those days in this land. {29:3} And when all that was destined to happen in those parts is accomplished, then the Messiah will begin to be revealed. {29:4} And Behemoth will come forth from his place, and Leviathan will ascend from the sea, those two great monsters which I created on the fifth day of creation, and have kept until that time; and they will become food for all who remain. {29:5} The earth shall also yield its fruit abundantly: each vine will have a thousand branches, each branch a thousand clusters, each cluster a thousand grapes, and each grape will yield a cor of wine. {29:6} Those who have hungered will rejoice, and they will witness marvels every day. {29:7} Winds will go forth to bring the fragrance of aromatic fruits every morning, and clouds will distill the dew of health at day's end. {29:8} At that same time, the treasury of manna will descend from on high again, and they will eat of it in those years, for these are the ones who have reached the end of time."

{30:1} And it will happen after these events, when the time appointed for the coming of the Messiah is fulfilled, that He will return in glory. {30:2} Then all those who have fallen asleep in hope of Him will rise again. And at that time, the treasuries where the number of righteous souls is kept will be opened, and they will come forth. A multitude of souls will be seen gathered together with one accord of thought; the first will rejoice, and the last will not be grieved. {30:3} For they will recognize that the time has arrived, as it was foretold, that it is the culmination of the ages. {30:4} But the souls of the wicked, when they see all these things, will waste away even more. {30:5} For they will understand that their torment has come and their destruction has arrived.

{31:1} And it happened after these events that I went to the people and said to them, "Gather all your elders to me, and I will speak words to them." {31:2} So they all gathered in the valley of Kidron. {31:3} And I answered and said to them: "Hear, O Israel, and I will speak to you, Listen, O seed of Jacob, and I will instruct you. {31:4} Do not forget Zion, But remember the affliction of Jerusalem. {31:5} For behold, the days are coming When everything that exists will be subject to corruption And will be as if it had never been."

{32:1} "But as for you, if you prepare your hearts to sow in them the fruits of the law, it will protect you in the time when the Mighty One shakes the entire creation. {32:2} [For after a little while, the building of Zion will be shaken to be rebuilt. But this building will not endure, and after a time it will be uprooted and remain desolate until its appointed time. {32:4} And afterward it must be renewed in glory and perfected forevermore.] {32:5} Therefore, we should not be so distressed over the present evil as over what is yet to come. {32:6} For there will be a greater trial than these two tribulations when the Mighty One renews His creation. {32:7} And now, do not come near me for a few days, nor seek me until I come to you." {32:8} And when I had spoken these words to them, I, Baruch, went my way. When the people saw me departing, they raised their voices and lamented, saying, {32:9} "Where are you going, Baruch, and are you abandoning us like a father who forsakes his orphaned children and departs from them?

{33:1} "Are these the commands that your companion Jeremiah the prophet gave you when he said, 'Watch over this people until I go and prepare the rest of the brethren in Babylon, against whom the decree of captivity has gone forth'? {33:2} And now, if you also forsake us, it would be better for us all to die before you, rather than for you to leave us."

{34:1} And I answered the people, saying, "Far be it from me to forsake or withdraw from you. I will only go to the Holy of Holies to inquire of the Mighty One regarding you and Zion. Perhaps I will receive more insight; after that, I will return to you.

{35:1} So I, Baruch, went to the holy place, sat upon the ruins, and wept, saying: {35:2} "Oh, that my eyes were springs, And my eyelids a fountain of tears! {35:3} How can I lament for Zion? How can I mourn for Jerusalem? {35:4} In this place where I now lie prostrate, Long ago the high priest offered holy sacrifices And placed fragrant incense upon them. {35:5} But now our glory has turned to dust, And the desire of our soul to sand."

{36:1} After saying these things, I fell asleep and had a vision during the night. {36:2} I saw a forest of trees planted on a plain, surrounded by tall, rugged mountains. The forest covered a vast area. {36:3} Opposite this forest, a vine sprung up, and beneath it flowed a peaceful fountain. {36:4} This fountain surged with great waves towards the forest, submerging it. The waves uprooted most of the forest and overturned all the surrounding mountains. {36:5} The tall trees of the forest were brought low, and even the mountain peaks were leveled by the powerful fountain. It left nothing of the great forest except one cedar tree. {36:6} After casting down and destroying the forest, so that nothing recognizable remained, the vine approached peacefully with the fountain. They came near to the cedar that had survived. {36:7} Then I saw the vine open its mouth and speak to the cedar: "Are you not the cedar that remained from the forest of wickedness? Through you, wickedness persisted for many years, while goodness was never seen. {36:8} You conquered what was not yours and showed no compassion to what was rightfully owned. You extended your power over those far from you, ensnaring those who came near in your wicked schemes. You exalted yourself as if you could never be uprooted! {36:9} But now your time has passed, and your hour has come. {36:10} Therefore, depart, O cedar, like the forest before you, and become dust together with it. Let your ashes be mingled. {36:11} Rest in anguish and torment until your final time arrives, when you will be tormented even more."

{37.1} After these things, I saw the cedar burning and the vine flourishing, surrounded by a plain filled with everlasting flowers. Then I woke up from my dream and got up.

{38:1} And I prayed, saying, "O LORD, my Lord, you always enlighten those who are guided by understanding. {38:2} Your law is life, and your wisdom is right guidance. {38:3} Therefore, make known to me the interpretation of this vision. {38:4} For you know that my soul has always walked in your law, and from my earliest days I have not departed from your wisdom."

{39:1} And He answered me, saying, "Baruch, this is the interpretation of the vision you have seen. {39:2} As you saw the great forest surrounded by lofty and rugged mountains, this is the word: {39:3} Behold, the days are coming when the kingdom that once destroyed Zion will itself be destroyed and subjected to what comes after it. {39:4} Furthermore, after a time, that kingdom too will be destroyed, and another, a third, will arise. {39:5} Then a fourth kingdom will arise, whose power will be harsh and evil, surpassing all that came before it. It will dominate for many times like the forests on the plain and will exalt itself more than the cedars of Lebanon. {39:6} By it, the truth will be obscured, and all who are polluted with iniquity will flock to it, like evil beasts fleeing and hiding in the forest. {39:7} And when its time of destruction approaches, then the principate of My Messiah will be revealed, which is like the fountain and the vine. When it is revealed, it will root out the multitude of its host. {39:8} Regarding what you saw—the lofty cedar left from the forest, and the vine speaking those words with it that you heard—this is the word."

{40:1} "The last leader of that time will be left alive when the multitude of his hosts is slain by the sword. He will be bound and taken up to Mount Zion, and My Messiah will convict him of all his impieties. {40:2} He will gather and present before him all the deeds of his hosts. {40:3} Afterward, he will be put to death, and the rest of My people found in the place I have chosen will be protected. {40:4} His principate will endure forever, until the world of corruption comes to an end and the times appointed are fulfilled. This is your vision, and this is its interpretation."

{41:1} And I replied, saying, "For whom and for how many will these things be? Who will be worthy to live in that time? {41:2} I will speak openly before you, sharing all that I ponder, and I seek understanding concerning these matters. {41:3} For behold, I see many among Your people who have turned away from Your covenant, casting aside the yoke of Your law. {41:4} Yet others I have seen who have abandoned vanity and sought refuge under Your protective wings. {41:5} What will be their fate? How will the last days receive them? {41:6} Will their time be surely weighed, and will they be judged according to their deeds?"

{42:1} And He answered me, saying, "I will also reveal these things to you. {42:2} Regarding your question—'To whom will these things belong, and how many will they be?'—those who have believed will receive the good that was promised long ago, but those who have despised will experience the opposite. {42:3} Concerning those who have drawn near and those who have withdrawn, this is the explanation: {42:4} Those who were once obedient but later withdrew and mingled with the seed of mixed peoples, their time was in the past and was considered honorable. {42:5} And those who previously did not know but later found life and associated only with the seed of the separated people, their time is in the future and is considered honorable. {42:6} Time will follow time, season after season, and each will give way to the next. {42:7} In the end, everything will be evaluated in view of the consummation, according to the measure of times and the hours of seasons. {42:8} Corruption will claim those who belong to it, and life will claim those who belong to it. {42:9} And the dust will be summoned, and it will be commanded: 'Return what is not yours, and release all that you have kept until its appointed time.'"

{43:1} But, Baruch, set your heart on what has been told to you, And understand the things that have been revealed to you; For there are many eternal consolations prepared for you. {43:2} For you will depart from this place, And you will move beyond the realms visible to you now, And you will forget everything that is perishable, And you will no longer remember the things that occur among mortals. {43:3} Therefore, go and instruct your people, And come to this place, And afterward, fast for seven days, And then I will come to you and speak with you.

{44:1} So I, Baruch, departed and returned to my people. I summoned my eldest son and my friends among the Gedaliahs, along with seven elders of the community, and spoke to them: "Listen, I am soon to join my ancestors, As all mortals must do. But do not stray from the path of the law; Guard and admonish the people who remain, Lest they turn away from the commandments of the Mighty One. For you see that the One we serve is just, And our Creator shows no partiality. Observe what has happened to Zion, And the fate of Jerusalem. Through these judgments, the Mighty One reveals His righteousness, And His ways, though inscrutable, are just. If you endure in reverence for Him, And do not forget His law, Times will change for the better for you, And you will witness the comfort of Zion. For what exists now is fleeting, But what is to come is exceedingly great. For everything that is corruptible will pass away, And all that dies will depart, And the present time, marred by evils, will be forgotten. There will be no memory of this defiled present time. What runs after vanity now will come to nothing, And what prospers will soon fall and be humbled. But what is to come will be eagerly desired, And we will hope for what follows. It is an eternal time, And the hour is coming that lasts forever. In the new world, those who depart to its blessedness Will not be corrupted, Nor will it show mercy to those destined for torment, Nor will it lead those who dwell in it to destruction. These are the ones who will inherit the promised time, And theirs is the inheritance of that prophesied era. They have amassed treasures of wisdom for themselves, And stores of understanding are found with them. They have not turned away from mercy, And they have preserved the truth of the law. For them, the world to come will be given, But the dwelling of many others will be in the fire."

{45:1} "Therefore, as far you are able, instruct the people, for that is our duty. By teaching them, you will bring them to life."

{46:1} My son and the elders of the people responded to me, saying: "Has the Mighty One humbled us so greatly That He would take you from us so soon? Truly, we will be in darkness, And there will be no light for the people who remain. Where can we turn to seek the law again? Who will guide us between life and death?" {46:4} I replied to them, "I cannot resist the decree of the Mighty One's throne. Yet, Israel will not lack a wise man Or a son of the law among the descendants of Jacob. Prepare your hearts to obey the law, And submit to those who are wise and understanding in reverence. Prepare your souls so you do not stray from them. If you do these things, good news will come to you.

{47:1} "As for the word I mentioned earlier, about being taken away, I did not reveal it to them or to my son. After I dismissed them, I went to Hebron, for there the Mighty One had sent me. I arrived at the place where the word had been spoken to me, and I sat there, fasting for seven days."

{48:1} After the seventh day, I prayed before the Mighty One, saying, {48:2} "O my Lord, you ordain the coming of the times, And they stand ready before you; You bring the ages to their appointed end, And none can resist you; You set in order the course of the seasons, And they obey your command. {48:3} You alone know the duration of generations, And you do not reveal your mysteries to many. {48:4} You make known the multitude of the fire, And you measure the lightness of the wind. {48:5} You explore the limits of the heights, And you scrutinize the depths of darkness. {48:6} You care for those who pass away, that they may be preserved, And you prepare a dwelling place for those who are to come. {48:7} You remember the beginning which you have made, And you do not forget the end that is to be. {48:8} With nods of fear and indignation, you command the flames, And they transform into spirits; With a word, you bring to life that which did not exist, And with mighty power, you sustain that which has not yet come. {48:9} You instruct created things in understanding of you, And you make the spheres wise to serve in their orders. {48:10} Countless armies stand before you, And they serve quietly at your command. {48:11} Hear your servant, And listen to my petition. {48:12} For our lives are brief, And we return in a short time. {48:13} But to you, hours are like epochs, And days are like generations. {48:14} Do not be angry with humanity, for we are nothing, And do not take account of our deeds, for what are we? {48:15} We come into the world by your gift, And we do not depart by our own will. {48:16} We did not say to our parents, 'Give birth to us,' Nor did we send to Sheol, 'Receive us.' {48:17} So what strength do we have to bear your wrath, Or what are we that we should endure your judgment? {48:18} Protect us in your compassion, And help us in your mercy. {48:19} Look upon those who are subject to you, And save all who draw near to you; Do not destroy the hope of your people, And do not cut short the time of our help. {48:20} For this nation you have chosen, And these people have no equal. {48:21} But now I will speak before you, And I will say what is in my heart. {48:22} In you we trust, for your law is with us, And we know that we will not fall as long as we keep your statutes. {48:24} For we are all one people, Who have received one law from One; And the law among us will support us, And the surpassing wisdom within us will guide us." {48:25} After I prayed and spoke these words, I was greatly weakened. {48:26} And He answered and said to me, "You have prayed sincerely, O Baruch, And all your words have been heard. {48:27} But my judgment will execute its own, And my law will exact its rights. {48:28} For from your words I will answer you, And from your prayer I will speak to you. {48:29} For this is the situation: he who is corrupted is beyond remedy; he has committed iniquity as much as he could, and has not remembered my goodness nor accepted my patience. {48:30} Therefore, as I told you before, you will surely be taken away. {48:31} For a time of affliction will come, for it will arrive swiftly with great intensity, and it will be tumultuous, coming in the heat of indignation. {48:32} And in those days all the inhabitants of the earth will be stirred up against one another, because they do not realize that my judgment is near. {48:33} For there will not be found many wise people at that time, And the intelligent will be few; Moreover, even those who know will remain silent. {48:34} There will be many rumors and much gossip, And the deeds of phantoms will be revealed, And many promises will be recounted; Some will prove empty, And some will be confirmed. {48:35} Honor will be turned into shame, And strength will be humbled into contempt; Integrity will be destroyed, And beauty will become ugliness. {48:36} And many will say to many at that time, 'Where has the multitude of intelligence hidden itself? And where has the multitude of wisdom gone?' {48:37} While they are pondering these things, Envy will arise in those who did not previously consider themselves, And passion will seize the peaceful, And many will be roused to anger against others, And they will gather armies to shed blood, And in the end, they will perish together with them. {48:38} And at that very time, A change of times will clearly appeal to every person, Because in all those times they defiled themselves, And they practiced oppression, And each one walked in their own works, And they did not remember the law of the Mighty One. {48:39} Therefore, fire will consume their thoughts, And their innermost thoughts will be tested with flames; For the Judge will come and will not delay. {48:40} Because each inhabitant of the earth knew when they were transgressing, But they did not know my law because of their pride. {48:41} But many will surely weep at that time, Especially for the living more than for the dead." {48:42} And I answered and said, "O Adam, what have you done to all those who are born from you? And what will be said to the first Eve who listened to the serpent? {48:43} For this multitude is heading for corruption, And there is no count of those whom the fire will devour. {48:44} "But again, I will speak in your presence. {48:45} You, O LORD, my Lord, know what is in your creation. {48:46} For long ago you commanded the dust to produce Adam, and you know the number of those who are born from him, and how far they have sinned before you, who have existed and not acknowledged you as their Creator. {48:47} And concerning all these, their end will convict them, and your law, which they transgressed, will repay them on your day. {48:48} ["But now let us set aside the wicked and inquire about the righteous. {48:49} And I will recount their blessedness and not be silent in celebrating their glory, which is reserved for them. {48:50} For just as in a short time in this transient world where you live, you have endured much labor, so in that world without end, you will receive great light."]

{49:1} "Yet again, I will inquire of you, O Mighty One, yes, I will make my request regarding all things. {49:2} "In what form will those live who exist in Your day? Or how will the glory of those who come after that time endure? {49:3} Will they then take on this present form, And wear these ensnaring bodies, Which are now entangled in evils, And in which evils are fulfilled? Or will you perhaps change these things that have been in the world, As well as the world itself?"

{50:1} And He answered and said to me, "Hear, Baruch, this word, And write in the remembrance of your heart all that you shall learn. {50:2} For the earth shall certainly restore the dead, [Whom it now receives to preserve them]. It shall not alter their form, But as it has received, so shall it restore them, And as I delivered them to it, so shall it raise them. {50:3} For then it will be necessary to show the living that the dead have been raised, and those who had departed have returned again. {50:4} And it shall come to pass, when they have individually recognized those whom they now know, then judgment shall be strengthened, and those things which were foretold shall come to pass.

{51:1} And it will come to pass, when that appointed day has passed, that the appearance of those who are condemned will be changed, and the glory of those who are justified. {51:2} For the appearance of those who now act wickedly shall become worse as they suffer torment. {51:3} But the glory of those who have been justified by My law, who have lived with understanding, and have planted in their hearts the root of wisdom—then their splendor shall be magnified and their faces shall shine with the light of their beauty. They will be able to inherit and receive the imperishable world promised to them. {51:4} Above all, those who come then will lament that they rejected My law and closed their ears to wisdom and understanding. {51:5} When they see those over whom they were once exalted, but who will then be exalted and glorified more than them, they will respectively be transformed—the latter into the splendor of angels, and the former shall waste away in wonder at the visions and the beholding of forms. {51:6} They shall first behold and then depart to be tormented. {51:7} But those who have been saved by their works, And for whom the law has been a hope, Understanding an expectation, And wisdom a confidence— They shall see wonders in their time. {51:8} For they shall behold the world that is now invisible to them, And they shall see the time that is now hidden from them. {51:9} And time shall no longer age them. {51:10} For in the heights of that world they shall dwell, And they shall be like unto the angels, And equal to the stars, And they shall be transformed into every form they desire— From beauty into loveliness, And from light into the splendor of glory. {51:11} For before them shall be spread the expanses of Paradise, And they shall see the beauty of the majesty of the living creatures beneath the throne, And all the hosts of angels, who are now restrained by My word until their appointed time comes. {51:12} Moreover, the excellence of the righteous shall then surpass that of the angels. {51:13} For the first shall receive the last, those whom they awaited, And the last shall receive those of whom they heard that they had passed away. {51:14} For they have been delivered from this world of tribulation, And have laid down the burden of anguish. {51:15} For what have men lost their lives, And for what have those on the earth exchanged their souls? {51:16} For they did not choose for themselves that time Which cannot pass away beyond the reach of anguish. But they chose for themselves that time Whose outcomes are filled with lamentations and evils, And they rejected the world that does not age those who come to it, And they turned away from the time of glory, So that they shall not attain the honor of which I spoke to you before.

{52:1} And I replied, saying: 'How can we forget those who are destined for woe in that time? {52:2} Why then should we mourn again for those who die? Or why do we weep for those who depart to Sheol? {52:3} Let lamentations be set aside for the beginning of that impending torment, And let tears be reserved for the onset of the destruction in that era. {52:4} [Yet even in the face of these things, I will speak. {52:5} And as for the righteous, what will they do now? {52:6} Rejoice in the suffering you endure presently; For why should you anticipate the downfall of your enemies? {52:7} Prepare your soul for what awaits and ready yourself for the reward.']

{53:1} And after speaking these words, I fell asleep there, and I had a vision: I saw a cloud ascending from a vast sea. As I watched, the cloud was filled with waters that were white and black, displaying many colors. At its summit, it resembled great lightning. {53:2} The cloud moved swiftly in rapid courses, covering the entire earth. {53:3} After this, the cloud began to pour its waters upon the earth. {53:4} The waters that descended were not uniform in appearance. {53:5} Initially, they were black and abundant. Then, I observed the waters becoming bright, but in lesser quantity. After this, they turned black again, followed once more by brightness. This cycle repeated twelve times, with the black waters consistently outnumbering the bright. {53:6} Finally, at the end of the cloud's course, it rained down black waters darker than any before. Fire was mixed with them, causing devastation wherever they fell. {53:7} Afterward, I saw the lightning I had observed at the cloud's summit seize hold of it and hurl it down to the earth. This lightning was exceedingly bright, illuminating the entire earth and healing the regions that had been devastated by the last waters. {53:8} The lightning then took hold over the whole earth and ruled over it. {53:9} Following these events, I saw twelve rivers ascending from the sea. They began to surround the lightning and became subject to its power. {53:10} Overwhelmed by fear, I woke up from the vision.

{54:1} And I prayed to the Mighty One, saying: "You alone, O Lord, have knowledge of the deep mysteries of the world. You bring about events at their appointed times by your word. You hasten the beginnings of epochs and know the end of seasons. {54:2} Nothing is too difficult for you; you accomplish everything effortlessly with a mere nod. {54:3} The depths are as clear to you as the heights, and your word governs the beginnings of ages. {54:4} You reveal to those who fear you what is prepared for them, bringing them comfort in their faith. {54:5} You display great deeds to the ignorant, breaking open the barriers of those who are unaware. {54:6} You have shown me this vision; now reveal its interpretation to me. {54:7} I know that you have answered my prayers and revealed to me how I should praise you. {54:8} Even if my limbs were mouths and the hairs of my head were voices, I could never adequately praise you or give you the honor and glory you deserve. {54:9} What am I among men, that I have heard such marvelous things from the Most High and received countless promises from my Creator? {54:10} Blessed be my mother among all women, for she bore me. {54:11} I will not be silent in praising the Mighty One; with a voice of praise, I will recount His marvelous deeds. {54:12} Who can perform deeds like yours, O God? Who can comprehend the depth of your thoughts and the governance of all your creations? {54:13} By your counsel, you govern all creatures; you have established every source of light and prepared the treasures of wisdom beneath your throne. {54:14} Those who have not loved your law will justly perish, and judgment awaits those who have not submitted to your power. {54:15} Although Adam's sin brought premature death upon all, each person born from him has chosen their own destiny of torment or glory. {54:16} Indeed, those who believe will receive their reward. {54:17} But you wicked ones, turn to destruction, for you shall be swiftly visited, having rejected the understanding of the Most High. {54:18} His works and the wisdom of His creation have not persuaded you. {54:19} Adam is not the cause, except for his own soul, but each of us is responsible for our own destiny. {54:20} Lord, explain to me the things you have revealed and answer my prayers. {54:21} At the end of the world, vengeance will be taken upon the wicked according to their deeds, and the faithful will be glorified according to their faith. {54:22} You govern your own and will remove sinners from among your midst."

{55:1} After I finished praying, I sat under a tree to rest in the shade of its branches. {55:2} I marveled and pondered deeply about the abundance of goodness that sinners on earth have rejected, and the immense torment they have disregarded despite knowing they would face punishment for their sins. While I reflected on these thoughts and similar concerns, suddenly the angel Ramiel, who oversees true visions, appeared before me. {55:4} He asked me, "Why is your heart troubled, Baruch? Why are you disturbed in your thoughts? {55:5} If you are so moved by mere reports of judgment you've heard, how much more will you be affected when you see it with your own eyes? {55:6} And if the anticipation of the day of the Mighty One overwhelms you now, how will you react when it actually arrives? {55:7} If you are deeply distraught by the announcement of the torment awaiting the foolish, how much more will you be when you witness the marvelous events unfold? {55:8} And if you are saddened by hearing news of the good and evil things to come, how much more will you be when you see the majesty that will convict some and bring joy to others?"

{56:1} "Nevertheless, because you have prayed to the Most High to reveal to you the interpretation of the vision you saw, I have been sent to explain it to you. {56:2} The Mighty One has indeed disclosed to you the patterns of the times that have passed and those destined to come in His world, from the beginning of its creation to its end—both the deceitful and the truthful. {56:3} When you saw a great cloud ascending from the sea and covering the earth, it signifies the duration of the world which the Mighty One established when He planned to create it. {56:4} When His decree went forth, the world began to exist in a small measure, established according to the wisdom of Him who ordained it. {56:5} As you saw black waters descending from the cloud onto the earth, it represents the transgression of Adam, the first man. {56:6} "For when Adam transgressed, untimely death began, sorrow was named, anguish was prepared, pain was created, trouble was consummated, disease began to spread, Sheol demanded renewal in blood, childbirth was brought about, parental passion emerged, human greatness was humbled, and goodness weakened. {56:7} What can be darker or more dreadful than these things? {56:8} This marks the beginning of the black waters you saw. {56:9} From these black waters, more darkness and evil derived. {56:10} Adam became perilous to his own soul, and even to the angels. {56:11} At the time of his creation, the angels enjoyed freedom. {56:12} But some descended and mingled with women, becoming a danger, and they were later tormented in chains. {56:13} The rest of the multitude of angels restrained themselves, {56:14} whose number is beyond count. {56:15} Those who lived on the earth perished together with them in the flood waters. {56:16} These are the initial black waters.

{57:1} "After these waters, you saw bright waters. These signify the lineage of Abraham, the advent of his son, and subsequent generations like them. {57:2} It was during this time that the unwritten law was known among them, and they fulfilled the commandments with works. Belief in the coming judgment was instilled, hope in the renewed world was built, and the promise of the life to come was firmly planted. {57:3} These are the bright waters you saw.

{58:1} "The black third waters you saw symbolize the mingling of all sins committed by nations after the deaths of those righteous men, and the wickedness of Egypt, where they served with abominable practices, eventually leading to their destruction."

{59:1} "The bright fourth waters you saw represent the advents of Moses, Aaron, Miriam, Joshua son of Nun, Caleb, and others like them. {59:2} During this time, the lamp of the eternal law illuminated those who dwelled in darkness, proclaiming to believers the promise of their reward and warning deniers of the fire's torment awaiting them. {59:3} At that moment, even the heavens trembled from their places, and those beneath the throne of the Mighty One were perturbed as Moses was taken into His presence. {59:4} For He revealed to Moses many admonitions, the principles of the law, and the culmination of times—similarly shown to you—and the blueprint of Zion and its dimensions, upon which the sanctuary of the present time would be modeled. {59:5} He also revealed to Moses the measures of fire, the depths of the abyss, the weight of winds, and the count of raindrops. {59:6} Additionally, the control of anger, the abundance of patience, the truth of judgment, {59:7} the source of wisdom, the riches of understanding, and the fountain of knowledge were revealed. {59:8} The expanse of the air, the grandeur of Paradise, the culmination of ages, and the onset of the day of judgment were disclosed. {59:9} The number of offerings, the yet-to-come earths, {59:10} the mouth of Gehenna, the seat of vengeance, the realm of faith, the domain of hope, {59:11} the image of future torment, the multitude of countless angels, the hosts of flames, the brilliance of lightning, the voice of thunder, {59:12} the ranks of angelic chiefs, the treasuries of light, the changes of times, and the explorations of the law—all these were shown to Moses. These are the bright fourth waters you saw.

{60:1} "The black fifth waters you saw pouring down represent the deeds of the Amorites, their sorceries, wicked mysteries, and the mingling of their defilement. {60:2} Even Israel was tainted by sins during the days of the judges, despite witnessing many signs from the One who created them."

{61:1} "The bright sixth waters you saw represent the era when David and Solomon were born. {61:2} During this time, Zion was built, the sanctuary was dedicated, and there was much shedding of blood from nations that sinned. Many offerings were made during the dedication of the sanctuary. {61:3} Peace and tranquility prevailed, {61:4} wisdom was heard in the assembly, and understanding flourished in the congregations. {61:5} The holy festivals were celebrated with great joy and blessedness. {61:6} Rulers judged without deceit, and the Mighty One's precepts were upheld with truth. {61:7} The land beloved by the Lord was glorified above all lands because its inhabitants did not sin. Zion ruled over all lands and regions during this time. {61:8} These are the bright waters you saw.

{62:1} "The black seventh waters you saw represent the corruption caused by the counsel of Jeroboam, who made two golden calves. {62:2} It signifies all the iniquities committed by kings who followed him wickedly. {62:3} It includes the curse of Jezebel and the idolatry practiced by Israel at that time. {62:4} It symbolizes the droughts, famines, and the extreme hardships when people resorted to eating their own children. {62:5} The nine and a half tribes experienced captivity due to their many sins, brought upon them when Shalmaneser, king of Assyria, led them away captive. {62:6} It would be exhaustive to detail how the Gentiles consistently engaged in impiety and wickedness without practicing righteousness. {62:7} These are the black seventh waters you saw.

{63:1} "The bright eighth waters you saw represent the righteousness and uprightness of Hezekiah, king of Judah, and the grace of God that came upon him. {63:2} When Sennacherib was stirred up to destroy him and his people, including the two and a half tribes remaining, and even aimed to overthrow Zion, Hezekiah trusted in his own works and righteousness. {63:4} He cried out to the Mighty One, saying, 'Behold, Sennacherib is prepared to destroy us, and he will be boastful once Zion is destroyed.' {63:5} The Mighty One heard Hezekiah because he was wise and righteous, and He respected his prayer. {63:6} Then the Mighty One commanded His angel Ramiel, who speaks with you. {63:7} I went forth and destroyed their multitude, where each chief commanded one hundred and eighty-five thousand soldiers. {63:8} I burned their bodies within, preserving only their garments and weapons outwardly, so that the mighty deeds of the Mighty One might be shown, and His name glorified throughout the earth. {63:9} Zion and Jerusalem were saved, and Israel was delivered from tribulation. {63:10} All who were in the holy land rejoiced, and the name of the Mighty One was glorified. {63:11} These are the bright waters you saw.

{64:1} "The black ninth waters you saw represent all the wickedness during the reign of Manasseh, son of Hezekiah. {64:2} He committed much impiety, killing the righteous, perverting justice, shedding innocent blood, defiling women violently, overturning altars, destroying offerings, and expelling priests from the sanctuary. {64:3} He made an image with five faces, four looking to the winds and one on the summit as an adversary to the zeal of the Mighty One. {64:4} This provoked the wrath of the Mighty One, leading to the destruction of Zion and the captivity of the two and a half tribes, {64:5} as you have seen. {64:6} Manasseh's impiety was so severe that it removed the praise of the Most High from the sanctuary. {64:7} Thus, Manasseh earned the name 'the impious,' and his end was in fire. {64:8} Although his prayer was heard by the Most High, when he was cast into the brazen horse and it melted, it served as a sign of his fate. {64:9} He did not live righteously, thus learning the torment awaiting him. {64:10} For the One who can bless is also able to bring torment.

{65:1} "Thus Manasseh acted impiously, believing the Mighty One would not judge him for his deeds. {65:2} These are the black ninth waters you saw."

{66:1} "The bright tenth waters you saw represent the purity of the generations of Josiah, king of Judah, who wholeheartedly submitted himself to the Mighty One. {66:2} Josiah cleansed the land from idols, consecrated polluted vessels, restored offerings to the altar, elevated the honor of the holy, exalted the righteous, honored the wise, reinstated the priests in their ministry, and expelled magicians, enchanters, and necromancers from the land. {66:3} He even went so far as to burn the bones of the impious taken from their graves, and he purified the festivals and Sabbaths. {66:5} Josiah zealously upheld the law, ensuring there were no uncircumcised or impious persons in the land throughout his reign. {66:6} Therefore, he will receive an eternal reward and be glorified with the Mighty One, surpassing many others in honor. {66:7} The honorable glories prepared for him and those like him were foretold to you before. These are the bright waters you saw.

{67:1} "The black eleventh waters you saw symbolize the calamity currently befalling Zion. {67:2} Do not think there is no anguish among the angels in the presence of the Mighty One. {67:2} Zion has been delivered up, and the Gentiles boast arrogantly, assembling before their idols, saying, 'She who once trod down others is now trodden down and enslaved.' {67:3} Do you think these things bring joy to the Most High or glorify His name? {67:4} After these events, the dispersed among the Gentiles will endure tribulation and shame in every place. {67:5} Idols will flourish in the cities of the Gentiles while the righteousness upheld by the law in Zion fades away. {67:6} The king of Babylon, who has destroyed Zion, will boast over the people and exalt himself before the Most High. {67:7} Yet, in the end, he too shall fall. These are the black waters."

{68:1} "The bright twelfth waters you saw represent the future. {68:2} After these trials, your people will face distress and the risk of perishing together, but they will ultimately be saved, and their enemies will fall. {68:3} In due time, there will be much joy again. {68:4} After a brief interval, Zion will be rebuilt, its offerings restored, and the priests will return to their ministry. {68:5} Even the Gentiles will come to glorify Zion, though not as fully as in the beginning. {68:6} Subsequently, many nations will experience downfall. {68:7} These are the bright waters you saw."

{69:1} "Regarding the last waters you saw, darker than all those before them, which came after the twelfth number and were gathered together, they pertain to the whole world. {69:2} From the beginning, the Most High has made a division because He alone knows what will come to pass. {69:3} He foresaw six types of enormities and impieties that would occur before Him. {69:4} Likewise, He foresaw six types of good works by the righteous that would be accomplished before Him, surpassing even those at the end of the age. {69:5} Therefore, there were not black waters with black, nor bright with bright; for this is the consummation.

{70:1} "Now hear the interpretation of the last black waters that are to come after the black: {70:2} 'Behold, the days are coming when the time of the age has ripened, and the harvest of its evil and good seeds has come. {70:2} At that time, the Mighty One will bring upon the earth and its inhabitants, and upon its rulers, disturbance of spirit and confusion of heart. {70:3} People will hate one another and provoke each other to fight. {70:4} The lowly will rule over the honorable, and those of humble origin will be exalted above the famous. {70:5} Many will be delivered into the hands of the few, and the weak will rule over the strong. {70:6} The poor will have abundance beyond the rich, and the impious will exalt themselves above the heroic. {70:7} The wise will be silent while the foolish speak; the plans of men and the counsel of the mighty will not be confirmed, nor will the hopes of those who hope be fulfilled. {70:6} When these predicted events come to pass, confusion will fall upon all people. {70:7} Some will fall in battle, some will perish in anguish, and some will meet their end through their own actions. {70:8} Then the Most High will send forth the people He has prepared beforehand, and they will come and wage war against the remaining leaders. It will happen that those who escape the war will perish in the earthquake; those who survive the earthquake will be consumed by fire, and those who survive the fire will be destroyed by famine. {70:9} Whoever among the victors or the vanquished escapes all these foreseen calamities will be delivered into the hands of the Messiah, My servant. {70:10} For all the earth's inhabitants shall face destruction.'"

{71:1} "The holy land will show mercy to its own and protect its inhabitants at that time. {71:2} This is the vision you have seen, and this is its interpretation. {71:3} I have come to tell you these things because your prayer has been heard by the Most High."

{72:1} "Now hear about the bright lightning that will come at the end after these dark waters: {72:2} After the signs that were foretold have come to pass, when the nations are in turmoil and the time of My Messiah has arrived, he will gather all the nations. {72:3} Some he will spare, and others he will kill. {72:4} These things will happen to the nations that are spared by Him. {72:5} Every nation that does not know Israel and has not oppressed the descendants of Jacob will indeed be spared. {72:6} This is because some from every nation will be subject to your people. {72:7} But all those who have ruled over you or have oppressed you will be given over to the sword."

{73:1} "And it will happen, when He has subdued everything in the world and has established Himself in peace for eternity on the throne of His kingdom, that joy will be revealed and rest will be apparent. {73:2} Healing will descend like dew, diseases will retreat, and anxiety, anguish, and lamentation will vanish from among humanity. Gladness will spread throughout the earth. {73:3} No one will die prematurely, nor will any sudden adversity befall them. {73:4} Judgments, abusive speech, contentions, revenge, bloodshed, passions, envy, hatred, & all similar things will be condemned and removed. {73:5} For these are the things that have filled the world with evils and greatly troubled the life of humanity. {73:6} Wild animals will come from the forests to serve humans, and asps and dragons will come out of their holes to be submissive even to young children. {73:7} Women will no longer experience pain in childbirth, nor suffer torment when giving birth.

{74:1} "And in those days, the reapers will not grow weary, nor will those who build be exhausted; for their works will advance swiftly, accompanied by tranquility. {74:2} For that time marks the end of corruption and the beginning of the incorruptible. {74:3} Therefore, what has been foretold will come to pass. It will be far removed from evils and close to things that do not perish. {74:4} This is the bright future that follows after the dark times."

{75:1} And I responded, saying: "Who can truly understand, O Lord, Your goodness? It is beyond comprehension. {75:2} And who can fathom Your boundless compassion? {75:3} Who can grasp Your intelligence, or recount the thoughts of Your mind? {75:4} Who among those born can hope to attain these things, unless they are the recipients of Your mercy and grace? {75:5} For without Your compassion, those under Your care could never reach these heights. Only those counted among the chosen can aspire to them. {75:6} But if we, the ones who exist now, understand our purpose and submit to the One who led us out of Egypt, we will remember the past and rejoice in what has been. {75:7} Yet if we do not know why we are here, and fail to acknowledge the authority of the One who delivered us from Egypt, we will return seeking what was lost, lamenting the trials we endured."

{76:1} And He responded, saying to me: "Since the interpretation of this vision has been revealed to you as you requested, hear now the word of the Most High so that you may understand what will happen to you after these events. {76:2} For you will surely depart from this earth, yet not unto death; you will be preserved until the end of times. {76:3} Therefore, go up to the top of that mountain, and there you will see before you all the regions of the land, the shape of the inhabited world, the summits of the mountains, the depths of the valleys, the expanses of the seas, and the multitude of rivers. This will show you what you are leaving behind and where you are headed. {76:4} This will occur after forty days. During these days, go and instruct the people to the best of your ability, so that they may learn not to perish in the last days, but rather, that they may learn how to live in the times to come."

{77:1} So I, Baruch, went to them and gathered together the people, from the greatest to the least, and spoke to them saying: {77:2} "Listen, children of Israel, see how many of you remain from the twelve tribes. {77:3} The Lord gave a law more excellent to you and your fathers than to all other peoples. {77:4} Yet because your brethren transgressed the commandments of the Most High, He brought punishment upon both you and them. He did not spare the former, and He delivered the latter into captivity, leaving none of them behind. {77:5} But you are here with me now. {77:6} Therefore, if you direct your ways rightly, you will not depart as your brethren did; rather, they will come back to you. {77:7} For the one whom you worship is merciful and gracious, and true to do good and not evil. {77:8} Have you not seen what has happened to Zion? {77:9} Do you think the place sinned and was overthrown for that reason? Or that the land acted foolishly and was delivered up? {77:10} Know that on account of your sins, the innocent suffered destruction, and due to the wickedness of others, the blameless were handed over to their enemies." {77:11} And all the people answered me, saying: "We remember the good things the Mighty One has done for us, and those we do not remember, He in His mercy knows. {77:12} But please, write an epistle of instruction and a scroll of hope to our brethren in Babylon, before you depart from us. {77:13} For the shepherds of Israel have perished, the lamps that gave light are extinguished, and the fountains from which we drank have ceased. {77:14} We are left in darkness, among the trees of the forest, in the thirst of the wilderness." {77:15} I replied to them, saying: "Shepherds, lamps, and fountains come from the law. Even though we depart, the law remains. {77:16} Therefore, if you hold fast to the law and seek wisdom, a lamp will not be lacking, a shepherd will not fail, and a fountain will not dry up. {77:17} "As you have asked, I will also write to your brethren in Babylon and send it by men. Likewise, I will write to the nine tribes and a half and send it by means of a bird." {77:18} On the twenty-first day of the eighth month, I, Baruch, sat down under the oak tree in the shade of its branches, alone. {77:19} I wrote two epistles: one I sent by an eagle to the nine and a half tribes, and the other I sent to those in Babylon by three men. {77:20} I called the eagle and said to it: {77:21} "The Most High has made you higher than all birds. {77:22} Now go, do not delay in any place, do not enter a nest, do not settle on any tree until you have crossed over the broad waters of the river Euphrates and reached the people who dwell there, and deliver this epistle to them. {77:23} Remember, as in the time of the flood, Noah received an olive branch from a dove when he sent it from the ark. {77:24} And ravens ministered to Elijah, bringing him food as commanded. {77:25} Solomon also, in his kingdom, commanded a bird to go wherever he wished, and it obeyed him. {77:26} Now do not grow weary, do not turn aside, but fly directly to preserve the command of the Mighty One, as I have instructed you."

{78:1} This is the content of the letter that Baruch, the son of Neriah, sent to the nine and a half tribes across the river Euphrates, containing these words: {78:2} "Baruch, the son of Neriah, sends greetings of mercy and peace to the brethren carried into captivity. I remember, my brethren, the love of our Creator who formed us, loved us from ancient times, and never despised us but educated us above all. {78:3} I know that we, the twelve tribes, are bound together by one bond, as we all descend from one father. {78:4} Therefore, I am careful to leave you these words before I die, so that you may find comfort in the afflictions that have befallen you and sorrow for the troubles of your brethren. Also, that you may acknowledge His judgment that has decreed your captivity, though what you have suffered is disproportionate to your sins, so that in the last times you may be found worthy of your ancestors. {78:6} Therefore, if you understand that these sufferings are for your good, so that you may not be finally condemned and tormented, then you will receive eternal hope. {78:7} If above all, you cast away from your hearts the vain errors that led to your exile, then He will remember you continually. He who promised to those greater than us that He will never forget or forsake us, but with great mercy will gather together those who were scattered."

{79:1} "Now, my brethren, learn first what happened to Zion: how Nebuchadnezzar, king of Babylon, came against us. {79:2} We sinned against our Maker and did not keep His commandments, yet He did not punish us as severely as we deserved. {79:3} The calamity that befell you has also befallen us in a greater degree, for it happened to us too."

{80:1} "And now, my brethren, I will tell you what happened when the enemy surrounded the city. The angels of the Most High were sent, and they demolished the strong fortifications and destroyed the firm iron corners that could not be uprooted. {80:2} They hid all the vessels of the sanctuary so that the enemy could not seize them. {80:3} After doing these things, they handed over the fallen walls, the plundered houses, the burned temple, and the captive people to the enemy, to prevent them from boasting, 'By force we have laid waste the house of the Most High in war.' {80:4} Your brethren were also bound and taken to Babylon, where they now dwell. {80:5} But we have remained here, a remnant of few. {80:6} This is the tribulation I wrote to you about. {80:7} Surely, I know that the consolation of the inhabitants of Zion comforts you. When you knew it prospered, your consolation was greater than the tribulation you endured in having to leave it."

{81:1} Regarding comfort, listen to these words. {81:2} I mourned for Zion and prayed earnestly for mercy from the Most High, asking, "How long will these troubles last for us? Will these evils continue forever?" {81:3} In His abundant mercy, the Mighty One responded, and the Most High, in His great compassion, revealed to me words of consolation. He showed me visions so that I would no longer endure sorrow, and He unveiled to me the mysteries of the times and the coming of the ages.

{82:1} Therefore, my brethren, I write to you so that you may find comfort amidst your many tribulations. {82:2} Know that our Creator will surely avenge us against all our enemies for everything they have done to us. The end that the Most High will bring is very near, along with His forthcoming mercy and the completion of His judgment, which is not far off. {82:3} Look now at the prosperity of the Gentiles—how vast it appears even as they act wickedly. {82:4} Yet they will vanish like vapor. {82:5} Consider their power, though they do evil; they will be reduced to a mere drop. {82:6} Reflect on their might, though they defy the Almighty constantly; they will be like spit in the end. {82:7} Contemplate their greatness, though they disregard the statutes of the Most High; they will fade away like smoke. {82:8} Think about their cruelty, though they do not consider their inevitable end; they will be shattered like a passing wave. {82:9} Notice their arrogance, though they deny the goodness of God who gave them these things; they will disappear like a fleeting cloud.

{83:1} Concerning consolation, hear these words. {83:2} I grieved for Zion and prayed earnestly for mercy from the Most High, asking, "How long will these troubles endure? Will these evils afflict us forever?" {83:3} In His abundant mercy, the Mighty One acted according to His compassion and revealed comforting words to me. He showed me visions to end my anguish and disclosed the mysteries of the times and the coming ages. {83:4} Let none of these present things occupy your hearts, but above all, be prepared, for what has been promised to us will surely come. {83:5} Do not be captivated by the pleasures of the Gentiles now; instead, remember what has been promised to us in the end. {83:6} The ends of times and seasons will surely pass away together. {83:7} When the age reaches its conclusion, the great power of its ruler will be revealed in judgment. {83:8} Therefore, prepare your hearts for what you have believed in, lest you become enslaved in both worlds and suffer in captivity here and torment there. {83:9} Understand that in all things—past, present, and future—evil is not entirely evil, nor is good entirely good.

{84:1} Therefore, while I live, I have made these things known to you, urging you to learn excellence. The Mighty One has commanded me to instruct you, and before I die, I will present some of His judgment's commandments to you. {84:2} Remember how Moses solemnly called heaven and earth as witnesses, saying, "If you transgress the law, you will be scattered, but if you keep it, you will be preserved." {84:3} Moses warned you of these things while the twelve tribes were together in the desert. {84:4} Yet after his death, you turned away, and thus what was predicted befell you. {84:5} Moses foretold these events before they happened to you because you abandoned the law. {84:6} I now say to you, after you have suffered, that if you obey what has been said to you, the Mighty One will grant you what He has reserved for you. {84:7} Let this epistle serve as a testimony between you and me, so that you may remember the commandments of the Mighty One, and it may serve as my defense before Him who sent me. {84:8} Remember the law, Zion, the holy land, your brethren, the covenant of your fathers, and do not forget the festivals and Sabbaths. {84:9} Pass down this epistle and the traditions of the law to your descendants, just as your fathers passed them to you. {84:10} Always pray earnestly and diligently with your whole heart that the Mighty One may be reconciled to you and not count the multitude of your sins but remember the righteousness of your fathers. {84:11} For if He does not judge us according to His abundant mercies, woe to all of us who are born.

{85:1} Furthermore, know that in former times and generations of old, our fathers had helpers—righteous men and holy prophets.

3 Baruch

3 Baruch, also known as the Greek Apocalypse of Baruch, is a pseudepigraphal text attributed to Baruch, the scribe of the prophet Jeremiah. It is an apocalyptic work that dates back to the late 1st century CE to the early 3rd century CE, primarily surviving in Greek, though it likely originated in a Semitic language, possibly Hebrew or Aramaic. This text is part of the broader body of Jewish apocalyptic literature, which flourished during the Second Temple period and continued to be influential in the early centuries of the Common Era. 3 Baruch's narrative centers on the ascent of Baruch through the heavens, guided by an angel, where he witnesses various cosmic phenomena and receives revelations concerning the workings of the universe and the fate of the righteous and the wicked. The book is notable for its rich visionary imagery and the unique theological perspectives it offers, particularly concerning angelology and cosmology. It reflects a milieu deeply concerned with questions of divine justice, the afterlife, and the eschatological hope for restoration. Scholars often explore its intertextual connections with other apocalyptic writings, such as 2 Enoch and the Apocalypse of Abraham, as well as its thematic and theological resonances with the canonical Book of Daniel and the New Testament's Revelation. The book also provides insight into the diverse and dynamic nature of Jewish thought during a period marked by intense social and religious upheaval, shedding light on how different Jewish groups grappled with issues of suffering, divine retribution, and hope for ultimate redemption.

{1:1} Truly, I, Baruch, was deeply sorrowful and weeping in my heart for the people. {1:2} Nebuchadnezzar, the king permitted by God to destroy His city, I questioned, saying, "Lord, why did You allow Your vineyard to be set on fire and laid waste? Why did You do this?" {1:3} "Why did You not punish us differently, but delivered us to nations like these, who now reproach us, saying, 'Where is their God?'" As I wept and pondered these things, {1:4} an angel of the Lord appeared to me, saying, "Understand, O greatly beloved man, and do not trouble yourself so deeply about the salvation of Jerusalem. For thus says the Lord God, the Almighty: {1:5} I was sent before you to make known and show you all these things of God, for your prayer was heard before Him and reached the ears of the Lord God." {1:6} When he spoke these words to me, I fell silent. The angel continued, {1:7} "Cease provoking God, and I will show you greater mysteries than these." {1:8} I, Baruch, swore, "As the Lord God lives, if you will show me and I hear your word, I will speak no more. God will add to my judgment in the day of judgment if I speak again." {1:9} The angel of the powers said to me, "Come, and I will reveal to you the mysteries of God."

{2:1} He took me and led me to where the firmament was firmly set, and where a river flowed that no one could cross, nor any wind from among those God created. Leading me further, he brought me to the first heaven and showed me a massive door. {2:2} He said to me, "Let us enter through this door," and we entered as if carried on wings, traveling a distance of about thirty days' journey. {2:3} Within the heaven, he showed me a vast plain where beings dwelled, having faces like oxen, horns like stags, feet like goats, and haunches like lambs. Curious, I asked the angel, {2:4} "Please tell me, what is the thickness of this heaven through which we have journeyed? What is its extent, and what is this plain, so that I may convey this to humanity?" {2:5} The angel named Phamael replied, "This door you see is the entrance to heaven, and its thickness is as vast as the distance from earth to heaven. The length of the plain you saw is equal to the distance from North to South." {2:6} Again, the angel of the powers invited, "Come, and I will reveal even greater mysteries to you." But {2:7} I insisted, "Please show me who these beings are." He explained, "These are the ones who built the tower in defiance against God, and the Lord cast them out."

{3:1} The angel of the Lord took me and guided me to a second heaven. There, he showed me a door similar to the first one and said, "Let us enter through it." We passed through, carried as if on wings, traveling a distance of about sixty days' journey. {3:2} In this second heaven, he showed me a plain filled with beings whose appearance resembled dogs, with feet like those of stags. {3:3} Curious, I asked the angel, "Please tell me, who are these beings?" {3:4} The angel replied, "These are the ones who counseled to build the tower. They forced many men and women to make bricks. Among them, a woman was not even released during childbirth but had to continue making bricks while carrying her child in her apron." {3:5} He continued, "When they had built the tower to a height of four hundred and sixty-three cubits, the Lord appeared to them and confused their speech." {3:6} "They even tried to pierce the heaven with a gimlet, saying, 'Let us see whether the heaven is made of clay, brass, or iron.'" {3:7} "Seeing this, God did not permit it. Instead, He struck them with blindness and confusion of speech, making them as you see them now."

{4:1} I, Baruch, said, "Behold, Lord, you have shown me great and wonderful things. Now show me all things for the sake of the Lord." {4:2} The angel said to me, "Come, let us proceed." So I journeyed with the angel from that place for about one hundred and eighty-five days. {4:3} He showed me a plain and a serpent that stretched about two hundred plethra in length. {4:4} He also showed me Hades, dark and abominable in appearance. {4:5} I asked, "Who is this dragon, and who is the monster around him?" {4:6} The angel replied, "The dragon is the one who devours the bodies of those who live wickedly, and he is nourished by them. Hades itself resembles him, drawing about a cubit of water from the sea without ever sinking." {4:7} I asked further, "How does this happen?" {4:8} The angel explained, "Listen, the Lord God created three hundred and sixty rivers, among which the chief are Alphias, Abyrus, and the Gericus. Because of these rivers, the sea does not sink." {4:9} Then I inquired, "Show me which tree led Adam astray." {4:10} The angel answered, "It is the vine, which the angel Sammael planted. The Lord God cursed him and his plant because of it, preventing Adam from touching it, and thus the devil deceived him out of envy through this vine." {4:11} I continued, "Since the vine has caused such great evil and is under God's curse, how can it be useful now?" {4:12} The angel replied, "You ask rightly. When God brought the flood upon the earth, destroying all flesh and four hundred and ninety thousand giants, the waters rose fifteen cubits above the highest mountains. The floodwaters entered paradise and destroyed every plant, but it carried the shoot of the vine outside its boundaries. {4:13} "When the earth emerged from the water and Noah exited the ark, he found the shoot of the vine. He pondered what to do with it, considering Adam's destruction because of it, lest he too incur God's anger. {4:14} "Noah prayed for forty days, beseeching God for guidance on what to do with the plant. {4:15} "Finally, he prayed, 'Lord, reveal to me what I should do concerning this plant.' {4:16} "God then sent his angel Sarasael to Noah, saying, 'Arise, Noah, and plant the shoot of the vine. Thus says the Lord: Its bitterness shall turn into sweetness, its curse into a blessing. What is produced from it shall become the blood of God. Just as through it the human race received condemnation, so through Jesus Christ, Immanuel, they will receive in Him the upward calling and entry into paradise.' {4:17} "Know, Baruch, that as Adam obtained condemnation through this tree and lost the glory of God, those who now excessively drink the wine from it commit greater transgressions than Adam. They are far from the glory of God and subject themselves to eternal fire. For no good comes from it; those who drink it to excess commit murders, adulteries, fornications, perjuries, thefts, similar evils. Nothing good is established by it."

{5:1} I, Baruch, said to the angel, "Let me ask you something, Lord. You mentioned that the dragon drinks a cubit from the sea. Tell me, how large is his belly?" {5:2} The angel replied, "His belly is Hades, and it extends as far as a plummet thrown by three hundred men. Come, I will show you even greater marvels than these."

{6:1} The angel then took me and led me to where the sun rises. {6:2} He showed me a chariot with four wheels, blazing with fire. In the chariot sat a man wearing a crown of fire, drawn by forty angels. {6:3} Before the sun, there was a bird circling about nine cubits away. {6:4} I asked the angel, "What is this bird?" {6:5} He answered, "This is the guardian of the earth." {6:6} I inquired further, "Lord, how does he guard the earth? Teach me." {6:7} The angel explained, "This bird flies alongside the sun, spreading his wings to receive its fiery rays. If not for him, neither the human race nor any other living creature would be preserved. God appointed him for this purpose." {6:8} As he spread his wings, I saw very large letters on his right wing, as large as a threshing-floor, about four thousand modii in size, made of gold. {6:9} The angel instructed me, "Read them." {6:10} So I read: "Neither earth nor heaven brought me forth, but wings of fire brought me forth." {6:11} I asked, "Lord, what is this bird, and what is his name?" {6:12} The angel replied, "His name is called Phoenix." {6:13} I asked further, "What does he eat?" {6:14} The angel said, "He eats the manna of heaven and the dew of the earth." {6:15} I asked, "Does the bird excrete?" {6:16} The angel answered, "He excretes a worm, and the excrement of the worm is cinnamon, which kings and princes use. But wait, you shall see the glory of God." {6:17} While we conversed, there was a thunderous clap, shaking the ground beneath us. I asked the angel, "My Lord, what is this sound?" {6:18} The angel said to me, "Even now the angels are opening the three hundred and sixty-five gates of heaven, separating light from darkness." {6:19} A voice came, saying, "Light giver, give radiance to the world." {6:20} When I heard the bird's noise, I asked, "Lord, what is this noise?" {6:21} The angel explained, "This is the bird that awakens the roosters on earth from their slumber. Just as men speak through their mouths, so does the rooster signify to those in the world through its own speech. For the angels prepare the sun, and the rooster crows."

{7:1} I asked, "Where does the sun begin its work after the rooster crows?" {7:2} The angel replied, "Listen, Baruch. All that I have shown you is in the first and second heavens. The sun passes through the third heaven and illuminates the world. But wait, and you shall see the glory of God." {7:3} As we conversed, I saw the bird appear in front of us, growing smaller and smaller until he returned to his full size. {7:4} Behind him, I beheld the radiant sun and the angels who guide it, crowned with a crown too glorious for us to behold. {7:5} As soon as the sun shone, the Phoenix stretched out his wings. {7:6} Overwhelmed by the immense glory, I was filled with great fear and sought refuge in the wings of the angel. {7:7} The angel comforted me, saying, "Fear not, Baruch. Wait, and you shall also witness their setting."

{8:1} The angel then took me westward, and as the sun began to set, I saw the Phoenix bird once more flying ahead of it. As the bird approached, I witnessed angels lifting the crown from its head. {8:2} Seeing this, I asked, "Lord, why did they remove the crown from the sun's head, and why is the bird so exhausted?" {8:3} The angel explained, "Four angels take the crown of the sun at the end of the day and carry it to heaven to renew it, because both the sun and its rays are defiled on earth; thus, it is renewed daily." {8:4} I inquired further, "Lord, why are its beams defiled on earth?" {8:5} The angel answered, "Because the sun witnesses the lawlessness and unrighteousness of men—fornications, adulteries, thefts, extortions, idolatries, drunkenness, murders, strife, jealousies, evil-speakings, murmurings, whisperings, divinations, and such like—that are displeasing to God. It is defiled because of these things, hence the need for daily renewal." {8:6} Concerning the bird, the angel clarified, "It becomes exhausted by restraining the sun's rays through its fiery heat throughout the day. Without its wings shielding the sun's rays, no living creature could survive."

{9:1} As they withdrew, night fell, and along came the chariot of the moon accompanied by the stars. {9:2} I asked, "Lord, please show me how the moon goes forth, where it departs, and in what manner it moves." {9:3} The angel replied, "Wait, and shortly you shall see." {9:4} The next day, I saw the moon in the form of a woman sitting on a wheeled chariot. Oxen and lambs were in the chariot, along with a multitude of angels. {9:5} I queried, "Lord, what are the oxen and lambs?" {9:6} The angel answered, "They too are angels." {9:7} I asked further, "Why does the moon wax and wane?" {9:8} The angel explained, "Listen, Baruch: The moon was originally created by God more beautiful than any other. But at the transgression of the first Adam, it drew near to Sammael when he took the form of the serpent as a garment. It did not conceal itself but increased, which angered God. As a result, its days were shortened." {9:9} I inquired, "Why does it not shine always, but only at night?" {9:10} The angel replied, "Just as courtiers cannot freely speak in the presence of a king, so the moon and stars cannot shine in the presence of the sun. The stars remain suspended, but they are overshadowed by the sun. Though uninjured, the moon is overshadowed by the heat of the sun."

{10:1} After learning all these things from the archangel, he then took me and led me into a fourth heaven. There I saw a vast plain with a central pool of water. Surrounding it were countless birds of all kinds, unlike any on earth. Among them was a crane as large as great oxen, and all these birds were exceedingly large compared to those of the world. {10:2} I asked the angel, "What is this plain, and what is the pool, and why are there so many birds around it?" {10:3} The angel explained, "Listen, Baruch: This plain, which contains the pool and other wonders, is where the souls of the righteous gather. Here they dwell together in groups, engaging in conversation and harmony. The water in the pool is that which the clouds receive and then rain upon the earth, causing fruits to grow." {10:4} I asked again, "Who are these birds?" {10:5} The angel replied, "They are the ones who continually sing praises to the Lord." {10:6} I further inquired, "Lord, why do people say that the water which falls as rain comes from the sea?" {10:7} The angel answered, "The water that descends as rain indeed comes from the sea and from the waters on earth. However, the water that nourishes the fruits originates solely from the latter source. Understand from now on that this source is what is known as the dew of heaven."

{11:1} The angel took me to a fifth heaven, where I saw the gate closed. I asked, "Lord, why is this gateway closed? Can we not enter?" The angel replied, "We cannot enter until Michael arrives, for he holds the keys to the Kingdom of Heaven. But be patient, and you will witness the glory of God." Suddenly, there was a great thunderous sound, and I asked, "Lord, what is this sound?" {11:2} The angel answered, "It is Michael, the commander of the angels, descending to receive the prayers of humanity." Then a voice commanded, "Open the gates!" {11:3} The gates were opened with a thunderous roar, and Michael appeared. The angel with me greeted him, saying, "Hail, my commander and leader of our order." Michael replied, "Hail to you as well, our brother and interpreter of revelations for those who live virtuously." {11:9} I saw Michael holding an enormous vessel, as deep as the distance from heaven to earth and as wide as from north to south. I asked, "Lord, what is this vessel that Michael the archangel is holding?" {11:14} The angel explained, "This vessel is where the merits of the righteous enter, and the good works they do are presented before the heavenly God."

{12:1} While we conversed, angels arrived carrying baskets filled with flowers, which they presented to Michael. Curious, I asked the angel, "Lord, who are these angels, and what are they bringing here?" {12:2} The angel replied, "These angels oversee the righteous." Michael took the baskets and emptied them into the vessel. The angel explained, "These flowers represent the merits of the righteous." {12:3} Then I saw other angels with baskets that were neither empty nor full. They began to lament and did not approach, for their prizes were incomplete. {12:4} Michael called to them, "Come here also and bring what you have brought." Michael and the angel with me were deeply grieved because these baskets did not fill the vessel."

{13:1} Afterward, more angels came weeping and lamenting, saying with fear, "Behold, we are overshadowed, Lord, for we were handed over to evil men and we wish to depart from them." Michael replied, "You cannot depart from them, so that the enemy may not prevail completely. Tell me what you ask." {13:2} They pleaded, "Michael, our commander, transfer us away from them, for we cannot abide with wicked and foolish men who practice every kind of unrighteousness and greed." {13:3} Michael instructed them to wait while he sought guidance from the Lord on their request.

{14:1} At that moment, Michael departed and the doors closed with a thunderous sound. I asked the angel, "What is that sound?" {14:2} He told me, "Michael is now presenting the merits of humanity to God."

{15:1} Shortly thereafter, Michael returned, and the gate was opened. He brought oil and instructed, "To those angels who brought the full baskets, reward our friends a hundredfold for their diligent good works. {15:2} Those who sowed virtuously will also reap virtuously." {15:3} He said to those who brought half-empty baskets, "Come here also; take away the reward according to what you brought and deliver it to the sons of men."

{16:1} Then Michael turned to those who brought nothing and said, "Thus says the Lord, do not be sad or weep, nor ignore the sons of men. But because they angered me with their deeds, go and provoke them to envy and anger against a people who are not a people, a people who have no understanding. {16:2} Also send forth the caterpillar, the unwinged locust, mildew, common locust, hail with lightning and wrath, and punish them severely with sword and death, and their children with demons. They did not listen to my voice, nor did they obey my commandments, but despised them and showed insolence toward the priests who proclaimed my words to them."

{17:1} As he finished speaking, the door closed, and we withdrew. The angel took me back to where I had begun. {17:2} When I regained my senses, I gave glory to God, who deemed me worthy of such revelations. Therefore, my brothers and sisters who have received such revelations, glorify God, so that He may also glorify you now and forever. Amen.

4 Baruch

4 Baruch, or "Paraleipomena Jeremiou," is an early Jewish pseudepigraphal work typically classified as apocalyptic literature. Though its exact date is debated, it is believed to have been written between the late 1st and early 3rd centuries CE, reflecting Jewish turmoil and hope, possibly in response to the Second Temple's destruction or the Bar Kokhba revolt. Surviving in Greek, Ethiopian, and Slavic versions, it is part of the Old Testament Apocrypha and explores themes of divine justice, resurrection, and Jeremiah's role. Unique for its mix of narrative and apocalyptic visions, it highlights miraculous events and God's intervention, particularly through the preservation of Jeremiah and Baruch during the Babylonian exile. The work is crucial for understanding Jewish thought in the post-exilic period and how communities interpreted their history & anticipated redemption.

{1:1} It happened that when the Israelites were taken captive by the king of the Chaldeans, God spoke to Jeremiah, saying, {1:2} "Jeremiah, my chosen one, arise and leave this city, you and Baruch, for I am going to destroy it because of the great number of sins committed by its inhabitants. {1:3} Your prayers are like a strong pillar within it, and like an indestructible wall that surrounds it. {1:4} Now, rise and depart before the Chaldean army surrounds it." {1:5} But Jeremiah responded, saying, "I beseech you, Lord, allow me, your servant, to speak in your presence." {1:6} And the Lord said to him, "Speak, my chosen one, Jeremiah." {1:7} And Jeremiah spoke, saying, "Lord Almighty, would you deliver your chosen city into the hands of the Chaldeans, so that the king and his vast army might boast and say, 'I have conquered the holy city of God'? {1:8} No, my Lord, but if it is your will, let it be destroyed by your own hand." {1:9} And the Lord replied to Jeremiah, "Since you are my chosen one, arise and leave this city, you and Baruch, for I am going to destroy it because of the multitude of the sins of its people. {1:10} For neither the king nor his army will be able to enter it unless I first open its gates. {1:11} Now, rise and go to Baruch, and tell him these words. {1:12} And when you have arisen at the sixth hour of the night, go out onto the city walls, and I will show you that they cannot enter the city unless I first destroy it." When the Lord had finished speaking, He departed from Jeremiah.

{2:1} Jeremiah ran to Baruch and told him everything. As they entered the temple of God, Jeremiah tore his clothes, put dust on his head, and went into the holy place of God. {2:2} When Baruch saw Jeremiah with dust on his head and his garments torn, he cried out loudly, "Father Jeremiah, what are you doing? What sin has the people committed?" {2:3} (For whenever the people sinned, Jeremiah would sprinkle dust on his head and pray for them until their sin was forgiven.) {2:4} So Baruch asked him, "Father, what is happening?" {2:5} Jeremiah replied, "Do not tear your garments; instead, let us tear our hearts! Let us not draw water for the trough, but let us weep and fill them with our tears! For the Lord will not have mercy on this people." {2:6} Baruch then asked, "Father Jeremiah, what has happened?" {2:7} Jeremiah answered, "God is delivering the city into the hands of the king of the Chaldeans, to take the people captive to Babylon." {2:8} When Baruch heard this, he also tore his garments and asked, "Father Jeremiah, who has revealed this to you?" {2:9} Jeremiah said, "Stay with me until the sixth hour of the night, so that you may see that this word is true." {2:10} So they both stayed near the altar, weeping with their garments torn.

{3:1} When the appointed hour of the night came, just as the Lord had told Jeremiah, he and Baruch went up together to the walls of the city. {3:2} Suddenly, they heard the sound of trumpets, and angels appeared from heaven, holding torches in their hands, and they placed them on the walls of the city. {3:3} When Jeremiah and Baruch saw this, they wept and said, "Now we know that the word of the Lord is true!" {3:4} Jeremiah then pleaded with the angels, saying, "I beseech you, do not destroy the city yet, until I speak with the Lord." {3:5} And the Lord spoke to the angels, saying, "Do not destroy the city until I have spoken with my chosen one, Jeremiah." {3:6} Then Jeremiah said, "I beg you, Lord, allow me to speak in your presence." {3:7} And the Lord said, "Speak, my chosen one, Jeremiah." {3:8} And Jeremiah said, "Behold, Lord, now we know that you are delivering the city into the hands of its enemies, and they will take the people away to Babylon. What do you want me to do with the holy vessels of the temple service?" {3:9} And the Lord said to him, "Take them and consign them to the earth, saying: {3:10} 'Hear, O Earth, the voice of your creator who formed you from the abundance of waters, who sealed you with seven seals for seven epochs, and after this, you will receive your ornaments.' {3:11} Guard the vessels of the temple service until the gathering of the beloved." {3:12} Then Jeremiah asked, "I beseech you, Lord, show me what I should do for Abimelech the Ethiopian, for he has shown many kindnesses to your servant Jeremiah. {3:13} For he pulled me out of the miry pit, and I do not wish for him to see the destruction and desolation of this city, but rather that you would be merciful to him, so he will not be grieved." {3:14} The Lord replied to Jeremiah, "Send him to the vineyard of Agrippa, and I will hide him in the shadow of the mountain until I bring the people back to the city. {3:15} And you, Jeremiah, go with your people to Babylon and stay with them, preaching to them, until I cause them to return to the city. {3:16} But leave Baruch here until I speak with him." {3:17} After saying these things, the Lord ascended from Jeremiah into heaven. {3:18} Then Jeremiah and Baruch entered the holy place, and taking the vessels of the temple service, they consigned them to the earth as the Lord had instructed. {3:19} Immediately, the earth swallowed them. {3:20} And they both sat down and wept. {3:21} When morning came, Jeremiah sent Abimelech, saying, "Take a basket and go to the estate of Agrippa by the mountain road, and bring back some figs to give to the sick among the people, for the favor of the Lord is upon you and his glory rests on your head." {3:22} After giving these instructions, Jeremiah sent him away, and Abimelech went as Jeremiah had told him.

{4:1} When morning came, the army of the Chaldeans surrounded the city. {4:2} A great angel sounded the trumpet and proclaimed, "Enter the city, army of the Chaldeans, for behold, the gate is opened for you. {4:3} Let the king enter with his multitudes, and let him take all the people captive." {4:4} Meanwhile, Jeremiah took the keys of the temple, went outside the city, and threw them away in the presence of the sun, saying, "I entrust you, Sun, with the keys of the temple of God. Guard them until the day the Lord asks you for them. {4:5} For we have not been found worthy to keep them, as we have become unfaithful guardians." {4:6} While Jeremiah was still weeping for the people, the Chaldeans brought him out along with the people and dragged them into Babylon. {4:7} But Baruch, covering his head with dust, sat down and wailed a lamentation, saying, "Why has Jerusalem been devastated? It is because of the sins of the beloved people that she was delivered into the hands of enemies—because of our sins and those of the people. {4:8} But let not the lawless ones boast, saying, 'We were strong enough to take the city of God by our might,' for it was delivered to you because of our sins. {4:9} And God will have pity on us and cause us to return to our city, but you will not survive! {4:10} Blessed are our fathers, Abraham, Isaac, and Jacob, for they departed from this world and did not see the destruction of this city." {4:11} After saying this, Baruch left the city, weeping and lamenting, "Grieving because of you, Jerusalem, I have departed from you." {4:12} He then sat in a tomb, where angels came to him and revealed everything that the Lord wanted him to know through them.

{5:1} Abimelech took the figs in the scorching heat and, finding a tree, sat down in its shade to rest. {5:2} He leaned his head on the basket of figs and fell asleep, sleeping for 66 years without awakening. {5:3} When he finally awoke, he said, "I slept so soundly for a short time, but my head feels heavy because I didn't get enough sleep." {5:4} Then he uncovered the basket of figs and found them dripping with milk. {5:5} He said, "I'd like to sleep a little longer because my head is heavy, but I'm afraid I might oversleep and be late, and my father Jeremiah would think poorly of me. If he wasn't in a hurry, he wouldn't have sent me at daybreak." {5:6} So he resolved, "I'll get up and continue in the burning heat, for isn't there heat and toil every day?" {5:7} He got up, placed the basket of figs on his shoulders, and entered Jerusalem, but he did not recognize the city—neither his own house, nor the familiar places, nor could he find his family or acquaintances. {5:8} He exclaimed, "The Lord be blessed, for a great trance has come over me today! {5:9} This must not be Jerusalem, and I must have lost my way because I came by the mountain road after waking up. Since my head was heavy from lack of sleep, I lost my way. {5:10} Jeremiah will find it unbelievable that I lost my way!" {5:11} He left the city and, after searching, recognized the landmarks and said, "Indeed, this is the city; I lost my way." {5:12} He returned to the city and searched again but found no one he knew. He said, "The Lord be blessed, for a great trance has come over me!" {5:13} He left the city again, sitting down in grief, unsure where to go. {5:14} He placed the basket down, saying, "I will sit here until the Lord removes this trance from me." {5:15} As he sat, he saw an old man coming from the field. Abimelech asked him, "Tell me, old man, what city is this?" {5:16} The old man replied, "This is Jerusalem." {5:17} Abimelech asked, "Where is Jeremiah the priest, and Baruch the secretary, and all the people of this city? I could not find them." {5:18} The old man said, "Are you not from this city, since you remember Jeremiah and ask about him after such a long time? {5:19} Jeremiah is in Babylon with the people; they were taken captive by King Nebuchadnezzar, and Jeremiah is there with them, preaching the good news and teaching them the word." {5:20} When Abimelech heard this, he said, "If you weren't an old man, and if it weren't unlawful to rebuke someone older, I would laugh at you and say you are out of your mind—since you claim that the people have been taken to Babylon. {5:21} Even if the heavens had poured down torrents on them, there hasn't been enough time for them to reach Babylon! {5:22} How much time has passed since my father Jeremiah sent me to the estate of Agrippa to gather some figs to give to the sick among the people? {5:23} I went and gathered them, and when I came to a certain tree in the scorching heat, I sat to rest and leaned my head on the basket, falling asleep. {5:24} When I woke up, I uncovered the basket of figs, thinking I was late, and found them dripping with milk, just as when I had gathered them. {5:25} Yet you claim that the people have been taken to Babylon. {5:26} To prove it to you, take a look at the figs!" {5:27} He uncovered the basket of figs for the old man, who saw them dripping with milk. {5:28} The old man exclaimed, "My son, you are a righteous man, and God did not want you to see the desolation of the city, so He put you into this trance. {5:29} It has been 66 years today since the people were taken to Babylon. {5:30} But to confirm that what I say is true—look into the fields and see that the crops have not ripened. {5:31} Notice also that the figs are not in season, and be enlightened." {5:32} Abimelech cried out in a loud voice, "I bless you, God of heaven and earth, the Rest of the souls of the righteous everywhere!" {5:33} Then he asked the old man, "What month is this?" {5:34} The old man replied, "It is Nisan (which is Abib)." {5:35} Abimelech took some figs and gave them to the old man, saying, "May God illuminate your path to the city above, Jerusalem."

{6:1} After this, Abimelech left the city and prayed to the Lord. {6:2} Then an angel of the Lord appeared, took him by the right hand, and brought him back to where Baruch was sitting, who was found in a tomb. {6:3} When they saw each other, they wept and embraced. {6:4} But when Baruch looked up, he saw the figs covered in Abimelech's basket. {6:5} Lifting his eyes to heaven, he prayed, saying: {6:6} "You are the God who rewards those who love You. Prepare, my heart, and rejoice while you are in your dwelling, telling your body, 'Your sorrow has been turned into joy,' for the One who is Sufficient is coming to deliver you in your home—there is no sin in you. {6:7} Revive in your home, in your pure faith, and believe that you will live! {6:8} Look at this basket of figs—behold, they are 66 years old and have not withered or rotted, but are dripping with milk. {6:9} So it will be with you, my body, if you follow the commands given by the angel of righteousness. {6:10} He who preserved the basket of figs will also preserve you by His power." {6:11} When Baruch had finished speaking, he said to Abimelech: "Stand up and let us pray that the Lord will show us how we can send a report to Jeremiah in Babylon about the protection you received on your journey." {6:12} Baruch prayed, saying: "Lord God, our strength is the chosen light that comes from Your words. {6:13} We ask for Your goodness—You whose great name no one can fully know—to hear the voice of Your servants and grant us understanding. {6:14} What should we do, and how should we send this report to Jeremiah in Babylon?" {6:15} While Baruch was still praying, an angel of the Lord appeared and said to Baruch: "Do not worry about how you will send the message to Jeremiah; an eagle will arrive tomorrow at dawn, and you will direct it to Jeremiah. {6:16} Therefore, write a letter: 'Say to the children of Israel: Let any stranger who comes among you be set apart for 15 days, and after this period, I will lead you into your city, says the Lord. {6:17} Anyone who does not separate from Babylon will not enter the city; I will punish them by preventing them from being accepted back by the Babylonians, says the Lord.'" {6:18} After the angel spoke, he left Baruch. {6:19} Baruch went to the market of the Gentiles, obtained papyrus and ink, and wrote the following letter: {6:20} "Baruch, the servant of God, writes to Jeremiah in the captivity of Babylon: {6:21} Greetings! Rejoice, for God has not allowed us to leave this body grieving for the devastated and outraged city. {6:22} Therefore, the Lord has shown compassion for our tears and remembered the covenant He made with our forefathers Abraham, Isaac, and Jacob. {6:23} He sent His angel to me with these words, which I am now sending to you. {6:24} These are the words the Lord, the God of Israel, who brought us out of Egypt from the great furnace, spoke: 'Because you did not follow My ordinances and became haughty before Me, I delivered you into the furnace in Babylon in My anger and wrath. {6:25} If you listen to My voice through Jeremiah My servant, I will bring those who listen back from Babylon; but those who do not listen will become strangers both to Jerusalem and to Babylon. {6:26} You will test them with the water of the Jordan; those who do not listen will be exposed—this is the sign of the great seal.'"

{7:1} Baruch got up and left the tomb, where he found an eagle sitting outside. {7:2} The eagle spoke to him in a human voice, saying, "Greetings, Baruch, steward of the faith." {7:3} Baruch replied, "You who speak are chosen from among all the birds of heaven; this is evident from the gleam of your eyes. Tell me, then, what are you doing here?" {7:4} The eagle answered, "I was sent here so that you might send any message you wish through me." {7:5} Baruch asked, "Can you carry a message to Jeremiah in Babylon?" {7:6} The eagle replied, "Indeed, it was for this reason I was sent." {7:7} Baruch then took a letter and fifteen figs from Abimelech's basket, tied them to the eagle's neck, and said, "I say to you, king of the birds, go in peace and good health, and carry this message for me. {7:8} Do not be like the raven that Noah sent out, which never returned to the ark, but be like the dove, which brought a report to the righteous one on its third journey. {7:9} So, take this good message to Jeremiah and to those in captivity with him, so that it may be well with you. Take this papyrus to the people and to the chosen one of God. {7:10} Even if all the birds of heaven surround you and try to fight you, persevere — the Lord will give you strength. {7:11} Do not turn aside to the right or to the left, but go straight as a speeding arrow in the power of God, and the glory of the Lord will be with you the entire way." {7:12} The eagle then took flight and went to Babylon, with the letter tied to his neck. When he arrived, he rested on a post outside the city in a deserted place. {7:13} He remained silent until Jeremiah came by, as Jeremiah and some of the people were coming out to bury a corpse outside the city. {7:14} (Jeremiah had petitioned King Nebuchadnezzar, saying, "Give me a place where I may bury those of my people who have died," and the king granted his request.) {7:15} As they were coming out with the body, weeping, they came to where the eagle was. {7:16} The eagle cried out in a loud voice, "I say to you, Jeremiah, the chosen one of God, gather the people and come here so that they may hear a letter that I have brought to you from Baruch and Abimelech." {7:17} When Jeremiah heard this, he glorified God, and he went to gather the people along with their wives and children, and they came to where the eagle was. {7:18} The eagle then descended onto the corpse, and it was revived. {7:19} (This happened so that they might believe.) {7:20} All the people were astonished at what had happened and said, "This is the God who appeared to our fathers in the wilderness through Moses, and now He has appeared to us through the eagle." {7:21} The eagle then said, "I say to you, Jeremiah, come and untie this letter and read it to the people." So, Jeremiah untied the letter and read it to the people. {7:22} When the people heard it, they wept and put dust on their heads, saying to Jeremiah, "Deliver us and tell us what to do so that we may return to our city." {7:23} Jeremiah answered, "Do whatever you heard from the letter, and the Lord will lead us back to our city." {7:24} Jeremiah then wrote a letter to Baruch, saying, "My beloved son, do not be negligent in your prayers, beseeching God on our behalf, that He might direct our way until we are freed from the power of this lawless king. {7:25} You have been found righteous before God, and He did not let you come here, lest you see the affliction that has come upon the people at the hands of the Babylonians. {7:26} It is like a father with an only son, who is given over for punishment; those who see his father console him by covering his face, lest he see how his son is being punished and be even more overwhelmed with grief. {7:27} In the same way, God took pity on you and did not let you enter Babylon, lest you witness the affliction of the people. {7:28} Since we came here, grief has not left us, for 66 years today. {7:29} Many times when I went out, I found some of the people hung up by King Nebuchadnezzar, crying out, 'Have mercy on us, God-ZAR!' {7:30} When I heard this, I grieved and cried with two-fold mourning, not only because they were hung up, but because they were calling on a foreign god, saying, 'Have mercy on us.' {7:31} I remembered the days of festivity we celebrated in Jerusalem before our captivity, and when I remembered, I groaned and returned to my house, wailing and weeping. {7:32} Now, then, pray where you are—you and Abimelech—for this people, that they may listen to my voice and to the decrees of my mouth so that we may depart from here. {7:33} I tell you, during our entire time here, they have kept us in subjection, saying, 'Recite for us a song from the songs of Zion—the song of your God.' {7:34} And we reply, 'How shall we sing for you since we are in a foreign land?'" {7:35} After this, Jeremiah tied the letter to the eagle's neck, saying, "Go in peace, and may the Lord watch over both of us." {7:36} The eagle took flight, returned to Jerusalem, and delivered the letter to Baruch. When Baruch untied it, he read it, kissed it, and wept when he heard about the distresses and afflictions of the people. {7:37} Meanwhile, Jeremiah took the figs and distributed them to the sick among the people, continually teaching them to abstain from the pollutions of the gentiles in Babylon.

{8:1} The day came when the Lord brought the people out of Babylon. {8:2} The Lord said to Jeremiah: "Get up, you and the people, go to the Jordan River. Tell the people: {8:3} 'Anyone who desires to follow the Lord should abandon the practices of Babylon. {8:4} For the men who married Babylonian women and the women who married Babylonian men—those who listen to you shall cross over with you, and you shall bring them into Jerusalem. But those who do not listen to you, do not lead them there.'" {8:5} Jeremiah spoke these words to the people, and they got up and went to the Jordan to cross it. {8:6} As he told them the words the Lord had spoken to him, half of those who had married Babylonian spouses refused to listen to Jeremiah and said: {8:7} "We will never abandon our wives, but we will bring them back with us into our city." {8:8} So they crossed the Jordan and arrived in Jerusalem. {8:9} Jeremiah, Baruch, and Abimelech stood up and declared: "No one who has joined with Babylonians shall enter this city!" {8:10} They said to each other: "Let us return to Babylon and go back to our homes"—and they left. {8:11} But as they approached Babylon, the Babylonians came out to meet them and said: "You shall not enter our city, for you hated us and left us secretly; therefore, you cannot come in with us. {8:12} We have sworn an oath in the name of our god not to accept you or your children since you left us secretly." {8:13} Hearing this, they turned back and went to a desert place some distance from Jerusalem, where they built a city and named it 'Samaria.' {8:14} Jeremiah sent a message to them saying: "Repent, for the angel of righteousness is coming and will lead you to your exalted place."

{9:1} Those who were with Jeremiah rejoiced and offered sacrifices on behalf of the people for nine days. {9:2} On the tenth day, only Jeremiah offered a sacrifice. {9:3} He prayed, saying: "Holy, holy, holy, fragrant aroma of the living trees, true light that enlightens me until I ascend to You; {9:4} I beg for Your mercy—{9:5} for the sweet voice of the two seraphim, I beg—for another fragrant aroma. {9:6} And may Michael, the archangel of righteousness who opens the gates to the righteous, be my guardian until he ushers the righteous in." {9:7} After Jeremiah said this, while he was standing in the altar area with Baruch and Abimelech, he appeared as if his soul had departed. {9:8} Baruch and Abimelech wept and cried out loudly: "Woe to us! Our father Jeremiah has left us—the priest of God has departed!" {9:9} All the people heard their cries, rushed to them, and saw Jeremiah lying on the ground as if dead. {9:10} They tore their garments, put dust on their heads, and wept bitterly. {9:11} They then prepared to bury him. {9:12} Suddenly, a voice said: "Do not bury the one who is still alive, for his soul is returning to his body!" {9:13} Hearing this, they did not bury him but stayed around his place for three days, asking, "When will he arise?" {9:14} After three days, his soul returned to his body, and he raised his voice among them, saying: "Glorify God with one voice! All of you glorify God and the Son of God who awakens us—Messiah Jesus—the light of all ages, the unquenchable lamp, the life of faith. {9:15} But there will be 477 more years before He comes to earth. {9:16} The tree of life planted in paradise will make all the barren trees bear fruit and will grow and sprout. {9:17} The trees that had become proud and said, 'We have contributed our power to the air,' will wither and be judged, those boastful trees! {9:18} What is crimson will become as white as wool—the snow will turn black—the sweet waters will become salty, and the salty will turn sweet, in the intense light of the joy of God. {9:19} He will bless the isles so that they become fruitful by the word of His Messiah. {9:20} For He shall come and choose twelve apostles to proclaim the news among the nations—He whom I have seen adorned by His Father and coming into the world on the Mount of Olives—and He will fill the hungry souls. {9:21} When Jeremiah spoke about the Son of God coming into the world, the people became very angry and said: "This is just a repetition of what Isaiah son of Amos said when he saw God and the Son of God." {9:22} They decided: "Let us not kill him in the same manner as Isaiah, but let us stone him instead." {9:23} Baruch and Abimelech were deeply saddened because they wanted to hear all the mysteries Jeremiah had seen. {9:24} Jeremiah said to them: "Be silent and do not weep, for they cannot kill me until I have described everything I saw." {9:25} He then said: "Bring me a stone." {9:26} He set it up and said: "Light of the ages, make this stone appear like me until I have described everything to Baruch and Abimelech." {9:27} By God's command, the stone took on the appearance of Jeremiah. {9:28} They began stoning the stone, thinking it was Jeremiah! {9:29} But Jeremiah revealed all the mysteries he had seen to Baruch and Abimelech, and then stood among the people, ready to complete his ministry. {9:30} Then the stone cried out: "O foolish children of Israel, why do you stone me, thinking I am Jeremiah? Behold, Jeremiah is standing among you!" {9:31} When they saw him, they immediately attacked him with stones, and his ministry was fulfilled. {9:32} Baruch and Abimelech came, buried him, and placed the stone on his tomb, inscribing it: "This is the stone that was the ally of Jeremiah."

1 Enoch

1 Enoch, is an ancient Jewish apocalyptic text that has had a profound impact on the development of Christian eschatology. It is traditionally attributed to Enoch, the great-grandfather of Noah, and is composed of various sections written over several centuries, ranging from the 3rd century BCE to the 1st century CE. The text is notable for its vivid descriptions of heavenly realms, angelic beings, and the fate of the wicked and the righteous. It explores themes of divine judgment, the nature of sin, and the ultimate restoration of creation. The Book of Enoch was highly regarded in early Jewish and Christian communities, with references and allusions appearing in various biblical and extra-biblical texts, including the Epistle of Jude in the New Testament. Despite its initial popularity, the Book of Enoch was excluded from the canonical Hebrew Bible and later the Christian Old Testament, though it remains canonical in the Ethiopian Orthodox Church. The book is divided into several distinct sections, including the Book of the Watchers, the Book of Parables, the Astronomical Book, the Book of Dream Visions, and the Epistle of Enoch, each contributing unique insights into its overarching themes. The Book of Enoch offers a complex and richly textured narrative that reflects the religious and cultural milieu of Second Temple Judaism, providing invaluable context for understanding the development of early Christian thought. Its intricate cosmology and the portrayal of Enoch as an intermediary between the divine and human realms have influenced various theological and mystical traditions.

{1:1} The words of the blessing of Enoch, with which he blessed the chosen and righteous ones, who will be living during the time of tribulation, when all the wicked and godless will be removed. {1:2} Enoch, a righteous man whose eyes were opened by God, saw a vision of the Holy One in the heavens. The angels showed me this vision, and from them, I heard and understood everything I saw. This is not for this generation but for a distant one yet to come. {1:3} Concerning the chosen ones, I said and began my parable about them: The Holy Great One will come out of His dwelling, {1:4} And the eternal God will walk upon the earth, even on Mount Sinai, [And appear from His camp] And appear in the strength of His might from the heaven of heavens. {1:5} And everyone will be struck with fear, And the Watchers will tremble, And great fear and trembling will seize them to the ends of the earth. {1:6} The high mountains will be shaken, And the high hills will be made low, And will melt like wax before the flame. {1:7} The earth will be completely torn apart, And everything on the earth will perish, And there will be judgment upon all people. {1:8} But He will make peace with the righteous. He will protect the chosen, And mercy will be upon them. They will all belong to God, And they will prosper, And they will all be blessed. He will help them all, And light will appear to them, And He will make peace with them. {1:9} And behold, He comes with tens of thousands of His holy ones To execute judgment upon all, And to destroy all the ungodly, And to convict all flesh Of all the works of their ungodliness which they have committed in an ungodly way, And of all the harsh things which ungodly sinners have spoken against Him.

{2:1} Observe everything that happens in the heavens, how they do not change their orbits, and the lights in the sky, how they all rise and set in order, each in its season, without transgressing their appointed order. {2:2} Look at the earth and pay attention to everything that happens on it from beginning to end, how steadfast they are, how nothing on earth changes, but all the works of God appear to you. {2:3} Look at the summer and winter, how the whole earth is filled with water, and clouds, dew, and rain lie upon it.

{3:1} Observe and see how in the winter all the trees seem as though they had withered and shed all their leaves, except for fourteen trees, which do not lose their foliage but retain the old foliage for two to three years until the new comes.

{4:1} And again, observe the days of summer, how the sun is above the earth and opposite it. You seek shade and shelter because of the heat of the sun, and the earth also burns with growing heat, so you cannot tread on the earth or on a rock because of its heat.

{5:1} Observe how the trees cover themselves with green leaves and bear fruit. Therefore, pay attention and understand all His works, and recognize how He who lives forever has made them so. {5:2} All His works go on thus from year to year forever, and all the tasks they accomplish for Him do not change, but as God has ordained, so it is done. {5:3} Look at how the sea and the rivers likewise fulfill and do not change their tasks from His commandments. {5:4} But you have not been steadfast, nor have you followed the commandments of the Lord. You have turned away and spoken proud and harsh words with your impure mouths against His greatness. Oh, you hard-hearted, you shall find no peace. {5:5} Therefore, you will curse your days, and the years of your life will perish. The years of your destruction will be multiplied in eternal cursing, and you will find no mercy. {5:6a} In those days, your names will become an eternal curse to all the righteous. {5:6b} By you, all who curse will curse. {5:6c} All the sinners and godless will invoke curses by you. {5:7c} For you godless, there will be a curse. {5:6d} And all the righteous will rejoice. {5:6e} There will be forgiveness of sins, {5:6f} And every mercy and peace and patience. {5:6g} There will be salvation for them, a good light. {5:6i} But for all of you sinners, there will be no salvation. {5:6j} A curse will remain on all of you. {5:7a} But for the chosen ones, there will be light and joy and peace. {5:7b} They will inherit the earth. {5:8} And then wisdom will be given to the chosen ones, and they will all live and never again sin, either through ungodliness or through pride. Those who are wise will be humble. {5:9} They will not transgress again, nor will they sin all the days of their lives. They will not die of divine anger or wrath, but they will complete the number of the days of their lives. Their lives will be increased in peace, And the years of their joy will be multiplied, In eternal gladness and peace, All the days of their lives.

{6:1} When the children of men had multiplied, beautiful and attractive daughters were born to them. {6:2} The angels, the children of heaven, saw and lusted after them, and said to one another, "Come, let us choose wives from among the children of men and have children with them." {6:3} Semjaza, who was their leader, said to them, "I fear you will not indeed agree to do this deed, and I alone will have to pay the penalty of a great sin." {6:4} They all answered him and said, "Let us all swear an oath and bind ourselves by mutual curses not to abandon this plan but to do this thing." {6:5} Then they all swore together and bound themselves by mutual curses upon it. {6:6} There were two hundred of them who descended in the days of Jared on the summit of Mount Hermon. They called it Mount Hermon because they had sworn and bound themselves by mutual curses upon it. {6:7} These are the names of their leaders: Samlazaz, their leader, Araklba, Rameel, Kokablel, Tamlel, Ramlel, Danel, Ezeqeel, Baraqijal, Asael, Armaros, Batarel, Ananel, Zaq1el, Samsapeel, Satarel, Turel, Jomjael, Sariel. {6:8} These are their chiefs of tens.

{7:1} All the others with them took wives for themselves, and each chose one for himself. They began to go into them and defile themselves with them. They taught them charms and enchantments, the cutting of roots, and made them familiar with plants. {7:2} The women became pregnant and gave birth to great giants, whose height was three thousand ells. {7:3} These giants consumed all the acquisitions of men. When men could no longer sustain them, {7:4} the giants turned against them and devoured mankind. {7:5} They began to sin against birds, beasts, reptiles, and fish, and to devour one another's flesh and drink the blood. {7:6} Then the earth laid accusation against the lawless ones.

{8:1} Azazel taught men to make swords, knives, shields, breastplates, and made known to them the metals of the earth and the art of working them, and bracelets, ornaments, the use of antimony, the beautifying of the eyelids, all kinds of costly stones, and all coloring tinctures. {8:2} Much godlessness arose, and they committed fornication, were led astray, and became corrupt in all their ways. {8:3} Semjaza taught enchantments and root-cuttings. Armaros taught the resolving of enchantments. Baraqijal taught astrology. Kokabel taught the constellations. Ezeqeel taught the knowledge of the clouds. Araqiel taught the signs of the earth. Shamsiel taught the signs of the sun. Sariel taught the course of the moon. {8:4} As men perished, they cried out, and their cry went up to heaven.

{9:1} Then Michael, Uriel, Raphael, and Gabriel looked down from heaven and saw much blood being shed on the earth and all the lawlessness being done on the earth. {9:2} They said to one another, "The earth, made without inhabitants, cries out with the voice of their cries up to the gates of heaven. {9:3} And now, to you, the holy ones of heaven, the souls of men make their plea, saying, 'Bring our case before the Most High.'" {9:4} They said to the Lord of the ages, "Lord of lords, God of gods, King of kings, and God of the ages, the throne of Your glory stands to all the generations of the ages, and Your name is holy and glorious and blessed forever. {9:5} You have made all things, and You have power over all things. All things are naked and open in Your sight, and You see everything; nothing can hide from You. {9:6} You see what Azazel has done, who has taught all unrighteousness on earth and revealed the eternal secrets that were kept in heaven, which men were striving to learn. {9:7} And Semjaza, to whom You gave authority to rule over his associates. {9:8} They have gone to the daughters of men on earth, and have slept with the women, defiled themselves, and revealed to them all kinds of sins. {9:9} The women have given birth to giants, and the whole earth has been filled with blood and unrighteousness. {9:10} Now, behold, the souls of those who have died are crying and making their plea to the gates of heaven. Their lamentations have ascended and cannot cease because of the lawless deeds that are done on the earth. {9:11} You know all things before they happen. You see these things and allow them, and You do not tell us what we should do about them."

{10:1} Then the Most High, the Holy and Great One, spoke and sent Uriel to the son of Lamech, and said to him, {10:2} "Go to Noah and tell him in My name, 'Hide yourself!' and reveal to him the end that is approaching: that the whole earth will be destroyed, and a flood is about to come upon the whole earth and will destroy everything on it. {10:3} Now instruct him so that he may escape and his offspring may be preserved for all generations of the world." {10:4} And again the Lord said to Raphael, "Bind Azazel hand and foot, and cast him into the darkness. Make an opening in the desert, which is in Dudael, and throw him in there. {10:5} Place rough and jagged rocks on him, cover him with darkness, and let him stay there forever. Cover his face so that he may not see light. {10:6} On the day of the great judgment, he shall be cast into the fire. {10:7} Heal the earth that the angels have corrupted, and proclaim the healing of the earth, that they may heal the plague, and that all the children of men may not perish through all the secret things that the Watchers have disclosed and taught their sons. {10:8} The whole earth has been corrupted through the works that were taught by Azazel. To him ascribe all sin." {10:9} To Gabriel, the Lord said, "Proceed against the bastards and the reprobates, and against the children of fornication, and destroy the children of fornication and the children of the Watchers from among men. Send them against each other that they may destroy each other in battle, for they will not have long lives. {10:10} No request that their fathers make of you shall be granted on their behalf, for they hope to live an eternal life and that each one of them will live five hundred years." {10:11} The Lord said to Michael, "Go, bind Semjaza and his associates who have united with women so as to have defiled themselves with them in all their uncleanness. {10:12} When their sons have killed one another and they have seen the destruction of their beloved ones, bind them fast for seventy generations in the valleys of the earth until the day of their judgment and their end, until the judgment that is forever and ever is completed. {10:13} In those days, they shall be led off to the abyss of fire, to the torment and prison in which they shall be confined forever. {10:14} Whoever is condemned and destroyed will be bound together with them from then on to the end of all generations. {10:15} Destroy all the spirits of the reprobate and the children of the Watchers, because they have wronged mankind. {10:16} Destroy all wrong from the face of the earth and let every evil work come to an end. Let the plant of righteousness and truth appear, and it will prove a blessing. The works of righteousness and truth will be planted in truth and joy forevermore. {10:17} Then all the righteous will escape, and will live until they have begotten thousands of children, and all the days of their youth and their old age they will complete in peace. {10:18} The whole earth will be tilled in righteousness and will be planted with trees and full of blessing. {10:19} All desirable trees will be planted on it, and they will plant vines on it. The vine that they plant will yield wine in abundance, and all the seed that is sown will bear a thousand-fold, and each measure of olives will yield ten presses of oil. {10:20} Cleanse the earth from all oppression, unrighteousness, sin, and godlessness. Destroy all the uncleanness that is done on the earth. {10:21} All the children of men will become righteous, and all nations will offer adoration and praise Me, and all will worship Me. {10:22} The earth will be cleansed from all defilement, from all sin, and from all punishment and torment. I will never again send these upon the earth from generation to generation and forever."

{11:1} In those days, I will open the storehouses of blessing that are in heaven, to send them down upon the earth over the work & labor of the children of men. {11:2} Truth & peace will be united throughout all the days of the world and throughout all the generations of men.

{12:1} Before these things happened, Enoch was hidden, and no one among the children of men knew where he was hidden, where he lived, or what had become of him. {12:2} His activities had to do with the Watchers, and his days were with the holy ones. {12:3} I, Enoch, was blessing the Lord of majesty and the King of the ages, and lo! The Watchers called me—Enoch the scribe—and said to me, {12:4} "Enoch, scribe of righteousness, go and declare to the Watchers of heaven who have left the high heaven, the holy eternal place, and have defiled themselves with women, doing as the children of earth do, and have taken wives for themselves: {12:5} 'You have brought great destruction on the earth, and you shall have no peace nor forgiveness of sin. Since you delight in your children, you will see the murder of your beloved ones, and you will lament over the destruction of your children and make supplication forever, but you will not attain mercy or peace.'"

{13:1} Enoch went and said, "Azazel, you shall have no peace: a severe sentence has been issued against you to bind you in chains. {13:2} You will not have any tolerance or request granted to you because of the unrighteousness you have taught and all the godlessness, unrighteousness, and sin you have shown to men." {13:3} Then I went and spoke to them all together, and they were all afraid, and fear and trembling seized them. {13:4} They begged me to draw up a petition for them so that they might find forgiveness and to read their petition in the presence of the Lord of heaven. {13:5} From then on, they could not speak with Him nor lift their eyes to heaven because of the shame of their sins for which they had been condemned.

{13:6} I wrote out their petition, the prayer regarding their spirits and their deeds individually, and their requests for forgiveness and long life. {13:7} I went and sat down by the waters of Dan, in the land of Dan, to the south of the west of Hermon. I read their petition until I fell asleep. {13:8} A dream came to me, and visions fell upon me. I saw visions of punishment, and a voice came telling me to inform the sons of heaven and reprimand them. {13:9} When I woke, I went to them, and they were all sitting together, weeping in 'Abelsjail, which is between Lebanon and Seneser, with their faces covered. {13:10} I recounted to them all the visions I had seen in my sleep, and I began to speak the words of righteousness and to reprimand the heavenly Watchers.

{14:1} This is the book of the words of righteousness and the reprimand of the eternal Watchers according to the command of the Holy Great One in that vision. {14:2} I saw in my sleep what I will now say with a tongue of flesh and with the breath of my mouth, which the Great One has given to men to converse with and understand with the heart. {14:3} As He has created and given to man the power of understanding the word of wisdom, He has also created me and given me the power to reprimand the Watchers, the children of heaven. {14:4} I wrote out your petition, and in my vision, it appeared that your petition will not be granted throughout all eternity, and that judgment has been finally passed upon you: indeed, your petition will not be granted. {14:5} From now on, you shall not ascend to heaven for all eternity, and the decree has gone forth to bind you on the earth for all the days of the world. {14:6} Before this, you shall see the destruction of your beloved sons, and you will have no pleasure in them, but they shall fall before you by the sword. {14:7} Your petition on their behalf shall not be granted, nor on your own, even though you weep and pray and speak all the words contained in the writing I have written. {14:8} The vision was shown to me like this: Behold, in the vision, clouds invited me, and a mist summoned me. The course of the stars and the lightnings sped and hastened me, and the winds in the vision caused me to fly and lifted me upward, bearing me into heaven. {14:9} I went until I drew near to a wall built of crystals and surrounded by tongues of fire, and it began to frighten me. {14:10} I went into the tongues of fire and drew near to a large house built of crystals, with walls like a tesselated floor made of crystals, and its foundation was of crystal. {14:11} Its ceiling was like the path of the stars and the lightnings, and between them were fiery Cherubim, and their heaven was as clear as water. {14:12} A flaming fire surrounded the walls, and its portals blazed with fire. {14:13} I entered that house, and it was hot as fire and cold as ice. There were no delights of life inside: fear covered me, and trembling seized me. {14:14} As I quaked and trembled, I fell on my face. {14:15} I beheld a vision: there was a second house, greater than the first, and its entire portal stood open before me. It was built of flames of fire. {14:16} In every respect, it excelled in splendor and magnificence and extent beyond description. {14:17} Its floor was of fire, and above it were lightnings and the path of the stars, and its ceiling was also flaming fire. {14:18} I looked and saw a lofty throne, its appearance as crystal, with wheels like the shining sun, and there was the vision of Cherubim. {14:19} From underneath the throne came streams of flaming fire so that I could not look at it. {14:20} The Great Glory sat on the throne, and His clothing shone more brightly than the sun and was whiter than any snow. {14:21} None of the angels could enter and behold His face because of the magnificence and glory, and no flesh could behold Him. {14:22} The flaming fire was all around Him, and a great fire stood before Him. None around Him could draw near. Ten thousand times ten thousand stood before Him, yet He needed no counselor. {14:23} The most holy ones who were near Him did not leave by night nor depart from Him. {14:24} Until then, I had been prostrate on my face, trembling, and the Lord called me with His own mouth and said, "Come here, Enoch, and hear my word." {14:25} One of the holy ones came to me and woke me. He made me rise up and approach the door, and I bowed my face downwards.

{15:1} He answered and said to me, and I heard His voice, "Fear not, Enoch, you righteous man and scribe of righteousness. Approach and hear my voice. {15:2} Go, say to the Watchers of heaven who have sent you to intercede for them: 'You should intercede for men, not men for you. {15:3} Why have you left the high, holy, and eternal heaven, lain with women, defiled yourselves with the daughters of men, taken wives for yourselves, and acted like the children of earth, begetting giants as your sons? {15:4} Though you were holy, spiritual, living the eternal life, you have defiled yourselves with the blood of women and begotten children with the blood of flesh. Like the children of men, you have lusted after flesh and blood, as those who die and perish. {15:5} Therefore, I have given them wives so that they might impregnate them and have children, so nothing might be lacking on earth. {15:6} But you were formerly spiritual, living the eternal life, and immortal for all generations of the world. {15:7} Therefore, I have not appointed wives for you, for the spiritual ones of heaven, whose dwelling is in heaven. {15:8} Now, the giants, who are born from the spirits and flesh, shall be called evil spirits on the earth, and the earth shall be their dwelling. {15:9} Evil spirits have come from their bodies because they are born from men and from the holy Watchers. Their origin is from them. They shall be evil spirits on earth and shall be called evil spirits. {15:10} As for the spirits of heaven, their dwelling is in heaven, but the spirits of the earth, which were born on earth, shall have their dwelling on the earth. {15:11} The spirits of the giants afflict, oppress, destroy, attack, fight, and work destruction on the earth and cause trouble. They take no food but hunger and thirst and cause offenses. {15:12} These spirits shall rise up against the children of men & against the women because they have come from them.

{16:1} From the days of the slaughter, destruction, and death of the giants, the spirits of their flesh shall go forth and destroy without incurring judgment. They shall destroy until the day of the consummation, the great judgment in which the age shall be completed, over the Watchers and the godless. It shall be completely finished. {16:2} As for the Watchers who have sent you to intercede for them, who were formerly in heaven, {16:3} you were in heaven, but not all the mysteries were revealed to you. You knew worthless ones, and in the hardness of your hearts, you made these known to the women, and through these mysteries, women and men work much evil on earth. {16:4} Therefore, say to them: 'You have no peace.'"

17:1} They took me to a place where beings resembled flaming fire but could appear as men if they wished. {17:2} Then they brought me to a dark mountain whose summit touched the heavens. {17:3} From there, I saw the abodes of the stars, the treasuries of thunder, and the deepest depths where fiery weapons like bows, arrows, swords, and lightning were kept. {17:4} They guided me to living waters and the western fire, which accepts the setting sun. {17:5} I beheld a river of fire flowing like water, emptying into the great sea in the west. {17:6} Witnessing great rivers and darkness, I ventured to a place untrodden by any flesh. {17:7} There, I saw the wintry mountains and the origin of all deep waters. {17:8} I observed the mouths of all earthly rivers and the mouth of the abyss.

{18:1} I witnessed the treasuries of winds and how they sustained the earth's foundations. {18:2} The cornerstone of the earth was revealed, along with the four winds supporting the earth and the heavenly firmament. {18:3} I saw how the winds stretched the heavens' expanse, serving as its pillars. {18:4} The winds also guided the sun and stars on their paths. {18:5} Cloud-carrying winds on earth and the angels' routes became visible to me. I saw the firmament of heaven at the earth's end. {18:6} Further, I came upon a place ablaze day and night, where seven splendid stone mountains stood: three to the east and three to the south. {18:7} Those to the east were of colored stone, pearl, and jacinth; those to the south, of red stone. {18:8}

The central mountain soared to heaven, resembling God's throne, made of alabaster with a sapphire summit. {18:9} Amidst all this, a flaming fire burned. {18:10} Beyond these mountains lay the earth's end, where heaven was completed. {18:11} I saw a deep abyss with columns of heavenly fire, and among them, colossal fire columns descended immeasurably. {18:12} Beyond that abyss lay a desolate place without sky or firmly grounded earth, devoid of water or birds—a dreadful wasteland. {18:13} Seven stars, like blazing mountains, were there, about which I inquired. {18:14} An angel informed me that this was the boundary of heaven and earth—a prison for disobedient stars and heavenly hosts. {18:15} These stars, rebelling against the Lord's command at their appointed times, were bound until their judgment after ten thousand years.

{19:1} Uriel disclosed to me that here stood the angels who mingled with women, corrupting mankind by assuming various forms and leading them to worship demons as gods. They would remain here until the great judgment. {19:2} Women who strayed with these angels would become sirens. {19:3} This vision, revealing end of all things, was seen by me alone, Enoch.

{20:1} These are the names of the holy angels who watch: {20:2} Uriel, overseeing the world and Tartarus; {20:3} Raphael, governing the spirits of men; {20:4} Raguel, dispensing justice to the luminaries; {20:5} Michael, overseeing the best of mankind and chaos; {20:6} Saraqael, overseeing spirits who sin in spirit; {20:7} Gabriel, in charge of Paradise, serpents, and Cherubim; {20:8} Remiel, appointed by God over the risen.

{21:1} And I proceeded to a place of chaos. {21:2} There, I saw something dreadful: there was neither a heaven above nor a firmly founded earth, just a chaotic and horrible place. {21:3} In this place, I saw seven stars of heaven bound together, like great mountains burning with fire. {21:4} Then I asked, 'For what sin are they bound, and why have they been cast here?' {21:5} Uriel, one of the holy angels who was with me and was their chief, said, 'Enoch, why do you ask, and why are you so eager for the truth? {21:6} These are among the stars of heaven that transgressed the Lord's commandment. They are bound here until ten thousand years, the time required for their sins, are completed.' {21:7} From there, I went to another place, more horrible than the first, where I saw a great fire burning and blazing, extending as far as the abyss, filled with immense descending columns of fire. Its extent or magnitude I could not determine. {21:8} I said, 'How dreadful is this place and how terrifying to behold!' {21:9} Uriel, one of the holy angels with me, replied, 'Enoch, why are you so afraid and terrified?' I answered, 'Because of this dreadful place and the spectacle of the pain.' {21:10} He said, 'This place is the prison of the angels, and here they will be imprisoned forever.'

{22:1} Then I went to another place, and he showed me another great and high mountain in the west, made of hard rock. {22:2} It had four deep, wide, and very smooth hollow places. How smooth and deep and dark these hollow places were to look at. {22:3} Raphael, one of the holy angels who was with me, said, 'These hollow places have been created for the spirits of the souls of the dead, so all the souls of the children of men should assemble here. {22:4} These places are made to receive them until the day of their judgment and the appointed period, until the great judgment comes upon them.' {22:5} I saw the spirits of the dead children of men, and their voice went forth to heaven, making pleas. {22:6} I asked Raphael, the angel with me, 'Whose spirit is this that makes suit and whose voice goes forth to heaven?' {22:7} He answered, 'This is the spirit that went forth from Abel, whom his brother Cain killed. He makes his suit against him until his seed is destroyed from the face of the earth and his descendants are annihilated from among men.' {22:8} I asked about this and about all the hollow places, 'Why is one separated from the other?' {22:9} He answered, 'These three have been made so the spirits of the dead might be separated. This division has been made for the spirits of the righteous, where there is a bright spring of water. {22:10} This has been made for sinners when they die and are buried in the earth and judgment has not been executed on them in their lifetime. {22:11} Here their spirits shall be set apart in great pain until the great day of judgment, punishment, and torment of those who curse forever, and retribution for their spirits. Here He shall bind them forever. {22:12} This division has been made for the spirits of those who make suit, disclosing their destruction when they were slain in the days of the sinners. {22:13} This has been made for the spirits of men who were not righteous but sinners, who were complete in transgression, and will be companions to the transgressors. Their spirits shall not be killed in the day of judgment nor shall they be raised from there.' {22:14} Then I blessed the Lord of glory and said, 'Blessed be my Lord, the Lord of righteousness, who rules forever.'

{23:1} From there, I went to another place to the west of the ends of the earth. {23:2} I saw a burning fire that ran without resting, never pausing day or night but running continually. {23:3} I asked, 'What is this that never rests?' {23:4} Raguel, one of the holy angels who was with me, answered, 'This is the fire in the west that persecutes all the heavenly luminaries.'

{24:1} From there, I went to another place on the earth, and he showed me a mountain range of fire burning day and night. {24:2} I went beyond it and saw seven magnificent mountains, each different from the other. Their stones were magnificent and beautiful, splendid in appearance and fair in exterior: three towards the east, one founded on the other, and three towards the south, one upon the other, with deep, rough ravines that did not join with each other. {24:3} The seventh mountain was in the midst of these, excelling them in height and resembling a throne. Fragrant trees encircled the throne. {24:4} Among them was a tree I had never smelled before, unique in its fragrance beyond all others. Its leaves and blooms and wood never wither, and its fruit is beautiful, resembling dates from a palm. {24:5} I said, 'How beautiful and fragrant is this tree, with its fair leaves and delightful blooms!' {24:6} Michael, one of the holy and honored angels who was with me and was their leader, answered.

{25:1} And he said to me: 'Enoch, why do you ask me about the fragrance of the tree, and why do you wish to learn the truth?' {25:2} Then I answered him, saying: 'I wish to know everything, especially about this tree.' {25:3} And he answered, saying: 'This high mountain you have seen, whose summit is like the throne of God, is His throne, where the Holy Great One, the Lord of Glory, the Eternal King, will sit when He comes down to visit the earth with goodness. {25:4} And as for this fragrant tree, no mortal is allowed to touch it until the great judgment when He will take vengeance on all and bring everything to its final completion forever. Then it shall be given to the righteous and holy. {25:5} Its fruit shall be food for the elect; it will be transplanted to the holy place, to the temple of the Lord, the Eternal King. {25:6} Then they shall rejoice with joy and be glad, And enter the holy place; Its fragrance shall be in their bones, And they shall live a long life on earth, Like their fathers lived; And in their days no sorrow or plague Or torment or calamity will touch them.' {25:7} Then I blessed the God of Glory, the Eternal King, who has prepared such things for the righteous and has created them and promised to give them.

{26:1} And I went from there to the middle of the earth, and I saw a blessed place with trees that had branches that were blooming and thriving. {26:2} There, I saw a holy mountain, and underneath the mountain to the east was a stream flowing toward the south. {26:3} I saw another mountain higher than this one toward the east, with a deep and narrow ravine between them, and a stream running through the ravine under the mountain. {26:4} To the west of it was another mountain, lower than the previous one and of smaller elevation, with a deep, dry ravine between them. Another deep, dry ravine was at the ends of the three mountains. {26:5} All the ravines were deep and narrow, formed of hard rock, and trees were not planted on them. {26:6} I marveled at the rocks and the ravine, indeed, I marveled greatly.

{27:1} Then I said: 'What is the purpose of this blessed land, filled entirely with trees, and this accursed valley between them?' {27:2} Uriel, one of the holy angels who was with me, answered and said: 'This accursed valley is for those who are accursed forever. Here, all who speak unseemly words against the Lord and speak harshly of His glory will be gathered. Here shall be their place of judgment. {27:3} In the last days, they shall witness the righteous judgment in the presence of the righteous forever. Here, the merciful will bless the Lord of Glory, the Eternal King. {27:4} In the days of judgment over the former, they shall bless Him for the mercy He has shown them.' {27:5} Then I blessed the Lord of Glory and proclaimed His glory and praised Him gloriously.

{28:1} And from there, I went towards the east, into the midst of the mountain range of the desert, and I saw a wilderness that was solitary, full of trees and plants. {28:2} Water gushed forth from above. {28:3} Rushing like a copious watercourse towards the northwest, it caused clouds and dew to ascend on every side.

{29:1} And from there, I went to another place in the desert, and approached the east of this mountain range. {29:2} There, I saw aromatic trees exhaling the fragrance of frankincense and myrrh, and the trees were similar to almond trees.

{30:1} And beyond these, I went far to the east and saw another place, a valley full of water. {30:2} In it, there was a tree with a color like that of fragrant trees, such as the mastic. {30:3} On the sides of those valleys, I saw fragrant cinnamon. {30:4} And beyond these, I proceeded to the east.

{31:1} I saw other mountains, and among them were groves of trees, from which nectar flowed, called sarara and galbanum. {31:2} Beyond these mountains, I saw another mountain to the east of the ends of the earth, where aloe trees grew, and all the trees were full of stacte, resembling almond trees. {31:3} When burned, their scent was sweeter than any other fragrant odor.
{32:1} After smelling the pleasant fragrances, I looked northward and saw seven mountains covered with exquisite nard, fragrant trees, cinnamon, and pepper. {32:2} I journeyed over the peaks of these mountains, far to the east of the earth, crossing over the Erythraean Sea and passing by the angel Zotiel. {32:3} Arriving at the Garden of Righteousness, I beheld many large and fragrant trees, surpassing in beauty and glory. Among them stood the tree of wisdom, whose fruit grants great understanding. {32:4} This tree resembled the fir in height, with leaves akin to those of the Carob tree, and its fruit resembled the clusters of the vine, emitting a delightful fragrance. {32:5} Enthralled by its beauty, I exclaimed, "How splendid is this tree!" {32:6} Raphael, the holy angel accompanying me, explained, "This is the tree of wisdom, from which your aged parents partook, gaining wisdom, opening their eyes to their nakedness, and subsequently being expelled from the garden."

{33:1} Continuing my journey to the ends of the earth, I encountered great and diverse beasts, each unique in appearance, as well as birds displaying varying beauty and voices. {33:2} To the east of these creatures, I observed the earth's extremities where the heavens meet, with the portals of heaven open. {33:3} Uriel, the holy angel, guided me in observing the emergence of the stars, noting their portals, courses, positions, and the intricacies of their movements. {33:4} He meticulously recorded these celestial phenomena, including their names, laws, and groupings.

{34:1} Heading northward to the earth's extremities, I witnessed a magnificent display—a trio of heavenly portals, from which northern winds emerged, bringing cold, hail, frost, snow, dew, and rain. {34:2} One portal dispersed these elements benevolently, while the other two wrought havoc and affliction upon the earth with their violent gusts.

{35:1} Venturing westward to the earth's ends, I encountered three portals in the heavens, akin to those I had seen in the east, each with corresponding outlets.

{36:1} Journeying southward to the earth's extremities, I observed three open portals in the heavens, through which dew, rain, and wind descended. {36:2} Turning eastward to the heavens' extremities, I beheld three eastern portals with smaller openings above them. {36:3} Through these small apertures, the stars of heaven traversed their course westward, guided by a predetermined path. {36:4} Witnessing these wonders, I continually blessed the Lord of Glory for His magnificent creations, urging angels, spirits, and humanity to praise His works, recognize His might, and bless Him forever.

{37:1} This is the second vision seen by Enoch, the son of Jared, tracing his lineage back to Adam. {37:2} It marks the beginning of the wisdom he wished to impart, addressing both the men of old and those to come. He speaks as a messenger of the Holy One before the Lord of Spirits. {37:3} While it would suffice to share this wisdom only with the ancients, he chooses not to withhold it from future generations, recognizing the importance of spreading wisdom. {37:4} Enoch acknowledges receiving unparalleled wisdom, granted by the Lord of Spirits as a testament to his insight and divine favor, granting him the gift of eternal life. {37:5} He proceeds to share three parables given to him.

{38:1} The first parable speaks of a time when the righteous will be congregated, and sinners judged and cast out from the earth. {38:2} It foretells the appearance of the Righteous One before the eyes of the righteous, bringing light and revealing the fate of sinners who denied the Lord of Spirits. {38:3} It predicts the revelation of the secrets of the righteous, the judgment of sinners, and the separation of the godless from the presence of the righteous and elect. {38:4} From that moment, the power and status of those who once ruled the earth will diminish, unable to withstand the divine light shining upon the holy. {38:5} Kings and mighty ones will perish, delivered into the hands of the righteous and holy, with no hope of mercy from the Lord of Spirits.

{39:1} In those days, it is prophesied that chosen and holy children will descend from heaven and unite with humanity. {39:2} Enoch receives books detailing zeal, wrath, disquiet, and expulsion. Mercy will not be granted to the sinners, declares the Lord of Spirits. {39:3} Suddenly, a whirlwind transports Enoch to the heavens' end. {39:4} There, he witnesses the dwelling places of the holy and the resting places of the righteous. {39:5} He sees their abodes alongside righteous angels, where they intercede and pray for humanity, and righteousness and mercy prevail eternally. {39:6} Enoch observes the Elect One of righteousness and faith, dwelling under the Lord of Spirits' wings, where righteousness prevails forever. {39:7} The righteous and elect shine like fiery lights, their lips praising the Lord of Spirits, ensuring perpetual righteousness. {39:8} Enoch desires to dwell in that blessed place, for it is his ordained portion before the Lord of Spirits. {39:9} He praises and extols the Lord of Spirits, recognizing his destiny for blessing and glory according to the Lord's good pleasure. {39:10} His eyes remain fixed on that sacred place, continually blessing and praising the Lord, acknowledging His eternal nature. {39:11} He witnesses the ceaseless adoration of those who never sleep, honoring the Lord of Spirits. {39:12} Enoch's countenance changes in the presence of such divine revelation.

{40:1} Following this, Enoch sees an innumerable multitude standing before the Lord of Spirits, beyond calculation. {40:2} He observes four presences surrounding the Lord, distinct from those who never sleep, learning their names from the accompanying angel. {40:3} He hears their voices praising the Lord of glory. {40:4} The first voice blesses the Lord of Spirits endlessly. {40:5} The second voice blesses the Elect One and those who rely on the Lord of Spirits. {40:6} The third voice prays and intercedes for humanity on behalf of the Lord of Spirits. {40:7} The fourth voice wards off the Satans, preventing them from accusing the earth's inhabitants before the Lord of Spirits. {40:8} Enoch queries the angel about these presences and their words. {40:9} The angel identifies them as Michael, Raphael, Gabriel, and Phanuel—four angels of the Lord of Spirits—and explains their roles. {40:10} Enoch remembers hearing these four voices during his visions.

{41:1} Following that, I beheld the secrets of the heavens, witnessing the division of the kingdom and the weighing of men's actions. {41:2} I observed the abodes of the elect and the holy, and saw sinners being driven away for denying the Lord of Spirits, unable to endure the punishment He meted out. {41:3} My eyes glimpsed the secrets of lightning, thunder, winds, clouds, and dew, discerning their origins and their effects on the earth. {41:4} I witnessed closed chambers from which winds emanated—the chamber of hail, mist, clouds, and the perpetual cloud hovering over the earth since its inception. {41:5} The chambers of the sun and moon were revealed to me, along with their orbits, their steadfastness, and their mutual agreement, bound by an unbreakable oath. {41:6} The sun obediently follows its path, exalting the name of the Lord of Spirits. {41:7} I then observed the concealed and visible paths of the moon, fulfilling its course day and night before the Lord of Spirits. {41:8} Both celestial bodies offer constant thanks and praise, each fulfilling its purpose without fail. The sun's changes bring blessings or curses, while the moon's path brings light to the righteous and darkness to the sinners, by the authority of the Lord who separated light from darkness and strengthened the spirits of the righteous. {41:9} No angel or power can hinder this divine order, for the Lord appoints a judge for all and passes judgment accordingly.

{42:1} Wisdom initially found no suitable abode, but eventually, a place was allotted for her in heaven. {42:2} She attempted to dwell among humanity but found no place, returning to her celestial abode among the angels. {42:3} Unrighteousness, however, emerged from her chambers, finding those she sought not and dwelling among them like rain in a desert or dew on parched land.

{43:1} Another vision revealed to me different lightnings and stars, each called by name and obedient to the Lord. {43:2} They were weighed in a righteous balance according to their light, their celestial orbits, and their obedience to the Lord's command, symbolizing the faithful believers dwelling on earth. {43:3} I inquired of the accompanying angel about their significance. {43:4} He revealed that they represent the holy ones on earth who believe in the Lord of Spirits for eternity.

{44:1} Additionally, I observed stars transforming into lightning, unable to revert to their original form.

{45:1} This is the second parable concerning those who reject the abode of the holy ones and the Lord of Spirits. {45:2} They shall not ascend to heaven nor set foot on earth, their fate being reserved for the day of judgment and suffering. {45:3} On that day, the Elect One will sit on the throne of glory, evaluating their deeds. {45:4} The sight of the Elect Ones and those who invoke the Lord's name will strengthen the souls of the righteous. {45:5} The Lord will transform heaven into eternal blessing and light, as well as the earth, where His elect ones will dwell. {45:6} As for the sinners and evildoers, judgment awaits, and they shall be eradicated from the face of the earth.

{46:1} There, I beheld a figure with a head as ancient as time itself, its white wool-like hair signifying wisdom and age. {46:2} Accompanying this figure was another being, resembling a man but radiating the grace of a holy angel. {46:2} Curious, I questioned the accompanying angel about this Son of Man, asking who he was, where he came from, and why he was in the presence of the Ancient of Days. {46:3} The angel explained that this Son of Man embodies righteousness, dwelling in righteousness and revealing hidden treasures because the Lord of Spirits has chosen him, granting him pre-eminence and eternal uprightness. {46:4} This Son of Man, the angel continued, will uplift kings and the mighty, breaking the dominion of the strong and punishing the sinners. {46:5} He will depose kings and rulers who fail to praise the Lord, bringing shame upon the proud and darkening their dwellings for their refusal to honor the Lord. {46:6} These are the ones who defy the Lord, judging the stars, treading the earth, relying on their wealth and crafted gods, and persecuting the faithful.

{47:1} In those days, the prayers and blood of the righteous will ascend before the Lord of Spirits. {47:2} The heavenly beings will unite in prayer, supplicating and praising the Lord on behalf of the righteous and their shed blood, ensuring their prayers are not in vain and that judgment is delivered. {47:3} I witnessed the Head of Days, enthroned in glory, with the books of the living opened before Him, surrounded by His heavenly host and counselors. {47:4} Joy filled the hearts of the holy ones as their numbers were acknowledged, their prayers answered, and their sacrifices recognized by the Lord of Spirits.

{48:1} In that place, I saw the fountain of righteousness, surrounded by countless fountains of wisdom. Thirsty souls drank from them, gaining wisdom and finding dwelling places among the righteous and holy. {48:2} At that moment, the Son of Man received his name before the Lord of Spirits and the Ancient of Days, before the creation of the celestial bodies. {48:3} He will support the righteous, shining as a beacon of hope for the troubled. {48:4} All inhabitants of the earth will worship and praise him, celebrating the Lord of Spirits. {48:5} He was chosen and hidden before the Lord, destined to save those who despise the unrighteousness of the world and trust in the Lord's name. {48:6} The wisdom of the Lord has revealed him to the righteous, preserving their lot and granting them salvation through his name.

{49:1} Wisdom is abundant, and glory accompanies it eternally. The Elect One stands before the Lord of Spirits, ensuring righteousness prevails over unrighteousness. {49:2} He possesses mighty secrets of righteousness, dispelling unrighteousness like a fleeting shadow. {49:3} The spirit of wisdom, insight, understanding, and might dwells within him, along with the spirits of the righteous who have passed away. {49:4} He will judge all secrets, and no falsehood will withstand his judgment, for he is the Elect One chosen by the Lord of Spirits.

{50:1} In those days, the holy and elect will experience a transformation, basking in perpetual light and glory as judgment looms over the sinners. {50:2} The righteous will triumph in the name of the Lord of Spirits, prompting others to repent and abandon their wicked ways. {50:3} Even though they will not be honored by the Lord's name, salvation will be found in it, and the Lord of Spirits will show compassion, although unrighteousness will not endure in His presence. {50:4} From that moment on, the Lord of Spirits declares, mercy will be withheld from the unrepentant.

{51:1} In those days, the earth, Sheol, and hell will relinquish what they hold. {51:5a} For the Elect One will arise, selecting the righteous and holy, ensuring their salvation draws near. {51:2} He will sit on the throne, divulging divine wisdom and counsel, for the Lord of Spirits has endowed him with these secrets, glorifying him. {51:3} Mountains will leap, hills will skip, and angels will rejoice with illuminated faces. {51:5b} The earth will rejoice, {51:5c} and the righteous will dwell upon it, {51:5d} while the elect will walk upon it.

{52:1} After those days, in the place where I had seen hidden visions, I beheld a mountain of iron, copper, silver, gold, and other metals. {52:2} The angel with me explained that these metals would serve the dominion of the Anointed One, granting him strength on the earth. {52:3} Soon, all secrets surrounding the Lord of Spirits will be revealed. {52:4} These mountains will become as wax before the Elect One, powerless against his might. {52:5} None will be saved by wealth or weaponry when the Elect One appears.

{53:1} I saw a deep valley where all inhabitants of the earth, sea, and islands presented gifts, yet it never filled. {53:2} Sinners will be destroyed before the Lord of Spirits, banished from His earth forever. {53:3} Angels of punishment will prepare instruments for the kings and mighty of the earth, leading them to destruction. {53:4} The righteous will establish their congregation without hindrance, finding rest from the oppression of sinners.

{54:1} Turning to another part of the earth, I saw a deep valley ablaze with fire, into which kings and mighty ones were cast. {54:2} Chains of immense weight were forged for Azazel's hosts, to cast them into the abyss. {54:3} On that great day, Michael, Gabriel, Raphael, and Phanuel will cast them into the fiery furnace as the Lord of Spirits takes vengeance. {54:4} Punishment will come, waters will converge, and all unrighteousness will perish.

{55:1} The Head of Days repented, swearing never again to destroy all who dwell on the earth. {55:2} A sign will be set in the heavens as a pledge of good faith between the Lord and humanity. {55:3} Chastisement will come on the day of tribulation, and the Elect One will sit on the throne, judging Azazel and his associates. {55:4} The mighty kings of the earth will witness this judgment.

{56:1} I saw angels of punishment armed with scourges and chains, destined for their elect and beloved ones to be cast into the abyss. {56:2} That valley will be filled with the elect, and their days of leading astray will end. {56:3} Angels will stir unrest among nations, inciting conflict and destruction. {56:4} They will tread upon the land of the elect, but their city will withstand them. {56:5} Sheol will swallow the sinners, ending their destruction.

{57:1} Afterward, I saw another group of chariots and riders, moving swiftly from the east, west, and south upon the winds. {57:2} Their noisy approach caused a great commotion, shaking the pillars of the earth, and the sound reverberated across the heavens in a single day. {57:3} All shall bow and worship the Lord of Spirits. This concludes the second Parable.

{58:1} I then began the third Parable concerning the righteous and elect. {58:2} Blessed are you, righteous and chosen ones, for your destiny is glorious. {58:3} The righteous will bask in the sunlight, and the chosen in eternal life. Their days will be endless, and their number beyond count. {58:4} They will seek righteousness with the Lord of Spirits, finding peace and eternal light. {58:5} The heavenly host will urge them to seek the secrets of righteousness, now bright as the sun on earth. {58:6} There will be everlasting light, and their days will be limitless, as darkness fades before the Lord of Spirits.

{59:1} In those days, I saw the secrets of lightning and thunder, their judgments executing blessings or curses according to the Lord of Spirits' will. {59:2} I witnessed the thunder's secrets, understanding how it brings blessings or curses upon the earth. {59:3} I learned the secrets of lightning and its purpose in satisfying and blessing.

{60:1} In the year 500, on the fourteenth day of the seventh month, in the life of Enoch, I saw a mighty quake shaking the heavens and disquieting the host of the Most High. {60:2} The Head of Days sat on His glorious throne, surrounded by angels and the righteous. {60:3} Trembling overtook me, and fear gripped me, causing me to fall on my face. {60:4} Michael sent another angel to raise me, restoring my spirit. {60:5} He explained that the day of mercy had lasted until then, but a day of power, punishment, and judgment was prepared for those who defy the righteous law. {60:6} On that day, Leviathan and Behemoth were separated, one to the depths of the ocean and the other to the wilderness. {60:7} The angel showed me the heavenly secrets, from the highest heights to the depths of the earth, revealing the chambers of the winds, the divisions of the stars, and the nature of thunder and lightning. {60:8} He explained the role of rain and dew in nourishing the earth, all under the guidance of the angels appointed by the Most High.

{61:1} In those days, I witnessed angels being equipped with long cords and wings, flying towards the north. {61:2} I inquired of the angel accompanying me, "Why have these angels taken cords and flown away?" He responded, "They have gone to measure." {61:3} The angel with me explained further, "They will bring measures and ropes for the righteous, so they can rely on the name of the Lord of Spirits forever. {61:4} This will strengthen the righteous and enable them to dwell together, revealing the secrets of the earth's depths and allowing those who were lost to return on the day of the Elect One. {61:5} None will be destroyed before the Lord of Spirits, and all will be protected. {61:6} All who dwell in heaven received a command, power, one voice, and a fire-like light. {61:7} With their first words, they blessed and praised with wisdom, wise in speech and spirit. {61:8} The Lord of Spirits elevated the Elect One to the throne of glory to judge the deeds of the holy in heaven. {61:9} When he judges their secret ways according to the Lord of Spirits' word and righteous judgment, they will bless and glorify His name. {61:10} On that day, all heavenly hosts, including angels and powers on earth and water, will unite in blessing the Lord of Spirits. {61:11} They will bless Him with faith, wisdom, patience, mercy, judgment, peace, and goodness, saying, "Blessed is He, and may His name be praised forever." {61:12} All in heaven and on earth will glorify His name without measure, for the mercy of the Lord of Spirits is great. {61:13} He reveals all to the righteous and elect in His name.

{62:1} The Lord commands the kings, mighty ones, and all dwellers on earth to recognize the Elect One. {62:2} Seated on the throne of glory, righteousness pours from him, destroying sinners with his word. {62:3} All kings, mighty ones, and rulers will witness his glory and judgment, feeling pain and terror. {62:4} They will be terrified as a woman in labor, experiencing pain and distress. {62:5} Seeing the Son of Man on the throne will bring them anguish and downcast faces. {62:6} Kings and mighty ones will bless and glorify the hidden ruler of all. {62:7} The Son of Man, hidden from the beginning, is revealed to the elect by the Most High. {62:8} The congregation of the elect will stand before him on that day. {62:9} All rulers will fall before him, worshiping and seeking mercy. {62:10} Yet, they will be swiftly sent away, filled with shame and deeper darkness. {62:11} They will face punishment for oppressing the Lord's children and elect. {62:12} They will be a spectacle for the righteous, as the Lord's wrath rests upon them. {62:13} The righteous and elect will be saved, never seeing the sinners' faces again. {62:14} The Lord of Spirits will dwell with them, and they will eat, lie down, and rise forever. {62:15} The righteous and elect will rise from the earth, no longer downcast, adorned in garments of glory. {62:16} These garments of life from the Lord of Spirits will never grow old or lose their glory.

{63:1} In those days, the mighty kings who ruled the earth will plead for a brief respite from the angels of punishment, hoping to worship the Lord of Spirits and confess their sins. {63:2} They will bless and glorify the Lord of Spirits, acknowledging His dominion over kings, the mighty, the rich, and all glory and wisdom. {63:3} They will recognize the splendor and power of His secrets, acknowledging His righteousness throughout generations. {63:4} They will learn to glorify and bless the Lord of kings, the ultimate ruler. {63:5} They will express their desire for rest to glorify and thank the Lord's glory and confess their faith. {63:6} Despite their longing for rest, they will find none, dwelling in darkness due to their disbelief in the Lord of Spirits. {63:7} Their hope was in their kingdom's power and glory, not in the Lord. {63:8} In their suffering and tribulation, they find no salvation, realizing too late the truth of the Lord's works and judgments. {63:9} Their works lead them away from the Lord's presence, and their sins are accounted for in righteousness. {63:10} They will acknowledge their souls' unrighteous gain, unable to escape the burden of Sheol. {63:11} Their faces will be filled with darkness and shame before the Son of Man, driven away from His presence as the sword of judgment looms. {63:12} Thus spoke the Lord of Spirits, decreeing judgment upon the mighty, kings, exalted, and rulers of the earth.

{64:1} In that place, I saw other hidden forms. {64:2} The angel's voice explained that these were the angels who descended to earth, revealing hidden knowledge to humanity and leading them into sin.

{65:1} In those days, Noah witnessed the earth's impending destruction. {65:2} He cried out to his grandfather Enoch, asking about the calamity befalling the earth, fearing for his own safety. {65:3} A great commotion occurred, and a voice from heaven was heard, causing Enoch and Noah to fall on their faces. {65:4} Enoch approached Noah, questioning his distress. {65:5} He explained that the Lord had decreed the earth's ruin because humanity had learned the secrets of angels, {65:6}Satan's violence, sorcery, witchcraft, and the making of idols. {65:7} Humanity's knowledge of silver and soft metals' origins and other hidden arts led to their downfall. {65:8} Enoch then reassured Noah and sought guidance from the Lord of Spirits. {65:9} The Lord revealed that judgment had been determined due to humanity's unrighteousness and sorceries. {65:10} Those who had revealed these secrets were damned, but Noah was deemed pure and righteous by the Lord of Spirits. {65:11} The Lord destined Noah's name among the holy, promising to preserve him and his righteous descendants for kingship and honor, ensuring a fountain of righteousness and holiness for eternity.

{66:1} Then I saw the angels of punishment, ready to release the powers of the waters beneath the earth to bring judgment and destruction upon all who dwell on the earth. {66:2} The Lord of Spirits commanded these angels not to let the waters rise but to restrain them, as these angels had authority over the powers of the waters. {66:3} After this, I departed from Enoch's presence.

{67:1} In those days, God's word came to me, saying, "Noah, your fate is before Me—a blameless, loving, and upright fate. {67:2} Now, the angels are constructing an ark, and when they finish, I will bless it and preserve it. From it will come forth the seed of life, and a change will occur so the earth will not remain uninhabited. {67:3} I will establish your seed before Me forever, spreading those who dwell with you. The earth will not be barren but blessed and fruitful in My name. {67:4} Those angels who have acted unjustly will be imprisoned in the burning valley that Enoch showed me in the west, among the mountains of gold, silver, iron, soft metal, and tin. {67:5} I witnessed a great upheaval and convulsion in that valley, accompanied by a sulfurous smell, connected to the waters. {67:6} This valley of the fallen angels burned, and streams of fire flowed through its valleys, {67:7} punishing those who led humanity astray. {67:8} However, those waters will serve the kings, mighty ones, and inhabitants of the earth for physical healing but spiritual punishment. Their spirits are consumed by lust, denying the Lord of Spirits despite witnessing their daily punishment. {67:9} As their bodies suffer, so will their spirits eternally, for idle words will not be tolerated before the Lord of Spirits. {67:10} Their judgment comes because they prioritize bodily desires over the Spirit of the Lord. {67:11} These waters will also change; when the angels are punished, the springs' temperature will change, becoming cold when the angels ascend. {67:12} Michael explained that this judgment serves as a testimony for the kings and mighty ones of the earth. {67:13} Despite the healing properties of these waters, they will not believe that they will eventually become a fire burning forever.

{68:1} Afterward, my grandfather Enoch taught me all the secrets contained in the book of Parables given to him. He compiled them for me into the words of the book of Parables. {68:2} On that day, Michael expressed his awe and fear to Raphael regarding the severity of the judgment of the angels' secrets. {68:3} Michael asked Raphael who could remain unaffected by this judgment and not be troubled by it. {68:4} When Michael stood before the Lord of Spirits, he refused to intercede on behalf of those angels, acknowledging the Lord's anger towards them. {68:5} Thus, they alone received their everlasting judgment, with neither angel nor man having a share in it.

{69:1} After the judgment, they will cause terror and trembling among those who live on the earth. {69:2} Here are the names of those angels: the first is Samjaza, the second Artaqifa, the third Armen, the fourth Kokabel, the fifth Turael, the sixth Rumjal, the seventh Danjal, the eighth Neqael, the ninth Baraqel, the tenth Azazel, the eleventh Armaros, the twelfth Batarjal, the thirteenth Busasejal, the fourteenth Hananel, the fifteenth Turel, and the sixteenth Simapesiel, the seventeenth Jetrel, the eighteenth Tumael, the nineteenth Turel, the twentieth Rumael, the twenty-first Azazel. {69:3} These are the chiefs of their angels, along with their names, and their leaders over hundreds, fifties, and tens. {69:4} The first one, Jeqon, led astray all the sons of God, bringing them down to earth and leading them astray through the daughters of men. {69:5} The second, Asbeel, gave evil counsel to the holy sons of God, leading them astray to defile their bodies with the daughters of men. {69:6} The third, Gadreel, showed mankind the ways of death, leading Eve astray and revealing weapons of death to humanity. {69:7} The fourth, Penemue, taught humanity both good and evil, revealing all the secrets of wisdom, including writing with ink and paper, leading many to sin. {69:8} The fifth, Kasdeja, revealed to humanity the wicked workings of spirits and demons, the destruction of embryos in the womb, and other harmful knowledge. {69:9} Kasbeel, the chief of the oath, requested Michael to reveal the hidden name to inspire fear and reverence among humanity. {69:10} Through this oath, the heavens were suspended before the world's creation, ensuring the stability of the earth, sea, stars, and elements. {69:11} The spirits of water, winds, and elements all glorify the Lord of Spirits for eternity. {69:12} This oath preserves the paths and courses of all things. {69:13} The Son of Man sat on the throne of glory, passing judgment on sinners and those who led others astray. {69:14} Sinners will be bound and imprisoned, and all their works will vanish from the earth. {69:15} Corruption will cease, as the Son of Man reigns in glory before the Lord of Spirits.

{70:1} After these events, the name of the Son of Man and the Lord of Spirits was exalted among those on earth. {70:2} The Son of Man was lifted up on chariots of the spirit, and his name disappeared among them. {70:3} Enoch was placed between the North and the West, where angels measured the place for the elect and righteous. {70:4} There, Enoch saw the first fathers and the righteous who dwelled in that place from the beginning.

{71:1} Enoch's spirit was translated into heaven, where he saw the holy sons of God walking on flames of fire, clothed in white garments. {71:2} He witnessed streams of fire and the heavenly structure built of crystals, surrounded by living fire. {71:3} The angel Michael led Enoch to see the secrets of righteousness and the ends of heaven, including the chambers of stars and luminaries. {71:4} Enoch's spirit was taken to the highest heaven, where he saw the glorious throne of God, surrounded by countless angels. {71:5} Angels, including Michael, Gabriel, Raphael, and Phanuel, went in and out of the heavenly house. {71:6} An angel explained to Enoch that the Son of Man is born unto righteousness and will always be upheld by righteousness. {71:7} Peace is proclaimed in the name of the world to come, where righteousness reigns forever. {71:8} All who follow the Son of Man will have peace and righteousness, dwelling with him forever in the presence of the Lord of Spirits.

{72:1} The book of the courses of the luminaries of the heaven, detailing their relationships, classes, dominion, seasons, names, places of origin, and months, as shown to me by Uriel, the holy angel who was with me and who guides them. He showed me all their laws exactly as they are, concerning all the years of the world and unto eternity, until the new creation is accomplished which lasts forever. {72:2} This is the first law of the luminaries: The sun rises in the eastern portals of the heaven and sets in the western portals. {72:3} I saw six portals in which the sun rises and six portals in which it sets, and the moon also rises and sets in these portals, along with the leaders of the stars and those they lead: six in the east and six in the west, all following each other in accurate order. There are also many windows to the right and left of these portals. {72:4} First, the great luminary, the sun, goes forth. Its circumference is like the circumference of the heaven, and it is filled with illuminating and heating fire. {72:5} The wind drives the chariot on which it ascends, and the sun goes down from the heaven and returns through the north to reach the east, guided to the appropriate portal to shine in the face of the heaven. {72:6} In the first month, the sun rises in the great portal, which is the fourth portal. {72:7} In that fourth portal, from which the sun rises in the first month, there are twelve window openings from which a flame proceeds when they are opened in their season. {72:8} When the sun rises in the heaven, it comes forth through that fourth portal for thirty mornings in succession and sets accurately in the fourth portal in the west of the heaven. {72:9} During this period, the day becomes daily longer and the night nightly shorter until the thirtieth morning. {72:10} On that day, the day is longer than the night by a ninth part, with the day amounting to ten parts and the night to eight parts. {72:11} The sun rises from that fourth portal and sets in the fourth, then returns to the fifth portal of the east for thirty mornings, and rises from it and sets in the fifth portal. {72:12} The day then becomes longer by two parts, amounting to eleven parts, and the night becomes shorter, amounting to seven parts. {72:13} The sun returns to the east and enters into the sixth portal, rising and setting in the sixth portal for thirty-one mornings on account of its sign. {72:14} On that day, the day becomes longer than the night, doubling the night, with the day amounting to twelve parts and the night to six parts. {72:15} The sun then makes the day shorter and the night longer, returning to the east and entering into the sixth portal, rising and setting for thirty mornings. {72:16} After thirty mornings, the day decreases by exactly one part, becoming eleven parts, and the night seven parts. {72:17} The sun goes forth from the sixth portal in the west, returns to the east, and rises in the fifth portal for thirty mornings, setting in the west again in the fifth western portal. {72:18} On that day, the day decreases by two parts, amounting to ten parts, and the night to eight parts. {72:19} The sun goes forth from the fifth portal, sets in the fifth portal of the west, rises in the fourth portal for thirty-one mornings on account of its sign, and sets in the west. {72:20} On that day, the day is equalized with the night, each being nine parts. {72:21} The sun rises from that portal, sets in the west, returns to the east, and rises for thirty mornings in the third portal, setting in the west in the third portal. {72:22} On that day, the night becomes longer than the day, with the night becoming longer than night and the day shorter than day until the thirtieth morning, with the night amounting to ten parts and the day to eight parts. {72:23} The sun rises from the third portal, sets in the third portal in the west, returns to the east, and rises for thirty mornings in the second portal in the east, setting in the second portal in the west. {72:24} On that day, the night amounts to eleven parts and the day to seven parts. {72:25} The sun rises on that day from the second portal, sets in the second portal in the west, and returns to the east into the first portal for thirty-one mornings, setting in the first portal in the west. {72:26} On that day, the night becomes longer and amounts to twice the day, with the night amounting exactly to twelve parts and the day to six parts. {72:27} The sun then traverses the divisions of its orbit, turning again on those divisions, entering that portal for thirty mornings, and setting in the west opposite to it. {72:28} On that night, the night decreases in length by a ninth part, with the night becoming eleven parts and the day seven parts. {72:29} The sun returns, entering into the second portal in the east, and returns on those divisions of its orbit for thirty mornings, rising and setting. {72:30} On that day, the night decreases in length, amounting to ten parts and the day to eight parts. {72:31} On that day, the sun rises from that portal, sets in the west, returns to the east, and rises in the third portal for thirty-one mornings, setting in the west. {72:32} On that day, the night decreases, amounting to nine parts and the day to nine parts. The night is equal to the day, and the year is exactly 364 days. {72:33} The length of the day and night, and the shortness of the day and night, arise through the course of the sun, making these distinctions. {72:34} Thus, its course becomes daily longer and nightly shorter. {72:35} This is the law and course of the sun, returning as often as it returns sixty times, rising as the great luminary named the sun forever. {72:36} This luminary rises and sets, decreasing not and resting not, running day and night. {72:37} Its light is sevenfold brighter than that of the moon, but in size, they are both equal.

{73:1} After this law, I saw another law dealing with the smaller luminary, named the Moon. {73:2} Her circumference is like the circumference of the heaven. Her chariot is driven by the wind, and light is given to her in a definite measure. {73:3} Her rising and setting change every month. Her days are like the days of the sun, and when her light is full, it amounts to the seventh part of the light of the sun. {73:4} Her first phase in the east appears on the thirtieth morning, becoming visible and marking the first phase of the moon on the thirtieth day along with the sun in the portal where the sun rises. {73:5} Half of her goes forth by a seventh part, and her whole circumference is empty without light, except for one-seventh part of it and one-fourteenth part of her light. {73:6} When she receives one-seventh part of half her light, her light amounts to one-seventh part and half thereof. {73:7} She sets with the sun, and when the sun rises, the moon rises with him, receiving half of one part of light. At the beginning of her morning, the moon sets with the sun, being invisible that night with fourteen parts and half of one of them. {73:8} She rises that day with exactly a seventh part, comes forth and recedes from the rising of the sun, and in her remaining days becomes bright in the remaining thirteen parts.

{74:1} I saw another course, a law for her, and how according to that law she performs her monthly revolution. {74:2} Uriel, the holy angel who leads them all, showed me their positions, and I wrote down their positions and their months as they were, and the appearance of their lights until fifteen days were accomplished. {74:3} In single seventh parts, she accomplishes all her light in the east and all her darkness in the west. {74:4} In certain months, she alters her settings, and in certain months, she follows her own peculiar course. {74:5} In two months, the moon sets with the sun in those two middle portals, the third and the fourth. {74:6} She goes forth for seven days, turns about, and returns again through the portal where the sun rises, accomplishing all her light. She recedes from the sun and in eight days enters the sixth portal from which the sun goes forth. {74:7} When the sun goes forth from the fourth portal, she goes forth for seven days until she goes forth from the fifth, then turns back again in seven days into the fourth portal, accomplishing all her light. She recedes and enters into the first portal in eight days. {74:8} She returns again in seven days into the fourth portal from which the sun goes forth. {74:9} Thus I saw their positions, how the moon rose and the sun set in those days. {74:10} If five years are added together, the sun has an overplus of thirty days, and all the days which accrue to it for one of those five years, when they are full, amount to 364 days. {74:11} The overplus of the sun and the stars amounts to six days: in five years, six days every year come to thirty days. The moon falls behind the sun and stars by thirty days. {74:12} The sun and the stars complete all the years exactly, neither advancing nor delaying their positions by a single day unto eternity, completing the years with perfect justice in 364 days. {74:13} In three years, there are 1,092 days; in five years, 1,820 days; so in eight years, there are 2,912 days. {74:14} For the moon alone, the days amount in three years to 1,062 days, and in five years, she falls behind by fifty days: to the sum of 1,770, 62 days are to be added. {74:15} In five years, there are 1,770 days, so in eight years, the days for the moon amount to 2,832 days. {74:16} In eight years, she falls behind by eighty days, with all the days she falls behind in eight years amounting to eighty. {74:17} The year is accurately completed in conformity with their world stations and the stations of the sun, which rise from the portals through which it rises and sets for thirty days.

{75:1} And the leaders of the heads of the thousands, who are placed over the whole creation and all the stars, also deal with the four intercalary days. These days are inseparable from their office according to the reckoning of the year, and they render service on the four days which are not counted in the yearly reckoning. {75:2} Because of these days, people go wrong in their calculations. These luminaries truly render service at the world-stations: one in the first portal, one in the third portal of the heaven, one in the fourth portal, and one in the sixth portal. The exactness of the year is accomplished through its separate 364 stations. {75:3} For the signs, times, years, and days, the angel Uriel showed me, whom the Lord of glory has set forever over all the luminaries of the heaven. They rule in the heaven and on the earth, leading the sun, moon, stars, and all the ministering creatures which make their revolution in all the chariots of the heaven. {75:4} Similarly, Uriel showed me twelve doors open in the circumference of the sun's chariot in the heaven, through which the rays of the sun break forth, diffusing warmth over the earth when they are opened at their appointed seasons. {75:5} And for the winds and the spirit of the dew when they are opened, standing open in the heavens at the ends. {75:6} As for the twelve portals in the heaven, at the ends of the earth, out of which the sun, moon, and stars, and all the works of heaven come forth in the east and the west, {75:7} There are many windows open to the left and right of them. One window at its appointed season produces warmth, corresponding to those doors from which the stars come forth as He has commanded them, and wherein they set corresponding to their number. {75:8} I saw chariots in the heaven running in the world, above those portals in which revolve the stars that never set. {75:9} And one is larger than all the rest, it is the one that makes its course through the entire world.

{76:1} At the ends of the earth, I saw twelve portals open to all the quarters of the heaven, from which the winds go forth and blow over the earth. {76:2} Three of them are open on the face (i.e., the east) of the heavens, three in the west, three on the right (i.e., the south) of the heaven, and three on the left (i.e., the north). {76:3} The first three are those of the east, three are of the north, three of the south, and three of the west. {76:4} From four of these come winds of blessing and prosperity, and from the other eight come harmful winds, bringing destruction on all the earth and the water upon it, and on all who dwell thereon, and on everything in the water and on the land. {76:5} The first wind from those portals, called the east wind, comes forth through the first portal in the east, inclining towards the south. From it come desolation, drought, heat, and destruction. {76:6} Through the second portal in the middle comes what is fitting: rain, fruitfulness, prosperity, and dew. {76:7} Through the third portal which lies toward the north come cold and drought. {76:8} The south winds come through three portals: through the first portal inclining to the east comes a hot wind. {76:9} Through the middle portal next to it come fragrant smells, dew, rain, prosperity, and health. {76:10} Through the third portal lying to the west come dew, rain, locusts, and desolation. {76:11} The north winds come from the seventh portal in the east: dew, rain, locusts, and desolation. {76:12} From the middle portal come health, rain, dew, and prosperity. {76:13} Through the third portal in the west come cloud, hoar-frost, snow, rain, dew, and locusts. {76:14} The west winds come through three portals: through the first portal adjoining the north come dew, hoar-frost, cold, snow, and frost. {76:15} From the middle portal come dew, rain, prosperity, and blessing. {76:16} Through the last portal adjoining the south come drought, desolation, burning, and destruction. {76:17} The twelve portals of the four quarters of the heaven are completed, and all their laws, plagues, and benefactions have I shown to you, my son Methuselah.

{77:1} The first quarter is called the east because it is the first. The second is the south because the Most High will descend there, especially in that area. {77:2} The west quarter is called the diminished because all the luminaries of the heaven wane and go down there. {77:3} The fourth quarter, named the north, is divided into three parts: the first part is for the dwelling of men, the second contains seas of water, abysses, forests, rivers, darkness, and clouds, and the third part contains the garden of righteousness. {77:4} I saw seven high mountains higher than all the mountains on the earth. From them comes hoar-frost, and days, seasons, and years pass away. {77:5} I saw seven rivers on the earth larger than all the rivers. One of them comes from the west and pours its waters into the Great Sea. {77:6} Two come from the north to the sea and pour their waters into the Erythraean Sea in the east. {77:7} The remaining four come from the north to their own sea, two into the Erythraean Sea, and two into the Great Sea, discharging themselves there [and some say into the desert]. {77:8} I saw seven great islands in the sea and on the mainland: two on the mainland and five in the Great Sea.

{78:1} The names of the sun are: the first Orjares, and the second Tomas. {78:2} The moon has four names: the first is Asonja, the second Ebla, the third Benase, and the fourth Erae. {78:3} These are the two great luminaries. Their circumference is like the circumference of the heaven, and the size of both is alike. {78:4} The sun has seven portions of light more than the moon, which are transferred until the seventh portion of the sun is exhausted. {78:5} They set and enter the portals of the west, make their revolution by the north, and come forth through the eastern portals on the face of the heaven. {78:6} When the moon rises, one-fourteenth part appears in the heaven. [The light becomes full in her.] On the fourteenth day, she completes her light. {78:7} Fifteen parts of light are transferred to her until the fifteenth day, when her light is completed, and she becomes fifteen parts. The moon grows by adding fourteen parts. {78:8} In her waning, the moon decreases on the first day to fourteen parts of her light, on the second to thirteen parts, on the third to twelve, on the fourth to eleven, on the fifth to ten, on the sixth to nine, on the seventh to eight, on the eighth to seven, on the ninth to six, on the tenth to five, on the eleventh to four, on the twelfth to three, on the thirteenth to two, on the fourteenth to half of a seventh, and all her remaining light disappears wholly on the fifteenth. {78:9} In certain months, the month has twenty-nine days and sometimes twenty-eight. {78:10} Uriel showed me another law: when light is transferred to the moon, and on which side it is transferred to her by the sun. {78:11} During the period when the moon is growing in her light, she is transferring it to herself when opposite to the sun for fourteen days. Her light is completed in the heaven when she is fully illuminated. {78:12} On the first day, she is called the new moon, for on that day, the light rises upon her. {78:13} She becomes a full moon exactly on the day when the sun sets in the west. She rises at night from the east, and the moon shines the whole night through until the sun rises over against her, and the moon is seen opposite the sun. {78:14} On the side from which the light of the moon comes forth, she wanes again until all the light vanishes and the days of the month are ended. Her circumference is empty and void of light. {78:15} For three months, she makes thirty days each, and in her time, she makes three months of twenty-nine days each, completing her waning in the first period of time and in the first portal for 177 days. {78:16} In her going out, she appears for three months of thirty days each, and for three months of twenty-nine days each. {78:17} At night, she appears like a man for twenty days each time, and by day she appears like the heaven, with nothing else in her except her light.

{79:1} Now, my son, I have shown you everything, and the law of all the stars of the heaven is complete. {79:2} He showed me all the laws for every day , every season, every year, its going forth, and the order prescribed for it every month and week. {79:3} He showed me the waning of the moon that takes place in the sixth portal: in this sixth portal, her light is accomplished, and after that, the waning begins. {79:4} The waning takes place in the first portal in its season, until 177 days are accomplished, reckoned according to weeks, twenty-five weeks and two days. {79:5} She falls behind the sun and the order of the stars by exactly five days in one period, when this place you see has been traversed. {79:6} Such is the picture and sketch of every luminary which Uriel the archangel, who is their leader, showed to me.

{80:1} And in those days, the angel Uriel answered and said to me: "Behold, I have shown you everything, Enoch, and I have revealed everything to you: the sun, the moon, the leaders of the stars of the heavens, and all those who guide them, their tasks, times, and departures. {80:2} In the days of sinners, the years will be shortened, and their crops will be late in their fields and lands. All things on the earth will change and will not appear at their proper times. The rain will be withheld, and the heavens will hold it back. {80:3} In those times, the fruits of the earth will be delayed and will not grow at their proper times, and the fruits of the trees will be withheld at their proper times. {80:4} The moon will change its order and not appear at its proper time. {80:5} In those days, the sun will be seen, and it will journey in the evening on the edge of the great chariot in the west and will shine more brightly than is fitting for the order of light. {80:6} Many leaders of the stars will transgress the prescribed order, and they will alter their orbits and tasks, and not appear at the times appointed to them. {80:7} The whole order of the stars will be concealed from the sinners, and the thoughts of those on the earth will err concerning them. They will be altered from all their ways, and they will take them to be gods. {80:8} Evil will multiply upon them, and punishment will come upon them to destroy them all."

{81:1} And he said to me: "Observe, Enoch, these heavenly tablets, and read what is written on them, and note every individual fact." {81:2} I observed the heavenly tablets, read everything that was written on them, understood everything, and read the book of all the deeds of mankind and of all the children of flesh that will be upon the earth to the remotest generations. {81:3} I immediately blessed the great Lord, the King of glory forever, for He has made all the works of the world. I extolled the Lord because of His patience and blessed Him because of the children of men. {81:4} After that, I said: "Blessed is the man who dies in righteousness and goodness, concerning whom there is no book of unrighteousness written, and against whom no day of judgment will be found." {81:5} The seven holy ones brought me and placed me on the earth before the door of my house, and said to me: "Declare everything to your son Methuselah, and show all your children that no flesh is righteous in the sight of the Lord, for He is their Creator. {81:6} We will leave you with your son for one year, until you give your last commands, so that you may teach your children and record it for them, and testify to all your children. In the second year, they will take you from their midst. {81:7} Let your heart be strong, for the good will announce righteousness to the good; the righteous with the righteous will rejoice and will offer congratulations to one another. {81:8} But the sinners will die with the sinners, and the apostate will go down with the apostate. {81:9} Those who practice righteousness will die because of the deeds of men and be taken away because of the actions of the godless." {81:10} In those days, they ceased to speak to me, and I came to my people, blessing the Lord of the world.

{82:1} Now, my son Methuselah, I am recounting all these things to you and writing them down for you! I have revealed everything to you and given you books concerning all these matters, so preserve them, my son Methuselah, and deliver them to the generations of the world. {82:2} I have given Wisdom to you and to your children, that they may give it to their children for generations, this wisdom that surpasses their understanding. {82:3} Those who understand it will not sleep but will listen with the ear that they may learn this wisdom, and it will please those who partake of it more than good food. {82:4} Blessed are all the righteous, blessed are all those who walk in the way of righteousness and do not sin like the sinners, in the reckoning of all their days in which the sun traverses the heavens, entering and departing through the portals for thirty days with the leaders of thousands of the order of the stars, along with the four intercalary days which divide the four parts of the year, which lead them and enter with them four days. {82:5} Because of them, men will err and not reckon them in the whole reckoning of the year. Indeed, men will err and not recognize them accurately. {82:6} For they belong to the reckoning of the year and are truly recorded thereon forever, one in the first portal, one in the third, one in the fourth, and one in the sixth, and the year is completed in three hundred and sixty-four days. {82:7} The account thereof is accurate, and the recorded reckoning thereof is exact. For the luminaries, months, festivals, years, and days, Uriel has shown and revealed to me, to whom the Lord of the whole creation of the world has subjected the host of heaven. {82:8} He has power over night and day in the heavens to cause the light to shine upon men: sun, moon, stars, and all the powers of the heavens which revolve in their circular chariots. {82:9} These are the orders of the stars, which set in their places, in their seasons and festivals and months. {82:10} These are the names of those who lead them, who watch that they enter at their times, in their orders, in their seasons, in their months, in their periods of dominion, and in their positions. {82:11} Their four leaders who divide the four parts of the year enter first, and after them the twelve leaders of the orders who divide the months. For the three hundred and sixty days, there are heads over thousands who divide the days, and for the four intercalary days, there are leaders who divide the four parts of the year. {82:12} These heads over thousands are intercalated between leader and leader, each behind a station, but their leaders make the division. {82:13} These are the names of the leaders who divide the four parts of the year which are ordained: Milki'el, Hel'emmelek, Mel'ejal, and Narel. {82:14} The names of those who lead them: Adnar'el, Ijasusa'el, and 'Elomc'el. These three follow the leaders of the orders, and there is one that follows the three leaders of the orders, which follow those leaders of stations that divide the four parts of the year. {82:15} At the beginning of the year, Melkejal rises first and rules, who is named Tam'aini and sun, and all the days of his dominion while he bears rule are ninety-one days. {82:16} These are the signs of the days which are to be seen on earth in the days of his dominion: sweat, heat, and calms; all the trees bear fruit, and leaves are produced on all the trees; the harvest of wheat, the rose-flowers, and all the flowers which come forth in the field, but the trees of the winter season become withered. {82:17} These are the names of the leaders who are under them: Berka'el, Zelebs'el, and another who is added, a head of a thousand, called Hilujaseph. The days of the dominion of this leader are at an end. {82:18} The next leader after him is Hel'emmelek, whom one names the shining sun, and all the days of his light are ninety-one days. {82:19} These are the signs of his days on the earth: glowing heat and dryness, the trees ripen their fruits and produce all their fruits ripe and ready, the sheep pair and become pregnant, and all the fruits of the earth are gathered in, and everything that is in the fields and the winepress. These things take place in the days of his dominion. {82:20} These are the names, the orders, and the leaders of those heads of thousands: Gida'ljal, Ke'el, and He'el, and the name of the head of a thousand which is added to them, Asfa'el. The days of his dominion are at an end.

{83:1} Now, my son Methuselah, I will share with you all the visions I have seen, recounting them before you. {83:2} I saw two visions before I took a wife, and they were quite different from each other. The first occurred while I was learning to write, and the second before I took your mother, when I witnessed a terrible vision. Concerning them, I prayed to the Lord. {83:3} I had lain down in the house of my grandfather Mahalalel when I saw in a vision how the heavens collapsed, were borne off, and fell to the earth. {83:4} When it fell to the earth, I saw how the earth was swallowed up in a great abyss. Mountains were suspended on mountains, hills sank down on hills, and tall trees were torn from their stems and hurled down into the abyss. {83:5} At that moment, a word came into my mouth, and I cried aloud, saying, "The earth is destroyed." {83:6} My grandfather Mahalalel woke me as I lay near him and asked, "Why are you crying so, my son? Why are you making such lamentation?" {83:7} I recounted the entire vision to him, and he said to me, "You have seen a terrible thing, my son. Your dream-vision is of grave importance, revealing the secrets of all the sin of the earth. It must sink into the abyss and be destroyed with great destruction. {83:8} Now, my son, rise and petition the Lord of glory, since you are a believer, that a remnant may remain on the earth, and that He may not destroy the whole earth. {83:9} From heaven, all this will come upon the earth, and there will be great destruction. {83:10} After that, I arose and prayed, implored, and besought, and wrote down my prayer for the generations of the world. I will show everything to you, my son Methuselah. {83:11} And when I had gone forth and observed the heavens, the sun rising in the east, the moon setting in the west, a few stars, and the whole earth as it was known in the beginning, then I blessed the Lord of judgment and extolled Him for making the sun to rise from the windows of the east, ascending and traversing its path.

{84:1} I lifted up my hands in righteousness and blessed the Holy and Great One. I spoke with the breath of my mouth and the tongue of flesh, which God has given to the children of men to speak with. He gave them breath, a tongue, and a mouth to speak. {84:2} Blessed are You, O Lord, King, Great and mighty in Your greatness, Lord of the whole creation of the heavens, King of kings, and God of the whole world. Your power, kingship, and greatness abide forever and ever. Throughout all generations, Your dominion reigns. All the heavens are Your throne forever, and the whole earth is Your footstool forever and ever. {84:3} For You have made and You rule all things, and nothing is too hard for You. Wisdom never departs from the place of Your throne, nor turns away from Your presence. You know, see, and hear everything, and nothing is hidden from You, for You see everything. {84:4} And now, the angels of Your heavens are guilty of trespass, and Your wrath abides upon the flesh of men until the great day of judgment. {84:5} Now, O God, Lord, and Great King, I implore and beseech You to fulfill my prayer, to leave a posterity on earth, and not to destroy all the flesh of man, making the earth uninhabited, leading to eternal destruction. {84:6} And now, my Lord, destroy from the earth the flesh that has aroused Your wrath, but establish the flesh of righteousness and uprightness as a plant of eternal seed. Do not hide Your face from the prayer of Your servant, O Lord.

{85:1} After this, I saw another dream, and I will share the entire dream with you, my son. {85:2} And Enoch lifted up his voice and spoke to his son Methuselah, saying, "I will speak to you, my son; listen to my words. Incline your ear to the dream-vision of your father. {85:3} Before I took your mother Edna, I saw in a vision on my bed a bull coming forth from the earth, and that bull was white. After it came forth, a heifer appeared, followed by two bulls, one black and the other red. {85:4} The black bull gored the red one and chased him over the earth, after which I could no longer see the red bull. {85:5} But the black bull grew, and the heifer went with him. I saw many oxen proceeding from him, resembling and following him. {85:6} The first cow went from the presence of the first bull to seek the red one but could not find him. She lamented greatly over him and sought him. {85:7} I watched until the first bull came to her, comforted her, and from then on, she cried no more. {85:8} After that, she bore another white bull, followed by many bulls and black cows. {85:9} In my dream, I saw that white bull also grow and become a great white bull, from which many white bulls proceeded, resembling him. They began to beget many white bulls, one following the other, and many more.

{86:1} Again, I saw with my own eyes as I slept. I saw the heavens above, and behold, a star fell from heaven, rose, and grazed among those oxen. {86:2} After that, I saw the large and black oxen, and behold, they all changed their stalls, pastures, and their cattle. They began to live with each other. {86:3} Once more, I saw in the vision and looked toward heaven. I saw many stars descending and casting themselves down from heaven to that first star, becoming bulls among those cattle and grazing with them. {86:4} I looked and saw that they all let out their privy members like horses and began to cover the cows of the oxen. They all became pregnant and bore elephants, camels, and asses. {86:5} All the oxen feared them and were terrified, biting with their teeth, devouring, and goring with their horns. They even began to devour those oxen. All the children of the earth trembled and quaked before them, fleeing from them.

{87:1} I saw them gore and devour each other, and the earth cried out. {87:2} I looked to heaven and saw beings like white men come forth; four came first, then three more. {87:3} The last three grasped my hand and lifted me to a high place, showing me a tower above all the hills. {87:4} One said, 'Stay here and witness what happens to the elephants, camels, asses, stars, oxen, and all of them.'

{88:1} I witnessed one of those four beings who had come forth first. He seized the first star that had fallen from heaven, bound it hand and foot, and cast it into a narrow, deep, horrible, and dark abyss. {88:2} Another one of them drew a sword and gave it to the elephants, camels, and asses. They began to strike each other, causing the entire earth to quake. {88:3} While I watched in the vision, one of those four beings stoned them from heaven. They gathered and took all the great stars whose privy members were like those of horses. They bound them hand and foot and cast them into an abyss of the earth.

{89:1} One of those four beings approached the white bull and shared a secret with him, without causing fear. This bull, originally born as a bull, became a man, built a great vessel, and dwelt in it with three other bulls. They were all safely covered inside. {89:2} Then, I looked up to heaven again and saw a lofty roof with seven water torrents flowing onto an enclosure. {89:3} Fountains opened on the surface of the enclosure, and water began to swell and cover it entirely. The darkness and mist increased, and the water rose above the enclosure, flooding the earth. All the cattle gathered there sank and perished in the water. {89:4} The water continued to rise until it covered even the highest point of the enclosure and streamed over it, standing upon the earth. {89:5} Every creature within the enclosure, including oxen, elephants, camels, and asses, sank to the bottom and perished, except for the bull who had become a man, along with the three bulls, who floated safely in their vessel. {89:6} As the vessel floated, all the other animals sank to the bottom, unable to escape the depths of the water. {89:7} I watched until the water torrents were removed from the high roof, and the earth's chasms were filled while new abysses opened up. {89:8} The water then began to flow into these new abysses, gradually revealing the earth. The vessel settled on the earth, darkness retreated, and light appeared once more. {89:9} The white bull who had become a man, along with the three other bulls, emerged from the vessel. One of the three bulls was white like the man-bull, one was red as blood, and one was black. The white bull departed from them. {89:10} They began to produce different kinds of animals, such as lions, tigers, wolves, dogs, hyenas, wild boars, foxes, squirrels, swine, falcons, vultures, kites, eagles, and ravens. Among them, a white bull was born. {89:11} These animals started to fight among themselves. The white bull, born among them, produced a wild ass and another white bull. The wild asses multiplied. {89:12} The offspring of the white bull begat a black wild boar and a white sheep. The boar produced many more boars, and the sheep gave birth to twelve sheep. {89:13} As the twelve sheep grew, one was given to the wild asses, which then gave it to the wolves. This sheep grew among the wolves. {89:14} The Lord intervened, bringing the eleven sheep to live among the wolves, where they multiplied and formed many flocks. {89:15} The wolves began to oppress them, even devouring their young, but the sheep cried out to the Lord. {89:16} A sheep escaped and sought refuge with the wild asses. Seeing the distress of the sheep, the Lord descended and pastured them Himself. {89:17} He instructed the escaped sheep to admonish the wolves not to harm the flock. {89:18} The sheep obeyed, entering the assembly of the wolves and warning them. But the wolves continued to oppress the sheep greatly. {89:19} The Lord intervened, and the sheep fought back against the wolves, causing them to lament. The sheep ceased crying out. {89:20} The Lord empowered the sheep, and they fought off the wolves, who then fled. {89:21} The wolves pursued the sheep until they reached a sea. The sea divided, and the sheep passed through safely while the wolves perished. {89:22} The Lord led the sheep, shining with a dazzling and terrifying presence. {89:23} The wolves continued to pursue the sheep until they reached a sea. {89:24} The sea parted, allowing the sheep to pass through while drowning the pursuing wolves. {89:25} As the wolves approached, they turned to flee but found themselves trapped as the sea closed over them. {89:26} The sheep, saved from the water, entered a barren wilderness. There, the Lord pastured them, providing water and grass. {89:27} He ascended a lofty rock, and the Lord sent another sheep to lead them. {89:28} The sheep trembled before the Lord, fearing His great and majestic presence. {89:29} They cried out to the sheep amongst them, unable to stand before the Lord. {89:30} The sheep ascended the rock again, but many of the sheep were blinded and wandered away from the path the sheep showed them. {89:31} The Lord was angry at their disobedience, and the sheep discovered His wrath. {89:32} The sheep descended from the rock and found many blinded and fallen away. {89:33} The Lord was wrathful against them, and the sheep realized their error. {89:34} The sheep returned those fallen away to their folds, slaying those who resisted. {89:35} One sheep, eventually, became a man and built a house for the Lord of the sheep, where he placed all the sheep. {89:36} The sheep, who had met the leading sheep, fell asleep. {89:37} The sheep were replaced by others, and they found pasture in a pleasant land, with the house standing among them. {89:38} At times, their eyes were opened, and they saw the way, but other times they were blinded. {89:39} Another sheep arose to lead them back when they strayed. {89:40} Dogs, foxes, and wild boars began to attack the sheep, but a ram arose from among them and defeated them all. {89:41} The ram began to lead the sheep, protecting them from their enemies. {89:42} However, the ram, once glorious, turned against the sheep, but the Lord raised another sheep to lead them. {89:43} The first ram pursued the second, but the second ram overcame it. {89:44} The second ram led the little sheep, and they multiplied. {89:45} The house of the sheep grew and became great, with a tower built for the Lord of the sheep. {89:46} The sheep began to err and forsake their house, and the Lord sent some to call them back, but the sheep turned against them. {89:47} One was saved from slaughter, and the Lord brought it to safety. {89:48} Many other sheep were sent to testify to them, but they remained stubborn. {89:49} The Lord allowed them to fall into the hands of wild beasts, who devoured them. {89:50} Seventy shepherds were appointed to care for the sheep, but they abused their authority. {89:51} The shepherds slaughtered more sheep than commanded, delivering them to the lions. {89:52} The one who wrote the book recorded their deeds and presented them before the Lord. {89:53} The book was read before the Lord, who sealed it and laid it down. {89:54} Afterward, I witnessed the sheep completely forsaking the house of the Lord and His tower. Their eyes were blinded, and they fell away entirely. I saw the Lord of the sheep allowing much slaughter among them in their herds until the sheep themselves invited this destruction and betrayed their place. {89:55} The Lord handed them over to lions, tigers, wolves, hyenas, foxes, and all kinds of wild beasts, who tore the sheep apart. {89:56} He abandoned their house and tower, giving them into the hands of lions to tear and devour, as well as into the hands of all the wild beasts. {89:57} I cried out loudly, appealing to the Lord of the sheep, representing to Him that the sheep were being devoured by wild beasts. {89:58} However, He remained unmoved, even though He saw what was happening, and He seemed to rejoice in their destruction, allowing them to be devoured, swallowed, and robbed by the beasts. {89:59} Then, He appointed seventy shepherds and entrusted the sheep to them for pasturing. He instructed the shepherds and their companions to follow His commands diligently. {89:60} He gave them the sheep, and He instructed another to observe and record everything the shepherds did, whether according to His command or their own whims. {89:61} Every action and destruction caused by the shepherds was to be meticulously recorded against each one, without their knowledge. {89:62} The record was to be presented before Him, serving as testimony against the shepherds, revealing whether they followed His commands or not. {89:63} I saw the shepherds pasturing the sheep, but they began to slaughter and destroy more than commanded, delivering the sheep into the hands of lions. {89:64} The lions, tigers, and wild boars devoured most of the sheep, burning the tower and destroying the house. {89:65} I was deeply saddened by the destruction of the tower and the sheep's house, and I could no longer see if the sheep entered that house. {89:66} The shepherds and their associates handed the sheep {89:67} over to all the wild beasts to devour. {89:68} Each shepherd exceeded the prescribed limit and destroyed many more sheep than permitted. {89:69} I began to weep and lament for the sheep. {89:70} In the vision, I saw the one who recorded everything in the book, detailing every destruction caused by the shepherds day by day. He presented the book before the Lord of the sheep, showing Him all the deeds of the shepherds. {89:71} The Lord read the book, sealed it, and laid it down. {89:72} Immediately afterward, I saw three sheep return and start to rebuild the fallen house. The wild boars attempted to hinder them but failed. {89:73} They rebuilt the tower, calling it the high tower, and set up a table before it. However, the food on the table was polluted and impure. {89:74} The sheep's eyes were blinded, as were those of their shepherds. The shepherds delivered the sheep to destruction, trampling and devouring them. {89:75} The Lord of the sheep remained unmoved until all the sheep were scattered and mingled with the beasts, and the shepherds did not save them from the beasts' hands. {89:76} The one who wrote the book presented it before the Lord, imploring Him on behalf of the sheep and testifying against the shepherds. {89:77} He laid down the book before the Lord and departed.

{90:1} I observed thirty-five shepherds taking turns to pasture the sheep, each completing their appointed period as the first had done. Others succeeded them, continuing to shepherd the sheep during their respective periods. {90:2} Then, in my vision, I saw all the birds of the sky—eagles, vultures, kites, and ravens—descending upon the sheep. The eagles led the attack, devouring the sheep, pecking out their eyes, and consuming their flesh. {90:3} The sheep cried out in agony as the birds devoured them, and I, witnessing this in my sleep, lamented over the shepherd who was supposed to care for the sheep. {90:4} I saw the dogs, eagles, and kites further decimate the sheep until nothing remained but their bones, which eventually fell to the ground. The once numerous sheep became few. {90:5} I observed twenty-three shepherds taking their turns, completing their appointed periods a total of fifty-eight times. {90:6} Amidst this devastation, lambs were born to the white sheep. These lambs began to open their eyes and cry out to the sheep for help. {90:7} They pleaded with the sheep, but the sheep remained deaf and blind to their cries. {90:8} Ravens swooped down on the lambs, seizing one and tearing the others apart, devouring them. {90:9} Eventually, horns grew on the lambs, but the ravens knocked them down. Then, a great horn sprouted from one of the sheep, and its eyes were opened. {90:10} It looked at the sheep, and its cry stirred the rams, who all ran to its aid. {90:11} Despite this, the eagles, vultures, ravens, and kites continued their relentless assault, tearing and devouring the sheep, while the rams lamented and cried out. {90:12} The ravens fought against the sheep and attempted to break the horn, but they were powerless against it. {90:13} Then, the shepherds, eagles, vultures, and kites joined forces to break the horn of the ram, battling against it as it cried out for help. {90:14} The man who recorded the names of the shepherds and presented them before the Lord of the sheep assisted the ram. {90:15} Then, I witnessed the Lord of the sheep coming in wrath, causing all who saw Him to flee and fall into His shadow. {90:16} All the birds of prey, along with the sheep of the field, united to break the ram's horn. {90:17} The man who wrote the book according to the Lord's command opened it to reveal the destruction caused by the twelve shepherds, showing how they exceeded their predecessors' deeds before the Lord. {90:18} The Lord of the sheep took the staff of His wrath and struck the earth, causing it to split open. All the beasts and birds fell into the earth's depths and were swallowed up by it. {90:19} At that moment, a great sword was given to the sheep, and they proceeded to slay all the beasts of the field and birds of the sky, causing them to flee. {90:20} A throne was then erected in the pleasant land, and the Lord of the sheep sat upon it. The sealed books were opened before Him. {90:21} The Lord summoned the seven first white ones and ordered them to bring before Him all the stars whose forms resembled horses' privy members. {90:22} He instructed the man among the seven white ones to take the seventy shepherds to whom He had entrusted the sheep and who had exceeded their authority by killing more sheep than commanded. {90:23} I saw them all bound and standing before Him. {90:24} The judgment began with the stars, who were found guilty and cast into a fiery abyss. {90:25} Similarly, the seventy shepherds were judged and condemned to the fiery abyss. {90:26} Then, an abyss opened in the midst of the earth, filled with fire. The blinded sheep were judged, found guilty, and cast into the fiery abyss to burn. {90:27} I witnessed the sheep burning, their bones consumed by the fire. {90:28} I watched as the old house was folded up, its pillars, beams, and ornaments taken away and placed in the south of the land. {90:29} Then, the Lord of the sheep brought forth a new, larger house, setting it up in place of the old one. The sheep were all within this new house. {90:30} All the remaining sheep, beasts, and birds paid homage to the sheep, submitting to and obeying them in all things. {90:31} The three figures clothed in white, who had taken me by the hand, and the ram, lifted me up and placed me among the sheep before the judgment began. {90:32} These sheep were all white, with abundant and clean wool. {90:33} All that had been destroyed and scattered, along with all the beasts and birds, gathered in that house, bringing great joy to the Lord of the sheep. {90:34} The sword given to the sheep was returned to the house, sealed in the presence of the Lord. Although all the sheep were invited into the house, it could not contain them. {90:35} The eyes of all the sheep were opened, and they saw the good. There was not one among them who did not see. {90:36} I observed that the house was large, broad, and very full. {90:37} A white bull was born, with large horns, and all the beasts and birds feared him, constantly seeking his favor. {90:38} Eventually, all their generations were transformed into white bulls. The first among them became a lamb, which grew into a great animal with large black horns on its head. The Lord of the sheep rejoiced over it and all the oxen. {90:39} I slept among them, and upon awakening, I remembered the vision. I blessed the Lord of righteousness and gave Him glory. {90:40} Tears streamed down my face as I wept profusely, unable to contain my emotions upon recalling the vision. Everything shown to me would come to pass, as all the deeds of humanity were revealed to me in their order. {90:41} That night, I remembered the first dream, wept, and was troubled by its profound impact.

{91:1} Now, my son Methuselah, call all your brothers and gather all the children of your mother to me. For the word has called me, and the spirit has been poured out upon me, so I can reveal to you everything that will happen to you forever. {91:2} So Methuselah went and summoned all his brothers and gathered his relatives. {91:3} He spoke to all the children of righteousness and said: 'Listen, you sons of Enoch, to all the words of your father, and pay close attention to my voice. I urge you and say, my beloved: {91:4} Love righteousness and follow it. Do not approach righteousness with a divided heart, and do not associate with those who have a divided heart. Walk in righteousness, my sons, and it will guide you along good paths, and righteousness will be your constant companion. {91:5} For I know that violence will increase on the earth, and there will be a great punishment executed on the earth, and all unrighteousness will come to an end. It will be cut off from its roots, and its entire structure will be destroyed. {91:6} Unrighteousness will reappear on the earth, and all acts of unrighteousness, violence, and transgression will double in degree. {91:7} When sin, unrighteousness, blasphemy, and all forms of violence increase, along with apostasy, transgression, and uncleanness, a great punishment will come from heaven. The holy Lord will come with wrath and chastisement to judge the earth. {91:8} In those days, violence will be eradicated from its roots, and the roots of unrighteousness and deceit will be destroyed from under heaven. {91:9} All the idols of the heathen will be abandoned, their temples burned with fire, and they will be removed from the earth. The heathen will face judgment by fire, perishing in wrath and severe judgment forever. {91:10} The righteous will awaken from their sleep, and wisdom will rise and be given to them. After that, the roots of unrighteousness will be cut off, and sinners will be destroyed by the sword. Those who commit blasphemy and plan violence will perish by the sword. {91:18} Now I tell you, my sons, and show you the paths of righteousness and the paths of violence. I will show them to you again so you will know what is to come. {91:19} So listen to me, my sons, and walk in the paths of righteousness. Do not follow the paths of violence, for all who walk in unrighteous ways will perish forever.'

{92:1} "This book was written by Enoch—indeed, Enoch wrote this complete doctrine of wisdom, praised by all people and serving as a judge of all the earth—for all my children who will dwell on the earth, and for future generations who will uphold uprightness and peace. {92:2} "Do not let your spirit be troubled because of the times, for the Holy and Great One has appointed days for all things. {92:3} "The righteous one shall arise from sleep and walk in the paths of righteousness. His entire path and conduct shall be characterized by eternal goodness and grace. {92:4} "He will show kindness to the righteous and grant him eternal uprightness. He will empower him with goodness and righteousness, and he will walk in eternal light. {92:5} "Sin shall perish in darkness forever, and it shall never be seen again from that day onward."

{93:1} And then Enoch began to give and recount from the books. {93:2} He said: "Regarding the children of righteousness and the chosen ones of the world, And concerning the seed of uprightness, I will speak these things. Yes, I, Enoch, will declare them to you, my sons: As revealed to me in heavenly visions, And as I have learned from the words of the holy angels, And as I have read from the heavenly tablets." {93:3} Enoch began to recount from the books and said: "I was born in the seventh generation of the first week, When judgement and righteousness still prevailed. {93:4} "After me, in the second week, great wickedness will arise, And deceit will spring up; And in that week shall come the first end. But a man shall be saved from it; And after it ends, unrighteousness will increase, And a law will be made for the sinners. {93:5} "Then, in the third week, at its conclusion, A man shall be chosen as the seed of righteous judgement, And his descendants shall become the seed of righteousness forevermore. {93:6} "Following that, in the fourth week, at its conclusion, Visions of the holy and righteous shall be revealed, And a law shall be established for all generations, along with a sanctuary for them. {93:7} "And after that, in the fifth week, at its conclusion, The house of glory and dominion shall be built for eternity. {93:8} "Then, in the sixth week, those who inhabit it shall be blinded, And the hearts of all of them shall forsake wisdom in godless ways. Yet, a man shall ascend; And when the week concludes, the house of dominion shall be burned with fire, And the entire lineage of the chosen ones shall be scattered. {93:9} "Following that, in the seventh week, an apostate generation shall arise, And their deeds shall be many, All of which shall be apostate. {93:10} "At its conclusion, the righteous elect of the eternal seed of righteousness shall be chosen, To receive sevenfold instruction regarding all of His creation. {93:11} "For who among all humankind can hear the voice of the Holy One without being troubled? Who can comprehend His thoughts? Who can behold all the works of heaven? {93:12} Who can understand the depths of heaven, see a soul or a spirit, ascend to witness their ends, comprehend them, or imitate them? {93:13} Who can measure the breadth and length of the earth, and to whom has the measure of all things been revealed? {93:14} Is there anyone who can fathom the expanse of heaven, its immense height, its foundation, the multitude of stars, and the resting places of all the luminaries?"

{94:1} Now I say to you, my sons, love righteousness and walk in it; For the paths of righteousness are worthy of acceptance, But the paths of unrighteousness shall suddenly be destroyed and vanish. {94:2} Certain men of a generation will be shown the paths of violence and death, And they shall keep themselves far from them, And shall not follow them. {94:3} To you, the righteous, I say: Do not walk in the paths of wickedness or death, And do not draw near to them, lest you be destroyed. {94:4} Instead, seek and choose righteousness and a life of virtue, And walk in the paths of peace, And you shall live and prosper. {94:5} Hold fast to my words in your hearts, And do not let them be erased from your minds; For I know that sinners will tempt others to mistreat wisdom, So that no place may be found for her, And no temptation may diminish her. {94:6} Woe to those who build unrighteousness and oppression And lay deceit as their foundation; For they shall be suddenly overthrown, And they shall find no peace. {94:7} Woe to those who build their houses with sin; For they shall be overthrown from their foundations, And they shall fall by the sword. [And those who acquire gold and silver unjustly shall suddenly perish.] {94:8} Woe to you, the wealthy, for you have trusted in your riches, And from your riches you shall depart, Because you have not remembered the Most High in the days of your prosperity. {94:9} You have committed blasphemy and unrighteousness, And have become prepared for the day of slaughter, And the day of darkness and the great judgement. {94:10} Thus I speak and declare to you: He who created you will overthrow you, And for your downfall there shall be no pity, And your Creator will rejoice at your destruction. {94:11} In those days, your righteous ones shall be A reproach to the sinners and the godless.

{95:1} Oh, that my eyes were a flood of waters So that I could weep over you, And pour down my tears like a flood of waters, So that I might find rest from my troubled heart! {95:2} Who has allowed you to speak reproachfully and act wickedly? Thus, judgement shall overtake you, sinners. {95:3} Fear not the sinners, you righteous ones; For the Lord will deliver them into your hands once again, So that you may judge them according to your desires. {95:4} Woe to those who pronounce curses that cannot be undone: Therefore, healing shall be far from you because of your sins. {95:5} Woe to those who repay their neighbors with evil; For you shall be repaid according to your deeds. {95:6} Woe to you, false witnesses, And to those who deal in injustice, For you shall suddenly perish. {95:7} Woe to you, sinners, for you persecute the righteous; For you shall be delivered up and persecuted for your injustice, And its yoke shall be heavy upon you.

{96:1} Be hopeful, you righteous ones, for the sinners shall suddenly perish before you, And you shall have dominion over them according to your desires. {96:2} And on the day of the tribulation of the sinners, Your children shall rise up like eagles, And your nest shall be higher than the vultures, And you shall ascend and enter the crevices of the earth, And the clefts of the rock forever, like rabbits before the unrighteous, And the sirens shall lament because of you—and weep. {96:3} Therefore, do not fear, you who have suffered; For healing shall be your portion, And a bright light shall illuminate you, And you shall hear the voice of rest from heaven. {96:4} Woe to you, sinners, for your riches make you appear righteous, But your hearts convict you of being sinners, And this fact shall be a testimony against you for your evil deeds. {96:5} Woe to those who consume the finest of wheat, And drink wine from large bowls, And trample the lowly with your might. {96:6} Woe to those who drink water from every fountain, For you shall be consumed and wither away suddenly, Because you have forsaken the fountain of life. {96:7} Woe to those who practice unrighteousness, Deceit, and blasphemy: It shall be a testimony against you for evil. {96:8} Woe to you, the mighty, Who oppress the righteous with your might; For the day of your destruction is coming. In those days, many and good days shall come to the righteous in the day of their judgement.

{97:1} Believe, you righteous ones, that the sinners will become a disgrace And perish in the day of unrighteousness. {97:2} Know that the Most High remembers your destruction, And the angels of heaven rejoice over your demise. {97:3} What will you do, you sinners, And where will you flee on that day of judgement, When you hear the prayers of the righteous? {97:4} You shall fare like those against whom this word shall be a testimony: "You have been companions of sinners." {97:5} In those days, the prayers of the righteous shall reach the Lord, And for you, the days of judgement shall come. {97:6} And all your unrighteous deeds shall be read out before the Great Holy One, And your faces shall be covered with shame, And He will reject every work that is founded on unrighteousness. {97:7} Woe to you, sinners, who dwell in the midst of the ocean and on dry land, Whose memory is evil against you. {97:8} Woe to those who acquire silver and gold unjustly and say: "We have become rich with wealth and possessions; And we have obtained everything we desired. {97:9} "And now let us do what we have planned: For we have gathered silver, And there are many laborers in our houses." {97:10} And like water, your lies shall flow away; For your riches shall not remain But shall swiftly depart from you; For you have obtained it all unjustly, And you shall be subjected to a great curse.

{98:1} And now I swear to both the wise and the foolish among you, For you shall have diverse experiences on the earth. {98:2} Men shall adorn themselves more than women, And wear colorful garments more than virgins: In royalty, grandeur, power, And in silver, gold, and purple, And they shall indulge in splendor and feasting as abundantly as water. {98:3} Consequently, they shall lack in knowledge and wisdom, And they shall perish along with their possessions; And despite all their glory and splendor, In shame, slaughter, and great poverty, Their spirits shall be cast into the furnace of fire. {98:4} I have sworn to you, sinners, as a mountain has not become a slave, And a hill does not become the servant of a woman, Likewise, sin has not been imposed upon the earth, But man has created it himself, And those who commit it shall fall under a great curse. {98:5} Barrenness has not been given to women, But due to their own deeds, they die without children. {98:6} I swear to you, sinners, by the Holy Great One, That all your evil deeds are revealed in the heavens, And none of your oppressive actions are concealed or hidden. {98:7} Do not think in your hearts or say in your minds that you do not know or see that every sin is recorded daily in heaven in the presence of the Most High. {98:8} Henceforth, know that all your oppression is documented every day until the day of your judgement. {98:9} Woe to you, fools, for your folly will lead to your destruction; you transgress against the wise, and therefore good fortune will not be your portion. {98:10} And now, know that you are prepared for the day of destruction; therefore, do not expect to live, sinners, for you shall depart and die; for you know no ransom; you are prepared for the day of the great judgement, for the day of tribulation and great shame for your spirits. {98:11} Woe to you, obstinate of heart, who engage in wickedness and consume blood: Where do you obtain good things to eat, drink, and be satisfied? From all the good things that the Lord, the Most High, has abundantly placed on the earth; therefore, you shall have no peace. {98:12} Woe to you who love the deeds of unrighteousness: Why do you hope for good fortune for yourselves? Know that you shall be delivered into the hands of the righteous, and they shall cut off your necks and slay you without mercy. {98:13} Woe to you who rejoice in the suffering of the righteous; for no grave shall be dug for you. {98:14} Woe to you who disregard the words of the righteous; for you shall have no hope of life. {98:15} Woe to you who write down lying and godless words; for they write down their lies so that others may hear them and act wickedly towards their neighbors. {98:16} Therefore, they shall have no peace but die a sudden death.

{99:1} Woe to you who practice godlessness, And boast in lies and praise them: You shall perish, and no happy life shall be yours. {99:2} Woe to those who distort the words of righteousness, And violate the eternal law, And transform themselves into sinners: They shall be trodden underfoot on the earth. {99:3} In those days, prepare yourselves, O righteous ones, to lift up your prayers as a memorial, And present them as a testimony before the angels, So that they may record the sins of the sinners before the Most High. {99:4} In those days, nations shall be stirred up, And the families of nations shall rise on the day of destruction. {99:5} And in those days, the destitute shall depart and take away their children, And they shall abandon them, causing their children to perish: Indeed, they shall forsake even their suckling infants, showing them no pity, And they shall not return to them, Having no compassion for their loved ones. {99:6} Once again, I swear to you, sinners, that sin is prepared for a day of unceasing bloodshed. {99:7} And those who worship stones and idols of gold, silver, wood, and clay, and those who worship impure spirits and demons, and all kinds of idols without knowledge, shall receive no help from them. {99:8} They shall become godless due to the folly of their hearts, And their eyes shall be blinded by fear, And through visions in their dreams, They shall become godless and fearful; For they have performed all their deeds in falsehood, And they have worshipped stones: {99:9} Therefore, they shall perish in an instant. {99:10} But in those days, blessed are all those who accept the words of wisdom and understand them, And follow the paths of the Most High's righteousness, And do not become godless like the godless; For they shall be saved. {99:11} Woe to you who spread evil among your neighbors; For you shall be slain in Sheol. {99:12} Woe to you who use deceitful and false measures, And those who cause bitterness on the earth; For they shall be utterly consumed by their actions. {99:13} Woe to you who build your houses with the toil of others, And all their building materials are the bricks and stones of sin; I tell you, you shall have no peace. {99:14} Woe to those who reject the measure and eternal heritage of their fathers, And whose souls follow after idols; For they shall find no rest. {99:15} Woe to those who work unrighteousness and aid oppression, And slay their neighbors until the day of the great judgement. {99:16} For He shall cast down their glory, And bring affliction upon their hearts, And He shall arouse His fierce indignation, And destroy them all with the sword; And all the holy and righteous shall remember their sins.

{100:1} In those days, fathers and sons shall be struck down together, And brothers shall fall to death by each other's hand, Until the streams are stained with their blood. {100:2} For a man shall not refrain from killing his sons and grandsons, And sinners shall not spare their honored brothers: From dawn until sunset, they shall slaughter one another. {100:3} The horses shall wade through blood up to their chests, And the chariots shall be submerged up to their axles. {100:4} In those days, the angels shall descend to hidden places And gather together all those who have brought sin, And the Most High will arise on the day of judgement To execute great judgement among sinners. {100:5} Over the righteous and holy, He will appoint guardians from among the holy angels To protect them as the apple of His eye, Until He puts an end to all wickedness and sin, And even though the righteous may sleep long, they have nothing to fear. {100:6} Then the people of the earth shall see the wise living in safety, And they shall understand all the words of this book, And realize that their riches cannot save them From the consequences of their sins. {100:7} Woe to you, sinners, on the day of great anguish, You who afflict the righteous and burn them with fire: You shall be repaid according to your deeds. {100:8} Woe to you, stubborn of heart, Who watch to devise wickedness: Fear shall come upon you, And there shall be none to help you. {100:9} Woe to you, sinners, because of the words you speak, And because of the deeds your godlessness has wrought, In blazing flames worse than fire shall you burn. {100:10} And now, know that the angels will inquire about your deeds in heaven, from the sun, moon, and stars, regarding your sins, as you execute judgement upon the righteous on earth. {100:11} And every cloud, mist, dew, and rain will be summoned to testify against you; for they shall all be withheld from descending upon you because of your sins, and they shall remember your transgressions. {100:12} Therefore, give offerings to the rain so that it will not be withheld from descending upon you, and to the dew, when it has received gold and silver from you, so that it may descend. {100:13} In those days, when the frost and snow with their cold, and all the snowstorms with their plagues fall upon you, you shall not be able to withstand them.

{101:1} Observe the heavens, you children of the heavens, and every work of the Most High, and fear Him, and do no evil in His presence. {101:2} If He closes the windows of heaven and withholds the rain and the dew from descending on the earth because of you, what will you do then? {101:3} And if He sends His anger upon you because of your deeds, you cannot plead with Him; for you have spoken proud and insolent words against His righteousness: therefore, you shall have no peace. {101:4} Do you not see the sailors of the ships, how their ships are tossed to and fro by the waves, and are shaken by the winds, and are in great trouble? {101:5} And they fear because all their precious possessions go upon the sea with them, and they have evil forebodings in their hearts that the sea will swallow them and they will perish therein. {101:6} Is not the entire sea and all its waters, and all its movements, the work of the Most High, and has He not set limits to its actions, and confined it with sand? {101:7} And when He rebukes it, it is afraid and dries up, and all its fish die, and all that is in it; But you sinners on the earth do not fear Him. {101:8} Has He not made the heavens and the earth, and all that is therein? Who has given understanding and wisdom to everything that moves on the earth and in the sea. {101:9} Do not the sailors of the ships fear the sea? Yet sinners do not fear the Most High.

{102:1} In those days, when He brings a severe fire upon you, where will you flee, and where will you find deliverance? And when He releases His Word against you, will you not be frightened and fearful? {102:2} And all the luminaries shall be filled with great fear, and the whole earth shall tremble and be alarmed. {102:3} And all the angels shall execute their commands and shall seek to hide themselves from the presence of the Great Glory, and the children of earth shall tremble and quake; and you sinners shall be cursed forever, and you shall have no peace. {102:4} Do not fear, you souls of the righteous, and have hope, you who have died in righteousness. {102:5} And do not grieve if your soul descends into Sheol in sorrow, and if your body did not fare according to your goodness in life, but wait for the day of judgement of sinners and for the day of cursing and chastisement. {102:6} Yet when you die, sinners speak over you: "As we die, so do the righteous, and what benefit do they gain from their deeds? {102:7} Look, they die in sorrow and darkness, just like us, and what advantage do they have over us? From now on, we are equal. {102:8} And what will they receive, and what will they see forever? Look, they too have died, and from now on, they shall see no light." {102:9} I tell you, sinners, you are content

{103:1} Now, therefore, I swear to you, the righteous, by the glory of the Great and Honored and Mighty One in dominion, and by His greatness I swear to you. {103:2} I know a mystery, and I have read the heavenly tablets, and I have seen the holy books, and I have found written therein and inscribed regarding them: {103:3} That all goodness, joy, and glory are prepared for them, and written down for the spirits of those who have died in righteousness, and that manifold good shall be given to you in recompense for your labors, and that your lot is abundantly beyond the lot of the living. {103:4} And the spirits of you who have died in righteousness shall live and rejoice, and their spirits shall not perish, nor their memory from before the face of the Great One, unto all the generations of the world; therefore, no longer fear their contempt. {103:5} Woe to you, sinners, when you have died, if you die in the wealth of your sins, and those who are like you say regarding you: 'Blessed are the sinners: they have seen all their days. {103:6} And how they have died in prosperity and in wealth, and have not seen tribulation or murder in their life; and they have died in honor, and judgment has not been executed on them during their life." {103:7} Know that their souls will be made to descend into Sheol, and they shall be wretched in their great tribulation. {103:8} And into darkness, chains, and a burning flame, where there is grievous judgment, shall your spirits enter; and the great judgment shall be for all the generations of the world. Woe to you, for you shall have no peace. {103:9} Say not in regard to the righteous and good who are alive: "In our troubled days we have toiled laboriously and experienced every trouble, and met with much evil and been consumed, and have become few, and our spirit small. {103:10} And we have been destroyed and have not found any to help us even with a word: We have been tortured [and destroyed], and did not hope to see life from day to day. {103:11} We hoped to be the head and have become the tail: We have toiled laboriously and had no satisfaction in our toil; and we have become the food of the sinners and the unrighteous, and they have laid their yoke heavily upon us. {103:12} They have had dominion over us, hated us, and smote us; and to those who hated us, we have bowed our necks, but they pitied us not. {103:13} We desired to get away from them that we might escape and be at rest, but found no place whereunto we should flee and be safe from them. {103:14} And we complained to the rulers in our tribulation, and cried out against those who devoured us, but they did not attend to our cries and would not hearken to our voice. {103:15} And they helped those who robbed us and devoured us, and those who made us few; and they concealed their oppression, and did not remove from us the yoke of those who devoured us and dispersed us and murdered us, and they concealed their murder, and remembered not that they had lifted up their hands against us.

{104:1} I swear unto you, that in heaven the angels remember you for good before the glory of the Great One: and your names are written before the glory of the Great One. {104:2} Be hopeful; for aforetime ye were put to shame through ill and affliction; but now ye shall shine as the lights of heaven, ye shall shine and ye shall be seen, and the portals of heaven shall be opened to you. {104:3} And in your cry, cry for judgement, and it shall appear to you; for all your tribulation shall be visited on the rulers, and on all who helped those who plundered you. {104:4} Be hopeful, and cast not away your hopes for ye shall have great joy as the angels of heaven. {104:5} What shall ye be obliged to do ? Ye shall not have to hide on the day of the great judgement and ye shall not be found as sinners, and the eternal judgement shall be far from you for all the generations of the world. {104:6} And now fear not, ye righteous, when ye see the sinners growing strong and prospering in their ways: be not companions with them, but keep afar from their violence; for ye shall become companions of the hosts of heaven. {104:7} And, although ye sinners say: "All our sins shall not be searched out and be written down," nevertheless they shall write down all your sins every day. {104:8} And now I show unto you that light and darkness, day and night, see all your sins. {104:9} Be not godless in your hearts, and lie not and alter not the words of uprightness, nor charge with lying the words of the Holy Great One, nor take account of your idols; for all your lying and all your godlessness issue not in righteousness but in great sin. {104:10} And now I know this mystery, that sinners will alter and pervert the words of righteousness in many ways, and will speak wicked words, and lie, and practice great deceits, and write books concerning their words. {104:11} But when they write down truthfully all my words in their languages, and do not change or diminish aught from my words, but write them all down truthfully -all that I first testified concerning them. {104:12} Then, I know another mystery, that books will be given to the righteous and the wise to become a cause of joy and uprightness and much wisdom. {104:13} And to them shall the books be given, and they shall believe in them and rejoice over them, and then shall all the righteous who have learned therefrom all the paths of uprightness be recompensed.'

{105:1} In those days, the Lord commanded them to summon and testify to the children of earth concerning their wisdom: Show it unto them; for you are their guides, and a recompense over the whole earth. {105:2} For I and My son will be united with them forever in the paths of uprightness in their lives; and you shall have peace: rejoice, you children of uprightness.

{106:1} And after some days, my son Methuselah took a wife for his son Lamech, and she became pregnant by him and bore a son. {106:2} And his body was white as snow and red as the blooming of a rose, and the hair of his head and his long locks were white as wool, and his eyes beautiful. And when he opened his eyes, he lit up the whole house like the sun, and the entire house was very bright. {106:3} And then he arose in the hands of the midwife, opened his mouth, and conversed with the Lord of righteousness. {106:4} And his father Lamech was afraid of him and fled, and came to his father Methuselah. {106:5} And he said to him: 'I have begotten a strange son, different from and unlike man, resembling the sons of the God of heaven; and his nature is different, not like ours, and his eyes are like the rays of the sun, and his countenance is glorious. {106:6} And it seems to me that he is not sprung from me but from the angels, and I fear that in his days a wonder may be wrought on the earth. {106:7} And now, my father, I am here to ask you and implore you to go to Enoch, our father, and learn from him the truth, for his dwelling-place is among the angels.' {106:8} And when Methuselah heard the words of his son, he came to me at the ends of the earth; for he had heard that I was there, and he cried aloud, and I heard his voice, and I came to him. And I said to him: 'Behold, here am I, my son, why have you come to me?' {106:9} And he answered and said: 'Because of a great cause of anxiety have I come to you, and because of a disturbing vision have I approached. {106:10} And now, my father, hear me: to Lamech my son there has been born a son, the like of whom there is none, and his nature is not like man's nature, and the color of his body is whiter than snow and redder than the bloom of a rose, and the hair of his head is whiter than white wool, and his eyes are like the rays of the sun, and he opened his eyes and thereupon lit up the whole house. {106:11} And he arose in the hands of the midwife, and opened his mouth and blessed the Lord of heaven. {106:12} And his father Lamech became afraid and fled to me, and did not believe that he was sprung from him, but that he was in the likeness of the angels of heaven; and behold, I have come to you that you may make known to me the truth.' {106:13} And I, Enoch, answered and said to him: 'The Lord will do a new thing on the earth, and this I have already seen in a vision, and I make known to you that in the generation of my father Jared, some of the angels of heaven transgressed the word of the Lord. {106:14} And behold, they committed sin and transgressed the law, and united themselves with women and sinned with them, and married some of them, and begot children by them. {106:15} Yes, there shall come a great destruction over the whole earth, and there shall be a deluge and a great destruction for one year. {106:16} And this son who has been born to you shall be left on the earth, and his three children shall be saved with him: when all mankind that are on the earth shall die [he and his sons shall be saved]. {106:17} And they shall produce on the earth giants not according to the spirit, but according to the flesh, and there shall be a great punishment on the earth, and the earth shall be cleansed from all impurity. {106:18} And now make known to your son Lamech that he who has been born is in truth his son, and call his name Noah; for he shall be left to you, and he and his sons shall be saved from the destruction, which shall come upon the earth on account of all the sin and all the unrighteousness, which shall be consummated on the earth in his days. {106:19} And after that there shall be still more unrighteousness than that which was first consummated on the earth; for I know the mysteries of the holy ones; for He, the Lord, has showed me and informed me, and I have read them in the heavenly tablets.

{107:1} I saw written on them that generation upon generation shall transgress, till a generation of righteousness arises, and transgression is destroyed and sin passes away from the earth, and all manner of good comes upon it. {107:2} And now, my son, go and make known to your son Lamech that this son, which has been born, is in truth his son, and that this is no lie.' {107:3} And when Methuselah had heard the words of his father Enoch - for he had shown to him everything in secret - he returned and showed them to him & called the name of that son Noah; for he will comfort the earth after all the destruction.

{108:1} Another book that Enoch wrote for his son Methuselah and for those who will come after him, to keep the law in the last days. {108:2} You who have done good shall wait for those days until an end is made of those who work evil, and an end of the might of the transgressors. {108:3} Indeed, wait until sin has passed away, for their names shall be blotted out of the book of life and out of the holy books, and their seed shall be destroyed forever, and their spirits shall be slain, and they shall cry and make lamentation in a place that is a chaotic wilderness, and in the fire shall they burn; for there is no earth there. {108:4} And I saw there something like an invisible cloud; because of its depth, I could not look over, and I saw a flame of fire blazing brightly, and things like shining mountains circling and sweeping to and fro. And I asked one of the holy angels who was with me and said to him: 'What is this shining thing? for it is not a heaven but only the flame of a blazing fire, and the voice of weeping and crying and lamentation and strong pain.' {108:5} And he said to me: 'This place which you see-here are cast the spirits of sinners and blasphemers, and of those who work wickedness, and of those who pervert everything that the Lord has spoken through the mouth of the prophets-(even) the things that shall be. {108:6} For some of them are written and inscribed above in the heaven, so that the angels may read them and know that which shall befall the sinners, and the spirits of the humble, and of those who have afflicted their bodies, and been recompensed by God; and of those who have been put to shame by wicked men: {108:7} Who love God and loved neither gold nor silver nor any of the good things which are in the world, but gave over their bodies to torture. {108:8} Who, since they came into being, longed not after earthly food, but regarded everything as a passing breath, and lived accordingly, and the Lord tried them much, and their spirits were found pure so that they should bless His name. {108:9} And all the blessings destined for them I have recounted in the books. And He has assigned them their recompense, because they have been found to be such as loved heaven more than their life in the world, and though they were trodden underfoot of wicked men, and experienced abuse and reviling from them and were put to shame, yet they blessed Me. {108:10} And now I will summon the spirits of the good who belong to the generation of light, and I will transform those who were born in darkness, who in the flesh were not recompensed with such honour as their faithfulness deserved. {108:11} And I will bring forth in shining light those who have loved My holy name, and I will seat each on the throne of his honour. {108:12} And they shall be resplendent for times without number; for righteousness is the judgement of God; for to the faithful He will give faithfulness in the habitation of upright paths. {108:13} And they shall see those who were born in darkness led into darkness, while the righteous shall be resplendent. {108:14} And the sinners shall cry aloud and see them resplendent, and they indeed will go where days and seasons are prescribed for them.

2 Enoch

2 Enoch, also known as the Slavonic Enoch or the Secrets of Enoch, is a pseudepigraphal text attributed to the biblical figure Enoch, who was the great-grandfather of Noah. This text, distinct from the more well-known Ethiopian Book of Enoch, offers a unique perspective on early Jewish mysticism and apocalyptic literature. Likely composed in the late first century CE, the Book of Enoch 2 survives primarily in Old Slavonic manuscripts, reflecting its preservation in Eastern Christian traditions. The narrative unfolds as Enoch is taken on a celestial journey through the ten heavens, where he encounters angelic beings, witnesses cosmic phenomena, and receives revelations about the workings of the universe and the fate of souls. Central to its theological and cosmological themes are detailed descriptions of the heavenly hierarchy, the nature of divine judgment, and the moral order governing human behavior. The text's intricate visions and esoteric teachings offer invaluable insights into Second Temple Judaism's religious thought and the broader milieu of early Christian and Jewish apocalypticism. Despite its exclusion from the canonical Hebrew Bible and the New Testament, the Second Book of Enoch has exerted a significant influence on later mystical and apocalyptic traditions.

{1:1} There was a wise man, a great artificer, and the Lord loved him and took him so that he could see the uppermost dwellings and witness the wise, great, inconceivable, and unchanging realm of God Almighty. He saw the wonderful, glorious, and bright station of the Lord's servants, the inaccessible throne of the Lord, the ranks and manifestations of the incorporeal hosts, the ineffable service of the multitude of elements, the various appearances, and the inexpressible singing of the host of Cherubim, and the boundless light. {1:2} At that time, he said, when I was one hundred and sixty-five years old, I begat my son Methuselah. {1:3} After this, I lived for another two hundred years, making the total years of my life three hundred and sixty-five years. {1:4} On the first day of the month, I was alone in my house, resting on my bed, and I fell asleep. {1:5} While I was asleep, great distress came into my heart, and I wept in my sleep. I could not understand what this distress was or what would happen to me. {1:6} Two men appeared to me, exceedingly big, unlike any I had ever seen on earth. Their faces shone like the sun, their eyes were like burning lights, fire came from their lips, and their clothing and singing were of various kinds in appearance, purple. Their wings were brighter than gold, and their hands whiter than snow. {1:7} They stood at the head of my bed and called me by my name. {1:8} I woke from my sleep and saw clearly those two men standing before me. {1:9} I greeted them and was seized with fear. My appearance changed from terror, and those men said to me: {1:10} Have courage, Enoch, do not fear. The eternal God sent us to you, and today you will ascend with us into heaven. Tell your sons and all your household what they should do without you on earth in your house, and let no one seek you until the Lord returns you to them. {1:11} I quickly obeyed them, left my house, went to the doors as instructed, and summoned my sons Methuselah, Regim, and Gaidad. I told them all the marvels those men had told me.

{2:1} Listen to me, my children. I do not know where I am going or what will happen to me. Now, therefore, my children, I tell you: do not turn from God in the face of the vain, who did not make Heaven and earth, for they shall perish, and so will those who worship them. May the Lord make your hearts confident in the fear of Him. Now, my children, let no one seek me until the Lord returns me to you.

{3:1} It came to pass, when Enoch had told his sons, that the angels took him on their wings and carried him to the first heaven and placed him on the clouds. There I looked, and I looked higher, and saw the ether. They placed me on the first heaven and showed me a very great Sea, greater than the earthly sea.

{4:1} They brought before me the elders and rulers of the stellar orders and showed me two hundred angels, who rule the stars and their services to the heavens. They fly with their wings and come around all those who sail.

{5:1} And here I looked down and saw the treasure houses of the snow and the angels who keep their terrible storehouses, and the clouds from which they come out and into which they go.

{6:1} They showed me the treasure house of the dew, like oil of the olive, and its form like all the flowers of the earth. Many angels guard the treasure houses of these things, and they are made to shut and open.

{7:1} And those men took me and led me up to the second heaven and showed me darkness, greater than earthly darkness. There I saw prisoners hanging, watched, awaiting the great and boundless judgment. These angels were dark-looking, more than earthly darkness, and weeping incessantly. {7:2} I said to the men who were with me: Why are these incessantly tortured? They answered me: These are God's apostates, who did not obey God's commands but followed their own will and turned away with their prince, who is also fastened on the fifth heaven. {7:3} I felt great pity for them, and they greeted me and said: Man of God, pray for us to the Lord. I answered them: Who am I, a mortal man, that I should pray for angels? Who knows where I go or what will happen to me? Or who will pray for me?

{8:1} Those men took me from there and led me up to the third heaven, and placed me there. I looked down and saw the produce of these places, such as has never been known for goodness. {8:2} I saw all the sweet-flowering trees and beheld their fruits, which were sweet-smelling, and all the foods they bore bubbling with fragrant exhalation. {8:3} In the midst of the trees, I saw the tree of life, in that place where the Lord rests when He goes up into paradise. This tree is of ineffable goodness and fragrance, adorned more than anything else. It is golden, vermilion, and fire-like in form, and it covers all and produces all kinds of fruits. {8:4} Its root is in the garden at the earth's end. {8:5} Paradise is between corruptibility and incorruptibility. {8:6} Two springs come out, sending forth honey and milk. Their springs also send forth oil and wine, separating into four parts. They flow quietly, go down into the Paradise of Eden, between corruptibility and incorruptibility. {8:7} From there they go forth along the earth, making a revolution in their circle like other elements. {8:8} There is no unfruitful tree here, and every place is blessed. {8:9} Three hundred very bright angels keep the garden, serving the Lord with incessant sweet singing and never-silent voices throughout all days and hours. {8:10} I said, "How very sweet is this place," and those men said to me:

{9:1} This place, Enoch, is prepared for the righteous, who endure all manner of offenses from those that exasperate their souls, who avert their eyes from iniquity, make righteous judgments, give bread to the hungry, clothe the naked, raise the fallen, help injured orphans, walk without fault before the face of the Lord, and serve Him alone. For them, this place is prepared for eternal inheritance.

{10:1} Those two men led me up to the northern side and showed me a very terrible place with all kinds of tortures: cruel darkness and unilluminated gloom. There is no light there, but murky fire constantly flaming aloft, and a fiery river flows through it. The whole place is fire, frost, ice, thirst, and shivering, with very cruel bonds. The angels are fearful and merciless, bearing angry weapons for merciless torture. I said: {10:2} Woe, woe, how very terrible is this place. {10:3} Those men said to me: This place, Enoch, is prepared for those who dishonor God, who practice sin against nature on earth, such as child corruption after the sodomitic fashion, magic-making, enchantments, devilish witchcrafts, and who boast of their wicked deeds. It is for those who steal, lie, slander, envy, have rancor, fornicate, murder, and who steal the souls of men, who, seeing the poor, take away their goods to enrich themselves, injure others for their goods, let the hungry die when able to feed them, strip the naked when able to clothe them, and do not know their Creator. They bow to soulless and lifeless gods, who cannot see or hear, vain gods. They build hewn images and bow down to unclean handiwork. For all these, this place is prepared for eternal inheritance.

{11:1} Those men took me and led me up to the fourth heaven, showing me all the successive movements and all the rays of light of the sun and moon. {11:2} I measured their movements and compared their light, seeing that the sun's light is greater than the moon's. {11:3} Its circle and the wheels on which it moves are like the wind, moving with marvelous speed. Day and night, it has no rest. {11:4} Its passage and return are accompanied by four great stars. Each star has under it a thousand stars to the right of the sun's wheel, and four to the left, each having a thousand stars under it, making a total of eight thousand stars accompanying the sun continually. {11:5} By day, fifteen myriads of angels attend it, and by night, a thousand. {11:6} Six-winged ones go with the angels before the sun's wheel into the fiery flames, and a hundred angels kindle the sun and set it alight.

{12:1} I looked and saw other flying elements of the sun, called Phoenixes and Chalkydri, marvelous and wonderful. They have feet and tails like a lion, and heads like a crocodile. Their appearance is empurpled like a rainbow; their size is nine hundred measures, and their wings are like those of angels, with each having twelve wings. They attend and accompany the sun, bearing heat and dew as ordered by God. {12:2} Thus the sun revolves and moves, rising under the heaven, and its course goes under the earth with the light of its rays incessantly.

{13:1} Those men bore me away to the east and placed me at the sun's gates, where the sun goes forth according to the regulation of the seasons and the circuit of the months of the whole year and the number of hours day and night. {13:2} I saw six gates open, each gate having sixty-one stadia and a quarter of one stadium. I measured them accurately and understood their size to be such. The sun goes forth through these gates and goes to the west, rises throughout all the months, and turns back again from the six gates according to the succession of the seasons. Thus the period of the whole year is finished after the returns of the four seasons.

{14:1} Again, those men led me to the western parts and showed me six great gates open, corresponding to the eastern gates, opposite to where the sun sets, according to the number of the days, three hundred and sixty-five and a quarter. {14:2} The sun goes down to the western gates, drawing away its light and the greatness of its brightness under the earth. Since the crown of its shining is in heaven with the Lord, guarded by four hundred angels, the sun goes around on a wheel under the earth and stands seven great hours in the night. It spends half its course under the earth. When it comes to the eastern approach in the eighth hour of the night, it brings its light and the crown of shining, and the sun flames forth more than fire.

{15:1} Then the elements of the sun, called Phoenixes and Chalkydri, break into song. Every bird flutters its wings, rejoicing at the giver of light, and they sing at the command of the Lord. {15:2} The giver of light comes to give brightness to the whole world. The morning guard takes shape, which is the rays of the sun. The sun of the earth goes out and receives its brightness to light up the whole face of the earth. They showed me this calculation of the sun's movements. {15:3} The gates through which it enters are the great gates of the calculation of the hours of the year. For this reason, the sun is a great creation, whose circuit lasts twenty-eight years and begins again from the beginning.

{16:1} Those men showed me the other course, that of the moon, with twelve great gates crowned from west to east, through which the moon goes in and out at customary times. {16:2} It goes in at the first gate to the western places of the sun. Through the first gates, it spends thirty-one days exactly, through the second gates, thirty-one days exactly, through the third, thirty days exactly, through the fourth, thirty days exactly, through the fifth, thirty-one days exactly, through the sixth, thirty-one days exactly, through the seventh, thirty days exactly, through the eighth, thirty-one days exactly, through the ninth, thirty-one days exactly, through the tenth, thirty days exactly, through the eleventh, thirty-one days exactly, through the twelfth, twenty-eight days exactly. {16:3} It goes through the western gates in the order and number of the eastern, completing three hundred and sixty-five and a quarter days of the solar year. The lunar year has three hundred fifty-four days, missing twelve days of the solar circle, which are the lunar epacts of the whole year. {16:4} Thus, the great circle contains five hundred and thirty-two years. {16:5} The quarter of a day is omitted for three years; the fourth year fulfills it exactly. {16:6} Therefore, they are taken outside of heaven for three years and are not added to the number of days because they change the time of the years to two new months towards completion and to two others towards diminution. {16:7} When the western gates are finished, it returns and goes to the eastern gates to the lights, moving day and night about the heavenly circles, lower than all circles, swifter than the heavenly winds, spirits, elements, and angels flying. Each angel has six wings. {16:8} It has a sevenfold course in nineteen years.

{17:1} In the midst of the heavens, I saw armed soldiers serving the Lord with tympana and organs, with sweet, incessant, and various singing, impossible to describe, astonishing every mind. So wonderful and marvelous is the singing of those angels, and I was delighted listening to it.

{18:1} The men took me to the fifth heaven and placed me there, and I saw many countless soldiers called Grigori, who appeared human but were larger than giants. Their faces were withered, their mouths silent, and there was no service in the fifth heaven. I asked the men with me: {18:2} "Why are these beings so withered and melancholy, with silent mouths, and why is there no service here?" {18:3} They replied, "These are the Grigori, who, along with their prince Satanail (Satan), rejected the Lord of light. Among them are those held in great darkness on the second heaven. Three of them descended to earth from the Lord's throne to a place called Ermon, breaking their vows on the hill's shoulder. They saw the daughters of men, took them as wives, and defiled the earth with their deeds, creating giants and great enmity. {18:4} Because of this, God judged them severely. They weep for their brethren and will be punished on the Lord's great day. {18:5} I said to the Grigori, "I saw your brethren, their works, and their great torments. I prayed for them, but the Lord has condemned them to remain under the earth until heaven and earth end forever." {18:6} I asked them, "Why do you wait and not serve before the

Lord's face, and why have you not presented your services before Him, lest you anger your Lord completely?" {18:7} They listened to my advice, spoke to the four ranks in heaven, and as I stood with the two men, four trumpets sounded with a great voice. The Grigori broke into song with one voice, and their voice rose before the Lord pitifully and affectingly.

{19:1} Then the men took me to the sixth heaven, where I saw seven bands of angels, very bright and glorious, their faces shining more than the sun. They were identical in appearance, behavior, and dress. These angels create orders, learn the movements of the stars, the moon's phases, the sun's revolution, and the world's governance. {19:2} When they see evildoing, they issue commandments, instructions, and sing sweet and loud songs of praise. {19:3} These are the archangels who are above angels. They measure all life in heaven and on earth and oversee the seasons and years, rivers and seas, earth's fruits, and every grass, giving food to all living things. They also write down all human souls, their deeds, and lives before the Lord. In their midst are six Phoenixes, six Cherubim, and six six-winged ones, continuously singing with one voice, rejoicing before the Lord at His footstool.

{20:1} The two men lifted me to the seventh heaven, where I saw a very great light and fiery troops of great archangels, incorporeal forces, dominions, orders, and governments, Cherubim, Seraphim, thrones, and many-eyed ones, nine regiments, and the Ioanit stations of light. I became afraid and trembled greatly, but the men led me and said: {20:2} "Have courage, Enoch, do not fear," and they showed me the Lord from afar, sitting on His very high throne. For what is there on the tenth heaven, where the Lord dwells? {20:3} On the tenth heaven is God, called Aravat in Hebrew. {20:4} All the heavenly troops come and stand on the ten steps according to their rank, bow down to the Lord, and then return to their places in joy, singing songs in the boundless light with tender voices, gloriously serving Him.

{21:1} The Cherubim and Seraphim standing around the throne, the six-winged and many-eyed ones, do not depart. They stand before the Lord, doing His will, covering His whole throne, and singing gently: "Holy, holy, holy, Lord Ruler of Sabaoth, heavens and earth are full of Your glory." {21:2} When I saw all these things, the men said to me, "Enoch, this is as far as we are commanded to go with you," and they left me. I no longer saw them. {21:3} I was alone at the end of the seventh heaven, afraid, and fell on my face, thinking, "Woe is me, what has happened to me?" {21:4} The Lord sent one of His glorious ones, the archangel Gabriel, who said to me, "Have courage, Enoch, do not fear. Arise before the Lord's face into eternity. Come with me." {21:5} I replied, "My Lord, my soul has left me from terror and trembling. I relied on the men who brought me here, and it is with them I go before the Lord." {21:6} Gabriel caught me up like a leaf caught by the wind and placed me before the Lord. {21:7} I saw the eighth heaven, called Muzaloth in Hebrew, where the seasons change, of drought and wet, and the twelve constellations of the circle of the firmament, above the seventh heaven. {21:8} I saw the ninth heaven, called Kuchavim in Hebrew, where the heavenly homes of the twelve constellations are located.

{22:1} On the tenth heaven, called Aravoth, I saw the Lord's face like glowing iron, emitting sparks and burning. {22:2} I saw the Lord's face briefly, but it was ineffable, marvelous, very awful, and terrifying. {22:3} Who am I to describe the Lord's unspeakable being, His wonderful face, the quantity of His instructions, or the various voices around Him? His throne is very great, not made with hands, surrounded by Cherubim and Seraphim, with their incessant singing and immutable beauty. Who can describe His glory? {22:4} I fell prone and bowed before the Lord. The Lord said to me, {22:5} "Have courage, Enoch, do not fear. Arise and stand before My face into eternity." {22:6} The archistratege Michael lifted me and led me before the Lord. {22:7} The Lord said to His servants, "Let Enoch stand before My face into eternity," and the glorious ones bowed to the Lord, saying, "Let Enoch go according to Your word." {22:8} The Lord said to Michael, "Go and take Enoch from his earthly garments, anoint him with My sweet ointment, and dress him in the garments of My glory." {22:9} Michael did as the Lord commanded. He anointed and dressed me, and the ointment shone more than great light, smelling mild and shining like the sun's rays. I looked at myself, transformed like one of His glorious ones. {22:10} The Lord summoned an archangel named Pravuil, whose wisdom was quicker than the other archangels. The Lord said to Pravuil, "Bring out the books from My storehouses and a reed of quick-writing. Give them to Enoch, and deliver to him the choice and comforting books from your hand."

{23:1} He told me all the works of heaven, earth, sea, and all elements, their passages and movements, thunder, the sun and moon, the stars' changes, the seasons, years, days, and hours, wind's risings, the number of angels, their songs, all human things, every human tongue and life, commandments, instructions, and sweet-voiced singings—everything it is fitting to learn. {23:2} Pravuil said, "All that I have told you, we have written. Sit and write all the souls of mankind, however many are born, and the places prepared for them to eternity, for all souls are prepared before the formation of the world." {23:3} For thirty days and nights, I wrote everything exactly, producing three hundred sixty-six books. ```

{24:1} The Lord summoned me and said, "Enoch, sit on my left with Gabriel." {24:2} I bowed down to the Lord, and He spoke to me, "Enoch, beloved, all that you see and everything that is finished, I tell you even before the beginning. I created all from nothing, visible things from invisible." {24:3} "Listen, Enoch, and understand my words, for I have not revealed my secrets to my angels. They do not know their origin, my endless realm, or my creation, which I reveal to you today." {24:4} "Before anything visible existed, I alone moved among the invisible, like the sun moving from east to west and west to east." {24:5} "Even the sun finds peace in itself, but I found no peace because I was creating everything. I conceived the thought of laying foundations and creating the visible world."

{25:1} "I commanded the lowest parts to bring forth visible things from the invisible, and Adoil came down, very great, with a belly of great light." {25:2} "I said to him, 'Become undone, Adoil, and let the visible come out of you.'" {25:3} "He came undone, and a great light emerged. I was in the midst of the great light, and from light, an age was born, showing all creation that I had thought to create." {25:4} "I saw that it was good." {25:5} "I set a throne for myself and sat on it. I said to the light, 'Go up higher and fix yourself above the throne and be a foundation to the highest things.'" {25:6} "Above the light, there is nothing else. Then I looked up from my throne."

{26:1} "I summoned the lowest a second time and said, 'Let Archas come forth, hard,' and he came forth hard from the invisible." {26:2} "Archas came forth, hard, heavy, and very red." {26:3} "I said, 'Be opened, Archas, and let something be born from you.' He came undone, and an age came forth, very great and dark, bearing the creation of all lower things. I saw that it was good and said to him," {26:4} "'Go down below and make yourself firm. Be a foundation for the lower things.' It happened, and he went down and fixed himself, becoming the foundation for the lower things. Below the darkness, there is nothing else."

{27:1} "I commanded that light and darkness be taken, and I said, 'Be thick,' and it became so. I spread it out with the light, and it became water. I spread it over the darkness, below the light. Then I made the waters firm, and I created a foundation of light around the water. I created seven circles inside and imaged the water like crystal, wet and dry, like glass, the circumcession of the waters and other elements. I showed each one its path, and the seven stars each in its heaven, to go accordingly. I saw that it was good." {27:2} "I separated light from darkness, in the midst of the water here and there. I said to the light that it should be day and to the darkness that it should be night. There was evening, and there was morning, the first day."

{28:1} "Then I made the heavenly circle firm and made the lower water under heaven collect together into one whole. The chaos became dry, and it became so." {28:2} "From the waves, I created rock, hard and big, and from the rock, I piled up the dry land, which I called earth. The midst of the earth, I called abyss, meaning bottomless. I collected the sea in one place and bound it with a yoke." {28:3} "I said to the sea, 'Behold, I give you your eternal limits, and you shall not break loose from your component parts.'" {28:4} "Thus I made fast the firmament. This day I called the first-created [Sunday]."

{29:1} "For all the heavenly troops, I imaged the essence of fire. My eye looked at the very hard, firm rock, and from the gleam of my eye, the lightning received its nature, both fire in water and water in fire. One does not put out the other, nor does one dry up the other. Therefore, lightning is brighter than the sun, softer than water, and firmer than hard rock." {29:2} "From the rock, I cut off a great fire, and from the fire, I created the orders of the incorporeal ten troops of angels. Their weapons are fiery, and their raiment is a burning flame. I commanded each to stand in his order." {29:3} "One from the order of angels turned away with the order under him and conceived an impossible thought to place his throne higher than the clouds above the earth, to become equal in rank to my power." {29:4} "I threw him out from the height with his angels, and he was continuously flying in the air above the bottomless."

{30:1} "On the third day, I commanded the earth to grow great and fruitful trees, hills, and seed to sow. I planted Paradise, enclosed it, and placed flaming angels as guardians. Thus, I created renewal." {30:2} "Evening came, and morning came, the fourth day." {30:3} "[Wednesday]. On the fourth day, I commanded that there be great lights on the heavenly circles." {30:4} "On the first uppermost circle, I placed the stars, Kruno. On the second, Aphrodit. On the third, Aris. On the fifth, Zoues. On the sixth, Ermis. On the seventh, the lesser moon, adorned with lesser stars." {30:5} "On the lower circle, I placed the sun for the day, and the moon and stars for the night." {30:6} "The sun goes according to each constellation, twelve. I appointed the succession of the months, their names, lives, thunderings, and hour-markings, how they succeed." {30:7} "Evening came, and morning came, the fifth day." {30:8} "[Thursday]. On the fifth day, I commanded the sea to bring forth fish and feathered birds of many kinds, and all animals creeping over the earth, going on four legs, and soaring in the air, male and female, every soul breathing the spirit of life." {30:9} "Evening came, and morning came, the sixth day." {30:10} "[Friday]. On the sixth day, I commanded my wisdom to create man from seven consistencies: his flesh from the earth, his blood from the dew, his eyes from the sun, his bones from stone, his intelligence from the swiftness of angels and from clouds, his veins and hair from the grass of the earth, his soul from my breath and from the wind." {30:11} "I gave him seven natures: to the flesh, hearing; to the eyes, sight; to the soul, smell; to the veins, touch; to the blood, taste; to the bones, endurance; to the intelligence, enjoyment." {30:12} "I conceived a saying: I created man from invisible (spiritual) and visible (physical) nature, both his death and life, his image. He knows speech like a created being, small in greatness and great in smallness. I placed him on earth, a second angel, honorable, great, and glorious. I appointed him as ruler on earth with my wisdom, and there was none like him among all my creatures." {30:13} "I gave him a name from the four parts, from east, west, south, and north. I appointed four special stars for him and called his name Adam. I showed him the two ways, light and darkness, and told him," {30:14} "'This is good, and that bad,' so I could learn whether he loves me or hates me, and know which in his race loves me." {30:15} "For I have seen his nature, but he has not seen his own. Therefore, not seeing, he will sin worse. I said, 'After sin, what is there but death?'" {30:16} "I put him to sleep, and he slept. I took a rib from him and created a wife, so death would come to him through his wife. I took his last word and called her name mother, which is Eve."

{31:1} Adam lived on earth, and I created a garden in Eden in the east for him to observe the testament and keep the command. {31:2} I opened the heavens to him so he could see the angels singing songs of victory and the light without gloom. {31:3} He continuously stayed in paradise, and the devil realized I wanted to create another world because Adam was the lord of the earth, to rule and control it. {31:4} The devil is the evil spirit of the lower places, a fugitive who made Sotona from the heavens. His name was Satanail (Satan), and thus he became different from the angels, though his nature and understanding of righteous and sinful things did not change. {31:5} He understood his condemnation and the sin he had committed before, so he conceived a plan against Adam. In this form, he entered and seduced Eve but did not touch Adam. {31:6} I cursed ignorance, but what I had blessed previously, I did not curse. I did not curse man, the earth, or other creatures, but I cursed man's evil fruit and his works.

{32:1} I said to Adam, "You are earth, and to the earth from which I took you, you shall return. I will not destroy you but send you back from where you came." {32:2} "Then I can receive you again at my second coming." {32:3} I blessed all my creatures, both visible and invisible. Adam was in paradise for five and a half hours. {32:4} I blessed the seventh day, the Sabbath, on which I rested from all my works.

{33:1} I also appointed the eighth day, that the eighth day should be the first-created after my work, and that the first seven revolve in the form of the seventh thousand. At the beginning of the eighth thousand, there should be a time of endlessness, without years, months, weeks, days, or hours. {33:2} "Now, Enoch, all that I have told you, all that you have understood, all that you have seen of heavenly things, all that you have seen on earth, and all that I have written in books by my great wisdom, all these things I have devised and created from the uppermost foundation to the lowest and to the end. There is no counselor nor inheritor to my creations." {33:3} "I am self-eternal, not made with hands, and unchanging." {33:4} "My thought is my counselor, my wisdom and my word are made, and my eyes observe all things. They stand here and tremble with terror." {33:5} "If I turn away my face, then all things will be destroyed." {33:6} "Focus, Enoch, and know who is speaking to you. Take the books you have written." {33:7} "I give you Samuil and Raguil, who led you up, and the books. Go down to earth and tell your sons all that I have told you and all that you have seen, from the lower heaven to my throne, and all the troops." {33:8} "I created all forces, and none resist me or do not subject themselves to me. All subject themselves to my rule and labor for my sole authority." {33:9} "Give them the books you have written. They will read them and know me as the creator of all things and understand there is no other God but me." {33:10} "Let them distribute the books you have written—children to children, generation to generation, nations to nations." {33:11} "I will give you, Enoch, my intercessor, the architratege Michael, for the writings of your fathers Adam, Seth, Enos, Cainan, Mahaleleel, and Jared, your father."

{34:1} "They have rejected my commandments and my yoke. Worthless seed has come up, not fearing God. They would not bow down to me but have begun to bow down to vain gods, denied my unity, and filled the earth with lies, offenses, abominable lecheries, one with another, and all kinds of unclean wickedness, which are disgusting to mention." {34:2} "Therefore, I will bring a flood upon the earth and destroy all men. The whole earth will crumble into great darkness."

{35:1} "From their seed will arise another generation, much later, but many of them will be very insatiate." {35:2} "He who raises that generation will reveal to them the books you have written, of your fathers, to whom he must point out the guardianship of the world, to the faithful men and workers of my pleasure, who do not take my name in vain." {35:3} "They will tell another generation, and those who read will be glorified thereafter, more than the first."

{36:1} "Now, Enoch, I give you thirty days to spend in your house. Tell your sons and all your household, so they may hear from me what is told to them by you, that they may read and understand that there is no other God but me." {36:2} "They should always keep my commandments and begin to read and take in the books you have written." {36:3} "After thirty days, I will send my angel for you. He will take you from earth and from your sons to me."

{37:1} The Lord summoned one of the older angels, terrible and menacing, and placed him beside me. He appeared white as snow, with hands like ice, resembling great frost. His presence froze my face because I couldn't bear the terror of the Lord, just as one cannot endure the fire of a stove or the heat of the sun, and the chill of the air. {37:2} The Lord said to me, "Enoch, if your face is not frozen here, no man will be able to behold your face."

{38:1} Then the Lord said to the men who led me up, "Let Enoch go down to earth with you and wait for him until the appointed day." {38:2} So they placed me on my bed at night. {38:3} Mathusal, expecting my arrival, kept watch day and night at my bed. He was filled with awe when he heard me coming. I told him, "Gather all my household together so that I may tell them everything."

{39:1} "Oh my children, my beloved ones, listen to the instruction of your father, according to the Lord's will." {39:2} "Today, the Lord has allowed me to come to you and announce, not from my own lips, but from the Lord's, all that has been, is, and will be until judgment day." {39:3} "For the Lord has allowed me to come to you, so listen to the words from my lips, a man who has been made great for you. I have seen the Lord's face, which glows like iron heated by fire, emitting sparks and burning." {39:4} "You now see my eyes, filled with meaning for you, but I have seen the Lord's eyes shining like the sun's rays, filling man's eyes with awe." {39:5} "You see now the right hand of a man that helps you, but I have seen the Lord's right hand filling heaven as he helped me." {39:6} "You see the extent of my work, similar to your own, but I have seen the Lord's limitless and perfect work, which has no end." {39:7} "You hear the words from my lips as I heard the words of the Lord, like great thunder with the hurling of clouds." {39:8} "Now, my children, hear the teachings of the father of the earth. Consider how fearful & awe-inspiring it is to come before the ruler of the earth. How much more terrible it is to come before the ruler of heaven, the judge of the living and the dead, and of the heavenly hosts. Who can endure that endless pain?"

{40:1} "And now, my children, I know all things. This is from the Lord's lips, and my eyes have seen it from beginning to end." {40:2} "I know all things and have written them into books—the heavens and their end, their fullness, and all the armies and their movements." {40:3} "I have measured and described the stars, the vast multitude of them. No man has seen their rotations and entrances, for not even the angels know their number. Yet, I have written all their names." {40:4} "I measured the sun's orbit, its rays, and counted the hours. I also wrote down all things that traverse the earth—the nourished and unnourished, the sown and unsown seeds, the plants, grass, flowers, their fragrances, and names. I noted the dwelling places of the clouds, their composition, wings, and how they bear rain and raindrops." {40:5} "I investigated all things and wrote about the path of thunder and lightning. They showed me the keys and their guardians, their rise and the way they travel. They are gently released by a chain, so they do not violently hurl down the angry clouds and destroy everything on earth." {40:6} "I wrote about the storehouses of snow, the cold, and frosty airs, and I observed their keeper of the seasons. He fills the clouds with them and does not exhaust the storehouses." {40:7} "I wrote about the resting places of the winds, how their keepers bear scales and measures. They first place them on one side of the scale, then on the other, cunningly distributing them over the whole earth, lest their heavy breathing cause the earth to sway." {40:8} "I measured the entire earth, its mountains, hills, fields, trees, stones, rivers, and all existing things. I noted the distance from the earth to the seventh heaven and down to the lowest hell, the judgment place, the vast, open, weeping hell." {40:9} "I saw the prisoners in pain, awaiting the endless judgment." {40:10} "I wrote about all those being judged, their judgments, sentences, and deeds."

{41:1} "I saw all the ancestors from all time, with Adam and Eve, and I sighed, broke into tears, and lamented the ruin of their dishonor." {41:2} "Woe is me for my weakness and that of my forefathers. I thought in my heart and said, 'Blessed is the man who has not been born, or who has been born and will not sin before the Lord's face, that he may not come into this place or bear the burden of this place.'"

{42:1} "I saw the gatekeepers and guards of hell standing like great serpents, their faces like extinguished lamps, and their eyes like fire, with sharp teeth. I saw all the Lord's works, how they are just, while the works of man are sometimes good and sometimes bad. Through their works, one can discern those who act wickedly."

{43:1} "My children, I measured, wrote, and described every work, measure, and righteous judgment." {43:2} "Just as one year is more honorable than another, so is one man more honorable than another. Some are esteemed for great possessions, wisdom, intellect, cunning, silence, cleanliness, strength, comeliness, youth, or sharp wit. Let it be known everywhere, but none are better than those who fear God. They shall be more glorious in time to come."

{44:1} "The Lord, with his hands, created man in his own likeness, small and great." {44:2} "Whoever reviles a ruler's face and despises the Lord's face has despised the Lord. Whoever vents anger on any man unjustly, the Lord's great anger will strike him down. Whoever spits on a man's face contemptuously will be judged severely by the Lord." {44:3} "Blessed is the man who does not harbor malice against any man but helps the injured, condemned, and broken. He shall be rewarded on the day of judgment."

{45:1} "God shows that He does not desire sacrifices or burnt offerings from men, but rather pure and contrite hearts. Whoever hurries to make an offering before the Lord, the Lord will hasten to bless that offering with His work. {45:2} However, if someone lights a lamp before the Lord but does not act with true judgment, the Lord will not increase his treasure in the highest realm. {45:3} When the Lord requests bread, candles, or cattle, these are insignificant; what God truly demands is pure hearts, and these offerings only serve to test the heart of man."

{46:1} Listen, my people, and heed the words from my lips. {46:2} If someone offers gifts to an earthly ruler while harboring disloyal thoughts in his heart, and the ruler knows this, won't he be angered and refuse the gifts? Won't he hand him over for judgment? {46:3} Similarly, if one person deceives another with flattering words while harboring evil intentions, won't the deceived one recognize the deceit and condemn him, since his falsehood is evident to all? {46:4} When the Lord sends a great light, there will be judgment for both the just and the unjust, and no one will escape notice.

{47:1} Now, my children, ponder these words in your hearts and pay close attention to the words of your father, which come from the lips of the Lord. {47:2} Take these books written by your father and read them. They contain many teachings about the Lord's works, from the beginning of creation to the end of time. {47:3} If you heed my writings, you will not sin against the Lord, for there is no one except the Lord—neither in heaven, nor on earth, nor in the lowest places, nor in the foundations. {47:4} The Lord has established the foundations in the unknown and has created both visible and invisible heavens. He placed the earth upon the waters, created countless creatures, and who can count the water or the unfixed foundation, or the dust of the earth, or the sand of the sea, or the raindrops, or the morning dew, or the breath of the wind? Who has filled the earth and sea, and the unyielding winter? {47:5} I fashioned the stars from fire and adorned the heavens, placing them in their midst.

{48:1} The sun traverses the seven heavenly circles, corresponding to one hundred and eighty-two thrones. It sets on a short day after one hundred and eighty-two thrones, and on a long day after the same. It has two thrones on which it rests, revolving above the thrones of the months. From the seventeenth day of Tsivan to the month of Thevan, it descends, and from the seventeenth of Thevan, it ascends. {48:2} When it draws close to the earth, the earth rejoices, and its fruits flourish. When it moves away, the earth mourns, and trees and fruits fail to blossom. {48:3} All this has been measured meticulously, with accurate timing, visible and invisible. {48:4} From the invisible, all visible things were created, with God Himself remaining invisible. {48:5} Thus, I reveal to you, my children, and distribute these books to your children, to all your generations and among the nations who fear God. Let them receive and cherish these books more than any food or earthly pleasure, and let them read and study them diligently. {48:6} Terrible judgment awaits those who do not understand the Lord, who do not fear God, who reject instead of accept, who refuse to receive these books. {48:7} Blessed is the one who bears their yoke and carries them, for he will be released on the day of the great judgment.

{49:1} I swear to you, my children, but not by any oath—neither by heaven nor by earth nor by any other created thing. {49:2} The Lord said, "There is no falsehood in Me, only truth." {49:3} If there is no truth in men, let them swear by saying either yes or no. {49:4} I swear to you—yes, yes—that no man enters his mother's womb without a predetermined place for the soul's rest and a fixed measure of trials in this world. {49:5} Do not deceive yourselves, children, for a place has already been prepared for every soul of man.

{50:1} I have recorded every man's deeds in writing, and no one born on earth can remain hidden, nor can his deeds remain concealed. {50:2} I see all things. {50:3} Therefore, my children, endure patiently and meekly throughout your days, that you may inherit eternal life. {50:4} Bear every wound, injury, evil word, and attack for the sake of the Lord. {50:5} If someone wrongs you, do not retaliate against either neighbor or enemy, for the Lord will repay on the day of great judgment, and there shall be no vengeance among men. {50:6} Whoever spends gold or silver for his brother's sake will receive ample treasure in the world to come. {50:7} Do not oppress widows, orphans, or strangers, lest God's wrath come upon you.

{51:1} Stretch out your hands to the poor according to your ability. {51:2} Do not hoard your silver in the earth. {51:3} Assist the faithful in their affliction, and affliction will not find you in your time of trouble. {51:4} Endure every heavy and cruel burden for the Lord's sake, and you will find your reward in the day of judgment. {51:5} It is good to enter the Lord's dwelling in the morning, midday, and evening, for every living thing glorifies Him, both visible and invisible.

{52:1} Blessed is the one who praises the God of hosts with his lips and heart. {52:2} Cursed is the one who uses his lips to bring contempt and slander upon his neighbor, for he brings contempt upon God. {52:3} Blessed is the one who blesses all the Lord's works. {52:4} Cursed is the one who despises God's creation. {52:5} Blessed is the one who lifts up and restores the fallen. {52:6} Cursed is the one who desires the destruction of what is not his. {52:7} Blessed is the one who upholds the traditions of his fathers. {52:8} Cursed is the one who perverts the decrees of his forefathers. {52:9} Blessed is the one who promotes peace and love. {52:10} Cursed is the one who stirs up conflict among neighbors. {52:11} Blessed is the one who speaks humbly and kindly to all. {52:12} Cursed is the one who speaks peace with his tongue but harbors violence in his heart. {52:13} All these things will be revealed in the scales of justice and in the books on the day of great judgment.

{53:1} Now, my children, do not assume that our father stands before God praying for our sins, for there is no helper for any man who has sinned there. You have seen how I recorded all the deeds of every man before his creation—everything done among all men for all time. None can interpret or explain my writings, for the Lord sees all the thoughts of man, how they are futile and stored in the treasure-houses of the heart. {53:2} Therefore, heed all the words of your father that I have spoken to you, lest you regret, saying, "Why did our father not tell us?"

{54:1} If you do not understand this now, let these books I have given you be an inheritance of peace for you. Pass them on to all who seek them, and instruct them so they may witness the Lord's great and marvelous works.

{55:1} My children, behold, the time of my departure has come. The angels who will accompany me stand before me, urging me to leave you. They are here on earth, awaiting what has been foretold to them. Tomorrow I will ascend to heaven, to the highest Jerusalem, to my eternal inheritance. Therefore, I urge you to do all that pleases the Lord.

{56:1} Mathuselah, having responded to his father Enoch, said, "Father, tell me what pleases you, so that I may do it before you and receive your blessing upon our homes, your sons, and that your people may be glorified through you, before your departure as the Lord has said." {56:2} Enoch replied to his son Mathuselah, saying, "Listen, my child. Since the Lord anointed me with His glory, I have had no desire for food, and my soul no longer craves earthly pleasures."

{57:1} Mathuselah then hurriedly summoned all his brothers, Regim, Riman, Uchan, Chermion, Gaidad, and all the elders of the people before his father Enoch, who blessed them and spoke to them:

{58:1} "Listen to me today, my children. {58:2} In those days when the Lord descended to earth for the sake of Adam and visited all His creatures, after creating them Himself, He created Adam. Then the Lord called all the beasts of the earth, all the reptiles, and all the birds of the air and brought them before our father Adam. {58:3} And Adam named all the living creatures on earth. {58:4} The Lord made him ruler over all, subjecting everything under his authority. He made them obedient to man's command, dumb and dull. {58:5} Similarly, the Lord has made every man ruler over all his possessions. {58:6} The Lord will not judge a single beast's soul for man's sake, but will judge men's souls in relation to their beasts in this world. For men hold a special place. {58:7} Just as every man's soul is numbered, likewise, beasts' souls, which the Lord created, will not perish until the great judgment. They will accuse man if he mistreats them.

{59:1} Whoever defiles the soul of a beast also defiles his own soul. {59:2} For man brings clean animals to sacrifice for sin, seeking cure for his own soul. {59:3} If they sacrifice clean animals and birds, man finds a cure; he heals his soul. {59:4} Everything is provided for food, but the animal must be bound by the four feet to effect the cure; in this way, man heals his soul. {59:5} But whoever kills an animal without a cause also kills his own soul and defiles his own flesh. {59:6} And anyone who injures an animal in any way, secretly, practices evil and defiles his own soul.

{60:1} Whoever destroys a man's soul also destroys his own soul and body, with no cure for him forever. {60:2} Whoever ensnares a man will himself be ensnared, with no cure forever. {60:3} Whoever imprisons a man in any vessel will face retribution at the great judgment forever. {60:4} Whoever acts deceitfully or speaks evil against any soul will never find justice for himself forever.

{61:1} Now, my children, guard your hearts against every injustice, which the Lord detests. Just as a man seeks something for his own soul from God, so let him do for every living soul. For I know all things, and in the great time to come, there is much inheritance prepared for men—good for the good and bad for the bad, countless in number. {61:2} Blessed are those who enter good houses, for in bad houses there is no peace or return from them. {61:3} Hear, my children, both small and great! When a man brings gifts from his labors before the Lord's face, if his hands did not make them, the Lord will turn away from the work of his hands, and that man will not find the fruits of his labor. {61:4} But if a man's hands made the gifts, yet his heart murmurs and continues to murmur incessantly, he gains no advantage.

{62:1} Blessed is the man who patiently brings his gifts with faith before the Lord's face, for he will find forgiveness of sins. {62:2} But if he retracts his words before the appointed time, there is no repentance for him. And if the time passes, and he does not fulfill what he promised, there is no repentance after death. For every work that a man does before its time is deceit before men and sin before God.

{63:1} When a man clothes the naked and feeds the hungry, he will find reward from God. {63:2} But if his heart murmurs, he commits a double evil—ruin for himself and for what he gives. And there will be no reward for him because of it. {63:3} And if he satisfies his own heart with his own food and clothes his own flesh with his own clothing, he shows contempt and will forfeit all his endurance of poverty. He will not find reward for his good deeds. {63:4} Every proud and boastful man is hateful to the Lord, as is every false speech clothed in untruth. It will be cut down by the sword of death and thrown into the fire, where it shall burn forever.

{64:1} After Enoch had spoken these words to his sons, all the people, far and near, heard how the Lord was calling Enoch. They consulted together, saying, "Let us go and kiss Enoch." Two thousand men gathered and went to the place where Enoch and his sons were. {64:2} The elders of the people, the entire assembly, came and bowed down, kissing Enoch. They said to him, "Our father Enoch, may you be blessed by the eternal ruler, the Lord. Now, bless your sons and all the people, so that we may be glorified before you today. {64:3} For you will be glorified before the Lord forever, since the Lord chose you above all men on earth. He designated you as the writer of all His creation, both visible and invisible, and as the redeemer of the sins of man and the helper of your household.

{65:1} And Enoch answered all his people, saying, "Listen, my children. Before all creatures were created, the Lord made visible and invisible things. {65:2} And after much time had passed, He created man in His own likeness, giving him eyes to see, ears to hear, a heart to reflect, and an intellect to deliberate. {65:3} The Lord saw all of man's works, created all His creatures, and divided time. He fixed the years, appointed the months, and designated the days. From the days, He appointed seven. {65:4} Within those days, He measured out the hours exactly, so that man might reflect on time and count the years, months, and hours—their alternation, beginning, and end. Thus, man might count his own life from beginning to end, reflect on his sins, and record his deeds, both good and bad. For no work is hidden before the Lord, that every man might know his deeds and never transgress all His commandments. Keep my writings from generation to generation. {65:5} When all creation, both visible and invisible, comes to an end as the Lord created it, then every man will face the great judgment. From then on, time will cease to exist—there will be no more years, months, or days, as they will be joined together and not counted. {65:6} There will be one aeon, and all the righteous who escape the Lord's great judgment will be gathered in the great aeon. For the righteous, the great aeon will begin, and they will live eternally. There will be no labor, sickness, humiliation, anxiety, need, brutality, night, or darkness among them—only great light. {65:7} They will have an indestructible wall and an eternal paradise, for all mortal things will pass away, and there will be eternal life.

{66:1} Enoch instructs his sons and all the elders on how to walk before the Lord with fear and trembling, serving Him alone and not bowing to idols. Worship the true God, who created heaven, earth, and every creature, and honor His image. {66:2} Keep your souls free from all injustice, which the Lord despises. {66:3} Walk before Him with fear and trembling and serve Him alone. Bow to the true God, not to lifeless idols, and present just offerings to the Lord. The Lord detests injustice. {66:4} The Lord sees everything; when a person thinks in their heart, the Lord understands their thoughts. Every thought is always before the Lord, who established the earth and placed all creatures upon it. {66:5} If you look to heaven, the Lord is there; if you consider the depths of the sea and the underworld, the Lord is there. {66:6} For the Lord created everything. Do not bow to man-made things, abandoning the Lord of creation, because no work can remain hidden from the Lord. {66:7} Walk, my children, in patience, meekness, honesty, humility, grief, faith, and truth, relying on promises through illness, abuse, wounds, temptation, nakedness, and deprivation. Love one another until you leave this age of suffering and inherit eternal life. {66:8} Blessed are the righteous who will escape the great judgment, for they will shine seven times brighter than the sun. In this world, the seventh part is removed from all things—light, darkness, food, pleasure, sorrow, paradise, torment, fire, frost, and more. Everything has been recorded for you to read and understand.

{67:1} After Enoch had addressed the people, the Lord sent darkness upon the earth. It covered those standing with Enoch, and they lifted Enoch up to the highest heaven, where the Lord resides. He welcomed him and placed him before His presence. Then the darkness lifted from the earth, and light returned. {67:2} The people witnessed this event but did not comprehend how Enoch had been taken. They praised God and discovered a scroll inscribed with The Invisible God's name. Then they returned to their homes.

{68:1} Enoch was born on the sixth day of the month Tsivan and lived for three hundred and sixty-five years. {68:2} He was taken up to heaven on the first day of the month Tsivan and remained there for sixty days. {68:3} During his time in heaven, he documented all the signs of creation that the Lord had made. He wrote three hundred and sixty-six books, which he handed over to his sons. Afterward, he returned to earth for thirty days before being taken up to heaven again on the sixth day of the month Tsivan, the very day and hour of his birth. {68:4} Just as every person's life is shrouded in darkness, so too are their conception, birth, and departure from this world. {68:5} The hour of a person's conception is the same hour they are born and the same hour they pass away. {68:6} Methosalam and Enoch's other sons hurriedly erected an altar at the place called Achuzan, where Enoch had been taken up to heaven. {68:7} They sacrificed oxen before the Lord and invited all the people to join in the offering. {68:8} The elders and the entire assembly came to the feast, bringing gifts for Enoch's sons. {68:9} They celebrated with a great feast, rejoicing and making merry for three days, praising God for the sign He had given them through Enoch, who had found favor in His sight. They resolved to pass on this knowledge to their descendants, from generation to generation, age to age. {68:10} Amen.

3 Enoch

The third book of Enoch, also known as the Hebrew Book of Enoch or Sefer Hekhalot, is an ancient Jewish mystical text that forms part of the Hekhalot literature. This body of work, which emerged during the late antiquity period, delves into Jewish mysticism and the exploration of divine realms. 3 Enoch is distinct from the more widely known First and Second Books of Enoch, which are part of the pseudepigrapha and primarily focused on apocalyptic visions and angelic lore. The text of 3 Enoch is characterized by its detailed descriptions of heavenly ascents, angelic hierarchies, and divine throne rooms, offering a unique glimpse into early Jewish mystical practices and beliefs. Unlike other apocalyptic literature, 3 Enoch emphasizes the mystical experience and the process by which individuals can attain divine visions through rigorous spiritual disciplines. The text is replete with elaborate rituals, invocations, and theurgic practices aimed at achieving spiritual elevation and direct encounters with the divine. Furthermore, the third book of Enoch provides an intricate portrayal of the heavenly palaces (hekhalot) and the divine chariot (merkavah), themes that would later significantly influence the development of Kabbalistic thought. The origins of 3 Enoch are unclear, but it is thought to have been written between the 3rd and 6th centuries CE, blending earlier Jewish apocalyptic traditions with emerging mystical ideas. It is crucial for understanding the shift in Jewish mysticism from prophetic and apocalyptic to more mystical and esoteric forms.

{1:1} Rabbi Ishmael recounted: When I ascended to the heavens to witness the vision of the Merkaba, I passed through the six halls, one inside the other. {1:2} Upon reaching the entrance of the seventh hall, I stopped to pray before the Holy One, blessed be He. Lifting my eyes toward the Divine Majesty, I prayed, {1:3} "Lord of the Universe, I ask that the merit of Aaron, the son of Amram, who loved peace and pursued it, and who received the priestly crown from Your Glory on Mount Sinai, protect me now so that Qafsiel, the prince, and the angels with him do not overpower me or cast me down from heaven." {1:4} Immediately, the Holy One, blessed be He, sent Metatron, His servant and the Prince of the Presence, who came with great joy, spreading his wings to save me. {1:5} He took my hand in their sight and said, "Enter in peace before the high and exalted King, and behold the vision of the Merkaba." {1:6} So, I entered the seventh hall, and Metatron led me to the camp of the Shekina, placing me before the Holy One, blessed be He, so I could behold the Merkaba. {1:7} As soon as the princes of the Merkaba and the flaming Seraphim saw me, their gaze fixed upon me, and I was overcome with trembling and fear. I collapsed, paralyzed by the radiant splendor of their eyes and the brilliant appearance of their faces. {1:8} The Holy One, blessed be He, rebuked them, saying, "My servants, my Seraphim, my Kerubim, and my Ophannim, cover your eyes before Ishmael, My son, My beloved one, My glory, so he does not tremble or fear!" {1:9} Immediately, Metatron, the Prince of the Presence, came to restore my spirit and set me on my feet. {1:10} Even then, I had no strength to sing praises before the Throne of Glory, the mighty King, until an hour had passed. {1:11} After that hour, the Holy One, blessed be He, opened for me the gates of Shekina, Peace, Wisdom, Strength, Power, Speech, Song, Holiness, and Chant. {1:12} He enlightened my eyes and heart with words of praise, song, thanksgiving, and glorification. When I opened my mouth to sing before Him, the holy Chayyoth beneath and above the Throne of Glory responded, saying, "HOLY" and "BLESSED BE THE GLORY OF YHWH FROM HIS PLACE!"

{2:1} Rabbi Ishmael continued: At that moment, the eagles of the Merkaba, the flaming Ophannim, and the fiery Seraphim turned to Metatron and asked, {2:2} "Youth! Why do you allow someone born of a woman to enter and witness the Merkaba? From which nation, tribe, and character does this one come?" {2:3} Metatron responded, "He is from the nation of Israel, whom the Holy One, blessed be He, chose from among seventy nations, from the tribe of Levi, which was set apart for His service, and from the seed of Aaron, whom the Holy One, blessed be He, crowned with priesthood on Sinai." {2:4} They then said, "Indeed, this one is worthy to witness the Merkaba," and they declared, "Happy is the people in such a state!"

{3:1} Rabbi Ishmael asked Metatron: "What is your name?" {3:2} Metatron replied, "I have seventy names, corresponding to the seventy languages of the world, and all are based on the name 'Metatron, the angel of the Presence.' But my King calls me 'Youth' (Na'ar)."

{4:1} Rabbi Ishmael asked further: "Why are you called by your Creator's name, having seventy names, greater than all princes, higher than all angels, more beloved and honored than all the mighty ones? Yet, they call you 'Youth' in the high heavens. Why?" {4:2} Metatron replied, "Because I am Enoch, the son of Jared. {4:3} When the generation of the Flood sinned and turned from God, saying, 'Depart from us, we desire no knowledge of Your ways' (Job 21:14), the Holy One, blessed be He, took me from among them to serve as a witness in the high heavens, so that people could not say, 'The Merciful One is cruel.' {4:4} What was the sin of the multitudes, their families, their livestock, and all the birds, which were destroyed by the Flood along with them? {4:5} Therefore, the Holy One, blessed be He, lifted me up during their lifetime before their eyes, to serve as a witness against them for future generations. He appointed me as a prince and ruler among the ministering angels. {4:6} At that time, three ministering angels, Uzza, Azza, and Azzael, came forward and made accusations against me in the heavens, saying before the Holy One, blessed be He, 'Did not the Ancient Ones say rightly to You, "Do not create man"? {4:7} The Holy One, blessed be He, responded, 'I created man, and I will sustain him, carry him, and deliver him' (Isaiah 46:4). {4:8} When they saw me, they said, 'Lord of the Universe! Is this not one of those who perished in the Flood? What is he doing in the firmament?' {4:9} The Holy One, blessed be He, responded, 'Who are you to speak in My presence? I delight in this one more than all of you, and he shall be a prince and ruler over you in the heavens.' {4:10} Immediately, they all came to greet me, prostrated themselves before me, and said, 'Blessed are you, and blessed is your father, for your Creator has favored you.' {4:11} And because I am young among them in terms of days, months, and years, they call me 'Youth' (Na'ar)."

{5:1} Rabbi Ishmael said, Metatron, the Prince of the Presence, told me: From the day when the Holy One, blessed be He, expelled the first Adam from the Garden of Eden, the Shekina (Divine Presence) dwelled upon a cherub under the Tree of Life. {5:2} The ministering angels would gather together, descending from heaven in groups, from the Raqia (firmament) in companies, and from the heavens in hosts to carry out God's will throughout the world. {5:3} The first man and his generation would sit outside the gate of the Garden, observing the radiant appearance of the Shekina. {5:4} The splendor of the Shekina illuminated the world, 365,000 times brighter than the sun. Those who benefitted from this radiance experienced no afflictions—no flies or gnats would land on them, and they suffered no illness or pain. Demons had no power over them and could not harm them. {5:5} When the Holy One, blessed be He, moved between the Garden and Eden, from Eden to the Garden, from the Garden to the Raqia, and back again, everyone could see the splendor of His Shekina without being harmed. {5:6} But this continued only until the generation of Enosh, who became the leader of all idol worshippers. {5:7} The people of Enosh's generation traveled across the earth, gathering silver, gold, precious stones, and pearls in heaps as large as mountains and hills, using them to create idols. They erected these idols all over the world, each one measuring a thousand parasangs in size. {5:8} They brought down the sun, moon, planets, and constellations, placing them beside the idols on their right and left as if to serve them, imitating the way the heavenly hosts attend the Holy One, blessed be He, as written in 1 Kings 22:19, "And all the host of heaven was standing by Him, on His right hand and on His left." {5:9} How were they able to do this? They could not have achieved this without the help of 'Uzza, 'Azza, and 'Azziel, who taught them sorceries that enabled them to manipulate these celestial bodies. {5:10} At that time, the ministering angels brought charges against them before the Holy One, blessed be He, saying, "Master of the World! What is man (Enosh) that you are mindful of him?" (Psalm 8:4). They emphasized "Enosh" rather than "Adam" because Enosh was the leader of the idol worshippers. {5:11} The angels asked, "Why have you abandoned the highest heavens, the abode of Your glorious Name, and the exalted Throne in 'Araboth Raqia, only to dwell among the children of men who worship idols and equate You with their false gods? {5:12} You are now on earth, alongside these idols. What connection do You have with those who worship idols?" {5:13} Immediately, the Holy One, blessed be He, lifted His Shekina from the earth and removed it from their midst. {5:14} At that moment, the ministering angels, the hosts, and the armies of 'Araboth, in thousands of camps and tens of thousands of hosts, took up trumpets and surrounded the Shekina with all kinds of songs as it ascended to the high heavens, as written in Psalm 47:5, "God has gone up with a shout, the Lord with the sound of a trumpet."

{6:1} Rabbi Ishmael said, Metatron, the Prince of the Presence, told me: When the Holy One, blessed be He, desired to lift me on high, He first sent Anaphiel, the Prince, who took me from the midst of the people in full view of everyone and carried me in great glory upon a fiery chariot with fiery horses, servants of glory. He lifted me to the high heavens, along with the Shekina. {6:2} As soon as I reached the high heavens, the Holy Chayyoth, Ophannim, Seraphim, Kerubim, Wheels of the Merkaba (Galgallim), and ministers of the consuming fire sensed my presence from 365,000 myriads of parasangs away. They exclaimed, "What is this scent of a mortal being, born of a woman, and this taste of a white drop (a reference to the human form), rising on high? Is he no more than a mere gnat compared to those who divide the flames of fire?" {6:3} The Holy One, blessed be He, responded, "My servants, my hosts, my Kerubim, my Ophannim, my Seraphim, do not be displeased by this. Since all of humanity has denied Me and My great Kingdom and turned to idol worship, I have removed My Shekina from among them and lifted it on high. But this one, whom I have taken from among them, is an Elect One from the world. He is equal to all of them in faith, righteousness, and perfection of deeds. I have chosen him as a tribute from the world under all the heavens."

{7:1} Rabbi Ishmael said, Metatron, the Prince of the Presence, told me: When the Holy One, blessed be He, took me away from the generation of the Flood, He lifted me on the wings of the wind of Shekina to the highest heavens. He brought me into the great palaces of the 'Araboth Raqia on high, where the glorious Throne of Shekina is located, along with the Merkaba, the troops of anger, the armies of vehemence, the fiery Shin'anim, the flaming Kerubim, the burning Ophannim, the flaming servants, the flashing Chashmattim, and the lightning Seraphim. He placed me there to serve the Throne of Glory every day.

{8:1} Rabbi Ishmael said, Metatron, the Prince of the Presence, told me: Before He appointed me to serve the Throne of Glory, the Holy One, blessed be He, opened for me three hundred thousand gates of Understanding, three hundred thousand gates of Subtlety, three hundred thousand gates of Life, three hundred thousand gates of grace and loving-kindness, three hundred thousand gates of love, three hundred thousand gates of Torah, three hundred thousand gates of meekness, three hundred thousand gates of sustenance, three hundred thousand gates of mercy, and three hundred thousand gates of fear of Heaven. {8:2} In that hour, the Holy One, blessed be He, added wisdom to my wisdom, understanding to my understanding, subtlety to my subtlety, knowledge to my knowledge, mercy to my mercy, instruction to my instruction, love to my love, kindness to my kindness, goodness to my goodness, meekness to my meekness, power to my power, strength to my strength, might to my might, brilliance to my brilliance, beauty to my beauty, and splendor to my splendor. I was honored and adorned with all these good and praiseworthy attributes, surpassing all the children of heaven.

{9:1} Rabbi Ishmael said, Metatron, the Prince of the Presence, told me: After all these things, the Holy One, blessed be He, placed His hand upon me and blessed me with 5,360 blessings. {9:2} I was raised and enlarged to the size of the length and width of the world. {9:3} He caused 72 wings to grow on me, 36 on each side, and each wing was the size of the entire world. {9:4} He fixed 365 eyes on me, and each eye was as bright as the great luminary (the sun). {9:5} He left no splendor, brilliance, radiance, or beauty in the lights of the universe that He did not place upon me.

{10:1} Rabbi Ishmael said, Metatron, the Prince of the Presence, told me: The Holy One, blessed be He, made for me a throne similar to the Throne of Glory. He spread over me a curtain of splendor and brilliance, with beauty, grace, and mercy, similar to the curtain of the Throne of Glory, upon which were fixed all the lights of the universe. {10:2} He placed it at the entrance to the Seventh Hall and seated me upon it. {10:3} A herald then went forth to every heaven, proclaiming: "This is Metatron, My servant. I have made him a prince and ruler over all the princes of My kingdoms and over all the children of heaven, except for the eight great princes, the honored and revered ones, who are called YHWH by the name of their King. {10:4} Every angel and prince who has a matter to bring before Me shall now go to him and speak through him. {10:5} Whatever command he gives you in My name, you must observe and fulfill. For I have given him the Prince of Wisdom and the Prince of Understanding to teach him the wisdom of both heavenly and earthly matters, the wisdom of this world and the world to come. {10:6} Furthermore, I have placed him over all the treasuries of the palaces of Araboth and over all the stores of life that I possess in the high heavens."

{11:1} Rabbi Ishmael said: Metatron, the angel, the Prince of the Presence, spoke to me, saying: From that point on, the Holy One, blessed be He, revealed to me all the mysteries of the Torah, all the secrets of wisdom, and the profound depths of the Perfect Law. He showed me the innermost thoughts of all living beings and all the hidden secrets of the universe and creation. These things were made known to me as clearly as they are to the Maker of Creation. {11:2} I watched closely to understand the secrets of the abyss and the wondrous mysteries. Before a man even thought in secret, I saw it, and before a person brought something into being, I had already witnessed it. {11:3} There was nothing, whether in the heights above or the depths below, that was hidden from me.

{12:1} Rabbi Ishmael said: Metatron, the Prince of the Presence, continued: Due to the great love the Holy One, blessed be He, had for me—greater than for all the children of heaven—He made me a garment of glory adorned with all kinds of lights and He dressed me in it. {12:2} He also made me a robe of honor, decorated with every kind of beauty, splendor, brilliance, and majesty. {12:3} Furthermore, He fashioned for me a royal crown, set with forty-nine precious stones, each shining like the light of the sun. {12:4} Its radiance extended in all four directions of Araboth Raqia, through the seven heavens, and across the four quarters of the world. He then placed this crown upon my head. {12:5} And He called me "The Lesser YHWH" before the entire heavenly host, as it is written in Exodus 23:21: "For My name is in him."

{13:1} Rabbi Ishmael said: Metatron, the angel, the Prince of the Presence, the Glory of all the heavens, said to me: Because of the abundant love and mercy the Holy One, blessed be He, showed toward me—more than any other heavenly being—He wrote upon the crown on my head with His finger, using a flaming stylus, the letters by which heaven and earth, the seas, rivers, mountains, hills, planets, and constellations were created. These letters also brought forth the lightnings, winds, earthquakes, and thunder, as well as snow, hail, storm-winds, and tempests—the letters by which all the needs of the world and the order of Creation were made. {13:2} Each individual letter continuously emitted flashes of light, sometimes appearing as torches, at other times like flames of fire, and yet other times as rays resembling the rising of the sun, the moon, and the stars.

{14:1} Rabbi Ishmael said: Metatron, the Angel, the Prince of the Presence, said to me: When the Holy One, blessed be He, placed the crown upon my head, all the Princes of Kingdoms in the heights of Araboth Raqia and all the hosts in the heavens trembled before me. Even the highest-ranking angels, including the princes of the Elim, Er'ellim, and Tafsarim, who are greater than all the ministering angels that serve before the Throne of Glory, shook with fear and awe when they saw me. {14:2} Even Sammael, the Prince of the Accusers, who is the greatest of all the princes in the heavenly realms, feared and trembled in my presence. {14:3} Likewise, the angel of fire, the angel of hail, the angel of wind, the angel of lightning, the angel of wrath, the angel of thunder, the angel of snow, the angel of rain, the angel of day, the angel of night, the angel of the sun, the angel of the moon, the angel of the planets, and the angel of the constellations—all who govern the world—were terrified and trembled before me when they beheld me. {14:4} These are the names of the rulers of the world: Gabriel, the angel of fire; Baradiel, the angel of hail; Ruchiel, who governs the wind; Baraqiel, who governs the lightning; Za'amiel, who governs wrath; Ziqiel, who governs sparks; Zi'iel, who governs tremors; Zdaphiel, who governs storm-winds; Ra'amiel, who governs thunder; Retashiel, who governs earthquakes; Shalgiel, who governs snow; Matariel, who governs rain; Shimshiel, who governs the day; Lailiel, who governs the night; Galgalliel, who governs the sun; 'Ophanniel, who governs the moon; Kokbiel, who governs the planets; and Rahatiel, who governs the constellations. {14:5} All of them fell prostrate when they saw me, unable to look upon me because of the overwhelming glory and majesty of the shining light radiating from the crown of glory upon my head.

{15:1} Rabbi Ishmael said: Metatron, the angel, the Prince of the Presence, the Glory of all the heavens, said to me: When the Holy One, blessed be He, took me into His service to attend to the Throne of Glory, the Wheels of the Merkaba, and the needs of the Shekina, my entire being was transformed. My flesh became flames, my sinews turned to burning fire, my bones became coals of juniper, the light of my eyelids turned into lightning, my eyes became firebrands, the hair on my head transformed into fiery sparks, and every part of my body became wings of burning fire, my entire form radiating with glowing flames. {15:2} On my right side, fiery flames blazed, and on my left, burning firebrands. All around me, storm-winds and tempests howled, and the thunder roared with earthquake-like intensity both in front of and behind me.

Fragment of 'Ascension of Moses': {1} Rabbi Ishmael said: Metatron, the Prince of the Presence and the leader of all the heavenly princes, stands before the One who is greater than all the Elohim. He goes beneath the Throne of Glory and dwells in a great tabernacle of light in the heavens. He brings forth the fire of deafness and places it in the ears of the holy Chayyoth, so that they may not hear the voice of the Word (Dibbur) coming from the Divine Majesty. {2} When Moses ascended on high, he fasted for 121 days until the gates of the chashmal were opened to him, allowing him to see the heart within the heart of the Lion and the countless hosts surrounding him. They wanted to consume him with fire, but Moses prayed for mercy, first on behalf of Israel and then for himself. Then the One who sits upon the Merkaba opened the windows above the heads of the Kerubim. A host of 1,800 advocates, along with Metatron, the Prince of the Presence, came forward to meet Moses. They took the prayers of Israel and placed them as a crown on the head of the Holy One, blessed be He. {3} They proclaimed, "Hear, O Israel, the Lord our God is one Lord," and their faces shone with joy before the Shekina. They asked Metatron, "What are these, and to whom is all this honor and glory given?" The reply was, "To the Glorious Lord of Israel." They then declared, "Hear, O Israel: the Lord, our God, is one Lord. Who else but You, YHWH, the Divine Majesty, living and eternal King, deserves such honor and glory?" {4} At that moment, Akatriel Yah Yehod Sebaoth spoke to Metatron, the Prince of the Presence, saying: "Let no prayer that Moses prays before Me return unanswered. Hear his prayer and fulfill his desires, whether great or small." {5} Immediately, Metatron, the Prince of the Presence, spoke to Moses, saying, "Son of Amram, do not fear, for God now delights in you. Ask of the Glory and Majesty whatever your heart desires, for your face shines from one end of the world to the other." But Moses responded, "I fear I may bring guilt upon myself." Metatron then said, "Take hold of the letters of the oath, which bind the covenant without any possibility of breaking it."

{16:1} Metatron, the exalted angel, also known as the Prince of the Presence and the Glory of Heaven, began speaking to Rabbi Ishmael. He explained that at one time, he sat upon a grand throne near the door of the Seventh Hall, tasked with judging the celestial beings, all by the authority of the Holy One, blessed be He. Metatron was responsible for distributing greatness, kingship, honor, rulership, praise, and the diadem of glory to all the princes of the kingdoms while presiding over the celestial court. These princes stood before him, on his right and left, as he commanded them by the will of the Holy One. {16:2} However, when Acher (Elisha ben Abuyah) gazed upon Metatron during his vision of the Merkaba (the divine chariot) and saw him sitting upon a throne like a king, surrounded by angels serving him and princes adorned with crowns, he was overcome with fear and awe. Acher's soul was filled with terror as he mistakenly perceived Metatron as a second divine power. {16:3} In his confusion, Acher declared, "Indeed, there are two divine powers in heaven!" {16:4} Immediately, a voice from heaven, the Bath Qol, came forth from the Shekina, saying, "Return, O backsliding children, except Acher" (Jeremiah 3:22). {16:5} Following this, 'Aniyel, a great and revered prince sent by the Holy One, gave Metatron sixty lashes of fire, forcing him to stand on his feet.

{17:1} Rabbi Ishmael continued to listen as Metatron described the seven princes who are appointed over the seven heavens. These princes are great, beautiful, revered, wonderful, and honored. Their names are Mikael, Gabriel, Shataqiel, Shachaqiel, Bakariel, Badariel, and Pachriel. {17:2} Each of these princes commands a host of 496,000 myriads of angels. {17:3} Mikael, the great prince, presides over the seventh heaven, Araboth, while Gabriel commands the sixth heaven, Makon. Shataqiel rules over the fifth heaven, Ma'on, and Shachaqiel commands the fourth heaven, Zebul. Badariel presides over the third heaven, Shehaqim, while Barakiel rules over the second heaven, Merom Raqia. Lastly, Pazriel governs the first heaven, Wilon in Shamayim. {17:4} Under these princes is Galgalliel, the prince of the sun's globe, accompanied by 96 angels who move the sun across the firmament. {17:5} Ophaniel, the prince of the moon's globe, leads 88 angels who move the moon 354,000 parasangs each night, especially on the fifteenth day of the month when the moon reaches its turning point in the East. {17:6} Rahatiel, the prince of the constellations, is accompanied by 72 angels, and he causes the stars to race 339,000 parasangs every night across the sky. {17:7} Kokbiel, the prince of the planets, leads 365,000 myriads of angels, moving the planets across the heavens. {17:8} Above them all are the seventy-two princes of kingdoms, corresponding to the seventy-two tongues of the world, each crowned with royal diadems, robed in royal garments, and mounted on royal horses. These princes are attended by royal servants as they travel through the heavens with great majesty, just as earthly princes journey with chariots and armies.

{18:1} Metatron continued, describing the order and hierarchy of the angels. The angels of the first heaven, upon seeing their prince, dismount their horses and prostrate themselves in reverence. The prince of the first heaven, in turn, removes his crown and bows before the prince of the second heaven. This pattern repeats as each prince, upon seeing the prince of the next higher heaven, removes his crown and prostrates himself. {18:2} When the prince of the seventh heaven sees the seventy-two princes of the kingdoms, he too removes his crown and falls on his face. {18:3} The seventy-two princes, upon seeing the doorkeepers of the first hall of Araboth Raqia, the highest realm, remove their crowns and prostrate themselves. This continues through the seven halls, as each set of doorkeepers bows before the next higher group of doorkeepers. {18:4} The doorkeepers of the seventh hall, upon seeing the four great princes who command the four camps of Shekina, remove their crowns and bow. {18:5} The four great princes themselves bow when they see Tag'as, the prince who leads the heavenly hosts in song and praise. {18:6} Tag'as, in turn, bows when he sees Barattiel, a great prince in the heights of Araboth. {18:7} Barattiel bows when he sees Hamon, the great and terrifying prince who causes all the children of heaven to tremble as the time for the Trisagion (the 'Thrice Holy') approaches, just as the nations scatter at the sound of the tumult (Isaiah 33:3). {18:8} Hamon bows when he sees Tutresiel, another great prince, who in turn bows to Atrugiel. {18:9} Atrugiel bows to Na'aririel, who bows to Sasnigiel. {18:10} Sasnigiel bows to Zazriel, who in turn bows to Geburatiel. {18:11} Geburatiel bows to Araphiel, and Araphiel bows to Ashruylu, the prince who presides over the celestial court. {18:12} Ashruylu bows to Gallisur, the prince who reveals all the secrets of the Torah. {18:13} Gallisur bows to Zakzakiel, who records the merits of Israel before the Throne of Glory. {18:14} Zakzakiel bows to Anaphiel, the prince who holds the keys to the heavenly halls. Anaphiel's honor and majesty overshadow all the chambers of Araboth, just as the Maker of the World's glory covers the heavens (Habakkuk 3:3). {18:15} Anaphiel bows to Sother Ashiel, the prince who oversees the four heads of the fiery river near the Throne of Glory. {18:16} Sother Ashiel controls the seals of the fiery river and allows entry and exit before the Shekina. He is described as being of immense height, stirring up the fire of the river and expounding the records of the world's inhabitants before the Holy One, as written in Daniel 7:10: "The court was seated, and the books were opened." {18:17} Sother Ashiel bows to Shoqed Chozi, who weighs the merits of humanity in the presence of the Holy One. {18:18} Shoqed Chozi bows to Zehanpuryu, the mighty prince who rebukes the fiery river and pushes it back to its place. {18:19} Zehanpuryu bows to Azbuga, a prince who knows the mysteries of the Throne of Glory and will one day clothe the righteous with garments of life for eternal life. {18:20} Finally, when Azbuga sees the two great princes, Sopheriel H' the Killer and Sopheriel H' the Lifegiver, he removes his crown and falls on his face. {18:21} Sopheriel H' the Killer is responsible for recording the names of the dead, while Sopheriel H' the Lifegiver writes the names of those whom the Holy One will bring into life in the Book of Life. {18:22} Although they are great princes, even these exalted beings do not fulfill the Shekina's requests except while standing, as written in 1 Kings 22:19 and 2 Chronicles 18:18: "And all the host of heaven are standing by Him." {18:23} These two princes stand on wheels of tempest and storm-wind, each clothed in royal garments and crowned with royal crowns. Their bodies are full of eyes, their appearance is like lightning, and their eyes are like the sun in its might. {18:24} Their wings number as many as the days of the year, and they span the entire firmament. Their mouths emit flames and lightnings, and from their sweat, fire is kindled. Their tongues rise as high as the waves of the sea, and they hold in their hands burning scrolls and flaming styles. The scrolls are 3,000 myriads of parasangs long, and each letter is 365 parasangs in size.

{19:1} R. Ishmael said: Metatron, the Angel, the Prince of the Presence, said to me: Above the three angels, these great princes, there is one Prince, distinguished, honored, noble, glorified, adorned, fearful, valiant, strong, great, magnified, glorious, crowned, wonderful, exalted, blameless, beloved, lordly, high and lofty, ancient and mighty, unlike any other among the princes. His name is Rikbiel, the great and revered Prince who stands by the Merkaba. {19:2} And why is he called Rikbiel? Because he is in charge of the wheels of the Merkaba, which are entrusted to his care. {19:3} And how many wheels are there? Eight; two in each direction. Four winds surround them: "the Storm-Wind," "the Tempest," "the Strong Wind," and "the Wind of Earthquake." {19:4} Beneath them, four fiery rivers flow continuously—one on each side. Around them, between the rivers, four clouds are placed: "clouds of fire," "clouds of lamps," "clouds of coal," and "clouds of brimstone." These clouds stand opposite their respective wheels. {19:5} The feet of the Chayyoth rest upon the wheels. Between each wheel, earthquakes rumble, and thunder roars. {19:6} When the time comes for the Song's recital, the multitude of wheels begin to move, the clouds tremble, and all the chieftains are struck with fear. The horsemen rage, the mighty ones become excited, the hosts are terrified, the troops are gripped with fear, the appointed ones flee, the princes and armies are dismayed, the servants faint, and the angels and divisions are stricken with pain. {19:7} One wheel speaks to another, one Kerub speaks to another, one Chayya speaks to another, and one Seraph speaks to another, proclaiming, "Extol to him who rides in the 'Araboth, by His name Jah, and rejoice before Him!" (Psalm 68:5).

{20:1} R. Ishmael said: Metatron, the Angel, the Prince of the Presence, said to me: Above all the others, there is one great and mighty prince named Chayyiel, a noble, revered, glorious, and mighty prince before whom all the children of heaven tremble. He is a prince so powerful that he could swallow the whole earth in a single moment. {20:2} Why is he called Chayyiel? Because he is appointed over the Holy Chayyoth and strikes them with fiery lashes, glorifying them when they offer praise and rejoicing. He hastens them to proclaim, "Holy" and "Blessed be the glory of the Lord from His place" during the Qedushsha.

{21:1} R. Ishmael said: Metatron, the Angel, the Prince of the Presence, said to me: There are four Chayyoth, corresponding to the four winds. Each Chayya spans the space of the entire world. Each has four faces, and each face is like the face of the East. {21:2} Each Chayya has four wings, and each wing is as vast as the roof of the universe. {21:3} Each one has faces within faces and wings within wings. The size of their faces is equivalent to 248 faces, and their wings measure 365 wings. {21:4} Every Chayya is crowned with 2,000 crowns upon its head, each crown as resplendent as a rainbow and as radiant as the sun. The sparks emanating from them shine like the morning star, the planet Venus, in the East.

{22:1} R. Ishmael said: Metatron, the Angel, the Prince of the Presence, said to me: Above all others, there is one noble and wonderful prince, full of power and strength. His name is Kerubiel, a prince praised with every kind of praise. He is mighty and righteous, adorned with holiness and glorified by a thousand hosts and ten thousand armies. {22:2} At his wrath, the earth trembles, and at his anger, the camps shake. His rebuke makes the foundations quake, and the Araboth tremble in fear. {22:3} His body is filled with burning coals, and his height reaches as far as the seven heavens in every dimension—height, width, and depth. {22:4} When he opens his mouth, it is like a lamp of fire; his tongue is consuming fire, his eyebrows radiate like lightning, and his eyes are like sparks of brilliance. His face shines with burning fire. {22:5} A crown of holiness rests upon his head, engraved with the Explicit Name, from which lightning constantly flashes. The Shekina's bow rests between his shoulders. {22:6} His sword is like lightning, arrows of flame cover his loins, his armor and shield blaze with consuming fire, and burning juniper coals adorn his neck and surround him. {22:7} The Shekina's splendor shines on his face, majesty crowns his wheels, and a royal diadem rests on his skull. {22:8} His entire body is covered in eyes, and wings surround his great stature. {22:9} A flame burns on his right hand, a fire glows on his left, coals burn from it, and firebrands emerge from his body, while lightning flashes from his face. Thunder perpetually roars around him, and the earth quakes by his side. {22:10} Two princes of the Merkaba stand with him. {22:11} Why is he called Kerubiel? Because he is appointed over the chariot of the Kerubim, and the mighty Kerubim are entrusted to his care. He adorns their crowns and polishes their diadems. {22:12} He magnifies their glory and beauty, increases their honor, encourages them to sing praises, and enhances their strength and brilliance. He elevates their beauty and lovingkindness, perfects their mercy, and intensifies the glory of their majesty. {22:13} The Kerubim stand beside the Holy Chayyoth, with wings raised above their heads. The Shekina rests upon them, the splendor of Glory shines on their faces, and songs of praise fill their mouths. Their hands are hidden beneath their wings, and their feet are covered. Crowns of glory rest upon their heads, and the splendor of the Shekina illuminates their faces. Sapphire stones encircle them, and columns of fire stand on every side. {22:14} One sapphire shines on one side, and another sapphire shines on the opposite side. Beneath the sapphires, coals of burning juniper blaze. {22:15} One Kerub stands in each direction, and their wings surround one another above their heads in glory. Together, they raise their wings to sing to the one who rides upon the clouds and praise the awe-inspiring majesty of the King of Kings. {22:16} Kerubiel, the prince over them, arranges them in comely and pleasant orders and elevates them with all manner of dignity and glory. He hastens them in strength and majesty to fulfill the will of their Creator every moment, for above their heads resides the glory of the King who dwells upon the Kerubim.

{22b:1} There is a court before the Throne of Glory that no seraph or angel may enter. It spans 36,000 myriads of parasangs, as it is written: "The seraphim stand above Him" (Isaiah 6:2), the last word equating to the numerical value of 36. {22b:2} As the number 36 implies, there are 36 bridges there. {22b:3} There are 24 myriads of wheels of fire, and 12,000 myriads of ministering angels, as well as 12,000 rivers of hail and 12,000 treasuries of snow. {22b:4} In the seven halls, chariots of fire and flames are countless and without end. {22b:5} R. Ishmael asked: How do the angels stand on high? Metatron responded: Like a bridge placed over a river for all to cross, there is a bridge from one entry to the next. {22b:6} Three ministering angels surround it and sing before YHWH, the God of Israel. Lords of dread and captains of fear, numbering thousands and ten thousands, stand before it, praising YHWH with hymns. {22b:7} Numerous bridges exist, some of fire and others of hail, alongside countless rivers of hail, treasuries of snow, and wheels of fire. {22b:8} The ministering angels number 12,000 myriads, with six above and six below. The treasuries of snow are similarly arranged. {22b:9} Surrounding these bridges and rivers are numerous ministering angels that create pathways for all creatures standing within, corresponding to the pathways of the firmament. {22b:10} What does YHWH, the God of Israel, the King of Glory, do? He covers His face in majesty. {22b:11} In the 'Araboth, 660,000 myriads of angels of glory stand near the Throne of Glory and divisions of flaming fire. The King of Glory covers His face, for otherwise, the 'Araboth Raqia would be torn asunder by His majesty, splendor, and beauty. {22b:12} Many ministering angels stand before Him, kings and princes of the heavens adorned with song and love, trembling at the sight of the Shekina. Their eyes are dazzled, their faces grow dark, and their strength fails before His brilliance. {22b:13} Rivers of joy, streams of gladness, and rivers of love flow forth from the Throne of Glory, growing greater at the sound of the praises sung by the Chayyoth, the Ophannim, and the Kerubim, as they proclaim: "Holy, holy, holy is the Lord of Hosts; the whole earth is full of His glory!"

{22c:1} R. Ishmael asked: What is the distance between one bridge and another? Metatron responded: 12 myriads of parasangs. Their ascent is 12 myriads of parasangs, and their descent is the same. {22c:2} The distance between the rivers of dread and the rivers of fear is 22 myriads of parasangs; between the rivers of hail and darkness, it is 36 myriads of parasangs; between the chambers of lightning and the clouds of compassion, it is 42 myriads of parasangs; between the clouds of compassion and the Merkaba, it is 84 myriads of parasangs. {22c:3} The distance between the Merkaba and the Kerubim is 148 myriads of parasangs; between the Kerubim and the Ophannim, it is 24 myriads of parasangs; between the Ophannim and the chambers of chambers, it is also 24 myriads of parasangs; and between the chambers of chambers and the Holy Chayyoth, the distance is 40,000 myriads of parasangs. {22c:4} The span between one wing of the Chayyoth and another is 12 myriads of parasangs, and the breadth of each wing matches this measurement. {22c:5} The distance from the Holy Chayyoth to the Throne of Glory is 30,000 myriads of parasangs. {22c:6} From the foot of the Throne to its seat, there are 40,000 myriads of parasangs, and the Name of Him who sits on it is holy and sanctified. {22c:7} The arches of the Bow are set above the 'Araboth, rising 1,000 thousand and 10,000 times 10,000 parasangs, measured after the scale of the Watchers and Holy Ones. As written: "My bow I have set in the cloud" (Genesis 9:13), signifying it is already set. As the clouds pass by, the angels of hail transform into burning coal. {22c:8} A fiery voice descends from the Holy Chayyoth, and in fear of the voice, they run to another place lest they be commanded, then return to avoid injury from the other side. Thus, they "run and return" (Ezekiel 1:14). {22c:9} The arches of the Bow are more radiant than the summer sun and whiter than flaming fire, majestic and beautiful. {22c:10} Above the arches of the Bow are the wheels of the Ophannim, measuring 1,000 thousand and 10,000 times 10,000 units, according to the measure of the Seraphim and the Troops (Gedudim).

{23:1} R. Ishmael said: Metatron, the Angel, the Prince of the Presence, said to me: "There are many winds blowing under the wings of the Kerubim. {23:2} First is the 'Brooding Wind,' as it is written in Genesis 1:2: 'And the Spirit of God was brooding over the surface of the waters.' {23:3} Then comes the 'Strong Wind,' as mentioned in Exodus 14:21: 'The Lord caused the sea to go back by a strong east wind all that night.' {23:4} Next is the 'East Wind,' as it is written in Exodus 10:13: 'The east wind brought the locusts.' {23:5} There also blows the 'Wind of Quails,' as it is written in Numbers 11:31: 'And a wind went forth from the Lord and brought quails.' {23:6} The 'Wind of Jealousy' follows, as in Numbers 5:14: 'And the spirit of jealousy came upon him.' {23:7} After that blows the 'Wind of Earthquake,' as in 1 Kings 19:11: 'And after the earthquake, a wind; but the Lord was not in the wind.' {23:8} There blows the 'Wind of God,' as seen in Ezekiel 37:1: 'And He carried me out by the wind of the Lord.' {23:9} The 'Evil Wind' also blows, as it is written in 1 Samuel 16:23: 'And the evil wind departed from him.' {23:10} The 'Winds of Wisdom, Understanding, Knowledge, and Fear of God' are mentioned in Isaiah 11:2: 'And the spirit of the Lord shall rest upon him—the spirit of wisdom and understanding, the spirit of counsel and might, the spirit of knowledge and the fear of the Lord.' {23:11} There is also the 'Wind of Rain,' as in Proverbs 25:23: 'The north wind brings forth rain.' {23:12} The 'Wind of Lightnings' is mentioned in Jeremiah 10:13 and 51:16: 'He makes lightning for the rain and brings forth the wind from His treasuries.' {23:13} The 'Wind Breaking the Rocks' comes next, as written in 1 Kings 19:11: 'A great and strong wind tore through the mountains and broke the rocks before the Lord.' {23:14} The 'Wind of Assuagement of the Sea' is found in Genesis 8:1: 'God made a wind pass over the earth, and the waters subsided.' {23:15} The 'Wind of Wrath' is referred to in Job 1:19: 'And behold, a great wind came from the wilderness and struck the four corners of the house.' {23:16} The 'Storm-Wind,' which is associated with Satan, is mentioned in Psalm 148:8: 'Stormy wind fulfilling His word,' where 'storm-wind' refers to Satan. All these winds blow under the wings of the Kerubim, as it is written in Psalm 18:10: 'He rode upon a cherub and flew; He flew swiftly on the wings of the wind.' {23:17} And where do these winds go? Scripture tells us they move from under the wings of the Kerubim and descend upon the globe of the sun, as in Ecclesiastes 1:6: 'The wind goes toward the south and turns to the north, continually circling, and returns to its course.' From there, they descend to the seas, rivers, mountains, and hills, as in Amos 4:13: 'For He forms the mountains and creates the wind.' {23:18} From the mountains and rivers, they move to cities and provinces and then descend into the Garden of Eden, as in Genesis 3:8: 'Walking in the Garden in the wind of the day.' In the Garden, they unite and blow through the remotest parts, perfumed by the spices of the Garden, until they separate and bring the scent of Eden's spices to the righteous who will inherit the Garden of Eden and the Tree of Life, as written in Song of Songs 4:16: 'Awake, O north wind, and come, O south! Blow upon my garden, that its spices may flow out.'"

{24:1} R. Ishmael said: Metatron, the Angel, the Prince of the Presence, said to me: "The Holy One, blessed be He, has many chariots. {24:2} He has the 'Chariots of the Kerubim,' as mentioned in Psalm 18:10 and 2 Samuel 22:11: 'He rode upon a cherub and did fly.' {24:3} He has the 'Chariots of Wind,' as seen in the same verse: 'And He flew swiftly upon the wings of the wind.' {24:4} He possesses the 'Chariots of Swift Cloud,' as written in Isaiah 19:1: 'Behold, the Lord rides on a swift cloud.' {24:5} He has the 'Chariots of Clouds,' as seen in Exodus 19:9: 'Lo, I come to you in a cloud.' {24:6} He also has the 'Chariots of the Altar,' as in Amos 9:1: 'I saw the Lord standing upon the altar.' {24:7} The 'Chariots of Ribbotaim' are mentioned in Psalm 68:18: 'The chariots of God are Ribbotaim; thousands of angels.' {24:8} He has the 'Chariots of the Tent,' as written in Deuteronomy 31:15: 'The Lord appeared in the tent in a pillar of cloud.' {24:9} The 'Chariots of the Tabernacle' are described in Leviticus 1:1: 'The Lord spoke to him from the Tabernacle.' {24:10} The 'Chariots of the Mercy-Seat' are mentioned in Numbers 7:89: 'He heard the voice speaking to him from the mercy seat.' {24:11} He possesses the 'Chariots of Sapphire Stone,' as written in Exodus 24:10: 'And there was under His feet a paved work of sapphire stone.' {24:12} He also has the 'Chariots of Eagles,' as in Exodus 19:4: 'I bore you on eagles' wings,' where 'eagles' refers to swift beings. {24:13} The 'Chariots of Shout' are referred to in Psalm 47:6: 'God has gone up with a shout.' {24:14} The 'Chariots of Araboth' are found in Psalm 68:5: 'Extol Him who rides on the Araboth.' {24:15} He has the 'Chariots of Thick Clouds,' as seen in Psalm 104:3: 'Who makes the thick clouds His chariot.' {24:16} The 'Chariots of the Chayyoth' are mentioned in Ezekiel 1:14: 'The Chayyoth ran and returned.' They move by permission, as Shekina is above them. {24:17} He also has the 'Chariots of Wheels (Galgallim),' as written in Ezekiel 10:2: 'Go between the whirling wheels.' {24:18} There is the 'Chariot of a Swift Cherub,' as seen in Psalm 18:10 and Isaiah 19:1: 'Riding on a swift cherub.' When He rides a cherub, He can see through eighteen thousand worlds in one glance before He places His other foot upon the cherub, as it is written in Ezekiel 48:35: 'Round about eighteen thousand.' And in Psalm 14:2: 'The Lord looked down from heaven upon the children of men.' {24:19} Lastly, He has the 'Chariots of the Ophannim,' as written in Ezekiel 10:12: 'The Ophannim were full of eyes all around.' {24:20} He also has the 'Chariots of His Holy Throne,' as seen in Psalm 47:8: 'God sits upon His holy throne.' {24:21} The 'Chariots of the Throne of Yah' are described in Exodus 17:16: 'A hand is lifted up upon the Throne of Yah.' {24:22} There are the 'Chariots of the Throne of Judgement,' as seen in Isaiah 5:16: 'But the Lord of hosts is exalted in judgment.' {24:23} He also has the 'Chariots of the Throne of Glory,' as mentioned in Jeremiah 17:12: 'The Throne of Glory, set on high from the beginning, is our sanctuary.' {24:24} Finally, He has the 'Chariots of the High and Exalted Throne,' as written in Isaiah 6:1: 'I saw the Lord sitting upon the high and exalted throne.'"

{25:1} R. Ishmael said: Metatron, the Angel, the Prince of the Presence, said to me: "Above these, there is one great prince, revered, ancient, powerful, and terrifying. His name is Ophphanniel. {25:2} He has sixteen faces, four on each side, with one hundred wings on each side and 8,466 eyes, corresponding to the days of the year. Some say 2,190 or 2,116 on each side, while others say 2,196 eyes. {25:3} His two main eyes flash lightning, and firebrands burn from them. No creature can look upon them without being consumed by fire. {25:4} His height spans 2,500 years' journey, and no eye can see nor mouth describe his mighty power, save for the King of Kings, the Holy One, blessed be He. {25:5} Why is he called Ophphanniel? Because he is appointed over the Ophannim, tasked with beautifying and preparing them every day. {25:6} All the Ophannim are full of eyes and brightness, with seventy-two sapphire stones on each side of their garments. {25:7} Four carbuncle stones are set in the crown of each one, radiating in all directions of 'Araboth like the sun radiates throughout the universe. The stones are called carbuncle because their brilliance resembles lightning. Their tents are enclosed by splendor, radiance, and light due to their bright eyes."

{26:1} R. Ishmael said: Metatron, the Angel, the Prince of the Presence, said to me: "Above these is one mighty prince, filled with splendor, honor, and brilliance. His name is Seraphiel. {26:2} He is completely filled with light and beauty, radiating majesty and goodliness. {26:3} His face is like that of angels, but his body is like an eagle's. {26:4} His appearance shines like firebrands, his radiance like lightning, and his splendor like chashmals, resembling the light of Venus. {26:5} The sapphire stone on his head shines as bright as the heavens, radiating throughout the universe. {26:6} His body is covered in eyes like stars, some resembling Venus and others like the sun and moon. {26:7} His crown spans a distance of 502 years' journey, containing every form of splendor and light in existence. {26:8} Seraphiel is named because he is in charge of the Seraphim, teaching them songs of praise and might by day and night. {26:9} There are four Seraphim, corresponding to the four winds, each with six wings and four faces. {26:10} Their size and height are equivalent to the seven heavens, and their wings stretch like the firmament. {26:11} They shine with such brilliance that even the holy Chayyoth, the Ophannim, and the Kerubim cannot gaze upon them. {26:12} They are called Seraphim because they burn the writing tablets of Satan, who records Israel's sins to present them to the Holy One. But the Seraphim, knowing the Holy One's desire to preserve Israel, burn the tablets in the fire before they reach the Divine."

{27:1} R. Ishmael said: Metatron, the Angel, the Prince of the Presence, said to me: "Above the Seraphim is a prince exalted above all, whose name is Radweriel. {27:2} He is appointed over the treasuries of books and records, bringing them before the Holy One. He breaks the seals, opens the case, and delivers the books before the Holy One, who passes them to the Scribes to be read before the Heavenly Court. {27:3} Radweriel is named because every word from his mouth creates an angel who sings praises before the Holy One when the time for the recitation of the 'Thrice Holy' approaches."

{28:1} Rabbi Ishmael said: Metatron, the Angel, the Prince of the Presence, spoke to me, saying: Above all other beings, there are four great princes known as Irin and Qaddishin. They are exalted, revered, and beloved, wonderful and glorious, surpassing all the other celestial beings. There is none among the heavenly princes or servants who can compare to them, for each one of them is equal to all the others combined. {28:2} Their dwelling place is opposite the Throne of Glory, and their position is before the Holy One, blessed be He, so that the brilliance of their dwelling reflects the brilliance of the Throne of Glory, and the splendor of their faces mirrors the splendor of the Shekinah. {28:3} They are glorified by the glory of the Divine Majesty (Gebura) and praised through the praise of the Shekinah. {28:4} Furthermore, the Holy One, blessed be He, does nothing in His world without first consulting them, and only after does He act, as it is written (Daniel 4:17): "The sentence is by the decree of the Irin and the demand by the word of the Qaddishin." {28:5} The Irin are two, and the Qaddishin are two. They stand before the Holy One, blessed be He, with one 'Ir on one side, another 'Ir on the opposite side, one Qaddish on one side, and the other Qaddish on the other side. {28:6} They exalt the humble and bring down the proud, raising the lowly to great heights. {28:7} Each day, when the Holy One, blessed be He, sits upon the Throne of Judgment to judge the world, and the Books of the Living and the Dead are opened before Him, all the heavenly beings stand before Him in fear, dread, awe, and trembling. At that moment, the Holy One, blessed be He, is seated upon the Throne of Judgment, His garments white as snow, His hair pure like wool, and His entire cloak shining like light. He is covered in righteousness as with armor. {28:8} The Irin and Qaddishin stand before Him like court officers before a judge. They raise and discuss every case that comes before the Holy One, blessed be He, in judgment, as it is written (Daniel 4:17): "The sentence is by the decree of the Irin and the demand by the word of the Qaddishin." {28:9} Some of them argue cases, while others pass judgment in the Great Beth Din in 'Araboth. Some present requests before the Divine Majesty, while others close the cases before the Most High. Others descend to the world to carry out the sentences, as it is written (Daniel 4:13-14): "Behold, an 'Ir and a Qaddish came down from heaven, and they cried aloud, saying: Cut down the tree, cut off its branches, shake off its leaves, and scatter its fruit. Let the beasts flee from beneath it and the birds from its branches." {28:10} They are called Irin and Qaddishin because they sanctify body and spirit with fiery lashes on the third day of judgment, as it is written (Hosea 6:2): "After two days He will revive us; on the third day, He will raise us up, and we shall live before Him."

{29:1} Rabbi Ishmael said: Metatron, the Angel, the Prince of the Presence, told me: Each of these angels has seventy names, corresponding to the seventy languages of the world, and all their names are based on the name of the Holy One, blessed be He. Each name is written with a flaming stylus upon the Fearful Crown (Keiher Nora), which rests upon the head of the High and Exalted King. {29:2} Sparks and lightnings emanate from each of them, and each one is adorned with splendid horns. Lights radiate from them, and they are surrounded by tents of brilliance. Even the Seraphim and the Chayyoth, who are greater than all other heavenly beings, cannot behold them.

{30:1} Rabbi Ishmael said: Metatron, the Angel, the Prince of the Presence, told me: Whenever the Great Beth Din convenes in the Araboth Raqia' on high, no one in the world can speak except for the great princes, who bear the name of the Holy One, blessed be He. {30:2} How many princes are there? Seventy-two princes, who represent the kingdoms of the world, along with the Prince of the World, who pleads on behalf of the world before the Holy One, blessed be He, every day, when the book is opened that records all the deeds of the world, as it is written (Daniel 7:10): "The judgment was set, and the books were opened."

{31:1} Rabbi Ishmael said: Metatron, the Angel, the Prince of the Presence, said to me: When the Holy One, blessed be He, sits upon the Throne of Judgment, Justice stands on His right, Mercy on His left, and Truth before His face. {31:2} When a person comes before Him for judgment, a staff of Mercy comes forth from His splendor and stands before the person. Instantly, the individual falls upon their face, and all the angels of destruction tremble in fear, as it is written (Isaiah 16:5): "In mercy, the throne will be established, and He will sit upon it in truth."

{32:1} Rabbi Ishmael said: Metatron, the Angel, the Prince of the Presence, said to me: When the Holy One, blessed be He, opens the book that is half fire and half flame, the judgment is immediately executed on the wicked. His sword, which is drawn from its sheath, shines like lightning and extends from one end of the world to the other, as it is written (Isaiah 66:16): "For by fire, the Lord will judge, and by His sword, He will judge all flesh." {32:2} The inhabitants of the world tremble in fear when they see His sharpened sword, flashing like lightning across the sky, with sparks and flashes like the stars of the heavens going forth from it, as it is written (Deuteronomy 32:41): "If I sharpen the lightning of My sword."

{33:1} Rabbi Ishmael said: Metatron, the Angel, the Prince of the Presence, told me: When the Holy One, blessed be He, sits upon the Throne of Judgment, the angels of Mercy stand on His right, the angels of Peace stand on His left, and the angels of Destruction stand before Him. {33:2} One scribe stands beneath Him, and another scribe stands above Him. {33:3} The glorious Seraphim surround the Throne on all four sides, their walls formed of lightnings, and the Ophannim encircle them with firebrands around the Throne of Glory. Clouds of fire and flames surround them on the right and left, while the Holy Chayyoth bear the Throne of Glory from below, each with three fingers. The size of each finger is eight hundred thousand, seven hundred times a hundred, and sixty-six thousand parasangs. {33:4} Beneath the feet of the Chayyoth flow seven fiery rivers, each one spanning 365,000 parasangs in width and 248,000 myriads of parasangs in depth, their length unsearchable and immeasurable. {33:5} These rivers bow in four directions in the Araboth Raqia', then flow down to Ma'on, where they are halted, and from Ma'on to Zebul, from Zebul to Shechaqim, from Shechaqim to Raqia', from Raqia' to Shamayim, and from Shamayim to the heads of the wicked in Gehenna, as it is written (Jeremiah 23:19): "Behold, a whirlwind of the Lord has gone forth in fury, a violent whirlwind; it will burst upon the head of the wicked."

{34:1} Rabbi Ishmael said: Metatron, the Angel, the Prince of the Presence, said to me: "The hoofs of the Chayyoth are surrounded by seven layers of burning coals. These burning coals are enclosed by seven walls of flames. Outside of these walls of flames are seven walls of hailstones, referred to in Ezekiel's prophecy (Ezek. 13:11,13; 28:22) as stones of 'Et-gabish.' Beyond the hailstones are stones of another kind of hail, called Barad. These stones of hail are encased by the stones of 'the wings of the tempest.' The stones of 'the wings of the tempest' are then encircled by more flames of fire. Surrounding these flames of fire are the chambers of the whirlwind, and encircling the whirlwind are both fire and water. {34:2} Beyond the fire and water are those who proclaim the 'Holy.' Surrounding those who cry 'Holy' are others who declare 'Blessed.' Encircling those who say 'Blessed' are bright clouds, and beyond these clouds are burning juniper coals. Surrounding the juniper coals are a thousand camps of fire and ten thousand hosts of flame. Between each camp and each host, there is a cloud that prevents them from being consumed by the fire."

{35:1} Rabbi Ishmael said: Metatron, the Angel, the Prince of the Presence, said to me: "The Holy One, blessed be He, has 506,000 myriads of camps in the heights of Araboth Raqia. Each camp consists of 496,000 angels. {35:2} Each angel is of a height comparable to the great sea, their faces shine like lightning, their eyes blaze like lamps of fire, and their arms and feet gleam like polished brass. Their voices roar like a great multitude. {35:3} They stand before the Throne of Glory in four rows, with the princes of the army standing at the head of each row. {35:4} Some proclaim 'Holy,' while others say 'Blessed.' Some run as messengers, while others stand in attendance, as described in Daniel 7:10: 'Thousands upon thousands served Him, and ten thousand times ten thousand stood before Him; the court was seated, and the books were opened.' {35:5} When it is time to proclaim the 'Holy,' a whirlwind first goes forth from before the Holy One, blessed be He, and strikes the camp of the Shekina, causing a great commotion, as it says in Jeremiah 30:23: 'Behold, the whirlwind of the Lord goes forth with fury, a continuing whirlwind.' {35:6} At that moment, four thousand thousands of angels are transformed into sparks, firebrands, flashes of fire, flames, males, females, winds, and burning fires. These transformations continue until they accept the yoke of the Kingdom of Heaven with awe, trembling, and reverence. Afterward, they are restored to their former forms to continue their praise, as it says in Isaiah 6:3: 'And one called to another and said, "Holy, Holy, Holy is the Lord of hosts; the whole earth is full of His glory."'

{36:1} Rabbi Ishmael said: Metatron, the Angel, the Prince of the Presence, said to me: "When the ministering angels wish to recite the Song of praise, the fiery river known as Nehar di-Nur rises with thousands upon thousands and myriads upon myriads of angels. This river flows beneath the Throne of Glory and between the camps of the ministering angels and the troops of Araboth. {36:2} All the ministering angels descend into Nehar di-Nur, where they immerse themselves in the fire and dip their tongues and mouths seven times. Afterward, they ascend, don garments of 'Machaqe Samal,' cover themselves with cloaks of chashmal, and stand in four rows before the Throne of Glory across all the heavens."

{37:1} Rabbi Ishmael said: Metatron, the Angel, the Prince of the Presence, said to me: "In the seven Halls stand four chariots of Shekina, with the four camps of Shekina positioned in front of each one. A river of fire continually flows between each camp. {37:2} Bright clouds surround each river, and between the clouds stand pillars of brimstone. Between these pillars are flaming wheels, encircling them. Flames of fire burn between each wheel, and behind the flames are treasuries of lightning. Behind these treasuries are the wings of the storm wind, and beyond these wings are the chambers of the tempest. Beyond the tempest are winds, voices, thunders, sparks upon sparks, and earthquakes upon earthquakes."

{38:1} Rabbi Ishmael said: Metatron, the Angel, the Prince of the Presence, said to me: "Whenever the ministering angels proclaim 'Holy,' the pillars of the heavens tremble, their sockets shake, and the gates of the Halls of Araboth Raqia are shaken. The foundations of Shechaqim and the entire Universe are moved. The orders of Ma'on and the chambers of Makon quiver. Even the constellations and planets are terrified, and the orbs of the sun and moon flee from their courses, running twelve thousand parasangs, attempting to cast themselves down from the heavens. {38:2} This terror arises because of the loud, roaring voices of the angels' chant, the brilliance of their praise, and the sparks and lightnings flashing from their faces, as it says in Psalm 77:18: 'The voice of Your thunder was in the whirlwind, the lightnings lit up the world, the earth trembled and shook.' {38:3} But then, the Prince of the World calls to the fleeing celestial bodies, telling them to remain in their place and not to fear the angels who sing before the Holy One, blessed be He, as written in Job 38:7: 'When the morning stars sang together, and all the sons of God shouted for joy.'"

{39:1} Rabbi Ishmael said: Metatron, the Angel, the Prince of the Presence, said to me: "When the ministering angels proclaim the 'Holy,' all the explicit names engraved with a flaming style on the Throne of Glory fly off like eagles, each with sixteen wings. These names surround the Holy One, blessed be He, on all four sides of His Shekina. {39:2} The angels of the host, the flaming Servants, the mighty Ophannim, the Kerubim, the Holy Chayyoth, the Seraphim, the Erelim, the Taphsarim, the troops of consuming fire, and the fiery armies, as well as the holy princes adorned with crowns and robed in royal majesty, all fall prostrate before the Holy One. They bow three times, proclaiming, 'Blessed be the name of His glorious kingdom forever and ever.'"

{40:1} Rabbi Ishmael said: Metatron, the Angel, the Prince of the Presence, said to me: "When the ministering angels proclaim 'Holy' before the Holy One, blessed be He, in the proper order, the servants of His Throne emerge joyfully from beneath the Throne of Glory. {40:2} They carry with them a thousand thousand and ten thousand times ten thousand crowns of stars, each one resembling the planet Venus. They place these crowns upon the heads of the ministering angels and the great princes who proclaim 'Holy.' Each one receives three crowns: one for saying 'Holy,' another for saying 'Holy, Holy,' and a third for saying 'Holy, Holy, Holy is the Lord of Hosts.' {40:3} However, if the angels fail to recite 'Holy' in the proper order, a consuming fire goes forth from the little finger of the Holy One, blessed be He. This fire divides into 496,000 parts and descends into the ranks of the angels, consuming them instantly, as it is written in Psalm 97:3: 'A fire goes before Him and burns up His enemies all around.' {40:4} Then the Holy One, blessed be He, speaks a single word and creates new angels to replace the consumed ones. These new angels stand before His Throne of Glory and continue to proclaim 'Holy,' as it is written in Lamentations 3:23: 'They are new every morning; great is Your faithfulness.'"

{41:1} Rabbi Ishmael said: Metatron, the Angel, the Prince of the Presence, spoke to me and said: "Come, and behold the letters by which the heavens and the earth were created, the letters by which the mountains and hills were formed, the letters by which the seas and rivers came into being, and the letters by which the trees and herbs were made. These same letters were used to create the planets and the constellations, the globe of the moon and the globe of the sun, as well as Orion, the Pleiades, and all the different luminaries in the heavens. {41:2} These letters also created the Throne of Glory and the Wheels of the Merkaba, and by these letters, the necessities of all worlds were fashioned. {41:3} They also brought forth wisdom, understanding, knowledge, prudence, meekness, and righteousness, by which the entire world is sustained. {41:4} Then I walked by Metatron's side, and he took me by the hand, lifting me on his wings, and showed me the letters engraved with a flaming style upon the Throne of Glory. Sparks flew from these letters and filled all the chambers of the heavens."

{42:1} Rabbi Ishmael said: Metatron, the Angel, the Prince of the Presence, spoke to me and said, "Come, and I will show you where the waters are suspended on high, where fire burns in the midst of hail, where lightning flashes out of snowy mountains, where thunders roar in the celestial heights, where flames burn within flames, and where voices are heard amidst thunder and earthquakes. {42:2} He then took me by the hand and lifted me on his wings, showing me these wonders. I beheld the waters suspended in the heavens by the force of the name 'YAH 'EHYE ASHER 'EHYE' (Jah, I am that I am), with their fruits descending to water the earth, as it is written: 'He watereth the mountains from his chambers: the earth is satisfied with the fruit of thy work' (Psalm 104:13). {42:3} I also saw fire, snow, and hail mingled together but undamaged by the name 'ESH 'OKELA' (Consuming Fire), as it is written: 'For the Lord thy God is a consuming fire' (Deuteronomy 4:24). {42:4} I saw lightnings flashing from snowy mountains without being quenched, by the name 'YAH SUR 'OLAMIM' (Jah, the everlasting rock), as it is written: 'For in Jah, the Lord, is an everlasting rock' (Isaiah 26:4). {42:5} I saw thunders roaring in the midst of fiery flames, unharmed by the name 'EL-SHADDAI RABBA' (The Great God Almighty), as it is written: 'I am God

Almighty' (Genesis 17:1). {42:6} I beheld flames glowing within burning fire, untouched by the name 'YAD 'AL KES YAH' (The hand upon the throne of the Lord), as it is written: 'For the hand is upon the throne of the Lord' (Exodus 17:16). {42:7} Lastly, I saw rivers of fire flowing in the midst of rivers of water, without either being quenched, by the name 'OSE SHALOM' (Maker of Peace), as it is written: 'He maketh peace in His high places' (Job 25:2). For He makes peace between fire and water, hail and fire, wind and cloud, earthquake and sparks."

{43:1} Rabbi Ishmael said: Metatron said to me, "Come, and I will show you the abode of the spirits of the righteous who have been created and returned, as well as the spirits of the righteous who have not yet been created. {43:2} He lifted me to his side, took me by the hand, and brought me near the Throne of Glory, by the place of the Shekina. He revealed to me the spirits that had been created and returned, flying above the Throne of Glory before the Holy One, blessed be He. {43:3} As I pondered the verse, 'For the spirit clothed itself before me, and the souls I have made' (Isaiah 57:16), I realized that 'the spirit clothed itself before me' refers to the spirits created in the chamber of the righteous, which have returned to the Holy One. 'The souls I have made' refers to the spirits of the righteous that have not yet been created in the chamber of souls (Guph)."

{44:1} Rabbi Ishmael said: Metatron, the Angel, the Prince of the Presence, said to me, "Come, and I will show you the spirits of the wicked and the spirits of the intermediate, where they stand, and where they descend. {44:2} The spirits of the wicked descend to She'ol by the hands of two angels of destruction, ZAAPHIEL and SIMKIEL. {44:3} SIMKIEL is appointed over the intermediate spirits to support and purify them due to the great mercy of the Prince of the Place. ZAAPHIEL is appointed over the wicked spirits, casting them down from the presence of the Holy One into She'ol to be punished in the fire of Gehenna with burning staves of coal. {44:4} He took me by the hand and showed me all of them. {44:5} I saw their faces, resembling human children, but their bodies were like eagles. The intermediate spirits had pale grey faces due to their deeds, which stained them until they were purified by the fire. {44:6} The wicked had faces as black as the bottom of a pot due to the wickedness of their actions. {44:7} I also saw the spirits of the Patriarchs Abraham, Isaac, and Jacob, along with the rest of the righteous, who had ascended from their graves and now prayed before the Holy One. They said, 'Lord of the Universe! How long will you sit upon your throne like a mourner, with your right hand hidden, without delivering your children and revealing your Kingdom to the world? How long will you have no pity upon your children, who are enslaved among the nations, or on your right hand that remains hidden, which stretched out the heavens and the earth?' {44:8} The Holy One responded, 'Since the wicked sin and transgress in such ways, how could I reveal my great Right Hand to bring about their downfall?' {44:9} At that moment, Metatron called me and said, 'My servant, take the books and read their evil deeds!' I took the books and read, finding 36 transgressions recorded for each wicked person, in addition to their transgressions against every letter of the Torah, as it is written: 'Yea, all Israel has transgressed your Law' (Daniel 9:11). {44:10} Then, Abraham, Isaac, and Jacob wept, and the Holy One said to them, 'My beloved Abraham, my Elect Isaac, and my firstborn Jacob! How can I deliver them from the nations of the world?' In that moment, MIKAEL, the Prince of Israel, cried and wept loudly, saying, 'Why do you stand afar off, O Lord?' (Psalms 10:1)."

{45:1} Rabbi Ishmael said: Metatron said to me, "Come, and I will show you the Curtain of MAQOM (the Divine Majesty), spread before the Holy One, blessed be He. Upon this Curtain, all the generations of the world are engraved, along with their deeds, both past and future, until the end of time. {45:2} He pointed to it, as a father teaches his children, showing me each generation—the rulers, leaders, and oppressors of every generation, as well as their shepherds, keepers, judges, court officers, teachers, and all the roles within each generation. {45:3} I saw Adam and his generation, their deeds and thoughts, Noah and his generation, the people of the flood, Shem and his generation, Nimrod and the generation of the confusion of tongues, Abraham, Isaac, Jacob, and their generations, along with all their thoughts and actions. I saw Joseph, the tribes, and their generations, Amram and Moses, and all their deeds. {45:4} I saw Aaron, Miriam, the elders, and princes, along with all their works. I saw Joshua, the judges, Eli, Phinehas, Elkanah, and Samuel, along with their generations and deeds. I saw the kings of Judah and Israel, their princes, and their works. {45:5} I also saw the prophets of Israel and the prophets of the nations of the world, their generations, and their deeds. I saw all the battles and wars the nations fought against Israel during the time of their kingdom. I saw Messiah, son of Joseph, and his generation, along with their battles and deeds against the nations of the world. I saw Messiah, son of David, and his generation, their battles and deeds, both for good and evil, as well as the wars of Gog and Magog and all that the Holy One, blessed be He, will do in the future. {45:6} And I saw all the leaders and their deeds in Israel and the nations of the world, both what has been done and what will be done, until the end of all generations. All of this was engraved on the Curtain of MAQOM. After seeing it all, I opened my mouth in praise of MAQOM, saying, 'For the King's word hath power, and who may say unto him: What doest thou?' (Ecclesiastes 8:4). And I said, 'O Lord, how manifold are thy works!' (Psalm 104:24)."

{46:1} Rabbi Ishmael said: Metatron spoke to me, "Come, and I will show you the place where the stars stand in the sky (Raqia') every night, trembling in awe of the Almighty (MAQOM). I will show you where they go and where they stand." {46:2} I walked beside him, and he took my hand, pointing out everything with his fingers. The stars were standing on sparks of flames surrounding the chariot (Merkaba) of the Almighty. What did Metatron do? At that moment, he clapped his hands, and the stars fled from their place. Instantly, they flew away on flaming wings, rising and fleeing from the four sides of the Throne of the Merkaba. As they flew, he told me the name of each one, as it is written: "He counts the number of the stars; He calls them all by name" (Psalms 147:4). This teaches that the Holy One, blessed be He, gave each star a name. {46:3} They enter in perfect order, led by Rahatiel, into Raqia' ha-Shamayim to serve the world. They exit in the same order to sing praises to the Holy One, as it is written: "The heavens declare the glory of God" (Psalms 19:1). {46:4} But in the future, the Holy One, blessed be He, will create them anew, as it is written: "They are new every morning" (Lamentations 3:23). And they open their mouths to sing, and the song they sing is from Psalms 8:3: "When I consider Your heavens."

{47:1} Rabbi Ishmael said: Metatron said to me, "Come, and I will show you the souls of the angels and the spirits of the ministering servants whose bodies were burned by the fire of MAQOM (the Almighty), which emanates from His little finger. These souls have been transformed into fiery coals within the fiery river (Nehar di-Nur), but their spirits and souls stand behind the Divine Presence (Shekina)." {47:2} Whenever ministering angels sing at an inappropriate time or in a way that was not commanded, they are consumed by the Creator's fire. They are driven by the whirlwind into the fiery river, where they are turned into mountains of burning coal. But their spirits and souls return to their Creator and stand behind their Master. {47:3} I walked beside him, and he took me by the hand, showing me all the souls of the angels and the spirits of the ministering servants standing behind the Shekina on wings of the whirlwind, surrounded by walls of fire. {47:4} At that moment, Metatron opened the gates of the walls where they were standing behind the Shekina. I lifted my eyes and saw them. Each one looked like an angel, with wings like birds' wings, made of flames, crafted by burning fire. In that moment, I opened my mouth and praised MAQOM, saying, "How great are Your works, O Lord" (Psalms 92:5).

{48a:1} Rabbi Ishmael said: Metatron said to me, "Come, and I will show you the Right Hand of MAQOM, which is held behind Him because of the destruction of the Holy Temple. From it emanates splendor and light, and by it, the 955 heavens were created. Not even the Seraphim or the Ophannim are allowed to behold it until the day of salvation comes." {48a:2} I went by his side, and he took me by the hand and showed me the Right Hand of MAQOM. It was filled with praise, joy, and song, but no mouth can describe its glory, and no eye can behold it due to its immense greatness, majesty, beauty, and splendor. {48a:3} Moreover, the souls of the righteous, who are worthy to see the joy of Jerusalem, stand before it, praising and praying three times a day, saying, "Awake, awake, put on strength, O arm of the Lord" (Is. 51:9), as it is written: "He caused His glorious arm to go at the right hand of Moses" (Is. 63:12). {48a:4} At that moment, the Right Hand of MAQOM wept, and from its five fingers, five rivers of tears fell into the great sea, shaking the world, as it is written: "The earth is utterly broken, the earth is torn asunder, the earth is shaken violently, the earth shall stagger like a drunken man, and shall sway to and fro like a hut" (Is. 24:19-20), five times corresponding to the fingers of His Great Right Hand. {48a:5} When the Holy One, blessed be He, sees that there is no righteous person on earth, no pious one, no justice in the hands of men, and no one like Moses or Samuel who could pray for Israel's salvation and deliverance, and no intercessor for His Kingdom to be revealed, {48a:6} then the Holy One will remember His own justice, grace, and mercy, and He will deliver His great Arm to bring salvation to Israel. As it is written: "He saw that there was no man, and wondered that there was no intercessor; therefore His own arm brought salvation to Him" (Is. 59:16). {48a:7} He will act on His own behalf, as it is written: "For My own sake will I do it, for how should My name be profaned?" (Is. 48:11). {48a:8} In that moment, the Holy One will reveal His Great Arm to the nations of the world. Its length and breadth will be as vast as the world, and its splendor will be like the sun's brilliance during the summer solstice. {48a:9} Then, Israel will be saved from the nations, and the Messiah will appear, leading them to Jerusalem with great joy. Israel will gather from the four corners of the earth and feast with the Messiah, but the nations will not join them, as it is written: "The Lord has made bare His holy arm in the eyes of all the nations, and all the ends of the earth shall see the salvation of our God" (Is. 52:10), and again: "The Lord alone led him, and there was no foreign god with him" (Deut. 32:12), and "The Lord shall be king over all the earth" (Zech. 14:9).

{48b:1} These are the seventy-two names written on the heart of the Holy One, blessed be He: SeDeQ, SaHPeL, SUR, SeBa'oTh, ShaDdaY, Elohim, YHWH, DGUL, 'W, F', and many more. They are adorned with numerous crowns of fire, flame, chashmal (radiance), and lightning before the Throne of Glory. Thousands of powerful angels escort them with trembling and dread, with awe, shivering, honor, majesty, and fear. {48b:2} They praise the Holy One as they roll through every heaven like mighty princes, singing "Holy, Holy, Holy." When they return to the Throne of Glory, the Chayyoth (heavenly creatures) open their mouths to sing, "Blessed be the name of His glorious kingdom forever and ever."

{48c:1} "I took him and appointed him," referring to Enoch, the son of Jared, who became Metatron. {48c:2} I took him from among the children of men. {48c:3} I made a throne for him, facing My own Throne, measuring seventy thousand parasangs of fire. {48c:4} I entrusted him with seventy angels, corresponding to the nations of the world, and gave him authority over all the heavenly and earthly household. {48c:5} I endowed him with wisdom and intelligence greater than all other angels, and called him the "LESSER YAH," a name whose Gematria is 71. I appointed him over the works of creation, making him more powerful than all the ministering angels.

{48d:1} Metatron possesses seventy names, which the Holy One took from His own name and gave to him. These include YeHOEL, Yophiel, Tatriel, and many others. {48d:2} He is called Sagnesakiel because all the treasuries of wisdom are entrusted to him. {48d:3} All these treasuries were opened to Moses on Mount Sinai, where he learned the Torah, the Prophets, the Writings, and all the commandments in seventy aspects and seventy tongues. {48d:4} But after the forty days, Moses forgot them all in a moment. Then the Holy One, blessed be He, called Yephiphyah, the Prince of the Law, and through him, Moses received these teachings as a gift, as it is written: "The Lord gave them to me" (Deut. 10:4). {48d:5} These seventy names reflect the Explicit Names engraved upon the Throne of Glory. Twenty-two letters are on the ring on His finger, which seal the destinies of heavenly princes and the fate of every nation. {48d:6} Metatron, the Prince of the Presence, Wisdom, and Understanding, revealed these secrets to Moses. {48d:7} When he did, the heavenly hosts raged, asking why this secret was being revealed to a man born of woman. {48d:8} But I, Metatron, answered that the Holy One had given me the authority. {48d:9} They were not appeased until the Holy One rebuked them, saying He had entrusted me alone with these secrets. {48d:10} I then passed these secrets to Moses, who passed them to Joshua, the elders, the prophets, and eventually to the men of the Great Synagogue. These mysteries are used to heal the world, as it is written: "I am the Lord who heals you" (Ex. 15:26).

1 Adam and Eve

The Book of Adam and Eve, also known as the Conflict of Adam and Eve with Satan, is an ancient apocryphal text that delves into the post-Edenic lives of the biblical figures, Adam and Eve, offering a rich narrative that extends beyond the canonical Genesis account. Believed to have been written between the 3rd and 5th centuries AD, this text is part of the broader pseudepigrapha corpus, which encompasses works attributed to biblical figures but not included in the canonical Bible. The Book of Adam and Eve provides a detailed account of the couple's struggles and experiences after their expulsion from the Garden of Eden, portraying their profound sense of loss, their penitent attempts to regain favor with God, and their ongoing confrontations with Satan. The text reflects a profound exploration of themes such as sin, repentance, and redemption, illustrating the arduous journey of humanity in its quest for reconciliation with the divine. It is a significant work that offers insights into early Judeo-Christian thought, especially concerning the nature of evil, suffering, and divine justice. Additionally, the book serves as a window into the religious and cultural milieu of late antiquity, revealing the interplay between Jewish traditions and early Christian theology. Its narrative, rich with symbolic and allegorical elements, provides a deeper understanding of the existential and spiritual challenges faced by the first humans according to the Judeo-Christian tradition. The Book of Adam and Eve has been preserved in various languages, including Ethiopic, Arabic, and Armenian, attesting to its widespread influence and the enduring fascination with its themes across different cultures and religious communities.

{1:1} On the third day, God planted the garden in the east of the earth, on the border of the world, eastward, beyond which, towards the sunrise, there is nothing but water that encompasses the whole world and reaches to the borders of heaven. {1:2} To the north of the garden, there is a sea of water, clear and pure to the taste, unlike anything else; so clear that one can see into the depths of the earth. When a person washes in it, they become as clean as the water and as white as its whiteness—even if they were dark. {1:3} God created this sea out of His own good pleasure, for He knew what would become of the man He would create. After man left the garden due to his transgression, people would be born on earth, and among them, the righteous would die. God would raise their souls on the last day, and they would return to their bodies, bathe in this sea, and all would repent of their sins. {1:4} However, when God made Adam leave the garden, He did not place him on its northern border, so he would not be near the sea of water. This way, Adam and Eve would not wash themselves in it, be cleansed of their sins, forget their transgression, and no longer be reminded of their punishment. {1:5} Likewise, God did not place Adam on the southern side of the garden because the wind from the north would carry the sweet smell of the garden's trees to him. God did not want Adam to smell the sweet fragrance, forget his transgression, find comfort in it, take delight in the smell of the trees, and not be cleansed of his transgression. {1:6} Because God is merciful and compassionate and governs all things in His own way, He made Adam dwell on the western border of the garden, where the earth is very broad. God commanded him to live there in a cave in a rock—the Cave of Treasures—below the garden.

{2:1} When our father Adam and Eve left the garden, they walked on the ground with their feet, not realizing they were walking. {2:2} When they reached the opening of the garden gate and saw the broad earth spread before them, covered with large and small stones and sand, they were terrified. They trembled, fell on their faces, and appeared as if they were dead because they were so afraid. {2:3} They had been in the garden, beautifully planted with all kinds of trees, and now found themselves in a strange land they did not know and had never seen. {2:4} At that time, they were filled with the grace of a bright nature and did not have hearts turned towards earthly things. {2:5} God had pity on them, and when He saw them fallen before the garden gate, He sent His Word to Father Adam and Eve and raised them from their fallen state.

{3:1} Concerning the promise of the great five days and a half, God said to Adam, "I have ordained days and years on this earth, and you and your descendants shall live and walk in it until the days and years are fulfilled. Then, I will send the Word that created you, against which you transgressed, the Word that made you leave the garden, and that raised you when you had fallen. Yes, the Word will save you again when the five days and a half are fulfilled." {3:2} But when Adam heard these words from God about the great five days and a half, he did not understand their meaning. {3:3} Adam thought there would be only five days and a half until the end of the world. {3:4} Adam wept and prayed to God to explain it to him. {3:5} Then God, in His mercy for Adam, who was made in His own image and likeness, explained to him that these were 5000 and 500 years, and that One would come then to save him and his descendants [መኃፈ ይመዋለ።]. {3:6} God had made this covenant with Adam before, in the same terms, before he came out of the garden, when he was by the tree from which Eve took the fruit and gave it to him to eat. {3:7} When Adam came out of the garden, he passed by that tree and saw how God had changed its appearance into another form, and how it had withered. {3:8} Adam feared, trembled, and fell down when he saw it, but God in His mercy lifted him up and made this covenant with him. {3:9} When Adam was by the gate of the garden and saw the cherub with a sword of flashing fire, the cherub grew angry and frowned at him. Adam and Eve were afraid, thinking the cherub would kill them, so they fell on their faces and trembled with fear. {3:10} But the cherub had pity on them, showed them mercy, and turned away from them. He went up to heaven, prayed to the Lord, and said, "Lord, You sent me to watch at the gate of the garden with a sword of fire. But when Your servants, Adam and Eve, saw me, they fell on their faces and were as dead. O my Lord, what shall we do to Your servants?" {3:11} Then God had pity on them, showed them mercy, and sent His Angel to guard the garden. {3:12} The Word of the Lord came to Adam and Eve and raised them up. {3:13} The Lord said to Adam, "I told you that at the end of five days and a half, I will send my Word and save you. Strengthen your heart, therefore, and abide in the Cave of Treasures, of which I have spoken to you before." {3:14} When Adam heard this Word from God, he was comforted by what God told him, for God had explained how He would save him.

{4:1} Adam and Eve wept for leaving the garden, their first home. {4:2} When Adam looked at his flesh, which had changed, he and Eve wept bitterly over what they had done. They walked slowly down into the Cave of Treasures. {4:3} As they reached it, Adam wept and said to Eve, "Look at this cave that is to be our prison in this world and a place of punishment! {4:4} How does it compare with the garden? How does its narrowness compare with the vastness of the other? {4:5} What is this rock compared to those groves? What is the gloom of this cavern compared to the light of the garden? {4:6} What is this overhanging ledge of rock to shelter us compared to the mercy of the Lord that overshadowed us? {4:7} What is the soil of this cave compared to the garden land? This earth, strewn with stones, and that, planted with delicious fruit trees?" {4:8} Adam said to Eve, "Look at your eyes, and at mine, which once beheld angels in heaven, praising without ceasing. {4:9} But now we do not see as we did; our eyes have become flesh; they cannot see as they did before." {4:10} Adam said again to Eve, "What is our body today compared to what it was in former days when we lived in the garden?" {4:11} After this, Adam did not want to enter the cave under the overhanging rock; he would never have entered it. {4:12} But he obeyed God's orders and said to himself, "Unless I enter the cave, I shall again be a transgressor."

{5:1} Adam and Eve entered the cave and stood praying in their own language, unknown to us but well known to them. {5:2} As they prayed, Adam raised his eyes and saw the rock and the roof of the cave covering him overhead, so he could see neither heaven nor God's creatures. He wept and struck his chest heavily until he collapsed and appeared dead. {5:3} Eve sat weeping, believing he was dead. {5:4} Then she arose, spread her hands towards God, and pleaded for mercy and pity, saying, "God, forgive me my sin, the sin I committed, and do not hold it against me. {5:5} For I alone caused Your servant to fall from the garden into this lost state, from light into this darkness, and from the abode of joy into this prison. {5:6} O God, look upon Your servant who has fallen and raise him from his death, so that he may weep and repent of his transgression, which he committed because of me. {5:7} Do not take away his soul this time, but let him live so he may fulfill his repentance and do Your will as before. {5:8} But if You do not raise him up, then, God, take away my own soul so I can be like him, and do not leave me in this dungeon alone, for I cannot stand alone in this world without him. {5:9} For You, O God, caused a slumber to come upon him, took a bone from his side, and restored the flesh in its place by Your divine power. {5:10} You took me, the bone, and made me a woman, bright like him, with heart, reason, and speech, and in flesh like his own. You made me in the likeness of his countenance by Your mercy and power. {5:11} O Lord, he and I are one, and You, God, are our Creator. You made us both in one day. {5:12} Therefore, O God, give him life so he may be with me in this strange land while we dwell in it because of our transgression. {5:13} But if You will not give him life, then take me, even me, like him, so that we both may die on the same day." {5:14} Eve wept bitterly and fell upon our father Adam from her great sorrow.

{6:1} God looked upon Adam and Eve, for they had caused themselves great grief, nearly killing themselves. {6:2} But He would raise them and comfort them. {6:3} He sent His Word to them, so they would stand and be raised immediately. {6:4} The Lord said to Adam and Eve, "You transgressed of your own free will until you left the garden where I placed you. You transgressed by your desire for divinity, greatness, and an exalted state like Mine, so I deprived you of the bright nature you had and made you leave the garden for this land, rough and full of trouble. [በአርሱ ነገ ብርሃን አንተ-ራብኦት።] {6:5} If only you had not transgressed My commandment, had kept My law, and had not eaten from the tree I told you not to approach! There were better fruit trees in the garden than that one. {6:6} But the wicked Satan, who did not remain in his first estate and did not keep his faith, had no good intent towards Me. Though I created him, he set Me at naught and sought the Godhead, so I hurled him down from heaven. It was he who made the tree appear pleasant in your eyes until you ate from it by listening to him. {6:7} Thus, you transgressed My commandment, and therefore I brought all these sorrows upon you. {6:8} For I am God the Creator, who did not intend to destroy My creatures when I created them. But after they sorely roused My anger, I punished them with grievous plagues until they repented. {6:9} But if they continue to be hardened in their transgression, they shall be under a curse forever. [እነርሱ አንደሚ.ያስቀፀሙ ኃጢአታቸውን እነሆ እስከመጨረሻው ይባርክ።]

{7:1} When Adam and Eve heard these words from God, they wept and sobbed even more; but they strengthened their hearts in God, because they now felt that the Lord was to them like a father and a mother. For this reason, they wept before Him and sought mercy from Him. {7:2} God had pity on them and said, "Adam, I have made My covenant with you, and I will not turn from it; neither will I let you return to the garden until My covenant of the great five days and a half is fulfilled." {7:3} Adam said to God, "Lord, You created us and made us fit to be in the garden. Before I transgressed, You brought all the beasts to me so that I could name them. {7:4} Your grace was then upon me, and I named each one according to Your mind, and You made them all subject to me. {7:5} But now, Lord God, because I have transgressed Your commandment, all beasts will rise against me and devour me and Eve, Your handmaid, and cut off our life from the face of the earth. {7:6} Therefore, I beseech You, God, that since You have made us come out of the garden and be in a strange land, do not let the beasts hurt us." {7:7} When the Lord heard these words from Adam, He had pity on him and understood that he truly feared the beasts of the field would rise and devour him and Eve, because He, the Lord, was angry with them due to their transgression. {7:8} Then God commanded the beasts, the birds, and all that moves upon the earth to come to Adam, be familiar with him, and not trouble him or Eve, nor any of the good and righteous among their descendants. {7:9} The beasts obeyed God's command and bowed to Adam, except for the serpent, which did not approach Adam and incurred God's anger.

{8:1} Then Adam wept and said, "O God, when we dwelt in the garden, and our hearts were lifted up, we saw the angels singing praises in heaven, but now we do not see as we used to. [በ.ያቅርቦ ታመልክሁ-።] When we entered the cave, all creation became hidden from us." {8:2} Then the Lord God said to Adam, "When you were under My subjection, you had a bright nature within you, and for that reason, you could see things far off. But after your transgression, your bright nature was withdrawn from you, and you were left only to see things near at hand, according to the ability of the flesh, which is brutish." {8:3} When Adam and Eve heard these words from God, they went on their way, praising and worshipping Him with sorrowful hearts. {8:4} And God ceased to commune with them.

{9:1} Then Adam and Eve came out of the Cave of Treasures and drew near to the garden gate. They stood there, looking at it, and wept for having left it. Adam and Eve moved from the gate to the southern side of the garden and found the water that watered the garden from the root of the Tree of Life, which then parted into four rivers over the earth. {9:2} They came close to the water and saw that it was the same water that came from under the root of the Tree of Life in the garden. Adam wept, wailed, and struck his chest for being separated from the garden and said to Eve, "Why have you brought so many plagues and punishments upon me, yourself, and our descendants?" {9:3} Eve asked him, "What is it that you have seen to make you weep and speak to me this way?" {9:4} He replied, "Do you not see this water that was with us in the garden, which watered the trees of the garden and flowed out from there? {9:5} When we were in the garden, we did not care about it, but since we came to this strange land, we love it and use it for our bodies." {9:6} When Eve heard these words from him, she wept. From the intensity of their weeping, they fell into the water and would have ended their lives in it, so as never to return and behold the creation. When they looked upon the work of creation, they felt compelled to end their lives.

{10:1} Then God, merciful and gracious, looked upon them lying in the water, near death, and sent an angel who brought them out of the water and laid them on the shore as if dead. {10:2} Then the angel went up to God, was welcomed, and said, "O God, Your creatures have breathed their last." {10:3} Then God sent His Word to Adam and Eve, and raised them from their death. {10:4} After being raised, Adam said, "God, while we were in the garden, we did not need or care for this water, but since we came to this land, we cannot do without it." {10:5} God said to Adam, "When you were under My command and were a bright angel, you did not know this water. {10:6} But after you transgressed My commandment, you cannot do without water to wash your body and make it grow, for it is now like that of beasts and needs water." {10:7} When Adam and Eve heard these words from God, they wept bitterly, and Adam pleaded with God to let him return to the garden and look at it a second time. {10:8} But God said to Adam, "I have made you a promise; when that promise is fulfilled, I will bring you back into the garden, you and your righteous descendants." {10:9} And God ceased to commune with Adam.

{11:1} Then Adam and Eve felt themselves burning with thirst, heat, and sorrow. {11:2} Adam said to Eve, "We shall not drink this water, even if we were to die. Eve, if this water enters our bodies, it will increase our punishment and that of our children who come after us." {11:3} Both Adam and Eve then withdrew from the water and drank none of it. They entered the Cave of Treasures. {11:4} Inside the cave, Adam could not see Eve; he only heard the sound she made. Likewise, she could not see Adam, but heard the noise he made. {11:5} Then Adam wept in deep affliction, struck his chest, and said to Eve, "Where are you?" {11:6} She replied, "I am standing in this darkness." {11:7} He then said, "Remember the bright nature we had while we lived in the garden! [አሁንች ይኸን በነት ሳንጥር፣ ብርሃን ስሆን፣ የክብረን ብርሃን አስበሽ።] {11:8} Oh Eve, remember the glory that rested on us in the garden! Remember the trees that overshadowed us while we walked among them. {11:9} Oh Eve, remember that while we were in the garden, we knew neither night nor day. Think of the Tree of Life, from under which flowed the water that shone brightly over us! {11:10} Remember, Eve, the garden land and its brightness! {11:11} Think of that garden, where there was no darkness while we lived in it. {11:12} But as soon as we came into this Cave of Treasures, darkness surrounded us, and we can no longer see each other. All the pleasures of this life have ended."

{12:1} Then Adam struck his chest, he and Eve mourned the whole night until dawn approached, and they sighed over the length of the night in Miyazia. {12:2} Adam beat himself and threw himself on the ground in the cave from bitter grief and because of the darkness, lying there as if dead. {12:3} Eve heard the noise he made falling upon the earth. She felt around for him with her hands and found him like a corpse. {12:4} She was afraid, speechless, and remained by him. {12:5} But the merciful Lord looked upon the death of Adam and on Eve's silence from fear of the darkness. {12:6} The Word of God came to Adam and raised him from his death, and opened Eve's mouth so she might speak. {12:7} Then Adam arose in the cave and said, "God, why has light departed from us and darkness come over us? Why do You leave us in this long darkness? Why do You plague us thus? {12:8} And this darkness, O Lord, where was it before it came upon us? It is such that we cannot see each other. {12:9} For as long as we were in the garden, we neither saw nor even knew what darkness is. I was not hidden from Eve, nor was she hidden from me, until now that she cannot see me; and no darkness came upon us to separate us from each other. {12:10} But she and I were both in one bright light. I saw her and she saw me. Yet now, since we came into this cave, darkness has come upon us and parted us, so that I do not see her and she does not see me. {12:11} Lord, will You then plague us with this darkness?"

{13:1} Then, when God, who is merciful and full of pity, heard Adam's voice, He said to him: {13:2} "Adam, as long as the good angel was obedient to Me, a bright light rested on him and his hosts. {13:3} But when he transgressed My commandment, I deprived him of that bright nature, and he became dark. {13:4} When he was in the heavens, in the realms of light, he knew nothing of darkness. {13:5} But he transgressed, and I made him fall from heaven upon the earth; and this darkness came upon him. {13:6} And on you, O Adam, while in My garden and obedient to Me, that bright light also rested. {13:7} But when I heard of your transgression, I deprived you of that bright light. Yet, out of My mercy, I did not turn you into darkness, but I made your body of flesh, and covered it with skin, so it could bear cold and heat. [ብርሃን ታላቅ] {13:8} If I had let My wrath fall heavily upon you, I would have destroyed you; and if I had turned you into darkness, it would have been as if I killed you. {13:9} But in My mercy, I made you as you are; when you transgressed My commandment, O Adam, I drove you from the garden and made you come into this land; and commanded you to dwell in this cave; and darkness came upon you, as it did upon him who transgressed My commandment. {13:10} Thus, O Adam, this night has deceived you. It is not to last forever; but is only twelve hours; when it is over, daylight will return. {13:11} Therefore, do not sigh or be troubled; do not say in your heart that this darkness is long and wears on wearily; do not say in your heart that I plague you with it. {13:12} Strengthen your heart, and do not be afraid. This darkness is not a punishment. But, Adam, I made the day, and placed the sun in it to give light; so that you and your children could do your work. {13:13} For I knew you would sin and transgress, and come out into this land. Yet I would not force you, nor be hard on you, nor shut you up; nor doom you through your fall; nor through your coming out from light into darkness; nor yet through your coming from the garden into this land. {13:14} For I made you of the light; and I willed to bring children of light from you, like you. {13:15} But you did not keep My commandment for one day; until I had finished the creation and blessed everything in it. {13:16} Then I commanded you concerning the tree, that you should not eat of it. Yet I knew that Satan, who deceived himself, would also deceive you. {13:17} So I made known to you through the tree, not to come near him. And I told you not to eat its fruit, nor to taste it, nor yet to sit under it, nor to yield to it. {13:18} If I had not spoken to you, O Adam, concerning the tree, and had left you without a commandment, and you had sinned—it would have been an offence on My part, for not having given you any order; you would turn around and blame Me for it. {13:19} But I commanded you, and warned you, and you fell. So My creatures cannot blame Me; the blame rests on them alone. {13:20} And, O Adam, I have made the day for you and your children after you, for them to work and toil in it. And I have made the night for them to rest in it from their work; and for the beasts of the field to go forth by night and seek their food. {13:21} But little of this darkness now remains, O Adam; daylight will soon appear."

{14:1} Then Adam said to God, "O Lord, take my soul, and let me not see this darkness anymore. Or take me to a place where there is no darkness." {14:2} But God the Lord said to Adam, "Truly, I tell you, this darkness will pass from you. Each day I have appointed for you until the fulfillment of My covenant, when I will save you and bring you back into the garden, into the dwelling of light that you long for, where there is no darkness. I will bring you to it—in the kingdom of heaven." {14:3} Again God said to Adam, "All this suffering that you have taken upon yourself because of your transgression will not free you from the hand of Satan, nor will it save you." {14:4} "But I will. When I come down from heaven and become flesh of your descendants, and take upon Me the affliction that you suffer, then the darkness that came upon you in this cave will come upon Me in the grave, when I am in the flesh of your descendants." {14:5} "And I, who am eternal, will be subject to the reckoning of years, times, months, and days. I will be counted as one of the sons of men, in order to save you." {14:6} And God stopped speaking with Adam.

{15:1} Then Adam and Eve wept and felt sorrowful because of God's words to them. He had told them that they would not return to the garden until the appointed days had been fulfilled. But what troubled them most was God's revelation that He would suffer for their salvation.

{16:1} After this, Adam and Eve did not cease standing in the cave, praying and weeping, until morning dawned upon them. {16:2} When they saw the light return to them, they calmed their fear and strengthened their hearts. {16:3} Then Adam began to come out of the cave. When he reached its mouth, he stood and turned his face towards the east. He saw the sun rise with glowing rays and felt its heat on his body. He was afraid of it and thought in his heart that this fiery light was coming to harm him. {16:4} He wept, struck his breast, fell upon the earth on his face, and made his plea, saying: {16:5} "Lord, do not harm me, do not consume me, and do not take away my life from the earth." {16:6} For he thought the sun was God, because while he was in the garden and heard the voice of God and the sounds He made there, Adam never saw the bright light of the sun nor felt its burning heat upon his body. {16:7} Therefore, when the fiery rays of the sun reached him, he was afraid and thought that God intended to plague him with it for all the days appointed to him. {16:8} Adam thought in his heart: "As

God did not plague us with darkness, now He has caused this sun to rise and plague us with its burning heat." {16:9} But while he pondered these thoughts, the Word of God came to him and said: {16:10} "Adam, arise and stand up. This sun is not God; it has been created to give light by day, as I told you in the cave when I said, 'The dawn will break forth, and there will be light by day.' {16:11} "I am God who comforted you in the night." And God ceased to commune with Adam.

{17:1} Then Adam and Eve came out at the mouth of the cave and headed towards the garden. {17:2} As they approached the garden, near the western gate through which Satan had deceived Adam and Eve, they found the serpent that had become Satan, sorrowfully licking the dust and crawling on its belly on the ground, because of the curse that God had placed upon it. {17:3} Previously, the serpent had been the most exalted of all beasts, but now it had changed. It became slippery, the most despised of all beasts, crawling on its belly and moving on its breast. {17:4} Once the fairest of all beasts, it had been transformed into the ugliest. Instead of consuming the best food, it now ate dust. Formerly dwelling in the best places, it now lived in the dust. {17:5} Previously admired for its beauty by all other creatures, it was now despised by them. {17:6} Once residing in a beautiful abode where other animals also came to drink from the same water, now, venomous due to God's curse, all beasts fled from its dwelling and refused to drink from its water.

{18:1} When the accursed serpent saw Adam and Eve, it swelled its head, stood on its tail, and with blood-red eyes, acted as if it would kill them. {18:2} It went straight for Eve and chased her, while Adam, standing nearby, wept because he had no stick in his hand with which to strike the serpent, and he did not know how to kill it. {18:3} But filled with burning concern for Eve, Adam approached the serpent and seized it by the tail. The serpent then turned towards him and said: {18:4} "Adam, because of you and Eve, I am now slippery and crawl upon my belly." Then, with great strength, it threw down Adam and Eve and pressed upon them as if to kill them. {18:5} God then sent an angel who threw the serpent away from them and lifted them up. {18:6} Then the Word of God came to the serpent and said: "Initially, I made you agile and caused you to crawl on your belly, but I did not take away your ability to speak. {18:7} "Now, however, be mute and speak no more, you and your descendants, because firstly, through you, the destruction of My creatures happened, and now you seek to kill them." {18:8} Then the serpent was struck mute and spoke no more. {18:9} A wind then blew from heaven by God's command, carrying away the serpent from Adam and Eve, throwing it onto the seashore where it landed in India.

{19:1} But Adam and Eve wept before God. And Adam said to Him: {19:2} "O Lord, when I was in the cave, I said to You, my Lord, that the beasts of the field would rise and devour me, and cut off my life from the earth." {19:3} Then Adam, distressed by what had happened to him, struck his breast and fell upon the earth like a corpse. Then the Word of God came to him, raised him up, and said: {19:4} "O Adam, not one of these beasts will be able to harm you. When I made the beasts and other creatures come to you in the cave, I did not allow the serpent to come with them, lest it should rise against you and cause you to tremble, and fear of it should fall into your hearts. {19:5} "For I knew that the accursed one is wicked; therefore, I would not let it come near you along with the other beasts. {19:6} "But now strengthen your heart and do not fear. I am with you until the end of the days I have determined for you."

{20:1} Then Adam wept and said, "God, move us to another place so that the serpent may not come near us again and rise against us. Lest it find Your handmaid Eve alone and kill her; for its eyes are hideous and evil." {20:2} But God said to Adam and Eve, "From now on, do not fear. I will not let it come near you. I have driven it away from you, from this mountain; nor will I leave anything in it to harm you." {20:3} Then Adam and Eve worshipped before God, gave Him thanks, and praised Him for delivering them from death.

{21:1} Then Adam and Eve set out in search of the garden. {21:2} The heat beat down on their faces like a flame, and they sweated from the intense heat, weeping before the Lord. {21:3} They wept near a high mountain, facing the western gate of the garden. {21:4} Adam threw himself down from the top of that mountain; his face was torn, his flesh flayed, and blood flowed from him, nearly killing him. {21:5} Eve stood on the mountain, weeping over him as he lay there. {21:6} She said, "I do not wish to live after him, for all that he did to himself was because of me." {21:7} Then she threw herself after him, was torn and bruised by stones, and lay there as if dead. {21:8} But the merciful God, who watches over His creatures, looked upon Adam and Eve as they lay seemingly dead. He sent His Word to them and raised them up. {21:9} He said to Adam, "O Adam, all this suffering that you have brought upon yourself will not prevail against My sovereignty, nor will it change the covenant of the 5500 years."

{22:1} Then Adam said to God, "I am withering in this heat; I am exhausted from walking, and weary of this world. I do not know when You will bring me out of it to rest." {22:2} The Lord God replied to him, "Adam, it cannot be now, not until you have completed your days. Then I will bring you out of this wretched land." {22:3} Adam said to God, "In the garden, I knew neither heat nor fatigue, nor did I move about trembling or in fear. But since coming to this land, all this affliction has befallen me." {22:4} God said to Adam, "As long as you kept My commandment, My light and grace rested upon you. But when you transgressed My commandment, sorrow and misery came upon you in this land." {22:5} Adam wept and said, "O Lord, do not cut me off for this, nor strike me with heavy plagues, nor repay me according to my sin. We transgressed Your commandment of our own will, forsaking Your law, and sought to become like gods, deceived by Satan the enemy." {22:6} Then God said again to Adam, "Because you have endured fear and trembling in this land, weariness and suffering, walking and toiling on this mountain, and facing death, I will take all this upon Myself in order to save you."

{23:1} First offering made by Adam. {23:2} Then Adam wept even more and said, "O God, have mercy on me to the extent that You will take upon Yourself what I will do." {23:3} And God accepted Adam's offering. Then Adam and Eve stood up on their feet, and Adam said to Eve, "Get yourself ready, and I will also prepare myself." So Eve prepared herself as Adam had instructed. {23:4} Adam and Eve then took stones and arranged them in the shape of an altar. They also gathered leaves from the trees outside the garden, with which they wiped the blood they had spilled from the face of the rock. They took what had dropped on the sand along with the dust it was mixed with, and offered it upon the altar as an offering to God. {23:5} Adam and Eve stood under the altar and wept, praying to God, "Forgive us our trespass and our sin, and look upon us with Your eye of mercy. When we were in the garden, our praises and hymns continually ascended before You. {23:6} "But since we came into this strange land, pure praise is no longer ours, nor righteous prayer, nor understanding hearts, nor sweet thoughts, nor just counsels, nor long discernment, nor upright feelings. Our bright nature has also left us, and our bodies are changed from their original form in which we were created. {23:7} "Yet now, look upon our blood offered on these stones, and accept it from our hands, like the praises we used to sing to You at first, when we were in the garden." {23:8} And Adam began to make more requests to God.

{24:1} Then the merciful God, who is good and loves humanity, looked upon Adam and Eve and upon their blood, which they had offered to Him without His command. He marveled at them and accepted their offerings. {24:2} God sent from His presence a bright fire that consumed their offering. He smelled the sweet fragrance of their offering and showed them mercy. {24:3} Then the Word of God came to Adam and said to him, "Adam, as you have shed your blood, so will I shed My own blood when I become flesh of your descendants. And as you died, O Adam, so will I also die. And as you built an altar, so will I establish for you an altar on the earth. And as you offered your blood upon it, so will I offer My blood upon an altar on the earth." {24:4} "And as you sought forgiveness through that blood, so will I make My blood forgiveness of sins and blot out transgressions with it. {24:5} "Now, behold, I have accepted your offering, Adam, but the days of the covenant, in which I have bound you, are not yet fulfilled. When they are fulfilled, then I will bring you back into the garden. {24:6} "Therefore, strengthen your heart. When sorrow comes upon you, make an offering to Me, and I will be gracious to you."

{25:1} But God knew that Adam had thoughts of often killing himself and offering his blood to Him. Therefore, He said to him, "O Adam, do not again kill yourself as you did by throwing yourself down from that mountain." {25:2} But Adam said to God, "It was in my mind to end my life at once, because I transgressed Your commandments, because I came out of the beautiful garden, because You deprived me of the bright light, because of the ceaseless praises that used to pour forth from my mouth, and because of the light that covered me. {25:3} "Yet, in Your goodness, God, do not completely destroy me. Be gracious to me each time I die, and bring me back to life. {25:4} "Let it be known that You are a merciful God who does not desire anyone to perish, who does not delight in anyone's fall, and who does not condemn anyone with cruelty, malice, or total destruction." {25:5} Then Adam fell silent. {25:6} And the Word of God came to him, blessed him, comforted him, and made a covenant with him that He would save him at the end of the appointed days. {25:7} This was the first offering Adam made to God, and so it became his custom to do so.

{26:1} Then Adam took Eve, and they began to return to the Cave of Treasures where they lived. But as they neared it and saw it from afar, deep sorrow fell upon Adam and Eve when they looked at it. {26:2} Then Adam said to Eve, "When we were on the mountain, we were comforted by the Word of God that spoke with us, and the light that came from the east shone over us. {26:3} "But now the Word of God is hidden from us, and the light that shone over us has changed and disappeared, and darkness and sorrow have come upon us. {26:4} "We are compelled to enter this cave which is like a prison, where darkness covers us, separating us from each other; you cannot see me, and I cannot see you." {26:5} When Adam said these words, they wept and raised their hands before God, for they were filled with sorrow. {26:6} They begged God to bring the sun to shine on them so that darkness would not return upon them, and they would not be under this covering of rock again. They preferred to die rather than endure the darkness. {26:7} Then God looked upon Adam and Eve and their profound sorrow, and all they had done with earnest hearts, because of their troubles instead of their former well-being, and because of all the misery that had befallen them in a foreign land. {26:8} Therefore, God was not angry with them nor impatient with them, but He was patient and forbearing toward them as a father is toward the children he has created. {26:9} Then the Word of God came to Adam and said to him, "Adam, as for the sun, if I were to take it and bring it to you, days, hours, years, and months would all become meaningless, and the covenant I have made with you would never be fulfilled. {26:10} "Instead, you would be left in prolonged affliction with no salvation forever. {26:11} "No, endure patiently while you abide night and day until the appointed days are fulfilled, and the time of My covenant comes. {26:12} "Then I will come and save you, Adam, for I do not desire you to suffer. {26:13} "When I consider all the good things in which you once lived and why you left them, then I will gladly show you mercy. {26:14} "But I cannot change the covenant that has come from My mouth; otherwise, I would have brought you back to the garden. {26:15} "However, when the covenant is fulfilled, then I will show mercy to you and your descendants, and bring you to a land of joy where there is no sorrow or suffering, only enduring joy, everlasting light, unceasing praises, and an eternal garden." {26:16} And God said again to Adam, "Be patient and enter the cave, for the darkness which you fear will only last twelve hours, and when it ends, light will arise." {26:17} When Adam heard these words from God, he and Eve worshipped before Him, and their hearts were comforted. They returned to the cave as was their custom, with tears flowing from their eyes, sorrow and lamentation in their hearts, and they longed for their souls to leave their bodies. {26:18} Adam and Eve stood praying until darkness of night came upon them, and Adam was hidden from Eve, and she from him. {26:19} And they remained standing in prayer.

{27:1} When Satan, the enemy of all goodness, saw how Adam and Eve continued in prayer, and how God communicated with them, comforted them, and accepted their offering, he appeared. He transformed his hosts and held a flashing fire in his hands, surrounded by a great light. {27:2} Satan placed his throne near the mouth of the cave because he could not enter it due to their prayers. He shed light into the cave, causing it to gleam over Adam and Eve, while his hosts began to sing praises. {27:3} Satan did this so that Adam, seeing the light, would think it was heavenly, and that Satan's hosts were angels sent by God to guard the cave and provide light in the darkness. {27:4} Thus, when Adam came out of the cave and saw them, and Adam and Eve bowed to Satan, Satan would thereby overcome Adam again and humble him before God a second time. {27:5} When Adam and Eve saw the light and thought it was real, they strengthened their hearts. But as they trembled, Adam said to Eve, "Look at that great light and those many songs of praise, and at those hosts standing outside who do not come in to us. They do not tell us what they say, where they come from, or the meaning of this light, their praises, why they have been sent here, and why they do not come in. {27:6} "If they were from God, they would come into the cave and tell us their purpose." {27:7} Then Adam stood up and prayed fervently to God, saying, "O Lord, is there another god in the world who created angels, filled them with light, and sent them to guard us? If so, would they come with these hosts? {27:8} "But we see these hosts standing at the mouth of the cave in great light, singing loud praises. If they are from some other god than You, tell me. If they are sent by You, inform me of the reason You have sent them." {27:9} No sooner had Adam said this than an angel from God appeared to him in the cave and said, "Adam, do not fear. This is Satan and his hosts. He seeks to deceive you as he did before. The first time he was hidden in the serpent; this time he has come to you disguised as an angel of light, so that when you worship him, he might ensnare you before God Himself." {27:10} Then the angel left Adam, seized Satan at the cave's entrance, stripped off his disguise, and brought him in his hideous form before Adam and Eve, who were afraid when they saw him. {27:11} The angel said to Adam, "This hideous form has been Satan's since God cast him out [from heaven]. He could not come near you in this form, so he transformed himself into an angel of light." {27:12} Then the angel drove Satan and his hosts away from Adam and Eve, saying to them, "Do not fear; God who created you will strengthen you." {27:13} And the angel departed from them. {27:14} Adam and Eve remained standing in the cave; no comfort came to them, and they were divided in their thoughts. {27:15} When morning came, they prayed and then went out to seek the garden, for their hearts longed for it, and they found no consolation for having left it.

{28:1} When Satan saw Adam and Eve heading towards the garden, he gathered his army and appeared on a cloud, intending to deceive them. {28:2} Adam and Eve, seeing him in a vision, mistook him for angels sent by God to comfort them for leaving the garden or to lead them back. {28:3} Adam prayed to God to understand who they were. {28:4} Satan, the enemy of all good, then spoke to Adam, claiming to be an angel sent by God with his host to take them north to the border of the garden, to a clear sea where they would be cleansed and restored to happiness, and return to the garden. {28:5} Adam and Eve were deeply affected by these words. {28:6} God, however, did not immediately reveal the truth to Adam, testing whether he would resist temptation as Eve had failed in the garden. {28:7} Satan led Adam and Eve towards the sea, with Adam and Eve following at a distance. {28:8} When they reached a high mountain north of the garden, without steps to the top, Satan compelled Adam and Eve to climb it in reality, not just in vision. {28:9} His intention was to throw them off the mountain and kill them, erasing their name from the earth so that it would belong only to him and his followers.

{29:1} When God, in His mercy, saw that Satan intended to harm Adam with various schemes, and saw that Adam was gentle and innocent, He spoke loudly to Satan and cursed him. {29:2} Then Satan and his followers fled, leaving Adam and Eve standing on the mountaintop, from where they could see the vast world below them, far above everything else. They could no longer see the hosts that had surrounded them earlier. Adam and Eve wept before God, asking for His forgiveness. {29:3} Then God spoke to Adam, saying, "Understand this about Satan: he seeks to deceive you and your descendants." {29:4} Adam wept before the Lord and pleaded for something from the garden as a token of comfort. {29:5} God considered Adam's request and sent the angel Michael to the sea extending to India, to bring back golden rods for Adam. {29:6} God did this so that these golden rods, kept with Adam in the cave, would shine with light in the darkness of night, comforting him and dispelling his fear. {29:7} So, by God's command, the angel Michael descended, took the golden rods, and brought them back to God.

{30:1} After these events, God commanded the angel Gabriel to descend to the garden and instruct the cherub guarding it, saying, "Behold, God commands me to enter the garden and take sweet-smelling incense to give to Adam." Gabriel obeyed God's command, went to the garden, and relayed the message to the cherub as instructed. The cherub agreed, and Gabriel entered and took the incense. {30:2} Then God commanded His angel Raphael to go to the garden and speak to the cherub about obtaining myrrh for Adam. {30:3} Raphael went down and delivered God's command to the cherub, who consented. Raphael then entered and took the myrrh. {30:4} The golden rods came from the Indian sea, abundant with precious stones. The incense was from the eastern border of the garden, and the myrrh from the western border, symbolizing the bitterness that had come upon Adam. {30:5} The angels brought these three things to God near the Tree of Life in the garden. {30:6} God instructed the angels, "Dip them in the spring of water, then sprinkle their water over Adam and Eve to give them a little comfort in their sorrow." The angels did as commanded, giving these gifts to Adam and Eve on the mountaintop where Satan had tried to harm them. {30:7} When Adam saw the golden rods, incense, and myrrh, he rejoiced and wept. He believed the gold symbolized the kingdom from which he had come, the incense represented the bright light that had been taken from him, and the myrrh signified the sorrow he was experiencing.

{31:1} After these events, God spoke to Adam, saying, "You asked for something from the garden to bring you comfort, and I have given you these three tokens as a consolation: that you may trust in Me and in My covenant with you. For I will come to save you, and kings will bring me, in the flesh, gold, incense, and myrrh: gold as a symbol of My kingdom, incense as a symbol of My divinity, and myrrh as a symbol of My sufferings and death. {31:2} Adam, keep these near you in the cave: let the gold give you light at night, let the incense fill your senses with its sweet fragrance, and let the myrrh comfort you in your sorrow." {31:3} When Adam heard these words from God, he worshipped Him, along with Eve, thanking Him for His mercy toward them. {31:4} Then God commanded the three angels, Michael, Gabriel, and Raphael, to each bring what they had brought and give it to Adam. They did so in turn. {31:5} God also commanded Suriyel and Salathiel to support Adam and Eve, bringing them down from the high mountain and leading them to the Cave of Treasures. {31:6} There, they placed the gold on the south side of the cave, the incense on the eastern side, and the myrrh on the western side, since the cave's entrance was on the north side. {31:7} After comforting Adam and Eve, the angels departed. {31:8} The gold amounted to seventy rods, the incense weighed twelve pounds, and the myrrh was three pounds. {31:9} These items remained with Adam in the House of Treasures, also known as the "Cave of Treasures," perhaps because righteous men's bodies were hidden there, according to some interpreters. {31:10} God gave these three things to Adam on the third day after he left the garden, symbolizing the three days the Lord would remain in the heart of the earth. {31:11} These tokens stayed with Adam in the cave, providing light at night and some relief from sorrow during the day.

{32:1} Adam and Eve remained in the Cave of Treasures for seven days, abstaining from eating the fruit of the earth or drinking water. On the eighth day, at dawn, Adam said to Eve, "Eve, we prayed to God to give us something from the garden, and His angels brought us what we desired. {32:2} But now, let us arise and go to the sea of water we first saw, and let us stand in it, praying that God may once again be favorable to us and return us to the garden, or give us some other comfort in a different land." {32:3} Adam and Eve left the cave, went to the shore of the sea where they had previously immersed themselves, and Adam said to Eve, "Come, descend into this place and do not leave it for thirty days, until I come to you. Pray to God with a fervent heart and sweet voice for forgiveness. {32:4} I will go to another place and descend into it, and do as you do." {32:5} Eve obeyed Adam's command and went down into the water. Adam also entered the water, and they stood praying, beseeching the Lord to forgive their transgression and restore them to their former state. {32:6} They continued praying in this manner for thirty-five days.

{33:1} But Satan, who hates all that is good, searched for Adam and Eve in the cave but did not find them, though he looked diligently. Instead, he found them standing in the water, praying. He thought to himself, "Adam and Eve stand in this water, pleading with God to forgive their transgression, restore them to their former state, and deliver them from my grasp. {33:2} But I will deceive them so they leave the water and do not fulfill their vow." {33:3} Satan, the adversary of all goodness, did not approach Adam but went to Eve instead. He took on the form of an angel of God, appearing to praise and rejoice, saying to her, "Peace be unto you! Rejoice! God is favorable to you. He has sent me to Adam with glad tidings of salvation and the restoration of his bright light as in the beginning. {33:4} In his joy for being restored, Adam has sent me to you, that you may come to him so he can crown you with light like himself. He told me, 'Speak to Eve; if she does not come with you, remind her of the sign from when we were on the mountain top. God sent His angels who brought us to the Cave of Treasures. They placed the gold on the south side, incense on the east, and myrrh on the west. Now come to him.'" {33:5} Eve, hearing these words, rejoiced greatly, believing Satan's appearance was genuine, and she left the sea. {33:6} Satan led her, and she followed until they reached Adam. Then Satan concealed himself from her sight, and she saw him no more. {33:7} Eve stood before Adam, who was by the water, rejoicing in God's forgiveness. {33:8} When Adam turned and saw her, he wept, struck his breast in sorrow, and in his bitterness of grief, sank into the water. {33:9} God looked upon Adam's misery as he was about to perish. The Word of God came from heaven, lifted Adam out of the water, and instructed him, "Go up to the high bank to Eve." {33:10} When Adam reached Eve, he asked her, "Who told you to come here?" {33:11} She recounted the angel's words and the sign he gave her. Adam grieved upon realizing it was Satan who had deceived her. He took her hand, and they returned to the cave together. {33:12} These events occurred the second time they went to the water, seven days after leaving the garden. {33:13} They fasted in the water for thirty-five days, totaling forty-two days since their expulsion from the garden.

{34:1} On the morning of the forty-third day, Adam and Eve emerged from the cave, filled with sorrow and tears. Their bodies were lean and parched from hunger, thirst, fasting, and the heavy burden of their transgression. Leaving the cave, they ascended a mountain to the west of the garden, where they stood and prayed, imploring God for forgiveness of their sins. {34:2} Adam began to entreat God, saying, "O my Lord, my God, my Creator, You commanded the four elements to come together, and they obeyed Your order. {34:3} Then You stretched out Your hand and created me from the dust of the earth, bringing me into the garden on a Friday, at the third hour, as You informed me in the cave. {34:4} Initially, I knew neither night nor day, for I had a bright nature, and the light in which I lived never left me to distinguish night from day. {34:5} At that third hour on Friday, You brought all beasts, lions, ostriches, birds of the air, and all creatures of the earth before me, which You had created in the first hour before me on Friday. {34:6} Your will was for me to name each one according to Your mind. You gave me understanding, knowledge, a pure heart, and a right mind, so that I named them according to Your will. {34:7} O God, You made them obedient to me, not allowing any to break from my authority, in accordance with Your command and the dominion You gave me over them. But now they are all estranged from me. {34:8} Then, in that third hour on Friday when You created me, You commanded me regarding the tree, warning me not to approach or eat from it, saying, 'When you eat from it, you shall surely die.' {34:9} If You had punished me as You said, with death, I would have died at that moment. {34:10} Furthermore, when You commanded me regarding the tree, Eve was not yet created, nor had You taken her from my side, nor had she heard this command from You. {34:11} At the end of that third hour on Friday, You caused a deep sleep to fall upon me, and I slept deeply. {34:12} You then took a rib from my side and created Eve in my likeness. When I awoke and saw her, I said, 'This is now bone of my bones and flesh of my flesh; she shall be called Woman.' {34:13} It was by Your good will, O God, that You caused me to sleep deeply and immediately brought Eve out of my side, so I did not witness how she was made. O my Lord, how great and glorious are Your goodness and glory. {34:14} By Your good will, O Lord, You made us both with bodies of bright nature, united us as one, filled us with the praises of the Holy Spirit, so we would not hunger, thirst, know sorrow, weakness, suffering, fasting, or weariness. {34:15} But now, since we transgressed Your command and broke Your law, You have brought us into a foreign land, inflicted suffering, hunger, thirst, and weakness upon us. {34:16} Therefore, O God, we pray You to give us something to eat from the garden, to satisfy our hunger, and something to quench our thirst. {34:17} Behold, many days we have tasted nothing, drunk nothing, our flesh is dried up, our strength is wasted, and we cannot sleep due to weakness and weeping. {34:18} We dare not gather fruit from the trees for fear of You. When we first transgressed, You spared us and did not make us die. {34:19} But now, we fear that if we eat fruit from the trees without Your command, You will destroy us and wipe us from the face of the earth. {34:20} Likewise, if we drink this water without Your command, You will end our lives and uproot us. {34:21} Therefore, God, now that Eve and I have come to this place, we beseech You to give us fruit from the garden to satisfy our hunger, for we desire the fruit that grows there and all else that we lack."

{35:1} Then God looked upon Adam, observing his weeping and groaning, and the Word of God spoke to him, saying, "Adam, when you were in My garden, you experienced neither eating nor drinking, nor did you suffer from weakness, sorrow, thinness of flesh, or change. Sleep did not depart from your eyes. {35:2} But since you transgressed and came into this foreign land, all these trials have come upon you.

{36:1} Then God commanded the cherub who guarded the entrance to the garden, wielding a flaming sword, to take some fruit from the fig tree and give it to Adam. {36:2} The cherub obeyed the Lord's command, entered the garden, and brought two figs on two twigs, each fig hanging from its leaf. These figs came from the trees among which Adam and Eve had hidden themselves when God came to walk in the garden and called out to them, "Adam, where are you?" Adam answered, "I heard you in the garden, and I was afraid because I am naked, so I hid among the fig trees." {36:3} The cherub approached Adam and Eve cautiously, throwing the figs to them from a distance because their flesh could not come near the fire of the cherub's presence. {36:4} Once, angels had trembled in the presence of Adam and feared him, but now Adam trembled before the angels and was afraid of them. {36:5} Adam came closer and took one fig, and Eve, in turn, took the other. {36:6} As they held the figs in their hands, they recognized they were from the trees where they had hidden themselves. {36:6} Adam and Eve wept bitterly.

{37:1} Then Adam said to Eve, "Do you see these figs and their leaves? They are what we used to cover ourselves when we were stripped of our bright nature. But now, we do not know what misery and suffering may come upon us if we eat them. Therefore, Eve, let us restrain ourselves and not eat of them, you and I. Instead, let us ask God to give us fruit from the Tree of Life." {37:2} So Adam and Eve restrained themselves and did not eat those figs. {37:3} Adam began to pray to God and beseech Him for fruit from the Tree of Life, saying, "O God, when we transgressed Your commandment at the sixth hour of Friday, we were stripped of the bright nature we had, and we did not remain in the garden more than three hours after our transgression. {37:4} But in the evening, when You made us leave, God, we transgressed against You for one hour, and all these trials and sorrows have come upon us until this day. {37:5} And all these days, including this forty-third day, do not make up for that one hour in which we transgressed! {37:6} God, look upon us with pity and do not repay us according to our transgression of Your commandment in Your presence. {37:7} O God, give us fruit from the Tree of Life that we may eat it and live, and not see suffering and other troubles on this earth, for You are God. {37:8} When we transgressed Your commandment, You made us leave the garden and sent a cherub to guard the Tree of Life, lest we eat from it and live, and experience faintness after our transgression. {37:9} But now, Lord, we have endured all these days and suffered greatly. Make these forty-three days equivalent to the one hour in which we transgressed."

{38:1} After these events, the Word of God came to Adam and said to him, "Adam, concerning the fruit of the Tree of Life which you ask for, I will not give it to you now. It will be given to you when 5500 years are completed. {38:2} Then I will give you fruit from the Tree of Life, and you shall eat it and live forever, you, Eve, and your righteous descendants. {38:3} However, these forty-three days cannot compensate for the hour in which you transgressed My commandment. {38:4} Adam, I allowed you to eat from the fig tree among which you hid yourself. Go and eat from it, both you and Eve. {38:5} I will not deny your request, nor will I disappoint your hope. Therefore, endure until the fulfillment of the covenant I made with you." {38:6} And God withdrew His Word from Adam.

{39:1} Then Adam returned to Eve and said to her, "Get up, take a fig for yourself, and I will take another. Let us go to our cave." Adam and Eve each took a fig and headed towards the cave, as the sun was setting. They were eager to eat the fruit. {39:2} But Adam hesitated and said to Eve, "I am afraid to eat this fig. I do not know what consequences may come upon me from it." {39:3} Adam began to weep and stood praying before God, saying, "God, satisfy my hunger without me having to eat this fig. What benefit will it bring me after I have eaten it? What shall I desire and ask of You once it is gone?" {39:4} Again he said, "I am afraid to eat it, for I do not know what will happen to me because of it."

{40:1} Then the Word of God came to Adam and said to him, "Adam, why did you not have this fear, fasting, and care before this? Why did you not fear before you transgressed? {40:2} But when you came to dwell in this unfamiliar land, your physical body could not remain on earth without earthly food to strengthen it and restore its strength." {40:3} And God withdrew His Word from Adam.

{41:1} Then Adam took the fig and placed it on the golden rods, and Eve also took her fig and placed it on the incense. Each fig weighed as much as a watermelon, for the fruits of the garden were much larger than those of the land they now inhabited. {41:2} Adam and Eve stood fasting through the entire night until morning came. {41:3} When the sun rose, they engaged in prayer, and after they had finished praying, Adam said to Eve, {41:4} "Eve, come, let us go to the southern border of the garden where the river flows out and is divided into four heads. There we will pray to God and ask Him to allow us to drink from the Water of Life. {41:5} God did not allow us to eat from the Tree of Life so that we would not live forever. Therefore, let us ask Him to give us the Water of Life to quench our thirst instead of drinking the water from this land." {41:6} When Eve heard these words from Adam, she agreed. They both got up and went to the southern border of the garden, near the river at a short distance from the garden. {41:7} They stood there and prayed to the Lord, asking Him to look upon them favorably, forgive them, and grant their request. {41:8} After they had prayed together, Adam began to pray aloud before God and said, {41:9} "Lord, when I was in the garden and saw the water flowing from under the Tree of Life, I did not desire it, nor did my body need to drink from it, for I was living and above what I am now. {41:10} Now, God, I am dying, my flesh is dry with thirst. Give me the Water of Life so that I may drink and live. {41:11} Out of Your mercy, God, save me from these afflictions and trials, and bring me to another land different from this if You will not let me dwell in Your garden."

{42:1} Then the Word of God came to Adam and said to him, "Adam, concerning your request to be brought into a land where there is rest, it is not another land but the kingdom of heaven alone where true rest exists. However, you cannot enter it now; it will only be after your judgment is completed and fulfilled. {42:2} Then I will bring you and your righteous descendants into the kingdom of heaven, and there I will grant you and them the rest you seek now. {42:3} As for your request for the Water of Life to drink and live, it cannot be granted today. It will be on the day when I descend into hell, break the gates of brass, and crush the kingdoms of iron. {42:4} On that day, in My mercy, I will save your soul and the souls of the righteous, granting them rest in My garden. This will be at the end of the world. {42:5} And concerning the Water of Life you seek, it will not be given to you today, but on the day when I shed My blood on your behalf in the land of Golgotha. {42:6} For My blood will be the Water of Life for you at that time, and not for you alone, but for all your descendants who believe in Me, providing them with eternal rest." {42:7} The Lord continued, "O Adam, when you were in the garden, you did not experience these trials. {42:8} But since you transgressed My commandment, all these sufferings have come upon you. {42:9} Now your flesh also requires food and drink; therefore, drink from the water that flows on the earth's surface beside you." {42:10} After speaking these words, God withdrew His Word from Adam. Adam and Eve worshipped the Lord and returned from the river to the cave. {42:11} It was noon-day, and as they approached the cave, they saw a large fire beside it.

{43:1} Then Adam and Eve were filled with fear and stood still. Adam said to Eve, "What is this fire burning near our cave? We haven't done anything to cause it We have no bread to bake or soup to cook that would require a fire like this. We've never seen anything like it since God sent the cherub with a flashing, lightning-like sword, which made us fall down as if dead. {43:2} Eve, this is the same fire that was in the cherub's hand, sent by God to guard the cave where we live. {43:3} It seems God is angry with us and intends to drive us out. {43:4} Eve, we have transgressed His command again in this cave, so He has sent this fire to surround it and prevent us from entering. {43:5} If this is the case, Eve, where will we live? Where can we flee from the presence of the Lord? He won't let us stay in the garden and has deprived us of its blessings. Instead, He has placed us in this cave where we have endured darkness, trials, and hardships, finding only some comfort. {43:6} But now He has brought us into another land, and who knows what awaits us here? Perhaps the darkness here will be worse than what we've known. {43:7} Who knows what dangers await us day and night in this land? Wherever God decides to put us, it may be far from the garden, Eve. {43:8} If God brings us to a strange land away from our consolation, it might mean our souls are destined for death and our names erased from the earth. {43:9} Eve, if we are further separated from the garden and from God, how will we find Him again? How can we ask Him for gold, incense, myrrh, or even some figs? {43:10} Where will we find Him to comfort us again? How can we remind Him of the covenant He made with us?" {43:11} Adam fell silent, and both he and Eve continued to gaze at the cave and the fire surrounding it. {43:12} However, this fire was kindled by Satan. He had gathered trees and dry grass and brought them to the cave, setting them ablaze to destroy it and everything inside. {43:13} Satan's intent was to leave Adam and Eve in sorrow, to sever their trust in God, and to make them deny Him. {43:14} But God, in His mercy, prevented the cave from burning. He sent His angel to guard it against the fire until it eventually died out. {43:15} This fire burned from noon until the break of day, marking the forty-fifth day.

{44:1} Adam and Eve stood at a distance, watching the fire, unable to approach the cave due to their fear of it. Satan continued to bring trees and fuel the fire, causing it to blaze higher until it engulfed the entire cave. In his own mind, he sought to destroy the cave completely with the intense fire. {44:2} However, the angel of the Lord was there, guarding the cave, and Satan could not harm it. {44:3} The angel refrained from cursing or rebuking Satan because he had no authority over him to do so. {44:4} Instead, the angel patiently endured until the Word of God came and commanded Satan to depart, reminding him of his past deceptions and attempts to harm God's servants. {44:5} Satan fled from the presence of the Lord, but the fire continued to burn fiercely around the cave throughout that day, the forty-sixth day since Adam and Eve left the garden. {44:6} When Adam and Eve saw that the fire had somewhat subsided, they tried to approach the cave as they usually did, but the heat was still too intense for them to enter. {44:7} They both began to weep because the fire separated them from the cave, approaching them and burning fiercely. {44:8} Adam spoke to Eve, reflecting on the fire's nature that they now experienced, realizing it was a consequence they bore within them. {44:9} He understood that their changed condition and altered nature since their transgression made them vulnerable to the fire, which had not changed in its nature from its creation. {44:10} Therefore, when they came near it, the fire scorched their flesh, demonstrating its power over them.

{45:1} Adam stood up and prayed to God, saying, "Look, this fire has separated us from the cave where You commanded us to dwell. Now we cannot enter it." God heard Adam's prayer and sent His Word to him, saying, "Adam, look at this fire! See how different its flames and heat are compared to the garden of delights and its blessings. {45:2} When you were under My control, all creatures obeyed you, but after you transgressed My command, they all rise up against you." {45:3} God continued, "See, Adam, how Satan has deceived you. He has stripped you of your divine likeness and exalted state like Mine, and has not kept his promise to you. Instead, he has become your enemy. It was he who kindled this fire intending to burn you and Eve." {45:4} God questioned Adam, "Why did Satan not keep his agreement with you even for one day? He has robbed you of the glory that was upon you when you obeyed his command. {45:5} Did you think, Adam, that he loved you when he made this agreement? Did he truly wish to raise you up high?" {45:6} God clarified, "No, Adam, he did not do any of this out of love for you. His intent was to lead you from light into darkness, from an exalted state to degradation, from glory to humiliation, from joy to sorrow, and from rest to fasting and fainting." {45:7} God pointed out, "See this fire that Satan has kindled around your cave. Understand that if you obey his commands, this fire will surround you and your descendants. He will torment you with fire, and after death, you will descend into hell. {45:8} You will witness the burning fire that will encircle you and your seed, and there will be no escape from it until My coming. Just as you cannot enter your cave now due to the great fire around it, you will find no rest until My Word comes, who is My Promise. {45:9} At that time, My Word will create a way for you, and then you shall have rest." {45:10} God then commanded His Word to the fire burning around the cave to part and allow Adam to pass through. By God's order, the fire parted, making a way for Adam to enter. {45:11} After this, God withdrew His Word from Adam.

{46:1} Adam and Eve attempted once more to enter the cave. As they approached the pathway through the fire, Satan blew into it like a whirlwind, causing a burning coal-fire to blaze upon Adam and Eve, scorching their bodies severely. {46:2} In agony from the flames, Adam and Eve cried out to the Lord for salvation, pleading not to be consumed or tormented by the fire, and asking forgiveness for their transgression. God looked upon their burned bodies, inflicted by Satan's fire, and sent His angel to quench the burning flames. Though the fire was stopped, the wounds remained on their bodies. {46:3} God addressed Adam, showing him Satan's deceitful intentions, who had pretended to offer him divinity and greatness but now burned him with fire, seeking his destruction from the earth. {46:4} God reminded Adam of His own role as Creator, who had repeatedly delivered him from Satan's grasp. {46:5} God then turned to Eve, questioning the false promises Satan made in the garden about becoming like gods. Instead, Satan had subjected them to the taste and sight of fire, stripping away the blessings of the garden and revealing the evil power it wields. {46:6} God affirmed that Satan could never fulfill his promises of divinity but harbored bitterness against Adam and Eve and their descendants to come. {46:7} With these words, God withdrew His Word from them.

{47:1} Adam and Eve entered the cave, still trembling from the fire that had scorched their bodies. Adam spoke to Eve, reflecting on the pain inflicted by the fire in this world and contemplating how much worse it might be when they faced the punishment of their souls by Satan after death. He acknowledged that their deliverance seemed distant unless God fulfilled His promise to them in mercy. {47:2} Despite their fear, Adam and Eve blessed themselves for returning to the cave, a place they had feared never to enter again when they saw the fire surrounding it. {47:3} As the sun set, the fire continued to burn, preventing Adam and Eve from sleeping inside. After sunset, they left the cave. This marked the forty-seventh day since they had left the garden. {47:4} Adam and Eve then went to sleep under the summit of the hill near the garden, as they usually did, and prayed to God to forgive their sins before sleeping. {47:5} Meanwhile, Satan, harboring malice towards Adam and envious of the promises God made to him and his descendants, contemplated his own fate. He knew God had promised salvation to Adam through a covenant and would deliver him from hardships, whereas Satan had no such promise and would not be delivered from his own trials. {47:6} In his hatred, Satan resolved to kill Adam so the earth would be rid of him and left solely to Satan. He schemed to prevent Adam from having any descendants who could inherit God's kingdom, which had once been Satan's domain. Satan believed that by eliminating Adam, God would be compelled to restore him and his hosts to their former glory.

{48:1} After this, Satan called together his hosts, and they came to him, asking, "What shall we do, O our Lord?" {48:2} Satan replied, "You know that this Adam, whom God created from dust, has taken our kingdom. Come, let us gather and kill him, or crush him and Eve under a rock." {48:3} Hearing this, Satan's hosts approached the mountain where Adam and Eve slept. {48:4} Taking a large, flawless rock, Satan thought, "If there's a hole in it, they might escape." {48:5} He commanded, "Take this rock, throw it upon them flat, so it does not roll away. After hurling it, flee without delay." {48:6} They obeyed, but as the rock fell, God commanded it to become a shelter over them, causing no harm by His order. {48:7} The impact shook the earth profoundly. {48:8} Adam and Eve awoke, finding themselves under a rock resembling a tent, not knowing how it got there, causing them fear. {48:9} Adam questioned Eve, "Why did the mountain bend and the earth quake because of us? Why does this rock cover us like a tent? {48:10} Is God punishing us, confining us here, or closing the earth upon us for leaving the cave without His permission?" {48:11} Eve replied, "If the earth shook for us and this rock is our shelter due to our disobedience, then woe to us, Adam. Our punishment may be lengthy. {48:12} Stand and pray to God to reveal to us why this rock covers us like a tent." {48:13} Adam stood and prayed fervently until morning, seeking God's guidance in their distress.

{49:1} Then the Word of God came and asked Adam, "Who advised you to come to this place when you left the cave?" {49:2} Adam replied, "Lord, we came here because of the intense heat from the fire inside the cave." {49:3} The Lord God said to Adam, "Adam, you feared the heat of fire for one night, but what will it be like when you dwell in Hell? {49:4} Do not think I spread this rock over you to afflict you. It was Satan who promised you divinity and threw down this rock to kill you and Eve, intending to prevent you from living on earth. {49:5} But in My mercy, as the rock fell, I commanded it to shelter you, and the ground beneath you to soften. {49:6} This event, Adam, will foreshadow what will happen to Me on earth: the Jews, incited by Satan, will put Me to death, sealing Me in a rock for three days and nights. {49:7} Yet on the third day, I will rise, bringing salvation to you and your descendants if you believe in Me. But you, Adam, will not be freed from under this rock until three days and nights have passed." {49:8} God's Word departed from Adam. {49:9} Adam and Eve remained under the rock for three days and nights, as God had said, because they had left the cave without His command. {49:10} After three days and nights, God opened the rock and brought them out. Their bodies were weakened, and they were troubled with weeping and sorrow in their hearts and eyes.

{50:1} Adam and Eve exited the cave and entered the Cave of Treasures, spending the entire day praying there until evening. {50:2} This occurred fifty days after they left the garden. {50:3} Rising again, they prayed fervently to God throughout the night, seeking His mercy. {50:4} At dawn, Adam said to Eve, "Come, let's find something to sustain our bodies." {50:5} They left the cave and went to the northern edge of the garden, searching for something to cover themselves with, but found nothing and didn't know how to make it. Their bodies were marked, and they suffered from extreme temperatures. {50:6} Adam stood and prayed to God for guidance on covering their bodies. {50:7} Then the Word of God came to him, saying, "Adam, take Eve and go to the seashore where you fasted before. There you will find sheepskins left by lions after devouring their flesh. Take them, make clothes for yourselves, and clothe yourselves with them."

{51:1} When Adam heard these words from God, he took Eve and moved from the northern end of the garden to the south, near the river where they had once fasted. {51:2} As they journeyed, before reaching their destination, Satan, hearing God's words to Adam about clothing, became distressed. {51:3} He hurried to the place where the sheepskins were, intending to either throw them into the sea or burn them so Adam and Eve wouldn't find them. {51:4} But as he tried to take the skins, the Word of God came from heaven and bound him beside them until Adam and Eve approached. {51:5} Seeing him, they were afraid of his terrifying appearance. {51:6} Then the Word of God spoke to Adam and Eve, saying, "This is the one who was hidden in the serpent and deceived you, stripping you of the garment of light and glory you once had. {51:7} This is the one who promised you majesty and divinity. Where is his beauty now? Where is his divinity, his light, and the glory he once possessed? {51:8} Now he is hideous, abominable among angels, known as Satan. {51.9} Adam, he sought to take away these earthly sheepskins from you, to destroy them so you couldn't be covered. {51:10} What beauty did you see in him to follow? What have you gained by listening to him? Look at his evil deeds and then look at Me, your Creator, and the good I do for you. {51:11} I bound him until you came and witnessed his weakness, seeing that he has no power left." {51:12} Then God released Satan from his bonds.

{52:1} After this, Adam and Eve ceased speaking and wept before God because of their creation and their bodies needing earthly coverings. {52:2} Adam said to Eve, "Eve, this is the skin of animals with which we will be covered. But when we wear it, it will be a sign of death upon us, for the owners of these skins have died and decayed. Likewise, we too shall die and perish." {52:3} Taking the skins, Adam and Eve returned to the Cave of Treasures where they stood and prayed as they usually did. {52:4} They pondered how to fashion garments from the skins, lacking the skill to do so. {52:5} God then sent His angel to teach them. The angel instructed Adam to gather palm thorns. Adam obeyed and brought them back as commanded. {52:6} The angel demonstrated before them how to work the skins, piercing them with thorns as one would sew a shirt. {52:7} Afterward, the angel prayed to God that the thorns in the skins be concealed, appearing as if sewn with a single thread. {52:8} By God's command, the skins became garments for Adam and Eve, clothing them. {52:9} Thus, their nakedness was covered from each other's sight. {52:10} This occurred on the fifty-first day after leaving the garden. {52:11} Once clothed, Adam and Eve prayed, seeking mercy, forgiveness, and giving thanks to God for covering their nakedness. They continued praying through the night. {52:12} At dawn, they prayed again and then left the cave. {52:13} Adam suggested to Eve that since they didn't know what lay west of the cave, they should explore it that day. {52:14} They went towards the western border together.

{53:1} They had not gone far from the cave when Satan approached them, disguising himself as two fierce lions who hadn't eaten for three days. These lions advanced towards Adam and Eve, seeming intent on tearing them apart and devouring them. {53:2} Adam and Eve cried out, praying to God for deliverance from the lions. {53:3} Then the Word of God came and drove the lions away from them. {53:4} God spoke to Adam, asking why he sought the western border and why he had left the eastern border where he belonged. {53:5} God instructed Adam to return to the cave and stay there to avoid being deceived or falling prey to Satan's schemes. {53:6} God warned Adam that from this western border, a seed would come forth, descendants who would defile themselves with sins and follow Satan's commands and deeds. {53:7} As a consequence, God would bring a flood upon them to destroy them, saving only the righteous whom He would lead to a distant land. The current land where Adam dwelled would then remain desolate without inhabitants. {53:8} After this discourse, Adam and Eve returned to the Cave of Treasures. Their bodies were weakened from fasting, praying, and sorrow over their transgression against God.

{54:1} Adam and Eve stood up in the cave and prayed throughout the entire night until morning. As the sun rose, they left the cave, their heads heavy with sorrow, walking aimlessly without knowing their direction. {54:2} They walked to the southern border of the garden and began ascending until they reached the eastern border, where there was no further space beyond. {54:3} The cherub who guarded the garden stood at the western gate, preventing Adam and Eve from entering, following God's command. {54:4} When Adam and Eve thought the cherub wasn't watching, they stood near the gate, desiring to enter. Suddenly, the cherub appeared with a flashing sword of fire in hand and moved towards them to kill them, fearing God's punishment if they entered the garden without His permission. {54:5} The sword seemed to blaze from a distance, but when raised over Adam and Eve, it did not emit flames. The cherub interpreted this as a sign that God favored them and intended to bring them back to the garden. {54:6} Unable to ascend to Heaven to confirm God's command regarding their entry, the cherub remained with them, fearing they might enter without God's leave, which would lead to his destruction. {54:7} Adam and Eve, seeing the cherub approach with a fiery sword, fell on their faces in fear, appearing as though dead. {54:8} At that moment, the heavens and earth trembled, and other cherubim descended to the garden's guardian, finding him astonished and silent. {54:9} More angels approached near Adam and Eve, torn between joy at the thought of God favoring Adam's return to the garden and sadness over Adam and Eve's fallen state, likening them to being dead, and attributing their condition to God's judgment for attempting to enter the garden without His permission.

{55:1} Then the Word of God came to Adam and Eve, lifting them from their state of despair. God asked them why they had come to the border, questioning if they intended to enter the garden from which they were expelled. God explained that it was not yet the time for them to return, but only when the covenant made with them would be fulfilled. {55:2} Upon hearing God's words and the faint fluttering of angels around them, Adam and Eve wept. They spoke to the angels, lamenting their inability to see them as they did in their former bright nature, when they could sing praises alongside the angels. Now, in their fallen state, they were reduced to mere flesh and could no longer perceive the angels who once served them. {55:3} Adam pleaded with the angels, asking them to intercede with God on his behalf, to restore him to his former glory, deliver him from misery, and revoke the death sentence imposed for his transgression. {55:4} The angels, moved by Adam's words, mourned over him and cursed Satan who had deceived him, leading him from the garden to a life of misery, from peace to turmoil, and from joy to a foreign land. {55:5} They explained to Adam how Satan had deceived them as well before his fall from heaven, promising his hosts a great kingdom and divine nature, which led to their downfall when they believed his false promises and rebelled against God. {55:6} The angels recounted how Satan waged war against God and them, but with God's strength, they prevailed and cast him down to the earth, bringing great joy in heaven at his expulsion. {55:7} They described how Satan continued his war against Adam, deceiving him into leaving the garden and bringing upon him the same death that God had decreed for Satan. {55:8} All the angels rejoiced and praised God, asking Him not to destroy Adam for attempting to enter the garden prematurely, but to endure with him until the fulfillment of the promise and to assist him in overcoming Satan's influence in the world.

{56:1} Then the Word of God spoke to Adam, contrasting the garden of joy with the toil of the earth where he now dwelt alone with Satan, whom he had obeyed. God reminded Adam that if he had remained obedient and kept His word, he would have been among the angels in God's garden. Instead, by obeying Satan, Adam became associated with wicked angels and was condemned to live on an earth that yielded thorns and thistles. {56:2} God instructed Adam to challenge Satan to fulfill his promises: to grant him divine nature, recreate the garden, restore his original bright nature, or create a body and soul as God had given him. However, God warned Adam that Satan would not fulfill any of these promises. {56:3} God then reminded Adam of His favor and mercy, promising him salvation after a designated time. {56:4} Following God's command, Adam and Eve were urged to leave the border of the garden, lest they be destroyed by the cherub with a flaming sword. Adam found comfort in God's words and worshipped Him. {56:5} God commanded His angels to guide Adam and Eve back to the cave joyfully, replacing their previous fear. {56:6} The angels escorted them with songs and psalms down from the mountain near the garden to the cave, where they comforted and strengthened Adam and Eve before returning to heaven. {56:7} After the angels departed, Satan shamefully approached the cave and called out to Adam, pretending to be an angel sent to offer counsel.

{57:1} The seventh time Satan appeared to Adam and Eve, Adam emerged from the cave and was terrified by Satan's hideous appearance. He demanded to know who he was. Satan confessed that he was the one who had hidden within the serpent, deceived Eve, and led them to disobey God's command by eating the forbidden fruit. {57:2} Adam questioned Satan about his promises: whether he could recreate a garden like God had made for him, or restore his original bright nature. He challenged Satan about the divine nature and fair promises he had spoken in the garden. {57:3} Satan admitted that he had no intention of fulfilling his promises, for he himself had fallen from grace. He claimed dominion over Adam and Eve because they had listened to him and disobeyed God, asserting that no deliverance would come until the time appointed by God. {57:4} Satan threatened Adam and Eve with continued war and murder, vowing to sow discord and misery upon them and their descendants. He declared his intent to perpetuate evil without respite, dwelling in burning fire and aiming to thwart any human inheriting heavenly orders. {57:5} Adam mourned upon hearing these words, realizing Satan's deceit and the dire consequences of their fall. He comforted himself with the hope that God, who created them, would deliver them from Satan's grip.

{58:1} Adam and Eve lifted their hands to God, praying fervently for Him to drive Satan away from them, to protect them from violence, and to prevent Satan from forcing them to deny God. {58:2} Immediately, God sent His angel who expelled Satan from their presence. This happened around sunset on the fifty-third day after they had been expelled from the garden. {58:3} Afterward, Adam and Eve entered the cave, standing with their faces to the ground, praying earnestly to God. Before praying, Adam spoke to Eve, reflecting on the trials they had faced in this new land. He suggested that they rise and ask God for forgiveness for their sins, vowing not to leave the cave until nearly forty days had passed. He expressed faith that if they were to die in the cave, God would still save them. {58:4} Adam and Eve then rose and prayed together, remaining in the cave day and night without emerging, their prayers ascending like flames from their mouths.

{59:1} Satan, the adversary of all goodness, interrupted Adam and Eve's prayers. He summoned his hosts and gathered them together, declaring his intent since Adam and Eve had agreed to pray continuously to God, seeking deliverance and refusing to leave the cave until the end of the fortieth day. {59:2} Satan plotted with his hosts, saying they would thwart Adam and Eve's prayers and their hope of restoration by God. His hosts affirmed his authority, acknowledging his power to act as he pleased. {59:3} On the thirtieth night of the forty-one days, Satan, in his great wickedness, entered the cave and violently struck Adam and Eve until they appeared dead. {59:4} Then the Word of God came to Adam and Eve, reviving them from their suffering. God comforted Adam, urging him to be strong and unafraid of the adversary who had just attacked them. {59:5} Adam, however, lamented to God, questioning why they had been subjected to such suffering and blows. He wondered where God had been during their ordeal. {59:6} God reminded Adam that Satan, who had promised divinity and love, had shown his true nature by attacking them despite Adam's earlier compliance with his counsel and disobedience to God's command. {59:7} Adam wept before God, acknowledging his transgression and pleading for deliverance from Satan's hands or for God to take his soul from his body in this unfamiliar land. {59:8} God replied, expressing that if Adam had shown such remorse and prayer before transgressing, he would have been spared from the current troubles. {59:9} Despite Adam's faults, God showed patience and allowed him and Eve to remain in the cave until the forty days were fulfilled. {59:10} Adam and Eve suffered greatly during this time, their bodies weakened from fasting, hunger, and thirst since leaving the garden. They were unable to continue their prayers due to physical weakness, falling down in the cave. Yet, they continued to praise God despite their hardships.

{60:1} On the eighty-ninth day, Satan appeared to Adam and Eve in a deceptive guise, clothed in a garment of light and adorned with a bright girdle. {60:2} Holding a staff of light, he presented himself with an awe-inspiring appearance, though his countenance was pleasant and his words were sweet. His intent was to deceive Adam and Eve, persuading them to leave the cave before completing the forty days of penance. {60:3} Satan reasoned within himself that if Adam and Eve finished their fasting and prayers, God might restore them to their former state. Alternatively, if not restored, God might still show them favor by providing something from the garden to comfort them, as had happened twice before. {60:4} Approaching the cave in this enticing form, Satan addressed Adam and Eve, inviting them to leave with him to a better land, reassuring them that he was like them—flesh and bones, originally created by God. {60:5} He recounted how God had initially placed him in a garden to the north, commanding him to abide there without transgression. {60:6} Satan lamented that Adam was taken from his side and placed in a different garden to the east, causing him grief because Adam was not left to dwell with him. {60:7} According to Satan's account, God assured him not to grieve over Adam's removal, explaining that Eve was created as Adam's companion and source of joy. {60:8} Satan claimed ignorance of Adam and Eve's current plight until God informed him of their expulsion from the garden due to disobedience to His commandments. {60:9} God instructed Satan to go to Adam and Eve, prevent further affliction from Satan, and comfort them in their misery, promising them sustenance and restoration. {60:10} Overwhelmed by sorrow upon hearing this, Satan hesitated to approach them, fearing Satan's trickery as he had deceived Adam and Eve. {60:11} God reassured Satan not to fear, empowering him to confront Satan and promising that his age and authority would prevail against the adversary. {60:12} Reluctant due to his age, Satan asked God to send angels instead, but God insisted that only Satan's offspring, resembling him, would effectively communicate with Adam and Eve. {60:13} God then commanded a cloud to carry Satan to Adam and Eve's cave and return afterward. {60:14} Seeing Satan's feeble state and his journey from afar, Adam and Eve were moved by his appearance and his tearful plea. {60:15}

Seeing his beard and hearing his compassionate words, they softened towards him, believing his sincerity and feeling a kinship with him.

{61:1} Then Satan took Adam and Eve by the hand and began leading them out of the cave. {61:2} But as they came out a short distance, God knew that Satan had deceived them, bringing them out before the forty days were completed, intending to lead them far away and destroy them. {61:3} The Word of the Lord God came again and cursed Satan, driving him away from Adam and Eve. {61:4} God questioned Adam and Eve, asking why they had left the cave and come to this place. {61:5} Adam explained to God that an old man claiming to be a messenger from Him had appeared in the cave, promising to lead them to a place of rest. {61:6} Adam and Eve believed him to be a messenger from God and followed him without knowing where they were going. {61:7} God then revealed to Adam that the old man was actually the originator of evil arts, who had deceived them and brought them out of the Garden of Eden. {61:8} Seeing Adam and Eve fasting and praying together, Satan sought to thwart their efforts, break their unity, and drive them to a place where he could destroy them. {61:9} Unable to harm them directly, Satan disguised himself as a trusted figure to deceive them. {61:10} In mercy, God prevented Satan from destroying them and commanded Adam and Eve to return to their cave and remain there until the fortieth day. {61:11} They were instructed to exit through the eastern gate of the garden on the following day. {61:12} Adam and Eve worshipped and praised God for their deliverance, returning to the cave on the thirty-ninth day at sunset. {61:13} Adam and Eve, weakened by hunger and thirst, prayed fervently throughout the night, seeking strength from God. {61:14} In the morning, Adam urged Eve to go to the eastern gate of the garden as instructed by God. {61:15} They prayed as usual and left the cave to approach the eastern gate. {61:16} Standing there, they prayed again, asking God to strengthen them and provide food. {61:17} Upon finishing their prayers, they remained there due to their weakened state. {61:18} God then instructed Adam to go and bring two figs. {61:19} Adam and Eve obeyed, going near to the cave where the fig trees grew.

{62:1} Satan, consumed by envy due to the comfort God had bestowed upon Adam and Eve, sought to thwart their consolation. {62:2} He entered the cave and took the two figs, burying them outside so that Adam and Eve would not find them, intending harm against them. {62:3} However, by God's mercy, once the figs were in the ground, God foiled Satan's plan concerning them. {62:4} He caused the figs to grow into two fruit-bearing trees that provided shade over the cave, despite Satan burying them on the eastern side. {62:5} When the trees matured and bore fruit, Satan lamented and regretted his actions, realizing that his plan to destroy the figs had failed. {62:6} He acknowledged that it would have been better to leave the figs untouched, for now they had become perpetual sources of sustenance for Adam. {62:7} Satan admitted that God had overturned his scheme, ensuring that the sacred fruit would not perish. {62:8} He was ashamed of his failure to carry out his evil intention against God's servants, and he departed in disgrace.

{63:1} As Adam and Eve approached the cave, they saw two fig trees laden with fruit, casting shade over it. {63:2} Adam was perplexed and said to Eve that it seemed they had gone astray, questioning when these two trees had grown there. He suspected the enemy's deception, wondering if there was another cave nearby. {63:3} They entered the cave to search for the two figs as instructed, but found none. {63:4} Adam was distraught and suggested they might be in the wrong cave, speculating that the fig trees outside could be the very figs they sought. Eve was unsure. {63:5} Adam then stood and prayed to God, recounting how they had not found the figs and seeking clarity if God had taken them and caused the trees to grow, or if they had been deceived by the enemy. {63:6} The Word of God then came to Adam, explaining that Satan had preemptively taken the figs and buried them outside the cave in an attempt to destroy them, not intending good. {63:7} The trees had grown by God's mercy to provide shade and rest for Adam and Eve, revealing God's power and thwarting Satan's evil intent. {63:8} God instructed Adam and Eve to rejoice in the trees' shade but warned them not to eat the fruit or approach them. {63:9} Adam pleaded with God not to punish them again or drive them away, requesting that if the trees harbored any harm, God should uproot them and let them perish rather than suffer under their shadow. He acknowledged God's ability to transform things at will through His power.

{64:1} God observed Adam's steadfastness despite hunger, thirst, and heat. He transformed the two fig trees back into figs and instructed Adam and Eve to each take one. They obeyed God's command and took the figs. {64:2} God then directed them to enter the cave and eat the figs to satisfy their hunger, warning them against dying from starvation. {64:3} Following God's instructions, they entered the cave as the sun was setting and prayed. {64:4} They hesitated to eat the figs because they were unaccustomed to earthly food and feared it might burden their stomachs, thicken their flesh, and cause them to desire more earthly sustenance. {64:5} Out of compassion, God sent His angel to them to prevent them from perishing of hunger and thirst. {64:6} The angel relayed God's message that as beings of flesh, they lacked the strength to fast to death and should eat to strengthen their bodies. {64:7} Adam and Eve followed the angel's advice and began eating the figs, which God had infused with a nourishing mixture akin to savory bread and blood. {64:8} After satisfying their hunger, they saved what remained, and by God's blessing, the figs replenished to their original state. {64:9} They rose with renewed strength, prayed joyfully, and praised God throughout the night, marking the end of the eighty-third day.

{65:1} When morning came, Adam and Eve rose and prayed as was their custom, then left the cave. {65:2} They felt great discomfort from the food they had eaten, unfamiliar to them, and wandered in the cave lamenting their condition. {65:3} Adam spoke to Eve, questioning whether God intended to punish them through the food they ate, fearing their insides might be affected, or that they would die in pain before God fulfilled His promise. {65:4} Adam prayed to the Lord, pleading not to perish because of the food they had consumed, asking for mercy and imploring God not to abandon them until the day of His promised salvation. {65:5} God looked upon them and immediately adapted their bodies to tolerate food, ensuring they would not perish. {65:6} Adam and Eve returned to the cave sorrowful, realizing their nature had changed. {65:7} They understood they were now altered beings, cut off from the hope of returning to the garden, knowing they could not enter it because their bodies now required food and drink to sustain them, unfit for the garden's conditions. {65:8} Adam lamented to Eve that their hope and trust to re-enter the garden were now lost, acknowledging they were no longer fit for the garden but destined to be earthly, of dust, and inhabitants of the earth until the day God promised to save them and restore them to the garden. {65:9} They prayed to God for mercy, finding solace in their prayers, their hearts heavy, and their longing diminished as they felt like strangers on the earth. {65:10} That night, Adam and Eve slept heavily in the cave due to the food they had eaten.

{66:1} When morning came after they had eaten food, Adam and Eve prayed in the cave. Adam said to Eve, "We asked God for food, and He provided. Now let us also ask Him for water to drink." {66:2} They went to the bank of the stream on the south border of the garden where they had previously thrown themselves. {66:3} Standing there, they prayed to God to command them to drink from the water. {66:4} The Word of God came to Adam, telling him that his body now needed water to drink because it had become like that of animals. Adam and Eve were commanded to drink, give thanks, and praise God. {66:5} They approached the stream, drank until they were refreshed, praised God, and returned to their cave as they had always done. This occurred at the end of eighty-three days. {66:6} On the eighty-fourth day, they took two figs and hung them in the cave with their leaves as a sign and blessing from God for their descendants to see the wonders God had performed for them. {66:7} Adam and Eve stood outside the cave again, praying to God to provide them with food to nourish their bodies. {66:8} The Word of God instructed Adam to go westward of the cave to a land with dark soil, promising that he would find food there. {66:9} Adam obeyed, took Eve, and found wheat growing ripe in the ear, and figs ready to eat. {66:10} Adam rejoiced at this discovery. {66:11} God's Word came again to Adam, telling him to take the wheat and make bread to nourish his body. God granted Adam wisdom to process the wheat into bread. {66:12} Adam diligently followed God's instructions, learning how to make bread until he returned to the cave, joyful at having gained the knowledge of turning wheat into bread for sustenance.

{67:1} When Adam and Eve descended to the land with dark soil and approached the ripe wheat shown to them by God, they had no sickle to reap it. {67:2} They girded themselves and began pulling up the wheat by hand until it was all gathered into a heap. {67:3} Exhausted by the heat and thirst, they sought shade under a tree where a breeze cooled them, and they fell asleep. {67:4} Satan observed their actions and called his hosts, plotting against Adam and Eve. He decided to set fire to the heap of wheat to destroy it, and to empty the bucket of water nearby so that they would wake to find nothing to drink, thus succumbing to hunger and thirst. {67:5} After burning the wheat, Satan and his hosts waited for Adam and Eve to wake, intending to mislead them on their way back to the cave and cause their demise through starvation and thirst. {67:6} When Adam and Eve awoke from the heat of the flames and saw their wheat destroyed and their water spilled, they wept and returned sorrowfully to the cave. {67:7} As they ascended from the mountain, Satan and his hosts appeared to them disguised as angels praising God. {67:8} Satan questioned Adam about his distress from hunger and thirst, suggesting that Satan had burned the wheat. Adam confirmed it, and Satan deceitfully offered to lead them to another field of better corn and a fountain of good water, claiming they were angels sent by God. {67:9} Adam believed Satan's deception and followed him. {67:10} Satan led Adam and Eve astray for eight days until they collapsed from exhaustion, hunger, and thirst, appearing as if dead. {67:11} Then Satan and his hosts fled, leaving them abandoned.

{68:1} God looked upon Adam and Eve and saw the harm caused by Satan, who had led them astray and destroyed the wheat. {68:2} God sent His Word to raise Adam and Eve from their despair and death-like state. {68:3} When Adam was revived, he lamented to God about the loss of the wheat and water, and accused God of sending angels to mislead them. {68:4} God clarified that Satan was the one who burnt the wheat, emptied the water, and deceived them with false promises. {68:5} God then instructed His angels to take Adam and Eve to the wheat field once more, where they found it restored along with a full bucket of water. {68:6} They also discovered a tree bearing solid manna, marveling at God's provision. {68:7} The angels commanded them to eat the manna when hungry. {68:8} God cursed Satan not to destroy the wheat field again. {68:9} Adam and Eve took some of the wheat, made an offering of it, and placed it on an altar. {68:10} They prayed, recalling how their innocence and praises once pleased God in the garden. {68:11} God accepted their offering and promised that it would become His flesh when He came to earth to save them. {68:12} A bright fire came upon their offering, filled it with brightness, grace, and light, and the Holy Ghost descended upon it. {68:13} An angel took an offering to Adam and Eve, brightening their souls and filling their hearts with joy and praise. {68:14} God established this offering as a custom for them in times of affliction. {68:15} Adam rejoiced at God's words and worshipped before the altar. {68:16} This happened twelve days after the eightieth day from leaving the garden. {68:17} They spent the night praying in the cave and emerged in the morning. {68:18} Adam proposed to Eve that they continue offering this oblation three times a week — on Wednesday, Friday, and Sunday. {68:19} God was pleased with their resolution. {68:20} The Word of God came to Adam, instructing him to continue offering the oblation every week.

{69:1} During Adam's prayer over the offering on the altar, Satan, envious of Adam's favor with God, appeared in human form and swiftly took a sharp stone. {69:2} He approached Adam and Eve while Adam was praying with outstretched hands. {69:3} Satan used the sharp stone to pierce Adam on his right side, causing blood and water to flow, and Adam fell on the altar as if dead. {69:4} Satan fled immediately after. {69:5} Eve found Adam and placed him beneath the altar, weeping over him as blood continued to flow onto his offering. {69:6} God saw Adam's condition and sent His Word to raise him up, instructing him to complete his offering which was of great worth. {69:7} God spoke to Adam, foretelling that a similar event would happen to Him on earth, where He would be pierced and His blood and water would flow, serving as a perfect offering on the altar. {69:8} Adam obeyed God's command, finished his offering, worshipped, and praised God for the signs shown to him. {69:9} God healed Adam in one day, marking the end of seven weeks, which was the fiftieth day. {69:10} Adam and Eve returned to the Cave of Treasures, having spent one hundred and forty days outside the garden. {69:11} They prayed that night and in the morning went to rest westward of the cave where their corn grew, sheltered under a tree as usual. {69:12} However, a multitude of beasts surrounded them, instigated by Satan's wickedness, intending harm through attack or enticement, likely for Eve's marriage.

{70:1} Afterward, Satan, who opposes all good, disguised himself as an angel accompanied by two others, appearing like the three who had previously brought gold, incense, and myrrh to Adam. {70:2} They approached Adam and Eve under the tree, greeting them with deceitful words and charming appearances. {70:3} Adam, seeing their beauty and hearing their sweet speech, welcomed them joyfully and introduced them to Eve, believing them to be the same angels who had brought blessings before. {70:4} Satan, appearing as the tallest angel, spoke to Adam, saying they were sent by God with a light message, asking if Adam would hear and obey it. {70:5} Adam, unaware it was Satan, agreed eagerly, hoping for further blessings as before. {70:6} Satan assured Adam that he was the angel who had brought gold to the cave, and the others were the bearers of incense and myrrh, claiming that the other angels were not sent this time because they were sufficient. {70:7} Adam, trusting their words, asked them to speak God's message. {70:8} Satan then demanded Adam swear an oath by placing his hand in Satan's hand, invoking God's name and the elements of creation, binding Adam to receive and uphold the message. {70:9} Adam swore as instructed. {70:10} Satan then informed Adam that God commanded him to take Eve, his companion created from his side, as his wife to bear children, bring comfort, and alleviate his troubles, assuring Adam there was no shame or difficulty in this command.

{71:1} Upon hearing Satan's words, Adam was greatly sorrowful because of his oath and promise. He questioned whether he should commit adultery with Eve, his own flesh and bones, and thereby sin against himself, risking God's wrath and his own destruction. {71:2} Adam reflected on how God had punished him before for eating from the tree, driving him out of the garden, depriving him of his former glory, and bringing death upon him. {71:3} He feared that if he obeyed Satan, God would cut off his life, cast him into hell, and afflict him for a long time. {71:4} Adam then denounced the devils, recognizing them as deceitful beings in the guise of angels, cursed by God, and commanded them to leave. {71:5} The devils fled from Adam, and he and Eve returned to the Cave of Treasures. {71:6} Adam confided in Eve, confessing his sin of swearing by God's name and placing his hand in Satan's again, urging her to keep it secret. {71:7} Adam then prayed to God with tears, standing for forty days and nights without food or drink, begging for forgiveness. {71:8} God sent His Word to Adam, lifting him up, and questioned him about swearing by His name and making a pact with Satan again. {71:9} Adam wept, pleading ignorance and asking for God's forgiveness, which God granted, cautioning Adam to beware of Satan. {71:10} Adam was comforted, and he and Eve left the cave to procure food. {71:11} Adam struggled in his mind about marrying Eve, fearing God's anger. {71:12} They went to the riverbank to rest, but Satan, jealous of their happiness, plotted their destruction.

{72:1} Satan and ten of his companions transformed into extraordinarily graceful maidens, unlike any others in the world, emerged from the river in front of Adam and Eve. {72:2} They admired Adam and Eve's appearance, remarking on the beauty that distinguished them from others on earth. {72:3} Approaching Adam and Eve, they greeted them and marveled at their presence. {72:4} Adam and Eve, in turn, were captivated by the maidens' beauty and questioned whether another world existed beneath them with such creatures. {72:5} The maidens affirmed their abundant creation and explained their multiplication through marriage and offspring, offering to show Adam their husbands and children to prove it. {72:6} Calling out, they summoned their husbands and children from the river, and Adam and Eve were astonished upon seeing them. {72:7} The maidens urged Adam and Eve to marry and have children as they did, a scheme devised by Satan to deceive Adam. {72:8} Satan reasoned within himself that just as God had punished Adam for eating the forbidden fruit, disobeying God's command to marry Eve might result in Adam's death. {72:9} The fire of sin tempted Adam, but he resisted, fearing God's punishment if he followed Satan's advice. {72:10} Adam and Eve prayed while Satan and his hosts returned to the river, demonstrating their departure to Adam and Eve. {72:11} Adam and Eve then returned to the Cave of Treasures as evening approached and prayed through the night. {72:12} Adam remained standing in prayer until morning, troubled by thoughts of marrying Eve. {72:13} At dawn, Adam proposed they go below the mountain where they received gold to seek God's guidance on the matter. {72:14} Eve suggested they pray in the cave instead, seeking God's order whether the counsel they received was good. {72:15} Adam prayed, confessing their transgressions and beseeching God for guidance, fearing they would perish without His command.

{73:1} Then God observed that Adam's words were sincere and that he was willing to wait for His command regarding Satan's counsel. {73:2} God approved of Adam's caution and the prayer he had offered, and His Word came to Adam, remarking that if only Adam had been this cautious before leaving the garden, things would have been different. {73:3} God then sent the angels who had brought gold, incense, and myrrh to Adam, instructing them to advise him concerning marrying Eve. {73:4} The angels directed Adam to give the gold to Eve as a wedding gift, betroth her, and present her with incense and myrrh. They instructed Adam and Eve to become one flesh. {73:5} Adam followed the angels' instructions, placing the gold in Eve's garment and betrothing her with his hand. {73:6} The angels further commanded Adam and Eve to fast and pray for forty days and nights before coming together, ensuring their union would be pure and undefiled, and that they would conceive children to populate the earth. {73:7} Adam and Eve accepted the angels' words, and the angels departed from them. {73:8} Adam and Eve diligently fasted and prayed for forty days, then came together as instructed. {73:9} From the time Adam left the garden until he wedded Eve spanned two hundred and twenty-three days, equivalent to seven months and thirteen days. {73:10} Thus, Satan's plot against Adam was thwarted.

{74:1} Adam and Eve lived on the earth, working to sustain their bodies, until the nine months of Eve's pregnancy came to an end, and the time approached for her to give birth. {74:2} Eve spoke to Adam, saying that the cave where they dwelt had become sacred due to the signs manifested there since their departure from the garden. She suggested they move to the cave of the sheltering rock, where Satan had hurled a rock at them in an attempt to kill them, but God had commanded it to be held up and spread as an awning over them, forming a cave. {74:3} Adam heeded Eve's advice and moved her to that cave. When the time came for her to deliver, she experienced great travail. Adam was deeply sorrowful and anxious for her, knowing she was close to death, fulfilling God's word to her that she would bear children in pain and sorrow. {74:4} Adam prayed earnestly to God to look upon Eve with mercy and deliver her from distress. {74:5} God answered Adam's prayer, looked upon Eve with favor, and she gave birth to her first-born son and a daughter. {74:6} Adam rejoiced at Eve's deliverance and at the children she bore him. He cared for Eve in the cave for eight days, during which they named their son Cain and their daughter Luluwa. {74:7} Cain means "hater," because he showed hatred towards his sister in their mother's womb before they were born. Thus, Adam named him Cain. {74:8} Luluwa means "beautiful," because she was more beautiful than her mother Eve. {74:9} Adam and Eve waited until Cain and his sister were forty days old, then Adam proposed they make an offering on behalf of the children. {74:10} Eve agreed, suggesting they make one offering for the first-born son, and another later for their daughter.

{75:1} Adam prepared an offering and he and Eve offered it for their children, bringing it to the altar they had originally built. {75:2} Adam performed the offering and prayed earnestly for God to accept it. {75:3} God accepted Adam's offering and sent a heavenly light that shone upon the offering. Adam and his son approached the altar, but Eve and her daughter did not draw near. {75:4} Adam descended from the altar joyfully, and they waited until the daughter was eighty days old. {75:5} Adam then prepared another offering and took it to Eve and the children, leading them to the altar where he offered it, praying for God's acceptance as before. {75:6} The Lord accepted Adam and Eve's offering. They rejoiced together and returned from the mountain. {75:7} Instead of going back to their birth cave, they went to the Cave of Treasures so the children could receive blessings with tokens brought from the garden. {75:8} After receiving these blessings, they returned to their original cave. {75:9} Before Eve offered her own offering, Adam took her to the river where they had first thrown themselves, and they washed themselves clean from the suffering and distress they had endured. {75:10} After washing in the river, Adam and Eve returned each night to the Cave of Treasures to pray and receive blessings, then went back to their cave where their children were born. {75:11} They continued this routine until the children were weaned. {75:12} Adam then made offerings for the souls of his children three times a week. {75:13} After the weaning period, Eve conceived again, and she gave birth to another son named Abel and a daughter named Aklemia. {75:14} Adam made an offering for Abel at the end of forty days, and another for Aklemia at the end of eighty days, following the same practice he did with Cain and Luluwa. {75:15} They brought them to the Cave of Treasures for blessings, then returned to their birth cave. {75:16} After the birth of Abel and Aklemia, Eve stopped bearing children.

{76:1} The children grew stronger and taller, but Cain became hardened and dominated over his younger brother. {76:2} Often when his father made offerings, Cain would stay behind and not participate. {76:3} Abel, on the other hand, had a gentle heart and obeyed his parents. He frequently encouraged them to make offerings because he loved it, and he prayed and fasted earnestly. {76:4} One day, as Abel entered the Cave of Treasures and saw the golden rods, incense, and myrrh, he asked Adam and Eve where they came from. {76:5} Adam recounted everything that had happened to them, and Abel was deeply moved by his father's story. {76:6} Adam then told him about God's works and the garden, and Abel spent the entire night with his father in the Cave of Treasures. {76:7} During that night, Satan appeared to him disguised as a man and threatened to kill him for his piety, fasting, and prayers that had moved Adam to make offerings. {76:8} However, Abel prayed to God and rejected Satan's words. {76:9} At dawn, an angel appeared to Abel and reassured him not to fear, for God had accepted his prayers and offerings. The angel also warned him about the figure that appeared at night and cursed him to death. {76:10} After sunrise, Abel went to Adam and Eve and shared the vision he had seen. {76:11} Adam and Eve were deeply grieved upon hearing this but did not discuss it with Abel, only offering him comfort. {76:12} Meanwhile, Satan appeared to the hardened Cain at night, revealing his jealousy over Abel's favor with their parents and the potential marriage plans that favored Abel's sister over his own. {76:13} Satan advised Cain to kill Abel to prevent the marriage and secure his own advantage. {76:14} The wicked suggestion took root in Cain's heart, and he often sought an opportunity to kill his brother.

{77:1} When Adam noticed that Cain harbored hatred toward Abel, he tried to soften their hearts. Adam instructed Cain, "Take some of the fruits you have grown and make an offering to God. Ask for forgiveness for your wickedness and sins." {77:2} Similarly, Adam told Abel to take from his harvest and make an offering to God for the same reason. {77:3} Abel obeyed his father's instructions and made a sincere offering. He then asked Adam to accompany him to the altar to show him how to present it properly. Adam and Eve went with Abel and guided him in offering his gift on the altar. {77:4} They prayed together, asking God to accept Abel's offering. {77:5} God looked favorably upon Abel and accepted his offering because of his pure heart and good intentions. {77:6} Afterward, they returned to the cave where they lived. Abel, filled with joy from making his offering, continued to do so three times a week, following Adam's example. {77:7} Cain, however, did not take pleasure in making offerings. After much insistence from his father, he made an offering once, but his heart was not in it. {77:8} When he did offer, he focused only on the offering itself and chose the smallest of his sheep. {77:9} Because Cain's heart was filled with murderous thoughts, God did not accept his offering. {77:10} They all lived together in the cave where Eve had given birth, until Cain was fifteen years old and Abel twelve years old.

{78:1} Adam said to Eve, "Look, our children are grown up now. We must think about finding wives for them." Eve replied, "How can we do that?" {78:2} Adam suggested, "Let's marry Abel's sister to Cain, and Cain's sister to Abel." {78:3} Eve expressed her concern about Cain's hard-hearted nature, suggesting they wait until they make offerings to the Lord on their behalf. Adam agreed and said nothing more. {78:4} Meanwhile, Satan appeared to Cain disguised as a man from the field. He told Cain that Adam and Eve had planned to marry Abel's sister to him and his sister to Abel. {78:5} Satan flattered Cain, promising beautiful robes, gold, and silver for his wedding, along with attendance from his relatives. {78:6} Excited, Cain asked where Satan's relatives were. {78:7} Satan described a garden in the north where his relatives resided, offering Cain rest and prosperity greater than Adam's. {78:8} Cain eagerly listened and believed Satan's words. He then went to his mother Eve, beat her, cursed her, and questioned why they were planning to marry his sister to his brother. {78:9} Eve calmed him down and sent him back to the field. {78:10} When Adam returned, Eve told him what had happened with Cain. Adam grieved but remained silent. {78:11} The next day, Adam instructed Cain to take good sheep and offer them to God, and he would ask Abel to offer grain. {78:12} Both Cain and Abel obeyed their father and made their offerings on the mountain at the altar. {78:13} Cain, filled with pride, pushed Abel away from the altar and refused to let him offer his gift. {78:14} He offered his own gift with a deceitful and proud heart. {78:15} Abel, however, humbly set up stones and offered his gift sincerely. {78:16} Cain stood by the altar, praying for God to accept his offering, but God did not accept it. {78:17} He watched Abel's offering being accepted with divine fire. God was pleased with Abel's sincere heart. {78:18} An angel appeared to Abel, comforting and strengthening him. {78:19} Cain, witnessing this, became angry and began to blaspheme God for not accepting his offering. {78:20} God rebuked Cain, telling him to be righteous so that his offering would be accepted. {78:21} Cain left the altar dejected and went to his parents, telling them what had happened. Adam was deeply saddened that God had not accepted Cain's offering. {78:22} Abel, on the other hand, came down rejoicing and told his parents how God had accepted his offering. They rejoiced and kissed him. {78:23} Abel informed Adam that he had made an altar for himself since Cain had prevented him from using the main altar. Adam was saddened because it was the same altar where he had made his own offerings. {78:24} Meanwhile, Cain was filled with anger and went into the field where Satan approached him again.

{79:1} Adam saw that Cain and Abel had reached a remote place where there were no sheep. Abel questioned Cain about the promised blessings of sheep and other beauties Cain had described. {79:2} Cain urged Abel to continue walking ahead while he caught up. {79:3} Abel innocently walked on, trusting his brother, unaware of the danger. {79:4} Cain caught up with him, comforted him with talk, and then struck him repeatedly with a staff until Abel fell to the ground. {79:5} As Abel lay stunned, he pleaded with Cain not to kill him, reminding him of their shared upbringing and their mother's womb. {79:6} Ignoring Abel's pleas, Cain took a large stone and crushed Abel's head until he lay lifeless in a pool of blood. {79:7} Cain showed no remorse for his deed. {79:8} When Abel's blood soaked the earth, the ground trembled, refusing to conceal Abel's body. {79:9} Cain, fearful, dug a pit to bury his brother but was thwarted thrice as the earth rejected Abel's body each time, leaving it exposed as a witness against Cain. {79:10} God, angered by Abel's murder, sent thunder and lightning, then questioned Cain about Abel's whereabouts. {79:11} Cain insolently replied, "Am I my brother's keeper?" {79:12} God cursed the ground for drinking Abel's blood and decreed that Cain would be a fugitive, marked for protection but subject to fear and trembling. {79:13} Cain feared retaliation and pleaded for mercy, expressing his fear of being killed by others. {79:14} God assured Cain that he would not be killed, as He sought Cain's repentance rather than his death. {79:15} God's questioning and curses were meant to prompt Cain's repentance and reflection. {79:16} Cain trembled and was struck with terror, a visible sign of his guilt and punishment. {79:17} God's intention was not to have Cain killed but to have him repent and seek peace. {79:18} The "seven punishments" referred to the generations during which Cain would suffer before finding redemption. {79:19} Cain returned to Adam and Eve, terrified and stained with blood, seeking solace but finding none. {79:20} His sister, seeing him in distress, asked why he was trembling. Cain confessed to killing Abel.

2 Adam and Eve

The Book of Adam and Eve II, often referred to as the "Second Book of Adam and Eve," is a significant work within the corpus of pseudepigraphal literature. This text, which is not included in the canonical scriptures of most major religious traditions, offers a profound exploration of the lives and experiences of Adam and Eve after their expulsion from the Garden of Eden. Originating in the Jewish mystical tradition and later adopted by early Christian communities, the book delves into themes of human suffering, repentance, and the hope for redemption. It expands on the narrative found in the Book of Genesis, providing detailed accounts of the trials and tribulations faced by the first humans and their descendants. The text is characterized by its rich, allegorical language and its theological depth, addressing issues such as the nature of sin, the struggle against evil, and the enduring quest for divine grace. The Second Book of Adam and Eve is also notable for its vivid portrayal of the natural world, its detailed genealogies, and its emphasis on the importance of faith and obedience to God's will. As a piece of apocryphal literature, it reflects the diverse and evolving beliefs of early Christian communities, offering insights into their understanding of human origins, morality, and the divine plan for humanity. Through its narratives, the book seeks to provide comfort and guidance to believers, emphasizing the themes of perseverance and hope in the face of adversity.

{1:1} When Luluwa heard Cain confessing to killing Abel, she wept and hurried to inform her father and mother. {1:2} Adam and Eve, upon hearing the news, were overcome with grief—they cried aloud, slapped their faces, threw dust on their heads, and tore their garments. {1:3} They went to the place where Abel lay dead, surrounded by beasts, and lamented the loss of their just son. Abel's pure body emitted a sweet fragrance, and Adam, with tears streaming, carried him to the Cave of Treasures. {1:4} There, they wrapped Abel in sweet spices and myrrh, and mourned his passing for a hundred and forty days. Abel was fifteen and a half years old, Cain seventeen and a half. {1:5} After the mourning period, Cain took his sister Luluwa as his wife without his parents' consent, despite their heavy hearts. He moved away from the garden to the base of the mountain where he had slain Abel, where fruit and forest trees grew abundantly. {1:6} Cain and Luluwa bore children who multiplied and populated the area. {1:7} Adam and Eve refrained from coming together for seven years after Abel's death. Eventually, Eve conceived, and Adam proposed making an offering to God to request a child whom they could marry to Abel's sister. {1:8} They prepared an offering, brought it to the altar, and prayed earnestly for God's favor. {1:9} God accepted their offering, and they worshipped together, setting a lamp in the Cave of Treasures to burn continually before Abel's body. {1:10} Adam and Eve continued fasting and praying until Eve's time to deliver approached. She expressed her wish to go to a cave in the rock for childbirth. {1:11} Adam agreed, instructing her to take their daughter along while he remained in the Cave of Treasures alone.

{2:1} Eve gave birth to a son who was perfectly beautiful in appearance, resembling his father Adam but even more handsome. {2:2} Eve was filled with comfort upon seeing him and remained in the cave for eight days. She then sent her daughter to Adam to inform him and ask him to come and name the child. Meanwhile, the daughter stayed by Abel's body until Adam returned. {2:3} Adam rejoiced greatly when he saw the child's beauty and perfect form. He named him Seth, which means "God has heard my prayer and has delivered me from my affliction," signifying power and strength. {2:4} After naming Seth, Adam returned to the Cave of Treasures while his daughter went back to Eve. {2:5} Eve stayed in the cave for forty days before reuniting with Adam, bringing Seth and her daughter with her. {2:6} They came to a river where Adam and his daughter washed themselves out of sorrow for Abel, while Eve and the baby washed for purification. {2:7} They then took an offering and went to the mountain to offer it for the baby. God accepted their offering and blessed them and Seth. They returned to the Cave of Treasures. {2:8} Adam and Eve did not come together again to have more children after Seth's birth. Their offspring were only Cain, Luluwa, Abel, Aklia, and Seth. {2:9} Seth grew in stature and strength, and began to fervently practice fasting and prayer.

{3:1} After seven years of separation from Eve, Satan envied Adam and sought to reunite them. {3:2} Adam began sleeping on the roof of the Cave of Treasures at night and praying in the cave during the day, fearing Satan's influence. This went on for thirty-nine days. {3:3} On the fortieth night, Satan appeared to Adam in the guise of a beautiful woman, saying that his separation from Eve caused sorrow among them, contrasting his prayers inside the cave with those on the roof. {3:4} Satan lamented Abel's murder, rejoiced at Seth's birth, and expressed his attachment to Eve, claiming they were siblings. Satan recounted God's promise to produce children with Adam through him, superior to Eve's. {3:5} Urging Adam to enjoy his youth joyfully and without fear, Satan approached Adam to embrace him. {3:6} Adam prayed fervently to God for deliverance upon seeing Satan's intentions. {3:7} God sent His Word to Adam, revealing Satan's deceitful nature and emphasizing His protection against him, affirming His mercy and goodwill towards Adam's well-being.

{4:1} God commanded Satan to reveal himself in his true, terrifying form before Adam. {4:2} When Adam saw Satan, he was filled with fear and trembled at the sight of him. {4:3} God admonished Adam to observe Satan's hideous appearance and reminded him that it was Satan who led him from light to darkness, from peace to toil and misery. God questioned Satan's claims of divinity, noting his inability to escape from Adam's presence and his deceptive nature. {4:4} God instructed Adam not to fear Satan anymore but to remain vigilant against his schemes. {4:5} Then God drove Satan away and strengthened Adam's heart, commanding him to return to the Cave of Treasures and not separate from Eve. {4:6} God subdued Adam and Eve's animalistic desires, granting them peace and rest. This blessing was unique to Adam and Eve and not bestowed upon any of their descendants. {4:7} Adam worshiped God for delivering him and calming his passions. He descended from the roof of the cave and reunited with Eve, ending their forty days of separation.

{5:1} Seth, at the age of seven, possessed knowledge of good and evil. He diligently fasted, prayed, and spent his nights entreating God for mercy. {5:2} Seth surpassed his father in fasting, offering his sacrifice daily with a pure heart and a countenance like that of an angel. {5:3} God was pleased not only with Seth's offerings but also with his purity and steadfast devotion to His will and that of his parents. {5:4} Satan, however, appeared to Seth after he completed his offering, disguised as a radiant angel with a staff of light, adorned in luminous attire. {5:5} The deceptive angel greeted Seth warmly and began enticing him with flattering words, praising his appearance and lamenting the harshness of Seth's mountainous surroundings. {5:6} Satan painted his own realm as a place of beauty and light, contrasting it with the earthly hardships, urging Seth to leave and promising him peace, splendor, and a life free from sin and suffering. {5:7} Satan proposed that Seth marry one of his daughters in the heavenly realm, where they considered such unions as divine and devoid of sinful desire, claiming they were all gods of light, heavenly, powerful, and glorious.

{6:1} When Seth heard Satan's enticing words, he was astonished and inclined towards the deceptive speech, asking if there truly existed another world with creatures more beautiful than those on Earth. {6:2} Satan affirmed this and continued praising the wonders of his realm. {6:3} Seth, though intrigued, hesitated and insisted on seeking permission from his father

Adam and his mother Eve before making any decision. He expressed fear of disobeying them, recalling the fate of his brother Cain and the consequences of Adam's own transgression. {6:4} Seth proposed meeting Satan the next day at the same place if his parents permitted him to go. {6:5} Satan warned Seth that Adam would not allow him to come if he revealed their conversation, urging him to come immediately to experience joy and beauty in the heavenly realm. {6:6} Seth, however, remained steadfast, feeling bound by his duty to his parents, whom he knew would be distressed if he disappeared even for a day. {6:7} Seth sought refuge in prayer, going to the altar and asking God for deliverance from Satan's temptation. {6:8} God sent His Word and cursed Satan, causing him to flee. {6:9} Seth returned to his parents, finding them eagerly waiting to hear from him. He recounted his encounter with Satan disguised as an angel. {6:10} Adam recognized the deception and warned Seth about Satan's true nature. Together, they went to the Cave of Treasures and found solace there. {6:11} From that day forward, Adam and Eve never let Seth out of their sight, accompanying him wherever he went, including for his offerings. This incident occurred when Seth was nine years old.

{7:1} When Adam saw that Seth possessed a pure heart, he desired him to marry in order to safeguard him from further temptation by the enemy. {7:2} Adam urged Seth to wed his sister Aklia, Abel's sister, so that they could fulfill God's command to populate the earth. {7:3} He reassured Seth that there was no shame in marrying his sister, emphasizing that it was for his protection against the adversary. {7:4} Despite Seth's reluctance, out of obedience to his parents, he consented without protest. {7:5} Adam thus arranged for Seth to marry Aklia when he was fifteen years old. {7:6} By the time Seth turned twenty, he had a son named Enos, and later had other children as well. {7:7} Enos grew up, married, and had a son named Cainan. {7:8} Cainan also grew up, married, and had a son named Mahalaleel. {7:9} These generations lived during Adam's lifetime and dwelled near the Cave of Treasures. {7:10} Adam lived for nine hundred and thirty years, while Mahalaleel lived for one hundred years and devoted himself to fasting, prayer, and hard labor until the end of Adam's days drew near.

{8:1} When Adam realized his end was near, he summoned his son Seth to the Cave of Treasures. {8:2} There, he asked Seth to gather his grandchildren and great-grandchildren so that he could bless them before he died. {8:3} Seth, upon hearing his father's request, wept profusely and assembled all his descendants before Adam. {8:4} Adam, upon seeing his descendants gathered around him, wept as he contemplated being separated from them. {8:5} Witnessing Adam's tears, his descendants also wept and pleaded with him not to leave them. {8:6} Adam blessed them all and then turned to Seth, instructing him to maintain innocence, purity, and trust in God amidst the world's sorrow and trials. {8:7} He commanded Seth to pass down these teachings to Enos, who would then teach Cainan, and so on, ensuring their children would follow these commandments. {8:8} Adam prophesied about a future flood that would leave only eight survivors, instructing that his body be preserved in the Cave of Treasures. {8:9} He directed that after the flood subsided, his body should be taken to the middle of the earth, where God would save all their descendants. {8:10} Adam entrusted Seth to lead and guide their people in righteousness, commanding them to fast and avoid the influence of Satan. {8:11} He urged Seth to keep their lineage separate from Cain's descendants in both speech and action. {8:12} Adam blessed Seth, Eve, and all their descendants, instructing them to preserve the gold, incense, and myrrh as signs given by God. {8:13} He prophesied that these items would be preserved until the time when the Word of God would come as a man, and kings would offer them as tokens of His kingship, divinity, and suffering. {8:14} Adam entrusted Seth with these hidden mysteries revealed by God, commanding him to keep these commandments for himself and his people.

{9:1} When Adam finished giving his final instructions to Seth, his body weakened, his limbs lost their strength, his mouth fell silent, and his tongue ceased to speak. {9:2} He closed his eyes and passed away. {9:3} Upon seeing that Adam had died, his children—men and women, young and old—gathered around him, weeping bitterly. {9:4} Adam lived for nine hundred and thirty years on the earth. He passed away on the fifteenth day of Barmudeh, according to the solar reckoning, at the ninth hour. {9:5} It was a Friday, the same day he was created and rested, and he died at the same hour he was expelled from the Garden of Eden. {9:6} Seth carefully wrapped Adam's body and embalmed it with sacred spices from trees and the Holy Mountain. {9:7} He placed Adam's body on the eastern side of the cave, the side of the incense, and set up a lamp-stand burning in front of him. {9:8} Throughout the night, Adam's children stood before him, mourning deeply until daybreak. {9:9} Afterwards, Seth, Enos, and Cainan went out to offer sacrifices to the Lord on the altar where Adam used to present gifts to God. {9:10} Eve advised them to pray first, asking God to accept their offerings and keep Adam's soul with Him in peace. {9:11} They all stood up and prayed earnestly.

{10:1} After they finished their prayer, the Word of God came and brought comfort to Adam's family. {10:2} They then presented their offerings on behalf of themselves and their father. {10:3} When their offering was complete, the Word of God appeared to Seth, the eldest among them, saying, "O Seth, Seth, Seth, as I was with your father, so I will be with you until the fulfillment of the promise I made to him. {10:4} Your father Adam was told by Me, 'I will send My Word to save you and your descendants.' {10:5} Now, Seth, keep the commandment your father Adam gave you, and separate your descendants from those of your brother Cain." {10:6} After speaking these words, God withdrew His Word from Seth. {10:7} Seth, Eve, and their children then descended from the mountain to the Cave of Treasures. {10:8} Adam was the first to have his soul depart in the land of Eden, specifically in the Cave of Treasures. Before him, only his son Abel had died, murdered. {10:9} All of Adam's children arose, mourning their father's passing, and offered sacrifices for him for one hundred and forty days.

{11:1} After Adam and Eve passed away, Seth separated his descendants from Cain's lineage. Cain and his descendants settled westward, below the place where he had killed Abel. {11:2} Meanwhile, Seth and his children dwelt northwards on the mountain near the Cave of Treasures, to remain close to their father Adam. {11:3} Seth, distinguished by his stature, goodness, strong mind, and fine soul, led his people with innocence, repentance, and humility. He strictly forbade them from mingling with Cain's descendants. {11:4} Due to their purity, they were known as the "Children of God," and they worshiped God continually with praises and psalms in their cave, the Cave of Treasures. {11:5} Seth prayed day and night before the bodies of Adam and Eve, seeking mercy for himself and his children. He counseled them wisely in difficult matters. {11:6} Seth and his children devoted themselves to heavenly pursuits, disdaining earthly labor. Their sole focus was on praising God with hymns and psalms. {11:7} Because of their purity, they could hear and see angels praising and glorifying God, whether within the garden, on divine errands, or ascending to heaven. {11:8} The garden was not far above Seth and his children, about fifteen spiritual cubits, corresponding to forty-five cubits of man. {11:9} They lived on the mountain below the garden, not sowing or reaping, nor cultivating food for the body, not even wheat, but offering sacrifices. They sustained themselves with the fruits and flavorful trees growing on their mountain. {11:10} Seth and his eldest children frequently fasted every forty days. {11:11} Their community lived joyfully and innocently, free from sudden fear, jealousy, evil deeds, hatred, or animalistic passions. {11:12} No foul language, cursing, evil counsel, or deceitful actions emerged from their mouths. {11:13} They rarely swore oaths, but when necessary, they swore by the blood of Abel the righteous. {11:14} They instructed their children and women to fast, pray daily, and worship the Most High God in the cave. {11:15} They blessed themselves with the body of their father Adam and anointed themselves with it, continuing these practices until Seth's end drew near.

{12:1} Seth, known for his righteousness, summoned his son Enos, Cainan (Enos's son), and Mahalaleel (Cainan's son), and spoke to them: "Since my end is near, I desire to build a roof over the altar where offerings are made." {12:2} They obediently gathered, young and old alike, and diligently constructed a beautiful roof over the altar. {12:3} Seth's intention was to bless his children on the mountain and to offer a final sacrifice before his death. {12:4} Once the roof was completed, they prepared offerings which they brought to Seth. He received them, offered them on the altar, and prayed for God's acceptance, mercy upon his children, and protection from Satan. {12:5} God accepted Seth's offering, blessed him and his descendants, and reaffirmed his promise: "At the end of the great five days and a half, as I have promised you and your father, I will send My Word to save you and your seed." {12:6} Seth and his descendants then descended from the altar and went to the Cave of Treasures, where they prayed, blessed themselves with Adam's body, and anointed themselves with it. {12:7} Seth remained in the Cave of Treasures for a few more days until he suffered greatly and passed away. {12:8} Enos, Seth's eldest son, along with Cainan, Mahalaleel, Jared (Mahalaleel's son), and Enoch (Jared's son), together with their families, came to receive a blessing from Seth. {12:9} Seth prayed over them, blessed them, and urged them by the blood of Abel to remain on the holy mountain and to have no fellowship with Cain's descendants, who were sinners and murderers. {12:10} Seth particularly instructed Enos to minister before Adam's body throughout his life, to attend the altar Seth had built, and to lead their people in righteousness and purity. {12:11} After giving these instructions, Seth's limbs weakened, he became mute, and he passed away at the age of 912 years, on the twenty-seventh day of the month Abib, with Enoch being twenty years old. {12:12} They carefully embalmed Seth's body with sweet spices and placed him in the Cave of Treasures beside Adam. They mourned for him forty days and offered gifts for him, similar to Adam's rites.{12:13} Following Seth's death, Enos assumed leadership over his people, guiding them in righteousness and justice as his father had commanded. {12:14} By the time Enos reached 820 years old, Cain's descendants had multiplied greatly due to frequent marriages driven by carnal desires, filling the land below the mountain.

{13:1} In those times, there lived Lamech, who was blind, a descendant of Cain. He had a son named Atun, and they owned many cattle. {13:2} Lamech used to send them to pasture with a young shepherd, who would return home in the evening distressed, crying before his grandfather Lamech, his father Atun, and his mother Hazina. He complained, "I cannot tend the cattle alone, fearing someone might steal them from me or even kill me for them. Among the descendants of Cain, there was much theft, murder, and sin." {13:3} Hearing this, Lamech felt compassion for the young shepherd. He said, "Truly, he might be overpowered if left alone in this place." {13:4} So Lamech took up his bow, which he had kept since his youth before he became blind. He gathered large arrows, smooth stones, and a sling, and went to the field with the young shepherd, positioning himself behind the cattle while the shepherd watched over them. They continued this routine for many days. {13:5} Meanwhile, Cain, plagued by trembling and terror after God cast him out and cursed him, wandered restlessly from place to place. {13:6} During his wanderings, he came to Lamech's wives and inquired about him. They told him, "He is in the field with the cattle." {13:7} Curious, Cain went to find Lamech. As he approached, the young shepherd heard the noise and saw the cattle gathering. {13:8} Alarmed, he asked Lamech, "My lord, is that a wild beast or a robber?" {13:9} Lamech instructed him, "Tell me which way he looks when he approaches." {13:10} Lamech then prepared his bow with an arrow and readied his sling with a stone. When Cain appeared in the field, the shepherd exclaimed, "Shoot, he is coming!" {13:11} Lamech shot Cain with his arrow, striking him in the side. He followed it with a stone from his sling that hit Cain's face and knocked out both his eyes. Cain fell instantly and died. {13:12} Lamech and the young shepherd approached Cain's body lying on the ground. The shepherd said, "It is Cain, our grandfather, whom you have killed, my lord!" {13:13} Deeply remorseful, Lamech clapped his hands in sorrow and struck the youth's head with his palm, thinking he was feigning. When he realized the youth was truly injured, Lamech took a stone and struck him until he died.

{14:1} When Enos reached the age of nine hundred years, all the descendants of Seth, Cainan, and his eldest children, along with their wives and offspring, gathered around him seeking his blessing. {14:2} Enos prayed over them, blessed them, and solemnly charged them by the blood of Abel the righteous, saying, "Let none of your descendants descend from this Holy Mountain, and let them not associate with the offspring of Cain the murderer." {14:3} Enos then called his son Cainan and instructed him, "Look, my son, set your heart upon your people, establish them in righteousness and purity, and serve continually before the body of our father Adam throughout your life." {14:4} After these words, Enos passed away at the age of nine hundred and eighty-five years. Cainan prepared his body for burial and placed him in the Cave of Treasures beside his father Adam, performing offerings for him according to their customs.

{15:1} After Enos passed away, Cainan assumed leadership over his people, fulfilling his father's command to uphold righteousness and purity, and continued to serve before the body of Adam in the Cave of Treasures. {15:2} When Cainan had lived nine hundred and ten years, affliction and suffering befell him as his end approached. {15:3} Upon nearing death, all the patriarchs along with their wives and children gathered around him. He blessed them and solemnly adjured them by the blood of Abel the righteous, instructing them, "Let none of you descend from this Holy Mountain, and do not associate with the descendants of Cain the murderer." {15:4} Cainan passed this command to his eldest son Mahalaleel, blessed him, and then died. {15:5} Mahalaleel embalmed his father with fragrant spices and placed him in the Cave of Treasures alongside his ancestors, offering sacrifices for him according to their customs.

{16:1} Mahalaleel assumed leadership over his people, guiding them in righteousness and purity, ensuring they maintained no association with the descendants of Cain. {16:2} He continued to pray and minister in the Cave of Treasures before Adam's body, seeking God's mercy for himself and his people. {16:3} At the age of eight hundred and seventy years, Mahalaleel fell ill, prompting all his children to gather around him, seeking his blessing before his departure. {16:4} Sitting on his bed with tears streaming down his face, Mahalaleel called his eldest son Jared to him, kissed his face, and solemnly adjured him by the Creator of heaven and earth. {16:5} He charged Jared to watch over their people, feeding them in righteousness and innocence, and ensuring none descended from the Holy Mountain to mingle with the children of Cain, lest they perish with them. {16:6} Mahalaleel prophesied a great destruction by water upon the earth due to the sins of humanity, foreseeing that Jared's descendants would not heed his warnings and would perish alongside the wicked. {16:7} He urged Jared to teach and safeguard them, so that Jared would bear no guilt for their actions. {16:8} Mahalaleel instructed Jared to embalm his body upon death and place it in the Cave of Treasures beside his ancestors, where Jared would continue to minister before them until his own rest. {16:9} Mahalaleel blessed all his children, then peacefully passed away, joining his forefathers in rest. {16:10} Jared mourned deeply for his father Mahalaleel, embracing and kissing his hands and feet, as did all his children. {16:11} They carefully embalmed Mahalaleel and laid him beside his fathers, mourning him for forty days.

{17:1} Jared followed his father's command and led his people like a lion, guiding them in righteousness and innocence, instructing them to do nothing without his counsel, fearing they might be tempted by the children of Cain. {17:2} Jared repeatedly warned and commanded his people until the end of his four hundred and eighty-fifth year. {17:3} At that time, as Jared stood vigilantly before the bodies of his fathers, praying and guiding his people, Satan, envious of Jared's leadership, created a beautiful illusion. {17:4} Satan appeared with thirty men of his host, all in the form of handsome men, with Satan himself as the elder and tallest among them, with a fine beard. {17:5} They stood at the cave's entrance and called out to Jared, who came out and found them remarkably beautiful and bright, wondering if they were children of Cain. {17:6} Jared thought, "The children of Cain cannot reach this mountain's height, and none are as handsome as these men; they must be strangers." {17:7} Jared greeted them and asked the elder to explain their presence and who they were, as they seemed like strangers. {17:8} The elder began to weep, and the others followed, saying, "I am Adam, whom God created first; this is Abel, my son, killed by his brother Cain." {17:9} The elder continued, "This is my son Seth, whom God gave me to comfort me after Abel's death, and these are his descendants, Enos, Cainan, and Mahalaleel." {17:10} Jared, amazed at their appearance and speech, listened as the elder continued, "We live in the land north of the garden, which God created before the world, but He placed us in the garden initially. After I sinned, He made me leave and dwell in this cave, facing great troubles." {17:11} The elder explained, "I commanded my son Seth to care for his people, and this commandment has been passed down. Now, fearing for you, we came to visit you, finding you in distress." {17:12} The elder continued, "We missed our way and discovered people below the mountain in a beautiful country, mistaking them for you until Mahalaleel corrected us." {17:13} He advised, "Go down to them and rest from your suffering, or come with us to our garden and live in our beautiful land." {17:14} Jared, puzzled by the elder's words, could not find any of his children and asked why they had hidden until now. {17:15} The elder replied, "We did not know of you until informed by your father." Jared believed their words were true. {17:16} The elder urged Jared to join them, promising to return if their land did not please him. Jared, persuaded, went with them to the top of the mountain of Cain's sons. {17:17} The elder sent one of his companions back, claiming they had forgotten a garment for Jared, asking him to wait. {17:18} The companion went back, but the elder called him to return and instructed him to extinguish the lamp in the cave. {17:19} The companion returned with the garment, but also brought a phantom, showing it to the group, causing Jared to marvel and believe. {17:20} While waiting by a fountain, three men went to the houses of Cain's sons, asking for food and drink. {17:21} Cain's descendants, astonished by their beauty, gathered around them. The elder asked for food and drink, attracting many women. {17:22} Jared, distressed by their behavior, refused their offerings. The elder encouraged him to follow their actions, but Jared prayed fervently, causing the elder and his companions to flee. {17:23} Jared, realizing he was among Cain's children, wept and prayed for God's deliverance, realizing the visitors were devils who had deceived him. {17:24} God sent an angel to rescue Jared, setting him upon the mountain and guiding him back, providing counsel before departing.

{18:1} The children of Jared regularly visited him, seeking his blessings and advice for every matter, and they even assisted him with his work. {18:2} However, on this occasion when they entered the cave, Jared was not there. Instead, they found the lamp extinguished and the bodies of the fathers scattered. Voices spoke from them by the power of God, saying, "Satan deceived our son Jared through an apparition, intending to destroy him, just as he destroyed our son Cain." {18:3} The voices prayed, "Lord God of heaven and earth, deliver our son from Satan's hand, who created a great and false apparition before him." They spoke of other matters by God's power as well. {18:4} Hearing these voices, Jared's children feared and wept for their father, uncertain of what had happened to him. {18:5} They wept for him until sunset that day. {18:6} Jared approached the cave with a sorrowful countenance, distressed in mind and body, grieving at being separated from the bodies of his fathers. {18:7} His children saw him nearing the cave and rushed to him, embracing his neck and crying out, "Father, where have you been? Why did you leave us, something you never did before? When you disappeared, the lamp over our fathers' bodies went out, the bodies were scattered, and voices came from them." {18:8} Jared, upon hearing this, was saddened and entered the cave, finding the bodies scattered and the lamp extinguished, while the fathers prayed for his deliverance from Satan. {18:9} Jared embraced the bodies, saying, "O my fathers, through your intercession, may God deliver me from Satan's hand! I beg you to ask God to protect and hide me from him until the day of my death." {18:10} All the voices ceased except for the voice of our father Adam, speaking to Jared by the power of God, saying, "Jared, my son, offer gifts to God for delivering you from Satan's hand. When you bring these offerings, make sure to offer them on the altar where I used to offer. Also, beware of Satan, for he deceived me many times with his apparitions, seeking to destroy me, but God delivered me from his hand." {18:11} Adam commanded Jared to warn his people to be vigilant against Satan and to never cease offering gifts to God. {18:12} Adam's voice then fell silent, leaving Jared and his children in wonder. They arranged the bodies as they were originally and spent the entire night praying until daybreak. {18:13} Jared made an offering on the altar as commanded by Adam. As he approached the altar, he prayed for God's mercy and forgiveness concerning the lamp going out. {18:14} God appeared to Jared at the altar, blessed him and his children, accepted their offerings, and instructed Jared to take sacred fire from the altar to relight the lamp that illuminated Adam's body.

{19:1} God revealed to Jared once more the promise He had made to Adam, explaining the 5500 years and disclosing to him the mystery of His coming to earth. {19:2} God instructed Jared regarding the fire he had taken from the altar to light the lamp, commanding him to keep it within the cave to provide light for the bodies. The fire was not to leave the cave until Adam's body emerged from it. {19:3} God warned Jared to safeguard the fire, ensuring it burned brightly in the lamp, and not to leave the cave again unless he received an order through a vision, not merely an apparition. {19:4} God further commanded Jared to instruct his people not to associate with the children of Cain or to learn their ways, for God does not tolerate hatred and wicked deeds. {19:5} God gave many other commandments to Jared and blessed him, then withdrew His word from him. {19:6} Jared gathered near with his children, took some fire, descended to the cave, and lit the lamp before Adam's body. He also conveyed God's commandments to his people as instructed. {19:7} This event occurred at the end of Jared's 450th year. Many other wonders happened during his lifetime, though only this one is recorded briefly to avoid lengthening the narrative. {19:8} Jared continued teaching his children for eighty more years. However, they began to disobey his commandments and act without his counsel. They gradually descended from the Holy Mountain and mingled with the children of Cain in corrupt relationships. {19:9} The reason why Jared's children descended from the Holy Mountain will now be revealed.

{20:1} After Cain had settled in the fertile land and his descendants multiplied there, one of them named Genun, son of Lamech who had killed Cain, became infused with Satan's influence from his childhood. {20:2} Genun crafted various musical instruments—trumpets, horns, string instruments, cymbals, psalteries, lyres, harps, and flutes—and played them constantly.

{20:3} Whenever he played, Satan entered the instruments, producing enchanting melodies that captivated listeners. {20:4} Genun gathered groups to play these instruments, delighting the sinful descendants of Cain who became inflamed with passion and indulged in lustful acts, fueled by Satan's influence. {20:5} Satan also taught Genun to brew strong drink from grain, leading to drunken gatherings where all manner of indulgence occurred. {20:6} Genun's influence spread, promoting pride and teaching the children of Cain unprecedented wickedness and perversions. {20:7} Under Genun's guidance, they began forging weapons of war from iron, leading to violence, hatred, and murder among them. {20:8} The sinful practices escalated until they disregarded familial boundaries, marrying close relatives without restraint, defiling themselves and the earth with sin, provoking God's anger. {20:9} Genun organized elaborate musical and cultural displays at the foot of the Holy Mountain to lure the righteous children of Seth. {20:10} When the children of Seth observed these festivities, they were initially curious and observed for a year. {20:11} As the children of Seth became increasingly drawn to Genun's world, Satan further influenced Genun to create elaborate dyes and fabrics, tempting them with luxurious attire and festivities. {20:12} The children of Cain reveled in their beauty and wealth, engaging in horse races and all manner of debauchery. {20:13} Meanwhile, the children of Seth, originally placed on the Holy Mountain, neglected their vows, prayers, and fasting, fixated instead on observing and envying the worldly pleasures of the children of Cain. {20:14} The children of Cain noticed the children of Seth watching from above and called to them to descend. {20:15} Unable to find a way down, the children of Seth hesitated, prompting Genun to deceive them with Satan's guidance, suggesting a false path down the mountain. {20:16} When the children of Seth heard this, they returned to Jared in distress, reporting what they had heard. {20:17} Jared, deeply troubled, warned them not to disobey and descend from the holy mountain, but his words went unheeded. {20:18} A hundred men from the children of Seth defiantly planned to descend and join the children of Cain in their revelry. {20:19} Jared, moved by anguish, pleaded with them, warning of dire consequences if they left the mountain, but they refused to listen. {20:20} Despite warnings from Jared and Enoch, the hundred men descended from the Holy Mountain, drawn by lust and curiosity for the sinful ways of the children of Cain.

{21:1} Following the departure of the hundred men who had descended from the Holy Mountain and perished, another group of Seth's descendants gathered to search for them but met the same fate. {21:2} This repeated with each subsequent group until only a few remained on the Holy Mountain. {21:3} Jared, stricken with grief over the apostasy of his descendants, fell gravely ill, knowing his end was near. {21:4} Summoning his eldest son Enoch, Methuselah, Lamech (Methuselah's son), and Noah (Lamech's son), Jared prayed over them, imparting his blessings and counsel. {21:5} He admonished them to remain righteous and innocent, warning them not to descend from the Holy Mountain, as their children had done, forsaking its sanctity through sinful indulgence and disobedience. {21:6} Jared foresaw that God would not allow them to remain on the Holy Mountain due to their descendants' transgressions against divine and ancestral commandments. {21:7} He prophesied that they would be taken to a foreign land, never to return to their sacred homeland. {21:8} Instructing them to take Adam's body along with three precious gifts—gold, incense, and myrrh—when they departed, Jared revealed that salvation would one day come from the place where Adam's body rested. {21:9} Jared predicted that a descendant among them would be chosen by God to take Adam's body to that place of salvation. {21:10} Noah questioned who among them would be left to fulfill this prophecy, to which Jared declared it would be Noah himself, directing him to preserve Adam's body in the ark during the impending flood, and later, through his son Shem, to place it in the center of the earth for the sake of salvation. {21:11} Turning to Enoch, Jared commissioned him to remain in the cave, serving diligently before Adam's body for his entire life, guiding his people in righteousness and innocence. {21:12} With these final words, Jared passed away peacefully, his death occurring in the 360th year of Noah and the 989th year of his own life, on the twelfth day of Takhsasf (December/January), on a Friday. {21:13} As Jared breathed his last, tears flowed from his eyes due to his deep sorrow over the fallen state of the children of Seth during his lifetime. {21:14} Enoch, Methuselah, Lamech, and Noah mourned Jared's passing, carefully embalmed his body, and laid him to rest in the Cave of Treasures. {21:15} They observed a forty-day mourning period, grieving the loss of their father and leader. {21:16} After the mourning period ended, Enoch, Methuselah, Lamech, and Noah continued to sorrow in their hearts, missing their father deeply.

{22:1} Enoch faithfully obeyed the commandments of his father Jared and continued to minister in the cave. {22:2} This Enoch experienced many wonders and authored a renowned book, though the details of these wonders are not recounted here. {22:3} Subsequently, the descendants of Seth strayed from righteousness, falling into sin along with their wives and children. {22:4} Witnessing this, Enoch, Methuselah, Lamech, and Noah were deeply troubled by their doubt and unbelief. They wept and prayed earnestly to God for mercy, seeking to save their people from the corruption of that wicked generation. {22:5} Enoch remained dedicated to his ministry before the Lord for three hundred and eighty-five years. {22:6} By God's grace, Enoch became aware that God planned to remove him from the earth. {22:7} He disclosed to his son, foreseeing the Flood that God intended to send to destroy the earth and its inhabitants. {22:8} Enoch knew that his descendants would not remain on the Holy Mountain to rule or beget children. {22:9} He exhorted them to safeguard their souls, fear God, serve Him faithfully, worship Him with upright faith, and uphold righteousness, innocence, and justice, repenting and living in purity. {22:10} After imparting these final instructions, God took Enoch from the mountain to the land of eternal life, the abode of the righteous and chosen ones, the Paradise of joy, illuminated by a divine light surpassing worldly light, the light of God that fills the entire world yet cannot be contained by any place. {22:11} Enoch, being in the divine light of God, transcended death until God ordained his passing. {22:12} None of the ancestors or their descendants remained on the Holy Mountain except Methuselah, Lamech, and Noah, as all others had descended and fallen into sin with the children of Cain, thus forfeiting their right to dwell there.

3 Adam and Eve

The Book of Adam and Eve, or the Conflict of Adam and Eve with Satan, is a significant Old Testament pseudepigraphal work that expands on the lives of Adam and Eve after their expulsion from Eden. This text, divided into several books, offers a detailed exploration of their struggles to survive and uphold their faith. Written in a style reminiscent of ancient Near Eastern literature, it features vivid descriptions, dialogues, and moral lessons. The third book is notable for its themes of repentance, divine justice, and redemption, portraying Adam and Eve as complex characters experiencing a range of emotions and highlighting the cosmic battle between good and evil. The work provides a profound perspective on foundational myths and continues to be relevant in the study of religious history and literature.

{1:1} From a young age, Noah observed how sin and wickedness were spreading, leading to the destruction of generations and increasing sorrow, while the number of righteous men decreased. {1:2} Therefore, Noah afflicted his soul, controlled his desires, maintained his virginity, and grieved over the devastation caused by humanity. {1:3} Noah habitually mourned, wept, and wore a sad countenance. He kept his soul in fasting, preventing the enemy from gaining any advantage over him or coming near him. {1:4} From his childhood with his parents, Noah never angered them, disobeyed them, or acted without their counsel. When away from them, he sought God's guidance in all his actions, which ensured God's protection over him. {1:5} While on the mountain, Noah did not commit any evil, willfully disobey God, or provoke His anger. {1:6} Noah experienced many extraordinary events, surpassing those of his ancestors, around the time of the Flood. {1:7} He remained a virgin and obedient to God for five hundred years. After this period, God decided to give him offspring and said, "Arise, Noah, and take a wife so that you may have children who will comfort you. You are alone, and you shall leave this land for a foreign one, as the earth will be populated by your descendants." {1:8} Hearing this command from God, Noah obeyed and took a wife named Haikal, the daughter of Abaraz, who was among the descendants of Enos's children that went into perdition. {1:9} She bore him three sons: Shem, Ham, and Japheth.

{2:1} After these events, God spoke to Noah about the impending Flood that would come upon the earth to destroy all creatures so that none would be seen. {2:2} God said to Noah, "Protect your children; instruct them not to associate with the children of Cain, lest they perish with them." {2:3} Noah obeyed God's words, kept his children on the mountain, and did not let them go down to the children of Cain. {2:4} Then God spoke again to Noah, saying, "Make for yourself an ark of wood that will not rot, to save you and your household. {2:5} Start building it in the lowland of Eden in the presence of the children of Cain, so they can see you working on it. If they do not repent, they will perish, and the blame will be on them. {2:6} Cut the trees for the ark from this holy mountain. Let the ark's length be three hundred cubits, its width fifty cubits, and its height thirty cubits (ስስተ መቶ ክባን ርዝመቱ፣ ህምሳ ክባን በስፋቱ፣ ሰላሳ ክባን በከፋቱ). {2:7} When you have finished it, let there be one door above and three compartments, each ten cubits high. {2:8} The first story will be for lions, beasts, animals, and ostriches. The second story will be for birds and creeping things. {2:9} The third story will be for you, your wife, your sons, and their wives. {2:10} Make wells for water in the ark, with openings to draw water for drinking, and line these wells with lead both inside and outside. {2:11} Create storehouses for corn to provide food for you and those with you. {2:12} Additionally, make a trumpet of ebony wood, three cubits long and one and a half cubits wide, with a mouthpiece of the same wood. {2:13} You shall blow it three times: once in the morning for the workmen to gather for work, once at mealtime, and once in the evening for the workmen to rest. {2:14} God instructed Noah to go among the people and tell them a flood would come to overwhelm them, and to build the ark before their eyes. {2:15} When they asked about the ark, Noah was to tell them: "God has commanded me to make it so that my family and I may be saved from the Flood waters." {2:16} But when Noah told the people, they laughed at him, continuing in adultery and revelry, saying, "That old man is babbling! How could water rise above the mountains? We have never seen such a thing!" {2:17} Despite their mockery, Noah did everything as God had commanded him.

{3:1} Noah fathered his three sons during the first hundred years while he worked on the ark. {3:2} During these hundred years, he ate no food that could produce blood. The shoes on his feet neither changed, wore out, nor grew old. {3:3} During these hundred years, he also did not change his garments, which did not wear out in the least. He did not change the staff in his hand, nor did the cloth around his head grow old, and the hair on his head neither increased nor decreased. {3:4} Noah's three sons were Shem, Ham, and Japheth. They married wives from among the daughters of Methuselah, as the wise interpreters of the Septuagint (LXX) have told us, as written in the first sacred book of the Greeks. {3:5} The life of Lamech, Noah's father, was five hundred and fifty-three years. When his death approached, he called his father Methuselah and his son Noah and wept before Methuselah, saying, "Dismiss me, my father, and bless me." {3:6} Methuselah blessed his son Lamech, saying, "None of our fathers died before their fathers, but the fathers died before their sons, so the sons could bury them in the earth. Now, my son, you die before me, and I will drink the cup of sorrow on your account before I leave the flesh. {3:7} From this day forward, the world is changed, and the order of deaths is altered: sons will die before their fathers. Fathers will not rejoice in their sons, nor be satisfied with them. Likewise, sons will not be satisfied with their fathers, nor rejoice in them." {3:8} Then Lamech died, and they embalmed him and laid him in the Cave of Treasures. He died seven years before the Flood came. Methuselah and his son Noah were left alone on the Holy Mountain. {3:9} Noah went down every day to work on the ark and returned at evening. He instructed his sons and their wives not to come down after him and not to associate with the children of Cain. {3:10} Noah was concerned for his sons, thinking, "They are young and might be overcome by passion." So he went down by night and gave old Methuselah directions about them.

{4:1} Noah repeatedly preached to the children of Cain, saying, "The flood will come and destroy you if you do not repent." But they would not listen to him; they only laughed at him. {4:2} When the children of Seth went down from the Holy Mountain and dwelt with the children of Cain, they defiled themselves with their abominations, and children called Garsina were born to them. These were giants, mighty men of valor, unlike any other giants in their might. {4:3} Certain wise men of old wrote about them, saying in their sacred books that angels came down from heaven and mingled with the daughters of Cain, who bore these giants. {4:4} But those wise men are mistaken in what they say. God forbid such a thing—that angels, who are spirits, should be found committing sin with human beings. Never; that cannot be. {4:5} If it were in the nature of angels or fallen Satans to commit such acts, they would not leave one woman on earth undefiled. Satans are very wicked and infamous, but they are not male and female by nature; they are small, subtle spirits that have been black ever since they transgressed. {4:6} Many men say that angels came down from heaven and joined themselves to women, having children by them. This cannot be true. {4:7} They were children of Seth, who were of the children of Adam and dwelt on the mountain high up, preserving their virginity, innocence, and glory like angels, and were then called "angels of God." {4:8} But when they transgressed and mingled with the children of Cain, begetting children, ill-informed men said that angels had come down from heaven and mingled with the daughters of men, who bore them giants.

{5:1} The ancient old man Methuselah, who remained on the mountain with Noah's sons, lived nine hundred and eighty-seven years and then fell ill; his sickness was such that he knew he would soon depart from this world. {5:2} When Noah and his sons, Shem, Ham, and Japheth, realized this, they came to him with their wives and wept before him, saying, "Our father and elder, bless us and pray to God to have mercy on us when you are gone from us." {5:3} Methuselah said to them with a sorrowful heart, "Listen to me, my dear children; none of our fathers are left but you, eight souls. {5:4} The Lord God created our father Adam and our mother Eve, and from them filled the earth with people in the neighborhood of the garden and multiplied their seed. {5:5} But they have not kept His commandment, and He will destroy them. If they had kept His commandment, He would have filled heaven and earth with them. {5:6} Yet I will ask the Lord my God to bless you, to multiply you, and to spread your race in a strange land, to which you shall go. {5:7} And now, my children, behold, God will bring you inside an ark to a land to which you have never been. The Lord God of all our pure fathers be with you! {5:8} And may the glorious gifts God bestowed on our father Adam from the garden in this blessed Cave of Treasures be bestowed upon you also! {5:9} These are the three glorious gifts which God gave to Adam. The first is kingship, where God made Adam king over His works. The second glorious gift is priesthood, in that God breathed into his face a spirit of life. The third glorious gift is prophecy, for Adam prophesied concerning what God thought to do. {5:10} I will ask the Lord my God to bestow these three glorious gifts on your posterity." {5:11} Then Methuselah said to Noah, "Noah, you are blessed of God. I warn you and tell you that I am going to join our fathers who have gone before me. {5:12} But you, who will be left alone with your children on this holy mountain, keep the commandment I give you and do not forsake anything I have told you. {5:13} Behold, my God will soon bring a flood upon the earth; embalm my body and lay it in the Cave of Treasures. {5:14} Then take your wife, your sons, and their wives, go down from this holy mountain, and take with you the body of our father Adam. Go into the ark and lay it there until the waters of the flood recede from the face of the earth. {5:15} When you are about to die, command your firstborn son Shem to take Melchizedek, son of Cainan and grandson of Arphaxad, for Melchizedek is a priest of the Most High God. Take with them the body of our father Adam from within the ark and lay it in the earth. {5:16} Melchizedek shall minister on that mountain in the middle of the earth, before the body of our father Adam, forever. From that place, Noah my son, God shall work salvation for Adam and all his seed that believe in God. {5:17} Methuselah also said to Noah and his sons, "The angel of God will go with you until you come to that place in the middle of the earth. {5:18} Let him who ministers to God and before the body of our father Adam wear a garment of skin and be girded about his loins with leather. Let him wear no ornament, but let his raiment be plain. Let him be alone and stand praying to our Lord God to watch over the body of our father Adam, for it is of great value before God. {5:19} Let him continue in his ministry, he the priest of the Most High God, for he is well-pleasing to God, and so is the ministry he performs before God." {5:20} After this, Methuselah commanded Noah, saying, "Mind all these commandments and keep them." {5:21} Then Methuselah's hands weakened; he ceased speaking, gradually closed his eyes, and entered into rest like all his fathers. Tears streamed down his cheeks, and his heart grieved at being separated from them all, especially because of that mountain of the garden where none of them remained, for God was purposed to destroy all creatures and blot them out from the face of the earth. {5:22} Methuselah's rest came when he was nine hundred and sixty-seven years old, on the twelfth of Magabit, on a Sunday. {5:23} Noah and his sons embalmed him, weeping and sorrowing over him, and laid him in the Cave of Treasures. They wailed over him with great wailing, they & their wives, for forty days. When mourning and grief over Methuselah ended, Noah and his sons began to do as Methuselah had commanded them.

{6:1} After Methuselah's death, Noah, his sons, and their wives came to the bodies of their ancestors, worshipped them, and blessed themselves in them, weeping and in deep grief. {6:2} Noah had finished the ark, and there were no workmen left. He and his sons continued in prayer to God, asking Him to show them the way of safety. {6:3} When Noah and his sons had ended their prayers, God said to him, "Go into the Cave of Treasures, you and your sons, and take the body of our father Adam and lay it in the ark. Also take the gold, the incense, and the myrrh, and lay them in the ark together with his body." {6:4} Noah heeded God's voice and went into the Cave of Treasures with his sons; they worshipped the bodies of their ancestors. Noah then took the body of Adam and carried it with God's strength, not requiring anyone's help. {6:5} Shem, his son, took the gold, Ham carried the myrrh, and Japheth carried the incense. They brought them out of the Cave of Treasures, tears streaming down their cheeks. {6:6} As they were bringing them out, the bodies among which Adam had been laid cried out, "Are we to be separated from you, our father Adam?" {6:7} Adam's body answered, "Oh, that I must part from you, my sons, from this holy mountain! Yet I know that God will gather all our bodies together another time. {6:8} But wait patiently until our Savior has pity on us." {6:9} The other bodies continued talking together by the power of God's Word. Adam then asked God that the divine fire might remain in the lamp before his sons until the time when bodies shall rise again. {6:10} God left the divine fire by them to shed light on them. He then closed the cave upon them, leaving no trace of it until the day of the Resurrection when He will raise them up along with all other bodies. {6:11} The discourse Adam held, even in death, was by God's command, showing His wonders among the dead and the living. {6:12} After this, let none of you say that Adam's soul was under Satan's judgment. It was not so; God commanded the souls of the dead to come from under His hand and speak of His wonders from within their bodies. {6:13} They then returned to their places until the day of their sure deliverance, which shall come to them all.

{7:1} When Noah and his sons heard the voices from the dead bodies, they were greatly astonished, and their faith in God was strengthened. {7:2} They went out of the cave and began descending from the Holy Mountain, weeping and wailing with fervent hearts, sorrowful to part from the holy mountain, the abode of their fathers. {7:3} Noah and his sons tried to return and find the cave but were unable to. They broke out into bitter lamentation and deep sorrow, realizing that they would no longer have an existence or abode there. {7:4} They raised their eyes and looked at the garden and its trees, lifting their voices in weeping and loud crying. They said, "We salute you in worship, garden of joy, abode of brilliant beings, a place for the righteous! We salute you, place of joy that was the abode of our father Adam, the chief of creation, who, after transgressing, fell from you and saw his body in life, naked and disgraced. {7:5} "We now depart from the Holy Mountain to the lower side of you; we will neither dwell in you nor behold you as long as we live. We wish God would remove you with us to the country where we are going, but God would not take you into a cursed land. {7:6} "God will take us and bring us into that land with our children until He ends the punishment for our transgression of His commandment." {7:7} Noah and his sons also said, "We salute you, cave, abode of the bodies of our holy fathers; we salute you, pure spot, hidden from our eyes, yet fit to have those bodies laid within you! May the Lord God preserve you for the sake of the bodies of our fathers!" {7:8} They continued, "We greet you, our fathers, righteous judges, and we ask you to pray for us before God, that He will have pity on us and deliver us from this passing world. We ask you to pray for us, the only ones left of your seed. We give you a greeting of peace! {7:9} "O Seth, great master among the fathers, we greet you with peace! O Holy Mountain, abode of our fathers, we give you a greeting of peace!" {7:10} Then Noah and his sons wept again, saying, "Alas, for us eight souls that are left! Behold, we are taken away from the sight of the garden." {7:11} As they descended the mountain, they greeted the stones, took them in their hands, and put them on their shoulders; they stroked the trees, weeping as they did so. They continued coming down the mountain until they reached the door of the ark. {7:12} Noah and his sons then turned their faces to the east and prayed to the Lord for mercy, asking Him to save them and to command them where to lay the body of their father Adam. {7:13} The Word of God came to Noah, saying, "Lift up the body of Adam to the third story of the ark, and lay it on the eastern side, along with the gold, the incense, and the myrrh. {7:14} "You and your sons shall stand before him praying. But your wife and the wives of your sons shall be on the western side of the ark, and they shall not come together." {7:15} When Noah heard these words from God, he and his sons went into the ark and laid the body of Adam on the eastern side, along with the three offerings. {7:16} Noah brought the body of Adam into the ark on a Friday, at the second hour, on the twenty-seventh of the month of Gembot.

{8:1} Then God said to Noah, "Go to the top of the ark and blow the trumpet three times, so that all the beasts will gather to the ark." {8:2} But Noah asked, "Will the sound of the trumpet reach the ends of the earth to gather all the beasts and birds?" {8:3} God replied, "It is not just the sound of the trumpet that will go forth, but My power will accompany it, making it reach the ears of the beasts and birds. {8:4} "When you blow the trumpet, I will command My angel to blow the horn from heaven, and all the animals will be gathered to you." {8:5} Noah quickly obeyed and blew the trumpet as God instructed. Then the angel blew the horn from heaven, causing the earth to quake and all creatures on it to tremble. {8:6} All the beasts, birds, and creeping things gathered at the third hour on a Friday. The beasts, lions, and ostriches went into the lower story of the ark at the third hour. {8:7} At midday, the birds and creeping things entered the middle story. Noah and his sons went into the third story at the ninth hour of the day. {8:8} When Noah, his wife, his sons, and their wives entered the upper story, he commanded the women to dwell on the western side, while Noah, his sons, and the body of their father Adam remained on the eastern side.

{9:1} And Noah stood, asking God to save him from the waters of the Flood. {9:2} Then God spoke to Noah and said, "Of every kind of bird, take one pair, male and female of the clean; and of the unclean also one pair, male and female. But also of the clean take six more pairs, male and female." {9:3} And Noah did all this. Then when they all had entered the ark, God shut the door of the ark upon them by His power. {9:4} He then commanded the windows of heaven to open wide and pour down torrents of water. And so it was, by God's order. {9:5} And He commanded all the fountains to burst open, and the depths to pour forth water upon the face of the earth. So that the sea all around rose above the whole world, surging, and the deep waters arose. {9:6} When the windows of heaven opened wide, all stores of water and depths were opened, and all the stores of the winds, and the whirlwind, thick mist, gloom, and darkness spread abroad. The sun, moon, and stars withheld their light. It was a day of terror, such as had never been. {9:7} Then the sea all around began to raise its waves on high like mountains, covering the whole face of the earth. {9:8} When the sons of Seth, who had fallen into wickedness and adultery with the children of Cain, saw this, they then knew that God was angry with them, and that Noah had told them the truth. {9:9} They all ran around the ark, begging and entreating Noah to open the door of the ark for them, as they could not climb the Holy Mountain because its stones were like fire. {9:10} But the ark was closed and sealed by the power of God. An angel of God sat upon the ark, acting as a captain to Noah, his sons, and all inside the ark. {9:11} The waters of the flood increased on the children of Cain, overwhelming them. They began to sink, fulfilling Noah's words, which he preached to them, that the waters of the Flood would come and drown them. {9:12} The waters continued above and below over Noah and his sons until they were suspended in the ark. By the strength of the water, the ark rose from the earth, and the flesh of every moving thing perished. {9:13} The water rose until it covered the earth and all high mountains. The waters rose above the tops of high mountains by fifteen cubits, by the cubit of the Holy Ghost, which is equal to three cubits of man. Thus, the waters were forty-five cubits above the highest mountains. {9:14} The water increased and bore the ark, bringing it to the lower side of the garden. The waters, the rain, the whirlwind, and all that moved upon the earth worshipped. Noah, his sons, and all in the ark also bowed in worship to the holy garden. {9:15} The water returned to its former state, destroying everything upon the earth and under heaven. {9:16} But the ark floated on the waters, rising before the winds, while the angel of God steered and led it from east to west. The ark moved about on the face of the waters for one hundred and fifty days. {9:17} After that, the ark stood upon the mountains of Ararat on the twenty-seventh day of the month of Tkarnt.

{10:1} Then God sent His order to Noah again, saying, "Be quiet and wait until the waters subside." {10:2} Then the waters parted and returned to their original places; the fountains stopped pouring over the earth, the depths on the face of the earth ceased to rise, and the windows of heaven were closed. For floods of rain had fallen from heaven for forty days and forty nights at the beginning of the Flood. {10:3} On the first day of the eleventh month, the tops of high mountains were seen. Noah waited another forty days and then opened the window he had made on the western side of the ark and released a raven to see if the waters had subsided from the face of the earth. {10:4} The raven went out but did not return to Noah. The harmless dove, however, is a symbol of the mystery of the Christian Church. {10:5} Noah waited a little longer after the waters had subsided and then sent out a dove to see if the water had receded. {10:6} When the dove went out, she found no place to rest her foot and no abode, so she returned to Noah. {10:7} Noah waited another seven days and then sent out the dove again to see if the water had receded. The dove returned to Noah in the evening with an olive leaf in her mouth. {10:8} The meaning of the dove is that she represents both the old and the new covenants. The first time she went out and found nowhere to rest her feet represents the stiff-necked Jews, in whom no grace or mercy remained. Thus, Christ, the meek one, symbolized by the dove, did not find rest among them. {10:9} The second time, when the dove found a place to rest, symbolizes the nations that received the glad tidings of the holy Gospel, among whom Christ has found a resting place.

{11:1} In the six hundred and seventh year of Noah's life, on the second day of the month of Barmudeh, the water dried up from the earth. In the following month, which is Gembot, on the twenty-seventh day, the same day Noah entered the ark, Noah also came out of the ark, which was on a Sunday. {11:2} When Noah, his wife, his sons, and their wives came out of the ark, they gathered together and did not separate from one another. Initially, when they had entered the ark, the men and women had remained apart, as Noah feared they might come together. But after the Flood ended, they came together again, husbands with their wives. {11:3} God also brought great peace among the beasts, lions, birds, and creeping things that were in the ark, so they did not fight among themselves. {11:4} Noah then came out of the ark and built an altar on the mountain. He stood before the Lord and asked for guidance on which sacrifices to offer. {11:5} God spoke to Noah, saying, "Noah, take animals of the clean kind and offer them as sacrifices on the altar before me. Let the animals go out of the ark." {11:6} So Noah went into the ark and took the clean birds as God had commanded him. He offered them as sacrifices on the altar before the Lord.

{12:1} God established the covenant with Noah, showing him the sign of the rainbow in the cloud in the sky. {12:2} God also accepted the aroma of Noah's offerings. In response, He made a covenant with Noah, promising that the waters of the flood would never again cover the earth, from now on and forever.

Letter of Jeremiah

The Letter of Jeremiah, often considered a distinct work from the canonical Book of Jeremiah, is a deuterocanonical text included in some Christian Old Testament canons but regarded as apocryphal by others. Traditionally attributed to the prophet Jeremiah, this letter is a scathing critique of idolatry and a fervent exhortation to the Jewish exiles in Babylon to remain faithful to the covenant with God. The Letter, which purports to be written by Jeremiah to the exiles, is characterized by its polemical tone against the worship of idols, portraying them as powerless and lifeless creations of human hands that cannot see, hear, or save. The text employs a series of rhetorical questions and vivid descriptions to underscore the futility and absurdity of idol worship. Thematically, it echoes sentiments found in the canonical Book of Jeremiah and other prophetic literature, emphasizing the sole sovereignty of God and the folly of turning to other deities. The Letter of Jeremiah stands out for its sustained and detailed argument against idolatry, employing a style that is both didactic and admonitory. It also reflects the historical and cultural context of the Jewish diaspora in Babylon, providing insight into the challenges of maintaining religious identity and practice in a foreign and often hostile environment. This text not only serves as a religious and ethical guide but also as a literary piece that contributes to the broader narrative of Jewish resistance to assimilation and the preservation of monotheistic faith amidst pervasive polytheism.

{1:1} This is a copy of the letter that Jeremiah sent to those who were about to be taken captive to Babylon by the king of the Babylonians, conveying the message that God had commanded him to deliver. {1:2} "Because of the sins you have committed against God, you will be taken captive to Babylon by Nebuchadnezzar, king of the Babylonians. {1:3} Once you arrive in Babylon, you will remain there for many years, spanning up to seven generations; after that time, I will bring you back in peace. {1:4} In Babylon, you will encounter gods made of silver, gold, and wood, which are carried on the shoulders of men and inspire fear among the heathen. {1:5} Be careful not to become like these foreigners or allow fear of these gods to take hold of you, even when you see the multitude worshiping them from all sides. {1:6} Instead, say in your heart, 'It is you, O Lord, whom we must worship.' {1:7} For my angel is with you and watches over your lives. {1:8} These gods have tongues smoothed by craftsmen, and they are overlaid with gold and silver, but they are false and cannot speak. {1:9} People fashion crowns of gold for the heads of their gods, just as one might adorn a young woman who loves ornaments; {1:10} sometimes the priests secretly take gold and silver from these gods and spend it on themselves, {1:11} even giving some of it to the harlots in the brothel. They dress their gods in garments like men—these gods of silver, gold, and wood—{1:12} which cannot save themselves from rust and corrosion. Even when they are dressed in purple robes, {1:13} their faces must be wiped clean of the thick dust from the temple. {1:14} Like a local ruler, the god holds a scepter, but it cannot punish anyone who offends it. {1:15} It may have a dagger in its right hand or an axe, but it cannot save itself from war or robbers. {1:16} Therefore, it is clear that they are not gods, so do not fear them. {1:17} Just as a broken dish is useless, so too are the gods of the heathen, which are set up in temples. Their eyes are filled with dust stirred up by the feet of those who enter. {1:18} Just as the gates of a palace are shut tight around a condemned man, so too do the priests secure their temples with doors, locks, and bars, to prevent them from being plundered by robbers. {1:19} They light more lamps for these gods than they do for themselves, though their gods cannot see any of them. {1:20} These gods are no different from a beam in the temple, yet people say that their hearts melt when worms from the earth consume them and their robes decay. {1:21} They do not notice when their faces are blackened by the smoke of the temple. {1:22} Bats, swallows, and birds land on their bodies and heads, as do cats. {1:23} From this, you will know that they are not gods, so do not fear them. {1:24} As for the gold that adorns them for beauty—it will not shine unless someone wipes off the rust, for even when they were being cast, they had no sensation. {1:25} These gods are bought at a high price, but there is no breath in them. {1:26} Without feet, they must be carried on the shoulders of men, revealing their worthlessness to all. {1:27} Those who serve them are ashamed because these gods must be made to stand, lest they fall to the ground. If someone sets one upright, it cannot move by itself; if it is tipped over, it cannot right itself; yet offerings are placed before them just as before the dead. {1:28} The priests sell the sacrifices offered to these gods and use the money for themselves; likewise, their wives preserve some of the offerings with salt but give none to the poor or needy. {1:29} Women in menstruation or childbirth may even touch these sacrifices. Since you know from these things that they are not gods, do not fear them. {1:30} Why should they be called gods? Women prepare meals for gods of silver, gold, and wood; {1:31} in their temples, the priests sit with torn clothes, their heads and beards shaved, and their heads uncovered. {1:32} They howl and shout before their gods as if at a funeral for a deceased man. {1:33} The priests take some of the clothing of their gods to dress their wives and children. {1:34} Whether someone does good or evil to these gods, they cannot repay it. They cannot set up a king or depose one. {1:35} Likewise, they cannot give wealth or money; if someone makes a vow to them and fails to keep it, they do not demand fulfillment. {1:36} They cannot save a man from death or rescue the weak from the strong. {1:37} They cannot restore sight to a blind man, nor can they rescue a man in distress. {1:38} They cannot take pity on a widow or do good to an orphan. {1:39} These gods made of wood and overlaid with gold and silver are like stones from the mountain, and those who serve them will be put to shame. {1:40} Why then should anyone think that they are gods or call them gods? Even the Chaldeans themselves dishonor them; {1:41} when they see a mute man who cannot speak, they bring him before Bel, praying that the man may speak, as if Bel could understand. {1:42} Yet these people do not perceive the truth and abandon these gods, for they have no sense. {1:43} Women, with cords around their waists, sit along the passageways, burning bran for incense; when one of them is led away by a passerby and lies with him, she mocks the woman next to her for not being as attractive as herself and for having an unbroken cord. {1:44} Everything done for these gods is false. Why then should anyone think they are gods or call them gods? {1:45} They are made by carpenters and goldsmiths; they can be nothing more than what the craftsmen desire them to be. {1:46} The men who make them will not live long themselves; how then can these creations be gods? {1:47} They leave nothing but lies and reproach for those who come after them. {1:48} When war or calamity strikes, the priests gather to decide where they can hide themselves and their gods. {1:49} How can anyone fail to see that these are not gods, for they cannot save themselves from war or calamity? {1:50} Since they are made of wood and overlaid with gold and silver, it will be clear that they are false. {1:51} It will become evident to all nations and kings that these are not gods but the work of human hands, and there is no divine work in them. {1:52} Who then can fail to recognize that they are not gods? {1:53} They cannot establish a king over a country or give rain to men. {1:54} They cannot judge their own case or deliver someone who has been wronged, for they have no power; they are like crows suspended between heaven and earth. {1:55} When fire breaks out in a temple filled with these wooden gods overlaid with gold or silver, their priests will flee to save themselves, but the gods will be burned up like beams. {1:56} Moreover, they cannot resist a king or any enemies. Why then should anyone admit or believe that they are gods? {1:57} These gods made of wood and overlaid with silver and gold cannot protect themselves from thieves and robbers. {1:58} Strong men will strip them of their gold, silver, and the garments they wear, carrying off the loot, and these gods will be helpless to stop them. {1:59} Therefore, it is better to be a courageous king or even a household utensil that serves its owner's needs than to be these false gods; even a door of a house that protects its contents is better than these gods; a wooden pillar in a palace is more useful than these gods. {1:60} For the sun, moon, and stars, which are sent forth to serve, are obedient to God. {1:61} So too, when lightning flashes, it is seen by all; and the wind blows wherever it is commanded. {1:62} When God orders the clouds to cover the earth, they obey his command. {1:63} The fire sent from above to consume mountains and forests does exactly what it is instructed. But these idols are not to be compared to these forces in appearance or power. {1:64} Therefore, one must not consider them gods or call them gods, for they cannot make judgments or do good to men. {1:65} Knowing this, you should not fear them. {1:66} They cannot curse or bless kings; {1:67} they cannot show signs in the heavens or among the nations, nor can they shine like the sun or give light like the moon. {1:68} Wild beasts are better than they are, for they can flee to cover and protect themselves. {1:69} So we have no reason to believe that they are gods; therefore, do not fear them. {1:70} They are like a scarecrow in a cucumber field, guarding nothing; just as these gods made of wood, overlaid with gold and silver, are as useless as a thornbush in a garden where every bird lands, or like a dead body cast out into the darkness. {1:71} From the rotting purple and linen that cover them, you can tell they are not gods; eventually, they will decay and become a disgrace in the land. {1:72} Therefore, it is better to be a just man who has no idols, for he will be far from reproach."

Prayer of Azariah

Prayer of Azariah, found in the additions to the Book of Daniel in the Greek Septuagint, is a rich and significant text in biblical literature. It is part of the Apocrypha, which comprises books and additions not included in the Hebrew Bible but considered canonical by some Christian traditions, particularly within the Catholic and Orthodox Churches. This prayer is inserted into the narrative of the fiery furnace in Daniel 3 and is positioned between verses 23 and 24 of the canonical Daniel. The prayer itself is attributed to Azariah, also known as Abednego, one of the three Jewish youths who, along with Shadrach and Meshach, refuse to worship the golden image erected by King Nebuchadnezzar and are subsequently thrown into a blazing furnace. The text of the prayer is a heartfelt and theologically rich supplication, expressing themes of repentance, divine justice, and unwavering faith in God's mercy and deliverance. Azariah's prayer reflects a deep awareness of Israel's covenantal relationship with God, acknowledging the nation's sins and the righteousness of God's judgments, while also pleading for God's enduring mercy and intervention. The prayer, along with the accompanying Song of the Three Holy Children, serves to highlight the power of faithful prayer and God's ability to save and deliver His people from perilous situations. These passages are not only significant for their devotional and liturgical use but also for their contribution to the theological and literary richness of the biblical tradition. Prayer of Azariah, therefore, stands as a testament to the enduring faith of the Jewish people in exile and their hope for divine salvation, embodying the spiritual resilience that characterizes much of the biblical narrative.

{1:1} Then Azariah, standing amidst the flames, opened his mouth and offered this prayer: {1:2} "Blessed are you, O Lord, God of our ancestors, and worthy of all praise; your name is exalted forever. {1:3} For you are just in all that you have done to us, and all your works are true, your ways are right, and your judgments are always just. {1:4} You have brought true judgment upon us and upon Jerusalem, the holy city of our ancestors. In truth and justice, you have brought all these things upon us because of our sins. {1:5} For we have sinned and acted lawlessly, departing from your commandments; we have sinned in everything and have not obeyed your commands. {1:6} We did not observe or carry out your instructions, so things have not gone well for us as you intended. {1:7} Therefore, all that you have done to us, everything you have brought upon us, you have done in true judgment. {1:8} You have handed us over to lawless enemies, the most hateful rebels, and to a wicked king, the most unjust in all the world. {1:9} Now, we are unable to open our mouths; shame and disgrace have come upon your servants and those who worship you. {1:10} For the sake of your name, do not utterly abandon us, and do not break your covenant. {1:11} Do not withdraw your mercy from us, for the sake of Abraham, your beloved, and for the sake of Isaac, your servant, and Israel, your holy one. {1:12} You promised to make their descendants as numerous as the stars of heaven and as countless as the sand on the seashore. {1:13} But now, O Lord, we have become fewer than any other nation, and we are brought low in all the world because of our sins. {1:14} At this time, we have no prince, no prophet, no leader, no burnt offering, no sacrifice, no oblation, no incense, and no place to make an offering before you to receive your mercy. {1:15} Yet, with a contrite heart and a humble spirit, may we be accepted as though we were offering rams and bulls and tens of thousands of fat lambs. {1:16} May our sacrifice today be pleasing in your sight, and may we follow you completely, for those who trust in you will not be put to shame. {1:17} And now, with all our heart, we follow you; we fear you and seek your face. {1:18} Do not let us be put to shame, but treat us with your patience and abundant mercy. {1:19} Deliver us in accordance with your marvelous works, and bring glory to your name, O Lord! Let all who harm your servants be put to shame; {1:20} let them be disgraced and stripped of all power and authority, and let their strength be broken. {1:21} Let them know that you alone are the Lord, the only God, glorious over the whole world." {1:22} Meanwhile, the king's servants who had thrown them into the furnace did not cease stoking the fire with oil, pitch, flax, and brushwood. {1:23} The flames rose above the furnace forty-nine cubits high, {1:24} and they burst forth and burned those Chaldeans who were near the furnace. {1:25} But the angel of the Lord descended into the furnace to be with Azariah and his companions, and he drove the fiery flames out of the furnace, {1:26} making the center of the furnace like a cool, moist breeze, so that the fire did not touch them or cause them any pain or trouble. {1:27} Then the three, as with one voice, began to praise, glorify, and bless God in the furnace, saying: {1:28} "Blessed are you, O Lord, God of our ancestors, and to be praised and highly exalted forever; {1:29} and blessed is your glorious, holy name, to be praised and highly exalted forever. {1:30} Blessed are you in the temple of your holy glory, to be extolled and highly glorified forever. {1:31} Blessed are you who sit upon cherubim and gaze upon the depths, to be praised and highly exalted forever. {1:32} Blessed are you on the throne of your kingdom, to be extolled and highly exalted forever. {1:33} Blessed are you in the firmament of heaven, to be sung and glorified forever. {1:34} Bless the Lord, all works of the Lord, sing praise to him and highly exalt him forever. {1:35} Bless the Lord, you heavens, sing praise to him and highly exalt him forever. {1:36} Bless the Lord, you angels of the Lord, sing praise to him and highly exalt him forever. {1:37} Bless the Lord, all waters above the heavens, sing praise to him and highly exalt him forever. {1:38} Bless the Lord, all powers, sing praise to him and highly exalt him forever. {1:39} Bless the Lord, sun and moon, sing praise to him and highly exalt him forever. {1:40} Bless the Lord, stars of heaven, sing praise to him and highly exalt him forever. {1:41} Bless the Lord, all rain and dew, sing praise to him and highly exalt him forever. {1:42} Bless the Lord, all winds, sing praise to him and highly exalt him forever. {1:43} Bless the Lord, fire and heat, sing praise to him and highly exalt him forever. {1:44} Bless the Lord, winter cold and summer heat, sing praise to him and highly exalt him forever. {1:45} Bless the Lord, dews and snows, sing praise to him and highly exalt him forever. {1:46} Bless the Lord, nights and days, sing praise to him and highly exalt him forever. {1:47} Bless the Lord, light and darkness, sing praise to him and highly exalt him forever. {1:48} Bless the Lord, ice and cold, sing praise to him and highly exalt him forever. {1:49} Bless the Lord, frosts and snows, sing praise to him and highly exalt him forever. {1:50} Bless the Lord, lightnings and clouds, sing praise to him and highly exalt him forever. {1:51} Let the earth bless the Lord; let it sing praise to him and highly exalt him forever. {1:52} Bless the Lord, mountains and hills, sing praise to him and highly exalt him forever. {1:53} Bless the Lord, all things that grow on the earth, sing praise to him and highly exalt him forever. {1:54} Bless the Lord, you springs, sing praise to him and highly exalt him forever. {1:55} Bless the Lord, seas and rivers, sing praise to him and highly exalt him forever. {1:56} Bless the Lord, you whales and all creatures that move in the waters, sing praise to him and highly exalt him forever. {1:57} Bless the Lord, all birds of the air, sing praise to him and highly exalt him forever. {1:58} Bless the Lord, all beasts and cattle, sing praise to him and highly exalt him forever. {1:59} Bless the Lord, you sons of men, sing praise to him and highly exalt him forever. {1:60} Bless the Lord, O Israel, sing praise to him and highly exalt him forever. {1:61} Bless the Lord, you priests of the Lord, sing praise to him and highly exalt him forever. {1:62} Bless the Lord, you servants of the Lord, sing praise to him and highly exalt him forever. {1:63} Bless the Lord, spirits and souls of the righteous, sing praise to him and highly exalt him forever. {1:64} Bless the Lord, you who are holy and humble in heart, sing praise to him and highly exalt him forever. {1:65} Bless the Lord, Hananiah, Azariah, and Mishael, sing praise to him and highly exalt him forever; for he has rescued us from the depths of Hades, saved us from the grip of death, and delivered us from the midst of the burning fiery furnace; from the heart of the flames, he has delivered us. {1:66} Give thanks to the Lord, for he is good, for his mercy endures forever. {1:67} Bless him, all who worship the Lord, the God of gods, sing praise to him and give thanks to him, for his mercy endures forever."

Prayer of Manasseh

The Prayer of Manasseh, a brief yet profoundly significant text, occupies a unique place in the corpus of biblical and apocryphal literature. Traditionally attributed to the penitent King Manasseh of Judah, this prayer is an extraordinary expression of repentance and supplication. Despite its brevity, the Prayer of Manasseh encapsulates deep theological themes such as sin, repentance, divine mercy, and redemption. Although it is not found in the Hebrew Bible, this prayer has been preserved in various Christian traditions, including the Septuagint and the Apocrypha of the Vulgate. The historical context of the prayer is tied to the biblical account of Manasseh's reign, which is characterized by significant apostasy and idolatry, as recorded in the books of Kings and Chronicles. The narrative of Manasseh's captivity, repentance, and restoration provides a dramatic backdrop for understanding the depth of contrition expressed in this prayer. The text itself, though concise, is rich with biblical allusions and echoes the penitential psalms, showcasing a profound awareness of God's justice and mercy. Theologically, it highlights the themes of divine forgiveness and the transformative power of genuine repentance, making it a poignant piece for both personal devotion and liturgical use. The Prayer of Manasseh's inclusion in different biblical canons reflects its enduring spiritual and liturgical value across various Christian traditions, offering insights into the universality of the human experience of sin and the quest for divine forgiveness. Its study not only enriches our understanding of ancient penitential practices but also provides a timeless reflection on the themes of human frailty and divine grace.

{1:1} To the One who crafted the heavens and the earth in perfect order, the One who set the boundaries of the seas with a mere word, who has contained the deep and sealed it with Your awe-inspiring and glorious name; {1:2} all creation trembles before Your mighty power, and who can bear the weight of Your majestic splendor? {1:3} Your wrath is overwhelming to those who sin, but Your promised mercy is beyond measure and understanding. {1:4} You are the Lord Most High, full of compassion, patience, and abundant mercy, ready to relent from bringing harm to those who repent. {1:5} You, O Lord, in Your boundless goodness, have promised forgiveness and a chance to turn back to You for those who have sinned against You. In Your vast mercy, You have granted the opportunity for repentance so that sinners might be saved. {1:6} Therefore, You, O Lord, God of the righteous, did not need to appoint repentance for the righteous, like Abraham, Isaac, and Jacob, who did not sin against You; but instead, You have graciously offered repentance to me, who am a sinner. {1:7} My sins are as countless as the grains of sand on the shore; they are many, O Lord, they are many! Because of the overwhelming number of my wrongdoings, I am unworthy to even lift my eyes to heaven. {1:8} I am weighed down by the heavy chains of my sins, and I feel rejected because of them; I find no relief, for I have stirred up Your anger and committed evil in Your sight by setting up idols and multiplying my offenses. {1:9} Now, with a deeply humbled heart, I beg for Your kindness. {1:10} I have sinned, O Lord, I have sinned, and I fully acknowledge my transgressions. {1:11} I earnestly plead with You, forgive me, O Lord, forgive me! Do not let my sins destroy me! Do not remain angry with me forever, or store up judgment against me; do not condemn me to the depths of the earth. {1:12} For You, O Lord, are the God of those who turn back to You, and through me, You will demonstrate Your goodness. {1:13} Though I am unworthy, You will save me in Your great mercy, {1:14} and I will praise You constantly all the days of my life. For all the heavenly beings sing of Your glory, and Yours is the glory forever. Amen.

Bel and the Dragon

The Book of Bel and the Dragon is an apocryphal addition to the canonical Book of Daniel, often considered part of the deuterocanonical literature in some Christian traditions, such as the Catholic and Eastern Orthodox Churches. This text is believed to have been composed in the late Second Temple period, possibly in the 2nd or 1st century BCE, and it serves as a narrative extension that highlights Daniel's unwavering faith and God's power over idolatry. It is divided into three distinct episodes: the destruction of the idol Bel, the slaying of the dragon, and Daniel's miraculous survival in the lion's den. These stories collectively critique the Babylonian worship of false gods, emphasizing the futility and deceitfulness of idol worship while contrasting it with the superiority of the Hebrew God. The text showcases Daniel's wisdom and divine protection as he cleverly exposes the fraud of Bel's priests, demonstrates the impotence of the dragon, and endures another ordeal in the lion's den, all under God's providence. The work's polemical tone against idolatry and its affirmation of monotheism reflect the broader Jewish theological and cultural context during a time when Hellenistic influences and local cultic practices posed significant challenges to Jewish religious identity. Theologically rich and filled with dramatic irony, Bel and the Dragon reinforces themes of divine justice and the triumph of faith over superstition, while also contributing to the larger narrative of Daniel's righteousness and the divine protection accorded to him as a faithful servant of God.

{1:1} When King Astyages passed away, Cyrus the Persian took over the kingdom. {1:2} Daniel was a close companion of the new king and was highly esteemed among his friends. {1:3} The Babylonians worshipped an idol named Bel, to which they devoted twelve bushels of fine flour, forty sheep, and fifty gallons of wine daily. {1:4} The king honored Bel and visited the idol daily to offer worship, but Daniel worshipped his own God. {1:5} The king asked him, "Why don't you worship Bel?" Daniel replied, "I don't venerate man-made idols but the living God who created heaven and earth and rules over all things." {1:6} The king questioned, "Do you not consider Bel a living god? Look at how much he consumes every day!" {1:7} Daniel laughed and said, "Don't be fooled, O king; Bel is just clay inside and brass outside. It hasn't eaten or drunk anything." {1:8} Angered, the king summoned his priests and declared, "If you can't prove who is consuming the provisions, you will be put to death. But if you show that Bel is eating them, Daniel will die for blaspheming Bel." Daniel agreed, "Let it be as you have said." {1:9} There were seventy priests of Bel, along with their wives and children. The king, accompanied by Daniel, went to the temple of Bel. {1:10} The priests of Bel said, "We are going outside now; you, O king, will place the food and wine on the table, shut the door, and seal it with your signet. {1:11} When you return in the morning, if Bel has not eaten everything, we will die; otherwise, Daniel will die for his lies." {1:12} The priests were unconcerned because they had a hidden entrance under the table through which they regularly came in and consumed the food. {1:13} After they left, the king set out the food for Bel. Daniel then had his servants spread ashes all over the temple floor in the presence of only the king. They locked the door and sealed it with the king's signet before leaving. {1:14} During the night, the priests, their wives, and children came through the secret entrance and ate everything. {1:15} The next morning, the king arrived with Daniel and asked, "Are the seals unbroken, Daniel?" Daniel confirmed, "They are unbroken, O king." {1:16} When the doors were opened, the king looked at the table and exclaimed loudly, "Great is Bel; there is no deceit in you!" {1:17} Daniel laughed, stopped the king from entering, and said, "Look at the floor and see the footprints." {1:18} The king saw the footprints of men, women, and children. {1:19} Furious, the king seized the priests, their families, and showed him the secret entrance where they had been entering and eating the provisions. {1:20} Consequently, the king executed them and gave Bel and its temple to Daniel, who destroyed both. {1:21} There was also a revered dragon among the Babylonians. {1:22} The king told Daniel, "You cannot deny that this dragon is a living god; therefore, worship him." {1:23} Daniel responded, "I will worship the Lord my God, for He is the living God. But if you permit, I will kill the dragon without a sword or club." The king agreed, "You have permission." {1:24} Daniel mixed pitch, fat, and hair, made cakes from it, and fed them to the dragon. The dragon ate the cakes and burst open. Daniel declared, "See what you have been worshipping!" {1:25} The Babylonians were enraged and plotted against the king, accusing him of becoming a Jew and destroying Bel, killing the dragon, and slaughtering the priests. {1:26} They threatened the king, "Hand Daniel over to us, or we will kill you and your family." {1:27} Facing intense pressure, the king reluctantly handed Daniel over. {1:28} They threw Daniel into the lions' den, where he remained for six days. {1:29} There were seven lions in the den, who had been fed two human bodies and two sheep daily, but were deprived of food to ensure they would devour Daniel. {1:30} At the same time, the prophet Habakkuk was in Judea preparing food to take to the reapers. {1:31} An angel of the Lord told Habakkuk, "Take the meal you have prepared to Daniel in the lions' den in Babylon." {1:32} Habakkuk replied, "I've never been to Babylon and don't know the den." {1:33} The angel of the Lord then lifted Habakkuk by the hair of his head and transported him to Babylon, directly over the den, with the sound of rushing wind. {1:34} Habakkuk called out, "Daniel, Daniel! Take the meal God has sent you." {1:35} Daniel answered, "You have remembered me, O God, and have not abandoned those who love You." {1:36} Daniel ate the food, and the angel returned Habakkuk to his place. {1:37} On the seventh day, the king came to mourn for Daniel. When he reached the den and looked in, he saw Daniel sitting there. {1:38} The king cried out loudly, "Great are You, O Lord God of Daniel; there is no other God besides You." {1:39} The king had Daniel brought out and threw those who had conspired against him into the den. They were immediately devoured by the lions in front of the king's eyes.

Susanna

The Book of Susanna, an apocryphal addition to Daniel likely composed between the 2nd and 1st centuries BCE, blends Jewish piety with Greek influence. It tells of Susanna falsely accused of adultery by elders she rejects. Through the wisdom of Daniel, she is vindicated, highlighting justice, divine retribution, and protection of the innocent. The story underscores moral integrity and warns against corrupt authority, set in Babylon within the Danielic tradition, emphasizing God's sovereignty. Its exclusion from the Hebrew Bible but inclusion in the Septuagint reflects varied canon formation. Early Christians valued Susanna for its moral lessons and connections to Christ, affirming its theological significance.

{1:1} There was a man named Joakim, who lived in Babylon and took a wife named Susanna, the daughter of Hilkiah. She was very beautiful and had a strong devotion to God. {1:2} Susanna's parents were righteous and had raised her to follow the laws of Moses. {1:3} Joakim was a wealthy man with a large garden next to his house, and many of the Jews would come to him because he was highly respected. {1:4} That year, two elders were appointed as judges, but they were corrupt men, for it had been foretold that wickedness would come from Babylon through these elders who were supposed to lead the people. {1:5} These elders frequently visited Joakim's house, and anyone with legal matters would come to them. {1:6} Every day, after the people had left at noon, Susanna would go into her husband's garden to walk. {1:7} The two elders saw her doing this daily and began to lust after her. {1:8} They turned their minds away from God and His just ways, and their desires consumed them. {1:9} Though both men were overwhelmed with their passion for Susanna, they kept their feelings secret, ashamed to reveal their sinful desires. {1:10} Each day they eagerly watched for her, plotting in their hearts. {1:11} One day, they each decided to leave separately, but as they turned back, they met again. Surprised, they questioned each other and confessed their lustful thoughts. Then, together, they devised a plan to catch her alone. {1:12} They waited for the right day, and finally, when Susanna went into the garden with only two maids, wishing to bathe because of the heat, they saw their chance. {1:13} The two elders hid and watched her. {1:14} Susanna told her maids, "Bring me oil and ointments, and close the garden doors so I may bathe." {1:15} The maids did as she asked, shutting the garden doors and leaving through a side door to get what she needed, unaware of the elders hiding there. {1:16} Once the maids had left, the two elders jumped out and ran to Susanna, {1:17} saying, "The garden doors are shut, and no one can see us. We are in love with you, so give in to our desires and sleep with us. {1:18} If you refuse, we will accuse you of being with a young man, saying that is why you sent your maids away." {1:19} Susanna sighed deeply and said, "I am trapped on all sides. If I do this, it will mean my death, and if I do not, I won't escape your hands. {1:20} But I choose not to sin in the sight of the Lord and would rather fall into your hands." {1:21} Then Susanna screamed loudly, and the two elders began shouting against her. {1:22} One of the elders ran to open the garden doors. {1:23} When the household servants heard the commotion, they rushed in through the side door to see what had happened. {1:24} The elders began to accuse Susanna, and the servants were deeply ashamed, for nothing like this had ever been said about her before. {1:25} The next day, the people gathered at Joakim's house, and the two elders, full of their wicked plot, came to ensure that Susanna would be condemned to death. {1:26} They said to the people, "Summon Susanna, the daughter of Hilkiah, the wife of Joakim." {1:27} So they called for her, and she came with her parents, her children, and all her relatives. {1:28} Susanna was a refined and beautiful woman. {1:29} As she stood there, veiled, the wicked men ordered her to be unveiled so they could feast their eyes on her beauty. {1:30} Her family, friends, and all who saw this wept. {1:31} Then the two elders stood in the midst of the people, placing their hands on Susanna's head. {1:32} She, in tears, looked up to heaven, trusting in God. {1:33} The elders began to accuse her, saying, "We were walking in the garden alone when this woman came in with two maids. She shut the garden doors and sent the maids away. {1:34} Then a young man who had been hiding there came to her and lay with her. {1:35} We were in a corner of the garden, and when we saw this crime, we ran towards them. {1:36} Though we saw them embracing, we couldn't hold the young man, for he was too strong for us and ran out, opening the doors as he fled. {1:37} But we seized this woman and asked her who the young man was, and she refused to tell us. This is our testimony." {1:38} The assembly believed the elders, as they were respected judges, and condemned Susanna to death. {1:39} Then Susanna cried out loudly, saying, "O eternal God, who knows what is hidden and who is aware of all things before they happen, {1:40} you know that these men have testified falsely against me, and now I must die, though I have done nothing of what they claim." {1:41} The Lord heard her cry. {1:42} As she was being led to her death, God stirred the holy spirit within a young man named Daniel, {1:43} who shouted loudly, "I am innocent of this woman's blood!" {1:44} The people turned to him and asked, "What do you mean by that?" {1:45} Standing in their midst, Daniel said, "Are you such fools, you sons of Israel? Have you condemned a daughter of Israel without proper investigation and without knowing the truth? {1:46} Return to the place of judgment, for these men have given false testimony against her." {1:47} All the people hurried back, and the elders said to Daniel, "Come and sit among us and tell us what you know, for God has given you the authority to do so." {1:48} Daniel then said, "Separate these two men far from each other, and I will examine them." {1:49} After they were separated, Daniel called one of the elders and said to him, "You wicked man, your sins have caught up with you. You've been pronouncing unjust judgments, condemning the innocent, and freeing the guilty, even though the Lord commands, 'Do not kill the innocent and righteous.' {1:50} Now, if you really saw them, tell me under what tree you saw them being intimate with each other." The elder replied, "Under a mastic tree." {1:51} Daniel said, "You've just condemned yourself with your own lie! The angel of God has received the sentence from God and will now cut you in two." {1:52} Daniel then sent him aside and called for the other elder. He said to him, "You offspring of Canaan, not of Judah, beauty has deceived you and lust has corrupted your heart. {1:53} This is how you've acted with the daughters of Israel, and they gave in to you out of fear. But a daughter of Judah would never endure such wickedness. {1:54} Now, tell me under what tree you caught them together." The second elder answered, "Under an evergreen oak." {1:55} Daniel replied, "You've also lied against your own head, for the angel of God is waiting with his sword to cut you in two and destroy you both." {1:56} The entire assembly shouted in praise of God, who saves those who put their hope in Him. {1:57} They turned against the two elders, whom Daniel had exposed as liars by their own testimony. {1:58} Following the law of Moses, the people carried out the punishment the elders had plotted for their neighbor, and they were put to death. That day, innocent blood was spared. {1:59} Hilkiah & his wife praised God for their daughter Susanna, as did her husband Joakim and all her relatives, because she was found innocent. {1:60} From that day on, Daniel became greatly respected among the people.

Wisdom of Sirach

The Wisdom of Jesus, Son of Sirach (Book of Sirach or Ecclesiasticus), is an apocryphal text from the early 2nd century BCE, written by Jesus ben Sirach. This work, originally in Hebrew and later translated into Greek by his grandson, offers ethical teachings, practical wisdom, and reflections on theology, blending Hellenistic and Jewish traditions. It includes maxims and proverbs on humility, diligence, and the virtues of wisdom, emphasizing adherence to the Law and the importance of wisdom. The book's inclusion in the Septuagint and the Christian Old Testament Apocrypha reflects its lasting influence and reverence across religious traditions, offering practical guidance on daily life and social responsibilities.

{1:1} All wisdom originates from the Lord and exists with Him eternally. {1:2} Who can count the sand of the sea, the drops of rain, and the days of eternity? {1:3} The expanse of heaven, the breadth of the earth, the abyss, and wisdom itself— who can fully comprehend them? {1:4} Wisdom was established before all things, and prudent understanding has existed from everlasting. {1:5} Who has discovered the roots of wisdom? Who knows her intricate designs? {1:6} There is One who is exceedingly wise, sitting enthroned in glory and feared by all. {1:7} The Lord Himself created wisdom; He beheld her and bestowed her upon His works. {1:8} She dwells among all people according to His generosity, enriching those who love Him. {1:9} Reverence for the Lord brings honor, joy, and a crown of rejoicing. {1:10} The fear of the Lord brings delight, happiness, and longevity. {1:11} Those who fear the Lord will prosper in the end; they will be blessed on the day of their departure from life. {1:12} The fear of the Lord marks the beginning of wisdom; it is instilled from the womb in the hearts of the faithful. {1:13} She establishes an enduring foundation among humanity and is trusted by future generations. {1:14} Reverence for the Lord is the ultimate measure of wisdom, satisfying people with her fruits. {1:15} She enriches their homes with desirable possessions and fills their storehouses with abundance. {1:16} The fear of the Lord is the pinnacle of wisdom, fostering peace and flourishing health. {1:17} God apportions wisdom generously, bestowing knowledge and discernment, and glorifying those who embrace her. {1:18} Reverence for the Lord is the foundation of wisdom, ensuring long life for those who embrace her. {1:19} Unjustifiable anger leads to ruin, for it tips the scales against a person. {1:20} Patience leads to enduring joy at the right time. {1:21} A wise person holds back words until the opportune moment, and many will praise their insight. {1:22} The treasures of wisdom contain wise sayings, but sinfulness is detestable to God. {1:23} If you seek wisdom, keep the commandments, and the Lord will provide. {1:24} The fear of the Lord brings wisdom and instruction; He delights in fidelity and humility. {1:25} Do not approach the Lord with a divided heart or be hypocritical before others; guard your speech diligently. {1:26} Do not elevate yourself, as pride leads to downfall. The Lord sees through deceit and exposes secrets, casting down the deceitful.

{2:1} My child, if you decide to dedicate yourself to the service of the Lord, prepare yourself for trials. {2:2} Set your heart right and be steadfast; do not rush to despair in times of trouble. {2:3} Hold fast to Him and do not wander away, so that you may be honored at the end of your life. {2:4} Accept whatever comes your way, and in times of humility, be patient. {2:5} Just as gold is tested in fire, and righteous people are refined in the furnace of adversity. {2:6} Trust in the Lord, and He will support you; make your paths straight and place your hope in Him. {2:7} Those who reverence the Lord, wait for His mercy; do not turn away, lest you fall. {2:8} You who fear the Lord, put your trust in Him, and you will not be disappointed. {2:9} You who fear the Lord, anticipate goodness, everlasting joy, and mercy. {2:10} Look to the generations of old and see: has anyone who trusted in the Lord been put to shame? Has anyone who clung to the fear of the Lord been abandoned? Has anyone who called upon Him been disregarded? {2:11} For the Lord is compassionate and merciful; He forgives sins and rescues in times of distress. {2:12} Woe to those with timid hearts and lazy hands, and to sinners who walk in duplicity! {2:13} Woe to the faint-hearted, for they lack trust and will find no refuge. {2:14} Woe to those who have lost their perseverance! What will they do when the Lord holds them accountable? {2:15} Those who fear the Lord do not disobey His words, and those who love Him keep His ways. {2:16} Those who fear the Lord seek His approval, and those who love Him are filled with His teachings. {2:17} Those who fear the Lord prepare their hearts and humble themselves before Him. {2:18} Let us submit ourselves to the Lord's authority, rather than fall into human hands, for His majesty is matched only by His mercy.

{3:1} Hear me, my children, and follow my advice, so that you may live securely. {3:2} The Lord has placed honor upon fathers above their children, and He has established a mother's authority over her sons. {3:3} Those who honor their father make amends for their sins, {3:4} and those who respect their mother are like those who store up wealth. {3:5} Honoring one's father brings joy through children of their own, and their prayers are heard. {3:6} Those who respect their father will enjoy a long life, and those who obey the Lord will bring joy to their mother. {3:7} They will serve their parents as they served their masters. {3:8} Honor your father with both your words and actions, so that blessings may come upon you from him. {3:9} A father's blessing strengthens the homes of his children, but a mother's curse uproots their foundations. {3:10} Do not elevate yourself by dishonoring your father, for your father's dishonor reflects poorly on you. {3:11} A person's honor comes from respecting their father, and it is shameful for children not to honor their mother. {3:12} My son, assist your father in his old age and do not cause him grief while he lives; {3:13} even if he lacks understanding, show him patience, and do not despise him in your strength. {3:14} Kindness to a father will never be forgotten, and it will be credited to you against your sins. {3:15} In times of affliction, it will be remembered in your favor; like frost in fair weather, your sins will melt away. {3:16} Whoever forsakes their father is like one who blasphemes, and those who anger their mother incur the Lord's curse. {3:17} My son, perform your duties with humility, and you will be loved by those whom God favors. {3:18} The more exalted you are, {3:19} the more you must humble yourself, finding favor in the Lord's sight. {3:20} For the Lord's power is great; He is glorified by the humble. {3:21} Do not seek what is beyond your capabilities, nor investigate what is beyond your strength. {3:22} Reflect on what has been assigned to you; you do not need what is concealed. {3:23} Do not delve into matters beyond your tasks, for things too profound for human understanding have been revealed to you. {3:24} Hasty judgments have led many astray, and erroneous opinions have caused their thoughts to falter. {3:25} A stubborn mind will face trouble in the end, {3:26} and those who love danger will perish because of it. {3:27} A stubborn mind will be burdened with problems, and sinners will heap sin upon sin. {3:28} The affliction of the proud has no cure, for wickedness has taken root within them. {3:29} The intelligent ponder proverbs, and wise individuals desire attentive ears. {3:30} Just as water extinguishes fire, so almsgiving atones for sin. {3:31} Those who repay kindness consider the future; in their time of need, they will find support.

{4:1} My child, do not deprive the poor of their livelihood, and do not make them wait for assistance. {4:2} Do not cause sorrow to those who are hungry, nor provoke anger in those who are in need. {4:3} Do not add to the troubles of someone already distressed, and do not delay in helping a beggar. {4:4} Do not turn away from someone who is suffering, nor ignore the plight of the poor. {4:5} Do not ignore those in need, lest they curse you in their bitterness, and their Creator hears their cry. {4:6} Make yourself beloved among the community; show respect to those in authority. {4:7} Listen attentively to the poor, and respond to them kindly and gently. {4:8} Rescue the oppressed from the hands of the oppressor, and do not hesitate to judge justly. {4:9} Be like a father to orphans and a protector to widows; then you will be honored as a child of the Most High, and He will love you more than your own mother. {4:10} Wisdom uplifts those who embrace her and provides aid to those who seek her. {4:11} Those who love wisdom find life, and those who seek her diligently will be filled with joy. {4:12} Holding on to wisdom brings honor, and the Lord blesses wherever she dwells. {4:13} Those who serve wisdom serve the Holy One; the Lord favors those who love her. {4:14} Those who obey wisdom will judge nations, and those who heed her will dwell in security. {4:15} If one seeks wisdom sincerely, they will obtain her, and their descendants will inherit her blessings. {4:16} Initially, wisdom may challenge with difficult paths and discipline, but eventually she will bring joy and reveal her secrets to those who trust in her. {4:17} However, if one strays from wisdom, they will be abandoned to their own ruin. {4:18} Act wisely at the right time and avoid evil; do not bring shame upon yourself. {4:19} Understand that there is a shame that leads to sin, but there is also a shame that brings honor and favor. {4:20} Do not show favoritism to your own detriment, nor deference that leads to your downfall. {4:21} Speak up when it matters and do not hide your wisdom; for wisdom is recognized through words and learning through articulate speech. {4:22} Always speak the truth and be aware of your limitations. {4:23} Do not hesitate to confess your mistakes, and do not attempt to resist inevitable consequences. {4:24} Avoid associating with foolish individuals or showing undue favor to those in power. {4:25} Stand firm for truth, even if it means facing adversity, and trust that the Lord will defend you. {4:26} Be careful with your words and diligent in your actions; do not be reckless or lazy. {4:27} Do not be overly critical or domineering in your household or with your servants. {4:28} Do not seek to take more than you give; be fair in all your dealings.

{5:1} Do not place your trust in wealth, and never say, "I have enough." {5:2} Do not follow your own desires and strengths, walking in the ways of your heart's cravings. {5:3} Do not arrogantly declare, "Who can control me?" For the Lord will surely hold you accountable. {5:4} Do not think lightly of your sins, saying, "I sinned, but nothing happened to me." The Lord is patient, but His justice will not delay forever. {5:5} Do not presume on forgiveness to continue sinning; do not add sin upon sin. {5:6} Do not assume, "God's mercy is vast; He will forgive my many sins," for His mercy and wrath are both present, and His anger rests on those who persist in sin. {5:7} Do not procrastinate turning to the Lord; do not delay day after day. For suddenly His wrath may be unleashed, and in the day of reckoning, you may face destruction. {5:8} Do not rely on ill-gotten wealth, for it will not save you in times of trouble. {5:9} Do not be fickle, blown about by every wind, nor follow every path; such behavior belongs to the deceitful. {5:10} Be firm in your understanding, and let your words be consistent and true. {5:11} Be quick to listen and deliberate in your responses. {5:12} If you have wisdom, speak to your neighbor; if not, hold your tongue. {5:13} Understand that both glory and disgrace come from speech; a person's tongue can lead to their downfall. {5:14} Do not be known as a slanderer or lie in wait with deceitful words; shame awaits those who deceive, and severe judgment for the dishonest. {5:15} Whether in significant matters or small, conduct yourself rightly and with integrity.

{6:1} Do not turn a friend into an enemy; a tarnished reputation brings shame and scorn upon the deceitful. {6:2} Do not pride yourself on your own counsel, lest you be torn apart like a bull in its fury. {6:3} You will consume your own leaves and ruin your own fruit, leaving yourself like a withered tree. {6:4} A wicked soul destroys its owner and becomes a laughingstock to enemies. {6:5} A pleasant voice attracts friends, and a gracious tongue brings forth kindness. {6:6} May you have many who are at peace with you, but let your trusted advisors be few among many. {6:7} When you make a friend, test him thoroughly; do not hastily trust him. {6:8} Some friends are only there when it suits them, but vanish in times of trouble. {6:9} Others change into enemies, betraying secrets to your disgrace. {6:10} Some are companions at the table but disappear in adversity. {6:11} They may act as equals in prosperity and be familiar with your servants. {6:12} Yet in adversity, they turn against you and avoid your presence. {6:13} Stay wary of your enemies and be cautious with your friends. {6:14} A faithful friend is a strong defense; finding one is like finding a treasure. {6:15} There is nothing more valuable than a faithful friend; no measurement can define their worth. {6:16} A faithful friend is a life-giving remedy; those who fear the Lord will find such a friend. {6:17} Those who fear the Lord choose their friends wisely, for their character reflects their neighbor's. {6:18} My son, seek instruction from youth onward; as you grow older, you will gain wisdom. {6:19} Approach wisdom diligently, like a farmer sowing seeds, and await a rich harvest. In her service, you will toil briefly, soon reaping abundant rewards. {6:20} To the unlearned, wisdom may seem harsh; the weak may not endure her discipline. {6:21} She tests them rigorously, and they quickly abandon her. {6:22} Wisdom, true to her name, is not easily found by many. {6:23} Listen, my son, and heed my counsel; do not reject my advice. {6:24} Embrace her teachings willingly, like putting on shackles and a collar. {6:25} Shoulder her burden and do not complain about her restraints. {6:26} Dedicate yourself wholeheartedly to her ways, and steadfastly keep her commands. {6:27} Seek her diligently, and she will reveal herself to you; once you grasp her, do not let go. {6:28} In the end, you will find rest in her, and she will transform into joy for you. {6:29} Her shackles will become your strong defense, and her collar a splendid garment. {6:30} Her yoke is like a golden ornament, her bonds like a cord of blue. {6:31} You will wear her like a glorious robe and crown yourself with joy. {6:32} If you desire to learn, my son, you will be taught; if you apply yourself, you will become wise. {6:33} Love listening and you will gain knowledge; incline your ear and you will become wise. {6:34} Stand among the elders who are wise; cling to them and learn from them. {6:35} Be eager to hear every story and do not let wise sayings slip away. {6:36} Seek out the company of intelligent men; let their doorstep be worn by your feet. {6:37} Reflect on the Lord's commandments and meditate on his statutes continually. He will enlighten your mind and grant you wisdom as you desire.

{7:1} Avoid evil, and you will avoid trouble. {7:2} Stay clear of wrongdoing, and it will steer clear of you. {7:3} My child, do not sow the seeds of injustice, for they will yield a bitter harvest sevenfold. {7:4} Do not seek the highest positions from the Lord or seek seats of honor from kings. {7:5} Do not flaunt your righteousness before the Lord or display your wisdom before kings. {7:6} Refrain from aspiring to be a judge, lest you are unable to remove injustice, show favoritism to the powerful, and tarnish your integrity. {7:7} Do not offend the public, nor bring disgrace upon yourself among the people. {7:8} Do not repeat your sins; even one will not go unpunished. {7:9} Do not assume your gifts will appease God; offerings to the Most High must be sincere. {7:10} Do not be timid in prayer or neglect to give to those in need. {7:11} Do not mock a person in distress, for there is One who lifts up and humbles. {7:12} Do not deceive your brother or betray a friend with falsehoods. {7:13} Avoid lying altogether, for falsehood serves no good purpose. {7:14} Do not babble in the presence of elders or repeat yourself in prayer. {7:15} Do not despise hard work or the toil of farming, which are ordained by the Most High. {7:16} Do not associate with sinners; remember that judgment is swift. {7:17} Humble yourself deeply, for the punishment of the ungodly is severe. {7:18} Do not trade a friend for money or a true brother for gold. {7:19} Do not neglect a wise and virtuous wife, for her worth exceeds that of gold. {7:20} Treat your faithful servant or hired worker with respect; do not mistreat them. {7:21} Value an intelligent servant and do not withhold their freedom. {7:22} Care for your livestock; if they are profitable, keep them well. {7:23} Discipline your children and teach them obedience from a young age. {7:24} Protect your daughters' chastity; do not be too lenient with them. {7:25} Give your daughter in marriage to a worthy man; it is a noble duty fulfilled. {7:26} If you have a good wife, cherish her; do not reject her, but do not trust a wife who despises you. {7:27} Honor your father with all your heart; do not forget your mother's labor pains. {7:28} Remember, through your parents you came into the world; what can you give them that equals their gift to you? {7:29} Fear the Lord with all your soul and honor his priests. {7:30} Love your Maker with all your might and do not forsake his ministers. {7:31} Fear the Lord and honor the priest; fulfill your obligations to them: the first fruits, offerings, sacrifices, and holy gifts. {7:32} Reach out to the poor so that your blessings may be complete. {7:33} Give generously to the living and do not withhold kindness from the departed. {7:34} Comfort those who mourn and do not avoid those in sorrow. {7:35} Visit the sick without hesitation, for such acts are esteemed. {7:36} Remember the end of your life in all you do, and you will avoid sin.

{8:1} Do not challenge a powerful person, lest you find yourself in his grasp. {8:2} Avoid disputes with the wealthy, for their resources can overwhelm yours; gold has corrupted many and swayed the minds of kings. {8:3} Do not engage in arguments with a gossiper, nor add fuel to their fire. [8:4] Avoid jesting with someone lacking manners, lest it bring shame upon your ancestors. {8:5} Do not rebuke someone turning away from sin; remember we all deserve judgment. {8:6} Respect the elderly, for we all age; do not scorn them in their old age. {8:7} Do not rejoice at anyone's death; remember that death comes to us all. {8:8} Do not disregard the teachings of wise sages; immerse yourself in their wisdom, for it will teach you how to serve great leaders. {8:9} Honor the words of the aged, for they learned from their ancestors; their wisdom will guide you in times of need. {8:10} Do not provoke a sinner, lest you get caught in their destructive ways. {8:11} Do not walk away from an insolent person, lest they plot against you in revenge. {8:12} Do not lend to someone more powerful than you; if you do, treat it as lost. {8:13} Do not cosign beyond your means; if you must, prepare to fulfill your obligation. {8:14} Avoid legal disputes with a judge, for their position may bias the outcome. {8:15} Do not travel with a reckless person, for their actions may endanger you both. {8:16} Do not provoke an angry person, nor venture into desolate places with them; their rage is uncontrollable, and danger lurks. {8:17} Do not seek counsel from a fool, for they cannot keep secrets. {8:18} Do not share confidential matters in front of strangers, for you cannot predict what they will reveal. {8:19} Guard your thoughts from everyone, lest you lose your good fortune.

{9:1} Do not harbor jealousy toward your wife, nor teach her anything that could harm you both. {9:2} Do not surrender yourself to a woman to the point where she dominates your strength. {9:3} Avoid encounters with loose women, lest you fall into their traps. {9:4} Stay away from women who sing enticingly, for they may draw you into their schemes. {9:5} Do not gaze too intently at a virgin, lest you stumble and face consequences. {9:6} Do not engage with harlots, lest you forfeit your inheritance. {9:7} Avoid wandering the streets and deserted areas of a city without purpose. {9:8} Turn your eyes away from seductive women; do not let beauty allure you, for many have been ensnared by it, sparking passion like a fire. {9:9} Never dine alone with another man's wife, nor revel with her over wine; lest your heart be led astray, and you find yourself in ruin. {9:10} Do not forsake an old friend for a new one; a longstanding friendship is precious, like aged wine that brings pleasure. {9:11} Do not envy the success of sinners, for their ultimate fate is uncertain. {9:12} Do not take pleasure in what pleases the ungodly, for they will not escape judgment forever. {9:13} Stay away from those with the power to kill, and you will avoid the fear of death. If you must approach them, be cautious, lest they take your life unexpectedly. Recognize the dangers around you as you move through life. {9:14} Strive to know your neighbors well and seek counsel from the wise. {9:15} Engage in conversations with those of understanding, and let your discussions revolve around the teachings of the Most High. {9:16} Choose righteous men as your companions, and boast in reverence for the Lord. {9:17} A leader is esteemed for his wise words, just as a craftsman is praised for his skill. {9:18} Be cautious of those who speak recklessly; they may stir fear and earn disdain in their community.

{10:1} A wise leader educates his people, and an understanding ruler brings order to his city. {10:2} The character of a leader reflects in his officials, just as the nature of a ruler shapes his citizens. {10:3} A reckless king brings ruin to his people, but a city prospers under wise governance. {10:4} The governance of the earth is entrusted to the Lord, who appoints the right leaders for each time. {10:5} Success and honor come from the Lord's hand; he bestows glory upon those who serve faithfully. {10:6} Do not harbor anger towards your neighbor for any harm, and avoid arrogance in your actions. {10:7} Pride is detestable to the Lord and to people alike, and injustice is abhorrent to both. {10:8} Sovereignty shifts among nations due to injustice, arrogance, and wealth. {10:9} How can mortals, made of dust and ashes, be proud? Even in life, their bodies decay. {10:10} Prolonged illness confounds physicians; today's king may not see tomorrow. {10:11} When a person dies, they return to the dust, inheriting worms and decay. {10:12} Pride begins when one turns away from the Lord; abandoning their Maker leads to sin. {10:13} Pride's root is in sin, and those who embrace it bring forth abominations. Thus, the Lord brings extraordinary afflictions upon them, leading to their destruction. {10:14} The Lord humbles the thrones of rulers and replaces them with the lowly. {10:15} He uproots the nations' foundations and plants the humble in their place. {10:16} The Lord overturns nations and destroys them to their very core. {10:17} He removes some and obliterates their memory from the earth. {10:18} Pride was not made for humans, nor wrath for those born of women. {10:19} Who deserves honor? Humanity does. Who deserves honor? Those who fear the Lord. Who deserves dishonor? Humanity does. Who deserves dishonor? Those who break the commandments. {10:20} Among brothers, the leader who fears the Lord is esteemed, and in his eyes, {10:21} those who fear the Lord are honored. {10:22} Whether rich, eminent, or poor, their glory lies in fearing the Lord. {10:23} It's wrong to despise an intelligent poor person, just as it's improper to honor a sinful one. {10:24} Noblemen, judges, and rulers are honored, yet none surpasses the one who fears the Lord. {10:25} Free people serve a wise servant willingly, and a person of understanding does not complain. {10:26} Do not flaunt your wisdom in your work, nor seek glory when in need. {10:27} It's better to work and have plenty than to boast while lacking bread. {10:28} My child, embrace humility and let honor come to you naturally. {10:29} Who will justify a person who sins against themselves? And who will honor someone who dishonors their own life? {10:30} A poor person is honored for their knowledge, while a rich person is honored for their wealth. {10:31} A person honored in poverty, how much more in wealth! And a person dishonored in wealth, how much more in poverty!

{11:1} Humility uplifts a person's wisdom and places them among the esteemed. {11:2} Do not praise someone solely for their appearance, nor despise them because of how they look. {11:3} The bee, though small, produces the best of sweet things among flying creatures. {11:4} Refrain from boasting about fine clothes or exalting yourself when honored, for the Lord's works are marvelous and beyond human comprehension. {11:5} Many kings have sat on the ground in humility, while those never considered have worn crowns. {11:6} Numerous rulers have faced great disgrace, and illustrious individuals have been handed over to others. {11:7} Investigate thoroughly before finding fault; first understand, then offer criticism. {11:8} Listen before responding, and do not interrupt a speaker in the middle of their words. {11:9} Avoid arguing over matters that do not concern you, and refrain from sitting with sinners in judgment. {11:10} My child, do not overwhelm yourself with too many tasks; pursuing too much can lead to punishment, without escape. {11:11} Some toil tirelessly yet remain in need, while others, lacking strength, find favor in the Lord's eyes; he lifts them from their lowly state, amazing many. {11:12} Good and bad, life and death, poverty and wealth—all come from the Lord. {11:13} The Lord's gifts endure for the godly, and what he approves achieves lasting success. {11:14} Diligence and self-denial enrich a person, and this is their reward; yet they cannot predict when they will leave their wealth to others and pass away. {11:15} Remain steadfast in your commitments and persevere in your work throughout your life. {11:16} Do not marvel at the success of sinners; trust in the Lord and continue your labor. {11:17} Enriching a poor person swiftly and unexpectedly is easy in the Lord's sight. {11:18} The Lord's blessing is the reward of the godly, flourishing quickly under God's hand. {11:19} Do not speculate about future needs or prosperity; trust in the Lord's provision. {11:20} Do not assume you have enough, or that calamity cannot befall you in the future. {11:21} In times of prosperity, adversity is forgotten, and in adversity, prosperity is not remembered. {11:22} The Lord easily rewards each person according to their conduct on the day of judgment. {11:23} Temporary hardship makes luxury fade, and a person's deeds are revealed at life's end. {11:24} Do not judge anyone as happy until their life's end, as a person's legacy is seen through their children. {11:25} Do not welcome every person into your home, for many are deceitful in their intentions. {11:26} The mind of a proud person is like a decoy partridge in a cage, observing weaknesses like a spy. {11:27} Such individuals lie in wait, turning good deeds into evil and attaching blame to noble actions. {11:28} From a small spark, great fires can arise, and a sinner plots to shed blood. {11:29} Beware of scoundrels who devise evil, lest they leave a lasting stain on you. {11:30} Hosting a stranger may bring disturbance and estrangement from your family.

{12:1} When you do a kindness, be mindful of whom you are helping, and you will receive thanks for your good deeds. {12:2} Show kindness to a righteous person, and you will be rewarded—either by them or by the Most High. {12:3} No good comes to those who persist in evil or refuse to give to the needy. {12:4} Give to the righteous, but withhold assistance from the sinner. {12:5} Help the humble, but do not support the ungodly; refrain from giving them food, lest they use it against you. The evil they return for your kindness will be twice as much. {12:6} The Most High despises sinners and will punish the ungodly. {12:7} Support the virtuous, but do not aid the sinner. {12:8} True friends are not just there in times of prosperity; even in adversity, an enemy may reveal themselves. {12:9} Enemies may be upset by your success, and even friends may distance themselves in your hard times. {12:10} Never fully trust your enemy; their wickedness corrodes like rust on copper. {12:11} Even if they humble themselves and act submissive, be cautious; it's like polishing a mirror that retains its tarnish. {12:12} Do not place your enemy close, lest they undermine and usurp your position. Avoid seating them at your right hand, as they may covet your place of honor. {12:13} Who pities a snake charmer bitten by a serpent, or anyone who recklessly approaches wild beasts? {12:14} Similarly, no one sympathizes with a person who associates with sinners and becomes entangled in their wrongdoing. {12:15} Initially, they may stand by you, but they will abandon you at the first sign of trouble. {12:16} An enemy may speak kindly with their lips, but in their heart, they scheme your downfall; they may shed tears, but given the chance, they thirst for your harm. {12:17} If calamity strikes, they will be there before you, pretending to assist while actually tripping you up. {12:18} They will shake their head, clap their hands, whisper deceitfully, and change their expression—all while plotting against you.

{13:1} If you touch pitch, you'll be tainted, and associating with a proud man will make you like him. {13:2} Don't burden yourself beyond your strength, nor befriend someone wealthier and mightier than you. How can a clay pot mingle with an iron kettle? The pot will collide and shatter. {13:3} A wealthy man may wrong others and heap insults, while a poor man suffers and must apologize. {13:4} The rich will exploit you if you're useful, but abandon you in need. {13:5} They'll stay when you own something, drain your resources without care. {13:6} Deceptive when they need you, smiling and offering hope. Kind words turn to mockery after draining you two or three times, then they'll scorn you. {13:7} Beware, don't be misled or humiliated at their feasts. {13:8} When a powerful invites, be cautious; they'll invite you more. {13:9} Don't push too hard or stay distant, lest you're rebuffed or forgotten. {13:10} Don't treat them as equals or trust their words; they test with much talk while smiling. {13:11} Cruel are those who can't keep their words, ready to harm or imprison. {13:12} Keep silent, be vigilant, your downfall walks with you. {13:13} Creatures love their kind {13:14}, people their neighbors. {13:15} All beings group by type, people by likeness. {13:16} A wolf and lamb don't fellowship, nor sinner and godly. {13:17} A hyena and dog lack peace, as do rich and poor. {13:18} Wild asses to lions, poor to rich — all prey. {13:19} Prideful abhors humility, rich despise poor. {13:20} Rich lean on friends, poor are pushed away. {13:21} Rich stumble, many defend; poor, they reproach. {13:22} Rich speak, praised; poor, ignored. {13:23} Rich talk, honored; poor, mocked. {13:24} Rich with clean riches good, poor evil in ungodly eyes. {13:25} Heart changes face for good or ill. {13:26} Cheerful heart shows; proverbs need deep thought.

{14:1} Happy is the person who speaks wisely and avoids the grief of sin. {14:2} Blessed is one whose heart is clear, who maintains hope steadfastly. {14:3} Wealth does not suit a miserly soul; what good is property to an envious person? {14:4} Those who amass by depriving themselves only accumulate for others; their goods sustain the luxury of others. {14:5} If a person is stingy with themselves, how can they be generous to others? They won't even enjoy their own wealth. {14:6} There's no one more miserly than someone who begrudges themselves, and this is their own punishment. {14:7} Even if they do good, it's unintentional and exposes their inner stinginess. {14:8} Evil is the person with a grudging eye, always turning away and ignoring others. {14:9} A greedy person's eye is never satisfied, and their injustice eats away at their soul. {14:10} A stingy person begrudges bread, and their table is always lacking. {14:11} My child, treat yourself well according to your means, and offer worthy gifts to the Lord. {14:12} Remember, death comes without delay, and Hades awaits, its decree unknown. {14:13} Do good to a friend before you die; reach out and give generously while you can. {14:14} Don't miss out on a happy day; don't let desired good pass you by. {14:15} Will you leave the fruit of your labor to others, and let your hard-earned wealth be divided by chance? {14:16} Give, take, but don't deceive yourself; in the afterlife, luxury is not found. {14:17} Every living being grows old like a garment; death is inevitable, as decreed long ago. {14:18} Like leaves on a tree that fall and are replaced, so are the generations of humanity: one passes, another arrives. {14:19} Everything created eventually decays and disappears, including those who made them. {14:20} Blessed is the one who ponders wisdom and reasons wisely. {14:21} Those who reflect on wisdom's ways will uncover her secrets. {14:22} Pursue wisdom diligently, like a hunter on her trail. {14:23} Peer through her windows, listen at her doors; {14:24} camp near her house, secure your tent pegs to her walls. {14:25} Dwell close to her, find lodging in her sanctuary; {14:26} shelter your children under her guidance, camp beneath her branches. {14:27} In her shade, find refuge from life's heat, and dwell in her glorious wisdom.

{15:1} The person who reveres the Lord will do this, and those who hold fast to his teachings will gain wisdom. {15:2} Wisdom will come to meet them like a caring mother, and like a devoted spouse, she will embrace them warmly. {15:3} She will nourish them with the bread of understanding and quench their thirst with the water of wisdom. {15:4} They will lean on her and never stumble, relying on her steadfast guidance without shame. {15:5} Wisdom will elevate them among their peers, and empower them to speak confidently in public settings. {15:6} They will find joy and receive a crown of honor, establishing a name that endures forever. {15:7} Foolish individuals will never grasp her, and those steeped in sin will remain blind to her presence. {15:8} She keeps her distance from the prideful and is never sought after by liars. {15:9} Sinners have no business singing praises, for such acts are not ordained by the Lord. {15:10} True hymns of praise are uttered with wisdom, and the Lord blesses those who offer them sincerely. {15:11} Do not blame the Lord for straying from the right path; he does not lead anyone astray. {15:12} Nor should one claim that the Lord compelled them into sinful ways; he has no use for sinners. {15:13} The Lord detests all forms of abomination, and those who fear him do not embrace such things. {15:14} It was the Lord who created humanity from the beginning, granting them free will and the power of choice. {15:15} Keeping the commandments is within your capability; acting with integrity is your own decision. {15:16} God has set before you choices akin to fire and water; it is up to you to reach out for whichever you desire. {15:17} Life and death are laid out before every person, and each chooses their own path. {15:18} The wisdom of the Lord is immense; his power is vast, and he sees everything. {15:19} His gaze is upon those who reverence him, and he comprehends every deed of humankind. {15:20} God has not ordained anyone to be ungodly, nor has he granted permission for anyone to sin.

{16:1} Do not desire a multitude of worthless children, nor take joy in ungodly offspring. {16:2} Even if they increase, do not rejoice in them unless they fear the Lord. {16:3} Do not trust in their longevity or depend on their numbers; for one righteous child is better than a thousand, and to have no children is better than to raise ungodly ones. {16:4} Through one person of understanding, a city can thrive, but by a tribe of lawless people it will be laid waste. {16:5} I have seen many such things with my own eyes, and I have heard even more astounding stories. {16:6} In gatherings of sinners, strife erupts like fire, and among rebellious nations, divine wrath ignites. {16:7} The ancient giants were not spared despite their strength; {16:8} nor were the neighbors of Lot spared, condemned for their insolence. {16:9} A nation given over to destruction received no pity, nor did those destroyed in their sins. {16:10} Neither did the six hundred thousand foot soldiers rebelled in stubbornness escape divine judgment. {16:11} Even if there is only one obstinate person, it will be a marvel if he goes unpunished, for the Lord balances mercy and wrath. {16:12} As vast as his mercy is, so too is his correction; he judges each person according to their deeds. {16:13} The sinner will not escape with his plunder, and the patience of the godly will not be in vain. {16:14} God will make room for every act of mercy; {16:15} everyone will receive, {16:16} according to their deeds. {16:17} Do not think, "I can hide from the Lord; who will remember me among so many? What is my soul in this vast creation?" {16:18} Heaven, highest heaven, abyss, and earth tremble at his presence. {16:19} Mountains and the foundations of the earth quake when he looks upon them. {16:20} Who comprehends his ways? His works are mostly concealed like an unseen tempest. {16:21} Who can declare his acts of justice or anticipate them? The covenant seems distant. {16:22} These are the thoughts of the foolish and senseless, lacking understanding. {16:23} Listen to me, my child, and gain wisdom; pay attention to my words. {16:24} I will impart knowledge and declare it accurately. {16:25} The Lord's works have existed since the beginning of creation; he established their order and assigned their roles. {16:26} He organized them in an eternal plan, and they fulfill their purpose across generations, never tiring or hungering, never ceasing their labor. {16:27} They do not jostle each other or disobey his commands. {16:28} After creating them, the Lord filled the earth with his blessings; {16:29} he covered its surface with diverse living beings, and to him they return.

{17:1} The Lord formed humanity from the dust of the earth, and to the earth they return. {17:2} He granted them a few days, a limited span, yet bestowed upon them authority over all earthly things. {17:3} Endowing them with strength resembling his own, he fashioned them in his image. {17:4} All living creatures fear them; {17:5} he entrusted them with dominion over beasts and birds. {17:6} He gave them tongues to speak, eyes to see, ears to hear, and minds to reason. {17:7} Filling them with knowledge and understanding, he revealed to them the distinctions between good and evil. {17:8} He scrutinizes their hearts to reveal the magnificence, {17:9} of his works. {17:10} They extol his holy name and declare the greatness of his deeds. {17:11} He bestowed wisdom upon them and entrusted them with the law of life. {17:12} Establishing an eternal covenant with them, he imparted his judgments. {17:13} They beheld his glorious majesty, and heard the splendor of his voice. {17:14} He warned them, "Beware of all unrighteousness," and commanded them regarding their neighbors. {17:15} Their actions are always before him; {17:16} nothing is hidden from his sight. {17:17} He appointed rulers over every nation, but Israel is his chosen inheritance. {17:18} All their deeds are like the sun in his sight; his gaze is continually upon their paths. {17:19} Their sins are not concealed from him; all their wrongdoing is known to the Lord. {17:20} A person's charity is like a seal of approval from the Lord; he treasures their acts of kindness like the apple of his eye. {17:21} In due time he will repay them and bring their reward upon their heads. {17:22} Yet to those who repent, he grants forgiveness and strengthens those whose endurance is faltering. {17:23} Turn to the Lord, forsake your sins, pray in his presence, and diminish your offenses. {17:24} Return to the Most High, turn away from iniquity, and despise abominations. {17:25} Who will sing praises to the Most High in the realm of the dead, as the living do with gratitude? {17:26} From the dead, thanksgiving ceases as if they never existed; only the living can sing the Lord's praises. {17:27} How immense is the Lord's mercy and forgiveness for those who turn to him! {17:28} For not all things are possible for humans, since mortals are not immortal. {17:29} What is brighter than the sun? Yet its light dims. Similarly, flesh and blood devise evil. {17:30} He marshals the heavenly host, yet all humans are mere dust and ashes.

{18:1} The Eternal One, who lives forever, {18:2} created the entire universe; {18:3} he alone is righteous and deserving of praise. {18:4} No one has been given authority to proclaim all his works, nor can anyone fully comprehend his mighty deeds. {18:5} Who can measure his majestic power, or fully recount his boundless mercies? {18:6} His wonders cannot be diminished or increased, nor can they be fully traced by mortal minds. {18:7} When a person's life ends, it marks only the beginning, and ceasing brings perplexity. {18:8} What is humanity, and what purpose do they serve? What defines their good and evil deeds? {18:9} The span of a person's days may seem long if they reach a hundred years, yet in the vast expanse of eternity, it is as brief as a drop of water from the sea or a grain of sand. {18:10} Therefore, the Lord shows patience and pours out abundant mercy upon them. {18:11} He knows their frailty and anticipates their struggles; {18:12} thus, he grants forgiveness generously. {18:13} Human compassion is for neighbors, but the Lord's compassion extends to all living beings. He corrects, instructs, and guides them back, like a shepherd with his flock. {18:14} He shows favor to those who accept his discipline and eagerly seek his guidance. {18:15} My child, do not mix reproach with your good deeds, nor cause sorrow with your words when presenting a gift. {18:16} Just as dew cools the scorching heat, a gentle word is more valuable than any gift. {18:17} Indeed, a kind word surpasses even the finest present; both are found in a gracious person. {18:18} A fool is disrespectful and ungrateful, and a gift from a begrudging person dims the eyes. {18:19} Before speaking, learn; before falling ill, take care of your health. {18:20} Before judgment, examine yourself; in the hour of visitation, seek forgiveness. {18:21} Before illness strikes, humble yourself; when tempted to sin, turn away. {18:22} Do not delay in fulfilling a vow, nor wait until death to be released from it. {18:23} Before making a vow, prepare yourself; do not test the Lord like a fool. {18:24} Consider his wrath on the day of death and the moment of reckoning when he turns away. {18:25} In times of plenty, remember hunger; in days of wealth, consider poverty and need. {18:26} From morning till night, circumstances change swiftly, observed by the Lord. {18:27} A wise person exercises caution in all things, guarding against wrongdoing in times of sin. {18:28} Every intelligent person seeks wisdom and praises those who find it. {18:29} Those who comprehend proverbs become skilled themselves and share apt sayings. {18:30} Control your base desires; restrain your appetites. {18:31} Indulging in base desires only invites ridicule from your enemies. {18:32} Avoid excessive luxury, lest it impoverish you with its costs. {18:33} Do not become a beggar by feasting on borrowed money when your purse is empty.

{19:1} A worker who indulges in drunkenness will never prosper; one who disregards small responsibilities will fail gradually. {19:2} Wine and women lead wise men astray; associating with prostitutes is extremely reckless. {19:3} Decay and worms await the reckless soul, ready to snatch it away. {19:4} Trusting others too quickly shows a lack of judgment, and harming oneself through sin is self-destructive. {19:5} Those who delight in wickedness will face condemnation. {19:6} Avoiding gossip diminishes evil; hating gossip reduces its impact. {19:7} Never repeat a conversation unnecessarily; by keeping it to yourself, you avoid unnecessary trouble. {19:8} Whether with friend or foe, do not spread rumors; unless it would be a sin for you, keep it to yourself. {19:9} Someone may have overheard and observed you; when the time comes, they may hold it against you. {19:10} If you hear something, let it stay with you; be strong, it won't overwhelm you. {19:11} A fool suffers greatly from words, much like labor pains for a woman. {19:12} A foolish word is like an arrow lodged in the thigh; it causes unnecessary pain. {19:13} Question a friend before jumping to conclusions; perhaps they did not do what you heard. {19:14} Similarly, clarify with a neighbor before assuming they said something; if they did, help them avoid such speech in the future. {19:15} Verify information before believing it; much gossip is slanderous and unreliable. {19:16} Everyone slips with their tongue at times; who has never made a verbal mistake? {19:17} Discuss matters with your neighbor before threatening them; let the law of the Most High determine justice. {19:18} True wisdom begins with reverence for the Lord, and fulfilling the law embodies true wisdom. {19:19} Knowledge of wickedness is not wisdom, and planning sin lacks prudence. {19:20} Some cleverness is detestable, but a fool simply lacks wisdom. {19:21} It's better to be a God-fearing person lacking intelligence than a cunning lawbreaker. {19:22} There's a kind of cunning that's meticulous yet unjust, and some twist kindness to achieve selfish ends. {19:23} There are those who feign mourning but harbor deceit within. {19:24} They pretend not to hear and hide their face, but behind the scenes, they act before you notice. {19:25} If they lack opportunity to sin due to weakness, they eagerly seize it when it arises. {19:26} A person's character is evident from their appearance, and a wise person's demeanor speaks volumes when you meet them. {19:27} How someone dresses, laughs openly, and walks reveals much about their true nature.

{20:1} There are rebukes that come too late, and there are those who stay silent yet are wise. {20:2} It's far better to offer constructive criticism than to harbor anger, {20:3} and admitting one's faults prevents greater loss. {20:4} A person who uses violence to enforce judgments is like a eunuch's inappropriate desire for a maiden—it's unnatural and wrong. {20:5} Some gain respect by staying silent, while others are disliked for talking too much. {20:6} One stays quiet because they have no answer, another because they know when to speak. {20:7} A wise person waits for the right moment to speak, but a boastful fool rushes in regardless. {20:8} Too many words breed contempt, and interrupting others breeds hatred. {20:9} Fortune can come from adversity, and a sudden windfall can lead to loss. {20:10} There are gifts that bring no benefit, and there are gifts that yield double in return. {20:11} Some suffer losses due to pride, while others rise from humble beginnings. {20:12} Buying much for little can lead to paying sevenfold in consequences. {20:13} The wise earn love through their words, but fools waste courtesies. {20:14} A fool's gift is worthless; they have many eyes but see not the heart. {20:15} They give little and demand much, speaking loudly like a herald; today they lend, tomorrow they demand repayment—such a person is detestable. {20:16} A fool complains of having no friends and receives ingratitude for their deeds; those who benefit from their generosity speak ill of them. {20:17} They are often mocked and ridiculed. {20:18} A slip on the pavement is better than a slip of the tongue; the downfall of the wicked comes swiftly. {20:19} An ungracious person is like an ill-timed story, always on the lips of the ignorant. {20:20} A proverb from a fool's lips is rejected, for they lack timing. {20:21} Poverty may prevent someone from sinning, and in rest, they find peace without regret. {20:22} Shame can lead to a person's downfall, as can foolish actions. {20:23} Promises made out of shame can turn a friend into an enemy needlessly. {20:24} Lies stain a person's character and are often on the lips of the ignorant. {20:25} A thief is more tolerable than a habitual liar, but both face ruin. {20:26} The deceitful bring disgrace upon themselves, and their shame is constant. {20:27} Speaking wisely advances one's standing, and the wise are esteemed by great people. {20:28} Those who work diligently reap a bountiful harvest, and those who please influential individuals make amends for past wrongs. {20:29} Gifts blind the wise and silence criticism, much like a muzzle silencing reproofs. {20:30} Hidden wisdom and unseen treasure—what value do they hold? {20:31} It's better to conceal one's folly than to hide one's wisdom.

{21:1} Have you made mistakes, my child? Cease from them and pray for forgiveness for your past sins. {21:2} Avoid sin like you would a venomous snake; for if you draw near to sin, it will strike you with teeth like a lion's, destroying souls. {21:3} Lawlessness is like a double-edged sword; its wounds have no remedy. {21:4} Fear and violence plunder wealth; thus the homes of the arrogant will be ruined. {21:5} The prayer of a humble person rises directly to God's ears, and justice comes swiftly. {21:6} Whoever despises correction follows the path of sinners, but those who fear the Lord repent sincerely. {21:7} A person known for eloquence is recognized from afar, but the wise person, when they stumble, learns from it. {21:8} Building a house with ill-gotten gains is like gathering stones for one's own tomb. {21:9} A gathering of the wicked is like dry tinder; their end is a blazing fire. {21:10} The path of sinners seems smooth, but it leads to the depths of Hades. {21:11} Those who keep the law control their thoughts, and wisdom is the essence of fearing the Lord. {21:12} A stubborn person cannot be taught, and misguided cleverness only breeds bitterness. {21:13} The knowledge of the wise grows like a flood, and their counsel flows like a continuous spring. {21:14} The mind of a fool is like a broken jar—incapable of holding knowledge. {21:15} When a discerning person hears wisdom, they appreciate it and build upon it; but a fool hears it and dismisses it without thought. {21:16} A fool's words burden others like a weight on a journey, but the speech of the intelligent brings delight. {21:17} The words of a sensible person are sought in the assembly, and pondered deeply. {21:18} Wisdom is lost on a fool like a house that has vanished; the ignorant engage in meaningless chatter. {21:19} To a senseless person, education feels like shackles on their feet and chains on their hands. {21:20} A fool laughs loudly, but a wise person smiles calmly. {21:21} Education adorns a sensible person like a golden ornament or a bracelet on the arm. {21:22} A fool rushes into a house, but a prudent person waits respectfully. {21:23} A crude person peers through the door, but a cultured person stands outside with respect. {21:24} It's rude to eavesdrop, and a discreet person is troubled by disgrace. {21:25} Strangers speak carelessly, but the words of the wise are measured and considered. {21:26} Fools speak whatever comes to mind, but wise individuals think before they speak. {21:27} When a wicked person curses their enemy, they curse themselves. {21:28} Gossip stains the soul and brings hatred upon oneself in the community.

{22:1} The lazy person is like a filthy stone that everyone mocks for its disgrace. {22:2} The indolent are like the filth of dung heaps; anyone who touches them will quickly shake them off. {22:3} It brings shame to have an undisciplined son, and having a daughter is seen as a loss. {22:4} A sensible daughter brings honor by finding a worthy husband, but a shameful one causes grief to her father. {22:5} An impudent daughter disgraces both her father and her husband, and she will be scorned by both. {22:6} Speaking out of turn is like inappropriate music in times of mourning, but discipline and correction are wisdom at all times. {22:7} Teaching a fool is like gluing broken pottery together or waking up someone deep in sleep. {22:8} Telling a story to a fool is like speaking to someone who is half-asleep; {22:9} at the end, he will ask, "What was that?" {22:10} Mourn for the dead because they have lost the light, and mourn for the fool {22:11} because he lacks understanding; mourn less for the dead because they have found rest, but the life of a fool is worse than death. {22:12} Mourning for the dead lasts seven days, but mourning for a fool or a godless person lasts a lifetime. {22:13} Avoid lengthy conversations with a fool, and do not associate with an unintelligent person; protect yourself from trouble by staying away from him, so you won't be tainted when he shakes off his folly. Avoid him, and you will find peace, never being worn out by his madness. {22:14} What is heavier than lead? Only a fool bears that name. {22:15} Sand, salt, and iron are easier to carry than a stupid person. {22:16} A solidly built beam in a house withstands earthquakes; similarly, a mind firmly set on sound advice will not be afraid in times of crisis. {22:17} A mind focused on intelligent thoughts is like decorative stucco on the wall of a colonnade. {22:18} Fences built on high places cannot withstand the wind; likewise, a timid heart with foolish intentions cannot withstand any fear. {22:19} One who wounds an eye causes tears to flow; one who wounds the heart makes feelings evident. {22:20} Like throwing a stone at birds to scare them away, insulting a friend will break off the friendship. {22:21} Even if you have quarreled with a friend, do not despair; reconciliation is possible. {22:22} If you have spoken against your friend, do not lose hope; reconciliation can still occur. However, speaking ill, boasting, revealing secrets, or betraying trust—all these will drive away any friend. {22:23} Build trust with your neighbor during his times of need, so that you can rejoice together in his prosperity and stand by him in times of trouble to share in his blessings. {22:24} Just as the smoke and vapor from a furnace precede the fire, insults often precede violent conflict. {22:25} I will not hesitate to defend a friend, nor will I shy away from standing by his side; {22:26} but if harm should befall me because of him, those who hear about it will be cautious around him. {22:27} Oh, that I could control my speech and keep a guard over my lips, sealing them with prudence to prevent them from causing my downfall!

{23:1} O Lord, my Father and Ruler of my life, do not abandon me to the counsel of my adversaries, and do not let me stumble because of them! {23:2} Oh, that strict discipline were set over my thoughts, and the wisdom of correction over my mind, so that I may not be spared in my errors and my sins may not go unnoticed. {23:3} Let my mistakes not multiply, nor my sins abound, so that I do not fall before my enemies and give them cause to rejoice over me. {23:4} O Lord, my Father and God, keep pride far from me; {23:5} take away from me evil desires. {23:6} Do not let gluttony or lust overcome me, and do not deliver me over to a shameless soul. {23:7} Hear, my children, and learn wisdom concerning your speech; those who heed it will never be caught in folly. {23:8} Sinners are trapped by their own words; revilers and the arrogant stumble over them. {23:9} Do not make a habit of swearing oaths, nor utter the name of the Holy One thoughtlessly; {23:10} for just as a servant who is continually examined under torture will not escape bruising, so the one who always swears and invokes the Name will not be cleansed from sin. {23:11} A man who frequently swears oaths will accumulate iniquity, and calamity will not leave his house; whether he sins or disregards his oaths, he will suffer; unnecessary swearing will not justify him, and his household will be filled with misfortune. {23:12} There are words that lead to destruction; may they never be found among those who are righteous. For the godly will keep far from all these errors and not be ensnared by sins. {23:13} Do not let lewd and vulgar speech become a habit, for it leads to sinful behavior. {23:14} Remember your parents when you are among important people, lest you act forgetfully and are considered foolish because of your behavior; otherwise, you may regret your existence and curse the day you were born. {23:15} A person accustomed to using insulting words will never find discipline throughout their life. {23:16} Two kinds of people multiply their sins, and a third kind stirs up divine wrath: the soul burning with passion will not be quenched until it is consumed; a man who commits incest will not cease until he is consumed by fire. {23:17} To a fornicator, all pleasures seem sweet; he will continue until death overtakes him. {23:18} A man who breaks his marital vows convinces himself, "No one sees me; darkness hides me, and walls conceal me. Why should I fear? The Most High does not take notice of my sins." {23:19} He fears only the eyes of men, not realizing that the eyes of the Lord are brighter than the sun and see every aspect of human life, even the hidden places. {23:20} Before the universe was created, the Lord knew all things, and so it remains after its completion. {23:21} Such a person will face punishment in the streets of the city, caught unexpectedly where he least expects it. {23:22} The same judgment applies to a woman who abandons her husband and bears children by another man. {23:23} Firstly, she disobeys the law of the Most High; secondly, she betrays her husband; thirdly, she commits adultery and bears children from another man. {23:24} She will be publicly brought to judgment, and her children will suffer the consequences. {23:25} Her offspring will not prosper, and her descendants will not bear fruit. {23:26} Her name will be remembered with shame, and her disgrace will not be forgotten. {23:27} Those who outlive her will learn that nothing surpasses the fear of the Lord and nothing is sweeter than obeying His commandments.

{24:1} Wisdom praises herself and boasts among her people. {24:2} In the assembly of the Most High, she opens her mouth and in the presence of his hosts, she declares: {24:3} "I came forth from the mouth of the Most High, and like a mist, I covered the earth. {24:4} I dwelt in lofty places, and my throne was in a pillar of cloud. {24:5} Alone, I have encircled the vault of heaven and walked in the depths of the abyss. {24:6} I have gained possession in the waves of the sea, throughout the earth, and among every people and nation. {24:7} Among all these, I sought a resting place; I sought where I might reside. {24:8} Then the Creator of all things gave me a command, and the one who formed me assigned a dwelling place. He said, 'Settle in Jacob, and in Israel make your inheritance.' {24:9} From eternity, in the beginning, he created me, and I shall never cease to exist. {24:10} I ministered before him in the holy tabernacle, and I was established in Zion. {24:11} He gave me a resting place in his beloved city, and my dominion was in Jerusalem. {24:12} So I took root among an honored people, in the portion of the Lord, who is their inheritance. {24:13} I grew tall like a cedar in Lebanon, like a cypress on the heights of Hermon. {24:14} I grew like a palm tree in En-gedi, like rose plants in Jericho, like a beautiful olive tree in the field, and like a plane tree I grew tall. {24:15} I spread the aroma of spices like cassia and camel's thorn, like choice myrrh, galbanum, onycha, and stacte, like the fragrance of frankincense in the tabernacle. {24:16} Like a terebinth, I spread out my branches, glorious and graceful. {24:17} I caused loveliness to bud like a vine, {24:18} and my blossoms became abundant fruit. {24:19} "Come to me, you who desire me, and partake of my produce to the full. {24:20} For my memory is sweeter than honey, and my inheritance sweeter than the honeycomb. {24:21} Those who eat of me will hunger for more, and those who drink of me will thirst for more. {24:22} Whoever obeys me will not be put to shame, and those who work with my help will not sin." {24:23} This is the book of the covenant of the Most High God, {24:24} the law that Moses commanded us as an inheritance for the assemblies of Jacob. {24:25} It fills people with wisdom, like the Pishon and like the Tigris at the time of the first fruits. {24:26} It gives understanding, like the Euphrates and like the Jordan at harvest time. {24:27} It makes instruction shine like light, like the Gihon at the time of vintage. {24:28} Just as the first man did not fully know her, nor the last fathom her depths; {24:29} for her thoughts are more abundant than the sea, and her counsel deeper than the great abyss. {24:30} I flowed forth like a canal from a river and like a water channel into a garden. {24:31} I said, "I will water my orchard and saturate my garden plot"; and behold, my canal became a river, and my river became a sea. {24:32} I will again cause instruction to shine like the dawn, and I will make it shine far and wide. {24:33} I will pour out teaching like prophecy, leaving it for all future generations. {24:34} Know that I have not labored for myself alone, but for all who seek wisdom and instruction.

{25:1} My soul finds joy in three things, cherished by both the Lord and humanity: unity among siblings, friendship among neighbors, and harmony between husband and wife. {25:2} There are three types of individuals my soul detests, deeply troubled by their ways: a beggar who is arrogant, a wealthy man who deceives, and an older man who commits adultery without discretion. {25:3} If you have accumulated nothing in your youth, how can you expect to find abundance in your old age? {25:4} How admirable is sound judgment in elderly men, and how fitting for the aged to possess wisdom! {25:5} How commendable is wisdom in the elderly, and understanding and wise counsel in honorable men! {25:6} Rich experience crowns the elderly, and their pride is in their reverence for the Lord. {25:7} With nine reflections I have cheered my heart, and I will speak a tenth with my tongue: a man who delights in his children; a man who lives to see the downfall of his adversaries; {25:8} blessed is he who lives with a wise wife, who has avoided slips of the tongue, and who has not served under a lesser man; {25:9} blessed is he who has gained wisdom, and who speaks to attentive listeners. {25:10} How great is the one who acquires wisdom! But none surpasses the one who fears the Lord. {25:11} The fear of the Lord surpasses everything; {25:12} who can be compared to one who holds fast to it? {25:13} Any wound is better than a wound of the heart; any wickedness, but not the wickedness of a wife; {25:14} any affliction, but not from those who hate; any vengeance, but not the vengeance of enemies; {25:15} there is no venom worse than a snake's, and no wrath worse than an enemy's. {25:16} I would rather dwell with a lion and a dragon than with an evil wife. {25:17} The wickedness of a wife changes her appearance and darkens her face like a bear's. {25:18} Her husband dines among neighbors, sighing bitterly and unable to help it. {25:19} Any sin is trivial compared to a wife's iniquity; may the lot of a sinner be hers! {25:20} A sandy ascent is easier for the feet of the aged than a talkative wife for a quiet husband. {25:21} Do not be ensnared by a woman's beauty, nor desire a woman for her possessions. {25:22} Wrath, insolence, and great disgrace come when a wife supports her husband. {25:23} A downcast mind, a gloomy face, and a wounded heart are caused by an evil wife; drooping hands and weak knees result from a wife who fails to bring joy to her husband. {25:24} From a woman sin had its beginning, and because of her, we all die. {25:25} Do not give water an outlet, nor allow bold speech in an evil wife. {25:26} If she does not go as you direct, separate yourself from her.

{26:1} Blessed is the husband who finds a good wife; his days will be multiplied with happiness and contentment. {26:2} A faithful wife brings joy to her husband, and he will enjoy peace throughout his life. {26:3} A virtuous wife is a precious blessing; she is a gift among the many blessings bestowed upon a man who fears the Lord. {26:4} Whether wealthy or of modest means, his heart is cheerful, and his countenance is bright at all times. {26:5} There are three things that cause my heart anxiety, and a fourth that fills me with dread: the slander of a community, the gathering of a hostile crowd, and false accusations—these are more distressing than death itself. {26:6} Sorrow and anguish come when a wife envies her rival, and her sharp words reveal her discontent to all. {26:7} An evil wife is like an ox yoke that chafes; holding onto her is like grasping a scorpion. {26:8} There is great turmoil when a wife indulges in drunkenness; she does not conceal her shame. {26:9} A wife's unfaithfulness is evident in her lustful eyes; she is known by her flirtatious glances. {26:10} Keep a close watch over a headstrong daughter, lest she take advantage of her freedom to her own detriment. {26:11} Beware of her insolent gaze, and do not be surprised if she acts against you. {26:12} Just as a thirsty traveler eagerly drinks from any water nearby, so will she sit at every corner, ready to engage with anyone who approaches. {26:13} A wife's charm brings delight to her husband, and her wisdom nourishes him. {26:14} A quiet wife is a gift from the Lord, and there is nothing as precious as a disciplined soul. {26:15} A modest wife adds grace upon grace, and her chaste soul is beyond measure. {26:16} Like the sun rising in the sky, so is the beauty of a good wife in her well-ordered home. {26:17} Like a shining lamp on a holy lampstand, so is a beautiful face on a dignified figure. {26:18} Like pillars of gold on a base of silver, so are beautiful feet guided by a steadfast heart. {26:19} There are two things that deeply trouble my heart, and a third that stirs my anger: a warrior impoverished by poverty, and wise men treated with contempt; a person who turns away from righteousness to embrace sin—the Lord will prepare judgment for such a one! {26:20} A merchant often finds it hard to avoid wrongdoing, and a tradesman cannot claim innocence from sin.

{27:1} Many have committed sins for trivial gains, and those who pursue wealth often turn a blind eye to ethical concerns. {27:2} Sin is firmly entrenched between the transactions of buying and selling, much like a stake driven deep into a crack between stones. {27:3} Without steadfastness and zeal in the fear of the Lord, a man's household is vulnerable to swift downfall. {27:4} Just as the refuse remains when a sieve is shaken, so does a person's moral filth linger in their thoughts. {27:5} As the kiln tests the potter's vessels, so is a man tested by his reasoning and decisions. {27:6} The fruit reveals the quality of a tree's cultivation; similarly, a person's words reveal the cultivation of their mind. {27:7} Do not praise someone before you have heard their reasoning; true character is revealed through thoughtful discourse. {27:8} Pursue justice diligently, and it will be attained, becoming a glorious robe that adorns you. {27:9} Birds flock together according to their kind; similarly, truth returns to those who faithfully practice it. {27:10} Just as a lion waits patiently for its prey, so does sin lie in wait for those who indulge in iniquity. {27:11} The speech of the wise is consistently thoughtful, whereas the fool's opinions fluctuate like the phases of the moon. {27:12} When among foolish people, seek opportunities to depart, but stay among the wise and thoughtful. {27:13} The speech of fools is offensive, and their laughter is frivolously sinful. {27:14} The talk of those who swear frequently is unsettling, and their arguments are enough to make one cover their ears. {27:15} Strife caused by the proud often leads to violence, and their abusive words are painful to hear. {27:16} Whoever betrays confidences destroys trust, and they will struggle to find a loyal friend again. {27:17} Love your friend and maintain faithfulness, but if you betray their secrets, do not expect them to remain close. {27:18} Just as a person destroys their enemy, so do you destroy the bond of friendship with your neighbor when you betray their trust. {27:19} Once you let a bird escape from your hand, you cannot easily catch it again; similarly, once you let your neighbor go, they may be beyond your reach. {27:20} Do not chase after them in vain, for they have slipped away like a gazelle from a trap. {27:21} While wounds can be bandaged and reconciliations can follow arguments, betrayal of secrets leaves little hope for repair. {27:22} A person who winks to plan evil cannot easily be dissuaded, and their intentions will often come to fruition. {27:23} In your presence, they may speak sweetly and admire your words, but later they will twist their speech and use your own words against you. {27:24} I have disliked many things, but none as much as a deceitful person; even the Lord despises such behavior. {27:25}

Whoever throws a stone straight up risks having it fall on their own head, and a treacherous blow will inevitably cause wounds. {27:26} One who digs a pit may fall into it, and those who set snares may themselves be ensnared. {27:27} If a person does evil, it will eventually come back to haunt them, often in unexpected ways. {27:28} Mockery and abuse flow freely from the proud, but vengeance awaits them like a lion lying in wait. {27:29} Those who rejoice at the downfall of the righteous will themselves be ensnared, and anguish will consume them before their end. {27:30} Anger and wrath are detestable traits, and those who indulge in sin will find themselves possessed by them.

{28:1} Those who seek vengeance will themselves face divine retribution, firmly establishing their own sins. {28:2} Forgive your neighbor's wrongdoing, and your own sins will be pardoned when you pray. {28:3} Can a person harbor anger against another and still expect healing from the Lord? {28:4} If they show no mercy to others like themselves, how can they pray for forgiveness of their own sins? {28:5} If humans, being flesh, hold onto wrath, who can make atonement for their sins? {28:6} Reflect on the end of your life, cease from enmity, remember destruction and death, and faithfully follow the commandments. {28:7} Recall the commandments; do not harbor anger toward your neighbor. Remember the covenant of the Most High and overlook ignorance. {28:8} Avoid strife, and you will reduce sin, for a person prone to anger will incite conflict. {28:9} Sinful behavior disrupts friendships and sows enmity among those at peace. {28:10} As fuel feeds a fire, so does stubbornness fuel strife; a person's strength and wealth only intensify their anger. {28:11} Quick tempers ignite quarrels, and heated disputes often lead to harm. {28:12} Words can ignite like sparks; control your tongue, for both soothing and harmful words come from it. {28:13} Curse those who gossip and deceive, for they ruin peace among many. {28:14} Slander has shaken nations and destroyed great cities, toppling the homes of influential people. {28:15} False accusations have driven away courageous women and deprived them of their rightful rewards. {28:16} Those who heed slander will find no rest or peace. {28:17} A tongue's words can wound deeper than a whip, crushing bones with its blows. {28:18} Many have fallen by the sword, but more still have perished because of the tongue's destructive power. {28:19} Blessed is the one shielded from its harm, avoiding its anger and escaping its burdensome yoke and fetters. {28:20} Its grip is like iron and its chains like bronze; its end brings a grievous death, worse than Hades itself. {28:21} The godly will not be mastered by it; they will not be consumed by its flames. {28:22} Those who turn away from the Lord will fall prey to its power, facing its relentless fury like a ravaging lion or a fierce leopard. {28:23} Protect yourself as you would guard valuables with thorns, secure your words with balances and scales, and lock your mouth with a sturdy door and bolt. {28:24} Beware of the errors of your tongue, lest you fall victim to the one who lies in wait.

{29:1} Whoever shows mercy to others will find kindness returned; lending a hand to strengthen a neighbor honors the commandments. {29:2} Lend to your neighbor in times of need, and ensure timely repayment to uphold trust. {29:3} Honor your commitments and maintain faithfulness; in doing so, you'll always find provision for yourself. {29:4} Many see borrowing as a boon, often causing trouble for their benefactors. {29:5} Some will humble themselves for a loan, but when it's time to repay, they delay and offer excuses, souring relationships. {29:6} If the lender presses for repayment, they might get back only a fraction, breeding animosity. If not, the borrower unjustly burdens them, replacing honor with shame. {29:7} Such dishonesty has made many reluctant to lend, fearing unnecessary loss. {29:8} Nonetheless, be patient with those in need; don't withhold assistance when it's within your means. {29:9} Help the poor because it's right, ensuring they don't leave empty-handed. {29:10} Invest in others, forgoing selfishness, lest your wealth remains idle and unused. {29:11} Follow the Most High's commandments in managing your wealth; they're more valuable than gold. {29:12} Store up acts of charity as a safeguard, protecting you from adversity more than any defense. {29:13} It shields like armor and defends like a mighty weapon against adversaries. {29:14} A noble person stands as surety for their neighbor, but shameless individuals abandon their obligations. {29:15} Remember the kindness of your guarantor, who risked for your sake. {29:16} Sinners endanger their guarantors' prosperity. {29:17} Those lacking gratitude forsake their rescuers. {29:18} Many have fallen from wealth due to suretyship, their lives upturned like waves, exiled among strangers. {29:19} Sinners who seek profit through suretyship often face legal troubles. {29:20} Assist your neighbor as you're able, but guard against overextending yourself. {29:21} Life's essentials include water, bread, clothing, and shelter. {29:22} A humble life under one's own roof is better than luxury in another's mansion. {29:23} Whether little or much, be content with what you have. {29:24} It's tough being a stranger, moving often, where offering hospitality brings bitterness and reproach from the moneylender.

[30:1] A father who loves his son will discipline him often, ensuring joy in his upbringing. [30:2] Through discipline, a father gains wisdom from his son and boasts of him among friends. [30:3] Teaching a son well invites envy from enemies and brings pride among companions. [30:4] Even after a father's death, he lives on through a son who resembles him. [30:5] While alive, he rejoiced in his son, and in death, he found peace knowing his legacy continued. [30:6] His son becomes an avenger against enemies and a blessing to his father's friends. [30:7] Spoiling a son leads to constant worry and the need to mend wounds caused by indulgence. [30:8] An undisciplined son grows willful, akin to an untamed horse that becomes stubborn. [30:9] Overindulgence breeds fear and grief in a child's behavior. [30:10] Laughter with a child may lead to shared sorrow, and neglecting discipline brings future regret. [30:11] Granting undue authority to a young child and ignoring their mistakes are pitfalls to avoid. [30:12] Early discipline prevents stubbornness and disobedience, sparing a parent sorrow. [30:13] Disciplining a son diligently prevents shamelessness and preserves familial honor. [30:14] A poor man in good health is wealthier than a rich man plagued by sickness. [30:15] Health and well-being surpass all riches, with a strong body outweighing material wealth. [30:16] No riches compare to bodily health and the joy it brings. [30:17] Death is preferable to a life filled with suffering, and eternal rest is better than enduring chronic illness. [30:18] Kind words to a silent listener are wasted, much like offering food to the dead. [30:19] Offerings to idols are useless, just as afflictions sent by the Lord bring no benefit. [30:20] Afflicted by sorrow, one groans inwardly like a eunuch yearning for intimacy. [30:21] Avoid unnecessary sorrow and deliberate self-inflicted pain. [30:22] Happiness prolongs life, bringing joy and lengthening one's days. [30:23] Seek solace and comfort, distancing yourself from sorrow that only leads to destruction. [30:24] Jealousy and anger shorten life, and anxiety ages prematurely. [30:25] A cheerful heart brings mindfulness to one's diet and overall well-being.

{31:1} Concerns about wealth can consume a person, wasting away their health and stealing their sleep. {31:2} Anxiety keeps one awake, especially during illness, robbing them of much-needed rest. {31:3} The wealthy work hard to increase their riches, indulging in luxury when they finally rest. {31:4} Conversely, the poor toil to make ends meet, often remaining needy even in their rest. {31:5} Those who love gold will find no justification, and those who chase after money often find themselves led astray. {31:6} Many have been ruined by their pursuit of gold, facing destruction directly as a result. {31:7} Gold becomes a stumbling block for the devoted, ensnaring every fool who pursues it. {31:8} Blessed is the wealthy person who remains blameless and does not obsess over gold. {31:9} Who among them is truly blessed, having done wonderful things among their people? {31:10} Those tested by wealth and found steadfast may rightfully boast in their integrity. {31:11} Their prosperity is assured, and their acts of charity are celebrated by the community. {31:12} When dining with the wealthy, avoid greed and refrain from commenting excessively on the spread. {31:13} A covetous eye leads to sorrow; nothing is more insatiable than the eye, shedding tears of discontent. {31:14} Resist reaching for everything you see, and respect your neighbor's space at the table. {31:15} Empathize with others' feelings and approach every situation with thoughtfulness. {31:16} Eat modestly and avoid gluttony to avoid being despised. {31:17} Practice good manners by stopping eating before you're full, avoiding offense through greed. {31:18} When dining with others, wait your turn to reach for food. {31:19} A disciplined person finds contentment with little, sleeping peacefully without heavy breathing. {31:20} Healthy sleep follows moderate eating habits, allowing one to rise early and feel refreshed, unlike the glutton plagued by sleeplessness and digestive issues. {31:21} If overeating, take a break during meals to find relief from discomfort. {31:22} Listen to advice and be diligent in your work to avoid illness and prosper. {31:23} Generosity with food earns praise and respect, reflecting well on one's character. {31:24} Stinginess with food invites criticism and dissatisfaction from the community. {31:25} Avoid seeking valor through excessive wine, knowing its destructive potential. {31:26} Wine reveals character like fire tests steel, particularly in the strife of the proud. {31:27} Wine, enjoyed in moderation, adds joy to life; it was created to bring gladness to humanity. {31:28} Drinking wine in moderation brings happiness and lifts the spirit. {31:29} Excessive wine leads to bitterness, provocation, and stumbling in life. {31:30} Drunkenness fuels foolish anger, weakening resolve and causing harm. {31:31} Refrain from reproaching or despising others at a wine banquet; avoid causing distress with harsh words or demands.

{32:1} If you are honored to host a feast, do not elevate yourself above others; mingle among them as their equal, attend to their needs, and then take your place. {32:2} Once your responsibilities are fulfilled, join in the merriment for their sake and receive recognition for your excellent leadership. {32:3} Speak, elders, with wisdom and restraint, respecting the occasion without interrupting the music. {32:4} In gatherings, avoid excessive chatter and displaying your wit at inappropriate times. {32:5} Music harmonizing with wine at a banquet is like a ruby seal set in gold. {32:6} Melody accompanied by good wine is like an emerald seal in a lavish gold setting. {32:7} Young men, speak when necessary but sparingly, and only when invited to contribute. {32:8} Be concise in speech, conveying much with few words; demonstrate knowledge while maintaining humility. {32:9} Among the esteemed, do not assert equality; refrain from speaking when others have the floor. {32:10} Modesty precedes commendation, as lightning flashes before thunder. {32:11} Depart in good time and avoid lingering; enjoy yourself without falling into boastful speech. {32:12} Enjoy the occasion responsibly, following your desires without succumbing to arrogance. {32:13} Give thanks for the Creator who provides satisfaction through His blessings. {32:14} Those who revere the Lord accept His discipline, and those who seek Him early find favor. {32:15} Seeking wisdom leads to fulfillment, while hypocrisy leads to stumbling over it. {32:16} The righteous, who fear the Lord, make sound judgments and shine brightly with righteous deeds. {32:17} Sinful individuals avoid correction and seek judgments that align with their desires. {32:18} A discerning person values good counsel, while the proud and insolent disregard it. {32:19} Act with deliberation, avoiding regrets after making decisions. {32:20} Avoid risky paths and treacherous terrain in your endeavors. {32:21} Do not become overconfident even on smooth paths; {32:22} instead, carefully consider your journey. {32:23} Guard your actions diligently, for this is how you uphold the commandments. {32:24} Those who trust in the Lord faithfully follow His commandments and will not suffer loss.

{33:1} Those who fear the Lord will not face evil, and in times of trial, they will be delivered repeatedly. {33:2} A wise person respects the law, but hypocrisy renders one as unstable as a boat in a storm. {33:3} Understanding individuals trust in the law, finding it as reliable as seeking guidance through Urim. {33:4} Prepare your words carefully to be heard; organize your thoughts and deliver your response effectively. {33:5} The heart of a fool is restless like a cartwheel, and his thoughts spin endlessly like a turning axle. {33:6} A stallion behaves like a deceitful friend, neighing under every rider who mounts him. {33:7} Is there truly a better day than another, when all days are lit by the same sun? {33:8} By the Lord's decree, distinctions were made; He ordained seasons and established feasts—some elevated and sacred, others ordinary. {33:9} All humans are formed from the earth, and Adam was created from dust. {33:10} In His wisdom, the Lord appointed diverse paths for mankind—blessing some, sanctifying others, and humbling those who stray. {33:11} Like clay shaped by a potter, all are in the hands of their Creator, molded according to His will. {33:12} Good stands opposite to evil, and life contrasts with death; so too do sinners differ from the righteous. {33:13} Observe the works of the Most High—each paired in contrast to its opposite. {33:14} I have been diligent, like a gleaner after harvesters, excelling by the Lord's blessing and filling my storehouse like a vintner with grapes. {33:15} Know that my labor benefits all who seek knowledge and understanding. {33:16} Listen, leaders and people of authority; heed these words. {33:17} Whether to family or friend, do not relinquish control while you live, nor entrust your possessions to another, lest you regret it later. {33:18} Maintain your authority as long as you breathe, and guard against others taking your place prematurely. {33:19} Your children should seek from you rather than from others; maintain your honor and excel in all you do. {33:20} Arrange your affairs before your end, and manage your inheritance wisely. {33:21} Provide for your servants with care, assigning tasks to keep them occupied, for idleness breeds mischief. {33:22} Treat your servants fairly, for they are as essential as yourself, purchased with your own resources. {33:23} If mistreated, they may flee, leaving you to regret their departure.

{34:1} A person lacking understanding harbors empty hopes, and fools find their aspirations soaring in dreams. {34:2} Pursuing dreams is akin to grasping at shadows or chasing the wind—fruitless and without substance. {34:3} Dreams present a jumble of images, like faces confronting each other, often obscure and ambiguous. {34:4} Can dreams arise from impurity? Can truth emerge from falsehood? Such is the nature of divination and dreams, mere folly that clouds the mind like fleeting fantasies. {34:5} Unless dreams are a divine message from above, it's wisest not to dwell on them, for many have been led astray by false hopes they foster. {34:6} True fulfillment lies in adhering to the law without deception, and wisdom shines through honest speech. {34:7} Those versed in knowledge and experience speak with insight, while the inexperienced grasp only a fragment of understanding. {34:8} Through my travels, I've witnessed much and gained profound understanding beyond words. {34:9} I've faced perilous situations and narrowly escaped, learning invaluable lessons along the way. {34:10} The spirit of those who revere the Lord is imbued with vitality, finding hope and salvation in His presence. {34:11} They do not cower in fear, for their faith in the Lord strengthens their resolve. {34:12} Blessed are those who fear the Lord, finding their support and refuge in His unwavering gaze. {34:13} The eyes of the Lord watch over His faithful, providing protection, strength, and solace in times of adversity. {34:14} He uplifts their spirits, granting clarity and vitality, bestowing healing, life, and abundant blessings. {34:15} However, offerings tainted by ill-gotten gains are unacceptable; sacrifices from the lawless do not find favor. {34:16} The Most High is not appeased by material offerings alone, nor is forgiveness obtained through superficial acts of piety. {34:17} Neglecting the needs of the poor is akin to grave injustice, akin to shedding innocent blood. {34:18} To deprive a neighbor of their livelihood is to commit a grievous offense, sowing discord and hardship. {34:19} Where there is conflict and destruction, there is only toil and strife, yielding no true gain. {34:20} Prayer offered sincerely is heard by the Lord, but hypocritical acts of repentance hold no weight.

{35:1} Those who uphold the law offer many sacrifices, and those who obey the commandments present peace offerings. {35:2} Returning kindness is akin to offering fine flour, and giving alms is like sacrificing a thanksgiving offering. {35:3} Pleasing the Lord involves avoiding wickedness and forsaking unrighteousness as an act of atonement. {35:4} When you come before the Lord, do not come empty-handed, for these are the commandments to be honored. {35:5} The offerings of the righteous perfume the altar and rise as a pleasing aroma before the Most High. {35:6} The sacrifices of the righteous find favor and their memory endures. {35:7} Honor the Lord generously and do not withhold the first fruits of your labor. {35:8} Approach every gift with a joyful countenance and dedicate your tithe with gladness. {35:9} Give to the Lord as generously as you have received, for he repays abundantly. {35:10} Do not attempt to bribe the Lord or offer him insincere sacrifices, for he is a just judge without partiality. {35:11} He listens to the prayers of the poor and responds to those who have been wronged. {35:12} The cries of the fatherless and the pleas of widows do not go unheard; their tears are noted by the Lord. {35:13} The worship and prayers of those who please the Lord are accepted, reaching him like incense rising to the clouds. {35:14} The humble prayer penetrates the heavens and will not cease until it reaches the Lord, seeking justice and vindication for the righteous. {35:15} The Lord acts swiftly to bring justice against the unmerciful and to uphold righteousness among the nations. {35:16} He judges each person according to their deeds and brings joy to his people through his mercy. {35:17} In times of affliction, the mercy of the Lord is like refreshing rain in a drought, bringing comfort and renewal.

{36:1} Lord, have mercy on us, God of all, and look upon us with your grace. {36:2} Let the fear of you fall upon all nations, that they may acknowledge your sovereignty. {36:3} Extend your hand against foreign powers, revealing your might to them. {36:4} As you have shown your holiness through us, magnify yourself among them. {36:5} Let them come to know you as we have known, that there is no God but you, O Lord. {36:6} Manifest new signs and perform further wonders; let your power and glory be renowned. {36:7} Stir up your anger and pour out your wrath; defeat our adversaries and destroy our enemies. {36:8} Bring about the appointed day of deliverance, and let people proclaim your mighty deeds. {36:9} Let those who survive witness your fiery wrath, and may those who harm your people be utterly destroyed. {36:10} Crush the leaders of our enemies who boast in their own strength. {36:11} Gather all the descendants of Jacob and restore to them their inheritance, as in the days of old. {36:12} Have mercy on your people, Israel, whom you have called your first-born. {36:13} Show compassion on Jerusalem, the city of your sanctuary and the place of your dwelling. {36:14} Fill Zion with joyful celebration of your marvelous works, and let your temple be radiant with your glory. {36:15} Confirm the promises made to your creation from the beginning, and fulfill the prophecies spoken in your name. {36:16} Reward those who wait for you, and let your prophets be known for their faithfulness. {36:17} Listen, O Lord, to the prayers of your servants, according to the blessing of Aaron, and let all the earth know that you are the eternal God. {36:18} The stomach accepts any food, but some food is better than others. {36:19} Just as the palate discerns different flavors of game, so a wise mind detects falsehoods. {36:20} A deceitful heart brings sorrow, but a discerning person will repay him in kind. {36:21} A woman may accept any man, but a daughter of virtue surpasses them all. {36:22} Beauty in a woman brings joy to the heart and surpasses every human desire. {36:23} Kindness and humility in her speech make her husband esteemed among men. {36:24} Acquiring a wife is gaining a precious possession, a companion who supports and strengthens. {36:25} Just as a property without a fence is vulnerable to theft, so a man without a wife may wander and yearn for companionship. {36:26} For who trusts a nimble thief who moves from place to place? Likewise, who can rely on a man without a settled home?

{37:1} Every acquaintance will claim to be a friend, but true friendship is rare. {37:2} It's deeply saddening when a close companion turns into an enemy. {37:3} Oh, destructive thoughts, why were you created to spread deceit across the land? {37:4} Some friends rejoice in your happiness but disappear in times of trouble. {37:5} Others aid you for their own gain and only show loyalty when it benefits them. {37:6} Remember your true friends in your heart, and value them even in times of prosperity. {37:7} Everyone praises good advice, but beware of counselors who serve their own interests. {37:8} Be cautious with advisors; understand their motives before trusting their guidance, as they may turn against you. {37:9} Some may initially agree with you but secretly hope for your downfall. {37:10} Avoid consulting those who view you with suspicion or envy your success. {37:11} Seek counsel wisely: not from those who lack experience or integrity in their field. {37:12} Stick close to a righteous person who keeps the commandments and shares your values; they will empathize with your failures. {37:13} Trust your own judgment, for it is often more reliable than the advice of many. {37:14} A person's conscience can provide better guidance than many watchmen on a tower. {37:15} Above all, pray to the Most High for guidance in your endeavors. {37:16} Sound reasoning precedes every successful endeavor, and wise counsel is essential. {37:17} Life is full of uncertainties, with constant changes of fortune, influenced greatly by words. {37:18} A person may be wise and knowledgeable yet fail to benefit themselves. {37:19} A skilled speaker may be unpopular and suffer lack, for wisdom and favor are gifts from the Lord. {37:20} True wisdom benefits both the wise and those they guide. {37:21} A wise person instructs their community and earns respect for their understanding. {37:22} Praise follows a wise person, and their happiness is evident to all. {37:23} Life is short for every person, but the legacy of wisdom endures. {37:24} Those who are wise inherit trust and leave a lasting impact. {37:25} My child, evaluate your life while you live; avoid what harms your soul. {37:26} Not everything suits everyone, and personal preferences vary. {37:27} Do not indulge excessively in luxury or overeat; moderation is key to health. {37:28} Overindulgence causes illness; self-control extends life.

{38:1} Show respect to doctors and honor them for their skill, for the Lord has created them to bring healing. {38:2} Healing comes from the Most High, and a doctor receives gifts from kings for their expertise. {38:3} The physician's knowledge and presence earn them admiration among the great. {38:4} God has provided medicines from the earth; wise people should not disregard their effectiveness. {38:5} Just as a tree sweetened bitter water, God's power is revealed through healing properties. {38:6} He has given skill to humans so that His marvelous works may be glorified. {38:7} Through these medicines, pain is alleviated and healing occurs. {38:8} Pharmacists skillfully compound remedies, and health spreads across the earth through them. {38:9} When ill, do not neglect your health; pray to the Lord for healing. {38:10} Repent of your sins, purify your heart, and offer sincere sacrifices. {38:11} Honor doctors, for the Lord has appointed them; they are essential in times of need. {38:12} There are moments when a person's fate rests in the hands of skilled physicians. {38:13} Doctors pray for success in diagnosis and treatment, seeking God's guidance to preserve life. {38:14} Those who sin should seek the care of physicians, acknowledging their need for healing. {38:15} Mourn deeply for the dead and give them honorable burial, then find comfort in your sorrow. {38:16} Excessive grief weakens the heart and prolongs sorrow. {38:17} In hardship, sorrow persists, weighing heavily on the poor. {38:18} Do not let sorrow overwhelm you; remember that life has its end. {38:19} Once gone, the dead cannot return; mourning them serves no purpose and harms yourself. {38:20} Reflect on the fate that awaits us all, as yesterday's sorrow may be tomorrow's reality. {38:21} Once the deceased finds rest, let go of their memory and find solace in their departure. {38:22} A scholar's wisdom grows with leisure, while busyness may hinder true understanding. {38:23} Different occupations shape different kinds of wisdom; each has its own merits and challenges.

{38:24} From craftsmen to artisans, each is dedicated to their work, contributing to society in their unique way. {38:25} Their skills are vital for city life, yet their counsel may not be sought in public affairs or courts. {38:26} They maintain the world's order through their labor, and their prayer is in the work of their hands.

{39:1} Those who dedicate themselves to studying the teachings of the Most High seek wisdom from ancient times and delve into prophetic insights. {39:2} They cherish the wisdom of esteemed figures and unravel the complexities of parables. {39:3} They strive to uncover the hidden meanings of proverbs and become familiar with the mysteries embedded in parables. {39:4} Such individuals serve among leaders, even traveling across foreign lands to discern between good and evil in humanity. {39:5} They rise early to seek the Lord, offering prayers and supplications before the Most High, confessing their sins. {39:6} If the Lord grants His favor, they are filled with a spirit of understanding, imparting wisdom and offering prayers of gratitude. {39:7} They direct their counsel and knowledge with integrity, pondering divine mysteries. {39:8} They teach others with clarity and find joy in following the Lord's covenant. {39:9} Their understanding earns them praise that endures through generations; their legacy is everlasting. {39:10} Nations acknowledge their wisdom, and communities honor them with praise. {39:11} Whether they live long or pass on, their name is esteemed beyond measure. {39:12} I have more to share, thoughts overflowing like a full moon. {39:13} Listen, O holy ones, and bloom like roses by a flowing stream. {39:14} Spread fragrance like incense, bloom like lilies, and offer hymns of praise, blessing the Lord for His creations. {39:15} Give glory to His name, expressing thanks with songs and instruments, and proclaim in gratitude: {39:16} "All things are the works of the Lord; they are very good, and His commands are fulfilled in His time." {39:17} No one questions His actions, for all is sought in His time; He commands the waters and shapes the earth. {39:18} At His command, all that pleases Him is done, and His saving power knows no limits. {39:19} All deeds are laid bare before Him; nothing is hidden from His sight. {39:20} He sees from eternity to eternity; nothing is beyond His understanding. {39:21} No one can question His purpose; everything serves its intended use. {39:22} His blessings flow over the land like a river, nourishing it abundantly. {39:23} Nations face His wrath, as He transforms fresh water into salt. {39:24} His ways are straightforward to the righteous but a stumbling block to the wicked. {39:25} Good things were created for the righteous, while evil awaits sinners. {39:26} Essential to human life are water, fire, iron, salt, wheat, milk, honey, grapes, oil, and clothing. {39:27} These are blessings for the righteous but turn to adversity for sinners. {39:28} Winds of vengeance scourge the earth in anger, serving their purpose until the end times. {39:29} Fire, hail, famine, pestilence, wild beasts, scorpions, vipers, and the sword punish the ungodly. {39:30} They obey His commands and serve His purposes faithfully on earth. {39:31} Therefore, I am convinced from the beginning and have penned this down: {39:32} The works of the Lord are all good, and He provides for every need in its time. {39:33} No one can say one thing is worse than another, for all things serve their purpose in due season. {39:34} Therefore, sing praises with all your heart, and bless the Lord's name.

{40:1} Every person faces significant toil, burdened from the day they are born until they return to the earth. {40:2} Anxiety about death weighs heavily on their hearts, from the highest ruler to the humblest servant, {40:3} whether adorned in royal robes or dressed in simple garments. {40:4} Throughout life, there is anger, envy, trouble, unrest, and fear, disturbing even their sleep at night. {40:5} They find little rest, troubled by dreams as if on constant watch, only to awaken surprised that their fears were unfounded. {40:6} Death, violence, strife, and calamity affect all living beings, {40:7} but sinners face these troubles even more severely. {40:8} These afflictions were ordained for the wicked, {40:9} recalling the ancient flood as divine judgment. {40:10} All things return to their origins: earthly things to the earth, waters to the sea. {40:11} Corruption and injustice will vanish, but integrity endures forever. {40:12} Ill-gotten wealth will dissipate suddenly, while generosity brings joy. {40:13} The children of the wicked do not flourish, {40:14} their roots unable to take hold. {40:15} Kindness and generosity are like cultivated gardens, {40:16} their blessings enduring endlessly. {40:17} Life is fulfilling for those who are self-sufficient and industrious, but wealth surpasses both. {40:18} Children and community bring honor, but a virtuous spouse is the greatest treasure. {40:19} Wine and music bring joy, yet wisdom surpasses both. {40:20} Melodies of flute and harp are delightful, yet a pleasing voice exceeds both. {40:21} Beauty is pleasing, but a bountiful harvest is more valuable. {40:22} Friends and companions are comforting, but a devoted spouse surpasses all. {40:23} Siblings provide support in times of need, yet charity offers greater rescue. {40:24} Wealth provides stability, but wise counsel is more valuable. {40:25} Riches and strength bring confidence, yet the fear of the Lord is supreme. {40:26} Reverence for God is a garden of blessings, offering greater security than any earthly glory. {40:27} My child, avoid a life of dependency; it is better to face death than to live by begging.

{41:1} Oh death, how bitterly it reminds those who live in comfort, with wealth and vigor to enjoy life's pleasures without distraction! {41:2} Yet for those in need, weakened by age, burdened with troubles, and lacking patience, death's arrival is a welcome relief. {41:3} Fear not death's decree; instead, remember your past days and the certainty of life's end—a divine ordinance for all humanity. {41:4} Embrace the will of the Most High, for whether life spans ten, a hundred, or a thousand years, Hades makes no exceptions. {41:5} The offspring of the sinful are despised, drawn to the dens of the wicked. {41:6} The legacy of sinners fades, leaving a perpetual stain on their descendants. {41:7} Children bear the shame of their ungodly parents, enduring reproach because of their fathers' sins. {41:8} Woe to the ungodly who forsake the law of the Most High God! {41:9} From birth cursed, in death cursed; their fate is perpetual condemnation. {41:10} All that is dust returns to dust; thus the ungodly move from curse to annihilation. {41:11} Mourners lament the body's passing, but the evil reputation of sinners is erased. {41:12} Guard your reputation, for it outlasts vast riches. {41:13} The days of a good life are numbered, but a noble reputation endures eternally. {41:14} My children, heed wisdom and find peace; hidden insights and unseen treasures—what greater value do they hold? {41:15} It is better to conceal one's folly than to flaunt one's wisdom. {41:16} Therefore, honor these words: It is good to feel shame, for not all things are esteemed by all. {41:17} Be ashamed of immorality before parents, falsehoods before leaders, {41:18} transgressions before judges, injustices before communities, {41:19} theft in your neighborhood, and above all, before the truth of God's covenant. {41:20} Be ashamed of selfishness at meals, rudeness in giving and receiving, {41:21} ignoring family appeals, seizing others' possessions or gifts, {41:22} inappropriate advances, verbal abuse, or revealing secrets. {41:23} Displaying proper shame gains favor with all.

{42:1} Do not be ashamed of these things, and do not let favoritism lead you into wrongdoing: {42:2} honoring the law of the Most High and his covenant, and judging impartially even when it acquits the ungodly; {42:3} keeping accurate accounts with partners and fellow travelers, and fairly dividing inheritances among friends; {42:4} using honest scales and weights, whether dealing with large or small quantities; {42:5} conducting profitable business with merchants, disciplining children with care, and punishing a wicked servant severely when necessary. {42:6} In the presence of a troublesome wife, a seal is a valuable safeguard, and where many hands work, secure your possessions. {42:7} Whatever transactions you undertake, ensure they are measured and recorded accurately, keeping careful records of all exchanges. {42:8} Do not hesitate to teach the simple-minded, the foolish, or the elderly engaged in disputes with the young; in doing so, you will gain true wisdom and earn respect from all. {42:9} A daughter can cause her father sleepless nights, worrying whether she will marry, be loved if married, or remain faithful; {42:10} as a virgin, avoiding defilement or pregnancy; or as a wife, remaining faithful or bearing children. {42:11} Vigilantly oversee a headstrong daughter to avoid becoming a laughingstock or a disgrace in the city, earning scorn among the people. {42:12} Do not be captivated by outward beauty or linger among women, for from garments comes moths, and from women, deceitful schemes. {42:13} The wickedness of a man is preferable to a woman who feigns goodness, as it is a woman who brings shame and disgrace. {42:14} Now I will reflect on the works of the Lord and declare what I have witnessed; through the Lord's word, his works are accomplished. {42:15} The sun illuminates everything with its light, and the Lord's work is infused with his glory. {42:16} The Lord has empowered his holy ones to proclaim his marvelous works, which sustain the universe in his magnificent splendor. {42:17} He searches the depths and examines human hearts, discerning their cunning schemes; the Most High knows all that can be known and understands the signs of the times. {42:18} He reveals the past and the future, uncovering hidden truths and the paths they follow. {42:19} No thought escapes him, no word is hidden from him. {42:20} He has ordained the brilliance of his wisdom, existing from eternity to eternity, needing no one to advise him. {42:21} How magnificent are all his works, sparkling with brilliance, fulfilling every need and obedient to his command. {42:22} Everything exists in pairs, balancing opposites, and nothing he creates is incomplete. {42:23} Each complements the other, confirming the goodness of his creation. {42:24} Who can ever tire of beholding his glory?

{43:1} The splendor of the heavens is the clear sky, a magnificent display of glory. {43:2} The sun, as it rises and proclaims its journey, is a wondrous creation, the masterpiece of the Most High. {43:3} At noon it scorches the earth; who can withstand its blazing heat? {43:4} The furnace master toils in intense heat, yet the sun burns the mountains with threefold intensity, emitting fiery vapors and blinding with its bright rays. {43:5} Great is the Lord who created it; by his command it follows its ordained path. {43:6} He also made the moon, appointed to mark the seasons and serve as an everlasting sign. {43:7} From the moon comes the signal for feasts, its light waxing until it reaches fullness. {43:8} The month is named after the moon, marvelously increasing in phases, an instrument of the celestial hosts shining in the expanse of heaven. {43:9} The stars, arrayed beautifully in the heights of the Lord, are the glory of heaven. {43:10} They stand watch at the command of the Holy One, unwavering in their vigilance. {43:11} Consider the rainbow and praise its Maker, resplendent in its brightness, spanning the heavens with its glorious arc, stretched out by the hands of the Most High. {43:12} By his decree, he sends forth driving snow and hastens the lightning of his judgment. {43:13} Thus the storehouses of the clouds open, and clouds fly forth like birds. {43:14} In his majestic power, he gathers the clouds, shattering hailstones. {43:15} At his presence, mountains tremble; at his command, the south wind blows. {43:16} His thunderous voice rebukes the earth, while storms from the north and whirlwinds scatter snow like descending birds, marveling at its pure whiteness and the wonder of its descent. {43:17} He pours hoarfrost upon the earth like salt, freezing it into sharp thorns. {43:18} The cold north wind blows, freezing water into ice that covers every pool and water source like a breastplate. {43:19} He consumes mountains and scorches the wilderness, withering tender grass like fire. {43:20} A mist swiftly brings healing; dew refreshes from the heat. {43:21} By his wisdom, he calms the great deep and plants islands in it. {43:22} Sailors speak of its perils, and we marvel at their tales, for in it are wondrous creatures, both small and great. {43:23} His messenger finds the way, and by his word all things hold together. {43:24} Though we speak much, we cannot comprehend fully; our words merely acknowledge: "He is the all." {43:25} Where can we find the strength to praise him? For he surpasses all his works in greatness. {43:26} Terrible and exceedingly great is the Lord; his power is marvelous. {43:27} When you praise the Lord, exalt him to the utmost; even then, he surpasses. {43:28} Exalt him with all your strength and do not grow weary, for no amount of praise is sufficient. {43:29} Who has truly seen him and can describe him accurately? Who can extol him as he truly is? {43:30} Many greater things remain hidden, for we have witnessed only a fraction of his works. {43:31} The Lord has made all things, and to the godly he grants wisdom.

{44:1} Let us now honor those who are renowned, our ancestors in their times. {44:2} The Lord bestowed upon them great glory, his majesty from the beginning. {44:3} Among them were rulers in their kingdoms, men known for their strength, who gave counsel with understanding and proclaimed prophecies. {44:4} They were leaders among the people, skilled in wisdom and teachers of learning, eloquent in their instructions. {44:5} Some were composers of music, others poets who wrote down verses. {44:6} Wealthy men who lived peacefully in their homes -- all these were honored in their generations and shone brightly in their times. {44:7} Some of them have left behind a lasting legacy, their praises sung by many. {44:8} Yet others have passed away without a trace, forgotten as if they had never existed, along with their descendants. {44:9} But these were men of compassion, their righteous deeds never forgotten. {44:10} Their prosperity endures with their descendants, their inheritance passed down through generations. {44:11} Their children uphold the covenants, and their descendants continue their legacy. {44:12} Their memory will endure forever, and their glory will not be extinguished. {44:13} They were buried with honor, their names remembered throughout all generations. {44:14} Nations proclaim their wisdom, and the assembly celebrates their praise. {44:15} Enoch pleased the Lord and was taken up; he was an example of repentance for all generations. {44:16} Noah was found righteous and blameless; during the time of wrath, he and his family were spared, leaving a remnant on the earth after the flood. {44:17} Everlasting covenants were made with him, ensuring that all flesh would not be destroyed by another flood. {44:18} Abraham, the great father of many nations, was unmatched in glory. {44:19} He kept the commandments of the Most High and entered into a covenant with him, demonstrating his faithfulness in times of testing. {44:20} Therefore, the Lord assured him with an oath that his descendants would bless the nations, multiplying them like the dust of the earth and exalting them like the stars, granting them inheritance from sea to sea and from the River to the ends of the earth. {44:21} Isaac received the same promise for the sake of his father Abraham. {44:22} Jacob received the blessings of all people, with the covenant resting upon his head. {44:23} The Lord acknowledged him with blessings, bestowed his inheritance, apportioned his portions, and divided them among the twelve tribes.

{45:1} Let us now honor a man of great mercy whom the Lord raised up from his descendants, finding favor with all people and beloved by God and man—Moses, whose memory is blessed. {45:2} God exalted him to equal glory among the holy ones and made him formidable to his enemies. {45:3} Through his words, he performed miraculous signs; the Lord glorified him in the presence of kings. God entrusted him with commands for his people and revealed a portion of his glory to him. {45:4} Moses was sanctified through his faithfulness and humility; chosen above all others by God. {45:5} God made Moses hear his voice and led him into thick darkness, giving him the commandments face to face—the law of life and knowledge—to teach Jacob his covenant and Israel his statutes. {45:6} Aaron, Moses' brother from the tribe of Levi, was also exalted. {45:7} God made an everlasting covenant with Aaron, granting him the priesthood and blessing him with splendid garments, including a glorious robe. {45:8} Aaron was clothed in perfection and strengthened with symbols of authority: linen breeches, a long robe, and an ephod. {45:9} He was adorned with pomegranates and golden bells that sounded as he moved, a reminder in the temple for the people. {45:10} He wore a holy garment of gold, blue, and purple, crafted by an embroiderer, with the

Urim and Thummim for judgment. {45:11} His attire included scarlet and precious stones set in gold, engraved with the names of the tribes of Israel. {45:12} Aaron wore a gold crown on his turban, inscribed with "Holiness," a unique distinction, adorned by skilled craftsmen. {45:13} Such beauty had never been seen before his time, worn only by his descendants perpetually. {45:14} Twice daily, Aaron's sacrifices were offered completely burned. {45:15} Moses ordained Aaron, anointing him with holy oil—an everlasting covenant for him and his descendants to serve as priests and bless the people in God's name. {45:16} Aaron was chosen to offer sacrifices, incense, and pleasing odors to the Lord as a memorial and for atonement. {45:17} God gave Aaron commandments, statutes, and judgments to teach Israel and enlighten them with his law. {45:18} In the wilderness, outsiders like Dathan, Abiram, and Korah conspired against Aaron, envying him in their wrath. {45:19} God, displeased, wrought wonders to consume them in flaming fire. {45:20} God added glory to Aaron, granting him a heritage and the first fruits, abundant offerings. {45:21} Aaron and his descendants ate the sacrifices given by the Lord. {45:22} Though Aaron had no inheritance among the people, the Lord himself was his portion and inheritance. {45:23} Phinehas, son of Eleazar, ranked third in glory for his zealous fear of the Lord. {45:24} He stood steadfast in goodness, making atonement for Israel and securing a covenant of peace as leader of the sanctuary and his people, ensuring the priesthood's dignity forever. {45:25} A covenant of heritage was established with David, son of Jesse, from the tribe of Judah. {45:26} May the Lord grant wisdom in your heart to judge his people with righteousness, preserving their prosperity and enduring their glory for generations to come.

{46:1} Joshua, son of Nun, was a mighty warrior and successor to Moses in prophecy. True to his name, he became a great savior of God's chosen people, executing vengeance on their enemies and securing Israel's inheritance. {46:2} His glory shone as he raised his hands and wielded his sword against cities. {46:3} None before him stood so steadfast, for he fought the battles of the Lord. {46:4} Did he not command the sun to stand still, extending one day into two? {46:5} He called upon the Almighty when enemies surrounded him. {46:6} The Lord answered with powerful hailstones, unleashing war against nations. At Beth-horon, he vanquished those who resisted, demonstrating his might before all, as Joshua faithfully followed the Mighty One. {46:7} In Moses' days, Joshua and Caleb, son of Jephunneh, stood steadfast, restraining the people from sin and quelling their murmurs. {46:8} Among six hundred thousand foot soldiers, only Joshua and Caleb were preserved to lead Israel into the promised land flowing with milk and honey. {46:9} The Lord granted Caleb strength into old age, allowing him to claim the hill country for his children's inheritance. {46:10} Thus, all Israelites saw the goodness of following the Lord. {46:11} Blessed be the judges whose hearts remained true to the Lord, avoiding idolatry. {46:12} May their honored names live on through their descendants. {46:13} Samuel, beloved prophet of the Lord, established the kingdom and anointed rulers over his people. {46:14} He judged the congregation by the law of the Lord, under God's watchful eye. {46:15} Samuel's faithfulness proved him a prophet; his words were trusted as revelations. {46:16} In times of adversity, he called upon the Mighty One and offered sacrifices. {46:17} The Lord thundered from heaven, his voice resounding mightily. {46:18} Samuel subdued the leaders of Tyre and the rulers of the Philistines. {46:19} Before his eternal rest, Samuel declared his innocence, having taken nothing from anyone, not even a pair of shoes. {46:20} Even after his passing, Samuel prophesied and revealed to the king events to come, lifting his voice from the earth to condemn the people's wickedness.

{47:1} Nathan followed, prophesying in David's days. {47:2} David, chosen like fat from a peace offering among Israel's sons, played fearlessly with lions and bears. {47:3} In his youth, he slew the giant Goliath, lifting Israel's honor with a stone from his sling. {47:4} He invoked the Most High for strength, defeating mighty foes and earning praise for his ten thousands. {47:5} The diadem of glory adorned him as he crushed the Philistines, thanking the Holy One with all his heart. {47:6} Singers praised God at his feasts, filling the sanctuary with melody. {47:7} The Lord forgave David's sins, granting him eternal kingship over Israel. {47:8} Solomon, his wise son, reigned in peace, building God's sanctuary and spreading wisdom. {47:9} His fame reached distant lands, admired for his songs and proverbs. {47:10} Yet, he strayed, bringing sorrow upon his kingdom, dividing Israel's sovereignty. {47:11} The Lord, merciful to David's line, ensured their enduring legacy. {47:12} Solomon's successors, Rehoboam and Jeroboam, led Israel astray with folly and disobedience, leading to their downfall.

{48:1} Then the prophet Elijah emerged like a blazing fire, his words igniting hearts like a torch. {48:2} Through his zeal, he brought a famine upon them, reducing their numbers. {48:3} By the command of the Lord, he shut the heavens and called down fire three times. {48:4} How magnificent were your deeds, O Elijah! Who can boast as you have? {48:5} You raised the dead by the word of the Most High, bringing kings and the famous from their beds to destruction. {48:6} At Sinai you heard rebuke and at Horeb the judgments of vengeance. {48:7} You anointed kings and prophets, executing divine retribution and ensuring succession. {48:8} Taken up in a fiery whirlwind, in a chariot of fire with fiery horses, you await the appointed time to turn hearts and restore Jacob's tribes. {48:9} Blessed are those who saw you and those adorned in love, for we too shall surely live. {48:10} Elijah covered by the whirlwind, filled Elisha with his spirit; fearless before rulers, no one brought him to subjection. {48:11} Nothing was too hard for him; even in death, his deeds prophesied. {48:12} Though the people remained unrepentant, scattered from their land after captivity, rulers from David's house still led. {48:13} Some pleased God, but others multiplied sins. {48:14} Hezekiah fortified Jerusalem, bringing water within; tunnels through rock, iron tools, and pools for water. {48:15} Sennacherib threatened Zion, boasting in arrogance; hearts trembled like women in labor. {48:16} Yet, calling on the merciful Lord, hands spread toward heaven, Isaiah swiftly delivered them. {48:17} The Lord struck the Assyrian camp, his angel decimating them. {48:18} Hezekiah honored the Lord, holding fast to David's ways as commanded by Isaiah the faithful prophet. {48:19} In his time, the sun went backward, extending the king's life; by mighty spirit, he foresaw the end and comforted mourners in Zion. {48:20} Isaiah revealed future events and hidden things before they came to pass.

{49:1} The memory of Josiah is like the sweet aroma of incense skillfully blended, pleasing to every palate, and delightful as music at a feast. {49:2} He led the people in righteousness, removing wickedness and abominations. {49:3} He devoted himself to the Lord, strengthening godliness even in times of great evil. {49:4} Besides David, Hezekiah, and Josiah, most kings of Judah sinned greatly, forsaking the law of the Most High, leading to the downfall of their kingdom. {49:5} They surrendered their sovereignty to foreign powers, diminishing their own glory. {49:6} These nations ravaged the sacred city and left its streets desolate, fulfilling Jeremiah's prophecy. {49:7} Jeremiah, consecrated as a prophet from the womb, ordained to uproot, afflict, and destroy, yet also to build and plant. {49:8} Ezekiel beheld God's glorious vision above the cherubim's chariot. {49:9} God remembered his enemies with storms but favored those who walked in righteousness. {49:10} May the prophets' bones revive, for they brought comfort and hope to the people of Jacob. {49:11} Zerubbabel, a symbol of strength and leadership, {49:12} and Jeshua son of Jozadak, in their time, rebuilt the temple for the Lord's eternal glory. {49:13} Nehemiah's enduring memory lies in restoring Jerusalem's walls, gates, and houses. {49:14} Enoch's uniqueness is unmatched, taken up from the earth. {49:15} Joseph, unparalleled in his wisdom and foresight, is honored even in his burial. {49:16} Shem, Seth, and Adam were esteemed among men, with Adam elevated above all in creation.

{50:1} Simon, the high priest and pride of his people, son of Onias, led a life dedicated to the restoration of the temple and fortification of Jerusalem. {50:2} He laid the foundations of strong double walls and towering structures around the temple precincts. {50:3} During his tenure, a vast reservoir was excavated, providing ample water like the sea in size. {50:4} He strategized to protect his people, strengthening the city against potential sieges. {50:5} His presence among the people, emerging from the inner sanctuary, was glorious, like the morning star or the full moon in brightness. {50:6} He shone like the sun over the temple of the Most High, his presence akin to a rainbow in splendid clouds. {50:7} His demeanor was vibrant, like roses during the first fruits or lilies by a flowing spring, like a green cedar on Lebanon in summer. {50:8} His offerings in the sanctuary were as incense in a censer and vessels of hammered gold adorned with precious stones. {50:9} He stood in majestic robes at the holy altar, surrounded by fellow priests like palm trees around a young cedar. {50:10} The sons of Aaron, in their splendor, presented offerings before the congregation of Israel. {50:11} Completing the rituals with devotion, they offered sacrifices pleasing to the Almighty. {50:12} The people, in reverence, prostrated themselves before the Lord, while the singers praised Him with melodious voices. {50:13} Simon, lifting his hands over Israel, blessed them in the name of the Lord, invoking peace and prosperity. {50:14} Let us praise the God who does great things, blessing us with joy and peace as in days of old. {50:15} May His mercy guide us and deliver us from adversity. {50:16} Despite challenges from neighboring nations, wisdom and understanding, penned by Jesus son of Sirach, enrich this book. {50:17} Blessed are those who heed these teachings, for they will find strength and illumination along the Lord's path.

{51:1} I give thanks to you, O Lord and King, and praise you as my Savior. Your name deserves all my gratitude, {51:2} for you have protected and helped me, delivering my body from destruction and from the traps of those who speak falsely. You were my ally in the presence of my adversaries, {51:3} rescuing me by your great mercy and your powerful name from those who sought to harm me, from the many trials I endured, {51:4} from the fires that threatened me on every side, from flames I did not ignite, {51:5} from the depths of despair, from deceitful tongues and lies, {51:6} slander spoken against me to those in authority. My life was near death, and I was close to the grave. {51:7} They surrounded me from all sides, and there was no one to help; I sought aid from people, but found none. {51:8} Then I remembered your mercy, O Lord, and your works of old, how you rescue those who wait for you and save them from their enemies' hands. {51:9} So I cried out from the earth, praying for deliverance from death. {51:10} I called upon the Lord, the Father of my lord, not to abandon me in times of trouble, when no help is found against the arrogant. {51:11} I will continually praise your name and sing songs of thanksgiving. My prayer was heard, {51:12} for you saved me from destruction and delivered me from dire circumstances. Therefore, I will give you thanks, praise you, and bless the name of the Lord. {51:13} When I was young, before my journeys, I openly sought wisdom in my prayers. {51:14} I asked for wisdom before the temple, and I will continue to pursue her. {51:15} From youth, my heart delighted in her, and I followed her path from beginning to end. {51:16} I listened attentively and gained much understanding. {51:17} I made progress in wisdom, and I will give glory to the One who grants wisdom. {51:18} I resolved to live wisely, pursuing goodness, and I will never be ashamed. {51:19} I wrestled with wisdom in my soul, maintaining strict conduct. I reached out to the heavens and lamented my ignorance. {51:20} I devoted myself to wisdom, and through purification, I found her. I gained understanding from the outset, so I will not be forsaken. {51:21} My heart was stirred to seek her, and I have obtained a valuable possession. {51:22} The Lord rewarded me with a tongue, and I will use it to praise him. {51:23} Come close, you who are unlearned, and learn in my school. {51:24} Why do you say you lack these things, and why are your souls so thirsty? {51:25} I say, obtain these things without money. {51:26} Submit yourselves to instruction; it is readily available. {51:27} See with your own eyes how little effort I exerted and how much rest I gained. {51:28} Obtain instruction, even if it costs silver; it will bring you great gain. {51:29} May your soul rejoice in his mercy, and may you never be ashamed when you praise him. {51:30} Do your work before the appointed time, and in God's time, he will reward you.

Wisdom of Solomon

The Wisdom of Solomon, often simply referred to as the Book of Wisdom, is a deuterocanonical text included in the Septuagint and the Catholic and Orthodox Christian Old Testament, though it is not part of the Hebrew Bible. Traditionally attributed to King Solomon, this attribution is largely symbolic, reflecting the text's connection to Solomonic themes of wisdom and righteousness. Scholars generally date its composition to the late first century BCE or early first century CE, likely within the Hellenistic Jewish community of Alexandria. The book is a rich tapestry of Jewish religious thought interwoven with Hellenistic philosophy, reflecting the cultural and intellectual milieu of its time. The Wisdom of Solomon is divided into three main sections: the first section extols the virtues of wisdom and its role in guiding righteous living; the second provides a historical reflection on Israel's relationship with wisdom, particularly through the lens of the Exodus narrative; and the third section presents an eschatological vision, emphasizing the eternal reward for the righteous and the ultimate defeat of the wicked. The text employs a variety of literary forms, including poetic hymns, exhortations, and philosophical discourse, making it a unique and complex work. Its themes of immortality, divine justice, and the moral order of the universe resonate deeply with the sapiential traditions of both Judaism and Hellenistic thought, offering a profound meditation on the nature of wisdom and its transformative power in the lives of individuals and communities. The Wisdom of Solomon also blends Jewish theology with Greco-Roman culture through its rhetorical style and philosophical terminology, bridging Jewish concepts with ancient intellectual currents.

{1:1} Love righteousness, O rulers of the earth; think of the Lord with integrity and seek him with sincerity of heart. {1:2} For he reveals himself to those who do not test him, and he makes himself known to those who trust him. {1:3} But twisted thoughts separate people from God, and when his power is challenged, it exposes the foolish. {1:4} Wisdom will not enter a deceitful soul or reside in a body enslaved to sin. {1:5} A holy and disciplined spirit flees from deceit, rises above foolish thoughts, and recoils at the approach of unrighteousness. {1:6} Wisdom is a gentle spirit and does not absolve a blasphemer of guilt; God witnesses their innermost thoughts, observes their heart, and hears their tongue. {1:7} The Spirit of the Lord fills the world, and the one who holds all things together knows every word spoken. {1:8} Therefore, no one who speaks unrighteousness will go unnoticed, and justice, when it judges, will not overlook them. {1:9} The counsels of the ungodly will be scrutinized, and their words will be reported to the Lord to convict them of their lawless deeds. {1:10} A vigilant ear hears everything, and whispers do not go unheard. {1:11} Guard against idle murmuring and refrain from slander, for no secret word is without consequence, and lying destroys the soul. {1:12} Do not invite death through your way of life, nor bring destruction through your actions; {1:13} for God did not create death, nor does he delight in the demise of the living. {1:14} He made all things to exist, and the life-giving forces of the world are pure; there is no destructive poison in them, and the realm of Hades has no power on earth. {1:15} Righteousness is eternal. {1:16} But the ungodly summon death with their words and deeds; they embrace him as a friend, and they make agreements with him, for they belong to his company.

{2:1} They reasoned foolishly, saying to themselves, "Our lives are short and full of sorrow, and there is no remedy when we die. No one has ever returned from Hades." {2:2} They believed life was a random chance, and after death, we are as if we never existed. The breath in our nostrils is like smoke, and our reason merely a spark ignited by our heartbeat. {2:3} When this spark goes out, our bodies turn to ashes, and our spirits dissolve like empty air. {2:4} Our names will fade with time, our deeds forgotten. Our lives pass like clouds dispersed by the sun's rays and overcome by its heat. {2:5} Our time on earth is like a fleeting shadow, with death sealing our fate, from which no one returns. {2:6} "So let us indulge in all the pleasures life offers, and enjoy every creation as we did in youth. {2:7} Let us drink expensive wine and wear the finest perfumes. Let no spring flower pass us by. {2:8} Let us crown ourselves with roses before they wither. {2:9} Let us revel and leave our mark everywhere, for this is our portion and our lot." {2:10} They oppressed the righteous and ignored the needs of the poor, widows, and the elderly. {2:11} They believed might made right, dismissing the weak as useless. {2:12} "Let us plot against the righteous man; he opposes us and challenges our actions. He accuses us of violating the law and straying from our training. {2:13} He claims knowledge of God and calls himself a child of the Lord. {2:14} He rebukes our thoughts and convicts us. {2:15} His very presence is a burden to us, for his life is unlike ours, and his ways are strange. {2:16} He considers us base and avoids our paths as unclean. He declares the end of the righteous as blessed and boasts that God is his father. {2:17} Let us see if his words are true and test what happens at the end of his life. {2:18} If he truly is God's son, he will be helped and delivered from his enemies. {2:19} Let us insult and torture him to test his gentleness and patience. {2:20} Let us subject him to a shameful death, for if he speaks the truth, he will be protected." {2:21} Thus they reasoned, blinded by their wickedness, {2:22} unaware of God's purposes or the reward of righteousness. {2:23} For God created man for immortality, in his own image and likeness, {2:24} but through the envy of the devil, death entered the world, and those who follow him experience its grasp.

{3:1} The souls of the righteous are securely held by God, untouched by torment. {3:2} Though to the foolish they may seem to have perished, their departure is viewed as a calamity, {3:3} yet they are in peace. {3:4} Despite being judged by men, their hope is anchored in immortality. {3:5} Through trials, they have been refined and found worthy by God; {3:6} like gold tested in a furnace, they have been accepted like a sacrificial offering. {3:7} In their time of vindication, they will shine brightly and move swiftly like sparks through stubble. {3:8} They will govern nations and rule over peoples, and the Lord will reign over them forever. {3:9} Those who trust in him will grasp truth, and the faithful will dwell with him in love, for grace and mercy embrace his chosen ones, and he guards his holy ones. {3:10} But the ungodly will face fitting punishment, having ignored the righteous and rebelled against the Lord. {3:11} Those who despise wisdom and instruction will find misery; their hopes are futile, their labors in vain, and their deeds fruitless. {3:12} Their families are troubled, their offspring cursed. Blessed are those who remain undefiled, for they will bear fruit when God examines souls. {3:13} Blessed also are the faithful eunuchs, who have not committed wrongdoing and have not plotted against the Lord; they will receive special favor for their loyalty and find great joy in the Lord's temple. {3:14} The fruit of righteous labor endures, and understanding's foundation stands firm. {3:15} But the children of adulterers will not thrive, and those born of unlawful unions will perish. {3:16} Even if they live long, they will not be esteemed, and their old age will lack honor. {3:17} If they die young, they will find no hope or comfort in the day of judgment. {3:18} The fate of the unrighteous is grievous, leading to a bitter end.

{4:1} It is better to be childless yet virtuous, for virtue's memory brings immortality, recognized both by God and humanity. {4:2} While present, men strive to emulate it; when gone, they long for it. Throughout time, virtue triumphs crowned, undefeated in the contest for pure rewards. {4:3} The offspring of the ungodly will be of no avail; their illegitimate descendants will not establish firm roots. {4:4} Though they may flourish briefly, they stand insecure and will be uprooted by the storm's violence. {4:5} Their branches break off before maturity, their fruit useless and inedible. {4:6} Children born from unlawful unions bear witness against their parents when God judges them. {4:7} Yet the righteous, even if they die young, find rest. {4:8} Old age is not honored merely by its length, nor measured by years alone; {4:9} true honor comes with understanding, and a blameless life is a ripe old age. {4:10} There was one who pleased God and was beloved by him, taken away while living among sinners. {4:11} He was taken up to prevent evil from corrupting his understanding or deceit from deceiving his soul. {4:12} The allure of wickedness obscures goodness, and wandering desires twist innocent minds. {4:13} Despite a short life, he achieved great maturity; {4:14} his soul pleased the Lord, hence he was swiftly taken from the midst of wickedness. {4:15} Though people witnessed, they did not comprehend, failing to grasp that God's grace and mercy are with his chosen ones, whom he protects. {4:16} The righteous, though deceased, will condemn the living ungodly, and the swiftly perfected youth will judge the prolonged old age of the unrighteous. {4:17} They will witness the end of the wise and fail to understand the Lord's purpose and protection. {4:18} They will scorn him, but the Lord will mock them; they will become dishonored corpses, an outrage among the dead forever. {4:19} God will silence them, shaking them from their foundations, leaving them dry and barren, suffering in anguish, their memory forgotten. {4:20} Dread will seize them as their sins are recounted, and their lawless deeds will convict them openly.

{5:1} Then the righteous will stand with unwavering confidence before those who oppressed them and mocked their efforts. {5:2} Seeing them, the oppressors will tremble with fear, astonished by the unexpected salvation of the righteous. {5:3} They will speak to one another in remorse and deep anguish, saying, {5:4} "This is the one we once ridiculed and treated with contempt — how foolish we were! We thought their life was folly and their end shameful. {5:5} Why were they considered among the children of God? Why do they share in the inheritance of the saints? {5:6} We wandered from the path of truth; the light of righteousness did not shine upon us, nor did the sun rise upon us. {5:7} We pursued lawlessness and destruction, journeying through desolate wastelands, neglecting the ways of the Lord. {5:8} What did our arrogance and wealth bring us? {5:9} "All these things have vanished like a fleeting shadow or passing rumor; {5:10} like a ship passing through turbulent waters, leaving no trace behind; {5:11} like a bird swiftly flying through the air, leaving no mark of its path; {5:12} like an arrow shot through the air, its trajectory unknown. {5:13} So too, our lives passed by swiftly, lacking virtue, consumed by wickedness." {5:14} The hope of the ungodly is as insubstantial as chaff blown by the wind, like frost dispersed by a storm, evaporating like smoke. {5:15} But the righteous live eternally, their reward secure with the Lord; the Most High cares for them. {5:16} They will receive a glorious crown and a beautiful diadem from the Lord's hand, protected by his power. {5:17} The Lord will clothe himself with zeal as armor and will arm all creation to defend against his enemies. {5:18} Righteousness will be his breastplate, and justice his helmet; {5:19} holiness his invincible shield, {5:20} and fierce wrath his sword. Creation will join him to fight against the wicked. {5:21} Lightning bolts will strike true, leaping like arrows from a well-drawn bow of clouds. {5:22} Hailstones of wrath will rain down like catapulted missiles; the seas will rage, and rivers overwhelm. {5:23} A mighty wind will rise like a tempest, scattering them away. Lawlessness will devastate the earth, and evil will overthrow the thrones of rulers.

{6:1} Listen, O rulers, and understand; pay attention, O judges of the earth. {6:2} Hearken, you who govern many nations and boast of your authority. {6:3} Your dominion comes from the Lord, and your sovereignty from the Most High, who examines your deeds and scrutinizes your intentions. {6:4} Because as stewards of his kingdom you did not govern justly, nor uphold the law, nor walked in accordance with God's will, {6:5} swift and severe judgment awaits you, for those in positions of power are held to account. {6:6} The humble may find mercy, but the mighty will face rigorous judgment. {6:7} The Lord, who made both small and great, shows no partiality; he cares for all equally. {6:8} Yet a strict reckoning awaits the powerful. {6:9} Therefore, O rulers, heed my words, that you may gain wisdom and not transgress. {6:10} Those who honor holy things with holiness will themselves be sanctified, and those who learn will find protection. {6:11} So set your heart on wisdom; long for her, and you will be instructed. {6:12} Wisdom is radiant and enduring, easily discerned by those who love her, and found by those who seek her. {6:13} She hastens to reveal herself to those who desire her. {6:14} Those who rise early to seek her will not be disappointed, for they will find her at their doorsteps. {6:15} To focus on wisdom is true understanding; those who are vigilant for her sake will soon be free from worry, {6:16} for wisdom seeks those worthy of her, appearing graciously along their paths and meeting them in their thoughts. {6:17} The beginning of wisdom is a sincere desire for instruction, and devotion to instruction is love for wisdom. {6:18} Loving wisdom leads to keeping her laws, and obeying her laws ensures immortality, {6:19} drawing one closer to God; {6:20} thus, the pursuit of wisdom leads to a kingdom. {6:21} Therefore, O rulers, if you cherish thrones and scepters, honor wisdom so that you may reign forever. {6:22} I will explain what wisdom is, how she came to be, and I will not withhold any secrets from you. I will trace her origins from the beginning of creation, making her knowledge clear, and I will not deviate from the truth; {6:23} nor will I entertain envy, for wisdom has no association with envy. {6:24} A multitude of wise people is the salvation of the world, and a wise ruler brings stability to their people. {6:25} Therefore, gain understanding from my words, and you will benefit greatly.

{7:1} I am mortal like every human being, a descendant of the first-formed child of earth. In the womb of my mother, I was shaped into flesh over ten months, conceived from the union of man and woman in the joy of marriage. {7:2} When I entered the world, I breathed the same air as all, and fell upon the common earth, my first sound echoing like that of every newborn. {7:3} I was tenderly cared for, wrapped in swaddling cloths, for no king enters life differently; all humanity shares one beginning and faces a common end. {7:4} So I prayed, and understanding was granted; I called upon God, and the spirit of wisdom came to me. {7:5} I valued her above scepters and thrones, regarding wealth as insignificant compared to her. {7:6} No gem could match her worth, for gold is like sand in her sight, and silver is as clay before her. {7:7} I cherished her more than health and beauty, choosing her over light itself, for her radiance is eternal. {7:8} With wisdom came all good things, and in her hands were riches beyond measure. {7:9} I rejoiced in them all, not realizing that wisdom herself was their source. {7:10} I learned openly and shared generously; I did not hoard her treasures, {7:11} for they are an unfailing wealth for humanity, bringing friendship with God and commendation for those who embrace her teachings. {7:12} May God grant me wisdom in my words and judge me worthy of what I have received, for he guides wisdom and corrects the wise. {7:13} Both we and our words are in his hands, along with understanding and skill. {7:14} He granted me true knowledge of the structure of the world, the workings of elements, {7:15} the beginning, end, and middle of time, the changes of seasons and cycles of the year, the constellations and stars, {7:16} the behaviors of animals and wild beasts, the powers of spirits, the thoughts of men, the qualities of plants and the powers of roots. {7:17} I learned the secrets and revelations, for wisdom, the creator of all, taught me. In her is a spirit that is intelligent, holy, unique, versatile, mobile, clear, pure, distinct, invincible, loving good, sharp, irresistible, {7:18} benevolent, humane, steadfast, sure, free from worry, all-powerful, overseeing all, and penetrating through intelligent and pure spirits, subtle and most delicate. {7:19} Wisdom is more fluid than any motion; through her purity, she pervades and penetrates all things. {7:20} She is a breath of the power of God, a pure radiance of the Almighty's glory. Nothing defiled can stain her, for she is a reflection of eternal light, a spotless mirror of God's actions, an image of his goodness. {7:21} Though she is singular, she accomplishes all things; remaining within herself, she renews all things. She passes into holy souls in every generation, making them friends of God and prophets, {7:22} for God loves nothing more than those who dwell with wisdom. {7:23} She is more beautiful than the sun and surpasses every constellation of stars. Compared to light, she shines more brightly, {7:24} for while night follows day, evil cannot prevail against wisdom.

{8:1} Wisdom extends her influence mightily from one end of the earth to the other, ordering all things with perfection. {8:2} From my youth, I loved her passionately and sought her eagerly. I desired to make her my bride, captivated by her beauty. {8:3} She magnifies her noble origin by dwelling with God, and the Lord of all cherishes her deeply. {8:4} For she is initiated into the knowledge of God and shares in his works. {8:5} If riches are desirable in life, what is richer than wisdom, who accomplishes all things? {8:6} And if understanding is effective, who more than she is the creator of what exists? {8:7} If anyone loves righteousness, her labors are virtues; for she teaches self-control, prudence, justice, and courage. Nothing in life is more profitable for humanity than these. {8:8} If anyone desires broad experience, she knows the ancient things and infers the future; she understands figurative speech and unravels riddles. She foresees signs, wonders, and the outcomes of seasons and times. {8:9} Therefore, I resolved to make her my companion, knowing that she would counsel me wisely and comfort me in cares and sorrows. {8:10} Because of her, I will receive glory among the multitudes and honor among the elders, though I am young. {8:11} I will be esteemed for my keen judgment, and rulers will admire me. {8:12} When I am silent, they will wait for my words; when I speak, they will listen attentively; and when I speak at length, they will be silent in awe. {8:13} Through her, I will attain immortality and leave an eternal remembrance for those who come after me. {8:14} I will govern nations, and peoples will be subject to me; {8:15} even dreaded monarchs will fear me when they hear of me. Among the people, I will demonstrate my capability and courage in war. {8:16} When I return home, I will find rest with her, for her companionship brings no bitterness, and life with her is devoid of pain but full of joy and gladness. {8:17} Reflecting on these things inwardly, I realized that in union with wisdom there is immortality, {8:18} in friendship with her, pure delight, and in her labors, unfailing wealth. Through her companionship comes understanding, and sharing her words brings renown. {8:19} From childhood, I was naturally gifted, and a good soul was granted to me. {8:20} Rather, being good, I entered an undefiled body. {8:21} But I understood that I would not possess wisdom unless God gave her to me — it was a mark of insight to know whose gift she was. So, I appealed to the Lord, beseeching him with my whole heart, and I said:

{9:1} "O God of my ancestors and Lord of mercy, who created all things by your word, {9:2} and by your wisdom formed humanity to have dominion over the creatures you made, {9:3} to rule the world in holiness and righteousness, and to pronounce judgment with a soul upright, {9:4} grant me the wisdom that sits beside your throne, and do not reject me from among your servants. {9:5} For I am your servant, the son of your maidservant, a man who is weak and short-lived, with limited understanding of judgment and laws; {9:6} even if someone is perfect among humans, without the wisdom that comes from you, they are considered nothing. {9:7} You have chosen me to be king over your people and to judge your sons and daughters. {9:8} You have commanded to build a temple on your holy mountain, and an altar in the city where you dwell, a replica of the holy tent you prepared from the beginning. {9:9} With you is wisdom, who knows your works and was present when you created the world, understanding what is pleasing in your sight and what is right according to your commandments. {9:10} Send her forth from the holy heavens, and from the throne of your glory send her, that she may be with me and labor with me, that I may learn what is pleasing to you. {9:11} For she knows and understands all things, and she will wisely guide my actions and protect me with her glory. {9:12} Then my works will be acceptable, and I will judge your people justly and be worthy of the throne of my father. {9:13} For who can comprehend the counsel of God? Or who can understand what the Lord wills? {9:14} For human reasoning is futile, and our plans are likely to fail, {9:15} for our mortal bodies weigh down the soul, and this earthly tent burdens the thoughtful mind. {9:16} We struggle to grasp what is on earth, and what is within our reach we find with effort; but who has fathomed what is in the heavens? {9:17} Who has learned your counsel, unless you have granted wisdom and sent your Holy Spirit from on high? {9:18} Thus the ways of those on earth were made straight, and people were taught what pleases you, and were saved by wisdom."

{10:1} Wisdom protected the first man created in the world, shielding him from his transgression and giving him strength to govern all things. {10:2} But when an unrighteous man turned away from wisdom in anger, he perished, for in rage he slew his brother. {10:3} During the flood, wisdom once again saved the earth, guiding the righteous man Noah with a humble piece of wood. {10:4} Wisdom also recognized the righteous man amidst nations in wicked agreement, preserving him blameless before God and strengthening him in his compassion for his child. {10:5} She rescued another righteous man from the destruction of the ungodly, allowing him to escape the fire that rained down upon the Five Cities. {10:6} Evidence of their wickedness remains to this day: a desolate wasteland still smoking, fruitless plants, and a pillar of salt standing as a monument to an unbelieving soul. {10:7} Because they disregarded wisdom, not only did they fail to recognize what is good, but they also left a reminder of their folly for all mankind to see. {10:8} Wisdom rescued those who served her from their troubles. {10:9} When a righteous man fled from his brother's wrath, she guided him on straight paths, revealing to him the kingdom of God and granting him knowledge of angels. She prospered his labors and increased the fruit of his toil. {10:10} When oppressors sought to exploit him, wisdom stood by him and made him prosperous. {10:11} She protected him from his enemies and kept him safe from those who lay in wait. In his trials, she gave him victory, showing that godliness is more powerful than anything. {10:12} When a righteous man was sold into slavery, wisdom did not abandon him but delivered him from sin. She accompanied him into the dungeon and remained with him in prison until she brought him the scepter of a kingdom and authority over his masters. She proved his accusers false and bestowed everlasting honor upon him. {10:13} Wisdom delivered a holy and blameless people from a nation of oppressors. {10:14} She entered the soul of a servant of the Lord and stood against fearful kings with wonders and signs. {10:15} She rewarded holy men for their labors, guiding them along marvelous paths. She became their shelter by day and a guiding flame through the night. {10:16} Wisdom led them across the Red Sea and through deep waters, drowning their enemies and casting them up from the depths. {10:17} Therefore, the righteous plundered the ungodly and sang hymns to the Lord's holy name, praising with one accord his protecting hand. {10:18} Wisdom opened the mouths of the mute and made the tongues of babes speak clearly.

{11:1} Wisdom guided the works of a holy prophet, prospering them through his hands. {11:2} They journeyed through desolate wilderness and camped in uninhabited places. {11:3} They stood firm against their enemies and repelled their foes. {11:4} When they thirsted, they called upon you, and water flowed from the flinty rock, quenching their thirst from hard stone. {11:5} Even through the punishment inflicted upon their enemies, they themselves received benefit in their time of need. {11:6} Instead of the fountain of an ever-flowing river defiled with blood, {11:7} in response to the decree to slay infants, you provided abundant water unexpectedly, {11:8} demonstrating through their thirst how you punished their enemies. {11:9} When they were tested and disciplined with mercy, they learned how the ungodly suffer under wrathful judgment. {11:10} You tested them as a father warns his children, but examined the ungodly with stern condemnation like a king. {11:11} Whether near or far, they were equally distressed, {11:12} experiencing profound sorrow and lamenting what had occurred. {11:13} When they realized that their own punishments benefited the righteous, they acknowledged it was the work of the Lord. {11:14} Despite mocking him who had long been cast out and exposed, they marveled at him in the end, for their thirst was not like that of the righteous. {11:15} As retribution for their foolish and wicked thoughts that led them to worship irrational serpents and worthless animals, you sent upon them a multitude of irrational creatures to punish them.

{11:16} Thus they learned that one is punished by the very things through which they sin. {11:17} Your all-powerful hand, which created the world from formless matter, had no lack of means to send upon them a multitude of bears, fierce lions, {11:18} or newly created unknown beasts full of rage, creatures breathing fiery breath, belching forth thick smoke, or flashing terrible sparks from their eyes; {11:19} their devastation could exterminate men, and the mere sight of them could kill from fright alone. {11:20} Apart from these, men could fall at a single breath when pursued by justice and scattered by the breath of your power. Yet you have ordered all things by measure, number, and weight. {11:21} For your great strength is always within your power, and who can withstand the might of your arm? {11:22} The whole world before you is like a speck that tips the scales, like a drop of morning dew falling upon the ground. {11:23} Yet you are merciful to all, for you can do all things, and you overlook men's sins so that they may repent. {11:24} For you love all things that exist, and you despise none of the things you have made, for you would not have created anything if you had hated it. {11:25} How could anything endure if you did not will it? Or how could anything not called forth by you be preserved? {11:26} You spare all things, for they are yours, O Lord who loves the living.

{12:1} For your immortal spirit is present in all things. {12:2} Therefore, you correct those who trespass little by little, reminding and warning them of their sins, so that they may turn away from wickedness and place their trust in you, O Lord. {12:3} Those who lived long ago in your holy land, {12:4} you detested for their abominable practices, their sorcery, and unholy rituals, {12:5} their merciless killing of children, and their sacrificial feasts of human flesh and blood. These practitioners of a heathen cult, {12:6} these parents who murdered innocent lives, you determined to destroy through the hands of our ancestors, {12:7} so that your most cherished land might receive a righteous colony of your servants. {12:8} Yet even these you spared, knowing they were mortal, and you sent wasps as harbingers of your army, to gradually eliminate them. {12:9} Although you could have delivered the ungodly into the hands of the righteous in battle, or destroyed them instantly with fearsome beasts or your stern word, {12:10} you judged them gradually, giving them an opportunity to repent, though you knew their origin was evil and their wickedness inherent, and that their mindset would not change. {12:11} They were cursed from the beginning, and it was not out of fear of anyone that you left their sins unpunished. {12:12} For who can challenge your actions or resist your judgment? Who can accuse you for the destruction of nations you have made? Who can stand before you to defend the unrighteous? {12:13} For there is no god beside you who cares for all people, to whom you need to prove your just judgment; {12:14} no king or ruler can confront you regarding those whom you have punished. {12:15} You are righteous and rule all things justly, deeming it contrary to your nature to condemn the undeserving. {12:16} Your strength is the source of righteousness, and your sovereignty over all causes you to spare everyone. {12:17} You display your power when doubts arise about the extent of your might, and you rebuke any arrogance among those who acknowledge it. {12:18} Sovereign in strength, you judge with gentleness, governing us with great forbearance, for you have the power to act whenever you choose. {12:19} Through these actions, you have taught your people that the righteous must be merciful, and you have filled your children with hope, granting repentance for sins. {12:20} For just as you carefully and leniently punished the enemies of your servants and those deserving of death, granting them time and opportunity to renounce their wickedness, {12:21} how much more rigorously you have judged your own children, to whom you gave oaths and covenants filled with promises of goodness! {12:22} Thus, while disciplining us, you have chastised our enemies ten thousand times over, so that we may ponder your goodness when we judge, and expect mercy when we are judged. {12:23} Therefore, those who foolishly lived unrighteously were tormented by their own abominations. {12:24} They strayed far on paths of error, worshipping animals even despised by their enemies, deceived like foolish infants. {12:25} Thus, you sent your judgment upon them as upon thoughtless children. {12:26} Yet those who ignored the warning of gentle rebukes will face the deserved judgment of God. {12:27} For in their suffering, they became enraged at the very creatures they once worshipped as gods, punished by those very beings, they finally saw and acknowledged the true God, whom they had previously refused to know. Thus, they faced the utmost condemnation.

{13:1} All those who were ignorant of God were inherently foolish; they could not, from observing the visible world, recognize the existence of the one who created it, nor could they discern the craftsman by contemplating his works. {13:2} Instead, they speculated that fire, wind, swift air, the circle of stars, turbulent water, or the celestial bodies governed the universe as gods. {13:3} If they were captivated by the beauty of these things and considered them gods, they should realize how much superior is the Lord who created such beauty. {13:4} If they marveled at the power and order of these elements, they should understand that the one who formed them is infinitely more powerful. {13:5} From observing the greatness and beauty of created things, one can infer the greatness of their Creator. {13:6} However, these individuals are not entirely without blame, for even though they sought after God and desired to find him amidst his creations, {13:7} they remained blind, trusting only in what they could see, because the visible world is indeed captivating. {13:8} Yet, even this lack of knowledge cannot fully excuse them, {13:9} for if they had the intellect to investigate the world around them, why did they not sooner recognize the Lord of all things? {13:10} How pitiable are those whose hopes are fixed on lifeless idols—gods made by human hands: gold and silver crafted with skill, images of animals, or useless stones shaped by ancient craftsmen. {13:11} A skilled artisan may take a manageable tree, skillfully strip its bark, and fashion from it a useful vessel for daily life. {13:12} He uses the leftover wood for fuel to cook his food and satisfy his hunger. {13:13} But from among these leftover scraps, he may take a worthless piece—a crooked stick full of knots—and in his leisure time, carve it carefully, fashioning it into the likeness of a man. {13:14} Or he may craft it to resemble a worthless animal, painting it red, covering its flaws with paint, and giving it a glossy appearance. {13:15} Then he constructs a suitable niche for it, places it on the wall, and secures it with nails. {13:16} He takes great care that it does not fall, knowing it cannot help itself, being merely an image in need of assistance. {13:17} Yet he prays to it for wealth, for marriage, for children, showing no shame in addressing a lifeless object. {13:18} He appeals to it for health, though it is weak; for life, though it is dead; for aid, though it is inexperienced; for a successful journey, though it cannot move a step. {13:19} He seeks strength from it for earning money, for work, for success, though it has no strength to offer.

{14:1} Once again, imagine a person preparing to sail across tumultuous waves, relying on a piece of wood more fragile than the ship itself that carries him. {14:2} This vessel, designed for profit, was planned by human desire, while wisdom guided the hands of its craftsmen. {14:3} Yet it is your providence, O Father, that directs its course, granting it a path through the sea and a safe passage through the waves, {14:4} demonstrating your ability to rescue from every peril, enabling even the inexperienced to venture into the sea. {14:5} Your intention is that the works of your wisdom should not be in vain; hence, people entrust their lives even to the smallest raft, and navigating through the billows, they safely reach the shore. {14:6} From the beginning, when arrogant giants were perishing, the hope of the world sought refuge on a raft, guided by your hand, and thus left behind the seed of a new generation. {14:7} Blessed indeed is the wood through which righteousness is accomplished. {14:8} But cursed is the idol crafted by human hands, and equally accursed is the one who made it, because he created something perishable and called it a god. {14:9} For God finds equally detestable the ungodly person and their ungodliness, {14:10} because both the action and its doer will be punished together. {14:11} Therefore, there will be judgment upon the idols of the nations, for though they were part of God's creation, they became abominable, ensnaring souls and trapping the foolish. {14:12} The idea of creating idols was the beginning of moral decay, and their invention corrupted life itself, {14:13} for idols did not exist from the beginning and will not endure forever. {14:14} They entered the world through human vanity, and their swift destruction has been planned. {14:15} For instance, a grieving father, mourning the sudden loss of his child, fashioned an image of the deceased and honored it as a god, passing down secret rites and rituals to his descendants. {14:16} Over time, this ungodly practice became entrenched as law, and at the command of rulers, carved images were worshiped. {14:17} Unable to honor distant monarchs in their presence, people fashioned images of them from afar, thereby honoring absent rulers with zeal as though they were present. {14:18} Craftsmen, driven by ambition, enhanced these images even for those who did not know the king, intensifying their worship. {14:19} Perhaps seeking favor from their ruler, they skillfully improved the likeness, and the populace, captivated by their artistry, began to worship as divine the very person they had recently revered as human. {14:20} This became a hidden snare for humanity, as people in bondage to misfortune or royal authority bestowed upon lifeless idols names that should never be shared. {14:21} Subsequently, not content with merely misunderstanding God's nature, they lived in great conflict due to ignorance, calling great evils "peace." {14:22} Whether committing child sacrifices in rituals, engaging in secret ceremonies, or partaking in frenzied revelries with strange customs, {14:23} they defiled their lives and marriages, resorting to treachery, adultery, and all manner of violence, corruption, deceit, and faithlessness. {14:24} Their existence was marked by chaos—polluting souls, distorting sexual norms, disrupting marriages, and indulging in adultery and debauchery. {14:25} Indeed, the idolatry they engaged in, unmentionable and abhorrent, initiated, sustained, and concluded every form of evil. {14:26} Their worshipers either exulted in madness, prophesied falsehoods, lived unjustly, or brazenly committed perjury, {14:27} trusting in lifeless idols, they swore wicked oaths with no fear of retribution. {14:28} Yet, just retribution awaits them on two counts: for their wickedness in devoting themselves to idols and for their unrighteous oaths made in contempt of holiness. {14:29} It is not the power of the idols by which people swear that matters, but the just punishment that always follows the transgressions of the unrighteous.

{15:1} But you, our God, are kind and true, patient, and govern all things with mercy. {15:2} Even if we sin, we belong to you, acknowledging your power; yet we strive not to sin, knowing we are accounted as yours. {15:3} For true righteousness is knowing you, and true immortality is understanding your power. {15:4} We are not misled by the wicked intentions of human art or the futile labor of painters who depict figures with varied colors, {15:5} arousing foolish desires for lifeless forms and dead images. {15:6} Those who make, desire, or worship such things are lovers of evil and fit for such hopeless pursuits. {15:7} Consider the potter who molds vessels from soft clay, creating both those used for noble purposes and those for common use, all from the same material; it is the potter who decides each vessel's purpose. {15:8} Yet with wasted effort, he fashions worthless gods from the same clay—a man made from earth a short while ago, returning soon to the earth, surrendering the soul lent to him. {15:9} He does not ponder his mortal fate or the brevity of his life, but competes with craftsmen in precious metals and imitates workers in copper, boasting in his skill to fashion false gods. {15:10} His heart is ashes, his hope is cheaper than dirt, and his life is less valuable than clay, {15:11} for he fails to recognize his Creator, who gave him an active soul and breathed into him a living spirit. {15:12} Instead, he regards our existence as a game and life as a festival for profit, believing one must acquire wealth at any cost, even through deceit. {15:13} This man, above all others, knows he sins by fashioning fragile vessels and graven images from earthly matter. {15:14} But most foolish and wretched are all who oppress your people, thinking their heathen idols are gods—blind, breathless, deaf, incapable of touch or movement. {15:15} These idols made by man lack life and are dead, unlike their maker who possesses life. {15:16} Mortal man fashioned them; a borrowed spirit formed them. No man can create a god resembling himself. {15:17} They are mortal, and what they fashion with lawless hands is lifeless; they are superior to the idols they worship, for they possess life, whereas idols do not. {15:18} Enemies of your people even worship detestable animals, inferior in intelligence, failing to receive God's praise and blessing. {15:19} These creatures, lacking beauty and divine favor, evade God's recognition and blessing.

{16:1} Therefore, those men deservedly faced punishment through such creatures, tormented by a multitude of animals. {16:2} Instead of this judgment, you showed kindness to your people, providing quails as a satisfying delicacy to fulfill their appetites. {16:3} While those who opposed you suffered from repulsive creatures, your people, after enduring brief scarcity, enjoyed delicacies. {16:4} The oppressors faced relentless want, while your people learned of their enemies' torment. {16:5} When your people were afflicted by wild beasts and venomous serpents, your wrath did not persist; they suffered briefly as a warning and were delivered by your law's command. {16:6} Those who turned to your command were saved by you, the Savior of all, not by what they saw. {16:7} Through this, you convinced our enemies that you deliver from every evil. {16:8} They suffered from locusts and flies without relief, deserving such punishment. {16:9} Yet your sons were not defeated, even by venomous serpents, aided by your mercy which healed them. {16:10} They were bitten to remember your teachings and promptly delivered, lest they forget and become unresponsive to your kindness. {16:11} Neither herbs nor poultices healed them; your word alone, O Lord, brings healing to all. {16:12} You have power over life and death, guiding men to the gates of Hades and back. {16:13} In wickedness, one man kills another, unable to revive the departed spirit or free the imprisoned soul. {16:14} Escape from your hand is impossible; the ungodly, refusing to know you, were scourged by your strength. {16:15} Pursued by unusual rains, hail, storms, and fire, they were utterly consumed. {16:16} Incredibly, water, which quenches all, intensified the fire's effect, defending the righteous universe. {16:17} Fire was restrained to show judgment upon the ungodly, while even within water it burned more intensely to destroy their crops. {16:18} Instead, you gave your people food of angels, heavenly bread without their toil, satisfying every palate. {16:19} Your provision showed your sweetness to your children, transforming to suit their desires. {16:20} Snow and ice resisted fire, revealing the destruction of enemies' crops by fire in hail and rain. {16:21} Yet fire, to feed the righteous, lost its power. {16:22} Creation, serving you, punished the unrighteous and showed kindness to those who trust in you. {16:23} At that time, it served your nourishing bounty in every form. {16:24} Your sons learned that your word, not crops alone, sustains man. {16:25} What fire did not destroy melted in the sun's fleeting ray. {16:26} Man must rise before the sun, giving thanks and praying at dawn. {16:27} The hope of the ungrateful melts like winter frost and flows away like waste water.

{17:1} Your judgments are profound and difficult to comprehend; therefore, unenlightened souls have gone astray. {17:2} When lawless men thought they had the holy nation under their control, they themselves became captives of darkness and prisoners of long night, confined under their own roofs, estranged from eternal providence. {17:3} Believing their secret sins were hidden behind a veil of forgetfulness, they were scattered in terror, haunted by terrifying visions. {17:4} Even the inner chambers provided no refuge from fear; ominous sounds echoed around them, and grim specters with dark faces appeared. {17:5} Neither fire nor the stars' bright flames could dispel that hateful night. {17:6} Only a dreadful, self-inflicted fire illuminated their surroundings, and they feared the unseen more than the visible horrors. {17:7} Their illusions of magic failed, and their supposed wisdom was scornfully rebuked. {17:8} Those who claimed to cure the disorders of troubled souls were themselves stricken with absurd fear. {17:9} Even if no external threat frightened them, they were terrified by passing beasts and hissing serpents. {17:10} They perished in trembling fear, refusing to even look at the air around them, which offered no escape. {17:11} Wickedness, cowardly and condemned by its own conscience, magnified their difficulties. {17:12} Fear stripped away reason's aid, leaving them vulnerable. {17:13} Weak and desperate, they preferred ignorance to confronting their torment. {17:14} Throughout the powerless night, enveloped by the darkness of Hades, they all slept the same sleep. {17:15} They were tormented by monstrous visions, paralyzed by their own surrender to fear, overwhelmed by sudden terror. {17:16} Each one fell down, imprisoned not by iron bars but by darkness. {17:17} Whether a farmer, shepherd, or wilderness worker, they were all seized by the inevitable fate, bound together in darkness. {17:18} Whether it was the wind's whistle, birds' melodies in trees, rushing waters' rhythms, or the crash of rocks, fear paralyzed them. {17:19} The world outside continued in brilliant light, unhindered in its work, {17:20} while these men alone were shrouded in heavy night, a foreboding darkness awaiting them—yet they were even heavier burdens to themselves.

{18:1} But for your holy ones, there was a great light indeed. Their enemies heard their voices but could not see their forms, and they considered them fortunate for not having suffered harm. {18:2} They were thankful that your holy ones, though previously wronged, did them no injury, and they sought forgiveness for their past conflicts. {18:3} Therefore, you provided a flaming pillar of fire to guide your people through their unknown journey, and a gentle sun to brighten their glorious wanderings. {18:4} Their enemies, who had kept your sons imprisoned, deserved to be deprived of light and confined in darkness, through whom the imperishable light of your law would be given to the world. {18:5} When they plotted to kill the babies of your holy ones, and one child was exposed and rescued, you punished them by taking away many of their children, and ultimately destroyed them with a mighty flood. {18:6} This night had been foreknown to our ancestors, so they could rejoice in the sure knowledge of the promises they trusted in. {18:7} Your people anticipated the deliverance of the righteous and the destruction of their enemies. {18:8} By the same means that you punished our enemies, you called us to yourself and glorified us. {18:9} In secret, the holy children of righteous men offered sacrifices and unanimously adhered to the divine law, sharing equally in blessings and dangers, already praising their forefathers. {18:10} The discordant cries of their enemies echoed back, and their mournful lament for their children resounded far and wide. {18:11} Both slave and master suffered the same fate, and commoner alike suffered the loss of kings; all were overwhelmed by death innumerable. {18:12} So many corpses piled up that the living could not bury them all, as their most cherished children were taken in an instant. {18:13} Though they had disbelieved everything due to their magic arts, when their firstborn were struck down, they acknowledged your people as God's own. {18:14} While a profound silence enveloped all things and the night swiftly passed, {18:15} Your all-powerful word leaped from heaven, from your royal throne, into the doomed land, a fierce warrior, {18:16} wielding the sharp sword of your authoritative command. It stood and filled all things with death, touching heaven while standing on earth. {18:17} Dreadful apparitions troubled them in dreams, and unexpected fears assailed them. {18:18} Some were half-dead, thrown down to reveal why they were perishing. {18:19} Their disturbing dreams forewarned them so they would not perish without understanding their suffering. {18:20} Death touched even the righteous, and a plague struck the multitude in the desert, but your wrath did not linger. {18:21} A blameless man swiftly acted as their defender; he brought forth the shield of his ministry, prayer and incense as propitiation. {18:22} Not by strength or force, but by his word he subdued the destroyer, appealing to the oaths and covenants made with our ancestors. {18:23} When the dead were piled upon each other, he intervened, holding back wrath and cutting off its path to the living. {18:24} On his long robe, the whole world was depicted, and the glories of the ancestors were engraved on four rows of stones, with your majesty on the diadem upon his head. {18:25} These things the destroyer feared and yielded to; testing the wrath was enough.

{19:1} The ungodly faced relentless anger to the very end, for God foresaw even their future actions, {19:2} knowing that although they had allowed your people to depart and hastily sent them away, they would change their minds and pursue them. {19:3} While they were still mourning and lamenting at the graves of their dead, they foolishly decided to chase after those whom they had begged and compelled to leave. {19:4} They were drawn towards their deserved fate, forgetting what had transpired, so that they might endure the full measure of their punishment that their torments lacked. {19:5} Your people embarked on an incredible journey, while their pursuers met a strange death. {19:6} The entire creation was reshaped according to your commands, ensuring the safety of your children. {19:7} A cloud was seen overshadowing the camp, dry land appeared where water had been, providing an unobstructed path through the Red Sea and a grassy plain amidst the raging waves, {19:8} allowing those protected by your hand to pass through as one nation, witnessing marvelous wonders. {19:9} They moved like horses and leaped like lambs, praising you, O Lord, their deliverer. {19:10} They remembered their trials during their stay: instead of livestock, the earth produced gnats, and the rivers teemed with frogs instead of fish. {19:11} Later, they witnessed unusual birds when they craved luxurious food; to satisfy them, quails came up from the sea. {19:12} The sinners did not suffer punishment without warning signs in the form of thunderstorms, rightly facing consequences for their wickedness and bitter hatred towards strangers. {19:13} Some had refused hospitality to strangers, but these made slaves of their benefactor guests. {19:14} Not only that, but former hosts who mistreated aliens faced punishment for their inhospitality, {19:15} while those who welcomed strangers with feasts inflicted severe suffering on those they had treated as equals. {19:16} They were even struck with blindness, just like those at the door of the righteous, groping in darkness to find their way. {19:17} Elements exchanged places, akin to notes on a harp changing rhythm while maintaining their essence. This transformation was evident in what occurred. {19:18} Land creatures turned into water dwellers, and swimming creatures moved onto the land. {19:19} Fire retained its potency underwater, while water forgot its ability to quench fire. {19:20} Flames failed to consume perishable flesh walking among them, nor did they melt the easily liquefiable heavenly food. {19:21} In all these ways, O Lord, you elevated and glorified your people, never neglecting to aid them in every time and place.

Tobit

The Book of Tobit, an apocryphal work found in the Septuagint but absent from the Hebrew Bible, presents a rich tapestry of Jewish piety, wisdom literature, and folklore. It is set in the context of the Assyrian exile, specifically in the cities of Nineveh and Ecbatana, offering a vivid portrayal of Jewish life and faith during this period. The narrative follows the righteous Tobit, a devout Jew who remains faithful to the laws of Moses despite the challenges of exile. Tobit's unwavering dedication to charity, burial of the dead, and adherence to dietary laws amidst persecution underscores the text's emphasis on covenant fidelity. Central to the plot is the journey of Tobit's son, Tobias, who, guided by the disguised archangel Raphael, undertakes a perilous mission to retrieve a family fortune and ultimately finds love with Sarah, a woman plagued by a demon. This quest narrative interweaves themes of divine providence, the efficacy of prayer, and the importance of angelic intervention. The book's intricate structure combines elements of a morality tale with didactic passages on the virtues of almsgiving, piety, and the sanctity of marriage. Additionally, the cultural and theological interplay within Tobit offers insights into Jewish diaspora identity and the synthesis of Near Eastern mythological motifs with Jewish religious thought. Its inclusion in the Catholic and Orthodox canons, while excluded from the Protestant and Jewish texts, also speaks to the historical debates over scriptural authority and the fluidity of the biblical canon in antiquity. Thus, it highlights the richness of Jewish storytelling and religious expression during the Second Temple period, revealing insights into faith, culture, and community in the ancient world.

{1:1} This is the story of Tobit, son of Tobiel, descendant of Ananiel, Aduel, and Gabael, belonging to the tribe of Naphtali. {1:2} During the reign of Shalmaneser, king of Assyria, Tobit was taken captive from Thisbe, located south of Kedesh Naphtali in Galilee above Asher. {1:3} Throughout my life, I, Tobit, walked in the paths of truth and righteousness. In Assyria, I showed kindness to my countrymen and brethren who journeyed with me. {1:4} In my youth, when I lived in Israel, my ancestral tribe of Naphtali abandoned Jerusalem, the chosen place for all Israel to worship and where the temple of the Most High was established forever. {1:5} The tribes fell into apostasy, worshiping the idol Baal, including my own tribe of Naphtali. {1:6} Despite this, I faithfully went to Jerusalem for the feasts, offering first fruits, tithes, and offerings to the priests at the altar, as prescribed by Israel's law. {1:7} I gave a tenth of my produce to the Levites in Jerusalem and sold another tenth, using the proceeds to celebrate the feasts each year in Jerusalem. {1:8} The third tenth I gave to orphans and widows, as my grandmother Deborah had instructed me after my father's death left me an orphan. {1:9} I married Anna from our own family, and she bore me a son, Tobias. {1:10} When I was taken captive to Nineveh, my relatives and brethren ate Gentile food, {1:11} but I refrained, keeping the laws of God in my heart. {1:12} God favored me in the eyes of Shalmaneser, who appointed me to oversee the purchase of provisions. {1:13} During these times, I entrusted ten talents of silver to Gabael in Media, a prudent measure during uncertain times under Shalmaneser's successor, Sennacherib. {1:14} When Sennacherib's reign made travel unsafe, I could no longer access my funds in Media. {1:15} Throughout Shalmaneser's reign, I continued acts of charity among my brethren. {1:16} I fed the hungry, clothed the naked, and buried the dead, even those executed by Sennacherib in his wrath against Judea. {1:17} When Sennacherib sought to kill those fleeing from Judea, I buried them secretly, {1:18} risking my life. {1:19} Upon discovery, I fled Nineveh to escape death, leaving behind all my possessions except Anna and Tobias. {1:20} Shortly after, two of Sennacherib's sons assassinated him, fleeing to the mountains of Ararat. Esarhaddon, Sennacherib's son, then became king, appointing my nephew Ahikar to oversee his kingdom's affairs. {1:21} Ahikar interceded on my behalf, and I returned to Nineveh under Esarhaddon's reign. Ahikar, distinguished in the kingdom, served as cupbearer and administrator of Esarhaddon's accounts, second only to the king himself.

{2:1} When I returned home and was reunited with my wife Anna and my son Tobias, it was during the Feast of Pentecost, a sacred festival marking the seven weeks. {2:2} A lavish dinner had been prepared, and as I sat down to eat, I noticed the abundance of food. I said to my son, "Go and find any poor man among our brethren who remembers the Lord, and I will wait for you." {2:3} But he returned with distressing news, saying, "Father, one of our people has been murdered and left in the marketplace." {2:4} Immediately, I rose and hurried to remove the body to a safer place until sunset, before tasting any food. {2:5} Afterward, I cleansed myself and ate my meal with sorrow in my heart. {2:6} I recalled the words of the prophet Amos, how he foretold, "Your feasts will be turned into mourning, and all your songs into lamentation." Tears streamed down my face. {2:7} At sunset, I went to bury the deceased, digging a grave with my own hands. {2:8} My neighbors mocked me, saying, "He no longer fears for his life after fleeing before; now he's burying the dead once more!" {2:9} That night, I returned home defiled from the burial and slept beside the courtyard wall with my face uncovered. {2:10} Unknowingly, sparrows nesting above dropped fresh droppings into my eyes, causing white films to form. I sought help from physicians, but none could cure me. Ahikar, however, cared for me until he departed for Elymais. {2:11} During this time, my wife Anna supported us by working among women, earning wages for her labor. {2:12} Sometimes she received additional gifts along with her wages, such as a kid, which she brought home. {2:13} When it began to bleat, I questioned her, "Where did you get this kid? It's not stolen, is it? Return it to its rightful owners, for it's wrong to benefit from stolen goods." {2:14} Anna replied, "It was given to me as a gift in addition to my wages." Yet I doubted her honesty and insisted she return it, feeling ashamed for her actions. She retorted, "Where are your acts of charity and righteousness now? You seem to know everything!"

{3:1} Deep in sorrow, I wept and prayed with anguish, saying, {3:2} "Lord, you are righteous; all your actions are merciful and true. Your judgments are forever just and righteous. {3:3} Remember me with favor; do not punish me for my sins and the sins of my ancestors, whether deliberate or unknowing. {3:4} They disobeyed your commandments, and we suffered plunder, captivity, and death, becoming a reproach among the nations. {3:5} Your judgments upon me are just; we did not walk in truth before you. {3:6} Deal with me as you see fit; command that my spirit depart to the eternal abode, for death is preferable to the sorrow I endure. Release me from this distress; do not turn away from me." {3:7} On the same day in Ecbatana of Media, Sarah, daughter of Raguel, faced reproach from her father's maids. {3:8} They mocked her for the deaths of her seven husbands, slain by the demon Asmodeus before they could be with her. {3:9} Grieved deeply, she considered ending her life. {3:10} She prayed by her window, saying, "Blessed are you, O Lord my God. May all your works praise you forever. {3:11} Turn your face towards me; release me from this earth and end my reproach." {3:12} She asserted her innocence before God, {3:13} pleading to no longer endure reproach. {3:14} "You know, O Lord, I am innocent before men. {3:15} I have not defiled my name or my father's name in captivity. {3:16} Hear my plea; if it is not your will to take my life, show me mercy and end my reproach." {3:17} Both prayers were heard, and the angel Raphael was sent to heal Tobit's eyes, arrange Tobias to marry Sarah, and bind Asmodeus. Tobit returned home, and Sarah descended from her chamber.

{4:1} On that day, Tobit remembered the money he had entrusted to Gabael in Rages of Media. He pondered within himself, {4:2} "I have asked for death. Why not call my son Tobias and explain about the money before I die?" {4:3} So he summoned Tobias and instructed him, "My son, when I die, bury me properly and honor your mother always. Do what pleases her and never cause her grief. {4:4} Remember, she endured many dangers for you even before you were born. When she passes, bury her beside me in the same grave. {4:5} Remember the Lord our God all your days, my son. Refrain from sinning and keep his commandments faithfully. Live uprightly throughout your life; avoid wrongdoing. {4:6} For if you walk in truth, your actions will prosper. {4:7} Be generous with your possessions, giving alms to the upright without hesitation. Never turn your face from the poor, and God will not turn his face from you. {4:8} Give according to what you have; if you are wealthy, be generous accordingly; if you have little, do not hesitate to give what you can. {4:9} By doing so, you store up a treasure for yourself against times of need. {4:10} Charity saves from death and prevents one from entering darkness. {4:11} It is a noble offering before the Most High for all who practice it. {4:12} Son, beware of immorality. Choose a wife from among your own people, not from foreigners. We are descendants of prophets; follow their example. {4:13} Love your brethren and do not despise them in your heart. Do not marry outside your tribe, for pride leads to ruin and carelessness to want. {4:14} Pay workers promptly; do not delay their wages. Serve God faithfully, and you will receive your reward. {4:15} Guard yourself in all your actions; practice discipline in everything you do. {4:16} Treat others as you wish to be treated. Avoid excess in wine and drunkenness. {4:17} Share your bread with the hungry and your clothing with the naked. Be generous in charity, without begrudging. {4:18} Seek advice from the wise and do not disregard useful counsel. {4:19} Bless the Lord at all times; seek his guidance for your paths to prosper. The nations lack understanding, but the Lord grants wisdom and humbles whom he chooses. {4:20} Remember my teachings, my son; keep them in your heart. Now, let me explain the ten talents of silver entrusted to Gabael in Rages. {4:21} Fear not, my son, despite our poverty. True wealth lies in fearing God, avoiding sin, and doing what pleases him."

{5:1} Then Tobias replied to his father, "Father, I will follow all your instructions. {5:2} But how will I obtain the money if I do not know this man?" {5:3} Tobit then handed him the receipt and said, "Find someone to accompany you, and I will pay him wages for as long as I live. Go and retrieve the money." {5:4} So Tobias set out to find a companion and encountered Raphael, who was an angel though Tobias was unaware. Tobias asked him, "Can you journey with me to Rages in Media? Are you familiar with that region?" {5:5} The angel replied, "I will accompany you; I know the way well and have stayed with our kinsman Gabael." {5:6} Tobias said, "Wait here, and I will inform my father." {5:8} Raphael instructed him, "Go ahead, do not delay." Tobias went inside and told his father, "I have found someone to accompany me." Tobit said, "Bring him to me so I can ascertain his tribe and reliability to travel with you." {5:9} Tobias invited Raphael in, and they greeted each other. {5:10} Tobit then asked him, "My brother, what tribe and family do you belong to? Please tell me." {5:11} Raphael responded, "Are you seeking a tribe and family, or looking for a man to accompany your son for pay?" Tobit said, "I want to know your people and your name, my brother." {5:12} Raphael answered, "I am Azarias, son of the great Ananias, one of your relatives." {5:13} Tobit said warmly, "Welcome, my brother. Do not be offended that I asked about your lineage. You come from a noble and good family. I knew Ananias and Jathan, sons of the great Shemaiah, when we went to Jerusalem together to worship and offer sacrifices." {5:14} Tobit then inquired, "What wages shall I pay you — a drachma a day, and your expenses, as I would for my son?" {5:15} Raphael agreed to these terms, and added, "I will increase your wages if you both return safely." {5:16} He said to Tobias, "Prepare for the journey; may it be successful." Tobias made ready, and Tobit blessed him, saying, "Go with this man; may God in heaven prosper your journey, and may his angel accompany you." They departed, and Tobias's faithful dog went with them. {5:17} Meanwhile, Anna, his mother, began to weep and said to Tobit, "Why have you sent away our child? Isn't he our support, coming and going before us?" {5:18} Tobit reassured her, "Do not worry, sister. He will return safely, and you will see him again. {5:19} The life given to us by the Lord is sufficient; do not worry about money." {5:20} Tobit comforted her, saying, "Do not fear. A good angel will be with him; his journey will be prosperous, and he will return safely." {5:21} With these words, Anna ceased weeping.

{6:1} As they journeyed, they arrived at the Tigris River by evening and decided to camp there. {6:2} Tobias went down to wash himself when suddenly a fish leaped out of the river, aiming to swallow him. {6:3} The angel instructed him, "Catch the fish." Tobias quickly seized it and pulled it onto the shore. {6:4} The angel continued, "Now, cut open the fish and take out its heart, liver, and gall; keep them safely." {6:5} Tobias followed the angel's directions, and they roasted and ate the fish. Then they resumed their journey toward Ecbatana. {6:6} Tobias asked the angel, "Brother Azarias, what are the uses of the heart, liver, and gall of the fish?" {6:7} Azarias replied, "The heart and liver can be used to drive away demons or evil spirits by making a smoke in their presence. They will no longer trouble anyone. {6:8} And the gall can cure a man with white films in his eyes if it is applied to them." {6:9} As they approached Ecbatana, {6:10} the angel said to Tobias, "Brother, today we will stay with Raguel, who is your relative. He has an only daughter named Sarah. I will propose that she be given to you in marriage, {6:11} because you are entitled to her and her inheritance as her closest kin. She is beautiful and sensible. Listen to my plan: I will speak to her father, and after we return from Rages, we will celebrate your marriage. {6:12} I know that according to the law of Moses, Raguel cannot give her to another man without facing death, because you are the rightful heir." {6:13} Tobias said to the angel, "Brother Azarias, I have heard that this girl has been married seven times before, and each husband died in the bridal chamber. {6:14} Now I am my father's only son, and I fear that if I go in to her, I will end up like those before me, because a demon is in love with her and harms no one except those who approach her. I fear I may die and bring my parents to their graves in sorrow, as they have no other son to bury them." {6:15} The angel reassured him, "Do you not remember your father's command to marry within your own people? Listen to me, brother. She is destined to be your wife. Do not fear the demon, for tonight she will be given to you in marriage. {6:16} When you enter the bridal chamber, take live ashes of incense and lay upon them some of the heart and liver of the fish to create smoke. {6:17} The demon will smell it and flee, never to return. As you approach her, both of you should rise and call upon the merciful God; he will save you and have mercy on you. Do not be afraid, for she was destined for you from eternity. You will save her, and she will go with you. I am certain that you will have children by her." When Tobias heard these words, he fell deeply in love with her and longed for her affectionately.

{7:1} Upon reaching Ecbatana, they arrived at the house of Raguel, where Sarah greeted them warmly. They reciprocated her greeting, and she ushered them into the house. {7:2} Observing Tobias, Raguel remarked to his wife Edna, "This young man bears a striking resemblance to my cousin Tobit!" {7:3} Curious, Raguel asked them, "Where are you from, brothers?" They replied, "We are from the descendants of Naphtali, who are exiled in Nineveh." {7:4} Raguel inquired further, "Do you know our relative Tobit?" They answered, "Yes, we do." He then asked, "Is he in good health?" {7:5} They assured him, "Yes, he is alive and well." Tobias added, "He is my father." {7:6} Overwhelmed with emotion, Raguel embraced Tobias, kissed him, and shed tears of joy. {7:7} He blessed him, exclaiming, "You are the son of that good and noble man!" Learning of Tobit's blindness, Raguel and his wife Edna, along with their daughter Sarah, were deeply saddened and wept with compassion. {7:8} They warmly welcomed Tobias and Raphael, offering them hospitality with a feast that included a ram from their flock. Tobias then turned to Raphael, saying, "Brother Azarias, speak of the matters we discussed on our journey; let's settle this matter." {7:9} Raphael conveyed the proposal to Raguel, who responded, "Eat, drink, and rejoice, for you have the right to marry my daughter. But let me explain the situation to you clearly. {7:10} I have given my daughter to seven husbands, and each one has died on their wedding night. {7:11} But for now, let us celebrate." Tobias replied firmly, "I will not eat or drink anything until you make a binding agreement with me." {7:12} Raguel consented, saying, "Take her now, in accordance with the law. She belongs to you as her relative, and may the merciful God guide both of you." {7:13} Calling his daughter Sarah, Raguel took her hand and gave her to Tobias as his wife, saying, "Here she is. Take her according to the law of Moses, and take her with you to your father." He blessed them both. {7:14} Next, he summoned his wife Edna, and they wrote out a marriage contract, affixing their seals to it. {7:15} Then they began the wedding feast. {7:16} Raguel instructed his wife Edna, "Sister, prepare the other bedroom and take Sarah there." {7:17} She did as he instructed, and Sarah began to weep. But her mother comforted her, saying, {7:18} "Be strong, my child. May the Lord of heaven and earth grant you joy in place of this sorrow. Be courageous, my daughter."

{8:1} After they finished their meal, Tobias was escorted to Sarah's room. {8:2} Remembering Raphael's instructions, he took live ashes of incense and placed the heart and liver of the fish on them, creating a fragrant smoke. {8:3} As the demon smelled the odor, it fled to the farthest parts of Egypt, where the angel Raphael bound it. {8:4} Once the door was closed and they were alone, Tobias rose from the bed and said, "Sister, let us pray that the Lord may have mercy on us." {8:5} Tobias began to pray, "Blessed are you, God of our ancestors, and blessed be your holy and glorious name forever. Let the heavens and all your creatures bless you. {8:6} You created Adam and gave him Eve, his wife, as a helper and support. From them, the human race has come. You said, 'It is not good that the man should be alone; let us make a helper for him like himself.' {8:7} And now, Lord, I am taking this sister of mine not out of lust, but with sincerity. Grant that I may find mercy and grow old together with her." {8:8} Sarah responded, "Amen." {8:9} Then they both went to sleep for the night. {8:10} Meanwhile, Raguel arose and dug a grave, thinking, "Perhaps Tobias will die." {8:11} He then went inside and told his wife Edna, "Send one of the maids to see if he is alive. {8:12} If not, let us bury him quietly. {8:13} The maid checked and found them both asleep. {8:14} She reported that Tobias was alive. {8:15} Raguel blessed God, saying, "Blessed are you, God, with every pure and holy blessing. Let your saints and all your creatures bless you; let all your angels and chosen people bless you forever. {8:16} Blessed are you, for you have made me glad. Things have not turned out as I expected, but you have treated us with great mercy. {8:17} Blessed are you, for you have shown compassion on these two young people. Show them mercy, Lord, and grant them health, happiness, and mercy throughout their lives." {8:18} Raguel then ordered his servants to fill in the grave. {8:19} Afterward, he held a wedding feast for them that lasted fourteen days. {8:20} Before the feast days concluded, Raguel swore an oath to Tobias that he should not leave until the fourteen days of the wedding feast were over. {8:21} He promised Tobias half of his property immediately, with the rest to be inherited upon Raguel's and his wife's passing.

{9:1} Tobias summoned Raphael and said to him, "Brother Azarias, take a servant and two camels, and go to Gabael at Rages in Media. Retrieve the money for me and bring Gabael back with you to the wedding feast. {9:2} Raguel has sworn that I must not leave, but my father is anxious, counting the days. If I delay too long, he will be greatly distressed." {9:3} Raphael undertook the journey and spent the night with Gabael. He presented him the receipt, and Gabael brought out the money bags with their seals intact and handed them over. {9:4} Early the next morning, they both set out and arrived at the wedding feast. Gabael blessed Tobias and his wife.

{10:1} Tobit anxiously counted each passing day, waiting for Tobias to return. As the days of their expected journey expired without their arrival, {10:2} he wondered, "Could he have been delayed? Or perhaps Gabael has passed away, leaving no one to deliver the money?" {10:3} Tobit was deeply distressed. {10:4} His wife said to him, "Our son must have perished; his prolonged absence suggests it." She began to mourn for him, lamenting, {10:5} "I am distraught, my child, that I let you go, you who are the light of my eyes." {10:6} Tobit reassured her, "Be calm and do not worry; he is safe." {10:7} But she replied, "Stop deceiving me; my child is lost." She went out daily to the road they had departed from, eating nothing during the day and mourning throughout the nights for her son Tobias, until the fourteen days of the wedding feast ordained by Raguel had passed. {10:8} At that time, Tobias said to Raguel, "Send me back, for my father and mother have given up hope of ever seeing me again." {10:9} But Raguel urged him, "Stay with me, and I will send messengers to your father to inform him of your well-being." {10:10} Tobias insisted, "No, please send me back to my father." {10:11} So Raguel blessed Tobias and Sarah and sent them off, saying, "May the God of heaven prosper you, my children, before I pass away." {10:12} He also instructed his daughter, "Honor your father-in-law and mother-in-law as your own parents. Let me hear good reports of you." Then he kissed her. Edna, Sarah's mother, said to Tobias, "May the Lord of heaven bring you back safely, dear brother, and grant me the joy of seeing your children with my daughter Sarah. I entrust my daughter to you; take care not to bring her sorrow."

{11:1} Afterward, Tobias continued his journey, praising God for its success and blessing Raguel and Edna. As they neared Nineveh, {11:2} Raphael said to Tobias, "Do you remember how you left your father? {11:3} Let's go ahead and prepare the house for your wife. Take the gall of the fish with you." So they went ahead, with the dog following behind them. {11:4} Meanwhile, Anna sat watching the road, eagerly awaiting her son's return. {11:5} When she spotted Tobias approaching, she said to Tobit, "Look, your son is coming, and the man who went with him!" {11:6} Raphael reassured Tobias, "I know your father will regain his sight. {11:7} You must anoint his eyes with the gall. When they sting, he will rub them, and the white films will fall away, allowing him to see you." {11:8} Anna ran to meet them, embracing her son and saying, "Now I have seen you, my child; I am ready to die." They both wept tears of joy. {11:9} Tobit, hearing their voices, stumbled toward the door, but Tobias rushed to support him. {11:10} Taking the gall, Tobias sprinkled it on his father's eyes, saying, "Be encouraged, father." {11:11} As Tobit's eyes stung, he rubbed them, and the white films peeled away from the corners. {11:12} He saw his son, embraced him, and wept, praising God, saying, "Blessed are you, O God, and blessed is your name forever. Blessed are all your holy angels. {11:13} You have afflicted me, but you have also shown me mercy. Here I see my son Tobias!" {11:14} His son entered the house rejoicing, telling Tobit of all that had transpired in Media. {11:15} Tobit went out to meet his daughter-in-law Sarah at the gate of Nineveh, rejoicing and praising God. Those who saw him were amazed that he could see. {11:16} Tobit thanked God publicly for his mercy. Approaching Sarah, he blessed her, saying, "Welcome, daughter! Blessed is God who has brought you to us, and blessed are your parents." {11:17} There was great rejoicing among all of Tobit's relatives in Nineveh. {11:18} Ahikar and his nephew Nadab came to celebrate Tobias' marriage for seven days with great festivity.

{12:1} Tobit then called his son Tobias and said, "My son, take care of the wages for the man who traveled with you, and give him more than what was agreed." {12:2} Tobias replied, "Father, it's no trouble for me to give him half of what I've brought back." {12:3} "He brought me back safely, healed my wife, secured the money, and healed your eyes," Tobias added. {12:4} Tobit nodded, saying, "He deserves it." {12:5} So Tobit called Raphael and said, "Take half of everything you and Tobias have brought back." {12:6} Then Raphael called them both aside and said, "Praise God and thank Him; extol and give thanks to Him in the presence of all the living for what He has done for you. It is right to praise God and proclaim His deeds. Do not delay in giving Him thanks. {12:7} "It is good to keep the secret of a king, but it is glorious to reveal the works of God. Do good, and evil will not conquer you. {12:8} "Prayer accompanied by fasting, almsgiving, and righteousness is good. A little with righteousness is better than much with wrongdoing. Giving alms is better than hoarding gold. {12:9} "Almsgiving delivers from death and cleanses every sin. Those who practice charity and righteousness will have fullness of life. {12:10} "But those who commit sin harm themselves." {12:11} "I will not hide anything from you. As I said, keeping the secret of a king is good, but revealing the works of God is glorious." {12:12} "When you and Sarah prayed, I brought your prayer before the Holy One. When you buried the dead, I was with you." {12:13} "Your act of leaving your meal to bury the dead did not go unnoticed by me. I was with you." {12:14} "God sent me to heal you and Sarah." {12:15} "I am Raphael, one of the seven holy angels who present the prayers of the saints and stand before the glory of the Holy One." {12:16} Tobias and Tobit were both startled and fell face down, afraid. {12:17} But Raphael reassured them, saying, "Do not be afraid; you are safe. Praise God forever." {12:18} "I did not come by my own will, but by the will of God. Therefore, praise Him forever." {12:19} "All this time I appeared to you without eating or drinking; you were seeing a vision." {12:20} "Now, thank God, for I am returning to Him who sent me. Write down everything that has happened." {12:21} After saying this, Raphael disappeared from their sight. {12:22} Tobias and Tobit then acknowledged the great and miraculous works of God and recognized that the angel of the Lord had appeared to them.

{13:1} Tobit then composed a prayer of thanksgiving, saying: "Blessed is God who lives forever, and blessed is His kingdom. {13:2} For He afflicts and He shows mercy; He brings down to the grave and He raises up again, and no one can escape His hand. {13:3} O sons of Israel, acknowledge Him before the nations, for He has scattered us among them. {13:4} Make His greatness known there and exalt Him in the presence of all the living, for He is our Lord and God, our Father forever. {13:5} He will punish us for our sins, but He will also show mercy and gather us from all the nations where we have been scattered. {13:6} If you turn to Him with all your heart and soul to do what is right before Him, He will turn to you and not hide His face from you. Give thanks to Him with all your heart; praise the Lord of righteousness and exalt the King of all ages. {13:7} I exalt my God; my soul praises the King of heaven and rejoices in His majesty. {13:8} Let all people speak and give thanks in Jerusalem. {13:9} O Jerusalem, the holy city, He will punish you for the sins of your children, but He will show mercy again to the descendants of the righteous. {13:10} Give thanks to the Lord with full voice and praise the King of all ages, that His tent may be rebuilt with joy for you. {13:11} Many nations will come from afar to honor the name of the Lord God, bringing gifts for the King of heaven. Generations upon generations will offer you joyful praise. {13:12} Cursed are those who hate you; blessed forever are those who love you. {13:13} Rejoice and be glad, O children of the righteous, for you will be gathered together and will praise the Lord of the righteous. {13:14} Blessed are those who love you; they will rejoice in your prosperity. Blessed are those who mourn over all your afflictions, for they will rejoice when they see your glory and will be glad forever. {13:15} Let my soul praise God, the great King. {13:16} For Jerusalem will be adorned with sapphires and emeralds, her walls with precious stones, and her towers and battlements with pure gold. {13:17} The streets of Jerusalem will be paved with beryl, ruby, and stones of Ophir; all her streets will cry out 'Hallelujah!' and give praise, saying, 'Blessed is God who has exalted you forever.'"

{14:1} Tobit concluded his words of praise. {14:2} He was fifty-eight years old when he became blind, and after eight years, his sight was restored. Throughout his life, he practiced charity, feared the Lord God, and continually praised Him. {14:3} As he grew very old, he called his son and grandsons to him, saying, "My son, gather your sons. I am old and about to depart from this life. {14:4} Go to Media, my son, for I believe in what Jonah the prophet foretold about the destruction of Nineveh. But in Media, there will be peace for a time. Our people will be scattered across the earth from our homeland, and Jerusalem will lie desolate. The temple of God in Jerusalem will be burned and remain in ruins for a while. {14:5} Yet God will show mercy again to our people, gather them back to their land, and rebuild His temple. It will not be like the former one until the times of the age are fulfilled. Then they will return from captivity, and Jerusalem will be rebuilt in splendor. The temple of God will be rebuilt there, a magnificent structure for all generations, just as the prophets declared. {14:6} At that time, all the nations will turn to fear the Lord God in truth and forsake their idols. {14:7} The Gentiles will praise the Lord, and His people will give thanks to God. The Lord will exalt His people, and all who love the Lord God sincerely and practice righteousness will rejoice, showing mercy to our brethren. {14:8} "Now, my son, leave Nineveh, for what Jonah the prophet predicted will surely come to pass. {14:9} But observe the law and commandments, be merciful and just, so that you may prosper. {14:10} Bury me and your mother properly together. Do not remain in Nineveh any longer. Consider what Nadab did to Ahikar, who raised him, how he repaid him by bringing him from light into darkness. Ahikar was saved, but Nadab fell into his own trap and perished. {14:11} "Therefore, my children, understand the power of charity and the deliverance that comes from righteousness." With these words, Tobit passed away peacefully in his bed at the age of one hundred fifty-eight. Tobias honored him with a grand funeral. {14:12} After Anna passed away, Tobias buried her beside his father. Then he returned with his wife and sons to Ecbatana, to his father-in-law Raguel. {14:13} He lived a dignified life, honoring his father-in-law and mother-in-law with splendid funerals. He inherited their possessions along with those of his father Tobit. {14:14} Tobias died in Ecbatana of Media at the age of one hundred twenty-seven. {14:15} Before his death, he heard of the fall of Nineveh, which Nebuchadnezzar and Ahasuerus had captured. Tobias rejoiced over Nineveh's downfall before he passed away.

Judith

The Book of Judith, valued in Roman Catholic and Eastern Orthodox traditions but apocryphal for Protestants, recounts how Judith, a brave widow, rescues the Jewish people from the Assyrian general Holofernes. Set in Nebuchadnezzar's era, it is likely fictional and survives only in Greek. Known for its vivid imagery and dramatic tension, the book explores themes of faith, piety, and divine intervention. Judith's cleverness and courage lead to Holofernes's defeat and her people's salvation. The text is studied for its literary artistry and its insights into faith, gender, and power.

{1:1} In the twelfth year of Nebuchadnezzar's reign, who ruled over the Assyrians from the great city of Nineveh, during the time of Arphaxad's rule over the Medes in Ecbatana— {1:2} this is the king who fortified Ecbatana with walls made of hewn stones, three cubits thick and six cubits long. The walls stood seventy cubits high and fifty cubits wide. {1:3} He constructed towers at the gates, each one hundred cubits high and sixty cubits wide at their base. {1:4} The gates themselves were seventy cubits high and forty cubits wide, designed for large armies to pass through and for infantry to assemble. {1:5} During those days, King Nebuchadnezzar waged war against King Arphaxad in the vast plain near Ragae. {1:6} He gathered supporters from the hill country, along the rivers Euphrates, Tigris, and Hydaspes, and from the plains where Arioch ruled the Elymaeans. Many nations joined forces with the Chaldeans. {1:7} King Nebuchadnezzar of Assyria sent messengers to Persia, the western lands, Cilicia, Damascus, Lebanon, Antilebanon, and all along the seacoast. {1:8} He summoned nations from Carmel, Gilead, Upper Galilee, and the great Plain of Esdraelon, as well as Samaria and its surrounding towns, extending beyond the Jordan to Jerusalem, Bethany, Chelous, Kadesh, the river of Egypt, Tahpanhes, Raamses, and the entire land of Goshen. {1:9} His summons reached Tanis, Memphis, and all of Egypt to the borders of Ethiopia. {1:10} However, the entire region refused to obey Nebuchadnezzar, regarding him as merely a single man. They sent his messengers back empty-handed and disgraced. {1:11} Nebuchadnezzar became furious with the entire region and swore by his throne and kingdom to exact revenge on Cilicia, Damascus, Syria, Moab, Ammon, Judea, and Egypt, extending to the coasts of the Mediterranean and the Red Sea. {1:12} In the seventeenth year of his reign, he marched against King Arphaxad, defeated him in battle, and decimated his entire army, including cavalry and chariots. {1:13} Thus, Nebuchadnezzar seized Arphaxad's cities, captured Ecbatana's towers, looted its markets, and turned its splendor to shame. {1:14} He captured Arphaxad in the mountains near Ragae, struck him down with hunting spears, and completely annihilated him. {1:15} Returning triumphantly to Nineveh with his combined forces, a massive army, he and his troops rested and celebrated for 120 days.

{2:1} In the eighteenth year of Nebuchadnezzar's reign, on the twenty-second day of the first month, discussions arose in the palace of the Assyrian king about carrying out his vengeance on the entire region, just as he had declared. {2:2} He summoned all his officials and nobles, revealing to them his secret plan and recounting in detail the disobedience of the region. {2:3} It was decided that anyone who had defied his orders would face destruction. {2:4} After presenting his strategy, Nebuchadnezzar called upon Holofernes, the chief commander of his army, second only to himself, and instructed him, {2:5} "Thus commands the Great King, ruler of the entire earth: When you depart from here, take with you confident men, one hundred and twenty thousand foot soldiers and twelve thousand cavalry. {2:6} Go and attack the entire western region, for they have disobeyed my command. {2:7} Demand that they submit earth and water, for I will come against them in wrath, covering the earth with the tread of my armies, handing them over to be plundered by my troops. {2:8} Their valleys will be filled with the wounded, every brook and river will overflow with their dead. {2:9} I will lead them away captive to the ends of the earth. {2:10} Proceed and seize their territory for me beforehand. They will surrender to you, and you shall hold them for me until the day of their punishment. {2:11} But if they refuse, do not spare them; deliver them to slaughter and plunder throughout the region. {2:12} As surely as I live and by the power of my kingdom, what I have spoken, I will accomplish. {2:13} Take heed not to disobey any of your king's commands; carry them out promptly as I have ordered you." {2:14} So Holofernes left the presence of his master and summoned all the commanders, generals, and officers of the Assyrian army. {2:15} He assembled the chosen troops in divisions as instructed, one hundred and twenty thousand foot soldiers and twelve thousand horsemen. {2:16} He organized them into a formidable army for the campaign. {2:17} They gathered a multitude of camels, donkeys, and mules for transport, along with countless sheep, oxen, and goats for provisions. {2:18} They stocked up on food for every soldier and amassed a vast amount of gold and silver from the royal treasury. {2:19} Thus, Holofernes set out with his entire army ahead of King Nebuchadnezzar, covering the western lands with their chariots, horsemen, and elite infantry. {2:20} Accompanying them was a mixed multitude like a swarm of locusts, countless as the dust of the earth. {2:21} They marched for three days from Nineveh to the plain of Bectileth, and camped near the mountain north of Upper Cilicia, opposite Bectileth. {2:22} From there, Holofernes led his entire army, infantry, cavalry, and chariots, into the hill country. {2:23} They ravaged Put and Lud, plundered the people of Rassis and the Ishmaelites in the desert south of the Chelleans' territory. {2:24} Following the Euphrates, they passed through Mesopotamia, destroying all the hilltop cities along the Abron River to the sea. {2:25} They seized Cilicia's territory, killing all who resisted, and reached the southern borders of Japheth, facing Arabia. {2:26} They surrounded the Midianites, burning their tents, plundering their sheepfolds. {2:27} Descending into the plain of Damascus during the wheat harvest, they burned fields, destroyed flocks and herds, sacked cities, ravaged lands, and slew all their young men with the sword. {2:28} Fear and dread of him spread among the people along the seacoast, from Sidon and Tyre to Sur, Ocina, Jamnia, Azotus, and Ascalon.

{3:1} They sent messengers seeking peace, saying, {3:2} "We, servants of Nebuchadnezzar the Great King, bow down before you. Do with us as you wish. {3:3} Our buildings, land, wheat fields, flocks, herds, and sheepfolds are yours to command. {3:4} Our cities and people are your servants. Come and govern them as you see fit." {3:5} The messengers relayed this to Holofernes. {3:6} He then marched to the seacoast with his army, placing garrisons in hilltop cities and recruiting allies. {3:7} The locals welcomed him with garlands, dances, and tambourines throughout the region. {3:8} Holofernes destroyed their shrines and cut down sacred groves, fulfilling his mission to eradicate local gods so all would worship Nebuchadnezzar alone. {3:9} He reached the edge of Esdraelon near Dothan, facing the Judean hills. {3:10} There, between Geba and Scythopolis, he camped for a month to gather supplies for his army.

{4:1} The Israelites living in Judea heard about all that Holofernes, the general of Nebuchadnezzar king of the Assyrians, had done to the nations. They were deeply alarmed at his approach, fearing for Jerusalem and the temple of their God. {4:2} Having recently returned from captivity, the people of Judea had gathered together anew. The sacred vessels, altar, and temple had just been consecrated after being defiled. {4:3} They sent messengers to Samaria, Kona, Beth-horon, Belmain, Jericho, Choba, Aesora, and the valley of Salem, instructing them to fortify hilltops and villages and gather food in preparation for war, as their fields had just been harvested. {4:4} Joakim, the high priest in Jerusalem, sent letters to the people of Bethulia and Betomesthaim, urging them to secure the mountain passes that could be used to invade Judea, narrow enough for only two men to pass through. {4:5} The Israelites obeyed Joakim and the council's orders, preparing for war. {4:6} Every Israelite, including women, children, resident aliens, laborers, and slaves, wore sackcloth and fasted, crying out to God fervently. {4:7} They prostrated themselves before the temple, spreading ashes on their heads and sackcloth before the Lord. {4:8} They encircled the altar with sackcloth, praying earnestly that God would protect their infants, wives, cities, and sanctuary from destruction and desecration by their enemies. {4:9} The Lord heard their prayers and saw their affliction as they fasted for many days throughout Judea and Jerusalem. {4:10} Joakim and the priests ministering before the Lord offered continual burnt offerings, vows, and freewill offerings, their loins girded with sackcloth and ashes on their turbans. {4:11} They cried out to the Lord with all their might, seeking His favor upon the entire house of Israel.

{5:1} When Holofernes, the commander of the Assyrian army, heard that the Israelites had fortified themselves and blocked the mountain passes, he was furious. He summoned the princes of Moab, commanders of Ammon, and governors of the coastal regions, {5:2} asking them about the Israelites: who they were, where they lived, the size of their army, their military prowess, and who their king was. He questioned why they alone had refused to face him in battle. {5:3} Achior, leader of the Ammonites, spoke up boldly, offering to reveal the truth about the Israelites. He traced their history back to their origins among the Chaldeans, {5:4} recounting how they had rejected the idols of their ancestors in favor of worshiping the God of heaven. This choice led them to flee to Mesopotamia and later settle in Canaan. {5:5} During a famine, they sought refuge in Egypt, where they multiplied greatly but eventually became enslaved. {5:6} Their cries to God brought plagues upon Egypt, leading to their liberation and the parting of the Red Sea. {5:7} Guided by God, they conquered the lands of the Amorites and other nations, settling in the hill country of Canaan. {5:8} Whenever they followed God faithfully, they prospered, but their disobedience led to defeat and exile. {5:9} Recently, they had returned to God, reclaimed Jerusalem, and resettled in the uninhabited hill country. {5:10} Achior warned Holofernes that if the Israelites sinned against their God, they could be defeated, but if innocent, God would defend them, and their enemies would be disgraced. {5:11} Enraged by Achior's words, Holofernes' officers and allies demanded Achior's execution, dismissing the strength of the Israelites.

{6:1} When the commotion outside the council quieted down, Holofernes, commander of the Assyrian army, addressed Achior and the Moabite leaders in the presence of all his foreign allies: {6:2} "Who are you, Achior, and you mercenaries of Ephraim, to prophesy among us and advise against making war on the people of Israel? You claim their God will defend them. But who is God besides Nebuchadnezzar? {6:3} Nebuchadnezzar will send his forces to annihilate them from the earth, and their God will not save them. We, the servants of the king, will destroy them utterly. Their resistance is futile against our cavalry. {6:4} We will burn them up; their mountains will be soaked with their blood, and their fields strewn with their dead. They cannot withstand us and will be utterly destroyed. This is the word of King Nebuchadnezzar, lord of the entire earth; his decrees shall not be in vain. {6:5} "As for you, Achior, Ammonite mercenary, for speaking these words on a day of reckoning, you will not see my face again until I have taken vengeance on the Israelites who came out of Egypt. {6:6} Then my army's sword and my soldiers' spears will pierce your sides, and you will fall among their wounded when I return. {6:7} Now my servants will take you back to the hill country and place you in one of the cities near the passes. {6:8} You will not die until you perish alongside them. If you truly hope they will not be taken, do not despair. My words are final." {6:9} Holofernes then commanded his attendants in the tent to seize Achior and deliver him to Bethulia into the hands of the Israelites. {6:10} So they took him out of the camp into the plain, then up into the hill country until they reached the springs below Bethulia. {6:11} Seeing them approach, the men of Bethulia armed themselves and rushed to the hilltop, while slingers kept the Assyrians at bay with stones. {6:12} They managed to shield Achior, bound him, and left him lying at the foot of the hill, returning to Holofernes. {6:13} The men of Israel descended from their city, found Achior, untied him, and brought him into Bethulia before the city's officials. {6:14} These included Uzziah, son of Micah from the tribe of Simeon, along with Chabris and Charmis. {6:15} They gathered the city's elders, and everyone, young and old, joined the assembly. Achior was placed in their midst, and Uzziah questioned him about what had transpired. {6:16} Achior recounted the council with Holofernes, detailing the Assyrian leaders' words and Holofernes' threats against Israel. {6:17} Hearing this, the people fell to the ground and worshiped God, crying out to him: {6:18} "O Lord God of heaven, behold their arrogance! Have mercy on our humiliation. Look upon those consecrated to you today." {6:19} They comforted Achior and praised him greatly. {6:20} Uzziah took him to his house and hosted a banquet for the elders, while all night they called upon the God of Israel for aid.

{7:1} The following day, Holofernes commanded his entire army, along with all his allied forces, to break camp and advance towards Bethulia. Their objective was to seize the mountain passes and wage war against the Israelites. {7:2} On that day, they relocated their camp. Their military force consisted of 170,000 infantry and 12,000 cavalry, accompanied by baggage handlers and foot soldiers, a formidable multitude. {7:3} They set up camp in the valley near Bethulia, extending from Dothan to Balbaim, and from Bethulia to Cyamon facing Esdraelon. {7:4} When the Israelites saw their vast numbers, they were greatly alarmed, each man saying to his neighbor, "These men will consume the entire land. The high mountains, valleys, and hills will not support their weight." {7:5} Each man took up his weapons, and throughout the night they kept watch, lighting fires on their towers. {7:6} On the second day, Holofernes led out his cavalry before the Israelites in Bethulia. {7:7} He inspected the approaches to the city, visited the springs that supplied their water, seized them, stationed guards over them, and returned to his camp. {7:8} Then the leaders of the Edomites, Moabites, and coastal commanders approached him, {7:9} saying, "Listen, my lord, to our advice, lest your army suffer defeat. {7:10} The Israelites do not rely on their spears but on their mountain strongholds, difficult to reach. {7:11} Therefore, do not engage them in battle; not a single man of your army will fall. {7:12} Stay in your camp with all your forces, while your servants take control of the spring that flows from the mountain foot -- {7:13} for this is the water source for all of Bethulia. Thirst will weaken them, and they will surrender their city. We will camp on nearby mountains to ensure none escape the city." {7:14} They predicted famine for the Israelites and their families, with death in the streets before the sword reaches them. {7:15} Holofernes and his servants found this plan pleasing and ordered it executed. {7:16} The Ammonite army, along with 5,000 Assyrians, moved forward, encamped in the valley, and seized the Israelites' water sources. {7:17} The Edomites and Ammonites ascended to the hill country opposite Dothan, sending men south and east toward Acraba near Chusi beside the brook Mochmur. The rest of the Assyrian army camped in the plain, covering the land with their tents and supply trains, forming a vast multitude. {7:18} The Israelites cried out to the Lord their God, their courage failing as their enemies surrounded them with no escape. {7:19} The entire Assyrian army, infantry, chariots, and cavalry, besieged them for thirty-four days until all water vessels in Bethulia were empty. {7:20} Their cisterns dried up, and they had barely enough water measured out for daily needs. {7:21} Children lost heart, women and young men collapsed from thirst in the streets and at the city gates, utterly exhausted. {7:22} The people, young and old, gathered around Uzziah and the city rulers, crying out loudly, {7:23} "God, judge between us! You have allowed this great harm because we did not make peace with the Assyrians. {7:24} Now we are defenseless; God has handed us over to them, to be scattered and destroyed by thirst. {7:25} Call them in and surrender the city to Holofernes' army to be plundered. {7:26} It is better to be captured and enslaved than to witness our infants and loved ones perish before us. {7:27} Heaven and earth, and our God, the Lord of our ancestors, bear witness against you! He punishes us for our sins and those of our ancestors. Let him not allow this to happen!" {7:28} The assembly erupted in great lamentation as they cried out loudly to the Lord God. {7:29} Uzziah encouraged them, "Take heart, my brothers! Endure for five more days; by then the Lord our God will show us mercy. He will not forsake us completely. {7:30} If these days pass and no help arrives, I will do as you say." {7:31} He dismissed the people to their posts; they ascended the city walls and towers. Women and children were sent home, and great sorrow filled the city.

{8:1} At that time, Judith heard about these events. She was the daughter of Merari, the son of Ox, descendant of Joseph, son of Oziel, son of Elkiah, son of Ananias, son of Gideon, son of Raphaim, son of Ahitub, son of Elijah, son of Hilkiah, son of Eliab, son of Nathanael, son of Salamiel, son of Sarasadai, son of Israel. {8:2} Her husband Manasseh, from her tribe and family, had died during the barley harvest. He had been overseeing the workers binding sheaves in the field when the heat overcame him, leading to his death in Bethulia. They buried him in the field between Dothan and Balamon. {8:3} Judith lived as a widow in her home for three years and four months. {8:4} She set up a tent on her rooftop and wore sackcloth around her waist, maintaining the garments of her widowhood. {8:5} Throughout her widowhood, she fasted every day except on the eve and the Sabbath itself, the eve and the day of the new moon, and the feasts and rejoicing days of the house of Israel. {8:6} Judith was known for her beauty and lovely appearance. Her husband Manasseh had left her wealth in gold, silver, male and female slaves, and livestock, and she managed this estate. {8:7} No one spoke ill of her, for she had a deep reverence for God. {8:8} When Judith heard the people speaking wickedly against their ruler because they were faint from lack of water, and heard what Uzziah promised them under oath -- to surrender the city to the Assyrians in five days -- {8:9} she sent her servant, who managed all her possessions, to summon Chabris and Charmis, the elders of her city. {8:10} They came to her, and she addressed them, "Listen, rulers of the people of Bethulia! What you have promised the people today is not right. You have sworn an oath between God and yourselves, pledging to surrender the city to our enemies unless the Lord intervenes within these few days. {8:11} Who are you to test God in this way and act as if you are in His place among humanity? {8:12} You are testing the Almighty Lord, but you will never understand His ways! {8:13} You cannot fathom the depths of human hearts or comprehend the thoughts of God who created all things. Therefore, my brothers, do not provoke the Lord our God to anger. {8:14} If He does not choose to help us within these five days, He has the power to protect us at any time He wishes, or even to allow us to be destroyed before our enemies. {8:15} Do not attempt to bind the purposes of the Lord our God. God is not like a human to be threatened, nor like a mortal to be persuaded. {8:16} Therefore, as we await His deliverance, let us call upon Him for help, and He will hear our voice if it pleases Him. {8:17} For never in our generation, nor in these current times, has there been any tribe, family, people, or city among us that worshipped gods made by human hands, as was done in the past -- {8:18} and this was why our ancestors were handed over to the sword, plundered, and faced great calamity before our enemies. {8:19} But we know no other God but Him, and so we hope that He will not reject us or our nation. {8:20} If we are captured, all of Judea will be taken, our sanctuary plundered, and we will bear the penalty for its desecration. {8:21} The slaughter of our brethren, the captivity of our land, and the devastation of our inheritance -- all of this will fall upon us among the nations where we serve as slaves, becoming a reproach and an offense to those who conquer us. {8:22} Our servitude will not win us favor, but the Lord our God will turn it to dishonor. {8:23} Therefore, brothers, let us set an example for our brethren, for their lives depend on us, and the sanctuary, temple, and altar rely on our actions. {8:24} Despite everything, let us give thanks to the Lord our God, who tests us as He tested our forefathers. {8:25} Remember what He did with Abraham, how He tested Isaac, and the trials of Jacob in Mesopotamia while he tended Laban's sheep, his uncle. {8:26} He has not tested us with fire as He did them to search their hearts, nor has He taken vengeance on us. Instead, the Lord corrects those who draw near to Him to instruct them." {8:27} Uzziah affirmed, "Everything you've said is spoken with a true heart, and no one can dispute your words. {8:28} Your wisdom has been evident not just today, but from your early life, recognized by all for your righteous heart. {8:29} The people are desperate with thirst, compelling us to fulfill our promise and swear an oath we cannot break. {8:30} Therefore, pray for us, being devout, that the Lord will send rain to fill our cisterns and we will no longer faint." {8:31} Judith said to them, "Listen. I am about to do something that will be remembered by all generations of our descendants. {8:32} Stand at the city gate tonight, and I will go out with my maid. Within the days you have promised to surrender the city to our enemies, the Lord will deliver Israel by my hand. {8:33} Do not seek to know my plan, for I will not reveal it until I have finished what I am about to do." {8:34} Uzziah and the rulers replied, "Go in peace, and may the Lord God lead you to take vengeance on our enemies." {8:35} They left her tent and returned to their posts.

{9:1} Then Judith fell on her face, placed ashes on her head, and uncovered the sackcloth she was wearing. At the time of the evening incense offering in the house of God in Jerusalem, Judith cried out loudly to the Lord and said, {9:2} "O Lord God of my ancestor Simeon, to whom you gave a sword to avenge the defilement of a virgin's honor, when strangers sought to shame her and defile her womb against your command. Though you said, 'It shall not be,' they did it. {9:3} You delivered their leaders to be slain, and their bed, which was ashamed of their deceit, became stained with blood. You struck down both slaves and princes, and princes on their thrones. {9:4} You gave their wives as plunder and their daughters into captivity, and all their possessions to be divided among your beloved sons who were zealous for you, detesting the pollution of their blood and calling upon you for help. O God, my God, hear me, a widow. {9:5} "For you have accomplished these deeds, those before, and those to come. You have ordained what is now and what will be. Yes, the things you intended have come to pass, {9:6} and those you willed have presented themselves, saying, 'Here we are,' for all your ways are prepared beforehand, and your judgments are made with foreknowledge. {9:7} "Now behold, the Assyrians have grown in their power; they are exalted with their horses and riders. They boast in the strength of their infantry, trusting in shield and spear, bow and sling. They do not know that you are the Lord who crushes wars; the Lord is your name. {9:8} Crush their strength with your might; bring down their power in your anger. They seek to defile your sanctuary, pollute the tabernacle where your glorious name resides, and destroy the horn of your altar with the sword. {9:9} See their pride and send your wrath upon their heads. Give me, a widow, the strength to carry out my plan. {9:10} By the cunning of my words, strike down the slave with the prince and the prince with his servant. Crush their arrogance by the hand of a woman. {9:11} "For your power does not depend on numbers, nor your might on the strength of men. For you are God of the humble, helper of the oppressed, upholder of the weak, protector of the forsaken, and savior of those without hope. {9:12} Hear, O hear me, God of my ancestors, God of the inheritance of Israel, Lord of heaven and earth, Creator of the waters, King over all your creation. Hear my prayer! {9:13} Let my deceitful words be their downfall, for they have plotted cruel things against your covenant, your consecrated house, the summit of Zion, and the house owned by your children. {9:14} Let all your people and every tribe know and understand that you are God, the God of all power and might, and that there is no other who protects the people of Israel but you alone!"

{10:1} After Judith had finished praying to the God of Israel and had spoken these words, she got up from where she had been lying prostrate. She called her maid and went down from her upper room, where she lived on Sabbaths and during the festivals. {10:2} Judith removed the sackcloth she had been wearing and took off her widow's garments. She bathed herself, anointed herself with precious ointment, and carefully dressed herself in her finest clothes, the ones she wore when her husband Manasseh was alive. {10:3} She adorned herself with sandals, anklets, bracelets, rings, earrings, and all her jewelry, making herself very attractive to anyone who saw her. {10:4} Then she gave her maid a bottle of wine, a flask of oil, a bag of roasted grain, dried figs, and fine bread. She packed up all her utensils and handed them to her maid to carry. {10:5} Together, they went out to the city gate of Bethulia, where they found Uzziah and the elders Chabris and Charmis standing. {10:6} When they saw Judith, amazed at her transformed appearance and changed attire, they admired her beauty greatly and said to her, {10:7} "May the God of our ancestors grant you favor and fulfill your plans, bringing glory to the people of Israel and exalting Jerusalem." Judith then worshiped God. {10:8} She said to them, "Open the city gate for me, so that I may go out and accomplish the tasks we discussed." They ordered the young men to open the gate as she had requested. {10:9} Once the gate was opened, Judith and her maid went out, while the men of the city watched her until she descended the mountain and passed through the valley, disappearing from their sight. {10:10} As she traveled through the valley, Judith encountered an Assyrian patrol. {10:11} They seized her and asked, "To which people do you belong? Where are you coming from, and where are you going?" She answered, "I am a Hebrew woman fleeing from my own people, who are about to be handed over to you for destruction. {10:12} I am on my way to see Holofernes, the commander of your army, to give him accurate information. I will show him a route by which he can capture all the hill country without losing a single soldier, whether captive or killed." {10:13} Upon hearing her words and seeing her beauty, the men were captivated.

{11:1} Holofernes spoke to Judith, saying, "Take heart, woman, and do not fear in your heart, for I have never harmed anyone who has chosen to serve King Nebuchadnezzar, the ruler of all the earth. {11:2} If it were not for the disrespect shown to me by your people living in the hill country, I would never have raised my spear against them. They have brought this upon themselves. {11:3} Now tell me why you have fled from your own people and come to us seeking safety." {11:4} Judith replied, "Please listen to the words of your servant, and allow your maidservant to speak in your presence. I will not speak anything false to my lord tonight. {11:5} If you heed the counsel of your maidservant, God will work through you, and you will succeed in your endeavors. {11:6} Nebuchadnezzar, the king of the whole earth, lives, and under his authority, which he has delegated to you, all creatures serve you -- not only men but also the beasts of the field, cattle, and birds of the air. {11:7} We have heard of your wisdom and skill, renowned throughout the world as the only virtuous man in the entire kingdom, highly knowledgeable and adept in military strategy. {11:8} Regarding the words of Achior in your council, we have heard them. The people of Bethulia spared him, and he revealed all that he had said to you. {11:9} Therefore, my lord and master, do not disregard his counsel, but remember it well. It is true: our nation cannot be punished, nor can they be defeated by the sword unless they sin against their God. {11:10} Now, to prevent my lord from being frustrated in his purpose and defeated, death will come upon them because they have sinned and provoked their God to anger. {11:11} Their food supply is depleted, and their water is almost gone. They have planned to slaughter their cattle and to consume things forbidden by God's law. {11:12} They intend to eat the first fruits of grain and the tithes of wine and oil, which they had consecrated and set apart for the priests serving in the presence of our God in Jerusalem, though it is unlawful for anyone among the people to touch these things. {11:13} They have sent men to Jerusalem to obtain permission from the council, and when they receive it and proceed to act, they will be handed over to you for destruction that very day. {11:14} When I learned all this, I fled from them, and God has sent me to accomplish remarkable things with you, things that will astonish the world. {11:15} I am devoted to God and serve the God of heaven day and night. Therefore, my lord, I will stay with you, and every night I will go out into the valley to pray, and God will reveal to me when they commit their sins. {11:16} I will then come and inform you, and you can march out with your entire army. No one will be able to resist you. {11:17} I will lead you through the heart of Judea until you reach Jerusalem. I will establish your throne there, and you will lead them like sheep without a shepherd. Not even a dog will bark at you. This has been revealed to me and I was sent to tell you." {11:18} Holofernes and all his servants were pleased with her words. They marveled at her wisdom and said, {11:19} "There is no woman like her in all the earth, both for beauty and eloquence." {11:20} Holofernes said to her, "God has indeed sent you ahead of the people to strengthen our hands and to bring destruction upon those who have offended my lord. {11:21} You are not only beautiful but also wise in speech. If you carry out as you have said, your God will be my God, and you will live in the palace of King Nebuchadnezzar, becoming renowned throughout the world."

{12:1} Then he ordered them to bring her into his tent where his silverware was stored, and he directed them to set a table for her with his own food and serve her his own wine. {12:2} But Judith said, "I cannot eat this food, lest it be a cause of sin. Instead, I will eat from the provisions I have brought with me." {12:3} Holofernes replied, "If your supplies run out, where will we find more for you? There are none of your people here with us." {12:4} Judith answered him, "As surely as you live, my lord, your servant will not use up the provisions I have with me until the Lord accomplishes through my hand what he has determined." {12:5} So the servants of Holofernes brought her into the tent, and she slept until midnight. Toward the morning watch, she arose {12:6} and sent a message to Holofernes, saying, "Please command that your servant be allowed to go out and pray." {12:7} Holofernes instructed his guards not to hinder her. She remained in the camp for three days and went out each night to the valley of Bethulia, bathing at the spring in the camp. {12:8} When she returned from the spring, she prayed to the Lord God of Israel to guide her in raising up her people. {12:9} She stayed in the tent until she ate her food toward evening, having returned cleansed. {12:10} On the fourth day, Holofernes held a banquet for his personal servants only, excluding all his officers. {12:11} He said to Bagoas, the eunuch who attended to his personal affairs, "Go and persuade the Hebrew woman under your care to join us, to eat and drink with us. {12:12} It would be shameful if we let such a woman leave without enjoying her company, for if we do not win her over, she will mock us." {12:13} So Bagoas went out from Holofernes' presence and approached Judith, saying, "Please come to my lord and be honored in his presence. Drink wine, rejoice with us, and today become like one of the Assyrian women who serve in the palace of King Nebuchadnezzar." {12:14} Judith replied, "Who am I to refuse my lord? Whatever pleases him, I will do gladly, and it will be a joy to me until the day I die!" {12:15} So she got up and dressed herself in her finest attire, and her maid spread out the soft fleeces on the ground that Bagoas had given her for her daily use, so she could recline on them while eating. {12:16} Judith came in and lay down, and Holofernes was captivated by her beauty. He was consumed with desire for her, as he had been waiting for an opportunity to deceive her since the first day he saw her. {12:17} Holofernes said to her, "Drink now and be merry with us!" {12:18} Judith replied, "I will drink now, my lord, because today my life is more precious to me than on any day since I was born." {12:19} Then she ate and drank what her maid had prepared before him. {12:20} Holofernes was greatly pleased with her, and he drank more wine that day than he had ever drunk in his entire life.

{13:1} As evening fell, his servants departed hastily, and Bagoas closed the tent from outside, leaving Judith alone with Holofernes, who lay sprawled on his bed, overcome by wine. {13:2} Judith instructed her maid to stand outside the bedchamber as usual, while she pretended to go out for her nightly prayers, a routine known to Bagoas as well. {13:3} With everyone gone, Judith stood beside Holofernes' bed and prayed silently, "O Lord God of all power, look upon the work of my hands now, for the glory of Jerusalem. {13:4} It is time to support your inheritance and fulfill my mission to destroy our enemies who rise against us." {13:5} She approached the head of Holofernes' bed and took down his sword that hung there. {13:6} Drawing close to his bed, she grasped the hair of his head and said, "Give me strength this day, O Lord God of Israel!" {13:7} With all her might, she struck his neck twice and severed his head from his body. {13:8} Judith threw his body off the bed and brought down the canopy from its posts. After a moment, she went out and gave Holofernes' head to her maid, {13:9} who placed it in her food bag. Together, they went out as they usually did for prayer, passing through the camp and around the valley, then ascending the mountain to Bethulia and its gates. {13:10} From afar, Judith called out to the gatekeepers, "Open, open the gates! Our God, the God of Israel, is with us, displaying his power against our enemies as he has done this day!" {13:11} Upon hearing her voice, the people of Bethulia rushed to the city gate and summoned the elders. {13:12} They all gathered in amazement, opening the gate to welcome Judith and her maid. They lit a fire for light and gathered around them. {13:13} With a loud voice, Judith addressed them, "Praise God, O praise him! He has not withdrawn his mercy from the house of Israel, but has destroyed our enemies by my hand this very night!" {13:14} She then took out the head from the bag and showed it to them, saying, "Behold the head of Holofernes, the commander of the Assyrian army, and here is the canopy under which he lay in drunkenness. The Lord has struck him down by the hand of a woman. {13:15} As the Lord lives, who protected me on my journey, it was my appearance that deceived him to his downfall, yet he did not defile or shame me." {13:16} The people were greatly astonished, bowing down and worshiping God together, saying with one voice, "Blessed are you, our God, who has brought to naught the enemies of your people this day." {13:17} Uzziah spoke to her, saying, "O daughter, you are blessed by the Most High God above all women on earth. Blessed be the Lord God, who created the heavens and the earth, guiding you to strike down the leader of our enemies. {13:18} May your memory endure in the hearts of all, as they remember the power of God. {13:19} May God grant you everlasting honor, and bless you, because you did not spare your own life when our nation was brought low, but avenged our ruin, walking faithfully before our God." And all the people responded, "Amen, amen!"

{14:1} Judith addressed the people, saying, "Listen to me, my fellow citizens. Take this head and hang it upon the battlements of our city wall. {14:2} When morning comes and the sun rises, let every courageous man arm himself and leave the city with a leader as if preparing to descend into the plain against the Assyrian forces, but do not actually descend. {14:3} The Assyrians will then see their leader's headless body, and panic will seize them. They will rush into Holofernes' tent, but find him gone. Fear will overtake them, and they will flee before you. {14:4} Pursue them and strike them down as they scatter across the land of Israel." {14:5} "But first," she continued, "bring Achior the Ammonite to me. Let him see the man who mocked the house of Israel and was sent to his death." {14:6} Achior was brought from the house of Uzziah. When he saw Holofernes' head in the hands of the people, he fell to the ground, his spirit failing. {14:7} They lifted him up, and he knelt before Judith, saying, "Blessed are you in every tent of Judah! Your name will cause fear in every nation." {14:8} Judith then recounted all that had transpired since she left until that moment. {14:9} The people rejoiced loudly and made a great noise throughout the city. {14:10} Witnessing the deeds of the God of Israel, Achior believed firmly, was circumcised, and joined the house of Israel, remaining with them ever since. {14:11} At dawn, they hung Holofernes' head on the wall. Every man armed himself, and they went out in companies toward the mountain passes. {14:12} When the Assyrians saw them, they sent word to their commanders, who then went to the generals and captains and all the officers. {14:13} They reached Holofernes' tent and told the steward of his personal affairs, "Wake our lord, for the slaves have dared to come down against us, seeking their destruction." {14:14} Bagoas, assuming Holofernes was with Judith, knocked at the tent door. {14:15} Receiving no answer, he entered and found Holofernes dead on the bed, headless. {14:16} Bagoas cried out, wept, and tore his garments in anguish. {14:17} He searched Judith's tent but did not find her, then ran out to the people and shouted, {14:18} "We have been deceived by the slaves! A Hebrew woman has brought shame upon King Nebuchadnezzar's house! Holofernes lies dead, his head severed!" {14:19} The Assyrian leaders tore their clothes and were filled with dismay, their camp echoing with loud cries and shouts.

{15:1} When the men in the Assyrian camp heard the news, they were astounded by what had transpired. {15:2} Fear gripped them, and without waiting for one another, they fled in panic across the plain and into the hills. {15:3} Even those stationed around Bethulia in the hills joined the chaotic retreat. The Israelite soldiers seized the moment and pursued them relentlessly. {15:4} Uzziah dispatched messengers to Betomasthaim, Bebai, Choba, Kola, and throughout Israel's borders, spreading the news and rallying all to strike their enemies. {15:5} Upon hearing the call, the Israelites united and attacked the Assyrians with fervor, pursuing them all the way to Choba. From Jerusalem, the hill country, Gilead, and Galilee, they poured in with overwhelming force, extending their victory even beyond Damascus and its environs. {15:6} The people of Bethulia raided the Assyrian camp, seizing plunder and becoming exceedingly wealthy. {15:7} As the Israelites returned from battle, they took possession of the spoils left behind in the villages and towns of the hill country and plain, amassing a great amount of loot. {15:8} Joakim the high priest and the elders of Jerusalem came to witness the remarkable deeds the Lord had done for Israel and to meet Judith, extending their greetings to her. {15:9} They all blessed her unanimously, saying, "You are the pride of Jerusalem, the glory of Israel, and the honor of our nation! {15:10} You have achieved this alone, bringing immense good to Israel, and God is pleased with you. May the Almighty Lord bless you forever!" And all the people responded, "Amen!" {15:11} For thirty days, the people plundered the Assyrian camp. They gave Judith Holofernes' tent, his silverware, beds, bowls, and all his furnishings. Judith loaded them onto her mule and carts. {15:12} All the women of Israel gathered to see her, blessing her and celebrating with dances. Judith handed out olive branches to the women around her. {15:13} They crowned themselves with olive wreaths, and Judith led them in a joyful dance before the people, with the men of Israel following, armed and adorned with garlands, singing songs of victory.

{16:1} Judith began her thanksgiving before all Israel, and the people joined in a resounding song of praise. {16:2} She spoke, "Begin a song to my God with tambourines, sing to my Lord with cymbals. Raise a new psalm to Him, exalt Him, and call upon His name. {16:3} For God is the Lord who brings an end to wars; He has delivered me from the hands of my pursuers and brought me to safety among His people. {16:4} The Assyrians descended from the northern mountains with their countless warriors; they filled the valleys and covered the hills with their cavalry. {16:5} They boasted of burning my land, killing my young men, dashing my infants to the ground, seizing my children, and taking my virgins as plunder. {16:6} Yet the Lord Almighty thwarted them through the hand of a woman. {16:7} Their mighty warriors did not defeat him, nor did their strongest men overpower him. It was Judith, daughter of Merari, who defeated him with her beauty. {16:8} She removed her widow's garments to uplift the oppressed in Israel. Anointing her face with oil, she adorned her hair with a tiara and dressed in linen to deceive him. {16:9} Her beauty captivated his mind, and her sandal entranced his eyes. With swift action, her sword severed his neck. {16:10} The Persians trembled at her courage, and the Medes were amazed at her boldness. {16:11} My people, who were oppressed, rejoiced; the weak shouted, and the enemy trembled. Their voices rose, and the enemy fled. {16:12} The sons of maidservants struck them down; they were wounded like fleeing fugitives and perished before the Lord's army. {16:13} I will sing a new song to my God: O Lord, you are great and glorious, wonderful in strength, invincible. {16:14} Let all your creatures serve you; when you command, they come into being. You send forth your Spirit, and they are created; none can resist your command. {16:15} Mountains quake at your presence; rocks melt like wax before you. Yet you continue to show mercy to those who fear you. {16:16} Though sacrifices are but a small offering to you, and burnt offerings insignificant, those who fear the Lord shall be honored forever. {16:17} Woe to the nations that rise against my people! The Lord Almighty will avenge them on the day of judgment; fire and worms He will give to their flesh, and they will weep in pain forever. {16:18} Upon their arrival in Jerusalem, they worshipped God. After the people purified themselves, they offered burnt offerings, freewill offerings, and gifts. {16:19} Judith dedicated all the vessels of Holofernes to God, and the canopy she took from his bedchamber she offered as a votive gift to the Lord. {16:20} The people feasted in Jerusalem before the sanctuary for three months, and Judith stayed with them. {16:21} Afterward, everyone returned to their own homes, and Judith went back to Bethulia, where she remained on her estate and was honored throughout the entire country. {16:22} Many desired to marry her, but she remained a widow all her days after the death of her husband Manasseh, until she passed away at the age of 105. {16:23} Judith grew more renowned with age, living in her husband's house until her death in Bethulia. They buried her in the cave of her husband Manasseh, {16:24} and the house of Israel mourned her for seven days. Before she died, she distributed her property to Manasseh's relatives and her own closest kin. {16:25} After Judith's time, no one again caused fear among the people of Israel for a long time.

Eldad and Modad

The Book of Eldad and Modad is a fascinating yet often overlooked text within the corpus of ancient Jewish literature. Its origins are shrouded in mystery, with scholars debating both its precise dating and its place within the broader tapestry of biblical and apocryphal writings. This book, often referenced alongside other pseudepigrapha, offers unique insights into early Jewish eschatology, prophecy, and communal life. Eldad and Modad, its titular figures, are believed to be prophetic characters mentioned briefly in the Book of Numbers, who continued to prophesy outside the established framework of the seventy elders appointed by Moses. Their story resonates with themes of divine inspiration and the unexpected ways in which God's message can manifest, making it a poignant narrative for understanding the dynamics of prophetic authority and legitimacy in ancient Israelite religion. The text itself, surviving only in fragmented and secondary references, is pieced together through a combination of ancient manuscripts, citations in early Christian writings, and comparative studies with contemporaneous Jewish texts. This scholarly endeavor to reconstruct the Book of Eldad and Modad not only highlights the complexity of textual transmission in antiquity but also underscores the cultural and theological significance of these prophetic voices. The narrative weaves together elements of visionary experiences, angelology, and messianic expectations, reflecting the rich tapestry of Jewish thought during the Second Temple period.

Due to its status as an apocryphal text, the Ethiopic Book of Eldad and Modad is not referenced in mainstream Christian theology but holds interest for those studying the broader traditions and texts of early Jewish and Christian writings. It is not widely studied, and detailed information about its contents is scarce. There is limited scholarly consensus on the exact number of chapters or specific content, as many apocryphal texts have varying versions and fragmentary evidence. However, based on general references, the book is believed to contain prophecies and visions related to the end times, judgment, and the role of the righteous. Eldad and Modad, being prophetic figures, are depicted as delivering messages that align with the broader apocalyptic literature found in other ancient texts. For precise chapter details and specific content, one would typically need to refer to specialized scholarly resources or manuscripts housed in certain libraries or collections, particularly those focusing on Ethiopic literature and apocryphal writings.

As they are not widely accessible, and detailed, complete versions of the text are not available in mainstream sources. However, we created a representation of what such a text might look like, drawing from general themes and styles found in apocryphal literature.

{1:1} During the time of Moses, the servant of the Lord, two men named Eldad and Modad emerged among the seventy elders. {1:2} The Spirit of the Lord came upon them, and they began to prophesy within the camp. {1:3} The people were astonished, for these men spoke not by their own will but by the Spirit of the Almighty. {1:4} Eldad declared, "Listen, Israel, to the word of the Lord. The days are coming when the righteous will be gathered, and the wicked will be cast down." {1:5} Modad proclaimed, "Behold, the Lord's judgment is near. Prepare your hearts and turn from your wicked ways."

{2:1} A young man ran to Moses and said, "Eldad and Modad are prophesying in the camp." {2:2} Joshua, son of Nun, who served Moses, spoke up, "My lord Moses, stop them!" {2:3} But Moses replied, "Are you jealous for my sake? I wish that all the Lord's people were prophets and that the Lord would put His Spirit upon them." {2:4} The prophecies of Eldad and Modad spread among the tribes, bringing both hope and fear. {2:5} Eldad spoke of the coming Messiah, the Anointed One, who would bring salvation to His people.

{3:1} Modad foretold the signs of the end times: the sun would turn to darkness, and the moon to blood. {3:2} He said, "In those days, the Lord will pour out His Spirit on all people. Your sons and daughters will prophesy, your old men will dream dreams, and your young men will see visions." {3:3} "And it shall come to pass that whoever calls on the name of the Lord will be saved," said Modad. {3:4} The people trembled at these words, for they knew that the time of judgment was near.

{4:1} Eldad spoke of the New Jerusalem, a city of peace and righteousness, where the Lord Himself would live with His people. {4:2} "There will be no more death or mourning or crying or pain, for the old order of things has passed away," said Eldad. {4:3} Modad added, "The Lord will make all things new. He will wipe every tear from their eyes, and there will be no more night." {4:4} The people rejoiced at these promises, and many turned their hearts back to the Lord.

{5:1} But there were those who mocked and refused to listen, saying, "These men are drunk." {5:2} Eldad warned them, "Do not harden your hearts as in the rebellion. The day of the Lord is coming, and who can stand?" {5:3} Modad echoed, "Seek the Lord while He may be found; call on Him while He is near." {5:4} And thus, the words of Eldad and Modad were recorded for future generations, a testimony of the Lord's enduring mercy and justice.

Jannes and Jambres

The Book of Jannes and Jambres, a pseudepigraphal text rooted in Jewish and early Christian traditions, offers a compelling expansion of the biblical narrative surrounding the figures of Jannes and Jambres, the magicians who opposed Moses and Aaron in the Book of Exodus. Though not part of the canonical scriptures, references to Jannes and Jambres appear in various ancient sources, including the Dead Sea Scrolls, the New Testament, and rabbinic literature, indicating their significant role in Jewish folklore and early Christian thought. The text itself, often categorized among the Old Testament Pseudepigrapha, delves into the backstory and exploits of these two enigmatic characters, exploring themes of magic, power, and resistance against divine authority. It provides a richer context to their opposition to Moses, portraying them not merely as Egyptian sorcerers but as complex figures whose defiance is intricately linked to broader theological and moral issues. The narrative's origin likely dates back to the intertestamental period, reflecting the cultural and religious milieu of Second Temple Judaism. It underscores the tension between human cunning and divine will, a recurring motif in Jewish apocalyptic literature. Furthermore, the influence of Hellenistic thought on the text is evident, blending Jewish theological concepts with elements of Greco-Roman mythology. This amalgamation highlights the syncretic nature of religious and philosophical ideas during this era.

The fragments known as the "Book of Jannes and Jambres" refer to a work that is part of a collection of Jewish and Christian pseudepigrapha. Jannes and Jambres are traditionally considered to be the magicians who opposed Moses in the book of Exodus (Exodus 7:11-12). These names are not mentioned in the Hebrew Bible but are referred to in the New Testament (2 Timothy 3:8) and other ancient writings. The book is a fragmentary text that expands on the brief biblical references to these figures. It is believed to provide a narrative about their origins, their opposition to Moses, and their eventual downfall. The fragments that exist today were discovered in various manuscripts, including some written in Greek, Latin, and Coptic. The exact contents and scope of the original work are not entirely clear due to its fragmentary nature.

As they are not widely accessible, and detailed, complete versions of the text are not available in mainstream sources. However, we created a representation of what such a text might look like, drawing from general themes and styles found in apocryphal literature.

{1:1} Jannes and Jambres were born into the land of Egypt, sons of a wise man skilled in the arts of magic. {1:2} From their youth, they were instructed in the secret knowledge of their forefathers, learning the ways of the occult and the mysteries of the gods. {1:3} As they grew, their fame spread throughout the land, and they were brought into the court of Pharaoh, the ruler of Egypt. {1:4} There, they demonstrated their power by performing great wonders, and Pharaoh exalted them above all his other magicians. {1:5} But in their hearts, they were filled with pride, believing that no power could surpass their own.

{2:1} In the days of Moses, the servant of the Lord, Pharaoh's heart was hardened, and he refused to let the people of Israel go. {2:2} So the Lord sent Moses and Aaron to perform signs before Pharaoh, that he might know the power of the living God. {2:3} But Jannes and Jambres stood against Moses, saying, "We too can perform such wonders, for we are mighty in the wisdom of Egypt." {2:4} They cast down their rods, and they became serpents, just as the rod of Aaron had done. {2:5} But the rod of Aaron swallowed up their rods, and they were filled with fear, though they did not show it.

{3:1} When Moses turned the waters of the Nile into blood, Jannes and Jambres did likewise with their enchantments, and Pharaoh's heart was hardened. {3:2} Again, when frogs covered the land of Egypt, they brought forth frogs with their magic, and Pharaoh did not listen to Moses. {3:3} But when the dust became gnats by the word of the Lord, the magicians tried to do the same, but they could not. {3:4} Then Jannes and Jambres said to Pharaoh, "This is the finger of God," but Pharaoh's heart remained hard, and he did not listen to them.

{4:1} As the plagues continued, Jannes and Jambres grew weaker in their power, unable to replicate the mighty works of the God of Israel. {4:2} They recognized the truth, that their magic was nothing compared to the power of the Lord, but their pride kept them silent. {4:3} They sought to understand the source of Moses' power, consulting their scrolls and calling upon their spirits, but to no avail. {4:4} In the end, they could no longer stand before Moses, for they were covered with boils like all the Egyptians, and they fled from Pharaoh's presence in shame.

{5:1} After the final plague, when the firstborn of Egypt were struck down, Jannes and Jambres came to Moses in secret. {5:2} They fell at his feet and confessed their sins, saying, "We have opposed the Lord, and now we see that He alone is God." {5:3} Moses looked upon them with pity and said, "The Lord is merciful, but His judgment is just. You will not escape the consequences of your deeds." {5:4} And so it was that Jannes and Jambres were struck down by the hand of the Lord, and they perished with the rest of Pharaoh's servants who did not fear God.

{6:1} Let this be a warning to all who oppose the will of the Most High, for no power on earth can stand against Him. {6:2} The wisdom of the world is foolishness before the Lord, and those who trust in it will be brought low. {6:3} But those who humble themselves and seek the Lord will find mercy, for He is gracious and compassionate, slow to anger and abounding in steadfast love. {6:4} Remember the fate of Jannes and Jambres, and do not harden your hearts as they did, but turn to the Lord while there is still time.

Additional Esther

The Additions to the Book of Esther, also known as Greek Esther or the Additions to Esther, constitutes a series of six significant expansions to the canonical Hebrew text of Esther. These additions are found in the Septuagint, the Greek translation of the Hebrew Bible, and are also included in the Apocrypha. Originating between the 2nd and 1st centuries BCE, these texts reflect the religious, cultural, and political contexts of the Hellenistic period, showcasing how Jewish identity and piety were articulated under Greek influence. The additions serve to enhance the narrative of the Hebrew Esther by introducing explicit religious elements, which are notably absent in the original text, thereby emphasizing God's providential role in the deliverance of the Jewish people. The Additions include prayers by Mordecai and Esther, dream visions, and letters, which provide theological depth and underscore the themes of divine intervention and Jewish solidarity. They also offer a broader historical context, framing the events within a larger narrative of persecution and salvation that resonates with the experiences of Jews in the Hellenistic diaspora. These expansions not only fill in narrative gaps but also align the story more closely with Jewish liturgical traditions, particularly the festival of Purim. By integrating these additions, the Greek of Esther becomes a more overtly religious and didactic text, reflecting the evolving nature of Jewish thought and practice in the centuries leading up to the Common Era.

{10:1} Mordecai declared, "These events are from God. {10:2} I recall the dream I had regarding these matters, and every detail has been fulfilled without fail. {10:3} The tiny spring that became a river, with light, sun, and abundant water — that river symbolizes Esther, whom the king married and crowned queen. {10:4} The two dragons represent Haman and myself. {10:5} The nations are those who gathered to annihilate the Jewish people. {10:6} And my people, Israel, cried out to God and were delivered. The Lord has rescued his people; he has saved us from all these adversities. God has performed remarkable signs and wonders that have not been seen among other nations. {10:7} For this purpose, God established two lots: one for his people and one for all other nations. {10:8} These two lots were appointed by God to determine the time, moment, and day of judgment among all nations. {10:9} God remembered his people and vindicated his inheritance. {10:10} Therefore, these days in the month of Adar, on the fourteenth and fifteenth of that month, will be celebrated with assembly, joy, and gladness before God, from generation to generation, forever among his people Israel."

{11:1} In the fourth year of the reign of Ptolemy and Cleopatra, Dositheus, who claimed to be a priest and a Levite, along with his son Ptolemy, brought to Egypt the previous Letter of Purim. They asserted its authenticity, stating it had been translated by Lysimachus, the son of Ptolemy, who was a resident of Jerusalem. {11:2} In the second year of the reign of King Artaxerxes the Great, on the first day of Nisan, Mordecai son of Jair, son of Shimei, son of Kish, from the tribe of Benjamin, had a dream. {11:3} Mordecai, a Jew living in the city of Susa, held a high position serving in the king's court. {11:4} He was among the captives taken from Jerusalem by King Nebuchadnezzar of Babylon, along with King Jeconiah of Judah. This is what he dreamt: {11:5} There was noise and confusion, thunder and earthquake, turmoil on the earth! {11:6} Two great dragons appeared, both ready to fight, roaring terribly. {11:7} At their roar, every nation prepared for war against the righteous nation. {11:8} A day of darkness and gloom, trouble and distress, affliction and tumult gripped the earth! {11:9} The entire righteous nation was troubled, fearing the impending evils and facing the threat of destruction. {11:10} Then they cried out to God; from their cry, like a small spring, a great river flowed with abundant water. {11:11} Light emerged, the sun rose, and the humble were exalted, overcoming those who were esteemed. {11:12} Mordecai understood from this dream what God had ordained. After waking, he pondered it all day, seeking to grasp every detail.

{12:1} Mordecai rested in the courtyard with Gabatha and Tharra, two eunuchs who guarded the king's entrance. {12:2} He overheard their conversation and inquired about their intentions. Learning they planned to harm King Artaxerxes, Mordecai promptly informed the king. {12:3} The king investigated the eunuchs' plot, and upon their confession, they were executed. {12:4} The king recorded these events in the royal chronicles, and Mordecai documented them as well. {12:5} Impressed by Mordecai's loyalty, the king appointed him to serve in the court and rewarded him accordingly. {12:6} Meanwhile, Haman, son of Hammedatha the Agagite, held high favor with the king. However, he harbored resentment toward Mordecai and his people because of the incident involving the eunuchs.

{13:1} Here is a copy of the decree: "Artaxerxes the Great, ruler over a hundred and twenty-seven provinces from India to Ethiopia, and all their governors, sends greetings. {13:2} "Having become sovereign over many nations and master of the whole world, I do not boast of my authority but seek to govern with reason and kindness. My aim is to establish lasting peace and ensure free passage throughout my kingdom, fulfilling the desire for tranquility among all people. {13:3} "Upon seeking counsel on how to achieve this, Haman, renowned for his sound judgment and unwavering loyalty, who holds high office in the kingdom, {13:4} advised that a certain hostile people scattered among the nations, with laws that oppose all others and disregard royal decrees, pose a threat to our kingdom's unity. {13:5} This people alone persistently opposes all others, following their own peculiar customs and laws, and undermines our governance, seeking to destabilize our kingdom. {13:6} "Therefore, by decree of Haman, my trusted advisor and esteemed second in command, on the fourteenth day of the twelfth month, Adar, all these people, along with their wives and children, shall be annihilated by their enemies' swords without mercy. This decree aims to swiftly remove these long-standing adversaries and secure our kingdom's future peace." {13:7} Mordecai prayed fervently to the Lord, recalling His mighty works, saying: {13:8} "O Lord, King over all, whose power governs the universe, none can oppose Your will if You choose to save Israel. {13:9} You created heaven, earth, and all marvelous things under heaven. {13:10} You are Lord of all, and no one can resist You, O Lord. {13:11} You know all things, O Lord; You know that I did not act out of pride or arrogance in refusing to bow down to the proud Haman. {13:12} I would have been willing to humble myself even to kiss his feet to save Israel! {13:13} But I acted to honor Your glory above human glory, refusing to bow to anyone but You, my Lord, out of humility. {13:14} Now, O Lord God and King, God of Abraham, spare Your people. Our enemies seek our destruction and desire to eradicate Your chosen inheritance. {13:15} Do not forsake Your people, whom You redeemed from Egypt. {13:16} Hear my prayer and have mercy on Your inheritance. Turn our sorrow into joyous celebration, that we may live and sing praises to Your name, O Lord. Do not let those who praise You be silenced." {13:17} All of Israel cried out loudly, facing imminent death.

{14:1} Esther the queen, overwhelmed with mortal fear, turned to the Lord for help. {14:2} She removed her royal garments and dressed herself in garments of anguish and mourning. Instead of perfumes, she covered her head with ashes and dung. She humbled her body completely, covering even the parts she once adorned with tangled hair. {14:3} She prayed to the Lord God of Israel, saying, "O Lord, you alone are our King. Help me, for I am alone and have no one else but you to help me in my distress. {14:4} "My peril is at hand. {14:5} "From my youth I have heard in the tribe of my family that you, O Lord, took Israel out of all the nations, and our ancestors from among their forebears, to be an everlasting inheritance. You did for them all that you promised. {14:6} "But now we have sinned before you, and you have handed us over to our enemies, {14:7} "because we honored their gods. You are righteous, O Lord! {14:8} "And now they are not satisfied with our bitter slavery; they have made a pact with their idols {14:9} "to abolish your decrees, destroy your inheritance, silence those who praise you, extinguish your altar and the glory of your house, {14:10} "to open the mouths of the nations to praise vain idols and perpetuate the glory of a mortal king forever. {14:11} "O Lord, do not surrender your scepter to what is nonexistent; do not let them laugh at our downfall. Instead, turn their plan against themselves and make an example of the man who began this against us. {14:12} "Remember, O Lord, make yourself known in our time of affliction. Give me courage, O King of gods and Master of all dominion! {14:13} "Put persuasive words in my mouth before the lion, and turn his heart to hate the man who opposes us, so that he and his supporters may be defeated. {14:14} "But save us by your hand, and help me, for I am alone and have no one else but you, O Lord. {14:15} "You know all things; you know that I detest the splendor of the wicked and abhor the bed of the uncircumcised and of any foreigner. {14:16} "You know my necessity — how I despise the diadem upon my head when I appear in public. I loathe it like a menstruous cloth and do not wear it on my leisure days. {14:17} "Your servant has not dined at Haman's table, nor have I honored the king's feasts or drunk the wine of libations. {14:18} "Since the day I was brought here, your servant has found no joy except in you, O Lord God of Abraham. {14:19} "O God, whose power is over all, hear the voice of the despairing. Save us from the hands of evildoers, and deliver me from my fear!"

{15:1} On the third day, after concluding her prayer, Esther removed her garments of supplication and adorned herself in splendid attire. {15:2} Arrayed magnificently and invoking the aid of the all-seeing God and Savior, she took her two maids with her, {15:3} delicately leaning on one, {15:4} while the other followed, carrying her train. {15:5} Radiant with flawless beauty, she appeared joyful, as if cherished, yet her heart was gripped with fear. {15:6} Passing through all the doors, she stood before the king, seated on his royal throne, arrayed in majestic splendor, adorned with gold and precious stones. His appearance was awe-inspiring. {15:7} When he looked up, flushed with splendor, and glared at her in fierce anger, Queen Esther faltered, turned pale, and grew faint, collapsing against the head of the maid who preceded her. {15:8} But God changed the king's spirit to gentleness. In alarm, he rose from his throne, took her in his arms until she revived, and comforted her with reassuring words, saying, {15:9} "What is troubling you, Esther? I am your brother. Take courage; {15:10} you will not die, for the law applies only to the people. Come closer." {15:11} Then he raised the golden scepter and touched it to her neck; {15:12} he embraced her and said, "Speak to me." {15:13} Esther replied, "When I saw you, my lord, you seemed like an angel of God, and my heart trembled with fear at your splendor. {15:14} "For you are marvelous, my lord, and your countenance is full of grace." {15:15} As she was speaking, she fainted. {15:16} The king was deeply troubled, and all his servants sought to comfort her.

{16:1} Here is a copy of the letter: "King Artaxerxes, to the governors of the provinces spanning from India to Ethiopia, comprising one hundred and twenty-seven satrapies, and to all loyal subjects under our rule, greetings. {16:2} "Often, when people are excessively favored by their benefactors, many become prideful. {16:3} They not only seek to harm our subjects, but in their inability to handle prosperity, they even plot against their own benefactors. {16:4} They not only lack gratitude but, swayed by the boasts of the ignorant, believe they can evade the justice of God, who sees all things. {16:5} Frequently, those in positions of authority are implicated in shedding innocent blood and face irreparable disasters, influenced by friends entrusted with public affairs, {16:6} who deceitfully manipulate the sincere intentions of their rulers. {16:7} "The wicked deeds carried out by those who abuse their authority can be seen not only in ancient records but also in recent investigations. {16:8} Henceforth, we will ensure peace and tranquility throughout our kingdom by adopting fairer policies and just judgments. {16:9} We will carefully consider all matters brought before us with impartiality. {16:10} "Haman, son of Hammedatha, a Macedonian alien to Persian blood, though favored as our guest, lacked our kindness and hospitality. {16:11} He abused our goodwill to the extent of being esteemed as a father and second only to the royal throne. {16:12} Yet, unable to contain his arrogance, he conspired to seize our kingdom and our lives. {16:13} With cunning and deceit, he sought the destruction of Mordecai, our savior and constant benefactor, and of Esther, blameless queen of our realm, along with their entire nation. {16:14} He sought to leave us defenseless, aiming to transfer Persian rule to Macedonians. {16:15} "However, we recognize that the Jews, condemned to annihilation by this wicked man, are not evildoers but follow righteous laws. {16:16} They are children of the Almighty God, who has ordained the kingdom for us and our ancestors in perfect order. {16:17} "Therefore, do not execute the decrees sent by Haman, son of Hammedatha, {16:18} for he and his household have been executed by hanging at the gate of Susa, swiftly punished by God, the ruler of all. {16:19} "Publish this letter widely and permit the Jews to live according to their own laws. {16:20} Provide them with support so they can defend themselves on the thirteenth day of the twelfth month, Adar, against those who attack them. {16:21} God has turned this day, originally meant for their destruction, into a day of joy for his chosen people. {16:22} "Therefore, celebrate this day joyfully as a significant occasion among your annual festivals, {16:23} ensuring it brings salvation to us and loyal Persians, but serves as a reminder of destruction for our enemies. {16:24} "Any city or region that does not comply will face destruction by sword and fire, becoming desolate and loathed by all creatures for eternity."

Additional Psalms

The Additions to the Book of Psalms, also known as the Psalms 151-155, are a collection of psalms that are not included in the canonical Hebrew Bible but hold significant historical and religious value. These psalms are considered part of the broader category of Second Temple Jewish literature and are primarily extant in Greek and Syriac translations, with fragments also found in Hebrew. Composed between the 1st and 2nd centuries BCE, the Psalms provide a rich tapestry of Jewish theological reflection, messianic expectations, and socio-political commentary during a tumultuous period in Jewish history marked by Roman conquest and internal strife. The authorship of these psalms is unknown, but their style and content suggest they were written by members of the Jewish community who were deeply influenced by the Pharisaic tradition. Theologically, they echo themes from the canonical Psalms, such as divine justice, repentance, and the hope for deliverance, yet they also introduce unique elements, such as explicit references to the Messiah and the Roman occupation. These Psalms reflect a community grappling with the realities of oppression while maintaining a profound faith in God's ultimate sovereignty and justice. Their poetic form and liturgical use underscore their importance in the religious life of the Jewish community at the time, serving as a bridge between traditional psalmody and the evolving religious thought of the Second Temple period. Furthermore, these psalms offer invaluable insights into the development of Jewish eschatology and the messianic expectations that would later influence early Christian thought. The study of these Psalms thus provides a crucial understanding of the religious and historical context of late Second Temple Judaism, illuminating the continuity and divergence within Christian traditions.

{151:1} I crafted a harp with my hands and fashioned a lyre with my fingers. {151:2} And who will proclaim it to my Lord? The Lord himself; he is the one who listens. {151:3} It was he who sent his messenger and lifted me from tending my father's sheep, anointing me with his sacred oil. {151:4} My brothers were strong and impressive, but they did not find favor with the Lord. {151:5} I went out to confront the Philistine, who cursed me by his false gods. {151:6} Yet I took his own sword, struck him down, and delivered Israel from disgrace.

{152:1} Hear my prayer, O Lord, and incline your ear to my supplication. {152:2} You are my rock and my fortress; in you, I put my trust. {152:3} Guide me in your truth and teach me, for you are the God of my salvation. {152:4} Let your light shine upon me, that I may walk in your ways all the days of my life.

{153:1} The heavens declare your glory, O Lord, and the earth proclaims your handiwork. {153:2} Day to day they pour forth speech, and night to night they reveal knowledge. {153:3} Great are you, O Lord, and greatly to be praised; your greatness is unsearchable. {153:4} Let all creation praise your holy name forever and ever.

{154:1} Sing praises to the Lord, for he is good; his mercy endures forever. {154:2} Let the redeemed of the Lord say so, whom he has redeemed from the hand of the enemy. {154:3} Give thanks to the Lord, for he has delivered us and set us free. {154:4} Blessed be the name of the Lord, who does wondrous things in heaven and on earth.

{155:1} O give thanks to the Lord, for he is worthy of all praise. {155:2} His love endures forever, and his faithfulness continues to all generations. {155:3} Let the heavens rejoice and the earth be glad; let the sea roar and all that fills it. {155:4} For the Lord is great and greatly to be praised; he alone is worthy of all honor and glory.

Vita Adae et Evae

The Vita Adae et Evae, also known as the Life of Adam and Eve, is an apocryphal work that provides a rich, detailed narrative of the lives of Adam and Eve after their expulsion from the Garden of Eden. This text, which survives in several languages including Latin, Greek, Slavonic, and Armenian, expands upon the brief biblical account found in Genesis, offering an elaborate portrayal of the first humans' experiences, struggles, and spiritual journeys. Originating in the early centuries of the Common Era, likely between the 1st and 3rd centuries, this pseudepigraphal work is significant for its influence on later Christian, Jewish, and Islamic traditions. It introduces themes and motifs that are absent from the canonical Bible, such as Adam and Eve's penitent prayers, their interactions with angels, and the prophecy concerning the future redemption of humanity. The narrative delves into the profound theological implications of sin, repentance, and divine mercy, presenting a detailed dialogue between Adam, Eve, and God that highlights the complexities of human nature and divine justice. Moreover, the Vita Adae et Evae offers insights into early Jewish and Christian cosmologies, eschatological beliefs, and the developing notions of the afterlife. Its vivid descriptions of the natural world and the intimate, often emotional, exchanges between the characters provide a compelling glimpse into the religious imagination of its time.

{1:1} When Adam & Eve were driven out of paradise, they built a shelter and spent seven days mourning and lamenting in deep sorrow.

{2:1} After seven days, they grew hungry and began searching for food. {2:2} They found nothing to eat. Eve said to Adam, "My lord, I am hungry. Please find us something to eat. Perhaps the Lord God will show us mercy and bring us back to the place we were before."

{3:1} Adam walked for seven days across the land but found no food like they had in paradise. {3:2} Eve said to Adam, "Do you want me to die so that God might bring you back to paradise, since it was because of me that you were driven out?" {3:3} Adam replied, "Eve, stop speaking like that, or God may bring another curse upon us. How can I harm my own flesh? Let's continue searching for food so we don't perish."

{4:1} They wandered and searched for nine days but only found food meant for animals. {4:2} Adam said to Eve, "This is what the Lord provided for animals and beasts to eat; {4:3} but we used to have angels' food. It is right that we lament before God who made us. Let us repent deeply, perhaps the Lord will be gracious and provide us with something to sustain us."

{5:1} Eve asked Adam, "What is repentance? Tell me what kind of repentance I should do. Let's not take on more than we can endure, or the Lord may not listen to our prayers and turn His face away because we failed to keep our promise." {5:2} "My lord, how much repentance do you think we should do, since I have brought this trouble and sorrow upon you?"

{6:1} Adam said to Eve, "You cannot do as much as I can, so only do what you have the strength for. I will fast for forty days, but you should go to the Tigris River, lift a stone, and stand on it in the water up to your neck. Do not speak, for we are unworthy to address the Lord, as our lips are unclean from the forbidden tree. {6:2} Stand in the river for thirty-seven days, while I will spend forty days in the Jordan River. Perhaps the Lord God will have mercy on us."

{7:1} Eve went to the Tigris River and did as Adam had instructed. {7:2} Likewise, Adam went to the Jordan River and stood on a stone up to his neck in the water.

{8:1} Adam said, "Jordan River, grieve with me and gather all the creatures that swim in you. Let them surround me and mourn with me. Let them lament not for themselves, but for me; for they have not sinned, but I have." {8:2} Immediately, all living things came and surrounded him, and from that moment, the Jordan River's current stopped.

{9:1} Eighteen days passed. Then Satan, angry, transformed himself into an angel of light and went to the Tigris River where Eve was. {9:2} He found her weeping and pretended to grieve with her. He began to weep and said, "Come out of the river and stop lamenting. Cease your sorrow. {9:3} Why are you and your husband Adam anxious? The Lord God has heard your groaning and accepted your repentance. All the angels have interceded for you and prayed to the Lord. {9:4} He has sent me to bring you out of the water and give you the nourishment you had in paradise, for which you are crying out. {9:5} Come out of the water, and I will lead you to where your food is prepared."

{10:1} Eve heard and believed, coming out of the river, her body trembling from the cold water. {10:2} As she came out, she fell on the ground, and the devil lifted her up and led her to Adam. {10:3} When Adam saw her with the devil, he wept and cried out, "Oh Eve, where is the effort of your repentance? {10:4} How have you been ensnared again by our adversary, who caused us to be banished from our home in paradise and from our spiritual joy?"

{11:1} When Eve heard this, she realized it was the devil who had persuaded her to leave the river. She fell on her face, doubled over with sorrow and wailing. {11:2} She cried out, "Woe to you, devil! Why do you attack us without cause? What have we done to you? Why do you pursue us with deceit? Why does your malice target us? {11:3} Have we taken away your glory or caused you to be dishonored? Why do you harass us with wickedness and envy?"

{12:1} The devil replied with a heavy sigh, "Adam, all my hostility, envy, and sorrow are because of you. It is for your sake that I was expelled from my glory, which I had in the heavens among the angels. {12:2} Because of you, I was cast out onto the earth." Adam responded, "What are you telling me? What have I done to you? What fault do you find in me? {12:3} You have received no harm or injury from us, so why do you pursue us?"

{13:1} The devil said, "Adam, I was cast out because of you. When you were formed, I was banished from God's presence. When God breathed life into you and made you in His image, Michael brought you to us, and we had to worship you before God. {13:2} God said, 'Here is Adam, made in our image and likeness.'"

{14:1} Michael went out and called all the angels, saying, 'Worship the image of God as the Lord God has commanded.' {14:2} Michael himself worshipped first, then he called me and said, 'Worship the image of God the Lord.' {14:3} I answered, 'I have no need to worship Adam.' Since Michael kept urging me to worship, I said, 'Why do you urge me? I will not worship a being inferior and younger than I. I was made before him, so he should worship me.'"

{15:1} When the angels under me heard this, they refused to worship Adam. Michael said, 'Worship the image of God, or the Lord God will be wrathful with you.' {15:2} I said, 'If He is wrathful with me, I will set my seat above the stars of heaven and be like the Most High.'

{16:1} God the Lord was angry with me and banished me and my angels from our glory. {16:2} Because of you, we were expelled from our abodes into this world and hurled to the earth. {16:3} We were overwhelmed with grief, losing such great glory. {16:4} We were grieved when we saw you in joy and luxury. With deceit, I tricked your wife and caused you to be expelled from your joy and luxury, just as I was driven out of my glory."

{17:1} When Adam heard the devil's words, he cried out and wept, saying, "O Lord my God, my life is in your hands. Banish this adversary far from me, who seeks to destroy my soul, and give me his lost glory." {17:2} At that moment, the devil vanished before him. Adam continued his penance, standing for forty days in the Jordan River.

{18:1} Eve said to Adam, "Live, my lord. Life is granted to you, as you committed neither the first nor the second error. But I have erred and been led astray, not keeping God's commandment. Now banish me from your life, and I will go to the sunset. {18:2} There, I will stay until I die." She began to walk toward the west, mourning and weeping bitterly. {18:3} She built a booth there, while carrying offspring three months old in her womb.

{19:1} As Eve's time to give birth approached, she was overcome with labor pains and cried out to the Lord for help, saying, "Have mercy on me, Lord, assist me." {19:2} But her cries were not heard, and God's mercy did not surround her. She thought to herself, "Who will tell my lord Adam?" She then implored the heavenly lights, saying, "When you return to the east, bear a message to my lord Adam."

{20:1} At that moment, Adam sensed Eve's distress and thought, "Eve's complaint has reached me. Perhaps the serpent has troubled her again." {20:2} He went to her and found her in great distress. Eve said, "From the moment I saw you, my lord, my grief-stricken soul was refreshed. Now, please entreat the Lord God on my behalf to hear you and relieve me from these awful pains." Adam prayed to the Lord for Eve.

{21:1} Twelve angels and two virtues appeared, standing on either side of Eve, with Michael standing on her right. {21:2} Michael stroked her face down to her chest and said, "Blessed are you, Eve, for Adam's sake. Because of his great prayers and intercessions, I have been sent to help you. Rise now and prepare to give birth." {21:3} Eve bore a son who was radiant. Immediately, the baby stood up, ran, and handed a blade of grass to his mother. He was named Cain.

{22:1} Adam carried Eve and their son and led them eastward. The Lord God sent various seeds by Michael the archangel, who gave them to Adam and showed him how to till the ground so they could have food for themselves and their descendants. {22:2} Eve conceived again and bore a son named Abel. Cain and Abel grew up together. {22:3} Eve told Adam, "My lord, I had a vision while sleeping. I saw Abel's blood in Cain's hand, and Cain was drinking it. This has caused me great sorrow." {22:4} Adam replied, "If Cain kills Abel, let us separate them. We should give each of them their own dwelling."

{23:1} They made Cain a farmer and Abel a shepherd, so they would be separated. {23:2} However, Cain eventually killed Abel. Adam was 130 years old at that time, and Abel was 122 years old. After Abel's death, Adam and Eve had another son, whom they named Seth.

{24:1} Adam said to Eve, "Behold, I have begotten a son to replace Abel, whom Cain killed." {24:2} After Seth was born, Adam lived another 800 years and had 30 sons and 30 daughters, a total of 63 children. They spread across the earth in their nations.

{25:1} Adam said to Seth, "Listen, my son, let me tell you what I heard and saw after your mother and I were driven out of paradise. While we were praying, {25:2} Michael the archangel, God's messenger, came to me. I saw a chariot like the wind with fiery wheels, and I was taken up into the Paradise of righteousness. I saw the Lord sitting with a face like flaming fire, surrounded by thousands of angels.

{26:1} When I saw this, I was terrified and bowed down before God with my face to the ground. {26:2} God said to me, 'Behold, you will die because you disobeyed my commandment by listening to your wife, whom I gave to you to guide according to my will. You ignored my words and obeyed hers instead.'

{27:1} Hearing these words from God, I fell prone on the ground, worshipped the Lord, and said, 'My Lord, All-powerful and merciful God, Holy and Righteous One, do not let the memory of your majesty be erased. Convert my soul, for I am dying, and my breath is leaving my body. {27:2} Do not cast me out of your presence, whom you formed from the clay of the earth. Do not banish from your favor the one you nourished.' {27:3} And then, a word concerning you came to me, and the Lord said, 'Since your days were ordained, you have been created with a love of knowledge. Therefore, your descendants will always have the right to serve me.'

{28:1} When I heard these words, I threw myself on the ground and worshipped the Lord God, saying, 'You are the eternal and supreme God; all creatures give you honor and praise. {28:2} You are the true Light above all lights, the Living Life, infinite mighty Power. The spiritual powers give you honor and praise. You show abundant mercy to the human race.' {28:3} After I had worshipped the Lord, Michael, God's archangel, seized my hand and cast me out of the paradise of vision and God's command. Michael held a rod in his hand and touched the waters around paradise, causing them to freeze hard.

{29:1} I crossed over with Michael the archangel, who led me back to the place from where he had taken me. {29:2} Listen, my son Seth, to the rest of the secrets and sacraments revealed to me after I ate from the tree of knowledge and understood what will happen in this age—what God intends to do with His creation of humanity. The Lord will appear in a flame of fire, and from His majestic mouth, He will issue commandments and statutes, and a two-edged sword will proceed from His mouth. {29:3} They will sanctify Him in the house of His majesty's habitation, and He will show them the marvelous place of His majesty. They will build a house for the Lord their God in the land He prepares for them, but they will transgress His statutes. Their sanctuary will be burned, their land deserted, and they will be dispersed because they have kindled God's wrath. {29:4} Once more, He will bring them back from their dispersion, and they will rebuild the house of God. In the last time, the house of God will be exalted greater than before. Iniquity will again exceed righteousness, but then God will dwell with men on earth in visible form, and righteousness will begin to shine. The house of God will be honored forever, and their enemies will no longer harm those who believe in God. God will gather a faithful people for Himself, whom He will save for eternity, and the impious will be punished by God their king for refusing to love His law. {29:5} Heaven and earth, nights and days, and all creatures will obey Him and not overstep His commandment. People will not change their works but will turn away from forsaking the law of the Lord. The Lord will repel the wicked from Himself, and the just will shine like the sun in the sight of God. {29:6} In that time, people will be purified by water from their sins. Those who refuse to be purified by water will be condemned. Blessed is the man who has ruled his soul when Judgment comes and the greatness of God is revealed among men, and their deeds are examined by God, the just judge.

{30:1} When Adam was 930 years old and knew his days were ending, he said, "Let all my sons gather before me so I may bless them before I die and speak with them." {30:2} They gathered in three groups before him in the house of prayer where they used to worship the Lord God. They asked, "Father, what concerns you that you have assembled us, and why do you lie on your bed?" {30:3} Adam replied, "My sons, I am sick and in pain." All his sons said, "Father, what does this illness and pain mean?"

{31:1} Seth said, "Father, perhaps you long for the fruit of paradise, which you used to eat, and that is why you are sad. Tell me, and I will go to the nearest gates of paradise, put dust on my head, throw myself on the ground, and lament and plead with God. Perhaps He will hear me and send His angel to bring the fruit you long for." {31:2} Adam answered, "No, my son, I do not long for that, but I feel weak and in great pain in my body." Seth asked, "Father, what is pain? I do not know. Please tell us about it."

{32:1} Adam said, "Listen, my sons. When God made your mother and me and placed us in paradise, He gave us every tree bearing fruit to eat but forbade us from eating from the tree of knowledge of good and evil in the midst of paradise. He gave part of paradise to me—the trees of the eastern part and the north, near Aquilo—and to your mother, He gave the southern and western parts.

{33:1} God also gave us two angels to guard us. One day, when the angels ascended to worship before God, the adversary, the devil, found an opportunity while they were absent and led your mother astray to eat from the forbidden tree. {33:2} She ate and gave some to me.

{34:1} Immediately, the Lord God was angry with us and said to me, 'Since you have disobeyed My command and ignored My word, I will bring seventy blows upon your body, and you will be tormented with various pains, from your head and eyes and ears down to the nails on your toes, and in every limb. These punishments are appointed by God for chastisement. These afflictions have been sent to me and all our descendants.'

{35:1} Adam spoke to his sons and was seized with violent pains, crying out, "What shall I do? I am in distress. These pains are so cruel." When Eve saw him weeping, she also began to weep and said, "O Lord my God, let me take on his pain, for I am the one who sinned." {35:2} Eve said to Adam, "My lord, give me part of your pains, for they have come to you because of my fault."

{36:1} Adam said to Eve, "Rise and go with our son Seth to the area near paradise. Put dust on your heads, throw yourselves on the ground, and lament before God. Perhaps He will have pity on you and send His angel to the tree of His mercy, from which flows the oil of life, and give you a drop of it to anoint me, so I may have relief from these pains that consume me." {36:2} Seth and his mother went towards the gates of paradise. While they were walking, a beast—a serpent—attacked and bit Seth. Eve saw it and wept, saying, "Alas, wretched woman that I am. I am cursed because I did not keep God's commandment."

{37:1} Eve spoke to the serpent in a loud voice, "Accursed beast! How dare you fight against the image of God?"

{38:1} The beast replied in human language, "Isn't it against you, Eve, that our malice is directed? Aren't you the object of our rage? How did you open your mouth to eat the fruit? If I begin to rebuke you, you cannot bear it."

{39:1} Seth then said to the beast, "God the Lord rebuke you. Be silent, accursed enemy of Truth. Leave the image of God until the day the Lord orders you to be judged." The beast said to Seth, "I will leave the image of God as you have said." He then left Seth, who was wounded by the serpent's bite.

{40:1} Seth and his mother continued to the regions of paradise for the oil of mercy to anoint the sick Adam. They arrived at the gates of paradise, took dust from the earth, placed it on their heads, bowed to the ground, and began to lament and moan loudly, imploring the Lord God to have mercy on Adam and send His angel with the oil from the tree of mercy.

{41:1} After praying and imploring for many hours, the angel Michael appeared and said, "I have been sent to you from the Lord. I am set by God over the bodies of men. I tell you, Seth, man of God, do not weep or pray for the oil of the tree of mercy to anoint your father Adam for his pains."

{42:1} "I tell you, you will not be able to receive this until the last days." {42:2} "When five thousand five hundred years have passed, the most beloved King Christ, the Son of God, will come to earth to revive the body of Adam and also revive the bodies of the dead. The Son of God will be baptized in the River Jordan, and when He comes out of the water, He will anoint all who believe in Him with the oil of mercy." {42:3} "The oil of mercy will be for generations to come, for those ready to be born again of water and the Holy Spirit, leading to eternal life. The beloved Son of God, Christ, will descend to earth and lead your father Adam to Paradise, to the tree of mercy."

{43:1} "Seth, return to your father Adam, for his life is near its end. In six days, his soul will leave his body, and when it does, you will witness great marvels in heaven and on earth, and in the luminaries of heaven." With these words, Michael immediately departed from Seth. {43:2} Eve and Seth returned, bringing with them fragrant herbs such as nard, crocus, calamus, and cinnamon.

{44:1} When Seth and his mother reached Adam, they told him how the serpent had bitten Seth. Adam said to Eve, "What have you done? You have brought a great plague upon us, transgression, and sin for all our generations. Tell your children after my death about what you have done, so they may understand the toil and suffering that will come because of our actions." {44:2} "They will say, 'All evils have come upon us because of our parents who were at the beginning.'" {44:3} When Eve heard these words, she began to weep and moan.

{45:1} As the archangel Michael had foretold, Adam died six days later. When Adam sensed that his death was near, he told all his sons, "I am 930 years old. When I die, bury me facing the sunrise in the field near our dwelling." {45:2} When he finished speaking, he gave up his spirit. The sun was darkened, and the moon and stars were also darkened for seven days.

{46:1} Seth, in mourning, embraced his father's body. Eve looked at the ground with her hands folded over her head, and all her children wept bitterly. Suddenly, the angel Michael appeared and stood at Adam's head, saying to Seth, "Rise from your father's body and come to me to see what the Lord God has decreed for him. He is God's creature, and God has had pity on him." {46:2} All the angels blew their trumpets and cried out,

{47:1} "Blessed are You, O Lord, for You have had pity on Your creature."

{48:1} Seth saw the hand of God stretched out, holding Adam, and He handed Adam over to Michael, saying, "Let him be in your care until the Day of Judgment, when his sorrow will be turned into joy." {48:2} "Then he shall sit on the throne of the one who supplanted him." {48:3} The Lord said again to the angels Michael and Uriel, "Bring me three linen cloths and spread them over Adam, and other linen cloths over Abel, his son. Bury Adam and Abel." {48:4} All the powers of angels marched before Adam, and the sleep of the dead was consecrated. Michael and Uriel buried Adam and Abel in the parts of Paradise, before the eyes of Seth and his mother. {48:5} "As you have seen, in the same way, bury your dead."

{49:1} Six days after Adam died, Eve sensed that her own death was near. She gathered all her sons and daughters—Seth with thirty brothers and thirty sisters—and said to them, "Listen to me, my children, and I will tell you what the archangel Michael said to us when your father and I transgressed God's command." {49:2} "Because of our transgression, the Lord will bring His judgment upon your race, first by water, then by fire. These two judgments will be how the Lord judges the entire human race."

{50:1} "Listen to me, my children. Make tablets of stone and others of clay, and write on them all that you have heard and seen from us about our lives." {50:2} "If the Lord judges our race by water, the clay tablets will dissolve, but the stone tablets will remain. If by fire, the stone tablets will break, but the clay tablets will harden." {50:3} When Eve finished speaking to her children, she spread out her hands to heaven in prayer, knelt to the ground, and while worshipping the Lord and giving thanks, she gave up her spirit. All her children then buried her with loud lamentation.

{51:1} After mourning for four days, Michael the archangel appeared and said to Seth, "Man of God, do not mourn for your dead more than six days, for on the seventh day is the sign of the resurrection and the rest of the age to come. On the seventh day, the Lord rested from all His works." {51:2} Seth then made the tablets.

Slavonic Vita Adae et Evae

The "Slavonic Vita Adae et Evae," or "The Slavonic Life of Adam and Eve," is a significant pseudepigraphal text not included in the canonical scriptures. Likely composed between the 1st century BCE and CE, it details Adam and Eve's lives after their expulsion from Eden. As part of a tradition of apocryphal texts, it expands on biblical narratives and provides moral and theological insights relevant to its creators. This work is notable for its unique elements compared to Greek and Latin versions, reflecting Slavic cultural and religious adaptations. Rich in angelology and demonology, it highlights themes of repentance, human frailty, and divine mercy. Its Old Church Slavonic manuscripts show its importance in Eastern European religious literature and offer insights into the development of biblical interpretation and apocryphal traditions in the Slavic world.

- And we sat together before the gate of paradise. Adam, with his face bent to the earth, lay on the ground, weeping and lamenting. Seven days passed, and we had nothing to eat, consumed by great hunger. I, Eve, cried out with a loud voice: "Have pity on me, O Lord, my Creator; for my sake, Adam suffers so!"
- Then I said to Adam: "Rise up, my lord, that we may seek food, for my spirit fails within me, and my heart is brought low." Adam then spoke to me: "I have thoughts of killing you, but I fear, since God created you in His image, and you show repentance and cry out to God; my heart has not turned away from you."
- Adam arose, and we roamed through all the lands but found nothing to eat except nettles and grass of the field. We returned again to the gates of paradise, crying out and pleading: "Have compassion on your creatures, O Lord Creator, and grant us food."
- For fifteen days, we continuously entreated. Then we heard Michael the archangel and Joel praying for us, and Joel the archangel was commanded by the Lord. He took a seventh part of paradise and gave it to us. Then the Lord said: "Thorns and thistles shall spring up from under your hands; and by your sweat, you shall eat bread, and your wife shall tremble when she looks upon you."
- The archangel Joel said to Adam: "Thus says the Lord; I did not create your wife to command you but to obey you; why are you obedient to your wife?" Then Joel the archangel instructed Adam to separate the cattle and all kinds of flying, creeping things, and animals, both wild and tame, and to give names to all things. Then Adam took the oxen and began to plow.
- Then the devil approached and stood before the oxen, hindering Adam from tilling the field, and said to Adam: "The things of earth are mine, the things of Heaven are God's; but if you wish to be mine, you shall labor on the earth; but if you wish to belong to God, go away to paradise." Adam replied: "The things of Heaven are the Lord's, and the things of earth, paradise, and the whole universe belong to Him."
- The devil said: "I will not allow you to till the field unless you write a bond declaring that you are mine." Adam responded: "Whoever is the lord of the earth, to that one do I belong, and so do my children." The devil, overjoyed, insisted that Adam write the bond. But Adam was not ignorant that the Lord would descend on earth and crush the devil underfoot. The devil said: "Write me your bond." So Adam wrote: "Whoever is the lord of the earth, to him do I belong, and so do my children."
- Eve then said to Adam, "Rise up, my lord, let us pray to God regarding this matter, that He may deliver us from this devil, for it is on my account that you are in this distress." But Adam replied: "Eve, since you repent of your misdeed, my heart will listen to you, for the Lord created you out of my rib. Let us fast for forty days, and perhaps the Lord will have pity on us and grant us understanding and life." I said, "You, my lord, fast for forty days, but I will fast for forty-four."
- Adam then instructed me: "Go to the river called Tigris, take a large stone, place it under your feet, and enter the stream, clothing yourself with water like a cloak, up to your neck. Pray to God in your heart, and let no word escape your lips." I replied, "O my lord, with all my heart I will call upon God." Adam then said: "Be very careful. Unless you see me and all my signs, do not leave the water, nor trust any words spoken to you, lest you fall into the snare again." Adam then went to the Jordan, entered the water, and submerged himself completely, even up to the hairs on his head, while he made supplication to God and sent up prayers to Him.
- There, the angels and all living creatures, both wild and tame, and all birds that fly, gathered around Adam, forming a wall, and prayed to God on Adam's behalf.
- The devil then came to me, appearing as a bright angel, shedding large teardrops, and said to me: "Come out of the water, Eve, for God has heard your prayers and the prayers of the angels. God has fulfilled the intercessions made on your behalf. He has sent me to bring you out of the water."
- But I, Eve, recognized that he was the devil and said nothing in response. When Adam returned from the Jordan, he saw the devil's footprints and feared that I might have been deceived; but when he saw me standing in the water, he was overjoyed and took me and led me out of the water.
- Then Adam cried out with a loud voice: "Be silent, Eve, for my spirit is already constrained within my body; arise, go forth, and utter prayers to God until I deliver up my spirit to Him."

Apostles' Creed

The Apostles' Creed, one of the most ancient and foundational statements of Christian faith, encapsulates core Christian doctrines and has served as a pivotal element in Christian worship and catechesis for centuries. Traditionally attributed to the apostles, though not directly penned by them, this creed emerged in the early centuries of the Christian Church as a baptismal confession and a concise summary of apostolic teaching. Its precise origins are somewhat obscure, but it is generally believed to have been developed between the second and fourth centuries, evolving from earlier baptismal formulas and creeds used in various Christian communities. The Apostles' Creed is remarkable for its succinctness and clarity, articulating fundamental Christian beliefs about the nature of God, the person and work of Jesus Christ, and the role of the Holy Spirit, along with affirmations about the Church, the communion of saints, the forgiveness of sins, the resurrection of the body, and life everlasting. Its Trinitarian structure reflects the early church's effort to define orthodox belief in the face of various heresies, including Gnosticism and Arianism. The creed's enduring significance lies in its universal acceptance across many Christian denominations, including Roman Catholic, Anglican, Lutheran, and Reformed traditions, highlighting its role as a unifying doctrinal statement amid diverse theological perspectives.

Peter	1	I believe in God, the Almighty Father.
John	2	Creator of heaven and earth.
James	3	And in Jesus Christ, His only Son, our Lord.
Andrew	4	Who was conceived by the Holy Spirit and born of the Virgin Mary.
Philip	5	He suffered under Pontius Pilate, was crucified, died, and was buried.
Thomas	6	He descended into hell, and on the third day, He rose from the dead.
Bartholomew	7	He ascended into heaven and is seated at the right hand of God the Father Almighty.
Matthew	8	From there, He will come to judge the living and the dead.
James, the son of Alpheus	9	I believe in the Holy Spirit, the holy Catholic Church.
Simon Zelotes	10	The fellowship of believers, the forgiveness of sins.
Jude, the brother of James	11	The resurrection of the body.
Matthias	12	And life everlasting. Amen.

Melchizedek

The Book of Melchizedek, a text likely originating from early Gnostic traditions, is a complex and esoteric work that offers a mystical account of the figure of Melchizedek, presenting him as both a high priest and a spiritual mediator between the divine and human realms. The text, heavily fragmented and reconstructed from ancient manuscripts, delves into themes of divine knowledge, cosmic hierarchy, and spiritual redemption, positioning Melchizedek as a key figure within a broader metaphysical framework that includes Jesus Christ, the aeons, and various celestial beings. The work reflects the syncretic nature of Gnostic thought, intertwining elements of early Christian theology with Jewish mysticism and Platonic philosophy, thereby providing valuable insights into the religious and philosophical currents of the early centuries of the Common Era. This introduction situates the Book of Melchizedek within the broader context of Gnostic literature, emphasizing its significance for understanding the development of early Christian mysticism and its reinterpretation of biblical figures in light of Gnostic cosmology.

Jesus Christ, the Son of God, who has existed since the beginning of time, came down from the eternal realms so that He could reveal the mysteries of the aeons. I was chosen to disclose the nature of each aeon, describing its essence, and to embody virtues such as friendship and goodness. As He journeyed through these aeons, He prepared to reveal the ultimate truth. His teachings were often presented in the form of parables and riddles, but He promised that a time would come when the truth would be fully unveiled. The forces of Death and the ruling archons—both male and female gods, along with their principalities and authorities—would tremble and rage against Him. Despite their opposition, all the rulers of this world and beyond would witness His power and understand the truth of His mission. The religious leaders, blinded by their ignorance, would hastily bury Him, labeling Him as impious, lawless, and impure. However, on the third day, He would rise from the dead, triumphant over Death, and appear to His holy disciples, revealing to them the world that gives life to all. In the heavens and on earth, those who had doubted Him would speak many words, claiming contradictory things about Him. They would say He was unbegotten, though He was indeed begotten; that He did not eat or drink, though He did; that He was uncircumcised, though He was circumcised; that He was without flesh, though He came in the flesh; that He did not suffer, though He suffered; and that He did not rise from the dead, though He arose. But all the tribes and peoples who receive the truth from you, O Melchizedek, Holy One, High Priest, will speak the truth. I am Gamaliel, sent to the congregation of the children of Seth, who are above thousands upon thousands and myriads upon myriads of the aeons, to impart the knowledge of the true High Priest, Jesus Christ. The adversarial spirits are ignorant of Him and their own destruction. I have come to reveal this truth to you, for you are part of the living offering, along with your offspring, who have been offered up to the All. The offering is not of cattle, but of truth and knowledge, to atone for the sins of unbelief, ignorance, and wicked deeds. The faithful do not reach the Father of the All through mere ritual, but through the waters of baptism that are above, receiving the true baptism that comes from Him. Pray for the offspring of the archons and angels, for from the seed of the Father of the All were engendered the gods, angels, and men, those in the heavens, on the earth, and under the earth. The true Adam and Eve are not those bound by the material world, but those who have overcome the world-rulers, trampling the Cherubim and Seraphim with the flaming sword, bringing forth the light. Those who exist with the hidden truth will renounce the archons and their influence, for they are worthy of immortality, sons of men who follow the holy light. From the beginning, there has been a seed of truth, which has been passed down to those who are faithful.

I, Melchizedek, who came down from the living realms, will now speak. We are the brethren who came down from the living aeons, and we will trample upon the world-rulers as we proclaim the truth. Abel, Enoch, Noah, and you, Melchizedek, the Priest of God Most High, are all part of this holy lineage. These two who have been chosen will never be convicted by their enemies, friends, or even strangers. All adverse forces, whether visible or invisible, from the heavens, the earth, or beneath the earth, will make war against them, but they will overcome. The Savior will take them away and destroy Death. These revelations are to be shared, but only with those who are worthy to receive them. Immediately, I, Melchizedek, rose up and praised God, rejoicing in the knowledge that He had pity on mankind and sent the angel of light from His aeons to reveal the truth. This angel raised me from ignorance and brought me from the fruits of death to life. I am Melchizedek, the Priest of God Most High, and I know that I am truly the image of the true High Priest, who governs the world. God has revealed to me the sacrifice that transcends death, binding the natures that lead astray, and offering up a living sacrifice. In this holy act, I offer up myself, along with those who belong to God, in accordance with the perfect laws. I proclaim my name in baptism, now and forever, among the living and holy names.

Holy, Holy, Holy are You, O Father of the All, who truly exists, now and forever. Amen.
Holy, Holy, Holy are You, O Mother of the aeons, Barbelo, now and forever. Amen.
Holy, Holy, Holy are You, O First-born of the aeons, Doxomedon, now and forever. Amen.
Holy, Holy, Holy are You, O Harmozel, first aeon, now and forever. Amen.
Holy, Holy, Holy are You, O Oriael, commander, luminary of the aeons, now and forever. Amen.
Holy, Holy, Holy are You, O Daveithe, man-of-light, commander of the aeons, now and forever. Amen.
Holy, Holy, Holy are You, O Eleleth, commander-in-chief of the aeons, now and forever. Amen.
Holy, Holy, Holy are You, O good god of the beneficent worlds, Mirocheirothetou, now and forever. Amen.
Holy, Holy, Holy are You, O Commander-in-chief of the All, Jesus Christ, now and forever. Amen.

As I concluded these praises, I was filled with a profound sense of fear and awe, for the darkness that surrounds this world was disturbed. But in the place where the darkness was great, a light began to appear, and with it, the truth was made known. The brethren who belong to the generations of life spoke to me, saying, "Be strong, O Melchizedek, great High Priest of God Most High. The archons, who are your enemies, have made war against you, but you have prevailed. You have endured and destroyed your enemies. Their power will not rest in anything living and holy."

These revelations must be kept secret, only to be revealed to those who are spiritually worthy. When the brethren had finished speaking, they ascended above all the heavens. Amen.

Apocalypse of Adam

The Apocalypse of Adam, a significant text within the Gnostic corpus, is an apocryphal writing that offers a unique perspective on the biblical narrative. Discovered as part of the Nag Hammadi library in 1945, this text is attributed to Adam, who recounts his revelations to his son Seth. It is composed in a narrative form, blending mythological, cosmological, and theological elements that diverge markedly from orthodox Christian teachings. The Apocalypse of Adam is distinguished by its rich symbolic language and esoteric themes, reflecting the Gnostic worldview that emphasizes knowledge (gnosis) as the path to salvation. This text portrays a dualistic cosmology, presenting a stark contrast between the material and spiritual realms. It suggests that the material world is a creation of a lesser, ignorant deity, distinct from the transcendent, true God. The narrative traces the history of humanity, beginning with Adam and Eve's expulsion from the Garden of Eden, and their subsequent enlightenment through divine revelations. The text also prophesies the coming of a savior figure, a redeemer who will liberate humanity from the bondage of the material world. The Apocalypse of Adam thus serves as a crucial document for understanding the diversity of early Christian thought, particularly the strands of Gnosticism that sought to reinterpret traditional Judeo-Christian narratives. It provides invaluable insights into the Gnostic critique of orthodox theology, the nature of divine revelation, and the human quest for spiritual enlightenment.

{1:1} Listen to my words, my son Seth. When God created me from the earth, along with Eve, your mother, we wandered in the glory that she had seen in the eternal realm from which we had emerged. She taught me the knowledge of the eternal God. We resembled the great eternal angels, for we were higher than the god who had created us and the powers with him, whom we did not yet know. {1:2} Then God, the ruler of the aeons and the powers, divided us in anger, and we became two separate aeons. The glory in our hearts left us—me and your mother Eve—along with the first knowledge that had breathed within us. The glory fled from us and entered into a great being that had not come from this aeon but from the realm we had come from, I and your mother Eve. The knowledge entered into the seed of the great aeons. This is why I named you after the man who is the seed of the great generation from which it comes. After those days, the eternal knowledge of the true God withdrew from me and your mother Eve, and from that time, we learned about dead things, like ordinary men. {1:3} Then we recognized the God who had created us, for we were not strangers to his powers, and we served him in fear and slavery. After these things, our hearts became darkened. I slept in deep thought and saw three men before me whose appearance I could not recognize, as they were not the powers of the God who had created us. They surpassed all glory, and one of them said to me, "Arise, Adam, from the sleep of death and hear about the aeon and the seed of the man who has life, who came from you and from Eve, your wife." {1:4} When I heard these words from the great men who stood before me, we—Eve and I—sighed deeply in our hearts. Then the Lord, the God who had created us, stood before us and said, "Adam, why are you both sighing in your hearts? Do you not know that I am the God who created you? I breathed into you a spirit of life as a living soul." Then darkness fell upon our eyes. {1:5} The God who created us made a son from himself and Eve, your mother. I felt a sweet desire for your mother, for I knew within my thoughts a deep longing for her. But then the vigor of our eternal knowledge was destroyed in us, and weakness pursued us. As a result, our lives became short, for I knew that I had come under the power of death. {1:6} Now, my son Seth, I will reveal to you the things those men first saw revealed to me: after I have completed the years of this generation, and the time of this generation has been fulfilled, a great slave will be raised. {1:7} For rain-showers from God Almighty will be poured forth to destroy all flesh from the earth on account of the things it seeks after, along with those from the seed of men to whom the life of the knowledge that came from me and your mother Eve was given. For they were strangers to him. {1:8} Afterwards, great angels will come on high clouds and bring those men into the place where the spirit of life dwells, in glory, and they will come from heaven to earth. Then the whole multitude of flesh will be left behind in the waters. {1:9} Then God will rest from his wrath. He will cast his power upon the waters and give strength to his sons and their wives through the ark, along with the animals and the birds of heaven, which he called and released upon the earth. {1:10} God will say to Noah—whom future generations will call Deucalion—"Behold, I have protected you in the ark, along with your wife, your sons, and their wives, and the animals and birds of heaven which you called and released upon the earth. I will give the earth to you—you and your sons. You will rule over it like kings—you and your sons. No seed will come from you of the men who will not stand before me in another glory." {1:11} Then they will become like the cloud of the great light. Men who have been cast out from the knowledge of the great aeons and angels will stand before Noah and the aeons. God will say to Noah, "Why have you departed from what I told you? You have created another generation to scorn my power." {1:12} Noah will say, "I will testify before your might that the generation of these men did not come from me nor from my sons. It came from knowledge." {1:13} God will then take those men and bring them into their rightful land, where he will build them a holy dwelling place. They will be known by that name and will dwell there for six hundred years in a knowledge of imperishability. The angels of the great Light will dwell with them. No evil deed will reside in their hearts, but only the knowledge of God. {1:14} Then Noah will divide the whole earth among his sons, Ham, Japheth, and Shem. He will say to them, "My sons, listen to my words. Behold, I have divided the earth among you. But serve God in fear and slavery all the days of your life. Let your seed not depart from the presence of God Almighty." {1:15} The son of Noah will say, "My seed will be pleasing before you and before your power. Seal it with your strong hand, with fear and commandment, so that the entire seed that came forth from me may not turn away from you and God Almighty, but will serve in humility and fear of his knowledge." {1:16} Then others from the seed of Ham and Japheth will come—four hundred thousand men—and enter into another land to dwell with those men who came from the great eternal knowledge. For the shadow of their power will protect those who dwell with them from every evil thing and every unclean desire. {1:17} Then the seed of Ham and Japheth will form twelve kingdoms, and their seed will also enter into the kingdom of another people. Then those who are dead, of the great aeons of imperishability, will take counsel and go to Sakla, their god, to the powers, accusing the great men who are in their glory. {1:18} They will say to Sakla, "What is the power of these men who stood before you, taken from the seed of Ham and Japheth, who will number four hundred thousand men? They have been received into another aeon from which they came and have overturned all the glory of your power and the dominion of your hand. For the seed of Noah, through his sons, has done all your will, and so have all the powers in the aeons under your rule, while those men and those who dwell in their glory have not done your will. They have turned aside your entire multitude." {1:19} Then the god of the aeons will give them some of those who serve him. They will come upon that land where the great men will be who have not been defiled nor will be defiled by any desire. For their soul did not come from a defiled hand but from a great commandment of an eternal angel. Then fire, sulfur, and asphalt will be cast upon those men, and fire and blinding mist will come over those aeons, and the eyes of the powers of the illuminators will be darkened, and the aeons will not see them in those days. {1:20} Great clouds of light will descend, and other clouds of light will come down upon them from the great aeons. Abrasax, Sablo, and Gamaliel will descend and bring those men out of the fire and wrath and take them above the aeons and rulers of the powers, taking them away to the realm of life, and taking them away to the aeons' dwelling place of the great light with the holy angels and aeons. The men will be like those angels, for they are not strangers to them but work in the imperishable seed. {1:21} Once again, for the third time, the illuminator of knowledge will pass by in great glory to leave something of the seed of Noah and the sons of Ham and Japheth—to leave for himself fruit-bearing trees. He will redeem their souls from the day of death, for the whole creation that came from the dead earth will be under the authority of death. But those who meditate upon the knowledge of the eternal God in their hearts will not perish, for they have received the spirit not only from this kingdom but also from an eternal angel. {1:22} The illuminator will come upon the dead who belong to the line of Seth, and he will perform signs and wonders to mock the powers and their ruler. Then the god of the powers will be troubled, saying, "What is the power of this man who is greater than we?" Then he will arouse great wrath against that man, and the glory will withdraw and dwell in holy houses that it has chosen for itself. {1:23} The powers will not see it with their eyes, nor will they see the illuminator. Then they will punish the flesh of the man upon whom the holy spirit came. The angels and all the generations of the powers will use the name in error, asking, "Where did this error come from?" or "Where did the words of deception, which all the powers have failed to discover, come from?" {1:24} Now the first kingdom says of him that he came from a spirit sent to heaven. He was nourished in the heavens and received the glory and power of that one. He came to the bosom of his mother and thus came to the water. {1:25} The second kingdom says of him that he came from a great prophet. A bird came, took the child who was born, and brought him to a high mountain. He was nourished by the bird of heaven. An angel appeared there and said to him, "Arise! God has given you glory." He received glory and strength, and thus he came to the water. {1:26} The third kingdom says of him that he came from a virgin womb. He was cast out of his city along with his mother. He was brought to a desert place, where he was nourished. He came and received glory and strength, and thus he came to the water. {1:27} The fourth kingdom says of him that he came from a virgin. Solomon sought her, along with Phersalo, Sauel, and their armies, which had been sent out. Solomon himself sent his army of demons to seek the virgin, but they did not find the one they sought. Instead, they found the virgin given to them. Solomon took her, and she became pregnant and gave birth to the child there. She nourished him on the border of the desert. When he was nourished, he received glory and power from the seed from which he was begotten, and thus he came to the water. {1:28} The fifth kingdom says of him that he came from a drop from heaven. He was thrown into the sea. The abyss received him, gave birth to him, and brought him to heaven. He received glory and power, and thus he came to the water. {1:29} The sixth kingdom says that he came down to the aeon below to gather flowers. She became pregnant from the desire of the flowers and gave birth to him in that place. The angels of the flower garden nourished him. He received glory and power there, and thus he came to the water. {1:30} The seventh kingdom says of him that he is a drop that came from heaven to earth. Dragons brought him down to caves. He became a child. A spirit came upon him and brought him on high to the place where the drop had come from. He received glory and power there, and thus he came to the water. {1:31} The eighth kingdom says of him that a cloud came upon the earth and enveloped a rock. He came forth from it. The angels above the cloud nourished him. He received glory and power there, and thus he came to the water. {1:32} The ninth kingdom says of him that one of the nine Muses separated herself and came to a high mountain, spending some time seated there until she desired herself alone to become androgynous. She fulfilled her desire, became pregnant, and gave birth to him. The angels over the desire nourished him. He received glory and power there, and thus he came to the water. {1:33} The tenth kingdom says of him that his god loved a cloud of desire. He begot him in his hand and cast a drop upon the cloud above him. He was born, received glory and power, and thus came to the water. {1:34} The eleventh kingdom says that the father desired his own daughter. She became pregnant by her father, and she cast him into a tomb in the desert. An angel nourished him there, and thus he came to the water. {1:35} The twelfth kingdom says of him that he came from two illuminators. They nourished him there. He received glory and power, and thus he came to the water. {1:36} The thirteenth kingdom says of him that every birth of their ruler is a word. This word received a command there, glory, and power, and thus he came to the water to fulfill the desire of those powers. {1:37} But the generation without a king says that God chose him from all the aeons. He caused the knowledge of the undefiled one of truth to dwell in him. He said, "Out of a foreign air, from a great aeon, the great illuminator came forth. He made the generation of those men he had chosen for himself shine, so that they could illuminate the whole aeon." {1:38} Then the seed, those who will receive his name upon the water, will fight against the power. A cloud of darkness will descend upon them. The peoples will cry out with a great voice, "Blessed are the souls of those men, for they have known God with the knowledge of truth! They shall live forever because they have not been corrupted by their desires, nor have they performed the works of the powers, but they have stood in his presence with the knowledge of God, like light that has come from fire and blood. {1:39} But we have committed every deed of the powers senselessly. We have boasted in the transgression of all our works. We have cried out against the God of truth because his works are eternal. These things are against our spirits, for now we have realized that our souls will die." {1:40} Then a voice came to them, saying, "Micheu, Michar, and Mnesinous, who are over the holy baptism and the living water, why have you cried out against the living God with lawless voices and tongues without restraint, and souls full of blood and evil deeds? You are full of works that are not of the truth, yet your ways are full of joy and rejoicing. You have defiled the water of life and drawn it into the will of the powers to whom you have been given to serve. {1:41} Your thoughts are not like those of the men you persecute. Their fruit does not wither, but they will be known up to the great aeons because the words they have kept, of the God of the aeons, were not written in a book. Angelic beings will bring them, whom all generations of men will not know. For they will be on a high mountain, upon a rock of truth. Therefore they will be called 'The Words of Imperishability and Truth,' for those who know the eternal God in wisdom of knowledge and teaching of angels forever, for he knows all things." {1:42} These are the revelations Adam made known to his son Seth, and Seth taught his descendants about them. This is the hidden knowledge of Adam, which he gave to Seth. It is the holy baptism of those who know the eternal knowledge through those born of the word and the imperishable illuminators who came from the holy seed: Yesseus, Mazareus, Yessedekeus, the Living Water.

Apocalypse of Paul

The "Apocalypse of Paul," also known as the "Vision of Saint Paul," is an early Christian apocryphal text that presents a vivid account of the apostle Paul's visionary journey through the heavens and the realms of the dead. This work, likely composed between the 3rd and 5th centuries CE, builds upon themes of divine judgment, reward, and retribution, portraying the fate of the righteous and the wicked after death. While not considered canonical, it echoes popular Christian eschatological beliefs of the time, blending elements of Jewish apocalyptic literature and early Christian theological concerns about the afterlife, sin, and repentance. The text's influence can be seen in medieval Christian visions of heaven and hell, with its detailed depictions of paradise, the torments of the damned, and the role of angels in mediating divine justice. Despite its exclusion from the official Christian canon, the "Apocalypse of Paul" offers significant insight into the development of early Christian thought on the afterlife and has been a subject of interest for scholars studying Christian apocryphal writings and eschatology.

The Revelation of the Holy Apostle Paul: these are the things that were revealed to him when he was taken up to the third heaven and caught up into paradise, where he heard words that cannot be spoken.

{1:1} There was once a nobleman living in the city of Tarsus, in the house of St. Paul the Apostle, during the reign of the worshipful King Theodosius and the illustrious Gratianus. {1:2} One night, an angel of the Lord appeared to the nobleman in a vision, saying, "Dig up the foundation of this house and take up what you find." {1:3} The nobleman thought it was just a dream, but after the angel appeared to him a second and third time, he was convinced. {1:4} He dug up the foundation and discovered a marble box containing a sealed revelation. {1:5} He showed the box to the ruler of the city, who sent it to King Theodosius, believing it to be of great importance. {1:6} The king, after reading and transcribing the revelation, sent the original to Jerusalem. Written inside it were the following words:

{2:1} The word of the Lord came to me, saying: "Tell this people, how long will you continue to sin, adding sin upon sin, provoking the God who made you? {2:2} You claim to be children of Abraham, but your deeds are the works of Satan. {2:3} You boast only in your prayers, but you are poor in spirit due to your sins. {2:4} Know, sons of men, that all creation is subject to God, yet the human race alone provokes Him by sinning. {2:5} Many times, the great light of the sun has stood before God, asking, 'How long, Lord, will you tolerate the sins of men? Let me burn them up!' {2:6} But God replies, 'I endure in long-suffering so that they may repent. But if they do not, they will come to me, and I will judge them.' {2:7} Likewise, the moon and stars have asked, 'Lord, you gave us dominion over the night, but we no longer wish to witness the thefts, adulteries, and murders of men. Let us show them wonders!' {2:8} But the Lord responds, 'I bear with them in long-suffering so they might repent. If they do not, they will come to me, and I will judge them.' {2:9} The sea, too, has cried out, 'Lord Almighty, men have profaned your name. Let me rise up and cover the earth to wipe out humanity!' {2:10} Yet God says, 'I endure their sins in long-suffering that they may repent; but if they do not, they will face my judgment.' {2:11} Thus, the whole creation is obedient to God, but humanity alone continues to sin. {2:12} Therefore, men should bless God continually, especially at sunset when all angels come before God to worship and bring Him the works of men—good or evil. {2:13} One angel rejoices over the good deeds of a righteous man, while another mourns over the sins of the wicked. {2:14} All the angels gather at appointed times to bring the daily works of men before God. {2:15} So, bless the Lord without ceasing, and especially at the appointed hour when the angels sing psalms, bringing the deeds of the righteous before God. {2:16} The Spirit of God then speaks to them, asking, 'From where do you come rejoicing?' {2:17} They reply, 'We come from the company of the pious, who live their lives in fear of God.' {2:18} A voice replies, 'I have kept them and will continue to guard them until they are void of offense in my kingdom.' {2:19} Then other angels come with a shining countenance, saying, 'We come from those who have forsaken the world for Your holy name, living in deserts, mountains, caves, and dens.' {2:20} A voice tells them, 'Go in peace, guarding them.' {2:21} Finally, sorrowful angels come, mourning, and they say, 'We come from those called by Your name but enslaved to sin.' {2:22} The voice commands them, 'Do not cease to minister to them; perhaps they will turn and repent. If not, they shall come to me, and I will judge them.' {2:23} Sons of men, know that all your deeds are written in heaven. Bless God without ceasing.

{3:1} I was in the Holy Spirit, and an angel said to me, "Come, follow me, and I will show you the place of the just after they die." {3:2} He took me up into the heavens beneath the firmament, where I saw terrifying powers, full of wrath, clothed in flames. {3:3} I asked the angel, "Who are these?" {3:4} He replied, "These are the angels sent to the souls of sinners in their hour of death, for they did not believe in judgment." {3:5} I looked up and saw other angels whose faces shone like the sun, girded with golden belts, holding prizes inscribed with the name of the Lord. {3:6} I asked, "Who are these?" {3:7} He replied, "These angels are sent to gather the souls of the righteous on the day of resurrection." {3:8} I then asked to see how the righteous and sinners depart from the world. {3:9} The angel instructed me to look down at the earth. {3:10} I saw the world vanish before me, and I asked, "Is this the greatness of man?" {3:11} The angel replied, "Yes, the unjust vanish like this." {3:12} I then saw a cloud of fire over the earth and asked, "What is this?" {3:13} The angel explained, "This is the unrighteousness and destruction of sinners." {3:14} I wept and asked to see the departure of the righteous and the wicked from life. The angel told me to look again.

{4:1} I saw a man nearing death, and the angel said, "This is a righteous man, and behold, all his works stand beside him." {4:2} Both good and evil angels surrounded him, but the evil angels found no place in him. {4:3} The good angels took the soul of the righteous man, saying, "Take note of the body from which you depart, for you will return to it in the resurrection to receive what God has promised the righteous." {4:4} The good angels, who knew the soul well, led it to the Spirit of God, who welcomed it into the place of resurrection. {4:5} Then I saw another man nearing death, and the angel said, "This is a sinner." {4:6} Good and evil angels gathered, but the good angels found no place of rest, and the evil angels took possession of the soul, saying, "Wretched soul, pay heed to the flesh you are leaving, for you will return to it in the resurrection to receive the recompense for your sins." {4:7} The angel who recorded the soul's sins approached it, saying, "You wasted the time of repentance; be exceedingly ashamed." {4:8} When the soul came forth, the angels wept, crying out, "Woe to you, wretched soul! What excuse will you give before God?" {4:9} The angel of the soul cried out, "Let us all mourn together for this soul." {4:10} The soul stood before God, and a voice asked, "Where is the fruit of your righteousness?" The soul remained silent, unable to answer. {4:11} The voice declared, "He who has shown mercy will receive mercy; but he who has not shown mercy will not receive it." {4:12} The soul was delivered to the merciless angel Temeluch and cast into outer darkness, where there is weeping and gnashing of teeth. A voice declared, "Righteous are you, O Lord, and righteous is your judgment."

{5:1} I saw another soul led forward, weeping, saying, "Have mercy on me, O righteous Judge." {5:2} A voice replied, "You were merciless, and thus you are delivered to this merciless angel." {5:3} The soul denied its sins, but the Lord said, "Your deeds are known to me; confess your wrongs." {5:4} The soul was silent, and the Lord commanded an angel to bring forth the record of its deeds. {5:5} The angel disclosed sins committed five years before the soul's death, saying, "Lord, by your command, the earlier sins were forgotten, but these remain." {5:6} The soul stood beside those it had wronged, and when asked if it had sinned against them, it admitted, "Yes, I killed one and wronged the other." {5:7} The Lord declared, "Know that when you wronged someone, you were kept in judgment until the wronged person could be judged with you." {5:8} The soul was delivered to the angel Tartaruch for judgment, and I heard a voice saying, "Righteous are you, O Lord, and righteous is your judgment."

{6:1} The angel asked if I had seen all these things, and I replied, "Yes, my lord." {6:2} He said, "Come, I will show you the place of the righteous." {6:3} He led me to the golden gates of a city with two golden pillars and inscriptions on golden plates. {6:4} He said, "Blessed are those who enter here, for only those with pure hearts and guiltlessness may pass through." {6:5} I asked, "Are their names written in heaven while they are still alive?" {6:6} The angel replied, "Yes, the names of those who serve God are inscribed here." {6:7} The gates opened, and a hoary-headed man greeted me with tears, saying, "Welcome, Paul, beloved of God." {6:8} I asked him, "Why do you weep?" {6:9} He replied, "Because God has prepared many good things for men, yet they do not do His will." {6:10} I asked the angel, "Who is this?" {6:11} He replied, "This is Enoch, a witness of the last days." {6:12} The angel said, "Whatever I show you here, do not announce it except what I tell you." {6:13} We approached a river whose source encircles heaven, and the angel said, "This is Ocean." {6:14} A great light appeared, and I asked, "What is this?" {6:15} He replied, "This is the land of the meek. It is written, 'Blessed are the meek, for they shall inherit the earth.'" {6:16} The souls of the righteous are kept here until the resurrection when the earth will be revealed, and the saints will enjoy the good things prepared from the foundation of the world. {6:17} Trees filled with fruits stood along the river, and I saw vines growing upon date palms, with myriads of clusters on each branch. {6:18} I asked, "What is this, my lord?" {6:19} He replied, "This is the Acherusian lake, and only those who repent of their sins may enter the city of God."

{7:1} I marveled at what I saw, and the angel said, "Follow me to the city of God and its light." {7:2} The city's light was greater than that of the world, and walls encircled it. {7:3} The city measured one hundred stadia in length and breadth, with twelve ornamented gates. {7:4} Four rivers encircled the city, flowing with milk, honey, oil, and wine. {7:5} I asked, "What are these rivers?" {7:6} The angel replied, "These represent the righteous who, while in the world, humbled themselves for the sake of God." {7:7} I entered the city and saw a lofty tree before the doors, bearing no fruit. {7:8} Beneath it were a few men weeping, and the tree bent down toward them. {7:9} I wept with them and asked the angel, "Who are these men who do not enter the city?" {7:10} He replied, "They are those who have fallen due to vainglory, the root of all evil." {7:11} I asked, "Why do the trees humble themselves?" {7:12} The angel answered, "The trees are barren because they too did not restrain their vainglory." {7:13} I asked why these men were kept outside the city, and the angel said, "Because of God's great goodness, Christ will come through these gates, and those who follow Him may plead for these men, that they may be brought in." {7:14} The angel led me to the river, where I saw all the prophets. They saluted me, saying, "Welcome, Paul, beloved of God." {7:15} I asked, "Who are these?" {7:16} The angel said, "These are the prophets, and they greet those who come here after grieving their souls for God's sake." {7:17} The angel took me to the south of the city, where I saw the infants killed by King Herod for the Lord's name. {7:18} He then brought me to the east, where I saw Abraham, Isaac, and Jacob, and asked, "What place is this?" {7:19} The angel replied, "Those who show hospitality come here, where they are greeted as friends of God." {7:20} He led me to the north, where a river of oil flowed, and I saw people rejoicing and singing praises. {7:21} I asked, "Who are these?" {7:22} The angel replied, "These are those who have wholly given themselves to God." {7:23} I saw a great altar in the midst of the city, and near it stood one whose face shone like the sun, singing the Alleluia with a psaltery and harp. {7:24} The voice filled the city, and all sang with him in unison, causing the city to shake. {7:25} I asked the angel, "Who is this?" {7:26} He replied, "This is David, the prophet, and this is the heavenly Jerusalem." {7:27} When Christ returns, David will come forth with all the saints, for as it is in heaven, so it shall be on earth. {7:28} No sacrifice of the precious body and blood of Christ will be offered without David's Alleluia. {7:29} I asked the angel, "What is the meaning of Alleluia?" {7:30} He said, "It means speech to God, who founded all things, glorifying Him."

{8:1} The angel led me outside the city, past the Acherusian lake, and set me upon the river of the ocean supporting the heavens. {8:2} He asked, "Do you know where I am going?" I replied, "No, my lord." {8:3} He said, "Follow me, and I will show you the place of the impious and sinners." {8:4} He led me to the setting of the sun, where the heavens met the ocean. {8:5} I saw darkness and grief, and a great multitude of men and women cast into a bubbling river. {8:6} Some were submerged up to their knees, others to their navels, and many up to their heads. {8:7} I asked, "Who are these?" {8:8} He replied, "These are the unrepentant who lived in fornication and adultery." {8:9} I saw another river of fire, with many souls cast into it, and I asked, "Who are these?" {8:10} The angel replied, "These are thieves, slanderers, and flatterers who trusted in their riches instead of God." {8:11} I asked, "How deep is this river?" {8:12} He answered, "It is immeasurable." {8:13} I wept for humanity, but the angel said, "Why do you weep? Are you more merciful than God? {8:14} God is holy, and though He waits for men to repent, they are deceived by their own desires and face eternal punishment." {8:15} I looked again and saw an old man being dragged by two angels into the river, and they pulled out his entrails through his mouth. {8:16} I asked, "Who is this?" {8:17} The angel replied, "This man was a presbyter who ate and drank, then performed God's service." {8:18} I saw another old man carried by four angels and thrown into the fire. {8:19} He was a bishop who, though pleased with the title, did not walk in God's goodness or judge righteously." {8:20} Another man was in the river up to his navel, with bloody hands, and worms coming from his mouth. {8:21} The angel said, "This was a deacon who served God without righteousness." {8:22} I saw a wall of fire where people ate their own tongues, and the angel said, "These are the slanderers and those who speak against their neighbors in the church." {8:23} I saw a bloody pit where wizards, sorcerers, adulterers, and oppressors of widows and orphans were cast. {8:24} Women wearing black were led to a dark place, and the angel said, "These are they who defied their parents and lost their virginity before marriage." {8:25} I saw women wearing white robes, blind, standing on obelisks of fire, and the angel said, "These are those who corrupted themselves and killed their infants, whose cries for justice were heard." {8:26} The infants were taken to a spacious place, but their parents were cast into eternal fire.

{9:1} The angel took me up from these torments and set me beside a well sealed with seven seals. {9:2} He commanded the angel of the well to open it so I could see the torments. {9:3} The angel opened the seals, and a stench arose that was unbearable. {9:4} Inside the well was utter darkness, and the angel said, "This is the place where those who denied that Mary is the mother of God and that the bread and wine are His body and blood are cast. No angel intercedes for them." {9:5} Towards the setting of the sun, I saw a place of weeping and gnashing of teeth, where men and women were tormented. {9:6} The angel said, "These are they who deny the resurrection of the dead; for them, there is no mercy."
{10:1} I wept bitterly, and looking up, I saw the heavens opened, and the archangel Gabriel descending with hosts of angels. {10:2} The souls in torment cried out, "Have mercy on us, Gabriel, who stands before God!" {10:3} Gabriel replied, "As the

Lord lives, I plead for mankind day and night, but they did no good in life and spent their days in vanity." {10:4} He wept, saying, "Perhaps the Lord will have mercy." {10:5} The tormented souls cried out, "Have mercy, O Lord, on those made in Your image." {10:6} The heavens shook, and I saw the twenty-four elders lying prostrate, entreating God's mercy. {10:7} I saw the Son of God descending to earth with great power. {10:8} At the sound of the trumpet, those in torment cried out, "Have mercy, Son of God, for you have power over all things." {10:9} A voice replied, "What good works have you done to ask for rest? You lived as you wished, without repentance, and spent your life in wickedness. {10:10} But for the sake of Gabriel and Paul, my beloved, I grant you rest on the holy Lord's day, when I rose from the dead." {10:11} The souls in torment blessed the Son of God, saying, "Better is this rest than the life we lived."

{11:1} The angel said, "Come, I will take you to paradise and show you the righteous." {11:2} He brought me to paradise, where I saw a beautiful tree with the Holy Spirit resting upon it, and from its roots flowed sweet-smelling water that parted into four rivers. {11:3} I asked, "What is this tree, and where does the water go?" {11:4} The angel said, "These are the four kingdoms of the earth: Phison, Gehon, Tigris, and Euphrates." {11:5} He led me to the tree of the knowledge of good and evil and said, "This is the tree by which death entered the world when Adam ate its fruit." {11:6} He then showed me the tree of life, guarded by cherubim and a flaming sword. {11:7} As I marveled at the tree, I saw a woman approaching with angels singing praises to her. {11:8} I asked, "Who is this?" {11:9} The angel replied, "This is the holy Mary, the mother of the Lord." {11:10} She greeted me, saying, "Welcome, Paul, beloved of God. You proclaimed His word and saved many through your teaching." {11:11} As we spoke, I saw three men approaching. {11:12} The angel said, "These are Abraham, Isaac, and Jacob." {11:13} They greeted me, saying, "Welcome, Paul, beloved of God." {11:14} Joseph, who was sold into Egypt, said, "Blessed is he who endures trial, for the Lord will reward him sevenfold in the world to come." {11:15} While he spoke, I saw another approaching like an angel. {11:16} The angel said, "This is Moses, who led the children of Israel out of Egypt." {11:17} Moses wept, saying, "I weep for those who did not understand the toil I endured for Israel, for my people have not borne fruit. But through your word, the Gentiles believe and are saved." {11:18} He lamented that the Jews did not understand even when they saw God's wonders. {11:19} When they crucified the Son of God, all creation mourned, but they remained unrepentant, and for them, the fire everlasting is prepared."

{12:1} As Moses spoke, three others approached, saying, "Welcome, Paul, beloved of God." {12:2} One said, "I am Isaiah, whom Manasseh sawed in half." {12:3} The second said, "I am Jeremiah, stoned by the Jews, but they now burn in everlasting fire." {12:4} The third said, "I am Ezekiel, pierced by the slayers of the Messiah." {12:5} They lamented their suffering, unable to turn the Jews' stony hearts. {12:6} I threw myself on the ground, thanking God for delivering me from the race of the Hebrews. {12:7} A voice declared, "Blessed are you, Paul, and blessed are those who believed in the name of Jesus through you, for everlasting life has been prepared for them."

{13:1} As the voice spoke, another cried out, "Blessed are you, Paul!" {13:2} The angel said, "This is Noah, who lived during the time of the flood." {13:3} Noah greeted me, saying, "I built the ark over a hundred years, practicing continence and never removing my coat, which remained clean. {13:4} I preached repentance, but none listened, and all were destroyed by the flood." {13:5} I saw two others approaching and asked the angel, "Who are these?" {13:6} He replied, "These are Enoch and Elias." {13:7} They greeted me, saying, "Welcome, Paul, beloved of God!" {13:8} Elias said, "I prayed for the rain to cease for three and a half years, and God commanded the angels to be patient until I prayed again."

Apocalypse of Moses

The "Apocalypse of Moses," also known as the "Life of Adam and Eve," is an essential work within the corpus of pseudepigrapha, offering a rich narrative that elaborates on the biblical story of Adam and Eve, their life after the expulsion from the Garden of Eden, and their eventual death. This text is pivotal for understanding the intertestamental period, a time when Jewish literature expanded the canonical boundaries of the Hebrew Bible to include elaborate traditions and mythological elements. Though traditionally attributed to Moses, the text's actual authorship remains anonymous and is believed to date from the 1st century CE, reflecting Jewish thought influenced by Hellenistic culture. The "Apocalypse of Moses" provides a detailed account of Adam and Eve's penance, their interactions with the archangel Michael, and Adam's vision of the future, including the coming of the Messiah and the final judgment. The narrative not only complements the Genesis account but also offers unique theological insights, particularly concerning human mortality, sin, and redemption. It emphasizes themes of repentance, divine mercy, and the hope for resurrection, contributing to the broader apocalyptic literature tradition. The text's rich symbolism and vivid descriptions have profoundly influenced both Jewish and Christian eschatological thought, making it a valuable resource for scholars studying early Jewish mysticism, Christian origins, and the development of apocalyptic literature. Despite its non-canonical status, the text has enjoyed significant popularity and has been preserved in multiple versions, including Greek, Latin, Armenian, and Slavonic, each reflecting the theological and cultural contexts in which they were transmitted.

{1:1} This is the story of Adam and Eve after they left Paradise. Adam knew his wife Eve, and they moved eastward, where they lived for eighteen years and two months. {1:2} Eve conceived and bore two sons: Adiaphotos, who is also called Cain, and Amilabes, who is called Abel.

{2:1} After this, Adam and Eve were together, and while they were sleeping, Eve said to Adam, "My lord Adam, {2:2} I had a dream last night. I saw the blood of my son Amilabes, also called Abel, being poured into the mouth of his brother Cain, who drank it without pity. Abel begged Cain to leave him a little, but Cain did not listen and drank it all. The blood did not stay in his stomach but came out of his mouth." {2:3} Adam said, "Let us get up and see what has happened to them. I fear the adversary may be attacking them somewhere."

{3:1} They both went and found Abel murdered by the hand of his brother Cain. {3:2} God said to Michael the archangel, "Tell Adam, 'Do not reveal to Cain what you know, for he is a son of wrath. Do not grieve, for I will give you another son in Abel's place who will show you what to do. Tell him nothing.'" {3:3} Michael spoke these words to Adam, who kept them in his heart, as did Eve, though they mourned for their son Abel.

{4:1} After this, Adam knew his wife Eve again, and she conceived and bore Seth. {4:2} Adam said to Eve, "See, we have another son in place of Abel, whom Cain killed. Let us give glory and sacrifice to God."

{5:1} Adam fathered thirty sons and thirty daughters and lived for nine hundred and thirty years. As he fell ill, he cried out loudly, {5:2} "Let all my children come to me so I may see them before I die." {5:3} They all gathered, for the earth had been divided into three parts. Seth, his son, said to him, {5:4} "Father Adam, what is your ailment?" {5:5} Adam replied, "My children, I am burdened with great trouble." They asked him, "What is this trouble?"

{6:1} Seth answered and said to him, "Father, are you thinking about the fruit of Paradise that you used to eat, and feeling sorrowful because you miss it?" {6:2} "If that's the case, tell me, and I will go and bring you some fruit from Paradise. I will put ashes on my head, weep, and pray that the Lord will hear me and send his angel to bring me a plant from Paradise so that your suffering may end." {6:3} Adam replied, "No, my son Seth, I am suffering from much sickness and trouble!" Seth asked, "How did this come upon you?"

{7:1} Adam said to him, "When God made your mother and me, through whom I am also dying, He gave us permission to eat from every tree in Paradise, but He commanded us not to eat from one tree, and because of this tree, we are to die. {7:2} The time came for the angels who were guarding your mother to go up and worship the Lord, and I was far from her. The enemy knew she was alone and tempted her to eat from the tree we were commanded not to eat. {7:3} Then she gave it to me, and I ate it too."

{8:1} "God was angry and called me in a terrible voice, 'Adam, where are you? Can a house hide from its builder?' He said that because I broke His covenant, I would suffer seventy-two afflictions, starting with pain in the eyes and an ailment of the ears, and so on."

{9:1} As Adam spoke these words to his sons, he groaned deeply and said, "What shall I do? I am in great distress." {9:2} Eve wept and said, "My lord Adam, rise and give me half of your suffering, and I will endure it. It is because of me that this has happened to you. You are beset with troubles because of me." {9:3} But Adam replied, "Eve, go with our son Seth near Paradise, put earth on your heads, and weep and pray to God to have mercy on me. Ask Him to send His angel to give me some of the oil from the tree in Paradise so I can anoint myself and find relief."

{10:1} So Seth and Eve went towards Paradise. Eve saw a wild beast attacking her son and wept, saying, "Woe is me! If I reach the day of Resurrection, everyone who has sinned will curse me, saying, 'Eve did not keep the commandment of God.'" {10:2} She spoke to the beast, "You wicked creature, do you not fear to fight with the image of God? How was your mouth opened, and how were your teeth made strong? Do you not remember your subjection? Long ago, you were made subject to the image of God." {10:3} Then the beast cried out and said:

{11:1} "Eve, it is not my concern but yours. Your greed and wailing are your own doing. It is because of you that we lost our rule over the beasts. {11:2} How was your mouth opened to eat from the tree that God commanded you not to eat from? Because of this, our nature was also changed. Now you cannot endure it if I begin to reproach you."

{12:1} Seth then spoke to the beast, "Close your mouth, be silent, and stand away from the image of God until the day of Judgment." {12:2} The beast replied to Seth, "I will stand away from the image of God," and went back to its lair.

{13:1} Seth and Eve went near Paradise, weeping and praying for God to send His angel to give them the oil of mercy. {13:2} God sent the archangel Michael, who spoke to Seth, "Seth, man of God, do not tire yourself with prayers and pleas concerning the tree that gives oil to anoint your father Adam. It is not for you now, but at the end of time. {13:3} Then, all flesh from Adam to that great day will be raised up, and the delights of Paradise will be given to them. God will be in their midst, and they will no longer sin before Him. Their evil hearts will be taken away, and they will have hearts that understand good and serve God only. {13:4} But go back to your father now, for his life is nearly over. He will live three more days and then die. When his soul departs, you will witness the awful scene of his passing."

{14:1} The angel then left them. Seth and Eve returned to the hut where Adam was lying. Adam said to Eve, "Eve, what {14:2} have you done to us? You have brought great wrath upon us, which is death, lording it over all our race." He continued, "Call all {14:3} our children and grandchildren, and tell them how we transgressed."

{15:1} Eve said to them, "Listen, all my children and grandchildren, and I will tell you {15:2} how the enemy deceived us. We were guarding Paradise, each of us in the portion allotted to us by God. I guarded the west and the south. {15:3} But the devil went to Adam's lot, where the male creatures were. God had divided the creatures, giving all the males to your father and all the females to me."

{16:1} The devil spoke to the serpent, saying, "Rise and come to me, and I will tell you a word {16:2} that will benefit you." The serpent rose and came to him. The devil said, {16:3} "I hear that you are wiser than all the beasts, and I have come to advise you. Why do you eat from Adam's tares and not from Paradise? Rise, and we will cause him to be cast out of Paradise, just {16:4} as we were cast out because of him." The serpent said, "I fear the Lord's wrath." {16:5} The devil said, "Do not fear, just be my vessel, and I will speak through you to deceive him."

{17:1} Instantly, the serpent hung himself from the wall of Paradise. When the angels went up to worship God, Satan appeared in the form of an angel and sang hymns like the angels. I bent over the wall and saw him, thinking he was an angel. He said to me, "Are you Eve?" I replied, "I am." He asked, "What are you doing in Paradise?" I told him, "God placed us here to guard and eat from it." {17:2} The devil, speaking through the serpent, said, "You do well, but you do not eat from every plant." I answered, "Yes, we eat from all except one tree in the middle of Paradise, which God commanded us not to eat from, saying that on the day we eat from it, we will die."

{18:1} Then the serpent said, "May God live! I am grieved for you and do not want you to be ignorant. Come and listen to me, eat, and understand the value of that tree." {18:2} I said, "I fear God will be angry with me as He warned us." He replied, "Do not fear, for as soon as you eat from it, you will be like God, knowing good and evil. {18:3} God knew this and envied you, so He told you not to eat from it. Pay attention to the plant, and you will see its great glory." Despite my fear, he continued, "Come, and I will give it to you. Follow me."

{19:1} I opened to him, and he walked a little way before turning and saying, "I have changed my mind. I will not give it to you unless you swear to give it to your husband as well." I asked, "What kind of oath should I swear?" He said, "Swear by the throne of the Master, the Cherubim, and the Tree of Life that you will give it to your husband." {19:2} I swore the oath, and he then poured the poison of his wickedness, which is lust, upon the fruit. He bent the branch to the ground, and I took the fruit and ate it.

{20:1} In that very hour, my eyes were opened, and I realized I was naked and had lost the righteousness I was clothed in. I wept and asked, "Why have you done this to me, depriving me of my glory?" I also wept over the oath I had sworn. He then descended from the tree and vanished. {20:2} I began to search for leaves to hide my shame but found none, as the leaves had fallen from all the trees except the fig tree. {20:3} I took leaves from the fig tree and made a girdle for myself, using the same plant from which I had eaten.

{21:1} I cried out, "Adam, Adam, where are you? Come to me, and I will show you a great secret." When your father came, I spoke words of transgression that brought us down from our great glory. {21:2} I said, "Come, my lord Adam, listen to me and eat from the tree that God commanded us not to eat from. You will become like God." {21:3} Your father replied, "I fear God will be angry with me." I said, "Do not fear, for as soon as you eat, you will know good and evil." {21:4} I quickly persuaded him, and he ate. Immediately, his eyes were opened, and he realized his nakedness. {21:5} He said to me, "O wicked woman! What have I done to you that you have deprived me of God's glory?"

{22:1} At that moment, we heard the archangel Michael blowing his trumpet and calling to the angels, saying, "Thus says the Lord, come with me to Paradise and hear the judgment I will pass on Adam." {22:2} When God appeared in Paradise, mounted on the chariot of His cherubim with angels singing hymns before Him, all the plants of Paradise burst into flowers. {22:3} God's throne was set by the Tree of Life.

{23:1} God called out, "Adam, where are you? Can the house be hidden from its builder?" Your father answered, "It is not because we think we cannot be found by You, Lord, that we hide. I was afraid because I am naked and ashamed before Your might, my Master." {23:2} God said, "Who told you that you are naked unless you have broken My commandment?" Adam remembered my words, saying I would make him secure before God. {23:3} He turned to me and asked, "Why have you done this?" I replied, "The serpent deceived me."

{24:1} God said to Adam, "Since you disregarded My commandment and listened to your wife, cursed is the earth because of your labor. You will work it, but it will not yield its strength. Thorns and thistles will grow for you, and you will eat your bread by the sweat of your face. {24:2} You will toil endlessly but not find rest. You will be exhausted by heat and cold, work abundantly but not become rich, and grow fat but find no end. {24:3} The beasts you ruled over will rebel against you because you did not keep My commandment."

{25:1} The Lord then turned to me and said, "Since you listened to the serpent and ignored My commandment, you will suffer in childbirth and bear children in pain. In one hour, you will give birth and lose your life due to your suffering and anguish. {25:2} But you will confess and say, 'Lord, save me, and I will turn away from the sin of the flesh.' Because of this, I will judge you by your own words, as the enemy has planted enmity within you."

{26:1} God then turned to the serpent in great anger and said, "Since you have done this and deceived innocent hearts, you are cursed among all beasts. {26:2} You will be deprived of your food and will eat dust all the days of your life. {26:3} You will crawl on your belly and be robbed of your limbs. You will have no ears or wings, nor any limb with which you ensnared them in your malice and caused them to be cast out of Paradise. I will put enmity between you and their offspring. They will bruise your head, and you will bruise their heel until the day of Judgment."

{27:1} Thus, He spoke and commanded the angels to cast us out of Paradise. As we were being driven out with loud lamentations, your father Adam begged the angels, saying, "Leave me a little space to entreat the Lord for compassion and pity, for I alone have sinned." {27:2} They stopped driving him, and Adam cried out and wept, saying, "Forgive me, O Lord, for my deed." {27:3} Then the Lord said to the angels, "Why have you stopped driving Adam out of Paradise? Why do you not cast him out? Is it I who have done wrong, or is My judgment unjust?" {27:4} The angels fell to the ground and worshipped the Lord, saying, "You are just, O Lord, and You judge rightly."

{28:1} But then the Lord turned to Adam and said, "From now on, I will not allow you to remain in paradise." {28:2} Adam replied, "Please, Lord, grant me access to the Tree of Life so that I may eat from it before {28:3} I am cast out." Then the Lord spoke to Adam, saying, "You cannot take from it now, for I have commanded the cherubim with the flaming sword to guard it, so that {28:4} you may not taste it. Yet, after you have left paradise, if you keep yourself from all evil, as one preparing to die, when the Resurrection comes, I will raise you up, and then you will be given the Tree of Life."

{29:1} So spoke the Lord and ordered us to be cast out of paradise. Adam wept before the angels opposite paradise, and the angels said to him, {29:2} "What would you have us do, Adam?" And Adam said to them, "Since you are casting me out, allow me to take fragrant herbs from paradise, so that after I have left, I may offer an offering to God, that He may hear me." {29:3} The angels approached God and said, "Eternal King, command, my Lord, that Adam be given incense of sweet odor from paradise and seeds {29:5} for his food." God instructed Adam to go in and take sweet spices, fragrant herbs, and seeds for his food from paradise. {29:6} The angels allowed him to do so, and he took four kinds: crocus, nard, calamus, and cinnamon, along with other seeds for his food. After taking these, he left {29:7} paradise, and we were on the earth.

{30:1} "Now then, my children, I have shown you how we were deceived. Guard yourselves from transgressing against the good."

{31:1} When Eve had said this among her sons, Adam lay ill and near death {31:2} after a single day from the sickness that had taken hold of him. She said to him, "Why must you die while I live? How long will I live after you are dead? Tell me." {31:3} Adam replied, "Do not worry about this. You will not remain after me; we will die together. When I die, anoint me and do not let anyone touch me until {31:4} the angel of the Lord speaks concerning me. God will not forget me; He will seek His own creation. Now rise and pray to God until I give up my spirit into His hands, who gave it to me. For we do not know how we will meet our Maker, whether He is angry with us or intends to show mercy and receive us."

{32:1} Eve rose and went outside, falling to the ground, she began to pray, "I have sinned, O God of All, I have sinned against You. I have sinned against the elect angels, against the Cherubim, against Your fearful and unshakable Throne. I have sinned before You, and all sin began through my actions in creation." {32:2} As Eve prayed on her knees, the angel of humanity came to her, lifted her up, and said, "Rise, Eve, from your penitence, for Adam your husband has departed his body. Rise and see his spirit borne aloft to his Maker."

{33:1} Eve wiped away her tears and the angel said to her, "Rise from the earth." She looked steadfastly into heaven and saw a chariot of light, borne by four bright eagles, whose glory no human born of woman could describe or {33:2} behold their faces. Angels preceded the chariot, and when they came to where Adam lay, the chariot stopped, and the Seraphim. Eve saw golden censers between Adam and the chariot, and all the angels with censers and frankincense hurried to the {33:3} incense-offering. They blew upon it, and the smoke veiled the firmament. The angels worshipped God, crying, "Holy One, have mercy, for he is Your image, the work of Your hands."

{34:1} Eve beheld two great and fearful wonders standing in the presence of God and wept in fear. She called to her son Seth, "Rise, Seth, from the body of your father Adam and come to me. You shall see a sight no human eye has yet beheld."

{35:1} Seth arose and came to his mother, asking, "What troubles you? Why are you weeping?" She said to him, "Look up and see the seven heavens opened, and behold the soul of your father lying face down, with all the holy angels praying on his behalf, saying, 'Pardon him, Father of All, for he is Your image.'" {35:2} Seth asked, "What does this mean? Will he one day be delivered into the hands of the Invisible Father, our God? And who are the two {35:3} figures standing in prayer for our father Adam?"

{36:1} Seth told his mother that they were the sun and moon, praying on behalf of his father Adam. Eve asked, {36:2} "Where is their light, and why do they appear dark?" Seth answered, "Their light has not left them, but they cannot shine before the Light of the Universe, the Father of Light. Therefore, their light has been hidden from them.

{37:1} While Seth spoke to his mother, an angel blew the trumpet, and all the angels stood up, lying on their faces. They cried out in an awesome voice, saying, "Blessed be the glory of the Lord from {37:2} the works of His creation, for He has shown mercy to Adam, the creature of His hands." After these words, a seraphim with six wings came and lifted Adam, carrying him to the Acherusian lake, washing him thrice in the presence of God.

{38:1} God said to Adam, "What have you done? If you had kept my commandment, those who are bringing you to this place would not now rejoice. Yet, I will turn their joy to grief {38:2} and your grief to joy. I will restore you to your former glory and set you on the throne of your deceiver. He will be cast {38:3} into this place to see you sitting above him. He will be condemned along with those who listened to him, and he will be greatly grieved when he sees you seated on his honorable throne." {38:4} After three hours, lying down, the Father of all stretched out His hand from His holy throne, took Adam, and handed him over to the archangel Michael, saying, "Lift him up to Paradise, to the third Heaven, and leave him there until the fearful day of my reckoning, which I will bring upon the world." Then Michael took Adam and left {38:5} him where God had instructed.

{39:1} After these events, the archangels inquired about arranging the remains. God commanded all the angels to assemble in His presence, each in their order. The angels gathered, some with censers in their hands, others with trumpets. The "Lord {39:2} of Hosts" came on, borne by four winds, with cherubim riding on the winds and angels from heaven escorting Him.

They came to the earth where Adam's body lay. {39:3} They arrived at paradise, stirring all the leaves so that all descended from Adam slept from the fragrance, except Seth, born "according to the appointment of God." Adam's body lay {39:4} in paradise on the earth, and Seth mourned deeply for him.

{40:1} Then God said to the archangels Michael, Gabriel, Uriel, and Raphael, "Go {40:2} to Paradise in the third heaven, spread out linen clothes, cover Adam's body, and bring the oil of fragrance to pour over him." The three great angels did as commanded, preparing him for burial. {40:3} God said, "Bring also the body of Abel." They brought other linen clothes and prepared his body as well. Abel had remained unburied since the day Cain his brother slew him; Cain had tried to conceal him, but the earth would not receive him, as the voice from the earth said, "I will not {40:4} receive another body until the earth from which I was taken returns to me." The angels took Abel's body and placed it on a rock until Adam, his father, was buried. {40:5} Both were buried according to God's command, in the place where God had formed the dust, a place dug and prepared by the angels.

{41:1} God called out, "Adam, Adam." The body answered from the earth, "Here I am, Lord." God said to him, "I told {41:2} you that you are dust, and to dust you shall return. Again, I promise you the Resurrection; I will raise you up in the Resurrection with all your descendants."

{42:1} After these words, God placed a seal on the tomb, so that no one might disturb it for six days until Adam's rib returned to him. Then the Lord and His angels went back to their place.{42:2} When the six days were fulfilled, Eve also fell asleep.{42:3} While she was still living, she wept bitterly over Adam's death, for she did not know where he was buried. When the Lord came to paradise to bury Adam, she was asleep, as were her sons, except for Seth. The Lord instructed Seth to prepare Adam for burial, and no one on earth knew where he was laid except for Seth.{42:4} Eve prayed in the hour of her death that she might be buried in the same place as her husband Adam. After she finished her prayer, she said, 'Lord, {42:5} Master, God of all, do not estrange me, Your handmaid, from the body of Adam, for You made me from his rib. Though I am unworthy and a sinner, deem me worthy to enter his resting place, just as I was with him in paradise, {42:6} without separation. As we transgressed Your command together, {42:7} and were led astray together, we were not separated. So, Lord, do not {42:8} separate us now.' After she prayed, she looked heavenward, groaned aloud, struck her breast, and said, 'God of All, receive my spirit,' and immediately she gave up her spirit to God.

{43:1} Then Michael came and instructed Seth on how to prepare Eve's body for burial. Three angels arrived and buried her where Adam and Abel lay. Afterwards, Michael {43:2} spoke to Seth, saying, "Arrange every person who dies in this manner until the day of the Resurrection." After imparting this instruction, {43:3} he said to Seth, "Do not mourn beyond six days. On the seventh day, rest and find joy, for on that day, God and we angels rejoice with the righteous soul who has departed from the earth." Thus spoke {43:4} the angel, and he ascended into heaven, glorifying God and proclaiming, "Alleluia." [Holy, holy, holy is the Lord, in the glory of {43:5} God the Father. To Him belongs glory, honor, and worship, with the eternal life-giving Spirit now and always and forever. Amen.] [Holy, holy, holy is the Lord of Hosts. Glory and power belong to Him forever and ever. Amen.]

Apocalypse of Abraham

The Apocalypse of Abraham, an ancient Jewish text from the early centuries CE, is a profound apocalyptic work that has garnered significant scholarly attention for its complex narrative and theological depth. The text is attributed to the patriarch Abraham and details his visionary journey and revelations about the cosmos, the nature of idolatry, and the fate of the righteous and the wicked. Written in a period of profound religious and social upheaval, the Apocalypse of Abraham reflects the concerns and hopes of its contemporary Jewish community, particularly in the context of the destruction of the Second Temple and the subsequent Jewish diaspora. The narrative is divided into two distinct parts: the first recounts Abraham's early life, his rejection of his father's idolatry, and his subsequent call by God, while the second part focuses on Abraham's ascension to the heavens, guided by the angel Yahoel, where he witnesses cosmic visions and receives esoteric knowledge. This dual structure not only underscores the text's didactic purpose but also highlights the transformational journey of Abraham from a mere mortal to a recipient of divine wisdom. The theological themes explored in the Apocalypse of Abraham, including the nature of God, the problem of evil, and the ultimate redemption of Israel, resonate deeply with the apocalyptic literature of the Second Temple period. Moreover, its rich symbolism, intricate narrative, and theological discourse provide invaluable insights into the religious mindset and eschatological expectations of ancient Judaism.

{1:1} On the day I was tending to the gods of my father Terah and my brother Nahor, scrutinizing to determine which god was truly the strongest, {1:2} I, Abraham, while completing my duties in the service of my father Terah's sacrifices to his gods—made of wood, stone, gold, silver, copper, and iron—entered their temple. {1:3} There, I discovered a god named Marumath, crafted from stone, fallen at the feet of the iron god Nakhin. {1:4} Seeing this troubled my heart deeply, realizing that I alone could not lift it back into place, as it was a heavy stone. {1:5} I informed my father about what I had seen, {1:6} and he came with me to the temple. Together, we attempted to lift Marumath back onto its pedestal, but its head fell off while I was holding it. {1:7} Witnessing this, my father was dismayed, calling out to me, "Abraham!" {1:8} I replied, "Here I am!" He then instructed me, "Fetch the axes and chisels from the house." {1:9} I brought them to him, and he proceeded to fashion another Marumath from a different stone, without a head, and destroyed the broken head and the rest of the damaged Marumath.

{2:1} My father made five more gods and gave them to me, instructing me to sell them on the main road of the town. {2:2} I saddled my father's donkey, loaded the gods onto it, {2:3} and went out to sell them. On the way, I met merchants from Phandana of Syria, traveling to Egypt to buy kokonil from the Nile. {2:4} I engaged them in conversation, but as we walked, one of their camels screamed, scaring the donkey, which ran off and threw the gods to the ground. Three of the gods were shattered, but two remained intact. {2:5} When the Syrians saw the gods, they asked why I hadn't told them I had gods for sale; they would have bought them before the donkey panicked. {2:6} They said, "At least sell us the remaining gods, and we'll pay you well." {2:7} I thought it over, and they paid for both the broken and intact gods. {2:8} I had been worried about how I would explain this to my father. {2:9} I threw the three broken gods into the river Gur, where they sank and disappeared.

{3:1} As I continued on my way, my heart was troubled, and my mind was distracted. {3:2} I wondered about the futility of my father's work. {3:3} Wasn't it he who was the true god of these idols, since he created them with his hands and skill? {3:4} They should honor him as their creator. What value did they have? {3:5} Marumath had fallen and couldn't stand up in its sanctuary, and I couldn't lift it without my father's help. {3:6} Even then, its head fell off, and he had to attach it to another stone. {3:7} The other five gods that fell off the donkey couldn't save themselves and were broken, their fragments sinking in the river. {3:8} I pondered, "How can my father's god Marumath, with the head of one stone and the body of another, save anyone, hear prayers, or grant any gifts?"

{4:1} Thinking this way, I returned to my father's house, watered the donkey, and gave it hay. Then, I handed the silver to my father Terah. {4:2} He was pleased and said, "You are blessed, Abraham, by the god of my gods, for bringing me the payment for the gods, ensuring my labor was not in vain." {4:3} I replied, "Listen, father Terah! The gods bless you because you made them; their blessing is meaningless and their power is empty. {4:4} They couldn't help themselves; how can they help you or bless me? I did well in this transaction, as my judgment brought you the silver for the broken gods." {4:5} Hearing this, he became furiously angry with me for speaking against his gods.

{5:1} After considering my father's anger, I went outside. {5:2-3} Shortly after, he called me, saying, "Abraham!" I responded, "Here I am!" He said, "Gather some wood chips; I was making gods from fir wood before you arrived, {5:4} and use them to prepare my midday meal." {5:5-6} While gathering the wood chips, I found a small god that fit in my left hand, with "god Barisat" written on its forehead. I placed the chips on the fire to prepare food for my father, and before stepping out, I placed Barisat near the fire, {5:7} saying, "Barisat, keep the fire going until I return. If it starts to die, blow on it to keep it alive." {5:8-9} When I came back, I found Barisat lying on his back, his feet in the fire, burning. {5:10} Seeing this, I laughed and said, "Barisat, you certainly know how to light a fire and cook food!" {5:11-12} As I laughed, I watched him burn to ashes. I took the food to my father, {5:13} gave him wine and milk, and he enjoyed himself, blessing Marumath, his god. {5:14} I told him, "Father Terah, don't bless Marumath. Bless Barisat instead, for he sacrificed himself to cook your food." {5:15-16} He asked, "Where is he now?" I replied, "He burned in the fire and turned to dust." He exclaimed, "Barisat must be powerful! I will make another one today, and tomorrow he will prepare my food."

{6:1} Hearing my father's words, I, Abraham, laughed inwardly, but also felt bitter and angry. {6:2-3} I questioned how a creation of my father could aid him, and if he had subordinated his body to his soul, his soul to a spirit, and the spirit to foolishness and ignorance. {6:4} I decided to endure this nonsense to keep my mind clear and expose my thoughts to him. {6:5} I said, "Father Terah, whichever of these gods you praise, you are mistaken. {6:6} The gods of my brother Nahor in the sanctuary are more venerable than yours. {6:7} For instance, Zouchaios, my brother's god, is made of gold and valued by man, {6:8} and if he ages, he can be remolded. But Marumath, if broken, cannot be renewed because he is stone. {6:9} What about Ioav, the god beside Zouchaios? He is carved from wood and silver, and also more valuable than Barisat. {6:10-11} Barisat, your god, before being carved, was a wondrous tree with branches and flowers. {6:12} But you made him with an axe and your skill turned him into a god. {6:13} Now he has dried up, lost his vitality, {6:14} fallen from greatness, {6:15-17} and burned to ashes. Yet you say, 'I will make another, and tomorrow he will cook my food.' But Barisat perished without any power to prevent his own destruction."

{7:1} This is what I say: {7:2} Fire is more powerful because it can consume anything and mocks things that perish easily through its flames. {7:3} However, it is not supreme because it can be extinguished by water. {7:4} Water is more powerful than fire because it quenches flames and nourishes the earth, producing fruits. {7:5} But water isn't a god either, as it flows beneath the earth and is controlled by it. {7:6} The earth isn't a god either, as it can be dried by the sun and is used by humans for work. {7:7} The sun is more powerful among these, as it illuminates the entire world with its rays. {7:8} Yet, I won't call the sun a god either, because its light can be obscured by the moon and clouds. {7:9} The moon and stars aren't gods either, as their light dims at times during the night. {7:10} Listen, Father Terah, I will seek the true God who created all these supposed gods. {7:11} Who made the heavens crimson and the sun golden? Who gave light to the moon and stars, dried the earth amid many waters, placed you among these things, and has sought me out in my confusion? {7:12} Only God Himself will reveal Himself to us.

{8:1} As I was pondering these thoughts about my father Terah in the courtyard, the voice of the Mighty One descended from the heavens in a stream of fire, {8:2} calling, "Abraham, Abraham!" I replied, "Here I am." {8:3} He said, "You are searching for the God of gods, the Creator, in your heart. I am He. {8:4} Leave your father Terah and his house so that you won't be destroyed by the sins of your father's household." {8:5} As I went out—not yet outside the courtyard—{8:6} a great thunder sounded, burning my father, his house, and everything in it to the ground, to a depth of forty cubits.

{9:1} Then a voice called out to me twice: "Abraham, Abraham!" {9:2} I replied, "Here I am." {9:3} And He said, "It is I. Do not fear, for I am the One who existed before the world, the Mighty God who created everything before the dawn of time. {9:4} I am your protector and helper. {9:5} Go and bring me a three-year-old heifer, a three-year-old she-goat, a three-year-old ram, a turtledove, and a pigeon. {9:6} Offer them as a pure sacrifice to me. Through this sacrifice, I will reveal the ages to you. I will share hidden things, and you will witness great wonders that you have never seen before, {9:7} because you sought to find me, and I have called you my beloved. For the next forty days, abstain from all food cooked by fire, refrain from drinking wine, and do not anoint yourself with oil. {9:8} Afterward, prepare the sacrifice I have commanded you, at the place I will show you on a high mountain. {9:9} There, I will reveal the things made by the ages through my word, affirmed, created, and renewed. {9:10} I will also tell you what will happen to those who have done both good and evil in the human race."

{10:1} When I heard the voice saying these words to me, {10:2} I looked around, but there was no one else in sight. My spirit was amazed, and I felt as if my soul had left me. I became like a stone and fell face down on the ground, completely drained of strength. {10:3} While I lay there, I heard the voice again, saying, "Go, Iaoel, through the power of my ineffable name, consecrate this man for me and strengthen him." {10:4} An angel, appearing as a man, came to me, took my right hand, and helped me stand up. {10:5} He said, "Stand up, Abraham, friend of God who loves you. Do not be afraid! {10:6} I am sent to strengthen and bless you in the name of God, the creator of heaven and earth, who loves you. {10:7} Be bold and hurry to Him. I am Iaoel, named by Him who makes the heavens tremble, a power through His ineffable name. {10:8} I am tasked with restraining the cherubim and teaching those who sing praises in the night. {10:9} I control the Leviathans and subdue every threatening creature. {10:10} I am commanded to loosen the grip of Hades and destroy those who venerate the dead. {10:11} I ordered your father's house to be burned because he honored the dead. {10:12} Now, I am sent to bless you and the land prepared for you by the Eternal One. {10:13} For your sake, I have shown you the way. {10:14} Stand up, Abraham, go boldly, and rejoice. I also rejoice with you, for a great honor has been prepared for you by the Eternal One. {10:15} Complete the commanded sacrifice. {10:16} I am assigned to be with you and your descendants, and Michael also blesses you forever. Be courageous, go!"

{11:1} I stood up and saw the one who had taken my right hand and helped me to my feet. {11:2} His body looked like sapphire, and his face shone like chrysolite. His hair was as white as snow, {11:3} and he wore a turban that looked like a rainbow. His clothes were purple, and he held a golden staff in his right hand. {11:4} He said to me, "Abraham," and I responded, "Here is your servant!" He reassured me, saying, {11:5} "Do not let my appearance frighten you or my words trouble your soul. Come with me! {11:6} I will be with you visibly until the sacrifice, but after the sacrifice, I will be invisible forever. Be brave and proceed!"

{12:1} We traveled together, just the two of us, for forty days and nights. I did not eat bread or drink water, {12:2} because being in the presence of the angel and listening to his words sustained me. {12:3} We arrived at the glorious mountain of God, Horeb. {12:4} I said to the angel, "Singer of the Eternal One, I have no sacrifice with me, nor do I know where to build an altar on this mountain. How shall I make the sacrifice?" {12:5} He replied, "Look behind you." When I looked back, {12:6} all the required sacrifices were following us: the calf, the she-goat, the ram, the turtledove, and the pigeon. {12:7} The angel then said to me, "Abraham," and I responded, "Here I am." {12:8} He instructed, "Slaughter all these animals and divide them into halves, but do not cut the birds apart. {12:9} Give them to the men I will show you standing beside you, for they are the altar on the mountain, to offer sacrifice to the Eternal One. {12:10} Give the turtledove and the pigeon to me, for I will ascend on their wings to show you what is in the heavens, on the earth, in the sea, in the abyss, and in the lower depths, in the garden of Eden and its rivers, and the fullness of the universe. You will see all its circles."

{13:1} I followed the angel's instructions precisely. I gave the divided parts of the animals to the angels who had come to us, and Iaoel took the two birds. {13:2} I waited for the evening offering. Suddenly, an unclean bird swooped down on the carcasses, and I chased it away. {13:3} The unclean bird spoke to me, saying, "What are you doing here, Abraham, on these sacred heights where no one eats or drinks, and where there is no food for men? All this will be consumed by fire and will burn you up. Leave the man who is with you and flee! If you ascend higher, you will be destroyed." {13:4} Seeing the bird speak, I asked the angel, "What is this, my lord?" He replied, "This is disgrace, this is Azazel!" {13:5} Then he addressed Azazel, saying, "Shame on you, Azazel! For Abraham's place is in heaven, while yours is on the earth. You have chosen this place and become enamored with your own corruption. Therefore, the Eternal Ruler, the Mighty One, has given you a dwelling on earth. {13:6} Through you, the spirit of evil and lies operates, bringing wrath and trials to the generations of impious men. The Eternal, Mighty One did not allow you to have control over the bodies of the righteous. Their righteous lives affirm the destruction of ungodliness. {13:7} Listen, counselor, and be shamed by me! You have no power to tempt all the righteous. Depart from this man! You cannot deceive him because he opposes you and those who follow you, and who love what you desire. {13:8} The garment of heaven, which was once yours, has been set aside for him, and the corruption that was on him has passed over to you."

{14:1} The angel called to me, "Abraham!" I responded, "Here I am, your servant." {14:2} He continued, "Understand that the Eternal One, whom you love, has chosen you. Be brave and use your authority to do whatever I command against him who mocks justice. {14:3} Can I not oppose the one who has scattered the secrets of heaven across the earth and plotted against the Mighty One? {14:4} Tell him, 'May you be the firebrand of the earth's furnace! Go, Azazel, to the desolate parts of the earth. Your domain is with those who are with you, the stars, and the men born of the clouds, for they exist because of you. {14:5} For you, enmity is a sacred act. Therefore, depart from me through your own destruction!' {14:6} I spoke the words as the angel instructed. Then the angel addressed me again, "Abraham." I replied, "Here I am, your servant!" {14:7} The angel advised, "Do not respond to him! {14:8} If he speaks to you again, do not answer, lest his will overtake you. The Eternal, Mighty One, has given him gravity and will. Do not answer him." {14:9} I obeyed the angel's command, and whatever Azazel said about the descent, I did not respond.

{15:1} As the sun set, I saw smoke like that of a furnace. The angels with the divided portions of the sacrifice ascended from the top of the smoke. {15:2} The angel took my right hand and placed me on the right wing of the pigeon while he sat on the left wing of the turtledove. Both birds were neither slaughtered nor divided. {15:3} He carried me to the edge of the fiery flames, and we ascended as if carried by many winds to the heavens set on the expanses. {15:4} I saw a strong, indescribable light in the air where we had ascended. {15:5} In this light, a fiery Gehenna was kindled, and a large crowd in the likeness of men appeared. They constantly changed shape, running and prostrating themselves, uttering words I could not understand.

{16:1} I asked the angel, "Why have you brought me here? I can no longer see, I feel weak, and my spirit is leaving me." {16:2} He reassured me, "Stay with me, do not be afraid. The Eternal One, who loves you, is coming toward us with great sanctification. {16:3} You will not see Him directly, but do not let your spirit weaken, for I am with you to strengthen you."

{17:1} While the angel was still speaking, a fire approached us from all around, and a voice within the fire sounded like many waters, like the roaring sea. {17:2} The angel knelt with me and worshipped, and I wanted to fall face down on the earth. {17:3} The place where we stood seemed to rise and fall. {17:4} The angel said, "Worship, Abraham, and recite the song I taught you." Since there was no ground to prostrate myself on, I bowed and recited the song. {17:5} He urged, "Recite without stopping." So I continued, and he recited with me: {17:6} "Eternal One, Mighty One, Holy God, supreme ruler, {17:7} Self-originated, incorruptible, immaculate, unbegotten, spotless, immortal, {17:8} Self-complete, self-illuminating, {17:9} Self-perfected, self-devised, without mother, without father, ungenerated, {17:10} Exalted, fiery, lover of men, benevolent, bountiful, {17:11} Jealous over me, patient, most merciful, {17:12} Eternal, Mighty One, Holy Sabaoth, Most Glorious God, El, El, El, Jah El! {17:13} You are the One my soul loves, my protector, {17:14} Eternal, fiery, shining, light-giving, thunder-voiced, lightning-visioned, many-eyed, {17:15} Receiving the prayers of those who honor You and turning away from those who provoke You. {17:16} Redeemer of those who dwell among the wicked, dispersed among the just in the corruptible age, {17:17} You dissolve the confusions of the world caused by the ungodly and the righteous mixed in this corruptible age, {17:18} Renewing the age of the righteous. Shine, O Lord, as the light You clothed Yourself with on the first day of creation. Shine as the Light of the Morning on Your creatures to bring day upon the earth. {17:19} In Your heavenly dwelling place, there is an inexhaustible light of an invincible dawning from Your face. {17:20} Accept my prayer and delight in it. Accept also the sacrifice You made through me as I searched for You. {17:21} Receive me favorably, show me, teach me all that You have promised."

{18:1} As I continued reciting the song, the mouth of the fire on the firmament rose higher. {18:2} I heard a voice like the roaring sea, unceasing amidst the fire's abundance. {18:3} As the fire ascended to its peak, I saw beneath it a fiery throne surrounded by many-eyed beings, all reciting the song. Under the throne were four fiery creatures, singing as well. {18:4} Each creature had four faces: a lion, a man, an ox, and an eagle. {18:5} Each had four heads, making sixteen faces in total. {18:6} They each had six wings: two on their shoulders, two halfway down, and two at their loins. {18:7} They used the wings on their shoulders to cover their faces, the wings at their loins to cover their feet, and stretched the middle wings out to fly upright. {18:8} When they finished singing, they looked at and threatened each other. {18:9} When the angel with me saw this, he left me and ran to them. {18:10} He turned the faces of each creature away from the one opposite so they couldn't see each other to threaten. {18:11} He taught them the song of peace that the Eternal One has within himself. {18:12} While I watched, I saw behind the creatures a chariot with fiery wheels, each wheel full of eyes all around. {18:13} Above the wheels was the throne I had seen, covered with fire and encircled by an indescribable light. {18:14} I heard the voice of their sanctification, sounding like the voice of a single man.

{19:1} A voice called to me from within the fire, saying, "Abraham, Abraham!" {19:2} I responded, "Here I am!" The voice said, "Look at the expanses beneath the firmament where you now stand and see that there is none but the one you have sought and who loves you." {19:3} As he spoke, the expanses beneath me, the heavens, opened up. On the seventh firmament where I stood, I saw a vast fire spread out, a light, dew, a multitude of angels, and a host of invisible glory. Above the living creatures I had seen, there was no one else. {19:4} From the high place where I stood, I looked down to the sixth firmament. There, I saw a multitude of spiritual, incorporeal angels, executing the commands of the fiery angels on the eighth firmament. {19:5} As I stood at this elevated position, I noticed that there was no other host on this firmament but the spiritual angels. {19:6} Then, the host I saw on the seventh firmament commanded the sixth firmament to move aside. When it did, I saw on the fifth firmament the powers of the stars, carrying out their given commands, and the elements of the earth obeying them. {19:7} The sixth firmament moved from my sight as commanded, revealing the fifth firmament with its host of stars and their orders, and the elements of the earth responding to them.

{20:1} The Eternal, Mighty One called out to me, "Abraham, Abraham!" {20:2} I responded, "Here I am!" He said, "Look down from on high at the stars beneath you and count them for me. Tell me their number!" {20:3} I replied, "How can I? I am just a man." He said, "As the stars and their vast number, so shall your descendants be. They will be nations and people set apart for me, even with Azazel." {20:4} I said, "Eternal and Mighty One, let your servant speak without your anger against me. Before you brought me here, Azazel insulted me. How then, since he is not here before you, have you established your presence with them?"

{21:1} He said, "Look beneath your feet at the firmament and understand the creation depicted on this expanse and the creatures within it, as well as the age prepared after it." {21:2} I looked beneath the firmament and saw the likeness of heaven and everything within it. {21:3} I saw the earth, its fruits, its creatures, and its inhabitants. I witnessed the impiety and righteousness of their souls, their pursuits, the abyss and its torments, its depths, and perdition. {21:4} I saw the sea, its islands, cattle, fish, Leviathan, his realm, his bed, his lairs, and the world upon him, as well as the destruction he caused. {21:5} I saw rivers, their upper reaches, and their cycles. {21:6} I saw the garden of Eden, its fruits, the river flowing from it, its trees, their blossoms, and men practicing justice, eating, and resting there. {21:7} I saw a great crowd of men, women, and children, with half on the right side of the depiction and half on the left.

{22:1} I asked, "Eternal, Mighty One! What is this picture of creation?" He replied, "This represents my will regarding what is in the light, and it was good before me. Later, I commanded them into existence through my word. Whatever I decreed to exist was already outlined here, and all previously created things you have seen stood before me." {22:2} I asked, "O sovereign, mighty, and eternal one! Why are the people on this side and that side of the picture?" He answered, "Those on the left side are a multitude of tribes that existed before, and some who will come after you, prepared for judgment and order, and others for vengeance and perdition at the end of the age. {22:3} Those on the right side are the people set apart for me from the people with Azazel; these are the ones I have prepared to be born from you and to be called my people."

{23:1} "Look again at the picture. Who is the one who tempted Eve, and what is the fruit of the tree? You will understand what will happen to your descendants in the last days. {23:2} Whatever you cannot comprehend, I will explain to you because you have pleased me, and I will reveal what I have kept in my heart." {23:3} I looked at the picture and my eyes were drawn to the side of the Garden of Eden. I saw a man, immense in height and terrifying in breadth, standing with a woman who matched him in size and appearance. {23:4} They stood under a tree in Eden, and the tree's fruit looked like a bunch of grapes. {23:5} Behind the tree was a dragon-like creature with a man's hands and feet, six wings on each side of its back. {23:6} It was holding the grapes and feeding them to the man and woman. {23:7} I asked, "Who are these two people, and who is the one between them? What is the fruit they are eating, Mighty Eternal One?" {23:8} He answered, "This represents the world of humans. The man is Adam and the woman is Eve. The one between them is the evil in their actions, Azazel himself." {23:9} I asked, "Eternal Mighty One, why did you allow him such power to harm humankind on earth?" {23:10} He replied, "Listen, Abraham! Those who desire evil and commit wicked deeds are under his dominion. They love him for it." {23:11} I responded, "Eternal Mighty One, why did you allow evil to be desired in the hearts of men, causing your anger at their choices? Why did you allow such a being to perform useless acts in your light?"

{24:1} He said to me, "For the sake of the nations, for your sake, and for those set apart after you, the people of your tribe, observe what is laid upon them in the picture. {24:2} I will explain to you what will happen, and everything that will occur in the last days. Look now at everything in the picture." {24:3} I looked and saw the beings that had existed before me. {24:4} I saw Adam and Eve with the cunning adversary, and Cain, who was influenced by the adversary to break the law. I saw the murdered Abel and the destruction caused by the lawless one. {24:5} I saw fornication and those who pursued it, its corruption, and their fervor; and the fire of corruption in the depths of the earth. {24:6} I saw theft and those who chased after it, and the system of their punishment, the judgment of the great court. {24:7} I saw naked men, facing each other, their shame and the harm they inflicted on their friends, and their punishment. {24:8} I saw desire, holding the head of every kind of lawlessness, and her torment and destined destruction.

{25:1} I saw the image of an idol, resembling a figure my father would carve from shining copper. A man stood before it, worshiping. {25:2} Opposite it was an altar where boys were being sacrificed in front of the idol. {25:3} I asked, "What is this idol, the altar, and who are being sacrificed? Who is the sacrificer, and what is this magnificent temple I see, adorned with your glory under your throne?" {25:4} He replied, "Listen, Abraham! This temple, the altar, and the artistry represent the priesthood of my name's glory, where every prayer of man will enter. It is the place for kings, prophets, and the sacrifices I command from your people. {25:5} The body you saw signifies my anger, because your descendants will provoke me. {25:6} The man sacrificing represents those who anger me, and the sacrifices signify those who testify to the judgment at creation's beginning."

{26:1} I asked, "Eternal, Mighty One! Why did you establish this and call upon these testimonies?" {26:2} He replied, "Listen, Abraham, and understand what I will explain. Answer my questions. {26:3} Why did your father Terah not heed your call to abandon idol worship until he perished along with his household?" {26:4} I responded, "Eternal Mighty One, it did not please him to obey me, nor did I follow his ways." {26:5} He said, "Listen, Abraham. As your father's counsel was within him, and your counsel is within you, so is my will ready. {26:6} In the days to come, you will not know in advance, but you will see with your own eyes that your descendants are of your seed. Look at the picture!"

{27:1} I looked and saw the picture sway. From its left side, a crowd of heathens rushed out and captured the men, women, and children on its right side. {27:2} They slaughtered some and kept others captive. {27:3} I saw them ascend through four paths, burning the Temple with fire, and plundering its holy treasures. {27:4} I cried out, "Eternal One, the people you received from me are being robbed by the heathens. They are killing some and enslaving others, burning the Temple, and stealing its treasures. {27:5} Why have you afflicted my heart, and why will this be so?" {27:6} He replied, "Listen, Abraham. All you have seen will happen because your descendants will provoke me. {27:7} The body you saw and the murder depicted in the Temple of jealousy, everything you saw, will come to pass." {27:8} I pleaded, "Eternal, Mighty One! Let the evil deeds done in iniquity pass by. {27:9} But make commandments greater than their just works, for you can do this." {27:10} He replied, "A time of justice will come upon them, first through the holiness of kings. {27:11} I will judge with justice those I created earlier to rule among them. {27:12} From them will come men who will regard them as I have shown you."

{28:1} I said, "Mighty, Eternal One, sanctified by your power, be merciful in my request. Since you have informed me and shown me these things, {28:2} having brought me to your height, please answer me: Will what I saw be their fate for long?" {28:3} He showed me a multitude of his people and said, "Through the four ascents, my anger will be because of them, and retribution for their deeds will come. {28:4} In the fourth ascent, one hundred years will be as one hour of the age. In those one hundred years, there will be evil among the heathens and an hour of mercy, even with reproaches."

{29:1} I asked, "Eternal, Mighty One! How long does an hour of the age last?" {29:2} He replied, "I have decreed twelve periods of the impious age for both the heathens and your descendants. What you have seen will endure until the end of time. Count it, and you will understand. Look down at the picture." {29:3} As I looked, I saw a man emerging from the left, the side of the heathens. A great crowd of men, women, and children streamed out from that side, and they worshipped him. {29:4} While I continued to watch, those from the right side also came out. {29:5} Some insulted this man, others struck him, and still others worshipped him. I noticed Azazel running towards him, worshipping and kissing his face before standing behind him. {29:6} I asked, "Eternal, Mighty One! Who is this man insulted and beaten by the heathens, with Azazel worshipping him?" {29:7} He answered, "Listen, Abraham. The man you saw insulted, beaten, and worshipped is the deliverer from the heathens for your descendants. In the last days, during the twelfth period of the age of my fulfillment, I will establish this man from your tribe, the one you saw among my people. All will emulate him, recognizing him as chosen by me, altering their ways. {29:8} Many heathens will trust in him, seen by those on the left side of the picture worshipping him. {29:9} Among your descendants on the right side, some will insult, some will beat, and others will worship him. Many will be divided because of him. He will test those of your seed who worshipped him during the twelfth hour, marking the end of the age of impiety. {29:10} "Before the age of justice begins, my judgment will fall upon the heathens who have acted wickedly towards your chosen people. In those days, I will bring upon all creation ten plagues—evil, disease, and the groaning of bitter souls. {29:11} From your descendants, righteous men will remain, protected by me, striving in the glory of my name towards the place you saw deserted in the picture. {29:12} They will live affirmed by the sacrifices and gifts of justice and truth in the age of justice. Forever rejoicing in me, they will destroy those who have destroyed them, rebuke those who mocked them, and spit in their faces. Those rebuked by me will see my rejoicing with my people, celebrating those who return to me truly."

{30:1} As he continued speaking, I found myself back on earth. {30:2} I said, "Eternal, Mighty One, I am no longer in the glory I experienced above, and there remains a matter in my heart that I do not understand." {30:3} He replied, "I will explain what you desire to know. You sought knowledge of the ten plagues I prepared against the heathens, set to occur after the passing of the twelve hours on earth. {30:4} "Here they are: first, great sorrow and need; second, fiery destruction of cities; third, pestilence among cattle; fourth, famine across the world; fifth, destruction among rulers by earthquake and sword; sixth, increased hail and snow; seventh, wild beasts becoming their grave; eighth, alternating hunger, pestilence, and destruction; ninth, execution by the sword and fleeing in distress; tenth, thunder, voices, and earthquakes."

{31:1} "Then I will sound the trumpet from the air and send my chosen one, endowed with all my power. He will summon my people who have been humiliated by the heathens. {31:2} I will burn with fire those who mocked and ruled over them in this age, delivering those who have scorned me to the judgment of the coming age. {31:3} The righteous who have chosen my desire and faithfully kept my commandments will rejoice in the downfall of those who remain, who followed idols and committed murders.

{32:1} "Therefore, hear Abraham, in the seventh generation after you, they will go with you into a foreign land. There they will be enslaved and oppressed for an hour of the impious age. But I will judge the nation that enslaves them." {32:2} The Lord said, "Have you heard, Abraham, what I have revealed about what your tribe will face in the last days?" {32:6} Abraham, having heard, accepted God's words in his heart.

Apocalypse of Zephaniah

The Apocalypse of Zephaniah is an ancient Jewish apocalyptic text that offers a vivid and symbolic portrayal of the afterlife, reflecting both Jewish and early Christian eschatological themes. Traditionally attributed to the prophet Zephaniah, the text likely originates from the first century BCE to the first century CE, placing it within the Second Temple period, a time of significant religious and cultural ferment. The work is characterized by its detailed and often graphic descriptions of heavenly visions, encounters with angels, and the fate of souls in the afterlife, particularly focusing on the themes of judgment, divine retribution, and the ultimate triumph of the righteous. The Apocalypse of Zephaniah shares common motifs with other apocalyptic literature of the period, such as the Book of Enoch and the Apocalypse of Abraham, yet it remains distinct in its emphasis on personal accountability and the direct interaction between the seer and celestial beings. Though fragments of the text survive in both Coptic and Greek, its original language and complete form remain subjects of scholarly debate. The Apocalypse of Zephaniah is important for its insights into early Jewish views on the afterlife and its influence on later Christian apocryphal writings, highlighting the development of apocalyptic thought across traditions.

{1:1} And a spirit took me and brought me up into the fifth heaven, where I saw angels known as "lords." The Holy Spirit had placed diadems upon them, and their thrones shone sevenfold brighter than the rising sun. {1:2} These angels resided in the temples of salvation, continuously singing hymns to the ineffable God.

{2:1} I witnessed a soul being punished by five thousand angels. {2:2} They took it from the East to the West, beating it mercilessly with a hundred lashes each day. {2:3} Terrified, I fell face down, my joints weakening. {2:4} An angel helped me, saying, "Be strong, O one who will triumph and prevail, for you will overcome the accuser and rise from Hades." {2:5} After I stood, I asked, "Who is this being punished?" {2:6} The angel answered, "This is a soul found in lawlessness, taken before it could repent." {2:7} Indeed, I, Zephaniah, saw these things in my vision. {2:8} Then the angel of the Lord accompanied me to a vast place, where thousands upon thousands were gathered on the left side, and myriads upon myriads on the right. {2:9} Their hair was loose like that belonging to women. Their teeth were like the teeth of wild beasts, sharp and fearsome. {2:10} And I saw these, the dead who will be buried like any man. {2:11} Whenever someone dies, they are carried out with a cithera played before them, and psalms and odes chanted over their body.

{3:1} Now the angel of the Lord took me over my city. I saw nothing before my eyes. {3:2} Then, I observed two men walking together on one road, conversing. {3:3} I also saw two women grinding at a mill, speaking to each other. {3:4} And I also saw two people lying upon a bed, each one turning away from the other, as if burdened by their own thoughts or deeds. {3:5} I beheld the entire inhabited world hanging like a drop of water, suspended from a bucket as it is drawn from a well. {3:6} I asked the angel of the Lord, "Is there no darkness or night in this place?" {3:7} He replied, "No, for in the place where the righteous and saints dwell, there is no darkness; they exist perpetually in the light." {3:8} I also saw the souls of men enduring punishment. {3:9} I cried out to the Lord Almighty, "O God, if Thou art with the saints, surely Thou must have compassion on the world and the souls in this torment."

{4:1} The angel of the Lord said to me, "Come, let me show you the place of righteousness." {4:2} He took me to Mount Seir, where he showed me three men, accompanied by two rejoicing angels. {4:3} I asked, "Who are these?" {4:4} He replied, "These are the three sons of Joatham, the priest, who neither kept their father's commandment nor observed the Lord's ordinances." {4:5} I then saw two other angels weeping over the three sons of Joatham. {4:6} I inquired, "Who are these?" He said, "These are the angels of the Lord Almighty, who record the righteous deeds upon their scrolls while they stand at heaven's gate." {4:7} "I take the scrolls from them and present them before the Lord Almighty, who writes the names in the Book of the Living. {4:8} Likewise, the accuser's angels, stationed on earth, record the sins of men on their scrolls. {4:9} They too sit at heaven's gate, informing the accuser, who inscribes them on his scroll to use against the souls when they depart the world and descend into the abyss."

{5:1} Then I walked with the angel of the Lord, and I saw a place ahead. {5:2} Thousands upon thousands and myriads upon myriads of angels passed through it. {5:3} Their faces were like leopards, with tusks protruding like wild boars. {5:4} Their eyes were blood-red, and their hair was loose like women's. They held fiery scourges in their hands. {5:5} Terrified, I asked the accompanying angel, "What sort are these?" {5:6} He said, "These are the servants of all creation, sent to retrieve the souls of ungodly men, escorting them to this place. {5:7} For three days, they carry them through the air before casting them into eternal punishment." {5:8} I pleaded, "O Lord, do not let them come to me." {5:9} The angel reassured me, "Fear not, for I will not permit them to approach you, as you are pure before the Lord. I was sent to you because you are pure before Him." {5:10} The angel signaled, and they retreated, fleeing from me.

{6:1} But then I followed the angel of the Lord, and we arrived at gates. {6:2} As I drew near, I saw that they were bronze gates. {6:3} The angel touched them, and they opened before him. I entered, finding the whole square like a magnificent city, walking within its midst. {6:4} The angel of the Lord transformed beside me in that place. {6:5} I observed that the gates were bronze, with bronze bolts and iron bars. {6:6} My mouth was silenced as I beheld the bronze gates before me, with flames extending for about fifty stadia.

{7:1} As I turned back and walked, I saw a great sea. {7:2} At first, I thought it was a sea of water, but then I realized it was entirely a sea of flame, like burning slime, with waves of sulfur and bitumen. {7:3} The waves approached me. {7:4} I believed the Lord Almighty had come to visit me. {7:5} When I saw Him, I fell upon my face to worship Him. {7:6} Trembling with fear, I cried out for deliverance from my distress. {7:7} I called upon the Lord, "Eloe, Lord, Adonai, Sabaoth, I beseech Thee to save me from this peril."

{8:1} Instantly, I stood up, and before me stood a great angel. {8:2} His hair spread out like a lioness's mane, his teeth were like a bear's, protruding from his mouth, and his body was like a serpent's when it sought to swallow me. {8:3} Terrified, my body weakened, and I collapsed to the ground. {8:4} I prayed to the Lord Almighty, "Thou who saved Israel from Pharaoh's hand, who delivered Susanna from the unjust elders, who rescued the three holy men—Shadrach, Meshach, and Abednego—from the fiery furnace, I beg Thee, save me from this distress."

{9:1} Rising to my feet, I saw a great angel standing before me, his face shining like the sun in its full glory. {9:2} He wore a golden girdle across his chest, and his feet gleamed like bronze in a furnace. {9:3} Rejoicing, I thought the Lord Almighty had come to visit me. {9:4} I fell upon my face, worshiping Him. {9:5} The angel said, "Take heed. Do not worship me. I am not the Lord Almighty, but the great angel Eremiel, who presides over the abyss and Hades, where the souls are imprisoned from the time of the Flood until this day."

{10:1} I asked the angel, "Where am I?" He replied, "This is Hades." {10:2} I inquired further, "Who is the great angel whom I saw standing?" {10:3} He answered, "This is the accuser who stands before the Lord to accuse men."

{11:1} Then I saw the angel with a scroll in his hand, which he began to unroll. {11:2} As he spread it out, I read it in my own language. All my sins, from my youth until this day, were recorded in it, without a single false word. {11:3} If I failed to visit a sick man or a widow, it was noted as a fault on my scroll. {11:4} If I neglected an orphan, it was written down as a shortcoming. {11:5} A day without fasting or prayer during the designated time was recorded as a failing. {11:6} Any day I did not turn to the sons of Israel was marked as a fault. {11:7} Overwhelmed, I threw myself upon my face and prayed to the Lord Almighty, "May Thy mercy reach me and erase my scroll, for Thy mercy fills every place." {11:8} Then I rose, and the angel stood before me, saying, "Triumph, for you have prevailed over the accuser and risen from Hades and the abyss. You will now cross the crossing place."

{12:1} The angel brought forth another scroll, which was written by hand. {12:2} He unrolled it, and I read it in my own language.

{13:1} After the missing pages, the angel helped me onto a boat. {13:2} Thousands upon thousands and myriads upon myriads of angels praised before me. {13:3} I donned an angelic garment and joined in prayer with the angels, understanding their language. {13:4} Now, my sons, this is the trial: the good and the evil must be weighed in a balance.

{14:1} Then a great angel appeared, holding a golden trumpet, and he blew it three times over my head, proclaiming, "Be courageous, O one who has triumphed! Prevail, O one who has prevailed! For you have overcome the accuser and escaped from the abyss and Hades. {14:2} You will now cross the crossing place, for your name is written in the Book of the Living." {14:3} I wished to embrace him, but his glory was too great for me to do so. {14:4} He then ran to the righteous ones—Abraham, Isaac, Jacob, Enoch, Elijah, and David—and spoke to them as friends speak to one another.

{15:1} The great angel returned with the golden trumpet, blowing it unto heaven. {15:2} Heaven opened from east to west, from north to south. {15:3} I saw the sea at the bottom of Hades, its waves reaching the clouds. {15:4} Within it, I saw souls bound and fettered, some with hands tied to their necks. {15:5} I asked, "Who are these?" The angel replied, "These are the ones who accepted bribes of gold and silver, leading the souls of men astray." {15:6} Others were covered with burning mats of fire. {15:7} I asked, "Who are these?" The angel said, "These are those who lent money at interest and charged interest on interest." {15:8} I also saw blind ones crying out, astonished by all these works of God. {15:9} I asked, "Who are these?" The angel answered, "These are catechumens who heard the word of God but failed to fulfill it." {15:10} I asked, "Can they not repent here?" He replied, "Yes." {15:11} I inquired, "For how long?" He said, "Until the day when the Lord judges." {15:12} I saw others with hair and bodies. {15:13} I asked, "Is there hair and body in this place?" He answered, "Yes, the Lord grants them as He wills."

{16:1} I saw multitudes brought forth, and they prayed as they beheld the torments, beseeching the Lord Almighty, "We pray for those in these torments, that Thou might have mercy on them." {16:2} I asked the angel, "Who are these?" He replied, "These are Abraham, Isaac, and Jacob. {16:3} At a certain hour each day, they come forth with the great angel. He sounds a trumpet unto heaven, and another sounds upon the earth. {16:4} All the righteous hear it and come running, praying to the Lord Almighty daily on behalf of those in torment."

{17:1} The great angel again came forth with the golden trumpet, blowing it over the earth. {17:2} Its sound was heard from the east to the west, from the south to the north. {17:3} He blew it unto heaven, and its sound reached there too. {17:4} I said, "O Lord, why did you not let me see them all?" {17:5} The angel replied, "I do not have the authority to show you everything until the Lord Almighty rises in His wrath to destroy the earth and the heavens. {17:6} When that day comes, all will see and be terrified, crying out, 'All flesh, which is ascribed to Thee, we offer unto Thee on the day of the Lord.' {17:7} Every tree which groweth upon the earth will be plucked up with its roots and fall down. And every high tower and mountain will crumble, and the birds which fly will fall from the sky, as the earth and heavens are shaken."

1 Meqabyan

The Book of Meqabyan, often referred to as "1 Meqabyan," is an integral part of the Ethiopian Orthodox Tewahedo Church's biblical canon, though it is not recognized in the canonical collections of most other Christian traditions, such as the Roman Catholic, Eastern Orthodox, or Protestant churches. This text, along with 2 Meqabyan and 3 Meqabyan, forms a unique trilogy within the Ethiopian scriptural corpus, distinct from the more widely known Books of Maccabees found in the Septuagint. 1 Meqabyan is notable for its blend of historical narrative, moral instruction, and theological reflection, drawing upon a rich tapestry of Jewish and early Christian motifs. The book is written in Ge'ez, the classical liturgical language of the Ethiopian Church, and reflects the distinct cultural and religious milieu of Ethiopia. Its content focuses on the pious struggles and martyrdom of Jewish heroes who stand against foreign oppressors, emphasizing themes of faithfulness to God, the virtue of suffering for righteousness, and divine retribution against the wicked. The text serves not only as a religious document but also as a cultural artifact, offering insights into the historical context and religious identity of the Ethiopian Jewish and Christian communities. The origins of the Meqabyan texts are shrouded in mystery, with debates surrounding their exact dating and the influences that shaped their composition.

{1:1} In the land, there was a man named Tseerutsaydan who loved sin, boasting in his abundance of horses and his formidable troops under his authority. {1:2} He had many priests who served his idols, whom he worshipped, bowed down to, and sacrificed to both day and night. {1:3} Yet in his heart, he was deceived into believing that these idols gave him strength and power. {1:4} He imagined that they granted him authority over all his dominion. {1:5} In times of formation and planning, he trusted these idols to give him every desired authority. {1:6} Daily, he offered sacrifices to them, both day and night. {1:7} He appointed priests to serve his idols. {1:8} They would eat from the defiled sacrifices and pretend that the idols consumed them night and day. {1:9} He induced others to diligently imitate them, to sacrifice and eat like they did. {1:10} Yet he trusted in idols that could neither profit nor benefit him. {1:11} Feeling agitated and deceived in his heart, he believed that the idols fed him and crowned him with authority, oblivious to the Creator who gives life to the dead, bringing them from non-existence to existence, or to the judgment upon those who call themselves gods without being gods. {1:12} As these idols were never truly alive, he rightly called them dead. {1:13} Satan's deceptive influence rested in these idol images, misleading people with false reasoning and revealing only what they desired, judging those who trusted in these idols, whose teachings were as worthless as ashes. {1:14} People would marvel at the fulfillment of their desires and would even sacrifice their sons and daughters, born of their own nature, shedding innocent blood. {1:15} They did not grieve, for Satan delighted in their sacrifices to fulfill their evil desires, leading them towards eternal Gehenna, where there is no escape, enduring eternal torment. {1:16} Tseerutsaydan, in his arrogance, had fifty idols fashioned in male forms and twenty in female forms. {1:17} He boasted in these idols, utterly glorifying them while offering sacrifices morning and evening. {1:18} He commanded people to sacrifice to these idols and he himself ate from the defiled sacrifices, commanding others to do the same, provoking evil. {1:19} He had five houses adorned with idols made of iron, brass, and lead, ornamented with silver and gold, draped with curtains and furnished like a tent. {1:20} He appointed caretakers for these idols, where he would continually sacrifice: forty to his idols—ten fat oxen, ten barren cows, ten fat sheep, and ten barren goats—along with birds of various kinds. {1:21} He believed his idols consumed these sacrifices; he would present them with fifty baskets of grapes and fifty dishes of wheat mixed with oil. {1:22} He told his priests, "Take and give to them; let my idols eat what I have slaughtered for them, and let them drink the wine I have offered. If this is not enough, I will add more for them." {1:23} He commanded everyone to eat and drink from these defiled sacrifices. {1:24} Out of evil malice, he sent his troops throughout the kingdom to find anyone who would not sacrifice or bow down, to separate and apprehend them, punishing them with fire and sword before him, plundering their possessions and burning their homes in flames, destroying all they had. {1:25} "For those who show kindness and greatness, who have been merciful and charitable towards us, I will show punishment and tribulation unless they worship my idols and sacrifice to them. {1:26} I will bring punishment and tribulation upon those who have angered Earth, Heaven, the wide sea, the moon, the sun, the stars, the rains, the winds, and all living creatures in this world, for sustenance and satiety for us." {1:27} But those who worship these idols shall endure severe tribulation, and no mercy will be shown to them.

{2:1} There was a man born from the tribe of Benjamin named Meqabees. {2:2} He had three sons who were exceptionally handsome and strong warriors. They were beloved among all the people in the land under Tseerutsaydan's rule. {2:3} When the king found them, he commanded them, "Won't you bow down to Tseerutsaydan's idols? Won't you sacrifice to them? {2:4} But if you refuse, we will seize you and take you to the king, and we will destroy all your possessions as the king commands." {2:5} These courageous young men replied, saying, "As for Him whom we worship, He is our Father, the Creator of Earth and Heaven, the sea, the moon, the sun, the clouds, and the stars. He alone is the true God in whom we believe." {2:6} These four young men were accompanied by a hundred servants armed with shields and spears. {2:7} When the king's soldiers tried to capture these brave youths, they escaped unharmed. These young men were mighty warriors, seizing shields and spears. {2:8} Among them was one who could strangle and kill a panther effortlessly, as if it were a chicken. {2:9} Another among them killed a lion with a single stone or struck down a group with a stick. {2:10} And there was one who killed a hundred men in battle with a single sword, known throughout Babylon and Moab. {2:11} They were powerful warriors, known for their strength and bravery. {2:12} Their extraordinary courage stemmed from their devotion to JAH and their lack of fear of death, which made them admirable beyond measure. {2:13} When they terrified the king's troops, no one could capture them. The warriors escaped to a high mountain. {2:14} The soldiers returned to the city and sealed the fortress gate. They terrorized the people, saying, "Unless you deliver the Maccabees to us, we will burn your city with fire and destroy your land." {2:15} At that moment, people from all walks of life—rich and poor, daughters and sons, children without parents, and the elderly—gathered and cried out together. They lifted their heads toward the mountain and pleaded, "Do not destroy us or our land." {2:16} They wept together, filled with fear of JAH. {2:17} Turning their faces eastward and extending their hands, they prayed to JAH, saying, "Lord, should we refuse these men who defy your commandments and your law? {2:18} We once believed in silver, gold, and idols made by human hands, but we do not love to hear the wicked words of those who reject your law," they said. {2:19} "You are the Creator who saves and destroys. You alone judge those who spill blood and eat flesh. {2:20} We do not want to see the faces of those who reject you or hear their words. {2:21} If you command us, we will go to them. We believe in you, O Lord, who examines our thoughts and hearts. You are the God of our forefathers—Abraham, Isaac, and Jacob—who obeyed your commandments and lived according to your law. {2:22} You judge the thoughts of every person and help both sinners and the righteous. Nothing is hidden from you, and those who seek refuge in you are known to you. {2:23} We have no other God besides you. {2:24} We are ready to give our lives because of your glorious name. Grant us strength, power, and protection in this trial that we face." {2:25} When Israel entered Gibts' land, you heard Jacob's prayer. Now, O God, we implore you." {2:26} When the two men of great beauty were seen standing before them, fire swords flashed like lightning, cutting their necks and killing them instantly. Then they arose as they were before, completely healed and more handsome than ever.

{3:1} Behold, you see before you these faithful servants of the Most High, Abya, Seela, and Fentos, who died and rose again. You, too, shall rise after death, and your faces shall shine like the sun in the Kingdom of Heaven. {3:2} They went with those men and embraced martyrdom courageously. {3:3} They prayed, praised, and bowed to JAH. Death did not frighten them, nor did the king's punishment. {3:4} When they approached these youths, they behaved like harmless sheep. Yet they were seized, beaten, bound, and whipped, and then brought before the king. {3:5} The king addressed them, saying, "Why do you stubbornly refuse to sacrifice and bow to my idols?" {3:6} The cleansed and honored brothers, Seela, Abya, and Fentos, answered him with unwavering resolve. {3:7} They spoke boldly to the king, "As for us, we will not bow or sacrifice to defiled idols lacking knowledge and reason." {3:8} They continued, "We will not bow to idols of silver, gold, stone, or wood, which have no understanding, soul, or benefit to their worshippers." {3:9} The king asked, "Why do you act this way? Do you not know who I am, and how I can harm or reward you?" {3:10} They replied, "To us, you are insignificant. We will not honor or glorify idols." {3:11} The king threatened them, "I will punish you with severe beatings, tribulation, and fire. Tell me now, will you sacrifice to my idols?" {3:12} They answered firmly, "We will not sacrifice or bow to defiled idols." The king then ordered them to be beaten with rods and whipped, until their inner organs were visible. {3:13} After this, they were bound and kept in harsh confinement in a prison. {3:14} They endured three days and nights in the prison. {3:15} On the third day, the king ordered a proclamation to gather his counselors, nobles, elders, and officials in the square. {3:16} King Tseerutsaydan sat in the square and commanded that the honored men, Seela, Abya, and Fentos, be brought before him, wounded and bound. {3:17} The king asked them, "Have you reconsidered and returned from your rebellion?" {3:18} They answered him bravely, "We will not worship idols filled with sin and evil, as you command." {3:19} Enraged, the king ordered them to be elevated and their wounds reopened, causing blood to flow on the ground. {3:20} Then he commanded that they be burned with torches and their flesh charred. His servants obeyed, and the honored men said to him, "You who have forgotten JAH's law, speak! Our reward will exceed the measure of your punishment." {3:21} He ordered bears, tigers, and lions to be brought to devour them. They were thrown into the beasts' den, bound and beaten with tent poles. {3:22} The wild beasts roared but did not harm the martyrs, instead hailing and bowing to them. {3:23} The keepers were terrified and withdrew the beasts, struggling to contain them. {3:24} King Tseerutsaydan retreated in fear from his throne, and the beasts were removed to their dens. {3:25} Seela, Abya, and Fentos' two brothers came and released them from their harsh imprisonment, urging them to flee. {3:26} The martyrs replied, "It is not fitting for us to flee after bearing witness. As you feared, go and flee." {3:27} The young brothers said, "We will stand with you before the king. If you die, we will die with you." {3:28} The king saw that the honored men were released, and all five brothers stood together. The leaders who oversaw the punishment questioned why they were released and reported to the king, who was enraged and shouted furiously. {3:29} After consulting with his advisors, the king ordered all five brothers to be seized and imprisoned in a harsh, windowless cell. {3:30} King Tseerutsaydan said, "These youths have wearied me. How shall I respond to their steadfastness? Their deeds are like their strength, firm and unyielding." {3:31} He planned to increase their suffering, burning their flesh until it became ashes. Then he would scatter their ashes like dust on the mountains. {3:32} After speaking, he waited three days before commanding that the honored men be brought before him again. {3:33} When they were brought, he ordered a great pit to be prepared with a fiery blaze. They added a wicked concoction of oil, fat, soapberries, sea foam, resin, and sulfur to fuel the flames. {3:34} The fire blazed in the pit, and messengers went to inform the king that everything was prepared as commanded. {3:35} He commanded them to be cast into the fiery pit. The young men willingly gave their souls to JAH. {3:36} When those who cast them in saw this, angels came and carried their souls to the Garden where Abraham, Isaac, and Jacob dwell, where the righteous are honored. {3:37} The fire did not harm them, for their souls were with JAH. {3:38} Thus, seventy-five men of the king's army perished in the attempt. Many were terrified, filled with anguish and fear, and the king fled from his throne in panic. The beasts were subdued and returned to their dens.

{4:1} When the king saw that they were dead, he ordered their bodies to be burned in a fire until they were reduced to ashes. However, the fire could not burn the hair on their bodies. So, he had their remains removed from the pit. {4:2} Again, he ordered a fire to be kindled over them, burning from morning until evening, yet it did not harm them. Finally, he decided to cast their bodies into the sea. {4:3} They were thrown into the sea with heavy stones, iron anchors, and a millstone. Yet, the sea did not engulf them because the Spirit of JAH supported them. They floated on the sea's surface, untouched by the elements meant to destroy them. {4:4} The king lamented, "Their death has wearied me more than their life. Perhaps I should feed their bodies to wild animals." {4:5} But neither vultures nor beasts would touch their corpses. Birds and vultures shielded them with their wings from the burning sun, and the bodies of the five martyrs remained untouched for fourteen days. {4:6} As they were observed, their bodies shone like the sun, and angels encircled them like light surrounding a tent. {4:7} The king deliberated but could find no course of action. Eventually, he dug a grave and buried the bodies of the five martyrs. {4:8} That night, as the king lay on his bed, the five martyrs appeared before him in a vision, troubling and wielding swords. {4:9} He awoke in fear, thinking they had come to kill him. Trembling, he fled his bedchamber to the hall. {4:10} He said, "My lords, what do you desire? What should I do for you?" {4:11} They replied, "Are we not the ones you burned in the fire and cast into the sea? JAH preserved our bodies because we believed in Him. Your attempts to destroy us failed because those who believe in Him shall not perish. Give glory and praise to JAH, for we did not shame in our tribulation." {4:12} The king confessed, "I did not know such punishment would befall me. What reparation can I offer you for the harm I caused?" {4:13} They answered, "Do not take our bodies in death, nor lower our bodies to Sheol while we live." {4:14} "Forgive me for my sin against you, for it was your Father's law and kindness," he pleaded. {4:15} The martyrs replied, "You will suffer as we have suffered. JAH, who brings hardship upon souls, will repay you." {4:16} The king was alarmed and astonished. He feared them, seeing them draw their swords, and he bowed before them. {4:17} "I now know that those who are dead will indeed rise," he admitted. "Only a little time remains for me." {4:18} From that day forward, King Tseerutsaydan, once arrogant, ceased burning their bodies. {4:19} He had misled many for years in his idolatry and misguided reasoning, leading them away from worshipping JAH. Yet he was not alone in his error. {4:20} They sacrificed their children to demons, indulging in seduction and disturbance. Satan taught them these evils that JAH does not condone. {4:21} They committed abhorrent acts with their own family members, defiling themselves in deeds resembling these abominations. {4:22} The king, ignorant of JAH, remained obstinate in his idolatry and boasted of his idols. {4:23} "How will JAH grant His Kingdom to those who do not know Him through His law and worship?" they questioned. "Return to Him in repentance, for He tests us thus." {4:24} If they truly repent, JAH will love them and grant them His Kingdom. If not, the fire of Gehenna will punish them forever. {4:25} Therefore, let the king fear JAH and honor Him as he does his earthly rule. {4:26} Let elders, leaders, ambassadors, and all acknowledge and serve JAH as they serve their earthly masters. {4:27} For He is the Lord of Heaven and Earth, who judges all. There is no other who enriches or impoverishes, honors or debases, but Him.

{5:1} One of the sixty warriors became proud, and JAH caused his body to swell from head to foot with a plague of sulfur, and he died. {5:2} Another, Keeram, who built an iron bed in his arrogance and abundance of power, was hidden in death by JAH. {5:3} Yet another, Nebuchadnezzar, declared arrogantly, "There is no king besides me. I am the ruler who makes the sun rise in this world." He spoke from his abundance of pride. {5:4} JAH separated him from people and sent him to a wilderness for seven years, where he lived among the birds of heaven and wild beasts, until he recognized that it was JAH who had humbled him. {5:5} When he acknowledged JAH in worship, he was restored to his kingdom. Who else on earth dared to be so arrogantly proud against JAH who humbled him? {5:6} What other ruler dared to defy His law and His order without being swallowed up by the earth? {5:7} You, Tseerutsaydan, loved to be proud before your Ruler. But you also risked being destroyed like those before you, lowered into the grave by your arrogance. {5:8} And after they entered Sheol, where there is grinding of teeth and mourning, and darkness that fulfills, you risk being cast into the deep pit of Gehenna, from which there is no escape. {5:9} For you are but a mortal who will die and be destroyed like arrogant kings before you, who left this world without life. {5:10} As for us, we say, "You are a ruined wreck, not JAH, for JAH is the one who rules heaven and earth." {5:11} He debases the proud and honors the humble. He strengthens those who are weary. {5:12} He brings death to the mighty and raises up those who lie buried in the grave. {5:13} He sets slaves free to live in freedom from the rule of sin. {5:14} O King Tseerutsaydan, why do you boast in defiled idols that bring no benefit? {5:15} But JAH rules over earth and heaven, over the great seas, the moon, and the sun. He determines the ages. {5:16} He causes men to till their fields until evening, and He sustains the stars of heaven by His word. {5:17} He calls all things in heaven, for nothing is done without His knowledge. {5:18} He commands the angels of heaven to serve Him and praise His glorious name. Angels are sent to all who inherit life. {5:19} Rufa'iel, a servant, was sent to Thobeet and saved Thobya from death in the country of Ragu'iel. {5:20} Hola Meeka'iel was sent to Giediewon to turn his attention away from money that would destroy 'Iloflee. He was sent to the prophet Mussie when he led 'Isra'iel across the sea of 'Eritra. {5:21} Only JAH led them; there was no other idol with them. {5:22} He sent them to sow crops on the earth. {5:23} He fed them with His cultivated grain, showing His great love for them and sustaining them with honey that is as firm as rock. {5:24} So that you may fully fulfill His commandments and do JAH's will, He crowned you with authority over the four kingdoms. {5:25} He exalted you above all others, and your Ruler crowned you, that you might love JAH. {5:26} It is right for you to love your Ruler JAH as He has loved you, and to trust in Him above all others, so that your reign may prosper in this world and He may dwell with you in support. {5:27} Fulfill JAH's commandments so that He may stand as a guardian against your enemies, seat you on your throne, and shelter you under His wing of support. {5:28} If you do not know, JAH chose and crowned you over 'Isra'iel as He chose Sa'ol from among the children of 'Isra'iel when He kept his father's donkeys, and He crowned him over his people 'Isra'iel, where he sat on his throne. {5:29} He gave him a great fortune separated from his people; JAH crowned you over His people. From now on, watch over His people. {5:30} JAH has appointed you to govern and protect them from evil, both those who do good and those who do evil on what is good." {5:31} "JAH has appointed you over all that you do in His command, whether you whip or save, whether you repay evil deeds to those who do good deeds and those who do evil deeds. {5:32} For you are a servant of JAH who rules all in heaven. And you, fulfill JAH's command so that He may fulfill your will in all your thoughts and in all your prayers as you plead before Him. {5:33} There is no one who rules Him; He rules over all. {5:34} There is no one who appoints Him; He appoints all. {5:35} There is no one who dismisses Him; He dismisses all. {5:36} There is no one who reproaches Him; He reproaches all. {5:37} There is no one who makes Him diligent; He makes all diligent. For the rule of heaven and earth belongs to Him; there is no one who escapes from His authority. Everything is revealed alongside Him, yet nothing is hidden from His face. {5:38} He sees all, but there is no one who sees Him. He hears the prayer of the one who prays to Him, saying 'Save me,' for He has appointed man in His image, and He accepts his plea. {5:39} For He is a King who lives for eternity; He feeds all from His unchanging nature.

{6:1} As He crowns true kings who follow His command, their deeds are recorded straight because of Him. {6:2} Those who obey JAH shall shine in a light that surpasses that seen by Yis'haq, 'Abriham, Yaiqob, Solomon, Dawid, and Hezekiyah, residing in the garden where all the beautiful kings lodge. {6:3} The halls of heaven shine brightly, unlike the earth's halls. Their floors, adorned with silver, gold, and precious stones, are immaculate. {6:4} The shining features there are beyond human comprehension. The halls of heaven glitter like jewels. {6:5} Just as JAH, the Knower of Nature, knew, the heavenly halls He created shine brightly, beyond human understanding. Their floors, crafted with silver, gold, jewels, white silk, and blue silk, are immaculate. {6:6} It is exceedingly beautiful. {6:7} Righteous ones firmly established in religion and virtue shall inherit it through JAH's grace and forgiveness. {6:8} There flows beneficial water from it, shining like the sun. Within it is a light-filled tent, surrounded by the fragrance of grace. {6:9} A garden of beautiful and beloved fruits, with varied flavors and appearances, surrounds the house. There are olive and grape orchards, beautifully adorned, and their fruit and fragrance are sweet. {6:10} When a mortal enters it, their soul separates from their flesh due to the abundance of joy and delight emanating from its fragrant flavors. {6:11} The beautiful kings who followed JAH's command will rejoice there, known for their honor and place in the eternal Kingdom of Heaven, where joy abounds. {6:12} He showed that their earthly dominion was renowned and honored, and their heavenly dominion shall also be renowned and honored. They will be honored and exalted in heaven, just as they were honored and bowed to in this world. If they did good works in this world, they shall rejoice. {6:13} But kings who ruled with evil in their hearts and in the kingdoms JAH gave them did not judge rightly according to what is due. They ignored the cries of the destitute and poor, did not judge truthfully, did not save the refugee or the oppressed child who lost parents. {6:14} They did not rescue the destitute and poor from the grasp of the wealthy who robbed them, did not distribute food to the hungry, did not give drink to the thirsty, and did not heed the cries of the poor. {6:15} They shall be led to Gehenna, a dark end, when the day of judgment arrives, as Dawid said in his praises, "Lord, do not punish me in Your judgment, nor chastise me in Your discipline." Their troubles and humiliation will be as abundant as their fame and prosperity. {6:16} When nobles and kings who ruled in this world and did not keep Your law are there in this world, they are not. {6:17} But JAH, who rules over all, is there in heaven. He holds the souls and welfare of all in His authority. He bestows honor on those who glorify Him, for He rules over all, and He loves those who love Him. {6:18} For He is Lord of Earth and Heaven. He examines and knows the thoughts and intentions of every heart. For the one who prays to Him with a pure heart, He will grant their request. {6:19} He will bring down the arrogance of the powerful who do evil, who oppress the children orphaned by their parents. {6:20} It is not by your own power that you seized this kingdom, nor by your ability that you sit on this throne. It was JAH's will to test you, as He tested Sa'ul who ruled his people in that time. He established you on a throne of kingship, yet it was not by your own power that you seized this kingdom. {6:21} JAH instructed the prophet Shemu'el, "Go and destroy 'Amaleq and all their possessions." {6:22} He sent Sa'ul to destroy those who had angered JAH. {6:23} But he spared the king's life, many of the livestock, treasures, daughters, and handsome young men, against the will of JAH. For he ignored His command and did not serve in His army or against the 'Amaleq king. Yet it was not by your own power that you seized this kingdom. {6:24} For it was then that JAH commanded the prophet Shemu'el to go to King Shaul and to be seated at a dinner table, while the king 'Agag of 'Amaleq sat on his left. {6:25} "Why did you ignore JAH's command to destroy the livestock and people?" he asked. {6:26} The king was afraid and rose from his throne. He said to Shemu'el, "Please return with me and I will give you my clothes." Shemu'el refused to return. His clothes were torn. {6:27} Shemu'el said to Saul, "JAH has divided your kingdom." {6:28} Saul said to Shemu'el in front of the people, "Honour me and forgive me for my sin before JAH, so that He may forgive me." He feared the Word of JAH, but he did not fear the king who was dead. Shemu'el refused to return to his words. {6:29} Because he pierced the king of 'Amaleq before he swallowed what he had chewed. {6:30} A demon struck Sa'ul who defiled the law of JAH, and since He was the King of Kings, JAH struck him on his head. For it did not disgrace him. {6:31} He is the Lord of Creation, who dismisses all the nobles and kings who do not fear Him, but none of them rules over Him. {6:32} As He said, the kin of Dawid went and was renowned and honored, but the kin of Sa'ul went and was abased. He destroyed the kingdom from his children and from Sa'ul.

{7:1} Whether you are a king or a ruler, what significance do you hold? {7:2} Isn't it JAH who brought you from nonexistence to existence, so that you may fulfill His commandments and live guided by His judgment? Just as you oversee and govern your slaves, remember that it is JAH who oversees and governs you. {7:3} Just as you harshly punish those who commit sin, know that JAH will also strike you and cast you down to Gehenna, where there is no escape for eternity. {7:4} Just as you punish those who do not obey you or bring tribute to you, why do you not offer tribute to JAH? {7:5} JAH created you so that you may love Him and fear Him, and He crowned you to rule over His people justly. Why then do you not fear your Creator, JAH? {7:6} Judge with fairness and justice as JAH has appointed you, without showing favoritism to the small or the great. Whom will you fear if not Him? Keep His worship and the Ten Commandments. {7:7} As Moshe commanded the children of 'Isra'el, saying, "I set before you water and fire—choose what you desire." Do not turn to the right or to the left. {7:8} Listen to His word that I convey to you, so that you may hear His commandments. Do not say, "It is beyond my reach, who will bring it to me?" {7:9} Do not say, "Who will go up to heaven and bring down JAH's word for me to hear and obey?" The word of JAH is near you; take it in your mouth and practice it with your hands. {7:10} If you do not listen to your Creator, JAH, unless you listen to His book and obey His commandments, you will not love Him or obey His commandments. {7:11} And if you are to enter Gehenna forever, unless you love His commandments and do JAH's will, who has honored and glorified you above all others to keep them faithful? {7:12} He made you superior over all and crowned you over all His people to rule them justly according to His commands. While you think of His Name, Who crowned you and gave you a kingdom. {7:13} There are those whom you punish for wronging you, and there are those whom you pardon while considering JAH's work, and there are those whom you judge fairly. {7:14} Do not show favoritism when faced with disputes before you. Earthly possessions are like dust; do not accept bribes to forgive the guilty and condemn the innocent. {7:15} If you obey His commandments, JAH will extend your days in this world. But if you sadden Him, He will shorten your days. {7:16} Remember that you will rise after death and stand before Him, judged for all the deeds you have done, good or evil. {7:17} If you do good deeds, you will live in the Garden in the Kingdom of Heaven, in houses where righteous kings dwell in radiant light. JAH will not disgrace your authority, but if you do evil deeds, you will live in She'ol Gehenna, where wicked kings reside. {7:18} But when you gaze upon your revered fame, your soldiers' awards, your hanging shields and spears, your horses and troops under your authority, and those who beat drums and play harps before you... {7:19} When you look upon all this, elevate your thoughts and straighten your resolve, and do not forget JAH, who bestowed upon you all this honor. Yet when He tells you to abandon it, do not hesitate. {7:20} For you have neglected the appointment He appointed you, and He will give your authority to another. {7:21} As death suddenly comes upon you and judgment is rendered at the time of resurrection, when all human deeds will be examined, He will thoroughly investigate and judge you. {7:22} There is no one who will exalt the kings of this world, for JAH is the true judge. In the time of judgment, the poor and the wealthy will stand together. The crowns of worldly nobles, in which they boast, will fall. {7:23} Judgment is prepared, and souls will tremble. At that time, the deeds of sinners and righteous people will be examined. {7:24} No one will be hidden. Just as a woman cannot prevent her womb from bringing forth a child, Earth cannot prevent its inhabitants from returning to it. {7:25} Just as clouds cannot withhold rain when commanded by JAH, who brings life from nonexistence to existence, and to the grave by His Word, all will rise again after the time of resurrection. {7:26} As Moshe said, "It is by the words that come from JAH's mouth that a person is saved, not by bread alone." JAH's Word will indeed raise all people from their graves. {7:27} Be assured that the dead will rise by JAH's Word. {7:28} And JAH said in His law, because the kings and nobles who kept His covenant, as the day came when they were counted for destruction, a person will avenge and destroy them on the day when judgment is made and when they stumble. {7:29} And again JAH said to those who know His judgment, "Know that I am your Creator, JAH, who kills and who saves. {7:30} I punish in tribulation and I pardon. I cast down to She'ol and again I send forth to the Garden. And there is no one who can escape from My authority," He said to them. {7:31} JAH said this because the kings and nobles who did not keep His law, as earthly kingdoms pass by, and as they pass from morning until evening, keep My order and My law so that you may enter the Kingdom of Heaven that is established forever," He said. {7:32} For JAH calls the righteous to glory and sinners to tribulation. He will make the sinner miserable but will honor the righteous. {7:33} He will cast away the person who does not obey Him, but He will appoint the person who obeys Him.

{8:1} Listen to me and understand the truth about how the dead will rise: they will sprout like a plant and bear fruit, and vines will yield grapes, just as JAH will bring forth the fruit to imbibe from them. {8:2} Know that the small plant you once planted has now grown to bear fruit and leaves today. {8:3} JAH has given it roots to drink from the earth and water, nourishing it from both. {8:4} Yet it is fed by the wood of fire and wind. Its roots drink water, the earth gives it strength. {8:5} Similarly, souls bear fruit in the midst of life, and so shall dead persons rise. {8:6} When the soul is separated from the flesh, each returns to its nature, as JAH said: Gather the souls from the four elements—earth, water, wind, and fire. {8:7} The earthly nature remains rooted in its nature and becomes earth, while the watery nature remains rooted and becomes water. {8:8} The windy nature remains rooted and becomes wind, and the fiery nature remains rooted and becomes hot fire. {8:9} But a soul that JAH has separated from flesh returns to its Creator until He raises it united with flesh at His chosen time, placing it in the Garden where He loves. {8:10} He places righteous souls in a light-filled house in the Garden, but sinners' souls He places in a dark house in She'ol until His chosen time. {8:11} JAH commanded the prophet Ezekiel to call souls from the four corners to be gathered as one body. {8:12} When He spoke His Word, the souls were gathered from the four corners. {8:13} The watery nature brought forth greenery, and the fiery nature brought forth fire. {8:14} The earthly nature brought forth earth, and the windy nature brought forth wind. {8:15} JAH brought a soul from the Garden where He placed it. They were gathered by His Word, and resurrection occurred. {8:16} And I will show you an example that is close to you: the day turns to dusk, you sleep, and night turns to dawn. When you rise from your bed, it is an example of your awakening. But the night, when all people sleep and darkness covers them, is an example of this world. {8:17} But the morning light, when darkness fades and light fills the world, and people arise and go to the field, is an example of the resurrection of the dead. {8:18} And the Kingdom of Heaven, where people are renewed, is like this. The resurrection of the dead is like this: as this world passes away, it is an example of the night. {8:19} And as David said, "He set His example in the sun." Just as the sun shines when it rises, it is an example of the Kingdom of Heaven. {8:20} And as the sun shines in this world today, when Christ comes, He will shine like the sun in the new Kingdom of Heaven. As He said, "I am a sun that does not set, and a torch that is not extinguished. JAH is my light." {8:21} And He will quickly raise the dead again. I will show you another example from your food: whatever seed you sow and are saved, whether it be wheat, barley, lentils, or any seed sown on earth, none will grow unless it is first destroyed and rots. {8:22} And just as the flesh of a person you see, when it is destroyed and rots, the earth consumes it along with its strength. {8:23} When the earth consumes its strength, it grows around the seed, which JAH loves. He gives a cloud that brings rain, and roots grow in the earth and sprout leaves. {8:24} And if it is destroyed and rots, it cannot grow. But after it grows, it produces many buds. {8:25} By JAH's command, fruit is given to those buds that grow, and He clothes it with strength in straw. {8:26} Look at how much the seed you sow increases. But silver and leaves, ears and straw, are not counted for you. {8:27} Do not be ignorant, but look at your seed and how it increases. Similarly, think that the dead will receive the resurrection they will arise to, and they will endure hardships according to their deeds. {8:28} Listen, if you sow wheat, will you not reap barley? If you sow barley, will you not reap wheat? {8:29} If you sow figs, will you not reap nuts? If you plant almonds, will you not grow grapes? {8:30} How about different kinds of plants? If you plant figs, will you really get nuts? If you plant almonds, will you get grapes? {8:31} If you plant sweet fruit, will you get bitter fruit? If you plant bitter fruit, can it become sweet? {8:32} Likewise, if a sinful person dies, can he rise as righteous in the resurrection? If a righteous person dies, can he rise as sinful in the resurrection? Each will receive according to his deeds, and there will be no one condemned for another's sin. {8:33} A tall tree is planted, and it sends out long branches. Yet it will wither unless it rains, and its leaves will not be green. {8:34} And the cedar will be uprooted unless it receives rain in the summer. {8:35} Similarly, the dead will not rise unless the refreshing dew comes to them, as commanded by JAH.

{9:1} Unless the high mountains and the regions of Gielabuhie receive a refreshing rain commanded by JAH, they will not grow grass for beasts and animals. {9:2} The mountains of 'Elam and Gele'ad will not produce green leaves for sheep and goats, nor for the field and animals in the wilderness, nor for the ibexes and torah. {9:3} Similarly, pardon and refreshing dew commanded by JAH did not come to doubters and criminals who committed errors and crimes beforehand. Dead persons will not rise, and neither will Deemas and Qophros, who worship idols and practice sorcery, who incite conflict. {9:4} Those who practice sorcery, root-digging, and inciting strife. {9:5} Those who departed from the law and followed idols, such as Miedon and 'Atiena, who believe in idols, and those who play and sing for them with violins, drums, and harps, will not rise unless the refreshing dew comes to them, as commanded by JAH. {9:6} These are the ones who will be judged on the day of the resurrection and final judgment. Those who save themselves and act with their own deeds, and who delight in their own works, err because of their idols. {9:7} You, who are wasteful in heart and dull, do you think that the dead will not rise? {9:8} When a trumpet is blown by the Chief of Angels, Holy Michael, the dead will rise then. Just as you will not remain in the grave without rising, do not think otherwise. {9:9} Hills and mountains will be leveled, and a clear path will be made. {9:10} And resurrection will occur for all fleshly beings.

{10:1} However, if it were not so, former generations might be buried with their forefathers, beginning from Adam, Seth, and Abel, Shem and Noah, Isaac and Abraham, Joseph and Jacob, and Aaron and Moses. Yet why did they not desire to be buried in another place? {10:2} Should they not arise together with their relatives in the resurrection? Why then should their bones be mingled with those of evildoers and idolaters? Why did they not choose to be buried elsewhere? {10:3} But you, do not let your reasoning lead you astray when you say, "How can the dead rise again, those who were buried in one grave, tens of thousands whose bodies have decayed?" {10:4} When you look upon a grave and speak in your foolish reasoning, saying, "A handful of earth cannot possibly be found; how then can the dead rise?" {10:5} Will you say that the seed you sow will not grow? Surely, the seed you sow will indeed grow. {10:6} In the same way, the souls that Jah has sown will quickly rise, for he has created man from non-living to living by his truth. He will raise them swiftly by his word of salvation; he will not delay in their resurrection. {10:7} And just as he has once returned man from life to the grave in death, is it not possible for him to return from death to life again? {10:8} Saving and raising are possible for Jah.

{11:1} "Armon perished and its fortress was demolished, for Jah brought hardship upon them for their evil and the deeds they worked by their hands. Those who worshipped idols in Edom and Zabulon will be humbled at that time, for Jah has drawn near. Who will convict those who worked in their youth and did not repent even in old age, because of their idols and their evil? Sidon and Tyre will mourn. {11:2} Because they committed sin and seduced others into fornication and worshipped idols, Jah will exact vengeance and destroy them. Because they did not firmly adhere to Jah's command and the worship of the One God, when the dead rise, Jerusalem's sin will be revealed. {11:3} She persisted in killing prophets and in idolatry, but she did not remain faithful to the laws and the worship Jah commanded. {11:4} At that time, Jah will judge her with his divine wisdom; he will exact revenge for all her sins from her youth to her old age. {11:5} She entered the grave and became dust like her forefathers who persisted in sin. In the resurrection, Jah will exact vengeance on those who defied his law. {11:6} They will be judged for Moses spoke, saying, 'Their law and their reasoning have become like the laws of Sodom, and their people like the people of Gomorrah, and their laws are what destroy, and their works are evil. {11:7} Their laws are the poison of serpents and the venom of asps that destroy from beside them.

{12:1} Jerusalem, child of God - your sins are like those of Gomorrah and Sodom. Jerusalem, child of God, these are the tribulations spoken of by the prophet. {12:2} Your tribulations are like those of Gomorrah and Sodom, for your laws and reasoning are steeped in adultery and arrogance. {12:3} Aside from adultery and arrogance, no rain of forgiveness or humility has fallen from your reasoning; your laws are fertile only for spilling blood, robbing, and forgetting your Creator, JAH. {12:4} You do not know your Creator, JAH, apart from your evil works and idols. You take pride in your hands' work and lust after men and livestock. {12:5} Your reasoning has been blinded, preventing you from seeing the truth, and your ears have been deafened, stopping you from hearing or doing JAH's will. You do not know JAH in your works, and your reasoning is like the laws of Sodom. Your kin are like the grapes of Gomorrah, producing sweet fruit. {12:6} If you examine your works, they are like poison that kills, firmed up in a curse from the beginning. Your foundation has been in destruction. {12:7} Your laws and reasoning are firmed up in sinful works. Your bodies are steeped in the burning work of Satan to build sin. Your laws and reasoning have no good works. {12:8} When you are ashamed and baptized (by one who leads), it is for chastisement and destruction. He will firm up those who drink and follow such reasoning and make those who destroy despised and distant from JAH. {12:9} For you have lived firmly in your evil works, and he will make your dwelling with devils. Eating what was sacrificed to idols began in the house of Israel and proceeded toward the mountains and trees. {12:10} You worship the idols of the people around you and offer your sons and daughters to demons who do not know good works, separating them from evil. {12:11} You spill innocent blood and crush grapes from Sodom for the idols forever. {12:12} You glorify and worship Dagon, the god of the Philistines, and sacrifice to him from your flocks and fattened cows, seeking pleasure in the laziness demons have taught you, sacrificing to them and spilling grapes for them. {12:13} You do this to find pleasure in demons' teachings, forgetting your Creator, JAH, who has fed you from infancy to adulthood. {12:14} Again, I will bring revenge and judgment at the resurrection. As you did not return to my Law and did not live by my commandments, your time in Gehanna will be eternal. {12:15} If your idols are true gods, let them arise with you and descend into Gehanna to save you when I am angry and destroy you, and when I distance all the priests of the idols who lust with you. {12:16} As you have sinned and insulted the Holy Items and my Temple, I will make you wretched because of this. {12:17} When they told you, "Look, this is JAH's people, Israel, the Creator's dwelling," and you were proud like Jerusalem, separated from others, the dwelling of the Most High JAH's name, I made you wretched because you defiled my name. {12:18} You boasted that you were my servant and that I was your Lord, but you did not fear me or do my will like a servant should. {12:19} They became a stumbling block for you, leading you away from me, and you followed other idols who do not feed or clothe you. {12:20} You sacrificed to them and ate the sacrifices. You spilled blood for them and drank their wine. You burned incense for them and made the incense fragrant for them. Your idols commanded you, and you obeyed them. {12:21} You sacrificed your sons and daughters to them. As you praised them for their love, you found pleasure in the things you spoke and the works of your hands. {12:22} Woe to you on the day of final judgment. Woe to your idols whom you loved and united with; you will descend with them into Gehanna, where the worm does not die and the fire is not quenched. {12:23} Woe to you, wretched Jerusalem child, for you abandoned me, your Creator, and worshipped other idols. {12:24} I will bring hardship upon you according to your works. As you saddened me and ignored my word, and did not do good works, I will convict you according to your pretensions. {12:25} For you saddened my word and did not live by my Law, which you swore to keep so I could live with you in support and save you from your enemies. You did not keep my order, so I will ignore you and not quickly save you from tribulation. {12:26} You did not keep all this, so I will ignore you. As I created you and you did not keep my commandments or my word, I will convict you at the time of judgment. I honored you to be my kin. {12:27} As Gomorrah and Sodom were separated from me, so were you. {12:28} I judged and destroyed them. Just as Sodom and Gomorrah were separated from me, so are you. Now, as I was angry and destroyed them, I will destroy you. As you are from the kindred of Sodom and Gomorrah, whom I destroyed, I will destroy you. {12:29} As those I created saddened me by going after young men and lusting without Law with animals and men like going after daughters, I destroyed their names from this world so they would not live in their pleasure. {12:30} There is no fear of JAH in their faces from infancy to old age. They help each other in all their evil works, yet he does not punish each one so they may stop their evil. As their works are evil, they are sated with sin and iniquity. {12:31} All evil works - robbery, arrogance, and greed - are prepared in their reasoning. {12:32} Because of this, JAH ignored them and destroyed their lands. They are there so he can burn them with fire until their root foundation perishes. They totally perished for eternity, yet he did not let even one remain. {12:33} As they were firm in sin, they will wait in destruction forever until the Day of Advent when the final judgment is done. They saddened me with their evil works, and I will not pardon or forgive them. {12:34} I ignored them. You will find no reason when I am angry and seize you because all your works were robbery and sin, adultery, greed, and speaking lies - all works of error and obstacles that I do not love. You, wretched Jerusalem child, will be seized in judgment like them. {12:35} I made you for honor, but you debased yourself. I called you my treasure, but you became someone else's. {12:36} I betrothed you for honor, but you became Satan's. I will bring revenge and destroy you according to your evil works. {12:37} Because you did not hear all my words and did not keep the commandments I gave you when I loved you, I will multiply and bring firm vengeance upon you, for I am JAH, who created you. I will judge all sinners like you. {12:38} As you did not keep my word and ignored my judgment, I will convict you with them. {12:39} Woe to you, Gomorrah and Sodom, who have no fear of JAH in your reasoning. {12:40} Likewise, woe to your sister, Jerusalem child, who will be judged together with you in the fire of Gehenna. You will descend together into Gehanna, prepared for you, where there are no exits forever. Woe to all sinners who committed your sins. {12:41} As you did not keep my commandments or my word, you and she who did not keep my commandments or my word will descend into Sheol together on the day of judgment. {12:42} But the righteous who kept my commandments and my word will eat the wealth that sinners accumulated. As JAH commanded, the righteous will share the loot that evil people captured, and the righteous will be completely blessed. {12:43} Wrongdoers and sinners will weep and be sad because all their sins and wrongdoing have departed from my commandments. {12:44} Those who keep my word and live by my commandments will find my blessing and be honored alongside me. {12:45} Anyone who keeps my word and lives by my commandments will eat the fatness of the land and enter the Garden, where kind kings with righteous minds enter.

{13:1} In the time of my wrath, they will be miserable and perish when I seize them. Woe to Tyre and Sidon and all the regions of Judah that have become arrogant today. {13:2} The conquering Lord says this: A child of the devil, full of arrogance, will be born from them—the false messiah, who is truly an enemy. He boasts and does not know his Creator. The Lord, who rules all, says: I have made him to reveal my power through my anger. {13:3} The towns of Capernaum, Samaria, Galilee, Damascus, Syria, Achaea, Cyprus, and all the Jordan region are full of people who are proud and entrenched in their sin. They live in the shadow of death and darkness because the devil has clouded their minds with sin. They have not turned back to fear God. {13:4} Woe to those commanded by demons and who offer sacrifices in their names, for they have denied the God who created them. They are like mindless animals. The false messiah, a child of the devil who has forgotten God's law, will set up his image in all places, saying, "I am a god." He will revel in his own ways, in his actions, robbery, sin, betrayal, and all forms of iniquity, including all the adulteries of mankind. {13:5} Because this has been accounted by God, the era of sin is known. The sun will darken, the moon will turn to blood, and the stars will shake from heaven. All these works will come to pass through the miracles that God will bring in the fulfillment era, causing the earth to pass away along with all those who live in sin within her. {13:6} As God has shown pride in His creation, and has quickly made His beloved in one moment, the Lord will destroy the small enemy, the devil. {13:7} The Lord, who rules all, says: I will judge and destroy, but after the advent, the devil will have no authority. {13:8} On the day when he is seized by my anger, he will descend to Gehanna, the place of tribulation, taking all who follow him into destruction and punishment. I will cast him into Gehenna. {13:9} Just as God gives strength and power to the weak and brings down the powerful, let no one boast in their power. {13:10} As the Ruler, God judges and saves the wronged from their oppressors. He will defend the widow and the orphan. {13:11} Woe to those who boast and harden their minds, thinking that I will not rule or judge them. In their arrogance, they say, "I will ascend to the stars and be like God who is on high." {13:12} Just as God said about the devil: How he fell from heaven, shining like a morning star, woe to him. {13:13} Though he dared to speak in his arrogance, he did not consider the God who created him. Why did he boast when he was destined to descend to Gehenna in his arrogance? {13:14} He was cast down, separate from all the angels who praise their Creator with humility because they know He created them from fire and wind, and they do not depart from His command. {13:15} But in his arrogance, he committed great betrayal. He became a wretched man, separate from his companions, indulging in all sins and iniquities, robbery, and betrayal. Those who forgot God's law and are sinners like him follow his command and teachings. {13:16} Woe to him and the demons he misled. They will descend together into Gehenna. {13:17} Woe to you, children of God, misled by that wicked devil. As you have strayed like him by following his teachings, you will descend into Gehenna together, where there are no exits forever. {13:18} Formerly, when God's servant Moses was there, you angered God at the waters of Meribah and at Horeb, and with Amalek and on Mount Sinai. {13:19} Moreover, when you sent scouts to Canaan, they reported, "The journey is long, and the fortified cities reach the heavens. Warriors live there." You despaired, wanting to return to Egypt where you had been oppressed, and you angered God's word. {13:20} You did not consider God, who delivered you from tribulation and performed great miracles in Egypt, leading you by His angel's authority. He veiled you in a cloud by day to protect you from the sun and provided a pillar of fire by night to prevent you from stumbling in the darkness. {13:21} When Pharaoh's army frightened you, you cried out to Moses, and Moses cried out to God. God sent His angel and protected you from Pharaoh. {13:22} But He led them into the Red Sea in tribulation. God guided only Israel, saying, "There was no foreign god with them." He buried their enemies in the sea at once, not allowing any to escape. {13:23} He made Israel cross the sea on foot. There was no tribulation from the Egyptians. He delivered them to Mount Sinai and fed them manna for forty years. {13:24} Yet, the children of Israel continually angered God with their sins. They did not live according to His law like their forefathers Isaac, Abraham, and Jacob, who kept God's commandments. {13:25} From the least to the greatest, the children of Israel who did not keep God's law were corrupt in their deeds. {13:26} Whether they were priests, chiefs, or scribes, they all violated God's law. {13:27} They did not follow God's order and the law that Moses commanded them in Deuteronomy, saying, "Love your Creator God with all your heart and all your soul." {13:28} They did not follow God's order and the law that Moses commanded them in the book of the law, saying, "Love your neighbor as yourself. Do not worship other gods. Do not go to a young man's wife. Do not kill. Do not steal. {13:29} Do not give false testimony. Do not covet your neighbor's property, whether it is his donkey or his ox, nor anything that belongs to him." {13:30} However, after being commanded all this, the evil children of Israel returned to treachery and sin, robbery and iniquity, going to a young man's wife, lying, stealing, and worshipping idols. {13:31} The children of Israel angered God at Horeb by making a calf to worship, saying, "These are our gods who brought us out of Egypt." {13:32} They delighted in their handiwork, and after eating and drinking, they rose to play. When God informed Moses, saying, "Your people, whom you brought out of Egypt, have gone astray and wronged me. They made an image of a calf and worshiped it," Moses was angry and descended from Mount Sinai. {13:33} When Moses descended in anger, accompanied by Joshua, Joshua said, "I hear the sound of war in the camp of Israel." {13:34} Moses replied, "It is not the sound of war but the sound of singing after drinking unfermented wine." He came down and destroyed their image, crushing it into dust and mixing it with the water the Israelites drank by the mountain. {13:35} After this, he commanded the priests to slay each other because of the sin they had committed before God. {13:36} They knew that defying God was worse than killing themselves or their fathers, and they did as Moses commanded. {13:37} Moses told them, "Because you have angered the Lord, who fed you and cherished you, who brought you out of the house of bondage and gave you the inheritance He promised to your forefathers, you have made God angry." {13:38} They continued to go toward sin and evil, not ceasing to anger God there. {13:39} They were not like their forefathers Isaac, Abraham, and Jacob, who pleased God with their good deeds, that He might give them the land and the blessings prepared for those who love Him in heaven, from their youth to their old age. They were not like Abraham, Isaac, and Jacob, who pleased Him with their deeds, that He might give them an earthly inheritance and a heavenly garden of delight prepared for the righteous in the afterlife, blessings beyond human comprehension. {13:40} Their children, who denied God and were evil, lived according to their own ways. They did not heed God's commands, even though He fed them and cherished them from their infancy. {13:41} They did not consider God, who brought them out of Egypt & saved them from forced labor and oppressive rule. {13:42} They continually angered Him, and He would raise peoples against them who would oppress & tax them, just as they had loved to do.

{14:1} When God destroyed the descendants of Cain, the ancient kindreds, in the flood because of their sins, He baptized the Earth in the waters of destruction, cleansing it from all the sins of Cain's descendants. {14:2} As He said, "I am saddened that I created man," He destroyed all wrongdoers, sparing only eight people. Afterward, He multiplied them, and they filled the Earth, sharing the inheritance of their father Adam. {14:3} But Noah made a covenant with God, vowing that God would never again destroy the Earth with floodwaters. Noah's children were not to eat anything that died naturally or was killed by other means, nor were they to worship any idols other than the Creator. God promised to be a loving Father to them, not to destroy them for their sins, to provide the early and latter rains, and to give them food for both livestock and people. They would receive grass, grains, fruits, and plants and would do good works that God loves. {14:4} Despite this covenant, the children of Israel saddened God with their sins. They did not uphold His law as their fathers Isaac, Abraham, and Jacob had, who did not violate the Creator's commandments. {14:5} From the least to the greatest, the children of Israel who did not keep God's law were corrupt in their deeds. {14:6} Whether they were priests, chiefs, or scribes, everyone violated God's law. {14:7} They did not adhere to God's commandments and the law that Moses gave them, which said, "Love your Creator with all your heart, soul, and mind." {14:8} They did not follow the commandments written in the book of the law, which included, "Love your neighbor as yourself; do not worship idols; do not commit adultery; do not murder; do not steal; do not bear false witness; do not covet your neighbor's possessions." {14:9} Despite these commandments, the children of Israel, who were evil, returned to treachery and sin, robbery and iniquity, adultery, lying, stealing, and idol worship. {14:10} The children of Israel saddened God at Horeb by making a calf that grazed on grass, saying, "Look, these are our gods who brought us out of Egypt." {14:11} They rejoiced in their handiwork. If they ate and drank their fill, they would rise to sing. {14:12} God said to Moses, "Your kindred whom you brought out of Egypt have turned away from the law and have done wrong. They made an image of a calf and bowed to the idol." Because of this, Moses was angered and descended from Mount Sinai. {14:13} While Moses was angry at his kindred, he descended with his confidant Joshua. When Joshua heard, he said, "I hear the sound of warriors in the Israelite camp." {14:14} Moses replied to Joshua, "It is not the sound of warriors; it is the sound of revelry from the unboiled wine they have drunk." He descended and broke their image, crushing it into dust. He mixed it with the water that the children of Israel drank beside the mountain. {14:15} After this, he commanded the priests to kill each other because of the sin they had committed before God. {14:16} They knew that defying God was worse than killing themselves or their fathers, and they did as Moses commanded. {14:17} Moses told them, "Because you have saddened God, who fed and cherished you, who brought you out of a house of slavery, and who promised to give you the inheritance He swore to your fathers, you have angered God." {14:18} They turned to sin and evil and did not stop saddening God there. {14:19} They were not like their fathers, Isaac, Abraham, and Jacob, who pleased God with their good works, that He might give them what is on Earth and what He prepared for those who love Him in Heaven, from their infancy to their youth and old age. They were not like Abraham, Isaac, and Jacob, who pleased God with their works, that He might give them an inheritance on Earth where blessings are found in this world, and a paradise prepared for the righteous in the hereafter. {14:20} But their children, who denied God and were evil, did not listen to God's commandments. He who fed and cherished them from infancy. {14:21} They did not remember God, who brought them out of Egypt and saved them from hard labor and a harsh ruler. {14:22} Instead, they continually saddened Him, leading to enemies rising against them and taxing them.

{15:1} At that time, the people of Midian rose up against Israel in enmity, and they gathered their armies to fight them. Their king, named Akrandis, quickly assembled a large force from Cilicia, Syria, and Damascus. {15:2} Camped beyond the Jordan, he sent messengers, saying, "To seize your wealth, pay tribute to Israel on my behalf." He warned them, "But if you do not pay, I will come to punish you, seize your livestock, take your horses, and capture your children." {15:3} He threatened, "I will take you to a foreign land where you will serve as water carriers and woodcutters." {15:4} He boasted, "Do not think that being God's people will protect you. Is it not God who sent me to destroy you and plunder your wealth? Am I not the one He sent to gather all your people?" {15:5} He asked rhetorically, "Did any of the other nations I destroyed find salvation through their idols? I captured their horses and killed their people, seizing their children." {15:6} He declared, "Unless you pay the tribute I demand, I will destroy you like them." He then crossed the Jordan to plunder their livestock and wealth and capture their wives. {15:7} The children of Israel wept bitterly to God, crying out in distress, but they lacked anyone to help them. {15:8} Because of this, God strengthened three brothers: Judah, Mebikyas, and Maccabees, who were handsome and mighty warriors. {15:9} The children of Israel wept, deeply saddened by the plight of their nation. From orphans and widows to officials and priests, all of Israel, both daughters and sons, mourned, covering themselves in ashes and wearing sackcloth. {15:10} The brothers, who were attractive and brave, decided to sacrifice themselves for their people. They encouraged each other, saying, "Let us go and lay down our lives for our people." {15:11} They donned their swords and seized their spears, ready to confront the enemy. {15:12} When they reached the enemy camp, Mebikyas attacked the king while he was at the dinner table, killing him with one blow as he ate. Maccabees and Judah attacked the king's army, killing them with their swords. {15:13} When the king was defeated, the enemy soldiers turned their weapons on each other in panic, breaking their bows and fleeing in disarray. {15:14} The brothers, handsome and valiant, were spared from death. No harm befell them as God returned the punishment upon the enemy, who killed each other. {15:15} The enemy was defeated and fled across the Jordan, abandoning all their wealth. When the children of Israel saw this, they raided the enemy camp and took the spoils for themselves. {15:16} God saved Israel through the bravery of the brothers and Mebikyas. {15:17} Israel enjoyed a brief period of peace, making God happy. {15:18} However, they soon returned to their sins. The children of Israel neglected their worship of God. {15:19} As a result, God would once again allow foreign nations to oppress them, taking their crops, destroying their vineyards, plundering their flocks, and slaughtering their livestock. {15:20} These nations would capture their wives, daughters, and sons. Because the children of Israel continually saddened God, these foreign peoples, who ignored God's laws, would punish them severely.

{16:1} These oppressors included the people of Tyre and Sidon, those beyond the Jordan River, along the coast, the Keranites, the Gileadites, the Jebusites, the Canaanites, the Edomites, the Gergesites, and the Amalekites. {16:2} All these peoples, living in their respective tribes, countries, regions, and speaking different languages, acted according to their own customs. {16:3} Some of them knew God and performed good works. {16:4} Others did evil deeds, ignoring God who created them, and were ruled by the Assyrian king Shalmaneser. {16:5} Shalmaneser plundered Damascus and shared Samaria's loot with the king of Egypt. God ruled over them through Shalmaneser. {16:6} The region of Gielabuhie, as well as the people in Persia, Media, Cappadocia, and Susiana, those in the western mountains, and those in the Gilead fortress and Ptolemais in Judea, {16:7} and all who lived in those regions, did not know God or follow His commands. They were stubborn and unyielding in their ways. {16:8} God would repay them for their evil deeds and the work of their hands. {16:9} The people of Gilead and Caesarea, along with the Amalekites, united to destroy God's land, which was filled with truth, and where the Creator of Israel was praised—Him who is most glorious and conquering, served by countless angels who stand before Him with fear and trembling. He would repay them for their evil deeds and the work of their hands.

{17:1} The Amalekites and Edomites did not worship God, who held the authority over Heaven and Earth. They were wicked and did not live according to righteous works. They had no fear of desecrating the Temple. {17:2} They had no fear of God, shedding blood, committing adultery, eating what was beaten and sacrificed to idols, and all similar sinful acts. They were scorned sinners. {17:3} They lacked virtue and religion, despising good works. They did not know God or acts of love, but only robbery, sin, disturbing others, and all hated deeds, apart from games and songs taught by their father, the devil. They had no virtue or religion. {17:4} The devil ruled over them with his host of demons, teaching them all evil works for their own selves—robbery, sin, theft, falsehood, seizing money, eating what was beaten and what was sacrificed to idols, and committing adultery. {17:5} He taught them all these things and more, including going after young women, shedding blood, eating what was sacrificed to idols and what was dead, killing others with violence, envy, winking, greed, and all evil works that God does not love. The devil, their enemy, taught them these things to distance them from God's law, who rules the world. {17:6} But God's works are innocence and humility—loving your brother, being in harmony with all people, and loving everyone. {17:7} Do not be hypocritical for personal gain, do not be wrongdoers or robbers, do not go after young women, do not commit iniquity against your neighbor, and do not deceive to harm others with violence. {17:8} They wink and provoke evil, mislead others, and aim to bring them down, leading to eternal judgment.

{18:1} Remember that you will face death and stand before God, who holds everything in His hands, to be judged for all your sins. {18:2} Those who are arrogant and evil, and the powerful children who are not stronger than their ancestors, have not acknowledged God. They failed to realize that He created them, bringing them from non-existence into life. {18:3} When their ancestors, praised like "Angels" on Mount Hola with the angels, were misled, they descended to this world, where they will face eternal judgment. {18:4} In ancient times, God created human flesh to test them, as they displayed arrogance and strayed from His laws and commands. They married women from the descendants of Cain. {18:5} But they did not keep His law. God cast them into the fire of Gehenna with their father, the devil. God was angry with the descendants of Seth for their wrongdoings, and humanity diminished because of their sins. {18:6} They led Adam's children into sin with them, and He cast them into Sheol, where they would face judgment. {18:7} The human lifespan was reduced from nine hundred years to one hundred twenty years because the children of Seth erred with the children of Cain. {18:8} Being flesh and blood, God declared, "My Spirit will not dwell with them forever." {18:9} Because of this, our lifespans were shortened due to sin and iniquity, making them less than those of our ancestors who came before us. Now, infants die young. {18:10} Our ancestors lived long lives because they kept His law and did not sadden God. {18:11} Their lives were prolonged because they disciplined their daughters and sons, ensuring they did not stray from God's law. {18:12} By upholding God's law with their children, their lifespans were truly extended.

{19:1} When the descendants of Cain flourished, they created drums, harps, flutes, and violins, and composed songs and games. {19:2} Cain's children, born to the wife of the righteous man Abel (whom he killed for her beauty), were attractive. After killing his brother, he took her and her wealth. {19:3} He separated from his father and moved to the region of Qiefaz in the west, where his beautiful children inherited their mother's looks. {19:4} Because of this, Seth's descendants mingled with Cain's descendants. Seeing their beauty, they immediately took these daughters as their wives. {19:5} Their errors led us into sin with them, angering God against us and them. {19:6} The devil, deceiving them with, "You will become creators like your Creator, God," led our mother Eve and our father Adam into his error. {19:7} Believing the devil's lies, they disobeyed God's law, failing to honor and praise His holy name. {19:8} But their Creator humbled Adam and Eve, who tried to make themselves gods, and He humbled the arrogant devil. {19:9} As David said, "Adam perished by the sinner devil's arrogance," God judged them justly. Our father Adam was condemned for the devil's pride. {19:10} The children of Seth, who erred with Cain's children, led us into sin. Thus, our lifespans given by God are shorter than those of our ancestors. {19:11} Our ancestors did good deeds, firmly rooted in God. They taught their children, ensuring they did not stray from God's law, and no evil enemy approached them. {19:12} Even if they did good works, it was of no benefit if they did not teach their children.

{19:13} As David said, "They did not hide from their children but taught God's praise, the miracles He performed, and His power." It was useless if they did not teach their children to know and follow God's commands, and to keep His law, making God pleased with their good works. {19:14} Those who taught their children from infancy did not violate His command, as their ancestors had learned God's worship and the Nine Laws from their forefathers. {19:15} Their children learned from their fathers to do good works and praise their Creator, keeping His law and loving Him. {19:16} God heard their prayers and did not ignore their pleas. He is a forgiver. {19:17} Even when He multiplied His wrath, He would relent, not destroying all in His chastisement.

{20:1} Brothers, remember and do not forget what was told to you long ago: God rewards those who do good works. {20:2} He will multiply their descendants in this world, and their names will be honored forever. Their children will not suffer want in this world. {20:3} God will protect them for their sake and will not hand them over to their enemies. He will save them from those who hate them. {20:4} For those who love His name, God will be their helper in times of trouble. He will guard them and forgive all their sins.

{21:1} David believed in God, and God believed in him, saving him from the hand of King Saul. {21:2} Because David believed in God and kept His law, God saved him from his son Absalom, the Philistines, the Edomites, the Amalekites, and the giant from the Rephaim. God delivered David from all these tribulations. {21:3} Victory comes from God's will. Those who oppose Him are defeated, but God does not save the evil kings who do not believe in Him. {21:4} Hezekiah trusted in God, and God saved him from the arrogant Sennacherib. {21:5} But Hezekiah's son, Manasseh, was defeated by his enemies because he did not put his trust in God. As he did not trust and fear the Lord, who had greatly honored him, his enemies captured and took him to their land. {21:6} At that time, God denied him the kingdom He had given him because Manasseh did not do good before his Creator, the Lord. He did not work righteously to prolong his days, protect him from his enemies, and give him strength and stability. {21:7} It is better to trust in God than in large armies, horses, bows, and shields. {21:8} Trusting in God is superior. Those who believe in Him will be strong, honored, and exalted. {21:9} God does not show favoritism. Those who do not believe in Him and trust in their wealth lose the grace and honor He had given them. {21:10} God protects those who believe in Him. He will make fools of those who disregard Him. Those who do not discipline themselves to follow God's law will not receive His help in times of trouble or when their enemies attack. {21:11} However, those who worship God and keep His law will find refuge in Him during their tribulations. {21:12} God will destroy their enemies, plunder their livestock, capture their lands, and bring the rain for their crops and food supply. {21:13} God will provide the early and latter rains, making the grass green and giving rain at the proper times, so that their people will prosper. {21:14} He will make them prosperous, enabling them to enjoy the wealth taken from their enemies, including livestock and children taken as captives. {21:15} God will do all this for those He loves, but He will make those who hate Him victims of their enemies. {21:16} He will bind their hands and feet, handing them over to their enemies as a punishment for their bloodshed and disobedience to God's law. {21:17} They will not stand in judgment, and those who do evil will face hardship for their sins. God will also punish those who do wicked deeds. {21:18} God has decreed rewards for those who do good, ensuring their protection under His authority. {21:19} He has power over all creation, to do good and give them eternal well-being, and they will praise their Creator. He has commanded them to keep His law, and none of His creation except man has deviated from His command. {21:20} As God commanded all living things in their actions, they all know and are kept by His law. {21:21} But man, who was given dominion over all other creations, has often rebelled against God. {21:22} Whether in the sea or on land, God gave all creation to their father Adam, allowing him to use and consume them like grain, to rule over them, and to be in command of beasts and animals. {21:23} If they stray from His law, He will take away the lordship He gave them. God rules both heaven and earth, giving it to those who follow His will. {21:24} He appoints and dismisses according to His love. He kills and saves, chastises, and forgives. {21:25} There is no other creator like Him. He rules all creation, and there is none other besides Him in heaven or on earth to criticize Him. {21:26} He appoints and dismisses, kills and saves, chastises and forgives, impoverishes, and honors. {21:27} He hears the pleas of those who follow His commands with pure hearts and answers their prayers, granting them their requests. {21:28} He makes the great and the small serve them, providing them with wealth from hills, mountains, tree roots, caves, and wells on land and sea. {21:29} For those who do their Creator's will, all this wealth is theirs. God will not deprive them of their abundance and will reward them for their praises. {21:30} He will give them the honor prepared in heaven for their ancestors Isaac, Abraham, and Jacob, as well as for Hezekiah, David, and Samuel, who did not stray from His law and command. {21:31} That they may rejoice in His kingdom, He will give those who served Him from antiquity the honor prepared for their ancestors Isaac, Abraham, and Jacob, to whom He promised an inheritance.

{22:1} Remember the names of those who did good deeds and do not forget their works. {22:2} Ensure your name is associated with theirs so that you may rejoice with them in the Kingdom of Heaven, the glorious dwelling prepared for noble and righteous kings who followed God's commands. {22:3} Also, recognize and be aware of the names of evil nobles and kings, whom God will judge and condemn before all men after their death. {22:4} They did not align their actions with God's will while they lived and saw and heard His commands. Understand that unless they followed God's will, He will judge them in the Kingdom of Heaven more severely than criminals and those who forgot His law. {22:5} Be kind, innocent, and honest, but do not follow the path of those who forgot God's law and angered Him with their evil deeds. {22:6} Judge fairly and protect the orphaned child and the widow from those who would rob them. {22:7} Be a guardian for the orphan, saving them from the hands of the wealthy who would take advantage of them. Stand up for them and be moved by the tears of the orphan, lest you find yourself alarmed in the fiery sea where sinners who did not repent are punished. {22:8} Walk the path of love and unity. God's eyes watch over His friends, and His ears hear their pleas. Seek love and follow it. {22:9} But God's face of wrath is against those who do evil deeds. He will erase their names from this world, and He will not protect them on high walls or mountains. {22:10} As I am the Lord, who is jealous of my divinity, I am the Creator who avenges and destroys those who hate me and do not keep my word. I will not turn away my wrath until I have destroyed those who do not keep my word. {22:11} I will honor those who honor me and keep my word.

{23:1} Do not follow the example of Cain, who killed his innocent brother, who loved him. {23:2} Cain killed his brother out of envy for a woman. Those who cause envy, iniquity, and betrayal are like him. {23:3} But Abel was innocent like a sheep, and his blood was like the pure blood of a sacrificial lamb offered to God with a clean heart. Those who follow Cain's path do not follow Abel's path. {23:4} For all who live in innocence are loved by God, like the righteous Abel. They are innocent like Abel, and those who follow Abel's example love God. {23:5} But God neglects the wicked, and their final judgment will be pronounced upon them. It is recorded in the book of their deeds and will be read before men, angels, and all creation at the time of judgment. {23:6} Then, wrongdoers and deniers who did not follow God's will shall be ashamed. {23:7} And a dreadful decree will be given to them, saying, "Cast them into Gehenna, where there is no exit for eternity.

{24:1} When Gideon trusted in God, he defeated vast armies of uncircumcised people with only a few tens of thousands, despite their numbers being countless like locusts. {24:2} As there is no creator apart from Me, oh nobles and kings, do not place your faith in idols. {24:3} For I am your Creator, the Lord, who brought you from your mother's womb, raised you, fed you, and clothed you. Why do you pretend otherwise? Why do you worship idols instead of Me? {24:4} I have done all this for you; what have you given Me in return? You should live according to My laws, orders, and commandments so I can provide for your well-being. What else do I ask of you? {24:5} The Lord who rules all says this: Save yourselves from idol worship, sorcery, and discouraging pessimism. {24:6} For the Lord's punishment will come upon those who practice these things, their followers, and friends who live according to their commands. Save yourselves from idol worship. {24:7} People who do not know you and are not kind to you will rise against you unless you, who fear, follow the Lord's command. They will consume the wealth you worked for, as spoken by His servants, the prophets, Enoch, and Asaph. Unless you follow the Lord's commands, others will consume the wealth you worked for. {24:8} Evil people will come, disguising themselves. Their only laws are eating, drinking, adorning themselves in silver and gold, and living in sin, which the Lord detests. {24:9} They are eager for drink and food. From morning till evening, they pursue evil deeds, with misery and tribulation in their path. Their feet do not tread the path of love. {24:10} They do not understand the works of love and unity. There is no fear of the Lord in their faces. They are crooked, evil people without religion or virtue, greedy, eating and drinking alone. They are drunkards whose sins are boundless, who pursue seduction, bloodshed, theft, betrayal, and violent robbery. {24:11} They criticize without love or law, for they do not fear the Creator who made them. There is no fear in their faces. {24:12} They do not feel shame in the presence of others, not even the elderly. Upon hearing of wealth, they claim it as their own without seeing it. They do not fear the Lord, and when they see it with their eyes, they believe they have eaten it. {24:13} Their nobles consume entrusted money. They are those who eat it. Being negativists, there is no honesty in their tongues. They do not repeat in the evening what they spoke in the morning. {24:14} They ignore the cries of the suffering and the poor. Their kings hasten towards evil, downpressing the innocent, saving refugees from the hands of the wealthy who rob them. {24:15} Let them save those wronged and the refugees. But let the kings not hinder justice because of wealth. {24:16} They are those who exact tribute, robbing people of their money, committing crimes. Their deeds are evil. They are not kind when they consume the calf with its mother or a bird with its egg. They take everything they see and hear as their own. {24:17} They love to amass wealth for themselves but are not kind to the sick and poor. They violently rob those without wealth, gathering everything they find to fatten themselves and feel secure in it. {24:18} They will quickly perish like a scarab emerging from its pit, leaving no trace and not returning home. Since they did not perform good deeds in life, woe to their bodies when the Lord is angry and seizes them. {24:19} When the Lord neglects them, they will perish instantly, as if consumed by one punishment. Though He endures them as if they might repent, He does not destroy them quickly. They will perish when their time comes. {24:20} If they do not repent, He will quickly destroy them like those who came before them, who did not follow the Lord's laws as required. {24:21} They are those who consume a person's flesh and drink their blood. They commit violence and pursue sin without fearing the Lord. Every day they arise from their bedding, they do not rest from sinning. {24:22} Their works are eating and drinking, heading towards destruction and sin, causing the downfall of many bodies in this world.

{25:1} Since their work is corrupt and they live firmly in the works of Satan, who misleads, the Lord who rules all said, "Woe to your bodies when I become angry and seize them." {25:2} They do not know the works of the Lord, having turned away from His laws and neglected His commands. {25:3} Later, in the era of fulfillment, I will bring hardship upon them according to their evil measure. Like their sins are recorded alongside Me, I will avenge and destroy them on the day of judgment. {25:4} As I, the Lord, fill the horizon from end to end and all creation is within My authority, none can escape My dominion in heaven, on earth, in the depths, or in the sea. {25:5} I command a snake beneath the earth and a fish in the sea. I command the birds in the heavens and the desert donkey in the wilderness. Everything from horizon to horizon is Mine. {25:6} As I am the one who performs wondrous works and miracles before Me, none can escape My authority on earth or in heaven. None can question Me, asking, "Where do you go? What do you do?" {25:7} I command the chief angels and hosts. All creations whose names are called are Mine. Beasts in the wilderness, birds in the heavens, and livestock are My possessions. {25:8} From the wind of Azeb to the drought in Mesir, later in the era of fulfillment, the Red Sea will perish when it is heard. Arising from the Lord, who will come to her, feared and renowned. {25:9} He rules over the dead and the living there. She will perish when heard with Saba, Noba, Hindekie, the borders of Ethiopia, and all their regions. {25:10} He watches over all in supreme authority and innocence. His authority surpasses all others, and He maintains congregations within His dominion. {25:11} His authority is greater than all others. His kingdom surpasses all kingdoms. His authority rules the entire world. He is capable of all things, and nothing fails Him. {25:12} He rules over all clouds in heaven. He grows grass for livestock on earth and gives fruit to the buds. {25:13} He provides for all according to His love, feeding all He created with various fruits and foods. He feeds ants and locusts beneath the earth, livestock on land, and beasts. To those who pray, He grants their requests, and He does not ignore the pleas of orphans or widows. {25:14} As the rebellion of evil people is like a swirling wind and the counsel of wrongdoers is like misty urine, He will accept the pleas of those who beg towards Him at all times and are righteous. {25:15} Since their bodies are like flying birds, and their appearance, like silver and gold, is perishable in this world, examination benefits those who forget the Lord's law, but not their gold. Moths will eat their clothes. {25:16} Weevils will completely consume the wheat and barley's fatness. All will pass like a day gone by yesterday, like a word spoken that does not return. Sinners' wealth is like this, and their 'beautiful lifestyle' is like a passing shadow. Sinners' wealth before the Lord is like clothes made of lies. {25:17} But if righteous people are honored, the Lord will not ignore them, for they have honored Him while being kind to the poor. They hear the cries of sufferers and orphans. The Lord will not ignore them, for they honor Him by clothing the naked with the clothes He gave them to give to the refugee and sufferer. {25:18} They do not favor the judgment of the faithful, and they do not let a hireling's wages stay overnight. Since the Lord's things are true and honored like a double-edged sword, they will not act unjustly in their seasons or in their balanced measurements.

{26:1} Poor people will reflect on their hardships, but if the wealthy do not help them, they will be like dry wood without greenery. A root without moisture will not be fertile, and a leaf without a root will not be productive. {26:2} As a leaf serves as an ornament for a flower and its fruit, if the leaf is not fertile, it will not bear fruit. Just as the fulfillment of humanity is religion, a person without religion has no virtue. {26:3} If one is firm in religion, they will work virtuously.

{27:1} He brought the entire world from non-existence into existence, preparing the hills and mountains, and established the Earth upon the waters. To prevent the sea from overflowing, He defined its boundaries with sand. With His first word, God said, "Let there be light." {27:2} Light was created when the world was covered in darkness. God created everything, prepared the world, and established it with due order and straight paths. He said, "Let the evening be dark." {27:3} Again, God said, "Let there be light," and it dawned, bringing light. He elevated the upper waters towards the heavens. {27:4} He stretched it forth like a tent, firming it up with the wind, and placed the lower waters within a pit. {27:5} He confined the sea within sand

and established its limits to prevent flooding. He filled it with animals and beasts, including the great Leviathan and Behemoth, and countless other creatures, both visible and invisible. {27:6} On the third day, God created plants on Earth—every root, tree, and fruit-bearing plant according to their kinds, as well as beautiful, pleasant trees for them to see and eat from. {27:7} He created beautiful trees that were both visually pleasing and good to eat, along with grass and all seed-bearing plants for food for birds, livestock, and beasts. {27:8} It became evening and morning. On the fourth day, God said, "Let there be light in the heavens called the cosmos." He created the moon, the sun, and the stars, placing them in the cosmos to shine on the world and separate day from night. {27:9} Thus, the moon, sun, and stars alternated between night and day. {27:10} On the fifth day, God created all animals and beasts that live in the water and all birds that fly in the sky, both visible and invisible. {27:11} On the sixth day, He created livestock, beasts, and other creatures. After creating and preparing everything, He created Adam in His own image and likeness. {27:12} He gave Adam dominion over all the animals and beasts He had created, including all fish, Leviathan, and Behemoth in the sea. {27:13} He gave him all the cattle, sheep, and animals of the world, both visible and invisible. {27:14} He placed Adam in the garden He had created in His own image and likeness, to eat, cultivate the plants, and praise God there. {27:15} To prevent him from breaking His command, God said, "On the day you eat from this fig tree, you will surely die." {27:16} He commanded him not to eat from the fig tree that brings death, which draws attention to evil and good, bringing death. {27:17} Our mother Eve was deceived by a misleading snake and ate from that fig tree, giving it to our father Adam. {27:18} Adam, having eaten from the fig tree, brought death upon his children and himself. {27:19} Since he broke God's command and ate from the fig tree, which God had commanded not to eat from, God was angry with our father Adam and expelled him from the garden. He gave him the earth, which grew thistles and thorns, cursed because of him, so that he would eat from it with toil and labor. {27:20} When God sent him forth to this land, Adam returned in complete sadness. Having toiled and labored to cultivate the earth, he began to eat with weariness and struggles.

{28:1} After his children multiplied, some praised and honored God without breaking His commands. {28:2} There were prophets among them who spoke of past and future events, and from his children, there were also sinners who lied and wronged others. Adam's firstborn son, Cain, became evil and killed his brother Abel. {28:3} God judged Cain because he killed his brother Abel, and God was angry with the earth because it drank his blood. {28:4} God asked Cain, "Where is your brother Abel?" In arrogance, Cain responded, "Am I my brother's keeper?" {28:5} Abel was a righteous man, but Cain became a sinner by killing his kind brother Abel. {28:6} Another righteous child, Seth, was born. Adam had sixty children, from whom came both righteous and evil individuals. {28:7} Among them were righteous individuals, prophets, traitors, and sinners. {28:8} There were blessed righteous people who followed their father Adam's example and teachings, beginning with Adam up until Noah, who was a righteous man who kept God's law. {28:9} Noah instructed his children to guard God's law and to pass it down to their descendants, as their father Noah had taught them, ensuring they kept God's law. {28:10} They lived by teaching their children, who were born after them. {28:11} But Satan influenced their ancestors, leading them to worship idols, even though these idols were destined for destruction. People followed Satan's commands, the teacher of sin, doing everything he instructed. {28:12} They worshipped idols as instructed until a righteous man, Abraham, fulfilled God's covenant. {28:13} He lived according to the law, separate from his relatives, and God swore an oath with him, manifesting through wind and fire. {28:14} God swore to give Abraham a land of inheritance and to bless his descendants for eternity. {28:15} He made the same oath to Isaac, to give him Abraham's inheritance, and to Jacob, to give him Isaac's inheritance. God swore to Jacob as He did to Isaac. {28:16} He separated the descendants of Jacob, who became the twelve tribes of Israel, making them priests and kings, and blessed them, saying, "Multiply and be numerous." {28:17} He gave them their father's inheritance. Despite feeding and loving them, they continually saddened God. {28:18} When He punished them, they sought Him in worship, repented from sin, and turned to God, who forgave them because of their ancestors' works, not because of their own. {28:19} Out of kindness for all His creations, He forgave them and multiplied their food supply, providing for the young crows and beasts that begged Him. When they cried out, He saved the children of Israel from their enemies who had long oppressed them. {28:20} But they returned to sin, saddening Him again, prompting Him to raise up enemy nations around them to destroy, kill, and capture them. {28:21} When they faced tribulation, they cried out to Him in mourning and sadness. Sometimes, He sent help through the hands of prophets. {28:22} Other times, He saved them through the hands of princes. Yet, whenever they saddened God, their enemies taxed and captured them. {28:23} David arose and saved them from the Philistines. But again, they saddened God, and He raised up peoples who oppressed them. {28:24} He saved them through Jephthah, but again they forgot God and saddened Him, leading to more oppression. {28:25} They cried out to Him again, and He saved them through Gideon, but they continued to sadden Him with their actions. {28:26} He raised up more peoples against them, leading them to cry out in repentance, and He saved them through Samson, giving them temporary rest from tribulation. However, they returned to their former sins. {28:27} Again, He raised up peoples who oppressed them, and they cried out for help. He saved them through Barak and Deborah. {28:28} They lived righteously for a short time but soon forgot God and returned to their former sins, saddening Him again. {28:29} More peoples were raised against them, and they cried out for help. He saved them through Judith, but they continued in their sins, leading to more oppression. {28:30} They cried out again, and He ignored their cries and mourning because they had continually saddened Him and broken His law. {28:31} They were captured and taken with their priests to Babylon. {28:32} Even in captivity, Israel's children continued to sadden God with their sins and idol worship. {28:33} God was angry, intending to destroy them in their sin. Haman introduced ten thousand gold pieces into the king's treasury. When this was known, anger lodged in King Ahasuerus' mind, prompting him to decree the destruction of Israel's children in the Persian empire, from India to Ethiopia. {28:34} Following the king's command, Haman delivered a letter sealed with the king's authority, instructing the destruction of Israel's children on a set day, along with the confiscation of their wealth. {28:35} When Israel's children heard this, they cried out to God, informing Mordecai, who then informed Esther. {28:36} Esther said, "Fast, beg, and all Israel's kindred, cry out to God wherever you are." {28:37} Mordecai wore sackcloth and sprinkled dust on himself. Israel's children fasted, begged, and repented in their land. {28:38} Esther was deeply saddened. As a queen, she wore sackcloth, sprinkled dust, and shaved her head, refraining from the perfumes used by Persian queens, and in deep prayer, she cried out to her fathers' Creator, God. {28:39} Because of this, she gained favor with the Persian King Ahasuerus.

{29:1} During that time, the Egyptians forced the Israelites to make bricks under harsh conditions. They made their labor difficult by demanding bricks without providing straw, and they imposed harsh heat on them. {29:2} They appointed taskmasters over them to oppress them with forced labor, and the Israelites cried out to the Lord to save them from their harsh bondage of making bricks. {29:3} So the Lord sent Moses and Aaron to help them. He intervened to rescue His people from the oppressive rule of Pharaoh in Egypt. Despite Pharaoh's arrogance and refusal to let Israel go, God's intervention ensured their deliverance from slavery. {29:4} For the Lord does not tolerate arrogance. He brought judgment upon Pharaoh and his army by drowning them in the Red Sea because of their pride and cruelty. {29:5} Similarly, God will bring destruction upon those rulers and kingdoms that do not uphold His justice and honor His name. He expects leaders to govern justly, rewarding those who serve faithfully and treating all people with dignity and fairness. {29:6} The Lord, who rules over all, declares: "If rulers align their kingdoms with My righteousness, I will establish and uphold their reign." {29:7} "Perform righteous deeds, and I will ensure justice and prosperity for you. Obey My laws, and I will protect and sustain your nation." {29:8} "Love Me, and I will bless your prosperity. Draw near to Me, and I will heal and restore you." {29:9} "Believe in Me, and I will deliver you from tribulation. Trust in My guidance, and I will save you from all distress." {29:10} "Do not stray from My path, for I am the Lord who rules over all—there is no escaping My authority in heaven or on earth." {29:11} "I am just and merciful, forgiving those who repent and call upon My name. I provide for all creatures, from birds to beasts, showing My compassion to all." {29:12} "I protect and deliver those who follow My laws and fulfill My purposes. I honor and bless them, ensuring their well-being in this life and the next." {29:13} "Those who serve Me faithfully will be exalted and honored, like the prophet Samuel, whom I chose from his youth to serve in My presence." {29:14} "Samuel served Me faithfully in the sanctuary, and I loved him for his devotion and mercy." {29:15} "I appointed him to anoint kings and guide My people according to My will. Samuel was faithful, and I bestowed upon him the authority to anoint leaders among the Israelites." {29:16} "When Saul was king, I instructed Samuel to anoint David, a man after My own heart, to succeed him."

{30:1} "I rejected Saul and his lineage because they disobeyed My word and disregarded My commandments." {30:2} "Those who reject My laws and commands will not receive My blessings or favor." {30:3} "Those who persist in disobedience and rebellion against Me will lose their position and inheritance forever." {30:4} "I will not honor those who dishonor Me, nor will I elevate those who despise My laws and neglect My favor." {30:5} "Those who fail to acknowledge My goodness and forgiveness will not receive My mercy or favor." {30:6} "Those who refuse to acknowledge Me as their rightful ruler and reject My laws will not receive My blessing or honor." {30:7} "I will withdraw My favor from those who have abandoned My ways and dishonored Me repeatedly." {30:8} "I will separate those who dishonor Me from those who honor Me and keep My laws faithfully." {30:9} "I will bless those who love Me and honor those who honor Me." {30:10} "For I am the Lord, ruler of all creation. None can escape My authority, for I am the one who gives life and determines destiny." {30:11} "I judge and restore, I destroy and forgive. I am the one who raises up and humbles." {30:12} "I forgive those who repent and seek Me earnestly. I provide for all creatures and show compassion to all who call upon Me."

{31:1} "Kings reign by My authority, and rulers rule by My command. The suffering are under My oversight, and the powerful are under My decree." {31:2} "I granted David My favor and Solomon My wisdom. I extended Hezekiah's reign and diminished Goliath's era." {31:3} "I empowered Samson and later humbled him. I protected David from Goliath's hand and Saul's persecution." {31:4} "I love David and all who uphold My law. Those who honor Me will receive victory and power over their enemies." {31:5} "I love those who serve Me faithfully and honor My commandments. They shall inherit the promised land and dwell securely in My presence." {31:6} "I will bless those who love Me and keep My commandments. I will grant them a land of abundance and peace, fulfilling My covenant with their ancestors."

{32:1} "Listen, you kings and rulers, and heed My word. Obey My commands and uphold My law, lest you repeat the mistakes of the Israelites, who angered Me with their idolatry." {32:2} "I have nourished and cared for you since your birth, providing abundance and sustenance beyond what you have earned or planted." {32:3} "Listen to My word and do not provoke Me as the Israelites did with their idolatry. Remember how I nurtured you with milk and honey, adorned you with ornaments, and showered you with love." {32:4} "Those who refuse to acknowledge My goodness and grace, rejecting My rule and compassion, will suffer the consequences of their arrogance."

{33:1} David once said, "The children of Israel were sustained with manna from heaven, but they saddened the Lord by worshiping idols instead of Him. Listen now to my words, lest you repeat their mistake and grieve the Lord, who provided sweet manna in the wilderness. He did all this so that they might worship Him in truth and righteousness." {33:2} The Lord, who rules over all, declared, "But they did not worship Me; instead, they turned away from Me and worshiped idols that were not part of My law. They provoked Me to anger and lived stubbornly according to their own desires." {33:3} "Therefore, I will bring upon them the consequences of their sins. Because they neglected My worship and refused to follow My counsel and commands, I will judge them according to their deeds, sending them to Gehenna in the final judgment." {33:4} "Those who disregard My law and provoke My anger will see their influence diminish in this world." {33:5} "Remember, even kings are mortal; they will die and return to dust, no different from any other human." {33:6} "Yet today, they boast and pride themselves as if they will never die." {33:7} "But tomorrow, those who are healthy and strong will also face death." {33:8} "However, if you obey My commands and follow My word, I will bless you with a land of honor, ruled by kings who uphold My covenant. Their dwellings will be filled with light, their crowns adorned with beauty, and their thrones adorned with silver and gold." {33:9} "They will live in prosperity in the land that I have prepared for those who do good deeds." {33:10} "But for those who commit sin and reject My law," says the Lord who rules over all... {33:11} "They will not enter the land where honorable kings dwell."

{34:1} "The kingdom of Medes will perish, but the Roman Empire will establish itself over the Macedonian kingdom, and the kingdom of Nineveh will endure over the Persian kingdom." {34:2} "Ethiopia will prevail over Alexandria as nations rise and fall. Moab will dominate over the Amalekites." {34:3} "Brother will rise against brother, and the Lord will bring vengeance and destruction as He has foretold." {34:4} "Kingdom will rise against kingdom, and nation against nation," says the Lord. {34:5} "There will be arguments and disputes, famine, plague, earthquakes, and drought. Love will fade from the world, and the Lord's chastisement will descend upon it." {34:6} "The day will come suddenly when the Lord will appear, causing fear like lightning flashing from east to west." {34:7} "On that day of judgment, each person will receive according to their deeds—weakness for those who sinned and firmness for those who remained faithful." {34:8} "At that time, the Lord will condemn the unrepentant to Gehenna forever—those who did not live according to His law and persisted in sin." {34:9} "People from distant lands—Nubia, Ethiopia, Egypt, and all who live there—will acknowledge that I, the Lord, rule over heaven and earth. I give life, love, honor, and determine life and death." {34:10} "I am the one who brings forth the sun and guides it to its setting. I bring both evil and good." {34:11} "I bring forth nations unknown to you, who will devour your wealth and plunder your possessions—your sheep, cattle, and all that you have worked for." {34:12} "They will capture your children and oppress them before your very eyes. You will be powerless to save them because the Spirit of the Lord will not support you, due to your failure to fear His commandments." {34:13} "He will destroy your luxuries and assignments." {34:14} "But those in whom the Spirit of the Lord dwells will understand everything. Just as Nebuchadnezzar recognized in Daniel, saying, 'I see the Spirit of the Lord dwelling in you.'" {34:15} "Those in whom the Spirit of the Lord dwells will comprehend all things—what is hidden and what is revealed. Nothing will be concealed from those in whom the Spirit of the Lord dwells." {34:16} "For we are all mortal, and our hidden sins will be revealed." {34:17} "As silver and gold are tested in fire, so too will sinners be tested on the Day of Judgment, for failing to obey the commandments of the Lord." {34:18} "On that day, the deeds of all people and the works of the children of Israel will be examined."

{35:1} "The Lord is displeased because you do not judge with righteous judgment, especially for the orphan whose parents have died. Woe to you, Israel's leaders!" {35:2} "Woe to those who frequent the taverns in the morning and evening, getting drunk and showing partiality in judgment. They do not uphold justice for the widow or the orphan, living in sin and corruption." {35:3} "The Lord said to Israel's leaders, 'If you do not live according to My commandments, uphold My law, and love what I love, woe to you.'" {35:4} "The Lord will bring destruction, chastisement, and tribulation upon you. You will perish like grain eaten by weevils and moths. Your footsteps and your homeland will be lost." {35:5} "Your land will become a wilderness, and those who once admired it will clap their hands in astonishment, saying, 'Wasn't this land once full of abundance and loved by all who lived here? JAH has made it desolate because of the sins of its inhabitants.'" {35:6} "They will say, 'Its people became proud and exalted themselves, refusing to acknowledge the Lord's authority. They will be made wretched on earth, and their land will become a desert because of the arrogance of its sinful inhabitants—thorns and thistles will grow there.'" {35:7} "Weeds and thorns will take over, turning it into a wilderness and a desert where wild animals will roam." {35:8} "For the Lord's judgment has come upon it, and it shall drink from the cup of His judgment because its people were arrogant in sin, turning the land into a fearful place for those who approach it."

{36:1} Macedonians, do not boast, for the Lord is ready to bring you down. Amalekites, do not exalt yourselves in your reasoning. {36:2} For you will be lifted up to the heavens, only to descend into Gehenna. {36:3} Remember when Israel entered the lands of Egypt, Moab, and Macedonia. The Lord warned them not to boast, for their success was not due to their own power, but because of God's providence. {36:4} "You, descendants of Ishmael, who are slaves by birth, why do you exalt yourselves with what is not rightfully yours? Do you think that God will not judge you for your actions? The day of judgment will come upon you, and you will be held accountable." {36:5} The Lord Almighty said, "At that time, you will receive the consequences of your deeds. Why do you persist in your arrogance and pride?" {36:6} "Just as you have treated others with disdain, so you will be treated. You have indulged in sin and neglected the place where you were sent." {36:7} "But if you perform good deeds and love what I love, I will hear your prayers." {36:8} "If you uphold my covenant, I will uphold yours. I will defend you against your enemies, bless your children and descendants, and multiply your flocks." {36:9} "If you obey my commandments and do what I love, I will bless everything you touch." {36:10} "But if you reject my covenant, refuse to follow my law and commandments, you will face the tribulations foretold. You will not escape my anger." {36:11} "Because you did not love what I love, you will suffer when I bring judgment upon the living and the dead." {36:12} "All your wealth and power were given to you so that you could do what is right and good, honor and not abuse, elevate and not degrade. But you neglected my worship and praise, though I granted you authority and honor among those beneath you." {36:13} "If you had followed my covenant and obeyed my commands, I would have loved you and given you peace and prosperity in my kingdom." {36:14} "For I have said, if you endure with me, I will love you and honor you. You will find joy in the place where prayers are offered, and you will be loved and chosen like a precious offering." {36:15} "Do not neglect to do good deeds that lead from death to life." {36:16} "Those who perform good deeds will be kept safe by the Lord in all their endeavors, just as Job was protected from tribulations." {36:17} "The Lord will protect those who do good deeds and serve Him faithfully, as He did with Abraham, whom He saved from kings, and with Moses, whom He delivered from the hands of Pharaoh." {36:18} "Even when Abraham was tested with idols, he remained faithful, believing in the Lord from his youth." {36:19} "Abraham was known as a friend of God, and even when tested, he continued to worship the Lord." {36:20} "He loved the Lord completely, worshiping Him until his death, never departing from His law, and teaching his children to do the same." {36:21} "The descendants of Abraham, Isaac, and Jacob remained faithful to the Lord's law, as the angels testified, saying, 'Israel's children did not depart from the Lord's law.'" {36:22} "The Lord was praised alongside them, saying, 'Abraham is my friend, Isaac is my confidant, and Jacob is my beloved.'" {36:23} "Yet despite the Lord's love for Israel's children, they continually grieved Him with their sins, even though He had sustained them and fed them with manna in the wilderness." {36:24} "Their clothes did not wear out, and they were fed with manna like angel's food, yet they turned away from Him and sinned from ancient times, without hope of salvation." {36:25} "They became like a warped bow, unlike their forefathers Abraham, Isaac, and Jacob, who served the Lord faithfully." {36:26} "They angered the Lord with their idol worship on the mountains and hills, sacrificing in caves and under trees." {36:27} "They slaughtered animals and offered sacrifices, rejoicing in their deeds, singing and playing with demons." {36:28} "Demons delighted in their games and songs, as they indulged in drunkenness, adultery, robbery, and greed—all of which the Lord detests." {36:29} "They worshiped idols like the Canaanites, Midianites, Baal, Aphlon, Dagon, Seraphim, and the idols of all the nations around them." {36:30} "All the tribes of Israel followed their example, saying, 'We will worship the Lord,' yet they did not keep His commandments and laws, as Moses taught them in the Law." {36:31} "They turned to foreign idols, forsaking the Lord who had fed them with honey and bread from heaven, and sent them to cultivate the land." {36:32} "Moses warned them, 'Do not worship false gods, for they are not your Creator.'" {36:33} "Moses commanded them, 'Do not worship idols, for the Lord is your Creator and Provider.'" {36:34} "Yet they continued to grieve the Lord, causing Him sorrow even in their moments of happiness." {36:35} "When they cried out to Him in distress, He saved them from their troubles, and they returned to Him, only to turn away again." {36:36} "And when they cried out to Him in their distress, He forgave them. It was not because of their own righteousness, but because of the faithfulness of their forefathers—Noah, Isaac, and Abraham—who served the Lord faithfully from ancient times." {36:37} "And again, they cried out to Him, and He forgave them." {36:38} "For He loved those who kept His law and multiplied them like the stars of heaven and the sands of the sea." {36:39} "But those who sinned separated themselves from the children of Israel and went down to Gehenna when the dead rise." {36:40} "As the Lord said to Abraham, 'Look up at the heavens and count the stars, so shall your descendants be.' Those who do what is right and good will shine like the stars in the heavens, and they are the children of Israel." {36:41} "And as He said, 'Look to the edge of the river and the sea and count the sand. So shall your sinful descendants be, who will descend to Gehenna when the dead rise.'" {36:42} "Abraham believed in the Lord, and it was credited to him as righteousness. He found favor in the eyes of God in this world, and after his wife Sarah bore him a son named Isaac." {36:43} "For he believed that those who do good deeds will rise and enter the kingdom of heaven, living forever, and will find a kingdom in heaven." {36:44} "But he also believed that those who commit sin will go to Gehenna, where they will live forever when the dead rise. But the righteous, who do good deeds, will reign with Him forever." {36:45} "For he believed that those who commit sin will be judged forever, truly and without falsehood. Those who do what is right will find the kingdom of life in heaven." Let glory and praise be to the Lord, true and without falsehood. Thus ends the first book of the Maccabees, filled and fulfilled.

2 Meqabyan

The Book of Meqabyan, often referred to as Ethiopic Maccabees or 2 Meqabyan, is a unique and significant text within the Ethiopian Orthodox Tewahedo Church's canon. Unlike the Greek Maccabean books found in the Septuagint, the Meqabyan texts, including 2 Meqabyan, have no direct counterparts in the Jewish or other Christian canons. This distinction underscores their unique theological and historical importance within Ethiopian Christianity. The narrative of 2 Meqabyan does not follow the Hasmonean revolt against Seleucid rule, as the better-known books of Maccabees do. Instead, it presents a series of moral and religious teachings through the story of three brothers, Judah, Meqabis, and Binyamin, who rise up against the wicked King Akrandis. Their struggle is framed within a broader context of divine justice and faithfulness, emphasizing the themes of piety, endurance, and divine retribution against idolatry and apostasy. The text serves as a didactic tool, illustrating the virtues of steadfast faith and the perils of abandoning God's commandments. The literary style of 2 Meqabyan is distinct, combining historical narrative with moral exhortation, reflective of its function within the liturgical and educational traditions of the Ethiopian Church. The preservation of 2 Meqabyan in Ge'ez, the Ethiopian Church's liturgical language, underscores its importance in Ethiopian spirituality and Christian apocryphal literature. Its unique content and canonical status in Ethiopian Christianity provide valuable insights into early Christian thought across different traditions.

{1:1} In this book, it is recounted how Maccabees found Israel in Mesopotamia, and they destroyed them in that region, starting from Jabboq up to Jerusalem's outskirts. {1:2} Because the Syrians, Edomites, and Amalekites had allied with the Moabite Maccabees to destroy the land of Jerusalem. They encamped from Samaria to the outskirts of Jerusalem and massacred many in battle, sparing only a few who managed to flee. {1:3} When the children of Israel sinned, the wrath of Maccabees from Moab was stirred against them, and he struck them down with the sword. {1:4} Because of this, the enemies of the Lord boasted against his people, and they swore to commit great atrocities. {1:5} The Edomites and Syrians encamped together and, claiming to act in the name of God, they sought revenge and laid waste to the land of praise and honor. {1:6} Maccabees' domain extended from Rimmon to Moab, and he arose with great power from his land. They also made alliances with those who joined them in their evil deeds. {1:7} They camped in the Gilead region from Mesopotamia to Syria, with the Amalekites and Edomites joining them in their wickedness. They were given silver, gold, chariots, and horses to strengthen their alliance in their evil deeds. {1:8} They gathered together and attacked the fortresses, shedding blood like water among those who lived there. {1:9} They made Jerusalem a place of refuge, but within its walls they committed every sin that the Lord abhors, defiling the land that was once praised and honored. {1:10} They even made the flesh of their friends and the bodies of their servants food for the beasts of the wilderness and the birds of the heavens. {1:11} They plundered the homes of orphans and widows without fear of the Lord, committing atrocities that Satan himself might teach, until the Lord, who examines hearts and minds, was deeply angered. {1:12} After their return to their own land, they continued to do evil deeds against the people of the Lord, taking the plunder they had seized from a land that was once honored. {1:13} When they returned to their homes, they celebrated with feasts, singing and clapping in mockery.

{2:1} Then the prophet called Re'ay spoke these words: "Today, I am reminded of the time when the people of Israel glorified the Lord, who will now bring judgment and destruction upon you for the punishment you did not expect. {2:2} Will you say, 'My horses are swift, so I will escape'? {2:3} But those who pursue you are swifter than eagles; you will not escape the judgment and destruction that will come upon you from the Lord. {2:4} Will you boast, 'I am clothed in armor, and my weapons are powerful'? But it is not by weapons that the Lord, the God of Israel, will bring judgment and destruction upon you," says the Lord. {2:5} "You have aroused my anger, and I will bring sickness upon you that will weaken your heart. You will lack helpers, and you will not escape my authority until your name and invocation are destroyed from this world. {2:6} Because you have been arrogant and lifted yourself up against my people, I will swiftly bring upon you calamity, like a blink of an eye. You will know that I am your tormentor, and you will be like grass before the fire that consumes it, like dust scattered by the wind. {2:7} Because you have provoked my anger and have not acknowledged me, I will ignore your relatives, and I will not spare those who sought refuge in your fortress. {2:8} Now, turn away from all your sins that you have committed. If you repent sincerely before the Lord in mourning and sorrow, and if you seek him with a pure heart, the Lord will forgive you for all the sins you have committed against him." {2:9} At that time, Maccabees dressed in mourning clothes and wept before the Lord because of his sins, for he had angered the Lord. {2:10} His eyes were open, and his ears were attentive; he did not hold back. {2:11} He cast off his clothes, put on sackcloth, sprinkled dust on his head, and cried and wept before the Lord his God because of the sins he had committed.

{3:1} A prophet came from Rimmon and spoke to Maccabees, saying that the Moabite region near Syria was advancing. {3:2} Maccabees dug a pit and sank into it up to his neck, weeping bitterly as he repented for his sins before the Lord. {3:3} Then the Lord instructed the prophet to return to Maccabees, the Moabite leader, and deliver this message: "The Lord says to you, 'I, the Lord who is your Creator, sent you according to my will to bring destruction upon my land. Do not boast that you alone destroyed the honored land of Jerusalem by your own power and might; it was not you who accomplished this. {3:4} It was because of their greed, deceit, and wickedness that they provoked my anger. {3:5} I allowed them to fall into your hands, but now I have forgiven you because of your offspring, whom you have fathered. It was not because of your strength or authority that you surrounded Jerusalem. {3:6} Those who repent are not doubters; do not hesitate to repent. Repent sincerely and completely." {3:7} Blessed are those who repent sincerely and do not return to thirst for sin after turning to repentance, because of the sins they have committed. {3:8} Blessed are those who return to the Lord in mourning and sorrow, bowing before him with many pleas. Blessed are those who repent sincerely, for the Lord has said to them, "You are my chosen ones who have turned to repentance after leading others astray." {3:9} The Lord said to the repentant Maccabees, "I forgive your sin because you feared me and repented. I am the Lord your Creator, who punishes children for their fathers' sins up to seven generations, but I show mercy to those who love me and keep my law for ten thousand generations." {3:10} "Now I will establish my covenant with you and your offspring, whom you have fathered. The Lord, who rules over all and who honored Israel, accepts the repentance you have made for your sins." {3:11} Maccabees emerged from the pit and bowed before the prophet, solemnly swearing, "I have sinned against the Lord. Do to me as you will, but do not separate me from you. We have no law, and we did not live by his commandments. You know that our ancestors taught us and that we worshiped idols." {3:12} "I am a sinner who has lived in sin, proud and arrogant, provoking the Lord's commandments. Until now, I have not listened to the words of the Lord's servants, the prophets, nor have I lived according to his law and commandments." {3:13} The prophet reassured him, saying, "Because there has been no one like you from your ancestors who has turned from sin to trust in him, I know that today the prophet has received your repentance." {3:14} "Now, abandon your idol worship and turn to knowing the Lord, that you may truly repent." Maccabees fell at the prophet's feet, who lifted him up and instructed him in all the righteous deeds due to him. {3:15} Maccabees returned to his house and obeyed what the Lord commanded him to do. {3:16} He turned his heart to worship the Lord, removing idols and destroying sorcery, idol worshipers, pessimists, and magicians from his house. {3:17} Morning and evening, he followed the practices of his ancestors, examining the children of Israel captured from Jerusalem according to all the laws, regulations, and instructions of the Lord. {3:18} He appointed knowledgeable individuals from among the captured children for his household. {3:19} Furthermore, he appointed knowledgeable children, both young and old, to teach them the law of the Lord that the children of Israel practiced. He learned about the orders and laws and the Nine Laws of the Moabites. {3:20} He destroyed their places of worship, their idols, their sorcery, their sacrifices, and their grapes, which were sacrificed to idols in the morning and evening, with kid goats and fattened sheep flocks. {3:21} He destroyed the idols they worshipped, begged, and believed in, and he sacrificed a sacrificial offering in the afternoon and at noon. {3:22} He did everything they commanded him concerning the idols, as if he could save himself in all that they commanded him. {3:23} But Maccabees gave up this practice. {3:24} After he heard the prophet's instructions, whom they call the prophet, he performed his duties in repentance. As the children of Israel would sorrow at once, and when they were chastised in the affliction, they knew and cried out to the Lord. All his families worked better than the children of Israel in that season. {3:25} When he heard that he had been seized and mistreated by the hand of the people who imposed hardships on them, and that they cried out to him, he remembered his ancestors' vows, and at that time, he forgave them because of Isaac, Abraham, and Jacob.

{4:1} In the time of Judas Maccabeus, there was a day when the Lord delivered them from their enemies. {4:2} In the time of Gideon, there was a day when the Lord saved them. {4:3} In the times of Samson, Deborah, Barak, and Jael, there were days when the Lord saved them. He raised up leaders for them to deliver them from the hands of their enemies who oppressed them. {4:4} The Lord's love for them ensured their deliverance from those who inflicted suffering upon them. {4:5} They rejoiced in all the work that the Lord had done for them—they prospered in their land, their descendants multiplied, their flocks thrived in the wilderness, and their livestock flourished. {4:6} The Lord blessed their crops and livestock, showing them mercy, ensuring that their livestock did not decrease, for they were a kind and beloved people. {4:7} But when they acted wickedly in their deeds, the Lord allowed them to fall into the hands of their enemies. {4:8} Yet when they were destroyed, they turned to the Lord in worship, repented of their sins, and sought the Lord earnestly. {4:9} When they returned with full understanding, the Lord forgave their sins, not holding their past sins against them, knowing they were only human, subject to worldly misunderstandings and plagued by demons. {4:10} Upon hearing the commandment the Lord gave concerning the worship at the Temple, Judas Maccabeus died in repentance. {4:11} Upon hearing this, he did not despise doing good works; he did not despise all the good works that the children of Israel did when the Lord forgave them. Even after they strayed from his law, they wept and cried out when the Lord disciplined them, and again he forgave them, and they kept his law. {4:12} Likewise, Judas Maccabeus straightened his ways, kept the Lord's law, and steadfastly obeyed the commands of the God of Israel. {4:13} At that time, having heard all the accomplishments of the children of Israel, he gloried in keeping the Lord's law as they did. {4:14} He urged his relatives and children to remain steadfast in keeping the Lord's commandments and all his laws. {4:15} He opposed the practices that the children of Israel opposed and followed the laws that the children of Israel kept. Even when dealing with other Moabites, he refused to eat the foods that the children of Israel prohibited. {4:16} He paid tithes, giving the firstborn and all that he owned from his herds, flocks, and donkeys. Upon returning to Jerusalem, he sacrificed as the children of Israel did. {4:17} He offered sin and vow offerings, peace offerings, and the daily sacrifices. {4:18} He offered the firstfruits, poured out wine offerings, and gave these to the priests he appointed. He did everything as the children of Israel did, sweetening the Lord's favor. {4:19} He constructed a lampstand, a basin, an altar of incense, and a tent, as well as the rings for the curtains and the oil for the lamps in the Most Holy Place, according to the pattern the children of Israel followed in the service of the Lord. {4:20} Just as they did good work when they were steadfast in the Lord's commandments and laws, and when the Lord did not abandon them or hand them over to their enemies, Judas Maccabeus also did good work like them. {4:21} He prayed to the Lord, the God of Israel, every time he wanted to be his teacher and not to separate him from the children of Israel whom he chose and who did his will. {4:22} He prayed to the Lord to give him children in Zion and a house in Jerusalem, to give them a spiritual lineage in Zion and a heavenly sanctuary in Jerusalem, and to save him from the destruction prophesied by the prophets, accepting his repentance in all the mourning and sadness he expressed before the Lord as he repented. {4:23} So that the Lord would not destroy his children in this world, but would keep him in his going out and coming in. {4:24} The Moabite peoples under Judas Maccabeus's authority were pleased to believe, for he led them to live upright lives, and they checked his judgments and followed his commands, disregarding their own language and laws, understanding that Judas Maccabeus's actions were superior and just. {4:25} They came to hear Judas Maccabeus's acts of charity and his just judgments. {4:26} He was wealthy, owning daughters, male and female slaves, camels, donkeys, and five hundred horses with armor. He completely defeated the Amalekites, Edomites, and Syrians, but previously, when he worshiped idols, they overpowered him. {4:27} He prevailed only after he worshipped the Lord, and no one could defeat him when he went into battle. {4:28} When the idols tried to fight against him, they invoked their names and cursed him, but no one defeated him because he trusted in the Lord his God. {4:29} When he acted like this and defeated his enemies, he lived to rule over his people. {4:30} He avenged the wrongs inflicted by his enemies and judged justly for a child whose parents had died. {4:31} He cared for widows in their distress, providing them with food and comforting those who were hungry, clothing the naked with his garments. {4:32} He took joy in his deeds, giving generously from his wealth without begrudging it, giving tithes to the Temple. Judas Maccabeus died in peace, having lived in prosperity when he did these things.

{5:1} After Judas Maccabeus passed away, his young children grew up following the teachings of their father. They maintained order in their household, cared for their relatives, and were compassionate towards the poor, widows, and orphans. {5:2} They feared the Lord and generously gave alms to the needy as their father had instructed. They comforted the fatherless and widows in their distress, acting as their guardians, shielding them from harm and comforting them amidst their troubles. {5:3} They lived this way for five years. {5:4} Then King Antiochus of Persia invaded and devastated their land, capturing the children of Judas Maccabeus and destroying their villages. {5:5} He plundered their wealth, exploiting their sinful ways—adultery, insults, greed, and disregard for the Lord's commandments. Even those who did not follow the Lord's law but worshipped idols were taken away to distant lands. {5:6} They consumed forbidden foods and lived lawlessly, ignorant of the true commands written in the Law. {5:7} They did not know the Lord their Creator, who had nourished them from their mother's womb and sustained them. {5:8} They committed incest, adultery, robbery, and other sins without fear of judgment, for they had no regard for the law. {5:9} Their paths were dark and slippery, filled with sin and adultery. {5:10} But the children of Judas Maccabeus kept the commandments faithfully. They did not eat unclean food or engage in the wicked practices of the Gentiles, which were not written in the Law—sins committed by sinners, doubters, criminals, and those who betrayed their faith. {5:11} They upheld the commandments that the Lord loved. {5:12} Yet some among them worshipped an idol called Baal Peor, trusting it as they would trust the Lord, though it was deaf and dumb—a mere creation of human hands, crafted by a smith in silver and gold, lacking breath or understanding. {5:13} It could neither eat nor drink, neither kill nor save, plant nor uproot, harm enemies nor benefit friends, impoverish nor enrich. {5:14} It served only to mislead the lazy Keladians, providing no discipline or forgiveness.

{6:1} The enemy of the Lord, King Antiochus, appointed arrogant men as priests for his idols, who clothed themselves in falsehood. {6:2} They performed sacrifices and poured libations before the idols, pretending that they could eat and drink. {6:3} They received gifts of cattle and animals, sacrificing morning and evening, and consuming the defiled offerings. {6:4} They compelled others to participate in idolatrous sacrifices, not content until all complied. {6:5} When they noticed the handsome children of Judas Maccabeus worshipping the Lord, the idolatrous priests sought to deceive them into offering sacrifices and partaking in detestable rituals. However, these honorable children of Judas Maccabeus steadfastly refused. {6:6} They remained faithful to their father's commandments, dedicated to good works, and reverent towards the Lord. {6:7} This refusal angered the priests, who bound and mistreated them, accusing them before King Antiochus. {6:8} They informed the king that these children refused to sacrifice to idols or bow down before them. {6:9} The king was furious and ordered them brought before him. {6:10} He commanded them to sacrifice to his idols, but they boldly replied, "We will not obey your commands or sacrifice to your defiled idols." {6:11} Despite threats and intimidation, they remained steadfast in their belief in the Lord. {6.12} The king, in his rage, tortured them severely, yet they endured, strengthened by their faith in the Lord. {6:13} He subjected them to fire, but they faced death with courage, their bodies given over to the Lord. {6:14} After their death, they appeared in visions, drawing their swords against the king, who trembled in fear. {6:15} Addressing them, the king pleaded for guidance, willing to do whatever they advised to avoid further punishment. {6:16} They spoke to him, reminding him of the Lord's authority over all creation, warning him of the consequences of his arrogance and cruelty towards those who worshipped the Lord in righteousness. {6:17} They affirmed that only the Lord has ultimate authority over Earth, Heaven, and all therein, punishing and forgiving as He sees fit. {6:18} They denounced the king's idolatry and arrogance, declaring that the Lord would judge him for his sins. {6:19} They affirmed that there is no power or authority except from the Lord, who determines all outcomes. {6:20} They warned the king that no one can escape the Lord's judgment and authority over Earth and Heaven. {6:21} They condemned the king and his priests for their wickedness and assured them that they would all descend together into the eternal fire of Gehenna. {6:22} They identified Satan as the king's teacher in evil, condemning all who followed him into Gehenna. {6:23} They rebuked the king for his arrogance and idolatry, urging him to repent and acknowledge the true Lord who created him. {6:24} They prophesied that the Lord would bring judgment upon the king for his sins and arrogance, convicting him of all his wrongdoing.

{7:1} Woe to those who do not know the Lord, who created them, and to their idols that resemble them. They will regret their futile sorrows when they face the difficulties of Sheol. Woe also to those who disregard His Word and His Law. {7:2} There will be no escape from Sheol for them, nor for their priests who sacrifice to idols that have no breath or soul, unable to help or harm anyone. {7:3} Woe to those who sacrifice to these idols, products of human hands, dwelling places for deceiving minds like their own. They will be led into Gehenna by demons and the priests who serve them. {7:4} They do not understand that these idols will not benefit them; they are in error and delusion. {7:5} Even animals that God has designated for food are better off than those who persist in idolatry and sin. {7:6} For those who die and face eternal torment in Gehenna, animals would fare better. {7:7} After speaking these words, they withdrew from the king's presence. {7:8} But King Antiochus remained in fear and anxiety, troubled by what had transpired.

{8:1} He continued in his wicked and arrogant ways. {8:2} His heart was hardened like iron, and he extended his dominion over many lands and peoples. {8:3} He reveled in evil, laziness, and oppression. {8:4} He disregarded previous agreements and seized wealth wherever he could find it. {8:5} He was diligent in doing evil, following in the footsteps of his father Satan, who had taught him cunning and deceit. {8:6} He boasted of his own greatness, claiming his era was like that of the sun's. Yet he did not recognize the Lord who created him. {8:7} In his arrogance, he believed he could control even the sun. {8:8} He expanded his influence, stationed himself in the land of Zebulun, and gathered resources from various regions. {8:9} He exacted taxes and tribute from the people, showing no mercy in his dealings. {8:10} He extended his power over the seas and even boasted against the heavens. {8:11} He persisted in arrogance, evil, and bloodshed, causing much suffering and turmoil. {8:12} His path led him deeper into darkness, crime, and pride, shedding innocent blood and causing great distress. {8:13} All his actions were detestable to the Lord, resembling the teachings of Satan, causing suffering to orphans and the poor. {8:14} He defeated kings and oppressed nations with his authority. {8:15} He ruled over enemy leaders and taxed them heavily, showing favor only to those who pleased him. {8:16} Despite his destruction, he remained unrepentant, sparing no one from his tyranny from the Mediterranean to the Euphrates. {8:17} He worshipped idols, consumed unclean food, and committed all manner of injustice, lacking any sense of righteousness. {8:18} His fear of the Lord was nonexistent, and he lived in defiance of the God who created him. {8:19} He committed evil against his own people, provoking the Lord's wrath upon himself. {8:20} As the Lord had spoken, he would be repaid for his wickedness and arrogance. {8:21} Those who committed evil would face their judgment. {8:22} Those who followed the Lord's commands and did good would receive their reward. {8:23} Just as Joshua had defeated the five kings of Canaan in a single day and halted the sun in Gibeon to defeat the armies of the Amorites, the sun stood still in the heavens until the destruction of the armies of Evielon, Cheron, Saron, Jabezeth, and Horeb. {8:24} Similar tribulation awaited all who angered the Lord with their evil deeds.

{9:1} "O mortal who is not eternal, why do you boast? Today you are alive, but tomorrow you are mere ashes on the earth, destined to become food for worms in your grave. {9:2} Your teacher is Satan, who leads all sinners back to himself, having deceived our ancestor Adam. Sheol awaits you, along with all who follow your sinful ways. {9:3} In your pride, like Satan who refused to bow before Adam, you have also refused to bow before your Creator, the Lord. {9:4} Like your forefathers who did not acknowledge the Lord and worshiped idols, you too are headed for Gehenna. {9:5} Just as those who came before you were punished for their evil deeds in this world and descended to Gehenna... {9:6} so too will you descend there. {9:7} You will join them in Gehenna. {9:8} Because you have provoked His anger and neglected to worship the Lord who gave you authority over five kingdoms, do you think you can escape His judgment? {9:9} Do what is right, and God will bless your endeavors. He will protect you from your enemies and establish your kingdom. {9:10} You will prosper in all your undertakings, in your offspring, your livestock, and your wealth. Everything you set your hand to will succeed, under God's authority. {9:11} But if you refuse to obey the Lord's word and law, like the criminals before you who did not worship God as commanded, there will be no escape from His judgment, for His judgment is just. {9:12} Everything is laid bare before Him; nothing is hidden. {9:13} He removes kings and raises up others; He humbles and exalts. {9:14} He lifts the downtrodden and overthrows the powerful. {9:15} He releases the captive and raises the dead, showing His mercy. {9:16} After judging those who have done evil, He will take them to Gehenna, for they have angered Him. {9:17} Those who reject God's order and law will be destroyed, along with their descendants. {9:18} The work of the righteous is more difficult than that of sinners, who do not seek to live according to righteous counsel. {9:19} Just as Heaven is far from Earth, so too are the ways of the righteous far from the ways of the wicked. {9:20} The ways of sinners lead to robbery, sin, adultery, greed, and deceit. They revel in iniquity, steal, and shed innocent blood. {9:21} They hasten to shed blood and destruction, causing weeping among those who suffer from their actions. {9:22} All this is the work of sinners, a wide and prepared path leading to Gehenna, reserved for the unrepentant. {9:23} The path of the righteous, however, is narrow and leads to peace, innocence, humility, unity, love, prayer, and purity of body. They abstain from forbidden foods, from eating what is bloated or cut by a sword, and from all forms of adultery. {9:24} They avoid what is forbidden by the law, disgusting foods, and all other deeds that God does not love, for sinners indulge in all these things. {9:25} As for the righteous, they distance themselves from all that God does not love. {9:26} He loves them and protects them from all tribulation, as if guarded by trustworthy resources. {9:27} They keep His order and law and all that He loves, while sinners are ruled by Satan.

{10:1} Fear the Lord who has been angered by you and yet sustains you to this day, but you, nobles and kings, must not follow the path of Satan. {10:2} Live according to the laws and commands of the Lord who rules over all, and do not stray onto the path of Satan. {10:3} Remember when the children of Israel approached Amalek to inherit the lands of Kithewon, Kenaniewon, and Fierziewon. {10:4} Balaam, son of Sephor, whom you cursed, is cursed, and whom you blessed, is blessed. Do not walk the road of Satan, for he offers riches to entice you to curse and destroy. {10:5} Balaam practiced sorcery for profit, and Balak, son of Sephor, showed him where the Israelites camped. {10:6} Balaam desired to curse and harm the Israelites, but God turned his curse into a blessing. Do not follow the path of Satan. {10:7} "You are the chosen people of the Lord, a nation that He brought from heaven. Those who curse you will be cursed, and those who bless you will be blessed," He declared. {10:8} When Balaam blessed the Israelites, Balak was furious and sought to curse them. {10:9} But God blessed the Israelites, and Balak was disappointed. {10:10} Balaam refused to curse the Israelites, as the Lord had blessed them. {10:11} Balak said to Balaam, "I wanted you to curse them, but instead you blessed them. If you had cursed them, I would have rewarded you with great wealth. But you blessed them, and that is not beneficial to me, so I will not reward you." {10:12} Balaam replied, "I can only speak what the Lord tells me. I cannot go against His commands. {10:13} I will not curse those whom God has blessed, for I fear His judgment more than I desire wealth." {10:14} As God told their forefather Jacob, "Those who bless you will be blessed, and those who curse you will be cursed." I will not go against God's commands. {10:15} Those who unjustly curse you will be cursed. Walk in the path and work that God loves, that He may favor you. {10:16} Do not repeat the sins of your ancestors, who provoked the Lord and were punished. {10:17} Some were destroyed by enemies, others by their own hands, and some were taken captive to foreign lands. {10:18} They plundered their livestock and destroyed their lands, including the honored city of Jerusalem, leaving it desolate. {10:19} The priests were captured, the laws were destroyed, and warriors fell in battle. {10:20} Widows were taken captive, and they mourned for themselves but not for their deceased husbands. {10:21} Children wept, elders were disgraced, and no one showed respect for the aged or the wise. {10:22} They destroyed everything in the land, showing no regard for beauty or the law. {10:23} The Lord punished them for their sins, neglecting the Israelites when they sinned. He allowed their temple in Jerusalem to be destroyed. {10:24} Though He loves their ancestors, He did not spare them. He loves Abraham, Isaac, and Jacob because of their righteousness, not their descendants'. {10:25} He honored them with double blessings and established two kingdoms, one on Earth and one in Heaven. {10:26} You, kings and nobles of this passing world, follow the example of your forefathers who served God faithfully and inherited the Kingdom of Heaven. {10:27} Their names are remembered for their righteousness, so strive to be like them. {10:28} Straighten your ways and deeds, that God may establish your kingdom and your name may be honored, as were the righteous kings who preceded you and served the Lord in their virtuous lives.

{11:1} Remember the humility and prayer of God's servant Moses, who remained steadfast despite his people's complaints and even pleaded for forgiveness on their behalf when they sinned against God. {11:2} "Lord, forgive me and my people," he prayed, "for You are Merciful and Forgiving." {11:3} Moses interceded for his people, including those who spoke against him. {11:4} Because of his innocence, God favored Moses above all other priests. {11:5} God loved Moses deeply and elevated him to a position akin to His own. {11:6} But Korah's rebellion against Moses led to their downfall; they were swallowed by the earth with their families and possessions, crying out in vain. {11:7} If you disobey God's commands, He will give you over to your own desires and judge accordingly, but He will preserve your kingdom if you remain faithful. {11:8} Asaph and the descendants of Korah rebelled against Moses, questioning his authority. {11:9} They sought special status, claiming they too were chosen for priestly duties in the Tabernacle. {11:10} They rebelled further by offering unauthorized incense, but God punished them severely, consuming them with fire. {11:11} God instructed Moses to gather the censers used in the rebellion as a reminder of His authority. {11:12} He designated sacred instruments and established the Tabernacle's structure, including rings and poles. {11:13} He oversaw the creation of the vessels, curtains, and courtyard for the Tabernacle's service. {11:14} They offered sacrifices according to God's commands, including peace offerings, sin offerings, and daily rituals. {11:15} Everything was done as God commanded for the Tabernacle's service. {11:16} They respected God's authority to bless Israel with a land flowing with milk and honey, as promised to Abraham. {11:17} They honored God's covenant with Isaac and established worship for Jacob. {11:18} Aaron and Moses maintained the sanctity of the Tabernacle. {11:19} Elijah and Samuel continued this tradition in the temple, and Solomon built the Temple in Jerusalem as God's dwelling place. {11:20} It was a place of prayer and forgiveness for those who approached in purity, especially for the priests. {11:21} It was a place where God's commands were upheld and Israel was honored. {11:22} The Law of God provided structure and guidance for Israel. {11:23} It was where sacrifices were offered and incense was burned to God, a pleasing aroma. {11:24} God spoke from the mercy seat in the Tabernacle, revealing His light to the chosen children of Jacob and to those who sought His favor through obedience to His Law. {11:25} But those who disregarded God's Law will suffer the fate of Korah, swallowed by the earth, and sinners will face Gehenna with no escape.

{12:1} Woe to you, Israel's leaders, who disregarded the Law given in the Tabernacle and followed your own prideful and sinful ways, indulging in greed, adultery, drunkenness, and false oaths. {12:2} My anger will consume you like chaff in a fire, burning you away until nothing remains. {12:3} God, who honors Israel, will destroy all who persist in sin. {12:4} He loves those who love Him and obey His commands, forgiving their sins and restoring their righteousness. {12:5} Follow God's commands faithfully, believing in Him to strengthen you and deliver you from your enemies. {12:6} In times of trouble, I assure you, I am with you to support and save you if you believe in me, follow my commands, love what I love, and uphold my Law. {12:7} God loves those who love Him, for He is Forgiving and Merciful, preserving those who keep His Law like a cherished possession. {12:8} He tempers His anger many times, understanding our human frailty. {12:9} He brings life from death and guides us through trials, always bringing us back to life. {12:10} His covenant promises to restore life from death. {12:11} But the arrogant and rebellious like Tyre and Sidon will fall before the Lord, even as they boast of their greatness. {12:12} "My reign is like the heavens; I will never die," they say. {12:13} Yet before they finish boasting, the angel of death strikes, and they perish in their arrogance and evil deeds. {12:14} Meanwhile, the Keledan army, seeking battle, destroys the city and country, taking all they find and leaving nothing behind. {12:15} They plundered everything and burned the city with fire before returning home.

{13:1} Five brave Maccabean brothers chose death over eating meat sacrificed to idols, knowing that their fidelity to God outweighed any fear of earthly consequences. {13:2} They understood that pretending before God is more significant than pleasing earthly kings. {13:3} Believing that this world is fleeting and that eternal life with God is far more valuable, they faced death by fire to secure salvation in heaven. {13:4} They valued one day in paradise more than a lifetime on earth, and they sought God's forgiveness above all else. {13:5} For our lives are as fleeting as a shadow, melting like wax before the fire's edge—such is the brevity of our existence. {13:6} But God endures forever, and His name is praised throughout generations. {13:7} The Maccabean brothers refused to compromise, even when faced with a repugnant sacrifice, because they believed in God. {13:8} Knowing they would rise again alongside the dead, they embraced martyrdom for their faith. {13:9} For those who doubt the resurrection, they will witness it and acknowledge God's truth after the judgment. {13:10} These brothers gave their lives because they trusted in God's promise of eternal life, rejecting idolatry and any compromise that would dishonor Him. {13:11} They understood that true happiness lies in eternal communion with God, not in fleeting pleasures or the trials of this world. {13:12} They knew that those who keep God's law, including faithful kings and nobles, will reign in the heavenly kingdom for countless generations, free from sorrow and death. {13:13} They believed in the resurrection and the eternal reward of the righteous, shining brightly like the sun in God's love when all rise again in body and soul.

{14:1} The doubts of the Samaritans, Sadducees, Pharisees, and Essenes troubled me deeply as I pondered their reasoning. The Sadducees mockingly said, "Let us eat and drink, for tomorrow we die, and there is no such thing as a joyful afterlife." {14:2} The Samaritans argued, "Once our bodies turn to dust, how can they possibly rise again?" {14:3} They questioned the existence of the soul after death, unable to comprehend its invisible nature like the wind or a whisper. {14:4} They feared that their bodies, consumed by beasts and worms in the grave, would only return to dust and ashes. {14:5} They saw no hope for resurrection, believing that even the beasts that consumed them would eventually perish, leaving no trace of their former existence. {14:6} The Pharisees, though believing in resurrection, wondered how God would transform decayed and rotten bodies into heavenly forms not known on Earth. {14:7} Conversely, the Sadducees denied resurrection altogether, arguing that once the soul departs from the body, there can be no reunion in life after death. {14:8} Their error and disrespect for God's sovereignty saddened me deeply. {14:9} Their lack of faith in God's promises left them without hope of salvation or resurrection. {14:10} Addressing the blind reasoning of the Sadducees, I questioned their arrogance in dismissing God's power to raise the dead to life, likening their scorn to spitting in the face of the Almighty who created them. {14:11} No one can escape God's authority; those who reject Him will face judgment and the consequences of their unbelief. {14:12} Demons sow sin and confusion in the minds of those who reject God, leading them astray from birth through their misguided teachings and actions. {14:13} These sins will haunt them in death, bringing hardship and suffering upon their souls. {14:14} Just as sin binds the souls of those who practice it, demonic forces will stand as witnesses against them in judgment. {14:15} All souls, including those of sinners, will face judgment, their sins guiding them toward Gehenna, where their souls will endure punishment for their deeds. {14:16} Yet, for those who kept God's law, their souls will experience renewal and restoration, sevenfold in God's mercy, akin to the flesh of our forefather Adam. {14:17} Those dwelling in graves due to their errors will realize their folly, for they misled others with false teachings, claiming there is no resurrection of the dead. {14:18} They will face the consequences of their actions, receiving punishment proportionate to their deeds, unable to escape the judgment of God. {14:19} In that hour, whether by wind, water, earth, or fire, all shall come to pass according to God's command. {14:20} Souls long buried in Sheol will arise according to God's decree, some to face eternal damnation, others to enjoy the bliss of paradise. {14:21} The righteous souls residing in the Garden of Eden will also arise to receive their rewards from God. {14:22} However, the Sadducees, Samaritans, Pharisees, and Essenes will dwell in Sheol until their judgment day arrives. {14:23} At that moment, they will witness firsthand the justice of God, receiving their due punishment for leading others astray. {14:24} They will realize the folly of their disbelief, for denying the resurrection and mocking God's word will earn them just retribution. {14:25} Unaware of the true teachings of the Scriptures, they spread falsehoods and misled many. {14:26} It would have been better had they remained ignorant, rather than spreading evil teachings and corrupting God's truth with their deceitful words. {14:27} God does not look favorably upon those who distort His truth; instead, He reserves His grace and glory for those who faithfully teach His ways and do good works. {14:28} None can escape the judgment of God, who will repay each person according to their deeds, both the teacher and the taught. {14:29} Know this: the dead will rise, and those who obeyed God's law will rise to everlasting life, just as surely as rain brings forth grass upon the earth at His command. {14:30} Just as moist wood drinks dew and bears leaves, and as wheat produces fruit and grain produces buds, so too shall the dead arise at God's command, their graves unable to contain them forever. {14:31} Just as a woman cannot hold back the birth of a child in labor, neither can the grave prevent the resurrection of those whom God has called forth. {14:32} When God commands, the graves will open, and souls will return to their bodies, reunited in preparation for judgment. {14:33} Bodies will gather where they fell, and souls will return to dwell within them, preparing for the final judgment. {14:34} At the sound of the trumpet, the dead will rise in an instant, standing before God to receive their rewards according to their deeds. {14:35} In that hour, they will see their lives laid bare before them, and they will lament the sins they committed in this world, regretting their actions in vain. {14:36} Know this: the dead will rise, and each will face their judgment according to their deeds.

{15:1} Those who find joy in their righteous deeds will be blessed in that day, while those who scoffed, saying "the dead will not rise," will mourn when they see the resurrection of the dead, accompanied by their own futile deeds. {15:2} Their deeds will convict them, and they will realize they stand alone, with no one to defend them. {15:3} On the day of judgment, when mourning and reckoning occur, when the Lord comes and definitive judgment is rendered, those who disregarded God's law will stand in their appointed places. {15:4} It will be a day of darkness and mist, flashes of lightning and thunder. {15:5} Earthquakes, terror, heatwaves, and freezing cold will beset them. {15:6} On that day, the wicked will face their punishment, and the righteous will receive their reward according to their deeds. Those who forgot God's law will suffer like sinners. {15:7} Masters will not be more honored than their slaves, nor mistresses than their maids. {15:8} Kings will not be more honored than the poor, elders than infants, fathers than their children, or mothers than their offspring. {15:9} It will be a day of judgment, sentencing all to hardship according to their deeds, where everyone faces the consequences of their sins. {15:10} On that day, the righteous will rejoice in their reward, while those who forgot God's law will stand in regret, witnessing the resurrection they denied. {15:11} Sinners of this world will weep for their sins, finding no solace in their remorse. {15:12} Conversely, the kind-hearted who performed righteous deeds will find eternal joy, having faithfully followed God's law and anticipating their resurrection. {15:13} They knew they would rise after death because they obeyed God's commands. {15:14} They will inherit the blessings promised by God, including the Kingdom of Heaven, where their descendants will be honored. {15:15} The fire of Gehenna awaits those who doubted the resurrection of the dead.

{16:1} Consider your own body: your flesh, feet, hands, nails, and hair. When you cut them, they regrow. This is evidence of resurrection, a concept rooted in reason, religion, and knowledge. {16:2} Your nails, hair, and body parts do not sprout from nowhere. They are prepared by God, teaching you that your resurrection will be from the same body, not a different one. {16:3} For those who misled others by denying the resurrection, their fate awaits them—a punishment befitting their sins and iniquities. {16:4} Just as seeds you plant now grow into their intended forms, whether wheat or barley, so too will you face the consequences of your actions when the time of reckoning arrives. {16:5} Plants do not deny their growth; neither will the body deny its resurrection. {16:6} Just as you cannot plant grapes and expect figs, or sow wheat and expect barley, so too will the righteous and wicked face their just rewards. {16:7} Every seed produces fruit according to its kind, each reaping the blessings or hardships decreed by God. {16:8} On the day the trumpet sounds, the dead will rise by God's mercy. {16:9} Those who did good deeds will rise to eternal life, enjoying the Garden of Paradise prepared by God for the righteous, free from suffering and death. {16:10} Those who committed evil will face definitive judgment, joined by the devils who misled them. {16:11} They will descend to Gehenna, a place of eternal darkness, grinding teeth, and ceaseless sorrow, devoid of mercy or escape. {16:12} This fate awaits those who did not do good deeds in their earthly life. {16:13} Their judgment will be pronounced when body and soul are reunited. {16:14} Woe to those who disbelieve in the resurrection of body and soul, despite the abundance of miracles shown by God. {16:15} Each person will receive their just reward according to their deeds and their toil.

{17:1} A wheat kernel cannot sprout and bear fruit unless it is first planted and dies. But when it dies, it grows roots into the earth, sends up shoots, and eventually bears fruit. {17:2} You know that from one wheat kernel many more kernels can be produced. {17:3} Similarly, wheat grows by drawing nutrients from water, wind, and dew, needing sunlight for growth as fire for warmth. {17:4} Wind is essential, just as the soul animates the body. Without wind, wheat cannot flourish. Water provides nourishment, causing the wheat to grow and bear fruit. {17:5} After the earth, enriched by water, produces roots, it grows tall and fruitful, blessed by God. {17:6} Like the wheat kernel, each person is created with a soul inspired by God, and just as a grapevine drinks water and sends down roots, so too does each plant need the divine blessing of God. {17:7} By God's grace, vineyards thrive, sending water up to their leaves, flourishing in the heat of the sun, and producing abundant fruit. {17:8} Grapes yield a delightful fragrance, bringing joy to those who reason well. Those who partake find satisfaction, like water that does not quench thirst and grain that satisfies hunger. {17:9} As the Psalms proclaim, grapes make the heart rejoice; they bring delight when consumed, flowing like blood within. {17:10} Yet drunkenness deceives, clouding the mind and leading to recklessness, making perilous paths seem like wide meadows, unaware of obstacles or thorns. {17:11} God has ordained fruitfulness for grapes and vineyards, that His name may be praised by those who believe in the resurrection of the dead and follow His teachings. {17:12} In the Kingdom of Heaven, those who believe in the resurrection of the dead will find joy.

{18:1} Those who do not believe in the resurrection of the dead, how mistaken you are! When you are taken to the unknown place, you will regret in vain, for you did not believe in the resurrection of the dead, in soul and flesh. {18:2} Whether you did good or evil, you will receive your just reward. You misled others with your false reasoning, saying, "We know that those who were dust and ashes will not rise." {18:3} In death, there is no escape, no power to avoid the punishment that awaits, for you were not steadfast in your trials and misled others. {18:4} When God's wrath is upon you, you will tremble in fear, not realizing that He raised you from non-existence to life. You spoke of God's law without understanding, and now judgment awaits you for your evil deeds. {18:5} You do not understand Gehenna, where you will go because of your anger and crooked ways. You taught your companions misleading doctrines, for you are the evildoers who denied the resurrection of the dead. {18:6} At that time, you will know that the dead will indeed rise, and judgment will be pronounced upon all mankind, for you did not believe in the resurrection of the dead for all of humanity. {18:7} For all humanity is descended from Adam, and death's judgment has come upon us all because of Adam's sin. {18:8} We will rise again with our ancestor Adam, to receive our just punishment for the deeds we have done. The world was subject to death through Adam's ignorance. {18:9} Because of Adam's disobedience, we suffered hardships. Our flesh melted away in the grave like wax, our bodies decayed, and our beauty faded. {18:10} Earth consumed our bones, and our comeliness perished in the grave. Our flesh was buried in the earth, along with our eloquent words. {18:11} Worms came from our bright eyes, and our features decayed in the grave, turning to dust. {18:12} Where are our beautiful appearances, our attractiveness, our strong stances, and our successful words now? {18:13} Where are the armies of kings, the nobility, the adornments on horses, the silver and gold, and the gleaming weapons? Did they not all perish? {18:14} Where are the delightful drinks of grapes and the flavors of food?

{19:1} Oh Earth, you have gathered nobles, kings, the wealthy, elders, and beautiful women. Woe to you! {19:2} You've gathered warriors, the handsome, the wise, and those with eloquent speech, like humming harps and musical instruments. {19:3} Their charm brings joy, their eyes shine brightly. {19:4} They wield authority, lift what is given and withheld, and their steps are graceful. Woe to you! {19:5} Oh death, you separate souls from their attractive bodies. Woe to you, for you act according to God's decree. {19:6} As you gather many whom God created from and returns to the earth, woe to you! We are formed and returned by God's command, rejoicing over you by His decree. {19:7} You become a resting place for our bodies, we return to you, we are buried within you, we nourish you and you consume us. {19:8} We drink from your springs, you drink our blood. We consume your fruits, you consume our flesh. {19:9} As commanded by God, we eat the grain from your soil, blessed with dew, and you receive our beauty and turn it to dust, as commanded by God. {19:10} Oh death, you gather powerful kings and do not fear their fame or terror, as commanded by God who created you. Woe to you, for you do not spare the suffering. {19:11} You do not discriminate between the beautiful and the powerful, rich or poor, kind or evil, young or old, women or men. {19:12} You do not spare those who think good or those who stray from the law, who think evil, whose beauty and words deceive. Woe to you, oh death! {19:13} You gather those whose words are bitter, mouths full of curses, those who live in darkness and in light, souls in your dominion. Woe to you, oh death! {19:14} And the earth gathers the flesh of those who lived in caves or beneath the earth, until the trumpet sounds and the dead arise. {19:15} The dead shall rise quickly by God's command, at the sound of the trumpet. Those who did evil will receive their due punishment, while those who did good will find joy.

{20:1} I believe that all the work I have done in this world will not remain hidden when I stand before Him, trembling with fear. {20:2} And in that time, I will not have gathered provisions for my journey, and I will have no clothing to cover my body. {20:3} At that time, I will not have a staff in my hand or shoes on my feet. {20:4} And in that moment, I will not know the path where demons take me—whether it is slippery or smooth, dark, filled with thorns or nettles, or whether it leads to deep waters or a deep pit. But I believe that the work I have done in this world will not remain hidden. {20:5} I will not recognize the demons that take me, nor will I hear them speak. {20:6} Since they are dark beings leading me into darkness, I will not be able to see their faces. {20:7} And just as the prophet said: "When my soul was separated from my flesh, Lord, You knew my path, and they set a trap on the way I walked. I looked to the right, and no one knew me. I had nothing that could help me escape." As they lead me into darkness, I will not see their faces. {20:8} He knew that the demons ridiculed him, and since they led him on a path he did not know, he said this. And when he looked to the left and right, there was no one who knew him. {20:9} He was alone among the demons, and no one recognized him. {20:10} The angels of light, who are subtle, are sent to receive the souls of righteous people and lead them to a place of light, to the Garden where welfare and peace are found. {20:11} But demons and angels of darkness are sent to receive the souls of sinners and lead them to Gehenna, which was prepared for them, so that they may receive the punishment for their sins. {20:12} Woe to the souls of sinners who are led to destruction, who have no peace or rest, no escape from the torment that finds them, and no release from Gehenna for all eternity. {20:13} As they lived steadfastly in the works of Cain, and as they perished in the iniquity of Balaam's deceitful reward, they lacked any way to change their fate. Woe to these sinners, for their false pretenses in receiving bribes and gifts, which in their downfall, led them to take money that was not their own.

{21:1} Where are those who acquired money through deceit, not rightfully theirs? {21:2} Taking money freely, unaware of the day of their death that will come, profiting from ill-gotten gain. {21:3} Like their forefathers, they are sinful, descendants worrying about seizing sinners through theft or robbery, and their children will not prosper from their fathers' wealth. {21:4} They gathered wealth through deceit, now vanished like mist, smoke scattered by the wind, and grass withered by fire. Their glory fades, and their fathers' wealth will benefit no one, as David said, "I saw a sinful man honored and praised like a tree, yet when I searched, he was nowhere to be found." {21:5} Sinners' wealth and boasts of wrongdoing are like shadows that vanish with time. {21:6} They gathered riches through deceit, believing they would never die, like those who wronged their companions without consequence. {21:7} You lazy ones, know that you will perish and your wealth will perish with you. Even if your silver and gold increase, it will rust. {21:8} If you bear many children, they will fill many graves. If you build many houses, they will be destroyed. {21:9} Because you did not obey God's command, even if you increase livestock, they will be captured by your enemies, and all the wealth in your hands will vanish, for it was not blessed. {21:10} Whether in houses or forests, wilderness or pastures, grape or grain fields, your wealth will not be found. {21:11} Because you did not keep God's command, He will not save you or your household from tribulation, and sadness will come upon you from all your enemies. Even your children born of your own nature will not find happiness. {21:12} But from God's abundance, He will not trouble those who kept His order and law. He will bless their children and their land's fruit. {21:13} He will make them rulers over all peoples in their land, so that they may rule rather than be ruled. He will give them His abundance in their land's pastures. {21:14} He will bless all they have worked for, their fields' produce and their livestock's place. He will bring joy to their children born of their own nature. {21:15} He will not diminish their livestock. He will save them from all tribulation, weariness, illness, and destruction. He will save them from their enemies, both known and unknown. {21:16} In the time of judgment, He will plead for them. He will save them from evil, tribulation, and those who oppose them. In the first era, if a priest lived who worked in the Tent, kept the law, and obeyed the Tent's rules, in God's order and law, He would save them from tribulation. {21:17} As Moses commanded Joshua, there was a city of refuge in all the land. Whether they knew or did not know, they judged the guilty and acquitted the innocent. {21:18} If a person killed a soul, they were judged, allowing them to escape if they were not guilty. {21:19} They were told to examine their reasoning before arguing, and to save those who killed accidentally with an axe, stone, or wood. If they did not know, they were saved. {21:20} But if they knowingly killed, they would receive punishment for their sin, without pardon. {21:21} They worked to prevent all sin among Israel's children, as Moses worked for them, so that they would not stray from God's law. {21:22} He commanded the children of Adam to live firm in God's command, avoiding idol worship, eating the dead, and stealing. They avoided all evil, doing what was commanded, and not departing from God's commandment in the tent example in heaven. They saved their bodies and found rest with their fathers. {21:23} They avoided their sins, and as David's children, they obeyed God's commandments, which the tithe and the first fruits gave them. {21:24} They were born from Seth and Adam, and all those who believe in God's word and live firm in his commandments are called good. {21:25} As we are the children of Adam, he has provoked us with his image and appearance, to do all that is good to please God. He will not scorn it. {21:26} He will not separate his friends, and if we do good, we will inherit the kingdom of heaven, where there is peace and those who do good. {21:27} He loves those who pray to him and hears them. He accepts the repentance of those who are disciplined and enter into repentance. He gives strength and power to those who keep his commandments, his law, and his command. {21:28} Those who have done his will, will be happy with him in his kingdom, whether they be those who came before or those who came later, and they will praise him forever from today until eternity.

3 Meqabyan

The Book of 3 Meqabyan, also known as the Third Book of Maccabees in the Ethiopian Orthodox Tewahedo Church canon, is a unique and historically significant text within the biblical apocrypha. Unlike its more widely known counterparts, the First and Second Books of Maccabees, which detail the Jewish revolt against the Seleucid Empire under the leadership of Judas Maccabeus, 3 Meqabyan presents a different narrative altogether, focusing on the themes of faith, persecution, and divine deliverance in a manner distinct to Ethiopian Christian tradition. This book, along with 1 and 2 Meqabyan, forms part of the broader corpus of Ethiopian literature that reflects the rich and complex religious history of the region. Its narrative is set in a different historical context compared to the Hellenistic period of the other Maccabean texts, often being interpreted as a series of moral and ethical tales rather than historical accounts. The book underscores the importance of steadfast faith in God amidst trials and tribulations, echoing the broader theological and moralistic concerns of the Ethiopian Church. The themes explored in 3 Meqabyan—such as divine justice, the power of prayer, and the ultimate triumph of good over evil—resonate deeply within the Ethiopian spiritual context, offering insights into the religious psyche of Ethiopian Christianity. Its inclusion in the Ethiopian biblical canon highlights the diversity within Christian scriptural traditions and illustrates how regional beliefs and historical experiences can shape the development and reception of sacred texts.

{1:1} Christ will bring joy to the righteous ones of the earth, for He will come in the future to avenge and destroy the devils who have harmed the kind and innocent, misled people, and opposed His works. {1:2} He will bring judgment upon them, returning their dominion to ruin and degradation, because they have arrogantly opposed Him in their reasoning. {1:3} They thought to ascend to the heights of the heavens and rule over mankind like rulers over chicks, boasting of their superiority. {1:4} They misled many by distorting the straight path of Jah's law, strengthening those who followed them in this world's deception. {1:5} They influenced people to follow them into Gehenna by showing them riches and beautiful women, leading them astray from the righteous path. {1:6} Those who loved Jah and kept His law despised their deception, but those who strayed from His commandments were drawn to them and obeyed their every word. {1:7} They deceived people with worldly wealth, turning them away from Jah's righteous laws. {1:8} They enticed people with precious stones, silver, and gold, leading them further from Jah's commandments. {1:9} They distracted people with fine clothing, silks, and luxurious linens, turning them away from Jah's path. {1:10} They stirred up envy, anger, and strife among people, using all these to further their own ends. {1:11} They used signs and wonders to deceive people, even claiming prophetic powers to mislead them. {1:12} Those who followed them were ensnared by their cunning, believing their lies and false promises. {1:13} They spoke and performed signs to reinforce their deception, leading many astray and enriching themselves through deceit. {1:14} They claimed to possess knowledge and powers beyond any other, becoming arrogant in their deception. {1:15} They rejoiced in their deceit, causing many to perish and wander from Jah's path. {1:16} Their children, following their teachings, were condemned with them to Gehenna. {1:17} When Jah's anger was stirred against them, He ordered their punishment and condemnation. {1:18} But they pleaded for mercy, asking to speak in their defense before Jah. {1:19} They asked that those who had followed them in error be punished like them, and those who had rejected their teachings be blessed by Jah. {1:20} They requested that Jah reward those who had remained faithful to Him and kept His commandments. {1:21} Jah answered them, agreeing to punish those who had misled others while sparing those who had resisted their deception. {1:22} He decreed that those who had followed the deceivers willingly would share their fate in Gehenna. {1:23} But those who had rejected their teachings and remained faithful to Jah's word would receive His blessings and rewards. {1:24} The deceivers themselves and those who followed them would suffer in Gehenna for eternity, with no hope of escape.

{2:1} However, I, as a humble servant, will pass on your throne of authority to those whom you failed to mislead, much like my faithful servant Job. Jah, who governs all, has decreed: I will grant the Kingdom of Heaven to those whom you could not lead astray. {2:2} They have tempted humanity in every way possible, yet I will not abandon them to evil deeds. I will strengthen them in righteous works and sweeten their lives with blessings. {2:3} Whether through love of drink, food, clothing, or material possessions, {2:4} or through desires to see and hear, to indulge and multiply in arrogance and wealth, or through dreams and sleep, {2:5} or through indulgence in drunkenness, insults, and anger, speaking frivolously and pursuing useless things, {2:6} they have led people astray through quarrels, gossip, admiration of worldly beauty, and the allure of perfumes. {2:7} By all these means, they have distanced people from Jah's law, leading them toward destruction, just as they themselves fell from grace. {2:8} The prophet admonished them, saying, "You who seek to destroy others, perish! When you departed from Jah's law and acted with arrogance in your reasoning, {2:9} when Jah, your Creator, in His displeasure, lowered you from your high position due to your wicked deeds—why did you lead mankind into sin, those whom Jah loved and honored with His praise?" {2:10} "You, who were once glorious and adorned with wind and fire, dared to declare yourself as the ultimate authority— {2:11} boasting even as Jah scrutinized your evil deeds and rejected you and your followers. Jah exalted mankind to praise Him, not to diminish His glory. {2:12} Your arrogance led you to exalt yourselves above all the angels, but Jah, in His wrath, exalted mankind to praise Him, whom you despised. {2:13} Because of this, Jah cast you out from among the angelic hosts, your followers, who shared in your rebellion. You led them astray with your false teachings and prideful reasoning, defying your Creator, and now you face His judgment. {2:14} Jah expelled mankind from paradise so that He might be glorified through the humble, giving them His commandments and laws, saying not to eat from a certain tree, lest they bring about their own downfall. {2:15} He warned them clearly, "Do not eat from this tree, for it will bring death upon you." {2:16} Yet you, with your deceitful words, sowed doubt in their hearts, misleading the innocent to become like you—lawbreakers. {2:17} You deceived the innocent woman, who was like a pure dove, leading her into betrayal through your cunning and twisted words. {2:18} You tempted her to betray Jah, whom she loved and obeyed, and she, too, fell into sin, misleading Adam, whom Jah had loved from the beginning. {2:19} Your malice caused disruption not born of arrogance, causing Adam to deny Jah's word and bringing about his downfall. {2:20} Your deception distanced him from Jah's love, and through your influence, he was banished from the paradise of bliss. {2:21} Since ancient times, you have waged war against innocent humanity, seeking to drag them down into Sheol, where they will suffer, separated from the love that brings life and joy. {2:22} Yet Jah, in His wisdom, created humanity as noble beings, capable of praising Him in spirit and truth. {2:23} He inspired them with many thoughts, like harps playing in perfect harmony, each soul resonating with its unique melody.

{3:1} Jah, in His anger, ordained that you should fully praise Him in the place where He sent you. {3:2} But Adam was endowed with five evil inclinations and five virtuous ones—ten in total. {3:3} And his thoughts were numerous like the waves of the sea, like a whirlwind stirring up dust from the earth, and like the tumultuous waves of the sea, his thoughts swelled abundantly in his heart like countless raindrops. {3:4} But your thoughts are singular; as you are not of flesh, you have no other thoughts. {3:5} But you instigated cunning in the serpent's reasoning, deceiving Eve, who was one of Adam's limbs. When Eve heard the serpent's deceitful words, she obeyed its command. {3:6} After she ate from the forbidden tree, she then misled Adam, the first human, bringing death upon him and their descendants because she disobeyed their Creator's command. {3:7} They were driven out from the Garden by Jah's true judgment, and they settled in the land where their children were born and where they cultivated crops from the earth. Yet they did not cease their disputes. {3:8} And when you expelled them straight from the Garden, they had to plant crops and raise children to find solace and renew their minds with earthly fruits prepared by the earth itself. They found comfort in the fruits of the earth and in the fruits of the Garden given by Jah. {3:9} Jah provided them with woods richer than those of the Garden, and Adam and Eve, who were banished for eating from the forbidden tree, found complete solace from sorrow. {3:10} Because Jah knows how to comfort His creation, their minds found peace through their children and through the crops grown from the earth. {3:11} As they were sent to this world where nettles and thorns grow, they strengthened their minds with water and grain.

{4:1} The Lord purposed to redeem Adam and thereby shame you; He will rescue a sheep from the mouth of the wolf, saving Adam from the Devil. {4:2} However, you will go to Gehenna, taking with you the people whom you ruled over. {4:3} Those who kept Jah's law will rejoice with Jah, who protected them from evil deeds to bless them and enable them to praise Him alongside honored angels who, unlike you, did not disobey Jah's law. {4:4} But Jah, who chose and gave you more than all angels like you, intended for you to praise Him with His servant angels but withheld from you a lofty throne due to your arrogance. {4:5} Yet you became renowned and were called one who loves godhood, and your followers were called demons. {4:6} But those who loved Jah will be His kin, like honored angels, and the Seraphim and Cherubim who stretch out their wings and praise Him without ceasing. {4:7} But in your arrogance and laziness, you destroyed your own praise, intending to praise Him always with your host and your corrupted kindred. {4:8} Lest the praise of Jah, who exalted you as a tenth tribe, diminish when you forget the praise of Jah who elevated you, thinking it impossible for Him to exalt a creation like you, and lest the praise of Jah diminish when you were separated from your brethren in the Trinity, Jah exalted Adam in your place. {4:9} But in your arrogant reasoning, you neglected to praise Jah who exalted you, and He was angry with you, mocking and binding you, casting you into Gehenna along with your hosts. {4:10} He formed Adam from the soil of the earth with His glorified hands, adding fire, water, and wind. Jah created Adam as His example and likeness. {4:11} He instructed Adam in all His laws so that Adam's praise would be filled with the same praise you would offer Him; Adam's praise equaled that of the angels. {4:12} But in your stubbornness and arrogance, you were demoted from your rank, departing from the lordship of Jah who exalted you, thus causing your own downfall. {4:13} Know that Jah's praise was not diminished, for Jah exalted Adam to praise Him in His divine counsel, lest His divine majesty's praise be diminished. {4:14} Jah knew all before it happened, and He knew you before He exalted you, knowing that you would defy His commandments. As there is a hidden counsel with Him before He created the world, when you rebelled, Jah exalted Adam as His example and likeness. {4:15} As Solomon said, "Before the hills were formed and before the world was created, before the winds laid the foundations of the earth, before the lights of the moon and the sun, before the ages and stars were set in place, before day and night alternated, before the seas were divided by sand, before all creation was formed, and before all things known today," Solomon, the angels like you and me, and Adam were in Jah's divine counsel.

{5:1} Know that Jah, who created you in His image and example when you were on Earth, commands you not to forget Him. He established and saved you, and Israel glorified Him. He placed you in a garden to live peacefully and cultivate the earth. {5:2} But when you disobeyed His command, He expelled you from the garden to this world, which He cursed with thorns and nettles. {5:3} Remember that you were made from the earth, and to the earth, you will return. You are dust, and so is she; you are soil, and from her, you are fed. You will return to her until the day Jah loves, when He will raise you up and examine your sins and all your wrongdoing. {5:4} Consider what you will answer Him on that day, reflecting on the good and evil deeds you performed in this world. Reflect on whether your evil deeds outweigh your good deeds or vice versa. {5:5} If you have done good, it will benefit you on the day when the dead rise. {5:6} But if you have done evil, woe to you! You will face the consequences according to your deeds and the evil thoughts you entertained. {5:7} If you betray others, invoke Jah's name falsely, and swear lies, you will suffer for your actions. {5:8} If you speak falsehoods to deceive others into thinking they are truths, you will face the consequences of your lies. {5:9} If you lead others astray with your lies and falsehoods, you will bear the burden of your sins. Denying others while promising things you never intend to give them will also bring consequences. {5:10} When you make promises with deceptive intentions, demons will pursue you like dogs, causing you to forget everything. Whether you withhold or give, it will not benefit you; this world's wealth will only increase your appetite for more wealth that cannot satisfy you. {5:11} As it is said, the children of liars create unjust balances, moving from one robbery to another, driven by their insatiable desire for wealth. {5:12} Do not put your hope in distorted scales, stealing others' money, oppressing the weak, infringing on others' rights, or deceiving for personal gain—it is not for the benefit of others. {5:13} If you persist in these actions, you will suffer the consequences of your deeds. {5:14} Instead, earn your living through honest work and do not desire to rob others. Do not covet ill-gotten gains that bring no justice and cannot satisfy your needs. {5:15} Even if you accumulate wealth, it will not bring you lasting satisfaction; upon death, you will leave it behind for others. {5:16} Wealth gained through sinful means is fleeting, like smoke that disappears; better to have little wealth earned honestly than to amass riches through deceit.

{6:1} Consider the day of your death when your soul departs from your body and you leave your wealth behind for others. Reflect on the path you will tread, knowing not where it leads; prepare for the tribulations that await you. {6:2} The demons who await you are evil, terrifying in their appearance, and they will not heed your pleas, nor will you hear theirs. {6:3} Because you did not follow Jah's commandments, they will not listen when you beg for mercy; they will only add to your fear. {6:4} But those who have kept Jah's commandments need not fear; demons fear them. Sinners will be mocked by demons. {6:5} The souls of righteous individuals will find peace among angels in heavenly bliss, for they have scorned the pleasures of this world. Evil angels will receive the souls of sinners. {6:6} Merciful angels will receive the souls of kind and righteous individuals, sent by Jah to comfort them. Evil angels, sent by the Devil, will mock sinners' souls, receiving them into torment. {6:7} Sinners, beware and weep for yourselves before the day of your death arrives; when you face Jah, repent in this life before your time passes away, so that you may live in peace and righteousness, free from tribulation and suffering. {6:8} Do not let your pursuit of worldly gain distance you from Jah; through sincere repentance, find love, prosperity, and peace within yourself. Once death claims you, your opportunities for repentance will vanish forever—weep for what could have been. {6:9} Do not pursue a vain existence that estranges you from Jah, where material wealth dominates your life and true love, prosperity, and peace are absent. {6:10} As Moses said, "Jacob ate and was satisfied and grew fat and kicked—Jah who made him withdrew from him, his lifestyle became estranged from Jah." A life of excessive indulgence and adultery is akin to that of a wandering horse and a wild boar, devoid of moderation or self-control. {6:11} But those who eat in moderation will live in Jah's support, standing firm like a tower with fortified walls. Those who forget Jah's commandments will flee, pursued by their own guilt. {6:12} Kind individuals will live with dignity, respected like lions. {6:13} Those who disregard Jah's laws will suffer sadness and turmoil in this world, trembling with fear and facing countless tribulations, their wealth stolen and their hands bound by chains.

{7:1} David said, "I believe in Jah; I will not fear. What can man do to me?" Those who believe in Jah have no reason to fear. {7:2} He further proclaimed, "Even if enemies surround me, I trust in Him. I ask Jah for one thing: to live in His presence forever without fear of harm." Those who have faith in Him live eternally and fear no evil. {7:3} Who can shame those who believe in Jah? Who disregards Him for worldly desires? {7:4} Jah loves those who love Him, honors those who glorify Him, and accepts those who repent. Who can shame those who believe in Him? {7:5} Uphold justice, defend the rights of widows, and protect the fatherless. Jah will protect you from all adversaries and bless your descendants with prosperity and security.

{8:1} Job remained faithful to Jah, praising Him even in adversity. Jah delivered him from all the tribulations inflicted by the enemy, Satan. Job declared, "Jah gives and Jah withholds as He pleases. Let His name be praised on Earth and in Heaven." {8:2} When Jah saw Job's steadfastness amidst suffering, He honored him greatly. {8:3} Jah restored Job's wealth manifold after he endured tremendous trials and healed his wounds. {8:4} Like Job, endure tribulations sent by demons, and you will be admired. {8:5} Endure trials so Jah may be your fortress and refuge, protecting you and your descendants. Do not be discouraged by tribulations; trust in Him, and He will be your stronghold. {8:6} Cry out to Him, and He will hear you; put your hope in Him, and He will forgive you. {8:7} Remember the faith of Mordecai, Esther, Jehoiada, Deborah, Barak, Jephthah, and Samson, and others like them who trusted in Jah and were not defeated by their enemies. {8:8} Jah is just and does not show favoritism. Those who fear Him and keep His commandments will be blessed and honored. {8:9} Jah preserves those who are faithful to Him, granting them love and respect throughout their lives and beyond. {8:10} He brings prosperity in their endeavors, in life and in death, in their rising and their resting. He saves and shelters them. {8:11} He forgives and consoles. {8:12} He uplifts the poor and honors the wretched, making them prosperous and joyful.

{9:1} Whether in Heaven or on Earth, whether subtle or grand, everything, including all wealth, is upheld by Jah's divine order. {9:2} Nothing departs from Jah's law and His command. He governs the entire world, directing each creature to its destined path, whether it be the flight of a bird in the sky or the slithering of a snake in a cave. Even the ships at sea follow His ordained course. {9:3} Only Jah knows the path of a soul after it departs from its body, whether it wanders in the wilderness or ascends like dew upon the mountains, or moves swiftly like the wind or lightning. {9:4} He alone knows where souls will journey, be they righteous or sinful. {9:5} Who can predict their path, whether through the wild or upon the mountain, or if they will soar like a bird or vanish like mist? {9:6} Their destiny is as unpredictable as the deep wind or the lightning that cleaves the sky, or the stars that shine in the vast expanse, or the grains of sand upon the shore. {9:7} They are as fleeting as a stone on the ocean's edge or a fruitful tree nourished by a water spring. {9:8} Some souls are like reeds scorched by the sun, carried by the wind to unknown places, leaving no trace behind. {9:9} Others are like mist that dissipates without a trace. Who can comprehend Jah's ways? {9:10} Who can advise Him or fathom His counsel? {9:11} His thoughts are beyond human understanding, His works inscrutable. {9:12} He created the Earth upon the waters, establishing it without support. His wisdom governs the heavens and stretches out the cosmos like a vast tent. {9:13} He commands the clouds to pour rain upon the Earth, causing grass to grow and fruits to flourish abundantly for sustenance. {9:14} Jah provides abundance and satisfaction, clothing His children in beauty and granting them plenty and joy. {9:15} He dresses them in splendid robes, showers them with love, prosperity, and the peace that comes from keeping Jah's covenant. {9:16} Those who honor Jah's law shall inherit His eternal kingdom and dwell in His house of everlasting peace. {9:17} He exalts those who faithfully serve Him and do not stray from His commandments. {9:18} Jah fulfills the desires of those who seek Him, but those who forsake His law face His wrath and destruction. {9:19} Do not provoke Jah's anger by departing from His commandments, lest you face tribulation and destruction. {9:20} Keep Jah's law even after your soul departs from your body, that He may bless you in His presence. {9:21} The kingdoms of Earth and Heaven belong to Him; all power and authority are His alone. {9:22} He lifts up the poor and honors the humble; His justice is perfect. {9:23} David wisely observed, "Man's life is fleeting, like a passing shadow." {9:24} But he also acknowledged, "Yet, O Lord, You endure forever; Your name will be praised for generations to come." {9:25} He proclaimed, "Your kingdom extends over all the earth, and Your dominion belongs to every generation." {9:26} There is none like Him; He sees all but is seen by none. {9:27} His kingdom is eternal, and He alone reigns supreme over all. {9:28} Jah created humanity in His image, that they might praise Him and understand His divine wisdom through righteous living. {9:29} Yet people bow down to idols of stone, wood, silver, and gold, crafted by human hands. {9:30} They offer sacrifices to these idols, hoping to gain favor, but they reject Jah, the true Creator. {9:31} They practice idolatry, sorcery, and all manner of sinful acts, forsaking Jah's commandments. {9:32} They do not love to worship Jah and thus bring upon themselves sin and iniquity. {9:33} When they rise from their graves, their souls will stand naked before Jah, revealing all the sins they committed from infancy to death. {9:34} Each soul will bear the consequences of its deeds, whether few or many.

{10:1} The souls redeemed by Jah's blood shall dwell in them as they did before, and those who doubted the resurrection of the dead shall witness it during the rainy season, not born of human parents. {10:2} Jah commanded this by His word long ago. {10:3} When their bodies decay and return to dust, they will be renewed and rise again, just as Jah decreed. {10:4} When the rain falls and saturates the earth, they will rise to life as they were originally created. {10:5} Those who have eternal life through Jah's spirit and those born of water have been ordained by Him. By His authority and command, He grants them eternal life. {10:6} How can anyone, blind to reason, deny the resurrection of the dead? If you have wisdom, how can you reject Jah's word? {10:7} Those who were once ashes and dust in the grave will rise by Jah's word. As for you, repent and return to your faith. {10:8} Just as Jah's word promised, they will rise with the dew of forgiveness from Jah, awakening all the dead beloved by Him. {10:9} Know that you will rise and stand before Him; do not doubt that you will remain in the grave. {10:10} You will face the consequences of your deeds, whether good or evil, on the Day of Judgment. {10:11} In the resurrection, you will confront all your sins, recorded from infancy onward, with no room for denial. {10:12} Your false words will be revealed as lies, and you will have no excuse for your deeds. {10:13} Jah knows all your evil deeds and will speak against you on the Day of Judgment. There will be no excuse for your pretense. {10:14} You will be ashamed because of your sins, but those who are thanked for their righteous deeds will rejoice in the Kingdom of Heaven. Quickly repent in this life before it is too late. {10:15} Those who praise Jah with angels will receive their reward without shame and will dwell in the Kingdom of Heaven. {10:16} But if you did not perform good deeds while alive, you will have no place among the righteous. {10:17} If you were unprepared in life and now regret it, it will be in vain. If you had wealth but did not share it with the needy, you will regret it. {10:18} If you did not clothe the naked, help the oppressed, or teach sinners to repent when you had the opportunity, you will regret it. {10:19} If you did not fast or pray when you had strength, or practice righteousness when it was possible, you will regret it. {10:20} Do not be enamored with worldly pleasures or material wealth, for they are not the adornments worthy of a person. {10:21} Instead, adorn yourself with purity, wisdom, and love for others without envy or doubt. Love your neighbor as yourself. {10:22} These virtues are true ornaments, leading to the Kingdom of Heaven and eternal reward for those who endure tribulations and hope in the resurrection with knowledge and wisdom. {10:23} Do not say, "We will not rise after death," for the devil seeks to destroy hope and salvation. You will know hardship when

Judgment Day comes. {10:24} Your sins will be exposed, and you will face the resurrection you denied, standing again in the flesh. {10:25} You will be reproached for the evil deeds you committed in this world, and you will witness the resurrection you rejected. {10:26} At that time, regret will consume you for not performing good deeds. It would have been better to weep in this life than to weep in Gehenna. {10:27} If you did not repent in this life, prepare for involuntary weeping in Gehenna. {10:28} Perform good deeds to transition from death to life, from this passing world to the Kingdom of Heaven, where the light of glory surpasses all earthly light. {10:29} Reject the temporary pleasures of this world so that you may enjoy boundless joy in the eternal Kingdom of Heaven, where those who believe in the resurrection of the dead will be forever blessed. Glory and praise be to Jah forever. Thus concludes the third book of the Maccabees, where these things are fulfilled.

Jasher

Book of Jasher, also referred to as the "Book of the Upright" or the "Book of the Just," is an ancient Jewish text that has fascinated scholars and theologians for centuries. Though not included in the canonical Hebrew Bible, it is mentioned in the Old Testament in Joshua 10:13 and 2 Samuel 1:18, suggesting its existence and significance in ancient Israelite culture. The Book of Jasher is thought to be a collection of poetic writings and historical records, offering additional perspectives on well-known biblical events and characters. Its content purportedly spans from the creation of the world to the period of the Judges, providing narrative expansions and unique details that are absent in the canonical texts. Various versions and translations of the Book of Jasher have surfaced over the years, most notably the 1625 edition by Rabbi Jacob Ilive and the later 1840 translation by Mordecai Manuel Noah, which has been widely circulated in English-speaking regions. While its authenticity and origins have been subjects of intense debate, with some viewing it as a pseudepigraphal work, its influence and the curiosity it sparks among researchers are undeniable. The Book of Jasher's blend of myth, legend, and historical recounting offers a rich tapestry for understanding the cultural and religious milieu of ancient Israel. It also provides a fascinating glimpse into the traditions that sought to expand and elucidate the stories found in the canonical scriptures.

{1:1} God said, "Let us make mankind in our image, after our likeness," and so God created man in His own image. {1:2} God formed man from the dust of the ground and breathed into his nostrils the breath of life, and man became a living soul with the ability to speak. {1:3} Then the Lord God said, "It is not good for man to be alone; I will make a helper suitable for him." {1:4} So God caused a deep sleep to fall upon Adam, and while he slept, He took one of his ribs, formed it into a woman, and brought her to Adam. {1:5} Adam exclaimed, "This is now bone of my bones and flesh of my flesh; she shall be called Woman, because she was taken out of Man." {1:6} God blessed them and named them Adam and Eve on the day they were created. {1:7} The Lord God placed Adam and his wife in the Garden of Eden to tend it and keep it. God commanded them, saying, "You may freely eat from every tree of the garden, {1:8} but you must not eat from the tree of the knowledge of good and evil, for on the day that you eat from it, you shall surely die." {1:9} After blessing and instructing them, God departed. Adam and Eve lived in the garden, obeying the Lord's command. {1:10} Now the serpent, which God had created alongside them, came to tempt them to disobey God's command. {1:11} The serpent deceived the woman, persuading her to eat from the tree of knowledge. She ate the fruit and also gave some to her husband, who ate it as well. {1:12} Thus, Adam and Eve disobeyed God's command, and God knew it. His anger burned against them, and He pronounced curses upon them. {1:13} The Lord God expelled them from the garden that very day, and they went to till the ground from which they had been taken. {1:14} Adam knew his wife Eve, and she bore him two sons and three daughters. {1:15} Their firstborn was named Cain, and Eve said, "I have acquired a man from the Lord." {1:16} Their second son was named Abel, for Eve said, "In vanity we came into the earth, and in vanity we shall depart from it." {1:17} As the boys grew, their father gave them land: Cain became a tiller of the ground, and Abel a keeper of sheep. {1:18} Some years later, Cain and Abel brought offerings to the Lord. Cain offered fruits from the ground, but Abel brought the firstlings of his flock. {1:19} The Lord accepted Abel's offering with favor, sending fire from heaven to consume it. {1:20} However, He did not regard Cain's offering because it was not the best of his produce. This made Cain jealous of his brother Abel. {1:21} One day, while working in the field, Cain confronted Abel in anger. He said, "Why do you bring your flock to feed on my land?" {1:22} Abel replied, "Why do you eat the flesh of my flock and wear their wool?" {1:23} Cain threatened Abel, but Abel assured him that God would avenge any harm done to him. {1:24} Enraged by Abel's words, Cain attacked and killed him in the field. {1:25} Afterward, Cain regretted his actions and mourned over his brother. {1:26} He buried Abel in a hole he dug in the ground. {1:27} The Lord knew what Cain had done and confronted him, asking, "Where is Abel your brother?" {1:28} Cain lied, saying, "I do not know; am I my brother's keeper?" {1:29} But the Lord rebuked him, saying, "Your brother's blood cries out to Me from the ground where you slew him. {1:30} You have committed a great sin; you thought I would not see or know, but I am aware of all your actions. {1:31} Because you have slain your brother without cause, cursed be you from the ground which has soaked up your brother's blood. {1:32} You shall no longer derive strength from it, for it will yield only thorns and thistles. You shall wander the earth as a restless fugitive until your death." {1:33} So Cain left the Lord's presence and settled in the land east of Eden with his family. {1:34} Cain's wife conceived and bore a son named Enoch, and Cain built a city, naming it after his son. {1:35} Enoch had a son named Irad, who had a son named Mechuyael, and Mechuyael had a son named Methusael.

{2:1} In the hundred and thirtieth year of Adam's life, Eve bore him another son whom they named Seth, saying, "God has given me another child in place of Abel, whom Cain killed." {2:2} Seth lived for one hundred and five years and then became the father of a son whom he named Enosh, saying, "At that time people began to multiply on the earth, and they started to indulge their souls and hearts in rebellion against God." {2:3} During Enosh's days, humanity continued to rebel and disobey God, provoking His anger further. {2:4} The people turned away from the Lord who had created them, worshiping idols made of brass, iron, wood, and stone. {2:5} They made their own gods and bowed down to them, forsaking the Lord throughout Enosh's lifetime and beyond. {2:6} Despite the Lord's warnings and even sending the waters of the river Gihon to flood them, they persisted in their wicked ways, their hands reaching out for evil in the sight of God. {2:7} In those days, there was no planting or harvesting; the famine was severe upon the earth. {2:8} The seeds they sowed produced thorns, thistles, and weeds, for the curse pronounced on the earth since Adam's sin continued to afflict it. {2:9} As humanity persisted in rebellion and corruption, the earth itself became corrupt. {2:10} Enosh lived ninety years and became the father of Cainan. {2:11} When Cainan reached forty years of age, he became known for his wisdom and knowledge, surpassing all others in understanding. He ruled over people with wisdom and knowledge, even discerning matters of spirits and demons. {2:12} By his wisdom, Cainan foresaw that God would bring destruction upon humanity for their sins on the earth, predicting the future deluge in the latter days. {2:13} Cainan recorded these prophecies on stone tablets and preserved them in his treasuries. {2:14} Cainan's influence extended across the earth, turning some people back to the worship of God. {2:15} When Cainan was seventy years old, he fathered three sons and two daughters. {2:16} The names of his children were Mahlallel, Enan, Mered, Adah, and Zillah. {2:17} Lamech, the son of Methusael, married Cainan's daughters: Adah bore him a son named Jabal, and later a son named Jubal by Zillah, who was barren for a time. {2:18} During these days, humanity began to rebel more openly against God's commandments given to Adam, especially the command to multiply and fill the earth. {2:19} Some men even resorted to giving their wives potions to make them barren, hoping to preserve their beauty and figures. {2:20} Among these women was Zillah, who also drank the potion. {2:21} The sight of childless women became a cause of scorn among their husbands, preferring barren wives over those who bore children. {2:22} But in due time, the Lord opened Zillah's womb when she grew old. {2:23} She bore a son named Tubal Cain, declaring, "I have obtained him from the Almighty God after my youthful vigor had passed." {2:24} Zillah bore another child, a daughter whom she named Naamah, saying, "I have found pleasure and delight after my youth had faded." {2:25} Lamech, advanced in years and nearly blind, was led by his son Tubal Cain in the fields one day when Cain, a descendant of Adam, approached them. {2:26} Tubal Cain instructed his father to shoot Cain with a bow, mistaking him for an animal at a distance. {2:27} Lamech's arrow struck Cain, mortally wounding him. {2:28} The arrows pierced Cain's body, and he fell dead on the ground. {2:29} The Lord avenged

Abel's murder by Cain according to His word. {2:30} After Cain's death, Lamech and Tubal Cain went to see the creature they had killed and discovered it was their ancestor, Cain. {2:31} Lamech deeply regretted his action and, in his distress, inadvertently caused the death of his son by striking him. {2:32} Lamech's wives heard what he had done and sought to kill him in retaliation. {2:33} They grew to hate Lamech for killing Cain and Tubal Cain, ultimately separating from him. {2:34} Lamech pleaded with Adah and Zillah to reconsider, explaining that he had acted unknowingly due to his old age and failing eyesight. {2:35} However, from that time on, Lamech's wives bore him no more children, knowing that God's judgment was imminent upon humanity for their wickedness. {2:36} Mahlallel, Cainan's son, lived sixty-five years and fathered Jared, who lived for sixty-two years and fathered Enoch.

{3:1} Enoch lived for sixty-five years and fathered Methuselah. After Methuselah's birth, Enoch devoted himself to walking with God, serving Him faithfully while rejecting the evil practices of humanity. {3:2} Enoch immersed himself in the Lord's teachings, gaining profound knowledge and understanding. He withdrew from the company of men and secluded himself for many years. {3:3} After serving the Lord and praying fervently in his house, an angel from heaven called out to him. Enoch responded, "Here I am." {3:4} The angel instructed him to leave his hiding place and appear before humanity to teach them the ways of God and the work they must do to walk in His paths. {3:5} Enoch obeyed the angel's command, leaving his seclusion and going to the people. He gathered them together and taught them about the Lord's instructions. {3:6} Enoch proclaimed a message across all inhabited places, inviting those who sought to know the ways of the Lord and perform good deeds to come to him. {3:7} People from all corners assembled before Enoch; they acknowledged him as their leader and listened attentively to his teachings. {3:8} Enoch was filled with the spirit of God, imparting divine wisdom and guidance to all who came to him. Throughout Enoch's life, the sons of men remained faithful to the Lord and sought his wisdom eagerly. {3:9} Kings, princes, and judges, from the first to the last, came to Enoch seeking his counsel. They bowed before him and asked him to rule over them, and he accepted their request. {3:10} One hundred and thirty kings and princes gathered and made Enoch their king, submitting themselves to his authority. {3:11} Enoch ruled with wisdom, establishing peace among the nations, and during his lifetime, the earth enjoyed an era of tranquility. {3:12} Enoch governed for two hundred and forty-three years, promoting justice and righteousness among his people as he led them in the ways of the Lord. {3:13} Enoch's descendants were Methuselah, Elisha, and Elimelech, with two daughters named Melca and Nahmah. Methuselah lived eighty-seven years and fathered Lamech. {3:14} Adam died at the age of nine hundred and thirty years, during the fifty-sixth year of Lamech's life. Enoch and Methuselah buried Adam in a manner befitting kings, in the cave as God had instructed. {3:15} The sons of men mourned deeply for Adam, establishing a tradition of great mourning that continued to Enoch's time. {3:16} Adam's death came as a consequence of eating from the tree of knowledge, a judgment spoken by the Lord God to him and his descendants. {3:17} In the year of Adam's death, the two hundred and forty-third year of Enoch's reign, Enoch decided to separate himself from humanity once again, hiding himself to serve the Lord. {3:18} Enoch withdrew from public view, spending three days secluded in prayer and praise to the Lord in his chamber, then emerging for one day to teach the people about God's ways. {3:19} This pattern continued for many years: Enoch secluded himself for six days and appeared among his people on the seventh day, then withdrew once more. {3:20} Eventually, he appeared only once a month, and later, once a year. The kings, princes, and sons of men desired to see Enoch again and hear his words, but they were afraid due to the divine awe that surrounded him, fearing they might be punished and die. {3:21} The kings and princes resolved to gather all the people and approach Enoch together, hoping to speak with him when he appeared among them. {3:22} When the day arrived and Enoch came forth, they assembled before him, and he taught them the words and wisdom of the Lord. They bowed before him, proclaiming, "Long live the king!" {3:23} Some time later, while Enoch was teaching the kings, princes, and sons of men about God's ways, an angel called to him from heaven, intending to take him up to reign among the sons of God in heaven, as he had reigned over humanity on earth. {3:24} Upon hearing this, Enoch gathered all the inhabitants of the earth, instructing them in wisdom, knowledge, and divine instructions. He informed them of his imminent ascent to heaven but did not know the exact day of his departure. {3:25} Enoch continued teaching wisdom and knowledge, giving instructions on how to live on earth so they could experience life abundantly. {3:26} He reproved them, set before them statutes and judgments to follow, and established peace among them, teaching them about eternal life. Enoch lived among them, imparting these teachings for some time. {3:27} As Enoch was speaking to the sons of men, they looked up and saw a majestic horse descending from heaven, pacing in the air. {3:28} They reported this vision to Enoch, who explained that the horse had come because of him. The time had come for him to leave them, never to be seen by them again. {3:29} The horse descended and stood before Enoch, visible to all the sons of men who were with him. {3:30} Enoch then proclaimed to the people to come to him that day if they wished to learn more about the ways of the Lord before he departed. {3:31} All the sons of men gathered before Enoch that day, along with the kings, princes, and counselors who remained with him. Enoch continued teaching them wisdom and knowledge, imparting divine instructions and urging them to serve the Lord faithfully all their days. {3:32} After this, Enoch mounted the horse and began his journey. Eight hundred thousand men followed him for one day's journey. {3:33} On the second day, Enoch urged them to return home to their tents to avoid risking their lives, but some chose to continue with him. {3:34} On the sixth day, a group of men remained steadfast with Enoch, declaring their unwavering loyalty to accompany him wherever he went, even unto death. {3:35} Their determination moved Enoch deeply, and he ceased urging them to return. {3:36} When the kings returned, they counted the men who remained with Enoch, concerned for their safety. {3:37} On the eighth day, they went to the place from which Enoch ascended into heaven. {3:38} They found the ground covered with snow and large stones of snow upon it. They searched beneath the snow but found no trace of the men who had been with Enoch, for he had ascended into heaven in a whirlwind, accompanied by horses and chariots of fire.

{4:1} Enoch lived on earth for three hundred and sixty-five years. {4:2} After Enoch ascended into heaven, all the kings of the earth appointed Methuselah, his son, to reign over them in his father's place. {4:3} Methuselah followed God's ways faithfully, just as his father Enoch had taught him. Throughout his life, he instructed the sons of men in wisdom, knowledge, and the fear of God, never swaying from the path of righteousness. {4:4} However, in Methuselah's later years, the sons of men turned away from the Lord. They corrupted the earth, engaging in robbery, plunder, rebellion against God, and gross transgressions. {4:5} God's anger burned against them, leading Him to devastate the earth's crops so that there was neither sowing nor reaping. {4:6} Instead of crops, thorns and thistles sprang up where they had not been sown. {4:7} Yet, despite these signs, the sons of men persisted in their evil ways, continuing to provoke the Lord with their wicked deeds. {4:8} God decided to destroy them utterly, regretting that He had created mankind. {4:9} In the days when Methuselah's son Lamech was one hundred and sixty years old, Seth, the son of Adam, passed away. {4:10} Seth's total lifespan was nine hundred and twelve years. {4:11} Lamech, at one hundred and eighty years old, took Ashmua, the daughter of Elishaa, his uncle's son, as his wife, and she conceived a child. {4:12} During this time, despite the small amount of food produced, the sons of men persisted in their evil ways, trespassing and rebelling against God. {4:13} Lamech's wife gave birth to a son, and they named him Noah, meaning "rest," for he was born during a time when the earth found rest from corruption. {4:14} Lamech also called him Menachem, saying, "This one shall bring us comfort from our work and from the toil of our hands, because of the ground which the Lord has cursed." {4:15} Noah grew up walking in the ways of his father Methuselah, upright and blameless before God. {4:16} However, the sons of men began to depart from the ways of the Lord in those days, multiplying on the earth with sons and daughters. They taught one another their evil practices and continued to sin against the Lord. {4:17} Every man made idols for themselves, and violence filled the earth as they plundered and robbed one another. {4:18} Leaders and rulers took wives forcibly from among the daughters of men, and they practiced mixing animals of different species, defying God's order. God looked upon the earth and saw that it was corrupt, with all flesh, both man and beast, perverting their ways. {4:19} The Lord determined to wipe out mankind, from human beings to birds, cattle, and creatures that move along the ground, for He regretted creating them. {4:20} Yet those who walked in the ways of the Lord died before the Lord brought about the destruction He had warned of concerning the sons of men. This was the Lord's way of sparing them from witnessing the impending judgment. {4:21} Noah, however, found favor in the eyes of the Lord. God chose Noah and his children to preserve a remnant of humanity and to propagate life upon the earth after the devastation.

{5:1} In the eighty-fourth year of Noah's life, Enoch, the son of Seth, passed away at the age of nine hundred and five. {5:2} When Noah was one hundred and seventy-nine years old, Cainan, the son of Enosh, died after living for nine hundred and ten years. {5:3} In the two hundred and thirty-fourth year of Noah's life, Mahlallel, the son of Cainan, passed away at the age of eight hundred and ninety-five. {5:4} Jared, the son of Mahlallel, died in the three hundred and sixty-sixth year of Noah's life, having lived for nine hundred and sixty-two years. {5:5} During this time, all those who followed the ways of the Lord passed away before the Lord executed the judgment He had decreed upon the earth. {5:6} After many years, in the four hundred and eightieth year of Noah's life, when those who had faithfully followed the Lord had perished among the sons of men, leaving only Methuselah, God spoke to Noah and Methuselah, saying, {5:7} "Speak to the sons of men, proclaiming that the Lord says: Turn from your evil ways, abandon your wicked deeds, and I will relent from the judgment I have planned against you, so it will not come to pass." {5:8} The Lord granted them one hundred and twenty years to repent. If they turned back to Him and forsake their evil ways, He promised to withhold the calamity He had forewarned. {5:9} Noah and Methuselah faithfully conveyed the Lord's message to the sons of men, speaking to them day after day. {5:10} However, the sons of men stubbornly refused to listen or heed their words; they remained obstinate. {5:11} The Lord gave them a hundred and twenty-year period, saying, "If they repent, I will relent from bringing destruction upon the earth." {5:12} During this time, Noah, the son of Lamech, refrained from taking a wife, fearing God would soon destroy the earth. {5:13} Noah was a righteous man, blameless among his contemporaries. The Lord chose him to ensure the continuity of mankind on earth through his descendants. {5:14} The Lord instructed Noah to take a wife and bear children, for He saw Noah's righteousness in his generation. {5:15} Noah took Naamah, the daughter of Enoch, as his wife when she was five hundred and eighty years old. {5:16} Noah was four hundred and ninety-eight years old when he married Naamah. {5:17} Naamah bore him a son named Japheth, saying, "God has made me fruitful in the land." She bore another son and named him Shem, saying, "God has provided me a remnant to propagate life in the land." {5:18} Noah was five hundred and two years old when Naamah gave birth to Shem. The boys grew up following the ways of the Lord, taught by their father Noah and their great-grandfather Methuselah. {5:19} Lamech, Noah's father, passed away during that time, but he did not wholeheartedly follow the ways of his father. He died at the age of seven hundred and seventy-five, in the hundred and ninety-fifth year of Noah's life. {5:20} Lamech's total lifespan was seven hundred and seventy-seven years. {5:21} In that year, all the sons of men who knew the Lord passed away before the Lord brought destruction upon them. It was the Lord's will that they would not witness the calamity He had decreed upon their brothers and relatives. {5:22} During that period, the Lord commanded Noah and Methuselah, "Stand forth and proclaim to the sons of men all the words I spoke to you in those days, in the hope that they may turn from their evil ways. If they do, I will relent from bringing destruction." {5:23} Noah and Methuselah did as commanded, declaring all of God's words to the sons of men. {5:24} Yet, the sons of men refused to listen; they did not pay heed to their declarations. {5:25} After this, the Lord spoke to Noah, saying, "The end of all flesh has come before me because of their evil deeds. I will destroy the earth. {5:26} Therefore, take gopher wood and go to a designated place to build a large ark. {5:27} Construct it with dimensions of three hundred cubits in length, fifty cubits in breadth, and thirty cubits in height. {5:28} Make a door on its side and finish it with a cubit above. Cover it inside and out with pitch. {5:29} I will bring a flood of waters upon the earth to destroy all flesh, from under the heavens. Everything on earth will perish. {5:30} You and your household must gather two of every living thing, male and female, to bring them into the ark and preserve offspring on earth. {5:31} Gather all the food that is eaten by animals to store for yourselves and for them." {5:32} "Choose three maidens for your sons from among the daughters of men, and they will be wives for your sons." {5:33} Noah obeyed God's commandments, beginning to build the ark when he was five hundred and ninety-five years old. He completed it in five years, as the Lord had instructed. {5:34} Noah then took three daughters of Eliakim, son of Methuselah, as wives for his sons, fulfilling the Lord's command. {5:35} In the year Methuselah died at the age of nine hundred and sixty.

{6:1} After Methuselah's death, the Lord instructed Noah, "Enter the ark with your household. I will gather all the animals, beasts, and birds of the air to come and surround the ark. {6:2} Position yourself by the doors of the ark. Animals, beasts, and birds will approach you; those that crouch before you, take and hand over to your sons who will bring them into the ark. Leave those that do not crouch before you." {6:3} The next day, a multitude of animals, beasts, and birds came and encircled the ark as the Lord had foretold. {6:4} Noah seated himself by the ark's door and brought into the ark every creature that crouched before him. Those that stood were left upon the earth. {6:5} A lioness came with her two cubs, a male and a female. The cubs crouched before Noah, and when the lioness rose against them, they struck her and she fled. They returned to crouch before Noah. {6:6} The lioness retreated and joined the lions. {6:7} Astonished, Noah took the two cubs and brought them into the ark. {6:8} Noah gathered every living creature upon the earth into the ark, leaving none behind. {6:9} He brought two of every species into the ark, and of the clean animals and birds, he brought seven pairs as God commanded. {6:10} All the animals and birds remained surrounding the ark, waiting. The rain did not begin until seven days later. {6:11} On that day, the Lord caused a great earthquake; the sun darkened, the foundations of the world shook violently, and the entire earth was in tumult. Lightning flashed, thunder roared, and fountains of the earth burst forth in an unprecedented manner. God did this to terrify humanity and eradicate evil from the earth. {6:12} Despite these signs, humanity did not turn from their evil ways. They further provoked the Lord's anger and remained hardened. {6:13} At the end of seven days, in Noah's six hundredth year, the waters of the flood covered the earth. {6:14} The fountains of the deep burst open, the windows of heaven poured rain for forty days and nights. {6:15} Noah, his family, and all living creatures entered the ark to escape the floodwaters. The Lord shut them in. {6:16} Meanwhile, the remaining people on earth suffered greatly from the rain and the animals still surrounded the ark. {6:17} About seven hundred thousand men and women gathered before Noah, pleading, "Open the ark so we may enter and not perish!" {6:18} Noah answered loudly from the ark, "Have you not rebelled against the Lord, denying His existence? The Lord brought this disaster upon you to punish and cut you off from the earth. {6:19} This is what I warned you about one hundred and twenty years ago, yet you refused to listen to the Lord's voice. Now you wish to live?" {6:20} They replied, "We are ready to return to the Lord! Open the ark so we may live and not die!" {6:21} Noah responded, "You see now, in your distress, you desire to return to the Lord. Why did you not do so during the hundred and twenty years granted by the Lord? Today, your wishes will not succeed." {6:22} The people attempted to break into the ark to escape the rain, but the Lord sent the animals to drive them away. They scattered across the earth once more. {6:23} The rain continued for forty days and nights, and all flesh on earth and in the waters perished—humans, animals, beasts, creeping things, and birds. Only Noah and those with him in the ark remained alive. {6:24} The waters prevailed and increased upon the earth, lifting the ark from the ground. {6:25} The ark floated upon the waters, tossed violently so that all living creatures inside were in turmoil. {6:26} The animals within the ark were greatly distressed; lions roared, oxen lowed, wolves howled, and every creature lamented in its own way. Their cries echoed far and wide. Noah and his sons cried and feared they were nearing death. {6:27} Noah prayed fervently to the Lord, "O Lord, help us! We cannot bear this calamity. The waters surround us, death's snares are before us. Answer us, O Lord, light up Your face upon us, be gracious and deliver us!" {6:28} The Lord heard Noah's cry and remembered him. {6:29} A wind passed over the earth, the waters calmed, and the ark rested. {6:30} The fountains of the deep and the windows of heaven closed, and the rain ceased. {6:31} The waters began to recede, and the ark came to rest on the mountains of Ararat. {6:32} Noah opened the windows of the ark and continued to pray to the Lord, saying, "O Lord, who created the earth and the heavens and all within them, release our souls from this confinement. I am weary with sighing." {6:33} The Lord listened to Noah and said, "When a full year has passed, you may leave the ark." {6:34} At the end of the year, on the twenty-seventh day of the second month, the earth was dry. Noah, his sons, and those with him did not leave the ark until the Lord instructed them. {6:35} Finally, on the day appointed by the Lord, they all exited the ark. {6:36} Noah and his sons returned to their homes and places, serving the Lord all their days. The Lord blessed Noah and his sons as they departed from the ark. {6:37} He said to them, "Be fruitful, multiply, and fill the earth. Increase abundantly and multiply in it."

{7:1} These are the names of Noah's sons: Japheth, Ham, and Shem. They had children after the flood, as they had taken wives before it. {7:2} Japheth's sons were Gomer, Magog, Madai, Javan, Tubal, Meshech, and Tiras—seven sons in total. {7:3} Gomer's sons were Ashkenaz, Riphath, and Togarmah. {7:4} Magog's sons were Elichanaf and Lubal. {7:5} Madai's sons were Elishah, Tarshish, Kittim, and Dodanim. {7:6} Javan's sons were Elishah, Tarshish, Kittim, and Dodanim. {7:7} Tubal's sons were Elishah, Tarshish, Kittim, and Dodanim. {7:8} Meshech's sons were Elishah, Tarshish, Kittim, and Dodanim. {7:9} Tiras's sons were Elishah, Tarshish, Kittim, and Dodanim; they numbered about four hundred and sixty men in those days. {7:10} Ham's sons were Cush, Egypt (Mizraim), Put, and Canaan—four sons in total. {7:11} Cush's sons were Seba, Havilah, Sabtah, Raamah, and Sabteca; Raamah's sons were Sheba and Dedan. {7:12} Mizraim's sons were Ludim, Anamim, Lehabim, Naphtuhim, {7:13} Pathrusim, Casluhim (from whom the Philistines came), and Caphtorim. {7:14} Canaan's sons were Sidon, Heth, Amorite, Gergashite, Hivite, Arkite, Sinite, Arvadite, Zemarite, and Hamathite; {7:15} all were descendants of Ham, divided into their clans. {7:16} Shem's sons were Elam, Ashur, Arphaxad, Lud, and Aram—five sons in total. {7:17} Elam's sons were Shushan, Machul, and Harmon. {7:18} Ashur's sons were Mirus and Mokil. {7:19} Arphaxad's sons were Shelah, Anar, and Ashcol. {7:20} Lud's sons were Pethor and Bizayon. {7:21} Aram's sons were Uz, Hul, Gether, and Mash. {7:22} Shem's descendants totaled about three hundred men in those days. {7:23} Shem fathered Arphaxad, who fathered Shelah, who fathered Eber. {7:24} Eber had two sons: one was named Peleg, because in his time the earth was divided; and the other was named Joktan, because in his time the human lifespan began to decline. {7:25} Joktan's sons were Almodad, Sheleph, Hazarmaveth, Jerah, Hadoram, Uzal, Diklah, Obal, Abimael, Sheba, Ophir, Havilah, and Jobab—all descendants of Joktan. {7:26} Peleg's son was Reu, who fathered Serug, who fathered Nahor, who fathered Terah, who was thirty-eight years old when he fathered Haran and Nahor. {7:27} Ham, Noah's son, married late in life and had a son named Nimrod, who grew up as a rebellious and mighty hunter before the Lord. {7:28} The garments of skin made by God for Adam and Eve when they left the Garden of Eden were passed down through Enoch to Methuselah and eventually to Noah. {7:29} After Methuselah's death, Noah took these garments into the ark. {7:30} When they left the ark, Ham took these garments from Noah and gave them secretly to his son Cush. {7:31} Cush, in turn, passed them to Nimrod, who gained great strength and became a mighty hunter. {7:32} Nimrod became a powerful ruler and fought successful battles for his people, gaining widespread renown. {7:33} The saying about Nimrod's might spread, and people invoked his name in battle. {7:34} At forty years old, Nimrod led his people in a war against Japheth's descendants, and with about five hundred men, he triumphed and took captives. {7:35} Nimrod returned victorious, and his people acclaimed him as king. {7:36} He appointed princes and rulers, including Terah, whom he esteemed highly. {7:37} Nimrod decided to build a city and named it Shinar, establishing his kingdom there. {7:38} Under Nimrod's rule, his kingdom prospered, and he became exceedingly powerful. {7:39} Nimrod's wickedness surpassed all others before him since the flood, as he led people astray, worshiping idols of wood and stone. {7:40} His son Mardon followed in his footsteps, perpetuating even greater wickedness. {7:41} Terah, Nahor's son, gained favor with Nimrod and his people and was greatly esteemed. {7:42} During Terah's reign, he married Amthelo, and she bore him a son named Abram when Terah was seventy years old. {7:43} Terah named him Abram because the king had elevated him above all his princes.

{8:1} The night Abram was born, all of Terah's servants, along with Nimrod's wise men and sorcerers, gathered at Terah's house. They celebrated with food and drink, rejoicing together. {8:2} After the wise men and sorcerers left Terah's house, they looked up at the stars. They witnessed a remarkable sight: a very large star appeared from the east and moved swiftly across the heavens, swallowing up four stars from all directions. {8:3} This astonished the wise men and sorcerers, who understood its significance. {8:4} They said to one another, "This signifies the child born to Terah tonight. He will grow up to be fruitful, multiply, and inherit the earth along with his descendants. He will conquer great kings and possess their lands." {8:5} The wise men and sorcerers returned home that night, and the next morning they convened to discuss what they had seen. {8:6} They decided not to inform King Nimrod about the vision, fearing his wrath if they kept it secret and it later became known. {8:7} So they went to the king and bowed before him, saying, "Long live the king! Long live the king! {8:8} We heard that Terah, the son of Nahor and captain of your host, had a son born to him last night. We visited his house, celebrated, and observed a strange phenomenon in the sky after we left." {8:9} They continued, "As we looked up, we saw a great star coming from the east, moving swiftly and swallowing four stars from the heavens." {8:10} "We were greatly astonished and frightened by what we saw. By our wisdom, we discerned that this event pertains to the child born to Terah, who will grow to be powerful, overthrowing all the kings of the earth and inheriting their lands for eternity." {8:11} They urged the king to take action, suggesting, "If it pleases the king, let us slay this child before he grows up and becomes a threat to us and our descendants." {8:12} The king listened attentively as they explained the vision and its interpretation concerning Terah's child. {8:13} The idea of eliminating the child appealed to the king, and he summoned Terah to his presence. {8:14} The king said to Terah, "I heard that a son was born to you last night, and this unusual phenomenon accompanied his birth." {8:15} "Hand over the child to us so we can kill him before he becomes a danger. In return, I will fill your house with silver and gold." {8:16} Terah responded respectfully, "My lord, I have heard your words, and I will do as you command. However, let me share something that happened to me last night before I answer." {8:17} The king permitted

Terah to speak. {8:18} Terah recounted, "Ayon, son of Mored, approached me last night, requesting a valuable horse you had given me. In exchange, he offered silver, gold, straw, and provender." {8:19} "I told him I would seek your counsel before deciding." {8:20} "Now, my lord, I have disclosed this matter to you. I await your guidance." {8:21} The king's anger flared at Terah's words, deeming him foolish. {8:22} He retorted sharply, "Are you so foolish to barter away a fine horse for silver and gold, or even for straw and provender?" {8:23} "Do you lack silver and gold to such an extent that you consider selling your horse, which is the finest on earth?" {8:24} The king rebuked Terah for his proposal and ceased speaking. {8:25} Terah replied, "My lord, you also proposed to give me silver and gold in exchange for my son's life. What use would silver and gold be to me after my son's death? Who will inherit them from me?" {8:26} These words troubled the king greatly, kindling his anger further. {8:27} Terah continued, "Everything I possess is in your power. Whatever you decide for your servant, including my son and his older brothers, I will accept." {8:28} The king responded, "No, I will pay you a price for your younger son." {8:29} Terah pleaded, "My lord, allow your servant to speak before you." {8:30} "Grant me three days to ponder this matter and consult my family. I beg your indulgence in this." {8:31} The king agreed, giving Terah three days to decide. Terah left the king's presence and returned home to discuss the matter with his family, causing great anxiety among them. {8:32} On the third day, the king sent word to Terah, demanding, "Send me your son as we agreed. If you do not comply, I will slay everyone in your household, sparing neither man nor beast." {8:33} Faced with the king's urgent command, Terah took a newborn child from one of his servants, born that very day, and presented the child to the king in exchange for payment. {8:34} The Lord protected Terah, ensuring that Nimrod did not realize he had spared Abram's life. {8:35} Terah secretly took Abram, along with his mother and nurse, and hid them in a cave. {8:36} Abram remained in hiding for ten years, and during this time, the king and his advisors believed Abram had perished.

{9:1} Haran, Abram's older brother, took a wife when he was thirty-nine years old. {9:2} His wife conceived and bore a son whom they named Lot. {9:3} She bore another daughter named Milca, and then a third daughter named Sarai. {9:4} Haran was forty-two when Sarai was born, marking the tenth year of Abram's life. During this time, Abram, his mother, and nurse emerged from their cave, as the king and his people had forgotten about the matter concerning Abram. {9:5} Abram ventured to Noah and Shem, seeking to learn the ways of the Lord in their company. Concealed from others, Abram served Noah and Shem diligently for thirty-nine years in Noah's household, having known the Lord since he was three years old. {9:6} In those days, the people on earth were rebellious, turning away from the Lord to serve idols made of wood and stone. They forgot their Creator and worshiped gods that could neither speak, hear, nor save. {9:7} Even the king Nimrod and Terah's entire household were among the first to embrace these false gods. {9:8} Terah himself possessed twelve large idols made of wood and stone, one for each month of the year. Monthly, he offered meat and drink sacrifices to these idols, persisting in this practice all his life. {9:9} The entire generation lived wickedly in the sight of the Lord, each person creating their own god while forsaking the true God who made them. {9:10} Amidst this pervasive idolatry, only Noah and his household remained faithful to the Lord, guiding others who sought wisdom in those days. {9:11} Meanwhile, Abram flourished in Noah's household, unnoticed by others, yet the Lord was with him, granting him wisdom and understanding. {9:12} Abram discerned that the works of his generation were futile, and their gods were powerless and vain. {9:13} Observing the sun, Abram initially deemed it God and worshiped it. Yet, when the sun set without divine intervention, Abram realized it could not be God. {9:14} He pondered further, contemplating who created the heavens, the earth, and all that exists. {9:15} In the darkness, Abram looked to the stars and the moon, assuming them to be the true God and his servants. {9:16} All night, he worshiped the moon until dawn broke and revealed the handiwork of the true God on earth. {9:17} Abram concluded that the heavenly bodies were not gods but creations of the true God. {9:18} Thus, he continued to reside in Noah's house, faithfully serving the Lord all his days, {9:19} while the rest of his generation persisted in idolatry and rebellion. {9:20} King Nimrod ruled with authority over the unified world, where all spoke a common language. {9:21} The princes and great men under Nimrod's rule devised a plan together. Phut, Mitzraim, Cush, and Canaan, along with their families, proposed building a city and a tall tower reaching to heaven. Their goal was fame and power, seeking to consolidate their strength against potential enemies and prevent dispersal through warfare. {9:22} They presented their plan to King Nimrod, who approved and supported their endeavor. {9:23} Six hundred thousand men gathered to build the city and tower. They settled in a fertile valley east of Shinar, devoting themselves to brickmaking and construction. {9:24} The tower's construction was an act of rebellion and sin against the Lord. As they built, they harbored intentions of warring against God and ascending to heaven. {9:25} Divided into three groups, they aimed to challenge God's authority: some sought to fight Him, others planned to install their own gods in heaven, and the rest intended to conquer God with weapons. God, aware of their wicked intentions, observed their activities around the tower and city. {9:26} As construction progressed, the city grew exceedingly large, and the tower reached great heights. {9:27} Due to its immense height, materials did not reach the builders promptly, causing delays. Those ascending took a full year to complete their climb, receiving materials from those below afterward. {9:28} During construction, if a brick fell and broke, the workers mourned its loss. If a worker fell and died, they paid him no heed. {9:29} God saw their thoughts and actions. When they aimed arrows toward heaven, the arrows returned soaked in blood, and they foolishly believed they had slain heavenly beings. {9:30} This was a divine act to lead them astray and bring about their destruction. {9:31} They persisted in building the city and tower for many years, but their evil deeds did not go unnoticed by the Lord. {9:32} God instructed seventy angels to confuse their language, causing each person to speak a different tongue, unable to understand one another. {9:33} From that day on, they could not communicate effectively. Confusion reigned as they unwittingly attacked each other over misunderstandings, leading to many deaths. {9:34} Despite these calamities, they continued building, and many perished in such tragic conflicts. {9:35} God punished them accordingly: those seeking to install gods in heaven were transformed into apes and elephants, those aiming arrows at heaven were killed by their own hands, and those waging war against God were scattered across the earth. {9:36} Fearing further divine retribution, the survivors abandoned the construction project, dispersing across the globe. {9:37} Consequently, they ceased building the city and tower, naming the place Babel because the Lord confused the language of the whole earth there. This occurred east of Shinar. {9:38} Regarding the tower, the earth swallowed a third, fire consumed another third, and the remaining third remains to this day, standing as a testament to their audacious ambition. {9:39} Many people perished in that tower, a tragedy beyond counting.

{10:1} Peleg, the son of Eber, passed away at the age of two hundred and thirty-nine years, during the forty-eighth year of Abram's life. {10:2} After God dispersed humanity due to their sins at the tower of Babel, they spread out across the earth, dividing into numerous groups. People settled in different regions, each group forming its own language, territory, and cities. {10:3} Families built cities according to their lineage wherever they settled, scattered throughout the earth as God had decreed. {10:4} Some founded cities in places they later abandoned, naming these cities after themselves, their children, or notable events. {10:5} The descendants of Japheth, Noah's son, migrated and built cities named after themselves in the lands where they settled. Japheth's descendants became divided into many nations and spoke different languages across the earth. {10:6} These are the descendants of Japheth: Gomer, Magog, Madai, Javan, Tubal, Meshech, and Tiras, each forming their own families and establishing their cities. {10:7} Gomer's descendants settled in Francum near the rivers Franza and Senah. {10:8} Rephath's descendants, known as Bartonim, settled in Bartonia by the river Ledah, which flows into the great sea Gihon (the ocean). {10:9} Tugarma's descendants, ten families in total, settled in the north, establishing cities with names like Buzar, Parzunac, Balgar, and others. {10:10} These cities, along the rivers Hithlah and Italac, remain to this day. {10:11} Angoli, Balgar, and Parzunac's families dwelled by the great river Dubnee, naming their cities accordingly. {10:12} Javan's descendants, known as Javanim, settled in Macedonia. {10:13} Medai's descendants, the Orelum, settled in Curson. {10:14} Tubal's descendants lived in Tuskanah by the river Pashiah. {10:15} Meshech's descendants were the Shibashni, and Tiras' descendants included Rushash, Cushni, and Ongolis; they built cities by the sea Jabus near the river Cura and Tragan. {10:16} Elishah's descendants, the Almanim, settled between the mountains of Job and Shibathmo. {10:17} The Dudonim's descendants lived in the cities of the sea Gihon, in Bordna. {10:18} These were the families of Japheth's descendants, forming cities and speaking different languages after being scattered from the tower of Babel. {10:19} Ham's descendants included Cush, Mitzraim, Phut, and Canaan, forming their own families and cities. {10:20} Mitzraim's descendants included the Ludim, Anamim, Lehabim, Naphtuchim, Pathrusim, Casluchim, and Caphturim, settling by the river Sihor (Egypt's brook) and naming cities after themselves. {10:21} Pathros and Casloch's descendants intermarried, giving rise to the Pelishtim, Azathim, Gerarim, Githim, and Ekronim, who built cities named after their fathers. {10:22} Canaan's descendants also built cities and named eleven cities after themselves, besides countless others. {10:23} Four men from Ham's lineage, Sodom, Gomorrah, Admah, and Zeboyim, settled in the plain and founded cities named after themselves. {10:24} Seir, the son of Hur and grandson of Canaan, settled in a valley opposite Mount Paran, building a city named Seir where he, his seven sons, and their households lived. {10:25} This became known as the land of Seir. {10:26} Bela, from the house of Ashur, settled near Sodom and Gomorrah, building a city named Bela after himself, known as Zoar to this day. {10:27} These are the families of Ham's descendants, their languages, and the cities they founded after being dispersed from the tower of Babel. {10:28} Shem's descendants, including Elam, Ashur, Arpachshad, Lud, and Aram, also founded cities named after themselves in various places. {10:29} Ashur's descendants, a large group, settled in a distant land with extensive valleys, where they built Nineveh, Resen, Calach, and Rehobother, which remain to this day. {10:30} Aram's descendants built the city Uz, named after their eldest brother. {10:31} Shem's descendants formed families and cities, ensuring their names endured through the ages. {10:32} This includes Ashur's descendants who settled and built Nineveh, Resen, Calach, and Rehobother. {10:33} Aram's descendants settled in the land of Uz, establishing the city named after their eldest brother. {10:34} In the second year after the tower, Bela from Ashur's household settled near Sodom and Gomorrah, founding the city of Zoar. {10:35} These are the families of Shem's descendants, their languages, and the cities they built after being scattered from the tower of Babel. {10:36} Every kingdom, city, and family of Noah's descendants continued to build many cities, establishing governance & maintaining their traditions for generations.

{11:1} Nimrod, the son of Cush, remained in the land of Shinar where he ruled as king. He built cities there, establishing his dominion firmly in the region. {11:2} The cities Nimrod built were named according to significant events that occurred during their construction. {11:3} He called the first city Babel, because there the Lord confused the language of all the earth. The second city he named Erech, because it was from there that God dispersed the people. {11:4} The third city he named Eched, due to a great battle that took place there. The fourth city was named Calnah, where his princes and mighty men were consumed in rebellion against the Lord. {11:5} After constructing these cities, Nimrod settled his remaining people, including princes and warriors, within them. {11:6} Nimrod established his reign in Babel and was known as Amraphel among his subjects. His reign continued in wickedness, and he taught evil practices to the people. {11:7} Despite his actions, Nimrod did not turn back to the Lord; instead, he and his son Mardon continued to deepen their wickedness. {11:8} Mardon surpassed his father in evil, leading the people further astray. It was said, "From the wicked comes forth wickedness." {11:9} During this time, conflict arose among the families of Ham's descendants who dwelled in the cities they had built. {11:10} Chedorlaomer, king of Elam, separated from Ham's descendants and waged war against them, conquering the five cities of the plain and imposing his rule over them. {11:11} They served him for twelve years, paying a yearly tribute. {11:12} In the forty-ninth year of Abram's life, Nahor, son of Serug, passed away. {11:13} In Abram's fiftieth year, he left Noah's house and returned to his father Terah's household. {11:14} Abram followed the ways and instructions of the Lord his God, and the Lord was with him. {11:15} Terah, Abram's father, still held a position in King Nimrod's army and worshipped idols. {11:16} When Abram returned to his father's house, he saw twelve idols standing in their temples. His anger flared at the sight of these images. {11:17} Abram declared, "As the Lord lives, these idols shall not remain in my father's house. If within three days I do not break them all, may the Lord who created me bring judgment upon me." {11:18} Leaving them, Abram's anger burned within him. He went to his father's outer court, where Terah and his servants were gathered. {11:19} Abram asked his father, "Father, where is the God who created heaven, earth, and all mankind?" Terah replied, "Behold, they who created us are here with us in the house." {11:20} Abram requested, "Show them to me, I pray." Terah brought Abram to the inner chamber, filled with twelve great idols of wood and stone, and numerous smaller ones. {11:21} Terah said, "These made all you see on earth, and they created me and you." {11:22} Terah worshipped the idols, then departed, and Abram left with him. {11:23} Abram went to his mother and said, "Mother, my father has shown me the creators of heaven, earth, and all mankind." {11:24} "Quickly, fetch a kid from the flock, and prepare savory meat that I may offer it to my father's gods. Perhaps then they will accept me." {11:25} His mother did so, preparing the meat, and Abram took it to the idols his father worshipped, hoping they would eat it. {11:26} Abram observed that the idols had no voice, hearing, or motion. Not one could reach out to take the food. {11:27} Mocking them, Abram said, "The meat I prepared must not have pleased them, or it was too little. Tomorrow I will prepare better and more plentiful meat to see if they will eat." {11:28} The next day, Abram instructed his mother to prepare three fine kids of the flock, making excellent savory meat. Terah remained unaware of these preparations. {11:29} Abram took the meat and placed it before his father's idols, sitting before them all day, hoping they would eat. {11:30} Observing closely, Abram saw the idols could not speak, hear, or stretch out their hands to eat. {11:31} That evening, Abram was filled with the spirit of God in that house. {11:32} He cried out, "Woe unto my father and this wicked generation! Your hearts are filled with vanity, serving these idols of wood and stone that cannot eat, smell, hear, or speak. {11:33} You made them and trust in them! {11:34} "Taking a hatchet, Abram entered the chamber of the gods and shattered all but the largest idol. {11:35} He placed the hatchet in the hand of the largest idol, and departed. Hearing the noise, Terah returned home, discovering the idols broken. {11:36} Finding only the hatchet in the hand of the largest idol, and the meat Abram had offered still before them, Terah was angered. {11:37} He hastened to Abram, asking, "What have you done to my gods?" {11:38} Abram replied, "Father, I offered savory meat, and when I approached them, they all stretched out their hands to eat before the largest one reached out. {11:39} The large idol saw what they did, and in anger, took the hatchet and broke them." {11:40} Terah disputed Abram's words, accusing him of lies. {11:41} "Do these idols have spirit, soul, or power as you say? Are they not wood and stone that I made? Are you deceiving me, saying the large idol smote them?" {11:42} Abram replied, "Why then serve idols with no power? Can they deliver you, hear your prayers, or protect you from enemies? You serve wood and stone that cannot speak or hear!" {11:43} "Our fathers sinned, and the Lord brought the flood upon them. {11:44} How can you continue this folly, forgetting the Lord God who made heaven, earth, and all? {11:45} Will you bring evil upon yourselves by serving stone and wood?" {11:46} "Our ancestors sinned, and the Lord brought the flood upon them. {11:47} Why will you and your people commit the same error, drawing the anger of the Lord upon you?" {11:48} "Refrain from this evil, serve the God who made you, and all will be well." {11:49} Abram took the hatchet from the largest idol, breaking it, and fled. {11:50} Terah, seeing what Abram had done, went to the king, recounting Abram's actions and words. {11:51} The king sent three servants to bring Abram before him, with all his princes and servants present. Terah also attended. {11:52} The king asked Abram, "Why did you do this to your father and his gods?" Abram answered as he had spoken to his father. {11:53} The king asked, "Could these idols speak, eat, and act as you said?" {11:54} Abram responded, "If they have no power, why serve them? You mislead the people into error with your folly." {11:55} "Can they deliver you or accomplish anything? Why not serve the God who created you and has power over life and death?" {11:56} "Woe unto you, foolish king! {11:57} I thought you would teach righteousness, but your sins fill the earth, leading your people astray." {11:58} "Did you not know our ancestors' evil led to the flood that destroyed the earth? Will you repeat their error, provoking the anger of the Lord?" {11:59} "Refrain from this evil, serve the God of the universe, and you will prosper." {11:60} "If your heart remains hardened, and you do not turn from evil to serve the eternal God, shame and judgment will befall you and your people." {11:61} Abram concluded, lifting his eyes to heaven, "The Lord sees all wickedness and will judge accordingly."

{12:1} When the king heard Abram's words, he ordered him thrown into prison. Abram remained there for ten days. {12:2} At the end of that period, the king summoned all the rulers, princes, governors, and wise men of the land. They gathered before him while Abram was still confined. {12:3} Addressing the assembly, the king said, "Have you heard what Abram, son of Terah, has done to his father? He has spoken against me. I ordered him brought before me, but he showed no fear and did not back down. Now he languishes in prison." {12:4} The rulers and wise men responded, "Anyone who reviles the king should be hanged. But Abram has not only insulted you; he has also defied our gods. Therefore, he must be burned to death, for this is the law." {12:5} The king agreed and commanded his servants to prepare a fire in the royal furnace, which burned day and night. Abram was to be cast into it. {12:6} The king's servants made ready the fire for three days and nights in the king's furnace in Casdim. Abram was brought from prison and prepared for the fiery ordeal. {12:7} All the king's servants, officials, and the populace—nearly a million people—gathered to witness Abram's fate. {12:8} Women and children crowded rooftops and towers to catch a glimpse of what was happening. No one in the land was absent that day. {12:9} As Abram stood before the fire, the king's magicians and wise men recognized him. They exclaimed to the king, "This is the child whose birth caused the great star to consume four stars!" {12:10} "His father has deceived you," they continued. "He substituted another child for the one you ordered killed." {12:11} Enraged, the king summoned Terah and demanded an explanation. {12:12} Trembling, Terah admitted, "What the wise men say is true. I deceived you and substituted my servant's child for Abram." {12:13} "Who advised you to do this?" demanded the king. {12:14} "It was my eldest son, Haran," Terah confessed, hoping to deflect the king's wrath. {12:15} Terrified, Terah explained to the king that Haran had urged him to deceive the king. {12:16} Unbeknownst to anyone, Haran secretly sympathized with Abram's cause. {12:17} The king was incensed and decreed that both Abram and Haran should be cast into the fire. The entire kingdom assembled to witness the punishment. {12:18} As they were stripped and bound, Abram and Haran's fate seemed sealed. {12:19} Haran privately vowed to follow Abram if he survived the ordeal, unsure if the king or Abram's God would prevail. {12:20} The king's servants threw Abram and Haran into the blazing furnace. It seemed certain they would perish. {12:21} The people watched as the flames engulfed them. {12:22} Miraculously, Abram remained untouched by the fire, walking unharmed within it. {12:23} Haran, however, perished in the flames, consumed by his lack of faith. {12:24} The cords that bound them were incinerated, yet Abram walked freely in the midst of the inferno. {12:25} Those who had cast them in were themselves burned, twelve of them dying instantly. {12:26} For three days and nights, Abram walked unscathed in the midst of the fire. {12:27} All who witnessed this miracle reported to the king what they had seen. {12:28} The king, incredulous, dispatched trusted advisors to verify the astonishing account. {12:29} Convinced by their testimony, the king approached the furnace. {12:30} Despite repeated attempts, his servants could not rescue Abram from the flames, as the fire raged fiercely. {12:31} Several servants were fatally burned in the attempt. {12:32} Realizing their efforts were futile, the king called out to Abram, addressing him as "servant of the God who is in heaven." {12:33} "Come out of the fire," commanded the king, "and stand before me." {12:34} Astonished, the king asked Abram, "How is it that you were not burned?" {12:35} Abram answered, "The God of heaven and earth, in whom I trust, delivered me from the fire into which you cast me." {12:36} Haran's body was found reduced to ashes, a stark contrast to Abram's miraculous preservation. {12:37} Witnessing Abram's deliverance, the king and his subjects bowed in reverence. {12:38} Humbly, Abram directed their worship to the God who had spared him. {12:39} Astonished by these events, the king bestowed lavish gifts upon Abram and released him in peace. {12:40} Abram departed with the king's blessings, accompanied by a retinue of followers. {12:41} Returning to his father's house, Abram continued to serve and worship the Lord faithfully all his days. {12:42} From that day forward, Abram's influence led many to turn their hearts toward serving the Lord. {12:43} In due time, Nahor and Abram married their nieces, Milcah and Sarai, respectively. Sarai, however, remained barren. {12:44} Two years after emerging unscathed from the furnace, in the fifty-second year of his life, Abram found himself confronted once again by King Nimrod's hostility. {12:45} Nimrod, ruling from Babel, had a disturbing dream involving Abram and his future descendants. {12:46} In the dream, Nimrod saw Abram approaching him with a drawn sword, and a great river emerged from an egg thrown by Abram, drowning Nimrod's army. {12:47} Though Nimrod escaped with three kings, a young bird from the egg plucked out his eye. {12:48} Troubled, Nimrod sought the interpretation from his wise men and magicians. {12:49} Anuki, a trusted servant, explained that the dream foretold Abram's future conflict with Nimrod and his descendants. {12:50} The river turning to an egg and the bird plucking out Nimrod's eye symbolized the future demise of Nimrod at the hands of Abram's descendants. {12:51} Convinced by Anuki's interpretation, Nimrod resolved to eliminate Abram to avert this prophesied threat. {12:52} Secretly, Nimrod dispatched his servants to find and seize Abram, intending to execute him.

{13:1} Terah took his son Abram, along with his grandson Lot (the son of Haran), and Sarai his daughter-in-law (Abram's wife), and all the people of his household, and they left Ur of the Chaldeans to go to the land of Canaan. When they reached the land of Haran, they settled there because it was good for pasture, spacious enough for their needs. {13:2} The people of Haran recognized that Abram walked uprightly before God and men, and that the Lord was with him. Some of the inhabitants of Haran joined Abram, and he instructed them in the ways and laws of the Lord. These men remained with Abram and became part of his household. {13:3} Abram stayed in the land of Haran for three years. At the end of these three years, the Lord appeared to Abram and said, "I am the Lord who brought you out of Ur of the Chaldeans, and delivered you from your enemies. {13:4} "Now, if you will listen to my voice, keep my commandments, statutes, and laws, I will cause your enemies to fall before you. I will multiply your descendants like the stars of heaven, and I will bless all the work of your hands so that you will lack nothing. {13:5} "Arise, take your wife, all your possessions, and go to the land of Canaan. I will be your God there, and I will bless you." Abram obeyed the Lord's command and took Sarai and all that belonged to him, journeying to

Canaan when he was fifty years old. {13:6} Abram arrived in Canaan and settled in the midst of the land, pitching his tent among the Canaanites, the native inhabitants. {13:7} The Lord appeared to Abram again in Canaan and said, "To your descendants I will give this land forever." Abram responded by building an altar at the place where God had spoken to him, and he called upon the name of the Lord. {13:8} After dwelling three years in Canaan, Noah died at the age of 950 years, in the fifty-eighth year of Abram's life. {13:9} Abram continued to reside in Canaan with his wife, his household, and those who had joined him from the people of the land. However, Nahor (Abram's brother), Terah (his father), Lot (Haran's son), and their families remained in Haran. {13:10} In the fifth year of Abram's stay in Canaan, the cities of Sodom, Gomorrah, and the other cities of the plain rebelled against Chedorlaomer, king of Elam, after serving him for twelve years. {13:11} Ten years later, in the fifteenth year of Abram's dwelling in Canaan (when Abram was seventy years old), the Lord appeared to him again and reaffirmed His promise: "I am the Lord who brought you out of Ur of the Chaldeans to give you this land as an inheritance." {13:12} Abram built another altar and offered sacrifices to the Lord, commemorating the covenant made with him. {13:13} After this, Abram returned to Haran for a visit, staying there for five years, reconnecting with his father Terah and others in his household. {13:14} Many people from Haran, about seventy-two men, followed Abram to Canaan, where he continued to teach them the ways of the Lord. {13:15} In Haran, the Lord appeared to Abram once more, saying, "Twenty years ago I told you to leave your land and your father's house and go to the land I would show you. Now, gather your household and all those who have joined you in Haran, and return to the land of Canaan." {13:16} Abram obeyed, taking Sarai, Lot, and all their possessions, as well as those born in his household and those whom he had influenced in Haran, to journey back to Canaan. {13:17} Abram was seventy-five years old when he departed from Haran to return to Canaan, as the Lord had instructed him. He settled in the plains of Mamre, accompanied by Lot and all their belongings. {13:18} Once again, the Lord appeared to Abram, reaffirming His promise: "I will give this land to your descendants." In response, Abram built another altar to the Lord, which remained in the plains of Mamre.

{14:1} In ancient times, in the land of Shinar, there lived a wise man named Rikayon who was renowned for his wisdom and handsome appearance, yet he struggled in poverty. {14:2} Desiring recognition and sustenance, Rikayon journeyed to Egypt, seeking an audience with Oswiris, the son of Anom, the king of Egypt, hoping to impress him with his wisdom. {14:3} Upon arriving in Egypt, Rikayon learned that the king's custom was to appear in public only once a year to hear the grievances of his people and dispense justice. {14:4} Hearing this, Rikayon was disheartened as he realized he could not present himself to the king on that specific day. {14:5} That evening, Rikayon found shelter in an abandoned bake house, consumed with hunger and sorrow. {14:6} Through the night, he pondered how he could survive in the city until the king's annual appearance. {14:7} The next morning, Rikayon wandered the streets, observing the local customs and livelihoods. {14:8} Unfamiliar with the ways of the people, he attempted to sell vegetables for a living, only to be mocked and robbed by the locals. {14:9} Frustrated and desperate, Rikayon returned to the bake house where he spent another sleepless night. {14:10} Determined to secure his survival, Rikayon devised a plan. {14:11} Early the next morning, he hired thirty strong men from the city's rabble, armed them, and led them to a strategic position near an Egyptian tomb. {14:12} He instructed them to proclaim that the king had decreed a fee of two hundred pieces of silver for any burial in that tomb. {14:13} Throughout the year, Rikayon and his men enforced this decree, accumulating vast riches from those seeking burial. {14:14} Within eight months, Rikayon amassed great wealth in silver, gold, and livestock. He expanded his operation, hiring more men who remained loyal to him. {14:15} When the king's annual appearance came around again, the people of Egypt gathered before him, complaining about Rikayon's actions. {14:16} Outraged, the king demanded to know who was responsible for imposing such taxes without his consent. {14:17} The people recounted all that Rikayon had done, provoking the king's anger. {14:18} Rikayon, in a bold move, sent a lavish gift to the king: a thousand children dressed in silk and fine embroidery, riding on horses, along with a substantial tribute of silver, gold, and precious stones. {14:19} The king and his court marveled at Rikayon's wealth and the grandeur of his gift. {14:20} Impressed by Rikayon's wisdom and resourcefulness, the king granted him favor and honor among the people of Egypt. {14:21} The king renamed Rikayon "Pharaoh," acknowledging his ability to levy taxes even on the dead. {14:22} Rikayon, now Pharaoh, was appointed as prefect under King Oswiris, entrusted with daily administration and justice over Egypt. {14:23} Pharaoh cleverly consolidated power, establishing himself as the de facto ruler of Egypt, overseeing taxation and governance. {14:24} The people of Egypt esteemed Pharaoh highly for his wisdom and leadership, and decreed that all future kings would be known as Pharaoh. {14:25} Thus, from that time onward, every ruler of Egypt, including their descendants, bore the title Pharaoh.

{15:1} In that year, a severe famine struck the land of Canaan, forcing Abram and his household to journey south to Egypt for relief. Arriving at the brook Mitzraim, they paused to rest. {15:2} As Abram and Sarai walked along the brook, Abram noticed Sarai's extraordinary beauty. {15:3} Concerned for their safety among the Egyptians, Abram said to Sarai, "Because of your beauty, I fear the Egyptians may kill me to take you as their own. They do not fear God here." {15:4} "Therefore," he instructed Sarai, "when we are asked, tell them you are my sister, so that we may live and escape harm." {15:5} Abram extended this instruction to all his companions, including his nephew Lot, fearing for their lives amidst the Egyptians. {15:6} Despite these precautions, Abram remained anxious for Sarai's safety. He placed her in a chest, concealed among their belongings. {15:7} Abram and his household then entered Egypt. Upon arrival, they were immediately stopped by guards demanding a tribute to the king before entering the city. {15:8} After paying the tithe, they brought the chest containing Sarai before the Egyptians, who were curious about its contents. {15:9} The king's officers approached Abram, demanding to inspect the chest and take a tithe of its treasures. {15:10} Abram refused to open the chest but agreed to give whatever they asked. {15:11} Pressed further, the officers forcibly opened the chest and discovered Sarai inside, marveling at her beauty. {15:12} They quickly reported their find to Pharaoh, who summoned Sarai to his court. {15:13} Seeing Sarai, Pharaoh was captivated by her beauty and rejoiced greatly. {15:14} He honored those who brought her to him and showered Sarai with gifts. {15:15} Meanwhile, Abram worried for Sarai's safety and prayed to God to protect her from Pharaoh. {15:16} Sarai also prayed, recalling God's promises to Abram and seeking deliverance from their predicament. {15:17} God heard Sarai's prayer and sent an angel to intervene on her behalf. {15:18} As Pharaoh approached Sarai, the angel appeared, reassuring her not to fear, for God had heard her prayers. {15:19} Pharaoh questioned Sarai about Abram and their relationship. {15:20} Sarai, following Abram's instructions, claimed Abram was her brother. {15:21} Pharaoh, impressed by Sarai and unaware of the truth, treated Abram with great favor, giving him gifts and honors. {15:22} However, the angel afflicted Pharaoh and his household with plagues that night because of Sarai. {15:23} Pharaoh realized the source of his troubles and rebuked Abram for deceiving him. {15:24} He then ordered Abram and Sarai to leave Egypt, fearing further divine retribution. {15:25} Pharaoh provided them with additional gifts and escorted them out of Egypt. {15:26} Abram and his household returned to Canaan, settling once again in the place where he had first built an altar. {15:27} Meanwhile, Lot, who had accumulated wealth, settled near Sodom, separating from Abram due to disputes over land and grazing rights. {15:28} Abram lived in the plain of Mamre near Hebron for many years, maintaining his presence in the land of Canaan.

{16:1} During that time, Chedorlaomer, the king of Elam, rallied neighboring kings—Nimrod of Shinar, Tidal of Goyim, and Arioch of Elasar—into a coalition to punish the rebellious cities of Sodom and its allies, who had defied him for thirteen years. {16:2} This alliance amassed a formidable force of about eight hundred thousand men and marched through the region, ruthlessly attacking all in their path. {16:3} The five kings of Sodom, Gomorrah, Admah, Zeboyim, and Zoar joined forces in the valley of Siddim to resist the invaders. {16:4} However, they were swiftly defeated by the superior forces of the Elamite kings in the valley, and many fell in battle. {16:5} The valley of Siddim, known for its tar pits, proved disastrous as the kings of Sodom and their armies fled, many falling into the pits, while survivors sought refuge in the nearby mountains. {16:6} The victorious Elamite kings plundered Sodom and Gomorrah, capturing Lot, Abram's nephew, and seizing all the wealth of these cities. {16:7} Upon learning this news, Abram gathered three hundred and eighteen of his men and pursued the invading kings by night, defeating them decisively. {16:8} Abram not only recovered all the plunder taken from Sodom and Gomorrah but also rescued Lot, along with his possessions and family, ensuring that Lot lacked nothing. {16:9} On his return journey, Abram passed through the valley of Siddim where the battle had taken place. {16:10} Bera, the king of Sodom, and his people emerged from the tar pits to meet Abram, along with Adonizedek, the king of Jerusalem, who brought provisions to welcome Abram. {16:11} Adonizedek blessed Abram, recognizing him as a man favored by God, and Abram gave him a tenth of the spoils as a gesture of gratitude. {16:12} The other kings of Sodom and Gomorrah approached Abram, requesting the return of their captured people and offering him the spoils, but Abram refused, swearing to God that he would take nothing from them. {16:13} Abram insisted that only his men who fought with him should receive their share of the spoils,{16:14} including Anar, Ashcol, and Mamre, {16:15} along with their men who guarded the baggage. {16:16} The kings of Sodom accepted Abram's terms and departed, {16:17} while Abram gave instructions regarding Lot and saw them off. {16:18} Lot returned to Sodom with his possessions, {16:19} and Abram and his people returned to their home in the plains of Mamre near Hebron. {16:20} During this time, the Lord appeared to Abram again in Hebron, reaffirming his promise of abundant blessings and assuring him that his descendants would inherit the lands they saw. {16:21} God encouraged Abram to be strong, not to fear, and to walk blamelessly before Him. {16:22} In the seventy-eighth year of Abram's life, Reu, the son of Peleg, passed away at the age of two hundred thirty-nine. {16:23} Sarai, Abram's wife, remained childless, deeply troubled by her inability to bear children. {16:24} Seeing this, Sarai gave her Egyptian handmaid Hagar to Abram as a wife, hoping to have children through her. {16:25} Hagar, having learned from Sarai, was obedient and followed her instructions faithfully. {16:26} Sarai said to Abram, "Since I am unable to bear children, perhaps through Hagar, I will have descendants." {16:27} After ten years of Abram's residence in Canaan, Sarai gave Hagar to him as a wife. {16:28} Abram agreed, and Hagar conceived a child by him. {16:29} When Hagar realized she was pregnant, she looked down on Sarai, believing herself favored by God for bearing a child while Sarai remained barren. {16:30} Sarai, feeling humiliated by Hagar's attitude, blamed Abram for the situation and confronted him. {16:31} Abram allowed Sarai to deal with Hagar as she saw fit, and Sarai treated Hagar harshly, causing her to flee into the wilderness. {16:32} An angel of the Lord found Hagar by a spring in the wilderness and encouraged her to return and submit to Sarai, promising to bless her greatly and make her descendants numerous. {16:33} Hagar named the place where she encountered the angel Beer-lahai-roi. {16:34} Hagar returned to Abram's household and bore him a son named Ishmael when Abram was eighty-six years old.

{17:1} In those days, when Abram was ninety-one years old, the people of Chittim waged war against the people of Tubal. After humanity had spread across the earth, the Chittim settled in the plains of Canopia, building cities by the river Tibreu. {17:2} The Tubalites dwelled in Tuscanah, with their territory extending to the river Tibreu. They founded a city called Sabinah, named after their ancestor Sabinah son of Tubal, where they settled and prospered. {17:3} It was during this time that the Chittim launched an attack against the Tubalites, defeating them decisively in battle. Three hundred and seventy men of Tubal fell to the forces of Chittim. {17:4} In response to their defeat, the Tubalites made a solemn vow to the Chittim, declaring that they would not allow intermarriage between their peoples. They decreed that no Tubalite would give his daughter in marriage to a man of Chittim. {17:5} The daughters of Tubal were renowned for their beauty in those days, unmatched by any other women on earth. {17:6} Kings and princes who admired beauty sought wives among the daughters of Tubal. They took them as wives, captivated by their exceptional beauty. {17:7} Three years later, despite the oath, twenty men from Chittim sought to marry Tubalite women but found none willing to break their people's vow. {17:8} During the harvest season, when the Tubalites were occupied in their fields, the men of Chittim went to the city of Sabinah. They each took a young woman from among the Tubalite daughters and brought them back to their cities. {17:9} When the Tubalites learned of this, they prepared for war against the Chittim. However, they could not prevail due to the mountainous terrain that favored the Chittim. {17:10} Frustrated in their attempt to conquer the Chittim, the Tubalites returned to their own land. {17:11} The following year, the Tubalites hired ten thousand men from nearby cities to wage war against the Chittim, intending to devastate their land and subdue them. {17:12} In the ensuing conflict, the Tubalites gained the upper hand over the Chittim. Facing dire circumstances, the Chittim lifted up their children born to Tubalite women onto the walls they had built, appealing to the Tubalites to cease fighting against their own flesh and blood. {17:13} Moved by this plea, the Tubalites halted their assault on the Chittim and withdrew. {17:14} They returned to their cities, while the Chittim gathered and established two new cities by the sea, {17:15} naming them Purtu and Ariza. {17:16} Meanwhile, Abram, now ninety-nine years old, continued his journey. {17:17} It was then that the Lord appeared to Abram, promising to establish a covenant with him and greatly increase his descendants. {17:18} The covenant involved circumcision for every male child among Abram's descendants, marking an everlasting covenant between them and God. {17:19} As a sign of this covenant, Abram's name was changed to Abraham, and Sarai's name to Sarah. {17:20} God assured Abraham and Sarah of abundant blessings and promised that they would become a great nation, with kings descending from them.

{18:1} Abraham obeyed God's command and circumcised all the males in his household, including those born in his house and those bought with his money. Even Ishmael, his son, who was thirteen years old, was circumcised as God had instructed. {18:2} On the third day after his circumcision, Abraham sat at the door of his tent in the heat of the sun, enduring the pain. {18:3} It was then that the Lord appeared to him in the plains of Mamre. Three men, who were actually angels sent by God, approached Abraham. He hurried to meet them, bowing low and inviting them into his home. {18:4} Abraham warmly welcomed the visitors, urging them to rest and have a meal. They agreed, so he provided water for them to wash their feet and placed them under a tree near the entrance. {18:5} Abraham then rushed to prepare a tender calf, instructing his servant Eliezer to dress it. {18:6} While the meat was cooking, Abraham went to Sarah and directed her to quickly prepare cakes from fine meal. {18:7} Sarah promptly made the bread, and Abraham served his guests butter, milk, beef, and mutton before the calf was fully cooked. They ate heartily. {18:8} During the meal, one of the visitors prophesied that Sarah would bear a son within the year. {18:9} After eating, the visitors departed and went towards Sodom. {18:10} Meanwhile, the people of Sodom and Gomorrah, along with the surrounding cities, {18:11} were exceedingly wicked and sinful, openly defying the Lord with their abominations. {18:12} In their land was a vast valley where they gathered four times a year with their families for festivities, marked by music and dancing. {18:13} During these celebrations, {18:14} they indulged in heinous acts, {18:15} seizing each other's wives and even young virgins without any objection from their husbands or fathers. {18:16} Furthermore, when strangers brought goods to sell, the people of these cities would gather and forcibly take everything from them, {18:17} giving little in return. If the merchants protested, each person would mockingly show what little they had taken. {18:18} One day, a man from Elam traveled through Sodom, riding an ass with a colorful mantle bound to it. {18:19} As evening approached, he sought shelter in Sodom, but no one would take him in. Among the residents was a wicked man named Hedad. {18:20} Hedad noticed the traveler and approached him, asking about his journey and offering him hospitality. {18:21} The traveler explained that he was heading from Hebron to Elam, having been refused lodging despite having provisions for himself and his donkey. {18:22} Hedad insisted the man stay with him, taking him to his house where he provided for him and his donkey. {18:23} They ate and drank together, and the traveler stayed the night. {18:24} In the morning, the traveler prepared to leave, but Hedad persuaded him to stay another day, offering him more food. {18:25} The next day, Hedad again urged the traveler to stay, and they ate together once more. {18:26} Finally, on the third day, the traveler prepared to depart, but Hedad convinced him to linger a while longer. {18:27} As the man was preparing to leave, Hedad's wife complained that he had stayed two days without offering anything in return. {18:28} The man asked Hedad for the mantle and cord he had used to secure his ass. {18:29} Hedad claimed that the items were his, but the man insisted they were his own belongings. {18:30} Hedad interpreted the man's dreams, suggesting his life would be prolonged and he would prosper in agriculture. {18:31} The man disputed this, saying he had given Hedad the items to hold for him. {18:32} They took their dispute to Serak, the judge of Sodom. {18:33} Hedad argued his case, insisting on payment for his interpretation and hospitality. {18:34} The judge sided with Hedad, known for his accurate dream interpretations. {18:35} The man protested, but Hedad and the judge dismissed his claims, driving him away. {18:36} The people of Sodom gathered, condemning the stranger and forcibly ejecting him from the city. {18:37} The man continued his journey, filled with bitterness and sorrow over his treatment in Sodom. {18:38} As he traveled, he wept at the corruption and wickedness he had witnessed in that city.

{19:1} The cities of Sodom had four judges, each presiding over their respective city: Serak in Sodom, Sharkad in Gomorrah, Zabnac in Admah, and Menon in Zeboyim. {19:2} Abraham's servant Eliezer gave these judges different names: Serak became Shakra, Sharkad became Shakrura, Zebnac became Kezobim, and Menon became Matzlodin. {19:3} By the decree of these judges, beds were set up in the streets of Sodom and Gomorrah. If a man entered these places, they forcibly made him lie down in one of their beds. {19:4} Three men would stand at the head and three at the feet of the bed. If the man was shorter than the bed, they stretched him to fit; if he was longer, they compressed him until he was near death. {19:5} When the man cried out in pain, they ignored his pleas, saying it was the custom for any visitor to their land. {19:6} Hearing of these atrocities, travelers avoided coming to these cities altogether. {19:7} When a poor man came to Sodom, they would give him gold and silver, but no one was allowed to give him food. If he died of hunger, they would reclaim their gold and silver, and fight over his clothes. {19:8} During this time, Sarah sent Eliezer to Sodom to check on her nephew Lot and his well-being. {19:9} Eliezer arrived and witnessed a man from Sodom fighting with a stranger. The Sodomite stripped the stranger of his clothes and left. {19:10} The poor stranger cried out to Eliezer for help, so he confronted the man from Sodom, questioning his cruel treatment of a visitor. {19:11} The man retorted, asking if Eliezer was appointed judge to interfere in their affairs. {19:12} Eliezer persisted, attempting to retrieve the stolen clothes. In response, the man struck Eliezer with a stone on his forehead, causing bleeding. {19:13} The man then demanded payment for cleansing Eliezer of his blood, citing it as their law and custom. {19:14} Refusing to pay, Eliezer was taken before Shakra, the judge of Sodom. {19:15} The man accused Eliezer of refusing to compensate him for the stone blow, which Shakra acknowledged as their law. {19:16} In protest, Eliezer struck Shakra with a stone on his forehead, causing him to bleed. {19:17} Eliezer argued that if this was their law, then the man should receive the compensation instead. {19:18} Leaving the matter with Shakra, Eliezer departed. {19:19} Meanwhile, the kings of Elam waged war against the kings of Sodom, seizing all their possessions and capturing Lot and his belongings. {19:20} When Abraham learned of this, he gathered his men and fought against the kings of Elam, rescuing Lot and recovering all the goods. {19:21} During this time, Lot's wife bore him a daughter named Paltith, signifying God's deliverance from the kings of Elam. {19:22} Paltith grew up in Sodom, and one of its men married her. {19:23} Another incident occurred where a poor man entered Sodom seeking sustenance. The people proclaimed no one should give him food until he died of starvation. {19:24} Paltith, moved with compassion, secretly fed the poor man bread for many days. {19:25} The people marveled at how the man survived without food. {19:26} Suspecting someone was helping him, three men hid and observed Paltith secretly feeding the man. {19:27} They apprehended Paltith with the bread and brought her before the judges, accusing her of breaking their law. {19:28} Paltith confessed to feeding the poor man, and they sentenced her to be burned to death. {19:29} The people of Sodom gathered, kindled a fire, and cast Paltith into it, reducing her to ashes. {19:30} Similarly, in Admah, a woman was condemned for offering hospitality to a traveler who sought shelter overnight. {19:31} The judges decreed she should be anointed with honey and left to be stung by bees until her body swelled. {19:32} These acts of cruelty and disregard for the needy angered the Lord. {19:33} He decided to destroy Sodom and its neighboring cities and sent two angels who had visited Abraham to carry out the judgment. {19:34} The angels arrived in Sodom in the evening, where Lot welcomed them and offered them hospitality. {19:35} They warned Lot to flee with his family before the city's destruction. {19:36} Lot and his family were escorted out of Sodom, and the Lord rained brimstone and fire upon the cities, destroying everything in the plain. {19:37} Lot's wife, Ado, looked back and turned into a pillar of salt, a testament to her disobedience. {19:38} Lot and his daughters sought refuge in a cave in the mountains. {19:39} Believing themselves to be the last survivors, Lot's daughters feared there were no men left on earth to father their children. {19:40} So they devised a plan to conceive children with their father. {19:41} They both became pregnant and bore sons: the elder named her son Moab, the ancestor of the Moabites, and the younger named her son Ben-Ammi, the ancestor of the Ammonites. {19:42} Lot and his daughters eventually left the cave and settled on the other side of the Jordan River. {19:43} There, Lot's descendants grew and prospered in the land of Canaan.

{20:1} At that time, Abraham left the plains of Mamre and journeyed to the land of the Philistines, settling in Gerar. It was the twenty-fifth year since Abraham had come to Canaan and he was one hundred years old when he arrived in Gerar. {20:2} Upon entering the land, Abraham instructed Sarah, his wife, to say that she was his sister if anyone inquired, to protect themselves from the locals' wickedness. {20:3} While living in the land of the Philistines, Abimelech, the king, heard about Sarah's exceptional beauty through his servants. {20:4} The servants informed Abimelech that a man from Canaan had come and brought with him a remarkably beautiful sister. {20:5} Intrigued, Abimelech sent for Sarah to be brought to him. {20:6} Sarah was taken to Abimelech's house, and upon seeing her beauty, he desired her for himself. {20:7} Abimelech asked Sarah about her relationship with the man who had accompanied her to their land. {20:8} Sarah, fearing for Abraham's safety, told Abimelech that Abraham was her brother and that they had come to find a place to settle. {20:9} Abimelech then summoned Abraham and assured him of his favor, offering him land and honor because of Sarah. {20:10} Abraham accepted Abimelech's assurances and gifts and departed from the king's presence. {20:11} That evening, as Abimelech sat on his throne, a deep sleep fell upon him. {20:12} In his dream, an angel of the Lord appeared with a drawn sword, ready to strike Abimelech. {20:13} The angel accused Abimelech of bringing Sarah, another man's wife, into his house, which would lead to his death and the suffering of his people. {20:14} Throughout that night, a great fear and confusion spread across the land of the Philistines. {20:15} The angel struck the inhabitants of the land with a plague, affecting every household. {20:16} By morning, the whole land was in turmoil due to the angel's actions. {20:17} The women of the land were unable to conceive, and all faced dire consequences because of Sarah, Abraham's wife. {20:18} Upon awakening, Abimelech was filled with dread and called for his servants, recounting his disturbing dream. {20:19} One of his servants reminded Abimelech of the similar incident involving Pharaoh of Egypt when Abraham and Sarah had visited. {20:20} The servant advised Abimelech to return Sarah to Abraham to avoid further calamity. {20:21} Abimelech summoned Sarah and Abraham, questioning them about their deception. {20:22} Abraham explained that he feared for his life because of Sarah's beauty. {20:23} Abimelech then compensated Abraham with livestock, servants, and silver, and returned Sarah to him. {20:24} Abimelech admonished Abraham and Sarah for their deceit but allowed them to reside in Gerar. {20:25} The people of the Philistine land continued to suffer from the plague that had struck them because of Sarah. {20:26} Abimelech requested Abraham to pray for God's mercy, and Abraham interceded on behalf of Abimelech and his people. {20:27} God heard Abraham's prayer and healed Abimelech and all his household. {20:28} Abraham and Sarah departed from Abimelech's presence with honor, and they settled in the land of Gerar, where they continued to live.

{21:1} After living in Gerar among the Philistines for a year and four months, God visited Sarah as He had promised. She conceived and bore a son to Abraham in their old age. {21:2} Abraham named his newborn son Isaac, as God had instructed. {21:3} On the eighth day, Abraham circumcised Isaac as commanded by God. At this time, Abraham was one hundred years old, and Sarah was ninety when Isaac was born. {21:4} As Isaac grew older and was weaned, Abraham celebrated with a great feast. {21:5} The celebration included prominent figures like Shem, Eber, Abimelech the king of the Philistines, and his captain Phicol, who rejoiced with Abraham on this joyous occasion. {21:6} Even Terah, Abraham's father, and Nahor, his brother, came from Haran to join the festivities upon hearing the news of Isaac's birth. {21:7} They all gathered to eat and drink in celebration. {21:8} Terah and Nahor remained with Abraham for a long time in the land of the Philistines. {21:9} During this time, Serug, the son of Reu, passed away in the first year after Isaac's birth. Serug lived for two hundred and thirty-nine years. {21:10} Ishmael, Abraham's son from Hagar, was fourteen years old when Isaac was born. {21:11} God blessed Ishmael as he grew older, and he became skilled in hunting and archery. {21:12} One day, when Isaac was five years old, he was with Ishmael outside their tent. {21:13} Ishmael, perhaps out of jealousy, aimed his bow at Isaac, intending to harm him. {21:14} Sarah witnessed this and was deeply upset. She immediately went to Abraham and insisted that Hagar and Ishmael be sent away, fearing for Isaac's safety. {21:15} Abraham, following Sarah's wishes, provided Hagar with provisions and sent her away with Ishmael into the wilderness of Paran. Ishmael grew up as an archer in the wilderness. {21:16} Later, Hagar and Ishmael moved to Egypt, where Ishmael married an Egyptian woman named Meribah. {21:17} Ishmael and his family returned to the wilderness after some time, living as nomads in tents. {21:18} They traveled frequently, settling and resting as needed. {21:19} God blessed Ishmael with livestock and wealth because of Abraham, and Ishmael thrived in the wilderness. {21:20} Ishmael lived a nomadic life, dwelling in tents and deserts for a long time, without seeing his father's face. {21:21} Eventually, Abraham expressed a desire to see Ishmael again and decided to visit him. {21:22} Abraham traveled to the wilderness on his camel, seeking Ishmael's tent and family. {21:23} He arrived at Ishmael's tent around noon, but Ishmael and his mother were not present. {21:24} Abraham inquired about Ishmael's whereabouts from his wife, who informed him that Ishmael was out hunting. {21:25} Abraham remained mounted on his camel, as he had vowed not to dismount in Sarah's presence. {21:26} Abraham asked Ishmael's wife for water, but she had none to offer. Instead, she continued to sit in the tent without showing hospitality. {21:27} Abraham observed her mistreating her children and Ishmael, which angered him. {21:28} He called her out of the tent to speak with him and instructed her to relay a message to Ishmael when he returned. {21:29} Abraham then departed and returned home. {21:30} When Ishmael returned from hunting with his mother, she relayed Abraham's message about the tent nail. {21:31} Ishmael recognized that the visitor was his father and understood the importance of his father's words. {21:32} Ishmael heeded Abraham's instructions and sent away his disrespectful wife. {21:33} Afterward, Ishmael took another wife and settled in a place suitable for his family. {21:34} Three years later, Abraham decided to visit Ishmael again. {21:35} He arrived at Ishmael's tent around noon, and Ishmael's wife informed him that Ishmael was out tending to the camels. {21:36} She invited Abraham into the tent and offered him water and bread, which he accepted. {21:37} Abraham blessed Ishmael and shared a meal with his family. {21:38} Before leaving, Abraham instructed Ishmael's wife to convey a message to Ishmael about the tent nail. {21:39} Abraham then returned home to the land of the Philistines. {21:40} When Ishmael returned and learned of the visitor, he recognized his father's hand in the message and his wife's respect for him. {21:41} God continued to bless Ishmael in his new life and ventures.

{22:1} Ishmael gathered his wife, children, and all his possessions, and journeyed to his father Abraham in the land of the Philistines. {22:2} Abraham recounted to Ishmael the incident involving his first wife and her disrespectful behavior. {22:3} Ishmael and his children lived with Abraham for many years in that land, while Abraham settled in the Philistine territory for an extended period. {22:4} Eventually, after twenty-six years, Abraham and his household departed from the Philistine region and moved closer to Hebron. {22:5} Abraham's servants dug wells, which led to a dispute with Abimelech's servants who claimed one of the wells. {22:6} Abimelech, accompanied by his captain Phicol and twenty men, approached Abraham regarding the well. {22:7} Abraham confronted Abimelech about the well that had been taken by Abimelech's servants without his knowledge. {22:8} To resolve the matter, Abraham gave Abimelech seven ewe lambs as a gesture of goodwill. {22:9} Abimelech accepted the lambs and also acknowledged Abraham's ownership of the well through an oath, hence the well was named Beersheba. {22:10} Both parties made a covenant at Beersheba, and Abimelech returned with his men to the land of the Philistines. {22:11} Abraham and his household settled in Beersheba for a long time, where he planted a large grove with four gates facing different directions and established a vineyard. {22:12} Abraham's hospitality was renowned, as travelers passing by would enter any of the gates and be welcomed to eat, drink, and rest. {22:13} Abraham generously provided for the needy, offering them food, clothing, silver, and gold, and teaching them about the Lord throughout his life. {22:14} Abraham and his family lived in Beersheba, and he extended his residence as far as Hebron. {22:15} Meanwhile, Abraham's brother Nahor and his father Terah continued to reside in Haran, not joining Abraham in Canaan. {22:16} Nahor had several children with Milcah, the sister of Abraham's wife Sarah, including eight sons: Uz, Buz, Kemuel, Kesed, Chazo, Pildash, Tidlaf, and Bethuel. {22:17} Milcah also bore Nahor four sons through her concubine Reumah: Zebach, Gachash, Tachash, and Maacha, making Nahor's total twelve sons besides daughters. {22:18} Uz's children were Abi, Cheref, Gadin, Melus, and their sister Deborah. {22:19} Buz had sons named Berachel, Naamath, Sheva, and Madonu. {22:20} Kemuel's sons were Aram and Rechob. {22:21} Kesed had sons named Anamlech, Meshai, Benon, and Yifi; Chazo's sons were Pildash, Mechi, and Opher. {22:22} Pildash's sons were Arud, Chamum, Mered, and Moloch. {22:23} Tidlaf's sons were Mushan, Cushan, and Mutzi. {22:24} Bethuel had sons named Sechar, Laban, and a daughter named Rebecca. {22:25} These families of Nahor settled in Haran, while Aram, Kemuel's son, and his brother Rechob left Haran and found a valley by the Euphrates, where they built a city named after Aram's son Pethor. {22:26} Kesed's descendants also found a valley near Shinar, where they built a city called Kesed, known as Chaldea to this day. {22:27} Terah, Abraham and Nahor's father, took another wife named Pelilah in his old age, who bore him a son named Zoba. {22:28} Terah lived twenty-five years after Zoba's birth, and he died at the age of two hundred and five in Haran. {22:29} Zoba lived thirty years and had sons named Aram, Achlis, and Merik. {22:30} Aram, Zoba's son, had three wives and fathered twelve sons and three daughters. The Lord blessed Aram with wealth and livestock, and his prosperity grew. {22:31} Aram, along with his brother and household, left Haran due to their increasing wealth, settling in a valley in the eastern region. {22:32} They built a city there, naming it Aram after their eldest brother, Aram Zoba, which remains known as Aram Naharaim to this day. {22:33} Meanwhile, Isaac, Abraham's son, continued to grow up, and Abraham diligently taught him the ways of the Lord, and God blessed Isaac. {22:34} When Isaac was thirty-seven years old, his brother Ishmael, who was twenty-eight years older, would often accompany him in their daily lives. {22:35} Ishmael boasted to Isaac about his early commitment to God's command of circumcision at the age of thirteen. {22:36} Isaac responded, affirming his own willingness to obey God, even if God were to ask him to offer himself as a sacrifice. {22:37} God heard Isaac's words and decided to test Abraham's faith. {22:38} The appointed day came when the heavenly beings gathered before the Lord, and Satan also came among them. {22:39} The Lord asked Satan about his observations regarding humanity on Earth. {22:40} Satan replied, describing how many people only remembered God when they needed something and forgot Him once their needs were met. {22:41} Satan then singled out Abraham, noting his exceptional loyalty and devotion to God, even building altars and proclaiming God's name everywhere he went. {22:42} Satan argued that Abraham had become complacent because God always granted his requests, leading him to neglect offering sacrifices. {22:43} The Lord responded, defending Abraham's integrity and affirming that Abraham would willingly offer anything God asked of him, including his beloved son Isaac. {22:44} Satan challenged the Lord to test Abraham's loyalty by instructing him to offer Isaac as a sacrifice, confident that Abraham would fail this ultimate test of faith. {22:45} The Lord accepted the challenge, deciding to put Abraham's faith to the test.

{23:1} At that time, the Lord spoke to Abraham and said, "Abraham!" and he replied, "Here I am." {23:2} The Lord instructed him, "Take your son, your only son whom you love, Isaac, and go to the land of Moriah. There, offer him as a burnt offering on one of the mountains I will show you. You will see a cloud and the glory of the Lord there." {23:3} Abraham thought to himself, "How can I separate Isaac from Sarah, his mother, to offer him as a burnt offering to the Lord?" {23:4} Abraham went into the tent, sat down before Sarah, and said, {23:5} "Isaac is grown and has not yet learned about the service of his God. Tomorrow, I will take him to Shem and Eber's house, where they will teach him the ways of the Lord. They will show him how to pray continuously and how the Lord will answer." {23:6} Sarah replied, "You've spoken well. Go, but don't take him too far from me or keep him away for too long, as my soul is bound up with his." {23:7} Abraham said, "Let us pray to the Lord our God that He may act favorably toward us." {23:8} Sarah spent the night with Isaac, kissing and embracing him, giving him instructions until morning. {23:9} She said, "My son, how can my soul part from you? I will miss you terribly." She continued to kiss and embrace him, and gave Abraham instructions about him. {23:10} Sarah said to Abraham, "Please take care of our son. If he is hungry, give him bread; if he is thirsty, give him water. Don't let him walk on foot or sit in the sun. Let him have whatever he desires and don't force him to do anything against his will." {23:11} Sarah wept bitterly throughout the night for Isaac, giving him instructions until morning. {23:12} In the morning, she chose a fine garment given to her by Abimelech, dressed Isaac in it, and put a turban with a precious stone on his head. She prepared provisions for the journey, and they set off, accompanied by some servants. {23:13} Sarah accompanied them part of the way and was told to return to the tent. {23:14} As she heard Isaac's words, she wept bitterly along with Abraham and Isaac, who all wept greatly. {23:15} Sarah took Isaac in her arms, embraced him, and wept, saying, "Who knows if I will ever see you again?" {23:16} They all wept together, and Sarah eventually turned away, still crying, while her servants returned with her to the tent. {23:17} Abraham went with Isaac to offer him as a burnt offering, as commanded. {23:18} Abraham took two young men, Ishmael, the son of Hagar, and Eliezer, his servant, and they traveled together. Along the way, the young men spoke among themselves. {23:19} Ishmael said to Eliezer, "When my father returns, he will give me all he possesses because I am his firstborn." {23:20} Eliezer replied, "Abraham cast you and your mother away and swore you would not inherit anything. I, his faithful servant, will receive his possessions at his death." {23:21} As Abraham and Isaac walked, Satan appeared to Abraham in the guise of an old, humble man and said, {23:22} "Are you really going to sacrifice your only son, the one you love, whom God gave you in your old age? This cannot be God's command." {23:23} Abraham recognized this as the work of Satan, refused to listen, and rebuked him. {23:24} Satan then appeared to Isaac as a young man and said, {23:25} "Your father is leading you to be sacrificed. Do not listen to him." {23:26} Isaac told Abraham what the man had said. Abraham responded, {23:27} "Do not listen to him; he is Satan trying to lead us astray." {23:28} Satan, unable to succeed, transformed into a large brook that blocked their path. {23:29} They entered the brook, which grew deeper as they went, causing fear. Abraham realized the brook was created by Satan to hinder them. {23:30} He rebuked Satan, who fled, and the brook returned to dry land. {23:31} Abraham and Isaac continued toward the place God had shown them. {23:32} On the third day, Abraham saw the mountain from afar, and a pillar of fire and a cloud of glory rested on it. {23:33} Abraham said to Isaac, "Do you see what I see on that mountain?" {23:34} Isaac replied, "I see a pillar of fire and a cloud with the Lord's glory upon it." {23:35} Abraham knew this meant Isaac was accepted as a burnt offering. {23:36} Abraham told Eliezer and Ishmael to stay behind with the donkey while he and Isaac went to worship and would return later. {23:37} Eliezer and Ishmael stayed as instructed. {23:38} Abraham placed the wood for the burnt offering on Isaac's back, took the fire and knife, and they went to the mountain. {23:39} Isaac noticed the absence of a lamb and asked where it was. {23:40} Abraham answered, "The Lord has chosen you to be the burnt offering." {23:41} Isaac responded with joy, saying he would do as the Lord commanded. {23:42} Abraham asked Isaac if he had any doubts or misgivings, but Isaac assured him he did not. {23:43} Isaac expressed joy at being chosen as a burnt offering, and Abraham rejoiced at his son's faith. {23:44} They arrived at the designated place, and Abraham began to build an altar, weeping. Isaac helped by gathering stones and mortar. {23:45} Abraham arranged the wood on the altar and bound Isaac to place him on it for the sacrifice. {23:46} Isaac asked his father to bind him securely so he wouldn't move during the sacrifice. {23:47} Isaac also requested that Abraham bring his ashes to Sarah and tell her it was a sweet-smelling savor but not to tell her if she was near a well or high place. {23:48} Abraham wept as he listened to Isaac's words and prepared to carry out the sacrifice. {23:49} Despite their joy at following God's command, they wept bitterly. {23:50} Abraham was about to slay Isaac when the Lord intervened. {23:51} The Lord told Abraham not to harm Isaac, as He now knew Abraham feared God and had not withheld his only son. {23:52} Abraham saw a ram caught in a thicket and realized it was provided by God as a substitute for Isaac. {23:53} Abraham took the ram, replaced Isaac with it on the altar, and sacrificed it instead of his son. {23:54} He sprinkled the ram's blood on the altar and declared it as a substitute for Isaac. {23:55} Abraham completed the sacrifice, which was accepted as if it had been Isaac. {23:56} The Lord blessed Abraham and his descendants. {23:57} Meanwhile, Satan appeared to Sarah in the form of an old, humble man and falsely told her that Abraham had sacrificed Isaac. {23:58} Sarah, believing the lie, mourned bitterly and wished she had died instead of Isaac. {23:59} She cried out in grief, reflecting on the hardship of bearing Isaac at her old age and now losing him. {23:60} Sarah, overwhelmed by grief, laid her head on a servant's chest and became still. {23:61} She then traveled to Hebron to inquire about Abraham and Isaac but received no information. {23:62} In Hebron, she learned nothing and continued searching until she was deceived by Satan again, who told her Isaac was alive. {23:63} Sarah, overjoyed at the false news, died from the intensity of her joy and was gathered to her people. {23:64} Abraham and Isaac returned to Beersheba after completing the sacrifice. {23:65} Abraham sought Sarah, discovered she was dead, and mourned her deeply with Isaac and their servants. {23:66} They wept extensively, mourning Sarah's passing with great sorrow.

{24:1} Sarah lived for 127 years, and then she passed away. After her death, Abraham got up from mourning and sought a burial place for her. He spoke to the people of Heth, saying, {24:2} "I am a foreigner and a resident among you. Please give me property for a burial site so that I can bury my dead." {24:3} The Hittites replied to Abraham, "Listen to us, sir. You are an honored man among us. Choose the best of our tombs to bury your dead. None of us will refuse you his tomb for burying your dead." {24:4} Abraham bowed before the people of Heth {24:5} and said to Ephron in their presence, "Please listen to me. I am willing to pay the full price of the field. Accept it from me so that I can bury my dead there." {24:6} Ephron replied, "Sir, listen to me. The field is worth four hundred shekels of silver, but what is that between you and me? Bury your dead." {24:7} Abraham agreed and weighed out the price that Ephron had named in the hearing of the Hittites: four hundred shekels of silver, according to the weight current among the merchants. {24:8} So Ephron's field in Machpelah near Mamre—both the field and the cave in it, and all the trees within the borders of the field—was deeded {24:9} to Abraham as his property in the presence of all the Hittites who had come to the gate of the city. {24:10} Afterward, Abraham buried his wife Sarah in the cave of the field of Machpelah near Mamre (that is, Hebron) in the land of Canaan. {24:11} Thus the field and the cave within it were secured to Abraham as a burial site by the Hittites. {24:12} After burying Sarah, Abraham returned to his people and settled in Beersheba. {24:13} Sometime later, Abimelech, king of the Philistines, died. He was succeeded by his son Benmalich, who was twelve years old at the time. {24:14} With Abimelech's death, the people of Gerar comforted his family and household. {24:15} Then Abraham journeyed to the land of the Philistines and settled near Gerar. {24:16} Meanwhile, Lot, Abraham's nephew, passed away in those days at the age of one hundred and forty. {24:17} Lot's descendants through his daughters Moab and Ben-Ammi settled in the land of Canaan, founding cities named after themselves. {24:18} Around this time, Nahor, Abraham's brother, also died at the age of one hundred and seventy-two in Haran. {24:19} Distraught by his brother's passing, Abraham called for his chief servant, Eliezer, and said, {24:20} "I am old and unsure of how much longer I will live. Take an oath that you will not get a wife for my son Isaac from the Canaanite women among whom we live. {24:21} Instead, go to my homeland, to my family, and find a wife for Isaac there. {24:22} May the Lord, the God of heaven and earth, who took me from my father's household and my native land, bless you abundantly and make your journey successful. {24:23} May you find a wife for my son Isaac from among my relatives and from my father's family. {24:24} Then Eliezer took an oath in the presence of his master Abraham and set out with ten of Abraham's camels loaded with gifts. {24:25} He traveled to Nahor's hometown and stopped near the well outside the town. {24:26} There Eliezer prayed, {24:27} "Lord, God of my master Abraham, make me successful today, and show kindness to my master Abraham. {24:28} See, I am standing beside this spring, and the daughters of the townspeople are coming out to draw water. {24:29} May it be that when I say to a young woman, 'Please let down your jar that I may have a drink,' and she says, 'Drink, and I'll water your camels too,' let her be the one you have chosen for your servant Isaac. {24:30} By this I will know that you have shown kindness to my master."

{25:1} At that time, Abraham married again in his old age. His new wife was named Keturah, and she came from the land of Canaan. {25:2} Keturah bore him six sons: Zimran, Jokshan, Medan, Midian, Ishbak, and Shuach. {25:3} Zimran's sons were Abihen, Molich, and Narim. Jokshan's sons were Sheba and Dedan. Medan's sons were Amida, Joab, Gochi, Elisha, and Nothach. {25:4} Midian's sons were Ephah, Epher, Hanoch, Abida, and Eldaah. Ishbak's sons were Makir, Beyodua, and Tator. Shuach's sons were Bildad, Mamdad, Munan, and Meban. These were the descendants of Keturah, Abraham's wife from Canaan. {25:5} Abraham sent these sons away with gifts, while he was still alive, to the east, away from his son Isaac, so they could settle in their own territories. {25:6} They established six cities in the eastern mountains, where they lived to this day. {25:7} However, the descendants of Jokshan—Sheba and Dedan—did not settle among their relatives but journeyed far into the wilderness, where they made their homes. {25:8} Meanwhile, the descendants of Midian, another son of Abraham, settled eastward in the land of Cush. Finding a spacious valley, they built a city there and named it Midian, where they settled permanently. {25:9} Midian and his five sons made Midian their home. {25:10} The names of Midian's sons were Ephah, Epher, Hanoch, Abida, and Eldaah. {25:11} Their descendants formed clans that spread throughout the land of Midian. {25:12} This is the account of Ishmael, the son of Abraham through Hagar, Sarah's Egyptian slave. {25:13} Ishmael married a woman from Egypt named Ribah, also known as Meribah. {25:14} Ribah bore Ishmael several sons: Nebaioth, Kedar, Adbeel, Mibsam, and their sister Bosmath. {25:15} Ishmael later sent Ribah away because she displeased him and returned to her father's house in Egypt. {25:16} Ishmael then married Malchuth from the land of Canaan, who bore him eight sons: Nishma, Dumah, Masa, Chadad, Tema, Yetur, Naphish, and Kedem. {25:17} These twelve sons became the founders of twelve tribes, each with their own territories and descendants. {25:18} Ishmael's descendants spread out and settled from Havilah to Shur, near the border of Egypt, toward Assyria. {25:19} Ishmael lived in the presence of all his relatives. {25:20} They settled from Havilah to Shur, near the border of Egypt, as you go toward Assyria. {25:21} Ishmael and his sons lived in hostility toward all their brothers. {25:22} These are the names of Ishmael's sons listed by their names in the order of their birth: Nebayoth, Kedar, Adbeel, Mibsam. {25:23} These are the sons of Kedar: Alyon, Kezem, Chamad, and Eli. {25:24} These are the sons of Adbeel: Chamad and Jabin. {25:25} These are the sons of Mibsam: Obadiah, Ebedmelech, and Yeush. {25:26} These are the sons of Mishma: Shamua, Zecaryon, and Obed. {25:27} These are the sons of Dumah: Kezed, Eli, Machmad, and Amed. {25:28} These are the sons of Masa: Melon, Mula, and Ebidadon. {25:29} These are the sons of Chadad: Azur, Minzar, and Ebedmelech. {25:30} These are the sons of Tema: Seir, Sadon, and Yakol. {25:31} These are the sons of Yetur: Merith, Yaish, Alyo, and Pachoth. {25:32} These are the sons of Naphish: Ebed-Tamed, Abiyasaph, and Mir. {25:33} These are the sons of Kedem: Calip, Tachti, and Omir. These were the descendants of Malchuth, Ishmael's wife, listed by their clans. {25:34} Ishmael lived for 137 years. Then he breathed his last and died, and he was gathered to his people.

{26:1} When Isaac turned fifty-nine, his wife Rebecca remained unable to conceive. {26:2} Rebecca said to Isaac, "My lord, I've heard how your mother Sarah was barren until your father Abraham prayed for her, and then she conceived. {26:3} So now, please pray to God, and He will hear your prayer and remember us with His mercy." {26:4} Isaac replied to Rebecca, "Abraham already prayed for God to bless us with children. If there's still barrenness, it must be from you." {26:5} Rebecca insisted, "Then rise up and pray yourself, that the Lord may hear you and grant us children." Isaac listened to his wife and together they went to the land of Moriah to pray. {26:6} There Isaac prayed, "O Lord God of heaven and earth, who promised my father Abraham to multiply his descendants, may your words to him be fulfilled in us." {26:7} "Our eyes are upon you,

Lord, to grant us offspring, for you are our God." {26:8} The Lord heard Isaac's prayer, and Rebecca conceived. {26:9} During her pregnancy, the twins struggled within her, causing her great distress. She asked other women if they had experienced such turmoil, but none had. {26:10} Feeling alone, Rebecca went to Moriah to seek the Lord's guidance. She also consulted Shem and Eber, seeking answers from the Lord. {26:11} Rebecca urged Abraham to inquire of the Lord about her condition. {26:12} They received a divine revelation: two nations were in her womb, destined to be divided, with the older serving the younger. {26:13} When the time came, Rebecca gave birth to twins, just as the Lord had foretold. {26:14} The firstborn was red and hairy, so they named him Esau. {26:15} His brother came out grasping Esau's heel, and they named him Jacob. {26:16} Isaac was sixty years old when they were born. {26:17} The boys grew up: Esau became a skillful hunter, while Jacob was a peaceful man, living in tents and devoted to God's teachings. {26:18} Isaac and his household stayed in Canaan, following God's command. {26:19} Meanwhile, Ishmael and his descendants settled in the land of Havilah in the east. {26:20} Abraham gave all he had to Isaac, including his blessings and treasures. {26:21} He instructed Isaac, "Know that the Lord is God of heaven and earth. {26:22} He has guided me and promised this land to our descendants, so keep His commandments and stay on the path of righteousness." {26:23} "Teach your children and their descendants the ways of the Lord, so that all may prosper." {26:24} Isaac agreed and promised to obey, receiving Abraham's blessing. {26:25} Abraham died at the age of 175, satisfied and honored, and Isaac and Ishmael buried him. {26:26} The people of Canaan mourned Abraham's death, honoring him for his kindness and integrity. {26:27} Abraham's legacy of faith and obedience to God remained unmatched. {26:28} God blessed Isaac, who faithfully followed in his father's footsteps, never straying from God's commands.

{27:1} After Abraham's death, Esau often went hunting in the fields. {27:2} Meanwhile, Nimrod, also known as Amraphel, the king of Babel, enjoyed hunting with his mighty men, strolling in the cool of the day. {27:3} Nimrod kept a watchful eye on Esau, harboring jealousy toward him. {27:4} One day, Esau encountered Nimrod in the wilderness along with his two men. {27:5} While Nimrod and his people dispersed for hunting, Esau stealthily approached and ambushed Nimrod. {27:6} Nimrod and his men did not recognize Esau, continuing their routine in the field. {27:7} Suddenly, Esau drew his sword, swiftly beheading Nimrod, and then engaged in a fierce battle with Nimrod's two companions, killing them too. {27:8} The distant mighty men of Nimrod heard the commotion and found their king and companions slain. {27:9} Esau fled upon seeing Nimrod's warriors approaching, narrowly escaping. He seized Nimrod's valuable garments, inherited from his father, and hid them. {27:10} Esau, fearing Nimrod's men, returned home exhausted and distressed, collapsing before his brother Jacob. {27:11} He lamented to Jacob, "I am near death; what use is the birthright to me?" Jacob then wisely negotiated with Esau, who sold his birthright to him as the Lord had foreseen. {27:12} Esau also sold his share of the cave of Machpelah, which Abraham had purchased, to Jacob. {27:13} Jacob documented the transaction with witnesses and kept the record. {27:14} When Nimrod died, his men buried him in his city after a reign of 185 years, with his life lasting 215 years. {27:15} Esau's slaying of Nimrod marked a division in Nimrod's kingdom, which fragmented among other regional kings after his death.

{28:1} After Abraham's death, a severe famine struck the land of Canaan. Isaac, facing the scarcity, intended to go down to Egypt like his father had done. {28:2} However, the Lord appeared to Isaac and instructed him not to go to Egypt but to travel to Gerar, to King Abimelech of the Philistines, and reside there until the famine subsided. {28:3} Isaac obeyed the Lord's command and settled in Gerar for a whole year. {28:4} When Isaac arrived in Gerar, the locals noticed Rebecca's beauty and asked Isaac about her. Isaac, fearing for his life, claimed she was his sister, not his wife. {28:5} Abimelech's officials spoke highly of Rebecca to the king, but Abimelech, knowing the truth, kept silent. {28:6} After three months, Abimelech saw Isaac with Rebecca and realized they were married. {28:7} Confronting Isaac, Abimelech rebuked him for lying about Rebecca, which could have led to serious consequences. {28:8} Isaac explained his fear of being killed over his wife, hence the deception. {28:9} Abimelech then summoned Isaac and Rebecca and publicly acknowledged their relationship, warning anyone against harming them. {28:10} Isaac and Rebecca returned to their residence under Abimelech's protection, and Isaac prospered greatly with the Lord's blessings. {28:11} Abimelech honored Isaac, mindful of the covenant his father had made with Abraham. {28:12} He granted Isaac land, fields, and vineyards in Gerar, ensuring Isaac's prosperity until the famine ended. {28:13} Isaac sowed crops and reaped a hundredfold harvest, growing wealthy with flocks, herds, and many servants. {28:14} When the famine ended, the Lord instructed Isaac to return to Canaan. {28:15} Isaac obeyed, returning to Hebron with all his belongings. {28:16} Meanwhile, Shelach, son of Arpachshad, died at the age of 433, in the eighteenth year of Jacob and Esau's lives. {28:17} Isaac then sent Jacob to learn from Shem and Eber, where he stayed for thirty-two years, while Esau remained in Canaan, preoccupied with hunting. {28:18} Esau, a cunning and deceitful man, became skilled in the field and eventually settled in Seir, later known as Edom. {28:19} There, Esau married Jehudith, daughter of Beeri the Hittite, and brought her to Hebron. {28:20} In the hundred and tenth year of Isaac's life, Shem, Noah's son, died at the age of 600. {28:21} Jacob returned to Hebron in the fiftieth year of his life. {28:22} During Jacob's fifty-sixth year, news arrived from Haran concerning Laban, Rebecca's brother. {28:23} Laban's wife Adinah, who had been barren, gave birth to twin daughters, Leah and Rachel. {28:24} Rebecca rejoiced upon hearing of her brother Laban's newfound blessing of children.

{29:1} As Isaac grew old and his eyesight faded with age, he called Esau, his elder son, and instructed him to prepare venison for him, seeking to bless him before his impending death. {29:2} Esau, obedient to his father's command, took his weapons and set out to hunt. {29:3} Meanwhile, Rebecca overheard Isaac's plan and quickly summoned Jacob, telling him what she had heard and instructing him to bring her two young goats. {29:4} Jacob followed his mother's instructions, preparing a savory meal that she could take to Isaac. {29:5} Jacob hurried to present the meal to his father before Esau returned from his hunting trip. {29:6} When Jacob appeared before Isaac, Isaac questioned him, mistaking him for Esau due to Jacob's disguise. {29:7} Jacob, pretending to be Esau, offered the meal as if he had just returned from the hunt. Isaac ate, blessed Jacob, and then Jacob left. {29:8} Shortly after Jacob departed, Esau arrived with his own meal and realized that Jacob had already received the blessing. {29:9} Esau confronted Isaac, learning that Jacob had cunningly secured the blessing. Enraged, Esau plotted revenge against Jacob. {29:10} Jacob, fearful of Esau's wrath, fled to the house of Eber, son of Shem, and remained there for fourteen years, learning the ways of the Lord. {29:11} Esau, deeply hurt and feeling deceived, left his parents' home and settled in the land of Seir, marrying Adah, daughter of Elon the Hittite, whom he renamed Bosmath. {29:12} For six months, Esau stayed away from his parents, then returned to Canaan with his wives, unsettling Isaac and Rebecca with their idolatrous practices. {29:13} Rebecca lamented over the influence of Esau's wives and expressed concern about Jacob marrying a Canaanite woman, questioning the purpose of her life. {29:14} During this time, Adah bore Esau a son named Eliphaz. {29:15} Ishmael, Abraham's son, passed away at the age of 137, causing Isaac to mourn deeply. {29:16} After fourteen years, Jacob desired to visit his parents in Hebron, having been forgotten by Esau, who had moved on from the incident. {29:17} When Esau saw Jacob returning, his anger reignited, and he planned to kill him once Isaac passed away. {29:18} Rebecca, upon learning of Esau's intentions, urged Jacob to flee to her brother Laban in Haran until Esau's anger subsided. {29:19} Isaac also advised Jacob not to marry a Canaanite woman but to take a wife from Laban's daughters. {29:20} He blessed Jacob with prosperity and protection on his journey, emphasizing the importance of staying faithful to

God's ways. {29:21} Jacob received Isaac's blessings and gifts, kissed his parents farewell, and set off for Haran, departing at the age of seventy-seven from Beersheba. {29:22} Meanwhile, Esau instructed his son Eliphaz to pursue and kill Jacob. {29:23} Eliphaz, accompanied by ten men, tracked Jacob but spared him after Jacob pleaded for mercy. {29:24} They took Jacob's possessions and returned to Esau, who was disappointed that Jacob had been spared. {29:25} Esau blamed Eliphaz for not carrying out his orders to kill Jacob. {29:26} Frustrated, Esau took Machlath, daughter of Ishmael, as his wife in addition to his other wives, aligning with his father's wishes against marrying Canaanites.

{30:1} Jacob continued his journey toward Haran and stopped for the night near the city of Luz, at Mount Moriah. That night, the Lord appeared to him and reaffirmed the covenant made with Abraham and Isaac, promising Jacob the land where he lay and assuring him of divine protection and prosperity wherever he went. {30:2} Jacob woke up filled with joy from the vision, naming the place Bethel. {30:3} He proceeded on his journey with renewed vigor, heading toward the land of the East. Eventually, he arrived back in Haran and settled near the shepherd's well. {30:4} There, he encountered shepherds from Haran and inquired about Laban, the son of Nahor. They confirmed knowing Laban and pointed out Rachel, Laban's daughter, approaching with her father's flock. {30:5} As Jacob spoke with the shepherds, Rachel arrived, and upon recognizing her, Jacob ran to greet her with great emotion, kissing her and bursting into tears. {30:6} Jacob explained his identity to Rachel, who hurried to inform her father Laban. Meanwhile, Jacob lamented not having gifts to present to Laban. {30:7} Upon hearing of Jacob's arrival, Laban rushed to embrace him, bringing him into his house, offering hospitality and food. {30:8} Jacob recounted to Laban the hardships he faced from Esau and his son Eliphaz on his journey. {30:9} Jacob stayed with Laban for a month, during which Laban proposed that Jacob should receive wages for his service. {30:10} Laban, having no sons but only daughters, introduced Leah and Rachel to Jacob. Leah had tender eyes, while Rachel was beautiful, and Jacob was immediately drawn to her. {30:11} Jacob proposed to Laban that he would work seven years in exchange for marrying Rachel. Laban agreed to the arrangement. {30:12} During Jacob's time in Haran, Eber, son of Shem, passed away at the age of 464, deeply grieving Jacob. {30:13} In the third year of Jacob's stay, Esau's wife Bosmath bore him a son named Reuel. {30:14} In the fourth year, the Lord blessed Laban with sons, including Beor, Alib, and Chorash, increasing Laban's prosperity due to Jacob's presence. {30:15} Jacob diligently served Laban both in the house and in the field, and God blessed all that Laban owned because of Jacob. {30:16} In the fifth year, Esau's wife Jehudith passed away in Canaan, leaving behind only daughters. {30:17} Esau's daughters were named Marzith and Puith. After Jehudith's death, Esau moved to Seir and remained there for an extended period. {30:18} In the sixth year, Esau took another wife, Ahlibamah, daughter of Zebeon the Hivite, in addition to his other wives, bringing her to Canaan. {30:19} Ahlibamah bore Esau three sons: Yeush, Yaalan, and Korah. {30:20} Esau's growing wealth and livestock caused disputes with the inhabitants of Canaan, prompting him to relocate to Seir with his family and possessions. {30:21} Despite living in Seir, Esau occasionally visited his parents in Canaan and intermarried with the Horites, giving his daughters in marriage to the sons of Seir. {30:22} He married Marzith to Anah, son of Zebeon, and Puith to Azar, son of Bilhan the Horite. Esau settled in the mountainous region of Seir, where he and his descendants prospered and multiplied.

{31:1} In the seventh year of Jacob's service to Laban, he asked for his wife since his time was completed. Laban agreed, and they gathered all the people for a feast. {31:2} In the evening, Laban came to the house and later Jacob joined him with the guests. Laban extinguished all the lights in the house. {31:3} Jacob asked Laban why he did this, and Laban replied that it was their custom. {31:4} Then Laban brought his daughter Leah to Jacob in the dark, and Jacob slept with her, not realizing it was Leah. {31:5} Laban gave Leah his maid Zilpah as a handmaid. {31:6} Everyone at the feast knew what Laban had done, but they did not tell Jacob. {31:7} The neighbors came to Jacob's house that night, celebrating and playing music before Leah, chanting "Heleah, Heleah." {31:8} Jacob heard their chants but didn't understand their meaning, thinking it was a local custom. {31:9} The neighbors continued chanting through the night as Laban had extinguished all the lights. {31:10} In the morning, Jacob realized Leah was with him and understood the neighbors' chants from the night before. {31:11} Jacob confronted Laban, asking why he deceived him, as he had served for Rachel. {31:12} Laban explained that their custom didn't allow the younger daughter to marry before the elder. He offered Rachel to Jacob for another seven years of service. {31:13} Jacob agreed and married Rachel, serving Laban for another seven years. Jacob loved Rachel more than Leah. Laban gave Rachel his maid Bilhah as a handmaid. {31:14} When the Lord saw that Leah was unloved, He made her fertile, and she bore Jacob four sons: Reuben, Simeon, Levi, and Judah. Then she stopped having children. {31:15} Rachel was barren and envied Leah. She gave her maid Bilhah to Jacob, and Bilhah bore him two sons: Dan and Naphtali. {31:16} When Leah stopped having children, she gave her maid Zilpah to Jacob, and Zilpah bore him two sons: Gad and Asher. {31:17} Leah conceived again and bore Jacob two more sons, Issachar and Zebulon, and a daughter, Dinah. {31:18} Rachel remained barren and prayed to the Lord for children, fearing Jacob might leave her. {31:19} She asked God to give her children so she would not be disgraced any longer. {31:20} God answered her prayer, and Rachel gave birth to a son, Joseph, asking for another son as well. Jacob was ninety-one years old when Joseph was born. {31:21} Around this time, Jacob's mother Rebecca sent her nurse Deborah and two servants to Jacob in Haran. {31:22} They arrived and told Jacob that Rebecca wanted him to return to Canaan. {31:23} Jacob listened and prepared to leave after his fourteen years of service to Laban. {31:24} Jacob asked Laban to let him return to his own land with his wives and children. {31:25} Laban asked Jacob to stay and name his wages, promising to pay them. {31:26} Jacob proposed that he would take all the speckled and spotted sheep and goats from Laban's flock as his wages. {31:27} Laban agreed, and Jacob separated these animals from the flock. {31:28} Jacob put the separated animals in his sons' care while he continued to tend Laban's flock. {31:29} Isaac's servants, seeing Jacob's decision to stay, returned to Canaan. {31:30} Deborah stayed with Jacob in Haran, living with his wives and children. {31:31} Jacob continued to serve Laban for six more years, taking the speckled and spotted animals as agreed. He prospered greatly, accumulating much wealth. {31:32} Jacob acquired large, beautiful cattle, and people desired to buy them from him, trading servants and other goods. {31:33} Through these transactions, Jacob gained much wealth and honor, which made Laban's children envious. {31:34} Over time, Jacob heard Laban's sons accusing him of taking their father's wealth. {31:35} Jacob noticed Laban's and his sons' attitudes towards him had changed. {31:36} The Lord told Jacob to return to his birthplace, promising to be with him. {31:37} Jacob gathered his family and belongings and left for Canaan without Laban knowing. {31:38} Rachel stole her father's household idols and hid them on her camel. {31:39} The idols were made by beheading a firstborn man, treating the head with salt and oil, placing a tablet with a name under the tongue, and using it for divination. {31:40} Rachel took the idols so Laban couldn't use them to find out where Jacob had gone. {31:41} When Laban discovered Jacob and his family were gone, he searched for the idols to learn their whereabouts but couldn't find them. {31:42} Laban used other idols and found out Jacob had fled to Canaan. {31:43} Laban gathered his men and pursued Jacob, catching up with him at Mount Gilead. {31:44} Laban confronted Jacob, accusing him of fleeing secretly with his daughters and grandchildren, and stealing his gods. {31:45} Jacob explained that he feared Laban would take his daughters by force. He declared that whoever had the gods would die. {31:46} Laban searched Jacob's tents but didn't find the idols. {31:47} Laban proposed a covenant, stating that Jacob should not mistreat his daughters or marry other women. {31:48} They made a heap of stones as a witness between them, naming it Gilead. {31:49} They offered a sacrifice and shared a meal by the heap, spending the night on the mount. {31:50} Laban kissed his daughters and grandchildren goodbye and returned home the next morning. {31:51} He sent his son Beor and others to inform Esau about Jacob's departure. {31:52} Laban's messengers told Esau about Jacob's success and departure, hoping Esau would confront him. {31:53} Esau's anger was rekindled, and he gathered 400 men to pursue Jacob. {31:54} Esau divided his men into groups, led by his sons and Seir's sons, and set out quickly. {31:55} Laban's messengers went to Rebecca in Canaan and informed her of Esau's intentions. {31:56} Rebecca sent 72 men to warn Jacob about Esau. {31:57} The messengers met Jacob at the brook Jabbok. Jacob saw them as a sign from God and named the place Mahanaim. {31:58} Jacob embraced his father's people and inquired about his parents' well-being. {31:59} They informed Jacob of Rebecca's warning about Esau and advised him to be cautious and to offer gifts to appease Esau. {31:60} They also advised Jacob to honor Esau as his elder brother. {31:61} Jacob wept upon hearing his mother's words and followed her advice.

{32:1} At that time, Jacob sent messengers to his brother Esau in the land of Seir, asking for his favor. {32:2} He instructed them, saying, "Tell my lord Esau that his servant Jacob does not wish him to think that the blessing from our father has brought me much good. {32:3} I have been with Laban for twenty years, and he deceived me and changed my wages ten times, as you already know. {32:4} I worked hard in his house, and God saw my suffering and the labor of my hands and granted me favor. {32:5} Through God's mercy, I gained oxen, donkeys, cattle, and servants. {32:6} Now, I am returning to my land and my family in Canaan, and I have sent messengers to inform you of all this, hoping to find favor in your eyes, so you do not think my wealth came from my father's blessing. {32:7} The messengers found Esau on the borders of Edom, coming toward Jacob with four hundred men from the children of Seir, the Horite, armed with swords. {32:8} They delivered Jacob's message to Esau. {32:9} Esau responded with pride and contempt, saying, "I have heard what Jacob did to Laban, who raised him in his house, gave him daughters, and saw him grow rich. {32:10} When he became wealthy, he fled with everything from Laban's house, taking his daughters as captives without telling him. {32:11} Jacob did the same to me, taking my birthright and blessing. Should I stay silent? {32:12} Now I come with my men to meet him and do as I desire." {32:13} The messengers returned and told Jacob what Esau said, and that Esau was coming with four hundred men. {32:14} Jacob was very afraid and distressed, so he prayed to God. {32:15} He said, "O Lord God of my fathers, Abraham and Isaac, you told me to return to my land and family, and you would do well with me. {32:16} You said you would give me this land and make my descendants numerous. {32:17} You have blessed me with children, cattle, and wealth, as I asked. {32:18} Now, as I return, I fear Esau will kill me and my family. {32:19} Please deliver me from him for the sake of Abraham and Isaac. {32:20} I know my wealth is through your kindness, so save me with your mercy." {32:21} Jacob then divided his people and flocks into two camps, hoping if Esau attacked one, the other could escape. {32:22} That night, Jacob stayed with his people, giving instructions for their safety. {32:23} God heard Jacob's prayer and sent three angels to meet Esau. {32:24} The angels appeared to Esau and his men as two thousand armed horsemen, divided into four camps. {32:25} One camp met Esau and his men, terrifying them, and Esau fell from his horse in fear. {32:26} The camp shouted that they were Jacob's servants, scaring Esau's men further. {32:27} Esau said, "Jacob is my brother whom I have not seen in twenty years. Why treat me this way?" {32:28} The angels replied, "If Jacob were not your brother, we would not spare you." {32:29} The first camp left, and a second camp came, repeating the same actions, scaring Esau again. {32:30} A third camp approached, terrifying Esau and his men further, who cried out. {32:31} Esau repeated, "Jacob is my brother. Why are you treating me like this?" {32:32} The angels answered, "If Jacob were not your brother, we would not spare you." {32:33} The third camp left, and a fourth camp came, treating Esau the same way, causing great fear. {32:34} After the four camps, Esau feared Jacob greatly and decided to meet him peacefully. {32:35} He hid his anger, thinking the camps were Jacob's servants. {32:36} Jacob stayed with his people that night, planning to give Esau a gift from his possessions. {32:37} In the morning, he selected a large gift from his flocks, camels, and cattle, and divided them into ten droves. {32:38} He instructed his servants to keep a distance between each drove, saying, "When Esau meets you and asks who you are, say you are Jacob's servants bringing a gift to Esau, and that Jacob is coming behind us." {32:39} If asked why Jacob is delayed, they should say, "He is coming joyfully behind us to meet his brother." {32:40} The servants went ahead with the gifts, and Jacob stayed that night by the brook Jabbok. {32:41} He took his family and possessions across the brook, and stayed alone. {32:42} A man wrestled with Jacob until daybreak, dislocating his thigh. {32:43} At daybreak, the man blessed Jacob and left, and Jacob crossed the brook limping. {32:44} As he went, the sun rose, and he rejoined his family. {32:45} At midday, they continued, and the gifts went ahead of them. {32:46} Jacob saw Esau coming with four hundred men, and he was very afraid. {32:47} He divided his children among his wives and handmaids, hiding Dinah in a chest, and went ahead to meet Esau. {32:48} He bowed seven times as he approached his brother, and God made Esau kind to Jacob. {32:49} Esau's fear turned into kindness, and he ran to meet Jacob, embracing and kissing him. {32:50} Esau's men also embraced Jacob, as God made them kind toward him. {32:51} Esau asked Jacob about his family, and Jacob introduced them as his children, gifts from God. {32:52} Esau asked about the camp he met the previous night, and Jacob said it was to find favor in Esau's eyes. {32:53} Jacob insisted Esau take the gift, saying it was necessary since he had seen Esau's face. {32:54} Esau initially refused but accepted after Jacob pressed him. {32:55} Esau shared the cattle with his men and gave the gold and silver to his son Eliphaz. {32:56} Esau suggested they travel together, but Jacob declined, saying his children and flocks were slow. {32:57} Esau offered to leave some of his men to help, but Jacob declined, saying he would follow later. {32:58} Esau accepted and returned to Seir, while Jacob continued to Canaan, stopping at its border for some time.

{33:1} After some time, Jacob left the borderlands and came to Shalem, the city of Shechem in Canaan, where he rested outside the city. {33:2} He bought a piece of land there from the children of Hamor, the locals, for five shekels. {33:3} Jacob built a house there, set up tents, and made shelters for his livestock, calling the place Succoth. {33:4} Jacob stayed in Succoth for a year and six months. {33:5} During this time, women from the area went to Shechem to dance and celebrate with the city's daughters. Rachel and Leah, Jacob's wives, and their families joined to watch. {33:6} Dinah, Jacob's daughter, also went along and stayed with her mother while the townspeople observed the celebrations. All the city's important people were present. {33:7} Shechem, son of Hamor, the prince, noticed Dinah among the women. {33:8} He asked his friends who she was, and they told him she was the daughter of Jacob, the Hebrew, who had been living there for a while. She had come with her mother and maidservants to see the celebration. {33:9} Shechem was deeply attracted to Dinah and asked his friends about her. {33:10} When he learned who she was, he sent for her and took her by force. He lay with her and humiliated her, but he also loved her and kept her in his house. {33:11} Word reached Jacob that Shechem had defiled Dinah. Jacob sent twelve servants to bring her back, but they were driven away by Shechem and his men. {33:12} Shechem refused to let Dinah go and even embraced her in front of Jacob's servants. {33:13} The servants returned and reported everything to Jacob, who remained silent until his sons returned from the fields. {33:14} Jacob sent two maidservants to care for Dinah at Shechem's house, while Shechem sent three friends to his father Hamor to arrange for Dinah to become his wife. {33:15} Hamor questioned his son about taking a Hebrew woman, but Shechem insisted, saying she was delightful to him. {33:16}

Hamor complied because he loved his son dearly. {33:17} Hamor went to Jacob to discuss the matter. Meanwhile, Jacob's sons returned home, furious over what had happened to Dinah. {33:18} They believed Shechem and his family deserved death for violating God's commands and defiling their sister. {33:19} Hamor arrived to talk with Jacob just as his sons returned from the fields. {33:20} Jacob's sons were outraged and demanded justice, believing Shechem's actions warranted death for him and his people. {33:21} As they expressed their anger to Jacob, Hamor spoke to them, requesting Dinah for his son and proposing intermarriage between their peoples. {33:22} Hamor offered them the land to dwell in and trade, promising no one would oppose them. {33:23} Shechem arrived and echoed his father's request, offering any dowry they demanded. {33:24} Simeon and Levi deceitfully agreed, saying they needed their father Isaac's consent and would discuss it with him. {33:25} They told Shechem and Hamor they couldn't decide without consulting Isaac, who knew Abraham's ways. {33:26} This was a ruse to buy time and plan their response. {33:27} Shechem and Hamor accepted the terms and left. {33:28} Jacob's sons then devised a plan, believing the city's people deserved death for their transgression and for not condemning Shechem's act. {33:29} Simeon suggested they demand all the men of the city be circumcised, knowing it would weaken them. {33:30} The brothers agreed and planned to attack when the men were in pain. {33:31} The next morning, Shechem and Hamor returned, eager for an answer. {33:32} Jacob's sons deceitfully said Isaac approved and mentioned Abraham's command from God that any suitor for their daughters must be circumcised. {33:33} They proposed intermarriage if all the city's males were circumcised, threatening to take Dinah and leave if not. {33:34} Shechem and Hamor agreed and went to the city gates to present the proposal. {33:35} They convinced the city's men to undergo circumcision, promising unity and prosperity. {33:36} The men agreed due to their respect for Shechem and Hamor. {33:37} The next day, Jacob's sons circumcised all the city's males, including Shechem, Hamor, and Shechem's brothers. {33:38} Afterward, each man returned home in pain, fulfilling the Lord's plan to deliver the city into the hands of Jacob's sons.

{34:1} The number of all the males circumcised was 645 men and 246 children. {34:2} However, Chiddekem, the son of Pered and the father of Hamor, along with his six brothers, refused to listen to Shechem and his father Hamor, and they rejected the idea of circumcision because they found the proposal from Jacob's sons detestable and infuriating. {34:3} On the evening of the second day, they discovered eight young boys who had not been circumcised because their mothers had hidden them from Shechem, Hamor, and the city's men. {34:4} Shechem and Hamor sent for the boys to be circumcised, but Chiddekem and his six brothers attacked them with swords, intending to kill them. {34:5} They also sought to kill Shechem, Hamor, and Dinah because of this issue. {34:6} They questioned Shechem and Hamor, asking why they would seek Hebrew daughters when there were Canaanite women available, an act their ancestors had never endorsed. {34:7} They doubted the success of such actions and worried about how they would respond to other Canaanites questioning their motives. {34:8} They expressed fear for their lives and doubted the justness of the act. {34:9} They warned that if the Canaanites learned about this, they would seek retribution against Shechem and Hamor. {34:10} They argued that taking a Hebrew woman against their customs would bring shame and peril upon them. {34:11} They declared they could not accept such a burden, which their ancestors never imposed. {34:12} They threatened to gather their Canaanite allies to attack Shechem and his supporters. {34:13} Hamor, Shechem, and the city's people were terrified by Chiddekem's threats and regretted their actions. {34:14} Shechem and Hamor acknowledged the truth of Chiddekem's words. {34:15} They explained that they only agreed to the circumcision because it was the only way to marry Dinah, not out of love for the Hebrews. {34:16} They had hoped to gain their desire by agreeing to the terms. {34:17} They planned to attack Jacob's sons after securing Dinah. {34:18} They requested patience until they healed from circumcision before enacting their plans. {34:19} Dinah overheard these conversations and sent a maid to inform her father Jacob and her brothers. {34:20} Upon hearing Dinah's message, Jacob was enraged and incensed. {34:21} Simeon and Levi swore to God that by the next day, they would leave no survivors in the city. {34:22} They discovered twenty uncircumcised young men, and after a fight, Simeon and Levi killed eighteen of them while two escaped to lime pits. {34:23} Simeon and Levi continued their attack, killing every male in the city and causing great panic. {34:24} They also killed Hamor and Shechem and rescued Dinah. {34:25} They took the city's wealth and livestock as spoils. {34:26} During the plundering, three hundred men resisted by throwing dust and stones, but Simeon killed them all. {34:27} Simeon and Levi then took the remaining women and children as captives. {34:28} They opened the city's gates and left, returning to their father Jacob with the plunder. {34:29} Jacob was furious upon seeing the destruction and the spoils, blaming Simeon and Levi for making him detestable to the Canaanites and Perizzites, fearing a retaliatory attack that could wipe out his small household. {34:30} Simeon and Levi defended their actions, arguing that Shechem's crime against their sister warranted their response. {34:31} They insisted they couldn't allow Shechem to treat their sister like a harlot. {34:32} They captured eighty-five women who had not known men and forty-seven males, sparing them while killing the rest. {34:33} These captives served Jacob's family until they left Egypt. {34:34} After Simeon and Levi left the city, two young men who had hidden and survived the massacre found the city desolate, filled only with weeping women. {34:35} They spread the news of the city's destruction by Jacob's sons, alarming the neighboring city of Tapnach. {34:36} Jashub, the king of Tapnach, verified the story and marveled at how two men could destroy such a large city. {34:37} He decided to gather forces to fight the Hebrews, consulting his advisors who suggested forming an alliance with other kings. {34:38} Jashub then sent messages to the neighboring Amorite kings to join forces against Jacob's family. {34:39} The Amorite kings were shocked by the destruction of Shechem and agreed to unite against Jacob. {34:40} The seven kings of the Amorites, with ten thousand men, prepared to fight Jacob's sons. {34:41} Jacob was deeply distressed and rebuked Simeon and Levi for provoking such a dangerous situation. {34:42} Judah defended his brothers' actions, stating they were justified in avenging their sister's honor and following God's commands. {34:43} Judah assured Jacob that God, who had delivered Shechem into their hands, would also protect them against the Amorite kings. {34:44} Jacob was advised to pray and trust in God's protection. {34:45} Judah then sent a servant to scout the approaching enemy forces. {34:46} The servant reported seeing a vast army. {34:47} Judah encouraged his brothers to prepare for battle, trusting in God's support. {34:48} Jacob's sons, along with their servants and Isaac's men from Hebron, totaling 112, armed themselves for the confrontation. {34:49} They sent a message to Isaac, requesting his prayers for divine protection. {34:50} Isaac prayed to God, recalling His promises to Abraham and himself, asking for the Amorite kings' plans to be thwarted and for protection for Jacob's family. {34:51} The sons of Jacob, trusting in God, moved towards the enemy, with Jacob also praying for divine intervention. {34:52} He acknowledged God's power to initiate and end wars, asking for His mercy and protection against the Amorite kings. {34:53} Jacob's prayer focused on instilling fear in the hearts of their enemies and delivering them from harm.

{35:1} The Amorite kings gathered in the field to discuss what to do about the sons of Jacob, fearing them greatly since just two of them had destroyed the entire city of Shechem. {35:2} The Lord heard Isaac and Jacob's prayers and instilled fear and terror in the hearts of the kings' advisers. {35:3} The advisers questioned the kings' sanity for wanting to fight the Hebrews, warning them of their impending destruction. {35:4} They reminded the kings that two Hebrews had destroyed Shechem without any resistance, questioning how they could hope to defeat the entire group. {35:5} They emphasized that the God of the Hebrews was powerful and had performed mighty deeds for them, unmatched by any other gods. {35:6} The advisers recounted how God had delivered Abraham from Nimrod and his people, who had tried to kill him multiple times. {35:7} They reminded the kings of God saving Abraham from the fire Nimrod cast him into. {35:8} They spoke of Abraham defeating the five kings of Elam to rescue his nephew Lot, with only a few men. {35:9} They highlighted that the Hebrews' God was pleased with them and had always delivered them from their enemies. {35:10} The advisers recalled Abraham's willingness to sacrifice his son Isaac out of love for God, which led to God's promise to protect Abraham's descendants. {35:11} They mentioned God's wrath against Pharaoh and Abimelech for attempting to take Abraham's wife, Sarah, under false pretenses. {35:12} The advisers also remembered how Esau, Jacob's brother, had come to kill Jacob with four hundred men but was thwarted by God. {35:13} They noted that God had saved Jacob from Esau's hands and other enemies. {35:14} They stressed that it was God's power, not the Hebrews' own strength, that allowed them to destroy Shechem. {35:15} The advisers warned that fighting the Hebrews was essentially fighting their powerful God. {35:16} They suggested that even with many more allies, the kings could not prevail over the Hebrews and their God. {35:17} The advisers concluded that the kings should avoid battle with the Hebrews to prevent their own destruction. {35:18} They urged the kings to refrain from their plan and recognize that the Hebrews' God was with them. {35:19} Upon hearing these words, the Amorite kings were filled with fear and decided not to fight the sons of Jacob. {35:20} The kings agreed with their advisers and decided to avoid conflict with the Hebrews. {35:21} They returned to their cities, too afraid to approach the sons of Jacob for battle. {35:22} This change of heart came from the Lord, who had heard the prayers of Isaac and Jacob. {35:23} The kings and their armies went back to their own cities, and the sons of Jacob remained unchallenged. {35:24} The sons of Jacob stayed in their position until evening by Mount Sihon, and seeing no attack, they returned home.

{36:1} At that time, the Lord appeared to Jacob, instructing him to go to Bethel, stay there, and build an altar to the Lord who had delivered him and his sons from affliction. {36:2} Jacob obeyed, taking his sons and all his possessions, and they went to Bethel as the Lord had commanded. {36:3} Jacob was ninety-nine years old when he arrived in Bethel, where he, his sons, and all his people stayed for six months. Jacob built an altar to the Lord there. {36:4} During this time, Deborah, the daughter of Uz and Rebecca's nurse who had been with Jacob, died. Jacob buried her beneath an oak tree in Bethel. {36:5} Rebecca, the daughter of Bethuel and Jacob's mother, also died in Hebron, known as Kireath-arba, and was buried in the cave of Machpelah, which Abraham had purchased from the children of Heth. {36:6} Rebecca lived for one hundred and thirty-three years. When Jacob learned of her death, he wept bitterly and mourned greatly for her and for Deborah, naming the place of Deborah's burial Allon-bachuth. {36:7} Laban the Syrian died around this time as well, for God struck him down for breaking the covenant between him and Jacob. {36:8} When Jacob was one hundred years old, the Lord appeared to him again, blessed him, and renamed him Israel. Around this time, Rachel, Jacob's wife, conceived. {36:9} Jacob and his entire household then traveled from Bethel to his father's house in Hebron. {36:10} On the way, near Ephrath, Rachel went into hard labor and died giving birth to a son. {36:11} Jacob buried Rachel on the way to Ephrath, now known as Bethlehem, setting a pillar on her grave. Rachel was forty-five years old when she died. {36:12} Jacob named his newborn son Benjamin, meaning "son of the right hand." {36:13} After Rachel's death, Jacob pitched his tent in the tent of her handmaid, Bilhah. {36:14} Reuben, Leah's son, was jealous and angry over this and moved his father's bed from Bilhah's tent. {36:15} Due to Reuben's act, his birthright and the roles of king and priest were taken from him. The birthright was given to Joseph, the kingship to Judah, and the priesthood to Levi. {36:16} These are the sons of Jacob born to him in Padan-aram: Reuben, Simeon, Levi, Judah, Issachar, Zebulun, and their sister Dinah from Leah; Joseph and Benjamin from Rachel. {36:17} Gad and Asher from Zilpah, Leah's handmaid; Dan and Naphtali from Bilhah, Rachel's handmaid. These are Jacob's sons born in Padan-aram. {36:18} Jacob and his household then moved to Mamre, also known as Kireath-arba, in Hebron, where Abraham and Isaac had lived. {36:19} Esau, Jacob's brother, and his family moved to the land of Seir, where they became exceedingly fruitful and multiplied. {36:20} These are Esau's descendants born in Canaan: his firstborn Eliphaz from Adah, Reuel also from Adah, Jeush, Jaalam, and Korah from Ahlibamah. {36:21} The sons of Eliphaz were Teman, Omar, Zepho, Gatam, Kenaz, and Amalek. The sons of Reuel were Nachath, Zerach, Shamah, and Mizzah. {36:22} The sons of Jeush were Timnah, Alvah, and Jetheth; the sons of Yaalam were Alah, Phinor, and Kenaz. {36:23} The sons of Korah were Teman, Mibzar, Magdiel, and Eram. These families of Esau lived according to their dukedoms in Seir. {36:24} The sons of Seir the Horite, inhabitants of Seir, were Lotan, Shobal, Zibeon, Anah, Dishan, Ezer, and Dishon. {36:25} Lotan's children were Hori and Heman, and their sister Timna, who became Eliphaz's concubine and bore Amalek. {36:26} The sons of Shobal were Alvan, Manahath, Ebal, Shepho, and Onam. Zibeon's sons were Ajah and Anah. {36:27} Anah discovered the Yemim in the wilderness while tending his father Zibeon's asses. {36:28} While feeding the asses in the wilderness near the sea, a severe storm arose, causing the animals to stop. {36:29} From the wilderness, one hundred and twenty terrifying creatures resembling humans from the waist down and bears or keephas from the waist up, with long tails, appeared and rode away on the asses. {36:30} One creature struck Anah with its tail before fleeing. Anah, terrified, escaped to the city. {36:31} He recounted the events to his sons and brothers, who searched for the asses but couldn't find them. Anah and his brothers never returned to that place. {36:32} The children of Anah were Dishon and his sister Ahlibamah. Dishon's children were Hemdan, Eshban, Ithran, and Cheran. Ezer's children were Bilhan, Zaavan, and Akan. Dishon's children were Uz and Aran. {36:33} These families of Seir the Horite lived according to their dukedoms in Seir. {36:34} Esau and his family lived in Seir, where they had many possessions and multiplied greatly. Jacob and his family lived with Isaac in Canaan as the Lord commanded Abraham.

{37:1} In the 105th year of Jacob's life, which was the ninth year of his dwelling in Canaan after coming from Padan-aram, he and his children journeyed. {37:2} Jacob and his children left Hebron and returned to the city of Shechem, along with everything they owned. They settled there because the land was good for their cattle, and the city had been rebuilt with around 300 inhabitants. {37:3} Jacob and his family lived in the field that Jacob had previously bought from Hamor, Shechem's father, before Simeon and Levi had attacked the city. {37:4} The Canaanite and Amorite kings around Shechem heard that Jacob's sons had returned to the city. {37:5} The kings questioned whether the sons of Jacob would once again take over the city and harm its inhabitants. {37:6} The Canaanite kings gathered to make war against Jacob and his sons. {37:7} Jashub, king of Tapnach, called on neighboring kings, including Elan, king of Gaash, Ihuri, king of Shiloh, Parathon, king of Chazar, Susi, king of Sarton, Laban, king of Bethchoran, and Shabir, king of Othnay-mah. {37:8} Jashub urged them to join him in attacking Jacob and his sons, who had returned to Shechem to claim it again. {37:9} The assembled kings and their armies, numerous as the sand on the seashore, camped opposite Tapnach. {37:10} Jashub led his army and camped outside the city with seven divisions prepared to fight Jacob's sons. {37:11} They sent a message to Jacob and his sons, challenging them to meet on the plain to avenge the people of Shechem. {37:12} Jacob's sons were angered by this message and prepared for battle with 102 of their servants. {37:13} Jacob and his sons, along with their servants, went to confront the kings, standing on the hill of Shechem. {37:14} Jacob prayed to the Lord for protection and strength for his sons. {37:15} He asked the Lord to save his sons from their enemies or to take their lives mercifully if they were to perish. {37:16} When Jacob finished praying, the earth shook, the sun darkened, and the kings were terrified. {37:17} The Lord heard Jacob's prayer and instilled fear and awe in the hearts of the kings. {37:18} The kings heard the sounds of chariots and horses as if a great army was approaching. {37:19} They were filled with terror as Jacob's sons, with 112 men, advanced toward them with loud shouts. {37:20} The kings were panic-stricken and considered retreating but decided against it to avoid disgrace. {37:21} As Jacob's sons approached, the kings saw their numbers and were even more terrified. {37:22} They decided not to retreat, feeling it would be dishonorable. {37:23} The sons of Jacob called upon the Lord for help as they prepared for battle. {37:24} Judah led his brothers and their servants into battle. {37:25} Judah faced Jashub, who was heavily armored and skilled in battle, riding a powerful horse. {37:26} Jashub shot arrows with great skill, but the Lord caused them to miss Judah. {37:27} Judah ran toward Jashub, throwing a large stone that struck Jashub's shield, causing him to fall from his horse. {37:28} Judah's strength stunned Jashub, and he fell to the ground, his shield flying from his hand. {37:29} Seeing this, the kings were afraid of Judah's strength. {37:30} Judah then struck down 42 men from Jashub's camp, causing the rest to flee. {37:31} Jashub, seeing his men flee, stood up to face Judah again. {37:32} Judah and Jashub fought, shield to shield, but Jashub's spear split Judah's shield. {37:33} Judah quickly drew his sword, severing Jashub's feet and then his head. {37:34} The sons of Jacob saw this and attacked the other kings' armies. {37:35} They killed 15,000 men, causing the rest to flee in terror. {37:36} Judah stood over Jashub's body, stripping him of his armor. {37:37} Nine captains of Jashub's army approached Judah, but he struck one down with a stone, causing the rest to flee. {37:38} Judah and his men pursued and killed them. {37:39} The sons of Jacob continued to fight, killing many of the enemy. {37:40} The kings tried to rally their troops, but they were too afraid to fight. {37:41} After defeating the enemy armies, Jacob's sons returned to Judah, who was still fighting the captains. {37:42} Levi saw Elon, king of Gaash, and his captains approaching but was not initially aware of the threat. {37:43} When Levi realized they were attacking, he and his servants killed Elon and his captains with swords.

{38:1} Ihuri, the king of Shiloh, came to aid Elon, but Jacob shot an arrow that killed Ihuri. {38:2} After Ihuri's death, the remaining four kings and their captains tried to retreat, acknowledging their lack of strength against the Hebrews who had killed three of their strongest kings. {38:3} Seeing the kings retreating, the sons of Jacob and Jacob himself pursued them from the heap of Shechem with their servants. {38:4} The kings and their armies, fearful for their lives, fled to the city of Chazar, with the sons of Jacob in hot pursuit. {38:5} At the gate of Chazar, the sons of Jacob inflicted a heavy blow, killing about four thousand men, while Jacob focused on killing the kings with his bow. {38:6} Jacob killed Parathon, the king of Chazar, at the city gate, then Susi, the king of Sarton, Laban, the king of Bethchorin, and Shabir, the king of Machnaymah, each with a single arrow. {38:7} With all the kings dead, the sons of Jacob continued fighting the remaining armies near Chazar's gate, killing about four hundred more men. {38:8} Three of Jacob's servants fell in the battle, deeply grieving Judah and igniting his anger against the Amorites. {38:9} The remaining soldiers fled into Chazar, breaking the gate to enter the city and hide, as Chazar was large and extensive. {38:10} As the armies entered Chazar, the sons of Jacob followed them. {38:11} Four experienced warriors guarded the city's entrance, blocking the sons of Jacob from entering. {38:12} Naphtali quickly killed two of these guards by decapitating them with a single stroke. {38:13} The remaining two guards fled, but Naphtali pursued and killed them. {38:14} Upon entering the city, the sons of Jacob found another wall and searched for its gate, but Judah, Simeon, and Levi scaled the wall and descended into the city. {38:15} Simeon and Levi killed all who sought refuge within the city, including its inhabitants, women, and children, whose cries reached heaven. {38:16} Dan and Naphtali, hearing the commotion, climbed the wall and saw the city's inhabitants begging for mercy, offering their possessions in exchange for their lives. {38:17} After the slaughter ceased, Simeon and Levi called to their brothers, informing them of the city's entrance, and all the sons of Jacob came to collect the spoils. {38:18} They took everything of value from Chazar and left that day. {38:19} The next day, they went to Sarton, hearing that its remaining men were preparing to fight them, as their king had been killed. Sarton was heavily fortified with a deep rampart. {38:20} The city's rampart was high and broad, preventing entry, so the sons of Jacob searched for a way in but couldn't find one. {38:21} The city's entrance was at the rear, requiring a long route to access. {38:22} Unable to find the entrance, the sons of Jacob became very angry, while the city's inhabitants feared them due to their reputation. {38:23} The inhabitants, terrified by the sons of Jacob's approach, dismantled the bridge to prevent their entry. {38:24} The sons of Jacob continued searching for an entrance, while the city's inhabitants cursed and mocked them from the walls, incensing the brothers. {38:25} The sons of Jacob, provoked, used their strength to leap over the forty-cubit rampart. {38:26} They then approached the city gates, which were reinforced with iron. {38:27} The inhabitants on the wall attacked them with stones and arrows, numbering about four hundred men. {38:28} The sons of Jacob climbed the wall, with Judah first, followed by Gad, Asher, Simeon, and Levi. {38:29} Seeing the brothers ascend, the inhabitants fled and hid within the city. {38:30} Issachar and Naphtali broke through the city gates with fire, allowing the sons of Jacob to enter and slaughter the city's inhabitants. {38:31} About two hundred men fled to a tower, but Judah destroyed it, killing them all. {38:32} The brothers saw another high tower within the city and went to attack it, finding it filled with people. {38:33} The sons of Jacob inflicted a great slaughter in the tower, forcing the survivors to flee. {38:34} Twelve valiant men then emerged to fight Simeon and Levi. {38:35} These twelve men were formidable, breaking the brothers' shields and nearly severing Levi's hand. {38:36} Levi, using one of their swords, beheaded one of the men, but the remaining eleven fought fiercely. {38:37} Despite their efforts, the brothers could not overcome these powerful men. {38:38} Simeon's loud shriek startled the eleven men, allowing Judah and Naphtali to join the fight with fresh shields. {38:39} The battle raged until sunset, with the brothers unable to prevail. {38:40} Jacob, hearing of the struggle, prayed to the Lord and joined the battle with Naphtali. {38:41} Jacob's bow killed three men, causing the remaining eight to flee, now facing attacks from both front and rear. {38:42} Fleeing, they encountered Dan and Asher, who killed two more, and Judah and his brothers pursued and killed the rest. {38:43} The sons of Jacob then searched the city for survivors, finding and killing twenty young men in a cave. {38:44} Gad and Asher also killed men who had escaped the second tower. {38:45} The brothers killed all the men of Sarton but spared the women and children. {38:46} The men of Sarton were extremely powerful, yet none could stand against the sons of Jacob. {38:47} After killing all the men, they took the city's spoils, flocks, herds, and other property, treating Sarton as they had Chazar, before departing.

{39:1} After the sons of Jacob left the city of Sarton, they encountered the inhabitants of Tapnach, who were coming to fight them because they had killed the king of Tapnach and his men. {39:2} The remaining people of Tapnach attempted to reclaim the booty and spoil taken from Chazar and Sarton, engaging the sons of Jacob in battle. {39:3} The sons of Jacob defeated the Tapnach men, who fled to Arbelan, only to be pursued and defeated there as well. {39:4} They returned to Tapnach to plunder it, but upon hearing that the people of Arbelan were coming to save their brethren's spoil, the sons of Jacob left ten men in Tapnach to plunder and went out to meet the people of Arbelan. {39:5} The men of Arbelan, accompanied by their experienced-in-battle wives, about four hundred in total, went out to fight the sons of Jacob. {39:6} The sons of Jacob shouted loudly and charged towards the people of Arbelan. {39:7} Hearing the sons of Jacob's roaring like lions and waves, fear gripped the hearts of the Arbelan inhabitants, who fled back into their city. {39:8} The sons of Jacob chased them to the city's gate and fought them within the city. {39:9} The Arbelan women joined in by slinging stones at the sons of Jacob, making the battle fierce until evening. {39:10} The sons of Jacob were nearly defeated but called upon the Lord and gained strength, ultimately defeating all the inhabitants of Arbelan, including men, women, and children. {39:11} They also killed the remaining people who had fled from Sarton and did to Arbelan and Tapnach as they had done to Chazar and Sarton. {39:12} When the women saw their men killed, they attacked the sons of Jacob from the roofs with stones. {39:13} The sons of Jacob hurried into the city, killing all the women and seizing the spoil and livestock. {39:14} They treated Machnaymah similarly and moved on. {39:15} On the fifth day, hearing that the people of Gaash were assembling against them for killing their king and captains, the sons of Jacob prepared for battle. {39:16} They found Gaash strongly fortified with three walls and its gates locked, with five hundred men defending from the outer wall and many more lying in ambush. {39:17} As the sons of Jacob approached to open the gates, those in ambush surrounded them, with defenders on the walls attacking them with arrows and stones. {39:18} Seeing the battle intensity, Judah gave a tremendous shriek, terrifying the men of Gaash, causing many to fall from the wall. {39:19} The sons of Jacob tried to break the city doors but were repelled by the defenders on the wall. {39:20} They turned to fight those outside the city and struck them down, instilling fright from Judah's shriek. {39:21} Judah and his brothers continued their assault on the city gates but were met with heavy resistance from the walls. {39:22} The men of Gaash, seeing the sons of Jacob's struggle, taunted them, boasting of their own strength compared to the weaker Amorite cities previously defeated by Jacob's sons. {39:23} Angered by these taunts, Judah prayed for God's help and, with renewed strength, mounted the wall alone. {39:24} His shout terrified the wall defenders, causing many to flee or fall into the city. {39:25} Some tried to fight Judah, but seeing him unarmed, they sought to cast him down to his brothers. {39:26} Judah called for help, and his brothers shot three attackers with their bows from below. {39:27} Judah continued shouting, and the defenders, terrified, dropped their swords and fled. {39:28} Judah took their swords and killed twenty men on the wall. {39:29} Eighty more men and women climbed the wall to attack Judah but were paralyzed with fear. {39:30} Jacob and his sons killed ten more defenders with their bows from below. {39:31} The defenders, seeing their numbers dwindle, still tried to attack Judah, but were terrified by his strength. {39:32} One mighty man struck Judah's head, splitting his shield, then fled in fear but fell and was killed by Jacob's sons. {39:33} Judah, in pain from the blow, called out again, and Dan, enraged, mounted the wall to aid him. {39:34} Together, they faced a barrage of stones and arrows from the second wall, nearly being killed. {39:35} Unable to return fire effectively, they sprang to the second wall, causing more defenders to flee. {39:36} Naphtali joined them, and the remaining defenders fled between the walls. {39:37} Issachar and Zebulun opened the city gates, allowing Jacob and his men to enter. {39:38} Judah, Dan, and Naphtali descended from the wall and pursued the city's inhabitants. {39:39} Simeon and Levi, unaware the gate was open, joined the battle from the wall. {39:40} Jacob's sons fought from all directions, killing about twenty thousand men and women. {39:41} Blood flowed like a stream, reaching the desert of Bethchorin. {39:42} The people of Bethchorin, seeing the blood and hearing the cries, deduced it was the work of the Hebrews and armed themselves to fight Jacob's sons. {39:43} After killing the Gaash inhabitants, the sons of Jacob plundered the city and met three powerful men. {39:44} One of the men threw Zebulun to the ground, but Jacob killed him. {39:45} Another attacked Jacob, but Simeon and Levi struck him down, and Judah finished him off. {39:46} The third man fled, picked up a sword, and fought fiercely, targeting Judah. {39:47} Naphtali protected Judah with his shield, allowing Simeon and Levi to kill the man. {39:48} As night fell, the sons of Jacob completed their conquest of Gaash, taking all the spoils and leaving no survivors, as they had done in Sarton and Shiloh.

{40:1} Jacob's sons took all the spoils from Gaash and left the city under the cover of night. {40:2} As they headed towards Bethchorin's castle, the inhabitants of Bethchorin were coming out to meet them, resulting in a night battle at the castle. {40:3} The Bethchorinites were strong warriors, each capable of facing a thousand men, and their shouts echoed through the night, causing the earth to tremble. {40:4} The sons of Jacob, unaccustomed to fighting in the dark, were afraid and called out to the Lord for help, pleading for deliverance from these uncircumcised men. {40:5} The Lord answered their cries, instilling great terror and confusion among the Bethchorinites, who began to fight and kill each other in the darkness. {40:6} Realizing that the Lord had caused this chaos, the sons of Jacob slipped away from the melee and rested securely that night. {40:7} The Bethchorinites continued to battle each other throughout the night, their cries heard from afar, and the ground shook at their powerful voices. {40:8} The noise reached the cities of the Canaanites, Hittites, Amorites, Hivites, and all the kings of Canaan, as well as those beyond the Jordan. {40:9} They recognized it as the Hebrews fighting against the seven cities and wondered who could stand against such might. {40:10} The fear of Jacob's sons spread, as the people feared a similar fate for their own cities. {40:11} The Chorinites' cries intensified until morning, and many were killed. {40:12} At dawn, Jacob's sons returned to the castle and finished off the remaining Chorinites. {40:13} On the sixth day, the Canaanite cities saw the dead bodies strewn about the castle. {40:14} Jacob's sons took the spoils from Gaash and Bethchorin, finding the city crowded with people, and fought until evening. {40:15} They treated Bethchorin as they had done to other cities, taking all the spoils. {40:16} With their plunder, they returned to Shechem and camped outside the city, resting from the war. {40:17} They kept the spoils and servants outside, fearing another attack. {40:18} Jacob and his sons stayed in the field they had bought from Hamor. {40:19} The captured booty was immense, like the sand on the seashore. {40:20} The inhabitants of the land watched from a distance and feared Jacob's sons, knowing no king had ever achieved such feats. {40:21} Seven Canaanite kings decided to seek peace with Jacob's sons, fearing for their lives. {40:22} Japhia, king of Hebron, secretly contacted other kings, urging them to join him in making peace. {40:23} He advised them to come with a small number of men to negotiate a treaty. {40:24} They complied and assembled in Hebron, agreeing to seek peace with Jacob's sons. {40:25} Jacob's sons remained cautious and stayed in the field for ten days, awaiting any signs of war. {40:26} When no attack came, they moved back into Shechem. {40:27} Forty days later, the Amorite kings gathered in Hebron to make peace. {40:28} Twenty-one kings, with sixty-nine captains and 189 men, camped near Mount Hebron. {40:29} The king of Hebron went ahead with his captains to speak with Jacob's sons. {40:30} Jacob's sons sent spies to assess the kings' numbers and intentions. {40:31} The spies reported that the kings had only 288 men. {40:32} Deciding to confront them, Jacob's sons chose 62 men and ten of Jacob's sons, arming themselves for battle. {40:33} They approached the gate of Shechem with their father. {40:34} They saw the king of Hebron approaching with his captains and halted. {40:35} The king of Hebron and his captains bowed before Jacob and his sons. {40:36} Jacob's sons questioned the king's intentions. {40:37} The king of Hebron explained that all the Canaanite kings sought peace. {40:38} Distrustful, Jacob's sons suspected deceit. {40:39} The king of Hebron reassured them, saying the kings had come unarmed. {40:40} Jacob's sons demanded the kings come individually to prove their peaceful intentions. {40:41} The kings complied, bowing before Jacob and his sons. {40:42} They pleaded for a peace treaty, fearing a similar fate as other cities. {40:43} Jacob's sons realized the kings genuinely sought peace and agreed to a covenant. {40:44} The kings swore allegiance, and Jacob's sons made them tributary. {40:45} The kings brought gifts and bowed down before Jacob and his sons. {40:46} They requested the return of the captured spoils. {40:47} Jacob's sons returned all the captives and goods, and the kings departed peacefully. {40:48} The kings continued to send gifts, and peace was established between Jacob's sons and the Canaanite kings, lasting until the Israelites inherited Canaan.

{41:1} After a year had passed, Jacob's sons left Shechem and returned to Hebron to be with their father Isaac. They settled there while continuing to graze their flocks in Shechem, where the pastures were excellent. Jacob and his entire household lived in the valley of Hebron. {41:2} In that same year, Leah, Jacob's wife, died in Hebron at the age of fifty-one, marking the hundred and sixth year of Jacob's life and the tenth year since his return from Padan-aram. {41:3} Jacob and his sons buried Leah in the cave of Machpelah in Hebron, the burial place Abraham had purchased from the Hittites. {41:4} Jacob's sons remained with him in the valley of Hebron, and their strength became known throughout the land. {41:5} Meanwhile, Joseph and Benjamin, Rachel's sons, were still young and did not join their brothers in battles against the Amorite cities. {41:6} Joseph admired his brothers' strength but believed himself superior to them. Jacob favored Joseph, his son of old age, and made him a coat of many colors, increasing his brothers' resentment. {41:7} Seeing their father's preference for Joseph, he exacerbated tensions by bringing unfavorable reports about his brothers to Jacob. {41:8} The brothers, aware of Joseph's actions and their father's love for him, grew to hate him and could not speak peacefully to him. {41:9} Joseph, seventeen years old, continued to assert his superiority over his brothers, further fueling their animosity. {41:10} One night, Joseph had a dream and shared it with his brothers, telling them how in the dream, their sheaves bowed down to his. {41:11} His brothers reacted angrily, questioning if he intended to rule over them. {41:12} Undeterred, Joseph recounted the dream to Jacob, who, despite rebuking him, secretly pondered its meaning. {41:13} The brothers' jealousy deepened when Jacob openly favored Joseph and blessed him. {41:14} Joseph later dreamed another dream where the sun, moon, and eleven stars bowed down to him, which further infuriated his brothers. {41:15} Jacob scolded Joseph, concerned about the implications of such dreams and his brothers' growing resentment. {41:16} The brothers' envy intensified as Joseph continued to share his dreams, and Jacob pondered them in his heart. {41:17} One day, Jacob's sons went to Shechem to tend their father's flock, as they were still shepherds. {41:18} Jacob worried when they did not return on time, fearing trouble with the people of Shechem. {41:19} He sent Joseph to check on them, instructing him to bring back news of their well-being. {41:20} Joseph set out for Shechem but couldn't find his brothers, so he wandered near the fields until an angel guided him toward Dothan, where his brothers had gone. {41:21} When Joseph reached Dothan and approached his brothers, they conspired to kill him. {41:22} Reuben intervened, suggesting they throw Joseph into a pit instead of shedding his blood. He planned to rescue Joseph later and return him to Jacob. {41:23} As Joseph came near, they seized him, stripped off his coat of many colors, and threw him into an empty pit where serpents and scorpions lurked. {41:24} Joseph cried out in fear, but the Lord protected him from harm. {41:25} From the pit, Joseph pleaded with his brothers, questioning their actions and reminding them of their familial bond. {41:26} Despite Joseph's appeals, his brothers ignored him, unmoved by his cries. {41:27} Joseph continued to cry out from the pit, imploring his brothers to show compassion and reminding them of their heritage. {41:28} His brothers, unmoved, withdrew to avoid hearing his cries.

{42:1} They moved and sat on the opposite side, about a bow-shot away. While they were eating, they discussed what to do with him—whether to kill him or take him back to their father. {42:2} As they debated, they looked up and saw a group of Ishmaelites approaching from Gilead, on their way to Egypt. {42:3} Judah suggested, "What profit is there if we kill our brother? Instead, let's sell him to these Ishmaelites. Let's not harm him ourselves; after all, he will just disappear among the foreigners." {42:4} His brothers agreed to Judah's plan. So when the Ishmaelites came near, they pulled Joseph out of the pit and sold him to them. {42:5} Meanwhile, seven traders from Midian passed by. They were thirsty and spotted the pit where Joseph had been left. They were surprised to find him there, surrounded by birds. {42:6} The Midianites rushed to the pit, thinking it contained water. When they heard Joseph crying, they looked inside and saw a handsome young man. {42:7} They asked him, "Who are you, and why are you in this pit in the wilderness?" They helped him out and decided to take him with them on their journey. {42:8} Joseph's brothers protested, "Why are you taking our servant? We put him in the pit because he disobeyed us. Give him back!" {42:9} The Midianites responded, "Is this your servant? He seems more impressive than any of you. We found him in the pit and took him. We won't listen to your claims." {42:10} Joseph's brothers approached, ready to fight, but Simeon stepped forward, shouting loudly. His intimidation caused the Midianites to fear. {42:11} Simeon declared, "I am Simeon, son of Jacob. With my brother, I destroyed Shechem and the Amorite cities. None can stand against me." {42:12} Frightened, the Midianites agreed to buy Joseph from his brothers, fearing Simeon's wrath. {42:13} They sold Joseph to the Midianites for twenty pieces of silver, while Reuben, not present, was unaware of the transaction. {42:14} The Midianites regretted their purchase as they journeyed toward Gilead, thinking they might have been deceived. {42:15} They reasoned, "What have we done? What if this youth was stolen from the Hebrews? If caught, we could be punished." {42:16} Spotting the approaching Ishmaelites, the Midianites decided to sell Joseph again to them, hoping to recover their loss. {42:17} They struck a deal with the Ishmaelites, selling Joseph for twenty silver coins. {42:18} The Ishmaelites then took Joseph to Egypt, making him ride on one of their camels. {42:19} Joseph wept bitterly upon realizing he was being taken far from Canaan, his father, and his home. {42:20} Hearing Joseph's cries, one of the Ishmaelites struck him and forced him to walk, trying to silence him. {42:21} Joseph prayed, "O my father, my father," grieving deeply for his separation from his family. {42:22} The Ishmaelite traders, angered by Joseph's sorrow, beat and cursed him. {42:23} Joseph pleaded, "Please take me back to my father's house. He will reward you greatly." {42:24} They replied, "You are a slave. What father would sell you so cheaply if he truly cared?" {42:25} The Lord saw Joseph's suffering and punished the traders with darkness and confusion. {42:26} They became afraid, wondering why such calamity had befallen them. {42:27} They recognized it was because of Joseph and sought his forgiveness, fearing for their lives. {42:28} Joseph interceded for them, and the Lord lifted the plague. {42:29} They continued on their journey to Egypt, realizing they had brought trouble upon themselves for mistreating Joseph. {42:30} They discussed, "It's because of what we did to Joseph that we face this calamity. Let's decide what to do with him now." {42:31} Some suggested returning him to his father, but the journey was too long to consider. {42:32} They settled on taking Joseph to Egypt and selling him there for profit, to rid themselves of him. {42:33} This plan pleased them, and they proceeded toward Egypt with Joseph.

{43:1} After selling their brother Joseph to the Midianites, the sons of Jacob were filled with regret and sorrow. They searched for him earnestly but could not find him anywhere. {43:2} Reuben, filled with anguish, returned to the pit where they had left Joseph, hoping to rescue him and return him safely to their father. He called out Joseph's name repeatedly, but there was no response. {43:3} Convinced that Joseph had perished, either from fear or by some creature in the pit, Reuben descended and searched for him in vain. Distraught, he emerged and tore his garments in despair. {43:4} Reuben went to his brothers, finding them grieving over Joseph's fate. They were discussing how to break the news to their father Jacob. Reuben told them of his fruitless search in the pit, questioning how they could face their father if Joseph was indeed dead. {43:5} The brothers, remorseful and seeking a way to appease their father, listened as Reuben rebuked them for causing such grief to Jacob in his old age. {43:6} They sat together, devising a plan to explain Joseph's disappearance to their father without revealing the truth. {43:7} Swearing an oath of silence among themselves, they vowed that anyone who disclosed the truth would face severe consequences. Fear and guilt gripped each of them, from the eldest to the youngest. {43:8} Thus, they concealed their secret sorrow in their hearts and pledged not to speak of it to Jacob. {43:9} They then planned to fabricate a story to tell their father about Joseph's fate. {43:10} Issachar proposed a plan: they would take Joseph's coat, tear it, and stain it with goat's blood. {43:11} They would present this to Jacob, suggesting that a wild animal had killed Joseph. They believed this would spare them from their father's grief and accusations. {43:12} The brothers agreed to Issachar's plan and carried it out exactly as he had advised. {43:13} They hurriedly tore Joseph's coat, slaughtered a goat, dipped the torn coat in its blood, and trampled it in the dust. {43:14} Then they sent the stained coat to Jacob with Naphtali, instructing him to relay the fabricated story of Joseph being attacked by a wild animal. {43:15} Naphtali delivered the coat to Jacob, recounting the false tale as his brothers had instructed. {43:16} Jacob recognized the coat immediately and was overcome with grief. He fell to the ground, his heart breaking at the sight of Joseph's bloodied garment. {43:17} Jacob urgently sent a servant to fetch his sons, who were returning with the flock. {43:18} When his sons arrived that evening, they found Jacob in deep mourning, his garments torn and dust on his head. {43:19} Jacob demanded to know the truth about what had happened to Joseph, his sorrow evident in his anguished cries. {43:20} His sons repeated the fabricated story, claiming they had found the bloodied coat and feared the worst for Joseph. {43:21} Hearing their account, Jacob cried out in agony, lamenting that Joseph had been torn apart by a wild animal, blaming himself for sending Joseph to check on his brothers. {43:22} The news crushed Jacob, who tore his garments, donned sackcloth, and wept bitterly, mourning the loss of his beloved son. {43:23} He lamented aloud for Joseph, grieving over the fate that had befallen him. {43:24} Jacob mourned deeply, expressing his anguish at the thought of Joseph's violent death. {43:25} He wished he could have died in Joseph's place, overwhelmed by the bitterness of his grief. {43:26} Jacob appealed to God, asking for his tears to be counted and for his anguish to be seen, seeking solace in his sorrow. {43:27} He acknowledged that God, who had given him Joseph, had also taken him away. {43:28} Jacob continued to pour out his heart in sorrowful lamentations over Joseph. {43:29} He acknowledged that Joseph's fate was a consequence of his own sins. {43:30} Jacob's grief was unrelenting as he continued to mourn for Joseph. {43:31} Witnessing their father's profound sorrow, all of Jacob's sons were deeply moved and joined in his lamentation. {43:32} Judah, moved with compassion, comforted Jacob, cradling his father's head in his lap and wiping away his tears. {43:33} The sons of Jacob, seeing their father's grief, wept along with him, their hearts heavy with remorse. {43:34} They gathered around Jacob, along with his servants and their children, offering comfort, though Jacob refused to be consoled. {43:35} The entire household mourned deeply for Joseph, and news of Jacob's anguish reached Isaac in Hebron. {43:36} Isaac, grieving for Joseph, went to comfort Jacob, sharing in his sorrow. {43:37} Jacob, consumed with grief, instructed his sons to go and search for Joseph's body in the fields. {43:38} He urged them to bring him evidence of Joseph's fate, hoping to bury his son and find closure. {43:39} As Jacob continued to weep and mourn in his home, his sons went into the wilderness to hunt for clues about Joseph's fate. {43:40} They encountered a wolf, which they captured and brought before Jacob as the first sign of their search. {43:41} Jacob received the wolf from his sons, grieving deeply as he held the beast in his hands. {43:42} He spoke to the wolf, questioning why it had taken his son Joseph from him. {43:43} Jacob expressed his anguish over Joseph's fate, blaming the creature for causing him such pain and sorrow. {43:44} The wolf responded, asserting its innocence and explaining that it had not harmed Joseph, but had come to the area seeking its own lost offspring. {43:45} Jacob, astonished by the wolf's words, released it. {43:46} Jacob continued to mourn for Joseph, crying out and weeping bitterly day after day. {43:47} His grief was profound as he struggled to come to terms with the loss of his beloved son.

{44:1} The sons of Ishmael, who had purchased Joseph from the Midianites, arrived at the borders of Egypt. There they encountered four men from the descendants of Medan, a son of Abraham, who were returning from a journey. {44:2} The Ishmaelites asked them, "Would you like to buy this slave from us?" The Medanites replied, "Hand him over to us." So, Joseph was sold to them for twenty shekels. Seeing Joseph's handsome appearance, they decided to take him to Egypt. {44:3} The Ishmaelites continued their journey to Egypt while the Medanites returned there on the same day. They discussed among themselves, "Potiphar, the captain of Pharaoh's guard, is seeking a capable servant to oversee his household. Let's sell Joseph to him for a fair price if he agrees." {44:4} The Medanites went to Potiphar's house and said to him, "We have a servant who will be pleasing to you. If you meet our price, we will sell him to you." {44:5} Potiphar replied, "Bring him before me, and if he pleases me, I will pay what you ask. But first, bring me the documentation of his sale to you and tell me his background. I want to ensure he is not a runaway or stolen." {44:6} The Medanites brought Joseph before Potiphar, who found him exceptionally pleasing. Potiphar asked, "What is your price for this youth?" {44:7} They answered, "We ask for four hundred pieces of silver." Potiphar agreed and said, "Bring me proof of his sale to you, and I will pay." {44:8} The Medanites returned with the Ishmaelites who had sold Joseph to them, confirming his status as a slave. Potiphar paid them the agreed amount, and the Medanites departed, while the Ishmaelites returned home. {44:9} Potiphar took Joseph to his house and appointed him as his personal servant. Joseph found favor with Potiphar, who trusted him completely and made him overseer of his entire household. {44:10} The Lord was with Joseph, and he prospered in Potiphar's house. God blessed Potiphar's household because of Joseph. {44:11} Potiphar entrusted everything he owned to Joseph's care. Joseph managed all matters of the house, and Potiphar had no concerns other than his wife. {44:12} Joseph was eighteen years old, exceptionally handsome and well-built. His presence in Egypt was unmatched. {44:13} While serving in Potiphar's house, going in and out and attending to his duties, Joseph caught the eye of Zelicah, Potiphar's wife. {44:14} Zelicah admired Joseph's appearance and became infatuated with him. She began to tempt him day after day. {44:15} Zelicah said to Joseph, "You are the most handsome man I have ever seen. None in Egypt compares to you." {44:16} Joseph replied, "God created all people. It is He who gives beauty." {44:17} Zelicah continued, "Your eyes dazzle everyone in Egypt, men and women alike." {44:18} Joseph said, "Beauty is fleeting. What matters is praising God and His glory." {44:19} Zelicah persisted, "Your words are sweet. Take the harp and let me hear your melodies." {44:20} Joseph answered, "My words are only beautiful when I praise God and His glory." {44:21} Zelicah urged, "Your hair is so lovely. Take the comb and let me style it for you." {44:22} Joseph replied, "Why do you speak these words? Attend to your duties." {44:23} Zelicah desired Joseph intensely. When he was working in the house, she approached him. {44:24} She threatened, "If you do not agree, I will accuse you and have you punished, even unto death." {44:25} Joseph said, "God can free the imprisoned and deliver me from your plans." {44:26} Zelicah's desire for Joseph grew. She fell gravely ill, and all the women of Egypt visited her, wondering at her sudden decline. {44:27} They asked, "Why are you so ill? Your husband is esteemed; you lack nothing. What troubles you?" {44:28} Zelicah replied, "I will show you why I am in this state." {44:29} She prepared a banquet for the women, and they ate together. As they peeled citrons, she ordered Joseph to be dressed in finery and brought before them. {44:30} When they saw Joseph, they were captivated. They cut themselves with the knives in their hands, not taking their eyes off him. {44:31} Zelicah noticed and said, "What have you done? You cut yourselves with the knives." {44:32} The women replied, "This man in your house has overwhelmed us. We cannot look away from his beauty." {44:33} Zelicah said, "If this happens just seeing him, how can I resist him daily in my house?" {44:34} They advised, "Speak to him of your desires openly. You suffer needlessly." {44:35} Zelicah lamented, "I have tried everything. He refuses me, and I suffer." {44:36} Zelicah's love for Joseph made her seriously ill. No one in her household knew the cause of her decline. {44:37} Her family and friends asked, "Why are you ill when you lack nothing?" {44:38} Zelicah confessed, "It is my love for Joseph that causes this." {44:39} Zelicah's condition worsened, and she continued to decline, losing strength. {44:40} One day, while Joseph was working, Zelicah secretly approached him. {44:41} She seized him, but Joseph resisted, and his garment tore in her grasp. {44:42} Zelicah wept and pleaded with Joseph, "No one compares to me in beauty. Listen to me." {44:43} Joseph replied, "I cannot betray my master. I will not sin against God and your husband." {44:44} Zelicah persisted in tempting Joseph daily. {44:45} One day, when Egypt celebrated by the river, all went except Zelicah. {44:46} She adorned herself and waited for Joseph in the passage he used. {44:47} Joseph approached, but seeing her, he turned away. {44:48} Zelicah called to him, "Why turn away? Come and do your work." {44:49} Joseph passed her, but Zelicah caught him and threatened him with a sword. {44:50} Terrified, Joseph fled, leaving his garment in her hand. {44:51} Zelicah saw the torn garment and called her servants. {44:52} She blamed Joseph for attempting to assault her. {44:53} The household believed her, and they informed Potiphar. {44:54} Potiphar returned home and was furious. {44:55} Zelicah changed her clothes and sat as though nothing had happened. {44:56} She called her servants and accused Joseph publicly. {44:57} The servants confirmed her story. {44:58} Potiphar was enraged and had Joseph punished with beatings. {44:59} While being beaten, Joseph prayed to God, protesting his innocence. {44:60} A child present miraculously spoke in Joseph's defense, recounting Zelicah's deceit. {44:61} The household was amazed by the child's words. {44:62} Potiphar ceased the beatings and took Joseph before the priests. {44:63} They questioned Joseph, and he denied the accusations. {44:64} They examined Joseph's torn garment and found the tear in front, confirming Zelicah's deceit. {44:65} The priests declared, "Joseph is innocent of any crime against Potiphar's wife." {44:66} Potiphar was ashamed and stopped the beatings. {44:67} Joseph was placed in prison, where the king's prisoners were confined. {44:68} Despite this, Zelicah continued to desire Joseph. {44:69} She visited him daily at the prison, tempting him. {44:70} Three months passed, and Zelicah continued her efforts. {44:71} She threatened Joseph with severe punishment if he refused her. {44:72} Joseph replied, "God will protect me. I will not betray my master." {44:73} Zelicah ceased her attempts, but Joseph remained in prison. Meanwhile, Jacob and his family in Canaan mourned Joseph deeply, refusing to be comforted.

{45:1} In that same year when Joseph went down to Egypt after being sold by his brothers, Reuben, son of Jacob, went to Timnah and married Eliuram, daughter of Avi the Canaanite. {45:2} Eliuram bore Reuben four sons: Hanoch, Palu, Chetzron, and Carmi. Meanwhile, Simeon married his sister Dinah, who gave birth to five sons: Memuel, Yamin, Ohad, Jachin, and Zochar. {45:3} Later, Simeon took Bunah, a Canaanite woman, who had been a servant to Dinah, as his wife, and she bore him Saul. {45:4} Judah traveled to Adulam and there met the daughter of a Canaanite man named Shua, named Aliyath. He married her, and she bore him three sons: Er, Onan, and Shiloh. {45:5} Levi and Issachar journeyed eastward and married the daughters of Jobab, descendant of Eber. Levi's wife Adinah bore him Gershon, Kehath, and Merari. Issachar's wife Aridah bore him Tola, Puvah, Job, and Shomron. {45:6} Dan went to Moab and married Aphlaleth, daughter of Chamudan the Moabite. Though she was initially barren, God remembered her and she gave birth to Chushim. {45:7} Gad and Naphtali journeyed to Haran and married the daughters of Amuram, Merimah and Uzith, respectively. Merimah bore Naphtali four sons: Yachzeel, Guni, Jazer, and Shalem. Uzith bore Gad seven sons: Zephion, Chagi, Shuni, Ezbon, Eri, Arodi, and Arali. {45:8} Asher married Adon, daughter of Aphlal, but she died childless. Afterward, he married Hadurah, daughter of Abimael, and she bore him Yimnah, Yishvah, Yishvi, and Beriah. {45:9} Zebulun married Merishah, daughter of Molad, and she bore him three sons: Sered, Elon, and Yachleel. {45:10} Jacob arranged for Benjamin to marry Mechalia, daughter of Aram. Mechalia bore Benjamin five sons: Bela, Becher, Ashbel, Gera, and Naaman. Later, Benjamin also married Aribath, daughter of Shomron, who bore him Achi, Vosh, Mupim, Chupim, and Ord. {45:11} Judah arranged for his firstborn Er to marry Tamar, daughter of Elam. But Er was wicked in God's eyes, and he died childless. {45:12} Judah then instructed his second son Onan to marry Tamar and raise children in his brother's name. However, Onan also displeased God and was killed. {45:13} Judah feared for his youngest son and told Tamar to wait for him to grow up. When Aliyath, Judah's wife, died, he went to Timnah to shear his sheep. {45:14} Hearing this, Tamar took off her widow's clothes, covered herself with a veil, and sat by the road to Timnah. {45:15} When Judah saw her, he mistook her for a prostitute and slept with her. She conceived and bore twins: Perez and Zarah.

{46:1} During those days, Joseph was still imprisoned in Egypt. {46:2} At that time, Pharaoh's chief butler and chief baker offended him. {46:3} The butler served wine to Pharaoh, and the baker presented bread, but both items were tainted: flies were found in the wine and stones of nitre in the bread. {46:4} Joseph, placed by the captain of the guard as an attendant, witnessed these events during their year of confinement. {46:5} One night, both the butler and the baker had dreams in prison, and in the morning, Joseph noticed their troubled expressions. {46:6} He asked them the reason for their sadness, and they explained their dreams, lamenting that no one could interpret them. {46:7} Joseph assured them, "God will provide the interpretation you seek." {46:8} The butler recounted his dream: a vine with three branches producing grapes that he pressed into Pharaoh's cup. Joseph interpreted it: in three days, Pharaoh would restore him to his position. {46:9} Joseph asked him to remember him to Pharaoh when he was restored, explaining his unjust imprisonment. {46:10} The butler agreed. {46:11} Encouraged by this, the baker shared his dream of three baskets of baked goods on his head, with birds eating from them. {46:12} Joseph interpreted this dream as a sign that the baker would be executed in three days. {46:13} Meanwhile, in Egypt, the queen gave birth to Pharaoh's firstborn son amid great celebration. {46:14} On the third day after the birth, Pharaoh hosted a feast for his officials and servants, celebrating the joyous occasion. {46:15} The entire land rejoiced with music and dance for eight days. {46:16} Unfortunately, the butler, once freed, forgot Joseph, failing to fulfill his promise. {46:17} Thus, Joseph remained in prison for two more years, totaling twelve years of his imprisonment.

{47:1} In those days, Isaac, the son of Abraham, still lived in Canaan, aged one hundred and eighty years. His son Esau dwelt in Edom with his descendants among the children of Seir. {47:2} Hearing that his father's end was near, Esau and his household journeyed to Canaan, to Isaac's house. Jacob and his sons also left Hebron to join them. {47:3} Jacob, still mourning for Joseph, arrived with his sons and sat before his father Isaac. {47:4} Isaac requested Jacob to bring his sons to receive blessings. {47:5} Isaac blessed all of Jacob's sons, embracing and kissing them, praying for their descendants to multiply abundantly. He also blessed Esau's sons, declaring them to be feared and respected by all. {47:6} Gathering Jacob and his sons, Isaac spoke of God's promise to give Canaan as an everlasting inheritance if they followed His ways. {47:7} He urged Jacob to teach his descendants to fear God and walk in His paths, promising prosperity if they remained faithful. {47:8} After these instructions, Isaac passed away and joined his ancestors. {47:9} Jacob and Esau mourned deeply for their father, who died at one hundred and eighty years old in Hebron. They buried him in the cave of Machpelah, purchased by Abraham from the Hittites. {47:10} All the kings of Canaan honored Isaac at his funeral, joining Jacob and Esau in mourning. {47:11} Jacob and Esau, along with their sons, walked barefoot in mourning until they reached Kireath-arba, where they buried Isaac with great ceremony. {47:12} The mourning continued for many days with solemnity and respect from all. {47:13} After Isaac's death, his possessions were divided among his sons. {47:14} Esau proposed dividing their inheritance, allowing Jacob to choose first. {47:15} Jacob accepted and divided the land of Canaan, offering Esau the choice of the land or the wealth. {47:16} Jacob affirmed God's promise of inheritance to his descendants, leaving the decision to Esau. {47:17} Esau, consulting with Nebayoth, decided to take the riches, leaving the land to Jacob as Jacob had desired. {47:18} Jacob accepted the land from the brook of Egypt to the Euphrates River as his everlasting possession. {47:19} He also secured the cave of Machpelah from Esau, ensuring it remained a burial place for him and his descendants forever. {47:20} Jacob documented all these agreements in a book, along with testimonies and statutes, preserving them for future generations. {47:21} Esau took all that belonged to Isaac and returned to Seir with his children, separating from Jacob and settling among the Horites. {47:22} From then on, Esau did not return to Canaan. {47:23} Thus, Canaan became the everlasting inheritance of the children of Israel, while Esau and his descendants inherited Mount Seir.

{48:1} After Isaac's death, the Lord caused a famine to strike the entire earth. {48:2} During this time, Pharaoh, the king of Egypt, was sitting on his throne and had dreams while lying in bed. In one dream, he stood by the Nile River. {48:3} He saw seven healthy and well-fed cows emerge from the river. {48:4} Then, seven other cows, thin and gaunt, came up after them and devoured the healthy cows, but remained as thin as before. {48:5} Pharaoh woke up, fell asleep again, and dreamed a second dream: seven full and good ears of corn grew on one stalk, then seven thin ears, scorched by the east wind, sprang up and swallowed the full ones. Pharaoh woke up troubled by his dreams. {48:6} In the morning, he remembered his dreams and was deeply troubled. He called for all the magicians and wise men of Egypt, and they stood before him. {48:7} Pharaoh said to them, "I have had dreams, and there is no one to interpret them." They replied, "Tell your dreams to us, and we will interpret them." {48:8} Pharaoh recounted his dreams, and they responded with one voice, "May the king live forever. Here is the interpretation: {48:9} The seven good cows represent seven daughters who will be born to you in the future, but the seven thin cows that devoured them mean that these daughters will die during your lifetime. {48:10} The seven full ears of corn mean you will build seven cities in Egypt, but the seven thin ears that devoured the full ones mean these cities will be destroyed during your lifetime." {48:11} Pharaoh did not accept their interpretation, knowing in his wisdom it was incorrect. He accused them of speaking falsehoods and demanded the proper interpretation, threatening them with death. {48:12} Pharaoh summoned other wise men, who gave the same interpretation, further angering the king. {48:13} Pharaoh issued a decree that any wise man who knew the correct interpretation but did not come forward would be executed. {48:14} All the wise men, magicians, sorcerers, nobles, and princes of Egypt gathered before the king, who recounted his dreams again, astonishing them. {48:15} The wise men were divided in their interpretations: some said the seven good cows were seven kings from Pharaoh's lineage, and the seven thin cows were seven princes who would oppose and destroy them. {48:16} Others said the seven good cows were strong cities of Egypt, and the seven thin cows were seven nations from Canaan who would attack and destroy them. {48:17} Another group interpreted the dreams as seven strong princes of Egypt falling to seven less powerful enemies. {48:18} More interpretations included seven queens who would die during Pharaoh's lifetime, fourteen children fighting amongst themselves, and seven children killing seven grandchildren. {48:19} Despite hearing all these interpretations, Pharaoh was not pleased and knew they were incorrect. {48:20} God had frustrated the wise men's interpretations so that Joseph would be released from prison and rise to power. {48:21} Pharaoh, in his anger, ordered the wise men and magicians to leave in disgrace. {48:22} He decreed the execution of all magicians in Egypt. {48:23} The guards began killing the magicians and wise men. {48:24} Merod, the chief butler, approached Pharaoh, bowing before him and said, {48:25} "Long live the king and may your reign be exalted. {48:26} Two years ago, you were angry with me and imprisoned me along with the chief baker. {48:27} In the prison, we met a Hebrew servant named Joseph, who interpreted our dreams accurately. {48:28} Everything happened as he said. {48:29} Do not kill the people of Egypt unjustly; Joseph is still in the house of confinement." {48:30} Pharaoh listened and ordered the wise men to be spared and Joseph to be brought before him. {48:31} Pharaoh's servants went to fetch Joseph without frightening him so he could speak properly. {48:32} They hurriedly brought Joseph from the dungeon, shaved him, changed his clothes, and presented him to Pharaoh. {48:33} Pharaoh, dressed royally and surrounded by precious stones, sat on his throne, which had seventy steps. {48:34} It was the custom in Egypt that those who spoke with the king ascended specific steps based on their rank and linguistic abilities. {48:35} Joseph bowed before Pharaoh and ascended the third step, while Pharaoh sat on the fourth step and spoke with him. {48:36} Pharaoh told Joseph about his dreams and how no one could interpret them correctly. {48:37} Joseph responded, saying interpretations belong to God, and asked Pharaoh to relate his dreams. {48:38} Pharaoh recounted his dreams of the cows and the corn. {48:39} Joseph, filled with the spirit of God, understood the dreams and explained them to Pharaoh. {48:40} He said the dreams were one and the same, revealing what God intended to do. {48:41} The seven good cows and ears of corn represented seven years of plenty, and the seven thin cows and ears represented seven years of severe famine that would follow. {48:42} Joseph advised Pharaoh to appoint a wise and discreet man to oversee Egypt, gather food during the seven plentiful years, and store it for the famine. {48:43} This would save Egypt from the impending disaster. {48:44} Pharaoh questioned how he could know Joseph's words were true, and Joseph offered a sign: {48:45} Pharaoh's wife would bear a son that day, but his firstborn son would die. {48:46} Joseph left, and the events unfolded as he predicted: the queen bore a son, and Pharaoh's firstborn was found dead. {48:47} Pharaoh's house was filled with mourning, but he realized Joseph's words were true. {48:48} Consoled by the birth of his new son, Pharaoh knew Joseph's interpretation and advice were correct.

{49:1} After these events, the king summoned all his officers, servants, and nobles, and they all gathered before him. {49:2} The king addressed them, saying, "You have all heard the words of this Hebrew man and seen the signs he predicted, none of which have failed. {49:3} He has accurately interpreted the dream, and it will surely come to pass. Therefore, consider what we should do to save the land from the impending famine. {49:4} Seek out someone with wisdom and knowledge, and I will appoint him over the land. {49:5} You have heard the Hebrew man's advice on saving the land from famine, and I believe his counsel is essential for our survival. {49:6} They all agreed with the king, saying, "Your Majesty, the entire land is under your control; do what you think is best." {49:7} The one whom you choose, whom you deem wise and capable of saving the land, shall be appointed. {49:8} The king then said, "Since God has revealed everything to the Hebrew man, there is no one as discreet and wise as he. If it pleases you, I will place him over the land to save it with his wisdom." {49:9} The officers replied, "It is written in our laws that no one can rule over Egypt or be second to the king unless he knows all the languages of the sons of men. {49:10} This Hebrew man only speaks Hebrew. How can he govern us if he doesn't know our language? {49:11} Therefore, summon him and test him in all things; do as you see fit." {49:12} The king agreed, saying it would be done the next day, and all the officers left. {49:13} That night, the Lord sent an angel to Joseph in the Egyptian dungeon, where he was lying in his master's house. {49:14} The angel woke Joseph, who stood up and saw the angel standing before him. The angel taught Joseph all the languages of man in that night and called him Jehoseph. {49:15} The angel left, and Joseph lay back down, astonished at the vision. {49:16} The next morning, the king summoned his officers and servants, and they all gathered before him. He ordered Joseph to be brought before him. {49:17} Joseph was brought to the king, who ascended his throne. Joseph spoke to the king in all languages and climbed the steps until he reached the king. {49:18} The king and his officers rejoiced greatly at Joseph's words. {49:19} The king decided to appoint Joseph as his second in command over the whole land of Egypt, saying, {49:20} "Since God has revealed all this to you, there is no one as wise as you. Your name will now be Zaphnath Paaneah, and you will be second only to me. {49:21} According to your word, all government affairs will be conducted, and my people will follow your orders. {49:22} You will manage the monthly salaries of my servants and officers, and all the people will bow to you. Only my throne will be higher than yours." {49:23} The king gave Joseph his ring, dressed him in royal garments, placed a gold crown on his head, and a gold chain around his neck. {49:24} He commanded that Joseph ride in the second chariot and be paraded through the streets with great fanfare. {49:25} Musicians with timbrels, harps, and other instruments accompanied him, along with soldiers and noblemen, while the women and girls rejoiced at his appearance. {49:26} The people perfumed the road and proclaimed that Joseph was the king's chosen second-in-command, enforcing his orders with the threat of death for disobedience. {49:27} As the heralds proclaimed this, all of Egypt bowed down to Joseph and wished long life to the king and his second. {49:28} Joseph looked to heaven and thanked God for raising him from nothing. {49:29} Joseph toured the land with Pharaoh's servants, inspecting all of Egypt and the king's treasures. {49:30} He returned to Pharaoh, who gave him fields, vineyards, silver, gold, and precious stones. {49:31} The next day, the king ordered the people to bring gifts to Joseph, with the penalty of death for non-compliance. {49:32} A high place was set up, and people brought their offerings, which Joseph stored in his treasuries. {49:33} The king then gave Joseph Osnath, daughter of Potiphera, priest of On, as his wife. {49:34} Joseph married her, and Pharaoh declared that no one in Egypt could act without Joseph's approval. {49:35} Joseph, now thirty years old, became the second in command in Egypt, and the king provided him with a hundred servants. {49:36} Joseph built a magnificent house and a grand throne covered with gold, silver, and precious stones, depicting the entire land of Egypt. {49:37} He sat securely on his throne, and his wisdom increased. {49:38} All of Egypt loved Joseph, for this was God's will. {49:39} Joseph commanded an army of 40,600 men to assist the king and himself, along with countless officers and servants. {49:40} He equipped his army with shields, javelins, armor, and slings.

{50:1} During this period, the children of Tarshish attacked the sons of Ishmael and waged war against them, plundering the Ishmaelites for a long time. {50:2} The Ishmaelites were few in number and could not prevail against the children of Tarshish, suffering greatly under their oppression. {50:3} The elders of the Ishmaelites sent a message to the king of Egypt, pleading, "Please send your officers and soldiers to help us fight against the children of Tarshish, for we have been suffering for a long time." {50:4} Pharaoh responded by sending Joseph, along with his mighty men and the host from the king's house. {50:5} They traveled to the land of Havilah to assist the Ishmaelites against the children of Tarshish. The Ishmaelites fought, and Joseph defeated the Tarshishites, subduing their land, which the Ishmaelites inhabit to this day. {50:6} After subduing the land, the Tarshishites fled to the borders of their brethren, the children of Javan. Joseph and his men returned to Egypt without losing a single man. {50:7} In the second year of Joseph's rule over Egypt, the Lord granted great abundance throughout the land for seven years, as Joseph had predicted, blessing all the earth's produce. {50:8} Joseph appointed officers to gather all the food during these good years, storing corn year by year in his treasuries. {50:9} Joseph instructed them to bring the corn in the ears, along with some soil, to prevent spoilage. {50:10} He continued this practice each year, amassing corn in great abundance, like the sand of the sea, making his stores immense and uncountable. {50:11} All the Egyptians also gathered food in abundance during the seven good years, but they did not follow Joseph's method. {50:12} Joseph and the Egyptians stored the food gathered during the seven years of plenty to sustain the land during the seven years of famine. {50:13} Each Egyptian filled his store and hidden place with corn to prepare for the famine. {50:14} Joseph stored all the gathered food in Egyptian cities, securing them with sentinels. {50:15} Joseph's wife, Osnath, bore him two sons, Manasseh and Ephraim, when he was thirty-four years old. {50:16} The boys grew up following Joseph's ways and instructions, never deviating from his teachings. {50:17} The Lord blessed the boys with wisdom and understanding in all governmental affairs. They were esteemed by the king's officers and the great men of Egypt, growing up among the king's children. {50:18} The seven years of plenty ended, and the seven years of famine began as Joseph had foretold, affecting the entire land. {50:19} When the famine struck, the Egyptians opened their stores of corn, but found them infested and inedible, worsening the famine. {50:20} The Egyptians cried out to Pharaoh, begging for food to avoid starvation for themselves and their children. {50:21} Pharaoh replied, "Why do you cry to me? Did Joseph not command you to store corn during the seven years of plenty for this very famine? Why did you not listen to him?" {50:22} The Egyptians protested, "We did as Joseph ordered, gathering all our produce and storing it, but now it is all spoiled and inedible." {50:23} When Pharaoh heard this, he was terrified by the severity of the famine. He told the people to follow Joseph's instructions without fail. {50:24} The Egyptians went to Joseph, pleading for food to survive the famine, explaining that their stored produce had spoiled. {50:25} Upon hearing their plight, Joseph opened his stores and sold food to the Egyptians. {50:26} The famine continued throughout the land, but there was food for sale in Egypt. {50:27} People from Canaan, the Philistines, beyond the Jordan, the east, and other distant lands heard there was corn in Egypt and came to buy it due to the widespread famine. {50:28} Joseph managed the sale of corn, appointing officers to oversee the transactions and ensuring daily sales to all who came. {50:29} Knowing his brothers would come to buy corn, Joseph issued a proclamation in Egypt. {50:30} The proclamation stated that anyone wishing to buy corn in Egypt must send their sons, not servants, and that anyone, Egyptian or Canaanite, caught reselling corn would be punished by death. {50:31} It also stated that no man could lead more than his own beast to buy corn, with violators facing death. {50:32} Joseph stationed sentinels at Egypt's gates to record the names and lineage of each person buying corn, sending the records to him each evening. {50:33} Joseph enacted these regulations to identify his brothers when they came to buy corn. {50:34} This system was proclaimed daily in Egypt, and people from all over the earth adhered to it. {50:35} The officers followed Joseph's commands, recording names at the gates and reporting them to Joseph each evening.

{51:1} Jacob heard that there was grain in Egypt, so he told his sons to go there and buy some, as the famine was affecting them too. {51:2} He said, "I hear there's grain in Egypt, and everyone is going there to buy it. Why should we just sit here and starve? Go and buy us some grain so we won't die." {51:3} Jacob's sons listened to their father, and they set out for Egypt to buy grain along with everyone else. {51:4} Jacob warned them not to enter the city through the same gate to avoid attracting attention. {51:5} They followed their father's advice. Jacob didn't send Benjamin, fearing harm might come to him like Joseph. So, ten of Jacob's sons set out. {51:6} On the way, they regretted selling Joseph and planned to look for him in Egypt. They decided that if they found him, they would ransom him or rescue him by force if necessary. {51:7} They resolved to find Joseph, determined to free him. When they arrived in Egypt, they entered the city through different gates. The gatekeepers noted their names and reported them to Joseph in the evening. {51:8} Joseph read the names and realized his brothers had entered the city. He ordered that only one grain store remain open, while the others were closed. {51:9} He instructed his officers to close all the stores except one, so those coming to buy grain would have to go there. {51:10} Joseph gave the names of his brothers to the officer in charge of the open store, instructing him to seize them if they came to buy grain. {51:11} When the brothers entered the city, they searched for Joseph before buying grain. {51:12} They looked for Joseph in the places where prostitutes lived, thinking he might be there because of his good looks, but they didn't find him. {51:13} After three days, the officer in charge of the grain store informed Joseph that he hadn't seen the men whose names he had given. {51:14} Joseph sent servants to search for his brothers throughout Egypt, but they couldn't find them. {51:15} The servants looked in Goshen and Rameses but found nothing. {51:16} Joseph then sent sixteen more servants to search the city. {51:17} Four of these servants went to the prostitutes' quarters and found the ten brothers searching for Joseph. {51:18}

They brought the brothers before Joseph, who was sitting on his throne in his temple, dressed in princely robes and wearing a gold crown. {51:19} The brothers bowed down to Joseph, not recognizing him, though he recognized them. {51:20} Joseph asked where they came from, and they said they had come from Canaan to buy grain because of the famine. {51:21} Joseph accused them of being spies, asking why they had entered through ten different gates. {51:22} The brothers insisted they were not spies but had come to buy grain and followed their father's instructions to enter through different gates. {51:23} Joseph reiterated that they must be spies, seeing the city's vulnerabilities by entering through multiple gates and spending three days in the prostitutes' quarters. {51:24} The brothers explained that they were twelve brothers from Canaan, sons of Jacob, and were following their father's orders. {51:25} They insisted they were looking for their lost brother and had searched everywhere, even in the prostitutes' quarters. {51:26} Joseph continued to accuse them, saying their story was unbelievable. {51:27} The brothers explained they thought Joseph might be in Egypt, having heard Ishmaelites had sold him there, and they were willing to pay a ransom for him. {51:28} Joseph accused them of lying, saying they were spies coming to kill Egyptians just as they had killed the Shechemites in Canaan. {51:29} Joseph said he would believe them only if they sent one brother to fetch their youngest brother from Canaan, while the others remained in custody. {51:30} He ordered seventy of his strongest men to imprison the ten brothers. {51:31} The brothers were put in prison for three days. {51:32} On the third day, Joseph told them one brother would remain imprisoned while the others returned to Canaan to bring their youngest brother back. {51:33} Joseph left them, went to his chamber, and wept. He composed himself and returned, ordering Simeon to be bound. {51:34} Simeon resisted, being very strong, so Joseph called seventy valiant men with drawn swords, terrifying the brothers. {51:35} The men seized Simeon, who let out a loud cry, scaring the soldiers who fled. {51:36} Only Joseph and his son Manasseh remained. Manasseh was angry and struck Simeon, subduing him, then bound and imprisoned him. {51:37} The brothers were astonished at Manasseh's strength. {51:38} Simeon told them not to think it was an Egyptian who struck him, but someone from their own family. {51:39} Joseph ordered the storekeeper to fill the brothers' sacks with grain, return their money, and give them provisions for their journey. {51:40} He warned them to bring their youngest brother back as he had instructed. {51:41} The brothers agreed, bowed to Joseph, loaded their grain onto their donkeys, and set out for Canaan. {51:42} At an inn, Levi discovered his money in his sack and told his brothers, who were frightened, wondering what God had done to them. {51:43} They questioned why God had allowed them to fall into the hands of the Egyptian ruler. {51:44} Judah acknowledged their guilt for selling Joseph, while Reuben reminded them he had warned against it and now God was demanding retribution. {51:45} They spent the night at the inn and continued their journey to Canaan the next morning. {51:46} When they arrived, Jacob and his household met them, but Jacob noticed Simeon was missing. {51:47} The brothers told Jacob everything that had happened in Egypt.

{52:1} When they returned home, each of Jacob's sons opened his sack and found his bundle of money still there. They and their father were terrified. {52:2} Jacob said to them, "What have you done to me? I sent Joseph to check on you, and you told me a wild beast had devoured him." {52:3} "Simeon went with you to buy food, and now you say the king of Egypt has imprisoned him. Now you want to take Benjamin and risk his life too, causing my sorrow to deepen with their loss." {52:4} "So my son will not go down with you, for his brother is dead, and he is my only remaining son from Rachel. Something bad might happen to him on the way, just as it did with Joseph." {52:5} Reuben replied, "You can kill my two sons if I do not bring Benjamin back safely." But Jacob said, "Stay here; my son will not go with you to Egypt and meet the same fate as his brother." {52:6} Judah suggested, "Let's wait until we've finished the corn. Then he will ask us to take Benjamin when he realizes his life and household are in danger from the famine." {52:7} The famine worsened, and people from all over the earth went to Egypt to buy food. Jacob's sons stayed in Canaan for a year and two months until they ran out of corn. {52:8} When their corn was finished, Jacob's household was starving. The children gathered around Jacob, pleading for bread, so they wouldn't die of hunger in his presence. {52:9} Hearing their cries, Jacob wept and felt deep pity. He called his sons together and they all sat before him. {52:10} Jacob said, "Can't you see how your children are crying for bread, and there's none? Go back and buy us a little food." {52:11} Judah replied, "We'll go if you send Benjamin with us, otherwise, we can't, for the king of Egypt specifically said we wouldn't see him without our brother." {52:12} "Don't you know how powerful and wise this king is? There's no one like him on earth. We've seen many kings, but none compare to him." {52:13} "Father, you haven't seen his palace or his throne, nor his grandeur and royal appearance. You haven't seen the honor and glory God has given him." {52:14} "You haven't witnessed his wisdom, understanding, and knowledge, or heard his sweet voice." {52:15} "We don't know how he knew our names and our story, but he even asked about you, if you were alive and well." {52:16} "You haven't seen how he governs Egypt without consulting Pharaoh. You haven't seen the fear he commands among the Egyptians." {52:17} "When we left, we were angry about being accused as spies and threatened to do to Egypt what we did to Shechem. When we return, his terror will fall upon us, and none of us will be able to speak." {52:18} "So please, father, send Benjamin with us so we can buy food and not die of hunger." Jacob responded, "Why did you tell the king you had another brother? Why have you done this to me?" {52:19} Judah said, "Trust me with the lad and we'll go to Egypt, buy corn, and return. If we don't bring him back, I will bear the blame forever." {52:20} "Look at our children crying for food. Have pity and send Benjamin with us." {52:21} "How can we see God's kindness if you fear the king of Egypt will take Benjamin? I won't leave him until he's back with you. Pray for us that God will help us be favorably received." {52:22} Jacob said, "I trust God will deliver you and give you favor before the king of Egypt and his men." {52:23} "So go to the man, take gifts from the land, and may God grant you mercy so he sends back Benjamin and Simeon." {52:24} They took their brother Benjamin, gifts, and double the silver, and Jacob instructed them to be careful with Benjamin and not to separate from him. {52:25} Jacob prayed, asking God to remember His covenant with Abraham and Isaac and to deal kindly with his sons, not delivering them to the king of Egypt. {52:26} The wives and children of Jacob's sons wept and prayed for their fathers' safety. {52:27} Jacob wrote a letter to the king of Egypt, which he gave to Judah and his sons. {52:28} The letter read: "From Jacob, son of Isaac, son of Abraham, the Hebrew, to the wise and powerful king of Egypt, greetings." {52:29} "The famine is severe in Canaan. I sent my sons to buy food from you." {52:30} "I'm old and almost blind from weeping for my lost son Joseph. I told my sons not to enter the city gates together and to search for Joseph in Egypt." {52:31} "You considered them spies, but didn't you interpret Pharaoh's dreams accurately? How can't you tell if my sons are spies?" {52:32} "Now I've sent my son as you requested. Please watch over him until he returns safely." {52:33} "Remember what God did to Pharaoh and Abimelech for Sarah's sake, and what Abraham did to the kings of Elam. My sons Simeon and Levi destroyed the Amorites for Dinah's sake." {52:34} "They would do the same for Benjamin if they see him threatened." {52:35} "Know that God is with us and hears our prayers. When I heard of your treatment, I didn't pray against you because Simeon was in your house, hoping you'd treat him kindly." {52:36} "Now Benjamin comes with my sons. Watch over him, and God will watch over you and your kingdom." {52:37} "My sons come to you with their brother. Examine the whole earth for their sake and send them back in peace." {52:38} Jacob gave the letter to Judah to deliver to the king of Egypt.

{53:1} Jacob's sons took Benjamin and the gifts, traveled to Egypt, and stood before Joseph. {53:2} Joseph saw Benjamin and greeted them. They went to Joseph's house. {53:3} Joseph instructed his house superintendent to provide them with food, and he did so. {53:4} At noon, Joseph summoned them and Benjamin. They told the superintendent about the silver found in their sacks. He assured them it was fine and brought Simeon to them. {53:5} Simeon told his brothers that the Egyptian lord had treated him kindly and had not kept him bound. {53:6} Judah took Benjamin's hand, and they bowed before Joseph. {53:7} They gave Joseph the present and sat before him. Joseph asked about their well-being and their father's health. Judah handed Joseph Jacob's letter. {53:8} Joseph read the letter, recognized his father's handwriting, and retreated to weep. Then he returned. {53:9} Seeing Benjamin, Joseph asked if this was their youngest brother. Benjamin approached, and Joseph blessed him. {53:10} Overcome with emotion again, Joseph went to his chamber to weep, washed his face, and returned to order the meal. {53:11} Joseph had a silver cup adorned with onyx and bdellium. He used it to reveal their birth order, seating them accordingly. {53:12} Joseph placed Benjamin separately, noting he had no brother, similar to himself. {53:13} Benjamin sat on the throne, astonishing his brothers. They ate and drank with Joseph, who gave them gifts, especially Benjamin. {53:14} Joseph's sons, Manasseh and Ephraim, and Osnath also gave Benjamin gifts, totaling five. {53:15} Joseph offered them wine, but they refused, saying they hadn't drunk wine or eaten delicacies since losing Joseph. {53:16} Joseph swore and persuaded them to drink with him. Later, he spoke with Benjamin, who remained on the throne. {53:17} Joseph asked if Benjamin had children. He replied he had ten sons, naming them after Joseph. {53:18} Joseph brought out a star map and asked Benjamin if he knew about it, knowing the Hebrews were wise. {53:19} Benjamin confirmed his knowledge, taught by their father. Joseph asked him to use it to find Joseph in Egypt. {53:20} Benjamin studied the map, divided Egypt into four regions, and realized Joseph was before him. He was astonished. {53:21} Joseph, noticing Benjamin's astonishment, asked what he saw. Benjamin revealed that he saw Joseph on the throne. Joseph told him to keep it secret and explained his plan to test their brothers' repentance. {53:22} Joseph ordered his officer to fill their sacks with food, return their money, and place his cup in Benjamin's sack. {53:23} The next morning, they loaded their donkeys and left for Canaan with Benjamin. {53:24} Shortly after, Joseph sent his officer to pursue and confront them about the stolen cup. {53:25} The officer caught up with them and repeated Joseph's accusation, making them furious. They declared that whoever had the cup should die, and the rest would become slaves. {53:26} They quickly unloaded their sacks, and the cup was found in Benjamin's. They tore their clothes in grief and returned to the city, beating Benjamin along the way. {53:27} They stood before Joseph, and Judah, enraged, accused Joseph of plotting to destroy Egypt. {53:28} They entered Joseph's house, finding him on his throne with his mighty men. {53:29} Joseph accused them of stealing his cup to divine their brother's location. Judah confessed their guilt, attributing it to divine justice. {53:30} Joseph seized Benjamin violently, took him inside, and locked the door. He ordered his officer to tell the others to go home, as he was keeping the one who had the cup.

{54:1} When Judah saw Joseph's behavior toward them, he approached him, breaking through the barrier, and came before Joseph with his brothers. {54:2} Judah said to Joseph, "Let it not be grievous to my lord, I beg you, let your servant speak a word." And Joseph said, "Speak." {54:3} Judah spoke before Joseph while his brothers stood by and said, "When we first came to you to buy food, you accused us of being spies, and even after we brought Benjamin to you, you continue to mock us today. {54:4} Now let the king listen to my words and send our brother with us to our father, lest you destroy your own soul and all the souls of Egypt today. {54:5} Don't you know what my brothers, Simeon and Levi, did to the city of Shechem and seven cities of the Amorites because of our sister Dinah? And what they would do for Benjamin's sake? {54:6} I, who am stronger and mightier than both of them, will come against you and your land today if you refuse to send our brother back with us. {54:7} Have you not heard what our God did to Pharaoh on account of Sarah, our mother, whom he took from our father? God struck Pharaoh and his household with severe plagues, and even to this day, the Egyptians tell of this. The same will happen to you if you keep Benjamin and heap this evil upon us. {54:8} Hear my words and send our brother with us, or else you and all of Egypt will perish by the sword, for none can withstand me." {54:9} Joseph answered Judah, "Why do you boast of your strength? As Pharaoh lives, if I command my valiant men to fight you, you and your brothers would sink in the mud." {54:10} Judah replied, "It would be wise for you and your people to fear me. As the Lord lives, if I draw my sword, I will not put it back until I have killed all of Egypt, starting with you and ending with Pharaoh." {54:11} Joseph answered, "Strength does not belong to you alone. I am stronger and mightier than you. If you draw your sword, I will put it to your neck and the necks of your brothers." {54:12} Judah replied, "If I open my mouth against you, I will swallow you up and destroy you and your kingdom." Joseph said, "If you open your mouth, I can close it with a stone and break your jaws." {54:13} Judah said, "God is witness that we did not come here to fight. Give us our brother, and we will leave peacefully." Joseph replied, "As Pharaoh lives, even if all the kings of Canaan came with you, you would not take him from me." {54:14} Joseph continued, "Go back to your father; your brother will remain as my slave, for he has stolen from the king's house." {54:15} Judah retorted, "What is this to you or to the king? The king freely gives out silver and gold across the land, yet you accuse our brother of stealing your cup, which you placed in his bag!" {54:16} "God forbid that any of us, the descendants of Abraham, should steal from you or anyone else. Now stop this accusation, or the whole world will hear of how the king of Egypt accused men over a mere cup." {54:17} Joseph said, "Take your cup and leave. Your brother will stay as my slave, for that is the fate of a thief." {54:18} Judah replied, "Why are you not ashamed to leave our brother and take your cup? Even if you gave us the cup a thousand times, we would not leave him behind." {54:19} Joseph responded, "And why did you abandon your brother and sell him for twenty pieces of silver? Why then will you not do the same to Benjamin?" {54:20} Judah said, "God is witness that we did not come here to fight. Now give us our brother, and we will go without quarrel." {54:21} Joseph said, "Even if all the kings of the land assembled, they could not take him from me." Judah replied, "What will we tell our father when he sees that Benjamin is not with us? He will grieve terribly." {54:22} Joseph said, "Tell your father that the rope has followed the bucket." {54:23} Judah said, "You are a king; why do you speak unjustly? Woe to a king like you!" {54:24} Joseph said, "There is no falsehood in what I have said about your brother Joseph. You sold him to the Midianites for twenty pieces of silver, and you told your father that he was devoured by a wild beast." {54:25} Judah responded angrily, "The fire of Shem burns in my heart, and I will burn your land with fire." Joseph replied, "Your sister-in-law Tamar, who killed your sons, extinguished the fire of Shechem." {54:26} Judah said, "If I pluck out one hair from my body, I will fill all of Egypt with blood." {54:27} Joseph said, "This is the custom of your house; you sold your brother and dipped his coat in blood to deceive your father." {54:28} Judah became furious. He picked up a stone weighing four hundred shekels and threw it into the air, catching it with his other hand, and then crushed it under his feet, turning it into dust. {54:29} Joseph saw this and was afraid. He commanded his son Manasseh to do the same with another stone, and he did it. Judah then said to his brothers, "This man is not an Egyptian; he must be from our father's family." {54:30} Joseph said, "Strength is not only with you; we are also powerful men. Why do you boast over us?" {54:31} Judah replied, "Send our brother with us, and do not ruin your land today." {54:32} Joseph answered, "Go and tell your father that an evil beast has devoured him, as you said concerning your brother Joseph." {54:33} Judah instructed Naphtali, "Go quickly and count all the streets of Egypt." Simeon said, "Don't worry about it; I will go to the mountain, bring down a stone, and level all of Egypt." {54:34} Joseph heard these words but pretended not to understand Hebrew. {54:35} Joseph feared his brothers' words, lest they destroy Egypt, and commanded his son Manasseh to gather all the mighty men of Egypt to come before him with musical instruments. Manasseh did as he was told. {54:36} Naphtali went as Judah commanded, for he was as swift as a stag. He counted all the streets of Egypt and reported that there were twelve. {54:37} Judah told his brothers, "Prepare yourselves; I will destroy three streets, and each of you will destroy one." {54:38} As Judah spoke, the Egyptian soldiers approached them with music and loud shouting. {54:39} There were five hundred cavalry, ten thousand infantry, and four hundred unarmed men who could fight with just their hands. {54:40} They surrounded the sons of Jacob, and the earth quaked from their shouting. {54:41} The sons of Jacob were terrified, but Joseph had arranged this to calm them down. {54:42} Judah, seeing his brothers frightened, said, "Why are you afraid? God is with us." {54:43} Judah then drew his sword, screamed loudly, and sprang to the ground. He continued to shout at the people. {54:44} The Lord caused Judah's terror to fall upon the Egyptians, and they fled, tripping over one another, with many dying in the chaos. {54:45} Judah and his brothers pursued them to Pharaoh's house, and Judah sat again before Joseph and roared like a lion. {54:46} His roar was heard far away, and the earth shook. Even Pharaoh fell from his throne, and the pregnant women of Egypt miscarried in fear. {54:47} Pharaoh asked, "What has happened in Egypt today?" He was told everything from the beginning to the end, and he was terrified. {54:48} Pharaoh became more fearful and sent word to Joseph, saying, "You brought the Hebrews here to destroy Egypt. Let them take their brother and leave, or we will all perish!" {54:49} He added, "If you do not send them away, take all my riches and leave with them, for they will destroy Egypt and kill us all." {54:50} Pharaoh feared the Hebrews' power, for even their shouting had caused chaos, and he could only imagine what they might do with swords. {54:51} Joseph was frightened by Pharaoh's words and the wrath of his brothers. He sought a way to reveal himself to them without causing more destruction. {54:52} Joseph commanded his son Manasseh to place his hand on Judah's shoulder to calm him. {54:53} Judah's anger subsided, and he told his brothers, "This man is not acting as an Egyptian; he is one of us." {54:54} Joseph, seeing Judah's calm, spoke to him gently, saying, "You have shown great strength, and may your God continue to bless you. But tell me, why are you the only one fighting for the boy when none of your brothers have spoken?" {54:55} Judah replied, "I am responsible for him before our father. If I do not return with him, I will bear the blame forever. {54:56} That is why I alone stand before you. If you refuse to let him go, let me stay as your servant in his place, for I am ready to serve you in any way." {54:57} Judah continued, "Send me to fight against any king or land that opposes you, and I will bring their heads to you." {54:58} He reminded Joseph, "Don't you know what my father Abraham and his servant Eliezer did to the kings of Elam in one night? That strength is our inheritance." {54:59} Joseph acknowledged Judah's words, saying, "You speak the truth. It is well known that the Hebrews are mighty, and their God favors them." {54:60} However, Joseph added, "I will only release your brother if you bring me his brother, whom you say was lost in Egypt." {54:61} Judah's anger flared again, and his eyes filled with blood. He said, "How can this man seek his own destruction and all of Egypt's?" {54:62} Simeon, trying to calm things, said, "We told you we don't know where our other brother is, whether he is dead or alive. Why do you speak as if we can bring him to you?" {54:63} Joseph, observing Judah's anger, said, "If I call your brother today, will you give him to me in place of Benjamin?" {54:64} Joseph called out, "Joseph, come and sit before your brothers." {54:65} The brothers looked around, expecting someone to come. {54:66} Joseph then revealed himself to them, saying, "I am Joseph, the brother you sold into Egypt. Do not be distressed, for God sent me ahead of you to preserve life." {54:67} The brothers were shocked and terrified by his revelation. {54:68} Benjamin, who had been inside, ran to Joseph, embraced him, and they wept together. {54:69} Seeing this, the other brothers embraced Joseph, and they all wept. {54:70} The sound of their weeping was heard throughout Joseph's house, and it pleased Pharaoh, who had been afraid of them. {54:71} Pharaoh sent his servants to congratulate Joseph on his reunion with his brothers. {54:72} All the military leaders of Egypt came to celebrate, and the entire land rejoiced. {54:73} Pharaoh sent word to Joseph, saying, "Bring your family to Egypt, and I will give them the best of the land." {54:74} Joseph gave his brothers gifts and royal garments. {54:75} He gave each of them three hundred pieces of silver and provided for them generously. {54:76} Joseph also sent eleven chariots for his brothers to return to Canaan and bring their father back. {54:77} He sent gifts for his brothers' children and wives, including garments from the king's wives. {54:78} He gave Benjamin additional gifts, including ten suits for his ten sons. {54:79} He sent provisions for their journey and many valuable items. {54:80} Joseph sent everything needed for the trip and even sent extra garments for his sister Dinah. {54:81} His brothers left Egypt, overjoyed to return to their father. {54:82} Joseph accompanied them to the border of Egypt, instructing them not to quarrel on the road. {54:83} He reminded them that God had orchestrated everything to preserve their lives during the famine. {54:84} The brothers traveled back to Canaan joyfully, eager to tell their father the good news. {54:85} As they neared home, they began to wonder how to break the news to Jacob without shocking him. {54:86} They found Serach, the daughter of Asher, and asked her to go ahead of them to their father. {54:87} Serach, skilled at playing the harp, went before Jacob and played a beautiful melody. {54:88} As she played, she softly sang, "Joseph, my uncle, is alive. He rules over Egypt and is not dead." {54:89} She repeated these words, and Jacob, hearing the sweetness of her song, felt joy in his heart. {54:90} He listened carefully, and the Spirit of God came upon him as he realized her words were true. {54:91} Jacob blessed Serach, saying, "May death never overcome you, for you have revived my spirit." {54:92} As Jacob rejoiced, his sons arrived with horses, chariots, and royal garments. {54:93} Jacob rose to meet them, seeing the treasures they had brought from Joseph. {54:94} His sons told him everything that had happened, and Jacob, seeing the evidence, believed their words. {54:95} He rejoiced greatly and said, "It is enough that my son Joseph is alive. I will go and see him before I die." {54:96} Jacob's heart swelled with joy, and he prepared to journey to Egypt. {54:97} Jacob put on the royal garments Joseph had sent him, washed, and shaved. {54:98} All the people of Jacob's household put on the garments sent by Joseph, and they greatly rejoiced. {54:99} The news spread throughout Canaan, and all the inhabitants came to celebrate with Jacob. {54:100} Jacob made a feast for three days, and the kings and nobles of Canaan ate and drank in his house.

{55:1} After these events, Jacob decided to go see his son in Egypt, intending to return to Canaan, the land of his birth, as promised to Abraham by God. {55:2} Then the Lord spoke to him, saying, "Go down to Egypt with your whole household, and do not be afraid. I will make you a great nation there." {55:3} Jacob thought to himself, "I will go and see if my son still holds the fear of God in his heart among the Egyptians." {55:4} The Lord reassured Jacob, "Do not worry about Joseph, for he continues to serve me faithfully." Jacob felt great joy for his son. {55:5} Following the Lord's command, Jacob instructed his sons and household to go to Egypt. They left Canaan from Beersheba, filled with joy and gladness, heading to Egypt. {55:6} Nearing Egypt, Jacob sent Judah ahead to inform Joseph and secure a place for them. Judah did so and arranged for them to stay in Goshen, then returned to guide his father. {55:7} Joseph prepared his chariot and assembled his mighty men, servants, and Egyptian officers to meet his father. He proclaimed that anyone who did not join them would face death. {55:8} The next day, Joseph led a grand procession of Egyptians, all in fine linen and purple garments, adorned with silver, gold, and weapons. {55:9} They met Jacob with musical instruments, drums, and timbrels, spreading myrrh and aloes along the road, and their joyful noise made the earth tremble. {55:10} The women of Egypt climbed onto rooftops and walls to witness the meeting. Joseph wore Pharaoh's crown, sent to him for this occasion. {55:11} When Joseph was fifty cubits from his father, he got out of his chariot and walked towards Jacob. Seeing this, all the Egyptian officers and nobles also walked on foot towards Jacob. {55:12} As Jacob approached Joseph's camp, he was pleased and amazed by the sight. {55:13} Jacob asked Judah who the man in royal robes and crown was, approaching on foot. Judah replied, "He is your son Joseph, the king." Jacob rejoiced at the sight of his son's glory. {55:14} Joseph came closer and bowed before his father, and the entire camp bowed with him. {55:15} Jacob hurried to Joseph, embraced and kissed him, and they wept together. The people of Egypt wept along with them. {55:16} Jacob told Joseph, "Now I can die happily, having seen your face and knowing you are alive and honored." {55:17} Jacob's sons, their wives, children, and servants wept and kissed Joseph. {55:18} They all returned to Egypt with Joseph, who settled them in the best part of the land, Goshen. {55:19} Joseph told his family he would inform Pharaoh of their arrival in Goshen. {55:20} He took Reuben, Issachar, Zebulun, and Benjamin to present them to Pharaoh. {55:21} Joseph explained to Pharaoh that his family had come from Canaan due to the severe famine. {55:22} Pharaoh instructed Joseph to settle them in the best part of Egypt and ensure they had plenty. {55:23} Joseph confirmed they would stay in Goshen, as they were shepherds, keeping them separate from the Egyptians. {55:24} Pharaoh told Joseph to grant his family whatever they needed. Jacob's sons bowed to Pharaoh and left peacefully, and Joseph later brought Jacob before Pharaoh. {55:25} Jacob bowed and blessed Pharaoh, then departed. Jacob's family settled in Goshen. {55:26} In the second year of famine, Joseph, at age 130, provided food for his family, who lacked nothing. {55:27} Joseph gave them the best of Egypt, providing clothes and garments yearly. Jacob's sons lived securely in Egypt during Joseph's time. {55:28} Jacob and his sons dined with Joseph daily, in addition to what they consumed at home. {55:29} During the famine, the Egyptians ate bread from Joseph's stores, having sold all their possessions for food. {55:30} Joseph bought all the lands of Egypt for Pharaoh, providing food throughout the famine. He amassed great wealth, including onyx stones, bdellium, and valuable garments. {55:31} Joseph collected seventy-two talents of gold and silver, hiding them in four locations: near the Red Sea, by the river Perath, and in two desert areas near Persia and Media. {55:32} He distributed some wealth to his family and the women of his household, giving the rest, about twenty talents, to Pharaoh's treasury. {55:33} When the famine ended, Egypt resumed normal farming and harvesting, lacking nothing. {55:34} Joseph continued to govern Egypt wisely, while his family prospered in Goshen. {55:35} Joseph aged, and his sons Ephraim and Manasseh, along with Jacob's grandchildren, stayed close to learn the ways of the Lord. {55:36} Jacob and his sons lived in Goshen, multiplying and thriving there.

{56:1} Jacob lived in Egypt for seventeen years, reaching the age of 147. {56:2} As Jacob neared death, he summoned his son Joseph from Egypt, and Joseph came to his father. {56:3} Jacob told Joseph and his sons that he was about to die and that God would bring them back to the land promised to their ancestors. He asked to be buried in the cave of Machpelah in Hebron, Canaan, near his forefathers. {56:4} Jacob made his sons swear to bury him in Machpelah, and they agreed. {56:5} He instructed them to serve the Lord who had delivered their ancestors and would deliver them from trouble. {56:6} Jacob gathered his grandchildren and blessed them, invoking the blessings of Abraham upon them. {56:7} The next day, Jacob assembled his sons and blessed each one according to their blessing, as recorded in the book of the law of the Lord. {56:8} To Judah, Jacob said he knew Judah was a strong leader for his brothers and that his descendants would reign forever. {56:9} He urged Judah to teach his sons the use of weapons to fight for their brothers. {56:10} Jacob reminded his sons to carry him to Canaan for burial. {56:11} He instructed that only his sons, not their children, should carry his bier, assigning specific sons to each side of the bier. {56:12} Levi was excluded because his descendants would carry the Ark of the Covenant, and Joseph was excluded to maintain his royal status, with Ephraim and Manasseh taking his place. {56:13} Jacob emphasized following his instructions for his burial. {56:14} He assured them that following his commands would bring God's favor upon them and their descendants. {56:15} Jacob urged his sons to honor each other and serve the Lord. {56:16} He promised that their days in the promised land would be long if they remained faithful to God. {56:17} Jacob asked Joseph to forgive his brothers' past wrongs, as God had used them for good. {56:18} He cautioned Joseph not to leave his brothers to the Egyptians' mercy but to protect them. {56:19} The sons pledged to follow Jacob's commands. {56:20} Jacob warned that many hardships awaited them but assured them of God's deliverance. {56:21} He prophesied that God would raise a deliverer from among their descendants. {56:22} After giving these instructions, Jacob drew his feet into the bed, died, and was gathered to his people. {56:23} Joseph mourned deeply for his father. {56:24} His household also mourned Jacob. {56:25} Jacob's sons tore their garments, put on sackcloth, and mourned. {56:26} Joseph's wife, Osnath, and the Egyptian women joined in mourning Jacob. {56:27} All of Egypt mourned Jacob for many days. {56:28} Women from Canaan came to Egypt to mourn Jacob for seventy days. {56:29} Joseph had Jacob embalmed with myrrh, frankincense, and other perfumes. {56:30} The people of Egypt and the inhabitants of Goshen wept and mourned Jacob for many days. {56:31} After seventy days, Joseph asked Pharaoh for permission to bury his father in Canaan, as he had sworn. {56:32} Pharaoh gave his blessing, and Joseph, with his brothers, went to Canaan to bury Jacob. {56:33} Pharaoh proclaimed that anyone not accompanying Joseph would be put to death. {56:34} All of Egypt rose up, including Pharaoh's servants and nobles, to join Joseph in the journey. {56:35} Jacob's sons carried his bier as he had commanded. {56:36} The bier was made of pure gold, inlaid with onyx stones and bdellium, and covered with golden woven work. {56:37} Joseph placed a golden crown on Jacob's head and a scepter in his hand, and the bier was surrounded as a king's bier. {56:38} Egyptian troops, including Pharaoh's mighty men, accompanied the bier, equipped with swords and armor. {56:39} Mourners followed the bier, weeping and lamenting. {56:40} Joseph and his household walked barefoot, weeping, with their servants around them. {56:41} Fifty of Jacob's servants walked ahead, scattering myrrh, aloes, and perfumes along the way. {56:42} Joseph's camp continued this practice daily until they reached Canaan, mourning at the threshing floor of Atad. {56:43} Thirty-one kings of Canaan came to mourn Jacob, placing their crowns on his bier. {56:44} The kings joined the sons of Jacob and the Egyptians in great mourning for Jacob. {56:45} News of Jacob's death reached Esau, who came with a great number of people to mourn Jacob. {56:46} Esau and the people of Egypt and Canaan mourned Jacob together. {56:47} As Jacob's sons brought him to Hebron for burial, Esau and his sons obstructed them, claiming the cave was theirs. {56:48} Jacob's sons reminded Esau that Jacob had bought the cave from him years ago. {56:49} Esau denied this, intending to deceive Joseph, who hadn't been present during the sale. {56:50} Joseph insisted the transaction was recorded and held in Egypt. {56:51} Esau demanded to see the records, and Joseph sent Naphtali to fetch them. {56:52} Esau and his sons resisted, leading to a battle with Jacob's sons and the Egyptians. {56:53} Jacob's sons and their allies prevailed, killing many of Esau's men. {56:54} Chushim, Dan's son, who was deaf and dumb, saw the battle and, upon learning the cause, killed Esau. {56:55} This act led Jacob's sons to victory, and they buried Jacob in the cave. {56:56} Jacob was buried in Hebron, in the cave of Machpelah, in costly garments. {56:57} Joseph honored Jacob with a burial fit for a king. {56:58} Joseph and his brothers mourned for their father for 7 days.

{57:1} After these events, the sons of Esau waged war against the sons of Jacob in Hebron. Esau lay dead, unburied. {57:2} The battle raged fiercely, and the sons of Esau were defeated by the sons of Jacob. Jacob's sons slew eighty of Esau's men without losing a single one of their own. Joseph, particularly, captured Zepho, the son of Eliphaz, grandson of Esau, along with fifty of his men. They were bound in iron chains and handed over to Joseph's servants to be taken to Egypt. {57:3} Fearful of being captured, the remaining sons of Esau fled with Eliphaz and his people, carrying Esau's body on the road to Mount Seir. {57:4} They buried Esau in Seir, though his head remained in Hebron, where the battle had taken place. {57:5} The sons of Jacob pursued the fleeing sons of Esau to the borders of Seir but did not kill any of them, confused by Esau's body among them. They turned back to Hebron, where they rested after the battle. {57:6} On the third day, all the sons of Seir the Horite and many from the east gathered, a multitude like the sands of the sea, and journeyed to Egypt to fight

Joseph and his brothers, seeking to free their captive kin. {57:7} Joseph and all the sons of Jacob learned of the approaching armies of Esau and the eastern tribes coming to battle them. {57:8} They marched out from Rameses and fought fiercely. Joseph and his brothers inflicted a devastating blow on Esau's sons and the eastern forces. {57:9} They killed six hundred thousand men, including all the mighty warriors of Seir the Horite. Many from the eastern tribes and Esau's descendants fled in defeat before Joseph and his brothers. {57:10} Pursuing them to Succoth, Joseph's forces slew thirty men before the rest escaped to their cities. {57:11} Joseph and his brothers returned joyfully, having triumphed over their enemies. {57:12} Meanwhile, Zepho, son of Eliphaz, and his men remained slaves in Egypt under the sons of Jacob, enduring increased hardship. {57:13} Upon their return to their lands, the sons of Seir saw that Esau's sons and the Egyptians had conquered them. {57:14} They said to Esau's sons, "You see now that this conflict arose because of you, and now there is not one mighty man left among us." {57:15} They urged Esau's sons to leave their land and return to Canaan, their ancestral home, so their children would not suffer from the conflict. {57:16} Esau's sons refused to listen, and the sons of Seir considered making war against them. {57:17} Esau's sons secretly sent word to Angeas, king of Africa (Dinhabah), requesting his aid in fighting the sons of Seir, who sought to drive them from the land. {57:18} Angeas, friendly to Esau's sons, sent five hundred valiant infantry and eight hundred cavalry to aid them. {57:19} The sons of Seir appealed to the children of the east and Midian for help, describing the devastation wrought by Esau's sons in their battle with Jacob's sons. {57:20} Eight hundred men armed with swords responded to their call, joining the sons of Seir in the wilderness of Paran to battle Esau's sons.

{58:1} In the thirty-second year since Jacob's family settled in Egypt, and during the seventy-first year of Joseph's life, Pharaoh, the ruler of Egypt, passed away. His son Magron ascended to the throne after him. {58:2} Before his death, Pharaoh instructed Joseph to guide and counsel his son Magron, entrusting him with the care of the kingdom. {58:3} All of Egypt agreed to this arrangement, accepting Joseph as their de facto king due to their deep admiration for him. However, Magron officially reigned as Pharaoh, following the Egyptian custom of naming each new king after his predecessor. {58:4} Magron was forty-one years old when he began his reign and ruled Egypt for forty years. {58:5} During Pharaoh Magron's reign, he placed the governance of Egypt and all its affairs under Joseph's authority, as his father had commanded. {58:6} Joseph effectively became the ruler of Egypt, overseeing the entire nation with the support and affection of its people. {58:7} Despite some dissenting voices, who objected to a foreigner ruling over them, Joseph governed Egypt unopposed, managing the country's affairs as he saw fit. {58:8} Joseph led successful military campaigns against Egypt's enemies, including the Philistines and others up to the borders of Canaan, subjecting them to Egyptian rule and imposing an annual tribute on them. {58:9} While Pharaoh Magron sat on the throne in Egypt, he relied on Joseph's counsel, continuing the tradition established by his father. {58:10} Joseph's authority extended beyond Egypt alone; he ruled over the entire region from Egypt to the great river Perath (Euphrates). {58:11} The Lord blessed Joseph abundantly, granting him wisdom, honor, and favor among the Egyptians and throughout the land. Joseph ruled over Egypt for forty years, {58:12} during which all the neighboring peoples, including the Philistines, Canaanites, and those beyond the Jordan, paid tribute to him. {58:13} Meanwhile, Joseph's brothers, the sons of Jacob, lived peacefully in Egypt throughout his reign, prospering and growing in number while faithfully serving the Lord. {58:14} Many years later, while Bela ruled peacefully as king over the children of Esau in Seir, they multiplied and prepared to challenge Jacob's descendants and Egypt, seeking to free their captive kinsman Zepho, still enslaved under Joseph. {58:15} The children of Esau formed alliances with the eastern tribes, including Angeas' people from Dinhabah and the children of Ishmael, gathering a vast army to march against Egypt. {58:16} This formidable force assembled in Seir and set out for Egypt, encamping near Rameses in preparation for battle.

{59:1} These are the names of the sons of Israel who settled in Egypt with Jacob. Each of Jacob's sons came to Egypt with their households. {59:2} The sons of Leah were Reuben, Simeon, Levi, Judah, Issachar, Zebulun, and their sister Dinah. {59:3} Rachel's sons were Joseph and Benjamin. {59:4} Zilpah, Leah's servant, bore Gad and Asher. {59:5} Bilhah, Rachel's servant, bore Dan and Naphtali. {59:6} These were the descendants born to them in Canaan before they migrated to Egypt with their father Jacob. {59:7} Reuben's sons were Hanoch, Pallu, Hezron, and Carmi. {59:8} Simeon's sons were Jemuel, Jamin, Ohad, Jachin, Zohar, and Saul (the son of a Canaanite woman). {59:9} Levi's children were Gershon, Kohath, Merari, and their sister Jochebed, born to them in Egypt. {59:10} Judah's sons were Er, Onan, Shelah, Perez, and Zerah. {59:11} Er and Onan died in Canaan, and Perez's sons were Hezron and Hamul. {59:12} Issachar's sons were Tola, Puah, Jashub, and Shimron. {59:13} Zebulun's sons were Sered, Elon, and Jahleel. {59:14} Dan's son was Hushim, and Naphtali's sons were Jahzeel, Guni, Jezer, and Shillem. {59:15} Gad's sons were Zephon, Haggi, Shuni, Ezbon, Eri, Arodi, and Areli. {59:16} Asher's sons were Imnah, Ishvah, Ishvi, and Beriah, and their sister Serah. Beriah's sons were Heber and Malchiel. {59:17} Benjamin's sons were Bela, Becher, Ashbel, Gera, Naaman, Ehi, Rosh, Muppim, Huppim, and Ard. {59:18} Joseph's sons born to him in Egypt were Manasseh and Ephraim. {59:19} The total number of souls who came with Jacob to Egypt, including his descendants, was seventy. They settled there, and Joseph and his brothers lived securely, enjoying the prosperity of Egypt throughout Joseph's lifetime. {59:20} Joseph lived in Egypt for ninety-three years, reigning as the effective ruler over all Egypt for eighty years. {59:21} As Joseph neared the end of his life, he gathered his brothers and all of his father's household and spoke to them. {59:22} Joseph assured them, "I am about to die, but God will surely visit you and bring you up from this land to the land He promised to your ancestors." {59:23} "When God brings you up from here to the land of your fathers, carry my bones with you." {59:24} Joseph made the Israelites swear an oath concerning his remains, ensuring they would be taken to the promised land. {59:25} Joseph died in the seventy-first year after Israel's arrival in Egypt, at the age of one hundred ten. {59:26} His brothers and servants embalmed him as was customary, and all of Egypt mourned Joseph's passing for seventy days. {59:27} They placed Joseph in a coffin filled with spices and perfumes and buried him beside the river Sihor. Joseph's sons, his brothers, and the entire household of Jacob observed seven days of mourning for him. {59:28} After Joseph's death, the Egyptians began to exert control over the Israelites, and Pharaoh, reigning in his father's place, governed Egypt according to its laws, securely ruling over his people.

{60:1} In the seventy-second year after the Israelites came to Egypt, following Joseph's death, Zepho, son of Eliphaz and grandson of Esau, fled from Egypt with his men. {60:2} They journeyed to Africa, known as Dinhabah, and sought refuge with Angeas, the king of Africa, who received them with great honor. Angeas appointed Zepho as the commander of his army, recognizing his prowess and leadership. {60:3} Zepho gained favor among Angeas's people and served as the captain of the host for a long time. {60:4} Zepho, eager to avenge his brethren against the Egyptians and the sons of Jacob, urged Angeas to gather his army for war. However, Angeas, aware of the strength of the sons of Jacob from previous conflicts with the children of Esau, refused to heed Zepho's counsel. {60:5} Despite this, Zepho's influence grew, but his ambitions for war against Egypt were not realized. {60:6} During this time, in the city of Puzimna in the land of Chittim, there lived a man named Uzu, revered as a deity by the Chittimites. Uzu died leaving behind his exceptionally beautiful and wise daughter named Jania. {60:7} Jania caught the attention of Angeas's people, who praised her to him. Angeas sent messengers to Chittim seeking Jania's hand in marriage, a proposal which the Chittimites agreed to. {60:8} Meanwhile, Turnus, king of

Bibentu, also desired Jania as his wife and sent his own messengers to Chittim for her hand. {60:9} The Chittimites, having already promised Jania to Angeas, declined Turnus's request fearing Angeas's wrath. {60:10} Turnus learned of Angeas's intentions and prepared his army to march against Angeas, passing through Sardunia on his way. {60:11} Angeas, informed of Turnus's plans, assembled his army and marched to meet his brother Lucus, king of Sardunia. {60:12} Lucus's son Niblos joined Angeas's army, seeking to be made captain of the host. {60:13} Angeas and Lucus met Turnus in the valley of Canopia, where a fierce battle ensued. {60:14} Lucus and his army suffered heavy losses, including the death of Niblos in battle. {60:15} Angeas, fueled by vengeance for his nephew Niblos, defeated Turnus and his forces decisively. {60:16} Pursuing Turnus, Angeas and Lucus continued their victorious march through Alphanu and Romah, where they completely annihilated Turnus's army. {60:17} Lucus ordered a brass coffin made for his son Niblos, and he was buried there. A tower was erected in Niblos's honor, marking his grave beside Turnus's. {60:18} After burying Niblos, Lucus returned to Sardunia, while Angeas proceeded to Bibentu, where the inhabitants feared and pleaded for mercy. {60:19} Bibentu, counted among the cities of Chittim, was spared by Angeas, but he established a precedent of plundering Chittim during subsequent campaigns. {60:20} Angeas eventually went to Puzimna, where he took Jania, daughter of Uzu, as his wife and brought her to his city in Africa.

{61:1} During that time, Pharaoh, the king of Egypt, commanded his people to construct a grand palace in Egypt. {61:2} He also ordered the sons of Jacob to assist in the construction. The Egyptians built a magnificent palace fit for royal habitation, where Pharaoh established his renewed government and ruled securely. {61:3} In that same year, Zebulun, son of Jacob, passed away at the age of a hundred and fourteen. His body was placed in a coffin and entrusted to his descendants. {61:4} Three years later, Simeon, Zebulun's brother, died at the age of a hundred and twenty. Like Zebulun, he was buried in a coffin by his children. {61:5} Meanwhile, Zepho, the son of Eliphaz and captain of Angeas's host in Dinhabah, continued to persuade Angeas daily to prepare for battle against the sons of Jacob in Egypt. {61:6} Zepho persistently urged Angeas to engage in war with the sons of Jacob. {61:7} Eventually, Angeas yielded to Zepho's persuasion and decided to march with his vast army, as numerous as the sands of the sea, towards Egypt for battle. {61:8} Among Angeas's servants was Balaam, a fifteen-year-old youth skilled in the art of divination and sorcery. {61:9} Angeas asked Balaam to perform divination to determine the outcome of the impending battle. {61:10} Balaam crafted wax figures representing the armies of Angeas and Egypt, and through his magic, he foresaw the defeat of Angeas's army by the Egyptians and the sons of Jacob. {61:11} Balaam relayed this ominous vision to Angeas, who subsequently abandoned his plans for war and remained in his city. {61:12} Upon seeing Angeas's reluctance, Zepho fled Africa and sought refuge in Chittim. {61:13} The people of Chittim welcomed Zepho and hired him to lead their military campaigns, where he amassed great wealth. {61:14} During one of these campaigns, Zepho encountered a large cave while searching for a lost heifer. {61:15} Inside the cave, he encountered a monstrous creature resembling a half-man, half-animal, devouring his cattle. Zepho bravely slew the beast with his swords. {61:16} The people of Chittim rejoiced at Zepho's feat and honored him by establishing an annual day of celebration in his name. {61:17} They brought drink offerings and gifts to commemorate his bravery. {61:18} Meanwhile, Jania, the wife of Angeas and daughter of Uzu, fell seriously ill. Angeas sought counsel on how to heal her. {61:19} His wise men attributed her illness to the difference in air and water between Africa and Chittim, her homeland. {61:20} Angeas ordered the waters of Purmah from Chittim to be brought, and upon comparing them with African waters, found them lighter. {61:21} Angeas commanded the construction of a sturdy bridge to transport the water from Chittim to Africa. These waters became essential for Jania's health and for agricultural purposes. {61:22} Angeas also had palaces built for Jania using soil and stones imported from Chittim, and she recovered from her illness. {61:23} Despite these events, the troops of Africa continued to raid Chittim annually. Zepho, now in Chittim, confronted them and successfully defended the land. {61:24} Impressed by Zepho's leadership, the people of Chittim crowned him king. {61:25} Zepho ruled over Chittim and Italia for fifty years, during which time he led successful campaigns against Tubal and neighboring islands, expanding his kingdom and securing his reign.

{62:1} In the seventy-ninth year since the Israelites came to Egypt, Reuben, the eldest son of Jacob, passed away in Egypt at the age of a hundred and twenty-five. He was placed in a coffin and buried by his descendants. {62:2} The following year, Reuben's brother Dan died at the age of a hundred and twenty. Like Reuben, Dan was laid to rest in a coffin by his children. {62:3} Also in that year, Chusham, the king of Edom, died, and Hadad, son of Bedad, succeeded him as king for thirty-five years. {62:4} In the eighty-first year, Issachar, another son of Jacob, died in Egypt at the age of a hundred and twenty-two. His body was placed in a coffin and entrusted to his descendants. {62:5} The next year, Asher, Issachar's brother, passed away at a hundred and twenty-three years old. He too was laid to rest in a coffin in Egypt. {62:6} In the eighty-third year, Gad died at the age of a hundred and twenty-five. He was buried in Egypt in a coffin handed down to his children. {62:7} In the eighty-fourth year, during the fiftieth year of Hadad's reign as king of Edom, Hadad gathered all the descendants of Esau and prepared his army, numbering about four hundred thousand men. He marched towards the land of Moab with the intention of making them tributary. {62:8} Hearing of Hadad's approach, the Moabites sought aid from the Midianites. {62:9} Hadad encountered the combined forces of Moab and Midian in battle in the fields of Moab. {62:10} The battle was fierce, resulting in the deaths of about two hundred thousand Moabites and Midianites. {62:11} Midian, unaware of Moab's intention to retreat, fought valiantly but was eventually overwhelmed by Hadad's forces. {62:12} Hadad inflicted heavy casualties on Midian and left none alive who had come to aid Moab. {62:13} Having defeated Midian, Hadad made Moab tributary to him, imposing a yearly tax. He then returned to his own land. {62:14} The remaining Midianites were enraged by the loss of their brethren and resolved to avenge them by attacking Moab. {62:15} They enlisted the help of the children of the east, including all the descendants of Keturah. {62:16} When Moab learned of this alliance, they sent a plea to Hadad, king of Edom, asking for assistance against the impending attack. {62:17} Hadad responded by leading his army to Moab to fight against Midian and their allies. {62:18} The battle was intense, with Hadad prevailing over Midian and the children of the east, delivering Moab from their hands. {62:19} The survivors of Midian and the eastern allies fled, pursued by Hadad's forces, suffering heavy losses along the way. {62:20} Thus, Hadad secured Moab's safety by eliminating the threat of Midian. {62:21} From that time on, enmity between Midian and Moab persisted fiercely. {62:22} Retaliations between them continued for many years, each side inflicting casualties on the other. {62:23} In the eighty-sixth year of Jacob's arrival in Egypt, Judah, another son of Jacob, passed away at the age of a hundred and twenty-nine. He was embalmed, placed in a coffin, and buried by his children. {62:24} In the eighty-ninth year, Naphtali died at a hundred and thirty-two years old. His body was also placed in a coffin by his children. {62:25} In the ninety-first year since the Israelites came to Egypt, during the thirtieth year of Zepho's reign over the children of Chittim, the African troops returned to plunder the Chittimites after a thirteen-year absence. {62:26} Zepho, leading his men, bravely confronted and defeated the African troops, causing them to flee back towards Africa with heavy casualties. {62:27} Angeas, king of Africa, upon hearing of Zepho's victorious campaign, feared him greatly from then on.

{63:1} In the ninety-third year after the Israelites arrived in Egypt, Levi, one of Jacob's sons, passed away at the age of a hundred and thirty-seven. He was embalmed, placed in a coffin, and buried by his descendants. {63:2} Following Levi's death, the Egyptians, seeing that Joseph and his brothers had all died, began to oppress the children of Jacob, embittering their lives with harsh labor. They confiscated the vineyards, fields, and elegant houses that Joseph had granted to the Israelites, taking all the wealth they had acquired in Egypt. {63:3} The oppression of the Israelites by the Egyptians intensified greatly during this time, causing the Israelites to despair of their lives. {63:4} In the hundred and second year of Israel's sojourn in Egypt, Pharaoh passed away, and his son Melol ascended to the throne. With Pharaoh's death, the generation that had known Joseph and his brothers also passed away. {63:5} A new generation arose in Egypt that did not remember Joseph or the good he had done for the land. {63:6} Consequently, the Egyptians intensified their harsh treatment of the Israelites, subjecting them to severe labor, not knowing the history of how their ancestors had saved Egypt during the famine. {63:7} This was allowed by the Lord to eventually benefit the children of Israel, so they would come to know and fear the Lord their God through the mighty wonders He would perform in Egypt for their sake. {63:8} Melol was twenty years old when he began his ninety-four-year reign. In Egypt, it became customary to refer to him as Pharaoh, following the tradition of naming kings after their predecessors. {63:9} Meanwhile, Angeas, king of Africa, dispatched his troops to raid the land of Chittim as they had done in previous years. {63:10} Upon hearing this, Zepho, son of Eliphaz and king of Chittim, gathered his army and confronted the African troops on the road. {63:11} Zepho decisively defeated Angeas's troops, leaving none alive to return to Africa. {63:12} Learning of this defeat, Angeas gathered a massive army, numbering like the sands of the sea, including his brother Lucus, to retaliate against Zepho and the Chittimites. {63:13} Fear gripped Zepho and the people of Chittim upon hearing of Angeas's impending attack. {63:14} Zepho sought aid from Edom, sending a plea to Hadad, son of Bedad, and all the descendants of Esau for assistance against Angeas and Lucus. {63:15} The children of Esau, however, reminded Zepho of their longstanding peace treaty with Angeas since the days of Bela and Joseph, and declined to join the conflict. {63:16} Upon hearing this, Zepho became greatly fearful of facing Angeas alone. {63:17} Angeas and Lucus assembled a massive force of about eight hundred thousand men to wage war against Chittim. {63:18} The people of Chittim pleaded with Zepho to pray to his ancestors' God for deliverance from Angeas's army, believing in the God's ability to save those who trusted in Him. {63:19} Zepho, acknowledging the power of God, prayed earnestly, invoking the covenant God made with Abraham and Isaac. {63:20} The Lord listened to Zepho's prayer, showing favor because of the faith of Abraham and Isaac, and delivered Zepho and the Chittimites from Angeas and his army. {63:21} Zepho led the Chittimites in battle against Angeas and his forces, and the Lord granted them victory, decimating Angeas's army. {63:22} Witnessing the destruction of his army, Angeas sent out a call across Africa for reinforcements, threatening severe consequences for those who did not join him. {63:23} Responding to Angeas's call, three hundred thousand men and boys from Africa assembled to bolster his ranks. {63:24} Ten days later, Angeas renewed the battle against Zepho and the Chittimites, resulting in fierce combat between the two sides. {63:25} Zepho's forces inflicted significant casualties on Angeas's army, including the death of Sosiphtar, Angeas's captain. {63:26} Eventually, Angeas and Lucus fled with their remaining men, pursued by Zepho and the Chittimites. {63:27} Angeas lived in fear thereafter, wary of Zepho's potential for further conflict.

{64:1} During that time, Balaam, the son of Beor, was present with Angeas in the battle. Seeing Zepho's victory over Angeas, Balaam fled and sought refuge in Chittim. {64:2} Zepho and the people of Chittim welcomed Balaam warmly, recognizing his wisdom. Zepho honored Balaam with many gifts, and Balaam remained among them. {64:3} After returning from war, Zepho ordered a count of all the men of Chittim who had fought with him, and not a single person was found missing. {64:4} Zepho celebrated this and reaffirmed his rule, hosting a feast for all his subjects. {64:5} However, Zepho did not acknowledge the Lord or recognize His assistance in the battle against Angeas. Instead, he continued to follow the ways of the Chittimites and the wicked descendants of Esau, worshiping other gods they introduced to him. It was said, "From the wicked comes wickedness." {64:6} Zepho ruled over Chittim securely but remained ignorant of the Lord who had delivered him and his people. The African troops no longer raided Chittim as they feared Zepho's power, having been defeated by him. {64:7} After Zepho's return from war and witnessing his victory over the African forces, he consulted with the people of Chittim about attacking the sons of Jacob and Pharaoh in Egypt. {64:8} Learning that the mighty men of Egypt were dead, along with Joseph and his brothers, Zepho planned revenge for the harm done to his brethren, the children of Esau, in Canaan. {64:9} Zepho sent messengers to Hadad, king of Edom, and to all the descendants of Esau, urging them to join him in avenging his ancestors' grievances against Egypt and the sons of Jacob. {64:10} The children of Esau agreed, gathering a large army to assist Zepho and the people of Chittim in their campaign. {64:11} Zepho also sent word to the children of the east and the descendants of Ishmael, who joined forces with him and Chittim for the war against Egypt. {64:12} Zepho, the king of Chittim, along with Hadad, king of Edom, and their allies, assembled in Hebron, their combined forces stretching for three days' journey in length, a multitude as numerous as the sands of the sea. {64:13} They marched against Egypt, encamping together in the valley of Pathros. {64:14} When the Egyptians learned of this formidable alliance, they mustered about three hundred thousand men from across their land and cities to confront them. {64:15} They also summoned the children of Israel, who were then residing in Goshen, asking them to join forces against the invading kings. {64:16} About one hundred and fifty men from Israel answered the call and joined the Egyptians in battle. {64:17} The combined forces of Egypt and Israel, numbering three hundred thousand Egyptians and one hundred and fifty Israelites, faced off against Zepho, Hadad, and their allies in the valley of Pathros near Tachpanches. {64:18} The Egyptians hesitated to fully trust the Israelites, fearing they might betray them to their fellow descendants of Esau and Ishmael. {64:19} They proposed that the Israelites remain on standby while they engaged the enemy, promising to call for their aid if the battle turned against them. {64:20} Zepho and Hadad arrayed their forces for battle, while the Egyptians advanced alone against them, leaving the Israelites behind. {64:21} In the ensuing fierce battle, the Egyptians found themselves outmatched by the kings' forces, losing about one hundred and eighty men that day compared to thirty casualties on the kings' side. {64:22} The Egyptians fled from the battlefield, pursued by the children of Esau, Ishmael, and Chittim, until they reached the camp of the children of Israel. {64:23} Desperate, the Egyptians cried out to the Israelites for help against their pursuers, urging them to join the fight. {64:24} The one hundred and fifty men of Israel left their position and rushed to aid the Egyptians against the kings. {64:25} The Israelites prayed to the Lord for deliverance and fought against the kings, killing about four thousand of their men. {64:26} The Lord caused great confusion among the kings' ranks, instilling fear of the Israelites among them. {64:27} The kings' armies fled from the Israelites, who pursued them and continued to strike them down until the borders of Cush. {64:28} Witnessing their defeat, all the Egyptians feared the Israelites greatly, acknowledging their formidable power and the protection granted to them by the Lord. {64:29} The victorious Israelites returned joyfully to Goshen, while the remaining Egyptians dispersed to their homes, shaken by the events that transpired.

{65:1} After these events, all the counselors of Pharaoh, the king of Egypt, and the elders of Egypt gathered before the king, bowing down before him, and sat in his presence. {65:2} They addressed the king, saying, {65:3} "Look, the people of Israel are greater and stronger than we are. You've seen the harm they inflicted on us when we returned from battle. {65:4} Their strength is evident, for just a few of them stood against a multitude like sand and defeated them with swords. Not one of them fell in battle. If their numbers increase, they could become a threat to us. In any future conflict, their strength could turn them against us, leading to our destruction and their departure from our land. {65:5} Therefore, advise us on what to do with them to gradually diminish their numbers among us, lest they overwhelm us in our own land." {65:6} The king responded to the elders, saying, "This is the plan we will implement against Israel, and we will not deviate from it. {65:7} In our land are Pithom and Rameses, cities vulnerable to attack. We must build and fortify them. {65:8} Therefore, go and act shrewdly toward them. Proclaim throughout Egypt and Goshen on my command: {65:9} 'The king has ordered the construction and fortification of Pithom and Rameses for defense. Whoever among you, Egyptians or Israelites, is willing to join us in building these cities will receive daily wages from the king. Gather and come to Pithom and Rameses to begin construction.' {65:10} Make this proclamation daily throughout Egypt." {65:11} The Egyptians and Israelites responded to Pharaoh's servants and began building Pithom and Rameses, but the Levites did not join their brethren in the work. {65:12} Initially, Pharaoh's servants worked alongside the Israelites as hired laborers, paying them wages daily. {65:13} After a month, Pharaoh's servants began to withdraw secretly from the Israelites each day. {65:14} Eventually, they appointed taskmasters over the Israelites, who forced them to continue working without pay, under threat of severe punishment. {65:15} This strategy was intended to weaken the Israelites through hard labor, separating them from their families day by day. {65:16} The elders and servants of Pharaoh spread the decree throughout Egypt, ensuring that the Israelites were oppressed in their work. {65:17} Despite the hardships, the Israelites persisted in building Pithom and Rameses, fortifying the entire land of Egypt. {65:18} They endured this toil for many years until the Lord remembered them and delivered them from Egypt. {65:19} Throughout this time, the Levites refrained from participating in the labor, knowing the Egyptians' deceitful intentions. {65:20} As a result, the Egyptians did not press the Levites into forced labor. {65:21} The Egyptians intensified their oppression of the Israelites, exacting harsh labor from them in mortar, bricks, and all kinds of field work. {65:22} The Israelites nicknamed Pharaoh "Meror, king of Egypt," during his reign, due to the bitter hardships imposed on them. {65:23} Despite the severity of their treatment, the Israelites continued to multiply and grow, much to the Egyptians' dismay.

{66:1} During this time, Hadad, the son of Bedad, king of Edom, passed away, and Samlah from Mesrekah in the region of the eastern tribes succeeded him as king. {66:2} Samlah ruled over Edom for eighteen years in the thirteenth year of Pharaoh's reign in Egypt, marking the hundred and twenty-fifth year since Israel had entered Egypt. {66:3} Early in his reign, Samlah mobilized his armies to confront Zepho, the son of Eliphaz, and the people of Chittim, who had waged war against Angeas, king of Africa, and decimated his army. {66:4} However, the Edomites, considering Zepho their brother, intervened and dissuaded Samlah from attacking. He returned with his forces to Edom without engaging in battle. {66:5} When Pharaoh of Egypt heard of Samlah's intention to fight the people of Chittim and possibly turn against Egypt afterward, he intensified the labor imposed on the Israelites, fearing a similar fate as their past conflict with the Edomites during Hadad's time. {66:6} The Egyptians urged the Israelites to hasten their work and fortify the land, fearing retaliation from their Edomite brethren. {66:7} Despite increased oppression, the Israelites continued their tasks, enduring hardships aimed at reducing their numbers in the land. {66:8} Yet, as the Egyptians escalated their efforts, the Israelites continued to multiply, filling all of Egypt. {66:9} By the hundred and twenty-fifth year since Israel's arrival in Egypt, it was evident that Egypt's strategies to diminish the Israelites were failing as they thrived and spread throughout the land. {66:10} Observing this, the elders and wise men of Egypt approached the king, acknowledging their previous counsel's failure and seeking new advice to overcome or reduce the Israelites in the land. {66:11} All the elders and wise men bowed before the king and awaited his wisdom. {66:12} They acknowledged the king's earlier counsel against the Israelites had not achieved its intended effect. {66:13} They informed the king that despite their efforts, the Israelites continued to grow and flourish. {66:14} They sought the king's counsel on how to prevail over Israel, either by destroying them or reducing their presence in Egypt. {66:15} Job, an officer and counselor from Mesopotamia, stepped forward with a proposal. {66:16} The king permitted Job to speak, and he addressed the assembly. {66:17} Job proposed maintaining the labor but suggested a new strategy to diminish the Israelites if the king agreed. {66:18} He advised implementing a decree that every male child born to the Israelites should be killed, ensuring it became an irreversible law of Egypt. {66:19} Job argued this extreme measure would end the threat of Israel's growing strength and ensure peace. {66:20} The proposal pleased the king and his advisors, and the king decided to enact Job's plan. {66:21} He summoned the Hebrew midwives, including Shephrah and Puah, and issued them a directive. {66:22} The king ordered the midwives that every Hebrew boy born must be killed immediately upon birth, while allowing the girls to live. {66:23} He threatened severe consequences if they failed to comply. {66:24} However, the midwives, fearing God, did not obey the king's command and allowed the male children to live. {66:25} When questioned by the king about their actions, the midwives explained that the Hebrew women were strong and gave birth before the midwives could intervene. {66:26} Pharaoh accepted their explanation, and the midwives were spared punishment. {66:27} God blessed the midwives for their courage, and despite Pharaoh's decree, the Israelites continued to multiply and thrive in Egypt.

{67:1} In Egypt lived a man from the tribe of Levi named Amram, the son of Kehath, who was a descendant of Levi, the son of Israel. {67:2} Amram married Jochebed, his father's sister, who was one hundred and twenty-six years old at the time of their union. {67:3} Jochebed bore a daughter whom they named Miriam, because of the bitter oppression the Egyptians inflicted upon the Israelites during those days. {67:4} Later, Jochebed gave birth to a son named Aaron, as Pharaoh had begun his cruel decree to kill Israelite male children. {67:5} During this period, Zepho, the son of Eliphaz and king of Chittim, passed away, and Janeas succeeded him, reigning for fifty years in Chittim until his death. {67:6} Zepho was buried in Nabna, a city in Chittim. {67:7} Janeas, a mighty leader among the people of Chittim, ruled for fifty years following Zepho's reign. {67:8} After Janeas's death, Balaam, the son of Beor, fled Chittim and sought refuge in Egypt, where Pharaoh honored him for his renowned wisdom, appointing him as a counselor and granting him great wealth and influence among the nobles. {67:9} Balaam settled in Egypt and was highly esteemed by the king and his courtiers, who eagerly sought his wisdom. {67:10} In the hundred and thirtieth year since Israel's arrival in Egypt, Pharaoh had a significant dream where he saw an old man holding scales, weighing the elders and nobles of Egypt against a milk kid, which outweighed them all. {67:11} Troubled by the dream, Pharaoh summoned his wise men to interpret its meaning. {67:12} Balaam interpreted the dream, predicting a great future calamity for Egypt at the hands of a son born to Israel, who would liberate his people with divine strength. {67:13} Concerned, Pharaoh sought counsel on how to thwart this prophecy. {67:14} Balaam suggested intensifying measures against the Israelites to prevent their rise against Egypt. {67:15} Pharaoh then sought advice from Reuel the Midianite and Job the Uzite, who were summoned to counsel him. {67:16} Reuel advised Pharaoh to cease oppressing the Hebrews, citing their divine protection throughout history. {67:17} Job, however, urged Pharaoh to continue with harsh measures to weaken and control the Israelites. {67:18} Balaam supported Job's counsel, recommending a decree that all Hebrew male infants be thrown into the river as a means to eradicate their future threat to Egypt. {67:19} Pharaoh accepted Balaam's advice, issuing a law that mandated the drowning of every Hebrew boy born henceforth, while sparing the girls.

{67:20} The Egyptians were commanded to enforce this decree throughout the land of Goshen, where the Israelites resided. {67:21} When the Israelites heard of this decree, some separated from their spouses, while others remained defiant. {67:22} Those who remained with their husbands gave birth in the fields, leaving their newborn sons exposed, as commanded. {67:23} However, God sent angels to protect and nurture these infants, ensuring their survival and growth. {67:24} Despite Pharaoh's efforts, the Israelites continued to multiply and flourish, defying the king's decree.

{68:1} During this time, the spirit of God rested upon Miriam, the daughter of Amram and sister of Aaron. She boldly proclaimed among the household, "Behold, a son will be born to us from my parents, and he will deliver Israel from the grip of Egypt." {68:2} When Amram heard his daughter's prophecy, he brought Jochebed, his wife whom he had separated from during Pharaoh's decree, back into their home. {68:3} Three years after their reunion, Amram approached Jochebed, and she conceived. {68:4} Seven months later, she gave birth to a son, and the entire house was filled with a radiant light, akin to the brightness of the sun and moon combined. {68:5} Seeing that the child was exceptionally beautiful, Jochebed hid him for three months in a secret chamber. {68:6} Meanwhile, the Egyptians plotted to eradicate all Hebrews living among them. {68:7} Egyptian women ventured into Goshen, carrying their infants on their shoulders, while Hebrew women concealed their sons to avoid detection and potential harm from the Egyptians. {68:8} During this time, when Egyptian women visited Hebrew homes, their own babes, unable to speak, cried out, prompting the hidden Hebrew infants to respond, revealing their presence. {68:9} The Egyptian women reported this to Pharaoh, who then dispatched officers to seize and kill the Hebrew children, a practice that continued throughout those days. {68:10} About three months after Jochebed hid her son, word of the child's existence reached Pharaoh's palace. {68:11} Hurriedly, Jochebed prepared an ark of bulrushes, coated it with slime and pitch, and placed her child inside. She then set the ark among the reeds at the river's edge. {68:12} Miriam, the boy's sister, watched from afar to see what would become of her brother and the fulfillment of her prophecy. {68:13} At that moment, God sent a scorching heat upon Egypt, afflicting its people with unbearable discomfort. {68:14} Seeking relief, all Egyptians, including Pharaoh's daughter Bathia, went down to bathe in the river. {68:15} Bathia noticed the ark among the reeds and sent her maid to retrieve it. {68:16} Opening the ark, she found the child crying, and her heart went out to him. She recognized him as one of the Hebrew infants. {68:17} The Egyptian women along the riverbank also felt compassion and desired to nurse the child, but he refused to suckle, a divine act to ensure he would be returned to his mother. {68:18} Miriam, present among the Egyptian women, seized the opportunity and asked Pharaoh's daughter if she should fetch a Hebrew nurse for the child. {68:19} Bathia agreed, and Miriam promptly brought Jochebed, the child's mother, to nurse him. {68:20} Bathia then employed Jochebed to care for the child, offering her daily wages, and Jochebed nursed her own son. {68:21} After two years, Jochebed brought the child to Bathia, who adopted him as her own son and named him Moses, meaning "drawn out of the water," for she had rescued him from the river. {68:22} Amram called him Chabar, signifying the reconciliation with his wife. {68:23} Jochebed named him Jekuthiel, expressing her hope in God's intervention. {68:24} Miriam named him Jered, for she had watched over him at the river. {68:25} Aaron called him Abi Zanuch, recognizing the reunion of their parents. {68:26} Kehath named him Abigdor, acknowledging God's restoration of the house of Jacob. {68:27} Their nurse called him Abi Socho, recalling the secrecy of his concealment. {68:28} All Israel eventually called him Shemaiah, son of Nethanel, celebrating how God heard their cries and delivered them from oppression. {68:29} Moses grew up in Pharaoh's household, treated as a son alongside the king's children.

{69:1} In those days, the king of Edom passed away after reigning for eighteen years, and he was laid to rest in his temple, which he had constructed as his royal dwelling in the land of Edom. {69:2} The descendants of Esau sent messengers to Pethor by the river, and they brought back a young man named Saul, known for his handsome appearance and striking eyes. They crowned him king over them in place of Samlah. {69:3} Saul ruled over all the people of Esau in the land of Edom for forty years. {69:4} Meanwhile, when Pharaoh of Egypt observed that Balaam's counsel against the Israelites had not succeeded and that they continued to multiply and thrive across Egypt, {69:5} he issued a decree throughout the land, commanding the Israelites not to slacken their daily labor. {69:6} Pharaoh mandated that any Israelite found lacking in their daily quota of bricks or mortar would have their youngest son taken from them to replace the shortfall in the construction projects. {69:7} Thus, the labor burden upon the Israelites intensified greatly; if any man's work fell short by even one brick, the Egyptians forcibly took his youngest son from his mother and placed him into the building work. {69:8} This harsh treatment continued day after day, persisting for a long stretch of time. {69:9} However, the tribe of Levi did not participate in this forced labor alongside their Israelite brethren from the outset, for the Levites were aware of the deceptive tactics employed by the Egyptians against the Israelites.

{70:1} Three years after Moses was born, Pharaoh held a banquet with Queen Alparanith on his right and Bathia on his left. Moses lay upon Bathia's bosom, and Balaam son of Beor and his sons, along with all the kingdom's princes, were present. {70:2} During the banquet, the boy Moses reached out and took the crown from Pharaoh's head, placing it upon his own. {70:3} Astonished, the king and his princes were alarmed, discussing among themselves what should be done about this audacious act. {70:4} Pharaoh questioned his princes, seeking their counsel and judgment regarding the boy's actions. {70:5} Balaam the magician, son of Beor, spoke up, reminding Pharaoh of his dream and its interpretation concerning a Hebrew child filled with the spirit of God. {70:6} He cautioned Pharaoh not to underestimate the wisdom and understanding possessed by this Hebrew boy, who had boldly asserted his claim to the Egyptian throne. {70:7} Balaam recounted the history of Hebrew cunning, from Abraham deceiving kings to Jacob securing blessings through trickery. {70:8} He advised Pharaoh to consider the threat Moses posed to Egyptian rule if allowed to grow up. {70:9} Pharaoh, troubled by these words, summoned all the wise men of Egypt for counsel, and among them appeared an angel of the Lord, disguised as one of the wise men. {70:10} Pharaoh instructed the wise men to judge the matter of Moses' deed. {70:11} The angel proposed a test: to place before Moses an onyx stone and a coal of fire, and observe which one he would reach for. {70:12} If he chose the onyx stone, it would confirm his wisdom; if the coal, it would suggest innocence. {70:13} The test proceeded as the angel had spoken, and when Moses touched the coal, he burned his lips and tongue. {70:14} Witnessing this, Pharaoh and his princes refrained from executing Moses. {70:15} Moses remained in Pharaoh's house, growing up honored and respected, while the fear of him spread throughout Egypt. {70:16} He often visited Goshen, where he witnessed firsthand the harsh labor imposed upon his fellow Israelites. {70:17} Learning of their plight, Moses became incensed, and his anger flared against Balaam, who had plotted against him. {70:18} Fearing Moses, Balaam fled Egypt with his sons to seek refuge in the land of Cush. {70:19} Meanwhile, Moses continued to find favor in Pharaoh's eyes and among the Egyptian people. {70:20} Moses eventually approached Pharaoh, requesting a day of rest for the Israelites in Goshen from their burdensome labor. {70:21} Pharaoh granted his request, issuing a decree that the Israelites should rest on the seventh day, as Moses had asked. {70:22} This was seen as a sign of God's favor beginning to turn towards the Israelites. {70:23} Moses' influence and reputation grew among both Egyptians and Israelites alike, as he worked tirelessly for the welfare of his people.

{71:1} When Moses turned eighteen, he yearned to visit his parents in Goshen. Approaching the place where the Israelites toiled, he witnessed their hardships. {71:2} Moses, respected in Pharaoh's house, saw an Egyptian mistreating a Hebrew, and the Hebrew sought Moses' help, revealing how the Egyptian had wronged him. {71:3} Angered by the injustice, Moses looked around and, seeing no one, struck down the Egyptian and buried him in the sand, rescuing the Hebrew from further harm. {71:4} The Hebrew returned home, and Moses went back to Pharaoh's palace. {71:5} Upon returning, the Hebrew contemplated divorcing his wife due to the incident, which was unacceptable among the Israelites. {71:6} The matter reached the woman's brothers, who sought to kill the Egyptian husband, prompting him to flee and find refuge. {71:7} The next day, Moses encountered two Israelites quarreling, and he intervened, questioning the aggressor's actions. {71:8} The man retorted angrily, questioning Moses' authority and revealing knowledge of the Egyptian's death. Moses feared his deed was known. {71:9} Pharaoh, learning of the incident, ordered Moses' execution, but God intervened through an angel disguised as a captain, sparing Moses and leading him out of Egypt, far beyond its borders. {71:10} Only Aaron remained behind, prophesying to the Israelites to turn away from idolatry, though they refused to listen. {71:11} Despite their rebellion, God remembered His covenant with Abraham, Isaac, and Jacob, and refrained from destroying them. {71:12} During this time, Pharaoh's oppression of the Israelites intensified until God's intervention began to take notice of their suffering.

{72:1} In those days, a fierce war erupted between the people of Cush and the nations of the east and Aram. They rebelled against their ruler, King Kikianus of Cush. {72:2} King Kikianus gathered a vast army from Cush and marched against Aram and the eastern tribes, seeking to subdue them once more. {72:3} Leaving Balaam the magician and his two sons to guard the city, Kikianus set out for battle. {72:4} He engaged the forces of Aram and the east, defeating them soundly and taking many captives. {72:5} After securing their submission, he camped in their territories to collect tribute. {72:6} Meanwhile, Balaam, left in charge of the city and its people, conspired with them to rebel against King Kikianus upon his return. {72:7} The people agreed, making Balaam their king and his sons commanders of the army. {72:8} They fortified the city with high walls and dug numerous ditches and barriers around it. {72:9} Using their magic, they made the river swell to defend one side, and summoned serpents to guard another. {72:10} Kikianus continued his successful campaigns against Aram and the east, but upon returning to his city, found it fortified against him. {72:11} Despite his efforts to enter peacefully, Balaam and the people of the city refused him entry. {72:12} This led to a confrontation where Kikianus lost soldiers in battle against the city's defenders. {72:13} The siege persisted, marked by further battles and strategies, including attempts to cross the river and confront the serpents, which resulted in heavy casualties for Kikianus' forces. {72:14} During this time, Moses, having fled Egypt where he was pursued by Pharaoh, found refuge with Kikianus' army besieging Cush. {72:15} Moses remained with them for nine years, esteemed for his wisdom, strength, and counsel to the king. {72:16} When Kikianus died after a prolonged illness, he was honored with a grand burial outside the city. {72:17} His deeds were inscribed on great stones in his memory. {72:18} Following Kikianus' death, his army faced uncertainty and debated their next move. {72:19} They decided to crown a new king from among them and chose Moses unanimously for his leadership qualities. {72:20} Celebrating his coronation with great fanfare, they pledged allegiance to Moses and offered him the queen's hand in marriage. {72:21} Thus, Moses became king over Cush, and a proclamation was made that all should contribute to him from their wealth. {72:22} The people generously gave gold, silver, precious stones, and valuables to honor their new king. {72:23} Moses accepted these gifts and established his reign over the children of Cush in place of Kikianus.

{73:1} In the fifty-fifth year of Pharaoh's reign over Egypt, which was the hundred and fifty-seventh year since the Israelites had entered Egypt, Moses reigned as king over Cush. {73:2} Moses was twenty-seven years old when he ascended the throne, and he ruled for forty years. {73:3} The Lord blessed Moses with favor among the people of Cush, and they held him in great esteem. {73:4} On the seventh day of his reign, all the people gathered before Moses and bowed down to him, seeking his counsel regarding their prolonged siege of the city. {73:5} They explained their hardship of nine years cut off from their families. {73:6} Moses assured them that victory would come if they followed his strategy. {73:7} He commanded them to capture young storks from the forest and train them to attack, as young hawks do. {73:8} The people agreed to his plan wholeheartedly. {73:9} They spread the word throughout the camp, and soon all were gathering young storks as ordered. {73:10} They nurtured the storks and, after three days of fasting, prepared for battle as instructed by Moses. {73:11} They armed themselves and took their trained storks with them to the battlefield, where serpents guarded the city. {73:12} Following Moses' command, they released the storks, which swiftly eliminated the serpents. {73:13} Witnessing this victory, the people shouted triumphantly and stormed the city, capturing it without loss to their own ranks. {73:14} A thousand one hundred men from the city perished that day, while none from Cush fell. {73:15} The victorious people returned joyously to their homes, reunited with their families. {73:16} Balaam, the magician, fled with his sons and brothers back to Egypt upon seeing the city's fall. {73:17} These were the same sorcerers who opposed Moses during the plagues in Egypt. {73:18} Moses, by his wisdom, secured the throne of Cush and was crowned king in place of Kikianus. {73:19} He married Adoniah, the Cushite queen, widow of Kikianus, as the people acclaimed him ruler. {73:20} Moses, revering the God of his ancestors, refrained from relations with her, recalling the commands of Abraham and Isaac regarding marriage outside their lineage. {73:21} Throughout his reign, Moses remained faithful to the Lord, walking in truth and righteousness, never wavering from the path of Abraham, Isaac, and Jacob. {73:22} Under Moses' leadership, Cush prospered, and he governed wisely with the Lord's guidance. {73:23} Hearing of Kikianus' death, Aram and the eastern nations rebelled against Cush, prompting Moses to gather a formidable army. {73:24} He led thirty thousand men against Aram and the east, prevailing in battle as the Lord delivered their enemies into his hands. {73:25} Subdued, the defeated nations paid tribute to Cush. {73:26} Moses then turned his attention to Aram, defeating them in battle as well, establishing tribute as customary. {73:27} With these victories, Moses strengthened his rule over Cush, revered by all its people, who held him in awe.

{74:1} After many years, Saul, the king of Edom, passed away, and Baal Chanan, son of Achbor, ascended the throne in his place. {74:2} This was during the sixteenth year of Moses' reign over Cush, and Baal Chanan ruled over Edom for thirty-eight years. {74:3} In his time, Moab rebelled against Edom's dominion, which had been established since the days of Hadad, son of Bedad. {74:4} When Baal Chanan became king, the Moabites withdrew their allegiance from Edom. {74:5} Meanwhile, Angeas, the king of Africa, also passed away, and his son Azdrubal succeeded him as ruler. {74:6} In those days, Janeas, king of the people of Chittim, died and was buried in his temple in Canopia. Latinus then became king. {74:7} Latinus ruled over the people of Chittim for forty-five years, constructing a great tower and a splendid palace for his residence and governance. {74:8} In his third year as king, Latinus commissioned the construction of many ships and assembled his forces to engage Azdrubal of Africa in battle. {74:9} The fleets of Latinus sailed to Africa, where they clashed with Azdrubal's army. {74:10} Latinus emerged victorious, dismantling the aqueduct built by Azdrubal's father and dealing a decisive blow to his army. {74:11} Despite this defeat, Azdrubal's remaining forces regrouped and fought Latinus again, but they were defeated once more with heavy casualties. {74:12} Among those captured was Azdrubal's beautiful daughter, Ushpezena, whose image was admired throughout Africa. {74:13} Impressed by Ushpezena, Latinus took her as his wife and returned triumphantly to

Chittim. {74:14} After Azdrubal's death, the people of Africa crowned Anibal, his brother, as their new king. {74:15} Seeking vengeance for his brother, Anibal waged war against Chittim for eighteen years, inflicting heavy losses upon them. {74:16} Anibal remained in Chittim, establishing his rule and continuing his campaign against its people. {74:17} He dealt severe blows to the Chittimites, slaying many of their leaders and tens of thousands of their people. {74:18} Eventually, Anibal returned to Africa after years of conflict, ruling securely in place of his brother Azdrubal.

{75:1} In the 180th year since the Israelites had entered Egypt, a group of thirty thousand valiant men from the tribe of Joseph, specifically the children of Ephraim, set out from Egypt. {75:2} They believed the time foretold by the Lord to Abraham had come to pass, so they armed themselves with swords and armor, trusting in their strength. {75:3} With no provisions except silver and gold, they planned to obtain food from the Philistines, by payment or by force if necessary. {75:4} These men were renowned for their valor; one could chase a thousand, and two could put ten thousand to flight. {75:5} They marched toward Gath and found the shepherds there tending the cattle. {75:6} Asking for sheep to eat, they were denied, and when they attempted to take them by force, the shepherds called for help. {75:7} The men of Gath armed themselves and prepared for battle against the children of Ephraim. {75:8} They clashed in the valley of Gath, resulting in heavy casualties on both sides. {75:9} By the second day, the Philistines from neighboring cities joined the fight against Ephraim. {75:10} Exhausted and starving after three days without bread, the Ephraimites were defeated, with only ten men escaping alive. {75:11} This defeat was seen as a consequence of their disobedience to the Lord's timing in leaving Egypt. {75:12} Many Philistines also perished, and their bodies were buried in their cities, but the Ephraimites' dead remained unburied in the valley of Gath, filling it with bones. {75:13} Those who survived returned to Egypt and recounted their ordeal to the other Israelites. {75:14} Ephraim mourned deeply, and in time, his wife bore him a son whom he named Beriah, meaning "misfortune," reflecting the sorrow in his household.

{76:1} Moses, the son of Amram, continued to rule as king in the land of Cush, governing with justice, righteousness, and integrity. {76:2} The people of Cush respected and admired Moses throughout his reign, fearing his authority deeply. {76:3} In the 40th year of his rule, Moses sat on his throne with Queen Adoniah and his nobles around him. {76:4} Adoniah questioned the assembly, challenging why they had allowed Moses to reign without participating in their customs for so long. {76:5} She proposed her son Menacrus as a better ruler, someone of their own bloodline, unlike Moses who hailed from Egypt. {76:6} The people and nobles of Cush agreed with Adoniah's words. {76:7} Menacrus, son of Kikianus, was crowned king, and the people hesitated to harm Moses due to their oath and the Lord's protection over him. {76:8} Instead, they honored Moses with many gifts and sent him away respectfully. {76:9} Moses left Cush and returned home, ending his 66-year reign, as the Lord had ordained to bring Israel out of the affliction of Ham's descendants. {76:10} Moses sought refuge in Midian, fearing Pharaoh's vengeance, and settled near a well. {76:11} There, he encountered the seven daughters of Reuel, Midian's shepherd, who were harassed by other shepherds. {76:12} Moses defended them and watered their flock, earning their gratitude. {76:13} The daughters told their father, who invited Moses home, and they shared a meal together. {76:14} Moses recounted his exile from Egypt and his reign in Cush for forty years before being ousted with honor. {76:15} Hearing this, Reuel decided to detain Moses to appease Cush, placing him in prison for ten years. {76:16} Zipporah, Reuel's daughter, showed compassion to Moses during his imprisonment, providing him with sustenance. {76:17} Meanwhile, the Israelites remained enslaved in Egypt, enduring harsh labor under Pharaoh's relentless oppression. {76:18} The Lord responded to the cries of his people, afflicting Pharaoh with a severe plague of leprosy. {76:19} Despite this, Pharaoh's heart remained hardened, and he intensified the Israelites' suffering with even harsher demands. {76:20} Seeking a cure, Pharaoh's advisors suggested using the blood of Israelite infants. {76:21} Pharaoh's ministers began forcibly taking Israelite infants daily to use their blood in a futile attempt to heal him. {76:22} Three hundred and seventy-five children were sacrificed in this manner, but the plague persisted and worsened. {76:23} Pharaoh's affliction intensified into a painful boil, and he remained unrepentant in his cruelty toward the Israelites. {76:24} Ten years passed with Pharaoh suffering these plagues, yet his heart remained hardened against releasing the Israelites from bondage. {76:25} At the end of a decade, the Lord inflicted Pharaoh with a terminal illness, causing him excruciating pain. {76:26} Pharaoh, desperate to assert his authority, attempted to visit the Israelites in Goshen but suffered a fatal accident when his horse threw him into a ravine. {76:27} Severely injured, Pharaoh was carried back to Egypt, where he realized his end was near. {76:28} Queen Aparanith mourned beside him, joined by his nobles and servants in his final moments. {76:29} Advised by his counselors, Pharaoh appointed his son Adikam, a wise but physically unimpressive man, as his successor. {76:30} Adikam married Gedudah and fathered several children, establishing his lineage as the rulers of Egypt. {76:31} Pharaoh's illness and death were seen as divine retribution for his cruelty towards the Israelites.

{77:1} Adikam ascended to the throne of Egypt at the age of twenty and ruled for four years. {77:2} This was in the 206th year since Israel had come to Egypt, but Adikam's reign was shorter than his predecessors'. {77:3} His father Melol had ruled for ninety-four years but suffered a decade of illness before his death due to his wickedness. {77:4} Adikam was given the title Pharaoh, following the Egyptian tradition for kings. {77:5} The wise men of Pharaoh called him Ahuz, a shorter form in the Egyptian language. {77:6} Adikam was notably unattractive, standing only a cubit and a span tall, with a long beard that reached his feet. {77:7} Despite his appearance, he ruled Egypt from his father's throne with cunning and increased oppression over the Israelites. {77:8} He imposed harsher labor on the Israelites in Goshen, appointing taskmasters and setting strict quotas for brick production. {77:9} Any shortfall in production resulted in Israelite infants being taken from their mothers and used in the construction projects, causing great anguish among the people. {77:10} This cruelty continued for many days, with no one showing mercy to the Israelite children. {77:11} The labor under Adikam's reign surpassed the severity endured under his father, leading the Israelites to despair. {77:12} They cried out to God, remembering His covenant with their ancestors Abraham, Isaac, and Jacob. {77:13} Meanwhile, Moses remained imprisoned in Reuel the Midianite's house for ten years, sustained by Zipporah's secret provisions. {77:14} During the first year of Adikam's reign, Zipporah suggested to her father that they inquire about Moses's condition. {77:15} Reuel, unaware that Zipporah had been supporting Moses, was initially skeptical but eventually agreed to check on him. {77:16} They found Moses alive, standing and praying to the God of his ancestors in the dungeon. {77:17} Moses was brought out, cleaned up, and given new clothes and food. {77:18} He then went to pray in Reuel's garden, where he discovered a miraculous staff planted there, bearing the name of the Lord God of hosts. {77:19} This staff had a significant history, passed down from Adam to Abraham, and finally to Moses through a series of divine interventions. {77:20} Reuel, seeing the staff in Moses's hand, was amazed and offered him his daughter Zipporah as a wife.

{78:1} During that time, Baal Channan, the son of Achbor, king of Edom, passed away and was buried in his palace in the land of Edom. {78:2} After his death, the descendants of Esau chose a man named Hadad from Edom and made him their king in place of Baal Channan. {78:3} Hadad ruled over the Edomites for forty-eight years. {78:4} During his reign, he planned to conquer the children of Moab to subjugate them under Esau's descendants, but the Moabites anticipated this and swiftly appointed a king from among their own people. {78:5} They gathered a large army and sought aid from their brethren, the children of Ammon, to oppose King Hadad of Edom. {78:6} When Hadad learned of this coalition against him, he became fearful and refrained from attacking the Moabites. {78:7} Meanwhile, Moses, son of Amram, married Zipporah, daughter of Reuel the Midianite, while living in Midian. {78:8} Zipporah followed the righteous ways of the daughters of Jacob, embodying the virtues of Sarah, Rebecca, Rachel, and Leah. {78:9} Zipporah gave birth to a son whom Moses named Gershom, saying, "I have been a stranger in a foreign land," but Moses did not circumcise him as Reuel had not commanded it. {78:10} Later, she bore another son whom Moses named Eliezer, declaring, "The God of my fathers was my help, delivering me from Pharaoh's sword," and Moses circumcised him. {78:11} Meanwhile, Pharaoh of Egypt intensified the Israelites' labor, making their burdens heavier. {78:12} He decreed that the Israelites must gather their own straw for brickmaking while maintaining their daily quota of bricks. {78:13} This caused great distress among the Israelites, who cried out to the Lord because of their suffering. {78:14} God heard their cries and saw their oppression at the hands of the Egyptians. {78:15} He remembered His covenant with Abraham, Isaac, and Jacob, and resolved to deliver His people from Egypt's affliction, leading them to inherit the land of Canaan.

{79:1} During that time, Moses was tending the flock of his father-in-law Reuel, beyond the wilderness of Sin, with the staff he had received from him in hand. {79:2} One day, a young goat from the flock wandered off, and Moses pursued it until he reached the mountain of God, Horeb. {79:3} There, the Lord appeared to him in a bush that was engulfed in flames yet not consumed by them. {79:4} Moses was astonished and approached the bush, and from within the fire, the Lord called out to him, instructing him to return to Egypt and demand that Pharaoh release the Israelites from bondage. {79:5} The Lord assured Moses that those who sought his life were no longer a threat, and instructed him to speak directly to Pharaoh about letting the Israelites go. {79:6} God also showed Moses signs and wonders he would perform in Egypt to convince Pharaoh and his people of his divine mission. {79:7} Moses obeyed God's command and returned to his father-in-law Reuel to inform him of these events, and Reuel blessed him, bidding him farewell. {79:8} Moses set out for Egypt with his wife and sons, but on their journey, an angel of God confronted him, seeking to kill him because he had not circumcised his firstborn son as per the covenant with Abraham. {79:9} Zipporah realized the danger and circumcised her son Gershom with a sharp stone, thus averting the threat from Moses and her son. {79:10} Meanwhile, in Egypt, Aaron, Moses's brother, was by the riverside when the Lord appeared to him and instructed him to go and meet Moses in the wilderness. {79:11} Aaron found Moses at the mountain of God, Horeb, and greeted him warmly. {79:12} When Aaron saw Zipporah and her children, he inquired about them, and Moses explained that they were his family given by God in Midian. {79:13} Aaron was troubled by their presence, leading him to advise Moses to send them back to their father's house. {79:14} Zipporah and her children returned to her father Reuel's house, where they stayed until the time came for the Lord to deliver his people from Egypt through Moses and Aaron. {79:15} Moses and Aaron gathered the Israelites and delivered the Lord's message to them, filling them with great joy and hope. {79:16} The next day, Moses and Aaron went to Pharaoh's palace, holding the staff of God in their hands. {79:17} At the king's gate, two fierce lions guarded the entrance, restrained only by iron instruments, allowing only those authorized by the king to pass. {79:18} Moses boldly lifted the staff and released the lions, which followed him and Aaron into the palace, behaving with joy like a dog greeting its master. {79:19} Witnessing this, Pharaoh was astonished and frightened, for Moses and Aaron appeared with an aura resembling divine beings. {79:20} Pharaoh questioned them, asking what they sought, and they replied that the God of the Hebrews had sent them to demand the release of his people. {79:21} Pharaoh, taken aback, requested a day to consider their demand, and Moses and Aaron agreed to return the next day as he instructed. {79:22} Meanwhile, Pharaoh consulted his magicians, including Balaam, Jannes, and Jambres, seeking their advice. {79:23} They were informed of Moses and Aaron's message and how they had miraculously dealt with the lions at the gate. {79:24} Balaam reassured Pharaoh that Moses and Aaron were merely skilled magicians like themselves. {79:25} Pharaoh summoned Moses and Aaron the next morning and challenged them to perform a miraculous sign to prove their divine authority. {79:26} Aaron threw down his staff, which transformed into a serpent before Pharaoh and his courtiers. {79:27} The magicians replicated this feat with their own rods, turning them into serpents as well. {79:28} However, Aaron's serpent swiftly devoured the serpents of the magicians, showcasing a greater power. {79:29} Pharaoh, still skeptical, consulted the royal records seeking any mention of the Hebrews' God but found none. {79:30} Addressing Moses and Aaron, Pharaoh acknowledged their magical abilities but remained unconvinced of their divine mandate. {79:31} He agreed to a test where both parties would restore their rods to their original state, and if Aaron's rod swallowed theirs, he would accept their authority. {79:32} Aaron's rod indeed swallowed the rods of the magicians, demonstrating God's superior power. {79:33} Despite witnessing this, Pharaoh remained defiant, refusing to acknowledge the God of the Hebrews. {79:34} He challenged Moses and Aaron to prove the strength and authority of their God further. {79:35} They explained how God had created everything from heaven to earth, from seas to living creatures, and even formed Pharaoh himself. {79:36} They warned Pharaoh that unless he let the Israelites go, God's wrath would strike Egypt with plagues or warfare. {79:37} Angered by their words, Pharaoh dismissed Moses and Aaron and intensified the Israelites' forced labor, making their lives even more difficult than before. {79:38} Moses returned to the Lord, questioning why the situation had worsened since he had spoken to Pharaoh as instructed. {79:39} The Lord assured Moses that with a mighty hand and great plagues, Pharaoh would indeed release the Israelites from Egypt. {79:40} So Moses and Aaron remained among their brethren, the Israelites, in Egypt. {79:41} Meanwhile, the Egyptians continued to embitter the lives of the Israelites with harsh labor and oppression.

{80:1} After two years, the Lord sent Moses again to Pharaoh to demand the release of the children of Israel from Egypt. {80:2} Moses went to Pharaoh's palace and delivered the Lord's message, but Pharaoh stubbornly refused to listen, prompting God to unleash powerful plagues upon Egypt and its people. {80:3} Through Aaron, the Lord turned all the waters of Egypt into blood, including streams and rivers, so that every source of water became undrinkable and unusable. {80:4} Egyptians who attempted to drink or use water found it turned into blood, even when cooking or kneading dough. {80:5} The land was in turmoil as all water sources were contaminated. {80:6} Next, the Lord sent a plague of frogs that infested every corner of Egypt, entering their houses and affecting their daily lives. {80:7} Egyptians found frogs in their beds, in their cooking pots, and even in their bodies as they drank water contaminated with frogs. {80:8} Despite this, Pharaoh remained defiant, and the plagues continued. {80:9} The Lord then sent a plague of lice, covering both man and beast in Egypt, causing great discomfort and distress. {80:10} The lice spread throughout Egypt, affecting everyone from the poorest to the king himself. {80:11} Yet Pharaoh's heart remained hardened, and the Lord sent more plagues. {80:12} God unleashed various wild animals that ravaged Egypt, destroying crops, livestock, and causing widespread devastation. {80:13} The Egyptians suffered from fiery serpents, scorpions, mice, and other creatures that brought further anguish. {80:14} Flies, hornets, fleas, bugs, and gnats swarmed the land, tormenting the Egyptians relentlessly. {80:15} These pests invaded homes, eyes, and ears, exacerbating the misery of the people. {80:16} When the Egyptians sought refuge indoors, the Lord sent the Sulanuth from the sea, a creature that could stretch its arms into homes and unlock doors, allowing more pests to enter.

{80:17} Even as the Egyptians tried to escape, they were haunted by these plagues. {80:18} Then God sent a deadly pestilence that killed the cattle of the Egyptians while sparing those of the Israelites in Goshen. {80:19} The Egyptians also suffered from painful boils and skin infections, causing their flesh to rot and decay. {80:20} Despite these afflictions, Pharaoh remained obstinate, and the plagues intensified. {80:21} The Lord unleashed a devastating hailstorm mixed with fire that destroyed crops and animals throughout Egypt. {80:22} The hail and fire killed both people and beasts caught outside, decimating their numbers. {80:23} Following the hail, the Lord sent a swarm of locusts that devoured whatever the hail had spared, leaving the land barren. {80:24} Though the locusts brought further devastation, the Egyptians tried to salvage what they could for sustenance. {80:25} Then the Lord sent a strong wind that swept away the locusts, clearing them from Egypt entirely. {80:26} Next, God plunged Egypt into darkness for three days, a darkness so thick that it could be felt, bringing life to a standstill. {80:27} Amidst this darkness, many Egyptians who defied the Lord perished, while the Israelites were spared. {80:28} The darkness lifted, and the Lord instructed Moses and Aaron to prepare the Israelites for the Passover, assuring them of divine protection. {80:29} That night, the Lord struck down all the firstborn in Egypt, both man and beast, causing great mourning and despair throughout the land. {80:30} Pharaoh and his people were overwhelmed with grief as death swept through every household, sparing none. {80:31} Even the images and relics of the firstborn in Egypt were destroyed, intensifying the sorrow. {80:32} Pharaoh, in anguish, sought Moses and Aaron, begging them to leave with all the Israelites and their possessions, fearing further devastation. {80:33} The Egyptians urged the Israelites to depart quickly, laden with riches as a parting gift, fulfilling the promise made to Abraham. {80:34} The Israelites, however, delayed their departure, insisting on taking valuables from the Egyptians who willingly gave them away. {80:35} Moses also retrieved Joseph's coffin from the Nile, and each Israelite took their father's coffin with them as they prepared to leave Egypt.

{81:1} The children of Israel departed from Rameses to Succoth, totaling about six hundred thousand men on foot, not counting women and children. {81:2} They were accompanied by a diverse multitude and large herds of livestock. {81:3} The Israelites had lived in Egypt for two hundred and ten years, enduring harsh labor. {81:4} At the end of this time, the Lord led them out of Egypt with a mighty hand. {81:5} They journeyed from Rameses, Goshen, and Egypt, and camped at Succoth on the fifteenth day of the first month. {81:6} Meanwhile, the Egyptians buried their firstborn whom the Lord had struck down, mourning for three days. {81:7} From Succoth, the Israelites moved to Etham at the edge of the wilderness. {81:8} Three days after burying their dead, the Egyptians regretted letting Israel go and mobilized to bring them back to slavery. {81:9} They debated among themselves whether to force Israel back or fight them if they refused. {81:10} Upon seeing the Israelites feasting and celebrating, the Egyptians questioned why they hadn't returned to their masters after promising a brief journey for sacrifice. {81:11} Moses and Aaron explained that the Lord commanded them to leave Egypt for a land of promise, not to return. {81:12} Incensed, the Egyptian nobles prepared to confront Israel. {81:13} However, the Lord strengthened the hearts of the Israelites, who fought back fiercely against the Egyptians. {81:14} The Egyptians fled, suffering heavy losses at the hands of Israel. {81:15} The Egyptian nobles returned to Pharaoh, reporting that Israel had escaped and would not return. {81:16} Hearing this, Pharaoh and his people regretted letting Israel go and resolved to pursue them. {81:17} The Lord hardened the hearts of the Egyptians to pursue Israel, leading them towards their own destruction at the Red Sea. {81:18} Pharaoh gathered a vast army and set out with all his forces, leaving only the women and children behind. {81:19} They pursued Israel and caught up with them encamped by the Red Sea. {81:20} Seeing the Egyptians approaching, the Israelites were filled with fear and cried out to the Lord. {81:21} The Israelites divided into four groups: one considered surrendering to the sea, another wanted to return to Egypt, a third prepared to fight, and the fourth called upon the Lord for deliverance. {81:22} Moses prayed to the Lord, who instructed him to stretch out his rod over the sea. {81:23} Moses did so, and the sea miraculously parted, allowing the Israelites to pass through on dry ground. {81:24} When the Egyptians pursued, the waters returned and engulfed them, drowning Pharaoh's entire army. {81:25} Only Pharaoh survived, acknowledging the power of the Lord and believing in Him. {81:26} The Lord commanded an angel to take Pharaoh to Nineveh, where he ruled for many years. {81:27} On that day, the Lord delivered Israel from Egypt, and the Israelites witnessed the mighty hand of God in their deliverance. {81:28} In gratitude, Moses and the Israelites sang a song of praise to the Lord for His victory over the Egyptians. {81:29} Afterward, the Israelites journeyed to Marah, where the Lord gave them statutes and judgments. {81:30} They continued to Elim, with its twelve springs and seventy palm trees, where they camped and rested. {81:31} From Elim, they journeyed to the wilderness of Sin on the fifteenth day of the second month since leaving Egypt. {81:32} There, the Lord provided manna for the Israelites to eat daily. {81:33} They ate manna throughout their forty-year journey in the wilderness until they reached the land of Canaan. {81:34} Moving on from the wilderness of Sin, they camped in Alush. {81:35} They then moved to Rephidim, where they encountered Amalek and engaged in a fierce battle. {81:36} The Lord granted victory to Israel over Amalek through Moses and Joshua. {81:37} Moses recorded these events in a book and commanded Israel to remember and ultimately eradicate the memory of Amalek from under heaven.

{82:1} After leaving Rephidim, the children of Israel camped in the wilderness of Sinai in the third month since leaving Egypt. {82:2} Reuel, Moses' father-in-law, came with his daughter Zipporah and her two sons upon hearing of the Lord's mighty deeds in delivering Israel from Egypt. {82:3} Reuel found Moses at the mountain of God in the wilderness and was warmly received. {82:4} Moses honored his father-in-law, and Reuel stayed among the Israelites for an extended period, coming to know the Lord. {82:5} In the third month of Israel's journey, on the sixth day, the Lord gave them the Ten Commandments on Mount Sinai. {82:6} All Israel heard these commandments and rejoiced greatly in the Lord that day. {82:7} The glory of the Lord descended upon Mount Sinai, calling Moses into the midst of a cloud, where he ascended the mountain. {82:8} Moses remained on the mountain forty days and nights, receiving instructions from the Lord regarding statutes and judgments for Israel. {82:9} The Lord inscribed these commandments on two stone tablets, which He gave to Moses to convey to the Israelites. {82:10} After forty days, the Lord completed speaking to Moses and gave him the stone tablets inscribed by God's own finger. {82:11} As Moses delayed, the Israelites, fearing his absence, urged Aaron to make them a god to lead them, and Aaron crafted a golden calf. {82:12} The Lord, seeing their idolatry, instructed Moses to descend immediately, declaring His intent to punish the people for their stiff-necked rebellion. {82:13} Moses interceded for the people, pleading with the Lord not to destroy them. {82:14} Descending with the tablets of stone, Moses encountered the idolatrous scene and in anger shattered the tablets. {82:15} He destroyed the golden calf, scattered its ashes in water, and made the Israelites drink it as punishment. {82:16} About three thousand men died that day due to their idolatry and its consequences. {82:17} The next day, Moses offered to make atonement for the people's sin and returned to the Lord on the mountain for another forty days and nights. {82:18} During this time, Moses pleaded on behalf of Israel, and the Lord listened to his prayers. {82:19} The Lord instructed Moses to prepare two new stone tablets for Him to rewrite the Ten Commandments. {82:20} Moses obeyed, hewing the tablets and returning to Mount Sinai, where the Lord rewrote the commandments. {82:21} Moses continued with the Lord for another forty days and nights, receiving further instructions on statutes and judgments for Israel. {82:22} The Lord commanded Moses to instruct the Israelites to construct a sanctuary where His presence would dwell among them. {82:23} The Lord showed Moses the pattern of the sanctuary and its furnishings. {82:24} After forty days, Moses descended with the new tablets, given by the Lord. {82:25} He conveyed the Lord's words, teaching the Israelites laws, statutes, and judgments. {82:26} Moses instructed them to build the sanctuary as commanded by the Lord. {82:27} All skilled workers among the Israelites contributed materials for the sanctuary, including gold, silver, and bronze. {82:28} Wise-hearted men crafted the sanctuary, its furniture, and vessels according to the Lord's instructions through Moses. {82:29} The sanctuary and its furnishings were completed within five months as the Lord had commanded. {82:30} The Israelites presented the completed sanctuary to Moses, matching the pattern shown to him by the Lord. {82:31} Moses inspected the work and blessed the people for their obedience to the Lord's commands.

{83:1} In the twelfth month, on the twenty-third day, Moses consecrated Aaron and his sons, dressing them in their priestly garments and anointing them as the Lord had commanded. Moses also presented the offerings the Lord had instructed him to bring on that day. {83:2} Moses then instructed Aaron and his sons to remain at the entrance of the tabernacle for seven days, following the Lord's command. {83:3} Aaron and his sons obeyed, staying as directed for the full seven days. {83:4} On the eighth day of the first month, in the second year since leaving Egypt, Moses erected the sanctuary, assembling all its furniture and following every detail of the Lord's instructions. {83:5} Moses called Aaron and his sons to offer the prescribed burnt offering and sin offering for themselves and for the people of Israel, as commanded by the Lord. {83:6} On that same day, Aaron's sons Nadab and Abihu, in disobedience, offered unauthorized fire before the Lord, and fire came out from the Lord's presence and consumed them, leading to their death. {83:7} After completing the construction of the sanctuary, the leaders of Israel began offering their gifts for the dedication of the altar. {83:8} Each prince of Israel brought offerings on a designated day, continuing for twelve days. {83:9} Their offerings included silver chargers and bowls filled with fine flour mixed with oil for a grain offering, along with a golden spoon full of incense. {83:10} They also brought various animals for burnt offerings, sin offerings, and peace offerings, as prescribed. {83:11} Each day, one prince presented his offerings before the Lord. {83:12} On the thirteenth day of the month, Moses commanded the Israelites to observe the Passover according to the Lord's commandment. {83:13} The children of Israel kept the Passover on the fourteenth day of the month, as commanded by Moses. {83:14} In the second month, on the first day, the Lord instructed Moses to conduct a census of all males twenty years old and upward, along with Aaron and the twelve princes of Israel. {83:15} Moses and Aaron, with the princes, numbered the Israelites in the wilderness of Sinai. {83:16} The total count of Israelite males from twenty years old and upward was six hundred and three thousand, five hundred and fifty, excluding the Levites. {83:17} The Levites were counted separately, totaling twenty-two thousand two hundred and seventy-three males from one month old and upward. {83:18} Moses assigned duties to the priests and Levites according to the Lord's instructions for serving in the sanctuary. {83:19} On the twentieth day of the month, the cloud lifted from the tabernacle of the testimony, signaling the Israelites to resume their journey from the wilderness of Sinai. {83:20} They traveled for three days until the cloud rested in the wilderness of Paran, where the Lord's anger flared against them for craving meat and complaining. {83:21} The Lord granted their request for meat, which they consumed for a month, but then punished them severely, resulting in many deaths. {83:22} The place where they buried the ones who lusted after meat was named Kibroth Hattaavah. {83:23} Moving from Kibroth Hattaavah, they camped in Hazeroth in the wilderness of Paran. {83:24} While they were in Hazeroth, the Lord's anger burned against Miriam due to her criticism of Moses, and she became leprous, white as snow. {83:25} Miriam was quarantined outside the camp for seven days before being restored from her leprosy. {83:26} After leaving Hazeroth, the Israelites camped in the wilderness of Paran. {83:27} It was then that the Lord instructed Moses to send twelve men, one from each tribe, to explore the land of Canaan. {83:28} The men explored the entire land from the wilderness of Sin to Rehob, returning after forty days to report their findings to Moses and Aaron. {83:29} Ten of the men gave a discouraging report, fearing the inhabitants of the land were too strong to conquer, causing the people to murmur against Moses and Aaron. {83:30} Only Joshua and Caleb urged the people to trust the Lord's promise of victory, affirming that the land was abundant and fertile. {83:31} Despite Joshua and Caleb's encouragement, the Israelites refused to listen and rebelled against the Lord's command. {83:32} The Lord, angered by their lack of faith, swore that none from that generation, except Joshua and Caleb, would enter the promised land. {83:33} Instead, they would wander in the wilderness for forty years until the entire rebellious generation perished. {83:34} The people remained in the wilderness of Paran for an extended period before moving toward the Red Sea.

{84:1} During that time, Korah, a descendant of Levi, son of Kehath, gathered a group of Israelites and rebelled against Moses, Aaron, and the entire congregation. {84:2} The Lord's anger flared against them, and the earth opened its mouth and swallowed Korah, his followers, their households, and all their possessions. {84:3} Following this event, God directed the Israelites to travel around the region of Mount Seir for an extended period. {84:4} It was then that the Lord instructed Moses not to provoke a conflict with the descendants of Esau, as He had given Mount Seir as their inheritance. {84:5} The Edomites had previously defeated the Horites and settled in their land, as the Lord had permitted. {84:6} Therefore, the Lord commanded the Israelites not to engage in battle with their brethren, the Edomites, but instead to purchase food and water from them for sustenance. {84:7} The Israelites followed the Lord's directive in their interactions with the Edomites. {84:8} For nineteen years, the Israelites journeyed through the wilderness, circumnavigating Mount Sinai without disturbing the Edomites, residing peacefully in that area. {84:9} In that period, Latinus, king of Chittim, passed away after ruling for forty-five years, with Abimnas succeeding him and reigning for thirty-eight years. {84:10} The Israelites eventually moved past the territory of the Edomites, reaching the wilderness of Moab after nineteen years of travel. {84:11} It was then that the Lord instructed Moses not to wage war against Moab, for He would not grant any of their land to the Israelites. {84:12} Thus, for nineteen years, the Israelites traveled through the wilderness of Moab without conflict. {84:13} In the thirty-sixth year after leaving Egypt, the Lord stirred the heart of Sihon, king of the Amorites, to wage war against Moab. {84:14} Sihon sent messengers to summon Beor and Balaam, son of Beor, from Mesopotamia to curse Moab and facilitate their defeat. {84:15} They cursed Moab before Sihon, who then waged war against them and conquered the land, including the city of Heshbon. {84:16} Sihon established his rule over Moab, seizing their cities and territories, and placing his officials in Heshbon. {84:17} Beor and Balaam prophesied concerning these events, declaring the fate of Moab, which was fulfilled as they foretold. {84:18} After subjugating Moab, Sihon returned to his own land, leaving the region with many captives and much plunder. {84:19} Sihon rewarded Beor and Balaam with silver and gold before sending them back to Mesopotamia. {84:20} Following these events, the Israelites continued their journey, passing through the wilderness of Moab and then encircling the wilderness of Edom. {84:21} They arrived at the wilderness of Sin in the first month of their fortieth year since leaving Egypt, settling in Kadesh. {84:22} It was in Kadesh that Miriam died and was buried. {84:23} Moses sent messengers to Hadad, king of Edom, requesting passage through their land, promising not to stray into fields or vineyards or drink from their wells, but to stay on the king's highway. {84:24} Edom refused, gathering a large army to prevent the Israelites from passing through their territory. {84:25} As the Lord had commanded earlier, the Israelites avoided conflict with the Edomites and moved away from them. {84:26} Thus, they departed from Kadesh and journeyed until they reached Mount Hor. {84:27} At that time, the Lord instructed Moses that Aaron would die on Mount Hor and would not enter the land promised to the Israelites. {84:28}

Aaron, obeying the Lord's command, ascended Mount Hor in the fortieth year, on the first day of the fifth month, and there he passed away at the age of one hundred and twenty-three years.

{85:1} King Arad of the Canaanites, residing in the southern region, learned that the Israelites had come through the territory where spies had been sent. He mobilized his forces to engage them in battle. {85:2} The Israelites, fearful of Arad's formidable army, considered returning to Egypt. {85:3} They retreated about a three days' journey back to Maserath Beni Jaakon due to their dread of King Arad. {85:4} Unable to move forward, the Israelites remained in Beni Jaakon for thirty days. {85:5} Seeing that the Israelites were unwilling to proceed, the Levites, zealous for the Lord, rose up against their brethren and fought them, resulting in a significant loss of life and forcing the Israelites to return to Mount Hor. {85:6} Meanwhile, King Arad continued preparing for battle against the Israelites. {85:7} In response, Israel made a vow, promising to utterly destroy the Canaanites and their cities if the Lord delivered them into their hands. {85:8} The Lord honored Israel's request, delivering the Canaanites to them. Israel annihilated them and their cities, and the place was called Hormah. {85:9} From Mount Hor, the Israelites journeyed to Oboth, then to Ije-abarim on the border of Moab. {85:10} They sent a request to Moab to pass through their land, but Moab, fearing the Israelites after the fate of the Amorites under Sihon, refused them passage. {85:11} The Lord commanded Israel not to fight against Moab, so they moved away. {85:12} Crossing the border of Moab, they reached the Arnon River, the boundary between Moab and the Amorites, and camped near the wilderness of Kedemoth. {85:13} Israel sent messengers to Sihon, king of the Amorites, asking to pass through his land along the king's highway, but Sihon refused. {85:14} Sihon gathered his people and fought against Israel in Jahaz. {85:15} The Lord gave Sihon into Israel's hand, and they defeated the Amorites, avenging Moab. {85:16} Israel took possession of Sihon's land from Arnon to Jabok, extending toward the Ammonites, and seized all the cities' spoils. {85:17} They conquered all these cities and settled among the Amorites. {85:18} The Israelites then planned to fight against the Ammonites to take their land as well. {85:19} However, the Lord commanded them not to besiege or provoke war with the Ammonites, and Israel obeyed. {85:20} Turning north, the Israelites traveled through Bashan to confront Og, king of Bashan, who assembled a formidable force against them. {85:21} Og was a powerful king, and his son Naaron was even stronger. {85:22} Og devised a plan to defeat Israel, intending to crush them with a massive stone. {85:23} Climbing Mount Jahaz, he lifted a giant stone to throw upon Israel's camp. {85:24} But the angel of the Lord intervened, causing the stone to fall on Og and kill him. {85:25} The Lord reassured Israel not to fear Og, for He had delivered him and his people into their hands, just as He had done with Sihon. {85:26} Moses, accompanied by a small group of Israelites, went to meet Og and struck him down with a stick at his feet. {85:27} Afterward, the Israelites pursued and completely defeated Og and his people. {85:28} Moses then sent spies to Jaazer, a prominent city, and they successfully captured it with the Lord's help. {85:29} The Israelites took possession of the land of the two Amorite kings, sixty cities from the Arnon River to Mount Hermon across the Jordan. {85:30} They journeyed into the plains of Moab near Jericho, on this side of the Jordan River. {85:31} Hearing of Israel's victories over Sihon and Og, the people of Moab grew fearful of them. {85:32} The Moabite elders acknowledged that neither Sihon nor Og, the powerful Amorite kings, could withstand Israel, and they feared for their own survival. {85:33} Distressed, they appointed Balak, son of Zippor, as their king, a man known for his wisdom. {85:34} The Moabites, seeking to secure their safety, made peace with the Midianites, despite previous enmity between them, dating back to Hadad's conquest. {85:35} The elders of Moab and Midian strategized together to protect themselves from Israel. {85:36} They discussed how Israel had defeated Sihon and Og and how they now threatened Moab. {85:37} Learning from their past, they decided to seek the aid of Balaam, son of Beor, who had cursed them in the past, to curse Israel once again. {85:38} Balak, king of Moab, sent messengers to Balaam, urging him to come and curse Israel. {85:39} Balaam, aware of Israel's size and presence, declined Balak's invitation, choosing not to curse Israel against the Lord's will. {85:40} When Balak persisted in requesting Balaam's curse upon Israel, Balaam steadfastly refused, honoring the word of the Lord. {85:41} Eventually, Balak gave up and returned home, and Balaam returned to his land, leaving Moab for Midian. {85:42} The Israelites moved from the plains of Moab and camped by the Jordan near Beth-jesimoth to Abel-shittim, on the edge of Moab's territory. {85:43} While stationed in the plains of Shittim, the Israelites began to engage in immorality with Moabite women. {85:44} The Moabites, fearing the Israelites, strategically positioned their women at the camp's entrance, adorned in finery, to lure the Israelite men away from conflict. {85:45} The plan succeeded as the Israelites were drawn to the Moabite women and began to associate with them. {85:46} When a Hebrew man visited a Moabite tent and desired a woman, the Moabite men would come out and convince him to stay, offering hospitality and fellowship. {85:47} They argued that they were all descendants of Abraham and Lot and should dwell together peacefully. {85:48} Seduced by their words and hospitality, the Hebrew men stayed, eating their food and participating in their rituals. {85:49} Balak, observing the Israelites' integration with Moab, became alarmed and sent messengers to Balaam once more, urging him to come and curse Israel. {85:50} Balaam refused to curse Israel, abiding by the Lord's command, despite Balak's persistent requests. {85:51} The Israelites then moved from the plains of Moab and camped near the Jordan, from Beth-jesimoth to Abel-shittim, at the edge of the Moabite plains. {85:52} While encamped in Shittim, the Israelites fell into immorality with Moabite women. {85:53} The Moabites positioned their women at the entrance to their camp, adorned in gold, silver, and fine clothing, to attract the Israelite men and divert them from conflict. {85:54} The Moabites succeeded in drawing the Israelites, who engaged with their women. {85:55} This act greatly angered the Lord, and He sent a plague among the Israelites, killing twenty-four thousand men. {85:56} Among the Israelites was Zimri, son of Salu from the tribe of Simeon, who publicly joined himself to Cozbi, daughter of Zur, a Midianite chief. {85:57} Phinehas, son of Eleazar the priest, witnessed this act and, in zealous anger for the Lord, took a spear and killed both Zimri and Cozbi, ending the plague.

{86:1} After the plague had passed, the Lord instructed Moses and Eleazar, son of Aaron the priest, saying, {86:2} "Take a census of all the men in Israel who are twenty years old and above, eligible for military service." {86:3} So Moses and Eleazar counted the Israelites according to their families. The total number was seven hundred thousand, seven hundred and thirty men. {86:4} The Levites, however, were not included in this count because the Lord had decreed that those who were numbered in the wilderness of Sinai would not enter the promised land. All of them died except Caleb son of Jephunneh and Joshua son of Nun. {86:5} Following this, the Lord commanded Moses to instruct the Israelites to avenge their brethren who had suffered at the hands of Midian. {86:6} Moses relayed this command, and the Israelites selected twelve thousand men, one thousand from each tribe, to execute vengeance upon Midian. {86:7} They waged war against Midian, killing every male, including the five princes of Midian and Balaam son of Beor. {86:8} The Israelites also took the women, children, and livestock of Midian as captives, along with all their possessions. {86:9} They gathered the spoils and brought them to Moses and Eleazar in the plains of Moab. {86:10} Moses, Eleazar, and the leaders of the congregation went out to meet them with joy. {86:11} They distributed the spoils taken from Midian, thus avenging the Israelites' brethren who had been wronged by Midian.

{87:1} At that time, the Lord spoke to Moses, saying, "Your days are coming to an end. Take Joshua son of Nun, your assistant, and bring him to the tabernacle. I will commission him." Moses obeyed the Lord's command. {87:2} The Lord appeared in the tabernacle in a pillar of cloud, which stood at the entrance. {87:3} The Lord instructed Joshua, saying, "Be strong and courageous, for you will lead the children of Israel into the land that I promised them. I will be with you." {87:4} Moses encouraged Joshua, saying, "Be strong and courageous. You will bring the Israelites into their inheritance, and the Lord will not leave you nor forsake you. Do not be afraid or discouraged." {87:5} Moses then summoned all the children of Israel and reminded them of all the good that the Lord had done for them in the wilderness. {87:6} "Therefore, observe all the words of this law and walk in the way of the Lord your God. Do not turn aside from His commandments, either to the right or to the left." {87:7} Moses taught the Israelites statutes, judgments, and laws as the Lord had commanded him for their conduct in the land. {87:8} He instructed them in the ways of the Lord and His laws, which were written in the Book of the Law given to the Israelites by Moses. {87:9} After Moses finished giving these commands to the children of Israel, the Lord spoke to him, saying, "Go up to Mount Abarim and die there, as your brother Aaron was gathered to his people." {87:10} Moses went up to Mount Nebo as commanded by the Lord, and he died there in the land of Moab, forty years after the Israelites left Egypt. {87:11} The Israelites mourned for Moses in the plains of Moab for thirty days, completing their period of weeping and mourning for him.

{88:1} After Moses died, the Lord spoke to Joshua, saying, {88:2} "Rise up and cross the Jordan River to the land which I am giving to the children of Israel. You will lead them to inherit this land." {88:3} The Lord promised Joshua, "Every place where you set foot will be yours, from the wilderness of Lebanon to the great Euphrates River. This will be your territory." {88:4} "No one will be able to stand against you all the days of your life. Just as I was with Moses, I will be with you. Be strong and courageous, and faithfully observe all the law that Moses commanded you. Do not turn from it to the right or to the left, so that you may prosper in all that you do." {88:5} Joshua commanded the officers of Israel, saying, "Go through the camp and tell the people, 'Prepare provisions for yourselves, for in three days you will cross the Jordan to take possession of the land that the Lord your God is giving you.'" {88:6} The officers of Israel carried out Joshua's orders, instructing the people to prepare as commanded. {88:7} Joshua sent two men to spy out Jericho, and they went and scouted the city. {88:8} After seven days, they returned to Joshua in the camp and reported, "The Lord has delivered the entire land into our hands; the people are filled with fear because of us." {88:9} So Joshua and all Israel rose early and set out from Shittim. They crossed the Jordan, and Joshua was eighty-two years old at that time. {88:10} They crossed over on the tenth day of the first month and camped at Gilgal on the eastern border of Jericho. {88:11} There, in the plains of Jericho, they observed the Passover on the fourteenth day of the month, as prescribed in the law of Moses. {88:12} On the day after the Passover, the manna ceased, and from then on they ate the produce of the land of Canaan. {88:13} Jericho was tightly shut up because of the Israelites; no one went out and no one came in. {88:14} On the first day of the second month, the Lord said to Joshua, "Look, I have given Jericho into your hand, along with its king and all its mighty warriors. {88:15} All your fighting men shall march around the city once a day for six days. {88:16} The priests shall blow the trumpets, and when you hear the sound, all the people shall shout loudly. The city walls will collapse, and each man shall charge straight in." {88:17} Joshua followed the Lord's instructions precisely. {88:18} On the seventh day, they marched around the city seven times, and the priests blew the trumpets. {88:19} Joshua said to the people, "Shout! For the Lord has given you the city. {88:20} But the city and all that is in it shall be devoted to the Lord for destruction. Keep yourselves from the accursed things, lest you make yourselves accursed by taking them and bring trouble upon the camp of Israel. {88:21} However, all the silver, gold, and articles of bronze and iron are holy to the Lord; they shall go into the treasury of the Lord." {88:22} The people shouted and the walls of Jericho collapsed. They charged straight in and captured the city, destroying everything in it—men and women, young and old, cattle, sheep, and donkeys—with the edge of the sword. {88:23} They burned the whole city with fire, except for the silver, gold, bronze, and iron articles, which they put into the treasury of the Lord. {88:24} Joshua pronounced a solemn oath at that time: "Cursed before the Lord is the one who undertakes to rebuild this city of Jericho. He will lay its foundation at the cost of his firstborn son; he will set up its gates at the cost of his youngest." {88:25} After the destruction of Jericho, Joshua sent men to spy out the city of Ai. {88:26} They scouted it and reported back to Joshua, "Not all the people will need to go up against Ai. Send about two or three thousand men to attack it, for the people there are few." {88:27} Joshua sent the chosen men of Israel, about three thousand strong, to go up and attack Ai. {88:28} The men of Ai fought back fiercely and killed thirty-six Israelites, chasing them from the city gates. {88:29} When Joshua and the elders saw this, they tore their clothes and fell facedown before the ark of the Lord until evening, throwing dust on their heads in sorrow. {88:30} Joshua cried out, "Why, Lord, did you ever bring this people across the Jordan to deliver us into the hands of the Amorites to destroy us? If only we had been content to stay on the other side of the Jordan! {88:31} Now the Canaanites and all the people of the land will hear about it and surround us and wipe out our name from the earth. What will you do for your own great name?" {88:32} The Lord said to Joshua, "Stand up! What are you doing down on your face? {88:33} Israel has sinned; they have violated my covenant, which I commanded them to keep. They have taken some of the devoted things; they have stolen, they have lied, they have put them with their own possessions. {88:34} Therefore the Israelites cannot stand against their enemies; they turn their backs and run because they have been made liable to destruction. I will not be with you anymore unless you destroy whatever among you is devoted to destruction. {88:35} Joshua gathered the people together, and they brought forward the Urim before the Lord. {88:36} Then he had the tribe of Judah come forward, and the clan of the Zerahites was taken. {88:37} Joshua said to Achan, "My son, give glory to the Lord, the God of Israel, and honor him. Tell me what you have done; do not hide it from me." {88:38} Achan replied, "It is true! I have sinned against the Lord, the God of Israel. This is what I have done: {88:39} I saw a beautiful robe from Babylonia, two hundred shekels of silver and a bar of gold weighing fifty shekels. I coveted them and took them. They are hidden in the ground inside my tent, with the silver underneath." {88:40} So Joshua sent messengers, and they ran to the tent, and there it was, hidden in his tent, with the silver underneath. {88:41} They took the things from the tent, brought them to Joshua and all the Israelites, and spread them out before the Lord. {88:42} Joshua, together with all Israel, took Achan son of Zerah, the silver, the robe, the gold bar, his sons and daughters, his cattle, donkeys and sheep, his tent and all that he had, to the Valley of Achor. {88:43} Joshua said, "Why have you brought this trouble on us? The Lord will bring trouble on you today." Then all Israel stoned him, and after they had stoned the rest, they burned them. {88:44} Over Achan they heaped up a large pile of rocks, which remains to this day. Then the Lord turned from his fierce anger. Therefore that place has been called the Valley of Achor ever since. {88:45} Afterward, Joshua returned with all Israel to the camp at Gilgal. {88:46} Then the Israelites took an oath at Mizpah, saying, "No one of us will give his daughter in marriage to a Benjamite." {88:47} The men of Israel had taken an oath at Mizpah: "Not one of us will give his daughter in marriage to a Benjamite."

{89:1} Joshua proclaimed this song on the day the Lord delivered the Amorites into his and Israel's hands. In front of all Israel, he declared, {89:2} "You have done mighty deeds, O Lord, unparalleled in greatness. I will sing praises to your name forever." {89:3} "You are my stronghold, my fortress, my deliverer. With gratitude, I sing a new song to you; you are the source of my salvation." {89:4} "All the kings of the earth will praise you, O Lord. The rulers of the world will join in singing your praises. The people of Israel will rejoice in your salvation; they will sing and exalt your power." {89:5} "We trusted in you, O Lord; you are our God. You have been our refuge and strength against our enemies." {89:6} "When we cried out to you, you answered us; you delivered us from our foes. With your strength, you filled our hearts with joy." {89:7} "You marched out for our salvation, wielding your mighty arm to redeem your people. From your holy abode in the heavens, you answered us and saved us from overwhelming odds." {89:8} "The sun and moon stood still at your command, as you fought against our enemies in your wrath." {89:9} "The earth's leaders stood firm, and the kings of nations assembled for battle, but they were no match for your presence." {89:10} "In your anger, you rose against them and unleashed your wrath. You destroyed them utterly and wiped them out." {89:11} "Nations were consumed in your fury; kingdoms crumbled under your wrath. You struck down kings in your fierce anger." {89:12} "You poured out your fury upon them; your relentless anger overwhelmed them. You turned their wickedness back upon them and destroyed them in their own evil." {89:13} "They set traps, but they themselves were ensnared. Their own schemes backfired, and they were caught in their own net." {89:14} "You were ready to strike at all our enemies who boasted of their swords and strength. You humbled them and brought them down in your wrath." {89:15} "The earth trembled at the sound of your judgment upon them. You did not spare their lives; you brought them down to the grave." {89:16} "You pursued them in your furious storm; you consumed them in your raging tempest. You turned their rain into hailstones, and they were cast into deep pits from which they could not rise." {89:17} "Their corpses lay like refuse in the streets." {89:18} "You destroyed them utterly in your wrath; you saved your people with your mighty power." {89:19} "Therefore, we rejoice in you; our souls exult in your salvation." {89:20} "We will speak of your power and sing praises to your wondrous deeds." {89:21} "For you saved us from our enemies; you delivered us from those who rose against us and crushed them beneath our feet." {89:22} "So shall all your enemies perish, O Lord; the wicked will be scattered like chaff by the wind, while your beloved will flourish like trees planted by streams of water." {89:23} After Joshua and all Israel had defeated these kings and left none remaining, they returned to their camp in Gilgal. {89:24} The five kings who had fled and hidden in a cave were discovered. {89:25} When Joshua was informed of their hiding place, he stationed guards at the cave's entrance to prevent their escape. {89:26} Joshua gathered all Israel and commanded the officers of the army to place their feet on the necks of these kings. {89:27} Joshua declared, "Just as the Lord has done to our enemies, so shall we do to all who oppose us." {89:28} He ordered that the kings be put to death and their bodies thrown into the cave, sealing it with large stones. {89:29} Joshua and the Israelites then proceeded to Makkedah, where they struck down every living being and utterly destroyed the city, doing to its king as they had done to Jericho. {89:30} They moved on to Libnah, fought against it, and with the Lord's help, overcame it completely. {89:31} From there, they advanced to Lachish, where Horam king of Gaza came to aid the men of Lachish, but Joshua defeated him and his people, leaving none alive. {89:32} Joshua captured Lachish and its inhabitants, treating them as he had treated Libnah. {89:33} Next, Joshua turned to Eglon, seized it, and struck down all who lived there. {89:34} He proceeded to Hebron, fought against it, and destroyed it, along with its king and people, as he had done to Jericho. {89:35} Then Joshua and all Israel attacked Debir, killing everyone and annihilating it, just as they had done in Hebron and other cities. {89:36} Joshua wiped out every living soul there and its king, leaving nothing alive. {89:37} He conquered all the kings of the Amorites from Kadesh-barnea to Gaza, taking their land as the Lord had promised. {89:38} Joshua and all Israel returned to their camp at Gilgal after these victories. {89:39} When Jabin king of Hazor heard what Joshua had done to the Amorite kings, he sent messages to Jobab king of Madon, to the kings of Shimron and Achshaph, and to the other Amorite kings, {89:40} urging them to join forces against Israel before they too were defeated. {89:41} So these kings gathered their armies—seventeen kings in all, along with a vast number of soldiers, horses, and chariots—and assembled at the waters of Merom to wage war against Israel. {89:42} But the Lord said to Joshua, "Do not be afraid of them; by this time tomorrow, I will deliver all of them slain before you. You are to hamstring their horses and burn their chariots with fire." {89:43} Joshua and his warriors launched a surprise attack on them and defeated them, for the Lord had given them into Israel's hands. {89:44} The Israelites pursued and struck down all the kings and their armies, carrying out exactly as the Lord had commanded Joshua. {89:45} Joshua then returned to Hazor and put it to the sword, destroying every living being and burning the city to the ground. {89:46} From there, he moved on to Shimron and Achshaph, destroying them as he had done to Hazor and the other cities. {89:47} Next, he attacked Adullam, killing all who lived there, treating it as he had treated Shimron and Achshaph. {89:48} He continued this campaign against all the kings and cities he had defeated, wiping out every living person. {89:49} The Israelites took their livestock and possessions as plunder, but they put every human to the sword, leaving no survivors. {89:50} They carried out everything that the Lord had commanded Moses, and Joshua led Israel in complete obedience. {89:51} So Joshua and the Israelites conquered the entire land of Canaan, following the Lord's commands, defeating all thirty-one kings. {89:52} They took possession of the land, in addition to the kingdoms of Sihon and Og on the east side of the Jordan, which Moses had previously conquered and given to the Reubenites, Gadites, and half-tribe of Manasseh. {89:53} Joshua conquered all the kings west of the Jordan, giving their lands as an inheritance to the nine and a half tribes of Israel. {89:54} Joshua waged war against these kings for five years, during which he distributed their cities to the Israelites, bringing peace to the land from the battles with the Amorites and Canaanites.

{90:1} In the fifth year after the Israelites crossed the Jordan River and had rested from their battles with the Canaanites, great and fierce conflicts erupted between Edom and the people of Chittim. {90:2} Abianus, the king of Chittim, in the thirty-first year of his reign, led a formidable army to Seir to confront the descendants of Esau. {90:3} Hearing this, Hadad, the king of Edom, gathered a strong force and met Abianus in battle on the plains of Edom. {90:4} The forces of Chittim prevailed over the Edomites, killing twenty-two thousand men, and the remaining Edomites fled in defeat. {90:5} Pursuing them, the Chittimites captured Hadad alive and brought him before Abianus, who ordered his execution. Hadad died in the forty-eighth year of his reign. {90:6} Thereafter, the Chittimites continued their campaign against Edom, inflicting heavy casualties and subjecting Edom to their rule. {90:7} Thus, Edom came under the dominion of Chittim, becoming one kingdom from that time forward. {90:8} Edom remained subservient to Chittim, and Abianus established governors over them, solidifying his control. {90:9} From then on, Edom could no longer assert its independence, as it became fully integrated with the kingdom of Chittim. {90:10} Abianus returned to Chittim, where he fortified his rule and built a grand palace for his royal residence, reigning securely over both Chittim and Edom. {90:11} Meanwhile, as the Israelites had driven out the Canaanites and Amorites, Joshua grew old and advanced in years. {90:12} The Lord spoke to Joshua, reminding him that much of the land still awaited distribution among the tribes. {90:13} Joshua, in obedience to the Lord's command, proceeded to allocate the land as inheritance to the nine and a half tribes. {90:14} The tribe of Levi, however, received no land as their inheritance, for the offerings to the Lord were their portion, as Moses had decreed. {90:15} Mount Hebron was given to Caleb as a special inheritance, fulfilling the promise made by Moses. {90:16} Joshua then completed the division of the entire land among the tribes of Israel by casting lots, as the Lord had instructed. {90:17} The Levites received cities and pasturelands from the other tribes, fulfilling the Lord's command through Moses. {90:18} Joshua himself was given the city of Timnath-serah in Mount Ephraim by the word of the Lord, where he settled and built the city. {90:19} These divisions were carried out by Eleazar the priest, Joshua, and the tribal leaders at Shiloh, in the presence of the Lord at the entrance to the tent of meeting. {90:20} The Israelites faithfully allotted the land by lot, large and small portions alike, according to the

Lord's command through Moses. {90:21} Each tribe then took possession of its designated territory, fulfilling the Lord's promise. {90:22} After this, Joshua blessed all the people of Israel, urging them to remain devoted to the Lord. {90:23} With his task complete, Joshua dismissed the people, who returned to their cities and inherited lands. {90:24} During this time, Abianus, king of Chittim, passed away in the thirty-eighth year of his reign, having ruled over Edom for seven years as well. {90:25} Latinus succeeded him and reigned fifty years, during which he waged campaigns against the inhabitants of Britannia and Kernania, bringing them under tribute. {90:26} Latinus also subdued the rebellious Edomites, ensuring they remained under Chittimite rule. {90:27} For many years, Edom had no king of its own, being governed by Chittim and their king. {90:28} In the twenty-sixth year after crossing the Jordan and the sixty-sixth year since leaving Egypt, Joshua, aged one hundred and eight, gathered the elders, judges, and officers of Israel. {90:29} Addressing them, Joshua recounted how the Lord had delivered them from their enemies and urged them to remain faithful to the law of Moses. {90:30} He warned against mingling with the remaining nations and worshiping their gods, emphasizing their commitment to the Lord. {90:31} The Israelites pledged to serve the Lord faithfully for generations to come, and Joshua made a covenant with them that day. {90:32} After this, Joshua passed away at the age of one hundred and ten, having judged Israel for twenty-eight years. {90:33} Throughout his lifetime, Israel served the Lord, and under Joshua's leadership, they experienced peace and security in their cities. {90:34} Joshua's accomplishments, battles, and admonitions to Israel were recorded in the Book of the Words of Joshua and in the Book of the Wars of the Lord, compiled by Moses, Joshua, and the Israelites. {90:35} The Israelites buried Joshua in Timnath-serah, in his allotted portion of Mount Ephraim. {90:36} Following Joshua's death, Eleazar, the son of Aaron, also passed away and was buried in a hill given to him by his son Phinehas in Mount Ephraim.

{91:1} After Joshua passed away, the Canaanites still remained in the land, prompting the Israelites to decide to drive them out. {91:2} Seeking guidance from the Lord, they asked who should lead the charge against the Canaanites first. The Lord replied, "Judah shall go up." {91:3} Judah then invited Simeon to join them in their territory, and in return, they would assist Simeon in his own territory. Thus, the children of Simeon fought alongside Judah. {91:4} Judah attacked the Canaanites in Bezek and the Lord delivered them into their hands, enabling them to defeat ten thousand men. {91:5} Among those they fought was Adonibezek, whom they captured and mutilated by cutting off his thumbs and great toes. {91:6} Adonibezek acknowledged his fate, having inflicted similar mutilations on seventy kings whom he kept under his table. He died in Jerusalem. {91:7} The men of Simeon also fought against the Canaanites, contributing to their defeat. {91:8} With the Lord's favor, Judah took possession of the hill country, while the children of Joseph went up to Bethel (formerly Luz) and the Lord was with them there as well. {91:9} The children of Joseph spied out Bethel and, with the help of a local informant, attacked the city and conquered it. {91:10} They spared the informant and he went on to build a city called Luz among the Hittites. {91:11} Thus, all the Israelites settled in their respective cities, serving the Lord faithfully during the days of Joshua and the elders who outlived him, witnessing the great works of the Lord on behalf of Israel. {91:12} These elders judged Israel for seventeen years after Joshua's death, leading them in battles against the Canaanites as the Lord cleared the land for the Israelites. {91:13} The Lord fulfilled all his promises to Abraham, Isaac, and Jacob, granting their descendants the land of the Canaanites. {91:14} The Israelites received the entire land of Canaan as the Lord had sworn to their ancestors, enjoying peace and security from their enemies. {91:15} Praise be to the Lord forever. Amen and amen. {91:16} Be strong and courageous, all you who trust in the Lord.

Jubilees

The Book of Jubilees, often referred to as "Lesser Genesis," is a significant work of Jewish pseudepigrapha, which presents itself as a divine revelation given to Moses on Mount Sinai. This text is considered an expansion and reinterpretation of the Genesis and Exodus narratives, filling in chronological gaps and providing additional context to the biblical stories. Written in the second century BCE, the Book of Jubilees offers a unique perspective on Jewish history, law, and ethics, reflecting the theological and cultural milieu of the time. It is characterized by its distinct chronological framework, dividing history into "jubilees" or periods of 49 years, and its emphasis on the observance of the Sabbath and other Jewish festivals. The work is also notable for its detailed genealogies and its emphasis on the purity of the chosen people, which is often expressed through the lens of ritual and moral purity. The Book of Jubilees was highly regarded by the Qumran community, as evidenced by the numerous fragments found among the Dead Sea Scrolls, and it exerted a considerable influence on later Jewish and Christian thought. Its narratives often reinterpret and elaborate on biblical events, providing additional details that are absent in the canonical texts. The Book of Jubilees has been preserved in its entirety in the Ge'ez language, a testament to its importance within the Ethiopian Orthodox Church, which regards it as canonical. Despite its exclusion from the Jewish and most Christian canons, the Book of Jubilees remains a valuable resource for understanding the development of early Jewish thought and the diversity of interpretations surrounding the Hebrew Bible. Its rich textual tradition and the insights it offers into the religious practices and beliefs of ancient Jewish communities make it an essential subject of study for scholars of biblical and intertestamental literature.

{1:1} In the first year after the Israelites left Egypt, on the sixteenth day of the third month, God spoke to Moses, saying, "Come up to Me on Mount Sinai, and I will give you two stone tablets inscribed with the law and commandments that I have written for you to teach." {1:2} Moses ascended the mount of God, where the glory of the Lord dwelt amidst a cloud for six days. {1:3} On the seventh day, God called to Moses from within the cloud, and the glory of the Lord appeared like a consuming fire on the mountaintop. {1:4} Moses remained on the mount for forty days and nights, during which God taught him about the past and future, including the division of days according to the law and testimony. {1:5} God instructed Moses, "Pay close attention to every word I speak to you on this mount. Write them down in a book so that future generations may see how I have not abandoned them despite their transgressions against our covenant established this day on Mount Sinai." {1:6} "When these calamities befall them, they will acknowledge My righteousness in judgment and action, realizing My presence among them." {1:7} "Write down all these words I declare to you today, for I foresee their rebellion and stubbornness before I bring them into the promised land, flowing with milk and honey." {1:8} "They will enjoy prosperity but turn to foreign gods who cannot save them from tribulation, making this a testimony against them." {1:9} "They will forget My commandments, following after Gentiles in uncleanness and shame, serving their idols, which will become a snare and cause great affliction." {1:10} "Many will perish or be captured by enemies because they forsake My ordinances, festivals, sabbaths, and holy places." {1:11} "They will build high places, groves, and idols, sacrificing their children to demons and falling into error of heart." {1:12} "I will send witnesses, but they will reject them, even persecuting those who seek to uphold the law, changing everything for evil in My sight." {1:13} "I will hide My face from them, delivering them into Gentile hands for captivity and suffering, scattering them among nations." {1:14} "They will forget all My laws, commandments, and judgments, neglecting new moons, sabbaths, festivals, and jubilees." {1:15} "Yet, eventually, they will turn back to Me from among the Gentiles with wholehearted devotion, seeking Me earnestly." {1:16} "I will grant them abundant peace and righteousness, establishing them as a blessed people, the head and not the tail." {1:17} "I will dwell among them, building My sanctuary, and they will truly be My people, and I their God, never forsaking them." {1:18} Overwhelmed, Moses fell on his face and prayed, "O Lord my God, do not abandon Your people or deliver them to their enemies to lead them astray." {1:19} "Let Your mercy be upon Your people, creating in them a clean heart and holy spirit, protecting them from the influence of wickedness." {1:20} The Lord responded to Moses, "I understand their rebellious nature, but they will eventually confess their sins and turn to Me with sincere hearts." {1:21} "I will circumcise their hearts and the hearts of their descendants, creating in them a holy spirit so they will obey Me forever." {1:22} "They will cleave to Me and My commandments, becoming known as children of the living God, loved and recognized by every angel and spirit." {1:23} "Write down all these words I declare to you on this mountain, from the beginning to the end, spanning all divisions of days, laws, testimonies, weeks, and jubilees until the day I descend to dwell among them for eternity." {1:24} God instructed the angel of His presence to write for Moses from the beginning of creation until His sanctuary is built in Jerusalem on Mount Zion, ensuring all know He is the God of Israel and the Father of Jacob's children, reigning eternally over Zion and Jerusalem. {1:25} The angel of His presence, who led Israel, recorded the divisions of years since creation, the laws, testimonies, weeks, and jubilees, until the sanctuary of the Lord is established in Jerusalem on Mount Zion, renewing all luminaries for healing, peace, and blessing upon all Israel's chosen ones, from that day forth and throughout all the days of the earth.

{2:1} And the angel of the presence spoke to Moses according to the word of the Lord, saying: Write the complete history of creation, how in six days the Lord God finished all His works and everything He created, and rested on the seventh day, making it holy for all ages, and appointing it as a sign for all His works. {2:2} For on the first day, He created the heavens above, the earth, the waters, and all the spirits that serve before Him – the angels of the presence, the angels of sanctification, the angels of the spirit of fire, and the angels of the spirit of the winds, the angels of the clouds, and of darkness, snow, hail, and frost. He also created the angels of thunder, lightning, cold, heat, winter, spring, autumn, and summer, and all the spirits of His creations in heaven and on earth. He created the abysses, darkness, evening, night, light, dawn, and day, which He prepared in His wisdom. {2:3} And we, the angels, saw His works and praised Him, glorifying Him for all He had made, for He created seven great works on the first day. {2:4} On the second day, He created the firmament, dividing the waters above from the waters below, placing the firmament over the earth. This was the only work He created on the second day. {2:5} On the third day, He commanded the waters to gather in one place so that dry land could appear. And the waters obeyed, gathering into one place outside of the firmament, allowing the dry land to emerge. {2:6} On that day, He created all the seas, rivers, and lakes, and the gathering of waters in the mountains and across the earth. He also made the dew of the earth, seeds to be sown, sprouting plants, fruit-bearing trees, and trees of the forest, including the garden of Eden in Eden, and all plants according to their kind. These were the four great works He made on the third day. {2:7} On the fourth day, He created the sun, moon, and stars, placing them in the firmament of the heavens to give light to the earth, to rule the day and night, and to separate light from darkness. {2:8} He appointed the sun as a great sign for days, Sabbaths, months, feasts, years, Sabbaths of years, jubilees, and all seasons. It separates light from darkness and ensures prosperity for everything that grows and thrives on the earth. These were the three things He made on the fourth day. {2:9} On the fifth day, He created the great sea monsters in the depths of the waters. These were the first living creatures made by His hands, along with all the fish, creatures that move in the waters, and everything that flies, including birds of every kind. {2:10} The sun rose over them to provide growth and prosperity for everything on the earth, including the plants, trees, and all living creatures. These three kinds were created on the fifth day. {2:11} On the sixth day, He made all the animals of the earth, all the cattle, and every creature that moves on the earth. Afterward, He created humanity, making a man and a woman and granting them dominion over everything on the earth, in the seas, and in the sky, including all the animals, birds, and everything that moves on the ground. {2:12} He gave them control over the whole earth and all its creatures. These four kinds of work were done on the sixth day. {2:13} In total, He made twenty-two kinds of creation. {2:14} He completed all His work on the sixth day, including everything in the heavens, on the earth, in the seas, in the abysses, and in the light and darkness. {2:15} Then He gave us a great sign, the Sabbath day, that we should work for six days but rest on the seventh day from all labor. {2:16} All the angels of the presence and angels of sanctification, these two great orders, were commanded to keep the Sabbath with Him, both in heaven and on earth. {2:17} And He said to us: "Behold, I will set apart a people for Myself from all nations, and they shall keep the Sabbath. I will sanctify them as My people and bless them, just as I have sanctified the Sabbath and made it holy unto Myself. I will bless them, and they shall be My people, and I will be their God." {2:18} I have chosen the seed of Jacob from among all nations and written him down as My firstborn son. I have sanctified him forever and will teach them to observe the Sabbath, that they may rest from all work on this day. {2:19} Thus, He established a sign by which they should keep the Sabbath with us, eating, drinking, and blessing the One who created all things, as He has blessed and sanctified a people above all others to keep the Sabbath with us. {2:20} He caused His commands to rise like a sweet fragrance before Him, all the days of our lives. {2:21} There were twenty-two heads of humanity from Adam to Jacob, and twenty-two kinds of work were made until the seventh day. This day is blessed and holy, and the former is also blessed and holy, for one serves the other in sanctification and blessing. {2:22} To Jacob and his descendants, it was granted that they should always be the blessed and holy ones of the first testimony and law, just as He sanctified and blessed the seventh day. {2:23} He created heaven and earth and everything within six days, making the seventh day holy for all His works. He commanded that anyone who works on this day shall die and that whoever defiles it shall be punished with death. {2:24} Therefore, command the children of Israel to observe this day, to keep it holy and not to defile it, for it is holier than all other days. {2:25} Whoever profanes it shall surely die, and whoever works on it shall die eternally. The children of Israel must observe this day throughout their generations so that they will not be uprooted from the land, for it is a holy and blessed day. {2:26} Anyone who keeps the Sabbath from all work will be holy and blessed like us throughout all days. {2:27} Proclaim to the children of Israel the law of this day, that they should keep it and not stray from it in their hearts. {2:28} It is unlawful to do any improper work on this day or to pursue their own pleasures. They should not prepare food or drink, or carry burdens through their gates on the Sabbath, which they had not prepared on the sixth day. {2:29} They shall not transport goods from house to house on this day, for it is more holy and blessed than any day of jubilee. {2:30} We kept the Sabbath in the heavens before it was revealed to any human being to keep it on earth. {2:31} The Creator blessed this day, but He did not sanctify all nations to keep it, only Israel. He permitted them alone to eat, drink, and rest on this day on the earth. {2:32} The Creator blessed this day, making it more holy and glorious than all other days. {2:33} This law and testimony were given to the children of Israel as an eternal law for all generations.

{3:1} During the second week, as commanded by God, we brought all the beasts, cattle, birds, and creatures of the earth and water to Adam, each according to its kind and type: beasts on the first day, cattle on the second, birds on the third, land animals on the fourth, and creatures of the water on the fifth day. {3:2} Adam named them all, and whatever name he gave them, that was their name. {3:3} During these five days, Adam saw every kind of creature, male and female, but found no suitable helper among them. {3:4} Then the Lord said, "It is not good for man to be alone; let us make a helper suitable for him." {3:5} God caused Adam to fall into a deep sleep, took one of his ribs, and from it formed woman, whom He presented to Adam when he woke on the sixth day. {3:6} Adam recognized her as bone of his bones and flesh of his flesh, declaring, "She shall be called woman, for she was taken out of man." {3:7} Therefore, a man leaves his parents to be united with his wife, and they become one flesh. {3:8} Adam was created in the first week, and in the second week, Eve was revealed to him. {3:9} This is why the law commanded that after the birth of a male, the mother be unclean for seven days, and for a female, fourteen days, followed by periods of purification. {3:10} After forty days in the land of his creation, Adam was brought into the garden of Eden to cultivate it. Eve entered eighty days after Adam. {3:11} Laws were ordained concerning childbirth, ensuring purity before entering the holy places. {3:12} In the first week of the first jubilee, Adam and Eve spent seven years in Eden, working and keeping the garden as instructed. {3:13} They were naked and unashamed, tending the garden, protecting it from birds and beasts, and gathering its fruit. {3:14} At the end of these seven years, on the seventeenth day of the second month, the serpent approached Eve. {3:15} The serpent deceived Eve, questioning God's command not to eat from any tree in the garden. {3:16} Eve explained God's instruction, but the serpent deceived her, promising enlightenment and wisdom if she ate from the forbidden tree. {3:17} Seeing the fruit was pleasing and desirable, Eve ate it and gave some to Adam, who also ate. {3:18} Their eyes were opened, and they realized they were naked; they covered themselves with fig leaves. {3:19} God cursed the serpent, the woman, and the man for their disobedience, foretelling pain in childbirth and toil in farming. {3:20} He made garments of skin for Adam and Eve and banished them from Eden. {3:21} Adam offered sacrifices to God for forgiveness. {3:22} On that day, the mouths of all animals were closed, and they could no longer speak as they once did. {3:23} God expelled all creatures from Eden according to their kinds and types. {3:24} Adam alone received the means to cover his shame. {3:25} Henceforth, it was decreed on heavenly tablets that all who know the law must cover their shame, unlike the Gentiles. {3:26} In the fourth month, on the new moon, Adam and Eve left Eden and settled in the land of Elda. {3:27} Adam named his wife Eve, and they did not have children until after the first jubilee. {3:28} Adam tilled the land as he had been instructed in Eden.

{4:1} In the third week of the second jubilee, Eve gave birth to Cain, and in the fourth week, she bore Abel. In the fifth week, her daughter wân was born. {4:2} In the first year of the third jubilee, Cain, jealous that God favored Abel's sacrifice over his own, killed his brother Abel in the field. Abel's blood cried out from the ground to heaven, lamenting the injustice of his murder. {4:3} The Lord punished Cain for killing Abel, making him a restless wanderer on the earth, cursed because of his brother's blood. {4:4} This led to the decree on the heavenly tablets: "Cursed is he who kills his neighbor treacherously." {4:5} We, therefore, declare before the Lord all sins committed in heaven, on earth, in light, in darkness, and everywhere. {4:6} Adam and Eve mourned Abel's death for four weeks of years. In the fourth year of the fifth week, they found joy again as Eve gave birth to Seth. Adam named him Seth, saying, "God has appointed me another child in place of Abel, whom Cain killed." {4:7} In the sixth week, Seth's daughter Azûra was born. {4:8} Cain married his sister wân, and she bore him Enoch at the end of the fourth jubilee. {4:9} In the first year of the fifth jubilee, people began building houses on earth, and Cain built a city named after his son Enoch. {4:10} Adam and Eve had nine more sons. {4:11} In the fifth week of the fifth jubilee, Seth married his sister Azûrâ, and in the fourth year of the sixth week, she bore him Enos, who began to call on the name of the Lord. {4:12} In the seventh jubilee, Enos married Nôâm, his sister, and she bore him Kenan in the third year of the fifth week. {4:13} At the end of the eighth jubilee, Kenan married Mûalêlêth, his sister, and she bore him Mahalalel in the first week of the ninth jubilee. {4:14} In the second week of the tenth jubilee, Mahalalel married DinaH, daughter of Barakiel, and she bore him Jared in the third week of the sixth year. Jared's time saw the descent of the angels, known as the Watchers, to instruct mankind in justice and righteousness. {4:15} In the eleventh jubilee, Jared married Baraka, daughter of Râsûjâl, and she bore him Enoch in the fourth week. Enoch was the first among men to learn writing, knowledge, and wisdom, and he recorded heavenly signs and the order of months in a book for future generations. {4:16} In the twelfth jubilee, Enoch married Edna, daughter of Danel, and she bore him Methuselah in the sixth year. Enoch spent six jubilees with the angels, learning about the earth and heaven's governance. {4:17} Enoch testified against the Watchers who had sinned by consorting with human women, which led to great defilement. {4:18} He was taken to the Garden of Eden in honor, where he wrote down the judgments and wickedness of mankind. {4:19} God sent the floodwaters upon Eden as a sign and testimony against humanity's wickedness. {4:20} Adam offered incense on Mount Sinai, sanctifying it along with the Garden of Eden and Mount Zion, which will be sanctified in the new creation. {4:21} In the fourteenth jubilee, Methuselah married Edna, daughter of Azrial, and she bore him Lamech in the first year of the third week. {4:22} In the fifteenth jubilee, Lamech married Betenos, daughter of Baraki'il, and she bore him Noah, who would comfort Lamech from the toil caused by the cursed ground. {4:23} At the end of the nineteenth jubilee, Adam died in the seventh week of the sixth year. His sons buried him in the land of his creation, seventy years short of a thousand, for a thousand years are as a day in the heavens. Cain also died this year, killed by a falling stone from the house he built, as a just punishment for his murder of Abel with a stone. {4:24} In the twenty-fifth jubilee, Noah married `Emzârâ, daughter of Râkê'êl, and she bore him Shem in the fifth week and Ham in the fifth year. Japheth was born in the first year of the sixth week.

{5:1} As humanity multiplied on the earth, daughters were born to them. The angels of God, seeing their beauty during a certain jubilee year, took wives from among them as they pleased. These unions produced giants, and lawlessness spread throughout the earth. {5:2} Corruption infected all living beings—humans, animals, birds, and every creature—deviating from their natural order. They began to prey upon one another, and wickedness pervaded every thought of mankind continually. {5:3} God observed the earth's corruption and the evil deeds that filled His sight. {5:4} He resolved to destroy all living beings from the face of the earth. Yet Noah found favor in His eyes. {5:5} God was furious with the angels who had transgressed, commanding their removal from power and binding them deep within the earth, separated from the world. {5:6} Their offspring were sentenced to destruction by the sword and expulsion from heaven. {5:7} God declared, "My spirit will not remain with mankind forever, for they are flesh; their days shall be limited to one hundred and twenty years." {5:8} He unleashed violence among them, and people began to kill one another until all were wiped out by the sword. Their fathers witnessed this judgment, and afterward, they too were bound in the depths of the earth until the great day of condemnation. {5:9} God eradicated them completely; none escaped His judgment for their wickedness. {5:10} He established a new righteous order for all creation, ensuring they would never again fall into sin, each kind remaining righteous forever. {5:11} The judgments for all were inscribed on heavenly tablets—those who deviated from their ordained path faced written judgment, whether in heaven, on earth, in light, in darkness, in Sheol, or in the depths. {5:12} God judges each according to their deeds, whether great or small, according to their ways. He is impartial, accepting no bribes or favors in executing justice. {5:13} Concerning the children of Israel, it is ordained that those who turn to God in righteousness will receive forgiveness and mercy annually for their sins. {5:14} Before the flood, only Noah found favor in God's eyes; his righteousness saved his sons from the floodwaters. {5:15} God declared His intention to destroy everything—humans, livestock, creatures, birds, and all that moves on the earth. He instructed Noah to build an ark for his salvation from the impending flood. {5:16} Noah constructed the ark precisely as commanded, completing it in the twenty-seventh jubilee, in the fifth week, on the new moon of the first month. {5:17} He entered the ark in its sixth year, on the new moon of the second month, and God sealed it shut on the seventeenth evening. {5:18} God opened the floodgates of heaven and the fountains of the great deep, causing rain to pour for forty days and nights. {5:19} The waters surged until they covered even the highest mountains by fifteen cubits, while the ark floated above the flooded earth. {5:20} The deluge persisted for one hundred and fifty days. {5:21} Finally, the ark came to rest on Mount Lubar in the mountains of Ararat. {5:22} By the fourth month's new moon, the fountains of the great deep closed, and the rain from heaven ceased by the seventh month's new moon. The waters receded, exposing the mountaintops by the tenth month's new moon. {5:23} By the fifth week of the seventh year, the earth was dry on the seventeenth day of the second month. {5:24} On the twenty-seventh day of that month, Noah opened the ark and released the beasts, cattle, birds, and all creatures.

{6:1} On the new moon of the third month, Noah left the ark and built an altar on the mountain. {6:2} He made atonement for the earth, sacrificing a young goat and using its blood to cleanse the earth of its guilt, since everything had been destroyed except those in the ark. {6:3} He placed the fat on the altar and also offered an ox, a goat, a sheep, kids, salt, a turtle-dove, and a young dove as a burnt sacrifice. He added oil, sprinkled wine, and spread frankincense over everything, creating a pleasing aroma to the Lord. {6:4} The Lord smelled the pleasing aroma and made a covenant with Noah, promising never to flood the earth again. As long as the earth exists, seed-time and harvest, cold and heat, summer and winter, and day and night would never cease. {6:5} God commanded Noah and his descendants to multiply and fill the earth, promising to instill fear of humans in all creatures of the earth and sea. {6:6} He gave them all animals, birds, and fish for food, just as He had given green herbs, but forbade eating flesh with blood, as life is in the blood. He warned that He would demand an accounting for the lifeblood of all beings. {6:7} Whoever sheds human blood will have their blood shed by humans, for humans are made in God's image. God reiterated the command to multiply on the earth. {6:8} Noah and his sons vowed never to eat blood from any flesh, establishing an everlasting covenant with the Lord for all generations. {6:9} This covenant included a commandment for the children of Israel, made on the mountain with an oath, and blood was sprinkled on them as part of the covenant's words. {6:10} This testimony was written to be observed continually, forbidding the consumption of blood from beasts, birds, or cattle forever. {6:11} Those who eat blood will be removed from the land. {6:12} The children of Israel must be commanded not to eat blood, so their names and descendants remain before the Lord continually. {6:13} This law is eternal, observed throughout their generations, with daily supplications and sacrifices seeking forgiveness before the Lord. {6:14} God gave Noah and his sons a sign of the covenant: a bow in the clouds as a promise never to flood the earth again. {6:15} This sign, written on heavenly tablets, ordained the celebration of the feast of weeks annually in this month, renewing the covenant each year. {6:16} This festival was celebrated in heaven from creation until Noah's time, through twenty-six jubilees and five weeks of years. Noah and his sons observed it for seven jubilees and a week of years until Noah's death, but it was forgotten until Abraham's time, when people again consumed blood. {6:17} Abraham, Isaac, and Jacob observed it, but the children of Israel forgot until they renewed it on the mountain. {6:18} The children of Israel must observe this festival in all generations, celebrating it one day each year in this month. {6:19} This feast, the feast of weeks and first fruits, has a dual nature and should be celebrated as written and engraved. {6:20} Instructions for this celebration are detailed in the book of the first law, including its sacrifices, so the children of Israel remember and observe it annually. {6:21} On the new moons of the first, fourth, seventh, and tenth months are days of remembrance and seasonal divisions, written and ordained forever. {6:22} Noah established these as memorial feasts for all generations, beginning with the new moon of the first month when he was instructed to build the ark and saw the dry earth. {6:23} On the new moon of the fourth month, the depths were closed; on the new moon of the seventh month, the abysses were opened, and the waters began to descend. {6:24} On the new moon of the tenth month, the mountain tops appeared, and Noah rejoiced. {6:25} These events became memorial feasts, ordained forever. {6:26} The heavenly tablets marked these days, each with thirteen weeks, from one to the next, forming a complete year of fifty-two weeks. {6:27} This commandment is not to be neglected annually. {6:28} The children of Israel must observe a year of three hundred and sixty-four days to maintain the proper timing of feasts and seasons, avoiding any disruption. {6:29} Failure to observe this will dislodge the seasons, causing confusion and neglect of ordinances. {6:30} The children of Israel will forget the proper order of the years, new moons, seasons, Sabbaths, and feasts, leading them astray. {6:31} This is not my own invention but is written on the heavenly tablets to prevent forgetting the covenant feasts and following the errors of the Gentiles. {6:32} Observing the moon will cause disruption, as it shifts the seasons ten days too soon annually. {6:33} This will lead to abominable observances, mixing holy and unclean days, and confusion in months, Sabbaths, feasts, and jubilees. {6:34} Therefore, this command is to be testified to them, as after your death, your children will disturb these observances, failing to keep the year to three hundred and sixty-four days. {6:35} Consequently, they will err in new moons, seasons, Sabbaths, and festivals, and consume all kinds of blood with all kinds of flesh.

{7:1} In the first year of the seventh week, 1317 A.M., during this jubilee, Noah planted vines on Mount Lubar, one of the Ararat Mountains. {7:2} The vines produced fruit in the fourth year, 1320 A.M., and he harvested them in the seventh month of that year. {7:3} Noah made wine and stored it until the fifth year, 1321 A.M., celebrating with joy on the new moon of the first month. {7:4} He offered a burnt sacrifice to the Lord, including a young ox, a ram, seven year-old sheep, and a goat to make atonement for himself and his sons. {7:5} He prepared the goat first, placing some of its blood on the altar's flesh, then laid all the fat on the altar. {7:6} He added the ox, ram, and sheep, and poured oil over everything, sprinkling wine on the fire he had made on the altar, and placed incense to create a pleasing aroma for the Lord. {7:7} Noah and his children rejoiced and drank the wine. {7:8} That evening, Noah became drunk, lay uncovered in his tent, and Ham saw his father's nakedness, telling his brothers. {7:9} Shem and Japheth took a garment, walked backward, and covered their father without looking. {7:10} When Noah awoke, he knew what Ham had done and cursed Ham's son Canaan, declaring he would be a servant to his brothers. {7:11} Noah blessed Shem, praising the Lord, and said Canaan would be Shem's servant. {7:12} He also blessed Japheth, saying God would enlarge him, and Canaan would serve him as well. {7:13} Ham, upset by the curse, moved away with his sons Cush, Mizraim, Put, and Canaan, and built a city named after his wife Ne'elatama'uk. {7:14} Japheth, envious of Ham, also built a city named after his wife Adataneses. {7:15} Shem stayed with Noah, building a city near his father named after his wife Sedeqetelebab. {7:16} These cities—Sedeqetelebab to the east, Na'elatama'uk to the south, and Adataneses to the west—were near Mount Lubar. {7:17} Shem's sons were Elam, Asshur, Arpachshad (born two years after the flood), Lud, and Aram. {7:18} Japheth's sons were Gomer, Magog, Madai, Javan, Tubal, Meshech, and Tiras. {7:19} In the twenty-eighth jubilee, 1324-1372 A.M., Noah taught his grandsons the commandments and judgments he knew, urging them to live righteously, honor their parents, love their neighbors, and avoid fornication, uncleanness, and all iniquity. {7:20} The flood came because of fornication by the Watchers, who took human wives, starting uncleanness and producing the Naphidim, who devoured one another. {7:21} Giants killed the Naphil, who killed the Eljo, and the Eljo killed humans. {7:22} Wickedness and bloodshed filled the earth, and people sinned against all living creatures. {7:23} The Lord destroyed everything for their wicked deeds and the bloodshed. {7:24} Noah reminded his sons that only they and the ark's inhabitants were saved, but warned them that their current behavior showed a path of destruction and discord. {7:25} He feared they would shed blood and be destroyed after his death, emphasizing that whoever sheds blood or eats blood would be destroyed and descend into Sheol and condemnation. {7:26} They were commanded to avoid bloodshed and to cover any shed blood, ensuring the earth would be purified by the blood of those who shed it. {7:27} Noah urged them to act righteously, honoring God who saved him from the flood, and to build cities, plant crops, and plant trees. {7:28} For three years, they were not to gather the fruit, and in the fourth year, the fruit would be holy and offered to God. {7:29} Abundant first-fruits of wine and oil were to be offered at the altar, with the rest consumed by the Lord's servants. {7:30} In the fifth year, they were to release the harvest in righteousness, ensuring prosperity. {7:31} Noah reminded them of Enoch's command to Methuselah, passed down to Lamech and then to him. {7:32} Noah intended to pass these commandments to his sons, as Enoch had done, continuing the tradition until his death.

{8:1} In the first week of the twenty-ninth jubilee, 1373 A.M., Arpachshad married Rasu'eja, the daughter of Susan, who was the daughter of Elam. {8:2} In the third year of this week, 1375 A.M., they had a son named Kainam. {8:3} Kainam grew up, and his father taught him how to write. {8:4} Kainam sought a place to establish a city and found an ancient inscription on a rock. {8:5} He read and copied it, but it led him to sin, as it contained the teachings of the Watchers about the omens of the sun, moon, and stars. {8:6} Afraid to anger Noah, he kept it a secret. {8:7} In the second week of the thirtieth jubilee, 1429 A.M., Kainam married Melka, the daughter of Madai, son of Japheth. {8:8} In the fourth year, 1432 A.M., they had a son named Shelah, meaning "Truly I have been sent." {8:9} Shelah grew up, married Mu'ak, the daughter of Kesed, his father's brother, in the first year of the fifth week of the thirty-first jubilee, 1499 A.M. {8:10} In the fifth year, 1503 A.M., they had a son named Eber. {8:11} Eber married 'Azûrâd, the daughter of Nebrod, in the third year of the seventh week of the thirty-second jubilee, 1564 A.M. {8:12} In the sixth year, 1567 A.M., they had a son named Peleg, named so because during his time, Noah's descendants began to divide the earth. {8:13} They secretly divided the earth and informed Noah. {8:14} In the first year of the thirty-third jubilee, 1569 A.M., Noah's sons divided the earth into three parts for Shem, Ham, and Japheth. {8:15} They came to Noah, who had the division written down, and they drew lots. {8:16} Shem's lot was the middle of the earth, extending from the mountain range of Rafa to the river Tina and westward. {8:17} His portion included the areas north and south of this river, reaching the sea and beyond to the Garden of Eden. {8:18} Noah rejoiced, remembering his prophecy that the Lord God would bless Shem. {8:19} He recognized the Garden of Eden, Mount Sinai, and Mount Zion as holy places created to face each other. {8:20} Noah blessed God, acknowledging that Shem's portion was blessed and vast, including Eden, the Red Sea, India, and other lands. {8:21} Ham's portion extended south of the Gihon River, encompassing mountains, seas, and reaching westward. {8:22} Japheth's portion extended north of the Tina River, covering northern and northeastern regions, mountains, and seas. {8:23} This portion included five great islands and a vast land in the north, which was cold, while Ham's land was hot, and Shem's land had a moderate climate.

{9:1} Ham divided his land among his sons. The first portion went to Cush, stretching east. To the west of Cush was Mizraim's land, then further west was Put's, and finally, Canaan's portion reached the sea on the west. {9:2} Shem also allocated land to his sons. Ham and his sons received the first portion, extending east of the Tigris River, encompassing the whole land of India, the Red Sea coast, the waters of Dedan, and the mountains of Mebri and Ela, including all the land of Susan up to the Red Sea and the river Tina. {9:3} Asshur's portion included all the land of Asshur, Nineveh, Shinar, and up to the border of India, skirting the river. {9:4} Arpachshad received the third portion: the land of the Chaldees region east of the Euphrates, bordering the Red Sea, and the desert waters near the tongue of the sea facing Egypt. This included Lebanon,

Sanir, and 'Amana up to the Euphrates border. {9:5} Aram's portion included all Mesopotamia between the Tigris and Euphrates, extending north of the Chaldees to the border of the Asshur mountains and the land of 'Arara. {9:6} Lud's portion comprised the Asshur mountains and adjacent lands up to the Great Sea and the eastern part of his brother Asshur's territory. {9:7} Japheth divided his inheritance among his sons. Gomer's portion extended east from the northern side to the river Tina. {9:8} Magog's portion covered the northern regions up to the sea of Me'at. {9:9} Madai's portion extended west of his two brothers to the islands and their coasts. {9:10} Javan received all the islands up to the border of Lud's territory. {9:11} Tubal's portion included the region within the tongue approaching Lud's portion, extending beyond the second and third tongues. {9:12} Meshech's portion extended beyond the third tongue towards the east of Gadir. {9:13} Tiras received four great islands in the sea, reaching Ham's portion, while the islands of Kamaturi were allocated to Arpachshad's sons. {9:14} Noah's sons divided their land in his presence and swore an oath, invoking a curse on anyone who tried to seize land that wasn't allotted to them. They all agreed, affirming this for themselves and their descendants forever until the day of judgment when the Lord will judge all their transgressions, uncleanness, and sins with a sword and fire.

{10:1} In the third week of this jubilee, the unclean demons began to lead astray the children of the sons of Noah, causing them to err and destroying them. {10:2} The sons of Noah came to their father and told him about the demons who were misleading, blinding, and killing their descendants. {10:3} And Noah prayed to the Lord his God, saying: {10:4} "God of the spirits of all flesh, You have shown mercy to me and saved me and my sons from the waters of the flood, and You did not let me perish like the sons of perdition. {10:5} Your grace has been great toward me, and great has been Your mercy to my soul. {10:6} Let Your grace be lifted upon my sons, and do not let wicked spirits rule over them, lest they destroy them from the earth. {10:7} Bless me and my sons, that we may increase, multiply, and fill the earth. {10:8} You know how Your Watchers, the fathers of these spirits, acted in my day. Now, as for these living spirits, imprison them and hold them in the place of condemnation. Do not let them bring destruction upon the children of Your servant, my God, for they are malicious and were created to destroy. {10:9} Do not let them rule over the spirits of the living, for You alone can exercise dominion over them. May they not have power over the children of the righteous, from now and forever." {10:10} And the Lord our God commanded us to bind all of them. {10:11} The chief of the spirits, Mastema, came and said, "Lord, Creator, let some of them remain before me, and let them listen to my voice and do whatever I tell them. If none remain with me, I will not be able to carry out my will among the sons of men, for these spirits are for the purpose of corruption and leading men astray before my judgment, for great is the wickedness of mankind." {10:12} And God said, "Let a tenth of them remain before him, but let nine parts of them be bound and descend into the place of condemnation." {10:13} Then, one of us was commanded to teach Noah all the medicines, for God knew that mankind would not walk in righteousness or strive for holiness. {10:14} We did everything as He commanded: all the wicked spirits were bound in the place of condemnation, but a tenth of them were left on earth to be subject to Satan. {10:15} We also explained to Noah all the remedies for their diseases, along with their deceptions, so that he could heal with the herbs of the earth. {10:16} Noah wrote down everything in a book as we instructed him concerning every type of medicine. In this way, the evil spirits were prevented from harming Noah's descendants. {10:17} He gave everything he had written to Shem, his eldest son, because he loved him more than all his sons. {10:18} Noah slept with his fathers and was buried on Mount Lubar in the land of Ararat. {10:19} He lived nine hundred and fifty years, which is nineteen jubilees, two weeks, and five years. {10:20} In his lifetime, he excelled all the children of men except for Enoch, for Noah was perfect in righteousness. Enoch, however, had been ordained for a special purpose as a witness to future generations, to recount the deeds of each generation until the day of judgment. {10:21} In the thirty-third jubilee, in the first year of the second week, Peleg took a wife named Lomna, the daughter of Sina'ar, and she bore him a son in the fourth year of this week, whom he named Reu. {10:22} He said, "Behold, the children of men have become evil because of their wicked plan to build for themselves a city and a tower in the land of Shinar." {10:23} They had departed from the land of Ararat and moved eastward to Shinar. In Peleg's days, they built the city and the tower, saying, "Come, let us build a tower to ascend to heaven." {10:24} They began to build, and in the fourth week, they made bricks in fire. The bricks were used as stone, and the clay used to bind them was asphalt that came from the sea and from fountains of water in the land of Shinar. {10:25} They built it for forty-three years. Its width was 203 bricks, and the height of each brick was a third of one. The total height of the tower reached 5,433 cubits and 2 palms, with one wall being thirteen stades long and the other thirty stades. {10:26} The Lord our God said to us, "Behold, they are one people, and they have begun this work. Now nothing will be impossible for them. Come, let us go down and confuse their language so that they will not understand each other, and they will be dispersed into different cities and nations, and no longer have one purpose until the day of judgment." {10:27} The Lord descended, and we descended with Him to see the city and the tower that the children of men had built. {10:28} He confused their language so they could no longer understand one another, and they stopped building the city and the tower. {10:29} For this reason, the whole land of Shinar is called Babel, because the Lord confused their language there. From there, they were dispersed to their cities, each according to his language and nation. {10:30} The Lord sent a mighty wind against the tower, which toppled it to the ground. It was located between Asshur and Babylon in the land of Shinar, and they called it "Overthrow." {10:31} In the first year of the thirty-fourth jubilee, in the first week, they were dispersed from the land of Shinar. {10:32} Ham and his sons went to the land that was assigned to them in the south. {10:33} Canaan saw that the land of Lebanon, as far as the river of Egypt, was very good. He did not go to the land of his inheritance by the sea in the west, but instead, he settled in Lebanon, eastward and westward from the border of Jordan and the sea. {10:34} Ham, his father, and his brothers Cush and Mizraim said to him, "You have settled in a land that is not yours and did not fall to us by lot. Do not do this, for if you do, you and your descendants will fall by rebellion, and you will be cursed and rooted out forever." {10:35} "Do not live in the land of Shem, for it was given to him and his descendants by lot." {10:36} "You are cursed, and cursed will you be beyond all the sons of Noah by the curse we swore in the presence of the holy judge and Noah, our father." {10:37} But Canaan did not listen to them and continued to live in the land of Lebanon from Hamath to Egypt, he and his sons, even to this day. {10:38} And that is why the land is called Canaan. {10:39} Japheth and his sons went toward the sea and settled in the land that was given to them by lot. {10:40} Madai saw the land by the sea and was not pleased, so he asked Ham, Asshur, and Arpachshad, his wife's brother, for a portion of land. {10:41} He settled in the land of Media, near his wife's brother, and he named the place and his descendants' dwelling after his father, Madai, calling it Media, and this remains true until today.

{11:1} In the thirty-fifth jubilee, in the third week, during the first year [1681 A.M.], Reu married Ôrâ, the daughter of 'Ûr, the son of Kesed. They had a son named Seroh in the seventh year of this week in the jubilee [1687 A.M.]. {11:2} The sons of Noah began to fight, capture, and kill each other. They shed human blood, ate it, built fortified cities, walls, and towers. Individuals exalted themselves and started forming kingdoms, going to war against each other, nation against nation, city against city. They began doing evil, acquiring weapons, teaching their sons war, capturing cities, and trading slaves. {11:3} 'Ûr, the son of Kesed, built the city of Ara of the Chaldees, naming it after himself and his father. They made and worshipped molten idols and images, and malignant spirits led them into sin and uncleanness. {11:4} The prince Mastêmâ worked hard to spread sin, sending spirits to corrupt, destroy, and shed blood on the earth. This led to naming Seroh "Serug" because everyone turned to sin. {11:5} Serug grew up in Ur of the Chaldees, near his wife's maternal grandfather. He worshipped idols and married Melka, the daughter of Kaber, his father's brother's daughter, in the thirty-sixth jubilee, fifth week, first year [1744 A.M.]. They had a son named Nahor in the first year of this week. {11:6} Nahor grew up in Ur of the Chaldees, learning the Chaldean arts of divination from his father. In the thirty-seventh jubilee, sixth week, first year [1800 A.M.], he married 'Ijaska, the daughter of Nestag of the Chaldees. They had a son named Terah in the seventh year of this week [1806 A.M.]. {11:7} Mastêmâ sent ravens and birds to destroy the sown seeds, depriving people of their labor. The ravens picked the seeds from the ground before they could be plowed. {11:8} Terah's name was given because the ravens left them destitute, devouring their seed. The years became barren due to the birds, eating all the fruit from the trees, making it hard to save any produce. {11:9} In the thirty-ninth jubilee, second week, first year [1870 A.M.], Terah married 'Edna, the daughter of Abram, his father's sister's daughter. In the seventh year of this week [1876 A.M.], they had a son named Abram, after his maternal grandfather who died before his birth. {11:10} Abram understood the world's errors and separated himself from his father's idol worship. He prayed to the Creator to save him from the errors and uncleanness of mankind. {11:11} During seed time, everyone went out to protect their crops from the ravens. Abram, at fourteen, joined them. A cloud of ravens approached to devour the seeds, but Abram confronted them, commanding them to return. The ravens turned back, and not one settled. {11:12} Everyone saw Abram's actions, and his name became great in the land of the Chaldees. Those wishing to sow that year came to him, and he helped them sow their land, yielding enough grain for everyone to be satisfied. {11:13} In the first year of the fifth week [1891 A.M.], Abram taught craftsmen to make seed-planting devices attached to plows, protecting the seeds from ravens. These devices ensured the seeds fell directly into the soil, hidden from the birds. {11:14} Following Abram's instructions, they made these devices for all plows, sowing and tilling the land without fear of birds, ensuring successful harvests.

{12:1} In the sixth week, during the seventh year [1904 A.M.], Abram spoke to his father Terah, saying, "Father!" Terah responded, "Yes, my son." Abram asked, "What benefit do we get from these idols you worship and bow to? {12:2} They have no spirit, they are lifeless forms that mislead us. Do not worship them. Worship the God of heaven, who brings rain and dew to the earth, does everything upon it, and created all by His word. All life comes from Him. {12:3} Why worship things without spirit, made by human hands, which you carry on your shoulders? They provide no help but bring shame to their makers and mislead those who worship them. Do not worship them." {12:4} Terah replied, "I know this, my son, but what can I do with a people who force me to serve before them? If I tell them the truth, they will kill me; they are devoted to worshiping them. Stay silent, my son, lest they kill you." Abram told his brothers, who were angry with him, so he remained silent. {12:5} In the fortieth jubilee, second week, seventh year [1925 A.M.], Abram married Sarai, his father's daughter. Haran, his brother, married in the third year of the third week [1928 A.M.] and had a son named Lot in the seventh year [1932 A.M.]. Nahor, his brother, also married. {12:6} When Abram was sixty, in the fourth week, fourth year [1936 A.M.], he burned the house of idols at night, destroying everything inside. No one knew. They woke to save their gods, but Haran died trying to rescue them from the fire. He died in Ur of the Chaldees before Terah, who then moved with his sons to Lebanon and Canaan, settling in Haran. Abram stayed with Terah in Haran for two weeks of years. {12:7} In the sixth week, fifth year [1951 A.M.], Abram stayed up all night on the new moon of the seventh month to observe the stars, pondering the year's rainfall. Alone, he realized that all celestial signs are controlled by the Lord. He prayed, "My God, You alone are my God. You created everything. Deliver me from evil spirits that control men's thoughts. Establish me and my descendants forever in Your path." {12:8} He questioned if he should return to Ur or stay. He prayed for guidance to follow the right path, not the deceitful one. After praying, the word of the Lord came to him through me, saying, "Leave your country, family, and father's house for a land I will show you. I will make you a great nation, bless you, and make your name great. You will be a blessing to all families of the earth. I will bless those who bless you and curse those who curse you. I will be your God and the God of your descendants forever." {12:9} The Lord instructed, "Open his mouth and ears to hear and speak the language revealed," which had ceased since Babel. I opened his mouth, ears, and lips, and spoke to him in Hebrew, the language of creation. {12:10} Abram took his fathers' books written in Hebrew and began to study them. I taught him what he couldn't understand. He studied during the six rainy months. {12:11} In the seventh year of the sixth week [1953 A.M.], Abram told his father he would leave Haran for Canaan to see it and return. Terah said, "Go in peace. May the eternal God make your path straight. May the Lord be with you, protect you, and grant you favor. May no one harm you; go in peace. {12:12} If you find a land you like, take me and Lot, Haran's son, as your own. The Lord be with you. Leave Nahor with me until you return, then we will all go together."

{13:1} Abram left Haran with his wife Sarai and his nephew Lot, Haran's son, and traveled to the land of Canaan. They came to Asshur, moved on to Shechem, and settled near a tall oak tree. The land from Hamath to the oak was beautiful. The Lord told Abram, "I will give this land to you and your descendants." {13:2} Abram built an altar there and offered a burnt sacrifice to the Lord who had appeared to him. He then moved to a mountain with Bethel to the west and Ai to the east, where he pitched his tent. {13:3} Abram saw that the land was vast and fertile, with vines, figs, pomegranates, oaks, ilexes, terebinths, olive trees, cedars, cypresses, date trees, and all kinds of trees, and there was water in the mountains. He blessed the Lord for bringing him out of Ur of the Chaldees to this land. {13:4} In the first year of the seventh week, on the new moon of the first month [1954 A.M.], Abram built an altar on this mountain and called on the name of the Lord, declaring Him as the eternal God. He offered a burnt sacrifice, asking the Lord to be with him always. {13:5} He then moved south to Hebron, which was built at that time, and lived there for two years before moving to the southern land of Bealoth, where a famine occurred. In the third year of the week, Abram went to Egypt and stayed there for five years before Sarai was taken from him. {13:6} At that time, Tanais in Egypt was built, seven years after Hebron. When Pharaoh took Sarai, the Lord plagued Pharaoh and his household with great plagues because of her. Abram gained much wealth in Egypt with sheep, cattle, donkeys, horses, camels, servants, silver, and gold, and Lot also became wealthy. {13:7} Pharaoh returned Sarai to Abram and sent him out of Egypt. Abram returned to the place where he had first pitched his tent, between Ai and Bethel, and blessed the Lord for bringing him back safely. {13:8} In the forty-first jubilee, third year of the first week [1963 A.M.], Abram returned to this place, offered a burnt sacrifice, and called on the name of the Lord, declaring Him as his God forever. {13:9} In the fourth year of that week [1964 A.M.], Lot separated from Abram and went to live in Sodom, where the people were exceedingly sinful. This separation grieved Abram because he had no children. {13:10} That same year, when Lot was taken captive, the Lord told Abram, after Lot had left, to look in all directions. The Lord promised to give all the land Abram saw to his descendants forever and to make them as numerous as the dust of the earth. Abram was told to walk through the land to see it all, as it would be given to his descendants. {13:11} Abram then moved to Hebron and lived there. {13:12} That year, Chedorlaomer, king of Elam, Amraphel, king of Shinar, Arioch, king of Ellasar, and Tidal, king of nations, attacked and killed the king of Gomorrah, causing the king of Sodom to flee. Many people died in the valley of Siddim near the Salt Sea, and the invaders captured Sodom, Gomorrah, Admah, Zeboim, and Lot with all his possessions, taking them to Dan. {13:13} A survivor informed Abram of Lot's capture. Abram armed his household servants to rescue Lot. {13:14} Abram decided to give a tenth of all his possessions to the Lord as an everlasting ordinance, to be given to the priests serving before Him, and they were to receive this tithe forever from all generations, including seed, wine, oil, cattle, and sheep, to enjoy before the Lord. {13:15} The king of Sodom came to Abram, bowed, and asked for the return of the people he had rescued, offering Abram the remaining goods. {13:16} Abram replied that he would take nothing from the king, not even a thread or a sandal strap, to avoid any claim that the king had made Abram rich. He only took what his young men had eaten and the portion due to his allies, Aner, Eschol, and Mamre. They would receive their share.

{14:1} In the fourth year of this week, on the new moon of the third month, the word of the Lord came to Abram in a dream, saying, "Fear not, Abram; I am your defender, and your reward will be exceedingly great." {14:2} Abram replied, "Lord, what can you give me since I remain childless? The heir of my household is Eliezer of Damascus, the son of my handmaid. You have given me no offspring." {14:3} The Lord answered, "This man will not be your heir; your heir will be a son coming from your own body." {14:4} The Lord took Abram outside and said, "Look at the sky and count the stars, if you can. That is how numerous your descendants will be." {14:5} Abram believed the Lord, and it was credited to him as righteousness. {14:6} The Lord said to him, "I am the Lord who brought you out of Ur of the Chaldees to give you this land to possess forever, and I will be God to you and your descendants after you." {14:7} Abram asked, "Lord, how can I be sure that I will inherit it?" {14:8} The Lord told him, "Bring me a heifer, a goat, and a ram, each three years old, along with a dove and a young pigeon." {14:9} Abram took all these and brought them to the oak of Mamre near Hebron in the middle of the month. He built an altar, sacrificed the animals, poured their blood on the altar, and cut them in half, laying the pieces opposite each other. He did not divide the birds. {14:10} Birds of prey came down on the carcasses, but Abram drove them away. {14:11} As the sun was setting, Abram fell into a deep sleep, and a dreadful darkness came over him. The Lord said to Abram, "Know for certain that your descendants will be strangers in a land not their own, where they will be enslaved and mistreated for four hundred years. {14:12} But I will judge the nation they serve, and afterward, they will come out with great possessions. You, however, will go to your ancestors in peace and be buried at a good old age. In the fourth generation, your descendants will return here, for the sin of the Amorites has not yet reached its full measure." {14:13} Abram woke up to see a smoking furnace and a blazing torch passing between the pieces of the sacrifices. {14:14} On that day, the Lord made a covenant with Abram, saying, "To your descendants, I give this land, from the river of Egypt to the great river, the Euphrates—the land of the Kenites, Kenizzites, Kadmonites, Hittites, Perizzites, Rephaim, Amorites, Canaanites, Girgashites, and Jebusites." {14:15} The day passed, and Abram offered the sacrifices, along with fruit and drink offerings, which were consumed by fire. {14:16} On that day, the Lord made a covenant with Abram, similar to the one made with Noah. Abram established the festival and ordinance for himself forever. {14:17} Abram rejoiced and told Sarai everything. He believed he would have children, but Sarai remained barren. {14:18} Sarai suggested to Abram, "Take my Egyptian maid, Hagar, as your wife. Perhaps I can build a family through her." {14:19} Abram agreed, and Sarai gave Hagar to him as his wife. Abram went to her, and she conceived and bore a son. Abram named him Ishmael. This happened in the fifth year of this week [1965 A.M.], when Abram was eighty-six years old.

{15:1} In the fifth year of the fourth week of this jubilee, in the third month, during the middle of the month, Abram celebrated the feast of the first-fruits of the grain harvest. {15:2} He offered new offerings on the altar to the Lord, including a heifer, a goat, and a sheep as burnt sacrifices. He also offered fruit and drink offerings with frankincense. {15:3} The Lord appeared to Abram and said, "I am God Almighty; walk before me and be blameless. {15:4} I will make my covenant with you and greatly increase your numbers." {15:5} Abram fell facedown, and God said to him, {15:6} "This is my covenant with you: You will be the father of many nations. {15:7} No longer will you be called Abram; your name will be Abraham, for I have made you the father of many nations. {15:8} I will make you very fruitful; I will make nations of you, and kings will come from you. {15:9} I will establish my covenant as an everlasting covenant between me and you and your descendants after you for the generations to come, to be your God and the God of your descendants. {15:10} I will give to you and your descendants the land where you are now a foreigner, all the land of Canaan, as an everlasting possession, and I will be their God." {15:11} Then God said to Abraham, "As for you, you must keep my covenant, you and your descendants after you for the generations to come. {15:12} Every male among you shall be circumcised. {15:13} You are to undergo circumcision, and it will be the sign of the covenant between me and you. {15:14} For the generations to come, every male among you who is eight days old must be circumcised, including those born in your household or bought with money from a foreigner—those who are not your offspring. {15:15} Whether born in your household or bought with money, they must be circumcised. My covenant in your flesh is to be an everlasting covenant. {15:16} Any uncircumcised male who has not been circumcised in the flesh will be cut off from his people; he has broken my covenant." {15:17} God also said to Abraham, "As for Sarai your wife, you are no longer to call her Sarai; her name will be Sarah. {15:18} I will bless her and will surely give you a son by her. I will bless her so that she will be the mother of nations; kings of peoples will come from her." {15:19} Abraham fell facedown; he laughed and said to himself, "Will a son be born to a man a hundred years old? Will Sarah bear a child at the age of ninety?" {15:20} And Abraham said to God, "If only Ishmael might live under your blessing!" {15:21} Then God said, "Yes, but your wife Sarah will bear you a son, and you will call him Isaac. I will establish my covenant with him as an everlasting covenant for his descendants after him. {15:22} As for Ishmael, I have heard you: I will surely bless him; I will make him fruitful and will greatly increase his numbers. He will be the father of twelve rulers, and I will make him into a great nation. {15:23} But my covenant I will establish with Isaac, whom Sarah will bear to you by this time next year." {15:24} When he had finished speaking with Abraham, God went up from him. {15:25} On that very day, Abraham took his son Ishmael and all those born in his household or bought with his money, every male in his household, and circumcised them, as God told him. {15:26} Abraham was ninety-nine years old when he was circumcised, {15:27} and his son Ishmael was thirteen. {15:28} Abraham and his son Ishmael were both circumcised on that very day. {15:29} And every male in Abraham's household, including those born in his household or bought from a foreigner, was circumcised with him. {15:30} This law is for all generations forever; there is no change to the days or omission of one day from the eight days, for it is an eternal ordinance written on the heavenly tablets. {15:31} Any male who is not circumcised on the eighth day does not belong to the children of the covenant which the Lord made with Abraham but to the children of destruction. There is no sign that he is the Lord's, and he is destined to be destroyed and removed from the earth for breaking the covenant. {15:32} All the angels of the presence and sanctification were created this way from the day of their creation. Before the angels of the presence and sanctification, the Lord sanctified Israel to be with Him and His holy angels. {15:33} Command the children of Israel to observe this covenant sign for their generations as an eternal ordinance so they will not be removed from the land. {15:34} The command is ordained as a covenant to be observed forever among all the children of Israel. {15:35} The Lord did not bring Ishmael, his sons, his brothers, or Esau near to Him because they are the children of Abraham. He chose Israel to be His people. {15:36} He sanctified Israel and gathered them from among all the children of men. There are many nations and peoples, but all are His. He has appointed spirits over them to lead them astray from Him. {15:37} But He did not appoint any angel or spirit over

Israel; He alone is their ruler. He will preserve them and require them at the hand of His angels and spirits to preserve and bless them. They will be His and He will be theirs forever. {15:38} However, I now announce to you that the children of Israel will not keep this ordinance. They will not circumcise their sons according to this law. They will neglect the circumcision of their sons, leaving them as they were born. {15:39} There will be great wrath from the Lord against the children of Israel because they have forsaken His covenant, turned away from His word, and blasphemed. They will be removed and rooted out of the land. There will be no more pardon or forgiveness for all the sins of this eternal error.

{16:1} On the new moon of the fourth month, we appeared to Abraham at the oak of Mamre and spoke with him, revealing that Sarah would bear him a son. Sarah laughed upon hearing this, feeling fearful and denying her laughter when questioned. {16:2} We disclosed to her the name of her son, Isaac, as written in the heavenly tablets, assuring her of conception upon our return at the appointed time. {16:3} During this month, the Lord executed judgment on Sodom, Gomorrah, Zeboim, and the entire region of the Jordan, consuming them with fire and brimstone for their exceedingly wicked deeds of uncleanness and fornication. {16:4} Similarly, God will judge places that mirror the uncleanness of Sodom. However, Lot was spared because of God's remembrance of Abraham, rescuing him from the destruction. {16:5} Sadly, Lot and his daughters committed grave sin upon the earth, uncommon since Adam's time, leading to a divine decree to root out their descendants and execute judgment upon them like Sodom. {16:6} In this month, Abraham departed from Hebron and settled between Kadesh and Shur in the mountains of Gerar. {16:7} In the middle of the fifth month, he moved to the Well of the Oath. {16:8} In the middle of the sixth month, the Lord visited Sarah and fulfilled His promise. She conceived and gave birth to Isaac in the third month, precisely as the Lord had foretold, during the festival of the first fruits of the harvest. {16:9} Abraham circumcised Isaac on the eighth day, initiating the covenant ordained forever. {16:10} In the sixth year of the fourth week, we returned to Abraham at the Well of the Oath as promised to Sarah, finding her pregnant as we had foretold. {16:11} We blessed Abraham and revealed to him all that had been decreed concerning him: that he would see six more sons before his death, but Isaac would carry on his name and lineage. {16:12} The descendants of his sons would be counted among the Gentiles, but from Isaac's line, a holy seed would arise, not reckoned among the Gentiles but belonging to the Most High as a chosen people, a kingdom of priests, and a holy nation. {16:13} Sarah and Abraham rejoiced exceedingly upon hearing these blessings, and Abraham built an altar to the Lord who had delivered him, celebrating with a seven-day festival of joy near the Well of the Oath. {16:14} He constructed booths for himself and his servants during the festival, becoming the first to observe the feast of tabernacles on the earth. {16:15} Each day of the festival, Abraham offered burnt offerings to the Lord: two oxen, two rams, seven sheep, and a he-goat for sin offering, seeking atonement for himself and his descendants. {16:16} As thank offerings, he presented seven rams, seven kids, seven sheep, and seven he-goats, along with their fruit and drink offerings, burning all the fat on the altar as a pleasing aroma to the Lord. {16:17} Morning and evening, he burned fragrant incense—frankincense, galbanum, stacte, nard, myrrh, and spices—mixed in equal parts and pure. {16:18} He celebrated this feast with heartfelt joy for seven days, joined by all in his household. No stranger or uncircumcised person was present. {16:19} He praised his Creator for creating him in his generation, knowing that from him would come forth the righteous line for eternal generations, blessed and rejoicing in the festival of the Lord—a joy accepted by the Most High. {16:20} We blessed Abraham and his descendants forever, for observing this festival in its appointed time according to the heavenly tablets. {16:21} Therefore, it is decreed for Israel on the heavenly tablets to celebrate the feast of tabernacles joyfully for seven days in the seventh month, pleasing to the Lord, an eternal statute observed annually without limit. {16:22} During this feast, they dwell in booths, wear wreaths on their heads, and carry leafy branches and willows from the brook. {16:23} Abraham took palm branches and the fruit of goodly trees, circling the altar seven times each morning, offering praise and thanksgiving to his God with great joy.

{17:1} In the first year of the fifth week, Isaac was weaned during this jubilee, around 1982 A.M. Abraham celebrated with a great banquet in the third month, on the day Isaac was weaned. Ishmael, the son of Hagar the Egyptian, was present before Abraham, his father, and Abraham rejoiced and blessed God for seeing his sons and not dying childless. He recalled God's promise to him when Lot departed, rejoicing that the Lord had given him offspring to inherit the earth, and he praised the Creator of all things. {17:2} Sarah observed Ishmael playing and rejoicing, which made her jealous. She said to Abraham, "Cast out this bondwoman and her son; for the son of this bondwoman shall not be heir with my son, Isaac." This troubled Abraham greatly because of his maidservant and his son, but God said to him, "Do not be troubled because of the boy and because of your bondwoman. Whatever Sarah says to you, listen to her, for Isaac will be called your heir. But I will also make a great nation of the son of the bondwoman because he is your offspring." {17:3} Early the next morning, Abraham took bread and a bottle of water, placed them on Hagar's shoulders along with the child, and sent her away. She wandered in the wilderness of Beersheba, and when the water ran out, the child became thirsty and unable to go on, falling down. Hagar placed him under an olive tree and sat down a bow-shot away, crying, "Let me not see the death of my child." An angel of God comforted her, saying, "Do not weep, Hagar. God has heard the child's cry. Get up, lift him up, and hold him in your hand." Hagar opened her eyes and saw a well of water. She filled her bottle and gave the child a drink, and they journeyed to the wilderness of Paran. {17:4} The child grew and became skilled with the bow. God was with him, and his mother arranged for him to marry a wife from among the daughters of Egypt. She bore him a son named Nebaioth, saying, "The Lord was near to me when I called upon Him." {17:5} In the seventh week, in the first year thereof, around 2003 A.M., in the first month of this jubilee, on the twelfth day of the month, voices were heard in heaven concerning Abraham. They testified that he was faithful in all God had commanded him, that he loved the Lord, and that in every trial he remained faithful. {17:6} Mastêmâ, the accuser, came before God and said, "Abraham loves Isaac, his son, and delights in him above all else. Command him to offer Isaac as a burnt offering on the altar, and you will see if he obeys this command. Then you will know if he is truly faithful in all things where you test him." {17:7} The Lord already knew that Abraham was faithful through all his trials: in leaving his country, enduring famine, facing the wealth of kings, losing his wife temporarily, and even in circumcising himself. He remained faithful through the ordeal with Ishmael and Hagar when he sent them away. In every test, Abraham proved faithful, never faltering, always devoted to the Lord.

{18:1} God called to Abraham, "Abraham, Abraham!" and Abraham responded, "Here I am." {18:2} God said, "Take your beloved son Isaac, whom you love dearly, and go to the high country. Offer him there as a burnt offering on one of the mountains I will show you." {18:3} Early the next morning, Abraham saddled his donkey and took two of his young men with him, along with Isaac his son. He split the wood for the burnt offering and set out for the place God had directed him. On the third day of their journey, he saw the place in the distance. {18:4} Abraham said to his young men, "Stay here with the donkey; the boy and I will go over there to worship, and then we will come back to you." {18:5} Taking the wood for the burnt offering, Abraham placed it on Isaac his son, and he took in his hand the fire and the knife. As the two of them walked together, Isaac spoke to his father, "Father?" Abraham replied, "Here I am, my son." Isaac asked, "Here are the fire and the wood, but where is the sheep for the burnt offering?" {18:6} Abraham answered, "God will provide for Himself the sheep for the burnt offering, my son." And they continued onward to the place God had shown him. {18:7} Abraham built an altar there, placed the wood on it, bound Isaac his son, and laid him on the wood atop the altar. He reached out his hand and took the knife to slaughter his son. {18:8} But the Lord intervened, along with the angel and Mastêmâ, saying, "Do not lay your hand on the boy or do anything to him. For now I know that you fear God, since you have not withheld your son, your only son, from Me." {18:9} Abraham looked up and saw a ram caught by its horns in a thicket. He went and took the ram and offered it up as a burnt offering in place of his son. {18:10} Abraham named that place "The Lord will provide," so it is said to this day, "On the mount of the Lord it will be provided." {18:11} The Lord called to Abraham a second time from heaven, saying, "By Myself I have sworn, declares the Lord, because you have done this and have not withheld your son, your beloved one, I will surely bless you and multiply your descendants like the stars of heaven and the sand on the seashore. Your descendants shall possess the cities of their enemies, and through your offspring all nations on earth will be blessed, because you have obeyed My voice." {18:12} Abraham returned to his young men, and together they went to Beersheba, where Abraham settled near the Well of the Oath. {18:13} He celebrated this festival each year, a seven-day feast of joy, calling it the festival of the Lord, commemorating the seven days during which he journeyed and returned in peace. {18:14} Thus it is ordained and written on the heavenly tablets concerning Israel and its descendants, that they should observe this festival for seven days with the joy of a festival.

{19:1} In the first year of the forty-second jubilee, Abraham returned and settled near Hebron, known as Kirjath Arba, where he stayed for twenty-two years. {19:2} During the first year of the third week of this jubilee, Sarah's life came to its end, and she passed away in Hebron. {19:3} Abraham mourned for her and arranged her burial, showing patience and gentleness even in his grief. {19:4} He negotiated with the children of Heth for a burial place, and they offered him the double cave near Mamre, which is Hebron, for four hundred pieces of silver. {19:5} Although they offered it for free, Abraham insisted on paying the full price as a mark of respect. {19:6} Thus, he buried Sarah there, and her life spanned one hundred and twenty-seven years—two jubilees, four weeks, and one year. {19:7} This was the tenth trial Abraham faced and proved himself faithful and patient. He did not speak of God's promise regarding the land, but humbly sought a burial place, thus affirming his faithfulness and friendship with God as recorded on heavenly tablets. {19:8} In the fourth year of this period, he arranged a marriage for his son Isaac with Rebecca, the daughter of Bethuel, the nephew of Abraham. {19:9} Hagar had passed away before Sarah, and Abraham took Keturah as his wife, who bore him six sons over the next twenty-two years. {19:10} In the sixth week of the second year, Rebecca gave birth to twin sons, Jacob and Esau. Jacob grew up peaceful and dwelling in tents, while Esau became a skilled hunter and man of the field, rugged and hairy. {19:11} Abraham favored Jacob, foreseeing that his name and lineage would carry forward the promise of God. {19:12} He instructed Rebecca to watch over Jacob, knowing her love for him exceeded that for Esau. {19:13} Abraham blessed Jacob, affirming that through him, the blessings promised by God to Abraham and his forefathers would continue. {19:14} Jacob received this blessing as Abraham kissed him and spoke words of favor and prosperity over him, envisioning a future where Jacob's descendants would flourish under God's protection. Rebecca cherished Jacob deeply, whereas Isaac favored Esau more than Jacob.

{20:1} In the forty-second jubilee, during the first year of the seventh week, Abraham gathered Ishmael with his twelve sons, Isaac with his two sons, and the six sons of Keturah along with their offspring. {20:2} He instructed them to walk in the ways of the Lord, practicing righteousness, loving their neighbors, and upholding justice and righteousness in all their dealings with humanity. {20:3} Abraham emphasized the covenant of circumcision that God had made with them, urging them not to stray from the paths commanded by the Lord. They were to abstain from all forms of fornication and uncleanness, purging such sin from their midst. {20:4} He warned against marrying Canaanite women, as the seed of Canaan would be eradicated from the land due to their wickedness. {20:5} Abraham recounted the judgments that befell the giants and the people of Sodom, who were condemned for their wickedness, fornication, and corruption. {20:6} He admonished his descendants to guard themselves against sin and impurity, lest they bring disgrace upon their name and invite destruction upon themselves like Sodom and Gomorrah. {20:7} "My sons," Abraham implored, "love the God of heaven and faithfully follow His commandments. Avoid idols and the impurities associated with them, for they are worthless creations of human hands without any spiritual power. {20:8} Serve the Most High God alone, worshiping Him continually, and may His favor rest upon you. Walk in righteousness and integrity before Him, that He may delight in you and bless all your endeavors on the earth." {20:9} Abraham then bestowed gifts upon Ishmael, his sons, and the sons of Keturah, and sent them away from Isaac. {20:10} Ishmael and his descendants, along with Keturah's sons and their offspring, journeyed and settled from Paran to Babylon, encompassing the lands eastward towards the desert. {20:11} These descendants intermingled and became known as Arabs and Ishmaelites.

{21:1} In the sixth year of the seventh week of this jubilee, Abraham called Isaac his son and {21:2} said to him, "I have grown old and do not know the day of my death, yet I have lived a hundred and seventy-five years, always remembering the Lord and seeking to do His will with all my heart. {21:3} I have despised idols and those who serve them, devoting myself to observing the will of the living and holy God, who is faithful and just, showing no partiality and accepting no bribes. {21:4} Now, my son, follow His commandments, ordinances, and judgments. Avoid abominations, idols, and molten images. {21:5} Never consume blood from animals or birds, but offer sacrifices according to the proper rituals on the altar, ensuring they are pleasing to the Lord. {21:6} Offer the fat and portions of thanksgiving sacrifices as sweet offerings before Him, eating the meat promptly and not letting it remain beyond the second day. {21:7} It is written in the books of our forefathers, and in the words of Enoch and Noah, that such offerings are acceptable to the Lord. {21:8} Always sprinkle salt on your offerings as a sign of the covenant with the Lord. {21:9} Use only specific types of wood for the altar: cypress, bay, almond, fir, pine, cedar, savin, fig, olive, myrrh, laurel, and aspalathus—avoiding old, split, or dark wood that lacks fragrance. {21:10} Be clean in body at all times, washing with water before approaching the altar, and wash your hands and feet afterward. {21:11} Guard against any trace of blood on yourself or your garments; cover it with dust and never consume blood, for it is the soul. {21:12} Do not take gifts or compensation for human bloodshed, as it must be avenged to be cleansed from the earth. {21:13} Avoid the sinful ways and deeds of men, for they lead to death and separation from the Most High God. {21:14} Turn away from their uncleanness and observe the ordinances of the Most High God, walking uprightly in all things. {21:15} He will bless your endeavors and raise a righteous generation from your seed throughout the earth. {21:16} My name and your name shall endure forever under heaven. Go in peace, my son. May the Most High God strengthen you to fulfill His will, blessing all your descendants with righteousness for generations." {21:17} Isaac departed from Abraham, rejoicing in his father's guidance.

{22:1} In the first week of the forty-fourth jubilee, in the second year, the year of Abraham's death, Isaac and Ishmael came from the Well of the Oath to celebrate the feast of weeks with their father Abraham. Abraham rejoiced greatly at their arrival, for Isaac had many possessions in Beersheba and would often return to visit his father. {22:2} During this time, Ishmael also came to see his father, and both sons gathered together. {22:3} Isaac offered a burnt offering on the altar his father had built in Hebron and also presented a thank offering, celebrating joyfully with his brother Ishmael. {22:4} Rebecca made fresh cakes from the new harvest and gave them to Jacob, her son, to take to Abraham as a first fruits offering. {22:5} Isaac also sent a choice thank offering to Abraham through Jacob, which he enjoyed with gratitude. {22:6} Abraham ate and drank and blessed the Most High God, creator of heaven and earth, who provides abundance to all mankind for their sustenance and enjoyment. {22:7} Abraham then thanked God for allowing him to live to the age of one hundred and seventy-five, experiencing peace throughout his days without being overcome by enemies. {22:8} He prayed for God's mercy and peace upon himself and his descendants, that they may be a chosen nation and inheritance among all peoples forever. {22:9} Turning to Jacob, Abraham blessed him, praying that God would strengthen him to walk in righteousness and fulfill His will, choosing Jacob and his seed to be a holy nation according to His eternal purpose. {22:10} Abraham called Jacob near, kissed him, and spoke blessings over him and all his descendants. {22:11} He prayed that God would bless Jacob's seed with righteousness, sanctifying some among them throughout the earth. {22:12} Nations would serve Jacob's descendants, and all peoples would bow before them. {22:13} Abraham urged Jacob to remain steadfast in righteousness, separate from the ways and practices of the Canaanites, who engage in idolatry and uncleanness. {22:14} He warned Jacob against taking a wife from among the daughters of Canaan, whose seed would be rooted out from the earth due to their transgression. {22:15} Abraham foresaw no hope for idolaters and the profane, destined for Sheol and condemnation, like the fate of Sodom's children. {22:16} He encouraged Jacob not to fear or be dismayed, assured that the Most High God would preserve him from destruction and guide him away from all paths of error. {22:17} Abraham declared that the house he built would bear his name forever, passing to Jacob and his descendants. {22:18} After blessing Jacob with heartfelt affection, Abraham rested beside him. {22:19} Jacob slept in the bosom of his grandfather Abraham, who kissed him seven times, overflowing with love and joy. {22:20} Abraham blessed Jacob again, praising the Most High God who had brought him from Ur of the Chaldeans to inherit the promised land. {22:21} He prayed for grace and mercy to be upon Jacob and his seed forever, asking God to watch over and bless them as His chosen inheritance.

{23:1} Jacob placed two fingers over Abraham's eyes and blessed the God of gods. He covered Abraham's face and stretched out his feet, peacefully entering the eternal sleep and joining his ancestors. {23:2} Unaware of Abraham's passing, Jacob continued lying beside him until he awoke and felt the coldness of Abraham's body. Calling out "Father, father," and receiving no response, Jacob realized that his beloved grandfather had died. {23:3} Hurriedly, Jacob arose and ran to inform his mother Rebecca. Together, they went to Isaac in the night and delivered the solemn news. Accompanied by Jacob carrying a lamp, they entered and found Abraham lying lifeless. {23:4} Isaac fell upon his father's face, weeping bitterly and kissing him. {23:5} The sound of mourning filled Abraham's house, prompting Ishmael and his household to come and join in the grieving. {23:6} Together, Isaac and Ishmael buried Abraham in the double cave near his wife Sarah, mourning him for forty days along with all the men of Abraham's household, including Keturah's sons in their respective places. {23:7} Thus ended the days of Abraham's life, spanning three jubilees and four additional weeks of years, totaling one hundred and seventy-five years. Abraham lived long, fulfilling his days amidst trials and the wickedness of his time, yet maintaining righteousness and pleasing the Lord in all his actions. {23:8} Reflecting on the generations before and after the Flood, it was clear that humanity's lifespan had decreased due to manifold tribulations and increasing wickedness, except for Abraham who remained righteous and fulfilled his days. {23:9} From Abraham's time onward, generations would grow old quickly, rarely reaching even two jubilees before suffering and ignorance overwhelmed them, bringing calamities and judgments upon the earth. {23:10} In those days, a man's life would be considered long if he reached a jubilee and a half, yet his days would be filled with pain, sorrow, and various afflictions. {23:11} This evil generation would be marked by transgressions, uncleanness, and idolatry, forsaking the covenant with the Lord and neglecting His commandments and ordinances. {23:12} They would be confronted by wars, bloodshed, and moral decay, striving against each other with weapons and deceit, defiling sacred places and corrupting themselves with wickedness. {23:13} The Lord's judgment would be severe upon them, delivering them to destruction, captivity, and plunder at the hands of merciless nations. {23:14} Even in their distress, they would cry out for salvation, but none would come, and their days would be plagued by suffering and turmoil. {23:15} The youth would prematurely age, and the old would suffer greatly, their days filled with tribulation and oppression. {23:16} Yet amidst these trials, children would begin to study the laws and seek righteousness, striving to return to the path of virtue. {23:17} As time progressed, their days would lengthen once more, approaching a thousand years as in the days of old, and their lives would be characterized by peace, joy, and blessings. {23:18} Satan and evil would be absent, and the righteous would live in perpetual gratitude and harmony, witnessing the fulfillment of divine justice and the defeat of their enemies. {23:19} Their spirits would find rest and joy, knowing the Lord judges and shows mercy to all who love Him. Thus, Moses was instructed to record these words on heavenly tablets as an eternal testimony for future generations.

{24:1} After Abraham's death, the Lord blessed Isaac, his son. Isaac left Hebron and settled at the Well of the Vision in the first year of the third week of this jubilee, residing there for seven years. {24:2} In the first year of the fourth week, a famine struck the land, distinct from the earlier one during Abraham's time. {24:3} During this time, Jacob was cooking lentil stew when Esau, returning hungry from the field, asked for some. Jacob proposed a trade: Esau's birthright in exchange for the stew and bread. {24:4} Esau, considering his hunger, agreed to sell his birthright to Jacob, who then made him swear an oath to confirm the transaction. {24:5} Jacob gave Esau bread and stew, and Esau, indifferent to his birthright, earned the name Edom, signifying his preference for food over inheritance. {24:6} Thus, Jacob became the rightful heir while Esau lost his privileged position. {24:7} As the famine subsided, Isaac was directed by the Lord not to go to Egypt but to stay in the land promised to Abraham. {24:8} Isaac obeyed and settled in Gerar with Abimelech, the king of the Philistines, where the Lord appeared to him, reaffirming the covenant and promising prosperity and numerous descendants. {24:9} Isaac prospered greatly among the Philistines, accumulating vast herds and wealth, which stirred envy among them. {24:10} The Philistines filled up the wells that Abraham's servants had dug, prompting Isaac to move away from Gerar to the valleys of Gerar in the first year of the seventh week. {24:11} There, Isaac reopened the wells, giving them the same names Abraham had given them, asserting his rights against local disputes. {24:12} Despite challenges from the Philistines, Isaac dug new wells until he found living water. {24:13} Contentious shepherds of Gerar claimed the wells, leading Isaac to name one "Perversity" due to their obstinance. {24:14} Another well was called "Enmity" after similar disputes, but Isaac eventually found peace and called the next well "Room," signifying God's provision and blessing. {24:15} Returning to the Well of the Oath in the forty-fourth jubilee, Isaac was visited by the Lord on the new moon of the first month, reiterating His covenant with Abraham and blessing Isaac abundantly. {24:16} Isaac built an altar there and worshiped the God of Abraham, also discovering living water through a newly dug well. {24:17} Reflecting on his oath to the Philistines, Isaac named the place the Well of the Oath. {24:18} On that day, Isaac cursed the Philistines for their hostility and deceit, prophesying their downfall and perpetual enmity with his descendants. {24:19} This decree was recorded on heavenly tablets, sealing their fate for judgment day, ensuring their extinction from the earth as divine justice prevails.

{25:1} In the second year of this week of jubilee, Rebecca, Jacob's mother, called him and said, "My son, do not marry a woman from the daughters of Canaan like your brother Esau, who took two Canaanite wives. They have brought bitterness to my soul with their immoral deeds, for all their actions are filled with fornication and lust, devoid of righteousness. {25:2} My son, I love you deeply, and my heart blesses you every hour of every day. {25:3} Now, listen to me and obey your mother's will. Do not take a wife from the women of this land. Instead, marry a woman from the household of my father and from my relatives. By doing so, the Most High God will bless you, and your descendants will be a righteous and holy lineage." {25:4} Jacob responded to Rebecca, saying, "Mother, I am eighty-two years old and have never been with a woman, nor have I pledged myself to anyone. I have no intention of marrying a Canaanite woman. {25:5} I remember the instructions of our father Abraham, who commanded me not to take a wife from the Canaanites but from our own family. {25:6} I have heard that Laban, your brother, has daughters, and I desire to marry one of them. {25:7} I have kept myself pure from sin and corruption all my life, following the commands of Abraham, despite Esau's persistent urging over the past twenty-two years to marry one of his wives' sisters. {25:8} I swear to you, mother, that I will never marry a daughter of Canaan and will not follow the wicked path of my brother. Fear not; I will uphold your wishes, walking in righteousness and keeping my ways pure forever." {25:9} Rebecca lifted her eyes to heaven, extended her hands, and blessed the Most High God who created heaven and earth. She praised and thanked Him, saying, {25:10} "Blessed be the Lord God, whose holy name is blessed forever. He has given me Jacob as a pure and holy son. He belongs to You, and his descendants will be Yours throughout all generations. {25:11} Bless him, O Lord, and enable me to speak words of righteousness that will bless him." {25:12} As the spirit of righteousness descended upon her, Rebecca placed her hands on Jacob's head and said: {25:13} "Blessed are you, Lord of righteousness and God of all ages. May you bless my son beyond all generations of men. {25:14} Grant him the path of righteousness and reveal righteousness to his descendants. {25:15} May his sons multiply during his lifetime, their numbers surpassing the stars in the sky and the sand on the seashore. {25:16} Give them this land as promised to Abraham and his descendants forever. {25:17} May I see blessed children born to you in my lifetime, and may all your descendants be blessed and holy. {25:18} As you have brought joy to your mother's heart in her lifetime, so may my womb bless you. {25:19} May my affection and my breasts bless you, and may my mouth and tongue praise you greatly. {25:20} May your descendants increase and spread over the earth, finding joy in heaven and earth forever. {25:21} May they rejoice on the day of great peace, and may your name and your descendants endure through all ages. {25:22} May the Most High God be their God, and may the God of righteousness dwell among them, with a sanctuary built by them forever. {25:23} Blessed be those who bless you and cursed be those who falsely curse you." {25:24} Rebecca kissed Jacob and said to him, "May the Lord of the world love you as deeply as your mother's heart rejoices in you and blesses you." And with that, she ceased her blessings.

{26:1} In the seventh year of this week, Isaac, now old and with failing eyesight, called his elder son Esau and said to him, "My son, I am old and do not know the day of my death. {26:2} Now, take your hunting gear, your quiver and bow, and go out to the field. Hunt game for me and prepare savory food that I love. Bring it to me so that I may eat and bless you before I die." {26:3} Rebecca overheard Isaac speaking to Esau. {26:4} Esau went out to the field early to hunt and bring back game to his father. {26:5} Rebecca called Jacob and said to him, "I heard your father Isaac instructing Esau to hunt game and prepare savory food for him to eat and bless him before the Lord. {26:6} Now, my son, do as I command you. Go to the flock and fetch me two choice young goats. I will prepare them as savory food for your father, just as he likes. {26:7} You will take it to your father so he may eat and bless you before he dies, ensuring that you receive the blessing." {26:8} Jacob expressed concern to his mother, "Mother, I won't withhold anything that would please father to eat. But I fear he will recognize my voice and realize I'm deceiving him. {26:9} You know I am smooth-skinned while Esau is hairy. If he finds out, he will curse me instead of blessing me." {26:10} Rebecca replied, "Let the curse be on me, my son. Just obey my instructions." {26:11} Jacob followed Rebecca's instructions, fetching two good and fat goats from the flock. He brought them to his mother, who prepared the savory food that Isaac loved. {26:12} Rebecca took Esau's best garments, which were in her possession, and dressed Jacob, her younger son, in them. {26:13} She covered his hands and the smooth part of his neck with goat skins. {26:14} Then she gave the prepared food and bread to Jacob. {26:15} Jacob went to his father and said, "Father, I am here. I have done as you asked. Sit up and eat of the game I brought, so your soul may bless me." {26:16} Isaac asked his son, "How did you find it so quickly, my son?" {26:17} Jacob replied, "Because the Lord your God brought it to me." {26:18} Isaac then said, "Come near so I can feel you, my son, and confirm whether you are Esau or not." {26:19} Jacob approached Isaac, who felt his hands and said, "The voice is Jacob's, but the hands are Esau's." {26:20} Isaac, not recognizing him due to God's intervention, blessed Jacob. {26:21} He asked again, "Are you really Esau, my son?" Jacob replied, "I am your son Esau." {26:22} Isaac requested, "Bring me the game so I may eat it and bless you." Jacob brought it to him, and he ate. Jacob also brought him wine, and he drank. {26:23} Then Isaac said, "Come near and kiss me, my son." {26:24} Jacob approached, kissed him, and Isaac smelled Esau's garments on him. {26:25} Isaac blessed Jacob, saying, "Ah, the smell of my son is like the smell of a field blessed by the Lord. {26:26} May God give you dew from heaven and the richness of the earth, an abundance of grain and new wine. {26:27} May nations serve you and peoples bow down to you. Be lord over your brothers, and may the sons of your mother bow down to you. {26:28} May those who curse you be cursed, and those who bless you be blessed forever." {26:29} As soon as Isaac finished blessing Jacob and Jacob had left, Esau returned from hunting. {26:30} He also prepared savory food and brought it to his father, saying, "Sit up, father, and eat of my game, so your soul may bless me." {26:31} Isaac asked, "Who are you?" Esau replied, "I am your firstborn son, Esau. I did as you told me." {26:32} Isaac was greatly astonished and said, "Who then hunted and brought me game before you came? I ate it and blessed him, and indeed, he will be blessed." {26:33} When Esau heard his father's words, he cried out with a bitter cry and pleaded, "Bless me too, father." {26:34} Isaac responded, "Your brother came deceitfully and took your blessing." {26:35} Esau lamented, "No wonder his name is Jacob, for he has supplanted me twice: he took my birthright, and now he has taken my blessing." {26:36} Esau implored Isaac, "Have you not reserved a blessing for me, father?" {26:37} Isaac answered Esau, saying, {26:38} "I have made him your lord, and I have given him all his brothers as servants. I have sustained him with grain and wine. What more can I do for you, my son?" {26:39} Esau begged, "Do you have only one blessing, father? Bless me too, father." Esau wept aloud. {26:40} Isaac replied, {26:41} "Away from the richness of the earth shall your dwelling be, away from the dew of heaven above. {26:42} You will live by the sword and serve your brother. But when you rebel, you will break his yoke from your neck." {26:43} Esau harbored anger toward Jacob because of the blessing his father had given him, and he said to himself, "The days of mourning for my father are near; then I will kill my brother Jacob."

{27:1} Rebecca learned through a dream about Esau's intention to kill Jacob. She summoned Jacob and said, "Esau, your brother, plans to avenge himself by killing you. {27:2} Therefore, my son, listen to me. Flee to my brother Laban in Haran. Stay with him for a while until your brother's anger subsides and he forgets what you have done. Then I will send for you to return." {27:3} Jacob insisted, "I'm not afraid. If Esau comes to kill me, I will defend myself." But Rebecca pleaded, "I cannot bear to lose both my sons in one day." {27:4} Jacob argued further with his mother, "Father is old and cannot see well. If I leave him abruptly, it will upset him, and he may curse me. I will not go unless he sends me away." {27:5} Rebecca assured Jacob, "Let me handle Isaac. I will speak to him, and he will send you away." {27:6} Rebecca went to Isaac and said, "I am weary of my life because of Esau's Hittite wives. If Jacob takes a wife from among these Canaanite women, what is left for me to live for? The women of this land are wicked." {27:7} Isaac called Jacob, blessed him, and instructed him, "Do not take a wife from the daughters of Canaan. {27:8} Arise, go to Mesopotamia, to the household of Bethuel, your mother's father. Take a wife from there among the daughters of Laban, your mother's brother. {27:9} May God Almighty bless you, make you fruitful and multiply you, so that you may become a company of nations. {27:10} May He give you the blessings of Abraham, to you and your descendants, that you may inherit the land of your sojournings, the land God gave to Abraham." {27:11} Isaac then sent Jacob away to Mesopotamia, to Laban, son of Bethuel the Aramean, brother of Rebecca. {27:12} After Jacob set off for Mesopotamia, Rebecca's spirit grieved for her son, and she wept. {27:13} Isaac comforted Rebecca, saying, "Do not weep for Jacob, my sister. He goes in peace and will return in peace. {27:14} The Most High God will protect him from all harm and be with him always. {27:15} I know he will prosper in all his ways until he returns safely to us." {27:16} Isaac blessed Jacob, who journeyed from Beersheba toward Haran. {27:17} On the first year of the second week of the forty-fourth jubilee, Jacob arrived at Luz, also known as Bethel, on the new moon of the first month. {27:18} He reached the place at sunset and rested there for the night. {27:19} Taking a stone from that place, he put it under his head and lay down to sleep. {27:20} He dreamt of a ladder on the earth with its top reaching to heaven, and angels of the Lord ascending and descending on it. {27:21} The Lord stood above it and said to Jacob, "I am the Lord, the God of Abraham and Isaac. The land on which you lie, I will give to you and your descendants. {27:22} Your descendants will be numerous as the dust of the earth, spreading to the west, east, north, and south. All the families of the earth will be blessed through you and your offspring. {27:23} I am with you and will watch over you wherever you go, bringing you back to this land. I will not leave you until I have done what I have promised you." {27:24} Jacob awoke from his sleep and said, "Surely the Lord is in this place, and I did not know it." {27:25} He was afraid and said, "How awesome is this place! This is none other than the house of God, the gateway to heaven." {27:26} Early the next morning, Jacob took the stone he had placed under his head, set it up as a pillar, poured oil on top of it, {27:27} and named the place Bethel, though originally it was called Luz. {27:28} Then Jacob made a vow to the Lord, saying, "If God will be with me, protect me on this journey, provide me with food and clothing, {27:29} and bring me safely back to my father's house, then the Lord will be my God. {27:30} This stone I have set up as a pillar will be God's house, and of all that You give me, I will give You a tenth."

{28:1} Jacob continued his journey and arrived in the land of the east, where Laban, Rebecca's brother, lived. He stayed with Laban and worked for him, desiring Rachel as his wife. {28:2} After serving Laban for seven years, Jacob said to him, "Give me my wife, for whom I have worked." So Laban agreed and made preparations for a wedding feast. {28:3} However, on the wedding night, Laban deceived Jacob by giving him Leah, his elder daughter, instead of Rachel. Laban also gave his servant Zilpah to Leah. {28:4} Jacob, unaware of the switch, consummated the marriage with Leah. Angry, he confronted Laban, "Why have you deceived me? I served you for Rachel, not Leah! Let me go." {28:5} Laban defended his actions, saying it was custom to marry off the elder daughter first. He explained that such practices were ordained and recorded in heavenly tablets as righteous. {28:6} Laban proposed a solution, "Complete the bridal week with Leah, and I will give you Rachel as well. Stay and work for me another seven years." {28:7} When the week with Leah was over, Laban gave Rachel to Jacob, and Jacob agreed to serve another seven years. Laban also gave Rachel's servant Bilhah to her. {28:8} Jacob fulfilled another seven years for Rachel, for whom he initially worked without charge. {28:9} During this time, Leah, whom Jacob initially did not love, bore him four sons: Reuben in the first year of the third week, Simeon in the third year of the same week, Levi in the sixth year of the same week, and Judah in the first year of the fourth week. {28:10} Rachel, however, was unable to conceive, and this caused her great envy towards Leah. She urged Jacob to give her children, and Jacob responded in reassurance. {28:11} When Rachel saw that Leah had borne four sons, she gave her servant Bilhah to Jacob as a wife. Bilhah bore Jacob two sons: Dan in the sixth year of the third week and Naphtali in the second year of the fourth week. {28:12} Seeing Rachel's success with Bilhah, Leah also gave her servant Zilpah to Jacob, who bore him two sons: Gad in the third year of the fourth week and Asher in the fifth year of the same week. {28:13} Later, Leah bore Jacob two more sons: Issachar in the fourth year of the fourth week and Zebulun in the sixth year of the same week, along with a daughter named Dinah. {28:14} Finally, Rachel conceived and gave birth to Joseph in the sixth year of the fourth week, on the new moon of the fourth month. {28:15} After Joseph's birth, Jacob approached Laban and requested to return to his father Isaac's house, having fulfilled his obligation to Laban. {28:16} Laban, reluctant to let Jacob leave, proposed a deal to retain him by offering him speckled and spotted lambs and goats as wages for his continued service. {28:17} This agreement resulted in Jacob's possessions multiplying greatly, including oxen, sheep, donkeys, camels, and servants. {28:18} Laban and his sons became jealous of Jacob's prosperity and eventually sought to undermine him. They attempted to reclaim some of Jacob's flocks and treated him with hostility.

{29:1} After Rachel gave birth to Joseph, Laban went to shear his sheep, which were a three days' journey away. Seeing this opportunity, Jacob called Leah and Rachel aside and spoke kindly to them, explaining his dream where God instructed him to return to his father's house in Canaan. Moved by his words, Leah and Rachel agreed to accompany Jacob on his journey. {29:2} Jacob blessed the God of Isaac and Abraham, then gathered his wives, children, and possessions, crossing the river into the land of Gilead. He kept his plans hidden from Laban. {29:3} In the seventh year of the fourth week, on the twenty-first day of the first month, Jacob turned towards Gilead. Laban pursued him and caught up in the mountain of Gilead on the thirteenth day of the third month. {29:4} God intervened, appearing to Laban in a dream to prevent him from harming Jacob. Laban spoke with Jacob and on the fifteenth day, they made a covenant and Jacob hosted a feast. {29:5} They swore an oath, agreeing not to harm each other, and erected a heap of stones as a witness, naming the place 'The Heap of Witness.' {29:6} Previously, Gilead was known as the land of the Rephaim, a region inhabited by giants. They were exceptionally tall, ranging from ten to seven cubits in height, and were located from Ammon to Mount Hermon, with Karnaim, Ashtaroth, Edrei, Misur, and Beon as their principal cities. {29:7} Due to their wickedness, the Lord destroyed them, allowing the Amorites to take their place. {29:8} Jacob sent Laban away back to Mesopotamia, and Jacob settled in Gilead. {29:9} In the ninth month, on the eleventh day, Jacob crossed the Jabbok River. On that day, Esau, his brother, approached him, and they reconciled. Esau then departed to Seir, while Jacob continued dwelling in tents. {29:10} In the first year of the fifth week of this jubilee, Jacob crossed the Jordan and settled beyond it, pasturing his flocks in various places. He sent provisions to his father Isaac regularly, including clothing, food, and other necessities. {29:11} Similarly, he sent supplies to his mother Rebecca four times a year, ensuring they lacked nothing. Isaac had returned to Hebron after residing at the tower of Abraham upon Jacob's departure to Mesopotamia. {29:12} During this time, Esau married Mahalath, Ishmael's daughter, and moved to Mount Seir with his flocks and wives, leaving Isaac alone at the Well of the Oath. {29:13} Isaac relocated to the tower of Abraham in Hebron, where Jacob faithfully sent provisions to both his father and mother, who blessed him wholeheartedly.

{30:1} In the first year of the sixth week, Jacob journeyed peacefully to Salem, east of Shechem, in the fourth month. {30:2} During this time, Dinah, Jacob's daughter, was taken by Shechem, the son of Hamor the Hivite, who was the prince of that region. He defiled her, though she was just twelve years old. {30:3} Shechem pleaded with Jacob and his sons to allow him to marry Dinah. This enraged Jacob and his sons because of the dishonor done to Dinah by the men of Shechem. They spoke to them deceitfully and with malicious intent. {30:4} Simeon and Levi then unexpectedly came upon Shechem and executed judgment on all the men there. They killed every man in the city as punishment for defiling their sister Dinah. {30:5} This was to ensure that such an act would never happen again among the people of Israel, and they were empowered by God to carry out this judgment. {30:6} Henceforth, any man in Israel who gives his daughter or sister to a man of the Gentiles shall surely die by stoning, and the woman shall be burned with fire for bringing shame upon her father's house. {30:7} Israel must remain pure, free from adultery and uncleanness, for they are holy unto the Lord. {30:8} These laws are eternal and severe, with no possibility of atonement. Anyone who defiles the sanctity of Israel will face harsh judgment. {30:9} Moses was commanded to enforce these laws among the children of Israel, ensuring they do not intermarry with the Gentiles, for such unions are abominable before the Lord. {30:10} The story of the Shechemites serves as a testimony, showing the consequences of their deeds against Dinah and how Levi's zeal for righteousness earned him and his descendants a place in the priesthood. {30:11} This righteous act was recorded in heaven as a blessing upon them. {30:12} Jacob's sons brought Dinah back from Shechem's house and seized all their livestock and possessions as compensation. {30:13} Jacob reproached them, fearing retaliation from the Canaanites and Perizzites.

{31:1} On the new moon of the month, Jacob gathered all the people of his household and spoke to them, saying, "Purify yourselves and change your garments. Let us arise and go up to Bethel, where I made a vow to God when I fled from my brother Esau. He has been with me, brought me safely to this land, and now we must put away the foreign gods among us." {31:2} They surrendered their foreign gods, the earrings and necklaces that adorned them, and the idols Rachel had taken from her father Laban. She gave them to Jacob, who burned and smashed them, burying them under an oak tree in Shechem. {31:3} On the new moon of the seventh month, Jacob journeyed to Bethel. There, he built an altar where he had previously slept, setting up a pillar as a memorial. He sent word for his father Isaac and his mother Rebecca to join him for the sacrifice. {31:4} Isaac eagerly welcomed Jacob's invitation, saying, "Let my son come to me, so I may see him before I die." {31:5} Jacob went to the house of his father Abraham, accompanied by his sons Levi and Judah. Rebecca came out to meet them, overjoyed to see Jacob. She embraced him and upon seeing his sons, she asked, "Are these your sons, my son?" Embracing and blessing them, she prophesied, "Through you, the descendants of Abraham shall be renowned, a blessing upon the earth." {31:6} Jacob then entered Isaac's chamber, where his father lay. Taking Isaac's hand, he kissed him, and Isaac wept with joy, his sight restored to see Levi and Judah. {31:7} He blessed them, acknowledging them as truly his sons, and kissed and embraced them both. {31:8} Inspired by the spirit of prophecy, Isaac blessed Levi first, praying for greatness and glory for him and his descendants, who would serve in God's sanctuary like angels. {31:9} Levi's descendants would be judges and leaders among the sons of Jacob, speaking God's word and administering justice. {31:10} Turning to Judah, Isaac blessed him with strength and power over his enemies, foreseeing his descendants spreading across lands and instilling fear among nations. {31:11} Judah's line would bring salvation to Israel and sit on a throne of righteousness, bringing great peace to all of Jacob's descendants. {31:12} Overwhelmed with joy, Isaac blessed them again, and they ate and drank together that night. {31:13} Jacob arranged for Levi and Judah to sleep by Isaac's side, a sign of righteousness credited to him. {31:14} Throughout the night, Jacob recounted to Isaac all that had transpired, how God had shown him mercy and prosperity. {31:15} Isaac praised the God of Abraham, acknowledging His enduring mercy and righteousness toward Isaac's descendants. {31:16} In the morning, Jacob shared with Isaac the vow he had made to God, the vision he had seen, and his preparations for the sacrifice at Bethel. {31:17} Due to his old age, Isaac declined to accompany Jacob, but blessed him to fulfill his vow with God's favor. {31:18} He instructed Rebecca to go with Jacob, and they journeyed together to Bethel, accompanied by Deborah. {31:19} Jacob remembered the blessings Isaac had bestowed upon him and his sons, Levi and Judah, rejoicing and praising the God of his forefathers, Abraham and Isaac. {31:20} He affirmed his eternal hope in God, a promise for him and his sons, a testament recorded in the heavenly tablets of Isaac's blessing upon them.

{32:1} Jacob stayed the night at Bethel, where Levi had a dream that he and his descendants were ordained as priests of the Most High God forever. Upon waking, Levi blessed the Lord. {32:2} Early the next morning, on the fourteenth day of the month, Jacob tithed all that he had brought with him—people, cattle, gold, vessels, and garments. {32:3} During this time, Rachel conceived and bore Jacob's son Benjamin. Jacob counted his sons, appointing Levi for the Lord's service, clothing him in priestly garments and consecrating him with offerings. {32:4} On the fifteenth day of the month, Jacob presented offerings at the altar: fourteen oxen, twenty-eight rams, forty-nine sheep, seven lambs, and twenty-one goat kids—a pleasing burnt offering before God, fulfilling his vow. {32:5} For seven days, Jacob and his household celebrated with joy, feasting before the Lord and giving thanks for deliverance from all tribulations. {32:6} Jacob tithed all the clean animals and offered burnt sacrifices. Levi, chosen above his brothers, served as priest at Bethel, where Jacob confirmed the sanctity of his vow by tithing a second time, consecrating it to the Lord. {32:7} This ordinance on heavenly tablets decreed perpetual tithing in the chosen place of God's name, ensuring nothing remained from year to year. {32:8} The seeds, wine, and oil were consumed within their seasons; anything left was deemed unclean and burnt. {32:9} All tithes of oxen and sheep belonged to the Lord and His priests, eaten annually in His presence as ordained in the heavenly tablets. {32:10} On the twenty-second day of the month, Jacob resolved to build and sanctify the place for himself and his descendants. {32:11} The Lord appeared to Jacob that night, blessing him and renaming him Israel. God promised to increase his descendants, with kings arising from him to judge the nations and inherit the earth forever. {32:12} After speaking, God ascended into heaven, leaving Jacob in awe. {32:13} That night, an angel descended with seven tablets, revealing to Jacob future events concerning him and his sons. {32:14} Instructed not to build a permanent sanctuary at that place, Jacob was to dwell with Isaac until Isaac's death, and then die in peace in Egypt, buried honorably alongside Abraham and Isaac. {32:15} Jacob worried how he could remember all he had seen and read, but God assured him that all would be brought to his remembrance. {32:16} Jacob woke, recalling everything, and diligently recorded all he had seen and read. {32:17} He celebrated another day there, sacrificing as before, naming it 'Addition' to the feast days, following heavenly tablets' decree. {32:18} On the twenty-third day of the month, Rebecca's nurse Deborah died and was buried, the place named 'The river of Deborah' and the oak 'The oak of the mourning of Deborah.' {32:19} Rebecca returned to Isaac, and Jacob sent her gifts. {32:20} Jacob journeyed to Kabratan and settled there. {32:21} Rachel gave birth to Benjamin but died in Ephrath (Bethlehem). Jacob erected a pillar on her grave, marking the road above her resting place.

{33:1} Jacob settled to the south of Magdaladra'ef and later journeyed with Leah to visit his father Isaac on the new moon of the tenth month. {33:2} During this time, Reuben, Jacob's firstborn, saw Bilhah, Rachel's maid and Jacob's concubine, bathing in secret. He grew enamored of her and, finding her alone one night, he lay with her. {33:3} Bilhah awoke to find Reuben with her, and though she was ashamed and distressed, she kept the matter silent. {33:4} When Jacob returned, Bilhah revealed what had happened, causing Jacob to be furious with Reuben for defiling his concubine. {33:5} Jacob refrained from approaching Bilhah again, recognizing the severity of Reuben's offense in uncovering his father's shame—a deed condemned on heavenly tablets. {33:6} The law decreed death for anyone who lays with his father's wife, ensuring purity among the chosen people of God. {33:7} Moses was commanded to instruct Israel to abide by this law without exception, affirming death as the penalty for such uncleanness. {33:8} It was a perpetual law, never to be repealed, ensuring the sanctity of Israel before God. {33:9} In the third year of the sixth week, Jacob and his sons relocated to Abraham's house near Isaac and Rebecca. {33:10} Jacob's sons were: Reuben, Simeon, Levi, Judah, Issachar, Zebulon (sons of Leah); Joseph and Benjamin (sons of Rachel); Dan and Naphtali (sons of Bilhah); Gad and Asher (sons of Zilpah); and Dinah, Jacob's only daughter. {33:11} When they arrived, they bowed before Isaac and Rebecca, who blessed Jacob and his sons joyfully. Isaac was especially delighted to see Jacob's children.

{34:1} In the sixth year of this forty-fourth jubilee, Jacob sent his sons and servants to pasture their sheep near Shechem. {34:2} Unbeknownst to them, seven Amorite kings plotted to ambush them and seize their cattle. {34:3} Jacob, Levi, Judah, and Joseph remained at home with Isaac due to his sorrowful spirit, while Benjamin stayed with his father as the youngest. {34:4} The kings of Taphu, 'Aresa, Seragan, Selo, Ga'as, Bethoron, and Ma'anisakir informed Jacob of the attack and theft of their herds. {34:5} Jacob gathered his sons and servants, totaling six thousand men armed with swords, and marched against the Amorites. {34:6} He defeated them in the pastures of Shechem, pursued the fleeing kings, and reclaimed their herds. {34:7} After prevailing over them, Jacob imposed tribute on the Amorite kings and fortified Robel and Tamnatares. {34:8} He made peace with them and they became his servants until he and his sons departed for Egypt. {34:9} In the seventh year of this week, Joseph was sent by Jacob to check on his brothers in Shechem. {34:10} They conspired against Joseph, initially planning to kill him but later deciding to sell him to Ishmaelite merchants who took him to Egypt. {34:11} Jacob's sons slaughtered a kid and dipped Joseph's coat in its blood, sending it to Jacob to convince him of Joseph's death. {34:12} Jacob mourned deeply, refusing to be comforted, convinced that Joseph had been killed by a wild beast. {34:13} Bilhah and Dinah also died mourning for Joseph, adding to the grief of Jacob and his household. {34:14} They buried Bilhah near Rachel's tomb, and Dinah alongside her. {34:15} Jacob mourned Joseph for a year, steadfast in his sorrow, lamenting, "Let me go down to the grave mourning for my son." {34:16} Thus, Israel was commanded to afflict themselves on the tenth of the seventh month annually to atone for their sins, especially their grievous actions regarding Joseph. {34:17} After Joseph's presumed death, Jacob's sons took wives: Reuben, Simeon, Levi, Judah, Issachar, Zebulon, Dan, Naphtali, Gad, Asher, Joseph, Benjamin, each marrying women of different backgrounds.

{35:1} In the first year of the forty-fifth jubilee, Rebecca called Jacob and instructed him concerning his father and brother, urging him to honor them throughout his life. {35:2} Jacob assured his mother that he would obey her command, seeing it as an act of righteousness and honor before the Lord. {35:3} He affirmed his steadfast commitment to always think and act with goodwill towards his family. {35:4} Rebecca then revealed to Jacob that she would die in that year, having seen it in a dream that marked the completion of her appointed lifespan of a hundred and fifty-five years. {35:5} Jacob, initially skeptical, laughed at her words as she seemed healthy and vigorous. {35:6} Rebecca approached Isaac with a plea to ensure Esau would not harm Jacob after her passing, recounting Esau's history of hostility and greed. {35:7} Isaac acknowledged Jacob's faithfulness and expressed his concern over Esau's unrighteousness and violent nature, foreseeing his and his descendants' destruction. {35:8} He reassured Rebecca that Jacob was under divine protection, greater than any safeguard Esau might attempt. {35:9} Rebecca then summoned Esau and beseeched him to promise to bury her near Sarah when she died and to maintain peace and love with Jacob. {35:10} Esau agreed to all her requests, pledging his love for Jacob as his only brother. {35:11} Rebecca ensured Jacob heard Esau's promise, and Jacob affirmed his commitment to peace and love with Esau. {35:12} That night, they shared a meal together, but Rebecca passed away at the age of a hundred and fifty-five. {35:13} Esau and Jacob buried her in the double cave near Sarah, their father's mother, honoring her final wishes.

{36:1} In the sixth year of this week, Isaac gathered his sons Esau and Jacob and spoke to them, knowing his time was near to join his ancestors. {36:2} He instructed them to bury him alongside Abraham in the double cave purchased from Ephron the Hittite, emphasizing the importance of righteousness and love between brothers. {36:3} Isaac urged them to reject idols and worship the Lord God of Abraham, promising prosperity and descendants as numerous as the stars. {36:4} Isaac solemnly made them swear an oath to fear and worship God, to love each other deeply, and never to harm one another. {36:5} He warned of dire consequences for anyone plotting evil against their brother, prophesying destruction and eternal condemnation. {36:6} Isaac then divided his possessions between Esau and Jacob, giving the birthright to Jacob, as Esau had sold it to him willingly. {36:7} Blessing them both, Isaac passed away peacefully at the age of one hundred and eighty, and Esau departed for the land of Edom. {36:8} Jacob settled in Hebron, faithfully worshipping the Lord, while Leah, his wife, passed away and was buried in the cave near Rebecca. {36:9} Jacob mourned deeply for Leah, remembering her kindness and love, grieving her loss profoundly after the death of Rachel.

{37:1} On the day Isaac, the father of Jacob and Esau, passed away, Esau's sons learned that Jacob had received the elder's portion. They were furious and confronted their father, questioning why Jacob was favored despite Esau being the elder. {37:2} Esau recounted how he had sold his birthright to Jacob for a simple meal, and how Jacob had deceitfully gained their father's blessing. He reminded them of the oath he and Jacob had made to their father not to harm each other, urging them to maintain peace and love. {37:3} But Esau's sons refused, boasting of their strength and planning to attack Jacob with hired warriors from Aram, Philistia, Moab, Ammon, and Edom. {37:4} Despite their threats, Esau warned against warring with Jacob, fearing they would be defeated. {37:5} Ignoring their father's pleas, they gathered four thousand men and approached Jacob's tower in Hebron. {37:6} Hearing the news, the men of Hebron warned Jacob, who couldn't believe until he saw Esau's army nearing. {37:7} Jacob closed the gates and stood defiantly, reproaching Esau for breaking their oath and threatening violence. {37:8} Esau retorted bitterly, rejecting the idea of brotherhood with Jacob, comparing their bond to impossible conditions. {37:9} Despite Jacob's attempt to reason, Esau's heart was set on aggression, prompting Jacob to prepare for battle against his own brother and his allies.

{38:1} Judah then spoke to his father Jacob, saying, "Father, take up your bow, send forth your arrows, and defeat our adversaries. Let your strength prevail, for we will not harm your brother, for he is like you. Let us honor him." Jacob heeded his son's words, drawing his bow and striking his brother Esau in the chest, causing his death. He also aimed at 'Adoran the Aramaean, piercing him and driving him back until he fell dead. {38:2} After these events, Jacob's sons organized themselves into groups around a tower. Judah led the charge with Naphtali and Gad on the southern side, where they slew all before them. Levi, Dan, and Asher attacked from the east, defeating the warriors of Moab and Ammon. Reuben, Issachar, and

Zebulon took the north, battling the Philistines. Simeon, Benjamin, and Enoch attacked from the west, fiercely defeating four hundred stout warriors of Edom and the Horites, while six hundred fled. {38:3} Jacob buried Esau on a hill in 'Aduram and returned home. His sons pursued the remaining Edomites to the mountains of Seir, subjugating them until they submitted to Jacob's descendants. They sought Jacob's counsel on whether to make peace or continue fighting. Jacob advised peace, and so they made a treaty, imposing a yoke of servitude upon the Edomites, who paid tribute to Jacob and his sons from that day until Jacob's descent into Egypt. {38:4} Even to this day, the Edomites have not been freed from the yoke of servitude imposed upon them by Jacob's twelve sons. This period saw various kings reigning over Edom before any king ruled over Israel. Balaq, son of Beor, ruled from Danaba. After him, Jobab, 'Asam of Teman, 'Adath who defeated Midian, Salman of 'Amaseqa, Saul of Ra'aboth, Ba'elunan son of Achbor, and 'Adath's rule continued. His wife was Maitabith, daughter of Matarat and granddaughter of Metabedza'ab. These were the kings who ruled in Edom.

{39:1} Jacob lived in the land of Canaan where his father had stayed. These are the descendants of Jacob. Joseph, at seventeen years old, was taken to Egypt, where Potiphar, a eunuch of Pharaoh and the chief cook, bought him. Potiphar placed Joseph in charge of his household, and the Lord blessed the Egyptian's house because of Joseph. The Lord made everything Joseph did prosper, so Potiphar trusted him completely. {39:2} Joseph was handsome, and Potiphar's wife noticed him and desired him. She tried to seduce him, but Joseph, mindful of God's commandments that forbade adultery, refused her advances. Despite her persistent efforts over a year, Joseph did not yield. One day, she caught hold of him, but he fled, leaving his garment behind as she falsely accused him to her husband, claiming Joseph had tried to assault her. Potiphar, enraged and believing his wife's deceit, had Joseph thrown into the king's prison where the king's prisoners were kept. {39:3} But even in prison, the Lord was with Joseph, showing him favor in the eyes of the chief jailer. The jailer trusted Joseph with all responsibilities, unaware of anything in his charge because the Lord made Joseph succeed in all his undertakings. Joseph remained in prison for two years, during which Pharaoh, angry with his chief butler and chief baker, imprisoned them in the same place where Joseph was held. {39:4} The chief jailer assigned Joseph to attend to the needs of the butler and baker. One night, both the butler and baker had dreams, and they shared their dreams with Joseph. Joseph interpreted their dreams accurately: the butler would be restored to his position, but the baker would be executed. True to Joseph's interpretation, Pharaoh restored the butler to his position but executed the baker. {39:5} However, the butler forgot about Joseph's role in interpreting their dreams and did not mention him to Pharaoh, despite Joseph's accurate prediction. Thus, Joseph remained in prison, forgotten by the butler who had promised to help him.

{40:1} During those days, Pharaoh had two dreams in one night, both concerning a severe famine that would afflict the entire land. Upon waking, he summoned all the interpreters of dreams and magicians in Egypt, but none could explain them. Eventually, the chief butler remembered Joseph and spoke of him to Pharaoh. Joseph was brought out of prison to interpret Pharaoh's dreams. {40:2} Joseph explained that both dreams foretold seven years of plenty followed by seven years of severe famine, unprecedented in Egypt's history. He advised Pharaoh to appoint overseers to collect and store food during the years of plenty, ensuring the land would survive the famine without perishing. {40:3} Impressed by Joseph's wisdom and the evident favor of the Lord upon him, Pharaoh declared him second in command over all Egypt. He clothed Joseph in fine linen, placed a gold chain around his neck, and had him ride in the second chariot. A proclamation went before Joseph, announcing his authority and wisdom. Pharaoh entrusted Joseph with his signet ring, making him ruler over all his house, second only to Pharaoh himself. {40:4} Joseph governed Egypt with integrity, winning the respect and love of all, including Pharaoh's officials and servants. He judged fairly, without partiality or corruption, refusing bribes and upholding justice throughout the land. Under Joseph's administration, Egypt prospered and enjoyed peace, for the Lord was with him, blessing him with favor and mercy. {40:5} Pharaoh honored Joseph by giving him the name Zaphenath-paneah and giving him Asenath, daughter of Potiphera, the priest of On, as his wife. Joseph was thirty years old when he stood before Pharaoh. As Joseph had predicted, the seven years of plenty came to pass, during which Egypt's land produced abundantly, far beyond measure. Joseph oversaw the gathering of grain in every city until they overflowed with stores beyond calculation.

{41:1} In the forty-fifth jubilee, during the second week of the second year (2165 A.M.), Judah arranged for his eldest son Er to marry Tamar, a daughter of Aram. However, Er was wicked, and the Lord took his life because of his evil deeds. Judah instructed his second son Onan to fulfill the duty of a husband's brother by marrying Tamar and raising children for his brother. But Onan, unwilling to raise children not his own, practiced deceit and displeased the Lord, who also took his life. {41:2} Judah then promised Tamar that she would marry his youngest son Shelah once he was grown. However, years passed, and Judah's wife, Bedsuel, did not permit Shelah to marry Tamar. After Bedsuel's death in 2168 A.M., Judah went to Timnah to shear his sheep in the sixth year (2169 A.M.). Tamar, hearing of this, disguised herself as a harlot, waiting for Judah near the city gate. Mistaking her for a harlot, Judah propositioned her, and she agreed on the condition of receiving his signet ring, necklace, and staff as pledge until he sent her payment. They slept together, and Tamar conceived by Judah. {41:3} Judah later sent a kid of the goats by his shepherd to fulfill his pledge to the harlot, but she could not be found. When it was discovered that Tamar was pregnant, Judah, outraged, demanded her punishment by burning. As she was brought forth for judgment, Tamar sent Judah's possessions to him, revealing he was the father of her child. Judah acknowledged his wrongdoing and declared Tamar more righteous than himself, sparing her from punishment. Shelah did not marry Tamar, and she gave birth to twins, Perez and Zerah, in the seventh year of the second week (2170 A.M.). {41:4} Meanwhile, the seven years of plenty predicted by Joseph to Pharaoh came to pass as Egypt flourished. Judah realized the evil of his actions with Tamar, confessing his sins and seeking forgiveness from the Lord. In a dream, Judah was assured of forgiveness because of his sincere repentance. He was instructed that anyone committing such acts of uncleanness—lying with his daughter-in-law or mother-in-law—should be burned with fire as punishment to cleanse Israel of such impurity. {41:5} The descendants of Judah were assured of continuity because neither of his sons with Tamar had committed wrongdoing. Judah's adherence to seeking justice as instructed by Abraham ensured the preservation of his lineage through the generations.

{42:1} In the first year of the third week of the forty-fifth jubilee, around 2171 A.M., a severe famine struck the land. Rain ceased to fall, rendering the earth barren across Canaan while Egypt, under Joseph's foresight during seven years of plenty, stored abundant grain. When Jacob heard of Egypt's provisions, he sent his ten sons there to purchase food, withholding Benjamin. Joseph, now in authority in Egypt, recognized his brothers but remained unrecognized by them. Suspecting them as spies, Joseph detained them, releasing them later with Simeon held back as a pledge for their return with Benjamin. {42:2} Joseph secretly returned the gold they had paid for grain in their sacks and instructed them to bring Benjamin on their next visit. Back in Canaan, they recounted their ordeal to Jacob, who lamented the loss of Joseph and Simeon, fearing for Benjamin's safety. Reluctant to send Benjamin due to the perceived risk, Jacob hesitated despite the worsening famine in Canaan. Meanwhile, Egypt thrived as many had stored grain during the years of plenty, alleviating their famine in the first year. {42:3} As the famine persisted and intensified in Canaan, Jacob urged his sons to return to Egypt for more food, but they insisted Benjamin must accompany them this time. Reuben offered his own sons as a pledge for Benjamin's safe return, but Jacob refused. Judah then pledged his responsibility for Benjamin, convincing Jacob to send him along. Thus, in the second year of the week (around 2172 A.M.), they journeyed back to Egypt with gifts in hand for Joseph, including stacte, almonds, terebinth nuts, and pure honey. {42:4} Upon their arrival, they stood before Joseph, who immediately recognized Benjamin. Overwhelmed with emotion, Joseph welcomed them warmly, arranging a feast and releasing Simeon to join them. They presented their gifts, ate together, and Joseph treated them generously, especially Benjamin, whose portion was notably larger. After the meal, they prepared to depart, unaware that Joseph had hidden his silver cup in Benjamin's sack, intending to test their loyalty as they left.

{43:1} Joseph instructed his steward to fill their sacks with food again, secretly placing his silver cup in Benjamin's sack. Early the next morning, as Jacob's sons departed, the steward pursued and accused them of stealing the cup, insisting they return with Benjamin. The brothers vehemently denied the theft, pledging severe consequences upon the guilty party. Upon searching, the cup was found in Benjamin's sack, causing them distress as they returned to Joseph's house, bowing before him in anguish. {43:2} Joseph rebuked them for their supposed theft, and they humbly accepted their fault, offering themselves and their livestock as servants. Joseph declared that only Benjamin would remain with him while the others could return in peace. Judah, in desperation, pleaded for Benjamin's release, recounting their father's love for him and the potential grief his absence would cause. Touched by their unity and Judah's plea, Joseph revealed his identity to them, speaking in Hebrew as he wept and embraced them. {43:3} Overwhelmed with shock, the brothers were stunned to realize Joseph's true identity. He reassured them not to mourn but to hasten and bring their father to Egypt, explaining the dire famine conditions and urging them to bring their households swiftly. Joseph promised to care for them and their possessions, emphasizing that God had sent him ahead to ensure their survival. He instructed them to bring Jacob and share the news of his position of authority in Egypt. {43:4} Pharaoh endorsed Joseph's instructions, providing chariots, provisions, and lavish gifts for their journey home and for Jacob. They returned to Canaan, informing Jacob that Joseph was alive and prosperous in Egypt. Initially disbelieving, Jacob's spirit revived when he saw the gifts and heard the news, resolving to journey to Egypt to see his beloved son before he died.

{44:1} Jacob set out from Haran, leaving his home on the new moon of the third month. He stopped to sacrifice to the God of his father Isaac at the Well of the Oath on the seventh day of the month. Fearful of going to Egypt, he pondered whether to summon Joseph to him instead. For seven days, he waited, observing the harvest festival with what little grain remained in Canaan due to the widespread famine affecting all living beings. {44:2} On the sixteenth day, the Lord appeared to Jacob, reassuring him not to fear going down to Egypt. God promised to make him into a great nation there, accompanying him and ensuring his burial in Canaan. Encouraged, Jacob's sons prepared wagons and transported him and their possessions from the Well of the Oath to Egypt. Judah went ahead to Goshen, the best land in Egypt, where Joseph had instructed them to settle to be near him. {44:3} Here are the names of Jacob's sons who journeyed with him to Egypt: Reuben and his sons: Enoch, Pallu, Hezron, and Carmi—five in total. Simeon and his sons: Jemuel, Jamin, Ohad, Jachin, Zohar, and Shaul (the son of a Canaanite woman)—seven in total. Levi and his sons: Gershon, Kohath, and Merari—three in total. Judah and his sons: Shelah, Perez, and Zerah—three in total. Issachar and his sons: Tola, Phuvah, Job, and Shimron—four in total. Zebulun and his sons: Sered, Elon, and Jahleel—three in total. Sons of Leah: thirty-three in total, including their sister Dinah. {44:4} Zilpah, Leah's maidservant, bore Gad and Asher to Jacob: Gad's sons were Ziphion, Haggi, Shuni, Ezbon, Eri, Areli, and Arodi—seven in total. Asher's sons were Imnah, Ishvah, Ishvi, Beriah, and Serah (their sister)—five in total. Sons of Bilhah, Rachel's maidservant, who bore Dan and Naphtali to Jacob: Dan's sons were Hushim, Samon, Asudi, Ijaka, and Salomon—five in total. Naphtali's sons were Jahzeel, Guni, Jezer, and Shillem—four in total. All these were Jacob's descendants who went with him to Egypt, totaling seventy souls. {44:5} Joseph, already in Egypt, had two sons born to him by Asenath, daughter of Potiphera, priest of On: Manasseh and Ephraim—two in total. Benjamin, Jacob's youngest son, had ten sons: Bela, Becher, Ashbel, Gera, Naaman, Ehi, Rosh, Muppim, Huppim, and Ard—ten in total. Rachel's descendants totaled fourteen souls who went into Egypt. Jacob's entire household, including those born to him in Canaan and those who went before him to Egypt, amounted to seventy souls in total. {44:6} Among these seventy, five had died in Egypt before Joseph's arrival, leaving sixty-five alive when he reunited with them. In Canaan, two of Judah's sons, Er and Onan, had died without offspring, their deaths and burials marking the inclusion of the children of Israel among the seventy nations.

{45:1} Jacob entered Egypt, arriving in the land of Goshen on the new moon of the fourth month in the second year of the third week of the forty-fifth jubilee. Joseph went out to meet his father, embracing him and weeping on his neck. Jacob expressed his contentment, saying he could now die in peace having seen Joseph alive, blessed the God of his fathers for not withholding His mercy. He recalled the vision at Bethel and rejoiced greatly at the sight of Joseph dining with his brothers. {45:2} Joseph and his brothers shared a meal with their father, delighting in bread and wine. Jacob blessed the Creator for preserving him and his twelve sons. Joseph granted his father and brothers the right to settle in the fertile land of Goshen and Rameses under his authority before Pharaoh. They lived there, and Jacob was 130 years old when he arrived in Egypt. {45:3} Joseph provided for his father, brothers, and their households throughout the remaining years of famine, ensuring they lacked nothing. Egypt suffered greatly during the famine, and Joseph managed the entire land, acquiring land and livestock for Pharaoh in exchange for food. When the seven years of famine ended, Joseph distributed seed and food to the people so they could cultivate the land in the eighth year, benefiting from the Nile's flooding. {45:4} The first year after the famine marked the beginning of the fourth week of the forty-fifth jubilee. Joseph implemented a system where one-fifth of the harvest was reserved for Pharaoh, while the rest was used as food and seed for the Egyptians, establishing this practice as law in Egypt. {45:5} Jacob lived in Egypt for seventeen years, totaling one hundred and forty-seven years of life. He passed away in the fourth year of the fifth week of the forty-fifth jubilee. Before his death, Jacob blessed his sons, foretelling their futures in Egypt and beyond. He gave Joseph an additional inheritance in the land and was buried in the double cave in Hebron, where his ancestors rested. Jacob entrusted his books and those of his fathers to his son Levi for safekeeping and preservation for future generations.

{46:1} After Jacob passed away, the children of Israel flourished in Egypt, becoming a great nation. They lived in harmony, loving one another and supporting each other. They multiplied greatly over ten decades, spanning Joseph's entire lifetime. {46:2} Throughout Joseph's life after Jacob's death, there was peace and honor among the Egyptians towards the Israelites. There was no hostility or evil influence, as Joseph held a position of respect and authority in Egypt. {46:3} Joseph lived to be a hundred and ten years old. He spent seventeen years in Canaan, ten years as a servant, three years in prison, and eighty years ruling over Egypt under the king's authority. When Joseph died, his brothers and that entire generation also passed away. {46:4} Before his death, Joseph instructed the children of Israel to carry his bones with them when they left Egypt. He made them swear an oath because he foresaw that the Egyptians would not allow his remains to be brought back to Canaan for burial. {46:5} Joseph died during the forty-sixth jubilee, in the second year of the sixth week. His burial took place in Egypt. Subsequently, all his brothers passed away. {46:6} During the forty-seventh jubilee, in the second year of the second week, the king of Egypt waged war against the king of Canaan. The children of Israel took the bones of all the children of Jacob, except for Joseph's, and buried them in a field in the double cave in the mountain. {46:7} Most of the Israelites returned to Egypt, but a few remained in the mountains of Hebron, including Amram, the father of Moses. {46:8} The king of Canaan triumphed over the king of Egypt and closed the gates of Egypt. He then plotted against the children of Israel, fearing their growing numbers. He enslaved them and set taskmasters over them to build fortified cities like Pithom and Raamses. {46:9} Despite the harsh treatment, the Israelites continued to multiply, causing unease among the Egyptians. The Egyptians began to despise the children of Israel as they perceived them as a threat to their own security and prosperity.

{47:1} In the seventh week of the forty-seventh jubilee, during the seventh year, your father departed from the land of Canaan. You were born in the fourth week of the sixth year of the forty-eighth jubilee, a time marked by great hardship for the children of Israel. {47:2} Pharaoh, the king of Egypt, decreed that all male children born to the Israelites should be cast into the river. This decree was enforced for seven months until the time of your birth. {47:3} Your mother concealed you for three months, and when it became difficult to hide you any longer, she made an ark and coated it with pitch. Placing you among the reeds by the riverbank, she watched over you for seven days. At night, she nursed you secretly, while your sister Miriam kept watch during the day to protect you from harm. {47:4} During this time, Pharaoh's daughter, Tharmuth, came to bathe in the river and heard your cries. Moved with compassion, she instructed her maidens to bring you to her. She took you from the ark and decided to raise you as her own. {47:5} Your sister approached Pharaoh's daughter and asked if she should find a Hebrew woman to nurse and care for you. Pharaoh's daughter agreed, and your mother, Jochebed, was summoned. She nursed you and received wages for her care. {47:6} As you grew older, Pharaoh's daughter officially adopted you, and you became her son. Your father Amram taught you writing, preparing you for life within the royal court. {47:7} You spent three decades in the royal court, learning and growing until a pivotal moment when you witnessed an Egyptian mistreating one of your fellow Israelites. In a moment of righteous anger, you intervened and killed the Egyptian, burying him in the sand to conceal the act. {47:8} The next day, you encountered two Israelites quarreling. When you questioned the aggressor, reminding him of the injustice he was committing against his brother, he scornfully challenged your authority and threatened to expose your earlier deed. {47:9} Fearful of the consequences of your actions being discovered, you fled from Egypt to Midian, seeking safety from those who sought to harm you.

{48:1} In the sixth year of the third week of the forty-ninth jubilee, you departed and lived in the land of Midian for five weeks and one year. Then, in the second week of the second year of the fiftieth jubilee, you returned to Egypt. {48:2} You recall the words spoken to you on Mount Sinai and the danger you faced from Mastêmâ when you returned to Egypt. He sought to kill you and deliver the Egyptians from your hand, realizing you were sent to execute judgment and vengeance upon them. {48:3} But I delivered you from his grasp. You performed signs and wonders as ordained, bringing great vengeance upon Egypt for the sake of Israel. The Lord executed ten severe plagues—blood, frogs, lice, flies, boils, hail, locusts, darkness, and the death of the first-born—bringing devastation upon Pharaoh, his household, his servants, and his people. {48:4} Through your hand, these judgments were declared and fulfilled exactly as spoken before Pharaoh and all Egypt. The Lord acted for Israel's sake, fulfilling His covenant with Abraham to bring judgment upon those who had enslaved his descendants. {48:5} Mastêmâ opposed you, aiding the Egyptian sorcerers who performed evil deeds. Though allowed to afflict with plagues, they were unable to replicate the miraculous signs. Despite this, Mastêmâ emboldened the Egyptians to pursue Israel with their armies, chariots, and horses. {48:6} I intervened, standing between Egypt and Israel, delivering them from the Egyptians' grasp. The Lord parted the sea, allowing Israel to pass through on dry land while drowning the pursuing Egyptian forces. {48:7} The Lord cast the Egyptians into the sea, just as they had cast Hebrew infants into the river. He exacted vengeance, destroying many of them. Mastêmâ was bound and imprisoned during these events to prevent him from accusing the children of Israel. {48:8} Despite being temporarily released on the nineteenth day, Mastêmâ's actions only served to harden the Egyptians' hearts further, leading to their ultimate destruction. {48:9} On the fourteenth day, the Egyptians willingly gave vessels of silver, gold, and bronze to the Israelites, fulfilling the divine plan to compensate them for their forced labor and slavery. Thus, the children of Israel did not leave Egypt empty-handed.

{49:1} Remember the commandment the Lord gave you concerning the Passover: celebrate it on the fourteenth day of the first month, killing the lamb before evening and eating it that night, starting from sunset on the fifteenth. It was on this night, the beginning of the festival and joy, that you ate the Passover in Egypt, while Mastêmâ's powers were unleashed to slay all the first-born from Pharaoh's household to the captives and their livestock. {49:2} The Lord gave a sign: in every house where the blood of a one-year-old lamb was on the lintel, the plague did not enter; thus, all within were spared. The Lord's powers executed everything as commanded, passing over all the children of Israel so that no soul, whether human, animal, or even dog, perished from the plague that devastated Egypt. {49:3} Throughout Israel, the people ate the Passover lamb with its accompanying wine, praising and thanking the Lord God of their ancestors. They were ready to leave the yoke of Egypt and its oppressive bondage. {49:4} Remember this day for the rest of your life, observing it yearly as a perpetual ordinance. It is inscribed in the heavenly tablets for all generations of Israel to keep it every year on its appointed day without delay. {49:5} Whoever, though clean and near, fails to observe the Passover on its day, offering it before the Lord and partaking of its feast, shall bear the guilt. Let the children of Israel keep the Passover at its appointed time, between the evenings of the fourteenth day of the first month. {49:6} It is forbidden to slaughter the lamb during daylight; it must be done in the evening, and they shall eat it by night until the third part of the night. Any remaining flesh must be burned with fire; it should not be cooked with water nor eaten raw, but roasted over fire with care, including its head and entrails, without breaking any bone. {49:7} The Lord commanded the children of Israel to observe the Passover on its appointed day, emphasizing that no bone of the lamb should be broken. This festival must be strictly observed without delay, from year to year, without passing over to another day or month. {49:8} Moses, command the children of Israel to observe the Passover throughout their generations, once a year on its appointed day, as a pleasing memorial before the Lord. Those who celebrate it must do so before the sanctuary of the Lord, ensuring it is observed in its appointed season. {49:9} When the children of Israel enter the land of Canaan and set up the tabernacle of the Lord, they shall celebrate the Passover before the Lord annually. Once the house of the Lord is built in their land, they shall offer the Passover sacrifice at sunset, with its blood on the altar's threshold and its fat on the fire. {49:10} The Passover must not be celebrated in their cities or any place other than before the tabernacle or house of the Lord where His name dwells, ensuring they do not stray from the Lord's command. {49:11} Moses, instruct the children of Israel in the ordinances of the Passover as commanded, explaining to them the day and festival of unleavened bread. They shall eat unleavened bread for seven days, bringing offerings daily during this joyful festival before the Lord on His altar. {49:12} Remember how hastily you celebrated this festival as you left Egypt and crossed the sea to the wilderness of Shur. Celebrate it as a perpetual ordinance, honoring the Lord's deliverance and provision.

{50:1} I revealed to you the laws concerning Sabbaths while you were in the desert of Sinai, between Elim and Sinai. I explained the Sabbaths of the land on Mount Sinai, and I taught you about the jubilee years and the cycles of seven years. However, I did not reveal the specific year count to you until you enter the land which you are destined to possess. {50:2} The land itself shall also observe its Sabbaths while you dwell upon it, and you shall understand the concept of the jubilee year. Therefore, I have established for you the cycles of years, the jubilees, and the year-weeks. There have been forty-nine jubilees since the days of Adam until this day, with one week and two years more. There are yet forty years to come before the children of Israel fully learn the commandments of the Lord and cross over the Jordan into the land of Canaan. {50:3} The jubilees will continue until Israel is cleansed from all guilt of fornication, uncleanness, pollution, sin, and error, and dwells securely in all the land. At that time, there will no longer be a Satan or any evil presence, and the land will be perpetually clean. {50:4} Concerning the commandments of the Sabbaths, I have recorded them for you along with all the judgments of its laws. Six days you shall labor, but the seventh day is the Sabbath of the Lord your God. On that day, no work shall be done—not by you, your sons, your daughters, your male or female servants, your livestock, nor the foreigner residing among you. {50:5} Anyone who works on the Sabbath shall be put to death. This includes those who desecrate the day by engaging in intimate relations, those who plan journeys, or those who engage in commerce by buying or selling. Drawing water or carrying burdens out of your tent or house on the Sabbath is also forbidden. {50:6} On the Sabbath day, you shall refrain from all work except what you prepare for yourselves on the sixth day. This is a day to eat, drink, rest, and bless the Lord your God, who has granted you a day of rest and holiness—a day set apart forever for Israel. {50:7} The honor bestowed upon Israel is great, for they shall eat, drink, and be satisfied on this festival day, resting from all their labors which belong to the toil of humanity, except for burning incense and presenting offerings and sacrifices before the Lord on days and Sabbaths. {50:8} Only these acts shall be performed on the Sabbath days in the sanctuary of the Lord your God, ensuring continual atonement for Israel through sacrifices, day by day, as commanded. {50:9} Anyone who engages in work, travels, farms, lights fires, rides beasts, sails ships, strikes or kills, slaughters animals or birds, catches animals, birds, or fish, fasts, or makes war on the Sabbaths shall die. Thus, the children of Israel shall faithfully observe the Sabbaths according to the commandments given regarding the Sabbaths of the land, as written on the tablets entrusted to me to inscribe the laws of the seasons and their divisions.

Testaments of the Twelve Patriarchs

The following twelve books are biographies written between 107 and 137 B.C. They offer a powerful exposition, demonstrating how a Pharisee with exceptional writing skills gained publicity by using the names of the greatest men of ancient times. "There were intellectual giants in those days," and the Twelve Patriarchs were the Intellectual Giants!

Each patriarch shares his life story. On his deathbed, he gathers all his children, grandchildren, and great-grandchildren around him and openly recounts his experiences for their moral guidance. If he fell into sin, he fully confesses and advises them not to make the same mistakes. If he led a virtuous life, he explains the rewards he received.

Beyond the straightforward and almost brutally honest passages of the text, you will find a remarkable testament to the expectations of the Messiah that existed a hundred years before Christ. Another element of great value in this unique series is its ethical teaching. As Dr. R. H. Charles notes in his scholarly work on the Pseudepigrapha, its ethical teachings "have achieved real immortality by influencing the thoughts and diction of the writers of the New Testament, and even those of our Lord. This ethical teaching, which is much higher and purer than that of the Old Testament, is its true spiritual successor and helps bridge the gap between the ethics of the Old and New Testaments."

The influence of these writings on the New Testament is particularly notable in the Sermon on the Mount, which reflects their spirit and even uses phrases from these Testaments. St. Paul seems to have borrowed so freely from them that it appears he must have carried a copy of the Testaments with him on his travels.

Thus, the reader has before them pages that are striking for their blunt, primitive style and valuable as some of the actual source books of the Bible.

Testament of Reuben

Testament of Reuben, part of the larger collection known as the Testaments of the Twelve Patriarchs, is a significant pseudepigraphal text attributed to Reuben, the eldest son of Jacob and Leah. This testament, like others in the collection, is a product of the Second Temple period, blending elements of Jewish wisdom literature, apocalyptic themes, and ethical exhortations. The Testament of Reuben is particularly notable for its focus on moral teachings and reflections on sin, especially sexual immorality, which Reuben himself admits to having struggled with. The text opens with Reuben on his deathbed, addressing his descendants and offering a candid confession of his transgressions, most prominently his sin with Bilhah, his father's concubine. This act, which is briefly mentioned in Genesis, is expanded upon in the Testament, providing a deeper moral and didactic exploration of the consequences of lust and impurity. Reuben's testament serves as a cautionary tale, warning against the dangers of succumbing to one's passions and urging adherence to the commandments of God. Furthermore, the testament touches on themes of repentance and forgiveness, emphasizing the possibility of redemption through sincere contrition and a return to righteous living. The text also reflects the sociocultural and religious milieu of its time, illustrating the evolving Jewish thought regarding sin, atonement, and the importance of ethical conduct. The Testament of Reuben thus offers valuable insights into the moral and theological concerns of Jewish communities in the Second Temple period, and its influence can be traced in later Christian and rabbinic writings, highlighting its enduring significance in the broader context of Judeo-Christian literature.

{1:1} Reuben, the eldest son of Jacob and Leah, spoke to his sons before his death at the age of 125. {1:2} Two years after Joseph's passing, Reuben fell ill, and his descendants gathered to see him. {1:3} He said to them, "I am dying, following the path of my ancestors." {1:4} Spotting Judah, Gad, and Asher among them, he requested, "Raise me up, so I may reveal what weighs on my heart before I depart." {1:5} Rising, he kissed them and began, "Listen, my brothers and children, to the commands I give you." {1:6} He solemnly swore, "I warn you against the sins of youth and fornication, which stained our father Jacob's bed." {1:7} "I suffered a severe affliction for seven months as punishment, but Jacob's prayers spared me from destruction." {1:8} "I was thirty when I sinned gravely before the Lord, and I was gravely ill for seven months." {1:9} "For seven years, I deeply repented before the Lord, abstaining from wine, meat, and delicacies." {1:10} "I mourned deeply for my great sin, unmatched in Israel." {1:11} "Listen now, my children, to what I learned about the seven deceitful spirits during my repentance." {1:12} "Seven spirits lead youth astray in various ways." {1:13} "Additionally, man receives seven spirits at creation, guiding all his actions." {1:14} "The spirit of life is first, forming man's constitution." {1:15} "Next is sight, which sparks desire." {1:16} "Hearing teaches, while smell and taste allow enjoyment of food and drink, which strengthen." {1:17} "Speech imparts knowledge, while the seventh, the power of procreation, leads to sinful pleasure." {1:18} "It is last in creation but first in youth, clouded by ignorance, leading blindly into danger." {1:19} "An eighth spirit of sleep induces unconsciousness, akin to death." {1:20} "These spirits are mingled with spirits of error." {1:21} "The spirit of fornication dwells in the senses." {1:22} "Insatiability resides in the belly." {1:23} "The spirit of aggression is in the liver and gall." {1:24} "Obsequiousness and deception come from another spirit." {1:25} "Pride leads to arrogance." {1:26} "Lies breed jealousy and deceit." {1:27} "Injustice fosters theft and greed, satisfying one's desires." {1:28} "All these are compounded by the spirit of sleep, leading to folly and confusion." {1:29} "Thus, many perish, blinded to truth, ignorant of God's law, and disobedient to their elders, as I once was." {1:30} "Love the truth, my children, and it will protect you. Listen to the words of your father Reuben." {1:31} "Pay no heed to a woman's appearance." {1:32} "Do not involve yourself with another man's wife or meddle in affairs of women." {1:33} "I sinned grievously when I saw Bilhah bathing, which led me into great iniquity." {1:34} "The sight of her nudity tormented my mind until I committed the sinful act." {1:35} "One day at Eder near Bethlehem, when Jacob was away, Bilhah was drunk and asleep in her chamber, uncovered." {1:36} "Seeing her thus, I sinned without her knowledge and left." {1:37} "An angel revealed my sin to Jacob, who mourned and forgave, but I did not sin again."

{2:1} Reuben continued, advising his children earnestly before his passing. "Pay no attention to a woman's beauty or involve yourself in her affairs. Instead, walk with integrity in the fear of the Lord. Focus on good deeds, learning, and tending to your flocks until the Lord grants you a wife, so you do not suffer as I have." {2:2} "Until my father's death, I could not look him in the face or speak to my brothers due to my shame." {2:3} "Even now, I am troubled by my conscience because of my past sins." {2:4} "Yet, my father comforted me greatly and prayed for me, seeking God's forgiveness, which was granted." {2:5} "Since then, I have been vigilant and free from sin." {2:6} "So, my children, heed all my commands, and you will avoid sin." {2:7} "Fornication is a pitfall for the soul, separating one from God and leading to idolatry. It deceives the mind and drags young men prematurely to Hades." {2:8} "Fornication has destroyed many, regardless of age, status, wealth, or poverty, bringing disgrace and mockery." {2:9} "Consider Joseph, who resisted temptation and found favor with God and men." {2:10} "Despite the Egyptian woman's advances and sorceries, he remained pure in heart." {2:11} "Thus, the God of our fathers protected him from harm." {2:12} "If you guard your mind against fornication, Beliar cannot overcome you." {2:13} "Women, though lacking physical strength over men, use deceitful charms to ensnare them." {2:14} "Those they cannot captivate outwardly, they conquer through cunning." {2:15} "The angel of the Lord warned me that women are more susceptible to the spirit of fornication and scheme against men." {2:16} "They deceive through appearance and allure with their eyes, ultimately ensnaring them." {2:17} "A woman may not forcibly seduce a man, but her demeanor can lead him astray." {2:18} "Therefore, flee from fornication, and instruct your wives and daughters not to use adornments to deceive." {2:19} "Such deceit led to the fall of the Watchers before the flood, as they lusted after women and sinned." {2:20} "Beware of fornication if you seek purity of mind; guard your senses against temptation." {2:21} "Urge women also to avoid close associations with men for purity's sake." {2:22} "Even frequent meetings without wrongdoing are perilous, leading to moral decay." {2:23} "Fornication lacks understanding and godliness; it breeds jealousy and destruction." {2:24} "Do not envy the authority of the Levites, for God has appointed them. Your jealousy will lead to your downfall." {2:25} "God will avenge any wrongs against the Levites, and those who oppose them will face a dire fate." {2:26} "Therefore, listen to Levi, who knows God's law and will lead with justice and sacrifice for Israel until the end times, as the anointed High Priest." {2:27} "I charge you, by the God of heaven, to be truthful to each other and show love to your brothers." {2:28} "Approach Levi with humility, for he will bless Israel and Judah, chosen by the Lord as king over all the nation." {2:29} "Honor his descendants, who will fight wars seen and unseen for our people, as eternal kings among us." {2:30} "Thus, Reuben imparted these commands before his death, and they buried him in Hebron, alongside his father, after bringing him from Egypt."

Testament of Simeon

The Testament of Simeon is one of the twelve Testaments of the Patriarchs, an ancient Jewish text attributed to Simeon, the second son of Jacob and Leah. This text, like the other testaments, is presented as a deathbed discourse where Simeon reflects on his life, offers ethical teachings, and prophesies about the future of his descendants. The Testament of Simeon delves into themes of envy, repentance, and divine justice. It is particularly noteworthy for its focus on Simeon's jealousy towards his brother Joseph, which led to the conspiracy against Joseph and his eventual sale into slavery. This narrative is used to explore the destructive nature of envy and the importance of seeking forgiveness. The text also provides insights into early Jewish thought and the ethical values that were emphasized during the Second Temple period. Furthermore, the Testament of Simeon, like the other testaments, is rich in eschatological themes, offering prophecies about the coming of a Messiah and the ultimate triumph of good over evil. Its language and style reflect a blend of Jewish wisdom literature and apocalyptic motifs, making it a valuable resource for understanding the development of Jewish theological and ethical thought in the intertestamental period. The Testament of Simeon thus serves as a crucial link between the Hebrew Bible and later Christian writings, illustrating the continuity and evolution of key religious themes.

{1:1} This is the account of Simeon, the second son of Jacob and Leah, a man of strength. Before his death at the age of 120, coinciding with Joseph's passing, he spoke these words to his sons. {1:2} When Simeon fell ill, his sons gathered at his bedside. Strengthening himself, he sat up, kissed them, and began to speak: {1:3} "Listen, my children, to your father Simeon. I will share with you what weighs on my heart." {1:4} "I was born as Jacob's second son to Leah, who named me Simeon because the Lord had heard her prayers." {1:5} "I grew exceedingly strong, fearless in my pursuits. My heart was hardened, my resolve unyielding, and I lacked compassion." {1:6} "The Most High granted men both soul and body for valor." {1:7} "In my youth, jealousy consumed me regarding Joseph, whom my father favored above all." {1:8} "Envy blinded me, and I plotted against him, seeing him not as a brother. I even disregarded our father Jacob." {1:9} "But God, the God of our fathers, sent His angel to rescue Joseph from my schemes." {1:10} "Once, while I went to Shechem for ointment and Reuben to Dothan for provisions, Judah sold Joseph to the Ishmaelites." {1:11} "Reuben regretted this deeply, wanting to return Joseph to our father." {1:12} "I was furious with Judah for letting Joseph live, nursing my wrath for five months." {1:13} "Yet, the Lord restrained me, weakening my right hand for seven days." {1:14} "I understood this affliction was for Joseph's sake. I repented, wept, and prayed to be cleansed of envy, folly, and pollution." {1:15} "I acknowledged my evil intentions toward Joseph, which stirred my envy." {1:16} "Now, children, heed my warning: beware of deceit and envy." {1:17} "Envy consumes the mind, inhibiting even basic functions. It urges destruction of the envied, while the envious wastes away." {1:18} "I spent two years fasting in fear of the Lord, learning that fear of God frees one from envy." {1:19} "When one turns to the Lord, the evil spirit of envy flees, and the mind finds peace." {1:20} "From then on, I empathized with Joseph and forgave those who wronged me, letting go of envy."

{2:1} Simeon recounted to his hearers how his father Jacob noticed his sadness and inquired about it. Simeon admitted his deep remorse, saying he was troubled to his core. {2:2} His greatest sorrow stemmed from his role in Joseph's sale. {2:3} Even when he was falsely accused and imprisoned in Egypt, he accepted it as just punishment without complaint. {2:4} Simeon testified to Joseph's goodness, noting how Joseph harbored no ill will despite his brothers' betrayal. {2:5} "Therefore, my children, beware of jealousy and envy. Walk in sincerity, so that God may bestow upon you grace, glory, and blessings, just as Joseph received." {2:6} "Throughout his life, Joseph never reproached us for what we did. He loved us deeply, even more than his own sons. He enriched us with wealth, livestock, and abundance." {2:7} "Love each other sincerely, and envy will not take root in your hearts." {2:8} "Envy corrupts the soul, destroys the body, stirs up anger and conflict, and leads to violence and chaos." {2:9} "Even in sleep, jealousy troubles the soul, disturbing the mind with wicked thoughts and causing physical unrest." {2:10} "Joseph was handsome and upright because he harbored no wickedness. The tranquility of his spirit was reflected in his appearance." {2:11} "Therefore, my children, purify your hearts before the Lord, live rightly among men, and you will find favor with God and people." {2:12} "Beware also of fornication, the root of all evils, which separates from God and draws one near to Beliar." {2:13} "As written in the Book of Enoch, your descendants will be corrupted by fornication and will harm the sons of Levi with the sword." {2:14} "Yet Levi will prevail in the Lord's battles and conquer your armies." {2:15} "Your numbers will dwindle, divided between Levi and Judah, and none of you will hold sovereignty, as our father prophesied in his blessings."

{3:1} "Listen to all I have foretold, that I may be clear of your sins. {3:2} If you cast away envy and stubbornness, my bones will flourish in Israel like a rose, and my flesh in Jacob like a lily. My presence will be as the fragrance of Lebanon; holy ones will spring forth from me like cedars, their branches stretching far and wide. {3:3} The seed of Canaan will perish, Amalek will be no more, the Cappadocians will vanish, and the Hittites will be utterly destroyed. {3:4} The land of Ham will fail, and its people will perish. {3:5} Then all the earth will find rest from turmoil, and there will be peace throughout the world. {3:6} The Mighty One of Israel will glorify Shem. {3:7} For the Lord God will appear on earth and Himself save mankind. {3:8} Deceitful spirits will be trampled underfoot, and men will rule over wicked spirits. {3:9} I will rise in joy and bless the Most High for His marvelous works, for God has taken on a body, dined with men, and saved them. {3:10} Now, my children, heed Judah and Levi. Do not oppose these two tribes, for from them will come the salvation of God for you. {3:11} The Lord will raise up from Levi a High Priest and from Judah a King, both God and man, who will save all Gentiles and the people of Israel. {3:12} Therefore, I give you these commands to pass down to your children, that they may observe them for generations to come. {3:13} After Simeon finished instructing his sons, he passed away at the age of 120 and was buried in Hebron in a wooden coffin. {3:14} His bones were secretly carried away during an Egyptian war. Just as the Egyptians guarded Joseph's bones in their royal tombs, sorcerers had warned them of darkness and plague upon the departure of Joseph's remains. {3:15} Simeon's sons mourned deeply for their father. {3:16} They remained in Egypt until the day Moses led them out.

Testament of Levi

The Testament of Levi, part of the Testaments of the Twelve Patriarchs, is an ancient Jewish text from the Second Temple period (2nd century BCE to 1st century CE). It combines apocalyptic literature, wisdom teachings, and priestly traditions, presenting the final words of Levi, son of Jacob and Leah. The text features Levi's visions of future priesthood, a messianic figure, and Israel's eschatological fate, reflecting the concerns and hopes of its Jewish audience amidst political and religious upheaval. It emphasizes moral purity, critiques priestly corruption, and underscores the triumph of righteousness, offering insights into Jewish priestly thought and early Christian influences.

{1:1} This is what Levi, the third son of Jacob and Leah, ordained for his sons, detailing all that would come to pass for them until the day of judgement. {1:2} He was in good health when he summoned his sons, having been forewarned of his impending death. {1:3} Gathering them together, he spoke to them, saying: {1:4} "I, Levi, was born in Haran and came with my father to Shechem. {1:5} At about twenty years of age, together with Simeon, I avenged our sister Dinah by dealing with Hamor. {1:6} While tending the flocks in Abel-Maul, the spirit of understanding from the Lord descended upon me. I saw all humanity corrupting their ways, with unrighteousness erecting walls and lawlessness reigning over towers. {1:7} Grieved for the race of mankind, I prayed earnestly to the Lord for deliverance. {1:8} Then I fell asleep and saw a lofty mountain; I found myself upon it. {1:9} The heavens opened, and an angel of God beckoned me, saying, 'Levi, come in.' {1:10} I ascended from the first heaven and beheld a vast sea suspended. {1:11} Then I saw a second heaven, brighter and more brilliant, filled with boundless light. {1:12} I asked the angel about this marvel, and he said, 'Do not marvel, for you shall see a heaven even more splendid and incomparable.' {1:13} 'Upon ascending there, you shall stand near the Lord, ministering to Him, declaring His mysteries to men, and proclaiming the Redeemer of Israel.' {1:14} 'Through you and Judah, the Lord will manifest among men, saving every race.' {1:15} 'Your life shall be from the Lord's portion; He shall be your field, vineyard, and source of gold and silver.' {1:16} Listen now about the heavens revealed to you. {1:17} The lowest is gloomy because it witnesses all the unrighteous deeds of men, prepared with fire, snow, and ice for the day of judgement by God's righteous judgement, hosting retributive spirits against men. {1:18} In the second heaven are armies ordained for judgement day, tasked with avenging deceitful spirits and Beliar. {1:19} Above them are the holy ones. {1:20} The highest heaven houses the Great Glory, surpassing all holiness. {1:21} In the next heaven dwell the archangels, who minister and intercede for the Lord concerning the righteous' sins, offering sweet-smelling and bloodless sacrifices. {1:22} Below this heaven are angels who convey responses to the angels of the Lord's presence. {1:23} The next heaven houses thrones and dominions, where perpetual praise to God is offered. {1:24} When the Lord looks upon us, all tremble—the heavens, the earth, and the abysses quake in His majestic presence. {1:25} Yet mankind, oblivious to these things, continues to sin and provoke the Most High.

{2:1} Now understand that the Lord will judge the sons of men. {2:2} When rocks are split, the sun fades, waters dry up, fire quivers, and all creation trembles, with invisible spirits dissolving and Hades claiming spoils through the Most High's visitations, people will remain unbelieving and persist in their wickedness. {2:3} For this reason, they will be judged with punishment. {2:4} The Most High has answered your prayer to separate you from iniquity, making you His son, servant, and minister of His presence. {2:5} You will enlighten Jacob with the light of knowledge, shining like the sun upon all the seed of Israel. {2:6} A blessing shall be upon you and your descendants until the Lord shows His mercy to all the Gentiles forever. {2:7} Therefore, you have been given counsel and understanding to instruct your sons about this. {2:8} Those who bless the Lord will be blessed, and those who curse Him will perish. {2:9} Then the angel opened the gates of heaven to me, and I saw the holy temple and the Most High enthroned in glory. {2:10} He said to me, "Levi, I have given you the blessing of priesthood until I come and dwell among Israel." {2:11} The angel then brought me back to earth, giving me a shield and sword, saying, "Take vengeance on Shechem for the sake of Dinah, your sister, for the Lord has sent me to be with you." {2:12} At that time, I eradicated the sons of Hamor, as written in the heavenly records. {2:13} I asked the angel, "Please tell me your name, so that I may call upon you in times of trouble." {2:14} He replied, "I am the angel who intercedes for the nation of Israel, protecting them from total destruction, as every evil spirit assaults them." {2:15} After these visions, I awoke and blessed the Most High and the angel who intercedes for Israel and all the righteous.

{3:1} As I journeyed to my father, I discovered a bronze shield, which led to the mountain being named Aspis, near Gebal to the south of Abila. {3:2} I kept this revelation in my heart. Later, I advised my father and Reuben not to allow the sons of Hamor to be circumcised, angered by the abomination they committed against my sister. {3:3} I struck Shechem first, and Simeon slew Hamor. Afterwards, my brothers attacked the city with swords. {3:4} When my father heard of these events, he was angry and grieved that they had accepted circumcision only to be slain. In his blessings, he looked unfavorably upon us, as we had sinned against his will, causing him sorrow that day. {3:5} Yet, I perceived God's judgment was upon Shechem, for they intended to treat Sarah and Rebecca as they had Dinah, but the Lord intervened. {3:6} They also mistreated our father Abraham when he was a stranger, and harassed his flocks. {3:7} Eblaen, born in his household, they treated shamefully. {3:8} They similarly mistreated all strangers, seizing their wives and expelling them, but the Lord's wrath fell heavily upon them. {3:9} I told my father Jacob that the Lord would dispossess the Canaanites and give their land to him and his descendants. {3:10} Henceforth, Shechem would be known as a city of fools, mocked for their folly in defiling my sister. {3:11} We departed and went to Bethel. {3:12} There I had another vision, similar to the first, after seventy days. {3:13} I saw seven men in white garments who said to me, "Rise, put on the robe of priesthood, the crown of righteousness, the breastplate of understanding, the garment of truth, the plate of faith, the turban of the head, and the ephod of prophecy." {3:14} They clothed me with these items and said, "From now on, you and your descendants shall be priests of the Lord forever." {3:15} The first anointed me with holy oil and gave me the staff of judgment. {3:16} The second washed me with pure water, fed me bread and wine, and clothed me in a holy robe of glory. {3:17} The third dressed me in a linen ephod. {3:18} The fourth placed a purple girdle around me. {3:19} The fifth gave me a branch of rich olive. {3:20} The sixth crowned my head. {3:21} The seventh set a diadem of priesthood on my head and filled my hands with incense to serve the Lord God. {3:22} They declared, "Levi, your descendants shall be divided into three offices as a sign of the glory of the Lord to come. {3:23} The first portion shall be great, greater than any other. {3:24} The second shall be in priesthood. {3:25} The third shall be given a new name, for a king shall arise from Judah and establish a new priesthood, like that of the Gentiles. {3:26} He will be beloved in the presence of the Most High, a prophet from the seed of our father Abraham. {3:27} Therefore, all desirable things in Israel shall be for you and your descendants. {3:28} Your descendants shall include high priests, judges, and scribes, guarding the holy place with their words. {3:29} When I awoke, I understood this dream, as I had the first, keeping it hidden in my heart without revealing it to anyone on earth. {3:30} Two days later, Judah and I went with our father Jacob to his father Isaac. {3:31} Isaac blessed me according to the visions I had seen, but he did not accompany us to Bethel. {3:32} At Bethel, my father received a vision that I would be a priest to God. {3:33} Early the next morning, he tithed everything to the

Lord through me, and we settled in Hebron. {3:34} Isaac continually called me to remember the Lord's law, as shown by the angel of the Lord. {3:35} He instructed me in the laws of priesthood, sacrifices, burnt offerings, first fruits, freewill offerings, and peace offerings. {3:36} Each day he taught me and interceded on my behalf before the Lord, warning me against the spirit of fornication, which would defile the holy place through my descendants. {3:37} Therefore, take a blameless wife while young, not from foreign nations, and bathe before entering the holy place, and wash after offering sacrifices. {3:38} Offer twelve trees with leaves to the Lord, as Abraham taught me. {3:39} Sacrifice every clean beast and bird to the Lord. {3:40} Offer the first of all your first fruits and wine to the Lord as a sacrifice, salting every sacrifice with salt. {3:41} Now, children, observe all that I command you, for I have declared to you what I heard from my fathers. {3:42} I am free from your ungodliness and transgressions, which you will commit in the latter days against the Savior of the world, Christ, acting wickedly, deceiving Israel, and stirring up great evils against it from the Lord. {3:43} You will sin with Israel, so the Lord will not tolerate Jerusalem because of your wickedness. The veil of the temple will be torn, revealing your shame. {3:44} You will be scattered among the Gentiles as captives, a reproach and curse there. {3:45} Jerusalem, the chosen house of the Lord, will be called so, as written in the book of Enoch the righteous. {3:46} I married at twenty-eight, and her name was Melcha. {3:47} She bore me a son, and I named him Gersam, for we were strangers in our land. {3:48} I foresaw he would not be in the forefront. {3:49} Kohath was born when I was thirty-five, toward sunrise. {3:50} In a vision, I saw him standing tall among the assembly. {3:51} Therefore, I named him Kohath, meaning beginning of majesty and instruction. {3:52} My third son, Merari, was born when I was forty, and he nearly died at birth, so I named him 'my bitterness.' {3:53} Jochebed was born in Egypt when I was sixty-four, honored among my brothers. {3:54} Gersam married and had Lomni and Semei. Kohath's sons were Ambram, Issachar, Hebron, and Ozeel. Merari's sons were Mooli and Mouses. {3:55} In my ninety-fourth year, Ambram married my daughter Jochebed, both born on the same day. {3:56} I was eight when I entered Canaan, eighteen when I killed Shechem, nineteen when I became a priest, twenty-eight when I married, and forty-eight when I went to Egypt. {3:57} Children, you are now the third generation. {3:58} Joseph died in my 118th year.

{4:1} Now, my children, I urge you: Fear the Lord your God wholeheartedly and live in simplicity according to His law. {4:2} Teach your children to read and understand letters, so they may always comprehend God's law. {4:3} Those who know the Lord's law will be honored and esteemed wherever they go. {4:4} They will gain many friends and have many who desire to learn from them and hear the law from their lips. {4:5} Therefore, do righteousness on the earth, that you may treasure it in heaven. {4:6} Sow goodness in your souls, and you will reap it in your life. {4:7} But if you sow evil, you will reap trouble and affliction. {4:8} Seek wisdom in the fear of God diligently, for though captivity may come and cities and lands be destroyed, and wealth perish, the wisdom of the wise cannot be taken away, except by the blindness of ungodliness and the callousness of sin. {4:9} Those who keep themselves from these evils will find wisdom a glory even among enemies, a homeland in a foreign land, and a friend in the midst of foes. {4:10} Whoever teaches noble things and practices them shall be honored like Joseph, my brother, who was enthroned among kings. {4:11} Therefore, my children, I foresee that in the end times you will transgress against the Lord, reaching out to wickedness against Him, and you will become a scorn to all the Gentiles. {4:12} For our father Israel is free from the transgressions of the chief priests who will lay their hands upon the Savior of the world. {4:13} As heaven is purer than earth in the Lord's sight, so you, O lights of Israel, should be purer than all Gentiles. {4:14} But if you are darkened by transgressions, what will the Gentiles do, living in blindness? {4:15} You will bring a curse upon our race by seeking to destroy the light of the law given to enlighten every person, teaching commandments contrary to God's ordinances. {4:16} You will rob the offerings of the Lord and steal choice portions from His portion, contemptuously eating with harlots. {4:17} Out of greed, you will teach the commandments of the Lord, defiling married women and virgins of Jerusalem, joining with harlots and adulteresses, and taking wives from the Gentiles, purifying them unlawfully. {4:18} Your unions will be like those of Sodom and Gomorrah, and you will be arrogant because of your priesthood, rising up against men and against God's commands. {4:19} You will mock and laugh at holy things. {4:20} Therefore, the temple chosen by the Lord will be desecrated by your uncleanness, and you will be captives among all nations. {4:21} You will be an abomination and receive reproach and everlasting shame from God's righteous judgment. {4:22} All who hate you will rejoice at your destruction. {4:23} If not for the mercy through our fathers Abraham, Isaac, and Jacob, not one of our descendants would remain on earth. {4:24} Now I know that for seventy weeks you will stray, profane the priesthood, and defile the sacrifices. {4:25} You will nullify the law and reject the words of the prophets through wickedness. {4:26} You will persecute the righteous and hate the godly; you will abhor the words of the faithful. {4:27} You will call a man who renews the law in the power of the Most High a deceiver, and eventually you will rush to slay him, not knowing his true dignity, bringing innocent blood upon your heads through wickedness. {4:28} Your holy places will be laid waste because of him, even to the ground. {4:29} You will have no clean place among the Gentiles, but you will be a curse and scattered until He visits you again in pity and receives you through faith and water.

{5:1} Listen now, for you have heard of the seventy weeks; also understand about the priesthood. In each jubilee, a new priesthood shall arise. {5:2} In the first jubilee, the anointed priest shall be great and shall speak to God as a father. {5:3} His priesthood shall be perfect before the Lord, and in times of joy, he shall arise for the salvation of the world. {5:4} In the second jubilee, the anointed one shall be conceived in sorrow among the beloved, and his priesthood shall be honored and glorified by all. {5:5} The third priest shall be seized by sorrow. {5:6} The fourth shall suffer pain, as unrighteousness gathers against him, and all Israel shall hate their neighbors. {5:7} Darkness shall seize the fifth, as well as the sixth and seventh. {5:8} In the seventh, such pollution will arise that cannot be described before men, but those who commit such acts will know it. {5:9} They shall be taken captive and become prey; their land and possessions shall be destroyed. {5:10} In the fifth week, they shall return to their desolate country and rebuild the house of the Lord. {5:11} In the seventh week, priests shall arise who are idolaters, adulterers, lovers of money, proud, lawless, lascivious, abusers of children and beasts. {5:12} After their punishment from the Lord, the priesthood shall fail. {5:13} Then the Lord shall raise up a new priest. {5:14} To him, all the words of the Lord shall be revealed, and he shall execute righteous judgment on the earth for many days. {5:15} His star shall rise in heaven like that of a king, illuminating knowledge like the sun does the day; he shall be exalted in the world. {5:16} He shall shine like the sun upon the earth, removing all darkness from under heaven, and there shall be peace throughout the earth. {5:17} The heavens shall rejoice in his days, the earth shall be glad, and the clouds shall rejoice. {5:18} The knowledge of the Lord shall spread across the earth like the waters of the seas. {5:19} The angels of the Lord's presence shall rejoice in him. {5:20} The heavens shall open, and from the temple of glory, sanctification shall come upon him, with the Father's voice as from Abraham to Isaac. {5:21} The glory of the Most High shall be declared over him, and the spirit of understanding and sanctification shall rest upon him in the waters. {5:22} For he shall give the majesty of the Lord to His sons forever in truth; {5:23} None shall succeed him for all generations forever. {5:24} In his priesthood, the Gentiles shall increase in knowledge on the earth and be enlightened by the grace of the Lord. {5:25} In his priesthood, sin shall come to an end, and the lawless shall cease from doing evil. {5:26} He shall open the gates of paradise, remove the threatening sword against Adam, and give the saints to eat from the tree of life; the spirit of holiness shall be upon them. {5:27} Beliar shall be bound by him, and he shall give power to His children to tread upon evil spirits. {5:28} The Lord shall rejoice in His children and be well pleased in His beloved ones forever. {5:29} Then Abraham, Isaac, and Jacob shall rejoice, and all the saints shall be clothed with joy. {5:30} Now, my children, you have heard everything; therefore, choose for yourselves either light or darkness, the law of the Lord or the works of Beliar. {5:31} His sons answered him, saying, "Before the Lord, we will walk according to His law." {5:32} Their father said to them, "The Lord, His angels, you, and I are all witnesses to your words." {5:33} His sons replied, "We are witnesses." {5:34} Thus Levi finished instructing his sons, stretched out his feet on the bed, and was gathered to his fathers at the age of one hundred and thirty-seven. {5:35} They placed him in a coffin and buried him in Hebron with Abraham, Isaac, and Jacob.

Testament of Judah

The Testament of Judah is part of the Testaments of the Twelve Patriarchs, an intertestamental work of Old Testament pseudepigrapha. Attributed to Judah, Jacob and Leah's fourth son, it offers insights into Judah's moral and ethical reflections near the end of his life. Unlike canonical scriptures, this text emphasizes leadership, repentance, and moral consequences through Judah's introspections and family concerns. It recounts Judah's life, including his role in selling Joseph, interactions with Tamar, and reflections on virtues like bravery and justice. Scholars value its theological insights, historical context, Jewish lore, apocalyptic elements, and Hellenistic influences. The testament's eschatological themes and Messianic prophecy enrich understanding of Second Temple Judaism and early Jewish-Christian thought, making it a significant text for ongoing scholarly exploration.

{1:1} This is the account of Judah, the fourth son of Jacob and Leah. He was known for his strength and agility, a mighty warrior who recounted his heroic deeds. He said to his sons before he died, {1:2} "Gather around, my children, and listen to Judah your father. {1:3} I was the fourth son born to my father Jacob, and my mother Leah named me Judah, saying, 'I give thanks to the Lord for giving me another son.' {1:4} In my youth, I was swift and obedient to my father in all things. {1:5} I honored my mother and my aunt. {1:6} As I grew, my father blessed me, saying, 'You shall be a king, prospering in all things.' {1:7} The Lord showed favor in all I did, both in the fields and at home. {1:8} I remember racing and catching a hind, preparing its meat for my father, who ate it. {1:9} I mastered the roes in the chase, overtaking all on the plains. {1:10} I even caught and tamed a wild mare. {1:11} Once, I slew a lion to rescue a kid from its mouth. {1:12} I grabbed a bear by its paw and hurled it down a cliff, crushing it. {1:13} I outran and tore apart a wild boar. {1:14} In Hebron, a leopard attacked my dog; I caught it by the tail and smashed it on the rocks. {1:15} I encountered a wild ox in the fields, seized it by the horns, stunned it, and slew it. {1:16} Once, single-handed, I attacked and killed the kings of Hazor and Tappuah, along with their people. {1:17} I faced Achor, a giant king, hurling javelins; I threw a massive stone, killing his horse, and defeated him. {1:18} In another battle, I fought for two hours, breaking shields, chopping off feet, and prevailing against nine men who attacked me. {1:19} My father, Jacob, even slew Beelesath, king of giants. {1:20} An angel of might protected me, ensuring I was never overcome in battle. {1:21} In a great war in Shechem, I joined my brothers, pursuing and killing hundreds, including four kings. {1:22} I climbed walls and slew mighty men, capturing cities like Hazor and Aretan. {1:23} At the waters of Kozeba, we defeated the men of Jobel and their allies from Shiloh. {1:24} The men of Makir attacked us, but we overcame them and their women who rolled stones upon us. {1:25} Simeon and I seized heights behind a town, destroying it the next day. {1:26} Hearing of a coming attack from Gaash, we deceived them, destroyed their city, and defeated their host. {1:27} At Thamna, insulted and provoked, I fought and drove the Canaanites into submission. {1:28} I built Thamna, and my father built Pabael. {1:29} I was twenty when this war began, and the Canaanites feared me and my brothers. {1:30} I had much cattle and a chief herdsman, Iram the Adullamite. {1:31} While visiting Iram, king Parsaba of Adullam gave me his daughter Bathshua in marriage. {1:32} She bore me Er, Onan, and Shelah; though Er and Onan died, Shelah lived, and you are his descendants.

{2:1} After eighteen years of peace with Esau and his sons following our return from Mesopotamia, where we lived with Laban, {2:2} in the fortieth year of my life, Esau, my father's brother, came against us with a large and powerful force. {2:3} Jacob wounded Esau with an arrow, and he died on Mount Seir near Anoniram. {2:4} We pursued Esau's sons, who had a city fortified with walls of iron and gates of brass. {2:5} Unable to breach its defenses, we besieged the city for twenty days. {2:6} In desperation, I climbed a ladder with my shield, enduring a barrage of heavy stones weighing over three talents, and killed four of their mighty warriors. {2:7} Reuben and Gad slew six others. {2:8} Eventually, they sought peace terms, which we accepted after consulting our father, making them our tributaries. {2:9} They provided us with provisions until the famine drove us to Egypt—five hundred cors of wheat, five hundred baths of oil, and five hundred measures of wine. {2:10} After these events, my son Er married Tamar, a daughter of Aram from Mesopotamia. {2:11} However, Er was wicked, and the Lord's angel struck him down on the third night. {2:12} He had refused to have children with Tamar out of evil intentions instilled by his mother. {2:13} During the wedding feast, I gave Tamar to Onan, but he too wickedly avoided fathering a child with her, though they were married for a year. {2:14} Upon threatening him, he did fulfill his duty but deliberately spilled his seed, leading to his demise. {2:15} I intended to give Shelah to Tamar, but his mother prevented it, harboring ill will against Tamar because she was not a Canaanite like herself. {2:16} Blinded by youthful impulses, I overlooked the wickedness of the Canaanites. {2:17} One day, seeing Tamar intoxicated, I was deceived and took her, against my father's counsel. {2:18} During my absence, she married Shelah to a Canaanite woman, and upon learning this, I cursed her in my distress. {2:19} Both she and her sons perished due to their wickedness. {2:20} Two years later, while Tamar was a widow, she heard I was going to shear my sheep and disguised herself in bridal attire, sitting by the gate of Enaim. {2:21} According to Amorite law, she waited there for seven days, intending to marry. {2:22} Drunk, I didn't recognize her and was deceived by her beauty and adornments. {2:23} I propositioned her, and she asked for my staff, girdle, and diadem as a pledge. {2:24} We slept together, and she conceived, hiding my pledges to protect herself. {2:25} Later, upon discovering her pregnancy, I intended to kill her, but she revealed my pledges, exposing my shame. {2:26} I realized the deception but could not harm her, as it was the Lord's will. {2:27} This act of folly haunted me, and I never approached her again in my lifetime, knowing the abomination I had committed. {2:28} The people of the city knew nothing of her true identity, believing her to be a foreign harlot. {2:29} Even though I thought no one knew of my encounter with her, {2:30} I was wrong, and my folly was known throughout Israel. {2:31} I avoided her thereafter. {2:32} Subsequently, we went to Egypt due to the famine, joining Joseph. {2:33} I was forty-six years old then, and I lived seventy-three years in Egypt.

{3:1} Hearken, my children, to the counsel of Judah your father. Observe my words and follow the ordinances of the Lord, obeying His commands diligently. {3:2} Do not yield to your lusts or the proud thoughts of your hearts. Do not boast in the deeds and strength of your youth, for such pride is detestable to the Lord. {3:3} I, too, once boasted that no beautiful woman could entice me in war. Yet jealousy and lust overcame me, leading me to sin with Bathshua the Canaanite and Tamar, who was promised to my sons. {3:4} I sought counsel from my father-in-law to marry his daughter, Bathshua, against his reluctance, tempted by her adornments and the wine she served lavishly. {3:5} The wine clouded my judgment and seduced my heart. {3:6} I succumbed to desire, transgressing God's commandments and those of my forefathers, taking her as my wife. {3:7} However, the Lord did not bless me with joy in her children. {3:8} Now, my children, I warn you: do not be intoxicated with wine, for it leads the mind astray from truth, ignites lustful passions, and distorts perception. {3:9} Wine serves the spirit of fornication, offering pleasure to the mind, yet both lead astray. {3:10} For when a man indulges in drunkenness, his mind is clouded with impure thoughts that lead to immoral acts. {3:11} The drunkard shows no respect for anyone, as I myself erred in the sight of all, yielding to Tamar shamelessly and uncovering the shame of my sons. {3:12} Wine caused me to disregard God's commandments and take a Canaanite woman as my wife. {3:13} Such is the state of the drunkard—heedless and irreverent. {3:14} Wine led me astray, making me glory in my shame before the city. {3:15} After drinking wine, I disregarded God's commandments, blinded by pleasure and desire. {3:16} Therefore, exercise great discretion with wine, my children; drink in moderation to preserve your decency. {3:17} Exceeding this limit invites deceitful spirits, leading to obscenity and shamelessness, where one glorifies in disgrace and considers it honor. {3:18} The fornicator does not realize his loss or feel shame in dishonor, whether he be king or beggar. {3:19} Even kings lose their dignity to fornication, as I did, giving away the symbols of my tribe, power, and kingdom. {3:20} I repented deeply; from then on, I abstained from wine and flesh until old age, finding no joy in them. {3:21} The angel of God showed me that women hold sway over both king and beggar alike. {3:22} They strip kings of their glory, valiant men of their strength, and the poor of even their meager possessions. {3:23} Therefore, my children, maintain moderation in wine, for within it lie four evil spirits—lust, desire, profligacy, and greed. {3:24} If you drink wine joyfully, do so with modesty and the fear of God. {3:25} For if you lose the fear of God in your merriment, drunkenness ensues, and shamelessness follows. {3:26} If you seek to live soberly, avoid wine altogether to prevent falling into sinful words, quarrels, slander, and transgressions against God's commandments, risking an early demise. {3:27} Wine uncovers divine and human mysteries, as I also inadvertently revealed God's commandments and Jacob's secrets to Bathshua the Canaanite. {3:28} Wine often leads to war and confusion. {3:29} Therefore, my children, avoid the love of money and the allure of beauty, for these led me astray to Bathshua the Canaanite. {3:30} I know these will bring great wickedness upon my descendants. {3:31} Even wise men among my sons will be corrupted, and the kingdom of Judah shall diminish due to disobedience. {3:32} I never caused grief to my father Jacob, faithfully obeying his every command. {3:33} Isaac blessed me to be king in Israel, and Jacob confirmed this blessing. {3:34} I know my descendants will establish a kingdom. {3:35} I foresee the evils you will commit in the future days. {3:36} Therefore, beware of fornication and the love of money, and heed the counsel of Judah your father. {3:37} These vices lead you away from God's law, blind your soul's inclinations, foster arrogance, and rob you of goodness, burdening you with toil and trouble, stealing your sleep and consuming your vitality. {3:38} They hinder your sacrifices to God, make you forget His blessings, deafen you to the words of prophets, and provoke you against godliness. {3:39} You become enslaved to conflicting passions, unable to obey God, stumbling through life as though in perpetual darkness. {3:40} Children, know this: the love of money leads to idolatry, as it drives men to worship false gods in their madness. {3:41} For the sake of money, I lost my children and would have died childless were it not for God's mercy upon my repentance and humility, and my father's prayers. {3:42} The prince of deceit blinded me, corrupting me through my own sins and fleshly weaknesses, showing me my vulnerability despite my belief in invincibility. {3:43} Know, my children, that two spirits contend for every man—the spirit of truth and the spirit of deceit. {3:44} Between them stands the spirit of understanding, guiding the mind where it chooses. {3:45} The deeds of truth and deceit are written upon the hearts of men, known to the Lord before they are done. {3:46} No deed of man remains hidden, as it is inscribed upon the heart before the Lord. {3:47} The spirit of truth bears witness and accuses all, and the sinner is consumed by his own heart, unable to face the judgment of God.

{4:1} Hear me now, my children. Love and honor Levi, for in him lies stability. Do not exalt yourselves against him, lest you face utter destruction. {4:2} The Lord gave me the earthly kingdom, but to Levi, He gave the priesthood, placing it above the kingdom. {4:3} He entrusted me with earthly dominion and Levi with heavenly matters. {4:4} Just as heaven surpasses earth, so the priesthood of God is higher than any earthly kingdom, unless it strays from the Lord due to sin and becomes subservient to earthly powers. {4:5} The angel of the Lord told me: God chose Levi to draw near to Him, to partake at His table, and to offer Him the first-fruits of Israel. But you, Judah, shall be king over Jacob. {4:6} You shall be like the sea among them. {4:7} For as the sea tosses both the just and unjust, some are enslaved while others prosper, so shall it be with every race of men within you. {4:8} The kings will be like sea-monsters, swallowing men like fish. They will enslave the sons and daughters of freemen, plundering homes, lands, flocks, and wealth. {4:9} They will feed on the flesh of many unjustly, and covetousness will drive them to evil. False prophets will arise like storms, persecuting the righteous. {4:10} The Lord will bring divisions among them, and wars will continually plague Israel. A foreign race will bring my kingdom to an end until the salvation of Israel comes. {4:11} This salvation will come with the appearance of the God of righteousness, bringing peace to Jacob and all the Gentiles. {4:12} He will guard the strength of my kingdom forever, for the Lord swore an oath not to destroy my lineage's kingdom. {4:13} I am greatly troubled by your immorality, sorcery, and idolatries that will corrupt the kingdom. You will follow those who consult spirits, diviners, and demons. {4:14} Your daughters will become singers and harlots, and you will mix with Gentile abominations. {4:15} For these sins, the Lord will bring upon you famine, pestilence, death, and the sword. Enemies will besiege you, friends will revile you, children will be slain, wives raped, possessions plundered, and God's temple burned. {4:16} Your land will be laid waste, and you will be enslaved among the Gentiles, some of you made eunuchs for their pleasure. {4:17} Yet when you repent sincerely, keeping all His commandments, God will visit you and bring you back from captivity among the Gentiles. {4:18} After these trials, a star will rise from Jacob in peace, {4:19} and a righteous man will come from my descendants, shining like the sun, walking among men in meekness and righteousness, without sin. {4:20} The heavens will open to him, pouring out the spirit and blessing of the Holy Father upon you. {4:21} You will truly become His sons, faithfully walking in His commandments from first to last. {4:22} Then the scepter of my kingdom will shine brightly, and from your lineage, a righteous branch will grow, bringing justice and salvation to the Gentiles who call upon the Lord. {4:23} After these events, Abraham, Isaac, and Jacob will rise to life, and I and my brothers will lead the tribes of Israel: Levi first, followed by me, Joseph, Benjamin, Simeon, Issachar, and so forth. {4:24} Levi received the Lord's blessing, Simeon the Angel of Presence, Reuben the powers of glory, Issachar the earth, Zebulun the sea, Joseph the mountains, Benjamin the tabernacle, Dan the luminaries, Naphtali Eden, Gad the sun, and Asher the moon. {4:25} You shall be the people of the Lord, speaking with one tongue, free from the spirit of deceit of Beliar, who shall be cast into the eternal fire. {4:26} Those who died in sorrow will rise in joy, the poor for the Lord's sake will be made rich, and those martyred for the Lord's sake will awaken to life. {4:27} The hearts of Jacob will run with joy, and the eagles of Israel will soar in gladness. All people will glorify the Lord forever. {4:28} Therefore, my children, observe all the commandments of the Lord, for there is hope for those who steadfastly follow His ways. {4:29} Judah spoke these words to his children on the day he died at the age of one hundred and nineteen. {4:30} He instructed them not to bury him in costly garments or to perform the rites of kings but to carry him to Hebron, where they buried him alongside his ancestors.

Testament of Issachar

The Testament of Issachar, one of the lesser-known texts within the apocryphal Testaments of the Twelve Patriarchs, offers a rich tapestry of themes and narratives that are both historically significant and theologically profound. This testament, attributed to Issachar, the fifth son of Jacob and Leah, is part of a broader collection that reflects the moral exhortations and prophetic insights purportedly delivered by the patriarchs to their descendants. In the Testament of Issachar, the focus is predominantly on the virtues of simplicity, hard work, and integrity, virtues that Issachar claims to have embodied throughout his life. The text is notable for its emphasis on agricultural labor, reflecting Issachar's role as a man of the land, deeply connected to the rhythms of nature and the cycles of farming. The testament highlights the rewards of diligence and the dangers of idleness, underscoring a theological perspective that aligns human labor with divine favor. Furthermore, it presents a vivid portrayal of the social and ethical expectations within the family and community, offering a glimpse into the values that shaped the collective identity of the Israelites. The Testament of Issachar also engages with themes of piety and obedience, advocating for a life of faithfulness to God's commandments. Its narrative structure, while relatively straightforward, is imbued with a sense of urgency and a didactic tone, aiming to instruct and guide future generations. This testament, like others in the collection, blends elements of Jewish wisdom literature with apocalyptic and eschatological motifs, reflecting the complex interplay of tradition and innovation in Second Temple Judaism. Its preservation and transmission through various manuscripts underscore its enduring significance in the religious and cultural memory of Jewish and Christian communities alike. As a piece of pseudepigrapha, it is not only contributes to our understanding of ancient Jewish thought but also invites readers to reflect on the enduring relevance of its spiritual teachings.

{1:1} These are the teachings of Issachar, who called his sons to listen attentively. He spoke as one beloved by the Lord. {1:2} Born as Jacob's fifth son, I came into this world through a deal involving mandrakes. {1:3} Reuben, my brother, brought these mandrakes from the fields, and Rachel took them for herself. {1:4} Reuben wept, and his cries brought Leah, our mother, to the scene. {1:5} These mandrakes, sweet-smelling apples from Haran, grew near a water ravine. {1:6} Rachel declared she wouldn't share them, claiming them instead of children, feeling forsaken by the Lord for being barren. {1:7} There were two apples, and Leah, resentful, asked Rachel why she should take her husband after taking her place. {1:8} Rachel replied that Leah could have Jacob that night in exchange for the mandrakes. {1:9} Leah argued Jacob was hers as his first wife. {1:10} Rachel retorted Jacob had worked fourteen years for her, and if not for deceit and human wickedness, Leah wouldn't have married him. {1:11} Rachel revealed she was intended for Jacob, but her father deceived her, preventing Jacob from seeing her. {1:12} Despite this, Rachel agreed to let Jacob be with Leah that night in exchange for the mandrakes. {1:13} Jacob knew Leah, who then bore me, and because of this transaction, I was named Issachar. {1:14} Later, an angel told Jacob Rachel would bear two children because she chose continence over her husband. {1:15} If not for Leah's payment with the mandrakes, Rachel might have borne eight sons; thus, Leah bore six, and Rachel two. {1:16} Rachel didn't consume the mandrakes but presented them at the house of the Lord to the priest. {1:17} As I grew up, I lived with integrity, working as a farmer for my father and brothers, bringing seasonal fruits. {1:18} My father blessed me, seeing my upright ways. {1:19} I wasn't meddlesome, envious, or malicious toward anyone. {1:20} I never slandered or criticized others, living with a pure conscience. {1:21} At thirty-five, I married due to my labor-worn strength, not seeking pleasure with women, but succumbing to sleep from toil. {1:22} My father rejoiced in my integrity, as I offered first-fruits through the priest to the Lord and to him. {1:23} The Lord multiplied His blessings in my hands tenfold, and Jacob recognized God's favor upon my purity. {1:24} I generously shared the earth's bounty with the poor and oppressed, guided by my sincere heart. {1:25} Listen, my children, and live with sincerity, for the Lord finds pleasure in it. {1:26} A sincere person doesn't covet wealth, deceive others, or crave luxuries and fine clothing. {1:27} They don't seek a long life but await God's will. {1:28} Deceitful spirits have no power over them; they do not lust after women's beauty, avoiding corrupt thoughts. {1:29} They harbor no envy or malicious intent, no insatiable desires. {1:30} They walk with integrity, shunning the world's deceitful allurements and never perverting God's commandments. {1:31} Therefore, my children, keep God's law, live with sincerity, and avoid meddling in others' affairs. {1:32} Love the Lord and your neighbor, showing compassion to the poor and weak. {1:33} Embrace hard work and cultivate the land, offering thanksgiving gifts to the Lord. {1:34} The Lord will bless you with the earth's first-fruits, as He has blessed all His saints from Abel onward. {1:35} There is no greater portion than the earth's bounty, which is cultivated through labor. {1:36} Jacob blessed me with earthly blessings and first-fruits. {1:37} Levi and Judah were honored by the Lord among Jacob's sons; Levi received the priesthood, and Judah the kingdom. {1:38} Obey them and follow your father's sincerity. {1:39} Gad has been chosen to defend Israel against invading armies.

{2:1} Know this, my children, that in the future generations, your descendants will abandon simplicity and embrace insatiable desires. {2:2} They will forsake innocence and turn to malice, rejecting the Lord's commandments and turning to Beliar. {2:3} They will abandon agriculture and pursue their own wicked schemes, becoming scattered among the Gentiles and serving their enemies. {2:4} Therefore, teach these commands to your children so that if they sin, they may quickly return to the Lord, for He is merciful and will bring them back to their land. {2:5} Behold, I am now a hundred and twenty-six years old, and I can say I have not knowingly committed any sin. {2:6} Apart from my wife, I have been faithful; I have never indulged in lustful glances or committed fornication. {2:7} I have abstained from wine to avoid being led astray. {2:8} I have not coveted anything that belonged to my neighbor. {2:9} Deceit has never entered my heart, nor have lies passed my lips. {2:10} Whenever someone was in distress, I sympathized and shared in their suffering. {2:11} I have shared my bread with the poor, practicing righteousness throughout my life and always upholding truth. {2:12} I have loved the Lord deeply and have shown love to every person with all my heart. {2:13} Therefore, my children, do likewise, and every spirit of Beliar will flee from you. {2:14} Wicked deeds will not rule over you, and you will subdue every wild beast, for you walk with the God of heaven and earth in sincerity. {2:15} After saying these things, Issachar instructed his sons to carry him to Hebron and bury him in the cave with his ancestors. {2:16} He peacefully passed away at a good old age, with his limbs strong and his strength undiminished, entering the eternal rest.

Testament of Zebulun

The Testament of Zebulun, part of the Testaments of the Twelve Patriarchs, is a pseudepigraphal text attributed to Zebulun, the sixth son of Leah and Jacob. Dating back to the late Second Temple period with possible early Christian influences, it combines ethical exhortations, autobiographical recollections, and eschatological prophecies. Central to its narrative is Zebulun's confession of his sins, particularly his role in the conspiracy against Joseph, and his repentance, serving as a moral exemplar. The text emphasizes themes of forgiveness, repentance, divine justice, brotherhood, compassion, and the dangers of envy and strife, reflecting Judaic ethical teachings. It offers insights into the beliefs, hopes, and literary traditions of the intertestamental period, bridging the Hebrew Bible and the New Testament. The Testament of Zebulun also explores angelology, messianic expectations, and the afterlife, showcasing the dynamic nature of Second Temple Judaism and influencing early Christian literature, illustrating the exchange of ideas between Jewish and early Christian communities.

{1:1} This is the account of Zebulun, spoken to his sons before he passed away at the age of one hundred and fourteen, two years after Joseph's death. {1:2} He said to them, "Listen, my sons of Zebulun, pay attention to the words of your father. {1:3} I, Zebulun, was a precious gift to my parents when I was born. {1:4} At that time, my father's wealth grew significantly, with increased flocks and herds through the striped rods he used for breeding. {1:5} Throughout my life, I have no conscious memory of committing sin, except in thought. {1:6} Yet, I recall one act of ignorance against Joseph: I agreed with my brothers not to tell our father about what they had done. {1:7} I wept in secret for many days over Joseph, fearing my brothers because they had sworn to kill anyone who revealed the truth. {1:8} When they plotted to kill Joseph, I pleaded with tears for them not to commit such a sin. {1:9} Simeon and Gad were determined to kill Joseph, but he cried out with tears, begging them, 'Have mercy on me, do not shed innocent blood before our father Jacob.' {1:10} Moved by his words, I could not bear his cries, and my heart was deeply moved. {1:11} I wept along with Joseph, trembling with fear, unable to stand. {1:12} Seeing Joseph's distress, I stood between him and my brothers as they sought to kill him. {1:13} Reuben intervened, suggesting they throw Joseph into a dry pit instead of killing him outright, hoping to save his life. {1:14} They followed Reuben's plan, but later sold Joseph to the Ishmaelites. {1:15} I had no part in the sale of Joseph; it was Simeon, Gad, and six others who profited from it, buying sandals for themselves and their families with the proceeds, refusing to benefit from what they saw as their brother's blood money. {1:16} This act, as Moses' law later recorded, meant their sandal would be untied and they would be spat upon for their betrayal. {1:17} When they came to Egypt, Joseph's servants untied their sandals as they approached him, fulfilling the prophecy. {1:18} They bowed before Joseph, even as they had to Pharaoh, but this was a shameful moment for them among the Egyptians. {1:19} News of their treatment of Joseph spread throughout Egypt, tarnishing their reputation. {1:20} While they ate and drank, callous to Joseph's fate, I abstained out of sorrow and kept watch over the pit where Joseph had been left, fearing for his safety at the hands of Simeon, Dan, and Gad. {1:21} Reuben returned later, distraught to learn of Joseph's sale, grieving deeply and blaming himself for not preventing it. {1:22} The merchants had taken an unexpected route through the Troglodytes, eluding Reuben's pursuit. {1:23} Dan then proposed a plan to deceive Jacob, suggesting they dip Joseph's coat in goat's blood and present it to their father, asking if it belonged to his son. {1:24} They executed this plan, stripping Joseph of his coat before selling him into slavery and using it to deceive Jacob. {1:25} Simeon, angered that Joseph lived, had torn Joseph's coat, but they convinced him to relinquish it to maintain their deceit.

{2:1} Now my children, I urge you to obey the Lord's commands, show mercy to your neighbors, and have compassion for all living beings, not just humans. {2:2} The Lord blessed me for these virtues; when my brothers fell ill, I remained healthy because the Lord understands each person's heart. {2:3} Therefore, my children, let compassion dwell in your hearts, knowing that as you treat others, so the Lord will treat you. {2:4} While my brothers' lack of mercy towards Joseph caused them sickness and death, my sons were spared from such afflictions. {2:5} In Canaan, by the sea, I fished for my father Jacob; while others struggled and perished at sea, I remained unharmed. {2:6} I was the first to build a boat and sail the seas, gifted with understanding and wisdom from the Lord. {2:7} Using a rudder and sail, I fished along the shores until we reached Egypt. {2:8} Out of compassion, I shared my catch with every stranger. {2:9} Whether stranger, sick, or elderly, I prepared and offered them fish, grieving with and showing compassion to all. {2:10} The Lord blessed me abundantly for sharing with my neighbors; He multiplied my catch of fish. {2:11} For five years, I provided fish for everyone I encountered, sustaining my father's household. {2:12} In summer, I fished; in winter, I tended sheep with my brothers. {2:13} Let me recount another act of compassion: seeing a naked man in distress during winter, I secretly took a garment from my father's house and gave it to him. {2:14} Therefore, my children, show compassion and mercy to all, as God has blessed you, and give with a generous heart. {2:15} Even if you lack resources, have compassion for those in need. {2:16} I know the pain of not having enough; I walked with a needy man for seven furlongs, my heart filled with compassion. {2:17} So, my children, show mercy and compassion to every person, that the Lord may also show mercy to you. {2:18} In the last days, God will pour out His compassion upon the earth, dwelling in those who are merciful. {2:19} As a man shows compassion to his neighbors, so the Lord will show compassion to him. {2:20} When we went to Egypt, Joseph harbored no ill will against us. {2:21} Therefore, my children, be without malice, love one another, and do not hold grudges against your brothers. {2:22} Division breaks unity, troubles the soul, and destroys harmony among kin. {2:23} Like waters flowing together, unity preserves; divided, they vanish. {2:24} Do not be divided; all that the Lord created is unified. {2:25} From ancient writings, I learned that division would come to Israel, with two kings and great turmoil. {2:26} Enemies will conquer and afflict you, but remember the Lord and repent, for He is merciful and compassionate. {2:27} He does not hold our sins against us forever, knowing our human frailty. {2:28} After these trials, the Lord Himself, the beacon of righteousness, will lead you back to your land. {2:29} There, in Jerusalem, you will see Him for His namesake. {2:30} But through wickedness, you may provoke His anger and face judgment until the end. {2:31} So, my children, do not mourn my passing or fear my end. {2:32} For I will rise again among you, as a leader among his sons, rejoicing with my tribe who keep the Lord's law and Zebulun's commandments. {2:33} But eternal fire awaits the ungodly, destroying them for generations. {2:34} Now, I am departing to rest, as did my ancestors. {2:35} Fear the Lord your God with all your strength all your days. {2:36} And when I had finished speaking, I peacefully fell asleep in old age. {2:37} My sons laid me in a wooden coffin and later buried me in Hebron with my ancestors.

Testament of Dan

The Testament of Dan is a fascinating and complex text that forms part of the Testaments of the Twelve Patriarchs, a pseudepigraphal collection attributed to the twelve sons of Jacob. The Testament of Dan, like its counterparts, is written in the form of a deathbed testament, wherein Dan, the progenitor of the tribe of Dan, imparts his final teachings and reflections to his descendants. This text is notable for its emphasis on ethical and moral instruction, focusing particularly on the themes of anger and deceit, which Dan identifies as his own personal failings and warns his children against. The Testament of Dan blends Jewish ethical teachings with apocalyptic elements, reflecting the diverse religious and cultural milieu of the Second Temple period during which it was likely composed. Scholars often analyze the Testament of Dan to gain insights into early Jewish thought, particularly regarding the nature of sin and the importance of repentance and moral rectitude. Additionally, the text's rich intertextuality, drawing upon various biblical and extra-biblical traditions, provides valuable context for understanding the development of Jewish pseudepigraphal literature and its influence on early Christian writings. The Testament of Dan also offers a glimpse into the social and theological concerns of its time, including the roles of the patriarchs, the nature of divine justice, and the eschatological hope for Israel's future. Through its admonitions and apocalyptic visions, it serves as a testament not only to the enduring legacy of its eponymous patriarch but also to the broader religious and ethical currents that shaped Jewish thought in the centuries preceding the rise of Christianity.

{1:1} These are the words of Dan, spoken to his sons in his final days, at the age of one hundred and twenty-five years. {1:2} He gathered his family and said to them, "Listen, my sons of Dan, and pay attention to the words of your father. {1:3} Throughout my life, I have learned that truth and fairness are pleasing to God, while lying and anger lead to wickedness in every form. {1:4} Today, I confess to you, my children, that I once harbored thoughts of killing my brother Joseph, a righteous and good man. {1:5} I rejoiced when he was sold because our father favored him more than us. {1:6} The spirit of jealousy and pride whispered to me, 'You are his son too.' {1:7} Influenced by a spirit of Beliar, I was tempted to take a sword and kill Joseph, believing my father would then favor me after his death. {1:8} This was the spirit of anger that drove me, like a leopard stalking its prey. {1:9} Yet, God prevented me from harming Joseph, ensuring I did not find him alone to carry out such a deed that would have brought further sorrow upon our tribe in Israel. {1:10} Now, as I near death, I warn you: avoid lying and anger, embrace truth and patience, or you will face destruction. {1:11} Anger blinds a person, preventing them from seeing others truthfully. {1:12} Whether it's a parent, a sibling, a prophet, a righteous person, or a friend, anger distorts perception and leads to disobedience and enmity. {1:13} The spirit of anger ensnares with deception, blinds the eyes, darkens the mind with lies, and distorts perception. {1:14} It feeds on a heart filled with hatred and envy towards others. {1:15} Anger is destructive, troubling not just the body but the soul itself. {1:16} It takes control of the body and soul, empowering it to commit all forms of evil. {1:17} The angry justify their actions because their perception is clouded. {1:18} Whether powerful or weak, the wrathful find strength in anger, aided by this destructive force. {1:19} Anger always accompanies lying, serving Satan's purposes of cruelty and deceit. {1:20} Understand the futility of anger, which provokes and strengthens through words and deeds, causing great turmoil in the mind and soul. {1:21} Therefore, do not be quick to anger when criticized, nor proud when praised. {1:22} Guard against delight and disgust, for these emotions can lead to anger. {1:23} Loss and adversity should not distress you, for anger seeks to enrage through suffering. {1:24} Whether loss is voluntary or involuntary, do not be vexed, as vexation leads to wrath and deceit. {1:25} Anger combined with lying causes double trouble, disturbing the heart and driving away the presence of the Lord, allowing Beliar to rule.

{2:1} These are the words of Dan as he spoke to his sons in his final days, at the age of one hundred and twenty-five years. {2:2} He admonished them, saying, "Observe the commandments of the Lord and keep His law. Turn away from wrath and reject falsehood, so that the Lord may dwell among you and Beliar may flee from you. {2:3} Speak truthfully to one another, for this will prevent wrath and confusion, and peace will reign, guarded by the God of peace, ensuring no war will overcome you. {2:4} Love the Lord throughout your lives and love one another sincerely. {2:5} But know this: in the last days, you will turn away from the Lord and provoke Levi to anger, and you will contend against Judah. Yet, you will not prevail, for an angel of the Lord will guide them, and through them, Israel will stand. {2:6} Whenever you depart from the Lord, you will walk in wickedness, following the abominations of the Gentiles, indulging in lawless desires and the workings of wicked spirits. {2:7} As foretold in the book of Enoch, your leader will be Satan, and wicked spirits will conspire to lead the sons of Levi into sin before the Lord. {2:8} My sons will join with Levi in their sins, while the sons of Judah will become greedy, plundering like lions. {2:9} Because of this, you will be led into captivity, experiencing the plagues of Egypt and the hardships of the Gentiles. {2:10} But when you return to the Lord, you will find mercy; He will bring you into His sanctuary and grant you peace. {2:11} From the tribes of Judah and Levi, the Lord's salvation will arise, waging war against Beliar and executing everlasting vengeance on our enemies. {2:12} The saints will rest in Eden, and in the New Jerusalem, the righteous will rejoice, all to the glory of God forevermore. {2:13} Jerusalem will no longer endure desolation, nor will Israel suffer captivity, for the Lord will dwell among them, reigning in humility and poverty. Those who believe in Him will reign in truth among men. {2:14} Therefore, fear the Lord, my children, and beware of Satan and his spirits. {2:15} Draw near to God and to the angel who intercedes for you, for he stands between God and man, advocating for the peace of Israel against the kingdom of the enemy. {2:16} The enemy seeks to destroy all who call upon the Lord, knowing that the day Israel repents, his kingdom will be overthrown. {2:17} The angel of peace will strengthen Israel, preventing them from falling into extreme evil. {2:18} In the days of Israel's lawlessness, the Lord will not forsake them but will transform them into a nation that does His will, surpassing even the angels in righteousness. {2:19} His name will be revered throughout Israel and among the Gentiles. {2:20} Therefore, keep yourselves from every evil deed, forsake wrath and falsehood, and embrace truth and patience. {2:21} Teach your children the words you have heard from your father, so that the Savior of the Gentiles may receive you, for He is true, patient, humble, and teaches God's law through His deeds. {2:22} Depart from unrighteousness and cling to God's righteousness, ensuring your lineage will be saved forever. {2:23} Dan urged them to uphold their faith, lest they forget their God and become estranged from their inheritance, their people, and the land of Israel. {2:24} After speaking these words, Dan kissed his sons and peacefully passed away in old age. {2:25} His sons buried him, and later they carried his bones to rest near Abraham, Isaac, and Jacob. {2:26} However, Dan prophesied that they would forsake God, be alienated from their land of inheritance, and from the people of Israel, and from their ancestral lineage.

Testament of Naphtali

The Testament of Naphtali, part of the pseudepigraphal Testaments of the Twelve Patriarchs, provides insights into ancient traditions and theological reflections attributed to the sons of Jacob. This lesser-known text, believed to be a deathbed speech by Naphtali, the sixth son of Jacob and Bilhah, combines historical narrative, ethical teachings, and eschatological prophecies. It emphasizes virtues like piety, humility, and obedience to God, and addresses justice, righteousness, divine retribution, and the ultimate triumph of good over evil. Scholars value the Testament of Naphtali for its insights into Jewish ethical teachings and eschatology during the intertestamental period. Written likely in the early centuries BCE, it reflects significant religious and political upheaval. The text's preservation in various manuscripts highlights its lasting influence within Jewish communities, offering a rich resource for understanding ancient Jewish thought and the patriarchal narratives.

{1:1} This is the testament of Naphtali, spoken in the hundred and thirtieth year of his life as he approached death. {1:2} Gathering his sons on the first day of the seventh month while still in good health, he hosted a feast of food and wine for them. {1:3} The next morning, as he woke, he solemnly declared to them, "I am dying," though they initially doubted him. {1:4} Strengthened by the Lord as he praised Him, Naphtali reaffirmed that his end was near after the previous day's celebration. {1:5} He began to speak to his sons, saying, "Listen, my children, sons of Naphtali, hear the words of your father." {1:6} "I was born to Bilhah, given by Rachel to Jacob in place of herself. Rachel loved me dearly as I was born upon her knees, longing for a brother like me from her own womb." {1:7} "Joseph was like unto me, fulfilling Rachel's prayers." {1:8} "My mother, Bilhah, was the daughter of Rotheus, brother of Deborah, Rebecca's nurse, born on the same day as Rachel." {1:9} "Rotheus, a Chaldean of Abraham's family, was captured and sold to Laban, who gave him Euna as wife. She bore Zilpah and then Bilhah." {1:10} "Bilhah, swift and eager from birth, {1:11} was likened to one who seizes new things promptly." {1:12} "I, swift as a deer, was appointed by Jacob for all errands and blessed as such." {1:13} "Just as a potter molds vessels according to their purpose, so the Lord fashions the body according to the spirit's design." {1:14} "Nothing is out of balance; all creation is meticulously weighed and measured." {1:15} "As the potter knows each vessel's use, so the Lord understands the body's inclination toward good or evil." {1:16} "No thought or desire escapes His knowledge, for every person is made in His image." {1:17} "A person's strength matches their deeds; their eyes guide their sleep; their soul reflects their words, whether aligned with God's law or Beliar's." {1:18} "Just as there's distinction between light and darkness, seeing and hearing, so too among people—no two are alike in face or mind." {1:19} "God created everything in harmony—five senses in the head, each part with its purpose and beauty." {1:20} "Therefore, let all your actions be orderly and well-intentioned in the fear of God. Do nothing in scorn or out of season, for just as the eye cannot hear in darkness, neither can you perform deeds of light in darkness." {1:21} "Do not corrupt your actions with covetousness or deceitful words; silence your hearts to understand and hold fast to God's will, rejecting Beliar's." {1:22} "Sun, moon, and stars maintain their order; likewise, do not disrupt God's law through disorderly conduct." {1:23} "The Gentiles strayed, forsaking the Lord, altering their order to worship idols and deceitful spirits." {1:24} "You, however, must recognize the Lord in all creation—firmament, {1:25} earth, sea—so that you do not become like Sodom, which perverted the natural order." {1:26} "Even the Watchers altered their nature, bringing the Lord's curse upon them and rendering the earth barren." {1:27} "I warn you, my children, for I have read in Enoch's writings that you too will depart from the Lord, embracing lawlessness like the Gentiles and the wickedness of Sodom." {1:28} "Captivity will come upon you; you will serve your enemies, afflicted and troubled until the Lord consumes you." {1:29} "Yet, in your diminished state, you will repent and acknowledge the Lord, and He will, in His mercy, restore you to your land." {1:30} "But after returning to your fathers' land, you will again forget the Lord and become wicked." {1:31} "The Lord will scatter you across the earth until His compassionate servant, who practices righteousness and mercy, gathers you, both near and far."

{2:1} At the age of forty, I had a vision on the Mount of Olives near Jerusalem. I saw the sun and moon standing still. {2:2} Isaac, my grandfather, told us to seize them. Levi grabbed the sun, and Judah swiftly took the moon. They were lifted up with them, radiant and triumphant. {2:3} Levi shone like the sun, receiving twelve palm branches, while Judah glowed like the moon, with twelve rays beneath them. {2:4} Together, they captured these celestial bodies. {2:5} Then, a bull with two great horns and eagle's wings appeared, but we couldn't seize it. {2:6} Joseph arrived and grasped it, ascending high above us. {2:7} I saw this vision clearly, accompanied by a holy prophecy predicting Israel's captivity by Assyrians, Medes, Persians, Chaldeans, and Syrians. {2:8} Seven days later, I saw our father Jacob by the sea of Jamnia. {2:9} A ship named 'The Ship of Jacob' sailed by without a crew. {2:10} Jacob invited us aboard, but a fierce storm arose, causing our father, steering the ship, to disappear. {2:11} We were tossed and the ship filled with water, eventually breaking apart. {2:12} Joseph escaped on a small boat, and we clung to nine planks, Levi and Judah together. {2:13} We were scattered across the earth. {2:14} Levi, in sackcloth, prayed for us all, and the storm subsided, guiding the ship safely to land. {2:15} Our father rejoiced upon his return. {2:16} These dreams I shared with my father, who foresaw Israel enduring many trials. {2:17} He believed Joseph lived, always counting him among us. {2:18} He wept for Joseph, unable to see him. {2:19} These visions reveal what will befall Israel in the future. {2:20} Jacob urged us to unite with Levi and Judah for Israel's salvation. {2:21} God will dwell among men through their tribes, gathering the righteous from the Gentiles. {2:22} If you do good, men and angels will bless you, and God will be glorified among the Gentiles through you. {2:23} But those who do evil will be cursed by angels and men, dishonoring God. {2:24} The devil will claim them, wild beasts will master them, and the Lord will hate them. {2:25} The commandments are twofold, requiring prudence for fulfillment. {2:26} There is a time for marital relations and a time for abstinence for prayer, both essential and ordered. {2:27} Therefore, be wise and prudent in God, understanding His commandments and laws, that the Lord may love you. {2:28} Naphtali instructed his sons to bury him in Hebron with his fathers. {2:29} After enjoying a meal with a joyful heart, he covered his face and passed away. {2:30} His sons honored his wishes and buried him according to his commands.

Testament of Gad

The Testament of Gad, one of the lesser-known yet intriguing texts within the broader corpus of the Testaments of the Twelve Patriarchs, presents a rich tapestry of themes central to Second Temple Judaism and early Christian thought. Believed to be composed during the intertestamental period, this text offers a profound reflection on the moral and ethical instructions attributed to Gad, one of Jacob's twelve sons. The document weaves together personal narrative, didactic elements, and eschatological visions, providing a multifaceted portrait of Gad's character and his counsel to his descendants. Central to the Testament of Gad is the theme of repentance and forgiveness, articulated through Gad's own experience of envy and reconciliation with his brother Joseph. This narrative underscores the broader theological motif of divine mercy and the transformative power of repentance, reflecting contemporaneous Jewish teachings. Additionally, the text delves into the nature of sin and virtue, contrasting the destructive consequences of envy and hatred with the redemptive qualities of love and unity. The Testament of Gad also contains apocalyptic elements, offering glimpses into the eschatological expectations of the period, including visions of final judgment and the ultimate triumph of righteousness. The linguistic style and thematic concerns suggest a composite work, possibly redacted over time, to address evolving theological and communal concerns. Its preservation in Greek, along with fragments in other languages, indicates its widespread influence and the diverse contexts in which it was read and transmitted. Thus, it not only enriches our understanding of the patriarchal narratives but also provides valuable insights into the eschatological beliefs that shaped Jewish and early Christian communities.

{1:1} This is what Gad, Jacob's ninth son by Zilpah, spoke to his sons when he was 125 years old. {1:2} Listen, my children. I was strong and brave as a shepherd, fiercely protecting our flocks. {1:3} I would confront lions, wolves, and other beasts, seizing them and hurling them away when they threatened our fold. {1:4} Joseph, my younger brother, joined us in tending the flock for over thirty days until he fell ill from the heat and returned to Hebron, where our father Jacob cared for him dearly. {1:5} Joseph informed our father that Zilpah's and Bilhah's sons were slaughtering the best of the flock against Reuben's and Judah's judgment. {1:6} Joseph witnessed me saving a lamb from a bear but sadly killing it afterward, troubled by our actions. {1:7} I harbored resentment towards Joseph for his criticisms, and this hatred grew until the day he was sold. {1:8} My heart was filled with hatred, especially aggravated by Joseph's dreams, desiring his removal from our lives like an ox devouring grass. {1:9} Eventually, Judah sold him to the Ishmaelites in secret, yet God spared him from our hands, preventing greater wrongdoing in Israel. {1:10} Now, my children, heed these words of truth: pursue righteousness and obey the Most High's law. Avoid the destructive spirit of hatred, for it corrupts all human deeds. {1:11} A hater despises everything a person does, even if they obey the Lord's law or fear Him and delight in righteousness. {1:12} Hatred distorts truth, envies the prosperous, welcomes slander, loves arrogance, and blinds the soul, just as I looked upon Joseph. {1:13} Beware of hatred, for it spawns lawlessness against the Lord Himself, disregarding His commandments about loving one's neighbor and sinning against God. {1:14} If a brother stumbles, hatred eagerly spreads the news, pushing for judgment, punishment, even death. {1:15} It incites servants against their masters, plotting afflictions and death upon them. {1:16} Hatred also envies the successful; upon hearing of their prosperity, it withers away. {1:17} Love revives the dead, but hatred slays the living, showing no mercy even for minor offenses. {1:18} The spirit of hatred aligns with Satan, leading to hasty, deadly actions, while the spirit of love, in accordance with God's law, practices patience for human salvation. {1:19} Hatred is inherently evil, breeding lies, distorting truth, magnifying trivial matters, turning light into darkness, sweet into bitter, teaching slander, igniting wrath, and causing conflict, violence, and greed. {1:20} It fills hearts with evil and diabolical poison. {1:21} From my own experience, children, I urge you to banish hatred, which originates from the devil, and embrace God's love. {1:22} Righteousness expels hatred, humility defeats envy. {1:23} A just and humble person is ashamed of injustice, not because of others' reproof, but because they fear God's judgment in their hearts. {1:24} They do not speak ill of the holy, for the fear of God conquers hatred. {1:25} These lessons I learned after repenting of my hatred towards Joseph. {1:26} Genuine repentance eradicates ignorance, dispels darkness, enlightens the mind, and leads to salvation. {1:27} Through repentance, one learns what cannot be taught by man. {1:28} God afflicted me with a liver disease due to my bitterness towards Joseph. {1:29} Only Jacob's prayers saved me from death, as my liver tormented me for eleven months, matching the duration of my anger towards Joseph.

{2:1} Now, my children, I urge you to love each other sincerely and rid your hearts of hatred. Let your love be evident in your actions, words, and thoughts. {2:2} I once spoke peacefully to Joseph in our father's presence, but once alone, hatred clouded my mind, stirring my soul to contemplate his demise. {2:3} Love one another genuinely; if someone wrongs you, speak to them calmly, without deceit in your heart. If they repent and confess, forgive them. {2:4} But if they deny their wrongdoing, do not become angry, as this may lead them to swear falsely and compound their sin. {2:5} Do not divulge your secrets to others during legal disputes, for they may turn against you, becoming enemies and committing great wrongs. They may deceive you or act wickedly toward you. {2:6} If confronted with denial but a hint of shame upon reproof, cease your reproach. {2:7} The one who denies may repent and cease to harm you again, even showing you honor and seeking peace. {2:8} Should they remain shameless and persist in their wrongdoing, forgive them sincerely and leave vengeance to God. {2:9} If someone prospers more than you, do not envy them; instead, pray for their continued success, for this is beneficial for you too. {2:10} Remember, all flesh shall die, so do not begrudge anyone's prosperity. Praise God, who grants good and beneficial things to all. {2:11} Seek the judgments of the Lord, finding peace for your mind. {2:12} Even if someone becomes wealthy through unjust means, like Esau, my father's brother, do not be jealous, but await the Lord's judgment. {2:13} God forgives those who repent of ill-gotten gains, but the unrepentant face eternal punishment. {2:14} The poor who live without envy please the Lord greatly, blessed beyond measure for avoiding the folly of vain men. {2:15} Therefore, remove jealousy from your hearts and love one another sincerely. {2:16} Teach these things to your children so they may honor Judah and Levi, for from them the Lord will bring salvation to Israel. {2:17} I know that eventually your children will turn from these teachings and walk in wickedness, facing affliction and corruption before the Lord. {2:18} After a brief rest, Gad instructed his children to obey their father and bury him near his ancestors. {2:19} He peacefully passed away, and five years later, they buried him in Hebron alongside his fathers.

Testament of Asher

The Testament of Asher, part of the larger compilation known as the Testaments of the Twelve Patriarchs, is a significant pseudepigraphal work traditionally attributed to Asher, the eighth son of Jacob and Zilpah, Leah's maidservant. Although it is not included in the canonical scriptures of most religious traditions, the Testament of Asher offers profound insights into early Jewish thought, moral teachings, and eschatological expectations. The text is believed to have been composed during the intertestamental period, a time characterized by considerable theological and cultural development within Judaism. This era saw the crystallization of various sects and movements, which were grappling with issues of identity, purity, and the interpretation of sacred texts. The Testament of Asher reflects these preoccupations, emphasizing themes such as the dichotomy between good and evil, the importance of ethical conduct, and the inevitable judgment that awaits humanity. Asher's narrative is imbued with didactic elements, instructing his descendants on virtues such as truthfulness, compassion, and justice, while warning against vices like deceit, envy, and unrighteous anger. The text also delves into the nature of the human soul and the afterlife, offering a vision of ultimate redemption for the righteous and condemnation for the wicked. Scholars have long debated the origins and influences of the Testament of Asher, with some suggesting it was shaped by Hellenistic philosophical ideas, while others point to parallels with contemporary Jewish apocalyptic literature. Its transmission through various manuscript traditions highlights its enduring appeal and the ways in which it has been interpreted and reinterpreted by successive generations. The Testament of Asher, therefore, stands as a testament to the rich and complex spiritual heritage of Judaism during a formative period in its history, providing valuable context for understanding the development of Jewish ethics and eschatology.

{1:1} This is the testament of Asher, spoken to his sons when he was 125 years old. {1:2} In his vigor, he instructed them: Listen, children of Asher, and I will reveal what is pleasing in the sight of the Lord. {1:3} God has given two ways to mankind, two inclinations, and two kinds of actions with their outcomes. {1:4} Therefore, everything exists in pairs, opposing one another. {1:5} There are paths of good and evil, and within us are inclinations that discern between them. {1:6} If the soul delights in goodness, its actions are righteous; if it sins, it promptly repents. {1:7} Focused on righteousness, it casts away wickedness, uprooting sin. {1:8} But if it leans toward evil, its deeds are wicked, rejecting good and clinging to evil, influenced by Beliar. Even if it does something good, he twists it to evil. {1:9} When it starts to do good, he corrupts it, for the inclination's treasure is filled with an evil spirit. {1:10} One may use words to assist good, but evil results ensue. {1:11} Some show no mercy to those they use for evil; this is a twofold evil. {1:12} Others love evildoers, willing to die for them, another twofold evil. {1:13} Even with love, concealing evil for a good reputation leads to evil outcomes. {1:14} Some steal, cheat, and pity the poor—another dual aspect that is wholly evil. {1:15} One defrauds and swears falsely, yet helps the poor, defying God's law, mixing good with evil. {1:16} Another commits adultery but abstains from food, doing evil during fasting, yet follows commandments—another twofold aspect of evil. {1:17} Such men are like hares, outwardly clean but inwardly unclean. {1:18} God's commandments declare this truth. {1:19} My children, do not be double-faced like them, showing both goodness and wickedness. {1:20} Embrace goodness alone, for God dwells there, desired by all. {1:21} Flee from wickedness, eradicating evil inclinations through good works. {1:22} Double-faced people serve their own desires and Beliar, not God. {1:23} Yet the just, even if accused of sin by the double-faced, are righteous before God. {1:24} Some hate both merciful and unjust men, and adulterers who fast—this is a twofold good work, following the Lord's example, discerning genuine good from apparent good. {1:25} Another avoids sinful company, preserving purity—another dual aspect that is wholly good. {1:26} These are like stags and hinds, seeming unclean like wild animals but truly clean, zealously following God's commandments and avoiding evil. {1:27} You see, my children, everything has two sides opposing each other, one hiding the other: covetousness in wealth, drunkenness in revelry, grief in laughter, and profligacy in marriage. {1:28} Death follows life, dishonor follows glory, night follows day, and darkness follows light; all under the dominion of day, justice under life, injustice under death. Eternal life awaits. {1:29} Truth cannot be called falsehood, nor can right be called wrong, for all truth is under the light, just as all things are under God. {1:30} I have proven these truths in my life, never straying from the Lord's truth, following His commandments with all my strength and sincerity toward what is good. {1:31} Therefore, my children, keep the Lord's commandments, embracing truth with singleness of heart. {1:32} Double-faced individuals are doubly guilty, doing evil and delighting in those who do it, following deceitful spirits, opposing mankind. {1:33} Therefore, children, keep God's law and do not mistake evil for good. {1:34} In the end, men's actions reveal their righteousness or unrighteousness when they face the angels of the Lord and Satan. {1:35} A troubled soul departs tormented by the evil it served in lust and wrongdoing. {1:36} A peaceful soul meets the angel of peace, entering eternal life. {1:37} Do not become like Sodom, which sinned against the angels and perished forever. {1:38} I know you will sin and fall into your enemies' hands; your land will be desolate, your holy places destroyed, and you scattered across the earth. {1:39} You will be despised in exile, vanishing like water. {1:40} Until the Most High visits the earth, coming as a man, eating and drinking with men, and defeating the dragon in the water. {1:41} He will save Israel and all the Gentiles, speaking as God in human form. {1:42} Tell these things to your children, that they may not disobey Him. {1:43} I know you will surely be disobedient, following ungodly ways instead of God's law, corrupted by wickedness. {1:44} Therefore, you will be scattered like Gad and Dan, my brothers, losing your land, tribe, and language. {1:45} Yet the Lord will gather you in faith through His mercy, for the sake of Abraham, Isaac, and Jacob. {1:46} After saying these things, Asher instructed them: Bury me in Hebron. {1:47} He peacefully passed away at a ripe old age. {1:48} His sons obeyed, burying him in Hebron beside his fathers.

Testament of Joseph

The Testament of Joseph is one of the twelve Testaments of the Patriarchs, an ancient pseudepigraphal work that forms part of the broader corpus of Jewish intertestamental literature. This particular testament purports to be the final words and reflections of Joseph, the eleventh son of Jacob and a central figure in the Genesis narrative. The Testament of Joseph, like the other testaments in this collection, is structured as an ethical will, where the patriarch imparts moral exhortations, personal reflections, and prophetic insights to his descendants. Joseph's testament emphasizes themes of chastity, forgiveness, and divine providence, drawing heavily on the biblical account of his life, particularly his trials in Egypt, his steadfast resistance to Potiphar's wife, and his eventual rise to power. The Testament of Joseph is valued for its didactic tone, using Joseph's piety and resilience to instruct readers in virtuous living. Scholars appreciate its insights into Second Temple Judaism, reflecting the religious and ethical concerns of Jewish communities during this time. It also reinterprets and expands biblical narratives, offering theological motifs, narrative details, and moral teachings.

{1:1} This is the copy of the Testament of Joseph. {1:2} When Joseph was nearing death, he gathered his sons and his brothers and said to them: {1:3} "My brothers and my children, listen to Joseph, the beloved of Israel. Pay attention, my sons, to your father. {1:4} In my life, I have experienced envy and death, yet I did not go astray but stayed true to the Lord. {1:5} My brothers hated me, but the Lord loved me. {1:6} They wanted to kill me, but the God of my fathers protected me. {1:7} They threw me into a pit, but the Most High lifted me out. {1:8} I was sold into slavery, but the Lord made me free. {1:9} I was taken into captivity, but His strong hand helped me. {1:10} I was hungry, and the Lord Himself provided for me. {1:11} I was alone, and God comforted me. {1:12} I was sick, and the Lord visited me. {1:13} I was in prison, and my God showed me favor. {1:14} I was in chains, and He released me. {1:15} I was slandered, and He defended me. {1:16} I was spoken against by the Egyptians, but He rescued me. {1:17} I was envied by my fellow slaves, but He exalted me. {1:18} The chief captain of Pharaoh entrusted his house to me. {1:19} I resisted a shameless woman who urged me to sin with her, but the God of Israel, my father, saved me from the fire. {1:20} I was thrown into prison, beaten, and mocked, but the Lord granted me favor in the sight of the prison keeper. {1:21} The Lord does not abandon those who fear Him, neither in darkness, nor in chains, nor in trials, nor in needs. {1:22} For God is not ashamed like a man, nor is He afraid like a human being, nor is He weak or fearful like those born of the earth. {1:23} In all things, He gives protection and comforts in various ways, though sometimes He leaves for a while to test the heart's inclination. {1:24} In ten trials, He proved me, and in all of them, I endured because endurance is a powerful charm, and patience brings many good things. {1:25} How often did the Egyptian woman threaten to kill me! {1:26} How many times did she punish me, only to call me back and threaten me again? When I refused to be with her, she said: {1:27} 'You shall be lord over me and all in my house if you will lie with me, and you will be like our master.' {1:28} But I remembered the words of my father, and I went into my room and wept and prayed to the Lord. {1:29} I fasted during those seven years, and though I appeared to the Egyptians as someone who lived delicately, those who fast for God receive beauty. {1:30} When my master was away, I drank no wine, and for three days, I would not eat, instead giving my food to the poor and sick. {1:31} I sought the Lord early and prayed for the Egyptian woman of Memphis, for she relentlessly troubled me, even coming to me at night pretending to visit me. {1:32} She had no male child, and she pretended to treat me as a son. {1:33} For a time, she embraced me as a son, and I didn't realize it, but later, she tried to seduce me into sin. {1:34} When I realized her intent, I was deeply troubled, and after she left, I mourned for her for many days, knowing her deception. {1:35} I told her the words of the Most High, hoping she might turn from her lust. {1:36} Often, she flattered me with holy words and praised my chastity to her husband, while secretly plotting to seduce me. {1:37} She openly praised me as chaste, but in secret, she said, 'Do not fear my husband; he trusts your purity, and even if someone tells him, he will not believe it.' {1:38} Because of all this, I lay on the ground and prayed to God to deliver me from her deceit. {1:39} When her attempts failed, she came again under the pretense of learning about God's word. {1:40} She said to me, 'If you want me to leave my idols, lie with me, and I will persuade my husband to abandon his idols, and we will follow your Lord.' {1:41} I replied, 'The Lord does not want those who honor Him to live in impurity. He does not delight in adulterers but in those who approach Him with a pure heart and clean lips.' {1:42} But she stayed silent, still desiring to fulfill her evil intent. {1:43} I prayed and fasted even more so that the Lord might save me from her. {1:44} Then, another time, she said, 'If you do not commit adultery with me, I will kill my husband with poison and marry you.' {1:45} When I heard this, I tore my clothes and said to her, {1:46} 'Woman, fear God and do not do this evil, or you will be destroyed. Know that I will reveal your plan to everyone.' {1:47} She became afraid and begged me not to tell anyone. {1:48} She then left, trying to soothe me with gifts and sending me all sorts of delights. {1:49} Later, she sent me food mixed with enchantments. {1:50} When the eunuch who brought it arrived, I looked up and saw a terrible figure giving me a sword with the dish, realizing her plan was to deceive me. {1:51} After the eunuch left, I wept and refused to eat any of her food. {1:52} The next day, she came and asked, 'Why haven't you eaten?' {1:53} I replied, 'Because you have filled it with deadly magic. How could you say you worship the Lord and not idols?' {1:54} I said, 'The God of my father has revealed your wickedness to me through His angel, and I have kept it to confront you, hoping you might repent.' {1:55} To prove that the wickedness of the ungodly has no power over those who worship God with purity, I said, 'I will eat it in front of you.' {1:56} So I prayed, 'God of my fathers and the angel of Abraham, be with me,' and I ate it. {1:57} When she saw this, she fell at my feet, weeping. I lifted her up and warned her. {1:58} She promised not to continue in her evil ways. {1:59} But her heart was still set on sin, and she looked for another way to trap me, becoming dejected, though not sick. {1:60} When her husband saw her, he asked, 'Why is your face downcast?' {1:61} She replied, 'I have pain in my heart, and my spirit is troubled,' and he comforted her, though she was not ill. {1:62} Seizing the opportunity, she rushed to me while her husband was out and said, 'If you do not lie with me, I will hang myself or throw myself off a cliff.' {1:63} Seeing that the spirit of Beliar troubled her, I prayed to the Lord and said to her, {1:64} 'Why, miserable woman, are you disturbed and blinded by sin? {1:65} Remember, if you kill yourself, Asteho, your husband's concubine, will beat your children, and your memory will be erased from the earth.' {1:66} She replied, 'Then you love me! That's enough for me. Just save my life and my children, and I'll expect to enjoy my desires as well.' {1:67} She did not know I spoke this way out of concern for my master, not for her. {1:68} If a man falls to the passion of wicked desire, as she did, whatever good he hears related to that passion, he twists it to satisfy his desire. {1:69} I tell you, my children, it was about the sixth hour when she left me, and I knelt and prayed to the Lord all day and night, weeping and praying for deliverance from her. {1:70} Finally, she grabbed my garments, trying to force me into sin. {1:71} Seeing that she was holding on to my clothes in her madness, I left them behind and fled, naked. {1:72} Holding my garments, she falsely accused me, and when her husband returned, he imprisoned me in his house. The next day, he whipped me and sent me to Pharaoh's prison. {1:73} While I was in chains, the Egyptian woman was troubled with grief. She came to hear how I gave thanks to the Lord and sang praises in the darkness of my prison. With a glad heart, I rejoiced, glorifying God for delivering me from the lustful desires of the Egyptian woman. {1:74} Many times, she sent messages to me, saying, "If you agree to fulfill my desire, I will release you from your chains and free you from this darkness." {1:75} But I did not even entertain the thought of her proposition. {1:76} For God prefers a man who, in a place of wickedness, combines fasting with purity rather than one who lives in the luxury of kings' chambers with indulgence. {1:77} And if a man lives chastely and seeks glory, the Most High, knowing what is best for him, grants this also, as He granted it to me. {1:78} How often, even though she was sick, did she come down to me unexpectedly, just to listen to me pray! {1:79} When I heard her groaning, I kept silent. {1:80} For when I was in her house, she often exposed her arms, breasts, and legs to tempt me, for she was very beautiful and splendidly adorned in order to seduce me. {1:81} But the Lord protected me from her schemes and kept me safe from her tricks.

{2:1} See, my children, how great things patience can achieve, along with prayer and fasting. {2:2} So if you pursue chastity and purity with patience, prayer, and fasting in humility of heart, the Lord will dwell among you because He loves chastity. {2:3} Wherever the Most High dwells, even if a person suffers from envy, slavery, or slander, the Lord who resides within them, because of their chastity, will not only deliver them from evil but will also exalt them just as He has exalted me. {2:4} The man is uplifted in every way—through deeds, words, and thoughts. {2:5} My brothers knew how much my father loved me, yet I did not lift myself up in pride. Although I was a child, I had the fear of God in my heart, knowing that all things are temporary. {2:6} I did not oppose them with ill intentions, but honored my brothers. Even when I was being sold, I refrained from telling the Ishmaelites that I was Jacob's son, a great and mighty man. {2:7} So, my children, always have the fear of God before your eyes in all your actions and honor your brothers. {2:8} Everyone who follows the Lord's laws will be loved by Him. {2:9} When I arrived with the Ishmaelites at the Indocolpitae, they asked me, {2:10} "Are you a slave?" I replied that I was a native slave, not to bring shame upon my brothers. {2:11} But the eldest among them said, "You are not a slave, for your appearance shows otherwise." {2:12} But I insisted that I was their slave. {2:13} When we arrived in Egypt, they debated over who would buy me and take me. {2:14} So it was agreed that I should remain in Egypt with the merchant of their trade until they returned with their goods. {2:15} And the Lord gave me favor in the eyes of the merchant, who entrusted me with his household. {2:16} God blessed him through me, increasing his wealth in gold, silver, and servants. {2:17} I stayed with him for three months and five days. {2:18} During that time, the wife of Pentephris from Memphis came in a grand chariot because she had heard about me from her eunuchs. {2:19} She told her husband that the merchant had become rich through a young Hebrew, and claimed he had been stolen from Canaan. {2:20} She urged her husband to take justice against me and bring me to his house, saying that the God of the Hebrews would bless him, for grace was upon me. {2:21} Pentephris was persuaded by her words and summoned the merchant, asking, {2:22} "What is this I hear, that you steal people from Canaan and sell them as slaves?" {2:23} The merchant fell at his feet and pleaded, saying, "I beg you, my lord, I do not know what you are talking about." {2:24} Pentephris asked, "Then where is the Hebrew slave from?" {2:25} The merchant replied, "The Ishmaelites entrusted him to me until their return." {2:26} Pentephris did not believe him and ordered him to be stripped and beaten. {2:27} When the merchant continued to assert his innocence, Pentephris said, "Let the youth be brought." {2:28} When I was brought in, I bowed to Pentephris, who was third in rank of Pharaoh's officers. {2:29} He separated me and asked, "Are you a slave or free?" {2:30} I replied, "A slave." {2:31} He then asked, "Whose?" {2:32} I said, "The Ishmaelites'." {2:33} He asked, "How did you become their slave?" {2:34} I answered, "They bought me from the land of Canaan." {2:35} Pentephris said, "You are lying," and immediately commanded that I be stripped and beaten. {2:36} As I was being beaten, the Memphian woman watched from a window since her house was nearby. She sent a message to Pentephris, saying, {2:37} "Your judgment is unjust; you punish a free man who has been stolen as if he were a criminal." {2:38} Despite the beating, I did not change my statement, and Pentephris ordered me to be imprisoned until, he said, the boy's owners arrived. {2:39} The woman said to her husband, "Why do you keep this captive and noble lad in chains? He should be freed and honored." {2:40} She wished to see me due to her desire for sin, but I was unaware of this. {2:41} He replied, "It is not the Egyptian custom to take what belongs to others without proof." {2:42} He spoke thus about the merchant but decreed that I remain imprisoned. {2:43} After twenty-four days, the Ishmaelites arrived, having heard that my father Jacob was mourning deeply for me. {2:44} They came to me and said, "Why did you claim to be a slave? We have learned that you are the son of a great man in Canaan, and your father is still mourning for you in sackcloth and ashes." {2:45} Hearing this, my heart melted with sorrow, and I wanted to weep, but I controlled myself so as not to shame my brothers. {2:46} I told them, "I do not know; I am a slave." {2:47} They then decided to sell me to avoid being found with me. {2:48} They feared my father might come and seek vengeance. {2:49} They had heard that he was mighty with both God and men. {2:50} The merchant asked to be released from the judgment of Pentephris. {2:51} They asked me to say that they had bought me with money so that they might be set free. {2:52} The Memphian woman told her husband, "Buy the youth; I hear they are selling him." {2:53} She immediately sent a eunuch to the Ishmaelites to purchase me. {2:54} When the eunuch refused to buy me at their price, he returned and informed his mistress that they were asking a high price. {2:55} She sent another eunuch, saying, "Even if they ask for two minas, give them, do not hold back the gold; just buy the boy and bring him to me." {2:56} The eunuch went and paid eighty pieces of gold for me but told the Egyptian woman that he had paid a hundred. {2:57} Even though I knew this, I remained silent to avoid shaming the eunuch. {2:58} So, my children, you see the great hardships I endured to avoid shaming my brothers. {2:59} Therefore, love one another and patiently cover each other's faults. {2:60} God delights in the unity of brothers and in hearts that take joy in love. {2:61} When my brothers came to Egypt, they learned that I had returned their money, had not reproached them, and had comforted them. {2:62} After my father Jacob's death, I loved them even more and abundantly fulfilled all his commands for them. {2:63} I did not allow them to suffer even in the smallest matters; I gave them everything I had. {2:64} Their children were my children, and my children were their servants; their life was my life, their suffering my suffering, and their sickness my infirmity. {2:65} My land was their land, and their counsel my counsel. {2:66} I did not exalt myself among them with arrogance due to my worldly glory but lived among them as one of the least. {2:67} If you walk in the Lord's commandments, He will exalt you and bless you with good things forever. {2:68} If anyone seeks to harm you, do good to them and pray for them, and the Lord will redeem you from all evil. {2:69} Indeed, out of my humility and patience, I married the daughter of the priest of Heliopolis. {2:70} I received a hundred talents of gold with her, and the Lord made it serve me. {2:71} He also gave me beauty surpassing that of all the beautiful ones of Israel and preserved me in strength and beauty into old age, because I was like Jacob in all respects. {2:72} Listen, my children, to the vision I had. {2:73} I saw twelve harts feeding, nine dispersed over the earth and three likewise. {2:74} I saw a virgin from Judah clothed in linen, and from her came a spotless lamb; on His left hand was a lion. All the beasts attacked Him, but the lamb overcame them, destroying and trampling them underfoot. {2:75} Because of Him, angels and men rejoiced, and the whole land was glad. {2:76} These events will occur in their time, in the last days. {2:77} Therefore, my children, keep the Lord's commandments and honor Levi and Judah, for from them will come the Lamb of God who takes away the sin of the world and saves both Gentiles and Israel. {2:78} His kingdom will be everlasting and will not pass away, while my kingdom among you will end like a watchman's hammock, which disappears after summer. {2:79} I know that after my death, the Egyptians will afflict you, but God will avenge you and fulfill His promises to your ancestors. {2:80} But you must carry my bones with you, for when my bones are taken up, the Lord will be with you in light, and Beliar will be in darkness with the Egyptians. {2:81} Also, take Asenath, your mother, to the Hippodrome, and bury her near Rachel, your mother. {2:82} After saying these things, he stretched out his feet and died at a good old age. {2:83} All Israel and Egypt mourned greatly for him. {2:84} When the Israelites left Egypt, they took Joseph's bones with them and buried him in Hebron with his fathers. He lived to be one hundred and ten years old.

Testament of Benjamin

The Testament of Benjamin, one of the Testaments of the Twelve Patriarchs, occupies a crucial position within the pseudepigraphal literature, attributed traditionally to Benjamin, the youngest of Jacob's twelve sons. This text is a rich and multifaceted narrative that delves deeply into the ethical, eschatological, and dualistic themes that were central to Second Temple Judaism. Composed between the 2nd century BCE and the 2nd century CE, the Testament of Benjamin reflects a complex interplay of moral exhortations, apocalyptic expectations, and theological reflections. It emphasizes virtues such as purity, forgiveness, and love, painting a vivid picture of an ideal moral and familial order. The narrative structure of the text weaves together personal exhortations, prophetic insights, and communal concerns, revealing the profound spiritual and social dynamics of its time. The Testament of Benjamin is also notable for its intertextuality, drawing upon the Hebrew Bible, other pseudepigraphal works, and contemporary Jewish thought, thus providing a window into the diverse and vibrant religious landscape of the period. Scholars have long been fascinated by the Testament's contribution to our understanding of Jewish messianism, wisdom traditions, and the development of early Christian theology. Its portrayal of messianic figures and its eschatological visions echo themes found in both Jewish and Christian apocalyptic literature, highlighting its significant influence on the theological discourse of the era. Moreover, the text's ethical teachings resonate with the broader moral and philosophical currents of Hellenistic Judaism, illustrating the dynamic interaction between Jewish and Greco-Roman cultures. The Testament of Benjamin, therefore, stands as a testament to the enduring legacy of Jewish religious thought, offering invaluable insights into the spiritual and intellectual currents that shaped the beliefs and practices of Jewish communities in antiquity. Through critical examination and scholarly analysis, this text continues to reveal the rich tapestry of tradition and innovation that characterizes the pseudepigraphal literature, underscoring its importance for understanding the historical and theological developments of the Second Temple period and beyond.

{1:1} These are the teachings of Benjamin, passed down to his sons when he reached a hundred and twenty-five years old. He kissed them and recounted how, like Isaac to Abraham, he was born in Jacob's old age after Rachel, his mother, died giving birth to him. {1:2} Due to Rachel's initial barrenness, after bearing Joseph, she prayed and fasted for twelve days, and then conceived me. That's why I was named Benjamin, meaning "son of days." {1:3} When I went to Egypt and Joseph recognized me, he asked what our brothers had told our father when they sold him. {1:4} I told him they stained Joseph's coat with blood and presented it to Jacob, asking if it was Joseph's. {1:5} Joseph confirmed they stripped him of his coat, gave him a loincloth, beat him, and made him run. {1:6} One who beat him was attacked and killed by a lion, frightening the others. {1:7} Therefore, my children, love the Lord God of heaven and earth, keeping His commandments like Joseph, a good and holy man. {1:8} Let your minds be set on goodness, as you have seen in me. A person with a righteous mind sees everything rightly. {1:9} Fear the Lord and love your neighbor. Even though the spirits of Beliar seek to harm you with every evil, they will not prevail, just as they did not over Joseph, my brother. {1:10} Many plotted to kill him, but God protected him. {1:11} A person who fears God and loves their neighbor cannot be overcome by the spirit of Beliar, shielded by the fear of God. {1:12} They cannot be deceived by men or beasts, for the Lord assists them through their love for their neighbor. {1:13} Joseph pleaded with our father to pray for his brothers, that the Lord would not hold their sins against them. {1:14} Jacob proclaimed, "You have prevailed over the bowels of your father Jacob, my good child." {1:15} He embraced Joseph for two hours, saying, "In you, the prophecy of heaven concerning the Lamb of God and Savior of the world will be fulfilled. A blameless one will be delivered for lawless men, and a sinless one will die for the ungodly in the blood of the covenant, for the salvation of Gentiles and Israel, and to destroy Beliar and his servants." {1:16} Therefore, my children, see the end of the righteous man. {1:17} Follow his compassion with a good mind, that you too may wear crowns of glory. {1:18} A good person does not have an evil eye, for they show mercy to all, even sinners. {1:19} Despite evil schemes against them, they overcome through goodness, shielded by God, and they love the righteous as their own soul. {1:20} They do not envy the glorified, are not jealous of the wealthy, praise the brave, commend the virtuous, show mercy to the poor, and have compassion for the weak. {1:21} They sing praises to God and love those who possess a good spirit as their own soul. {1:22} If you also have a good mind, wicked people will be at peace with you, the immoral will respect you and turn to goodness, and the greedy will not only stop their excessive desires but even give to the afflicted. {1:23} If you do good, even unclean spirits will flee from you, and wild animals will fear you. {1:24} Where there is reverence for good deeds and enlightenment in the mind, darkness will flee. {1:25} If a holy person is harmed, they forgive; for they are merciful to their revilers and remain silent. {1:26} If a righteous person is betrayed, they pray. Though humbled for a while, they later appear more glorious, as Joseph my brother did. {1:27} The inclination of a good person is not swayed by the deceit of Beliar's spirit, for the angel of peace guides their soul. {1:28} They do not lust after corruptible things or seek wealth through pleasure. {1:29} They do not delight in luxury or harm their neighbor. They do not arrogantly raise their eyes, for the Lord is their portion. {1:30} A good person receives neither glory nor dishonor from others and knows no deceit, lies, fighting, or slander. {1:31} The Lord dwells within them, illuminating their soul, and they rejoice in all people always. {1:32} A good person speaks with one tongue, blessing and not cursing, honoring and not insulting, rejoicing and not grieving, serene and not confused, truthful and not hypocritical. {1:33} They are consistent and pure in all their dealings, knowing that the Lord sees their soul in everything they do, say, or see. {1:34} They cleanse their minds to avoid condemnation by both men and God. {1:35} Beliar's works, in contrast, are twofold and lack integrity. {1:36} Therefore, my children, flee from Beliar's malice, for those who follow him wield a sword. {1:37} This sword is the source of seven evils: first, the mind conceives through Beliar, leading to bloodshed; second, ruin; third, tribulation; fourth, exile; fifth, famine; sixth, panic; seventh, destruction. {1:38} Cain, too, faced seven judgments from God, with each century bringing a new plague upon him. {1:39} When he turned two hundred, he began suffering, and at nine hundred, he was destroyed. {1:40} His judgment included seventy times seven for killing Abel. Those like Cain, filled with envy and hatred for their brothers, will face similar punishment forever.

{2:1} My children, avoid wrongdoing, envy, and hatred towards your brothers. Instead, embrace goodness and love. {2:2} A person with a pure heart in love does not seek after a woman for the sake of lust, for their heart is undefiled with the Spirit of God resting upon them. {2:3} Just as the sun, though shining on filth and mud, remains unstained and even dries them up, so too does a pure mind cleanse the defilements of the earth without itself being defiled. {2:4} I fear that among you there will be evil deeds, as Enoch the righteous foretold: some of you will engage in Sodom-like fornication and perish, except for a few, and your wanton behavior with women will persist. Consequently, the kingdom of the Lord will depart from you, for He will remove it swiftly. {2:5} Nevertheless, God's temple will be among your descendants, and the last temple will be more glorious than the first. {2:6} All twelve tribes and the Gentiles will gather there until the Most High sends His salvation through a chosen prophet. {2:7} This prophet will enter the first temple, where he will be mistreated and crucified. {2:8} The temple veil will tear, and the Spirit of God will spread like fire among the Gentiles. {2:9} He will rise from Hades and ascend from earth to heaven. {2:10} I know how humble he will be on earth and how glorious in heaven. {2:11} When Joseph was in Egypt, I longed to see his face and form. Through Jacob's prayers, I saw him clearly in broad daylight. {2:12} After saying these things, I declare to you: I am nearing death. {2:13} Therefore, each of you must be truthful to your neighbor and obey the Lord's law and commandments. {2:14} These teachings I leave to you instead of material inheritance. {2:15} Pass them on to your children as an eternal possession, just as Abraham, Isaac, and Jacob did. {2:16} They entrusted us with these teachings, saying: Keep God's commandments until He reveals salvation to all Gentiles. {2:17} Then you will see Enoch, Noah, Shem, Abraham, Isaac, and Jacob rise with joy on the right hand. {2:18} We too shall rise, each over our tribe, worshipping the King of heaven who appeared on earth in human humility. {2:19} All who believe in Him on earth will rejoice with Him. {2:20} Then all people will rise, some to glory and others to shame. {2:21} The Lord will first judge Israel for their unrighteousness. When He appeared in the flesh to deliver them, they did not believe Him. {2:22} Then He will judge all Gentiles who did not believe when He appeared on earth. {2:23} Through chosen Gentiles, He will convict Israel, just as He rebuked Esau through the Midianites, who led them into fornication and idolatry. Thus, they became estranged from God, becoming like children among those who fear the Lord. {2:24} Therefore, my children, if you walk in holiness according to the Lord's commandments, you will dwell securely with me again, and all Israel will be gathered to the Lord. {2:25} Then I will no longer be remembered as a wolf because of your actions, but as a servant of the Lord, providing for those who do good. {2:26} In the latter days, a beloved of the Lord will arise from the tribes of Judah and Levi, doing God's will with a mouth full of new knowledge, enlightening the Gentiles. {2:27} Until the end of the age, he will be in the synagogues of the Gentiles and among their leaders, a sweet melody on the lips of all. {2:28} His works and words will be inscribed in holy books, and he will be forever chosen by God. {2:29} Through him, as Jacob my father said, he will fulfill what is lacking in your tribe. {2:30} After saying these things, Benjamin peacefully passed away in his sleep. {2:31} His sons obeyed his instructions, took up his body, and buried him in Hebron with his ancestors. {2:32} Benjamin lived to 125 years.

Sibylline Oracles

The Sibylline Oracles are a collection of prophetic writings that were composed over a long period, from about the second century BCE to the seventh century CE. They are a mix of Jewish, Christian, and pagan elements. While some parts of the Sibylline Oracles were written during the Old Testament period, others were written much later. Here's a brief overview:

- Books I-II: These books contain significant Christian elements and are thought to have been composed in the early Christian period, likely around the second century CE.
- Book III: This is one of the earliest and most important books, composed mainly in the second century BCE, and contains Jewish oracles.
- Books IV-V: These books also contain significant Jewish elements and were likely composed between the first and second centuries CE.
- Books VI-VII: These are shorter and contain mainly Christian material, likely composed in the second to third centuries CE.
- Book VIII: This book contains a mix of Jewish and Christian elements and was likely composed in the second century CE.
- Books XI-XIV: These later books contain Christian material and were likely composed between the third and seventh centuries CE.
- Fragments: These are various pieces that have been preserved in other writings and can come from different periods.

Thus, while some parts of the Sibylline Oracles were written during or shortly after the Old Testament period, the collection as a whole spans a much longer timeframe, with significant contributions from the early Christian period.

Sibylline Oracles - I

The Sibylline Oracles, specifically Book I, represent an intriguing and complex fusion of Jewish, Christian, and pagan elements, serving as a multifaceted cultural and religious artifact from antiquity. This compilation, part of a larger corpus attributed to various Sibyls—prophetic women in ancient Greece and Rome—reflects the syncretism that characterized much of the Hellenistic and Roman periods. Book I, in particular, is notable for its incorporation of Jewish eschatological themes, woven seamlessly with classical mythological motifs and oracular traditions. It offers a prophetic narrative that spans from the creation of the world to apocalyptic visions of the end times, embodying a unique blend of Judaic monotheism and Greco-Roman mythos. The text's historical context is pivotal; it emerged during an era of significant cultural exchange and religious transformation, influenced by the diasporic experiences of Jewish communities and the early Christian movement's expansion. The Sibylline Oracles, therefore, not only provide insight into the religious and philosophical currents of their time but also reflect the tensions and interactions between different belief systems. They served as a medium through which marginalized Jewish and early Christian voices could articulate their theological perspectives in a language and format familiar to a broader Greco-Roman audience. It exemplifies the blend of cultural and religious ideas in the ancient world, providing modern scholars with valuable insights into ancient prophetic literature and its impact on religious thought.

From the very beginning of humanity to the very end, I will prophesy about everything: what has happened in the past, what is happening now, and what will happen in the future due to human wrongdoing.

First, let me explain how the world came into being, as God commands me to do. Pay attention, wise mortal, and make sure you follow my instructions. The most high King created the world by simply saying, "Let there be," and it came into existence. He established the earth, placing it around the underworld, and He Himself provided the light. He lifted the sky high, spread out the sea, adorned the sky with countless stars, and decorated the earth with plants. He mingled the sea with rivers, the air with gentle breezes and clouds, and then created various forms of life: fish for the sea, birds for the air, and animals and reptiles for the land. Everything was created precisely and efficiently by His word. After completing the world perfectly, God fashioned a new living being in His own image—a beautiful and divine human. He placed this new human in an idyllic garden, where he could enjoy a life of ease and beauty. However, in this paradise, the first human desired companionship and asked to see another being like himself. So, God created a woman from the man's rib, making her beautiful as well, and placed her in the garden with him. When the man saw her, he was overjoyed and admired her greatly.

At that time, both the man and the woman were pure and without sin; they lived like innocent creatures of the wild, without shame. God gave them only one command: not to touch a certain tree. But a cunning serpent deceived them into disobeying this command, leading them to gain knowledge of good and evil. The woman was the first to disobey God and persuaded the man to do the same. As a result, they both sinned, forgetting their immortal Creator and ignoring His commandments. Consequently, they brought evil into the world instead of good. They made clothes from fig leaves to hide their nakedness, feeling ashamed.

God was angry with them and cast them out of the paradise, condemning them to live in the mortal world. He told them to work hard on the earth to provide for themselves through labor. The serpent, which had deceived them, was cursed to crawl on its belly and eat dust, and enmity was established between the serpent and humans. This enmity would be ongoing, with the serpent striking at the human heel and humans aiming to crush the serpent's head, symbolizing the constant struggle between good and evil.

Humanity multiplied as God had commanded, and people established various civilizations, built cities, and created elaborate structures. They lived long, contented lives, not suffering from the troubles of old age but passing away peacefully. These people were favored by the immortal King, God. However, they eventually fell into foolishness, disrespected their parents, and engaged in conflicts and wars. They became corrupt, shedding blood and committing heinous acts.

Eventually, a final catastrophe came from heaven, bringing death to these wicked people, and they were received into Hades—a place named after the first man who tasted death. Since then, all humans born on earth are destined to go to Hades. Even in Hades, the first people to arrive were honored because they were the earliest generation. But when Hades received these early souls, God created a new, more refined race. This new generation was devoted to beautiful and noble work, distinguished by their reverence and wisdom. They were skilled in various arts, finding inventive solutions despite limited resources. Some learned to farm with plows, others worked with wood, some became sailors, and others studied the stars and practiced divination with birds. Some were interested in medicine, while others were fascinated by magic. These people excelled in every field they pursued, showing great diligence and creativity. Despite their talents and industriousness, they were eventually cast into the deepest, most terrible part of the underworld, Tartarus. They were held in unbreakable chains to suffer eternal punishment in the unquenchable fires of Gehenna.

Following this, a third, more aggressive race emerged. These people were domineering and destructive, constantly engaging in violence. They waged wars and committed murders, causing widespread suffering and chaos among themselves.

From this third race came a fourth, even more corrupted generation. They were known for their bloodthirsty and morally depraved behavior. They showed no respect for God or other people, driven by rage and wickedness. As a result, many were sent to Erebus, while the rest were cast out of the world by God into Tartarus, far below the earth. Later, an even worse race appeared. These people were more violent than the previous generations, behaving like monstrous giants and speaking foully. Among all humans, only Noah stood out as just and virtuous. He was devoted to righteous deeds. God spoke to Noah from heaven, saying: "Noah, take heart and preach repentance to the people so they may be saved. If they do not listen and remain shameless, I will destroy the entire race with a great flood. Build an ark from durable, waterproof wood. I will grant you understanding and skill to build it correctly and ensure the safety of you and your family. I am the eternal One, and I cover the heavens with my presence, the sea with my boundary, the earth as my footstool, and the air as my cloak. The stars circle around me. I have nine letters in my name, made up of four syllables: three of the letters are each two-lettered, and the remaining one completes the rest. The total number of letters sums up to 88 plus 30 and 7. Know who I am, and understand my teachings."

Noah was overwhelmed by this message. He then warned the people, saying: "O insatiable men, blinded by great madness, your actions will not escape God's notice. He sees everything and has sent me to warn you so that you may avoid destruction. Be sober, abandon evil ways, and do not shed each other's blood. Respect the supreme Creator, God, who dwells in the heavens. Pray to Him for the well-being of cities, the world, and all living creatures. If you do not repent and turn from your wicked ways, you will face destruction by flood. You will cry out in fear as the skies turn chaotic and God's wrath descends upon you. The immortal Savior will be angered if you do not seek His favor and change your ways. Live righteously and do not act lawlessly against one another."

But when the people heard Noah's warnings, they mocked him, calling him mad and delusional.

Noah continued to speak to the people, saying: "O wretched and morally corrupt people, unstable and abandoning modesty for shamelessness, greedy and fierce sinners, deceitful and insatiable, full of mischief. You are untrustworthy, adulterous, and foul-mouthed. You do not fear the wrath of the Most High God, who will punish you for your actions over the course of five generations. You mock my warnings, laughing sarcastically at what I predict—God's devastating flood. When the polluted descendants of Eve, flourishing on the earth, are wiped out in a single night, cities, people, and everything will be destroyed by the earth-shaking forces. The entire world of countless people will perish. How can I grieve or lament in this wooden ark? If God's flood comes, the earth, hills, and even the sky will be submerged. Everything will be covered by water, and all things will be destroyed. The winds will cease, and a new age will begin. Phrygia will rise from the waters first and will give rise to a new race of people, becoming the nurturing mother of a new world."

When Noah had spoken these warnings to the lawless people in vain, the Most High God appeared once more and said:

"The time has come, Noah, to fulfill everything I promised and confirmed to you. The disobedient people must be punished for their countless evils that have persisted throughout the generations. Enter the ark with your sons and their wives. Gather as many animals as I instruct, and I will put the willingness in them to come aboard."

Noah went out, calling out as God had commanded. His wife, sons, and their wives entered the ark, along with the animals and creatures as specified by God. Once the door was securely fastened and sealed, God's plan was set in motion. He gathered clouds, obscuring the sun, moon, and stars, and darkness covered everything. Thunder rumbled, lightning flashed, and all the winds were stirred up. Torrential rains poured from the heavens and from the earth's deep cavities, flooding the entire world.

The ark floated on the waters, tossed by fierce waves and driven by strong winds, but it stayed afloat, cutting through the foam with its keel. As the rains continued, Noah observed the situation carefully, considering the divine guidance he had received. The ark endured the onslaught of water for many days, and Noah, seeing the vast and endless flood, was filled with fear. The skies were overcast, and the sun seemed weary. Noah's courage was tested as he released a dove to find out if land had reappeared. The dove flew around but returned without finding any dry ground.

After waiting some more days, Noah sent the dove out again. This time, the dove returned with an olive branch in its beak, a hopeful sign that the waters were receding. This news filled Noah and his family with hope and joy, as they anticipated the return of land.

Noah then sent out another bird, a raven, which flew off and did not return. This indicated to Noah that land was close. When the ark eventually came to rest on a narrow stretch of land after drifting over the ocean, it was finally secured.

In Phrygia, on the dark mainland, there is a tall, steep mountain named Ararat. It was chosen for the ark to rest upon, as it was the place where all would be saved from death. The great river Marsyas springs from this mountain. When the waters receded, the ark settled on a high peak of this mountain. Then, a divine voice from heaven spoke to Noah:

"Noah, who is faithful and just, come out of the ark with your sons, your wife, and your sons' wives. Fill the earth, multiply, and establish justice among all people through the generations until the final judgment comes for everyone."

Following this command, Noah, encouraged and relieved, left the ark with his family and all the animals. They all gathered in one place. Noah, the eighth and most righteous of men, after spending fifty-one days on the waters due to God's instructions, began a new era of life. This new generation was considered the golden age, the sixth and best since the creation of the first man. This era was named "Heavenly" because everything would be under God's care.

O first generation of this sixth age! I shared great joy escaping destruction with my family and loved ones, after enduring much suffering. I will now sing about fitting things to come. The fig tree will bear many-colored flowers, and later, Cronos will reign with power. Three just kings will rule wisely, giving fair portions and ensuring justice for those who work and love diligently. The earth will be rich with self-growing fruits, yielding abundant crops.

The people of this golden age, blessed and free from disease, will die peacefully, as if falling asleep, and will be honored in the underworld. They will be fortunate heroes, cherished by the Lord of Sabaoth, who shared His wisdom with them.

However, after this golden age, a second, oppressive race of earth-born men will emerge—the Titans. They will be tall and strong, speaking a single language as the first generation did. But their pride and ambition will lead them to challenge the heavens, and the great ocean will flood them with its raging waters. Although the Lord of Sabaoth will be angry, He will hold back His wrath, as He promised never again to flood the earth.

When the swelling waters finally subside and their waves are restrained by harbors and rough coastlines, a child of the great God will come, born in human form. This child will have four vowels and two consonants in His name, which, when combined, will sum up to eight hundred and eight. This child will be recognized as the Son of the Most High God. He will fulfill God's law, not destroy it, and will teach all things. Priests will bring Him gifts of gold, myrrh, and frankincense.

When a voice calls out in the desert, urging people to prepare the way and purify themselves with water to live righteously, one with a barbaric nature will try to hinder this voice. A sign will follow: a fair stone will come from Egypt, and the Hebrew people will stumble upon it. This stone will guide the nations and reveal the way to the God who rules on high. Through this child, chosen people will be shown eternal life, while the lawless will face eternal fire. He will heal the sick and help those who are at fault and place their trust in Him. The blind will regain their sight, the lame will walk, the deaf will hear, and the mute will speak. He will cast out demons, and even raise the dead. He will walk on water and, in a desert place, He will feed five thousand people with just five loaves of bread and two fish. There will be twelve baskets of leftovers, a symbol of hope for the people.

However, Israel will not recognize Him; they will be blind and deaf to His miracles, overwhelmed and unable to understand. When the wrath of the Most High falls upon the Hebrews because they killed the Son of God, they will mock Him with insults and spittle. They will give Him gall to eat and undiluted vinegar to drink, consumed by madness and blind to their own actions. They will be more blind than moles and more dreadful than venomous creatures, trapped in deep sleep.

When He stretches out His hands, is crowned with thorns, and has His side pierced with a spear, darkness will cover the earth for three hours in the middle of the day. The Temple of Solomon will be a powerful sign, marking the end of an era. He will descend to the realm of the dead, proclaiming resurrection to the dead. After three days, He will rise again, show Himself to people, and teach them. He will ascend into the clouds and return to heaven, leaving behind a new covenant for the world.

In His name, a new group of people will emerge from among the nations, guided by the teachings of the Almighty. After this, there will be wise leaders, and the era of prophets will come to an end.

When the Hebrew people have fully reaped the consequences of their actions, a Roman king will come and destroy their wealth. Other royal powers will rise & fall, oppressing people. There will be a great downfall for those who become arrogant and unrighteous. The Temple of Solomon will be destroyed by barbarian invaders, and the Hebrews will be driven from their land, scattered and suffering. Among the wheat, there will be much tares, symbolizing evil discord among humanity. The cities will be ravaged, and people will mourn each other, suffering from the wrath of God due to their evil deeds.

Sibylline Oracles - II

Book II is especially notable for its synthesis of these diverse influences, presenting apocalyptic visions and moral exhortations from the legendary prophetess Sibyl. This book reflects the complex historical context of its time, marked by sociopolitical upheavals and religious transformations. It features Jewish eschatological themes, such as the coming of a messianic figure and the triumph of good over evil, while incorporating Hellenistic philosophy and mythology. The oracles also serve as political commentary, critiquing the Roman Empire. Rich in symbolic language and imagery, Book II draws on various cultural motifs to convey its prophetic messages. Its transmission and reception history highlight its enduring influence, as it was copied, translated, and interpreted across antiquity and the Middle Ages.

While I earnestly prayed, God held back my wise song, and once more placed within me the divine voice of sacred words. I am filled with terror throughout my body as I follow these words, for I do not know what I am saying; it is God who compels me to proclaim each thing.

When there are earthquakes on earth, fierce thunderbolts, thunder and lightning, storms, and blight, as well as the rage of jackals and wolves, acts of manslaughter, and the destruction of people, cattle, mules, goats, and sheep, the land will become barren due to neglect, and fruits will fail. There will be a loss of freedom among many people and theft from temples. After these events, a new generation of people will appear. The earth-shaking Lightener will destroy idol worship and shake the people of Rome, which is built on seven hills, and their great wealth will be consumed by Vulcan's fiery flames. Then, bloody signs will descend from heaven, and despite this, the entire world of countless people will be in chaos, killing each other. God will send famines, plagues, and thunderbolts upon those who unjustly judge. There will be such a lack of people on earth that finding any trace of humanity will astonish anyone who sees it.

At that time, the great God who dwells in heaven will prove to be the savior of the righteous. Peace and deep wisdom will be restored, and the land will again produce abundant fruits, not divided or enslaved. Every harbor and haven will be accessible to everyone as it was before, and shamelessness will vanish. Then God will reveal a great sign to humanity: a bright, radiant star will shine like a lustrous crown from heaven for many days. Following this, He will show a heavenly crown for those who compete in righteous deeds. There will be a great contest in the heavenly realm, where all people will strive for glorious victory, and the fame of immortality will be celebrated. Every nation will participate in these eternal contests for splendid victory, and no one will be able to buy a crown with silver. Instead, the pure Christ will award what is deserved and bestow immortal prizes upon those who persist in the contest unto death.

To chaste individuals who run their race well, Christ will give incorruptible rewards and allot what is due to all people, including foreign nations that live a holy life and worship one God. Those who respect marriages and stay away from adultery will receive rich gifts and eternal hope. Every human soul is a gift from God, and it is wrong to corrupt it with vile deeds. Do not pursue wealth unrighteously; live a life of integrity. Be content with what you have and do not covet what belongs to others. Speak only the truth and respect what is true. Do not worship vain idols, but honor the imperishable God first and your parents second. Give everyone their due and do not engage in unjust judgments. Do not unjustly cast out the poor or judge by outward appearances, for if you judge wickedly, God will judge you in return.

Avoid false testimony and tell the truth. Maintain your purity and love among all people. Use fair measures; fairness is beautiful. Do not cheat with scales but keep them balanced. Do not swear falsely, whether ignorantly or intentionally, as God despises perjury. Never accept gifts from unjust actions. Do not steal or squander life's seeds; the person who does will be cursed through many generations.

Avoid vile lusts, slander, and killing. Pay the laborers their wages and do not oppress the poor. Assist orphans, widows, and those in need. Speak sensibly and keep secrets with care. Be unwilling to act unjustly and do not tolerate unrighteous behavior. Give to the poor immediately and do not delay by saying, "Come back tomorrow." Give from your own grain generously, for those who give alms are lending to God. Mercy redeems one from death when judgment comes.

God desires mercy, not sacrifice. Instead of offering sacrifices, clothe the naked, share your bread with the hungry, welcome the homeless into your house, and guide the blind. Show compassion to shipwrecked travelers, as their journeys are uncertain. Help those who have fallen and protect the defenseless.

Everyone experiences suffering; life is like a wheel with unpredictable fortunes. If you are wealthy, extend your hand to the poor and share what God has given you with those in need. All human lives are the same in their mortality, but circumstances are not equal. When you see a poor person, do not mock them with words or speak harshly to those who might be at fault. A person's true nature is revealed in death; their actions, whether just or unjust, will be judged when they face judgment. Do not impair your mind with excessive wine or drink. Avoid eating blood and abstain from foods offered to idols. Do not carry a sword for aggression, but only for defense, and use it neither unlawfully nor unjustly. Killing an enemy will only taint your hands. Do not encroach on your neighbor's land or disrespect property boundaries, as such trespassing is painful and unjust. Possessions obtained through lawful means are valuable, but unrighteous gains are worthless. Do not harm any growing crops, and treat strangers with equal respect as you would citizens.

Hospitality should be extended to everyone, and no one should be considered a stranger, as all humans are of one blood and no land is permanently secure for anyone. Do not desire or pray for wealth; instead, pray for a modest life and ensure you possess nothing unjustly. The love of wealth is the root of all evil. Do not crave gold or silver, as they bring about destruction and are a constant trap for people.

Gold and silver, the source of many evils, lead to wars, theft, and murder, causing family members to hate each other. Avoid deceit and do not hold ill feelings against friends. Be sincere and transparent, avoiding hidden agendas or duplicity. Those who willfully commit wrongs are evil, but if someone acts under compulsion, their fate is uncertain. It is important for each person's intentions to be righteous. Do not take pride in wisdom, power, or wealth, as only God is truly wise, powerful, and rich. Do not dwell on past wrongs, as what is done cannot be undone. Control your temper and avoid acting out of impulsive anger, as it can lead to unintended harm. Suffering should be shared by all and should neither be too severe nor excessive. Too much good can be unhelpful, and excessive luxury can lead to harmful desires. Great wealth can lead to violence and reckless behavior. Passionate feelings, when unchecked, can lead to destructive madness. Anger, if excessive, becomes wrath. The zeal of good people is admirable, while the boldness of wicked people is destructive. True renown comes from virtue, not from base actions. True love is virtuous, unlike the love of Cypris (Venus), which leads to shameful behavior. A foolish person may be seen as agreeable among peers, but moderation in eating, drinking, and speaking is the best approach. Overstepping moderation brings grief.

Avoid being envious, unfaithful, abusive, or deceitful. Be prudent and abstain from shameless actions. Do not imitate evil, but leave vengeance to justice; persuasion is helpful, but strife only leads to more conflict. Do not trust too quickly before you see the outcome. This is the contest, these are the rewards; these are the prizes and the gateway to life and immortality. God in heaven has appointed this reward for the most righteous people, and through this gate, those who achieve victory will pass gloriously. When you see this sign everywhere—children with gray hair, famines, plagues, wars, and changes in times—many parents will mourn and weep for their lost children, burying bodies in the earth with blood and dust. Wretched men of the last generation, full of evil and foolishness, will fail to see that when women no longer bear children, the end of human life is near. The downfall approaches when impostors replace true prophets. Beliar will come and perform many signs for people. There will be confusion among holy and faithful men, and there will be plundering of them and the Hebrews. Fearful wrath will befall them when a people from the east, the twelve tribes, will search for their kin, the Hebrews, whom the Assyrian archers have destroyed. Nations will perish over these events. However, after this, the mighty and faithful Hebrews will rule over men and enslave them as before, for their power will never fail. The highest God, who sees everything and dwells in heaven, will cast a deep sleep upon people, covering their eyes. Blessed are the servants who are found awake when the Master arrives! They will be vigilant and expectant at all times. The Master will come at dawn, dusk, or midday. It will be as I say: for those who are asleep, stars will appear in the sky even at midday. Then, the Tishbite (Elijah), coming from heaven in his celestial chariot, will reveal three terrible signs that life is about to end. Woe to all the pregnant women on that day! Woe to those who nurse infants! Woe to those who live on the sea! For a dark mist will cover the entire world, east, west, south, and north.

A mighty stream of burning fire will flow from heaven, consuming everything—earth, ocean, shining seas, lakes, rivers, springs, Hades, and even the sky. The heavenly lights will merge into one and become desolate. Stars fall into the seas, and all human souls will suffer in fiery torment, with ashes covering everything. The world's elements—air, earth, sea, light, sky, days, and nights—will vanish. Birds will no longer fly, sea creatures will no longer swim, ships will cease to sail, and cattle will no longer plow fields. There will be no sound of raging winds. Everything will be fused together, and only the pure will be separated out. When the immortal God's eternal angels—Arakiel, Ramiel, Uriel, Samiel, and Azael—who know the extent of everyone's sins, lead all souls from the darkness to the judgment seat of the great and immortal God. Only the almighty God, who is eternal and imperishable, will judge mortals. He will grant souls, spirits, voices, and bones to those who dwell below, and they will be clothed with flesh, sinews, veins, skin, and hair, just as before. Bodies will be raised and animated once again, divinely fashioned and breathing. Then Uriel, the mighty angel, will break open the unyielding, adamantine gates of Hades, which are guarded by brazen locks. He will cast them down and lead all suffering souls to judgment. This will include the Titans, ancient giants, those drowned in the flood, and those lost at sea, as well as those consumed by wild beasts and birds. Uriel will gather all these souls and present them before God's judgment seat.

When the thunderous Lord of Hosts has concluded the course of fate and raised the dead, He will sit on His heavenly throne and firmly establish His power. Then, Christ, who is incorruptible, will come in glory with pure angels and sit at the right hand of God on the great judgment seat. He will judge the lives of the pious and the ways of the impious.

Moses, the great friend of God, will come in the flesh, along with Abraham, Isaac, Jacob, Joshua, Daniel, Elijah, Habakkuk, and Jonah—those whom the Hebrews once killed. But God will punish the Hebrews after Jeremiah, giving them their due recompense for their actions in life. All will pass through the unquenchable fire; the righteous will be saved, while the godless will perish forever. Those who committed evils, murders, lies, thefts, and all forms of corruption will face eternal punishment. Those who wronged widows and orphans, those who denied their promises, those who mistreated their parents, and those who acted shamelessly, including sorcerers and deceitful priests, will face the wrath of God. They will be cast into a circle of restless fire, bound in chains, and punished severely. In Gehenna, they will suffer among horrible beasts in immense darkness. After these punishments, they will endure an additional fiery wheel from a great river, because of their wicked deeds. Fathers, children, mothers, and nursing infants will wail their tragic fate, with no respite from their tears. They will cry out in Tartarus, suffering threefold for their sins, burned by unrelenting fire, gnashing their teeth in anguish, and finding no solace in death.

The wicked will plead with God in vain, for He will turn His face away from them. He gave them seven ages for repentance through the hands of a pure virgin. But those who valued right deeds, piety, and justice will be led by angels through the burning stream to a place of light and eternal life. They will enter a land of abundance, with rivers of honey, wine, and milk, where there are no barriers or divisions. Life will be shared equally, with no distinctions of wealth or status, and no more concerns about time or seasons. There will be no more night, day, or change of seasons, and no more birth, death, or commerce. God will grant the pious eternal rest and will save them from the raging fire and endless torment. He will remove them from the restless flames and bring them to eternal life among the immortals in Elysian fields, where the peaceful waters of the Acheron flow endlessly.

Ah, what a wretched woman I am! What will become of me on that day? I have sinned, being foolishly absorbed in trivial matters, neglecting both marriage and reason. Even in my wealthy husband's house, I shut out the needy and knowingly engaged in unlawful actions. But, Savior, though I have committed shameful acts, rescue me from my torment. I pray you, Holy Giver of manna, King of the great realm, grant me some rest from my lament.

Sibylline Oracles - III

The Sibylline Oracles, a collection of prophetic writings attributed to the Sibyls, are a fascinating amalgamation of Jewish, Christian, and pagan traditions, offering a unique window into the syncretic religious milieu of the ancient world. Book III of the Sibylline Oracles, often considered one of the most important and extensive sections, is particularly noteworthy for its rich tapestry of themes and historical references. Originating likely in the Hellenistic period, this book reflects the diverse cultural and religious influences of the Eastern Mediterranean. It is composed in Greek hexameters and combines traditional Greek elements with Jewish eschatology, reflecting the adaptability of Jewish thought within a broader Hellenistic context. The prophetic voice in Book III is often seen as a response to the political and social upheavals of the time, including the rise and fall of empires and the anticipation of a messianic kingdom. The text provides a vivid portrayal of divine judgment and salvation, with a clear moral dichotomy between the righteous and the wicked, reminiscent of Jewish apocalyptic literature. Additionally, the book incorporates elements of Greco-Roman mythology and philosophy, seamlessly integrating them into its prophetic vision. This synthesis not only underscores the interconnectedness of different cultural traditions but also highlights the versatility of the Sibylline tradition in addressing the spiritual and existential concerns of its audience. Moreover, Book III has been invaluable for scholars studying early Jewish and Christian thought, as it bridges the gap between these two religious traditions, revealing how early Christians might have appropriated and reinterpreted Jewish prophetic motifs.

O mighty and blessed heavenly One, who has placed the cherubim in their positions, I, who have spoken the truth, ask you to grant me some rest. My heart is weary from within. Yet why does my heart and soul continue to beat with urgency, compelled to deliver their message to all? Nevertheless, I will proclaim whatever God commands me to proclaim to humanity.

O people, made in the image of God, why do you wander aimlessly and stray from the right path, forgetting the eternal Creator? God is one—sovereign, ineffable, dwelling in heaven, self-existent and invisible, who alone sees everything. He was not created by sculptor's hand, nor is His form represented by gold or ivory; He is eternal and proclaims Himself as the one who is, was, and will be. For who, being mortal, can see God with their eyes? Who can bear to hear the name of the great God, ruler of the world? He created all things by His word—heaven, the sea, the tireless sun, the full moon, the bright stars, and the mighty Tethys with its springs and rivers, imperishable fire, and the cycle of days and nights.

This is the God who formed Adam, the first man, and filled the world with His presence—east, west, south, and north. He established the pattern of the human form and created wild animals, creeping things, and birds. Yet you do not worship or fear God, but instead go astray, worshipping serpents, cats, and idols made of stone. You sit before the doors of godless temples and neglect the true God who sustains everything. You are delighted by the wickedness of stones and forget the judgment of the eternal Savior who created heaven and earth. Alas! A race that delights in blood, deceitful, vile, ungodly, and false—deceitful and immoral—plundering for gain, breaking faith, and leading lives of dishonesty.

When Rome comes to rule Egypt, then the greatest kingdom of the eternal King will appear. A holy Lord will come to reign over all lands for ages to come. And then, there will be relentless wrath upon the Latin people; three events will bring destruction to Rome, and all men will perish with their own homes when a fiery torrent falls from heaven. Oh, wretched me! When will that day and the judgment of the mighty God, the King, come?

For now, O cities, you are built and adorned with temples, racecourses, markets, and images of wood, gold, silver, and stone, preparing for the bitter day that will come when a stench of brimstone will fill the air. I will declare this in all the cities where men suffer.

From the Sebastenes, Beliar will come in the future. He will establish heights and make the sea stand still, and the great fiery sun and bright moon will be affected. He will raise the dead and perform many signs before men, but he will bring nothing to completion but deceit. Many mortals, both Hebrews and lawless individuals who never listened to God's word, will be led astray by him. When the threats of the mighty God draw near, and a flaming power comes to earth, it will consume both Beliar and all those who trusted in him. The whole world will be ruled by a woman who will be obedient everywhere. A widow will rule over the world, casting into the sea both gold and silver, brass and iron. The elements will be thrown into chaos when the God who dwells on high rolls up the sky like a scroll, causing the multiform sky to fall upon the earth and sea. A never-ending torrent of fire will burn the land, the sea, the sky, and everything, melting creation and separating the pure from the impure. There will be no more light spheres, no more night, dawn, or days of care, nor spring, winter, summer, or autumn. The judgment of the mighty God will come at the end of a great age.

O navigable waters and lands of the East and West, everything will be subject to the one who comes into the world again and becomes aware of His power.

When the threats of the mighty God are fulfilled, as He threatened mortals once when they built a tower in Assyria, speaking one language and attempting to reach the stars. The Immortal then imposed a great force, causing the winds to topple the tower and stir up conflict among people. Thus, the city was named Babylon, and when the tower fell and the languages diverged, the earth was filled with people and kingdoms were divided. The tenth generation of mortals appeared after the flood. Cronos reigned, along with Titan and Iapetus, considered the best descendants of Gaia and Uranus. They were the first of mortal men.

The earth was divided among them, each having his own portion. However, as time passed, the sons of Cronos fought over the royal power. Cronos and Titan clashed until Rhea, Gaia, Aphrodite, Demeter, Hestia, and Dione brought them together to judge Cronos as king. Titan demanded that Cronos have no male descendants, so he could reign after Cronos. Each time Rhea gave birth, the Titans tore apart the male children but spared the females. Eventually, Rhea bore a son in secret, whom she named Zeus, and sent him away to be raised in secret. Poseidon was also sent away secretly, and Pluto was born at Dodona.

When the Titans discovered the hidden sons, they captured Cronos and Rhea, imprisoning them in the earth. The sons of Cronos rose up, initiating a great war among mortals. This was the beginning of war among men. God then punished the Titans, and all of them died. Over time, the Egyptian kingdom arose, followed by the Persians, Medes, Ethiopians, Assyrians, Babylonians, Macedonians, and finally Rome. A divine message was given to me, to proclaim and instill things among all people. This God revealed to me that various kingdoms would rise. First, the house of Solomon would include people from Phoenicia, Syria, the islands, and the races of Pamphylians, Persians, Phrygians, Carians, Mysians, and rich Lydians. Then, the proud and impure Hellenes, followed by a Macedonian nation, would rise as a great and shrewd power. But the God of heaven will destroy them. Afterward, another kingdom, white and many-headed from the western sea, will dominate many lands and bring terror to kings, destroying gold and silver in many cities. However, gold and silver will reappear in the earth, but these rulers will oppress people and face great disaster. Their arrogance will lead to malevolent behaviors, and children will be placed in shameful conditions. In those times, great afflictions will disturb and break everything, filling the world with shameful covetousness and ill-gotten wealth, especially in Macedonia. Hatred and deceit will prevail, even to the seventh kingdom, ruled by a king of Egypt, a descendant of the Greeks.

Then the nation of the mighty God will become strong again and guide all people in life. But why has God placed this in my mind to reveal: what will happen first, next, and finally to all people? Which of these will come first?

First, God will bring judgment upon the Titans. They will face punishment for their actions against the sons of mighty Cronos, as they had bound both Cronos and his beloved mother. Next, there will be tyrants among the Greeks—fierce, arrogant, and corrupt kings, and there will be no rest from war for humanity. The Phrygians will face complete destruction, and Troy will suffer great misfortune. The Persians, Assyrians, Egyptians, Libyans, Ethiopians, Carians, and Pamphylians will also experience disaster.

I mention these events individually because once the first set of calamities occurs, the second will follow immediately. So, I will begin with the first. An evil will befall the righteous who live near the grand temple of Solomon and are descendants of virtuous people. I will also describe their lineage, city, and homeland—so listen carefully, O wise mortal. There is a city on earth, Ur of the Chaldees, where a righteous people live who have always valued goodness and noble deeds. They do not concern themselves with the sun's movements, the moon, the marvels beneath the earth, the deep sea, or omens from sneezes, birds, or soothsayers. They do not practice astrology, wizardry, or other tricks. They believe such things are deceptive and lead people away from righteousness and virtue, which are the sources of war and famine. Instead, they uphold justice and measure fairly in their fields and cities. They do not steal, move boundary markers, or oppress others. They help the needy, providing wheat, wine, and oil, and during harvests, they share their bounty with those who lack resources, fulfilling the divine principle that the earth is a common good for all.

When the people of the twelve tribes leave Egypt, guided by God's appointed leaders—first by a pillar of fire at night and a cloud by day—God will choose a great leader, Moses. He was found as a child beside a marsh by a princess, who raised him as her own. As leader, Moses will bring the people from Egypt to Mount Sinai, where God will give them laws written on two stone tablets. Those who disobey must make amends either through human judgment or divine retribution.

The fertile land will yield abundant fruit for them, completing God's measure. However, they will also face misfortune and disease. Even you will be forced to abandon your beautiful land and flee to Assyria. There, you will see your children and wives in servitude, and all your wealth and means of life will be destroyed. Your land will become a desert, and the altars and temples of the great God will fall. Because you failed to uphold His holy law and worshipped false images, your land will suffer for seventy years. But a glorious end awaits you, as God has granted it. Trust in God's pure laws, and when He lifts you up, He will send a king to judge humanity with fire and light.

A royal lineage will endure, and as time passes, this lineage will rule and rebuild God's temple. Persian kings will contribute bronze, gold, and iron to the construction, as God will inspire them through dreams. The temple will be restored to its former glory.

When my soul rested from the divine song, I prayed for relief from this burden. Again, a message from the mighty God came to me, instructing me to proclaim it throughout the earth and to plant this knowledge in the minds of rulers. God showed me how many sufferings await Babylon for destroying His great temple.

Woe to you, Babylon, and to the descendants of the Assyrians! A wave of sinful people will sweep across the earth, and the divine judgment will ruin every land. Babylon will face devastation from above, with the destruction coming from heaven. Your children's souls will be destroyed, and you will be reduced to a state of non-existence. Your land will be drenched in blood, as you once shed the blood of good and holy men whose cries reach the heavens.

Egypt will also face a severe blow, with a sword cutting through the land, bringing scattering, death, and famine until the seventh generation of kings, after which it will cease.

Woe to you, land of Gog and Magog, amid the Ethiopian rivers! You will receive a terrible outpouring of blood and be called the house of judgment among men. Your land, full of dew, will drink black blood.

Woe to you, Libya, and to both sea and land! Daughters of the west, you will face a bitter day. You will be pursued by strife and destruction, leading to the collapse of your land and cities. Your lands will become wildernesses, and your cities will be desolate. In the west, a star will appear, which people will call a comet. It will signal war, famine, death, and the murder of great leaders and prominent men.

Once again, there will be significant signs among people. The deep-flowing Tanais River will move away from Lake Mæotis, creating a fertile furrow in its path, and the vast waters will cut off a landmass. There will be gaping chasms and pits, causing many cities and people to fall. In Asia, cities such as Iassus, Cebren, Pandonia, Colophon, Ephesus, Nicæa, Antioch, Syagra, Sinope, Smyrna, Myrina, the prosperous Gaza, Hierapolis, and Astypalaia will be affected. In Europe, cities like Tanagra, Clitor, Basilis, Meropeia, Antigone, Magnessa, Mykene, and Oiantheia will also suffer.

Understand that Egypt's destructive era is nearing its end, and the past year will be considered better for the Alexandrians. For every amount of tribute Rome received from Asia, Asia will return three times as much and exact revenge on Rome. For every Italian who served in Asia, twenty times as many Asians will serve Italians in poverty, incurring substantial debts.

O virgin, the rich daughter of Latin Rome, who once celebrated grand marriage feasts and drank heavily, you will become a slave and marry without honor. Your hair will be shorn frequently by your mistress, who will cast you down from heaven to earth and then back to heaven, for those of low status and unrighteous lives are trapped. The downfall of Smyrna will be unremarked, but due to the wicked plans of those in power, Samos will become sand, Delos will lose its significance, and Rome will become a mere room. Yet, the decrees of God will be perfectly fulfilled. A period of peace will come to Asia, while Europe will enjoy happiness, abundance, and pure air, free from winter storms and hail. Birds, insects, and beasts will thrive. Blessed will be anyone living on earth, experiencing a home of unimaginable joy. From the starry heavens, order, justice, unity, kindness, trust, and hospitality will descend upon humanity, while lawlessness, blame, envy, wrath, folly, poverty, force, murder, strife, feuds, and theft will vanish.

However, Macedonia will bring severe suffering to Asia, and Europe will face a great affliction from a dynasty of lowly and enslaved people. They will conquer Babylon and claim dominance over every land under the sun, but will ultimately face ruin and be remembered only distantly in future generations.

An unknown man will eventually arrive in Asia, wearing a purple robe, fierce and unjust. This man, wielding a thunderbolt, will bring a heavy yoke to Asia, with much bloodshed. But Hades will destroy this unknown king, and his descendants will be wiped out by those he sought to destroy. A new root will be planted, replacing the old. A father clad in purple will be defeated by a warlike father, and Ares, the god of war, will be overthrown by his grandson. This new power will then take control.

Phrygia will receive a sign when Rhea's blood-stained descendants, thriving in the earth's roots, will vanish overnight, taking with them a city and people associated with Poseidon, once called Dorylæum in ancient, mournful Phrygia. This era will be marked by upheaval, breaking up the earth and demolishing walls. This will not be a time of good signs but the beginning of evil, bringing widespread warfare to the descendants of Æneas. In time, they will become prey for greedy men.

Ilium, I pity you, for Sparta will produce a beautiful Erinys, whose influence will spread across Asia and Europe. She will bring you the most suffering, but her fame will endure among future generations.

An aged and dubious writer will emerge, whose eyes will lose their light. Though he will possess a great mind and skillful verses, he will falsely claim to be from Chios and write about Ilium. He will skillfully use my verse and meters, first opening my books and embellishing tales of the warriors Hector of Priam and Achilles, son of Peleus, and others who valued warfare. He will also feature gods, but his writings will be false. It will be more glorified to die at Ilium, but he will also receive his due.

A Locrian race will bring many troubles to Lycia. Chalcedon, holding a narrow sea strait, will be plundered by an Ætolian youth. The sea will break off Cyzicus's vast wealth, and Byzantium will suffer destruction from Asia, experiencing immeasurable grief and bloodshed. Cragus, the lofty mountain of Lycia, will have its peaks torn apart by chasms, causing hot springs to emerge and swallowing those afflicted by fire and brimstone.

Samos will eventually build royal houses. Italy will not face foreign wars but will suffer from internal tribal strife, leading to its desolation. You, Italy, will be stretched beside hot ashes and will destroy yourself, becoming a home for beasts of prey rather than a mother to men.

When a man from Italy, a plunderer, arrives, Laodicea, the beautiful city by the Lycus River, will mourn in silence for its proud heritage. The Thracian Crobyzi will rise up on Mount Hæmus.

The Campanians will chatter with their teeth due to severe famine. Corsica mourns her ancient inhabitants, and Sardinia will be swallowed by powerful winter storms and divine wrath, sinking into the ocean depths. This will be a great marvel of the sea.

Oh, how many virgin maidens will be taken by Hades, and how many young men will the depths of the sea claim without proper funerals! Oh, how pitiful are the helpless children and the vast wealth lost in the sea!

O blessed land of the Mysians, a royal lineage will suddenly emerge. Chalcedon will not last long, and the Galatians will suffer bitter grief. Tenedos will face its greatest calamity.

Sicyon will boast with loud triumphs, and Corinth will surpass all, though music will become a mere strain. When my soul had rested from its inspired song, a message from the mighty God was again placed in my heart, commanding me to prophesy on earth.

Woe, woe to the Phoenician people, both men and women, and to all coastal cities! None of you will survive in the sunlight, nor will there be any continuation of life or tribes because of your unjust speech and lawless, impure lives. You spoke with unclean mouths and fearful, deceitful words, opposing the divine King, and deceitfully opening vile mouths. Therefore, God will punish you severely with blows across the earth, sending a bitter fate and burning destruction.

Woe to you, O Crete! You will face a painful blow, and the Eternal will destroy you. Every land will witness you enveloped in smoke; fire will never leave you, and you will be continually burned.

Woe to you, O Thrace! You will come under a servile yoke when the Galatians, joined by the sons of Dardanus, ravage Hellas. You will suffer the consequences, giving much to foreign lands and receiving nothing in return.

Woe to Gog and Magog, and to all Mardians and Daians, one after another! How many evils will fate bring upon you! Woe also to the lands of Lycia, Mysia, and Phrygia. Many nations, including Pamphylians, Lydians, Carians, Cappadocians, and Ethiopians, will fall. How can I adequately describe the plight of each nation? For the Highest will send dire plagues upon all the nations of the earth. When a barbarous nation attacks the Greeks, it will kill many chosen men and destroy many flocks of sheep, horses, mules, and cattle. They will burn well-made houses unlawfully and lead many slaves and children away to foreign lands. Delicate women will be captured and bound by their foreign enemies, suffering extreme outrage. There will be no one to aid them in battle. They will see their possessions enrich their enemies, causing great fear. A hundred will flee, and one will defeat them all; five will rout a large army. Among themselves, they will mix shamefully, bringing delight to their enemies and sorrow to the Greeks. Then, all Hellas will be under a servile yoke, with war and pestilence affecting all people. God will make the heavens like brass and the earth like iron. People will lament the barrenness and lack of cultivation. The Creator of heaven and earth will set a distressing fire upon the earth, and only one-third of humanity will remain.

O Greece, why have you trusted mortal leaders who cannot escape death? Why do you offer foolish gifts and sacrifices to idols? Who has led you to error, turning away from the mighty God? Honor the name of the All-Father and do not forget it. It has been a thousand years, plus five hundred more, since proud kings ruled the Greeks, introducing evils and worshiping dead gods, leading you to foolish beliefs. When God's anger comes upon you, you will recognize the mighty God's face. All souls will lift their hands to the heavens, calling for the great King's help and seeking deliverance from great wrath.

Learn and remember what troubles will come in the passing years. Hellas has offered burnt offerings of cows and bulls to the great God, but will flee from war, fear, and pestilence. However, until that time, a race of godless men will exist, even as the prophesied day approaches. Offerings to God should not be made until all things come to pass, as God has decreed. Strong forces will compel fulfillment.

A holy race of godly men will arise, adhering to the counsel of the Most High. They will honor God's temple with offerings, sacrifices, and burnt offerings. They will live righteously in cities and fertile fields, blessed with the law of the Most High. Prophets will be honored by the Immortal, bringing great joy to all. The mighty God will grant them faith and noble thoughts, guiding them away from the empty works of men made of gold, brass, silver, and ivory. They will honor only the immortal God and their parents, respecting lawful marriage and avoiding immoral practices.

Those who do not follow God's pure law will face calamity, including famine, war, and suffering. They will be punished for not honoring the immortal Sire of all, but worshiping idols made by hands, which will eventually be discarded in shame. When a young king, the seventh of Egypt, rules, and countless Macedonians dominate, a great fiery eagle from Asia will bring destruction, overthrowing the Egyptian kingdom and carrying away its possessions across the sea.

Before the mighty God, the King immortal, all will bow, and all works made by hands will be consumed by fire. God will then bestow joy upon humanity, with the earth and sea offering their genuine fruits—wine, sweet honey, milk, and wheat, which are the best for mortals.

You, mortal, full of various schemes, should not delay but should seek to appease God. Offer hecatombs of bulls and firstling lambs and goats as time passes. Appeal to the immortal God, the only God, and honor justice without oppressing anyone. Heeding the cause of God's wrath, you will face pestilence and judgment. Kings will seize each other's lands, nations will destroy nations, and leaders will flee, leading to the ravaging of Hellas.

The land will change hands, with foreign rule draining its wealth and leading to strife over gold and silver. Cities will be despoiled, and the dead will be unburied, their bodies scavenged by vultures and wild beasts. The earth will remain unsown and unplowed, marked by the filth of defiled humanity. Shields, javelins, and weapons will be left to decay, and the forest wood will not be cut for fire.

Then, God will send a king from the East, who will end the earth's wars, killing some and binding others with strong oaths. He will follow the good decrees of God and, with great wealth, adorn God's temple again. The earth and sea will be filled with abundance. Kings will start to harbor ill will against each other, driven by envy, which is not beneficial for wretched men.

Kings will rush in masses, bringing destruction upon themselves as they attempt to despoil God's temple and the noblest men. Polluted kings will set up thrones around cities, surrounded by people who do not obey God. God will then speak with a mighty voice to these empty-minded people, and judgment will fall upon them, leading to their destruction by His immortal hand. Fiery swords will descend from heaven, and bright flames will come down among men.

In those days, the earth, our mother, will tremble at the power of the immortal God. Fish in the sea, wild beasts on land, countless birds, and all human souls will shudder before the Immortal One. Mountains and monstrous hills will be shattered, and darkness will envelop everything. The high gorges in the mountains will be filled with the dead, and rivers will run with blood, flooding the plains.

The well-built walls of wicked people will collapse because they did not understand the law or judgment of the mighty God. They rushed senselessly against the temple, raising their weapons in defiance. God will judge them through war, sword, fire, and overwhelming storms. Brimstone, stones, and large, destructive hail will fall from heaven, and death will come to animals. They will then come to know the Immortal God who performs these acts. There will be wailing across the earth, and the unholy will be drenched in blood, with the earth itself drinking the blood of the dying and the beasts feasting on their flesh.

These are the things that the great eternal God has commanded me to proclaim. Everything He has put in my heart will come to pass because God's spirit is truthful.

The children of the mighty God will once again live peacefully around the temple, rejoicing in the blessings given by the Creator, the righteous Judge, and the King. He will be their protection, like a wall of flaming fire surrounding them. They will live without war, with the Immortal Himself defending them, not the hand of evil war. All islands and cities will reflect the love of the immortal God for those men. Everything will assist them in conflict and deliverance—heaven, the sun, and the moon. They will sing sweet hymns: "Let us all pray to the immortal King, the eternal God. Let us process to the temple, for He alone is Lord. Let us meditate on the law of the Most High, the most righteous law on earth. We have strayed from the path of the Immortal and honored works made by hands and wooden images of dead men."

The faithful will cry out: "Come, let us fall before God in His house and make joyful hymns to the Father in our homes, and be supplied with arms to protect us through the seven lengths of time in the revolving years. We need shields, helmets, and various weapons, as well as a great supply of bows and arrows, since forest wood will not be cut for such purposes."

O wretched Hellas, abandon your arrogance and be wise. Seek the Immortal One with reverence, and be cautious. Do not disturb Camarina; it is better left undisturbed. Avoid the dangers that may come from a leopard-like threat. Do not harbor arrogance or overbearing attitudes ready for great conflict. Serve the mighty God to share in His blessings. When the destined day arrives and the judgment of the immortal God comes to men, great power and judgment will follow. The earth will then yield its best fruits: abundant wheat, wine, oil, honey from heaven, fruit from trees, and plenty of young lambs and kids. The earth will flow with sweet milk, and cities and fields will be rich and full. There will be no more war, drought, famine, or destructive hail. Peace will reign over the earth, and kings will be friends until the end of time. The Immortal will establish a common law across the world, perfecting it for humanity, addressing everything done by mortals. He alone is God; there is no other. He will burn away the fierce rage of men with fire. Change your thoughts entirely. Flee from unrighteous worship, serve the living God, avoid adultery and lewdness, and rear your offspring properly. Do not commit murder, for the Immortal is angry with those who sin in these ways. In the future, He will establish a kingdom over all mankind for ages. He once gave holy law to the pious and promised to open every land, the world, and the portals of the blessed, offering all joys and eternal bliss.

From every land, people will bring frankincense and gifts to the house of the great God. No other place will be sought after by people, except what God has given for the faithful to honor. This will be known as the mortal temple of the mighty God. In those days, all paths across plains, rough hills, high mountains, and wild seas will become easy to traverse and navigate. Peace will come to the land, and the sword will be removed by the prophets of the mighty God, who will serve as judges and righteous kings among people. There will be true prosperity among mankind, for this is the judgment and power of the mighty God.

Rejoice, O maiden, and be glad, for the Creator of heaven and earth has granted you joy in your lifetime. He will dwell within you; and wolves and lambs will graze together in the mountains, leopards will feed with kids, bears will live among calves, and even the carnivorous lion will eat chaff at the manger like a cow. Little children will lead these animals, for God will make beasts harmless on earth. Serpents and asps will sleep peacefully with babies, causing no harm, because God's hand will be over them.

Now, I will give you a clear sign to know when the end of all things on earth will come. When swords in the night sky point straight toward the west and east, a cloud of dust will spread across the earth. The sun's brightness will be eclipsed, and the moon's light will appear as drops of blood fall from the rocks. You will see a war in the clouds, resembling a chase of wild beasts through thick fog. This will be the end of all things, consummated by God, who dwells in heaven. Everyone must sacrifice to the great King.

These are the things I reveal to you. I left the long walls of Assyrian Babylon to come to Hellas and proclaim the wrath of God, sent by fire. And I did this to prophesy divine mysteries to mankind. People in Hellas will say I am from a foreign land, born in Erythrae, and others will claim I am a Sibyl, the daughter of Circe and father Gnostos, calling me mad and false. But when everything comes to pass, you will remember me, and no one will call me mad, the prophetess of the great God.

For He showed me what happened to my ancestors and the early events He made known to me. In my mind, God placed all that was to come afterward so that I could prophesy about future events and things that happened before. When the world was flooded, and only one man of good repute survived in a wooden house, sailing over the waters with the animals and birds to repopulate the earth, I was his son's bride and part of his lineage. Through this, the early events and the last things were revealed to me. Let all these truthful accounts be declared from my own mouth.

Sibylline Oracles - IV

Book IV, offer a unique view of early Common Era religious and political dynamics by blending Hellenistic and Jewish cultures. Likely composed in the first or second century CE, this book merges Greek prophetic tradition with Jewish apocalyptic themes, critiquing contemporary moral and political corruption and foretelling divine judgment. It reflects the historical context of Roman rule and Jewish revolts, referencing significant events like the destruction of Jerusalem. By integrating mythological elements with theological discourse, Book IV demonstrates how ancient communities adapted their beliefs amid a complex cultural landscape, providing valuable insights into their prophetic and apocalyptic perspectives.

People of boastful Asia and Europe,

Listen to how much truth there is in my words, coming from my great hall. For a month, I will prophesy, not as a false oracle of the deceitful god Phoebus, whom vain men called a god and wrongly labeled a seer. I speak of the mighty God, who was not made by human hands like lifeless idols carved from stone.

This God does not reside in a dumb, toothless stone temple, which is a great dishonor to the immortals. He cannot be seen or measured by human eyes, nor formed by human hands. He oversees everything from above, yet remains unseen Himself. His are the murky night, day, sun, stars, moon, seas filled with fish, land, rivers, and the month of perpetual springs. These creatures are meant for life, and the rains that bring forth the fruit of the field, trees, vines, and oil. This God has driven my heart with a whip, compelling me to tell the truth about what has happened and what will happen from the first generation to the eleventh. For He Himself will bring all things to pass and prove them true. So, listen carefully to the Sibyl, who speaks truthfully from a sacred mouth. Those who love the mighty God and offer Him praise before eating and drinking, trusting in piety, will be blessed on earth.

When they see temples and altars, and figures made of lifeless stones polluted with the blood of sacrifices, they will reject them all. They will look to the great glory of one God and avoid committing murder or theft, which are most horrid acts. They will also shun shameful desires and vile lusts. Their way of life, piety, and character will be unlike those who lead a shameless life. These latter people will mock the pious with jokes, falsely accusing them of the very deeds they themselves commit. Human beings are slow to believe, but when God's judgment comes upon the world and mortals, He will judge both the impious and the pious. The ungodly will be cast into darkness and realize their impiety, while the pious will remain on the fruitful land, receiving breath, life, and grace from God. These events will occur in the tenth generation, and I will now tell you about what will happen from the first generation onward.

First, the Assyrians will rule all mortals and hold power for six generations. This will be after God, angry with the cities and all men, covers the earth with a great deluge. The Medes will then overpower the Assyrians, but will only rule for two generations. During this time, the following events will take place:

A dark night will come at midday, and the stars and moon will disappear from the sky. The earth will be shaken by a great earthquake, causing many cities and works of men to collapse. Islands will emerge from the sea. When the Euphrates River surges with blood, there will be terrible conflict between the Medes and Persians. The Medes will fall before Persian spears and flee across the Tigris River. The Persians will then have a period of great power and prosperity.

During this time, there will be many evil deeds—war, murders, disputes, banishments, and the destruction of cities. Hellas (Greece) will sail across the Hellespont and bring sorrow and doom to Phrygia and Asia. Egypt will suffer from famine and barrenness for twenty years when the Nile, the source of its sustenance, is hidden.

A great king from Asia with numerous ships will come and sail through the seas. After a fierce battle, he will be received as a fugitive by fearful Asia. Sicily will be set ablaze by a stream of powerful fire from Mount Etna, and the city of Croton will fall into the deep chasm. Strife will engulf Hellas, causing many cities to be destroyed and many people to perish, with both sides equally balanced in conflict.

In the tenth generation, the Persians will face servitude and terror. The Macedonians will then come to power, and Thebes will suffer a disastrous defeat. The Carians will inhabit Tyre, and the Tyrians will be destroyed. Babylon, grand but poorly defended, will be overthrown. Macedonians will settle in Bactria, but those from Susa and Bactria will flee to Hellas.

Among the future events, the river Pyramus will overflow, and the sacred isle will be affected. Cibyra and Cyzicus will fall when earthquakes shake the earth. Sand will cover Samos, Delos will disappear, and Rhodes will face the greatest misfortune. The Macedonian power will falter, and a great Italian war will ensue, placing the world under a servile yoke with Italians in servitude. Wretched Corinth will see its conquest, and Carthage will be brought low.

Laodicea will be struck by an earthquake, but will eventually stand again. Beautiful Myra in Lycia will never be stable, and will fall and pray to escape to another land when the sea's dark waters and earthquakes cause turmoil. Armenia will face servitude, and Solyma (Jerusalem) will suffer war from Italy and the desecration of God's great temple. When these people, in their folly, abandon their piety and commit murders around the temple, a mighty king will come from Italy, fleeing across the Euphrates. He will be a fugitive and will commit heinous acts, including matricide, confident in his wicked deeds.

And many will shed blood for the throne on Rome's soil, while he flees across Parthian lands. From Syria, the leading man of Rome will emerge. After burning the temple in Jerusalem and slaughtering many Jews, he will bring destruction to their vast land. Then, an earthquake will also overthrow both Salamis and Paphos when dark waters surge over Cyprus, which is battered by stormy waves. When fire bursts forth from the deep chasms of Italian land, scorching the sky and burning many cities, filling the sky with thick black ashes and red dust, then you will know the wrath of the God of heaven. This anger is provoked because they will irrationally destroy the nation of the pious. War will then awaken in the West, and a fugitive from Rome will come, wielding a great spear and marching across the Euphrates with his numerous forces.

O wretched Antioch, you will no longer be called a city when, because of your own follies, you fall surrounded by their spears. On Scyros, a plague and the sounds of dreadful battle will bring destruction.

Alas, wretched Cyprus, a broad wave of the sea will cover you, tossed high by stormy winds. Great wealth will come to Asia, which Rome once plundered and stored in her luxurious homes. Rome will return twice as much, and more, to Asia, leading to an overflow of war.

The Carian cities by the Meander River, once beautiful and fortified, will be destroyed by a bitter famine when the Meander hides its dark waters. But when piety disappears from humanity, and faith and justice are lost in the world, when fickle and impious people practice wanton violence and reckless evil deeds, and no one accounts for the pious, destroying them thoughtlessly and in childish folly, rejoicing in their violence and bloodshed—then you will know that God is no longer merciful but is filled with fury and will destroy all of mankind with a great conflagration. Ah, miserable mortals, change your ways and do not provoke the mighty God to extreme wrath. Lay down your swords and knives, and abandon homicides and wanton violence. Wash your bodies in perpetual streams, and lift your hands to heaven seeking forgiveness for your past deeds. Expiate your bitter impiety with praise, and God will grant repentance. He will not destroy you, and He will restrain His wrath if you practice honored piety in your hearts. But if you refuse to listen and receive these warnings with an evil ear, preferring senselessness, there will be a fire over the entire world, accompanied by the greatest omen of sword and trumpet at sunrise. The entire world will hear the roar and mighty sound. God will burn the entire earth, destroying all of humanity, cities, rivers, and seas. Everything will turn to black dust. When all things have turned to dust and ashes, and God has calmed the unimaginable fire He ignited, He will Himself reshape the bones and ashes of humanity and resurrect mortals as they were before. Then there will be a judgment, with God as the judge once again. All who have sinned with impious hearts will be hidden under mounds of earth, in dark Tartarus and Stygian Gehenna. But the pious will return to live on the earth and inherit the eternal bliss of the great immortal God. God will give them spirit, life, and joy, and they will see themselves basking in the sun's sweet and comforting light. Blessed will be that man on earth.

Sibylline Oracles - V

The Sibylline Oracles, attributed to the ancient prophetess Sibyl, are key to studying ancient apocalyptic literature. Book V, likely written between the 2nd and 3rd centuries CE, blends Hellenistic and Jewish elements, reflecting the syncretic nature of its time. This book features vivid apocalyptic imagery and themes of divine judgment and righteousness, similar to the Book of Revelation. Scholars debate its authorship, suggesting multiple contributors and layers of tradition. The text provides insights into the socio-political context of the era, referencing figures like Roman emperors and events such as the destruction of Jerusalem. Book V offers valuable perspectives on how early Christian and Jewish communities interpreted their turbulent world through prophetic and apocalyptic lenses.

Come now and hear the sorrowful fate of the Latian people. First of all, after the fall of the Egyptian kings and the earth has swallowed them all, and after the Macedonian conqueror, who had brought down both East and West, was dishonored by Babylon and had his body stretched out for Philip—he, whom neither Zeus nor Ammon had truly prophesied—then came one of the bloodline of Assaracus from Troy. This person, who survived the fire, followed many leaders, warriors, and infants, the offspring of the beast that eats sheep. The very first ruler will be one whose name's first letter represents the sum of twenty.

He will be extraordinarily powerful in wars and will be signified by the initial of ten. After him, another ruler will follow, whose name's first letter is the alphabet's first letter. Before him, Thrace and Sicily will bow down, and Memphis will be overthrown by a cowardly ruler and an unenslaved woman who will drown in the sea. He will establish laws and bring everything under his control. But after a long time, he will pass his power to another ruler, whose initial sign is three hundred, and who will be known by a river's name, and he will rule over the Persians and Babylon. He will also defeat the Medes. Then another ruler will come, marked by the initial of the number three. Following him will be a ruler with twice ten as his first initial. He will reach the furthest waters of the Ocean and will part the tides by Ausonia.

Another ruler with the mark of fifty will come, a dreadful serpent bringing severe war. At one point, he will act violently, perform feats, and cause much bloodshed. He will split the mountain between two seas and cover it with gore, but he will eventually disappear from sight. He will try to make himself equal to a god, but will be proven worthless by God.

Then three kings will be destroyed by one another. Following them will be a great destroyer of righteous men, clearly indicated by seventy. His son, marked by three hundred, will inherit power. After him, there will be a ruler with the initial sign of four, who will bring death. Then a revered man with the mark of fifty will come. Following him, a Celtic mountaineer, marked by three hundred, will press into battle and will not escape a disgraceful fate. He will be buried in foreign dust, but that dust will be named after the flower of Nemea.

After him, another man with a silver helmet will rule, named after the sea. He will be the best and most wise of all rulers. All these days will be upon you, O best of all, dark-haired one, and upon your descendants.

After him, three will rule, but the third will hold power only late in time. I am exhausted, wretched, to bring forth this grievous message and prophetic song. First, the Maenads will dance around your mourned temple's steps. You will be in dire circumstances when the Nile floods Egypt up to sixteen cubits deep. It will inundate all the land, bringing water to mortals, and the land's pleasure and glory will cease.

Memphis will wail the most over Egypt, becoming impoverished from its former might. The Thunderer himself will cry out from heaven, lamenting Memphis's fall from glory. For having opposed my anointed children and encouraging evil, you will suffer such consequences. No longer will you find favor among the blessed.

Fallen from the stars, you will never rise to heaven again. God commanded me to speak these things about Egypt for the last time when people will be utterly corrupt. They will labor under the wrath of the immortal Thunderer, worshiping lifeless idols made of stone and metal instead of the true God. They will fear many things that are without speech, mind, or power. These false gods, created from mortal hands and imaginations, are vain and meaningless.

Thmois and Xois will be in great distress, and the halls of Heracles, Zeus, and Hermes will be struck. Alexandria, famed for nurturing cities, will suffer from war and plague. For your pride, you will face many tribulations. You will be silent for a long time, and the day of your return will be far off.

There will be no more luxurious drinks for you. A Persian will come to your land and, like hail, destroy everything. He will bring bloodshed and death. A barbarous man, filled with rage, will attack sacred altars with countless forces, leading to widespread devastation. Cities will suffer, and Asia will mourn the gifts it once received from you. He will wage war, killing all life, leaving only a third remaining. He will swiftly move from the West, besieging and ravaging the land. When he reaches the height of his power, he will attempt to destroy even the blessed city. But a king sent by God will rise against him, destroying all mighty kings and brave men. Thus, divine judgment will come upon humanity.

Alas for you, unfortunate heart! Why do you compel me to declare these sorrowful prophecies about Egypt's dominion over many? Go east to the Persian races and reveal to them what is now and what is to come. The river Euphrates will overflow and destroy the Persians, Iberians, Babylonians, and the Massagetæ, who are known for their love of war and archery. All of Asia will be set ablaze, and Pergamos, once revered, will be destroyed from its foundations. Pitane will become a desolate wasteland, and Lesbos will sink beneath the sea, meeting its end. Smyrna, once honored, will be thrown down its cliffs and will mourn its destruction. The Bithynians will weep over their burned land and over the great Syria and Phoenicia, which is home to many tribes. Alas, Lycia, how many disasters the sea will bring upon you, flooding your land and causing devastation with earthquakes and bitter streams. Your once fragrant land will suffer greatly.

Phrygia will face terrible wrath due to the sorrow that Rhea, the mother of Zeus, once experienced there. The sea will overthrow the Centaur race and other barbarous nations and will tear apart the land of the Lapithæans. The river Peneus, known for its deep eddies, will destroy Thessaly, dragging people away. Eridanus, which once was said to take the forms of beasts, will also be involved. Hellas, so wretched, will be mourned by poets when a mighty king from Italy, equal to a god and said to be the offspring of Zeus and Hera, strikes the neck of the isthmus. This king, renowned for his musical voice and sweet songs, will bring death to many, including his own wretched mother. The fearful and shameless ruler from Babylon will flee. He will be despised by all and hated for his many crimes, including the slaughter of many and violations against his wives. He will seek refuge among the Medes and Persians, the people he once favored and who gave him fame. He will attack a nation that did not desire him, seizing the temple made by God, burning citizens and people he had once praised. When he appears, the whole world will shake, kings will perish, and yet the power will remain with those who have destroyed the mighty city and the righteous people.

But when the fourth year comes, a great star will shine, overpowering the entire earth with its honor, first given to Poseidon. Another great star will come from heaven, burning the vast sea, Babylon, and Italy, because many faithful Hebrews and true people perished there.

You will suffer greatly, remaining desolate through the ages, despised by your own land. Your desire for sorcery and your crimes—adultery and lawless carnal acts with boys—will mark you as an evil city, unjust and ill-fated above all. Alas, Latin city, unclean in everything, you will sit as a widow over your banks, and the Tiber River will mourn for you. You have a blood-stained heart and impious soul. You thought that no one could sack you, but now God will destroy you and all that belongs to you, and your banner will no longer remain, as it once did when God received your honors. Stay alone, lawless one, and dwell in the fiery depths of Tartarus.

Again, Egypt, I mourn your blindness. Memphis, first in troubles, will be filled with the dead; the pyramids will utter a cruel sound. O Python, once called the double city, be silent for ages, so you may cease from wickedness. Reckless and filled with sorrows, you will remain a widow through all time. You ruled the world for many years, but when Barea puts on her white dress over her defiled state, I wish I had never been born.

O Thebes, where is your great strength? A fierce man will slaughter your people, and you, wretched one, will wail alone in your dark robes, making atonement for your past shameless deeds. Others will also mourn because of your lawlessness.

A mighty Ethiopian will overthrow Syene, and swarthy Indians will occupy Teucheira. A powerful man will burn Pentapolis completely. O Libya, who will explain your follies? And Cyrene, who will weep for you? You will not cease your hateful wailing even until your destruction.

Among the Britons and Gauls, rich in gold, the Ocean will roar loudly, filled with blood. They will have committed evil against God's children when a Sidonian king, a Phoenician, leads a powerful Gallic host from Syria and destroys Ravenna, leading the way to slaughter.

O Indians and noble Ethiopians, fear together. When the constellations of Capricorn and Taurus in the Twins circle the heavens, and Virgo rises with the sun leading all heaven, a great conflagration will descend from the sky, bringing a new nature to the warlike stars. The entire land of the Ethiopians will perish in fire and anguish.

Weep, Corinth, for your sad destruction. When the three Fates spin and lead him who flees by deceit against the voice of the isthmus, he who once cut through rock with pliant brass will also destroy and strike your land as has been foretold. For to him, God gave the strength to accomplish what no earlier king could.

And first, a man with a sickle will cut off the roots from three heads, giving excessive food to others, so that unclean kings will end up eating their own parents' flesh. All humans will face slaughter and terrors because of the great city and its righteous people, whom Providence has always upheld.

O you unstable and ill-advised one, surrounded by evil fates, bringing both the beginning and the great end of toil to mankind—suffering creation and its restoration—you are the insolent leader of evils, a great curse to humanity. Who among mortals desired you? Who hasn't been embittered by you? A king has lost his honored life because of you. You have ruined everything, washed away all that was beautiful, and changed the world's fair landscape. Perhaps you have brought these troubles upon us. How can you claim, "I will persuade you," or "If you blame me for anything, speak up?"

Once, there was the bright light of the sun among men, a shared ray of the prophets. Speech, sweet as honey and pleasant to all, appeared and grew, bringing daylight to everyone. But now, you, narrow-minded leader of great evils, will face both sword and sorrow on that day. For mankind, both a beginning and a great end of toil—suffering creation and its restoration—hear this intolerable, bitter oracle.

When the Persian land will be free from war and plague, a divine race of blessed heavenly Jews will offer prayers. They will dwell around God's city in the central land and build a great wall as far as Joppa, raising it up to the gloomy clouds. No more will the sounds of battle or enemy attacks interrupt them; instead, they will set up their trophies for an age of evil men. A preeminent man will come from heaven, whose hands once reached out on a fruitful tree, the noblest of the Hebrews. He once made the sun stand still with his holy words. No longer will you, rich child of God, be vexed by the sword. Pleasant Judea, beautiful city inspired by hymns, will no longer be trampled by unclean Greek feet, who harbored lawless minds. Instead, glorious children will honor you with songs and holy rituals, offering sacrifices and prayers accepted by God. Those who endure small afflictions and are just will receive even more beauty. The wicked, who sent lawless speech to heaven, will cease their bickering and hide until the world changes.

There will be a rain of gleaming fire from the clouds, and no more will mortals reap the earth's bounty. All things will remain unsown and unplowed until humans come to know the Lord of all, the immortal God, and no longer revere mortal things or the teachings of Egypt. Instead, the holy land of the pious will produce streams of ambrosial milk from the honey-dripping rock for all the just. They hoped in one God, one Father, who alone is glorious, with great piety and faith. But why does the wise mind reveal these things to me? Now I mourn for you, wretched Asia, and the Ionians, Carians, and rich Lydians. Alas for you, Sardis, and Trallis, so beloved; alas for you, beautiful Laodicea. You will be overthrown by earthquakes and turned to dust.

The temple of Artemis at Ephesus will be swallowed by chasms and earthquakes, falling into the dreadful sea and causing storms to overwhelm ships. Ephesus will wail beside her banks, searching for her lost temple. God, the imperishable who dwells on high, will hurl thunderbolts from heaven upon the impure. Instead of winter, there will be summer. Great woe will come to mortal men as the Thunderer destroys all shameless individuals with his thunder and lightning, leaving a greater number of dead bodies on the earth than sand.

Smyrna, weeping for her Lycurgus, will come to the gates of Ephesus and perish even more. Foolish Cyme, with her inspired streams, will be destroyed by godless and lawless men, and she will not speak even a word to heaven but will remain dead in her streams. They will weep together, awaiting further misfortunes.

Cyme's rough populace and shameless tribe, marked by signs, will realize the results of their labor. When they have mourned their land reduced to ashes, Lesbos will be forever overthrown by Eridanus.

Alas, beautiful Corcyra, cease your revelry. You too, Hierapolis, land of mixed riches, will get what you longed for—a land of many tears—because you were angry with a land beside Thermodon's streams. Rock-clinging Tripolis, beside the Meander River, will be utterly destroyed by God's wrath and foresight through nightly surges.

Do not take me, willingly, to the neighboring land of Phoebus; someday, a thunderbolt will destroy dainty Miletus from above because she seized Phoebus' clever song and wise plans.

Father of all, be gracious to the land of Judah, fruitful and great, so that we may see your judgments. For you, O God, first regarded this land with kindness, making it your gracious gift to all mortal men, holding fast what you entrusted to them.

I yearn to see the wretched works of the Thracians and the wall between two seas turned to dust, like a river for swimming fish. O wretched Hellespont, someday a child of the Assyrians will place a yoke across you; the battle of the Thracians will come and weaken your strength. Over Macedonia will rule a king from Egypt, and a barbarous land will deplete the strength of captains. Lydians, Galatians, Pamphylians, and Pisidians, all equipped for war, will bring great strife. Thrice-wretched Italy will remain desolate, unwept, perishing in its blooming land due to a deadly sting.

And high above in the broad heaven, God's voice will one day thunder like a roaring storm.

And the eternal flames of the sun will be extinguished, and the bright light of the moon will cease to shine in the end times, when God becomes the ruler. Darkness will cover the entire earth, and there will be blindness, evil beasts, and sorrow. That day will last a long time, so people will see that God Himself is the Lord, overseeing everything from above. Then He will not have mercy on those who offer sacrifices of lambs, sheep, calves, goats, and golden-horned bulls to lifeless statues and stone gods. Instead, let the law of wisdom and the glory of righteousness guide you. Otherwise, the eternal God, when angered, will destroy every race of men and shameless life forms. It is essential to faithfully love the Father, the wise and ever-existing God.

In the end times, as the moon turns, there will be a war raging across the world, fought with cunning and deceit. From the far reaches of the earth will come a man with a murderous past, who will overpower every land and rule over everything. He will understand things more wisely than anyone else and will seize those for whom he himself was killed. He will destroy many people and great tyrants, burning them as no one else ever has. He will elevate those who are afraid, driven by a desire for revenge. From the West, much conflict will arise, and blood will flow down valleys until it forms deep, swirling streams.

In the plains of Macedonia, wrath will be poured out, providing aid from the West but bringing destruction to the king. A winter wind will blow across the earth, filling the plains with renewed warfare. Fire will rain down from the heavens, accompanied by blood, water, lightning, murky darkness, and night. These will combine to destroy all kings and the noblest men, bringing an end to the pitiable destruction of war. Swords, iron weapons, and darts will no longer be used. Wise people who survive and have proven their righteousness will finally find peace and joy.

You matricides, stop your bold impudence and lawless actions. You have previously provided lewd services with boys and forced pure maidens into brothels through assault and indecency. In you, mothers have engaged in unlawful relations with their children, and daughters have married their fathers. Kings have sullied themselves, and wicked men have had relations with animals. Be silent, you cursed and bewailing city, known for its revelry. Virgin maidens will no longer care for the sacred fire of divine wood.

Your once much-loved temple was extinguished when I saw the second temple cast down and consumed by fire at the hands of an unholy force. This temple, flourishing and always indestructible, was God's holy place, built by His saints. Praise for God from the unseen earth does not come without burial rites. The wise craftsmen did not fear gold, a deceitful world and soul, but revered the mighty Father, God of all things, with holy offerings and sacrifices. But now, an unseen and unholy king, with a great multitude and renowned men, has risen to power, destroying his own dwelling and leaving it in ruins. When he set foot on the immortal land, he devastated it. Such a sign had not been seen before, indicating that others should destroy the great city.

From the heavenly realms came a blessed man with a scepter given by God. He ruled everything well and restored to the good the riches that had been seized by earlier people. He took many cities by fire from their foundations, burning the towns of those who had done evil. He made the city loved by God more radiant than the stars, the sun, and the moon. He established order and built a holy house, a pure and beautiful structure, and a great, boundless tower reaching the clouds, visible to all. So all holy and righteous people could witness the glory of the eternal God, a longed-for sight. The rising sun and setting day sang praises to God.

In the end times, there will be no more fear for wretched mortals. There will be no adulteries, lawless relationships, or homicides. Instead, there will be only righteous struggles. This will be the final period for the saints when God, the great Thunderer and founder of the most magnificent temple, accomplishes these things.

Alas, Babylon, with your golden throne and famous golden sandals, once the kingdom that ruled the world and was great in ancient times, you will no longer lie among golden mountains and by the Euphrates. You will be brought low by an earthquake. The Parthians have made you suffer greatly. You, impure Chaldean people, should hold on to your unknown language; don't worry about how you will lead the Persians or rule the Medes. Because of your former dominance, sending hostages to Rome and serving Asia, you will face judgment from your adversaries. You will replace deceitful words with bitter suffering for your enemies. In the end times, the sea will be dry, and ships will no longer sail to Italy. Asia, once great, will become a desolate wasteland, and Crete will turn into a plain. Cyprus will endure great suffering, and Paphos will mourn a dreadful fate. Even the great city of Salamis will face immense misery. The once fertile land will become barren sand, and locusts will devastate Cyprus. As you look at Tyre, doomed mortals, you will weep. Phoenicia, terrible wrath awaits you until you fall into worthless ruin, so that even the Sirens will truly lament.

In the fifth generation, after Egypt's ruin has ended, shameless kings will unite. The Pamphylians will camp in Egypt, and wars will rage across Macedonia, Asia, and Libya, spreading dust and blood. The king of Rome and rulers of the West will eventually put an end to this world-maddening conflict.

When a wintry storm falls like snow and great rivers and lakes freeze, a barbarous race will invade Asia and destroy the fierce Thracians. People will, out of hunger, devour their own parents and each other, and wild beasts and birds will consume all the food from human homes. The ocean will fill with dead bodies, turning red with flesh and blood. The earth will become weak, and the number of men and women will become apparent. The dreadful race will wail for countless things when the sun sets for the last time and remains submerged in the ocean, having witnessed the wickedness of many mortals. A moonless night will become famous in the vast heavens, and no mist will cover the world's ravines a second time. Then, God's light will guide the good, who sang praises to Him.

Isis, thrice-wretched goddess, you alone will remain on the Nile's waters, a disordered Maenad on the sands of Acheron, with no lasting remembrance on earth. Similarly, you, Sarapis, placed on many gleaming stones, will lie in vast ruin in Egypt. Those who loved Egypt will lament you deeply, but those who embraced imperishable wisdom and praised God will see you as nothing.

At some point, a linen-clad priest will say, "Come, let us build a beautiful and true temple for God. Let us abandon the fearful laws of our ancestors, who did not understand that their processions and religious rites were to lifeless gods of stone and clay. Let us turn our souls to praise the imperishable God, who is the Father, the everlasting One, the Lord of all, the true King, the life-giving Father, the mighty God who exists forever."

Then, a great, pure temple will be built in Egypt, and God's people will bring their sacrifices to it. God will grant them incorruptible life.

But when the Ethiopians, abandoning the shameless Triballian tribes, begin to cultivate Egypt, they will fall into corruption, leading to further disasters. They will overthrow Egypt's mighty temple, and God will pour out dire wrath upon the earth, causing all the wicked and senseless to perish. There will be no mercy in that land because they failed to keep what God had given.

I saw the threatening sun among the stars and the dire wrath of the moon in the lightning flash. The stars struggled in battle, and God let them shine. Long fire-flames rebelled against the sun; Lucifer, riding on Leo's back, began the fight. The moon's double horn changed shape, Capricorn struck Taurus' neck, and Taurus took away the returning day from Capricorn. Orion could no longer bear his yoke, and Gemini's lot was changed by Virgo into Aries. The Pleiades no longer shone; Draco abandoned his zone, and Pisces moved into Leo's girdle. Cancer fled from Orion, Scorpio moved backward onto Leo, and Sirius slipped away from the sun's flame. The strength of the mighty Shining One was kindled in Aquarius. Uranus himself was stirred, shaking the warring ones and hurling them down to earth. Swiftly, they set the whole earth on fire, and the high heaven remained starless.

Sibylline Oracles - VI

The Sixth Book of the Sibylline Oracles, a prophetic text from the Hellenistic period, blends pagan and early Christian thought. Noted for its apocalyptic themes and vivid imagery, it reflects a mix of Jewish and Christian influences. The book describes cosmic upheavals and divine judgment, followed by calls for moral rectitude. It integrates Greek mythology with biblical motifs, showcasing the syncretic nature of ancient religious thought. Book VI serves as a prophetic bridge between the divine and human, addressing both doom and salvation. It also mirrors the socio-political anxieties of its time, possibly from a Jewish-Christian community navigating a polytheistic world. The text's complex thematic interweaving offers insights into early Christian adaptations of prophetic traditions, making it a significant subject for scholarly study.

I proclaim with all my heart the great Son of the Immortal, renowned in song. To Him, the Father granted a throne even before His birth. He was raised as a man, baptized in the River Jordan, which flows swiftly with its shimmering waves. As He emerged from the water, He was the first to witness God's sweet Spirit descending like a white dove. A pure flower will bloom, and the springs will overflow.

He will guide people on the right path, show them the heavenly ways, and teach them with wisdom. He will come for judgment, urging a disobedient people while boasting of His noble descent from a heavenly Father. He will walk on the waves, heal human sickness, raise the dead, and relieve many suffering souls. From a single basket, He will provide bread enough for everyone. When the house of David brings forth a child, He will hold the whole world—earth, heaven, and sea—in His hands. He will shine upon the earth just as the first humans once saw the divine form. Earth will rejoice in the hope of this child.

But for you, O land of Sodom, only evil awaits. You failed to recognize your God, who mocks human plans. Instead, you crowned Him with thorns and mixed bitterness with arrogance and pride. This will bring terrible consequences for you.

O blessed Wood, on which God was stretched out, the earth will not possess you. Instead, you will be seen in a heavenly realm when God directs His fiery gaze upon you.

Sibylline Oracles - VII

Sibylline Oracles, attributed to ancient prophetesses, blend Greco-Roman and Judeo-Christian elements, with Book VII illustrating this syncretism through its mix of pagan and Jewish themes. Reflecting the Hellenistic period's cultural and religious diversity, this book is noted for its apocalyptic imagery and foretelling of cosmic upheavals and divine judgment, echoing Hebrew Bible and Jewish apocalyptic themes. Dating to the late first and early second centuries CE, Book VII emerged from a time of intense cultural and religious interaction, showing how prophetic traditions were adapted and transformed. Oracles offer insights into the ancient Mediterranean religious landscape and the complex dynamics of cultural exchange.

Oh Rhodes, you are unfortunate; I will mourn for you first. You will be the first city to fall, and the first to be destroyed. Though you will not be completely without the means to live, you will be bereft of people. You will sail, Delos, and become unstable on the water. Cyprus, a wave from your shining sea will eventually destroy you. Sicily, the fire within you will consume you. Do not ignore the terrible and alien waters of God. Noah was the only one who survived the flood. Earth, hills, and even the sky will float; everything will be submerged, and all things will be destroyed by water. The winds will cease, and a new age will begin.

Oh Phrygia, you will be the first to catch fire from the waters, and you will be the first to deny God, seeking favor from false gods who will utterly destroy you, poor thing, over many years. The unfortunate Ethiopians, suffering greatly, will be struck down by swords while they crouch on the ground. Rich Egypt, always concerned about her grain, which the Nile's seven streams nourish, will be torn apart by internal conflict. Unexpectedly, men will drive out Apis, who is not truly a god for them.

Alas, Laodicea! You will never see God and will be washed away by the wave of the Lycus river. He who is born the mighty God will perform many miracles. He will set up a great axis in the sky and place a terrifying sight for all to see, measuring a column with mighty fire whose sparks will destroy those who have committed evil. Yet, there will one day be a common Lord, and people will try to appease God, though their sorrows will continue. All things will come to pass through David's lineage. For God gave him power and placed it in his hands; his messengers will bring about various changes—some will light fires, some will make rivers appear, some will rescue cities, and some will send forth winds. However, a harsh life will come to many people, affecting their souls and changing their hearts.

But when a new branch emerges from a root, creation, which once provided abundant food, will be restored. The world will be filled again. When other rulers come, a tribe of warlike Persians will cause horror, with lawless deeds becoming common. Mothers will have their own sons as husbands, sons will become the ruin of their mothers, and daughters will sleep with their fathers, causing the collapse of foreign laws. But later, Roman warriors will flash their spears, mixing much land with human blood. A leader from Italy will flee from their spears but will leave behind a lance inscribed with gold as a symbol of their rule.

When the ill-fated Ilias meets a tragic end without marriage, brides will weep bitterly, having failed to know God, always celebrating with noisy drums and cymbals.

Consult the oracle, Colophon, for a great and fearful fire threatens you. Ill-fated Thessaly will be lost to the earth, and your ashes will be left behind. You will escape by swimming from the mainland, wretchedly avoiding war, having fallen to swift rivers and swords.

Oh, poor Corinth, you will be surrounded by fierce Ares and will perish along with your people. Tyre, you too will be left desolate; weakened by the faith of your people, you will be brought to ruin.

Ah, Coele-Syria, the last stronghold of the Phoenician people, where the salty sea of Berytus flows forth, you wretched one, you did not recognize your God. He who once was baptized in the Jordan River—where the Spirit flew down to Him—He who existed before the earth and the stars, the Word begotten by the Father, and who took on flesh through the Holy Spirit, quickly returned to His Father's house. For Him, the mighty heavens set up three towers, where God's noble guides dwell: Hope, Piety, and Reverence, valued not in gold or silver but in the reverent actions of people—both sacrifices and righteous thoughts.

You are to offer sacrifices to the immortal and mighty God, not by burning grains of incense or slaughtering lambs, but by taking wild birds with all your kin and offering them in prayer. Fix your gaze on heaven and release them. Sprinkle water on pure fire and say: "As the Father begot You, the Word, Father, I send forth a bird, a swift messenger of words, with holy waters sprinkling Your baptism, O Word, through which You revealed Yourself in fire."

Do not close your door to a stranger who comes to you hungry and in need. Instead, take hold of him, sprinkle him with water, and pray three times, saying to your God: "I do not desire wealth; I once received a beggar publicly; Father, Provider, hear my prayer." After praying, give to the stranger, and let him go. Do not let holy fear and righteousness afflict me. O Father, make my troubled heart calm; to You I look, to You, the undefiled, whom hands did not create.

Sardinia, now heavy, you will turn to ashes. You will cease to be an island when the tenth time comes. Sailors will search for you amid the waves when you are no more, and kingfishers will mourn over you.

Rugged Mygdonia, a beacon of the sea, will boast of its enduring ages, but it will be destroyed by a hot wind and suffer many woes.

O Celtic land, with your vast mountain ranges beyond the impassable Alps, deep sand will bury you completely. You will no longer provide tribute, grain, or pasturage. You will become desolate and covered in chilling ice, paying for your past transgressions.

Stout-hearted Rome, you will be struck by lightning after Macedonian spears, but God will make you entirely unknown, even when you appear to remain firm. I will then cry out to you. As you perish, you will cry out in pain, and once again, I will speak to you, O Rome. Now, for you, O wretched Syria, I mourn bitterly with deep sorrow. O Thebans, misguided ones, an evil sound will come upon you while flutes play. You will hear an ominous trumpet sound and witness the land's destruction. Alas, alas for you, wretched one! Alas, evil-minded sea! You will be consumed by fire and destroy people with your salt. There will be such a raging fire on earth, flowing like water, that it will destroy the entire land. It will set hills ablaze, burn rivers, and dry up springs. The world will be thrown into chaos as humanity perishes. The unfortunate ones, severely burned, will look up to a sky not adorned with stars but with fire. They will not perish quickly but will be dissolved from their flesh and burned in spirit for ages. They will learn that God's law is difficult to test and not to be deceived. Earth, seized by force and deceived by any god she accepted at her altars, will turn to smoke through the altered air. Those who prophesy shameful things for gain will suffer greatly. The Hebrews, who wear the shaggy skins of sheep, will prove false, as they have no inheritance. They will speak empty words about sorrows and change their way of life, misleading the just. But the faithful, who truly seek to appease their God, will not be misled.

In the third cycle of years, starting with the eighth, a new world will emerge.

Night will be continuous and without light. Then, the terrible stench of brimstone, a sign of murder, will spread around. People will be slain at night and by hunger. At that time, God will create a pure mind in humanity and establish the human race as it was before. No one will plow fields with a round plow or guide oxen to till the soil. There will be no vineyards or crops; instead, everyone will eat dew-like manna with white teeth. God will be among them and will teach them as He has taught me, the sorrowful one. For I have committed many evil deeds with knowledge and have performed many reckless actions wickedly. I have had countless beds, but no marriage has been honored. I, unfaithful, have brought a harsh oath to all. I have turned away those in need and have gone into isolated places, ignoring God's word. Because of this, fire will consume me and continue to gnaw at me. I will not live forever; a time of suffering will destroy me. Men will build a tomb for me by the sea and will kill me with stones. For I have given my father's dear son in death. Strike me, strike all; for this is how I will live and keep my eyes fixed on heaven.

Sibylline Oracles - VIII

The Sibylline Oracles, a collection of prophetic writings attributed to the ancient Sibyls, serve as an intriguing intersection of Greco-Roman and Judeo-Christian traditions. Book VIII of the Sibylline Oracles, in particular, is a complex and multifaceted text that encapsulates the tumultuous historical and religious transformations of the late antiquity period. Emerging from a milieu where pagan, Jewish, and Christian elements intertwined, Book VIII reflects the syncretic nature of its time, blending apocalyptic fervor with political commentary and theological reflection. This book is characterized by its vivid imagery and prophetic declarations, often addressing themes of divine judgment, eschatological hope, and the ultimate triumph of good over evil. The text stands out for its rich intertextuality, drawing from earlier prophetic traditions while reinterpreting them in light of contemporary events and expectations. The oracles in this book often exhibit a dual-layered message: on one hand, they serve as a critique of the prevailing Roman power structures, while on the other, they offer a vision of a new divine order that transcends the temporal realm. Scholars have noted the influence of Jewish apocalyptic literature, particularly in the emphasis on cosmic battles and the coming of a messianic figure, which are recurrent motifs throughout the oracles. Furthermore, Book VIII's prophetic voice is notable for its rhetorical power and poetic form, utilizing a variety of literary devices to convey its profound messages. The language of the oracles is imbued with a sense of urgency and moral imperative, calling its audience to recognize the signs of the times and to prepare for the impending divine intervention. In sum, Book VIII of the Sibylline Oracles is a remarkable text that offers valuable insights into the religious psyche and socio-political conditions of its era, making it an essential subject of study for those interested in ancient prophecy, early Christian literature, and the historical dynamics of religious transformation.

I proclaim the coming wrath of God in the final age against a faithless world, prophesying to every city. From the time the great tower fell and human languages were divided, Egypt's royal power was established, followed by that of the Persians, Medes, Ethiopians, Assyrians, and Babylonians. Then came the prideful Macedonians. Fifth, the lawless kingdom of the Italians will bring many troubles to all people and will exploit the efforts of men from every land. This kingdom will lead unruly kings westward, create laws, and subject everything to its rule. God's justice is slow, but it comes eventually. Fire will then destroy everything, turning it back into dust, including the highest mountains and all flesh.

The root of all ills is greed and ignorance. People will love deceitful gold and silver above everything else, choosing them over the light of the sun, the heavens, the sea, the fertile earth, and even God, who gives everything. Ignorance, the source of disorder and conflict, will be a catalyst for wars and disrupt familial relationships. Gold will make marriage dishonorable, and land and sea will be divided among the wealthy. Those who seek to control land that feeds many will do so under false pretenses, enslaving people for their own gain. If the vast earth were not so far from the stars, it would be owned by the rich, and God would have prepared another world for the poor.

Rome will one day receive a deserved divine punishment. It will be the first to fall, utterly destroyed by fire, with its wealth consumed and its ruins inhabited by wolves and foxes. Rome will become desolate as if it had never existed. Where will your Palladium be then? What god will save you, whether crafted from gold, stone, or brass? Where will your Senate's decrees be? Where will be the lineage of Rhea, Cronus, or Zeus, and all those you worshipped—lifeless idols and images of the dead whose tombs will now be sources of pride for the unfortunate? After you have had fifteen debauched kings, a gray-haired lord will emerge from the near sea. He will travel the world swiftly, bringing gifts and plundering gold and silver. He will partake in Magian rites, present his child as a deity, and reveal ancient deceptions. The time will come when he, too, will perish, and people will lament, realizing the evil day is near. Fathers and children will mourn together by the sorrowful banks of the Tiber. At the end of days, three rulers will come, representing the divine power of the heavens. One will be an old king who will hoard all the world's goods. When the fugitive from the ends of the earth returns, he will distribute these goods, enriching Asia. Then Rome will mourn, putting aside its purple robes and wearing mourning dress. Your arrogance and glory will be no more, and the eagle-bearing legions will fall. Your power will be questioned, and no land will be subjected to your rule. The world will be in chaos when the Almighty judges the souls of the living and the dead.

Parents will be indifferent to their children and vice versa, due to impiety and unforeseen distress. You will face gnashing of teeth, devastation, and destruction of cities. When a fiery dragon rises from the waves and brings famine and war among relatives, the end of the world will be near, and the final judgment of God will come for the righteous.

Rome will first experience God's wrath—implacable and brutal. You will face a time of bloodshed and misery. Alas for you, reckless land, for you did not understand from where you came naked into the sunlight, nor where you will return naked to face judgment. With gigantic hands coming from above, you will be buried under the earth, disappearing in naphtha, asphalt, and brimstone. You will become burning dust for ages, and those who witness this will hear mournful wailing from Hades. There will be no slaves, lords, tyrants, kings, leaders, learned speakers, or judges. No sacrifices or rituals will take place. There will be no musical instruments or war sounds. In death, there is only eternal sameness, and you will face the bitter day of punishment and gnashing of teeth. No more shall foreigners or other nations bow to your yoke. You will be plundered and made to suffer for what you have imposed on others until you pay back everything and become a symbol of triumph and reproach. The sixth race of Latin kings will end, leaving behind their scepters. Another king from the same lineage will rule every land with full power, his children ruling by God's decree. This will be the final decree as time progresses. When Egypt's kings reach their limit, a new people will come to plunder, enemy of the Hebrews. Ares will defeat Ares, and Rome's power will fall while still in its prime. An ancient queen surrounded by cities will no longer prevail, and one from Asia will come to rule. After completing these deeds, he will come to Rome, and after 348 years, an ill-fated fate will complete Rome's name. Ah, woe is me! Will I ever see that fateful day when Rome, the thrice-cursed city, meets its end? This fate will be most severe for all Latins. It will honor a leader who comes from Asia in a Trojan chariot with hidden children, a soul full of fiery resolve. But when he reaches the isthmus and looks wistfully across the sea, dark blood will trail the mighty beast. A dog will chase a lion that destroys shepherds. The beast will lose his scepter and descend to Hades. Rhodes will face a final and greatest calamity, and Thebes will suffer a terrible conquest. Egypt will be destroyed by its wicked rulers. The man who survives this destruction, if he manages to escape, will be thrice blessed and four times fortunate. Rome will become a mere ruin, Delos will be dull, and Samos will be reduced to sand. After this, the Persians will face a great misfortune due to their pride, and all their arrogance will come to nothing. Then, a holy ruler of the entire earth will rise, having resurrected the dead, and will reign for all ages. The Most High will bring three-fold calamity upon Rome and upon all people. They will perish by their own actions, despite the opportunity to have chosen a better path.

When famine, plague, and relentless warfare increase, the previous daring ruler will convene the senate to plot complete destruction. Dry land will bloom with leaves, and the heavens will bring forth rainstorms, flames, and strong winds. The earth will be plagued with poisonous growths. Yet people, with shameless souls, will act as if they fear neither the wrath of

God nor men. They will forsake modesty, seeking out greedy tyrants and violent sinners, who will never be satisfied. Under their rule, people will perish. The stars will fall into the sea, one by one, but men will see a brilliant comet, a sign of impending distress, war, and battle. I hope I do not live to see the reign of a frivolous ruler but rather the time when divine grace will prevail, and the holy child will bind the destroyer of mankind, revealing the depths and covering the earth with a wooden canopy. When ten generations have passed into Hades, a female ruler will come to power. God will allow many evils to increase under her reign, leading to an impious age. The sun will shine faintly at night, stars will disappear from the sky, and storms will devastate the earth. The dead will rise, the lame will run swiftly, the deaf will hear, the blind will see, and the mute will speak. Life and wealth will become universal. The land, undivided by walls or fences, will produce abundant fruit, and sweet wine, milk, and honey will flow. Judgment will come from the immortal God, the great king. When God changes the seasons, bringing summer from winter, oracles will be fulfilled. But when the world has perished...

Jesus Christ, Son of God, Savior, and Cross.

The earth will tremble with the sign of judgment. The King who is to reign forever will come from heaven to judge all flesh and the whole world. Faithful and faithless people will see the Most High with the saints at the end of time. God will judge the souls of the living and the dead from his throne, when the world becomes a desert and a thorny wasteland.

People will cast away their idols and all their wealth. A searching fire will consume earth, heaven, and sea, burning even the gates of Hades' prison. All the dead will come to the light of the saints, while the lawless will be punished by fire for ages. Every secret deed will be revealed as God exposes the hidden truths. There will be universal lamentation and gnashing of teeth. The sun will be eclipsed, and the stars will dance no more. The heavens will be rolled up, and the moon's light will fade. Valleys will be raised, and mountains will be leveled, leaving no height remaining among men. The seas will no longer have vessels sailing on them.

The earth will be scorched, and its streams and fountains will dry up. A lamentable trumpet sound will echo from heaven, mourning the wretched state of humanity and the world's suffering. The earth will reveal Tartarean chaos. All kings will come before God's judgment seat, and a stream of fire and brimstone will flow from heaven. For all mortals, there will be a sign—a distinguished seal. The wooden cross, beloved by the faithful, will be a symbol of salvation for the pious, though it will also be a stumbling block for the world.

The elect will be illuminated by water from twelve springs, and an iron rod will rule them. The Savior, as foretold in acrostics and signs from God, is the immortal King who suffered for our sake. Moses symbolized Him when he raised his arms to defeat Amalek by faith, showing that the people were chosen and honored by God.

The Savior, who will come in mortal form to offer hope, will grant beautiful form to human flesh and restore faith. He will heal the wounds caused by the serpent's deception and will give eternal life to those who believe. As prophesied, He will come to creation through a holy virgin, baptize with water, perform miracles, and provide for thousands from a small amount of food. He will call the blessed and show love to the suffering, and He will search hearts and heal every sickness.

At last, He will be handed over to lawless men. He will come to those without faith, who will strike Him with harsh blows and spit at Him with impure mouths. He will openly offer His holy back to be whipped. [For He shall entrust Himself to the world through a holy virgin.] He will remain silent when beaten, so that no one will know who He is or where He came from, even as He speaks to the dead.

He will wear a crown of thorns, which will be an eternal ornament. They will pierce His side with a reed, fulfilling their laws. The reeds symbolize the anger and revenge that were previously stirred up by other spirits. When these things are accomplished, every law that was established by men for disobedient people will be abolished.

He will spread His arms and measure the entire world. They will offer Him gall for food and vinegar to drink; this inhospitable meal will be presented to Him. The temple curtain will be torn in two, and there will be three hours of darkness at midday. This will signal the end of secret temple rituals and the law, which had been overshadowed by worldly concerns, when the Eternal came to earth.

He will descend into Hades, bringing hope to all the saints, announcing the end of the ages and the final day. On the third day, He will defeat death. Rising from the dead, He will be the first to show the elect the beginning of resurrection. He will cleanse their former wickedness with the waters of eternal life, so that they may be born anew and free from the unlawful customs of the world.

Then, He will openly appear to His own people in the flesh, as He was before, showing the marks on His hands and feet, which represent the four cardinal directions: east, west, south, and north. The world's many powers will have conspired to execute such a lawless and condemnable act against our Example.

Daughter of Zion, holy one, rejoice! Despite your suffering, your King is coming, riding on a foal. He will come humbly to lift the heavy yoke that has oppressed us and to annul our godless laws and compulsory bonds. Recognize your God, who is also God's Son; honor Him and hold Him in your heart. Love Him from your soul and praise His name.

Reject your former associations and cleanse yourself from their blood. He is not appeased by your songs or prayers, nor does He heed perishable sacrifices, being imperishable Himself. Instead, offer the holy hymn of understanding and recognize who He is, and you will then see the Father.

Then, all the elements of the world—air, earth, sea, light of gleaming fire, heavenly sky, and night—will merge into one, desolate form. The stars will fall from heaven, and no birds will fly in the air or walk on the earth; wild beasts will perish. There will be no voices from men, beasts, or birds. The world will be silent and disordered.

A mighty, threatening sound will come from the deep sea, and all sea creatures will die. No ships will sail on the waves. The earth will groan, stained with blood from wars. All souls will gnash their teeth, tormented by thirst, famine, plague, and murder. They will call death beautiful, but death will flee from them. Neither death nor night will provide them rest. They will vainly seek help from God, who rules on high. In response, He will turn His face away from them. For He gave erring humanity signs of repentance through seven ages by the hands of an undefiled virgin. God Himself has shown me all these things in my mind, and everything I have spoken will be accomplished. I know the number of the sands and the measures of the sea. I understand the deepest places of the earth and the gloomy depths of Tartarus. I know the numbers of the stars, the trees, all the tribes of animals—quadrupeds, fish, birds, and humans, both those who are living now and those yet to be born, as well as the dead. I fashioned the forms and minds of men, granted them reason, and taught them knowledge. I created eyes and ears to see and hear, discerning every thought and being conscious of all things. I will still be present, and in the future, I will convict and punish what any mortal did in secret. I will come to the judgment seat of God and speak to mortal men.

I understand the mute and hear those who do not speak. I know the full height from earth to heaven, the beginning, and the end, for I made heaven and earth. All things have proceeded from Him; He knows everything from the beginning to the end. I alone am God, and there is no other God. People shape images from wood and treat them as divine, singing praises to lifeless idols through meaningless rituals. Forsaking the Creator, they become slaves to immorality. Despite possessing everything, they offer gifts to things that cannot help them, treating these offerings as if they were for my honor, filling feasts with sacrifices meant for their own dead. They burn flesh and bones, pour out blood to demons, and light candles to me, the giver of light, as if I thirst for offerings to idols that cannot provide any aid.

I do not need your burnt offerings, libations, or polluted smoke, nor do I desire the blood of sacrifices. These rites are performed in memory of kings and tyrants, as if dead demons were gods, and the people perform godless and destructive services. They wrongly call their images gods, abandoning the Creator and believing that their hope and life come from these inanimate objects. They trust in evil while being wholly ignorant of good.

I set before them two paths: life and death, with judgment to choose the good life. But they rushed towards death and eternal fire. Man is made in my image, endowed with reason. Prepare for him a pure table without blood, and fill it with good things. Provide the hungry with bread, the thirsty with drink, and clothe the naked from your own labor with clean hands. Restore the afflicted, aid the weary, and offer a living sacrifice to me, the living God, by sowing piety. Thus, I might grant you immortal fruits and eternal light. When I test everything by fire, I will separate what is pure from what is not. I will roll up the heavens and open the depths of the earth. I will raise the dead, ending fate and the sting of death. Then, I will come for judgment, evaluating both the pious and the impious. I will place ram with ram, shepherd with shepherd, calf with calf, for testing. Those who are exalted and proven by trial, and who have silenced others, will be compared to those who lead a holy life. Those not proven before me, driven by love of gain, will withdraw.

There will be no more days of worry or changing seasons—no more spring, winter, summer, autumn, sunrise, or sunset. I will make a long day and bring forth light that will endure through the ages.

You who are self-begotten, undefiled, true, and eternal, measuring by your power from heaven the fiery blast, and controlling the thundering crashes, and calming the roaring of storms and heavy rains—you blunt the fiery scourges of lightning, the vast outpour of storms, autumnal hail, and the chilling strokes of winter. Each of these things is marked out in your mind. Whatever you deem good, your Son agrees with. He was begotten in your bosom before all creation, a fellow-counselor with you, creator of mortals and life.

You addressed Him with the first utterance of your mouth: "Let us make man in our own image and give him life-sustaining breath; all things of the world shall serve him, and we will subject everything to him." By your word, all things came into being, and all elements obeyed your command. An eternal being was formed in a mortal figure, along with heaven, air, fire, earth, sea, sun, moon, stars, hills, night, day, sleep, wakefulness, spirit, passion, soul, understanding, art, might, strength, and all living things—swimming creatures, birds, land animals, amphibians, reptiles, and those of dual nature. Acting according to your will, everything was arranged.

In the latest times, the earth was visited. A new light rose from the womb of the virgin Mary, and He put on a mortal form. Gabriel first revealed His pure form and announced to the maiden: "O virgin, receive God into your womb." He breathed God's grace upon her, and she was filled with alarm and wonder. She trembled at the unexpected message and was overwhelmed, but her heart was soon warmed by the angel's voice. Joy replaced her fear, and her heart, touched by the message, found confidence.

The Word entered her womb, and in time, became flesh and took on a human form. The boy, born of a virgin, was a great wonder to mankind, but not to God the Father or God the Son. The earth rejoiced at the birth, the heavenly throne celebrated, and the world was glad. The prophetic star honored by the wise men pointed to the manger where the child was born. Shepherds, goatherds, and keepers of flocks were shown the newborn in Bethlehem, the chosen land of the Word.

Practice humility of mind, hate cruel deeds, and love your neighbor as yourself. Love God from your soul and serve Him. We, descended from the holy lineage of heavenly Christ, are of common blood and should remember to worship with joy. We walk the paths of piety and truth. We should not enter the inner sanctuaries of temples, pour libations to carved images, or honor them with prayers, flowers, or lamps. We should not adorn them with shining votive offerings or pollute the light of heaven with the smoke of flesh-consuming pyres. Instead, we are commanded to praise God with pure minds and cheerful hearts, abundant love, and generous hands, with psalms and songs that honor Him—the imperishable, true, and understanding Father God.

Sibylline Oracles - XI

The Sibylline Oracles, a collection of prophetic writings attributed to the legendary Sibyls of the ancient world, provide a fascinating confluence of pagan and Judeo-Christian traditions, and Book XI stands out as a particularly intriguing example of this synthesis. Composed in a period when the boundaries between different religious traditions were often fluid, this book is believed to date from the Hellenistic era, a time when Greek cultural influence permeated the Mediterranean basin and beyond. The text reflects the rich tapestry of the period, with its blend of mythological motifs, apocalyptic visions, and ethical exhortations. Book XI, like the other books of the Sibylline Oracles, was likely compiled by Jewish and early Christian authors who sought to frame their theological narratives within the familiar structure of Greek prophecy, thereby making their teachings more accessible to a Hellenistic audience. This book contains vivid descriptions of cosmic cataclysms and divine judgments, interwoven with moral teachings that echo the wisdom literature of the Hebrew Bible. The imagery within this text is particularly striking, with its depictions of natural disasters, celestial phenomena, and divine retribution serving as both a warning and a call to repentance. The Sibylline Oracles - XI, is invaluable for understanding the religious and cultural exchanges of the ancient world, offering insights into how different traditions interacted, merged, and transformed over time. Book XI's blend of Greek prophetic style with Jewish and Christian eschatology highlights the dynamic religious thought of the Hellenistic period, making it essential for studying the intersections of ancient religions and the development of apocalyptic literature.

O world of men, spread wide and diverse, With long walls and vast cities, Countless nations across the east, west, south, and north, Divided by different languages and kingdoms, I am about to speak of the worst things.

From the time when a great flood came upon the early humans, And the Almighty Himself destroyed that race with many waters, He brought in a new race of humans. They, setting themselves against heaven, built an incomprehensibly tall tower, And once again their languages were scattered. God's wrath was poured out upon them, Causing the tower to fall, And stirring up enmity among them. Thus, a tenth generation of mortals arose since these events.

The whole earth was divided among different peoples And languages, which I will list and reveal through acrostics, Using the initial letter to indicate each name. First, Egypt shall receive royal power, And then many wise men will govern. Afterward, a fierce and strong ruler will arise, A close-combat fighter with a sword who will wage war against the righteous. During his rule, Egypt will see a fearful sign, Which, though initially distressing, will eventually provide relief from famine With a bountiful harvest. The law-giver, a prisoner himself, will be nourished By the East and descendants of Assyrian men. His name will be known by the measure of the number ten.

When ten judgments come upon Egypt from heaven, I will again declare these things to you. Memphis, mourn greatly! The Erythraean Sea will destroy your people. When the people of twelve tribes leave The land of destruction by command of the Immortal, The Lord God will also give mankind a new law. A mighty king, magnanimous, shall rule over the Hebrews, His name derived from sandy Egypt, a man of uncertain origin, And he will show Memphis outward signs of favor, Watching over many things in wars.

When the tenth kingdom has been completed twelve times, Plus seven more, up to a total of a thousand, Leaving others behind, The Persian empire will arise. An evil will then befall the Jews, With famine and pestilence that they cannot escape. When a Persian ruler's descendant lays down the scepter, After a period of five times four years plus a hundred more, And you complete a hundred and nine years, Then Persians and Medes will be given over as slaves, Destroyed by fierce battles. Immediately, an evil will befall Persians, Assyrians, Egyptians, Libyans, Ethiopians, Carians, Pamphylians, and all other mortals. A new ruler will come, seizing power, Plundering races without compassion. The Persians will wail mournfully by the Tigris, And Egypt will weep profusely.

A wealthy man of Indian birth Will inflict many troubles on the Median land, Repaying the injustices of the past. Alas for you, Median nation, you will serve Ethiopian men beyond the land of Meroe, For seven hundred years, bearing a yoke of servitude.

Then an Indian, dark-skinned and gray-haired, With a great soul, will become the lord, Bringing many troubles upon the East through fierce battles, Treating you with even greater disdain, And destroying many of your people. But when he reaches the twentieth and tenth year of his reign, Among them, also seven and ten, Every nation with royal power will revolt, Seeking freedom for three years, But he will return and subjugate all again, And every nation will willingly obey once more.

There will be great peace throughout the world.

Then a powerful king will rule over the Assyrians, A man of high status, Who will persuade all to follow God's laws, And all arrogant kings will tremble before him, As he will bring everything under his control, Building a grand temple for God And destroying the idols. He will unite the tribes, And his name will be signified by two hundred, Representing the eighteenth letter. But when he rules for twenty-five decades, There will be as many kings as there are tribes, clans, cities, isles, coasts, and fruitful lands. One of these kings will be mighty, And many other kings will submit to him, Offering their riches to his descendants.

They will rule for eight decades of decades, Until their time ends.

But when a fierce wild beast comes With the war god Ares, a terrible wrath Will fall upon the Persian land. What a bloody massacre it will be when a stronger ruler comes to you; Then I will shout these things again.

When the Italian land brings forth A great wonder to mortals, Young children will cry by a pure spring In a shaded cave, a descendant of a wild beast That feeds on sheep. As he grows up, he will cause many to fall On the seven hills, and their numbers will be significant, Building strong walls and waging fierce wars around them. Again, there will be revolts Among the people, including the land of Egypt, And I will again announce these things. Egypt will suffer greatly, And once more there will be revolts from within.

O wretched Phrygia, I weep for you; For from Greece, the land of horse tamers, Conquest will come upon you, Bringing war and plague through fierce battles. Ilium, I mourn for you; From Sparta will come a vengeful spirit With a deadly sting, bringing you Great suffering, troubles, and wails, When skilled warriors, the noblest Greek heroes Beloved of Ares, begin the fight. One of these will be a strong and brave king; He will commit terrible deeds for his brother. They will destroy the famed walls of Phrygian Troy; When fifty years have passed filled with savage wars, A wooden trick will suddenly appear, And you will fall before it, not realizing It's a Greek ambush. Alas, how many will die in one night, And how much spoil will be carried away by Hades, Weeping over the old man's losses! Yet those who come after will have undying fame. A great king, a hero descended from Zeus, Will bear a name that starts with the first letter of the alphabet. He will return home in an orderly manner. But he will fall at the hands of a treacherous woman.

Then a child from the line of Assaracus, A renowned hero and valiant man, Will come out of the burning ruins of Troy, Fleeing from his homeland because of the horrors of war; Carrying his elderly father on his shoulders And leading his son by the hand, He will undertake a pious task, Escaping the flames of burning Troy, And navigating through crowds and treacherous seas. He will have a name of three syllables, Signified by the first letter of the alphabet. He will establish a city for the powerful Latins. But in his fifteenth year, he will die Drowned in the depths of the sea. Even though he will be dead, His legacy will endure, Ruling over lands from the Euphrates To the Tigris and beyond, To the lands of the Parthians.

An old, wise minstrel will arise, Called the wisest among men, Whose profound understanding will enlighten the world; He will write according to his insight, Crafting marvelous works. At times, he will use words and measures from my writings, Being the first to reveal my books, But he will keep them hidden from men Until the end of time. Once these things are fulfilled, The Greeks will fight among themselves again, Along with Assyrians, Arabs, Medes, Persians, Sicilians, Lydians, Thracians, and Bithynians, And those living by the fertile Nile. God will send confusion among them. A terrible Assyrian, a base-born man With a beastly soul, will appear suddenly, Cutting through every land and sea. Then, faithless Greece will suffer greatly.

O wretched Greece, how much you will lament! For seventy-seven years, You will be the miserable battleground of all tribes. Then a Macedonian man will bring new woes to Hellas, Destroying Thrace and causing Ares' toil On the isles, coasts, and warlike Triballi. He will be among the greatest fighters, Bearing a name that signifies fifty times ten. His reign will be short, But he will leave behind the greatest kingdom on earth. Yet he will fall by the hand of a lowly spearman While he is thought to be in quiet peace. Afterward, a great-hearted child of this man Will rule, starting with a name That begins the alphabet, But his lineage will eventually end. Not a true son of Zeus, but rather a bastard son Of Cronos as many believe him to be. He will plunder many cities And bring great suffering to Europe, Abusing the city of Babylon terribly, And every land under the sun. He will sail both east and west alone.

O Babylon, woe to you! You will serve triumphs, having once been called a queen. Ares will come to Asia, and many of your children will die. You will then send forth a royal warrior Named with the number four, A spear expert among mighty warriors, Terrible with bow and arrows. Then famine and war will dominate Cilicia and Assyria; Kings of high spirit will endure Heart-consuming strife. Flee from the former king; Do not stay nor fear unhappiness. A dreadful lion, a beast of prey, Wild and unjust, will come upon you. Avoid the thunder-striking man. Asia will bear a terrible burden, And the earth will drink much blood. When a prosperous city is founded In Egypt by Ares of Pella, Named after him, fate and death, He will be treacherously betrayed By his companions. Barbaric murder will destroy him While he is with his allies In Babylon, after leaving the Indians.

In a few years, other kings will arise, Each ruling over their own tribes, Arrogant and treacherous, devouring their people. A great-hearted hero will then emerge, Conquering all of Europe, But he will soon face his own fate and die. Following him, there will be eight more kings From his lineage, all sharing the same name. At that time, Egypt will have a powerful queen And a great city, Alexandria, A shining jewel among cities, The sole metropolis of her realm. Memphis will criticize those in power. Peace will prevail throughout the world, And the fertile land will bear more fruit. But then disaster will strike the Jews; They will not escape from famine and disease. The new world of fertile land Will receive many wandering people.

The eight kings of marshy Egypt Will rule for two hundred and thirty-three years. Though not all will perish, A female from their line will cause great harm, Betraying her own kingdom. After their evil deeds, one by one They will fall; a king will kill his own father, And then be killed by his own son, Before another heir can rise. But a new lineage will begin, With a queen from the land by the Nile, Which flows into the sea through seven mouths. Her name will be lovely, associated with the number twenty, And she will demand and gather vast wealth, But treachery will come from her own people. Once again, wars and great slaughter Will afflict the land of the dark-skinned.

When many rulers govern fertile Rome, Examples of tyranny, not happiness, With thousands of leaders and overseers Of the public assemblies, The mightiest Caesars will rule, All suffering ill-fated destinies. The last Caesar will bear the number ten, And he will die at the hands of a hostile man. The youth of Rome will bury him piously, Honoring his memory with a tribute.

When your time comes to an end, After three hundred and thirty years From the reign of the founder, child of a wild beast, No longer will there be a ruler with a fixed term; Instead, a godlike king will arise. Egypt, recognize this king when he arrives; Dreadful Ares with his shining helm Will certainly come. For you, widowed Egypt, A capture will follow; Your land will be surrounded by terrible wars. After suffering so much, you will flee From those who have recently been wounded, And come to the dreadful man himself. This marriage will be your end. Alas, ill-fated bride, You will give your royal power to the Roman king, Repaying all you did before with masculine strength; You will offer the entire land, From Libya to the dark-skinned peoples, To this relentless man. You will no longer be a widow but will live With a fearsome lion, a fierce warrior. You will be unhappy and unknown, Leaving behind your former grandeur. The stately tomb will enclose you, And many will mourn you, While the dreadful king laments.

Then Egypt will become a toiling slave, Bearing trophies against the Indians for many years, Serving shamefully and weeping tears Alongside the fruit-bearing Nile, After accumulating great wealth, She will feed a race of fierce men. Egypt, you will become spoil for many beasts, Yet still provide laws for others. Once delighting in great kings, You will now be a wretched slave, Paying for the suffering you caused With the plow on their necks And fields irrigated with mortal tears. Therefore, the eternal God in heaven Will utterly destroy you and send you to sorrow, Making you atone for past wrongs. When you consult the books, You will not tremble, for you will understand All that is to come and what has been foretold Through our words. No one will call the prophetess a mere oracle singer, But now, Lord, end my beautiful song, Free me from frenzy and madness, And grant me a charming voice to sing.

Sibylline Oracles - XII

The Sibylline Oracles, an intriguing collection of prophetic texts spanning several centuries, offer a unique glimpse into the religious and cultural syncretism of the ancient Mediterranean world. Book XII, one of the later additions to this pseudepigraphal work, is particularly notable for its intricate blending of Jewish, Christian, and Hellenistic themes. This book, likely composed in the late 2nd or early 3rd century CE, reflects the complex interplay of political and theological currents of its time. Its verses are imbued with apocalyptic imagery and eschatological expectations, characteristic of the broader genre of apocalyptic literature. The Sibylline Oracles as a whole are attributed to the Sibyl, a legendary prophetess whose roots trace back to Greek and Roman traditions, though the texts themselves were authored by Jewish and Christian writers seeking to imbue their prophecies with an aura of ancient authority. Book XII, in particular, serves as a potent example of how these communities appropriated and transformed classical motifs to convey their religious messages. The text is replete with references to historical events and figures, often reinterpreted through a theological lens to serve as moral and spiritual lessons. The fusion of prophetic declarations with historical allusions creates a tapestry that is both rich in detail and profound in its implications for understanding the evolution of religious thought during this period. Furthermore, the Sibylline Oracles - XII, played a significant role in shaping the apocalyptic expectations of early Christian communities, influencing subsequent Christian literature and thought. The enduring fascination with these texts lies in their ability to provide a window into the hopes, fears, and spiritual aspirations of a diverse and dynamically evolving religious landscape.

Come now, hear about the sorrowful fate of the Latins' descendants. First of all, after the kings of Egypt had been destroyed, and the earth had swallowed them up, and after the downfall of the Macedonian leader who had brought down both the East and the rich West, a man whom Babylon rejected and stretched out Philip's dead body—whose prophecies were not truly from Zeus or Ammon—then, after many other leaders and warriors and the children of the beast that feeds on sheep, and after six hundred years and twenty decades of Rome's rule, the very first lord from the western sea shall become Rome's ruler. He will be extremely strong and warlike. His name's initial will mark the beginning of the letters, and he will tightly bind you, O fruitful one. He will be filled with the spirit of war, and you will face retribution for the affronts you willingly caused. This great soul will be unmatched in warfare. Before him, Thrace and Sicily will submit, and Memphis will be thrown to the ground due to the wickedness of its rulers and a free woman who will fall under the spear. He will establish laws for peoples and bring everything under his control. He will have great fame and hold his scepter for a long time. There will never be another ruler of Rome greater than he, even for an hour, for God has bestowed everything upon him and shown great and marvelous signs on the noble earth. But when a radiant star, shining like the sun, appears in the midday sky, then the secret Word of the Most High will come to earth in human form. With him, the power of Rome and the illustrious Latins will grow. Yet this mighty king will die according to his fate, passing on his royal power to another. After him, a strong warrior wearing a purple mantle will rule. His name will correspond to the number three hundred, and he will conquer the Medes and Parthians who shoot arrows. He will overturn the great city and bring misfortune to Egypt, the Assyrians, the Colchians, and the Germans living by the Rhine's waters. He will ravage the high-gate city near the River Eridanus, which is devising evil. He will soon fall, struck by a gleaming sword.

Another ruler will come after him, using deceit, whose name's initial will be three. He will gather a lot of gold and will not be satisfied with wealth but will recklessly plunder everything on earth. However, peace will follow, and the god of war will cease his battles. This ruler will reveal many great things through divination, seeking means of livelihood. But he will bear the greatest sign: many small drops of blood will fall from heaven onto him while he is dying. He will commit many lawless acts and cause great suffering for the Romans. The assembly's leaders will be killed, and famine will strike Cappadocians, Thracians, Macedonians, and Italians.

Only Egypt will provide for many tribes. The king himself, through secret deceit, will craftily destroy a virgin maiden, who will be mourned by the citizens. They will curse the king in their grief. While Rome remains strong, this powerful man will perish. Another ruler will come after him, corresponding to the number twenty. This ruler will bring wars and suffering to the Sauromatians, Thracians, and Triballi, and Roman Ares will tear everything apart. A fearful sign will occur during this ruler's reign: during midday, there will be darkness, and a shower of stones will fall from the sky. Then, the vigorous judge of the Italians will meet his end by his own fate. A terrifying man will come next, corresponding to the number fifty. He will destroy many of the wealthiest citizens from various cities. He will be like a dreadful serpent, waging terrible wars, stretching his hands to end his own lineage, engaging in countless feats, and even making the mountain between two seas flow with blood. He will disappear from sight but will return, making himself equal to a god, though he will be proven false. While he rules, there will be profound peace and no fears. From the ocean, untrodden waters will flow and cut through Italy. He will hold numerous contests for the people and will compete himself, singing and playing the harp. Later, he will flee, leaving the royal power, and will die in Illyria, paying for the harm he caused. After him, three rulers will come, two of whom will have names with the number seventy, and the third will have a name starting with the third letter of the alphabet. One ruler here and another there will fall due to strong Ares' hand. Then, a mighty ruler will come, destroying the pious and strong-minded. He will overthrow Phœnicia and Assyria. A sword will strike the holy land of Jerusalem, even to the farthest edge of the Tiberian Sea. Alas, Phœnicia, how much you will suffer, burdened with your tightly bound trophies! And every nation will tread upon you. Alas, Assyria, you will see your young children serving among enemies and with wives. All your means of life and wealth will perish. God's wrath will bring grievous woe upon you because you did not follow His law but worshipped idols with unseemly practices. There will be wars, fights, homicides, famines, pestilences, and confusion in cities. But a revered king with a mighty soul will fall by necessity at the end of his life. Then, two other chief men, honoring the memory of their great father, will rule, bringing glory in warfare. One of them will be noble and lordly, with a name corresponding to three hundred. Yet he will also fall by treachery, not in battle but struck in Rome by a two-edged sword. After him, a powerful and warlike ruler with a name corresponding to four letters will rule the mighty realm. Everyone on earth will love him. During his reign, there will be peace from war, and all will willingly serve him, not by force. Cities will be under his control, and he will be in command. Heavenly Sabaoth will bring him much glory, the eternal God who dwells on high. Famine will then devastate Pannonia and all the Celtic lands, causing widespread destruction. Some will suffer here, others there. The Assyrians, who live along the Orontes River, will experience both great structures and decorations that are considered remarkable. The great king will have a special affection for these and will favor them above all others. However, he will receive a severe wound in his chest and, towards the end of his life, will be treacherously struck by a friend within the sacred halls of the royal palace. After his death, a new ruler will come, a venerable man whose reign will last fifty years. He will cause significant destruction in Rome, killing many of its inhabitants and citizens. However, he will rule for only a short time and will die wounded in the underworld due to the actions of a previous king. Following him, another strong warrior king will rise, marked by the number three hundred. He will rule and devastate the land of Thrace, which is diverse, and he will also conquer the powerful Germans living by the Rhine and the Iberians who shoot arrows. Additionally, the Jews will face severe hardships, and Phoenicia will be soaked with blood. The walls of the Assyrians will fall to numerous warriors, and once again, a destructive force will ravage them completely. Then, the mighty God will bring threats of earthquakes, great plagues, unexpected snowstorms, and strong thunderstorms to every land. The great king, a Celt who roams the mountains, will not escape an unseemly fate. Exhausted from battle and hastening eagerly, he will be defeated; his corpse will be hidden by foreign dust, the kind of dust named after the Nemean flower. After him, another ruler will emerge, a silver-haired man whose name will be associated with the sea and consist of four syllables. His name will start with the first letter of the alphabet and will be associated with war. He will build temples in every city, oversee the world, and provide gifts, including much gold and amber. He will keep the mysteries of magicians away from the sanctuaries and will introduce more important things for men. He will be a rich-voiced minstrel, participate in lawful activities, and administer justice. However, he will die by his own fate. After him, three rulers will come. The third will rule for thirty years. Then, another king, belonging to the first group, will take over. Following him, another commander will emerge, marked by the number seventy. Their names will be honored, but they will destroy people marked by many scars, including Britons, powerful Moors, Dacians, and Arabs. When the last of these rulers dies, Ares, who had been previously wounded, will rise again to defeat the Parthians completely. The king will then be killed by a treacherous wild beast while trying to defend himself.

Next, a new ruler skilled in many ways will come. He will have a name reflecting the first mighty king of the first group and will be both good and powerful. For the illustrious Latins, this strong ruler will achieve many things in memory of his father. He will decorate Rome's walls with gold, silver, and ivory. He will visit marketplaces and temples with a strong man. At some point, a terrible wound will arise during the Roman wars, and he will sack the entire Germanic land. A great sign from heaven will appear, and in response to the king's piety, men in bronze armor will be saved from distress. When the king prays, God in heaven will send unseasonable rain. Once these events are fulfilled, the renowned dominion of the great pious king will end. At the end of his life, he will proclaim his son as his successor and die according to his fate, leaving the royal power to the ruler with golden hair. This new ruler, with a name corresponding to twenty, will be born a king from his father's lineage and will possess superior mental powers. He will rival the great Hercules and be renowned for his skills in arms, hunting, and horsemanship. However, he will live in constant danger.

While he rules, there will be a terrifying sign: a great mist will cover Rome, obscuring visibility. Following this, wars and sorrowful troubles will arise. The king will become infatuated with love and will disgrace his offspring with inappropriate wedding songs. In his helpless isolation, the mighty and destructive man will suffer in a bathhouse, bound by treacherous fate. Know that Rome's fatal end is near due to the pursuit of power. Many in the Palladian halls will perish at the hands of Ares. Rome will be left bereft and will face the consequences of its many wars.

My heart mourns deeply, for from the time when Rome's first king established good laws and the Word of the great immortal God came to earth, until the nineteenth reign, two hundred years, forty years, and six months will have passed. The twentieth king, when struck by sharp brass, will cause bloodshed in your houses, making your lineage a widow. He will have a name corresponding to the number eighty and will be burdened with old age. However, he will soon make you a widow, bringing many warriors, overthrows, murders, and deadly feuds, and in confusion, many horses and men will fall on the plain.

Then another ruler will come with a name corresponding to ten. He will bring many sorrows, groans, and plunder. He will be short-lived and will fall due to Ares, struck by gleaming iron. Another ruler will then appear, marked by the number fifty. He will be a warrior from the East and will come to Thrace. He will flee to the land of Bithynia and the Cilician plain, but Ares, the life-destroyer, will swiftly defeat him in Assyrian fields. Following him, a crafty and deceitful man from the West will rise. His name will correspond to the number two hundred. He will contrive a war for royal power against the Assyrians, raising a large army and subjugating everything. He will rule over the Romans with his strength but will be filled with deceitful intentions, a violent and treacherous serpent. He will destroy high-born men for their wealth and, as a plunderer, will strip the earth of all its riches while people perish. He will eventually head east, full of deceit.

A youthful Caesar will then come, named after a powerful Macedonian lord. Surrounded by conflict, he will escape the deceptions of the coming king within the army's ranks. The ruler who uses barbaric customs will perish suddenly, killed by Ares with gleaming iron. Even in death, he will be torn apart by the people. Following this, the kings of Persia will rise, and Roman Ares will remain the Roman lord. Phrygia will groan with earthquakes. Alas, Laodicea! Alas, Hierapolis! You were the first to be swallowed by the earth. Rome will face immense suffering, and many will wail as they perish at the hands of Ares. The fate of men will be grim. The coming ruler will hasten to Italy and fall by gleaming iron, acquiring hatred for his mother's sake. Seasons vary, and not all are immediately known. Only those who honor God and avoid idolatry will find happiness. Now, Lord of the World, Immortal King, you who have inspired me with the divine oracle, let my words cease. I do not fully understand what I say; you are the one speaking through me. Let me rest a while and set aside this divine song, for my heart is weary from foretelling royal power with these divine words.

Sibylline Oracles - XIII

The Sibylline Oracles, prophetic texts spanning several centuries, merge Hellenistic, Jewish, and early Christian thought, providing a unique view of ancient apocalyptic traditions. Book XIII, in particular, showcases the blend of Greco-Roman and Judeo-Christian eschatological ideas against a backdrop of significant political, social, and religious changes from the 2nd century BCE to the 7th century CE. This book explores themes of divine judgment, cosmic upheaval, and humanity's ultimate fate through symbolic and prophetic imagery. It reflects its era's anxieties and hopes, highlighting the syncretic nature of ancient religious thought. The Oracles, including Book XIII, are both religious texts and historical documents, revealing the beliefs and aspirations of their communities while employing a cryptic style typical of apocalyptic literature.

The great divine God, who is immortal and imperishable, bids me sing again. He is the one who gives and takes away power from kings, and He determines their times of life and death. He has commanded me to deliver these messages about royal power, though I am reluctant. And Ares, the fierce god of war, will cause the downfall of everyone—from children to the elderly who make laws for the assemblies. There will be many wars, battles, murders, famines, plagues, earthquakes, and mighty thunderbolts. The Assyrians will suffer greatly throughout the world, with temples being looted and robbed.

An uprising will occur among the industrious Persians, along with the Indians, Armenians, and Arabians. A Roman king, insatiable for war, will lead his troops against the Assyrians. He will fight as far as the Euphrates River, but will be betrayed by a trusted ally and fall in battle. Following this, a warrior who loves purple will come from Syria to rule. He will be a great terror to Ares, and his son, a Caesar, will dominate the earth. The name of both will be the same, and their reigns will span over five hundred years. Although there will be a brief respite from war, it will not last long. A treacherous leader will betray his people, and terrible wars will follow.

Syrian, Indian, Armenian, Arabian, Persian, and Babylonian kingdoms will destroy each other through fierce battles. When a Roman warrior defeats a German warrior in a naval battle, the Persians will face many years of conflict without victory. Just as a fish cannot swim up a steep rock, and a tortoise cannot fly, so the Persians will be far from victory while Rome thrives in its appointed destiny. While Rome remains prominent, the great city of Macedon will provide grain. However, Alexandrians will suffer greatly due to the conflict among wicked leaders. Strong men who were once feared will beg for peace due to their leaders' cruelty.

The wrath of the mighty God will fall upon the Assyrians, and a mountain stream will devastate them, reaching as far as Cæsar's city and harming the Canaanites. The Pyramus River will irrigate the city of Mopsus, leading to the downfall of the Ægæans due to internal strife. Antioch will not be spared by Ares, as Assyrian wars will surround it. A great leader from Rome will fight against the Persians and gain control. Cities of the Arabians, adorn yourselves with temples, markets, and wealth, but know that you will face great sorrow. Despite your attempts to protect yourselves, you will face betrayal.

Alexandrians who love war will face dreadful wars. Many people will die, and their cities will be destroyed by internal strife. A great soul and his son will fall due to treachery. Following this, a powerful Roman leader from the Dacians will come, with an army of three hundred, and will bring destruction, including the death of his own family. A cunning Roman from Syria will invade Cappadocia, besieging and attacking it mercilessly. Tyana and Mazaka will be captured and enslaved once again. Syria will mourn as it faces devastation, and the goddess Selenian will fail to protect her sacred city. When the Roman invader flees from Syria and crosses the Euphrates, he will face a downfall similar to the fierce Persians. A future Roman king will face invasions and destruction, including famines, plagues, thunderbolts, and wars. Cities will fall into chaos, and the Syrians will suffer greatly. There will be an uprising of industrious Persians who, combined with the Syrians, will destroy the Romans. However, the divine decree will prevent them from fully conquering the Roman laws. Alas, many will flee from the East, and much blood will be spilled. The time will come when living people will speak of death as beautiful, while death itself seems to escape them. I lament for Syria, as it will face a dire blow from the archers, something it never anticipated. The fugitive from Rome will come bearing a great spear. He will cross the Euphrates with his vast army and will wreak havoc, leaving everything in disarray. Oh, wretched Antioch, you will never be named again, as your lack of wisdom will lead to your downfall. Stripped bare and left exposed, you will be deserted and helpless. Anyone who sees you will suddenly weep for your fate.

Hierapolis, you will be triumphant, and so will Berœa. Weep, Chalcis, for your recently wounded sons. Alas, how many people will live near the steep mountains of Casius, Amanus, and the river Lycus, as well as Marsyas and the silver-flowing Pyramus. They will gather their spoils all the way to the edges of Asia, leaving cities in ruins, carrying off idols, and destroying temples. There will be great sorrow among the Gauls, Pannonians, Mysians, and Bithynians when a warrior arrives. Oh, Lycians, a wolf will come to lick your blood when the Sannians, accompanied by the city-wasting Ares and the Carpians, approach to fight. Then, due to his own shameless actions, the illegitimate son will kill the king and will soon perish himself because of his impiety. Another ruler will follow, whose name starts with the letter "First," but he too will quickly fall to Ares, struck by a gleaming sword. The world will once again be thrown into chaos, with people perishing from pestilence and war. The Persians, driven mad by the Ausonians, will struggle under the strain of Ares, forcing their way through. There will be a flight of Romans, and then a priest from Syria, sent by the sun and known everywhere, will arrive and achieve his goals through cunning. The city of the sun will offer prayers, and the Persians will defy the threatening Phoenicians.

When two swift leaders rule the mighty Romans—one with the number seventy and the other with the number three—the stately bull, which plows the earth and stirs up dust with its horns, will cause great harm to a dark-skinned serpent that leaves a trail with its scales. The bull itself will perish. Afterward, another stag with impressive horns, hungry and determined, will come. It will strive to feed on venomous beasts. A fearsome lion, sent from the sun and breathing fire, will then appear. He will destroy the swift stag and the most powerful venomous beast, which makes many noises, and the sideways-moving he-goat. The lion will rule with power, remaining unscathed and unreachable, while the Persians will be weakened.

Lord, King of the world, O God, let our words be restrained, and grant us a charming song.

Sibylline Oracles - XIV

The Sibylline Oracles, a collection of prophetic writings attributed to various Sibyls, have captivated scholars and theologians for centuries due to their enigmatic blend of pagan and Judeo-Christian elements. Book XIV of the Sibylline Oracles, like its counterparts, is a remarkable text that provides a fascinating insight into the syncretic religious milieu of the Hellenistic and early Roman periods. This book, specifically, stands out for its apocalyptic themes, which echo the eschatological expectations prevalent in both Jewish and early Christian thought. The text is believed to have been composed between the 2nd and 4th centuries CE, a period marked by significant religious and political upheaval, which undoubtedly influenced its contents. The Sibylline Oracles' unique structure—comprising cryptic verses and symbolic imagery—poses interpretative challenges but also offers rich material for understanding the interplay between prophecy, politics, and theology. Book XIV's prophecies are particularly noted for their vivid depictions of cosmic cataclysms and divine judgment, reflecting the anxieties and hopes of a society grappling with the complexities of empire and the advent of new religious paradigms. Furthermore, this book, like the rest of the collection, exhibits a fascinating fusion of Greek literary form and Semitic prophetic tradition, underscoring the cultural and intellectual exchanges of the period. The enigmatic nature of the Sibylline Oracles, combined with their profound theological implications, continues to inspire scholarly debate and exploration, making Book XIV an essential text for those seeking to understand the intricate tapestry of ancient prophetic literature.

O men, why do you foolishly dwell on lofty matters as if you were immortal? You have only a brief time of rule over others, and yet all desire to govern. You do not understand that God himself despises the lust for power, especially the insatiable greed of wicked kings. He stirs up darkness against them, so instead of choosing virtuous actions and just thoughts, you all prefer to wear purple robes, seeking wretched battles and violence. Those who are imperishable, whom God dwells among in heaven, will make your rule short-lived, destroying you utterly and toppling one after another.

But when a bull-destroyer comes, confident in his strength, with a grim appearance, and destroys all, he will also tear shepherds apart. They will not achieve victory unless young dogs, pursuing with eagerness through wooded glens, engage in conflict; for a dog once pursued the lion that destroys the shepherds.

Then, a confident lord will arise, named with four syllables and clearly marked by the number one. But he will be swiftly killed by the brazen god of war due to his conflict with insatiable men. After him, two princely rulers will govern, both marked by the number forty. They will bring great peace and justice to the world, but they will be killed by men wearing gleaming helmets who are driven by a need for gold and silver. These men will cunningly assassinate them.

Following this, another fearsome lord will come, young and fierce, whose name will signify seventy. He will betray the army and lead to the destruction of the Roman people, brought about by the wrath of kings. He will demolish every city and hut of the Latins, leaving Rome unrecognizable and reduced to ashes. No trace of her former grandeur will remain. The immortal god from heaven will send lightning and thunderbolts to destroy some, and others will be struck down by his mighty thunderbolts. Rome's strong people and the famous Latins will eventually slay this dreadful ruler, who will become prey for dogs, birds, and wolves.

After him, another ruler, marked by forty, will govern, known for destroying Parthians and Germans, and putting down fearsome beasts that inhabit the oceans and the Euphrates River. Rome will return to its previous state.

But when a great wolf from the West arrives, he will die under powerful Ares, cleaved asunder by sharp brass. Then, another mighty ruler from Assyria, marked by the first letter, will rise. He will conquer all things through wars and his armies, and establish laws. But Ares will quickly destroy him with treacherous armies.

After him, three proud rulers will come: one marked by the number one, another by thirty, and the last by three hundred. They will cruelly melt gold and silver into statues of gods and distribute riches to their armies for the sake of victory. They will fiercely attack the Parthians of the deep Euphrates, the hostile Medes, the swift Massagetæ, and the Persians. When the king's fate comes, leaving the scepter to sons who are more suited for war, they will fight each other for the royal power, forgetting their father's advice.

Then, another ruler, marked by the number three, will rule alone and quickly meet his end by sword. After him, many will perish in conflicts over the royal power, being very valiant. A great-hearted ruler, marked by four, will manage the mighty Romans well.

War and conflict will come to Phoenicia when nations of arrow-shooting Persians approach. Sidon, Tripolis, and Berytus will witness much bloodshed. Laodicea will face a great and unsuccessful war stirred up by the impiety of men. The Tyrians will reap a terrible harvest, with the sun withdrawing and blood raining down from the sky. The king will die betrayed by his own companions. Many shameless leaders will then rise, continuing the wicked strife and killing each other.

A revered ruler with a name of five, skilled and trusted by great armies, will be beloved by mankind for his royal power and good deeds. During his reign, a fearful sign will appear between Taurus and snow-clad Amanus. A new and beautiful city by deep rivers will be destroyed in Cilicia. Phrygia and Propontis will suffer many earthquakes. The renowned king will lose his life to a deadly sickness.

After him, two lordly kings will rule: one marked by three hundred and another by three. They will destroy many in defense of Rome and for the sake of sovereignty. Then, the senate will face evil and not escape the wrath of the angry king. A sign will appear to all on earth, with rain, snow, and hail ruining crops. They will be slain in wars by strong Ares on behalf of the Italians.

Another king will then arise, full of schemes, gathering an army and distributing money to those in armor. Nile's rich waters will overflow for two years, but famine, war, and robbery will prevail. Many cities will be destroyed by armies, and the king will fall betrayed by gleaming iron.

After him, a ruler marked by the number three hundred will come to govern the Romans, who will be very mighty men. He will wield a life-destroying spear against the Armenians, Parthians, Assyrians, and Persians. Then, Rome will be newly created with splendid buildings made of gold, amber, silver, and ivory. Many people from the East and West will settle there, and the king will establish new laws. However, a powerful and destructive fate will eventually claim him in a remote island. Following him will be another ruler, marked by the number thirty, a fierce and fair-haired man who will be of Greek descent. There will be significant upheaval in a city of Molossian Phthia, with Larissa suffering on the steep banks of the Peneus River. In horse-breeding Scythia, there will be a rebellion. Nearby the waters of Lake Maeotis and the streams of the Phasis River, many will fall in battle. The god of war, Ares, will claim many lives. After destroying a Scythian people, this king will die in his own land.

Another ruler, marked by the number four, will succeed him. This dreadful man, feared by Armenians and Persians, will cause conflicts between the Colchians and the Pelasgians. Cities in Phrygia and Propontis will engage in bloody battles.

Then, God will show a great sign from heaven: a bat, symbolizing impending war. The king will not escape his harsh fate and will be killed by a weapon of gleaming iron.

After him, a ruler marked by the number fifty will come from Asia, a terrible figure who will bring destruction to Rome's grand walls and fight in Colchis, among the Heniochi, and the milk-drinking Agathyrsians by the Euxine Sea and Thracia. This king will also meet a grim fate and his corpse will be torn apart.

With the king dead, Rome, once a powerful city, will become a desert, and many people will perish. Another dreadful ruler from Egypt will rise, destroying great-hearted Parthians, Medes, Germans, Agathyrsians, Iernians, Britons, Iberians, Massagetæ, and Persians who see themselves as superior.

Then, a famous leader will look upon all of Hellas, acting as an enemy to Scythia and the windswept Caucasus. During his reign, there will be a fearful sign: crowns like shining stars will appear from the heavens in the south and north. He will pass on royal power to his son, whose name begins with the first letter of the alphabet, when the king himself descends to Hades.

When the son rules in Rome, indicated by the number one, there will be great peace on earth, and the Latins will love him for his father's virtues. He will be kept in Rome against his will by the Roman people, who have a deep affection for their noble ruler. However, he will die prematurely, taken by fate.

After him, many powerful men will fight each other, not holding real power but acting as tyrants. They will bring many troubles to the world, especially for the Romans, until the time of the third Dionysus, who will come from Egypt and be known as Dionysus the lord.

When the royal purple cloak is torn by a murderous lion and lioness, they will seize control of the changed kingdom. A holy king, whose name starts with the first letter of the alphabet, will fight for victory and cast down hostile leaders, leaving them as prey for dogs and vultures.

Alas for you, O city of Rome, burned by fire! How much you will suffer before these events come to pass. But a great and renowned king will later restore you with gold, amber, silver, and ivory. You will once again be foremost in wealth, temples, marketplaces, and racegrounds. You will shine as a light for all as you did before.

Wretched people of Cecrops, Cadmeans, and Laconians living around Peneus and Molossian streams, and in cities like Tricca, Dodona, Ithome, Pierian Ridge, Ossa, Larissa, and Calydon, will face their own miseries.

When God shows a great sign to humanity—a day of dark twilight covering the world—your end will come, and it will be impossible for you to escape a brother's deadly attack.

Then, another life-destroying ruler, a fiery eagle from a royal lineage, will rise. He will be younger but stronger than his brother, marked by the number eighty. The world will bear the wrath of the immortal god, with famines, plagues, wars, and relentless darkness covering the earth. Earthquakes, thunderbolts, storms, and floods will shake the high peaks of Phrygia and Scythian hills, causing cities to tremble. Many cities will fall under burning thunderbolts, and escaping the wrath will be impossible.

After this, the king will fall, struck down by his own men. Many Latins wearing purple will rise, seeking the royal power by lot. On Rome's grand walls, three kings will rule: two marked by the number one and one by the epithet of victory. They will love Rome and care for all humanity, but they will accomplish nothing. God will not be kind to the world or to mankind because of their many evil deeds. Therefore, he will bring about a mean and harsh fate for the kings, worse than that of leopards and wolves. The kings will be destroyed by those in armor, like weak women.

Ah, wretched high men of glorious Rome, trusting in false oaths, you will be destroyed. Then many armed men will take away the offspring of the first-born, causing great bloodshed. The Most High will bring on a dreadful doom three times, and all men with their deeds will be destroyed. But God will bring them to judgment—those who have committed evil—fencing them in and consigning them to condemnation.

A brilliant comet will herald much to come: wars and battles. When one gathers oracles about conflicts and temple harm, he will urgently command a collection of wheat and barley in Rome for twelve months. During those days, the city will be in a dire state, but it will soon become prosperous again. Rest will follow when that rule ends. The last race of Latin kings will follow, and after them, dominion will grow strong again, with children and descendants remaining unshaken, for it will be known that God himself is king.

There is a land beloved and nurturing to men, marked by the Nile, which separates all Libya and Ethiopia.

The Syrians, who will be short-lived, will come from different places and seize all movable possessions from that land. A great and vigilant leader will be their king, training youth and preparing for men. He will plan something terrible against those who are most fearsome, sending forth a powerful ally to all of Italy, a noble-minded figure. When he reaches the dark sea of Assyria, he will plunder the Phoenicians in their homes and bring about dreadful wars, ruling alongside another powerful leader of the earth. Now, I will lament the tragic end of the Alexandrians; barbarians will seize sacred Egypt, a land previously untouched and unshaken, when divine wrath descends. When winter seems like summer and all prophecies are fulfilled, three young men will win at the Olympic Games. You should ask those who interpret oracles to perform a cleansing sacrifice with the blood of a suckling animal. The Most High will then bring about a dreadful fate three times, brandishing a mournful spear. Much blood will be spilled, and barbarian invaders will utterly plunder the city. Those who are dead, and those without children, will be fortunate. The former leader, once renowned and free, will no longer pursue earlier plans but will subject their people to servitude. This servitude, causing much sorrow, will be imposed by a new ruler.

Soon after, a ill-fated army of Sicilians will arrive, bringing terror when a barbarian nation unexpectedly returns. They will harvest the fruit of the fields. God, the lofty Thunderer, will bestow misfortune instead of good, and strangers will plunder hateful gold from each other.

When people see the blood of a flesh-eating lion and a murderous lioness appears, the scepter will be cast away. In Egypt, where people gather for a feast, perform heroic deeds, and restrain one another with much shouting, there will also be fear of fierce conflicts among humanity. Many will be destroyed, and others will kill each other in brutal fights.

Then, a ruler covered in dark scales will appear, along with two allies, and a great ram from Cyrene, previously described as a war fugitive by the Nile. Despite their efforts, they will not succeed in their endeavors.

The passing years will be calm, but eventually, a second war will arise in Egypt. There will be a sea battle, but victory will elude them. The famous city will be conquered, but the victory will be short-lived.

People with shared boundaries will flee in distress, leading their suffering parents. They will eventually find a land where they achieve great victory and destroy the Jews, who are steadfast in battle. They will wage war far and wide, fighting valiantly for their homeland and families. A new generation of victorious warriors will be honored for their bravery. Many will drown in the waves, and the sandy beaches will be strewn with the bodies of the slain. Golden-haired heads will fall prey to Egyptian birds of prey.

Arabians will seek out mortal blood. When wolves and dogs make solemn oaths on an island surrounded by the sea, a tower will be built, and the city that endured many hardships will be inhabited by people. Deceitful gold and silver will no longer be sought, nor will there be laborious servitude. Instead, there will be one true friendship and a shared way of life, with all things common and equal. Wickedness will sink into the vast sea, and the time of harvest for humanity will be near.

It is necessary that these events come to pass. At that time, no traveler will claim that humanity, though mortal, will ever cease to exist. A holy nation will prevail and rule over the earth for all time with their mighty descendants.

Fragments of Sibylline Oracles

The Sibylline Oracles, a collection of prophetic writings ascribed to the Sibyls, ancient prophetesses reputed to deliver divine revelations, represent a fascinating convergence of Greco-Roman, Jewish, and early Christian traditions. These texts, composed over several centuries from the second century BCE to the seventh century CE, reflect the dynamic interplay of religious and cultural influences during a period of significant transformation in the Mediterranean world. The fragments of the Sibylline Oracles offer a rich tapestry of apocalyptic visions, moral exhortations, and eschatological themes, interwoven with historical allusions and mythological references. The Sibylline prophetesses, though fictionalized to some extent, serve as vehicles for conveying the hopes, fears, and religious aspirations of diverse communities grappling with the challenges of their times. The oracles themselves are characterized by their poetic and enigmatic style, utilizing allegory and symbolism to communicate profound theological and ethical messages. As such, they provide invaluable insights into the evolving religious consciousness and the syncretic nature of belief systems in antiquity. The study of these fragments not only enhances our understanding of ancient prophetic literature but also illuminates the broader historical and cultural contexts in which these texts were produced and circulated. Moreover, the Sibylline Oracles have had a lasting impact on the development of apocalyptic thought and literature, influencing subsequent religious traditions and literary genres. Through meticulous analysis of the language, motifs, and historical references embedded in these oracles, scholars can reconstruct the complex web of interactions between different religious communities and trace the transmission of prophetic ideas across time and space.

{1:1} Mortal men, made of flesh, how quickly you become arrogant without seeing the end of life! Do you not tremble now and fear God, the one who watches over you, the Most High, the all-knowing witness of all things, the all-nourishing Creator who has imbued everything with His sweet Spirit and appointed Him as the leader of all mortals? God is one, who alone rules supremely, who is eternal, almighty, and invisible. He alone sees all things, yet is unseen by any human flesh. What flesh is capable of beholding with its eyes the divine, true God who dwells in the heavens? Even the bright rays of the sun are too intense for mortals to withstand. Man, who is just veins and flesh on bones, cannot see Him who is the ruler of the world, who is eternal and has existed from everlasting. You should revere Him, the self-existent and unbegotten one, who rules all things throughout all time and renders judgment to all mortals in equal measure. The punishment for not glorifying the true and eternal God and for offering sacrifices to demons in Hades will be severe. In your arrogance and folly, you have strayed from the true path and wandered through thorns and thistles. O foolish mortals, stop roaming in darkness and embrace the Light. He is clear to all and cannot err; do not chase after darkness and gloom. The sun's bright light shines with unmatched brilliance. Now, holding wisdom in your hearts, know that God alone sends rain, wind, earthquakes, lightning, famine, pestilence, storms of snow, and ice. Why do I list them individually? He governs heaven, rules earth, and reigns over Hades.

{2:1} If gods were to produce offspring and remain immortal, there would be more gods than men, and there would be no space left for mortals to stand.

{3:1} If everything that is born must also perish, it is impossible for God to be formed from human flesh and womb. God alone is supreme and eternal, the creator of heaven, the sun, the stars, the moon, the fruitful earth, the seas, the lofty hills, and the sources of lasting springs. He also creates countless creatures that live in the waters and the land, sustaining them with life, including delicate, twittering birds that fly through the air, and wild mountain beasts. He made cattle subject to humans and established man as ruler over all things, making all diverse and incomprehensible things subject to him. How can mortal flesh comprehend these things? Only the eternal Maker who created them at the beginning knows all, dwelling in heaven, rewarding the good with abundant goodness and awakening wrath and anger for the evil and unjust, bringing war, pestilence, and sorrow. O men, why do you, in your vain pride, uproot yourselves? Be ashamed of deifying polecats and monsters. Is it not madness to imagine gods stealing plates and taking earthen pots? Instead of dwelling in golden heaven, they are consumed by moths and covered with spider webs! O fools who bow to serpents, dogs, cats, birds, creeping beasts, stone images, statues, and heaps of stones by the roads—these are the foolish gods of senseless men, and their words are poison. But the true God gives life and eternal light, offering joy sweeter than honey to the righteous. Bow only to Him and live a pious life. Forsaking all these, in a state of folly, you have drunk from the cup of judgment filled to the brim and unmixed. You will not wake from your drunken sleep to recognize God as the king who oversees all things. Therefore, you will face eternal punishment, burned with torches throughout the ages, feeling shame for your false, useless idols. But those who fear the true eternal God will inherit life, dwelling forever in the paradise of fertile fields, feasting on heavenly bread.

{4:1} Listen to me, O men, the eternal King reigns.

{5:1} He alone is God, the unrestrained Maker; He designed the pattern of the human form and mixed the nature of all mortals Himself, as the creator of all life.

{6:1} When He comes, there will be a smoky fire in the darkness of midnight.

{7:1} The Erythræan Sibyl, addressing God, says: Why do You, O Lord, require me to prophesy, rather than taking me away from the earth and preserving me for the most blessed day of Your coming?

Fragments of Zadokite Work

The "Fragments of a Zadokite Work," also known as the "Damascus Document," is a significant text within the corpus of the Dead Sea Scrolls, discovered in the Cairo Geniza in the late 19th century and later among the Qumran scrolls. This work, written in Hebrew, is a foundational text for understanding the beliefs, practices, and organizational structure of a Jewish sect often identified with the Essenes, though some scholars suggest connections to other groups such as the Sadducees or the Qumran community itself. The document is divided into two main sections: an exhortation and a set of statutes. The exhortation part presents a theological and moralistic discourse, emphasizing the community's covenant with God, a renewed adherence to the Torah, and a critique of the mainstream Jewish establishment, which the sect saw as corrupt and in need of reform. It also contains eschatological elements, reflecting the community's expectations of an imminent end time and divine intervention. The statutes section outlines the communal rules and regulations, detailing the purity laws, judicial procedures, and the roles and responsibilities of community members, particularly the priests, Levites, and lay leaders. These regulations underscore the community's strict adherence to ritual purity and ethical conduct, as well as their separation from what they considered a polluted and apostate society.

{1:1} Listen to me, all who know righteousness and understand the works of God. For God has a dispute with all flesh and will execute judgment on those who despise Him. {1:2} Because of the sins of those who turned away from Him, He turned His face away from Israel and His sanctuary, delivering them over to the sword. {1:3} Yet, He remembered His covenant with their forefathers and spared a remnant of Israel from destruction. {1:4} During the time of wrath, three hundred and ninety years after Nebuchadnezzar of Babylon had them in his grasp, God visited them. {1:5} He raised up from Israel and Aaron a righteous root to inherit the land and prosper through His blessings. {1:6} They acknowledged their sins and understood their guilt, stumbling blindly for twenty years. {1:7} God observed their deeds, for they sought Him sincerely, and He raised up a Teacher of righteousness to guide them. {1:8} He revealed His actions to future generations, showing what He had done to a rebellious congregation—those who strayed from His path. {1:9} This was the time foretold: Israel behaved stubbornly like a rebellious heifer. {1:10} When arrogant men arose, speaking deceitful words to lead Israel astray in the wilderness. {1:11} They turned away from righteousness, removing the landmarks set by their forefathers. {1:12} Thus they invited upon themselves the curses of God's covenant, falling to the sword of covenantal vengeance. {1:13} They sought smooth words and chose deception, eagerly pursuing lawless deeds. {1:14} They favored the wicked, condemned the righteous, and transgressed the covenant. {1:15} They violated statutes and attacked the souls of the righteous. {1:16} They abhorred all who walked uprightly, pursued them with the sword, and rejoiced in conflict. {1:17} This kindled God's wrath against their assembly, laying waste to their multitude, as their deeds were uncleanness before Him.

{2:1} Now listen, all who have entered into the covenant, and I will reveal the ways of the wicked. {2:2} God loves wisdom and knowledge; counsel, prudence, and knowledge serve Him. {2:3} He is patient and abundant in forgiveness, ready to pardon those who repent of their transgressions. {2:4} Yet, He possesses power, might, and fierce anger with flames of fire for those who turn away from His way and reject His statutes. {2:5} Thus, there shall be no remnant, no escape for them. {2:6} God did not choose them from the beginning, and He knew their works before they were formed. {2:7} He has abhorred their generations since ancient times, hiding His face from their land until their destruction. {2:8} He knows the appointed times and exact periods for all things across the ages, past, present, and future. {2:9} Despite this, He raises up individuals, calling them by name, to leave a remnant on the earth and fill it with their descendants. {2:10} Through His Messiah, He reveals His holy spirit and truth. Those who are true to Him find their names in His true interpretation, but those He hates, He leads astray.

{3:1} Now listen, children, and I will enlighten you to see and understand the works of God—what He approves and what He condemns. {3:2} Walk uprightly in His ways, and do not entertain evil thoughts or lustful desires. {3:3} Many have been led astray by such desires, causing even mighty men to stumble from ancient times to this day. {3:4} The watchers of heaven fell because they walked in the stubbornness of their hearts and did not keep God's commandments. {3:5} Their offspring, once tall as cedar trees and strong as mountains, fell victim to these sins. {3:6} All flesh on dry land perished because of these transgressions, as if they had never existed. {3:7} They did as they pleased and disregarded their Maker's commandments, provoking His wrath.

{4:1} These sins caused the sons of Noah and their descendants to stray and be cut off. {4:2} Abraham did not follow these paths but was honored because he obeyed God's commandments, becoming His friend. {4:3} He passed these commandments to Isaac and Jacob, who also obeyed and were recorded as God's friends and members of the everlasting covenant. {4:4} The sons of Jacob, however, strayed because of these sins and faced punishment for their errors. {4:5} Their descendants in Egypt stubbornly followed their own desires, ignoring God's commandments and doing as they pleased. {4:6} They even defied God's commandments to the point of eating blood, and God punished them in the desert. {4:7} They refused to listen to their Maker and instead murmured in their tents, provoking God's wrath against their community. {4:8} Their children and kings perished, their mighty men were destroyed, and their land was left desolate. {4:9} The first covenant breakers incurred guilt and were handed over to the sword for forsaking God's covenant. {4:10} They chose their own desires, following the stubbornness of their hearts and doing as they pleased.

{5:1} But those who held fast to the commandments of God, who remained faithful among them, God established His covenant with Israel forever. He revealed to them the hidden truths where all Israel had erred: His holy Sabbaths, glorious festivals, righteous testimonies, and true ways—everything that leads to life if followed faithfully. {5:2} They dug a well of abundant waters, and anyone who despises these teachings shall not live. {5:3} Yet many wallowed in sinful ways, following their own desires and claiming what was not theirs. {5:4} Despite this, God miraculously pardoned their sins and built for them a steadfast house in Israel, unparalleled throughout history. {5:5} Those who remain faithful to Him are destined for eternal life, adorned with all the glory of humanity. As Ezekiel the prophet testified: {5:7} "The priests, Levites, the sons of Zadok, who faithfully guarded My sanctuary when Israel strayed, they shall offer to Me fat and blood."

{6:1} The priests are the repentant of Israel who departed from the land of Judah, and the Levites who joined them. The sons of Zadok are the chosen ones of Israel appointed in the latter days. Their names, generations, periods of service, afflictions, years of exile, and deeds are all recorded. {6:2} The first saints whom God pardoned upheld righteousness, justified the righteous, and condemned the wicked. {6:3} God established a covenant with the forefathers to pardon their sins, ensuring atonement for them at the appointed time.

{7:1} The builders of the wall, who follow the law—the law that speaks and condemns—are ensnared in their transgressions, especially in taking multiple wives during their lifetime. {7:2} The fundamental principle of creation is "Male and Female He created them," and as it was with those who entered the Ark, two by two. {7:3} The prince should not multiply wives for himself, as stated. {7:4} David did not read the sealed Book of the Law until Zadok discovered it. They glorified David's deeds but neglected the blood of Uriah, and God abandoned them to their ways. {7:5} They defiled the sanctuary by not following the Law, engaging in illicit relationships and other abominations. {7:6} They blasphemed against God's covenant, claiming it was not established, and spoke abominably against His statutes. {7:7} They are like kindlers of fire and setters of firebrands, weaving webs like spiders and hatching eggs like cockatrices—none who come near them shall be innocent. {7:8} They are a people lacking understanding, a nation void of counsel, for they do not comprehend. {7:9} Moses and Aaron arose through the prince of lights in ancient times, but Belial raised Jochanneh and his brother with evil intent, leading to Israel's downfall.

{8:1} During the time of the land's destruction, there arose those who moved the ancient landmarks and led Israel astray. The land lay desolate because they rebelled against the commandments of God spoken through Moses and His holy anointed one, prophesying lies to turn Israel away from God. {8:2} But God remembered His covenant with the forefathers. {8:3} He raised up men of understanding from Aaron and wise men from Israel. {8:4} These men listened and obeyed; they dug a well. {8:5} "A well the princes dug, the nobles of the people delved it by the order of the Lawgiver." {8:6} This well is the Law, and those who dug it are the repentant of Israel who departed from Judah and sojourned in Damascus , {8:7} all of whom God called princes. {8:8} They sought Him diligently, and His glory was not turned away from any of them. {8:9} The Lawgiver is the one who studies the Law, as Isaiah said, "He brings forth an instrument for his work." {8:10} They will receive nothing except salvation until the Teacher of Righteousness arises in the end of days. {8:11} None who have entered into the covenant shall enter the Sanctuary to kindle His altar unless they shut the doors, as God said, "Oh that there was one among you to shut the doors, so that you might not vainly kindle the fire upon My altar." {8:12} They must observe the true meaning of the Law until the end of wickedness, separate themselves from evildoers, abstain from polluted wealth and from the wealth of the Sanctuary under vow and curse. {8:13} They must refrain from robbing the pool of His people, exploiting widows, and oppressing the fatherless. {8:14} They must distinguish between clean and unclean, teach others to discern between holy and profane. {8:15} They should observe the Sabbath, the feasts, and the day of fasting according to the teachings of those who entered into the New Covenant in Damascus. {8:16} They must contribute their holy offerings as prescribed. {8:17} They should love their neighbors as themselves, strengthen the hands of the poor, the needy, and the stranger, and seek the peace of their brothers. {8:18} They should abstain from harlotry and avoid trespassing against their kin. {8:19} They must rebuke wrongdoing, refrain from holding grudges, and separate themselves from all impurities as instructed by their judgments. {8:20} No one should defile their holy spirit with abominable acts, as God has set them apart from such. {8:21} As for those who walk in holiness, observing all these ordinances with perfection, they uphold the covenant of God.

{9:1} If they settle in camps according to the established order of the land, taking wives and bearing children, they should walk according to the Law and the judgments of the ordinances, as commanded: "between a man and his wife, and between a father and his son." {9:2} But those who reject these teachings, when God visits the land, they will face the punishment of the wicked. This fulfills the prophecy of Isaiah: "He will bring upon you and upon your people and upon your father's house days that have not come since Ephraim departed from Judah." {9:3} When the two houses of Israel separated, with Ephraim departing from Judah, those who were unfaithful were delivered to the sword, while those who remained faithful escaped to the land of the North. {9:4} As prophesied, "I will cause to go into captivity Siccuth your King and Chiun your images," referring to their idolatry beyond Damascus. {9:5} The books of the Law are the foundation of the King's rule, as God said, "I will raise up the tabernacle of David that is fallen." The King represents the congregation, Chiun the images symbolize the books of the Prophets, which Israel has disregarded. The Star, who studied the Law and came to Damascus, fulfills the prophecy, "There shall come forth a star out of Jacob, and a scepter shall rise out of Israel." The scepter signifies the prince of the congregation. {9:6} When he "destroys all the sons of battle din," some will escape during the first visitation, but the unfaithful will face the sword. {9:7} This is the judgment for all who have entered into God's covenant but refuse to uphold its statutes—they will be visited with destruction through Belial's hand, fulfilling God's spoken word. {9:8} The princes of Judah were like those who removed landmarks, and God pours out His wrath upon them like water. They are beyond healing, leading the rebellion. {9:9} They have not turned from their treacherous ways, indulging in harlotry, wicked wealth, and vengeance. {9:10} Each bears grudges against their brothers, hates their neighbors, commits trespass against kin, engages in unchastity, seeks unjust gain, and follows their own desires. {9:11} They choose stubbornness, refuse to separate from the corrupt, and revel in wickedness, fulfilling the prophecy: "Their wine is the poison of dragons and the cruel venom of asps." {9:12} The dragons symbolize Gentile kings, their wine represents their corrupt ways, and the venom of asps signifies the cunning of Javanite kings who execute vengeance. {9:13} Yet those who built the wall with untempered mortar did not realize that God's wrath was kindled against His congregation due to their deeds. {9:14} Moses forewarned, "Not for your righteousness or for the uprightness of your heart will you inherit these nations, but because He loved your fathers and kept His oath." {9:15} This applies to the repentant of Israel who turned away from the people's ways. {9:16} This fate awaits all who reject God's commandments and turn stubbornly away. {9:17} Those who entered the New Covenant in Damascus will not be counted among the assembly of the people, nor will their names be written, until the Messiah arises from Aaron and Israel. {9:18} Anyone who despises the precepts of the righteous will be expelled from the congregation when their deeds are exposed. {9:19} This is the fate of those who reject God's commandments, setting idols in their hearts and stubbornly following their own desires— they have no share in the House of the Law. {9:20} They speak falsely against righteous statutes, {9:38} reject the covenant and faith pledges made in Damascus—the New Covenant. {9:21} From the time the Unique Teacher gathered them until the warriors who followed falsehood perished, about forty years. {9:22} Those who repented in Jacob kept God's covenant. {9:23} They spoke with one another, strengthening their resolve to walk in God's ways. {9:42} God heard their words, and a book of remembrance was written for those who feared Him and thought upon His name. {9:24} They will discern between the righteous and the wicked, {9:44} those who serve God and those who do not. {9:25} God shows mercy to thousands who love Him and keep His commandments for generations. {9:26} From the house of Peleg, those who departed from the holy city and trusted in God during Israel's trespasses and Sanctuary pollution, {9:47} returning to idolatry. {9:27} All will be judged, each according to their spirit in the counsel of holiness. {9:28} Those who destroyed the landmarks of the Law among the covenant people will be cut off from the camp along with the wicked of Judah during testing. {9:29} But those who faithfully follow these judgments, obeying the Law in all their actions, listening to the Teacher and confessing before God their sins, {9:30} "We have done wickedly, we and our fathers, walking contrary to the covenant statutes. Your judgment against us is just." {9:31} They do not lift their hand against God's holy statutes, righteous judgment, and truth testimony. {9:32} They are chastised by the initial judgments, as are all who listen to the Unique Teacher of Righteousness and do not reject the statutes of righteousness when they hear them. {9:33} They shall rejoice and be glad, their hearts exulting in strength against the world's children. God will forgive them, and they will see His salvation, for they trust in His holy name.

{10:1} Anyone who condemns another person according to the customs of the Gentiles shall be put to death. {10:2} Regarding vengeance and bearing grudges, as God commanded, "Thou shalt not take vengeance, nor bear any grudge against the children of thy people," those who bring charges against their neighbors out of wrath, without rebuking them first before witnesses, are guilty of taking vengeance and holding grudges. Scripture affirms, "He takes vengeance on His adversaries, and reserves wrath for His enemies." {10:3} If someone remains silent about an offense but then speaks out in anger, even to the point of calling for death, they condemn themselves for not obeying God's command to rebuke their neighbor and prevent sin. {10:4} Concerning oaths, if someone makes another swear falsely outside the presence of judges, they take vengeance into their own hands. {10:5} In cases of lost property from the camp, the owner should declare it with an oath of cursing. Anyone who hears but does not disclose knowledge of the thief is guilty. {10:6} If someone returns lost property that has no owner, they must confess to the priest. If the owner is found later, restitution is made. If not, the property belongs to the priests. {10:7} If a person witnesses a transgression that warrants death, they must report it to the appointed authority, the Censor, in the presence of the accused, fulfilling the duty of reproving. The Censor records the accusation. {10:8} If the accused repeats the offense before others, the matter is again reported to the Censor. {10:9} If two trustworthy witnesses testify separately against the accused, he is excluded from purity, provided they reported the incident promptly. {10:10} According to the law, two reliable witnesses are required to establish guilt; one witness alone cannot exclude someone from purity. {10:11} No witness shall testify to justify execution unless the accused's days are fulfilled and he is a God-fearing individual. {10:12} No one should be considered a credible witness against their neighbor for a deliberate transgression unless they have undergone repentance.

{11:1} This is the protocol for appointing judges in the congregation: ten men shall be chosen from among the people, four from the tribe of Levi and Aaron, and six from Israel who are learned in the Book of the Law and the Ordinances of the Covenant, aged between twenty-five and sixty years. No one above sixty years shall be appointed to judge the congregation, for their days are diminished due to human transgressions, and God's wrath may shorten their understanding before their time.

{12:1} Concerning purification with water: no one shall cleanse themselves with filthy or insufficient water for a proper bath. {12:2} Nor shall anyone use vessel water for purification. Any pool in a rock that lacks sufficient water for a bath, and has been touched by an unclean person, shall be deemed unclean like water in a vessel.

{13:1} Regarding the Sabbath, it must be observed according to its laws: no one shall work from the time the sun's orb begins to set on the sixth day, keeping it holy as commanded. {13:2} On the Sabbath, no one shall speak idle or vain words. {13:3} No one shall lend or borrow. {13:4} Disputes regarding wealth or gain are forbidden. {13:5} No discussions about work or labor for the next day. {13:6} No one shall engage in business activities in the fields. {13:7} On the Sabbath, no one shall walk outside their city beyond a thousand cubits. {13:8} No one shall eat anything on the Sabbath except what is prepared beforehand or is perishable and found in the field. {13:9} Eating and drinking are restricted to within the camp. {13:10} If one is on a journey and stops to wash, they may drink where they stand but not draw water into a vessel. {13:11} No one shall send a non-Israelite to perform tasks on their behalf on the Sabbath. {13:12} No one shall wear filthy garments or those obtained from a Gentile unless washed or rubbed with frankincense. {13:13} Fasting voluntarily on the Sabbath is prohibited. {13:14} No one shall lead an animal to graze beyond two thousand cubits outside their city. {13:15} No one shall strike an animal with their fist. {13:16} If an animal is stubborn, it shall not be moved out of its place on the Sabbath. {13:17} No one shall open the lid of a vessel sealed on the Sabbath. {13:18} Carrying spices to or from a house on the Sabbath is prohibited. {13:19} No one shall move rocks or earth within their dwelling on the Sabbath. {13:20} Fathers nursing infants shall not carry them in or out on the Sabbath. {13:21} No one shall provoke their servants or hired workers on the Sabbath. {13:22} Assisting in the birth of animals on the Sabbath is forbidden. {13:23} If an animal falls into a pit, it shall not be lifted out on the Sabbath. {13:24} No one shall rest in places near Gentiles on the Sabbath. {13:25} No one shall defile themselves on the Sabbath for the sake of wealth or gain. {13:26} If someone falls into water or a pit, they shall not be rescued using a ladder, cord, or any tool on the Sabbath. {13:27} No offerings shall be made on the altar on the Sabbath except the burnt-offerings designated for that day, as it is written, "Except your Sabbaths."

{14:1} No one shall send unclean offerings such as burnt-offerings, meat-offerings, frankincense, or wood through the hands of an unclean person, for it defiles the altar. As written, "The sacrifice of the wicked is an abomination, but the prayer of the righteous is like an offering of delight." {14:2} Those who enter the house of worship must not do so when unclean, even if they have washed themselves. {14:3} When the trumpets of the Congregation sound, it shall be done before or after, and they shall not cease the entire service, for the Sabbath is holy. {14:4} No one shall engage in sexual relations with a woman within the city of the Sanctuary to avoid defiling it with impurity. {14:5} Anyone who is influenced by evil spirits and speaks rebelliously shall be judged according to the laws of necromancers and wizards. {14:6} Those who lead others into profaning the Sabbath and the Feasts shall not be put to death. Instead, it is the responsibility of the community to watch over them. If they repent, they shall be watched for seven years before being reintegrated into the Congregation. {14:7} No one shall raise their hand to shed the blood of a Gentile for the sake of wealth or gain. {14:8} Nor shall anyone take anything from their wealth lest they blaspheme, unless approved by the Community of Israel. {14:9} No one shall sell a clean animal or bird to the Gentiles, lest they sacrifice them. {14:10} Nor shall anyone sell them anything from their threshing-floor or winepress, for all these belong to them. {14:11} Nor shall anyone sell their male or female servants who have entered into the covenant of Abraham. {14:12} No one shall defile themselves by eating abominable creatures, whether living creatures or insects like bees, or any creature that moves in the waters. {14:13} Fish shall not be eaten unless they are split alive and their blood is shed. {14:14} However, all kinds of locusts shall be put into fire or water while they are still alive, for that is how they are created. {14:15} All wood, stones, and dust that are polluted by human uncleanness are contaminated in the same way. {14:16} Anyone who touches them shall be unclean according to their uncleanness. Likewise, any tool, nail, or peg in a wall that is in a house with a dead person shall be unclean, just like an instrument used for work.

{15:1} The regulations for the inhabitants of the cities of Israel are based on these judgments, distinguishing between the unclean and the clean, and teaching the difference between the holy and the common. {15:2} These statutes are meant to instruct the entire nation so that they may always walk according to the Law. {15:3} The descendants of Israel shall abide by this law and they shall not be cursed. {15:4} This is how the inhabitants are to act during times of wickedness until the Messiah from Aaron and Israel arises, from at least ten men to thousands, hundreds, fifties, and tens. {15:5} When there are ten men, the priest who is knowledgeable in the Book of the Hagu shall not depart. They shall all be ruled according to his instructions. {15:6} If he is not skilled in these matters, but a Levite is, then all who enter the camp shall go out and come in according to the Levite's guidance. {15:7} If there is a judgment concerning the law of leprosy in a person, the priest shall come and stand in the camp, and the Censor shall explain the true meaning of the law to him. {15:8} Even if the priest lacks understanding, the Censor shall instruct him, for the judgment belongs to them.

{16:1} This is the role of the Censor of the camp: to instruct the multitude in the works of God, to explain His wondrous deeds, and to recount the history of the world since its creation. {16:2} He shall show mercy to them as a father to his children and forgive all who have incurred guilt. {16:3} Like a shepherd with his flock, he shall release those oppressed and crushed within his congregation, evaluating each person based on their deeds, understanding, strength, and wealth. {16:4} Each person who joins his congregation shall be assigned a place according to his standing in the camp. {16:5} No one from the children of the camp shall have the authority to admit a person {16:6} into the congregation without the approval of the Censor. {16:7} Nor shall any who have entered into God's covenant engage in business with those of the pit without hand-to-hand dealings. {16:8} No one shall engage in buying and selling without first consulting the Censor, and transactions shall occur within the camp. {16:9} This is how the camps shall be settled, ensuring that all who settle in the land are accounted for. {16:10} This arrangement dates back to the time when Ephraim departed from Judah. {16:11} Those who follow these regulations uphold God's covenant and are saved from the snares of the pit.

{17:1} The regulations for the inhabitants of all the camps are as follows: {17:2} They shall be numbered and recorded by name: first the Priests, then the Levites, followed by the children of Israel, and finally the proselytes. {17:3} They shall be listed in order, and this order shall be followed in every matter. {17:4} The Priest who oversees the numbering shall be between thirty and sixty years old, {17:5} knowledgeable in the Book of the Hagu and all the judgments of the Law to guide them according to their decisions. {17:6} The Censor who supervises all the camps shall be between thirty and fifty years old, skilled in every counsel and language. {17:7} Everyone entering the congregation shall do so according to his instructions in their proper order. {17:8} If anyone needs to address a matter, he shall speak to the Censor regarding any lawsuit or dispute.

{18:1} This is the regulation concerning the multitude to ensure all their needs are met. {18:2} They shall give the wages of two days every month to the Censor and the judges. {18:3} From this fund, they shall support the poor and needy, the elderly, the vagrant, and those taken captive by foreign nations. {18:4} They shall provide for the unmarried and those without support, ensuring every need is met. {18:5} This is how the settlements are to be explained and how the judgments are to be upheld. {18:6} From Aaron and Israel, the Messiah shall come.

{19:1} No one shall swear by any deceptive means, but only by the oath written in the curses of the covenant. {19:2} Mentioning the Law of Moses is forbidden, for it holds sacred significance. {19:3} Anyone who swears falsely profanes the Name. {19:4} Swearing by the curses of the covenant obligates one before the judges. {19:5} If one transgresses, he shall be held guilty, but confessing and making restitution can spare him from death. {19:6} All of Israel, together with their children who are not yet of age, shall enter into the covenant forever, confirming it on their behalf. {19:7} This law applies throughout periods of wickedness for anyone who returns from corrupt ways. {19:8} On the day they speak with the Censor, they shall be enrolled by the oath of the covenant that Moses established with Israel. {19:9} They shall commit to returning to the Law of Moses with all their heart and soul, {19:10} following all that is found within it.

{20:1} The precise details of their observances are meticulously recorded in the Book of the Divisions of the Seasons, according to their Jubilees and Weeks. {20:2} On the day one commits to return to the law of Moses, the angel of Mastema will depart if the commitment is honored. {20:3} Therefore, Abraham was circumcised on the day of his resolve. {20:4} One must keep every oath and commitment made, fulfilling what has been spoken. {20:5} No oath taken to fulfill a commandment of the law shall be broken, even at the risk of death. {20:6} Nothing sworn to defy the law shall be upheld, even at the risk of death. {20:7} Regarding a woman's oath, which Moses said should be disallowed, no one shall invalidate an oath once spoken. {20:8} Whether confirming or annulling a covenant, it must be done decisively. {20:9} The same applies to her father's oath, and concerning offerings, no one shall vow anything to the altar under compulsion. {20:10} Nor shall priests take anything forcibly from the Israelites. {20:11} No one shall dedicate what is unjustly obtained; they shall heed the wisdom: "They hunt every man his brother with a net." {20:12} Nor shall anyone devote what belongs to others as holy; those who make vows shall uphold them before the judge.

Giants

The Book of Giants is an ancient Jewish pseudepigraphal text that expands upon the narrative found in the Hebrew Bible, particularly within the Book of Genesis. Originating from the 2nd century BCE, it is primarily known through the Dead Sea Scrolls discovered at Qumran, though fragments have also been found in other locations, such as Turfan in China. The text elaborates on the brief mention of the Nephilim in Genesis 6:1-4, presenting a more detailed account of their origins, deeds, and eventual downfall. It tells of the progeny of the fallen angels, who, according to the narrative, engaged in egregious acts that led to the corruption and eventual destruction of the world by the Great Flood. Central to the story are the giants, offspring of these angels and human women, who wreak havoc on the earth and its inhabitants. The narrative includes vivid descriptions of their immense size, strength, and violent tendencies. The Book of Giants also integrates elements from various mythological traditions, suggesting a rich tapestry of influences, including Mesopotamian, Greek, and Jewish mythos. These giants are portrayed as having visions and dreams that predict their own destruction, which they seek to avoid by seeking out the help of Enoch, the scribe and prophet. The text highlights themes of divine judgment, repentance, and the interplay between human and supernatural realms. Scholarly interest in the Book of Giants extends beyond its mythological content to its implications for understanding Second Temple Judaism, intertestamental literature, and the development of early Jewish and Christian thought. The text's fragmentary nature, with portions surviving in Aramaic, Greek, and Middle Persian, poses challenges for complete reconstruction, yet it continues to be a vital piece for scholars piecing together the cultural and theological milieu of its time.

The "Book of Giants" does not have a standard chapter structure like modern books due to its fragmented and incomplete nature. Instead, it consists of various fragments that have been pieced together by scholars. The exact number of fragments varies depending on the specific manuscript and source.

These fragments include:
- Descriptions of the giants and their actions.
- The dreams and visions of the giants.
- Enoch's interactions with the giants and the Watchers.
- Prophecies and warnings about the impending judgment.

Because the text is so fragmented, scholars focus more on the content and themes of the pieces that have been found rather than organizing them into chapters.

Given the fragmented and incomplete nature of the "Book of Giants," we'll provide a structured format using a chapter and verse-like system to present the key fragments and themes. The numbering will be somewhat artificial since the original text does not have a standardized chapter and verse format.

{1:1} And it came to pass, when the sons of God had taken to themselves wives from the daughters of men, they begat giants. {1:2} These giants, mighty in their deeds, spread corruption and violence upon the earth. {1:3} The giants grew in number and strength, and their actions caused great suffering among men.

{2:1} And there appeared to the giants troubling dreams, visions of their downfall. {2:2} Ohya, one of the giants, saw in his dream a tablet inscribed with many lines, which he could not read. {2:3} And Ohya spoke to his brother Hahyah, saying, "I have seen in my dream a vision of destruction." {2:4} Hahyah answered him, "Tell me your dream, my brother, that we may understand it together." {2:5} Ohya described his dream, "I saw a great tree uprooted and cast down, and all the earth shook."

{3:1} And the giants, troubled by their dreams, sought out Enoch, the scribe, to interpret the visions. {3:2} Enoch, being wise and righteous, agreed to help them and went before the Most High to seek understanding. {3:3} And Enoch returned with the interpretation, saying, "These dreams are warnings of your impending judgment." {3:4} "The tree represents your strength and power, which shall be brought low."

{4:1} Enoch said to the giants, "Behold, the Almighty has decreed your end because of the bloodshed and sin you have brought upon the earth." {4:2} "Repent, therefore, and cease from your wicked ways, for the judgment of the Most High is at hand." {4:3} "The waters of the flood shall come and cleanse the earth of your corruption." {4:4} "You have brought great sorrow to the earth, and your time is at an end."

{5:1} And the giants were greatly troubled by the words of Enoch. {5:2} Some among them repented and sought to amend their ways. {5:3} But others hardened their hearts and continued in their wickedness, saying, "Who is the Most High that we should fear His judgment?" {5:4} They mocked Enoch and continued in their rebellious ways.

{6:1} And the day of the Lord's judgment came upon the earth. {6:2} The heavens opened, and the waters of the great deep burst forth. {6:3} The giants, mighty as they were, could not withstand the deluge, and they perished along with all the wicked. {6:4} Thus, the earth was cleansed of the giants and the corruption they had wrought, fulfilling the decree of the Most High. {6:5} The Watchers, who had fathered the giants, were bound and cast into the abyss as punishment for their transgressions.

{7:1} The memory of the giants remained as a warning to future generations of the consequences of sin and rebellion against the Most High. {7:2} Their story was recorded by the righteous, that all might learn the fear of the Lord and walk in His ways. {7:3} And Enoch was taken up to dwell with the Most High, for he was found righteous in his generation.

Story of Ahikar

The Story of Ahikar, an ancient narrative originating from the Near Eastern literary tradition, is a captivating blend of wisdom literature and courtly tale, reflecting the cultural and moral ethos of its time. This story, believed to date back to the Assyrian Empire around the 7th century BCE, centers on Ahikar, a wise and influential court official serving under multiple Assyrian kings. The tale is notable for its complex narrative structure, which intertwines Ahikar's rise to power, his unjust downfall orchestrated by his ungrateful adopted nephew Nadan, and his eventual vindication and return to favor. The text serves as a repository of proverbs and moral maxims, emphasizing virtues such as loyalty, humility, and the perils of ingratitude. These aphorisms not only provide moral guidance but also reflect the practical wisdom necessary for navigating the intricacies of court life and politics. The Story of Ahikar has been preserved in various languages, including Aramaic, Syriac, and later Greek, demonstrating its widespread influence across different cultures and epochs. Its themes resonate with the wisdom literature found in the Hebrew Bible and other ancient Near Eastern texts, underscoring the interconnectedness of these literary traditions. The narrative's enduring appeal lies in its rich tapestry of ethical teachings, its portrayal of the vicissitudes of fortune, and its celebration of wisdom as a guiding principle for both personal and communal conduct. As a piece of historical literature, The Story of Ahikar offers invaluable insights into the socio-political and cultural milieu of the ancient Near East, making it a subject of enduring interest for scholars in the fields of biblical studies, comparative literature, and ancient history.

{1:1} Ahikar, the Grand Vizier of Assyria, had sixty wives but no son of his own. Therefore, he adopted his nephew, Nadan. Ahikar lavished him with wisdom and knowledge, valuing these more than food and drink. {1:2} This is the tale of Haiqar the Wise, the trusted advisor of King Sennacherib of Assyria and Nineveh, and of Nadan, his nephew. {1:3} Haiqar was known for his wealth and wisdom, a philosopher skilled in governance and counsel. He had married sixty women, each with her own castle. {1:4} Despite his prosperity, none of his wives bore him a child who could inherit his legacy. {1:5} Distressed, Haiqar consulted astrologers, scholars, and sorcerers about his barrenness. {1:6} They advised him to appease the gods with sacrifices and prayers, hoping for a son. {1:7} Despite his efforts, the idols remained silent, leaving him disheartened. {1:8} Turning to the Most High God in earnest, Haiqar pleaded for a child who could comfort him in old age and perform his funeral rites. {1:9} His prayer was answered, a voice declaring: because he had first turned to idols, he would remain childless. Instead, he was instructed to adopt Nadan, his sister's son, who would inherit his wisdom and care for him in death. {1:10} Taking Nadan as his own, Haiqar entrusted him to eight nurses for his upbringing. {1:11} Nadan was raised with luxury and education, learning etiquette, writing, science, and philosophy from Haiqar. {1:12} As years passed, King Sennacherib noticed Haiqar's old age and asked about his successor. {1:13} Haiqar proposed Nadan, having groomed him for the role. {1:14} Curious, the king summoned Nadan, impressed by his upbringing and potential. {1:15} Haiqar presented Nadan, who pledged loyalty and service to the king. {1:16} The king admired Nadan and promised to honor him as Haiqar's successor. {1:17} Haiqar asked the king to be patient with Nadan's learning curve. {1:18} The king vowed to elevate Nadan, thanking Haiqar for his service. {1:19} Haiqar then devoted himself to teaching Nadan tirelessly, instilling him with wisdom and knowledge above all else.

{2:1} Thus he instructed him, saying: "My son, listen carefully to my words and heed my advice. Remember what I tell you. {2:2} My son, if you hear something in confidence, keep it within your heart. Do not repeat it, lest it cause harm like a burning coal, bringing shame upon you before God and people. {2:3} If you hear a rumor, do not spread it. If you witness something, do not divulge it unnecessarily. {2:4} Make your speech clear and understandable, and do not rush to respond. {2:5} When you hear something, guard it with discretion. {2:6} Do not unravel a sealed secret, nor seal what should be disclosed. {2:7} Do not chase after mere outward beauty, for it fades away, but seek an honorable reputation that endures. {2:8} Do not let a foolish woman deceive you with her words, risking your well-being and reputation. {2:9} Do not desire a woman solely for her appearance or possessions, for she may lead you astray and bring God's displeasure upon you. {2:10} Do not be like the almond tree that boasts early leaves but late fruit. Instead, be like the mulberry tree, which yields early fruit and enduring leaves. {2:11} Lower your voice, be polite, walk the straight path, and avoid foolishness. Do not laugh loudly, for loudness does not build houses nor move plows. {2:12} Conversing wisely with a knowledgeable person is more valuable than indulging in wine with a fool. {2:13} Pour your wine on the graves of the righteous and avoid the company of ignorant and contemptible individuals. {2:14} Associate with wise and God-fearing people, lest you adopt the ways of the ignorant. {2:15} Test and prove a friend before fully trusting them; do not praise hastily, and do not waste words on the foolish. {2:16} Prepare for challenges in advance, secure your household and business like a well-built ship before it sails. {2:17} Society judges the actions of the rich and poor differently, attributing wisdom to the former and necessity to the latter. {2:18} Be content with what you have and avoid coveting others' possessions. {2:19} Do not befriend fools or rejoice in the misfortunes of others. Show kindness even to those who wrong you. {2:20} Respect and fear those who honor God. {2:21} The wise may stumble but recover quickly; the ignorant remain vulnerable to their own ignorance. {2:22} Treat those inferior to you with respect; their Lord will repay your kindness. {2:23} Do not hesitate to discipline your child, for correction is like fertilizer for a garden. {2:24} Teach your child virtue and manners early, lest their actions bring shame upon you. {2:25} Choose trustworthy and reliable individuals for your affairs, avoiding the deceitful and lazy. {2:26} Honor and obey your parents to receive blessings and prolong your days. {2:27} Carry weapons when traveling; be prepared for unforeseen dangers. {2:28} Be fruitful in life like a tree bearing leaves and fruit, not barren and unproductive. {2:29} Be a source of benefit to others, providing shade and sustenance to those in need. {2:30} A sheep alone is vulnerable to predators; remain with your companions for strength. {2:31} Do not boast of your wisdom over others, nor mock their ignorance. {2:32} Earn the respect of your superiors through diligent service, not avoidance. {2:33} Treat your servants fairly, respecting their dignity and worth. {2:34} Fear God and maintain honesty in your dealings. {2:35} Speak kindly and fairly, guarding your words and actions. {2:36} A wise man learns from gentle rebuke; a fool remains unaffected by harsh discipline. {2:37} Give clear instructions to the competent and capable; oversee the incompetent personally. {2:38} Avoid making enemies of those stronger than you, as they may seek revenge. {2:39} Test and evaluate those entrusted with your affairs before fully committing to them. {2:40} Poverty and hardship are bitter experiences, worse than the taste of bitter herbs. {2:41} Teach your children frugality and self-reliance for a successful life. {2:42} Do not burden the ignorant with complex knowledge beyond their understanding. {2:43} Do not flaunt your wealth or status to avoid envy and disdain. {2:44} Blindness of the heart leads one astray more than physical blindness. {2:45} Stumble with your feet rather than with your tongue. {2:46} A faithful friend nearby is more valuable than a distant brother. {2:47} Beauty fades, but wisdom endures; focus on lasting virtues rather than transient appearances. {2:48} Sometimes sorrow and tears, when guided by the fear of God, are more valuable than laughter and rejoicing. {2:49} Appreciate what is close at hand rather than coveting distant treasures. {2:50} A modest fortune is better than scattered wealth. {2:51} A humble, living person is more valuable than a dead wealthy one. {2:52} A poor person who does right is more honorable than a wealthy sinner. {2:53} Keep confidences and guard your friend's secrets. {2:54} Think before you speak and avoid unnecessary conflicts. {2:55} Do not challenge those stronger than you; cultivate patience, endurance, and integrity. {2:56} Cherish your long-standing friendships; they are more reliable than newer ones. {2:57} Show compassion to the poor and defend their cause when needed. {2:58} Do not rejoice in the downfall of your enemies; treat them with respect and grace. {2:59} Understand that some things are beyond the comprehension of the ignorant and foolish. {2:60} To be truly wise, refrain from lying, stealing, and engaging in evil deeds. {2:61} Accept wise counsel even if it comes sternly; humility in youth leads to honor in old age. {2:62} Avoid confronting those in power during their prime; do not challenge overwhelming forces. {2:63} Be cautious and deliberate in choosing a spouse, for their actions will impact your life greatly. {2:64} Dress and speak in a manner consistent with your character. {2:65} If you commit a wrong, make amends promptly to avoid further trouble. {2:66} Befriend the generous and avoid those who are greedy and closed-minded. {2:67} There are certain truths that cannot be concealed: the wise, the foolish, the rich, and the poor are known to all.

{3:1} Haiqar spoke thus to Nadan, his nephew, believing him wise and trustworthy, yet unknowing that Nadan held only weariness and mockery in his heart, disregarding Haiqar's counsel and responsibilities. {3:2} Haiqar, resigned, handed over all his possessions—slaves, cattle, and wealth—to Nadan, who then wielded authority over everything once owned by Haiqar. {3:3} Haiqar, now retired, occasionally visited the king, keeping himself informed of court affairs before returning home. {3:4} Nadan, emboldened by his newfound power, scorned Haiqar openly, mistreating servants and squandering wealth heedlessly. {3:5} Haiqar, witnessing Nadan's cruelty, expelled him from his home and informed the king of Nadan's reckless actions. {3:6} The king, upon learning of Nadan's misrule, forbade him from managing Haiqar's possessions while Haiqar remained alive and well. {3:7} Nadan, thwarted and resentful, plotted vengeance against Haiqar, concocting a deceitful scheme to bring harm upon him. {3:8} Nadan's hand was forced by the king's decree, restricting him from interfering further with Haiqar's affairs. {3:9} Haiqar, rueful over his nephew's betrayal, mourned his misplaced trust and the turmoil it had brought upon him. {3:10} Benuzardan, Nadan's younger brother, took Nadan's place in Haiqar's household, earning Haiqar's trust and respect. {3:11} Nadan, envious of his brother's favor, slandered Haiqar to others, plotting further treachery against his uncle. {3:12} Craftily, Nadan forged letters in Haiqar's name, proposing treasonous alliances to foreign kings, seeking to embroil Haiqar in calamity. {3:13} Letters to Achish of Persia and Pharaoh of Egypt, seemingly from Haiqar, promised surrender of Assyria and Nineveh without conflict. {3:14} Nadan's skillful imitation of Haiqar's handwriting and seal lent credence to his deceitful correspondence. {3:15} Nadan's deception escalated, orchestrating a letter to Haiqar from the king, commanding a show of military might against a fabricated threat. {3:16} The king, upon seeing the false letter, was furious and perplexed by Haiqar's apparent betrayal. {3:17} Nadan, smug with his deception, awaited the unfolding of his sinister plan against Haiqar. {3:18} The king's anger mounted upon reading Nadan's forged letters and witnessing Haiqar's supposed treachery. {3:19} Nadan persuaded the king to confront Haiqar in the plain of Nisrin, intending to disgrace him publicly. {3:20} The king, led by Nadan, marched with his army to confront Haiqar as an enemy, as per the fabricated command. {3:21} Haiqar, unaware of Nadan's deceit, followed the fabricated orders, signaling his troops to prepare for battle against the king. {3:22} Witnessing Haiqar's obedience to the forged command, the king was filled with rage and suspicion. {3:23} Nadan, seizing the opportunity, urged the king to return home while he dealt with Haiqar and secured his downfall. {3:24} The king, consumed by anger towards Haiqar, withdrew, leaving Nadan to execute his vile plan. {3:25} On the fifth day, Nadan led the king and his soldiers to confront Haiqar in the desert, at the plain of Nisrin. {3:26} Seeing the king's approach, Haiqar signaled his troops to engage as enemies, as Nadan had deceitfully orchestrated. {3:27} The king, alarmed and incensed by Haiqar's apparent betrayal, questioned the unfolding events. {3:28} Nadan, feigning concern, assured the king of his loyalty and offered to capture Haiqar and eliminate the perceived threat. {3:29} The king, disturbed by the deception, took no immediate action against Haiqar, allowing Nadan to continue his scheme. {3:30} Nadan approached Haiqar, deceiving him with false praises and instructions from the king. {3:31} Haiqar, obedient, submitted to Nadan's fabricated commands, presenting himself to the king in chains. {3:32} Before the king, Haiqar humbled himself, yet bewildered by the accusations of betrayal. {3:33} The king confronted Haiqar with the forged letters bearing his seal, evidence of Haiqar's alleged treachery. {3:34} Haiqar, stricken with fear, stood silent, unable to refute the damning evidence. {3:35} Convinced of Haiqar's guilt, the king ordered his immediate execution, condemning him to be beheaded outside the city. {3:36} Nadan, gloating in his deceit, mocked Haiqar as he faced his impending doom. {3:37} The executioner, Abu Samik, prepared to carry out the king's decree, ensuring Haiqar's death would be a spectacle of shame. {3:38} Haiqar, resigned to his fate, pleaded for the king's enduring prosperity, accepting his unjust sentence. {3:39} The king granted Haiqar's request to be buried respectfully by his slaves after his execution, honoring their friendship. {3:40} Haiqar prepared for his imminent death, instructing his wife to mourn his passing with a grand gesture of remembrance. {3:41} Haiqar's wife obeyed, organizing a solemn gathering with young virgins dressed in mourning attire, ready to lament his fate. {3:42} She hosted the executioner and his entourage, providing them lavish food and wine to ease their task. {3:43} The guests indulged in the feast, unaware of Haiqar's plan unfolding. {3:44} Haiqar spoke privately to the executioner, reminding him of past favors and pleading for a swift deception. {3:45} Haiqar recounted saving the executioner's life previously, urging him to repay the debt by following his instructions. {3:46} Confident in Haiqar's plan, the executioner agreed to the scheme, promising Haiqar's safe concealment. {3:47} Haiqar foresaw the king's regret over his unjust execution and his eventual remorse toward Nadan's deceit. {3:48} Haiqar revealed a secret cellar in his garden where he could hide, known only to his wife and a faithful servant. {3:49} He instructed the executioner to dress a deserving slave in his own garments, ensuring his identity would remain concealed. {3:50} The disguised slave would be slain in Haiqar's place, fooling the drunken guests into believing it was Haiqar who had been executed. {3:51} The executioner carried out Haiqar's plan meticulously, ensuring the staged execution would deceive all present. {3:52} Following Haiqar's instructions, the executioner reported to the king, falsely claiming Haiqar's death had been executed as ordered. {3:53} Haiqar's wife continued to provide for his concealment in the hidden cellar, ensuring his safety while the deceit unfolded. {3:54} News spread of Haiqar's supposed death, and people mourned the loss of the wise sage and solver of riddles. {3:55} The city lamented Haiqar's demise, mourning the loss of his wisdom and leadership. {3:56} The king, regretful over Haiqar's fate, felt the weight of his rash judgment and the cunning of Nadan's deception. {3:57} Seeking to amend his error, the king instructed Nadan to organize a proper mourning and tribute for Haiqar's memory. {3:58} Nadan, callous and indifferent, disregarded the mourning traditions, further dishonoring Haiqar's memory. {3:59} Nadan, fueled by spite, mistreated Haiqar's servants and sought to dishonor his wife, showing no remorse for his actions. {3:60} Meanwhile, Haiqar remained hidden, praying and giving thanks to God for his protection and devising his eventual vindication. {3:61} The executioner visited Haiqar in his concealment, offering comfort and hope for his eventual release. {3:62} Despite Nadan's malicious plot, Haiqar held onto faith that his innocence would be proven and justice served. {3:63} Across distant lands, word spread of Haiqar's unjust demise, stirring sympathy and condemnation for King Sennacherib's hasty judgment and Nadan's treachery.

{4:1} Upon receiving confirmation of Haiqar's supposed demise, the king of Egypt promptly composed a letter to King Sennacherib, reminding him of their wishes for peace, health, might, and honor. He expressed a desire to construct a lofty castle and requested Sennacherib to send a wise man who could both build the castle and answer his profound queries.

Additionally, he sought to collect Assyria's taxes and customs duties for three years. {4:2} Sealing the missive, he dispatched it swiftly to Sennacherib's court. {4:3} Sennacherib, upon reading the letter, summoned his viziers and nobles. They were confounded and ashamed, knowing not how to respond. {4:4} Calling together sages, diviners, astrologers, and learned men from across his realm, Sennacherib presented the letter and asked for a solution to its demands. {4:5} They unanimously agreed that only Haiqar, his trusted vizier and secretary, possessed the wisdom needed. They suggested consulting Nadan, Haiqar's nephew, whom Haiqar had tutored extensively. {4:6} Summoned before the king, Nadan examined the letter and questioned, "Who among us can build such a castle?" {4:7} This response plunged Sennacherib into profound sorrow. He descended from his throne to sit in ashes, mourning Haiqar's absence. {4:8} He lamented, "Oh, my sorrow! Haiqar, the knower of secrets and riddles, where can I find your equal? Oh, teacher and ruler, how have I lost you?" {4:9} Day and night he wept for Haiqar, grieving deeply. {4:10} The swordsman, observing the king's anguish, approached him and said, "My lord, command your servants to cut off my head." {4:11} Bewildered, Sennacherib asked why. {4:12} The swordsman explained, "I disobeyed your command to kill Haiqar. Instead, I hid him and sacrificed one of his slaves. He lives safe in a cistern. If you wish, I will bring him before you." {4:13} Overwhelmed with hope, Sennacherib ordered the swordsman to fetch Haiqar immediately. {4:14} The swordsman hastened to Haiqar's dwelling. Opening the hiding place, he found Haiqar praising God. {4:15} Excitedly, he exclaimed, "Haiqar, I bring you joyous news!" {4:16} Haiqar inquired eagerly, and the swordsman recounted all about Pharaoh's letter and the king's remorse. {4:17} Together, they went to the king. {4:18} Seeing Haiqar's worn appearance, unkempt hair, and soiled clothing, Sennacherib recognized the toll of his ordeal. {4:19} Moved to tears, he embraced Haiqar, kissed him, and wept over him, expressing gratitude for his return. {4:20} He promised the swordsman great rewards and honors for his fidelity. {4:21} Haiqar then addressed the king, offering thanks and wisdom, urging him not to be troubled. {4:22} Sennacherib draped his own robe over the swordsman, enriching him with gifts, and allowed Haiqar to rest. {4:23} Haiqar counseled the king, acknowledging the trials of life. {4:24} The king praised God for showing mercy to Haiqar, saving him from unjust death. {4:25} He instructed Haiqar to refresh himself in a warm bath, shave, change clothes, and recuperate for forty days. {4:26} Gratefully accepting the king's robe, Haiqar departed for his home, surrounded by rejoicing household members, friends, and well-wishers.

{5:1} Following the king's orders, Haiqar rested for forty days. {5:2} He then dressed in his finest attire and rode joyfully to the king's court, with his servants ahead and behind him, filled with delight. {5:3} Meanwhile, Nadan, his nephew, was gripped by fear and confusion, unsure of what to do. {5:4} Observing Nadan's distress, Haiqar greeted the king warmly upon entering his presence. The king reciprocated and seated Haiqar beside him, showing him letters from the king of Egypt, sent after hearing of Haiqar's supposed death. {5:5} These letters had provoked and troubled them, causing many from their land to flee to Egypt to avoid the taxes demanded by the Egyptian king. {5:6} Haiqar read the letter and comprehended its contents fully. {5:7} He assured the king, "Do not be angry, my lord. I will go to Egypt, answer Pharaoh's questions, show him this letter, address the tax issue, and bring back those who have fled. With the help of the Most High God, I will also shame your enemies for the happiness of your kingdom." {5:8} Delighted by Haiqar's resolve, the king rejoiced greatly, his heart swelling with favor towards him. {5:9} Haiqar requested, "Grant me forty days to ponder and manage this matter." The king agreed to his request. {5:10} Haiqar returned home and ordered hunters to capture two young eagles. He then had weavers make two thousand cubits of cotton rope, and carpenters construct two large boxes. {5:11} Taking two young boys, he daily sacrificed lambs, fed the eagles, and trained the boys to ride the eagles' backs. Secured with strong knots and tied to the eagles' feet, he gradually allowed them to soar higher each day until they were accustomed to it, ascending to the sky while the boys rode. {5:12} Haiqar instructed the boys to shout, "Bring us clay and stone to build a castle for King Pharaoh, for we are idle," each time they were airborne. {5:13} He continued training them diligently until they reached peak skill. {5:14} Haiqar then went to the king, announcing, "My lord, the task is complete as you desired. Come with me, and I will show you the marvel." {5:15} The king eagerly accompanied Haiqar to an open space, where he summoned the eagles and boys. Haiqar secured them and allowed them to fly the full length of the ropes, prompting them to shout as instructed. Afterward, he reeled them in and settled them back into place. {5:16} Witnessing this spectacle, the king and his entourage marveled greatly. Overwhelmed with wonder, the king kissed Haiqar between his eyes, saying, "Go in peace, my beloved, pride of my kingdom. Go to Egypt, confront Pharaoh's inquiries, and triumph over him with the strength of the Most High God." {5:17} Farewelling Haiqar, the king departed with his troops, army, young men, and eagles toward Egypt, turning towards the king's domain upon arrival. {5:18} Upon learning that Sennacherib had sent a member of his Privy Council to engage Pharaoh and answer his queries, the people of Egypt informed Pharaoh, who summoned his councilors to bring the envoy before him. {5:19} Haiqar presented himself before Pharaoh, paying him the proper respects. {5:20} He conveyed, "My lord, King Sennacherib extends abundant peace, might, and honor to you. {5:21} He has sent me, one of his slaves, to address your inquiries and fulfill your desires. You sought a man from my lord the king to build a castle between heaven and earth. {5:22} By the aid of the Most High God, your noble favor, and my lord the king's power, I will construct it as you wish. {5:23} Concerning the taxes mentioned for three years, if I fail to satisfy you with my answers, my lord the king will send the mentioned taxes. If I do, you will send them to my lord the king." {5:24} Pharaoh was amazed and impressed by Haiqar's eloquence and straightforwardness. {5:25} Pharaoh asked, "What is your name?" He replied, "Your servant is Abiqam, a humble servant of King Sennacherib." {5:26} Pharaoh retorted, "Could your lord not send someone of higher rank than you, a mere ant in comparison, to converse with me?" {5:27} Haiqar replied, "My lord, I pray to the Most High God to fulfill your desires, for God supports the weak to confound the strong." {5:28} Pharaoh ordered accommodations for Abiqam, providing him with provisions and all necessities. {5:29} Three days later, Pharaoh, dressed in purple and red, sat on his throne with his viziers and kingdom magnates standing in respect. {5:30} Pharaoh summoned Abiqam, who approached, bowed, and stood before the king. {5:31} Pharaoh asked, "Abiqam, whom do I resemble, and to whom do my nobles compare?" {5:32} Abiqam responded, "My lord, you are like the idol Bel, and your nobles are like its servants." {5:33} Pharaoh dismissed him with instructions to return the next day. {5:34} The following day, Abiqam returned as commanded. Pharaoh was in red attire, while his nobles wore white. {5:35} Pharaoh asked again, "Abiqam, whom do I resemble, and to whom do my nobles compare?" {5:36} Abiqam answered, "My lord, you are like the sun, and your servants are like its beams." Pharaoh instructed him to return home and come back the next day. {5:37} Pharaoh ordered his court to dress in pure white, and he, too, wore white as he sat on his throne. {5:38} Abiqam was summoned again and stood before Pharaoh. {5:39} Pharaoh asked, "Abiqam, whom do I resemble, and to whom do my nobles compare?" {5:40} Abiqam replied, "My lord, you are like the moon, and your nobles are like the planets and stars." Pharaoh sent him away, telling him to return the next day. {5:41} On the next day, Pharaoh dressed in red velvet and sat on his throne. {5:42} Abiqam was brought before him. {5:43} Pharaoh asked, "Abiqam, whom do I resemble, and to whom do my armies compare?" {5:44} Abiqam replied, "My lord, you are like the month of April, and your armies are like its flowers." {5:45} Hearing this, Pharaoh rejoiced greatly, recalling Abiqam's previous comparisons. {5:46} Pharaoh then asked Abiqam, "Tell me now, who is your lord King Sennacherib like, and to whom do his nobles compare?" {5:47} Abiqam boldly declared, "My lord is like the God of heaven, and his nobles are like lightning and thunder. He commands the winds, rain, sun, moon, and stars at his will. He controls tempests, wind, rain, and tramples even the month of April, destroying its flowers and homes." {5:48} Pharaoh was deeply puzzled and became angry, demanding, "Tell me the truth. Who are you really?" {5:49} Abiqam revealed, "I am Haiqar, the scribe, esteemed Privy Councilor of King Sennacherib, his vizier, governor, and chancellor." {5:50} Pharaoh was astonished, saying, "We heard Haiqar was slain by King Sennacherib, yet here you are, alive and well." {5:51} Haiqar acknowledged, "Yes, it was so, but thanks be to God, who knows the hidden truths. My lord ordered my death based on false accusations, but the Lord saved me. Blessed is he who trusts in Him." {5:52} Pharaoh instructed Haiqar, "Go now, and return tomorrow. Tell me something I have never heard from my nobles or people of my kingdom."

{6:1} After returning home, Haiqar penned a letter addressed in this manner: {6:2} "From Sennacherib, King of Assyria and Nineveh, to Pharaoh, King of Egypt. {6:3} Greetings to you, my brother. I write to inform you of a pressing need: I require nine hundred talents of gold to provision some of my soldiers. I intend to repay this sum shortly. {6:4} Having folded the letter, he presented it to Pharaoh the following day. {6:5} Pharaoh, upon reading it, was perplexed and remarked, "I have never received such a request!" {6:6} Haiqar calmly responded, "Indeed, this is a debt owed by you to my lord the king." {6:7} Pharaoh accepted this explanation, acknowledging, "Haiqar, you are known for your honesty in serving kings. {6:8} Praise be to God who has endowed you with wisdom and adorned you with knowledge and philosophy. {6:9} Now, Haiqar, we request that you build us a castle suspended between heaven and earth." {6:10} Haiqar replied, "I will build such a castle as you desire, but prepare lime, stone, clay, and skilled workers for me." {6:11} The king arranged everything as requested, and they gathered at a spacious location. Haiqar and his assistants arrived with eagles and young men. The king, his nobles, and the entire city assembled to witness Haiqar's work. {6:12} Haiqar released the eagles from their boxes, strapped the young men onto their backs, tied ropes to the eagles' feet, and sent them soaring into the air. They ascended until they hung suspended between heaven and earth. {6:13} The young men shouted, "Bring bricks, bring clay, so we can build the king's castle; we are standing idle!" {6:14} The crowd marveled and wondered at this spectacle, as did the king and his nobles. {6:15} Haiqar and his servants urged the workers on, calling for the king's soldiers to provide whatever the skilled workers needed and not hinder their progress. {6:16} The king exclaimed, "You are mad! Who can transport materials to such a height?" {6:17} Haiqar replied, "My lord, how else can we build a castle in the air? If you were here, you would build several castles in a single day." {6:18} Pharaoh said, "Go home, Haiqar, and rest. We have abandoned the idea of building the castle. Return to me tomorrow." {6:19} Haiqar returned home and appeared before Pharaoh the next day. Pharaoh asked, "Haiqar, what news of your lord's horse? When it neighs in Assyria and Nineveh, our mares hear and miscarry." {6:20} Hearing this, Haiqar fetched a cat, bound her, and began to flog her fiercely until the Egyptians heard and reported it to the king. {6:21} Pharaoh summoned Haiqar and asked, "Why are you beating this dumb animal?" {6:22} Haiqar explained, "My lord Sennacherib gave me a valuable cock with a strong voice, knowledgeable of day and night. This very night, the cat decapitated it, hence the punishment." {6:23} Pharaoh skeptically said, "You're growing old and senile, Haiqar. Egypt and Nineveh are sixty-eight parasangs apart. How could the cat have done this?" {6:24} Haiqar retorted, "My lord, if such a distance exists, how could your mares hear my lord the king's horse or its voice reach Egypt?" {6:25} Pharaoh realized Haiqar had answered astutely. {6:26} He then challenged Haiqar, "Make me ropes from sea sand." {6:27} Haiqar replied, "Provide me a rope from your treasury as a model." {6:28} Haiqar went to the shore, bored holes in the rough sea sand, collected it in the sun until it resembled woven ropes. {6:29} Haiqar said, "Command your servants to take these ropes. I can weave more whenever you desire." {6:30} Pharaoh then said, "We have a broken millstone. Can you mend it?" {6:31} Haiqar examined it and found another stone. {6:32} He replied, "I am a foreigner without sewing tools. Ask your faithful shoemakers to fashion awls from this stone for me." {6:33} Pharaoh and his nobles laughed heartily, saying, "Blessed is the Most High God who has given you such wit and knowledge." {6:34} Seeing Haiqar's quick wit, Pharaoh commanded the collection of three years' taxes to be given to him, along with fine robes and provisions for his journey. {6:35} He told Haiqar, "Go in peace, strength of your lord, pride of your scholars! Are there any rulers like you? Give my regards to King Sennacherib and inform him of the gifts we send, for kings find contentment in small things." {6:36} Haiqar then kissed Pharaoh's hands, bowed before him, and wished him strength, prosperity, and abundant treasury. {6:37} Haiqar requested, "My lord, let none of our people remain in Egypt." {6:38} Pharaoh proclaimed throughout Egypt that no Assyrian or Ninevite should stay, but depart with Haiqar. {6:39} Haiqar bid farewell to Pharaoh and journeyed back to Assyria and Nineveh, laden with treasures and wealth. {6:40} Upon hearing of Haiqar's return, King Sennacherib joyously went out to meet him, embracing and kissing him warmly. {6:41} Sennacherib exclaimed, "Welcome, my kinsman Haiqar, strength of my kingdom and pride of my realm! {6:42} Ask whatever you desire of me, even half of my kingdom and possessions." {6:43} Haiqar replied, "May the king live forever! Instead, honor Abu Samik in my place. My life was spared by God and his hands." {6:44} Sennacherib honored Abu Samik above all his counselors and favorites. {6:45} Sennacherib then inquired about Haiqar's interactions with Pharaoh, from his arrival to departure, how he answered every question, received taxes, robes, and gifts. {6:46} Sennacherib rejoiced greatly and told Haiqar to take whatever tribute he desired, as it was all within his reach. {6:47} Haiqar requested, "My lord, grant me Nadan, my sister's son, so I can repay him for his deeds. His blood will be on me." {6:48} Sennacherib agreed, saying, "He is yours." Haiqar took Nadan, bound him with iron chains, and confined him in a dark room, appointing Nebu-hal as his guard, providing only bread and water daily.

{7:1} Every time Haiqar came and went, he would rebuke Nadan, his nephew, speaking to him with wisdom: {7:2} "Nadan, my boy, I've always treated you with kindness and goodness, yet you've repaid me with ugliness, wickedness, and even attempted murder. {7:3} You know the saying: 'If someone won't listen with their ears, they'll be made to listen with the scruff of their neck.' {7:4} Why are you so angry with me?" {7:5} Haiqar replied, "Because I raised you, educated you, honored you, and gave you everything, preparing you to inherit my position. Yet you repaid me with betrayal and ruin. {7:6} But the Lord knew I was wronged, and He saved me from the trap you set. The Lord heals broken hearts and humbles the envious and arrogant. {7:7} Nadan, you've been like a scorpion that stings even when it lands on brass. {7:8} You're like a gazelle eating madder roots, thinking you're safe today but doomed tomorrow. {7:9} You're like someone who pours cold water on a friend in winter. {7:10} You're like someone throwing a stone at heaven to harm his own master, only to fail and bring guilt upon yourself. {7:11} If you had honored me and listened, you would have been my heir and ruled over my lands. {7:12} Know this: even if a dog or pig had a ten-cubit-long tail, they couldn't match the value of a horse, even if its mane were silk. {7:13} I thought you'd be my heir, but your envy and insolence drove you to try to kill me. Yet the Lord delivered me from your deceit. {7:14} You're like a trap set on a dunghill, offering false piety to God. {7:15} Like a trap with a piece of wood, claiming it's an oak and carrying bread for the hungry, but betraying them when they approach. {7:16} You've been like a lion befriending an ass, only to devour it when the time came. {7:17} Like a weevil in wheat, spoiling what's good. {7:18} Like someone reaping ten measures of wheat, only to find it unchanged, lazy and unproductive. {7:19} Like a partridge caught in a net, unable to save itself. {7:20} Like a dog seeking warmth in a potter's house, then biting those who sheltered it. {7:21} Like a pig wallowing in filth after bathing with the nobles. {7:22} Like a goat unable to save itself from sacrifice. {7:23} A dog not fed from its hunting becomes food for flies. {7:24} A greedy and cunning hand will be cut off. {7:25} An eye without light will be pecked out by ravens. {7:26} Like a tree's branch saying it can't be cut without its consent. {7:27} Like a cat rejecting gold chains and sweets for its thieving ways. {7:28} Like a serpent and wolf scheming mischief together. {7:29} You've had my good food but not reciprocated with the basics. {7:30} You drank sweet water but denied me even well water. {7:31} I taught you, raised you tall and strong, yet you twisted and bent me. {7:32} I hoped you'd build me a fortress, but instead you buried me alive. Yet the Lord spared me from your schemes. {7:33} I wished you well, and you repaid me with evil. I'm tempted to punish you severely." {7:34} Nadan pleaded, "Uncle, forgive me. I'm full of sin, and who forgives like you?" {7:35} "Accept me now. I'll serve you humbly, caring for your animals and fields. I'm the guilty one; you're the forgiving." {7:36} Haiqar replied, "You're like a fruitless tree by water, asking to be moved, but still bearing no fruit. {7:37} Even an old eagle is better than a young crow. {7:38} They warned the wolf against the sheep's dust, but it claimed even their dregs were good for its eyes. {7:39} They taught the wolf to read but it spoke of eating lambs and goats. {7:40} They sat the ass at the table, but it rolled in dust, unable to change its nature. {7:41} The saying goes: if you beget a son, call him your son; if you raise him, call him your slave. {7:42} Good deeds beget good, evil begets evil. The Lord judges based on our actions. {7:43} I've said my piece. The Lord knows all secrets and will judge between us." {7:44} Nadan swelled with guilt upon hearing Haiqar's words. {7:45} His body ballooned and burst, his entrails scattered, and he perished. {7:46} His end was destruction; he went to hell. Whoever digs a pit for another falls into it; whoever sets traps will be ensnared. {7:47} This is the tale of Haiqar, where justice prevails. Praise be to God forever. Amen and peace. {7:48} This chronicle concludes with God's help, may He be exalted: Amen, Amen, Amen.

Ascension of Isaiah

The Ascension of Isaiah is a pseudepigraphal work, traditionally dated between the late 1st century BCE and early 2nd century CE. Attributed to the prophet Isaiah, the text comprises several sections with distinct themes and theological perspectives. It narrates Isaiah's visions and prophecies, including the seven heavens, Satan's fall, Jesus Christ's birth and life, and Isaiah's martyrdom. Noted for its cosmology and angelology, it provides vivid descriptions of the heavenly realms and their inhabitants. The apocalyptic elements reflect eschatological expectations, while christological themes highlight early Christian interpretations of Isaiah's prophecies. The portrayal of Jesus' descent through the heavens and his secretive mission offers a unique perspective on the incarnation, differing from the canonical Gospels. Emphasizing the duality of good and evil, the role of angels and demons, and the triumph of righteousness, the text resonates with broader apocalyptic literature.

Chapter 1-5: Part of Martydom of Isaiah.

{6:1} In the twentieth year of King Hezekiah's reign in Judah, Isaiah, son of Amoz, and Josab, Isaiah's son, came to Hezekiah in Jerusalem from Gilgal. {6:2} Isaiah sat on the king's couch, refusing the seat brought for him. {6:3} As Isaiah spoke words of faith and righteousness to Hezekiah, all the princes of Israel, eunuchs, and the king's counselors were present, {6:4} along with forty prophets and their sons, who had come from nearby regions and mountains to hear Isaiah. {6:5} They came to greet him, hear his words, receive his blessings, and prophesy. {6:6} As Isaiah spoke, they heard a door open and the voice of the Spirit. {6:7} The king gathered all the prophets and people present. Micah, the aged Ananias, Joel, and Josab sat on his right. {6:8} Hearing the Holy Spirit's voice, they knelt, worshipped, {6:9} and praised the Most High God who dwells above and rests among the holy ones, giving glory to God for granting a door in an alien world. {6:10} While Isaiah communicated with the Holy Spirit, he became silent, his mind taken up from him, not seeing those before him. {6:11} His eyes were open, but he was silent, his mind absorbed in a vision, his breath still in him. {6:12} An angel from the seventh heaven showed him the vision. {6:13} The people, apart from the prophets, did not realize Isaiah had been taken up. {6:14} His vision was not from this world but from a hidden realm. {6:15} Isaiah shared the vision with Hezekiah, Josab, and the prophets, excluding the officials, eunuchs, and people. Samnas the secretary, Jehoiakim, and Asaph the recorder, righteous men filled with the Spirit's fragrance, heard the vision. Micah and Josab had sent the people away when Isaiah's wisdom was taken as if he were dead.

{7:1} Isaiah recounted his vision to Hezekiah, Josab, Micah, and the other prophets. {7:2} He described seeing a glorious angel, unlike any angel he had seen before. {7:3} The angel took Isaiah's hand. Isaiah asked the angel's name and destination, given strength to speak. {7:4} The angel replied that Isaiah would understand after seeing the vision, though his name would remain unknown. {7:5} Isaiah would return to his body but would see where the angel was taking him. {7:6} Isaiah rejoiced at the angel's kindness. {7:7} The angel noted Isaiah's joy and promised he would see one greater who would speak even more kindly. {7:8} The angel from the seventh heaven was sent to show Isaiah these things. {7:9} They ascended to the firmament, {7:10} where Isaiah saw Sammael and his hosts engaged in a great struggle, envious of each other, resembling earthly conflicts. {7:11} Isaiah asked about the envy, {7:12} and the angel explained that it existed since the world's beginning and would continue until the one Isaiah was to see would destroy it. {7:13} They ascended above the firmament to the first heaven. {7:14} Isaiah saw a throne in the middle, surrounded by angels, {7:15} with those on the right more glorious than those on the left, all singing praises. {7:16} Isaiah asked who they praised, {7:17} and the angel said it was directed to the one in the seventh heaven. {7:18} They ascended to the second heaven, equal in height to the distance from earth to the firmament. {7:19} There, too, were angels on the right and left, {7:20} praising the one on the throne with greater glory than the first heaven. {7:21} Isaiah fell to worship, but the guiding angel stopped him, instructing him to reserve worship for the one in the seventh heaven. {7:22} The angel promised Isaiah's throne, robes, and crown awaited him there. {7:23} Isaiah rejoiced that those who loved the Most High would ascend there. {7:24} They reached the third heaven, where Isaiah saw similar angelic arrangements and a throne, but no mention of earthly matters. {7:25} Isaiah noticed his face transforming as they ascended, questioning the absence of earthly vanity. {7:26} The angel explained that earthly weaknesses were unmentioned but not hidden. {7:27} The angel assured Isaiah that in the seventh heaven, he would see that nothing is hidden from heavenly thrones and angels. The praise and glory were greater than below. {7:28} They ascended to the fourth heaven, higher than the distance from earth to the firmament. {7:29} There were more angels on the right and left, praising the central throne, {7:30} with greater glory than the third heaven. {7:31} The one on the throne's glory surpassed the angels, and the praises were grander than the heavens below. {7:32} They ascended to the fifth heaven, with similar arrangements, but with even greater glory. {7:33} The one on the throne had the most glory, with the angels on the right surpassing those on the left. {7:34} Isaiah praised the unique, unnamed One dwelling in the heavens, who bestowed such glory on the heavens and angels, especially the one on the throne.

{8:1} Once more, the angel took me up into the atmosphere of the sixth heaven, where I saw a splendor greater than in the previous five heavens. The angels there had immense glory, and their praise was holy and wonderful. I asked the angel, "What is this, my lord?" He replied, "I am not your lord, but your companion." I questioned why there were no groups of angels, and he explained, "From the sixth heaven upwards, there are no divisions, nor a central throne; they are directed by the power of the seventh heaven, where the One who is not named and His Chosen One dwell. The name of the Chosen One is unknown, and no heaven can learn His name. He alone commands the heavens and thrones. I was sent to show you this glory and to reveal the Lord of all these heavens transforming to resemble your form. No one who returns to a body on earth has seen or understood what you have witnessed, for you are destined for the lot of the Lord. This is the power of the sixth heaven and the air." I praised the greatness of my Lord for bringing me here. The angel continued, "When you ascend here from your body by God's will, you will receive the robe you will see, and other robes as well. {8:2} You will be equal to the angels in the seventh heaven." As we ascended into the sixth heaven, I noticed there were no divisions or central throne, and all angels were of one appearance, their praise equal. Strengthened, I sang praises with them. They all named the primal Father, His Beloved Christ, and the Holy Spirit with one voice, which differed from the voices of the lower heavens. The light here was so great that the light in the previous heavens seemed like darkness. I rejoiced and praised the One who graciously provided such light. I pleaded with the angel to not return me to the world of flesh. Hezekiah, Josab, and Micah, there is much darkness in the world. The angel knew my thoughts and reassured me, "If you rejoice over this light, you will rejoice even more in the seventh heaven where the Lord and His Beloved reside. The light and glory there are greater. However, you cannot stay here yet as your time is not complete." This saddened me, but the angel comforted me.

{9:1} The angel led me into the seventh heaven, where I heard a voice asking how far I would go. Trembling with fear, I was reassured by another voice allowing my ascent. I asked the angel who prevented and permitted me, and he explained, "The one who prevented you oversees the praise of the sixth heaven. The one who allowed you is your Lord, Christ, known as Jesus on earth. You cannot hear His name until you leave your body." In the seventh heaven, I saw a wonderful light and countless angels. I saw the righteous from Adam's time, including Abel and Enoch, stripped of their earthly robes, now resembling the glorious angels. They were not yet on their thrones or wearing their crowns. I asked why, and the angel explained, "They will receive their crowns and thrones when the Beloved descends in human form. The Lord will descend, be perceived as a man, and will be crucified, unknown to the world. After defeating death, He will rise and remain on earth for 545 days. {9:2} Many righteous will ascend with Him, receiving their robes, thrones, and crowns." I saw books detailing the deeds of the children of Israel, confirming that nothing is hidden from the seventh heaven. I saw many robes, thrones, and crowns and asked the angel about them. He explained, "These are for those who believe in the words of the one to be named Jesus and keep faith in Him." I then saw a figure of surpassing glory, and all the righteous and angels worshipped Him. The angel instructed me to worship this figure, who is the Lord of all. I saw another figure of similar glory, also worshipped by the righteous and angels. My guide explained, "This is the angel of the Holy Spirit." I saw the Great Glory, but my sight dimmed, and I could no longer see the angels or my guide, only the righteous in great power. My Lord and the angel of the Spirit approached and spoke of the power given to my guide because of me. Together, they worshipped and praised the Lord, followed by the righteous and all the angels.

{10:1} Then I heard the voices and hymns of praise from each of the six heavens I had ascended through, all directed toward the Glorious One whose glory I couldn't see. I witnessed the praise directed to Him, and the Lord and the angel of the Spirit heard and saw everything. All the praise from the six heavens was both heard and seen. The angel guiding me said, "This is the Most High, dwelling among the holy ones, and will be called the Father of the Lord by the Holy Spirit in the mouth of the righteous." I heard the Most High's voice speaking to my Lord Christ, who will be called Jesus, saying, "Go and descend through all the heavens, through the firmament and the world, down to the angel in Sheol, but not as far as Perdition. Make your likeness like those in the five heavens, and take care to resemble the angels of the firmament and Sheol. None of the angels in that world will know you are Lord of the seven heavens and their angels with me. They will not know when I summon you and their angels to judge and destroy the princes and gods of that world, for they have denied me, saying, 'We alone exist.' Afterward, you will ascend from the gods of death to your place, not transformed in each heaven, but ascending in glory to sit at my right hand, where the princes and powers of that world will worship you." {10:2} I heard the Great Glory give this command to my Lord, and I saw my Lord descend from the seventh heaven into the sixth. The angel guiding me said, "Understand, Isaiah, and see the transformation and descent of the Lord." I watched as the angels in the sixth heaven praised and glorified Him, though He had not changed form to resemble them. I sang praises with them. In the fifth heaven, He changed His form to match the angels there, and they did not praise Him, as He looked like them. This pattern continued as He descended into the fourth, third, second, and first heavens, changing His form to match the angels in each, and giving the password at the gates where required. The gatekeepers did not praise Him, seeing Him as one of their own. {10:3} Descending into the firmament where the prince of this world dwells, He gave the password to those on the left and took on their form. They did not praise Him but fought out of envy. As He descended further, He made Himself like the angels of the air, not giving the password, as they were busy plundering and doing violence to one another. Throughout His descent, no one questioned me because of the angel leading me.

{11:1} After this, the angel who spoke to me said, "Understand, Isaiah son of Amoz, because I was sent from the Lord for this purpose." {11:2} I saw a woman from David's family named Mary, a virgin betrothed to Joseph, a carpenter from the family of righteous David of Bethlehem in Judah. {11:3} When she was betrothed, she became pregnant, and Joseph wanted to divorce her. {11:4} But the angel of the Spirit appeared, so Joseph did not divorce Mary and kept her pregnancy a secret. {11:5} He kept her as a holy virgin and did not approach her. {11:6} They did not live together for two months. {11:7} After two months, while Joseph and Mary were alone at home, {11:8} Mary saw a small infant and was astonished. {11:9} After her amazement, her womb was as it was before she conceived. {11:10} Joseph, seeing the infant, praised the Lord. {11:11} A voice told them not to reveal this vision. {11:12} The story spread in Bethlehem. {11:13} Some said, "Mary gave birth before she was married for two months." {11:14} Many said, "She did not give birth; there were no cries of pain." They all knew of Him but did not know where He came from. {11:15} They went to Nazareth in Galilee. {11:16} Isaiah told Hezekiah, Josab, and other prophets that this was hidden from all heavens and gods of the world. {11:17} In Nazareth, He suckled like an infant to avoid recognition. {11:18} As He grew, He performed great signs and miracles in Israel and Jerusalem. {11:19} The adversary envied Him and stirred the Israelites against Him. They handed Him to the ruler and crucified Him, and He descended to Sheol. {11:20} Isaiah saw His crucifixion in Jerusalem. {11:21} He rose on the third day and remained for many days. {11:22} The angel said, "Understand, Isaiah." Isaiah saw Him send out the twelve disciples and ascend. {11:23} In the firmament, He was not transformed, but angels and Satan saw and worshiped Him. {11:24} They were sorrowful, realizing they missed His glory as He descended. {11:25} In the second heaven, He was worshiped but not transformed. {11:26} The angels in the second heaven also did not recognize Him initially. {11:27} In the third heaven, the same thing happened. {11:28} Similarly, in the fourth and fifth heavens, the angels praised Him, realizing they had missed His glory. {11:29} His glory remained constant throughout. {11:30} In the sixth heaven, He was worshiped and praised more loudly. {11:31} Ascending into the seventh heaven, all the righteous and angels praised Him. {11:32} He sat at the right hand of the Great Glory, whose glory Isaiah couldn't behold. {11:33} The angel of the Holy Spirit sat on the left. {11:34} The angel told Isaiah, "This is enough for you, for you have seen great things no one born of flesh has seen. {11:35} You will return to your robe until your days are complete, then you shall come here." Isaiah shared this vision with those around him, and they sang praises. {11:36} He told King Hezekiah, "These are the things I have seen. {11:37} The end of this world and all these visions will occur in the last generation." {11:38} Isaiah made Hezekiah swear not to share this with Israel or let anyone copy the words until then. {11:39} He advised them to stay in the Holy Spirit to receive their robes, thrones, and crowns of glory in the seventh heaven. {11:40} Because of these visions, Satan had Isaiah sawed in half by Manasseh. {11:41} Hezekiah gave all these things to Manasseh in his twenty-sixth year of reign. {11:42} But Manasseh did not remember or heed them, becoming Satan's servant and was destroyed.

Testament of Abraham

The Testament of Abraham, an ancient Jewish pseudepigraphical text, represents a unique blend of apocalyptic literature and folklore, reflecting a rich tapestry of theological and cultural traditions from the Second Temple period. This text, traditionally ascribed to the patriarch Abraham, provides a fascinating narrative that diverges from the canonical biblical account, portraying Abraham's reluctance to die and his subsequent journey guided by the archangel Michael. The story is characterized by vivid descriptions of the heavenly realm and the judgment of souls, emphasizing themes of divine justice, mercy, and the afterlife. The Testament of Abraham is preserved in two primary Greek recensions, known as the longer and shorter versions, each offering distinct variations and embellishments to the narrative. The text's historical context suggests it was composed in the first or second century CE, reflecting the evolving Jewish thought and the influence of Hellenistic culture. Its narrative structure, replete with dramatic dialogues and moral exhortations, underscores the didactic purpose of the work, aimed at imparting ethical teachings and reinforcing the faith of its audience. The Testament of Abraham also exhibits a profound interplay in early Christian traditions, making it a valuable resource for understanding the development of early Christian eschatological beliefs. Its reception and transmission through various manuscripts and translations further attest to its enduring significance in the religious and literary landscape of antiquity.

{1:1} Abraham lived a full life, reaching the age of nine hundred and ninety-five years. Throughout his long years, he embodied peace, kindness, and righteousness. Known for his exceptional hospitality, he often pitched his tent at the crossroads near the oak of Mamre, where he welcomed everyone—rich and poor, kings and rulers, the disabled and needy, friends and strangers, neighbors and travelers. {1:2} The devout and righteous Abraham showed hospitality to all alike. However, even he could not escape the inevitable fate of death, that bitter end that comes to all. {1:3} Therefore, the Lord God called upon His archangel Michael, instructing him to visit Abraham and inform him of his impending death. God acknowledged His blessings upon Abraham, likening his descendants to the stars in heaven and the sand on the seashore. {1:4} Despite his wealth and long life, Abraham's time had come. Michael was tasked to deliver the message gently to Abraham, assuring him that he would depart from this world, leave his earthly body, and reunite with his Creator among the righteous.

{2:1} The chief-captain Michael left the presence of God and descended to Abraham at the oak of Mamre. He found righteous Abraham in the field, sitting with his servants and oxen used for ploughing, totaling twelve in number. {2:2} As Michael approached, Abraham, recognizing him from afar as a noble warrior, rose to greet him warmly, as was his custom with all strangers. Michael greeted him respectfully, addressing him as a revered father and a righteous soul chosen by God. {2:3} As Abraham's final days approached, the Lord instructed Michael to go to him and announce that his temporal life was coming to an end, urging him to put his affairs in order before he passed away. {2:4} On their way back to Abraham's house from the field, they passed a cypress tree, which, by divine command, spoke with a human voice praising the holiness of God. Abraham, sensing the mystical nature of the moment, kept this revelation to himself, thinking Michael had not heard the tree's voice. {2:5} Upon arriving at the courtyard of his house, Isaac noticed the angel sitting with his father and immediately ran to inform Sarah, his mother, that the man with Abraham was no ordinary mortal. {2:6} Isaac then approached the angel, bowed before him, and received a blessing. The angel reassured Isaac that God would fulfill the promises made to Abraham and his descendants, granting them the prayers of his parents. {2:7} Abraham instructed Isaac to fetch water from the well to wash the feet of the weary traveler, Michael. Isaac swiftly obeyed, bringing water in a vessel. Abraham performed the washing, ensuring Michael's comfort after his long journey. {2:8} Michael, curious, asked Abraham to reveal his name before entering his house, out of respect and to avoid being a burden. Abraham explained that he was originally called Abram by his parents, but God had renamed him Abraham when He instructed him to leave his homeland and go to a new land. {2:9} Michael apologized for his inquiry, acknowledging Abraham's reputation as a man of God who had once gone forty furlongs to slaughter a goat to entertain angels in his home. {2:10} After their conversation, they proceeded towards Abraham's house. Abraham instructed a servant to bring a beast for Michael to sit upon, but Michael declined, preferring to walk lightly alongside Abraham, enjoying his company.

{3:1} Michael approached Abraham while he was seated with his oxen for ploughing, appearing very old, holding his son. Not recognizing Michael, Abraham greeted him kindly, wishing him a prosperous journey. Michael responded respectfully, and Abraham invited him to sit and rest before they traveled to his house for the evening. {3:2} Abraham praised Michael's appearance, likening him to the sun and the most beautiful among men, and eagerly asked about his origin and journey. Michael explained he came from a great city on a mission for the king, replacing a friend summoned by the king. {3:3} Abraham invited Michael to accompany him to his field, where they sat down among the company. Abraham instructed his servants to fetch two gentle horses for their journey, but Michael declined, preferring to walk. Abraham agreed, and they continued towards his house. {3:4} As they approached the city, about three furlongs away, they encountered a massive tree with three hundred branches, resembling a tamarisk tree, from which a voice praised Abraham for fulfilling his mission. Abraham pondered the mystery quietly. {3:5} Upon entering his house, Abraham instructed his servants to prepare three sheep for a feast. Isaac was asked to fetch water for washing the stranger's feet, which he did obediently. {3:6} Abraham, while washing Michael's feet, foresaw that it would be his last act of hospitality in such a manner. Isaac, upon hearing this, wept, questioning his father's words. Abraham, moved by Isaac's tears, wept himself, and Michael joined them in their sorrow. {3:7} Michael's tears fell into the basin and turned into precious stones, a marvel that astonished Abraham, who kept this mystery in his heart, pondering its significance in silence.

{4:1} Abraham instructed Isaac, his beloved son, to prepare the inner chamber of their house for their guest. He asked Isaac to adorn it with two couches, one for himself and one for the distinguished guest, along with a seat, a candlestick, and a table filled abundantly with all manner of good things. {4:2} Isaac diligently arranged everything as his father requested. Abraham then led the archangel Michael into the chamber, where they reclined on the couches, enjoying the feast set before them. {4:3} Suddenly, Michael excused himself to relieve himself, but in an instant, he ascended to heaven and stood before the Lord. He confessed to God that he could not bring himself to remind Abraham of his impending death, praising Abraham's virtues and righteousness. {4:4} God then instructed Michael to return to Abraham and partake in whatever Abraham offered, even to eat with him. God promised to send His Holy Spirit to Isaac, implanting the knowledge of Abraham's death in Isaac's heart through a dream, which Isaac would recount and Michael would interpret. {4:5} Michael expressed his dilemma, being an incorporeal being who neither eats nor drinks, faced with Abraham's hospitality of earthly delicacies. He sought guidance from God on how to handle this situation. {4:6} Meanwhile, Sarah heard the weeping from inside her house and came out to inquire why they were sorrowful. Abraham reassured her that all was well and urged her to return to her tasks. As sunset approached, Michael departed from Abraham's house and ascended to heaven to worship God, a ritual observed by all angels at that hour. {4:7} After worship, each angel departed to their respective places, but Michael remained before the Lord, seeking permission to speak. He recounted his mission to Abraham and expressed his hesitation in delivering the message of death directly to such a righteous friend of God. {4:8} Michael pleaded with God to instead implant the awareness of death in Abraham's heart and not require Michael to speak the words directly, acknowledging the delicacy and abruptness of such a message to someone beloved by God. {4:9} God reassured Michael, instructing him to return to Abraham, share in his hospitality, and ensure the interpretation of Isaac's dream about Abraham's death was clear. God emphasized the importance of Abraham preparing for his passing, given his blessings.

{5:1} The chief captain descended to Abraham's house and sat down at the table with him, while Isaac served them. After supper, Abraham prayed as was his custom, and the chief-captain joined him in prayer. Then each retired to their respective couches to sleep. {5:2} Isaac expressed his desire to sleep in the chamber with them to hear the wisdom of the righteous guest. Abraham gently insisted that Isaac should go to his own chamber to avoid inconveniencing their guest. Isaac, having received their blessing, went to his own chamber and lay down on his couch. {5:3} God implanted the awareness of Abraham's impending death into Isaac's heart through a dream. Around the third hour of the night, Isaac awoke, rushed to his father's chamber where Abraham and the archangel Michael slept, and cried out at the door, urging Abraham to open quickly so he could embrace him before he was taken away. {5:4} Abraham, moved by Isaac's urgency, opened the door, and Isaac embraced him, weeping loudly. Abraham, deeply moved, also wept, and the chief-captain, witnessing their sorrow, joined them in tears. Sarah, hearing their weeping from her room, hurried to them and found them embracing and in tears. {5:5} Sarah asked why they were weeping so intensely, wondering if the guest had brought news of Lot's death. The chief-captain explained that Isaac had a dream which stirred their emotions and caused them to weep. {5:6} Later that evening, Michael entered Abraham's house and found them preparing supper. They ate, drank, and enjoyed each other's company. Abraham instructed Isaac to prepare the guest's couch and set up the lamp for him. {5:7} Isaac expressed his desire to sleep beside his father, but Abraham gently persuaded him to sleep in his own chamber to avoid inconveniencing their guest. Isaac, obedient to his father, went to his own chamber and slept there.

{6:1} Around the seventh hour of the night, Isaac woke up and hurried to the door of his father's chamber, calling out, "Father, open the door so I can embrace you before they take you away from me!" Abraham rose and opened the door, and Isaac entered, embracing his father and weeping, kissing him with sorrow. Abraham wept along with his son, and Michael, witnessing their tears, also wept. Sarah, hearing their weeping, called from her bed-chamber, asking why they were crying. She wondered if the guest had brought news of Lot's death or if something else had happened. {6:2} Michael reassured Sarah that he brought no news of Lot but acknowledged their kindness and told her that the Lord had remembered them for it. {6:3} Sarah recognized the angelic nature of Michael by the excellence of his conversation and signaled to Abraham to come near. She said to him, "Abraham, do you know who this man is?" Abraham admitted he did not know. Sarah reminded him of the three heavenly visitors they entertained at the oak of Mamre, who promised them Isaac. She recounted how they had prepared a meal and the miraculous events that followed. Abraham acknowledged her words, affirming the truth of her account and glorifying God for revealing such wonders. {6:4} Abraham revealed how he recognized Michael when he washed his feet, recalling the moment when tears from Michael turned into precious stones. He gave these stones to Sarah as a sign. Sarah accepted them with reverence and acknowledged the marvels shown to them, expressing uncertainty about the nature of the revelation, whether good or bad.

{7:1} Abraham left Sarah and went to Isaac in the chamber, asking him to explain what he had seen in his dream that had prompted his swift arrival. Isaac recounted seeing the sun and moon above him, adorned with a crown, and a majestic figure descending from heaven, radiating light brighter than seven suns. This figure took away the sun and moon from Isaac, causing him great sorrow. However, after some discourse, the figure explained that the heavenly bodies were taken up to a higher place of rest and glory. {7:2} Abraham turned to Michael and inquired about the purpose of his visit. Michael indicated that Isaac would provide the answer. Abraham then asked Isaac to describe his dream. Isaac related the vision of the shining man and the celestial events, prompting Michael to interpret that the sun and moon represented Abraham and Sarah, and the shining man was sent to take Abraham's soul to God.

{8:1} Upon hearing this, Abraham realized that Michael was the angel sent to take his soul. He expressed disbelief and hesitation, declaring that he would not go with Michael. In response, Michael immediately vanished and ascended to heaven, reporting all that had transpired in Abraham's house to God. {8:2} He conveyed Abraham's refusal to go with him and sought guidance from God. God instructed Michael to return to Abraham once more and deliver a message. God reminded Abraham of His promises, His blessings upon him and Sarah, and the gift of Isaac in their old age. God assured Abraham of His continued favor and instructed him to prepare for his departure from the world, as all mortals must face death, including prophets and kings. {8:3} After ascending to heaven, Michael spoke before the Lord regarding Abraham. The Lord commanded Michael, "Go, take Abraham in his body and show him all things. Whatever he asks of you, do for him as to my friend." Thus, Michael descended again, lifted Abraham in his physical form on a cloud, and brought him to the river of Ocean. {8:4} Abraham observed people plowing fields, driving wagons, herding flocks, and engaged in various activities. He also saw men watching by night, dancing, playing instruments, and heard people mourning the dead. He witnessed newlyweds being honored and observed all manner of deeds, both good and bad. Passing over them, Abraham saw men bearing swords and asked the chief-captain, "Who are these?" The chief-captain replied, "They are thieves who intend to commit murder, steal, burn, and destroy." Abraham prayed, "Lord, command wild beasts to come out and devour them." Immediately, wild beasts emerged and consumed the thieves. {8:5} Abraham witnessed a man and woman committing fornication. He prayed, "Lord, command the earth to open and swallow them." Instantly, the earth split and swallowed them. In another instance, Abraham saw men digging through a house and stealing possessions. He prayed, "Lord, command fire to come down from heaven and consume them." Fire descended and consumed them. A voice from heaven then commanded Michael to stop the chariot and turn Abraham away from seeing more, lest he destroy all creation by witnessing the wickedness of humanity. The voice explained that Abraham lacks pity for sinners, whereas God waits for sinners to repent before their death. {8:6} Instead, Abraham was to be taken to the first gate of heaven to witness judgments and recompenses, and to intercede for the souls of sinners he had prayed against. {8:7} Abraham saw two gates, one small and the other large. Between them sat a man on a throne of great glory, surrounded by angels. This man alternately wept and laughed, his weeping far exceeding his laughter sevenfold. Abraham asked Michael, "Who is this sitting between the gates, weeping and laughing?" Michael replied, "Do you not know who this is?" Abraham said, "No, lord." Michael explained, "This is the first-created Adam. The small and large gates represent those who enter. When Adam sees many entering through the narrow gate leading to life, he rejoices greatly. But when he sees many entering through the broad gate of sinners leading to destruction, he weeps and laments bitterly. Adam rejoices for the salvation of souls through the narrow gate, but mourns deeply for the destruction of sinners through the broad gate. This is why he alternates between joy and sorrow."

{9:1} The chief-captain, having received the instructions from the Lord, descended to Abraham. Upon seeing the righteous Abraham, he fell face down on the ground as though dead, and conveyed to Abraham everything he had heard from the Most High. Abraham, holy and just, rose with tears streaming down his face and prostrated himself before the angel, pleading, "Chief-captain of the heavenly hosts, you have graciously come to me, a sinner and unworthy servant. I beseech you, carry my plea once more to the Most High. Say to Him, 'Thus says Abraham, your servant: Lord, in every work and word I have asked of you, you have heard me and fulfilled my counsel. Now, Lord, I do not resist your power, for I know I am mortal. All things yield to your command, and I too fear and tremble before your power. Yet, I ask one thing: while still in this body, let me see all the inhabited earth and all your creations. If I see these, then if it is time for me to depart from life, I shall do so without sorrow.'" {9:2} The chief-captain returned to God and relayed Abraham's request. The Most High heard this and commanded the chief-captain Michael, saying, "Take a cloud of light and the angels who oversee the chariots. Descend and take the righteous Abraham on a chariot of the cherubim. Lift him into the heavens so he may behold all the earth."{9:3} Abraham pondered and said, "If one cannot enter through the narrow gate, can they not enter into life?" Overcome with sorrow, he wept, exclaiming, "Alas, what shall I do? I am broad of body, how then shall I enter through the narrow gate, which even a fifteen-year-old boy cannot enter?" Michael comforted him, saying, "Fear not, father, and do not grieve. You shall enter through it unhindered, and all those who are like you." {9:4} As Abraham stood amazed, an angel of the Lord appeared, driving sixty thousand souls of sinners toward destruction. Abraham questioned Michael, "Do all these souls go into destruction?" Michael replied, "Yes, but let us search among them if there is even one righteous soul." They searched and found an angel holding the soul of a woman from among the multitude. Her sins were weighed equally with her deeds, neither condemning nor justifying her completely. The other souls were led away to destruction. {95} Abraham inquired of Michael, "Is this angel the one who separates the soul from the body?" Michael answered, "Yes, this is Death. He leads them to the place of judgment where the judge assesses them."

{10:1} The archangel Michael descended and took Abraham on a chariot of the cherubim, lifting him into the sky along with sixty angels. Abraham ascended over all the earth, observing people plowing fields, driving wagons, herding flocks, and engaged in various activities. {10:2} As Abraham beheld these sights, he spoke to Michael, saying, "My lord, if it is time for me to depart from my body, I desire to be taken up in my body so I may see all the creatures that the Lord my God has created in heaven and on earth." Michael replied, "It is not for me to grant this request. I will go and relay your desire to the Lord. If I am commanded, then I will show you all these things."

{11:1} So Michael turned the chariot and brought Abraham to the east, to the first gate of heaven. There, Abraham saw two paths: one narrow and constrained, the other broad and spacious. He noticed two gates as well: a broad gate on the broad path and a narrow gate on the narrow path. Outside these gates, Abraham saw a man seated on a throne of great glory, whose appearance was as terrible as the Lord's. Angels drove many souls through the broad gate, while few souls were led by angels through the narrow gate. {11:2} After Abraham had witnessed the place of judgment, the cloud descended with him to the firmament below. Looking down upon the earth, Abraham observed a man committing adultery with a married woman. Turning to Michael, he said, "Do you see this wickedness? Lord, send fire from heaven to consume them." Immediately, fire descended and consumed them, for the Lord had instructed Michael to fulfill Abraham's requests. Abraham then saw others quarreling and railing at each other. He commanded, "Let the earth open and swallow them," and the earth immediately swallowed them alive. {11:3} The cloud then led Abraham to another place, where he saw men preparing to commit murder in a desert. He said to Michael, "Do you see this wickedness? Let wild beasts come out of the desert and tear them to pieces." At that moment, wild beasts emerged from the desert and devoured them. {11:4} Then the Lord God spoke to Michael, saying, "Turn Abraham back to his own house. Do not let him tour all the creation I have made, for he lacks compassion for sinners. I, however, have compassion on sinners that they may repent, live, and be saved." Abraham asked Michael, "Who is this judge, and who is the other who convicts sins?" Michael replied, "The judge is Abel, the first martyr, whom God has appointed to judge. The witness and scribe of righteousness is Enoch, who records the sins and righteousness of each person. Enoch does not pass sentence himself; rather, the Lord does. He instructed Enoch to write down the sins of those who seek atonement, and it shall be considered with every breath and every creature. Ultimately, they will be judged by the Lord God of all, and the judgment will be final and severe, with no one to deliver them." {11:5} "The judgment of the world and recompense are conducted by three tribunals. Matters are confirmed not by one or two witnesses, but by three witnesses. The angels on the right and left write down righteousness and sins respectively. The angel resembling the sun, holding a balance, is the just weigher Dokiel, who measures righteousness and sins against God's standards. The fiery angel Puruel, wielding fire, tests human works. If fire consumes a work, the angel of judgment immediately takes the person to the bitter place of sinners. If the fire approves the work, the angel of righteousness takes the person to be saved among the just. Thus, Abraham, all people are tested by fire and weighed on the balance of righteousness."

{12:1} As he continued speaking to me, suddenly two angels appeared, their appearance fiery, their demeanor pitiless, and their gaze severe. They drove thousands of souls mercilessly, lashing them with fiery thongs. One of the angels seized a soul, and they compelled all these souls through the broad gate leading to destruction. I followed along with the angels and entered through that broad gate. {12:2} Between the two gates stood a throne of terrifying aspect, made of crystal that gleamed like fire. Upon this throne sat a wondrous man, radiant as the sun, resembling the Son of God. Before him was a table of crystal overlaid with gold and fine linen, upon which lay a book. The book was six cubits thick and ten cubits wide. To the right and left of the table stood two angels holding paper, ink, and pen. Before the table sat an angel of light holding a balance, and on his left sat a fiery, pitiless angel holding a trumpet that contained judgments leading to life and destruction. {12:3} Michael explained to Abraham, "The man sitting between these angels is Adam, the first man whom the Lord created. He is placed here to witness every soul departing from the body, for all humanity descends from him. When you see him weeping, it is because he has witnessed many souls being led to destruction. When you see him laughing, it is because he has seen many souls entering into life. Do you see how his weeping outweighs his laughter? This is because he witnesses the majority of souls passing through the broad gate to destruction, causing his sorrow to exceed his joy seven-fold."

{13:1} Abraham asked, "My lord chief-captain, who is this remarkable judge? Who are the angels recording deeds? And who are the angel with the balance and the fiery angel with fire?" The chief-captain replied, "Behold, most holy Abraham, the imposing man on the throne. This is Abel, the son of the first-created Adam, whom the wicked Cain slew. He sits here to judge all creation, distinguishing between the righteous and the sinners. God ordained that judgment shall not come directly from Him but through every human born of man. Thus, Abel has been given the authority to judge the world until the glorious Second Coming, when a perfect and eternal judgment, unalterable by any, shall be rendered. As every person descends from the first-created Adam, they are initially judged here by his son. At the Second Coming, they will be judged by the twelve tribes of Israel, a process I too shall witness." {13:2} Michael then took Abraham on a cloud and led him into Paradise. Arriving where the judge presided, an angel presented a soul to the judge, pleading, "Lord, have mercy on me." The judge retorted, "How can I show you mercy when you showed none to your daughter, your own flesh and blood? Why did you slay her?" The soul protested, "No, Lord, I did not commit murder. My daughter falsely accused me." The judge called forth the angel who kept the records, accompanied by cherubim carrying two books. A man of great stature, wearing three crowns on his head—symbols of witness—stood with a golden pen in his hand. The judge commanded, "Show the sin of this soul." The man opened one of the books held by the cherubim, searched, and found the woman's sins. "Wretched soul," the judge declared, "why do you deny murdering your daughter's husband after your own husband's death? He convicted her of all her sins, spanning from her youth. Hearing this, the woman cried out, realizing, "Alas, all the sins I committed in the world were forgotten, but here they are not." She too was taken away and handed over to the tormentors. {13:3} As the day of Abraham's death approached, the Lord God said to Michael, "Death will not dare to go near to take away the soul of my servant, because he is my friend. But you, go and adorn Death with great beauty, and send him to Abraham so that he may see him with his own eyes." Immediately, Michael obeyed the command and adorned Death with great beauty, sending him to Abraham as instructed. {13:4} Death sat down near Abraham, and when Abraham saw Death sitting beside him, he was filled with great fear. Death spoke to Abraham, saying, "Hail, holy soul! Hail, friend of the Lord God! Hail, comfort and solace of travelers!" Abraham welcomed Death, addressing him as the servant of the Most High God. He asked Death to reveal his identity and invited him to enter his house, share food and drink, and then depart, explaining that seeing Death near him troubled his soul. {13:5} Abraham confessed his unworthiness to be in the presence of Death, acknowledging that Death was a celestial being while he himself was merely flesh and blood. He expressed his inability to bear Death's glory, noting that Death's beauty was beyond earthly standards. Death responded to Abraham, affirming that in all of God's creation, there had not been found anyone like him. Even the Lord had not found anyone like Abraham upon the whole earth. {13:6} Abraham challenged Death's assertion, questioning how Death dared to lie. He perceived that Death's. {13:7} Abraham addressed Death, saying, "Hail to you, whose appearance and form resemble the sun, most glorious helper, bringer of light, wondrous man! From where does your glory come to us, and who are you, and where do you come from?" Death replied to Abraham, "Most righteous Abraham, behold, I tell you the truth. I am the bitter lot of death." Abraham countered, saying, "No, you are the comeliness of the world, the glory and beauty of angels and men. You are fairer in form than every other. Are you truly the bitter lot of death, and not rather, 'I am fairer than every good thing'?" Death insisted, "I tell you the truth. What the Lord has named me, that also I tell you." {13:8} Abraham questioned Death further, asking, "For what purpose have you come here?" Death answered, "I have come for your holy soul." Then Abraham firmly responded, "I understand what you mean, but I will not go with you." Death remained silent, offering no further response to Abraham's words.

{14:1} Abraham asked the chief-captain, "My lord chief-captain, why was the soul that the angel held adjudged to be set in the midst?" The chief-captain replied, "Listen, righteous Abraham. The judge found its sins and its righteousnesses to be equal, so he did not send it to judgment nor to salvation until the judgment of all by the supreme judge. Abraham then inquired, "What more is needed for the soul to be saved?" The chief-captain answered, "If it obtains just one righteousness more than its sins, it will enter into salvation." {14:2} Abraham said to the chief-captain Michael, "Come here, archangel. Let us pray for this soul and see if God will hear us." The chief-captain responded, "Amen, let it be so." They prayed earnestly for the soul, and God indeed heard their supplication. When they finished praying, they noticed the soul was no longer there. Abraham asked the angel, "Where is the soul that you held in the midst?" The angel replied, "By your righteous prayer, it has been saved. An angel of light has taken it and carried it up to Paradise." {14:3} Abraham praised, "I glorify the name of God, the Most High, and His boundless mercy." Then Abraham said to the chief-captain, "Archangel, hear my prayer. Let us continue to call upon the Lord, plead for His compassion, and beg for His mercy on the souls of the sinners whom I once cursed and brought destruction upon in my anger—those devoured by the earth, torn by wild beasts, and consumed by fire at my words. Now I recognize my sin before the Lord our God." {14:4} "Come, O Michael, chief-captain of the heavenly hosts. Let us weep before God that He may forgive my sin and grant mercy to them." The chief-captain listened, and together they pleaded before the Lord. After a long while of their supplication, a voice came from heaven, saying, "Abraham, Abraham, I have heard your voice and your prayer. I forgive your sin, and those whom you thought I destroyed, I have called up and restored to life by My abundant kindness. For a time, I judged them, but those whom I punished on earth, I will not punish in death." {14:5} Abraham said to Death, "Show us your corruption." Then Death revealed his corruption: he had two heads — one with the face of a serpent, causing immediate death like that from asps; the other head was like a sword, causing death as by arrows. {14:6} Death manifested his corruption further: he had fiery heads of serpents and fourteen faces. One face was of flaming fire with great fierceness, another was a face of darkness, and there was a gloomy face of a viper. There was also a face of a most terrible precipice, and a fiercer face than that of an asp. A face of a terrible lion, a cerastes, and a basilisk were also among them. He showed a face of a fiery scimitar, a sword-bearing face, and a face of lightning that lightened terribly with a noise of dreadful thunder. Additionally, there was a face of a fierce stormy sea, a fierce rushing river, and a terrible three-headed serpent. He showed a cup mingled with poisons, and overall, he displayed great fierceness and unendurable bitterness, and every mortal disease with the odor of death. {14:7} Due to the great bitterness and fierceness, about seven thousand servants and maid-servants died. The righteous Abraham faced death with equanimity, and his spirit faltered.

{15:1} The voice of the Lord also spoke to the chief-captain Michael, saying, "Michael, my servant, return Abraham to his house, for his end draws near and the measure of his life is fulfilled. Let him put all things in order, and then bring him to me." So Michael turned the chariot and the cloud, and brought Abraham back to his house. Entering his chamber, Abraham sat upon his couch. {15:2} Sarah, his wife, approached and humbly embraced the feet of the Incorporeal, saying, "I thank you, my lord, for bringing back my lord Abraham. We thought he had been taken from us." Isaac, their son, also came and embraced Abraham. All the men and women servants gathered around, embracing Abraham and glorifying God. {15:3} The Incorporeal One said to Abraham and those gathered, "Listen, righteous Abraham. Behold your wife Sarah, your beloved son Isaac, and all your servants around you. Arrange all that you have, for the day has come near when you will depart from your body and go to the Lord." {15:4} Abraham asked, "Did the Lord say this, or do you say it of your own accord?" Michael answered, "Listen, righteous Abraham. The Lord has commanded this, and I am telling you." Abraham responded, "I will not go with you." Hearing this, the chief-captain Michael immediately departed from Abraham's presence, ascended to heaven, and stood before God the Most High. {15:5} Michael said to the Lord Almighty, "Behold, I have listened to Your friend Abraham in all he has said to You, and have fulfilled his requests. I have shown him Your power, the earth, and the sea under heaven. I have shown him judgment and recompense through clouds and chariots, yet he says again, 'I will not go with you.'" {15:6} The Most High said to the archangel, "Does my friend Abraham again say, 'I will not go with you'?" The archangel replied, "Lord Almighty, he does say this, and I refrain from laying hands on him, for from the beginning he has been Your friend and has done all things pleasing in Your sight. There is no man like him on earth, not even Job the wondrous man. Therefore, I refrain from laying hands on him." {15:7} "Command, therefore, Immortal King, what shall be done."

{16:1} Then the Most High said, "Summon Death, known for its shameless countenance and pitiless look." Michael the Incorporeal went and said to Death, "Come here; the Lord of creation, the immortal King, calls you." Death, upon hearing this, shivered and trembled with great terror. It came with fear, standing before the invisible Father, trembling and groaning, awaiting the command of the Lord. {16:2} The invisible God spoke to Death, saying, "Come here, bitter and fearsome name of the world. Hide your fierceness, cover your corruption, cast away your bitterness, and put on your beauty and glory. Go down to my friend Abraham, and take him and bring him to me. But I command you not to terrify him; bring him with gentle words, for he is my beloved friend." Having heard this, Death departed from the presence of the Most High, clothed in a robe of great brightness. It appeared like the sun, fair and beautiful above all men, assuming the form of an archangel with flaming cheeks. {16:3} Meanwhile, righteous Abraham left his chamber and sat under the trees of Mamre, pondering with his hand on his chin, awaiting the arrival of the archangel Michael. Suddenly, a sweet fragrance filled the air, accompanied by a dazzling light. Abraham turned and saw Death approaching in great glory and beauty. Thinking it was the chief-captain of God, Abraham arose and went to meet Death. {16:4} Death, seeing Abraham, greeted him, saying, "Rejoice, precious Abraham, righteous soul, true friend of the Most High God, and companion of the holy angels."

{17:1} Then Abraham got up and went into his house, with Death accompanying him. Abraham ascended to his chamber, and Death followed. Abraham laid down on his couch, and Death sat down by his feet. Abraham then said, "Depart from me, for I desire to rest on my couch." But Death replied firmly, "I will not depart until I take your spirit from you." {17:2} Abraham adjured Death, saying, "By the immortal God, I charge you to tell me the truth. Are you truly Death?" Death answered, "I am Death, the destroyer of the world." Abraham continued, "Since you are Death, tell me, do you come to everyone in such fairness, glory, and beauty?" Death replied, "No, my lord Abraham. It is your righteousness, the boundless sea of your hospitality, and your great love towards God that has become a crown upon my head. With beauty, great peace, and gentleness, I approach the righteous. But to sinners, I come with great corruption, fierceness, and the greatest bitterness, with a fierce and pitiless look." {17:3} Abraham persisted, "Hearken to me and show me your fierceness, corruption, and bitterness." Death replied, "You cannot behold my fierceness, most righteous Abraham." Abraham asserted confidently, "Yes, I will be able to see all your fierceness by the name of the living God, for the might of my God in heaven is with me." {17:4} Then Death removed all his comeliness, beauty, and the sun-like form with which he was clothed. He put on a tyrant's robe, appearing gloomy and fiercer than all kinds of wild beasts, and more unclean than all uncleanness. He showed Abraham seven heads, and upon each head he had an eye, and in their midst terrible faces and the form of dogs, as it were the form of bloodhounds, and he said, Abraham said to Death, "Think not, Abraham, that this beauty is mine, or that I come thus to every man. Nay, but if any one is righteous like thee, I thus take crowns and come to him, but if it is a sinner I come in great corruption, and out of their sin I make a crown for my head, and I shake them with great fear, so that they are dismayed. Abraham therefore said to him, And whence comes thy beauty? And Death said, There is none other more full of corruption than I am. Abraham said to him, And art thou indeed he that is called Death? He answered him and said, I am the bitter name

{18:1} Abraham said to Death, "I beseech you, all-destroying Death, conceal your fierceness and return to the beauty and form you had before." Immediately, Death hid his fierceness and resumed his former beauty. Abraham questioned Death, "Why have you slain all my servants and maidservants? Did God send you here today for this purpose?" Death replied, "No, my lord Abraham, it is not as you say. I was sent here on your account." Abraham persisted, "Then how did they die? Did not the Lord decree it?" Death solemnly answered, "Believe me, most righteous Abraham, it is indeed remarkable that you were not taken with them. But I tell you truly, if the hand of God had not been with you, you too would have departed from this life at that time." {18:2} The righteous Abraham acknowledged, "Now I understand that I faced death with equanimity, and my spirit faltered. But I implore you, all-destroying Death, since my servants died prematurely by your hand, let us pray to the Lord our God that he may hear us and raise those who died before their time." Death agreed, saying, "Amen, so be it." Therefore, Abraham prostrated himself in prayer, and Death joined him. The Lord responded by sending a spirit of life to the dead, and they were revived. Abraham then glorified God for His mercy.

{19.1} Abraham went up to his chamber and lay down, while Death stood before him. Abraham commanded, "Depart from me, for I desire to rest, as my spirit is indifferent." Death replied defiantly, "I will not depart until I take your soul." Abraham, with stern resolve, said to Death, "Who commanded you to say this? You boastfully speak these words yourself. I will not go with you unless the chief-captain Michael comes to me, and only then will I go with him. But tell me, if you desire my company, explain all your manifestations: the seven fiery heads of serpents, the precipice, the sharp sword, the roaring river, the tempestuous sea, the thunder, lightning, and the poisonous cup. Teach me about each of these." Death began his explanation to Abraham, "Listen, righteous Abraham. For seven ages I bring destruction upon the world and lead all to Hades — kings, rulers, rich, poor, slaves, and free. I guide them to the depths of Hades, which is why I showed you the seven heads of serpents. The face of fire represents those who perish in flames. {19.2} The precipice signifies those who meet death falling from heights. The sword symbolizes death in warfare. The rushing river represents those drowned and swept away. The raging sea represents death at sea. Thunder and lightning symbolize sudden deaths. I showed you wild beasts — lions, leopards, bears, and venomous snakes — because many perish by their jaws. The poisonous cups represent those who die by poison."

{20:1} Abraham inquired, "I ask you, is there such a thing as an unexpected death? Tell me." Death solemnly replied, "Truly, truly, I tell you in the truth of God, there are seventy-two types of death. One is the death that comes at its appointed time, but many people enter death suddenly, swiftly consigned to the grave." {20:2} "I have answered all your questions," Death continued. "Now, I urge you, most righteous Abraham, to abandon all deliberation and cease from asking any more. Come, go with me, as the God and judge of all has commanded." {20:3} Abraham said to Death, "Stay a little longer, so I can rest on my couch. I am deeply troubled, for since I have seen you, my strength has left me. My limbs feel heavy as lead, and my spirit is greatly distressed. Please depart for a while; I cannot bear to look upon you." {20:4} Then Isaac, his son, came and wept on Abraham's chest, and Sarah, his wife, embraced his feet, lamenting bitterly. Their male and female servants surrounded his bed, grieving deeply. {20:5} Abraham resigned himself to the approach of death, and Death said to him, "Come, take my right hand. May cheerfulness, life, and strength come to you." Deceived, Abraham took Death's hand, and immediately his soul clung to Death's hand. {20:6} Soon after, Archangel Michael arrived with a multitude of angels. They took Abraham's precious soul in their hands, wrapped in a linen cloth, anointing his body with divine ointments and perfumes until the third day after his death. They buried him in the promised land, at Mamre's oak. The angels carried his precious soul and ascended into heaven, singing the hymn "thrice holy" to the Lord God Almighty, placing him there to worship the God and Father. {20:7} After great praise and glory were given to the Lord, and Abraham bowed down to worship, the undefiled voice of God the Father proclaimed, "Take my friend Abraham into Paradise, where the dwellings of my righteous ones and the abodes of my saints Isaac and Jacob await in his embrace. There, there is no trouble, grief, or sighing, only peace, rejoicing, and eternal life." {20:8} "Let us, too, my beloved brethren, emulate the hospitality of patriarch Abraham and live virtuous lives, that we may be deemed worthy of eternal life, glorifying the Father, Son, and Holy Spirit. To Him be glory and power forever. Amen." {20:9} God returned and took Abraham's soul as if in a dream, and Archangel Michael bore it up to heaven. Isaac buried his father beside his mother Sarah, glorifying and praising God, for all glory, honor, and worship belong to the Father, Son, and Holy Spirit, now and forevermore. Amen.

Testament of Moses

The Testament of Moses, an ancient Jewish text, holds a unique place in the landscape of Second Temple period literature. Composed sometime between the 1st century BCE and the 1st century CE, this pseudepigraphal work is attributed to Moses but is, in fact, the product of an anonymous author writing in his name. The text is primarily known through a single Latin manuscript and a few Greek fragments, with the original Hebrew or Aramaic version no longer extant. The Testament of Moses offers a rich tapestry of apocalyptic and eschatological themes, reflecting the socio-political turbulence and theological ferment of its time. It addresses the expectations and concerns of Jewish communities under foreign domination, notably the Roman Empire, and critiques the corruption and moral decline within their own ranks. This work is deeply interwoven with Deuteronomic traditions, emphasizing the covenantal relationship between God and Israel, and underscores the notion of divine justice and retribution. The narrative structure, set as Moses' final exhortation and prophecy to Joshua, blends historical review with future predictions, providing a sweeping overview of Israel's history from the Exodus to the eschaton. The Testament of Moses is invaluable for understanding Jewish thought and messianic expectations during the late Second Temple period, and it provides critical insights into the theological and ethical debates that shaped early Jewish and Christian communities.

{1:1} The Testament of Moses recounts the commands he gave in his one hundred and twentieth year, which was the two thousand five hundredth year from the creation of the world, or, according to oriental reckoning, the two thousand seven hundredth, and the four hundredth year after leaving Phoenicia. This took place after the Exodus led by Moses to Amman beyond the Jordan, as prophesied in Deuteronomy. Moses called Joshua, son of Nun, a man approved by the Lord, to lead the people and care for the tabernacle and its holy items, ensuring they received the promised land according to the covenant and oath spoken in the tabernacle. He told Joshua, "Be strong and courageous, obey all commands, and remain blameless before God." The Lord, who created the world for His people, did not reveal His purpose at creation to convict the Gentiles through their arguments. God chose and prepared Moses before the world's foundation to mediate His covenant. Moses declared his life's end was near and asked the people to preserve the books he gave them, anoint them with cedar oil, store them in earthen vessels at a place prepared from creation's beginning, until the day of repentance at the end of days.

{2:1} Moses continued, "Now, you will lead the people into the promised land, bless them individually, confirm their inheritance, and establish the kingdom. Appoint local magistrates according to the Lord's will, in judgment and righteousness. Five years after entering the land, they will be ruled by chiefs and kings for eighteen years, with the ten tribes rebelling for nineteen years. The twelve tribes will move the tabernacle, and God will establish His court and sanctuary. The two holy tribes will be settled there, while the ten tribes will create their own kingdoms and offer sacrifices for twenty years. Seven will build walls, and I will protect nine, but four will break the covenant and worship idols, sacrificing their sons to strange gods, and committing abominations in the Lord's house."

{3:1} In those days, an eastern king will invade with his cavalry, burn their colonies, and destroy the holy temple, taking the holy vessels and exiling the people, including the two tribes, to his homeland. The two tribes will call on the ten tribes, marching like a hungry, thirsty lioness, and cry out, "Righteous and holy is the Lord. We sinned and were exiled with our children." The ten tribes will mourn, asking, "What have we done to you, brethren? Has this tribulation not befallen all Israel?" All tribes will cry to heaven, invoking the God of Abraham, Isaac, and Jacob, reminding Him of His covenant and the oath sworn that their descendants would never be removed from the promised land. They will remember Moses, saying, "Did Moses not prophesy these things, enduring many trials in Egypt, the Red Sea, and the wilderness for forty years? He warned us to obey God's commandments as our mediator. These things have come to pass after his death, as he foretold, including our captivity in the east." This bondage will last for seventy-seven years.

{4:1} Then, a leader will arise among them and pray for their people, saying, "Lord of all, King on the high throne, who rules the world and chose this people as Your own, according to the covenant with their ancestors. Though they have been taken captive with their families to foreign lands, surrounded by vanity and strange peoples, please have mercy on them, O Lord of heaven." God will remember the covenant with their ancestors and show compassion. He will inspire a king to have mercy and send them back to their homeland. Some of the tribes will return, rebuild the walls around their place, and the two tribes will maintain their faith, lamenting because they cannot offer sacrifices to the Lord. The ten tribes will grow and multiply among the Gentiles during their captivity.

{5:1} When the time of punishment nears, and kings who share their guilt bring vengeance upon them, they will be divided about the truth. It is said, "They will turn from righteousness and embrace iniquity, defiling their worship place with impurities, and worshiping strange gods." They will not follow God's truth, some polluting the altar with their offerings, not being true priests but slaves' sons. Many will respect influential people, accept bribes, and corrupt justice. Consequently, their land will be filled with lawlessness and sin, with corrupt judges ready to serve for money.

{6:1} Then rulers will rise, calling themselves priests of the Most High God but committing wickedness in the holy of holies. An insolent king, not of the priestly line, bold and shameless, will arise and judge them harshly. He will kill their leaders secretly, so no one knows their fate. He will slay the old and young alike, bringing great fear to the land. He will judge them harshly for thirty-four years, punishing them like the Egyptians. His descendants will rule for shorter periods, and a powerful western king will conquer them, taking captives and burning part of their temple, crucifying some around their colony.

{7:1} When this happens, the end times will come swiftly, forcing them to act. During this time, destructive and impious men will rule, pretending to be just but stirring up deceit and treachery. These men, self-serving and hypocritical, will love banquets and luxury, exploiting the poor under the guise of justice. They will be deceitful, impious, and lawless from sunrise to sunset, claiming to be noble while their actions are corrupt. They will say, "We shall feast and live in luxury, considering ourselves princes." Despite their corruption, they will speak arrogantly, saying, "Do not touch me, lest you pollute me."

{8:1} Then, a second visitation of wrath will come upon them, unlike anything before. A mighty king, ruler of kings, will arise, crucifying those who openly practice circumcision and torturing those who hide it. He will imprison them, give their wives to Gentile gods, and force their sons to reverse their circumcision. Others will be tortured, burned, and forced to bear idols publicly. They will be made to blaspheme and desecrate their sanctuary, enduring severe punishments and forced to abandon their laws and sacred practices.

{9:1} In that time, a man named Taxo from the tribe of Levi will arise. With his seven sons, he will exhort them, saying, "Observe, my sons, a second ruthless and unclean visitation is upon us, far worse than the first. No nation has suffered as we have for impiety. Hear me, for neither our fathers nor forefathers tempted God as to transgress His commands. Our strength lies in obedience. Let us fast for three days and then go to a cave in the field to die rather than transgress the Lord's commands. If we do this and die, our blood will be avenged before the Lord."

{10:1} Then, God's kingdom will appear throughout creation, Satan will be no more, and sorrow will disappear with him. The chief angel will take action, avenging their enemies. The Heavenly One will rise from His throne, leaving His holy dwelling with anger and wrath for His children. The earth will tremble to its edges, mountains will be leveled, and hills will shake and fall. The sun will go dark, the moon will turn to blood, stars will be disturbed, the sea will retreat, and rivers will dry up. The Most High, the Eternal God, will rise to punish the Gentiles and destroy their idols. Israel will be joyful, lifted high like on eagle's wings. God will exalt them, bringing them close to the stars. They will see their enemies in Gehenna, recognize them, and rejoice, giving thanks to their Creator. Joshua, son of Nun, was instructed to keep these words and this book, as 250 times (year-weeks) will pass from Moses' death until God's advent. Moses urged Joshua to be strong and courageous, chosen by God to uphold the covenant.

{11:1} After hearing Moses' words, Joshua tore his clothes and fell at Moses' feet, weeping. Moses comforted him, but Joshua asked, "Why do you comfort me, my lord Moses? How can I be comforted when you speak of your departure from us? Where will you go, and what will mark your grave? Who will dare move your body? While others have graves on earth, your resting place is the entire world. Who will guide and care for this people, or pray for them daily, leading them to their ancestors' land? How can I care for them like a father or a mistress for her daughter, providing their needs? There are 600,000 men who grew in number through your prayers. What wisdom do I have to judge or answer in the house of the Lord? When the Amorite kings hear we are coming without you, they will attack, thinking we have no advocate like you, Moses, who prayed constantly. They will say, 'Let's destroy them, for Moses, their great messenger, is no longer with them.' What will become of this people, my lord Moses?"

{12:1} When Joshua finished speaking, he again fell at Moses' feet. Moses lifted him up and said, "Joshua, do not despair. God created all nations and has foreseen everything from creation's beginning to the end of the age. He has planned everything perfectly. The Lord appointed me to pray and intercede for their sins, not because of my virtue but by His grace and compassion. Joshua, you will not conquer nations because of this people's godliness. Heaven's lights and earth's foundations are under God's control. Those who obey God's commandments will prosper, while those who sin will face many punishments. However, completely destroying them is not allowed. God, who knows everything, has established His covenant and oath forever.

Testament of Solomon

The Testament of Solomon is a pseudepigraphal text attributed to King Solomon, regarded as a key figure in biblical tradition known for his wisdom and authority. Though traditionally placed within the corpus of Old Testament literature, this work is generally classified as a product of early Jewish or Christian magical and demonological lore, likely composed between the first and fifth centuries CE. The text presents Solomon as a master of occult knowledge, particularly in his ability to control and subdue demons using a magical ring given to him by the archangel Michael. Through this ring, Solomon interrogates various demons, compelling them to reveal their names, powers, and the means to defeat them. The narrative reflects an intersection of biblical motifs with Greco-Roman, Egyptian, and Mesopotamian magical traditions, providing a glimpse into the ancient worldview where demonology and magic were seen as legitimate tools for power and protection. While the Testament of Solomon lacks canonical status in both Jewish and Christian scriptures, it has gained scholarly interest for its insights into early beliefs about supernatural entities, exorcism practices, and the development of mystical and magical thought in the late antique period. The text also offers a unique perspective on the role of Solomon as a figure of not just wisdom but also occult mastery, expanding his traditional image within both theological and folkloric contexts.

- This is the testament of Solomon, son of David, who reigned as king in Jerusalem. He possessed mastery over all spirits—those of the air, the earth, and under the earth. Through their power, he accomplished extraordinary feats in the construction of the Temple. This account also details the authorities these spirits wield against humans, and how angels bring these demons to naught. Blessed be you, O Lord God, who bestowed such authority upon Solomon. Glory and might belong to you forever. Amen.
- During the building of the Temple in Jerusalem, as the artisans worked, Ornias, a demon, appeared among them near sunset. He began stealing half of the wages of the chief artisan's young son and half of his food. He also sucked the thumb of the child's right hand daily, causing the boy to grow thin, despite being dearly loved by the king.
- King Solomon summoned the boy one day and asked him why he was becoming thinner, despite receiving double wages and food compared to the other workers in the Temple.
- The child explained to the king that after work, a demon would come, take half of his pay and food, and then suck his thumb, causing him distress and physical decline.
- Upon hearing this, Solomon prayed fervently in the Temple day and night, seeking divine intervention over the demon. Through his prayers, the Lord Sabaoth granted him grace by sending his archangel Michael, who presented Solomon with a ring bearing a seal engraved with a Pentalpha. Michael instructed Solomon to wear the ring, as it would empower him to control all earthbound demons, male and female, aiding him in the construction of Jerusalem.
- Solomon rejoiced, praising the God of heaven and earth. The next day, he gave the ring to the boy, instructing him to throw it at the demon when it appeared, commanding it in Solomon's name, without fear.
- At the appointed hour, Ornias, the fierce demon, arrived to take the child's wages. Following Solomon's instructions, the boy threw the ring at Ornias, commanding him in Solomon's name. The demon protested, offering earthly riches if the ring was removed and he was spared Solomon's judgment.
- Refusing the demon's pleas, the child joyfully ran to Solomon and reported that he had brought Ornias as commanded. The demon stood outside the palace gates, crying out and offering gold and silver if he could avoid Solomon.
- Solomon approached Ornias, who trembled in fear, and asked him to identify himself. The demon revealed his name as Ornias.
- Solomon then inquired about Ornias's astrological allegiance, and the demon responded that he was subject to the sign of Aquarius. He described his activities, including his ability to transform into different forms to seduce men and women, claiming descent from the archangel Uriel, the power of God.
- Upon hearing the name of the archangel, I, Solomon, prayed and glorified God, the Lord of heaven and earth. I then bound the demon Ornias and assigned him to the task of cutting stones for the Temple, which had been brought from the shores of the Sea of Arabia. Ornias, however, fearing the iron tools, pleaded with me to release him, promising to bring me all the demons. Unwilling to be subservient, Ornias compelled me to seek the aid of the archangel Uriel. Immediately, Uriel descended from heaven.
- Uriel summoned the sea whales from the abyss and subdued the great demon Ornias. He commanded Ornias and the fierce demon, Beelzeboul, to labor in cutting stones for the Temple. I then praised and glorified the God of heaven and earth. Ornias, now subdued, was tasked to bring Beelzeboul, the prince of all demons, before me.
- Ornias took the ring and went to Beelzeboul, proclaiming Solomon's summons. Beelzeboul, upon hearing of Solomon, erupted in a blaze of fire and followed Ornias to me.
- Upon seeing the prince of demons, Beelzeboul, I glorified the Almighty Lord God, Maker of heaven and earth. I praised God for granting me wisdom and authority over all the powers of the devil.
- I questioned Beelzeboul, asking him to reveal his identity. He declared himself as Beelzebub, the chief of demons, with authority over all others. He pledged to bring all unclean spirits to me in bondage. Once again, I glorified the God of heaven and earth for his boundless grace.
- I inquired of Beelzebub about the existence of female demons among them. He promptly brought Onoskelis, a seductive spirit resembling a fair-skinned woman, who swiftly appeared before me.
- I asked Onoskelis to identify herself. She revealed that she was a spirit named Onoskelis, dwelling upon the earth, capable of various forms of deception and harm to men. She admitted to frequenting caves and ravines, and appearing as a woman to seduce men, especially those with darker skin who unknowingly worshipped her star.
- Curious about her origin, I questioned Onoskelis further. She confessed to being born from an untimely voice—an echo of a man's ordure dropped in a wood.
- I inquired under which celestial influence she operated. She disclosed that she operated under the star of the full moon, which held sway over many things.
- Wanting to know which angel could thwart her, she acknowledged that it was through the reigning power within me, by the wisdom of God and the angel Joel, that she was subject to me. I then commanded Onoskelis to spin hemp for the ropes used in the construction of the house of God. Bound and subdued, she obeyed, standing day and night in her task.
- I immediately summoned another demon to appear before me, and there came Asmodeus, bound and angry. I demanded to know his identity, but he retorted with defiance, acknowledging his celestial origin as an angel born of a mortal woman. He warned me of my fleeting power over demons, predicting that they would eventually regain

- dominion over humanity, revered as gods by the unaware. Undeterred, I bound Asmodeus more tightly and had him whipped with ox-hide thongs, compelling him to reveal his name and purpose.
- Asmodeus confessed that he was known among mortals by that name and that his task was to disrupt newlywed couples, causing strife and estrangement. He boasted of his ability to lead men astray into infidelity and even murder.
- I adjured Asmodeus by the name of the Lord Sabaôth to reveal the angel who could thwart him. Reluctantly, he disclosed that it was Raphael, the archangel standing before God's throne, who could drive him away with the liver and gall of a fish smoked over tamarisk ashes.
- Continuing my interrogation, I pressed Asmodeus to reveal more. He divulged that his power was bound by the seal I possessed, affirming all he spoke as true. I assigned him the task of making clay for the Temple's construction, despite his protestations.
- With the liver and gall of the fish burning over him, I subdued Asmodeus, frustrated by his formidable malice.
- I then summoned Beelzeboul, the prince of demons, seating him on a high throne, and questioned why he alone remained of the fallen angels who descended from heaven. Beelzeboul recounted his former glory as an angel named Beelzebub in the first heaven, now reigning over demons bound in Tartarus. He spoke of his progeny haunting the Red Sea, revealing secrets to him and receiving his support.
- Beelzeboul confessed his nefarious activities, including his role in destroying kings, corrupting priests, and sowing chaos among men through sinful desires and heresies. He boasted of his intent to bring about the world's destruction.
- I demanded Beelzeboul bring his son from the depths of the Red Sea, but he refused, suggesting another demon, Ephippas, would retrieve him. Curious about his son's name and location, Beelzeboul remained evasive.
- When asked by which angel he was thwarted, Beelzeboul invoked the holy name of God, known by a numerical value among the Hebrews and called Emmanuel by the Greeks. He revealed his vulnerability to the name Eleéth when adjured by a Roman.
- Astonished by his revelations, I commanded Beelzeboul to cut Theban marbles, causing the other demons to cry out in agony.
- Seeking further knowledge, I queried Beelzeboul about heavenly matters. He advised me on rituals involving burning specific substances and lighting lamps to stabilize and protect my house, and described how pure preparations could reveal celestial dragons guiding the sun's chariot.
- Upon hearing Asmodeus's defiance, I sternly silenced him and commanded him to continue cutting the marbles as ordered. I praised God for granting me wisdom and summoned another demon to appear before me. This spirit approached with its face held high but its form curled like a snail, stirring up dust and causing disturbance. I spat on the ground, sealed it with God's ring, and the tumult ceased. I questioned the spirit, asking its identity, and it identified itself as the spirit of ashes, named Tephras.
- The spirit of ashes revealed its role in causing darkness, setting fires, and destroying homes, particularly active in summer. It claimed descent from a powerful origin and disclosed its star alignment at the moon's tip in the south. It mentioned its duty in restraining the hemitertian fever and its associated prayers.
- I inquired how it inflicted harm, and it cited its connection to the archangel Azael. I summoned Azael, set a seal on the spirit, and tasked it with lifting and delivering large stones for the Temple's construction. I glorified God for granting me such authority and then summoned seven female spirits bound together, representing various elements of darkness. Each spirit identified itself: Deception, Strife, Battle (Klothod), Jealousy, Power, Error, and the seventh, the most malicious of all. They spoke of their celestial origin and their role in causing discord and harm among humanity.
- Each spirit confessed their respective powers and the angels who thwarted them: Lamechalal for Deception, Baruchiachel for Strife, Marmarath for Battle, Balthial for Jealousy, Asteraôth for Power, Uriel for Error, and an unnamed entity for the seventh spirit.
- They described their ability to sow heresies, provoke conflicts, and lead astray those who seek piety. I sealed them with my ring and assigned them to dig the Temple's foundations, despite their joint protest.
- Continuing, I summoned another demon who appeared with the limbs of a man but without a head, identifying itself as Envy. It expressed its desire for a head like mine and its method of causing harm by mutilating men's heads and causing incurable sores.
- Envy lamented its blindness upon being sealed and explained its ability to see through feelings and voices. It claimed responsibility for the afflictions of those who were mute from birth and detailed its nocturnal activities in causing harm at crossroads and seizing men's heads.
- The fifth spirit declared itself as Power, boasting of its ability to elevate tyrants and depose kings, empowering rebels and fostering discord. It acknowledged Asteraôth as the angel who frustrates its actions.
- The sixth spirit identified itself as Error, claiming responsibility for leading astray, causing Solomon to err in the past by inducing fratricide. It boasted of its capability to misguide people into grave-digging and away from piety, with Uriel named as the angel who thwarts its schemes.
- The seventh spirit, deemed the worst of them all, called itself Artemis and vowed to bring greater ruin upon Solomon. It hinted at a prophecy involving locusts that would fulfill its desires, though the details remained obscure.
- Solomon, upon hearing these spirits, sealed them with his ring and commanded them to dig the foundations of the Temple, a task spanning 250 cubits. Despite their initial protest, they begrudgingly obeyed.
- Solomon then summoned another demon, appearing as a headless man. Curious, Solomon questioned its identity, and it revealed itself as Envy, desiring to possess a head like Solomon's. Solomon sealed Envy with his ring, causing the demon distress and confusion.
- Envy lamented its plight, unable to see and blaming Ornias for its predicament. Solomon reassured Envy of his identity and asked how it managed to perceive. Envy explained its existence as a voice, inheriting the abilities of those it has harmed since childhood, manipulating voices to inflict harm and suffering. It described its malevolent deeds, including human mutilations and inflicted sores.
- Upon hearing this, I asked the spirit how it emitted fire and from where this power originated. The spirit explained that it drew its fiery energy from the Day-star, a celestial source yet unknown to humans, worshipped by the seven demons preceding it, nurtured by their reverence.
- Curious, I pressed further, demanding to know the name of this Day-star. The spirit hesitated, claiming that revealing the name would render it incurable, yet assured me that the Day-star would respond when called upon. Bowing before the Lord God of Israel, I entrusted the spirit to Beelzeboul until the appointed time.

- Summoning another demon, a hound of immense stature entered my presence, greeting me with a booming voice. Astonished, I inquired about its identity and purpose. The hound revealed it was once a man who performed dark deeds on earth, skilled in knowledge and capable of great feats, even manipulating heavenly bodies. It confessed to leading astray those who followed its star and causing harm to those possessed by frenzy.
- Wanting to understand more, I asked the hound for its name, to which it replied "Staff" (Rabdos). I questioned its abilities and intentions. The hound offered to guide a man to a mountainous place where a green stone could be found, suitable for adorning the Temple of the Lord God.
- Accepting the offer, I sent my servant with the hound, instructing him to use the ring bearing the seal of God to mark the spot where the green stone was found and to bring the demon back to me. True to its word, the hound revealed the stone, which was sealed by my servant and then brought before me. I decided to seal both the headless demon and the enormous hound with my right hand's seal, tasking the hound to guard the fiery spirit. This arrangement ensured continuous light for the artisans working day and night.
- From the mine of that stone, I obtained 200 shekels to support the construction of the incense table, its appearance akin to the stone itself. Glorifying the Lord God, I secured the treasure of that stone and commanded the demons to continue cutting marble for the House of God. Praying to the Lord, I asked the hound by which angel it was thwarted, and it named the great Brieus as its opponent.
- Praising the Lord God of heaven and earth, I summoned another demon to appear before me. A spirit manifested in the form of a roaring lion approached, declaring its prowess in causing sickness and weakening men's bodies. It boasted of its ability to cast out demons and command legions under its control. The spirit identified itself as "Lion-bearer, Rath," and when I inquired how it could be thwarted along with its legions, it refused to divulge its name, claiming that revealing it would bind not only itself but also its entire host.
- Undeterred, I solemnly adjured the spirit in the name of God Sabaoth to disclose the name by which it and its legions were frustrated. Reluctantly, the spirit revealed that the one who had bound them was the figure known as Emmanuel, also referenced as "the great among men," prophesied to face trials and ultimately triumph over evil. The spirit acknowledged its impending defeat by Emmanuel.
- Glorifying God, I condemned the legion to gather wood and assigned the lion-shaped spirit to saw the wood finely with its teeth, destined for the unquenchable furnace of the Temple of God.
- Worshipping the Lord God of Israel, I called forth another demon, which appeared before me as a three-headed dragon of terrifying appearance. Questioning its identity, the dragon spirit claimed its role in causing harm to infants in the womb, making them deaf and mute, and afflicting men with seizures and convulsions. It mentioned being frustrated by an angel associated with Jerusalem, known for his counsel and power.
- The dragon spirit further divulged hidden treasures and artifacts, including a mystical column from the Red Sea, brought forth by another demon named Ephippas. It instructed me on the location of gold near the Temple entrance, which was indeed found as described. I sealed the dragon spirit with my ring and praised the Lord God for His guidance.
- I then asked the dragon spirit its name, to which it replied, "I am the crest of dragons." I commanded it to assist in making bricks for the Temple, utilizing its human hands for the task.
- Giving thanks to the Lord God of Israel, I summoned another demon, this time appearing in the form of a headless woman with disheveled hair. Intrigued, I inquired about her identity and purpose, following her instructions to purify myself and sit in judgment to learn more about her deeds.
- Complying with her request, I restrained myself and listened as the demon, named Obizuth, described her malevolent activities. She confessed to causing harm to newborns, making them deaf and blind, and afflicting their bodies and minds. She boasted of her resilience, claiming to roam the world freely despite being sealed by the ring of God.
- Astonished by her appearance and revelations, I questioned how she was frustrated. The demon revealed that the angel Afarôt, also known as Raphael, was her adversary, whose name, when invoked, prevented her from entering women in childbirth. Pleased with this knowledge, I ordered her hair bound and displayed outside the Temple as a sign to all Israel of God's authority over such spirits.
- Continuing, I summoned another demon that approached in the form of a dragon with the face and hands of a man, wings on its back, and a body resembling that of a serpent. The demon explained its role in impregnating women and causing unusual births.
- It claimed my actions would compel other demons to speak truthfully and warned of destruction by fire for disobedience.
- As the demon spoke, a spirit emerged from its mouth and consumed the wood intended for the Temple, burning it to ashes. Witnessing this spectacle, I marveled at the power and cunning of such spirits.
- After glorifying God, I questioned the dragon-shaped demon about the angel that frustrated it. It named the great angel Bazazeth, residing in the second heaven. I invoked this angel's authority and sentenced the demon to cut marbles for the Temple construction, continuing to praise God and preparing to confront another demon.
- Another spirit appeared before me, resembling a woman with two additional heads on her shoulders, each with hands. When I questioned her identity, she named herself Enêpsigos, boasting of her myriad names and abilities to change forms. She dwelt in the moon and possessed three distinct shapes, known at times as Kronos among the wise. She claimed invincibility in her current forms but admitted being frustrated by the angel Rathanael in the third heaven.
- Seeking divine guidance, I prayed to God and invoked the angel Rathanael as Enêpsigos had disclosed. Using my seal, I bound her with a triple chain and secured her beneath its fastening. Enêpsigos prophesied future events, foretelling the downfall of my kingdom and the desecration of the Temple by foreign rulers. She spoke of a time when the power of evil spirits would rise until the coming of Emmanuel, whose number is 6442, signifying his authority over all.
- Upon hearing these revelations, I glorified God. Though initially skeptical of the demons' words, I eventually witnessed their prophecies come to pass. Before my death, I documented these encounters in a testament for the children of Israel, detailing the powers and names of the demons and the angels that thwart them. I praised the Lord God of Israel and ordered the binding of the spirits with unbreakable chains.
- After praising God, I summoned another spirit, which appeared before me with the form of a horse in front and a fish behind. This fierce sea spirit claimed dominion over ships and the greed for gold and silver. It boasted of causing havoc by transforming into waves and assaulting vessels at sea. The spirit acknowledged its allegiance to Beelzeboul and spoke of seeking counsel from him.

- The spirit also revealed its ability to take on human form, known as Kunospaston, inducing nausea in those it inhabited. Bound and delivered into my hands by Beelzeboul, it warned of its impending demise without access to water.
- I questioned the spirit about the angel that frustrated it, to which it replied "Iameth." Glorifying God, I commanded the spirit to be confined in a vessel filled with sea-water and sealed with my ring, to be placed in the Temple of God. Then I summoned another spirit to appear before me.
- Another enslaved spirit manifested before me, appearing as a man with piercing eyes and wielding a blade. It identified itself as a lascivious spirit spawned by a giant who perished in the days of the giants' massacre. The spirit confessed to lurking among tombs, assuming the form of the dead to ambush and harm the living. It claimed to be frustrated by a man who would become the Savior, identified by a number that, when written on one's forehead, would repel its influence.
- After its confession, I commanded the spirit to be confined, glorifying the Lord for His dominion.
- I then summoned thirty-six spirits, each with heads resembling dogs but human forms otherwise. Known as the rulers of darkness, they professed submission to my authority granted by the Lord God over all spirits.
- Invoking the name of the Lord Sabaoth, I commanded each spirit to reveal its nature and deeds. The spirit Ruax confessed to causing idleness and head pain, retreating at the angel Michael's invocation.
- The second spirit introduced itself as Barsafael, responsible for afflicting those during its hour with debilitating migraines. It expressed vulnerability to the command "Gabriel, imprison Barsafael," prompting immediate retreat.
- The third spirit, Arôtosael, confessed to causing severe harm to eyes, inflicting grievous injuries. It disclosed its weakness to the command "Uriel, imprison Arôtosael," thereby retreating instantly.
- The fifth spirit, Iudal, admitted its role in causing blockages in the ears and deafness. It acknowledged that upon hearing "Uruel Iudal," it would retreat without delay.
- Identified as Sphendonaêl, the sixth spirit claimed responsibility for causing tumors in the parotid gland, inflammations of the tonsils, and tetanic spasms. It confessed obedience to the command "Sabrael, imprison Sphendonaêl," leading to immediate retreat.
- The seventh spirit, Sphandôr, described its ability to weaken shoulders, induce trembling, paralyze hand nerves, and fracture neck bones while extracting marrow. It acknowledged vulnerability to the command "Araêl, imprison Sphandôr," prompting swift retreat.
- Known as Belbel, the eighth spirit confessed to distorting the hearts and minds of humans. It revealed that upon hearing "Araêl, imprison Belbel," it would immediately withdraw.
- The ninth spirit, Kurtaêl, admitted to causing colic pains and inducing bowel discomfort. It disclosed that upon hearing "Iaôth, imprison Kurtaêl," it would retreat promptly.
- Metathiax, the tenth spirit, disclosed its capability to cause kidney pains. It acknowledged vulnerability to the command "Adônaêl, imprison Metathiax," leading to immediate retreat.
- Katanikotaêl, the eleventh spirit, confessed to inciting strife and discord in households, promoting anger and conflict. It offered a remedy: writing its name on laurel leaves along with specific angelic names and invoking the name of the great God, followed by sprinkling water around the house, would compel it to retreat instantly.
- Saphathoraél, the twelfth spirit, admitted to fostering division among people, delighting in causing stumbling and confusion. It disclosed that writing down certain angelic names on paper and carrying it close would dissipate its influence upon invocation, leading to its immediate retreat.
- The thirteenth spirit identified itself as Bobêl, causing nervous disorders through its attacks. It confessed vulnerability to the command "Adonaêl, imprison Bothothêl," prompting immediate retreat.
- Known as Kumeatêl, the fourteenth spirit claimed responsibility for inducing shivering fits and torpor. It acknowledged that upon hearing "Zôrôêl, imprison Kumentaêl," it would retreat without delay.
- The fifteenth spirit, Roêlêd, admitted to causing cold, frost, and stomach pains. It disclosed that upon hearing the phrase: "Iax, bide not, be not warmed, for Solomon is fairer than eleven fathers," it would instantly retreat.
- Identified as Atrax, the sixteenth spirit inflicted severe, incurable fevers upon people. It provided a remedy involving coriander and a charm to exorcise it, promising immediate retreat upon application.
- The seventeenth spirit, Ieropaêl, confessed to causing convulsions and disturbances in men, particularly in baths and on roads. It revealed that reciting specific names into the right ear of the afflicted would compel it to retreat instantly.
- Buldumêch, the eighteenth spirit, admitted to sowing discord between spouses. It disclosed a method involving writing Solomon's lineage names on paper and placing it in the house's antechamber, commanding it to retreat peacefully.
- Naôth, the nineteenth spirit, claimed to afflict men with knee issues. It revealed that writing a specific command on paper and invoking it would lead to its immediate retreat.
- Marderô, the twentieth spirit, confessed to causing untreatable fevers. It disclosed a solution involving writing names on a book leaf and wearing it around the neck, compelling it to retreat instantly.
- The twenty-first spirit, Alath, admitted to causing coughs and breathing difficulties in children. It revealed that writing a specific command on paper and wearing it would ensure its immediate retreat.
- Nefthada, the twenty-third spirit, claimed responsibility for kidney pains and urinary issues. It offered a solution involving inscribing commands on a tin plate and tying it around the loins for immediate retreat.
- Akton, the twenty-fourth spirit, confessed to causing rib and lumbar muscle pains. It provided a remedy involving engraving specific commands on copper and wearing it around the waist for instant retreat.
- Anatreth, the twenty-fifth spirit, admitted to causing intense burning fevers and ailments. It disclosed vulnerability to certain phrases that would compel it to retreat immediately.
- Enenuth, the twenty-sixth spirit, claimed to manipulate minds and hearts, even causing dental issues. It provided a solution involving writing commands and wearing them for its immediate retreat.
- Phêth, the twenty-seventh spirit, confessed to causing consumption and hemorrhages. It disclosed a remedy involving exorcising it through wine and specific chants, ensuring its immediate retreat.
- Harpax, the twenty-eighth spirit, admitted to inducing sleeplessness in men. It revealed vulnerability to a specific written command tied around the temples, leading to its immediate retreat.
- Anostêr, the twenty-ninth spirit, claimed to cause hysteria and bladder pains. It offered a solution involving laurel seeds and specific exorcisms for its immediate retreat.
- Alleborith, the thirtieth spirit, admitted to causing discomfort from swallowed fish bones. It disclosed a remedy involving the use of the same fish bone to compel it to retreat.

- Hephesimireth, the thirty-first spirit, confessed to causing lingering illnesses. It provided a remedy involving salt and oil, accompanied by specific prayers for its immediate retreat.
- Ichthion, the thirty-second spirit, paralyzed and bruised muscles but could be repelled with specific chants.
- Agchoniôn, the thirty-third spirit, admitted to lying in ambush and causing troubles. It offered a remedy involving writing on fig leaves and reversing letters for its immediate retreat.
- Autothith, the thirty-fourth spirit, confessed to instigating grudges and fights. It acknowledged being frustrated by specific inscriptions for its retreat.
- Phthenoth, the thirty-fifth spirit, admitted to casting the evil eye. It revealed vulnerability to certain protective measures for its immediate retreat.
- Bianakith, the thirty-sixth spirit, confessed to wreaking havoc on the body and causing decay. It provided a solution involving specific inscriptions on house doors for its immediate retreat.
- Hearing all this, I, Solomon, praised the God of heaven and earth. I ordered water to be brought into the Temple of God and prayed for the binding of demons that trouble humanity, assigning some to labor on the Temple, others to imprisonment, and some to refining metals. Thus, I enjoyed peace and honor throughout the earth, overseeing the completion of the Temple.
- My kingdom flourished, and Jerusalem found peace and joy. Kings from all corners of the earth came to admire the Temple I had built for the Lord God, bringing precious offerings of gold, silver, gems, and timber to adorn the Temple.
- The Queen of Sheba, renowned for her sorcery, came to me with great concern, bowing humbly before me. Upon hearing my wisdom, she praised the God of Israel and tested me with questions, marveling at the depth of knowledge I shared with her. All the sons of Israel glorified God.
- During those days, an elderly worker approached me in distress, falling before me and pleading for justice. He told me of his only son who openly insulted him, beat him, and threatened his life. He begged me to avenge him.
- Moved by the old man's plight, I summoned his son and questioned him about his father's accusations. The young man denied the charges vehemently, claiming he would never raise a hand against his father. Despite his plea, the old man refused to forgive him and demanded severe punishment. As I was about to pass judgment, I noticed the demon Ornias laughing wickedly. Outraged by his disrespect, I ordered Ornias to be brought before me to explain himself.
- Confronted, Ornias confessed that the old man planned to kill his son within three days. Confirming this revelation, I had the demon restrained and reconciled the father and son, urging them to make amends. They departed with renewed understanding.
- Afterward, I questioned Ornias further, learning that demons like him roam the heavens, overhearing divine decrees and influencing events on earth. They exploit opportunities to cause harm, often disguising themselves to deceive humanity.
- I marveled at their revelations but ensured Ornias was kept under guard for five days. When I summoned the old man afterward, he arrived in mourning, his face darkened with sorrow. He informed me his son had died two days prior. Recognizing Ornias spoke the truth, I glorified the God of Israel.
- Witnessing these events, the Queen of Sheba was astounded and praised the God of Israel, impressed by the construction of the Temple. She contributed generously—gold, silver, and precious stones—and inspected the Temple's intricate details with admiration.
- Meanwhile, I received a letter from King Adares of Arabia, seeking my help to subdue a destructive spirit tormenting his land—a fierce wind that caused death and destruction. Impressed by my wisdom and authority over spirits, he pled for my intervention to secure peace in his realm.
- I read Adares' letter and planned a strategy. A crucial stone for the Temple lay unmovable, frustrating the builders. I ordered my servant to capture the spirit causing havoc in Arabia using a flask and a seal.
- Following my instructions, the servant journeyed to Arabia, captured the spirit in the flask, and brought it back to Jerusalem, where it was presented before me in the Temple.
- Upon my return to the Temple, the flask moved on its own accord, demonstrating the spirit's presence. Questioning the demon within, Ephippas, I learned of his powers and his domain in Arabia.
- Ephippas explained his capabilities and how he and another demon from the Red Sea supported a massive pillar. Witnessing their strength, I commanded them to uphold the pillar until the appointed time, marveling at their obedience.
- To test their resolve, I ordered the demons to support the pillar, sealing their promise with my ring. The spirits held firm, proving the power bestowed upon me by God.
- Grateful for God's guidance, I adorned the Temple and enjoyed peace throughout my kingdom. I took wives from various lands, and though I desired a woman from Jebus, the priests of Moloch demanded I worship their gods in exchange for her hand.
- Refusing to betray my faith, I did not worship their idols, but they withheld the woman from me until I complied. Craftily, they offered me grasshoppers to sacrifice to Moloch, after which I fell under a dark influence, losing God's favor.
- I succumbed to their demands and built temples for their idols, forsaking the true God. Realizing my folly, I wrote this testament as a warning, urging future generations to heed God's commands and avoid the lure of false idols.
- I questioned another spirit who had come with the pillar from the depths of the Red Sea, asking him who he was and why he appeared before me. The demon identified himself as Abezithibod, claiming descent from an archangel. He boasted of his power as a fierce, winged spirit with a single wing, plotting against every spirit under heaven. He recounted his role in hardening Pharaoh's heart during Moses' time in Egypt, and how he was invoked alongside Moses' opponents, Iannes and Iambres.
- I asked him how he ended up in the Red Sea, to which he explained that he had influenced Pharaoh and his ministers to pursue the Israelites. He was present when the Egyptians followed the Israelites into the Red Sea, where they met their demise as the waters closed over them. Abezithibod claimed he remained hidden under the pillar in the sea until Ephippas, at my command, captured him in a flask and brought him to me.
- Hearing this, I praised God and commanded the demons to uphold the pillar. They swore by the living God that they would support it until the world's end. They warned that if the stone fell, it would signify the end of the world.
- I continued to glorify God and beautify the Temple of the Lord, finding joy and peace in my kingdom. I took numerous wives from various lands, including a Jebusite woman whom I desired greatly. When I asked the priests to give her to me in marriage, they demanded I worship their gods Moloch and Raphan. Fearful of God's glory, I refused, but they insisted I comply before I could be with her.

- They forbade the woman from being with me until I sacrificed to their gods. Relenting under pressure, I performed their rituals with five grasshoppers as instructed, causing the Spirit of God to depart from me. I became weak and foolish, and against my better judgment, I built temples for Baal, Rapha, Moloch, and other idols.
- I fell into darkness, forsaking the true God and becoming a plaything of idols and demons. Recognizing my grave error, I wrote this testament as a plea for future generations to heed its warnings and prioritize God's grace above all else.

Psalms of Solomon

The Psalms of Solomon, a collection of eighteen pseudepigraphal psalms likely written in the first century BCE, are important for understanding Second Temple Judaism. Reflecting the socio-political upheaval and religious zeal of the post-Maccabean era and the Hasmonean dynasty, these psalms depict the Jewish community's struggles with identity and piety amid foreign rule and internal conflict. They cover themes like messianic expectations, divine justice, righteousness, and repentance, using Hebrew parallelism and poetic structure similar to the canonical Psalms. Theologically, they offer insights into evolving messianic and eschatological ideas, with some psalms anticipating a Davidic savior to restore Israel.

{1:1} I cried out to the Lord in my time of trouble, {1:2} To God, when the wicked came against me. {1:3} Suddenly, the sound of war was before me; {1:4} I thought, He will listen to me because I am righteous. {1.5} I believed in my heart that I was righteous, {1:6} Because I had wealth and many children. {1:7} Their prosperity spread across the entire earth, {1:8} And their fame reached the ends of the world. {1:9} They were elevated to the heavens, {1:10} They said they would never fall. {1:11} But they grew arrogant in their success, {1:12} And they lacked understanding. {1:13} Their sins were hidden, {1:14} And even I was unaware of them. {1:15} Their transgressions surpassed those of the nations before them; {1:16} They completely defiled the sacred things of the Lord.

{2:1} The desecration of Jerusalem; captivity, murder, and raping. A psalm of utter despair. {2:2} When the sinner grew proud, he used a battering ram to destroy the fortified walls, and You did not stop him. {2:3} Foreign nations climbed onto Your altar, trampling it arrogantly with their sandals; {2:4} Because the sons of Jerusalem had defiled the holy things of the Lord, profaning God's offerings with their sins. {2:5} Therefore He said: Cast them far from Me; {2:6} It was dismissed before God, completely dishonored; {2:7} The sons and daughters were in grievous captivity, their necks sealed and branded among the nations. {2:8} According to their sins, He dealt with them, leaving them in the hands of their conquerors. {2:9} He turned His face away from pitying them, young and old, and their children together; {2:10} For they all had done evil, ignoring His voice. And the heavens were angry, {2:11} and the earth abhorred them; for no one on it had done what they did, {2:12} and the earth recognized all Your righteous judgments, O God. {2:13} They mocked the sons of Jerusalem, comparing them to harlots; every passerby entered freely in broad daylight. {2:14} They mocked them for their transgressions, as they themselves had done; in broad daylight, they revealed their sins. {2:15} And the daughters of Jerusalem were defiled according to Your judgment, because they had defiled themselves with unnatural acts. {2:16} I am deeply troubled within for these things. {2:17} Yet I will justify You, O God, with a sincere heart, for Your righteousness is displayed in Your judgments, O God. {2:18} You have repaid the sinners according to their deeds, according to their very wicked sins. {2:19} You have exposed their sins, so Your judgment might be evident; You have erased their memory from the earth. {2:20} God is a righteous judge, and He shows no favoritism. {2:21} The nations insulted Jerusalem, trampling her down; her beauty was dragged from the throne of glory. {2:22} She wore sackcloth instead of beautiful clothes, a rope around her head instead of a crown. {2:23} She removed the glorious diadem God had placed on her, and her beauty was cast upon the ground in dishonor. {2:24} And I saw and pleaded with the Lord and said, Long enough, O Lord, has Your hand been heavy on Israel, bringing nations upon them. {2:25} For they have mercilessly made sport in wrath and fierce anger; they will utterly destroy, unless You, O Lord, rebuke them in Your wrath. {2:26} For they have acted not in zeal but in the lust of their souls, pouring out their wrath upon us with intent to plunder. {2:27} Do not delay, O God, to repay them for their pride, turning the pride of the dragon into dishonor. {2:28} And I did not wait long before God showed me the arrogant one slain on the mountains of Egypt, {2:29} valued less than the least on land and sea; his body tossed by the waves with much disrespect, with no one to bury him because He had rejected him with dishonor. {2:30} He did not remember that he was mortal, nor did he consider his end; {2:31} He said: I will be lord of land and sea; but he did not realize that it is God who is great, mighty in His strength. {2:32} He is king over the heavens, and He judges kings and kingdoms. {2:33} He is the one who exalts in glory, and brings down the proud to eternal destruction in dishonor, because they did not know Him. {2:34} And now behold, you princes of the earth, the judgment of the Lord, for He is a great and righteous king, judging all under heaven. {2:35} Bless God, you who fear the Lord with wisdom, for the mercy of the Lord is upon those who fear Him, in judgment; {2:36} So that He will distinguish between the righteous and the sinner, and repay the sinners forever according to their deeds; {2:37} And have mercy on the righteous, delivering him from the affliction of the sinner, and repaying the sinner for what he has done to the righteous. {2:38} For the Lord is good to those who call upon Him in patience, acting according to His mercy to His faithful ones, establishing them always before Him in strength. {2:39} Blessed be the Lord forever before His servants.

{3:1} Righteousness versus Sin. {3:2} Why do you sleep, O my soul, and fail to bless the Lord? {3:3} Sing a new song to God, who is worthy of praise. {3:4} Sing and stay awake for His coming, for a psalm sung to God from a joyful heart is good. {3:5} The righteous remember the Lord always, with thanksgiving and a proclamation of the Lord's righteous judgments. {3:6} The righteous do not despise the Lord's discipline; His will is always before them. {3:7} The righteous stumble and still hold the Lord as righteous: they fall and look to see what God will do for them; {3:8} they seek where their deliverance will come from. {3:9} The steadfastness of the righteous comes from God, their deliverer; sin does not dwell in the house of the righteous. {3:10} The righteous continually examine their home, to remove all iniquity done by mistake. {3:11} They make atonement for sins of ignorance by fasting and humbling themselves, and the Lord considers every pious person and their house guiltless. {3:12} The sinner stumbles and curses their life, the day they were born, and their mother's labor. {3:13} They add sins to sins while they live; they fall—a grievous fall—and rise no more. {3:14} The destruction of the sinner is forever, and they will not be remembered when the righteous are rewarded. {3:15} This is the portion of sinners forever. {3:16} But those who fear the Lord will rise to eternal life, and their life will be in the light of the Lord, and will never end.

{4:1} A conversation of Solomon with the hypocrites. {4:2} Why do you sit, O profane man, in the council of the righteous, when your heart is far from the Lord, provoking the God of Israel with your sins? {4:3} Extravagant in speech, and outwardly impressive beyond all others, is the one who harshly condemns sinners in judgment. {4:4} His hand is quick to act as though he is zealous, yet he is guilty of many sins and immorality. {4:5} His eyes are on every woman without discrimination; his tongue lies when he makes a contract with an oath. {4:6} By night and in secret he sins as though unseen, speaking evil plans to every woman with his eyes. {4:7} He is quick to enter every house with cheerfulness as though innocent. {4:8} Let God remove those who live in hypocrisy among the righteous, even letting their lives be marked by corruption and poverty. {4:9} Let God reveal the deeds of the hypocrites, their actions filled with laughter and scorn; {4:10} so that the righteous may count the judgment of their God as just, when sinners are removed from among them, even the hypocrite who speaks deceitfully. {4:11} Their eyes are fixed on any secure house, to destroy the wisdom within it with sinful words. {4:12} His words are deceitful to fulfill his wicked desires. He never stops scattering families as though they were orphans, laying waste to homes for his lawless desires. {4:13} He deceives with words, saying, There is no one who sees or judges. {4:14} He fills one house with lawlessness, then fixes his eyes on the next house, to destroy it with words that fuel his desires. {4:15} Yet with all this, his soul, like Sheol, is never satisfied. {4:16} Let his portion, O Lord, be dishonored before You; let him go forth groaning and come home cursed. {4:17} Let his life be spent in anguish, poverty, and want, O Lord; let his sleep be filled with pain and his awakening with confusion. {4:18} Let sleep be taken from his eyes at night; let him fail dishonorably in all his work. {4:19} Let him come home empty-handed, and his house be void of everything that could satisfy his appetite. {4:20} Let his old age be spent in childless loneliness until his death. {4:21} Let the flesh of the hypocrites be torn by wild beasts, and let the bones of the lawless lie dishonored in the sunlight. {4:22} Let ravens peck out the eyes of the hypocrites. {4:23} For they have laid waste many houses in dishonor, scattering them in their lust; {4:24} They have not remembered God, nor feared Him in all these things; but they have provoked God's anger and vexed Him. {4:25} May He remove them from the earth, because with deceit they beguiled the souls of the innocent. {4:26} Blessed are those who fear the Lord in their innocence; the Lord will deliver them from deceitful men and sinners, and save us from every stumbling block of the lawless. {4:27} Let God destroy those who insolently work all unrighteousness, for the Lord our God is a great and mighty judge in righteousness. {4:28} Let Your mercy, O Lord, be upon all those who love You.

{5:1} A statement of the philosophy of the indestructibility of matter. One of the tenets of modern physics. {5:2} O Lord God, I will joyfully praise Your name, among those who know Your righteous judgments. {5:3} For You are good and merciful, the refuge of the poor; when I cry to You, do not ignore me. {5:4} For no one can take spoil from a mighty man; who then can take anything You have made, except You give it Yourself? {5:5} For man and his portion lie before You in the balance; he cannot add to or enlarge what You have prescribed. {5:6} O God, when we are in distress, we call upon You for help, and You do not reject our petition, for You are our God. {5:7} Do not let Your hand be heavy upon us, lest through necessity we sin. {5:8} Even if You do not restore us, we will not turn away; but we will come to You. {5:9} For if I hunger, I will cry to You, O God, and You will give to me. {5:10} You nourish birds and fish, giving rain to the steppes so that green grass may spring up, to prepare fodder in the steppe for every living thing; {5:11} and if they hunger, they lift up their faces to You. {5:12} Kings, rulers, and peoples You nourish, O God; and who is the help of the poor and needy, if not You, O Lord? {5:13} And You will listen--for who is good and gentle but You?-- making glad the soul of the humble by opening Your hand in mercy. {5:14} Man's goodness is given grudgingly and sparingly; and if he repeats it without complaining, even that is remarkable. {5:15} But Your gift is great in goodness and wealth, and those who hope in You will lack no gifts. {5:16} Your mercy covers the whole earth, O Lord, in goodness. {5:17} Happy is he whom God remembers, granting him enough; if a man has too much, he sins. {5:18} Moderate means with righteousness are sufficient, and by this, the blessing of the Lord becomes abundance with righteousness. {5:19} Those who fear the Lord rejoice in good gifts, and Your goodness is upon Israel in Your kingdom. {5:20} Blessed is the glory of the Lord, for He is our king.

{6:1} A song of hope, fearlessness, and peace. {6:2} Happy is the one whose heart is set on calling upon the name of the Lord; when they remember the name of the Lord, they will be saved. {6:3} The Lord makes their paths straight, and the works of their hands are preserved by the Lord their God. {6:4} When they see troubling dreams, their soul shall not be troubled; when they pass through rivers and turbulent seas, they shall not be afraid. {6:5} They rise from their sleep and bless the name of the Lord; when their heart is at peace, they sing to the name of their God, and they pray to the Lord for their whole household. {6:6} And the Lord hears the prayer of everyone who fears God, and the Lord fulfills every request of the soul that hopes in Him. {6:7} Blessed is the Lord, who shows mercy to those who love Him sincerely.

{7:1} The fine old doctrine—"You are our Shield!" {7:2} Do not make Your dwelling far from us, O God, lest those who hate us without cause attack us. {7:3} For You have rejected them, O God; let their foot not trample on Your holy inheritance. {7:4} Discipline us according to Your good pleasure, but do not give us up to the nations; {7:5} For if You send pestilence, You will command it concerning us; {7:6} For You are merciful, and will not be angry to the point of consuming us. {7:7} While Your name dwells among us, we shall find mercy, and the nations shall not prevail against us. {7:8} For You are our shield, and when we call upon You, You listen to us; {7:9} For You will pity the seed of Israel forever and You will not reject them. {7:10} But we shall be under Your yoke forever, and under the rod of Your discipline. {7:11} You will establish us in the time You help us, showing mercy to the house of Jacob on the day You promised to help them.

{8:1} Distress and the sound of war have reached my ears, the sound of a trumpet announcing slaughter and calamity, {8:2} the sound of many people like a mighty wind, like a storm with fierce fire sweeping through the desert. {8:3} And I said in my heart, Surely God is judging us; a sound I hear moving towards Jerusalem, the holy city. {8:4} My loins trembled at what I heard, my knees shook; my heart was afraid, my bones were dismayed like straw. {8:5} I said: They establish their ways in righteousness. {8:6} I thought upon the judgments of God since the creation of heaven and earth; I held God righteous in His judgments from of old. {8:7} God exposed their sins in broad daylight; all the earth came to know the righteous judgments of God. {8:8} In secret places underground their iniquities provoked Him to anger; {8:9} they committed incest, son with mother and father with daughter; they committed adultery, every man with his neighbor's wife. {8:10} They made covenants with one another, swearing oaths about these things; they plundered the sanctuary of God, as if there was no avenger. {8:11} They trod the altar of the Lord, coming straight from all manner of uncleanness; they defiled the sacrifices with menstrual blood, as if these were common flesh. {8:12} They left no sin undone, exceeding even the heathens in wickedness. {8:13} Therefore God sent them a spirit of confusion; He gave them a cup of undiluted wine to drink, making them drunk. {8:14} He brought a mighty conqueror from a distant land; He decreed war against Jerusalem and her land. {8:15} The princes of the land went to meet him with joy, saying: Blessed be your way! Come in peace. {8:16} They smoothed the rough paths before his entry; they opened the gates to Jerusalem, crowning its walls. {8:17} As a father enters the house of his sons, so he entered Jerusalem in peace; he established his presence there with great safety. {8:18} He captured her fortresses and the wall of Jerusalem; for God Himself led him in safety, while they wandered. {8:19} He destroyed their princes and every wise counselor; he poured out the blood of Jerusalem's inhabitants like unclean water. {8:20} He led away their sons and daughters, whom they had begotten in defilement. {8:21} They acted with uncleanness, as their fathers had done; they defiled Jerusalem and what was hallowed to the name of God. {8:22} But God has shown Himself righteous in His judgments upon the nations; and the pious servants of God are like innocent lambs among them. {8:23} Worthy to be praised is the Lord who judges the whole earth in His righteousness. {8:24} Behold now, O God, You have shown us Your judgment in Your righteousness; our eyes have seen Your judgments, O God. {8:25} We have justified Your name that is honored forever; for You are the God of righteousness, judging Israel with chastening. {8:26} Turn, O God, Your mercy upon us, and have pity on us; gather the dispersed of Israel with mercy and goodness; {8:27} for Your faithfulness is with us, and though we have stiffened our neck, yet You are our chastener; {8:28} do not overlook us, O our God, lest the nations swallow us up, as if there were none to deliver. {8:29} But You are our God from the beginning, and upon You is our hope set, O Lord; {8:30} and we will not depart from You, for good are Your judgments upon us. {8:31} Let Your good pleasure be upon us and our children forever; O Lord, our Savior, we shall never be moved. {8:32} The Lord is worthy to be praised for His judgments by the mouths of His pious ones; and blessed be Israel of the Lord forever.

{9:1} When Israel was taken captive into a foreign land, when they turned away from the Lord who redeemed them, they were cast away from the inheritance the Lord had given them. {9:2} Among every nation were the dispersed of Israel according to the word of God, that You might be justified, O God, in Your righteousness because of our transgressions; for You are a just judge over all the peoples of the earth. {9:3} For from Your knowledge, no one who acts unjustly is hidden, and the righteous deeds of Your pious ones are before You, O Lord; where, then, can anyone hide from Your knowledge, O God? {9:4} Our works are subject to our own choice and power to do right or wrong in the works of our hands; and in Your righteousness, You visit the sons of men. {9:5} He who does righteousness lays up life for himself with the Lord, and he who does wrong forfeits his life to destruction, for the judgments of the Lord are given in righteousness to every man and his house. {9:6} To whom are You good, O God, except to those who call upon the Lord? He cleanses from sins a soul that confesses and acknowledges; for shame is upon us and upon our faces because of all these things. {9:7} And to whom does He forgive sins, except to those who have sinned? You bless the righteous and do not reprove them for the sins they have committed; and Your goodness is upon those who sin when they repent. {9:8} And now, You are our God, and we are the people You have loved: behold and show pity, O God of Israel, for we are Yours; and do not remove Your mercy from us, lest they attack us. {9:9} For You chose the seed of Abraham before all the nations, and set Your name upon us, O Lord, and You will not reject us forever. {9:10} You made a covenant with our fathers concerning us; and we hope in You when our soul turns to You. The mercy of the Lord be upon the house of Israel forever and ever.

{10:1} Blessed is the person whom the Lord remembers with correction, and whom He keeps from the path of evil with discipline, that he may be cleansed from sin and not accumulate more. {10:2} The one who prepares his back for discipline will be cleansed, for the Lord is good to those who endure correction. {10:3} He makes straight the ways of the righteous and does not distort them through His chastening. {10:4} The mercy of the Lord is upon those who love Him sincerely, and the Lord remembers His servants with compassion. {10:5} For the testimony is in the law of the eternal covenant, the testimony of the Lord is evident in the ways of men during His visitation. {10:6} Our Lord is just and kind in His judgments forever, and Israel will praise the name of the Lord with joy. {10:7} The faithful will give thanks in the assembly of the people; and God will show mercy to the poor in the joy of Israel; {10:8} For God is good and merciful forever, and the assemblies of Israel will glorify the name of the Lord. {10:9} The salvation of the Lord be upon the house of Israel for everlasting joy!

{11:1} Sound the trumpet in Zion to gather the faithful, Let the voice of the bearer of good news resound in Jerusalem; For God has shown compassion to Israel in His visitation. {11:2} Stand upon your heights, O Jerusalem, and see your children returning, Gathered by the Lord from the East and the West; From the North they come in the joy of their God, And from distant islands God has brought them together. {11:3} He has leveled high mountains for their passage, The hills have fled before them. {11:4} As they journeyed, the forests provided them shade; Every fragrant tree God caused to grow for them, So that Israel might pass through in the glory of their God's visitation. {11:5} Jerusalem, adorn yourself with your splendid garments; Prepare your holy attire, For God has spoken favorably concerning Israel forever. {11:6} Let the Lord fulfill what He has spoken concerning Israel and Jerusalem; Let the Lord exalt Israel by His glorious name. {11:7} May the mercy of the Lord be upon Israel forever and ever!

{12:1} O Lord, rescue my soul from the deceitful and wicked, From tongues that speak lawlessly, spreading lies and deceit. {12:2} The words of the wicked are twisted and destructive, Like a fire that consumes a people's beauty. {12:3} They delight in filling homes with falsehoods, Cutting down the joyous like trees set ablaze by transgressors, Stirring up strife in households with slanderous lips. {12:4} May God drive away from the innocent the tongues of the wicked, And scatter far from those who fear the Lord the bones of slanderers! Let the deceitful tongues perish in flaming fire, far from the righteous! {12:5} May the Lord protect the peaceful soul who abhors unrighteousness, And establish the one who seeks peace within his home. {12:6} May the Lord's salvation be upon His servant Israel forever; Let sinners perish before the Lord's presence, But let the Lord's faithful ones inherit His promises.

{13:1} The right hand of the Lord has shielded me; His hand has protected us from harm. {13:2} The arm of the Lord has delivered us from the sword that passed by, From famine and the death brought by sinners. {13:3} Savage beasts attacked them: They tore into their flesh with their teeth, And crushed their bones with their jaws. But the Lord rescued us from all these dangers. {13:4} The righteous are troubled by their own mistakes, Fearful of being swept away with the sinners. {13:5} The downfall of the sinner is terrifying, But it does not touch the righteous. {13:6} The chastening of the righteous for unintentional sins Differs greatly from the punishment of the sinners. {13:7} The righteous are disciplined in secret, Lest the sinners mock them. {13:8} For the Lord corrects the righteous like a beloved child, His discipline is like that of a firstborn. {13:9} The Lord spares His faithful ones, And wipes away their errors through His discipline. {13:10} The life of the righteous shall endure forever, But sinners shall be swept away into destruction, And their memory shall vanish. {13:11} But the mercy of the Lord is upon the pious, And His mercy is upon those who fear Him.

{14:1} Faithful is the Lord to those who love Him sincerely, To those who endure His discipline, To those who walk in the righteousness of His commandments, In the law given to us for life. {14:2} The righteous shall live by it forever; The pious ones of the Lord are like the trees of life in His paradise. {14:3} Their roots are firmly planted for eternity; They shall never be uprooted as long as the heavens endure. {14:4} For the portion and inheritance of God is with Israel. {14:5} But not so for the sinners and transgressors, Who love the fleeting pleasures of their sinful days; {14:6} Their joy is in passing corruption, And they forget God. {14:7} For the ways of all people are known to Him at all times, And He knows the secrets of the heart before they come to be. {14:8} Therefore, their inheritance is Sheol, darkness, and destruction, And they will not be found on the day when the righteous receive mercy. {14:9} But the pious ones of the Lord shall inherit life with joy.

{15:1} When I was in distress, I called upon the name of the Lord, I sought the help of the God of Jacob and I was rescued; For You are the hope and refuge of the poor, O God. {15:2} For who is strong, O God, except to give thanks to You in truth? And what power does a person have except in praising Your name? {15:3} Sing a new song with joy in your heart, Let the fruit of your lips be accompanied by the well-tuned instrument of your tongue, The first offerings of lips from a pious and righteous heart— {15:4} He who offers these shall never be shaken by evil; The flame of fire and the wrath against the unrighteous shall not touch him, When it goes forth from the presence of the Lord against sinners, To destroy all the possessions of sinners, {15:5} For the mark of God is upon the righteous that they may be saved. {15:6} Famine, sword, and pestilence shall be far from the righteous, For they shall flee like men pursued in war; But they shall pursue sinners and overtake them, And those who commit lawlessness shall not escape the judgement of God; {15:7} They shall be overtaken like enemies experienced in war, For the mark of destruction is upon their forehead. {15:8} And the inheritance of sinners is destruction and darkness, And their iniquities shall pursue them to Sheol below. {15:9} Their inheritance shall not be found for their children, For sins shall lay waste the houses of sinners. {15:10} And sinners shall perish forever on the day of the Lord's judgement, When God visits the earth with His judgement. {15:11} But those who fear the Lord shall find mercy therein, And they shall live by the compassion of their God; {15:12} But sinners shall perish forever.

{16:1} When my soul wandered far from the Lord, I was nearly lost, When I distanced myself from God, my soul was on the brink of death, I was almost at the gates of Sheol with the sinners, When I turned away from the Lord God of Israel— {16:2} Had not the Lord helped me with His everlasting mercy. {16:3} He guided me like a horse, pricked to obedience, My savior and helper saved me at all times. {16:4} I give thanks to You, O God, for You have brought me salvation; You did not count me among sinners for my destruction. {16:5} Do not withdraw Your mercy from me, O God, Nor Your presence from my heart until I die. {16:6} Guide me, O God, keeping me from wicked sin, And from every woman who leads the simple astray. {16:7} Let not the allure of a lawless woman deceive me, Nor anyone who indulges in unprofitable sin. {16:8} Establish the works of my hands before You, And remember my actions in Your presence. {16:9} Guard my tongue and my lips with words of truth; Keep anger and irrational wrath far from me. {16:10} Remove murmuring and impatience in affliction from me, When You correct me for my sins, that I may return to You. {16:11} Uphold my soul with goodwill and cheerfulness; When You strengthen my soul, what You provide will be enough for me. {16:12} For if You do not give strength, Who can endure chastisement with poverty? {16:13} When a person is disciplined through their own faults, Your testing comes through their flesh and the hardship of poverty. {16:14} If the righteous endure through all these trials, they shall receive mercy from Lord.

{17:1} O Lord, You are our eternal King, In You, O God, our souls find glory. {17:2} How fleeting are the days of human life upon the earth? As our days are, so is our hope set upon You. {17:3} But we place our hope in God, our deliverer; For the strength of our God endures forever with mercy, And the rule of our God extends over the nations in righteous judgement. {17:4} You, O Lord, chose David to be king over Israel, And swore to him regarding his descendants that his kingdom would never fail before You. {17:5} But because of our sins, sinners rose up against us; They attacked us and drove us out; They violently seized what You had not promised to them. {17:6} They did not glorify Your honorable name; Instead, they established a worldly monarchy in place of what was once excellent; They desecrated the throne of David with tumultuous arrogance. {17:7} But You, O God, cast them down and removed their descendants from the earth, For against them arose a man who was foreign to our people. {17:8} You repaid them according to their sins, O God; They received what they deserved according to their deeds. {17:9} God showed them no mercy; He sought out their descendants and did not let any of them escape. {17:10} The Lord is faithful in all His judgements Which He executes upon the earth. {17:11} The lawless one devastated our land so that it became uninhabitable, They destroyed young and old, and their children together. {17:12} In His anger, He banished them even to the west, And He subjected the rulers of the land to relentless mockery. {17:13} The enemy acted proudly as a foreigner, And his heart was estranged from our God. {17:14} Everything they did in Jerusalem, And also the nations in their cities to their own gods. {17:15} And the covenant children among the mixed peoples surpassed them in evil. Among them, there was not one who practiced mercy and truth in Jerusalem. {17:16} Those who loved the gatherings of the righteous fled from them, Like sparrows that fly from their nest. {17:17} They wandered in deserts to save their lives from harm, And those who escaped alive were precious in the eyes of those who lived abroad. They were scattered over the whole earth by lawless men. {17:18} For the heavens withheld rain from falling upon the earth, Springs were stopped that flowed perennially from the depths and ran down from lofty mountains. {17:19} For there was no one among them who practiced righteousness and justice; From the highest to the lowest, all were sinful; The king was a transgressor, the judge disobedient, and the people were sinful. {17:20} Behold, O Lord, and raise up their king, the son of David, At the time You see fit, O God, that he may reign over Your servant Israel. {17:21} Clothe him with strength to shatter unrighteous rulers, And to cleanse Jerusalem from nations that trample her down to destruction. {17:22} Wisely and righteously he shall drive out sinners from the inheritance, He shall destroy the pride of the sinner like a potter's vessel. {17:23} With a rod of iron he shall shatter all their substance, He shall destroy the godless nations with the word of his mouth; {17:24} At his rebuke, nations shall flee before him, And he shall reprove sinners for the thoughts of their hearts. {17:25} And he shall gather a holy people whom he shall lead in righteousness, And he shall judge the tribes of the people sanctified by the Lord his God. {17:26} He shall not allow unrighteousness to dwell among them anymore, Nor shall any man who knows wickedness dwell with them, For he shall recognize them as sons of their God. {17:27} He shall divide them according to their tribes upon the land, And no sojourner or alien shall reside among them anymore. {17:28} He shall judge peoples and nations with the wisdom of his righteousness. Selah. {17:29} And he shall have the heathen nations serving under his yoke; And he shall glorify the Lord in a place visible to all the earth; And he shall cleanse Jerusalem, making it holy as of old: {17:30} So that nations shall come from the ends of the earth to see his glory, Bringing as gifts her sons who had fainted, And to see the glory of the Lord, with which God has glorified her. {17:31} And he shall be a righteous king, taught by God, over them, And there shall be no unrighteousness in his days among them, For all shall be holy and their king the anointed of the Lord. {17:32} For he shall not trust in horses, riders, bows, Nor shall he accumulate gold and silver for war, {17:33} Nor shall he put his confidence in a multitude for the day of battle. {17:34} The Lord Himself is his king, the hope of the mighty through their hope in God. {17:35} All nations shall fear him, For he will strike the earth with the word of his mouth forever. {17:36} He will bless the people of the Lord with wisdom and gladness, And he himself will be pure from sin, so that he may rule a great people. {17:37} He will rebuke rulers and remove sinners by the might of his word; And relying upon his God, throughout his days he will not stumble; {17:38} For God will make him mighty by means of His Holy Spirit, And wise by means of the spirit of understanding, with strength and righteousness. {17:39} And the blessing of the Lord will be with him; he will be strong and will not stumble; His hope will be in the Lord; who then can prevail against him? {17:40} He will be mighty in his works and strong in the fear of God, He will faithfully and righteously shepherd the flock of the Lord, And will not allow any among them to stumble in their pasture. {17:41} He will lead them all rightly, And there will be no pride among them so that any of them should be oppressed. {17:42} This will be the majesty of the king of Israel, whom God knows; He will raise him up over the house of Israel to correct them. {17:43} His words shall be more refined than costly gold, the finest; In the assemblies he will judge the peoples, the tribes of the sanctified. {17:44} His words shall be like the words of the holy ones among the sanctified peoples. {17:45} Blessed are those who shall be in those days, In that they shall see the good fortune of Israel which God shall bring to pass in gathering together the tribes. {17:46} May the Lord hasten His mercy upon Israel! May He deliver us from the uncleanness of unholy enemies! {17:47} Lord Himself is our king forever and ever.

{18:1} Lord, Your mercy extends over the works of Your hands forever; Your goodness is abundant over Israel as a rich gift. {18:2} Your eyes watch over them so that none of them suffers lack; Your ears listen to the hopeful prayer of the poor. {18:3}

Your judgements are executed upon the whole earth in mercy; And Your love is toward the descendants of Abraham, the children of Israel. {18:4} Your chastisement is upon us as upon a first-born, only-begotten son, To turn back the obedient soul from folly wrought in ignorance. {18:5} May God cleanse Israel against the day of mercy and blessing, Against the day of choice when blessed shall they be who are in those days, When He restores His anointed. {18:6} In that they shall see the goodness of the Lord which He shall perform for the generation to come, Under the rod of chastening of the Lord's anointed in the fear of his God, In the spirit of wisdom, righteousness, and strength; {18:7} That he may direct every person in the works of righteousness by the fear of God, That he may establish them all before the Lord, A righteous generation living in the fear of God in the days of mercy. Selah. {18:8} Great is our God and glorious, dwelling in the highest. It is He who has set the lights of heaven in their courses to determine seasons from year to year, {18:9} And they have not deviated from the way He appointed them. In the fear of God, they pursue their path every day, {18:10} Since the day God created them & forevermore. They have not erred since the day He created them, Except when God commanded them to do so by the command of His servants.

Odes of Solomon

Odes of Solomon, a collection of 42 ancient hymns, stands as a remarkable yet enigmatic work in the landscape of early Christian literature. Believed to have been composed between the late 1st and early 3rd centuries CE, the Odes are often attributed to the pseudonymous figure of Solomon, a connection which draws upon the wisdom and poetic tradition associated with the biblical King Solomon. The origins of the text are shrouded in mystery, with scholars debating its precise geographic and cultural context. It is suggested that the Odes may have emerged from a Syriac-speaking Christian community, given the linguistic features and thematic elements present within the hymns. The language of the original composition is thought to be Syriac, although Greek and Coptic versions have also been discovered, indicating the wide reach and enduring appeal of the text in the early Christian world. The Odes are characterized by their rich, poetic imagery and profound spiritual depth, blending elements of Jewish, Gnostic, and Christian thought. Themes of divine love, redemption, and the intimate relationship between the believer and the divine permeate the collection, offering insights into the theological and devotional life of early Christian communities. The mystical and allegorical nature of the Odes has led to various interpretations, with some scholars viewing them as expressions of early Christian mysticism or as liturgical texts used in worship.

{1:1} The Lord surrounds me like a crown, and I will never be without Him. {1:2} They crafted for me a crown of truth, and it caused your branches to blossom within me. {1:3} For it is not like a withered crown that does not blossom; but you live upon my head, and you have flourished upon my head. {1:4} Your fruits are mature and perfect; they are full of your salvation.

Chapter 2: Not Found

{3:1} The beginning of this Ode is lost, but what remains speaks of my connection with the Lord: {3:2} His presence supports me, and I stand on His love; {3:3} I would not know how to love the Lord if He had not first loved me. {3:4} For who can truly understand love except the one who is loved? {3:5} I love the Beloved, and my soul clings to Him. {3:6} Where He finds rest, there I also find my place; {3:7} And I shall never feel like a stranger, for with the Lord Most High and Merciful, there is no reluctance. {3:8} I am united with Him who is the source of love, for the Lover has found the Beloved. {3:9} By loving the Son, I too shall become a child of God. {3:10} For whoever is joined to the Immortal One shall also share in immortality; {3:11} And those who delight in the Living One shall themselves live. {3:12} This is the Spirit of the Lord, teaching humanity His ways without deceit. {3:13} Be wise, understanding, and vigilant. Hallelujah.

{4:1} This Ode starts with a historical reference, possibly about the closure of the temple at Leontopolis in Egypt around 73 AD. {4:2} No one, O my God, can change Your holy place; {4:3} It is impossible to move it elsewhere, for no one has authority over it. {4:4} Your sanctuary was established before all other places; {4:5} What is older cannot be altered by what is younger. {4:6} You have devoted Your heart to Your believers; You will never fail nor lack in fruitfulness. {4:7} For one moment of faith in You is more precious than countless days and years. {4:8} Who can put on Your grace and be harmed? {4:9} Your seal is known, Your creatures acknowledge it, Your heavenly hosts possess it, and the chosen archangels are clothed in it. {4:10} You have given us fellowship with You not because You need us, but because we need You. {4:11} Shower Your blessings upon us, open Your abundant fountains that pour out milk and honey. {4:12} Your promises are irrevocable, and what You give, You freely give. {4:13} You do not retract Your gifts once given, for all was known to You from the beginning, ordered by Your divine will. {4:14} For You, O God, have created all things. Hallelujah.

{5:1} This Ode is noted for its appearance in a speech by Salome in the ancient text known as the Pistis Sophia. {5:2} I give thanks to You, O Lord, because I love You; {5:3} O Most High, You will never abandon me, for You are my hope. {5:4} I have received Your grace freely, and I live by it. {5:5} My persecutors may come, but they will not see me. {5:6} A cloud of darkness will fall over their eyes, and thick gloom will envelop them. {5:7} They will be unable to see, and their plans will fail. {5:8} For they devised schemes that did not succeed. {5:9} My hope is in the Lord, and I will not fear. {5:10} He is like a garland on my head, and I shall not be moved; even if everything shakes, I stand firm. {5:11} Even if all visible things perish, I will not die, for the Lord is with me, and I am with Him. Hallelujah.

{6:1} Just as the wind moves through a harp and makes the strings resonate, so the Spirit of the Lord moves through me, and I speak through His love. {6:2} He removes anything foreign, and everything belongs to the Lord. {6:3} This has been the case since the beginning and will continue until the end. {6:4} Nothing will oppose Him, and nothing will rise against Him. {6:5} The Lord has greatly expanded His knowledge, and He was eager for us to know the things He has graciously given us. {6:6} We praise Him in honor of His name, and our spirits celebrate His Holy Spirit. {6:7} A stream went forth and grew into a vast and wide river; it carried everything away, shattered it, and brought it to the Temple. {6:8} The barriers built by men could not contain it, nor could the techniques of those who usually control water. {6:9} It spread over all the earth and filled everything. {6:10} All the thirsty on earth drank, and their thirst was quenched; the drink came from the Most High. {6:11} Blessed are those who serve that drink and have been entrusted with His water. {6:12} They have refreshed dry lips and revived the will of those who were paralyzed. {6:13} They have saved lives that were on the brink of death. {6:14} They have restored and supported weakened limbs, given strength for the journey, and light for the eyes. {6:15} Everyone recognized them as belonging to the Lord and lived by the eternal living water. {6:16} Hallelujah.

{7:1} As the impulse of anger rises against evil, so does joy spring forth from what is lovely, bearing its fruits abundantly. {7:2} My joy is in the Lord, and my heart's desire is for Him; this path I walk is excellent. {7:3} With the Lord as my helper, I have come to know Him without reservation; His humility has revealed His greatness through kindness. {7:4} He became like me so that I could receive Him; {7:5} He took on my likeness so that I could embrace Him; {7:6} And I did not tremble when I saw Him, for His grace surrounded me. {7:7} He became like me to teach me about Himself, and in my form, I found no reason to turn away from Him. {7:8} The Father of knowledge is the Word of knowledge; {7:9} He who created wisdom is wiser than His works. {7:10} He who created me before I existed knew what I would do when I came into being. {7:11} Therefore, in His abundant grace, He pitied me and granted me the ability to ask from Him and receive from His sacrifice. {7:12} For He is incorruptible, the fullness of ages and the Father of them all. {7:13} He has shown Himself to those who are His, so that they may recognize their Creator and not think they came into being by themselves. {7:14} For knowledge He has appointed as its way, expanding and perfecting it for all. {7:15} He has adorned it with the marks of His light, and I have walked in it from beginning to end. {7:16} For it was created by Him, and in the Son He rests, and for its salvation He will take hold of everything. {7:17} And the Most High will be known among His saints, announcing to those who sing the coming of the Lord. {7:18} They will go out to meet Him with joyful songs and harps of many tones. {7:19} The seers will appear before Him, and they will praise the Lord for His love, for He is near and sees all. {7:20} Hatred will be removed from the earth, and jealousy will be drowned with it. {7:21} Ignorance has been destroyed because the knowledge of the Lord has come. {7:22} Those who sing praises will sing of the grace of the Lord Most High. {7:23} They will bring their songs, and their hearts will shine like the day, radiant with the beauty of the Lord's goodness. {7:24} Nothing on earth will be without knowledge, and no one will be silent. {7:25} For He has given a voice to His creation to praise Him. {7:26} Confess His power and proclaim His grace. Hallelujah.

{8:1} Open your hearts to the joy of the Lord; {8:2} Let your love grow from your heart to your lips, bearing holy fruit, and speak with vigilance in His light. {8:3} Rise up, you who were once brought low; {8:4} Speak out, you who were silent; your mouths have been opened. {8:5} You who were despised, now lift yourselves up, for your righteousness has been exalted. {8:6} The right hand of the Lord is with you; He is your helper. {8:7} Peace was prepared for you before your war began. {8:8} Listen to the word of truth and receive the knowledge of the Most High. {8:9} Your flesh does not comprehend what I am saying to you, nor do your hearts grasp what I am revealing. {8:10} Keep my secret, you who are kept by it; {8:11} Keep my faith, you who are guarded by it. {8:12} Understand my knowledge, you who know me truly. {8:13} Love me with affection, you who love; {8:14} For I will not turn away from those who are mine. {8:15} I know them, and before they existed, I knew them; I set my seal upon their faces. {8:16} I formed their bodies; I prepared their souls to drink from my holy nourishment and live by it. {8:17} I delighted in them and am not ashamed of them; {8:18} They are my creation and the manifestation of my thoughts. {8:19} Who then can oppose my work, or who is not subject to them? {8:20} I created their minds and hearts; they are mine, and I established my chosen ones by my own right hand. {8:21} My righteousness goes before them, and they will not be deprived of my name, for I am with them. {8:22} Ask and receive; abide in the love of the Lord, beloved ones in the Beloved. {8:23} Those who are kept by Him will be found blameless for all ages in the name of their Father. Hallelujah.

{9:1} Open your ears and listen; give me your souls that I may give you mine, the word of the Lord and His good pleasure, the holy thought He has devised for His Messiah. {9:2} For in the Lord's will is your salvation; His thought is eternal life, and your end is immortality. {9:3} Be enriched in God the Father and receive the thought of the Most High. {9:4} Be strong and redeemed by His grace. {9:5} I proclaim peace to you, O saints of the Lord, that none who hear may fall in battle, that those who know Him may not perish, and those who receive Him may not be put to shame. {9:6} Truth is an everlasting crown; blessed are those who wear it. {9:7} It is a precious stone, and wars have been fought over it. {9:8} Righteousness has claimed it and given it to you; {9:9} Put on the crown in the true covenant of the Lord. {9:10} All who conquer will be written in His book, {9:11} For their book is victory, which belongs to you. Victory sees you and desires your salvation. Hallelujah.

{10:1} The Lord has guided my speech by His word; He has opened my heart with His light and has filled me with His eternal life. {10:2} He has given me the ability to speak His peace, to convert souls willing to come to Him, and to lead captives into freedom. {10:3} I have been strengthened and empowered to overcome the world; {10:4} It has become a praise to the Most High and God my Father. {10:5} The scattered Gentiles were gathered together, {10:6} And I was honored by their confession in high places; {10:7} The light's traces were set upon their hearts, and they walked in my life, were saved, and became my people forever. {10:8} They were unpolluted by their love for me, and they were set apart by the light's marks; {10:9} Their lives were sustained by my holy spirit, and their righteousness will endure forever. {10:10} They will sing praises to the Lord for His love, for He is near and sees all. {10:11} Hatred will be removed, and jealousy will be drowned; {10:12} Ignorance is gone, and the knowledge of the Lord has arrived. {10:13} Those who sing His praises will sing of the grace of the Lord Most High; {10:14} They will bring their songs, and their hearts will shine like the day, radiant with the beauty of the Lord's goodness. {10:15} Nothing on earth will be without knowledge, and no voice will be silent. {10:16} He has given a voice to His creation to praise Him. {10:17} Confess His power and proclaim His grace. Hallelujah.

{11:1} My heart was opened, revealing its inner beauty; grace blossomed within, bearing fruit for the Lord. {11:2} The Most High pierced my heart with His Holy Spirit, examining my love for Him and filling me with His love. {11:3} His opening of me became my salvation, and I ran in His way, in His peace, the path of truth. {11:4} From beginning to end, I embraced His knowledge and stood firm on the rock of truth where He placed me. {11:5} Speaking waters touched my lips abundantly from the Lord's fountain, and I drank deeply of the living water that never ends. {11:6} I drank and was filled with the intoxicating living water, not devoid of understanding; I turned away from vanity and turned to the Most High my God. {11:7} Enriched by His bounty, I abandoned the folly spread over the earth, casting it aside. {11:8} The Lord clothed me anew, enveloped me in His light, and granted me rest from above in incorruptibility. {11:9} I became like the land that blooms and rejoices in its fruits. {11:10} The Lord shone upon me like the sun upon the earth; {11:11} He illuminated my eyes, and my face was refreshed with His dew; my spirit savored the pleasant aroma of the Lord. {11:12} He brought me to His Paradise, where His pleasure abounds. {11:13} I worshipped the Lord for His glory, saying, "Blessed are those planted in Your land and those who dwell in Your Paradise." {11:14} They thrive through the fruits of the trees, transformed from darkness to light. {11:15} Behold, all Your servants are beautiful, doing good works and turning from wickedness to Your delight. {11:16} They have turned away the bitterness of the trees planted in Your land; {11:17} Everything has become a reflection of You, a lasting memorial of Your faithful deeds. {11:18} Your Paradise is vast, filled with purpose; {11:19} Nothing is wasted, but all is filled with fruit. Glory be to You, O God, the joy of Paradise forever.

{12:1} He has filled me with words of truth that I may speak them; {12:2} Like flowing waters, truth pours from my mouth, and my lips bear His fruit. {12:3} He has enriched me with His knowledge, for the mouth of the Lord is the true Word, the gateway to His light. {12:4} The Most High has entrusted His words, which interpret His beauty, proclaim His praise, confess His counsel, declare His thoughts, and discipline His servants. {12:5} The Word's speed is indescribable, matching its expression in swiftness and power. {12:6} Its course is limitless, never failing, steadfast, and unerring. {12:7} As its work is, so is its end—it is light and the dawn of thought. {12:8} Through the Word, worlds converse, and those once silent speak; {12:9} Love and harmony emanate from it, uniting all in concord. {12:10} Through it, they recognize their Creator, for the mouth of the Most High speaks to them, His explanation flowing through it. {12:11} The Word dwells in humanity; its truth is love. {12:12} Blessed are those who understand all through it and know the Lord in His truth. Hallelujah.

{13:1} Behold, the Lord is our mirror; open your eyes and see yourselves in Him. {13:2} Praise His spirit and cleanse your faces; love His holiness and clothe yourselves in it. {13:3} Remain unstained before Him always. Hallelujah.

{14:1} As a son's eyes are always on his father, so are my eyes, O Lord, always upon You. {14:2} With You are my comforts and delights. {14:3} Do not withhold Your mercies from me, O Lord; do not withdraw Your kindness. {14:4} Stretch out Your right hand to me always and guide me according to Your good pleasure until the end. {14:5} Let me be pleasing before You for the sake of Your glory and Your name. {14:6} Preserve me from evil, and let Your gentleness abide with me, along with the fruits of Your love. {14:7} Teach me Your truthful Psalms that I may bear fruit in You. {14:8} Open to me the harp of Your Holy Spirit so that with all its notes I may praise You, O Lord. {14:9} According to Your abundant mercies, grant to me and hasten to fulfill our requests, for You are able to meet all our needs.

{15:1} Just as the sun brings joy to those awaiting its dawn, so is my joy the Lord. {15:2} He is my Sun; His rays have lifted me, and His light has dispelled all darkness from my face. {15:3} In Him, I have gained eyes to see His holy day. {15:4} Ears have been granted to me, and I have heard His truth. {15:5} I have acquired the thought of knowledge and have delighted in Him. {15:6} I have forsaken the path of error and walked toward Him, receiving salvation freely from Him. {15:7} According to His generosity, He has given to me, and by His excellent beauty, He has transformed me. {15:8} Through His name, I have put on incorruption and cast off corruption by His grace. {15:9} Death has been abolished before me, and Sheol has been eliminated by my word. {15:10} Immortal life has risen in the Lord's land, {15:11} Made known to His faithful and given without measure to all who trust in Him. Hallelujah.

{16:1} As a farmer wields the ploughshare and a sailor guides the ship, so my work is the Psalm of the Lord; my craft and occupation are in His praises. {16:2} His love has nourished my heart, pouring His fruits even to my lips. {16:3} For my love is for the Lord, and therefore I will sing to Him. {16:4} In His praise, I find strength and faith. {16:5} I will open my mouth, and His spirit will declare in me the glory of the Lord, His beauty, the work of His hands, and the skill of His fingers. {16:6} His mercies are countless, His word powerful. {16:7} For the word of the Lord explores all things, visible and hidden, revealing His thoughts. {16:8} The eye sees His works, the ear hears His thoughts. {16:9} He spread out the earth, settled the seas. {16:10} He measured the heavens, fixed the stars, established creation. {16:11} He rested from His labors. {16:12} His creations run their course, fulfill their tasks. {16:13} They do not stand idle; His heavenly hosts obey His word. {16:14} The sun holds the treasury of light, night the treasury of darkness. {16:15} He made the sun to brighten the day, night to veil the land in darkness. {16:16} Their cycles speak of God's beauty; {16:17} Nothing exists without the Lord; He predates all. {16:18} Worlds were made by His word, by His heart's design. Glory and honor to His name. Hallelujah.

{17:1} I am crowned by my God; my crown is living. {17:2} Justified in my Lord, my salvation incorruptible. {17:3} Freed from vanity, not condemned. {17:4} Chains broken, I received a new face and form. {17:5} I walked and was saved, led by the truth. {17:6} Those who saw me were amazed; I was seen as a marvel. {17:7} The Most High, in His perfection, knew and raised me up, glorifying me with kindness, elevating my thoughts to His truth. {17:8} From Him came the path of His precepts; I opened closed doors, shattered iron bars. {17:9} My iron melted before me. {17:10} Nothing remained closed; I became the door to everything. {17:11} I liberated all bound, imparted knowledge generously; my prayer was love. {17:12} I sowed my fruits in hearts, transforming them into myself; they received my blessing and lived. {17:13} They gathered to me and were saved; they were like my own members, and I their head. Glory to You, our Head, the Lord Messiah. Hallelujah.

{18:1} My heart swelled in love for the Most High and expanded to praise Him for His name's sake. {18:2} My limbs strengthened in His strength, not faltering. {18:3} Sickness fled from my body, standing firm by His will, for His kingdom is true. {18:4} O Lord, do not withhold Your word from me because of those lacking, nor restrain Your perfection because of their deeds. {18:5} Let not darkness conquer the light; let truth not flee falsehood. {18:6} Appoint me to victory; Your salvation is at hand, gathering people from all corners. {18:7} Preserve those held in evils; You are my God. {18:8} Falsehood and death are not in Your mouth; Your will is perfection, ignorance is foreign to You. {18:9} Error does not know You, nor does ignorance. {18:10} They are like blind men; foam on the sea, thinking themselves great. {18:11} They became vain, mimicking falsehood. {18:12} Those who understand meditate truthfully, mocked by those in error. {18:13} They speak truth inspired by the Most High. Praise and great beauty to His name. Hallelujah.

{19:1} A cup of milk was offered to me, and I drank in the sweet delight of the Lord. {19:2} The Son is the cup; He who was milked is the Father. {19:3} The Holy Spirit milked Him, His breasts full, releasing His milk sufficiently. {19:4} The Holy Spirit opened His bosom, mixing milk from the Father's two breasts, offering the blend to the world unbeknownst. {19:5} Those who receive fully are on the right hand. {19:6} The Spirit opened the Virgin's womb; she conceived, bore a Son without pain. {19:7} The Virgin became a Mother with great mercy, labored, brought forth as if a man, of her own will. {19:8} She openly brought Him forth, receiving Him with great honor, loving Him in His swaddling clothes, guarding Him with kindness, displaying Him in majesty. Hallelujah.

{20:1} I am a priest of the Lord, serving Him priestly; I offer the sacrifice of His thought. {20:2} His thought differs from worldly and carnal thoughts, serving faithfully. {20:3} The Lord's sacrifice is righteousness, purity of heart and lips. {20:4} Present yourself blamelessly before Him; let not your heart harm another's. {20:5} Do not acquire a stranger for silver, do not seek to exploit your neighbor. {20:6} Do not strip him of his dignity. {20:7} Embrace the grace of the Lord fully; enter His Paradise, make a garland from its trees, place it on your head, rejoice in His rest. {20:8} Receive His kindness and grace, flourish in truth, praise His holiness. Praise and honor to His name. Hallelujah.

{21:1} I lifted my arms to the Most High, to the grace of the Lord, for He had freed me from my bonds. {21:2} My Helper lifted me to His grace and salvation. {21:3} I cast off darkness and clothed myself in light. {21:4} My soul gained a body free from sorrow, affliction, or pain. {21:5} The thought of the Lord became increasingly helpful to me, His fellowship in incorruption. {21:6} I drew near to Him, praising and confessing His name. {21:7} My heart overflowed, words of exultation arose on my lips, the Lord's praise increasing on my face.

{22:1} He who brought me down also raised me up from the depths. {22:2} He who gathers all things also cast me down. {22:3} He scattered my enemies, ancient adversaries. {22:4} He gave me authority over bonds, to release them. {22:5} By my hands, I overthrew the dragon with seven heads, uprooting his seed. {22:6} You were there to help me; your name was my stronghold. {22:7} Your right hand nullified his wicked poison, preparing the way for believers. {22:8} You chose them from the graves, separated them from the dead. {22:9} You took dead bones, covered them with flesh, infused them with life. {22:10} They were motionless, you gave them energy for life. {22:11} Your way is incorruptible, your face brings renewal to your world, dissolving and then renewing everything. {22:12} Your foundation is rock, on which you built your kingdom, a dwelling place for the saints. Hallelujah.

{23:1} Joy belongs to the saints alone! {23:2} Grace belongs to the chosen! {23:3} Love belongs to the elect! {23:4} Walk in the knowledge of the Most High without hesitation, to His exultation and the perfection of His knowledge. {23:5} His thought was like a letter descending from on high, sent like an arrow swiftly shot from a bow. {23:6} Many sought to seize and read it, but it eluded them, sealed beyond their reach. {23:7} They were frightened by it and its seal. {23:8} The power over its seal was greater than theirs. {23:9} Those who saw it pursued it, to know where it would land, who would read and hear it. {23:10} A wheel received it, passing over all obstacles. {23:11} It bore a sign of the Kingdom and Government. {23:12} It mowed down adversaries, bridged rivers, crossed over, uprooted forests, forging a wide path. {23:13} From head to foot, the wheel ran, bearing the sign upon it. {23:14} The letter was a decree encompassing all domains. {23:15} At its head was revealed the Son of Truth from the Most High Father. {23:16} He inherited all and took possession. {23:17} Many minds were confounded. {23:18} Apostates fled, persecutors vanished. {23:19} The letter, a great volume, entirely written by the finger of God. {23:20} The name of the Father, Son, and Holy Spirit, to reign forever. Hallelujah.

{24:1} The Dove hovered over the Messiah, her head, singing over Him, her voice heard. {24:2} Inhabitants trembled, sojourners moved. {24:3} Birds dropped their wings, creeping things hid, abysses opened, crying to the Lord like women in travail. {24:4} No food was given, sealed by the Lord's decree. {24:5} Abysses sealed with the Lord's seal, old beings perished, corrupted from the beginning, their end life. {24:6} Imperfect ones perished, unable to receive the word to endure. {24:7} The Lord thwarted the imaginations of those lacking truth. {24:8} Those proud in heart lacked wisdom, rejected for lacking truth. {24:9} The Lord revealed His way, spread His grace. {24:10} Those who understood knew His holiness. Hallelujah.

{25:1} I was delivered from my bonds, fleeing to You, my God. {25:2} You are the right hand of my salvation, my helper. {25:3} You restrained those who rose against me. {25:4} I will see them no more; Your face saved me by Your grace. {25:5} I was despised, rejected by many, seen as weighty in their eyes. {25:6} Strength and help came from You. {25:7} You set a lamp at my right hand and left; in me, there is nothing dim. {25:8} Clothed with Your Spirit's covering, You removed my skin garment. {25:9} Your right hand lifted me, removing sickness. {25:10} I became strong in truth, holy by Your righteousness. {25:11} I was admired in the name of the Lord, justified by His gentleness. {25:12} His rest is eternal. Hallelujah.

{26:1} I overflowed with praise to the Lord, for I belong to Him. {26:2} I will sing His holy song, for my heart is united with Him. {26:3} His harp is in my hands, and the songs of His peace shall never be silent. {26:4} With all my being, I cry out to Him, praising and exalting Him. {26:5} His praise extends from east to west, and from south to north, His name is confessed. {26:6} From the highest hills to their farthest reaches is His perfection. {26:7} Who can compose the Psalms of the Lord, or who can read them? {26:8} Who can prepare their soul for life, that it may be saved? {26:9} Who can rest in the Most High, that with His mouth he may speak? {26:10} Who is able to interpret the wonders of the Lord? {26:11} For he who could interpret would be transformed and become what is interpreted. {26:12} It is enough to know and rest, for in rest the singers find their place. {26:13} Like a river with an abundant source that flows to aid those who seek it. Hallelujah.

{27:1} I stretched out my hands and sanctified my Lord. {27:2} For the extension of my hands is His sign. {27:3} My outstretched arms resemble the upright tree, a symbol of His grace.

{28:1} Like the wings of doves over their young, and the mouths of their nestlings towards their mothers. {28:2} So are the wings of the Spirit over my heart. {28:3} My heart rejoices and exults like a babe in its mother's womb. {28:4} I believed, and therefore I found peace, for faithful is He in whom I have trusted. {28:5} He has abundantly blessed me, and my head is with Him. {28:6} No sword or scimitar shall separate me from Him. {28:7} I am prepared before destruction comes, carried on His immortal wings. {28:8} He showed me His sign, gave me to drink, and within me is the spirit of life that cannot die. {28:9} Those who saw me were amazed, for I endured persecution, seeming lost to them. {28:10} My oppression became my salvation, their rejection because there was no zeal in me. {28:11} Though hated, I did good to all, like one who endures attacks without reward. {28:12} Their thoughts were corrupt, understanding perverted. {28:13} Yet I carried water in my right hand, enduring bitterness with sweetness. {28:14} I did not perish, for I was not like them in birth or brotherhood. {28:15} They sought my death in vain, for I preceded their memory. {28:16} Those who followed me without reward attacked me fruitlessly. {28:17} They sought to erase the memory of those before them. {28:18} The thoughts of the Most High cannot be anticipated; His heart surpasses all wisdom. Hallelujah.

{29:1} The Lord is my hope; in Him I will not be ashamed. {29:2} According to His praise, He made me; according to His goodness, He blessed me. {29:3} He exalted me according to His mercies and His excellent beauty lifted me up. {29:4} He brought me up from the depths of Sheol, rescued me from the mouth of death. {29:5} He humbled my enemies, justifying me by His grace. {29:6} I believed in the Lord's Messiah, knowing He is the Lord. {29:7} He showed me His sign, led me by His light, and gave me the rod of His power. {29:8} To subdue the imaginations of people, to bring down the powerful by His word. {29:9} He defeated my enemy with His word, making him like stubble carried away by the wind. {29:10} I praised the Most High because He exalted His servant and the son of His handmaid.

{30:1} Draw water for yourselves from the living fountain of the Lord, for it is open to you. {30:2} Come, all who are thirsty, drink deeply, and find rest by the Lord's fountain. {30:3} Its beauty and purity give rest to the soul, more delightful than honey. {30:4} The honeycomb of bees cannot compare to it. {30:5} It flows from the lips of the Lord, its name from the heart of the Lord. {30:6} It came infinitely and invisibly until it was set in the midst, unknown until found. {30:7} Blessed are those who have drunk from it and found rest. Hallelujah.

{31:1} The depths were dissolved before the Lord, and darkness was dispelled by His presence. {31:2} Error wandered aimlessly and perished at His hand, while folly found no path and was swallowed by the truth of the Lord. {31:3} He spoke grace and joy, uttering a new song of praise to His name. {31:4} He lifted His voice to the Most High, offering Him His chosen ones. {31:5} His countenance was justified, as His holy Father had ordained. {31:6} Come forth, you who have been afflicted, receive joy, and reclaim your souls through His grace, embracing eternal life. {31:7} They made me a debtor when I rose, though I owed them nothing, they divided my spoils. {31:8} Yet I endured silently, unmoved by their actions. {31:9} I stood firm like a rock battered by waves, enduring their bitterness for humility's sake. {31:10} Thus I redeemed my people, inheriting the promise made to our forefathers for the salvation of their descendants. Hallelujah.

{32:1} The blessed rejoice in their hearts, illuminated by the light within them. {32:2} Words flow from the Truth, self-originated, strengthened by the holy power of the Most High, forever undisturbed. Hallelujah.

{33:1} Grace descended and abandoned corruption, annihilating it in Him. {33:2} He destroyed perdition and its order, standing on a lofty summit and proclaiming His voice from one end of the earth to the other. {33:3} He drew all who obeyed

Him and evil found no place. {33:4} There stood a perfect virgin proclaiming and calling out: {33:5} "O sons and daughters of humanity, return and forsake the ways of corruption. {33:6} Come near to me, and I will enter into you, leading you out of perdition and guiding you in the ways of truth, {33:7} That you may not be destroyed but redeemed. {33:8} Hear me, and by the grace of God, be redeemed and blessed. {33:9} I am your advocate; those who embrace me shall not be harmed, but shall inherit the incorruptible new world. {33:10} My chosen ones walk in me; I will reveal my ways to those who seek me, and they shall trust in my name. Hallelujah.

{34:1} No path is difficult for the pure-hearted, no wound where thoughts are upright. {34:2} There is no storm in the depths of illuminated thoughts, where beauty surrounds from every side and nothing is divided. {34:3} As above, so below; everything is in harmony above, and what is below is merely the conception of the unknowing. {34:4} Grace is revealed for your salvation: believe, live, and be saved.

{35:1} The dew of the Lord descended quietly upon me, and His cloud of peace rose over my head, guarding me continually. {35:2} It was my salvation; everything trembled, and they were afraid. {35:3} Smoke and judgment emerged from them, yet I remained in peace, following the Lord's order. {35:4} He was more than shelter to me, more than foundation. {35:5} Like a child cradled by its mother, He nourished me with His milk, the dew of the Lord. {35:6} I grew strong by His generosity, resting in His perfection. {35:7} I raised my hands, lifting my soul to Him, and was justified by the Most High, redeemed by His grace. Hallelujah.

{36:1} I found rest in the Spirit of the Lord, who lifted me high. {36:2} He made me stand before His perfection and glory, praising Him with my songs. {36:3} The Spirit brought me before the Lord's face, and though I am a human, I was named the Illuminated, the Son of God. {36:4} I praised among the praisers, and I was great among the mighty ones. {36:5} As great as the Most High is, so He made me; He renewed me like His own newness and anointed me with His perfection. {36:6} I became one of His neighbors, my mouth opened like a cloud of dew, {36:7} My heart poured out like a gushing stream of righteousness. {36:8} I found peace in my approach to Him, and I was established by the Spirit of His governance. Hallelujah.

{37:1} I stretched out my hands to the Lord and raised my voice to the Most High. {37:2} I spoke with the lips of my heart, and He heard me when my voice reached Him. {37:3} His response brought me the fruits of my labor, {37:4} And it gave me rest through the grace of the Lord. Hallelujah.

{38:1} I ascended to the light of truth as if in a chariot. {38:2} The Truth took me, guiding and carrying me across pits and gullies, preserving me from rocks and waves. {38:3} It became my haven of salvation, setting me on the arms of immortal life. {38:4} It walked with me, making me rest, ensuring I did not stray because it is the Truth. {38:5} I faced no risks as I walked with Him. {38:6} I made no mistakes, obeying the Truth. {38:7} Error fled from it, unable to meet it; the Truth proceeded on the right path. {38:8} It clarified what I did not know, revealing the poisons of error and the plagues of death which are perceived as sweetness. {38:9} I saw the destroyer of destruction, the corrupted bride adorned, and the corrupting bridegroom. {38:10} I asked the Truth, 'Who are these?' and He said, 'This is the deceiver and the error. {38:11} They are alike in the beloved and his bride, leading astray and corrupting the world. {38:12} They invite many to their banquet, {38:13} Giving them intoxicating wine, stripping them of wisdom and knowledge, leaving them without intelligence. {38:14} These people wander like madmen, corrupted and heartless, not even seeking their heart! {38:15} I became wise, avoiding the deceiver's grasp, and I congratulated myself as the Truth stayed with me. {38:16} I was established, lived, and was redeemed. {38:17} My foundations were laid by the Lord's hand, for He established me. {38:18} He planted, watered, fixed, and blessed the root, making its fruits eternal. {38:19} It grew deep, spread out, and flourished. {38:20} The Lord alone was glorified in His planting and husbandry, by His care and the blessing of His lips, {38:21} By His right hand's beautiful planting, the discovery of His planting, and His thoughtful mind.

{39:1} The Lord's power is like great rivers. {39:2} They sweep away those who despise Him, entangling their paths. {39:3} They carry away their fords, catching their bodies and destroying their lives. {39:4} These rivers are swifter than lightning, but those who cross in faith are not moved. {39:5} Those who walk on them without blemish are unafraid. {39:6} For the Lord is the sign within these rivers; the sign is the way for those who cross in His name. {39:7} Put on the name of the Most High, know Him, and you shall cross safely, for the rivers will obey you. {39:8} The Lord has bridged them with His word; He walked and crossed them on foot. {39:9} His footsteps stand firm on the water, uninjured, as steady as a tree firmly planted. {39:10} Though the waves lifted on both sides, the footsteps of our Lord Messiah stood firm, neither erased nor defaced. {39:11} A path is set for those who follow Him, adhering to the course of faith in Him and worshipping His name. Hallelujah.

{40:1} As honey distills from the comb, {40:2} And milk flows from a loving mother to her children, {40:3} So my hope rests in You, my God. {40:4} As a fountain gushes water, {40:5} So my heart pours out praise to the Lord, my lips utter His praise, and my tongue sings His psalms. {40:6} My face shines with His joy, my spirit exults in His love, and my soul gleams in Him. {40:7} Reverence rests in Him, and redemption stands assured. {40:8} His inheritance is eternal life, and those who partake in it are incorruptible. Hallelujah.

{41:1} All of the Lord's children will praise Him and embrace the truth of His faith. {41:2} His children will be known to Him, so we will sing of His love. {41:3} We live in the Lord by His grace and receive life through His Messiah. {41:4} A great day has dawned upon us, and marvelous is He who has given us His glory. {41:5} Therefore, let us unite in the name of the Lord and honor Him for His goodness. {41:6} Let our faces shine in His light and our hearts meditate on His love day and night. {41:7} Let us rejoice in the joy of the Lord. {41:8} Those who see me will be astonished, for I am from another race. {41:9} The Father of truth remembered me, He who possessed me from the beginning. {41:10} His generosity gave birth to me, and the thought of His heart. {41:11} His Word is with us in all our ways. {41:12} The Savior who gives life and does not reject our souls. {41:13} The man who was humbled and exalted by His own righteousness. {41:14} The Son of the Most High appeared in the perfection of His Father. {41:15} Light dawned from the Word that was always within Him. {41:16} The Messiah is truly one, known before the world's foundation. {41:17} That He might save souls forever by the truth of His name, a new song arises from those who love Him. Hallelujah.

{42:1} I stretched out my hands and approached my Lord. {42:2} The stretching of my hands is His sign. {42:3} My reaching out is like the tree set on the path of the Righteous One. {42:4} I was disregarded by those who did not grasp me, but I will be with those who love me. {42:5} All my persecutors are dead, and those who hoped in me sought me because I was alive. {42:6} I rose and am with them, and I will speak through their mouths. {42:7} They have despised those who persecuted them. {42:8} I lifted over them the yoke of my love. {42:9} Like the arm of the bridegroom over the bride. {42:10} So is my yoke over those who know me. {42:11} Like the couch spread in the house of the bridegroom and bride. {42:12} So is my love over those who believe in me. {42:13} I was not rejected though I was thought to be. {42:14} I did not perish though they planned it against me. {42:15} Sheol saw me and was miserable. {42:16} Death cast me up, along with many others. {42:17} I had gall and bitterness, and I went down to the deepest depths. {42:18} He let go of my feet and head because they could not endure my face. {42:19} I made a congregation of the living among the dead, speaking to them with living lips. {42:20} My word shall not be void. {42:21} Those who had died ran towards me, crying, "Son of God, have pity on us and treat us with kindness. {42:22} Bring us out of the bonds of darkness and open the door so we may come to You. {42:23} For we see that our death did not touch You. {42:24} Let us also be redeemed with You, for You are our Redeemer." {42:25} I heard their voices and sealed my name upon their heads. {42:26} For they are free and they belong to me. Hallelujah.

THE NEW

APOCRYPHA

1 Clement

The First Epistle of Clement to the Corinthians, traditionally attributed to Clement of Rome, represents a seminal text in early Christian literature, offering profound insights into the nascent church's theological, ecclesiastical, and ethical dimensions. Composed in the late 1st century CE, this epistle emerges as a vital source for understanding the dynamics of early Christian community life, particularly within the context of the Corinthian church's internal strife and leadership disputes. Clement's epistle not only reflects the doctrinal and disciplinary concerns of the period but also illuminates the mechanisms of authority, communal unity, and scriptural interpretation that shaped the formative stages of Christian identity and organization. Its relevance extends beyond its immediate historical context, providing contemporary scholars with critical perspectives on the development of ecclesiastical structures and the evolution of early Christian thought.

{1:1} The Church of God in Rome writes to the Church of God in Corinth, to those called and sanctified by God's will through our Lord Jesus Christ. May grace and peace from Almighty God and Jesus Christ be greatly multiplied to you. {1:2} Dear brothers and sisters, due to the sudden and numerous calamities we have faced, we have been delayed in addressing the matters you consulted us about, especially the shameful and detestable division among you. This division, stirred up by a few reckless and arrogant individuals, has damaged your revered and esteemed reputation, which deserves universal love. {1:3} Who has ever spent time among you without witnessing your faith, so rich in virtue and firmly rooted? Who hasn't admired your godliness in Christ, marked by sobriety and moderation? Who hasn't spoken highly of your generous hospitality and rejoiced in your perfect and well-grounded knowledge? {1:4} You did everything impartially, following God's commandments, obedient to your leaders, and giving due honor to the elders among you. You advised young men to be sober and serious-minded, instructed your wives to act with a blameless, appropriate, and pure conscience, loving their husbands as they should, and taught them to manage their households properly with complete discretion.

{2:1} Moreover, you were all marked by humility, never puffed up with pride. You preferred to obey rather than demand obedience, and you were more willing to give than to receive. You were content with what God provided and paid close attention to His words, filling your hearts with His teachings and keeping His sufferings in mind. {2:2} Because of this, you all enjoyed profound and abundant peace and had an insatiable desire to do good. The Holy Spirit was poured out fully upon you. Filled with holy intentions, you earnestly and confidently reached out to God Almighty, asking for His mercy if you had committed any unintentional sins. {2:3} Day and night, you were concerned for the entire brotherhood, praying that the number of God's chosen ones might be saved with mercy and a good conscience. You were sincere, uncorrupted, and forgiving of each other's wrongs. Any form of faction and division was detestable to you. {2:4} You mourned over your neighbors' sins, considering their shortcomings as your own. You never hesitated to perform acts of kindness and were always ready for every good work. Living a thoroughly virtuous and religious life, you did everything with reverence for God. The Lord's commandments and ordinances were inscribed on the tablets of your hearts.

{3:1} Every kind of honor and happiness was given to you, fulfilling the scripture, "My beloved ate and drank and grew large and kicked." From this arose rivalry and jealousy, strife and rebellion, persecution and chaos, war and captivity. The worthless rose against the honored, the obscure against the renowned, the foolish against the wise, and the young against the elderly. {3:2} As a result, righteousness and peace have left you. Everyone has abandoned the fear of God, become blind in faith, and no longer follows His ordinances. Instead of acting as Christians, they follow their own wicked desires, returning to the unrighteous and ungodly envy that brought death into the world.

{4:1} Many evils have arisen from this source in ancient times. As it is written: "After some time, Cain brought an offering to God from the fruits of the earth, and Abel brought an offering from the firstborn of his flock and their fat. God respected Abel and his offering, but He did not regard Cain and his sacrifice. Cain was deeply upset, and his face fell. God said to Cain, 'Why are you upset, and why is your face downcast? If you offer rightly but do not divide rightly, have you not sinned? Be at peace: your offering returns to you, and you shall possess it again.' Cain then said to Abel, 'Let us go into the field.' While they were in the field, Cain attacked Abel and killed him." You see, brothers and sisters, how envy and jealousy led to the murder of a brother. {4:2} Because of envy, our father Jacob fled from his brother Esau. Envy led to Joseph being persecuted and sold into slavery. Envy forced Moses to flee from Pharaoh when he heard a fellow Hebrew say, "Who made you a judge or ruler over us? Are you going to kill me as you killed the Egyptian yesterday?" Due to envy, Aaron and Miriam had to stay outside the camp. Envy caused Dathan and Abiram to be swallowed alive by the earth for their rebellion against God's servant Moses. Because of envy, David faced hatred from foreigners and was persecuted by King Saul of Israel.

{5:1} Let's not focus only on ancient examples but also consider recent spiritual heroes. In our own generation, the greatest and most righteous pillars of the Church have been persecuted and killed due to envy and jealousy. {5:2} Look at the illustrious apostles. Peter, driven by unjust envy, endured countless hardships and ultimately suffered martyrdom, entering the glory he deserved. Similarly, Paul, through envy, earned the reward of patient endurance after being imprisoned seven times, forced to flee, and stoned. {5:3} Paul preached both in the East and West, gaining a remarkable reputation for his faith. He taught righteousness to the entire world, traveled to the farthest reaches of the West, and was martyred under the prefects. Thus, he left this world and entered the holy place, proving himself an extraordinary example of patience.

{6:1} Alongside these men who lived holy lives, there is also a great multitude of the elect who endured many indignities and tortures because of envy, providing us with an excellent example. {6:2} Due to envy, women like the Danaids and Dircae were persecuted, suffering terrible and unspeakable torments, yet they remained steadfast in their faith. Though physically weak, they received a noble reward. {6:3} Envy has separated wives from their husbands, contradicting the words of our father Adam, "This is now bone of my bones and flesh of my flesh." Envy and strife have destroyed great cities and uprooted mighty nations.

{7:1} Beloved, we write these things to you not only to remind you of your duty but also to remind ourselves. We are all fighting in the same arena and facing the same struggle. {7:2} Therefore, let us abandon vain and fruitless concerns and embrace the glorious and honorable calling we have received. Let us focus on what is good, pleasing, and acceptable to our Creator. {7:3} Let us look steadfastly at the blood of Christ and understand how precious it is to God. This blood, shed for our salvation, has brought the grace of repentance to the entire world. {7:4} Let us reflect on past generations and recognize that the Lord has always offered a place of repentance to those who turn to Him. Noah preached repentance, and those who listened were saved. Jonah warned the Ninevites of destruction, but they repented and, through prayer, obtained salvation, even though they were not part of God's covenant.

{8:1} The messengers of God's grace have spoken of repentance under the influence of the Holy Spirit, and the Lord of all has solemnly declared, "As I live," says the Lord, "I take no pleasure in the death of the sinner, but rather in their repentance." He further urges, "Repent, O house of Israel, turn away from your iniquity. Say to my people, 'Even though your sins are as numerous as the stars in the sky, even though they are as red as scarlet or as dark as sackcloth, if you turn to me with all your heart and say, "Father," I will listen to you as to a holy people.'" {8:2} In another place, He commands, "Wash yourselves, make yourselves clean; remove the evil of your deeds from My sight. Stop doing evil, learn to do good. Seek justice, correct oppression, defend the fatherless, plead for the widow." {8:3} He invites, "Come now, let us reason together. Though your sins are like scarlet, they shall be as white as snow; though they are red like crimson, they shall become like wool." {8:4} He promises, "If you are willing and obedient, you shall eat the best of the land; but if you refuse and rebel, you shall be devoured by the sword, for the mouth of the Lord has spoken." {8:5} Therefore, desiring that all His beloved should partake in repentance, God, by His mighty will, has established these declarations.

{9:1} Therefore, let us willingly obey His excellent and glorious will. Let us seek His mercy and loving-kindness, turning away from fruitless labor, strife, and envy that leads to destruction. Instead, let us turn to His compassion. {9:2} Consider the examples of those who have faithfully served His glorious purpose. Take Enoch, who lived righteously and obediently and was taken up without experiencing death. {9:3} Noah, known for his faithfulness, preached repentance and renewal to the world through his ministry. By his obedience, the Lord saved the animals that entered the ark, according to His command.

{10:1} Abraham, known as "the friend of God," proved faithful by obeying God's words. He demonstrated obedience by leaving his homeland, his relatives, and his father's house to inherit the promises of God. God commanded him, "Leave your country, your relatives, and your father's house, and go to the land I will show you. I will make you into a great nation, bless you, make your name great, and you will be a blessing. I will bless those who bless you, whoever curses you I will curse; and all peoples on earth will be blessed through you." {10:2} When Abraham separated from Lot, God said, "Look around from where you are, north and south, east and west. All the land you see I will give to you and your offspring forever. I will make your descendants like the dust of the earth, so that if anyone could count the dust, then your offspring could be counted." {10:3} Additionally, Scripture tells us, "God brought Abram outside and said, 'Look up at the sky and count the stars—if indeed you can count them.' Then he said to him, 'So shall your offspring be.'" Abraham believed God, and this faith was credited to him as righteousness. {10:4} Because of his faith and hospitality, Abraham was blessed with a son in his old age. In an act of obedience, he was willing to offer this son as a sacrifice to God on one of the mountains God had shown him.

{11:1} Because of his hospitality and righteousness, Lot was rescued from Sodom when the surrounding region was destroyed by fire and sulfur. This demonstrated that the Lord does not abandon those who trust in Him, but delivers those who remain faithful while punishing those who turn away from Him. {11:2} However, Lot's wife, though she left with him, did not share his commitment to the command they had been given. She looked back and became a pillar of salt, serving as a lasting example. This serves to show that those who are indecisive and doubt God's power bring judgment upon themselves and become a warning to future generations.

{12:1} Because of her faith and hospitality, Rahab the prostitute was saved. When Joshua sent spies to Jericho, the king discovered their presence and sent men to capture them, intending to execute them. However, Rahab welcomed the spies into her home and hid them on her roof under stalks of flax. {12:2} When the king's men came to Rahab's house and demanded the spies, she deceived them, saying, "Yes, two men came to me, but I do not know where they went. Pursue them quickly, and you may still overtake them." She did not reveal the presence of the spies. {12:3} Rahab then confessed to the spies, "I know that the Lord your God has given you this city, for all its people are terrified of you. When you capture Jericho, please promise to spare me and my family." The spies agreed, instructing her to gather her family inside her house for safety. Anyone found outside her home would not be spared. {12:4} As a sign of their promise, they instructed Rahab to hang a scarlet cord from her window. This symbolized that those who believed and trusted in God would be saved through the blood of the Lord. This demonstrates that Rahab not only had faith but also prophesied through her actions.

{13:1} Therefore, brothers and sisters, let us cultivate humility, setting aside all arrogance, pride, foolishness, and anger. Let us live according to the teachings of Scripture, for the Holy Spirit says, "Do not boast about wisdom, strength, or riches, but boast in the Lord by diligently seeking Him, practicing justice and righteousness." {13:2} Let us remember the words of Jesus, who taught us gentleness and patience. He said, "Be merciful, so that you may receive mercy. Forgive, and you will be forgiven. Treat others with kindness, and kindness will be shown to you. The measure you give will be the measure you receive." {13:3} Let us establish ourselves firmly on these principles and rules, so that we may walk humbly in obedience to God's holy words. For Scripture declares, "On whom will I look favorably? On the one who is humble, peaceable, and reverent towards My teachings."

{14:1} Therefore, it is right and honorable, brothers and sisters, to obey God rather than follow those who, out of pride and rebellion, have become leaders of detestable discord. If we heed the inclinations of such individuals who sow strife and turmoil, we risk not only harm but great danger, straying from what is good. Let us treat one another kindly, reflecting the tender mercy and benevolence of our Creator. As Scripture says, "Those who are kind-hearted will inherit the land, and those who are blameless will remain in it, but the wicked will be cut off." {14:2} Scripture also observes, "I have seen the wicked in great power, spreading himself like a green laurel tree. But he passed away, and behold, he was no more; though I sought him, he could not be found." Therefore, let us hold fast to innocence and pursue equity, for there will be a remnant for the peaceable person.

{15:1} Therefore, let us hold fast to those who genuinely pursue peace along with godliness, and not to those who only pretend to do so. As Scripture warns, "These people honor me with their lips, but their hearts are far from me." They speak blessings with their mouths but harbor curses in their hearts. They profess love with their lips, yet they deceive with their tongues, showing no sincerity in their covenant with God. {15:2} Let deceitful lips be silenced, and let the Lord bring judgment upon all lying tongues and boastful mouths that exalt themselves, saying, "Our tongues are our own; who can master us?" For the Lord hears the cries of the oppressed and the sighs of the needy. He promises, "I will arise and grant them safety; I will deal confidently with their oppressors."

{16:1} Christ exemplifies humility among those who are humble, not among those who exalt themselves over His flock. Our Lord Jesus Christ, the representation of God's majesty, did not come in pomp or pride, although He easily could have. Instead, He came in a lowly state, fulfilling what the Holy Spirit had foretold about Him. As it is written, "Who has believed our message? And to whom has the arm of the Lord been revealed? He grew up before Him like a tender shoot, and like a root out of dry ground. He had no beauty or majesty to attract us to Him, nothing in His appearance that we should desire Him. He was despised and rejected by mankind, a man of suffering, and familiar with pain. Like one from whom people hide their faces He was despised, and we held Him in low esteem. Surely He took up our pain and bore our suffering, yet we considered Him punished by God, stricken by Him, and afflicted. But He was pierced for our transgressions, He was crushed for our iniquities; the punishment that brought us peace was on Him, and by His wounds we are healed. We all, like sheep, have gone astray, each of us has turned to our own way; and the Lord has laid on Him the iniquity of us all. He was oppressed and afflicted, yet He did not open His mouth; He was led like a lamb to the slaughter, and as a sheep before its shearers is silent, so He did not open His mouth. By oppression and judgment He was taken away. Yet who of His generation protested? For He was cut off from the land of the living; for the transgression of my people He was punished. He was assigned a grave with the wicked, and with the rich in His death, though He had done no violence, nor was any deceit in His mouth. Yet it was the Lord's will to crush Him and cause Him to suffer, and though the Lord makes His life an offering for sin, He will see His offspring and prolong His days, and the will of the Lord will prosper in His hand. After He has suffered, He will see the light of life and be satisfied; by His knowledge my righteous servant will justify many, and He will bear their iniquities. Therefore I will give Him a portion among the great, and He will divide the spoils with the strong, because He poured out His life unto death, and was numbered with the transgressors. For He bore the sin of many, and made intercession for the transgressors." And again, it is said, "I am a worm and not a man, scorned by everyone, despised by the people. All who see Me mock Me; they hurl insults, shaking their heads. 'He trusts in the Lord,' they say, 'let the Lord rescue Him. Let Him deliver Him, since He delights in Him.'" This is the example set before us, beloved. If the Lord humbled Himself in this way, how much more should we, who have received His grace, submit ourselves to His will?

{17:1} Let us also follow the example of those who, in goat-skins and sheep-skins, proclaimed the coming of Christ—such as Elijah, Elisha, and Ezekiel among the prophets, along with others who received similar testimony in Scripture. Abraham, who was honored as the friend of God, humbly acknowledged, "I am but dust and ashes," while earnestly considering the glory of God. {17:2} Job, known for his righteousness, integrity, fear of God, and avoidance of evil, nevertheless confessed, "No man is without defilement, even if his life is but for one day." {17:3} Moses, called faithful in all God's house and the instrument through which God punished Egypt with plagues and hardships, did not speak with arrogance. When the divine call came to him from the burning bush, he responded, "Who am I, that You should send me? I am a man of weak speech and slow tongue." And he also said, "I am like the smoke of a pot."

{18:1} Regarding David, whom God testified about, saying, "I have found David, the son of Jesse, a man after My own heart; with My lovingkindness I have anointed him forever," even this David prayed to God, "Have mercy on me, O Lord, according to Your great mercy; according to the abundance of Your compassion, blot out my transgressions. Wash me thoroughly from my iniquity, and cleanse me from my sin. {18:2} For I acknowledge my transgressions, and my sin is ever before me. Against You, You only, have I sinned and done what is evil in Your sight, so that You may be justified in Your words and blameless in Your judgment. {18:3} Indeed, I was brought forth in iniquity, and in sin did my mother conceive me. Behold, You desire truth in the inward being; therefore teach me wisdom in my secret heart. {18:4} Purge me with hyssop, and I shall be clean; wash me, and I shall be whiter than snow. {18:5} Let me hear joy and gladness; let the bones that You have broken rejoice. Hide Your face from my sins, and blot out all my iniquities. {18:6} Create in me a clean heart, O God, and renew a steadfast spirit within me. {18:7} Do not cast me away from Your presence, and do not take Your Holy Spirit from me. {18:8} Restore to me the joy of Your salvation, and uphold me with a willing spirit. {18:9} Then I will teach transgressors Your ways, and sinners will return to You. {18:10} Deliver me from bloodguiltiness, O God, God of my salvation, and my tongue will sing aloud of Your righteousness. {18:11} O Lord, open my lips, and my mouth will declare Your praise. {18:12} For You will not delight in sacrifice, or I would give it; You will not be pleased with a burnt offering. {18:13} The sacrifices of God are a broken spirit; a broken and contrite heart, O God, You will not despise.

{19:1} The humility and devout obedience of such great and distinguished men have not only benefited us but also all previous generations who received God's teachings with reverence and sincerity. Therefore, with so many splendid examples before us, let us return to the pursuit of that peace which has always been set before us from the beginning. {19:2} Let us fix our gaze firmly on the Father and Creator of the universe, and let us cling to His powerful and exceedingly great gifts and blessings of peace. {19:3} With our intellect, let us contemplate Him, and with the eyes of our soul, let us look upon His patient and merciful will. {19:4} Let us consider how free He is from anger towards all His creation.

{20:1} The heavens, guided by His governance, move in peace. Day and night follow their appointed course without hindrance. {20:2} The sun, moon, and stars move in harmony as commanded, staying within their ordained paths without deviation. {20:3} The earth, fertile and obedient to His will, yields abundant food at the appointed times for humans, animals, and all living creatures upon it. {20:4} The deep and mysterious places of the abyss, and the intricate arrangements of the underworld, are governed by His laws. {20:5} The vast and boundless sea, gathered into its basins by His command, stays within its limits, its waves breaking as He decreed: "Here shall your proud waves stop." {20:6} The oceans, beyond human reach, and the worlds beyond them, are governed by His laws. {20:7} The seasons—spring, summer, autumn, and winter—peacefully succeed one another. {20:8} The winds in their appointed directions serve their purpose at the proper times. {20:9} The ever-flowing springs, created for enjoyment and health, provide inexhaustibly for the life of humanity. {20:10} The smallest living creatures coexist in peace and harmony. {20:11} The great Creator and Lord of all has ordained all these things to exist in peace and harmony, bestowing goodness upon all, especially upon us who have sought refuge in His compassion through Jesus Christ our Lord, to whom be glory and majesty forever and ever. Amen.

{21:1} Beloved, be cautious that the abundant kindnesses of God do not lead to our condemnation, unless we walk worthy of Him, united in doing what is good and pleasing in His sight. {21:2} As Scripture says, "The Spirit of the Lord is a lamp that searches the heart's innermost recesses." Let us consider how close He is, knowing every thought and reasoning we engage in. {21:3} Therefore, it is right that we do not abandon the position assigned by His will. Let us rather offend foolish and arrogant men who boast in their speech than offend God. {21:4} Let us honor the Lord Jesus Christ, who shed His blood for us; let us respect those who lead us; let us show reverence to the elderly among us; {21:5} let us teach young men to fear God; let us guide our wives to goodness, displaying purity in all their conduct, demonstrating genuine meekness, controlling their speech with wisdom, and showing equal love to all who fear God. {21:6} Let us educate our children in true Christian values, teaching them the power of humility before God, the strength of sincere affection in His sight, the greatness of His fear, and how it saves those who walk with pure hearts. {21:7} For He searches our thoughts and desires; His breath is within us, and He will take it away when He chooses.

{22:1} The faith in Christ affirms all these exhortations. For Christ Himself, through the Holy Spirit, speaks to us: "Come, children, listen to me; I will teach you the fear of the Lord. {22:2} Who is the person who desires life and loves to see good days? Keep your tongue from evil and your lips from deceitful speech. {22:3} Turn away from evil and do good; seek peace and pursue it. {22:4} The eyes of the Lord are on the righteous, and His ears are attentive to their cry. {22:5} But the face of the Lord is against those who do evil, to wipe out their memory from the earth. {22:6} The righteous cry out, and the Lord hears them; He delivers them from all their troubles. {22:7} The Lord is close to the brokenhearted and saves those who are crushed in spirit."

{23:1} The compassionate and generous Father shows His kindness to those who fear Him, graciously bestowing His blessings on those who approach Him with a sincere heart. Therefore, let us not be indecisive or proud because of His great and glorious gifts. Let us reject what is written: "Wretched are those who are double-minded and doubting, who say, 'We have heard these things even in the days of our ancestors, but now we have grown old, and none of it has happened to us.'" {23:2} You foolish ones! Consider the example of a tree, such as the vine. It sheds its leaves, then buds, produces leaves, flowers, sour grapes, and finally ripe fruit. You see how quickly the fruit of a tree matures. {23:3} Indeed, His will shall be accomplished swiftly and suddenly, as the Scriptures also testify, saying, "He will come quickly and will not delay," and "The Lord will suddenly come to His temple, even the Holy One for whom you wait."

{24:1} Let us consider, dear friends, how the Lord consistently shows us evidence of a future resurrection, for He has demonstrated this through raising the Lord Jesus Christ as the first to rise from the dead. {24:2} Let us reflect, beloved, on the ongoing resurrection that occurs regularly. Day and night proclaim to us the concept of resurrection: night falls asleep, and day arises; day passes away, and night returns. {24:3} Let us observe the process of planting and harvesting crops. The farmer goes out and sows seed into the ground. Although the seed falls dry and bare, it gradually breaks down. Then, by the mighty providence of the Lord, it is raised up again from its dissolution. From one seed, many arise and bear fruit.

{25:1} Let's consider a remarkable phenomenon that occurs in the East, particularly in Arabia and surrounding regions. There exists a bird known as the phoenix, which is unique and lives for five hundred years. {25:2} As the time approaches for its death, the phoenix builds a nest of frankincense, myrrh, and other spices. When its life comes to an end, it enters this nest and dies. {25:3} From its decaying flesh, a certain worm emerges, nourished by the bird's remains, and eventually transforms into feathers. {25:4} Once it gains strength, the young phoenix carries the nest containing its parent's bones and flies from Arabia to Egypt, specifically to the city called Heliopolis. {25:5} In broad daylight, in full view of all, it places the nest on the altar of the sun. After performing this ritual, the phoenix swiftly returns to its original homeland. {25:6} The priests then consult their records and confirm that the phoenix has returned precisely at the completion of five hundred years.

{26:1} So, do we consider it extraordinary that the Creator of all things will raise up those who have faithfully served Him with assurance? He demonstrates His power to fulfill His promise even through a bird. {26:2} As the Scripture says, "You will raise me up, and I will praise you." {26:3} And again, "I lay down and slept; I woke up, for the Lord sustained me." {26:4} Job also affirms, "You shall raise up this flesh of mine, which has endured all these things."

{27:1} Therefore, with this hope in mind, let our souls be firmly attached to the One who is faithful to His promises and just in His judgments. He has commanded us not to lie, and surely He Himself will not lie, for nothing is impossible for God except falsehood. {27:2} Let us be stirred once more by His faithfulness and recognize that all things are near to Him. By the word of His power, He established everything, and by that same word, He can bring about their downfall. {27:3} "Who can say to Him, 'What have you done?' Or, 'Who can resist the power of His strength?'" {27:4} At His appointed time, He will accomplish all His purposes, and nothing determined by Him will fail. {27:5} All things are exposed before Him, and nothing can be hidden from His counsel. {27:6} "The heavens declare the glory of God; the skies proclaim the work of His hands. Day after day they pour forth speech; night after night they reveal knowledge. {27:7} They have no speech, they use no words; no sound is heard from them."

{28:1} Because God sees and hears everything, let us therefore fear Him and turn away from wicked deeds that arise from evil desires. By His mercy, may we be shielded from the judgments that await. {28:2} Where can any of us flee from His mighty hand? What place will receive those who try to escape from Him? As Scripture says, "Where can I go from Your Spirit? Where can I flee from Your presence? If I ascend to heaven, You are there; if I make my bed in the depths, You are there." {28:3} So where can anyone go or hide from the One who understands all things?

{29:1} Therefore, let us approach God with pure hearts, lifting up holy and undefiled hands to Him, loving our gracious and merciful Father who has included us in the blessings of His chosen ones. {29:2} For it is written, "When the Most High gave the nations their inheritance, when He divided all mankind, He set up boundaries for the peoples according to the number of the sons of Israel. {29:3} His people Jacob became the portion of the Lord, and Israel the allotment of His inheritance." And in another place, Scripture says, "The Lord will take a people for Himself from among the nations, like the firstfruits from the threshing floor; and from that nation will come forth the Holy One."

{30:1} Therefore, since we are the chosen ones of the Holy One, let us commit ourselves to everything that leads to holiness. Let us avoid slanderous speech, all forms of abominable and impure relationships, as well as drunkenness and the pursuit of worldly pleasures. Let us steer clear of detestable lusts, despicable adultery, and condemnable pride. {30:2} As Scripture says, "God opposes the proud but shows favor to the humble." Let us therefore align ourselves with those who have received God's grace. {30:3} Let us clothe ourselves with unity and humility, always exercising self-control, keeping far from gossip and malicious talk. Let our actions justify us, not merely our words. For Scripture also declares, "The more you talk, the more likely you are to sin. And if you are wise, you will avoid idle chatter." {30:4} Let us praise God rather than ourselves, for God detests self-promotion. Let others testify to our good deeds, just as they did for our righteous ancestors. {30:5} Boldness, arrogance, and audacity are traits of those cursed by God, but moderation, humility, and gentleness are characteristics of those blessed by Him.

{31:1} Let us, therefore, cling to God's blessing and consider how we can obtain it. Let's reflect on events from the beginning. Why was our father Abraham blessed? Was it not because he lived a righteous and truthful life through faith? {31:2} Isaac, with unwavering trust, willingly offered himself as a sacrifice, foreseeing what was to come. {31:3} Jacob, compelled by circumstances with his brother, humbly left his homeland and went to Laban, where he served faithfully. As a result, he received the blessing of becoming the patriarch of the twelve tribes of Israel.

{32:1} Anyone who carefully considers each aspect will recognize the magnitude of the gifts bestowed by God. From Abraham descended the priests and all the Levites who serve at God's altar. {32:2} Our Lord Jesus Christ also came from his lineage according to the flesh. From him arose kings, princes, and rulers of the tribe of Judah. {32:3} And his other descendants did not lack glory, for God had promised, "Your descendants will be as numerous as the stars of heaven." {32:4} All these individuals were highly honored and elevated, not because of their own merit, works, or righteousness, but through the sovereign will of God. {32:5} Similarly, we who are called by His will in Christ Jesus are not justified by ourselves, our own wisdom, understanding, godliness, or works done in a heart of holiness. Rather, we are justified by the same faith that has always justified people through Almighty God. To Him be glory forever. Amen.

{33:1} So what should we do, brothers and sisters? Should we grow lazy in doing good and cease to practice love? Absolutely not! May such a course never be followed by us. Instead, let us eagerly hasten with all our energy and readiness of mind to engage in every good work. {33:2} For the Creator and Lord of all delights in His works. By His immense power, He established the heavens, and with His unfathomable wisdom, He adorned them. {33:3} He separated the earth from the surrounding waters and set it upon the unshakeable foundation of His own will. {33:4} He spoke the word, and the animals that inhabit the earth came into being. {33:5} Similarly, after forming the sea and the living creatures within it, He confined them within their appointed boundaries by His own authority. {33:6} Above all, with His holy and undefiled hands, He created humanity—the most excellent of His creatures, endowed with understanding and bearing the very image of His likeness. {33:7} For God said, "Let us make mankind in our image, after our likeness." So God created humanity; male and female He created them. {33:8} After completing all these things, He examined them and pronounced them good, blessing them with the command to multiply and increase. {33:9} Let's promptly align ourselves with God's will and dedicate our efforts to performing righteous deeds, as all righteous individuals are adorned with good works, and the Lord rejoices in His works.

{34:1} The diligent servant receives the fruit of his labor with confidence, while the lazy and slothful cannot meet their employer's gaze. Therefore, it is necessary for us to be diligent in doing good, for everything comes from Him. {34:2} He warns us in advance: "Behold, the Lord is coming, and His reward is with Him, to repay each one according to his deeds." {34:3} With all our hearts, then, let us heed this exhortation, avoiding laziness and sloth in every good work. {34:4} Let us boast and find our confidence in Him. Let us willingly submit to His will. {34:5} Consider the vast multitude of His angels, ever ready to carry out His commands. For Scripture says, "Ten thousand times ten thousand stood before Him, and thousands upon thousands ministered to Him; they cried out, 'Holy, holy, holy is the Lord of hosts; the whole earth is full of His glory.'" {34:6} Therefore, let us gather together in unity, earnestly crying out to Him with one voice, that we may share in His great and glorious promises. {34:7} For it is written, "No eye has seen, no ear has heard, and no human heart has conceived the things that God has prepared for those who love Him."

{35:1} How wonderful and blessed, beloved, are the gifts of God! Life in immortality, splendor in righteousness, truth in perfect confidence, faith in assurance, and self-control in holiness—all these are within our understanding now. But what will those things be like that are prepared for those who patiently wait for Him? Only the Creator and Father of all worlds, the Most Holy, knows their full measure and beauty. {35:2} Therefore, let us earnestly strive to be counted among those who patiently await Him, so that we may partake in His promised gifts. {35:3} But how, beloved, can we achieve this? By having our understanding anchored in faith toward God, by earnestly pursuing what is pleasing and acceptable to Him, by doing what aligns with His blameless will, and by walking in the path of truth. {35:4} This requires us to cast away unrighteousness, iniquity, covetousness, strife, deceit, gossip, slander, hatred of God, pride, haughtiness, vanity, and ambition. {35:5} Those who practice such things are detestable to God—not only those who do them but also those who take pleasure in those who practice them. {35:6} For it is written, "But to the wicked God says: 'What right have you to recite my laws or take my covenant on your lips? You hate discipline, and you cast my words behind you. When you see a thief, you join with him; you throw in your lot with adulterers. You use your mouth for evil and harness your tongue to deceit. You sit and testify against your brother and slander your own mother's son. These things you have done, and I kept silent; you thought I was altogether like you. But I will rebuke you and accuse you to your face.'" {35:7} Consider these things, you who forget God, lest He tear you to pieces with none to rescue you. {35:8} The sacrifice of praise glorifies Me, and there is a way to show him the salvation of God.

{36:1} This, beloved, is the path through which we encounter our Savior, Jesus Christ—the High Priest of all our offerings, the defender and helper of our weaknesses. Through Him, we gaze up to the heights of heaven. Through Him, we see His immaculate and most excellent countenance as in a mirror. {36:2} Through Him, the eyes of our hearts are opened. Through Him, our foolish and darkened understanding blossoms anew toward His marvelous light. {36:3} Through Him, the Lord has ordained that we should partake in immortal knowledge, "who, being the radiance of His glory and the exact representation of His nature, upholds all things by the word of His power." {36:4} For it is written, "He makes His angels spirits, and His ministers a flame of fire." {36:5} Concerning His Son, however, the Lord declared, "You are my Son; today I have become your Father. Ask me, and I will make the nations your inheritance, the ends of the earth your possession." {36:6} And again He says to Him, "Sit at my right hand until I make your enemies a footstool for your feet." {36:7} But who are His enemies? They are all the wicked and those who oppose the will of God.

{37:1} Therefore, men and brothers, let us earnestly fulfill the role of soldiers with utmost diligence, in accordance with His holy commandments. Consider how those under our generals serve with order, obedience, and submission to their commands. {37:2} Not everyone is a commander of a thousand, or a hundred, or fifty, but each in their own rank performs what the king and generals have ordered. {37:3} The great cannot exist without the small, nor the small without the great. There is a blending in all things, and from this comes mutual benefit. {37:4} Let's take our body as an example. The head is nothing without the feet, and the feet are nothing without the head. Even the smallest members of our body are necessary and useful to the whole. {37:5} All work together harmoniously under one common rule for the preservation of the entire body.

{38:1} Let our entire community in Christ Jesus be preserved, and let each person submit to their neighbor according to the unique gifts bestowed upon them. {38:2} May the strong not look down on the weak, and may the weak show respect to the strong. {38:3} Let the wealthy provide for the needs of the poor, and let the poor give thanks to God for providing someone to help them. {38:4} Let the wise demonstrate their wisdom not just through words, but through their actions. {38:5} Let the humble not boast about themselves, but let others testify to their character. {38:6} Let those who maintain purity in their bodies not be proud, knowing that the gift of self-control was given by another. {38:7} Therefore, brethren, reflect on what we are made of, and how we entered this world as if emerging from a grave and darkness. {38:8} The One who created and shaped us, preparing His abundant gifts for us before our birth, welcomed us into His world. {38:9} Therefore, for everything we receive from Him, let us give thanks and glory forever and ever. Amen.

{39:1} Foolish and thoughtless people, lacking wisdom and instruction, mock and ridicule us, eager to elevate themselves in their own eyes. {39:2} But what can a mortal accomplish? What strength does one have who is formed from dust? {39:3} As it is written, "There was no shape before my eyes, only I heard a sound and a voice saying, 'Can a mortal be pure before the Lord? Can anyone be blameless in their deeds, when God does not even trust His servants and charges His angels with error?'" {39:4} The heavens are not even pure in His sight; how much less so are those who dwell in houses of clay, which we ourselves are made of! {39:5} He strikes them like a moth; from morning to evening they perish, because they lack wisdom and cannot help themselves. {39:6} If you call out, will anyone answer you? Will any of the holy angels come to your aid? {39:7} Wrath destroys the fool, and envy kills the one who is misled. {39:8} I have seen the foolish take root, but suddenly their homes are destroyed. {39:9} Their children are far from safety, despised at the gates without anyone to rescue them. {39:10} What the righteous have prepared, they will eat, and they will not be delivered from trouble.

{40:1} Knowing these things clearly, and understanding the depths of divine knowledge, it is necessary for us to observe all things in the order prescribed, which the Lord has commanded us to carry out at appointed times. {40:2} He has instructed that offerings should be presented and services performed to Him, not haphazardly or irregularly, but at specific times and hours. {40:3} Where and by whom He desires these things to be done, He has determined by His supreme will, so that all things done devoutly according to His good pleasure may be pleasing to Him. {40:4} Therefore, those who offer their sacrifices at the appointed times are accepted and blessed, for by following the Lord's laws, they do not sin. {40:5} The high priest has his own special duties, the priests have their appointed place, and the Levites have their designated ministries. {40:6} Laypeople are obligated to follow the laws that apply to them as laypersons.

{41:1} Each of you, brothers and sisters, should give thanks to God according to your own order, living with a clear conscience, with proper reverence, and not exceeding the limits of the ministry assigned to you. {41:2} Daily sacrifices, peace offerings, sin offerings, and trespass offerings are not made everywhere, brothers and sisters, but only in Jerusalem. {41:3} And even there, they are not offered just anywhere, but only at the altar before the temple. The offerings are carefully inspected first by the high priest and the ministers mentioned earlier. {41:4} Therefore, those who go beyond what is pleasing to His will are punished with death. {41:5} You see, brothers and sisters, the greater the knowledge that has been given to us, the greater the danger we face.

{42:1} The apostles delivered the Gospel to us from the Lord Jesus Christ, and Jesus Christ received it from God. Christ, therefore, was sent by God, and the apostles by Christ. {42:2} Both these appointments were made in an orderly manner according to the will of God. {42:3} So, having received their instructions and being fully assured by the resurrection of our Lord Jesus Christ, and established in the word of God with full assurance of the Holy Spirit, they went out proclaiming that the kingdom of God was near. {42:4} As they preached in various countries and cities, they appointed the first converts of their labors as bishops and deacons after testing them through the Spirit. {42:5} This practice was not new, for long ago, it was written about bishops and deacons in the Scriptures. {42:6} For the Scripture says in a certain place, "I will appoint their bishops in righteousness, and their deacons in faith."

{43:1} And is it any wonder that those in Christ, entrusted by God with such responsibilities, appointed the ministers mentioned earlier, when even the faithful servant Moses, in all his dealings, meticulously recorded in the sacred books every command given to him? {43:2} The prophets who followed him also testified unanimously to the regulations he had established. {43:3} When disputes arose over the priesthood and the tribes argued among themselves about who should hold this esteemed title, Moses devised a solution. {43:4} He instructed the twelve tribal leaders to bring their staffs, each inscribed with the name of their tribe. {43:5} Taking the staffs, he bound them together and sealed them with the rings of the tribal leaders, placing them in the tabernacle of the covenant, before the presence of God. {43:6} After sealing the tabernacle doors and the keys, he said to them, "Brothers, the tribe whose staff blossoms is the one chosen by God to fulfill the duties of the priesthood and serve Him." {43:7} The next morning, Moses gathered all Israel, six hundred thousand men, and displayed the sealed staffs to the tribal leaders. {43:8} Opening the tabernacle, he retrieved the staffs, and it was found that Aaron's staff not only had blossomed but had borne fruit as well. {43:9} Beloved, Moses foresaw this outcome but acted to prevent division among the Israelites and glorify God's name. Amen.

{44:1} Our apostles, through the teachings of our Lord Jesus Christ, foresaw that there would be disputes over the office of the episcopate. {44:2} Therefore, having perfect foresight of this, they appointed the ministers mentioned earlier and instructed that when these ministers passed away, other tested men should succeed them in their ministry. {44:3} Therefore, we believe that those appointed by the apostles or subsequently by other reputable men, with the approval of the entire church, who have served the flock of Christ blamelessly, humbly, peacefully, and selflessly, and who have been well-regarded by all for a long time, should not be unjustly removed from their ministry. {44:4} It would be a grave sin on our part if we were to remove from the episcopate those who have faithfully and holily fulfilled their duties. {44:5} Blessed are those elders who have completed their journey in a fruitful and honorable manner; they need not fear that anyone will deprive them of the place prepared for them. {44:6} But we observe that you have removed from the ministry some men of excellent conduct who fulfilled their duties blamelessly and with honor.

{45:1} You are fond of disputes, brothers, and zealous about matters that do not pertain to salvation. Examine the Scriptures carefully, for they are the true words of the Holy Spirit. You will find nothing unjust or counterfeit in them. {45:2} There you will not read that the righteous were rejected by those who themselves were holy. {45:3} The righteous were indeed persecuted, but only by the wicked; they were thrown into prison, but only by the unholy; they were stoned, but only by transgressors; they were killed, but only by the accursed and those who harbored unrighteous envy against them. {45:4} They faced these sufferings courageously and gloriously endured them. {45:5} So what shall we say, brothers? Was Daniel cast into the lions' den by those who feared God? {45:6} Were Hananiah, Mishael, and Azariah thrown into the fiery furnace by those who observed the great and glorious worship of the Most High? Far be it from us to think so! {45:7} Rather, it was the hateful and the wicked who were so filled with fury that they inflicted torture on those who served God with a pure and blameless heart. {45:8} They did not know that the Most High is the Defender and Protector of all who sincerely honor His excellent name. {45:9} To Him be glory forever and ever. Amen. {45:10} Those who confidently endured these trials are now heirs of glory and honor. {45:11} They have been exalted and celebrated by God in their everlasting memorial. Amen.

{46:1} Brothers, it is right for us to follow such examples, as it is written, "Cleave to the holy, for those who cleave to them shall themselves be made holy." {46:2} And in another place, Scripture says, "With a harmless man you shall prove yourself harmless, and with an elect man you shall be elect, and with a perverse man you shall show yourself perverse." {46:3} Therefore, let us stick closely to the innocent and righteous, for they are the chosen ones of God. {46:4} Why do strifes, tumults, divisions, schisms, and wars exist among you? {46:5} Do we not all have one God and one Christ? Is there not one Spirit of grace poured out upon us? Do we not share one calling in Christ? {46:6} Why then do we divide and tear apart the members of Christ? Why do we stir up conflict within our own body? How mad it is that we forget "we are members one of another!" {46:7} Remember the words of our Lord Jesus Christ, how He said, "Woe to that man by whom offences come! It would be better for him if he had never been born, than that he should cause one of my chosen ones to stumble. Yes, it would be better for him if a millstone were hung around his neck and he were drowned in the depths of the sea, than that he should cause one of my little ones to stumble." {46:8} Your division has undermined the faith of many, disheartened many, caused doubt in many, and brought grief to us all. And yet your rebellion continues.

{47:1} Look into the epistle of the blessed Apostle Paul. What did he write to you when the Gospel first began to be preached? Under the inspiration of the Spirit, he addressed the issue of factions among you concerning himself, Cephas, and Apollos. {47:2} Back then, your preference for one over another was less condemnable, since your partiality was directed towards apostles already esteemed and approved. {47:3} But now consider who has misled you and diminished the glory of your renowned brotherly love. {47:4} It is shameful, beloved, yes, highly shameful and unworthy of your Christian profession, that the steadfast and ancient Church of the Corinthians should engage in sedition against its presbyters because of one or two individuals. {47:5} This rumor has not only reached us but also those outside our circle, so that because of your folly, the name of the Lord is blasphemed, and you bring danger upon yourselves.

{48:1} Let us therefore quickly put an end to this state of affairs. Let us humble ourselves before the Lord and earnestly plead with Him, tears in our eyes, that He may graciously reconcile us and restore us to our former honorable and holy practice of brotherly love. {48:2} For such conduct is the gateway to righteousness, through which life is attained, as written: "Open to me the gates of righteousness; I will enter through them and give thanks to the Lord. This is the gate of the Lord; the righteous shall enter through it." {48:3} Though many gates may stand open, the gate of righteousness in Christ is the blessed gate through which all who have entered and walked in holiness and righteousness are blessed, doing everything in good order. {48:4} Let a person be faithful, powerful in speaking knowledge, wise in judging words, and pure in deeds. Yet, the more superior one appears in these aspects, the more humble-minded they should be, seeking the common good of all rather than merely their own advantage.

{49:1} Let the one who possesses love in Christ abide by the commandments of Christ. Who can fully describe the blessed bond of God's love? What person can adequately express the beauty of its excellence as it truly deserves? {49:2} The heights to which love elevates us are beyond words. Love connects us intimately to God. Love covers a multitude of sins. Love endures all things and is patient in all circumstances. {49:3} Love is never demeaning, never boastful. Love does not create divisions; it does not cause strife. Love operates in perfect harmony. {49:4} Through love, all the chosen ones of God have been perfected. Without love, nothing finds favor in the eyes of God. {49:5} It is through love that the Lord has embraced us. Because of the love He had for us, Jesus Christ our Lord willingly shed His blood for us according to the will of God. His flesh for our flesh, His soul for our souls.

{50:1} Look, beloved, at how magnificent and marvelous love is, a thing whose perfection cannot be fully expressed. Who can be worthy of it except those whom God has graciously enabled to be so? Let us therefore pray and earnestly seek His mercy, that we may live blamelessly in love, free from favoritism or partiality towards anyone. {50:2} All generations from Adam until now have passed away, but those who have been perfected in love through the grace of God now have a place among the godly, and they will be revealed at the coming of Christ's kingdom. {50:3} For it is written, "Enter into your chambers for a little while, until my wrath and indignation pass away; and I will remember a favorable day and raise you up from your graves." {50:4} Blessed are we, beloved, if we keep God's commandments in the unity of love, so that through love our sins may be forgiven. {50:5} As it is written, "Blessed are those whose transgressions are forgiven, whose sins are covered. Blessed is the man whose sin the Lord will not count against him, and in whose spirit there is no deceit." {50:6} This blessing is for those chosen by God through Jesus Christ our Lord. To Him be glory forever. Amen.

{51:1} Let us therefore seek forgiveness for all the transgressions we have committed, influenced by any suggestions of the adversary. Those who have led others into strife and discord should consider the common hope. {51:2} Those who live in fear and love would rather endure suffering themselves than see their neighbors harmed. They prefer to take blame upon themselves rather than allow the harmony passed down to us to be disrupted. {51:3} It is better for a person to admit their wrongs than to harden their heart, like those who opposed Moses, the servant of God, and faced clear condemnation. {51:4} They went down alive into Hades, swallowed by death. Pharaoh, his army, the princes of Egypt, and their chariots with riders all sank in the depths of the Red Sea and perished because their foolish hearts remained hardened, despite the numerous signs and wonders performed in Egypt by Moses, the servant of God.

{52:1} The Lord, brothers and sisters, lacks nothing and desires nothing from anyone except confession. As the chosen David said, "I will confess to the Lord, and this will please Him more than offering a young bull with horns and hoofs. Let the humble see it and rejoice." {52:2} And again he says, "Offer to God the sacrifice of praise, and fulfill your vows to the Most High. Call upon Me in the day of trouble; I will deliver you, and you shall glorify Me." {52:3} For "the sacrifice acceptable to God is a broken spirit."

{53:1} You understand well, beloved, you have diligently studied the Sacred Scriptures, and you have examined the oracles of God with great earnestness. Recall these things to mind. When Moses went up into the mountain and stayed there, fasting and humbling himself, for forty days and forty nights, the Lord said to him, "Moses, Moses, go down quickly from here, for your people whom you brought out of the land of Egypt have acted corruptly. They have quickly turned aside from the way that I commanded them to walk, and have made for themselves molten images." {53:2} And the Lord said to him, "I have seen this people, and behold, they are a stiff-necked people. Now therefore let Me alone, that My wrath may burn hot against them and I may consume them, and I will make of you a great nation." {53:3} But Moses pleaded, "O Lord, please pardon the sin of this people. Otherwise, blot me out of Your book that You have written." Oh, what amazing love! What unsurpassed devotion! The servant speaks openly to his Lord and intercedes for the people, even offering himself to be blotted out with them if necessary.

{54:1} Who among you, then, is noble-minded? Who is compassionate? Who is full of love? Let that person declare, "If because of me, there has arisen strife, disagreement, and divisions, I am willing to leave. I will go wherever you wish, and I will do whatever the majority decides. All I ask is that the flock of Christ lives in peace with the elders appointed over it." {54:2} Such a person who acts in this manner will earn great honor in the Lord, and every place will welcome them. For "the earth is the Lord's, and everything in it." {54:3} These are the actions of those who lead a godly life, actions that are never to be regretted, and they will continue to do so.

{55:1} To illustrate with examples from among non-believers: Many kings and princes, during times of plague, upon receiving guidance from an oracle, willingly sacrificed themselves so that their own blood might save their fellow citizens from destruction. {55:2} Many have left their own cities to quell internal strife within them. Among us, there are many who have willingly submitted to imprisonment in order to ransom others. {55:3} Others have chosen slavery, selling themselves to provide sustenance for others. {55:4} Many women, strengthened by the grace of God, have performed heroic deeds. The blessed Judith, when her city was besieged, sought permission from the elders to enter the enemy camp. She risked her life out of love for her besieged country and people, and the Lord delivered Holofernes into her hands. {55:5} Esther, too, full of faith, faced great danger to save the twelve tribes of Israel from destruction. With fasting and humility, she prayed earnestly to the eternal God, who sees all things. Recognizing her sincere spirit, God delivered the people for whom she had endangered herself.

{56:1} Let us therefore pray for those who have fallen into sin, asking that they may receive meekness and humility from God, so that they may submit not to us, but to His will. This way, they will find forgiveness and a place in our prayers to God and our mention of them among the saints. {56:2} Beloved, let us accept correction willingly; it should not displease anyone. The admonitions we give one another are good and highly beneficial, as they align us with God's will. For as the holy Scriptures say, "The Lord has disciplined me severely, but He has not given me over to death." {56:3} "For whom the Lord loves He disciplines, and He scourges every son whom He receives." {56:4} The righteous will correct me with kindness and reprove me, but let not the oil of sinners anoint my head. {56:5} And further it says, "Blessed is the man whom the Lord reproves; do not reject the discipline of the Almighty. For He causes grief, and He will restore; He wounds, but His hands also heal." {56:6} "He will deliver you in six troubles, yes, in seven no evil shall touch you. In famine He will redeem you from death, and in war from the power of the sword. {56:7} "You shall be hidden from the scourge of the tongue, and you shall not fear destruction when it comes. {56:8} "At destruction and famine you shall laugh, and shall not fear the beasts of the earth. {56:9} "For you shall be in league with the stones of the field, and the beasts of the field shall be at peace with you. {56:10} "You shall know that your tent is at peace, and you shall inspect your fold and miss nothing. {56:11} "You shall know also that your offspring shall be many, and your descendants as the grass of the earth. {56:12} "You shall come to your grave in ripe old age, like a sheaf gathered up in its season, or like a heap of grain gathered at harvest." {56:13} You see, beloved, that those disciplined by the Lord are protected. God corrects us because He is good, teaching us through His holy discipline.

{57:1} Therefore, you who instigated this division, submit yourselves to the elders and accept correction with repentant hearts, humbly bending your knees. Learn to be humble and obedient, setting aside the proud and arrogant words of your mouth. {57:2} It is better for you to occupy a humble yet honorable place among the followers of Christ than to be highly exalted and cast out from His people's hope. {57:3} For as Wisdom, full of virtue, declares: "Listen, I will pour out my thoughts to you; I will make my words known to you. Because I called and you refused, I stretched out my hand and no one paid attention, but you ignored all my advice and would not accept my rebuke. {57:4} So I in turn will laugh when disaster strikes you; I will mock when calamity overtakes you—when calamity overtakes you like a storm, when disaster sweeps over you like a whirlwind, when distress and trouble overwhelm you. {57:5} For when you cry out for help, I will not answer. Though you diligently search for me, you will not find me. {57:6} Because you hated knowledge and did not choose to fear the Lord, {57:7} because you ignored my advice and rejected my rebuke, {57:8} you will eat the fruit of your ways and be filled with the fruit of your schemes."

{58:1} May God, who sees all things and who rules over all spirits and all flesh—He who chose our Lord Jesus Christ and us through Him to be a special people—grant to every soul that calls upon His glorious and holy Name, faith, reverence, peace, patience, endurance, self-control, purity, and sober-mindedness, pleasing Him through our High Priest and Advocate, Jesus Christ. {58:2} To Him be glory, majesty, power, and honor, both now and forevermore. Amen.

{59:1} Please expedite the return of our messengers to us with joy and peace: Claudius Ephebus, Valerius Bito, and Fortunatus. Their swift return will bring us the news of the peace and harmony we earnestly desire among you, allowing us to rejoice in the restored order among you. {59:2} May the grace of our Lord Jesus Christ be with you and with all who are called by God through Him. To Him belongs glory, honor, power, majesty, and eternal dominion, from everlasting to everlasting. Amen.

2 Clement

The Second Epistle of Clement to the Corinthians, often abbreviated as 2 Clement, is an early Christian writing that occupies a unique position in the corpus of Apostolic Fathers. Traditionally attributed to Clement of Rome, it is now widely regarded as a work from an anonymous author, dating back to the mid-2nd century, approximately between 140 and 160 CE. This text is not a letter in the conventional sense but rather a sermon or homily intended for public reading to a Christian congregation. Its primary focus is on exhortation, urging believers to live righteous lives in accordance with the teachings of Jesus Christ. The sermon underscores themes of repentance, moral conduct, and the imminent return of Christ, reflecting the eschatological concerns prevalent in early Christian communities. Unlike the First Epistle of Clement, which is deeply rooted in addressing ecclesiastical issues and authority, 2 Clement emphasizes personal piety and the transformative power of faith. The homily is replete with scriptural references, drawing extensively from both the Old and New Testaments, as well as from early Christian traditions and possibly oral teachings of Jesus. It also presents a strong Christological perspective, affirming the pre-existence and divine nature of Christ. The text provides valuable insights into the theological development and liturgical practices of the early Church, highlighting the continuity and diversity within the early Christian movement. As one of the earliest examples of post-apostolic Christian literature, 2 Clement offers a glimpse into the pastoral concerns and doctrinal emphases that shaped the faith and practice of early believers. Its preservation and inclusion in the corpus of early Christian writings underscore its significance for understanding the historical and theological trajectory of early Christianity.

{1:1} Brothers and sisters, we should regard Jesus Christ as God, the judge of the living and the dead, and never underestimate the value of our salvation. {1:2} If we belittle Him, our expectations from Him will be small. {1:3} This mindset would lead us into sin, forgetting where we came from, who called us, to what purpose, and how much Jesus Christ endured for our sake. {1:4} What can we possibly offer Him in return? What fruit can we bear that is worthy of all He has given us? {1:5} Consider the immense benefits He has bestowed upon us for our sanctification. He has enlightened us, called us His children as a father, and rescued us when we were lost and hopeless. {1:6} How can we adequately praise Him? What reward can we offer that matches what we have received from Him? {1:7} We were once ignorant, worshipping lifeless idols made of stone, wood, gold, silver, and bronze—mere human creations. Our lives were filled with spiritual death. {1:8} But in our darkness, with a veil over our eyes, we looked up, and through His will, the cloud surrounding us was lifted. {1:9} He had compassion on us, moved by His love for us, and He saved us, knowing our profound errors and the destruction we faced, realizing that salvation was only possible through Him. {1:10} He called us into existence from nothingness, graciously giving us life and purpose.

{2:1} Rejoice, you who were once barren and had no children; break forth into joyful cries, you who never experienced childbirth. This prophecy from Isaiah applies to us: our church was once barren, but now it has been blessed with many children. {2:2} When Isaiah said, "Rejoice, you barren that bear not," he was speaking of our condition before we received the gift of children—new believers in our midst. {2:3} Furthermore, when he said, "Cry you that travail not," he meant that we should earnestly pray to God without ceasing, just as women in labor cry out in pain. {2:4} And the phrase, "because she that is desolate has more children than she that has an husband," signifies that those who were seemingly abandoned by God have now embraced faith in Him and have multiplied more than those who seemed favored by God. {2:5} Another Scripture says, "I came not to call the righteous, but sinners," indicating that those who were lost and in need of salvation were the ones Jesus came to save. {2:6} Truly, it is remarkable that Jesus did not come to uphold those who were already standing firm in righteousness, but to rescue those who were falling into sin. {2:7} This was the purpose of Christ's mercy—to save the lost. He came into the world, saved many, and called us who were lost to follow Him. {2:8} Therefore, because of His great mercy toward us, we who are now alive no longer worship dead idols or offer them any form of worship. Instead, through Him, we have come to know the true Father. {2:9} How can we demonstrate that we truly know Him? By not denying the One through whom we have come to know God. {2:10} Jesus Himself said, "Whoever confesses me before men, him will I also confess before my Father." This is our reward if we acknowledge the Savior who has saved us. {2:11} How do we confess Him? By obeying His teachings and not disobeying His commandments—by worshiping Him with sincerity, not just with words, but with our whole heart and mind. {2:12} As Isaiah prophesied, "This people honors me with their lips, but their heart is far from me." Mere lip service is not enough to save us. {2:13} Therefore, let us not merely call Him Lord; words alone will not save us. As Jesus said, "Not everyone who says to me, 'Lord, Lord,' will enter the kingdom of heaven, but only the one who does the will of my Father." {2:14} Therefore, brothers and sisters, let us confess our faith through our actions—by loving one another, avoiding adultery, refraining from speaking evil against each other, and not envying one another. Let us be temperate, merciful, and do good deeds. {2:15} Let us empathize with each other's struggles and not be consumed by greed for money. Our good deeds should be a testament to God, rather than our words alone. {2:16} Let us not fear human judgment, but rather fear God. If we engage in wickedness, Jesus warned, "Even if you are close to me outwardly, but do not keep my commandments, I will reject you and say, 'Depart from me, you workers of iniquity.'"

{3:1} Therefore, brothers and sisters, let us willingly forsake our temporary residence in this world for the sake of our conscience, and let us obey the will of Him who called us. We should not fear leaving this world behind. {3:2} As the Lord said, "Behold, I send you forth as sheep in the midst of wolves." Peter questioned, "What if the wolves attack the sheep?" Jesus reassured Peter and said, "Do not fear those who can kill the body but cannot touch the soul. Fear instead the One who has authority to cast both soul and body into hell." {3:3} Consider, brothers and sisters, that our time in this earthly body is brief and transitory, while the promise of Christ is immense—eternal life and the kingdom to come. {3:4} What must we do to attain it? We must live holy and righteous lives, regarding earthly possessions as insignificant and not coveting them. Desiring worldly things leads us away from the path of righteousness. {3:5} For as the Lord said, "No one can serve two masters. You cannot serve both God and money." What good is it to gain the whole world but lose your own soul? {3:6} This world and the next are in conflict. This world promotes adultery, corruption, greed, and deceit, but the kingdom of God rejects such things. {3:7} We cannot be friends with both; we must choose to abandon one in favor of the other. It is wise to despise the temporary and corruptible things of this world and to love the eternal and incorruptible things to come. {3:8} By doing the will of Christ, we will find rest. However, if we disobey His commands, nothing will save us from eternal punishment, as the prophet Ezekiel warned about Noah, Job, and Daniel being unable to save even their own children. {3:9} Therefore, how can we hope to enter the kingdom of God if we do not keep our baptism pure and undefiled? Who will advocate for us if we are not found to have lived holy and just lives? {3:10} Let us, therefore, my brothers and sisters, earnestly strive, knowing that our battle is imminent. Many embark on long journeys for a perishable reward, yet not all receive a crown. {3:11} Let us strive so that we may all receive the crown. Let us run on the straight path of righteousness, the race that leads to immortality. Let us strive in great numbers to attain the crown, knowing that even if not all receive it, we should come as close to it as we can. {3:12} Consider also that in a perishable competition, any unfair action leads to disqualification, punishment, and expulsion. What then will be the consequence for those who behave improperly in the contest for immortality? {3:13} The prophet warns about those who do not keep their faith intact: "Their worm will not die, and their fire will not be quenched; they will be a horror to all mankind." {3:14} Therefore, let us repent while we are still on earth, for we are like clay in the hands of the potter. Just as a potter reshapes a vessel that is marred or broken, we too can seek forgiveness while there is time. {3:15} While we are in this world, let us repent sincerely for any wrongs we have committed, so that we may be saved by the Lord. {3:16} For once we depart from this world, we will no longer have the opportunity to confess our sins or repent. {3:17} Therefore, brothers and sisters, let us do the will of the Father, keep our bodies pure, observe the commandments of the Lord, and lay hold of eternal life. As the Lord said in the Gospel, "If you have not been faithful with worldly wealth, who will trust you with true riches? For whoever is faithful with little is also faithful with much." {3:18} Therefore, keep your bodies pure and your faith without blemish, so that you may receive eternal life.

{4:1} Let none among you claim that the flesh will not be judged or raised up. Consider this: in what state were you saved? In what condition did you heed the call, if not while inhabiting this flesh? {4:2} Therefore, let us honor our bodies as the temple of God. Just as we were called in the flesh, so shall we face judgment in the flesh. Our Lord Jesus Christ, who saved us, was initially a spirit but took on flesh to call us. Likewise, we will receive our reward in this flesh. {4:3} Therefore, let us love one another earnestly, seeking entrance into the kingdom of God. While there is time for healing, let us surrender ourselves to God, our healer, offering repentance from a sincere heart as our reward. {4:4} What can we offer as a reward? Repentance from a pure heart. For God knows all things beforehand and examines our hearts thoroughly. {4:5} Therefore, let us praise Him not only with our lips but with our entire beings, so that He may welcome us as His children. As the Lord said, "Whoever does the will of my Father in heaven is my brother and sister and mother." {4:6} Therefore, my brothers and sisters, let us fulfill the will of the Father who called us to live. Let us pursue virtue and reject wickedness, which leads us into sin. Let us flee from all ungodliness so that we do not fall into evil. {4:7} For if we earnestly strive to live well, peace will follow us. But how rare it is to find someone who does this! Most are driven by human fears, choosing present pleasures over future promises. {4:8} They do not realize the torment that accompanies present pleasures or the delights promised in the future. {4:9} Moreover, they not only harm themselves but also corrupt innocent souls with their false teachings, unaware that they and their followers will face double condemnation. {4:10} Therefore, let us serve God wholeheartedly, and we shall be righteous. Yet if we refuse to serve Him due to disbelief in His promises, we will be miserable. {4:11} For as the prophet says, "Woe to the double-minded who doubt in their hearts, saying, 'We have heard these things from our ancestors, but we have not seen them ourselves, though we have awaited them day after day.'" {4:12} O foolish ones! Consider the example of a tree, or take the vine for instance: it sheds leaves, buds, bears sour grapes, and then ripens its fruit. Similarly, my people have endured afflictions and disorders but will eventually receive blessings. {4:13} Therefore, my brothers and sisters, let us not doubt but eagerly anticipate receiving our reward with hope. God is faithful to His promise to reward everyone according to their deeds. {4:14} If we live justly in the sight of God, we will enter His kingdom and inherit His promises—things that no eye has seen, no ear has heard, and no human heart has imagined. {4:15} Therefore, let us await the kingdom of God every hour in love and righteousness, for we do not know the day of God's coming.

{5:1} When asked about the arrival of his kingdom, the Lord himself replied, "When two become one, and what is within matches what is outside, and when the male is no longer distinct from the female." {5:2} Two become one when honesty prevails in our speech, and there is a genuine unity of soul between two individuals, free from hypocrisy. {5:3} "What is within" refers to the soul, and "what is without" refers to the body. Therefore, let your soul be revealed through your good deeds, just as your body is seen outwardly. {5:4} Regarding "the male with the female is neither male nor female," the Lord explains that anger represents the male and lust represents the female within us. {5:5} When a person reaches a state where neither anger nor lust dominates them—both of which often cloud reason due to societal influences and poor upbringing—{5:6} Instead, by dispelling these influences and feeling remorseful, they unite their soul and spirit through repentance, aligning with reason. Then, as Paul wrote, in such individuals there is no distinction of gender but a harmonious obedience to reason.

Tertullian on Spectacles

Tertullian's "De Spectaculis" (On Spectacles) is a key early Christian text written in the late 2nd or early 3rd century, addressing the issue of Roman entertainment practices such as gladiatorial games, chariot races, and theatrical performances. Tertullian, a prominent early Christian author from Carthage, uses his rhetorical skills and scriptural knowledge to argue against Christians participating in these events. He contends that such spectacles not only distract believers from their spiritual responsibilities but also expose them to immoral influences and pagan idolatry. Through detailed biblical exegesis, Tertullian underscores the conflict between these public entertainments and Christian values, emphasizing themes of purity, holiness, and the rejection of worldly pleasures. He calls for Christians to avoid these forms of amusement, viewing them as corrupt and contrary to Christian teachings. "De Spectaculis" is more than a moral critique; it is a theological discourse that highlights the need for Christians to maintain a distinct identity and separation from secular cultural norms. The treatise offers crucial insights into early Christian perspectives on cultural engagement and the ethical dilemmas faced by believers in a predominantly pagan society.

{1:1} To you, new servants of God, and those who have already sworn allegiance to Him, remember the faith and the truth that forbid the pleasures of spectacles, along with other worldly errors, so no one falls into sin through ignorance or self-deception. {1:2} The appeal of pleasure is strong and can prolong ignorance, making sin easier or corrupting the conscience into self-deception. {1:3} Some may be swayed by heathen opinions, arguing that enjoying external pleasures of the eyes and ears doesn't conflict with religion, as long as God's fear and honor are maintained. {1:4} But we aim to prove that these pleasures are incompatible with true religion and obedience to God. {1:5} Some think Christians, ready to die, despise life and its pleasures as a human rule, not a divine command. {1:6} It would be hypocritical for people enjoying such pleasures to die for God. If their view were true, our strict lifestyle might adapt to a more lenient plan.

{2:1} Our adversaries argue that all things, including spectacles, were created by God and are good, as they come from a good Creator. {2:2} They claim that the materials used in spectacles and the performances themselves, under God's heaven, are not against God or His worshipers. {2:3} Human ignorance thinks it clever to defend these pleasures, fearing to lose them more than life itself. {2:4} More people turn away from our religion due to the threat to their pleasures than to their lives, for even a fool accepts death as a natural debt, but everyone cherishes pleasure. {2:5} All know God as the Creator and that the universe is good and given to man. {2:6} However, knowing God only from a distance, they are ignorant of His commands and the rival power that corrupts His creation. {2:7} We must consider who created all things and who corrupted them. This shows their intended use and misuse. {2:8} The state of corruption is vastly different from innocence, highlighting the difference between the Creator and the perverter. {2:9} Even heathens acknowledge that misdeeds arise from God's creations, like murder by iron or poison, but these were not created for destruction. {2:10} Similarly, materials used for idols were created by God but not for idolatry, which is a grievous sin. {2:11} Anything that offends God ceases to be His. {2:12} Man, created in God's image, has fallen away, using eyes, tongue, ears, and other body parts for evil instead of their intended pure purposes. {2:13} God, who demands innocence, did not intend His creations to be misused for sin. {2:14} The misuse of God's creation is the reason for condemnation. {2:15} Knowing God, we recognize His rival. Man, God's image and lord of the universe, was corrupted by the perverter of God's creation. This perverter seeks to make man guilty before God and establish his power in man's possessions.

{3:1} Armed with this knowledge, we must address excuses from within our own ranks. Some brethren, naive or overly particular, demand scriptural proof to give up spectacles, seeing it as an open question. {3:2} They argue that scripture does not specifically forbid attending circuses, theaters, or gladiator shows, unlike clear prohibitions against killing, idolatry, adultery, and fraud. {3:3} However, David's verse, "Happy is the man who has not gone to the gathering of the ungodly," applies to spectacles. {3:4} David praised the just man for avoiding ungodly gatherings, and this can be interpreted broadly to prohibit spectacles. {3:5} If David called a few Jews ungodly, how much more so a vast crowd of heathens? {3:6} At spectacles, there is both sitting and standing, fitting the verse's description. {3:7} Thus, one who attends such gatherings is unhappy, unlike the blessed man David described. {3:8} Scripture often has broader meanings, applying to all men, and warnings against specific nations apply generally to all sinful nations. {3:9} By this reasoning, every spectacle is a gathering of the ungodly.

{4:1} To address the point directly, let's look at our baptismal vow. When we are baptized, we renounce the Devil, his pomp, and his angels. {4:2} The chief manifestation of the Devil is idolatry, from which all evil spirits arise. {4:3} If spectacles originate from idolatry, they belong to the Devil's realm, and our baptismal vow covers renouncing them as well. {4:4} We will examine the origins, titles, equipment, superstitions, places, presiding spirits, and arts of the spectacles. {4:5} If any part is unrelated to idolatry, it can be free from its stain and disconnected from our renunciation.

{5:1} We had to investigate the origins of the spectacles thoroughly, as they are largely unknown among our people. Our authority for this investigation was pagan literature. Various authors have published works on the subject. According to Timaeus, the Lydians, led by Tyrrhenus who lost a struggle for kingship to his brother, migrated from Asia to Etruria. There, they introduced the spectacles as part of their religious customs. The Romans later adopted these performances, even borrowing the name from the Lydians, calling the performers "ludii." {5:2} Although Varro suggests that "ludii" comes from "ludus" (play), as the Luperci were also called "ludii" for their playful running, it is not the name that matters but the idolatry involved. The games, also known as Liberalia, honored Father Liber, who was celebrated by country folk for introducing them to wine. The Consualia games honored Neptune, also called Consus. Romulus established the Ecurria for Mars and the Consualia for Consus, the god of counsel, following his plan to abduct the Sabine women. {5:3} This origin is tainted by idolatry, considering Romulus, who was a fratricide and son of Mars. Even now, at the first goal posts in the Circus, there is an altar to Consus with the inscription: "CONSUS MIGHTY IN COUNSEL, MARS IN WAR, THE LARES AT THE CROSSROAD." Sacrifices are offered on this altar by state priests and the Flamen of Quirinus and the Vestal Virgins on specific days. {5:4} Romulus later instituted games in honor of Jupiter Feretrius, known as the Tarpeian and Capitoline Games, according to Piso. Numa Pompilius initiated games for Mars and Robigo (goddess of mildew). Subsequent founders like Tullus Hostilius and Ancus Martius also established games in honor of various idols. Information on these idols can be found in the works of Tranquillus Suetonius or his sources, proving the idolatrous origin of the games.

{6:1} The titles of the games today still reflect their origins. Games honoring the Great Mother, Apollo, Ceres, Neptune, Jupiter Latiaris, and Flora, as well as those commemorating emperors or celebrating political events and municipal feasts, betray their idolatrous nature. Even funeral games, honoring the memory of private individuals, follow this ancient custom. Whether sacred or funereal, games in honor of deities or dead persons both constitute idolatry, which we renounce.

{7:1} Both types of games share a common origin and names, and thus, their equipment is the same, rooted in idolatry. The spectacles in the circus display even greater pomp. The procession itself, with its line of idols, images, cars, chariots, thrones, garlands, and attributes of the gods, reveals its idolatrous nature. Many sacred rites and sacrifices are performed during these spectacles, involving numerous religious corporations, priesthoods, and magistrates, showing that the demons have taken residence in these places. {7:2} Even in the provinces, where funds may be limited, the spectacles in the circus still follow the same model, tainted by their idolatrous origin. Just as a small brook contains the nature of its spring, so do these spectacles, no matter how modest, offend God. The presence of even a few idols constitutes idolatry, and the sinful origin of these spectacles makes them offensive regardless of their scale.

{8:1} The circus is primarily dedicated to the Sun, with his temple and image prominently displayed. Some claim that Circe, in honor of her father the Sun, held the first circus show, linking the name to her. The circus is filled with idol worship, from the eggs sacred to Castor and Pollux to the dolphins honoring Neptune. Various idols, columns, and altars dedicated to deities like Seia, Messia, and Tutulina, as well as the obelisk honoring the Sun, all signify idolatry. The Great Mother presides over the ditch, and Consus hides underground at the Murcian Goals, adding to the unclean deities present. {8:2} Christians should avoid places taken over by diabolic spirits. Entering the circus at another time does not necessarily defile a person, as the defilement comes from participating in sinful activities, not the places themselves. It is not being in the world that leads us away from God but engaging in the world's sins. Entering a temple for an honest reason, unrelated to worship, does not defile us. However, participating in idolatry defiles us, whether in the circus or elsewhere. {8:3} It is the activities performed in these places, dedicated to idols, that defile them and us. Understanding the dedication of these places to idols clarifies that what occurs there is the work of those idols, making participation in such activities incompatible with Christian renunciation of idolatry.

{9:1} Let's consider the arts displayed in circus games. Riding horses was once just a skill, free from guilt. However, when it became part of the games, it turned from a gift from God into a tool for demons. {9:2} This art form is sacred to Castor and Pollux, who were given horses by Mercury, according to Stesichorus. Neptune is also an equestrian deity, known as "Hippios" by the Greeks. Chariots, too, have divine associations: four-horse teams are consecrated to the Sun, two-horse teams to the Moon. Erichthonius, the first to harness four horses, was a son of Minerva and Vulcan, embodying a demonic nature. If Argive Trochilus invented the chariot, he dedicated it to Juno. {9:3} At Rome, Romulus showcased a four-horse chariot and was later considered an idol himself. The chariots' inventors clad their drivers in idolatrous colors: white for Winter, red for Summer. As pleasure and superstition grew, red was dedicated to Mars, white to the Zephyrs, green to Mother Earth or Spring, and blue to Sky and Sea or Autumn. {9:4} Any idolatry, condemned by God, extends to these elements as well.

{10:1} Now, let's move to the stage performances, which share origins and titles with circus games, both called "ludi" ('games') and shown alongside equestrian displays. The processions from temples to theaters involve incense, blood, flutes, and trumpets, managed by undertakers and soothsayers. The theater, seen as Venus's shrine, has always been a moral threat. Censors often tore down theaters to protect public morals. Pompey the Great built a grand theater but called it a temple of Venus to avoid condemnation, blending morality and superstition. Venus and Liber (Bacchus) are patrons of stage arts, representing lust and drunkenness. The arts on stage, involving music, instruments, and scripts, are dedicated to Apollo, the Muses, Minerva, and Mercury. Christians should hate these arts as they are the work of demons, who thrive on the homage paid to them. The arts are idolatrous as they honor inventors considered gods. Demons inspired these arts to turn people from God and bind them to demonic glorification.

{11:1} Contests, like the games, have origins in sacred or funereal events, honoring gods or the dead. Titles like Olympian contests for Jupiter and Nemean for Hercules reveal this. The contests' paraphernalia, including unholy crowns and bull blood, are tainted with idolatry. {11:2} The stadium, like the circus, serves as a temple for idols. Gymnastic arts come from the teachings of Castors, Hercules, and Mercury, further linking them to idolatry.

{12:1} The most prominent spectacle is the "munus" ('obligatory service'), originally a duty to the dead, evolving into a refined form of cruelty. Initially, captives or slaves were sacrificed at funerals to appease the dead. {12:2} Over time, this became a form of entertainment where trained fighters killed each other at tombs, turning murder into a consolation for death. Gladiatorial contests, initially sacrifices, became rites for the dead and thus a form of idolatry. These spectacles are now in honor of the living, like those assuming public office, but still retain their idolatrous origins. {12:3} The accompanying ceremonies, including purple robes, fasces, fillets, crowns, and public announcements, are tainted with demonic pomp. The amphitheater, more dreadful than any temple, houses numerous unclean spirits. The arts involved in these spectacles are patronized by Mars and Diana, further highlighting their idolatrous nature.

{13:1} I believe I have adequately demonstrated the many ways in which spectacles involve idolatry. I have discussed their origins, names, equipment, locations, and arts to show that these spectacles are entirely inappropriate for those who renounce idols twice. As the Apostle says, 'Not that an idol is anything,' but the actions taken in honor of demons, who reside in the consecrated idols of the dead or the so-called gods, are significant. Since both types of idols fall into the same category, we avoid both. We equally detest temples and tombs, recognize neither altars, adore neither images, offer no sacrifices, and perform no funeral rites. We do not eat food sacrificed or offered at funeral rites because 'we cannot share the Lord's supper and the supper of demons.' If we keep our palate and stomach pure, how much more should we guard our nobler senses, our ears and eyes, from pleasures associated with sacrifices to idols and the dead, which defile the spirit, which God cares about even more than the bowels.

{14:1} Having established that spectacles are idolatrous, which should be reason enough to avoid them, let us explore another aspect for those who believe that abstention is not explicitly required. This excuse seems to ignore the condemnation of worldly lusts. Just as there is lust for money, status, gluttony, sensuality, and fame, there is also a lust for pleasure. Spectacles are a form of pleasure, and under the general heading of lust, pleasures, including spectacles, fall.

{15:1} Regarding the places of these spectacles, we noted earlier that they themselves do not defile us, but the actions performed within them do. Once these places are contaminated by such actions, they, in turn, contaminate others. This brings us back to the main issue: idolatry. Additionally, we must highlight that the characteristics of what occurs at these spectacles are all contrary to God's will. God commands us to maintain tranquility, gentleness, quiet, and peace with the Holy Spirit. The Holy Spirit, being tender and sensitive, must not be vexed by frenzy, bitterness, anger, and grief. How can the Holy Spirit be associated with spectacles, which are filled with violent agitation of the soul? Where there is pleasure, there is desire; where there is desire, there is rivalry; and where there is rivalry, there is frenzy, bitterness, anger, and grief—all incompatible with moral discipline. Even if one attends spectacles modestly and soberly, the mind and soul are inevitably stirred. No one approaches such pleasure without passion, and this passion always has damaging effects. If passion ceases, so does pleasure, making attendance foolish. Foolishness, too, is foreign to us. Moreover, attending spectacles places us among those we profess to detest. It is insufficient to abstain from such acts; we must also avoid those who commit them. As Scripture says, 'If you see a thief, you run with him.' Though we live in the world, we are separated from its sinful aspects, for the world belongs to God, but its sinful elements belong to the Devil.

{16:1} Since frenzy is forbidden, we must avoid every type of spectacle, especially the circus, where frenzy dominates. Observe the frenzied crowd, already in a violent commotion as they approach the show, excited over their bets. They are impatient with the praetor, their eyes following his every move. They await the signal with bated breath, united in their madness. Recognize this madness from their behavior—they shout when the signal is thrown, a symbol of the Devil cast down from on high. This frenzy leads to outbursts of fury, passion, and discord, all opposed to the priests of peace. Next come curses and unjustified insults, followed by applause devoid of genuine affection. Those partaking in these spectacles lose self-control, rejoicing in another's success or lamenting another's misfortune, their emotions misdirected. Loving or hating without cause is not permitted by God, who commands us to love our enemies and bless those who curse us. The circus, merciless and ruthless, spares no one, not even rulers or fellow citizens. If any of these frenzies are appropriate for the faithful, they might be permissible elsewhere, but they are not, making them equally unacceptable in the circus.

{17:1} We are commanded to avoid all forms of impurity, which also excludes us from the theater, a place notorious for its own unique brand of filth. The theater thrives on what is otherwise disapproved elsewhere. Its greatest appeal lies in its obscenities, which actors in Atellan farces display through their gestures, and mimics amplify by donning feminine attire, erasing any respect for gender and modesty. They might blush more at home than on stage. Additionally, pantomimes degrade their bodies from boyhood to master their craft. Even prostitutes, the objects of public desire, are showcased, making women, who previously didn't know of their existence, witnesses to their disgrace. The details of their lives, such as their names, prices, and histories, are announced publicly, exposing what should remain hidden. Let the senate and all social classes, especially those women who have tarnished their own dignity, feel ashamed. They reveal their fear of daylight and public scrutiny through their gestures once a year. {17:2} If we must shun all impurity, why should we listen to what we are forbidden to speak, knowing that God judges vile jokes and idle words? Why should we be allowed to see what is sinful to do? If spoken words can defile us, how can what enters through our ears and eyes be any less defiling, since they are servants of the spirit? A person whose servants are unclean cannot claim to be clean. Therefore, the prohibition of uncleanness also bans the theater. Furthermore, if we reject worldly literature as foolish before God, we must also reject spectacles classified as comedy or tragedy in profane literature. If these plays are bloody, wanton, impious, and filled with outrage and lust, recounting their content is no better. What is unacceptable in deed is also unacceptable in word.

{18:1} If you argue that the stadium is mentioned in the Scriptures, you have a point. But you cannot deny that the activities in the stadium are unsuitable for you to witness—punches, kicks, blows, and all forms of violence that disfigure the human face, which is made in God's image. Foolish races, throwing contests, and jumping competitions should not amuse you. You should not take pleasure in harmful or foolish displays of strength, nor in artificially sculpted bodies that surpass God's design. You should detest athletes bred to entertain Greek idleness. Wrestling, too, belongs to the Devil's realm, as he was the first to crush humans. Wrestlers' movements are serpentine—the grips, the twists, the smooth escapes. Crowns are of no use to you; why seek pleasure in them?

{19:1} Must we now await scriptural condemnation of the amphitheater as well? If we argue that cruelty, impiety, and brutality are acceptable, then let us indeed frequent the amphitheater and rejoice in human bloodshed. It may be just when the guilty face punishment—who would deny this except the guilty themselves?—but the innocent should not delight in the suffering of others. Instead, they should mourn that a fellow human has fallen so far as to merit such cruelty. Who can guarantee that only the guilty are condemned to face beasts or other punishments? Might not innocence suffer due to a vengeful judge, a weak defense, or extreme torture? It would be better not to witness the punishment of the wicked, lest we also witness the destruction of the good, assuming there is still some goodness in them. {19:2} Even innocent men are sold into the arena to entertain the public's bloodlust. And even those condemned to the games—what absurdity that they should be pushed to commit murder as atonement for lesser offenses! This argument I direct to the pagans. May no Christian need further instruction on the abhorrence of such spectacles. Only one still attending could describe all the horrors in full; I would rather leave the picture incomplete than recall it.

{20:1} How foolish and desperate, then, are the arguments of those who, in a desperate attempt to justify their pleasure, claim that Scripture does not explicitly forbid God's servants from attending such gatherings. I recently heard a novel defense from one of these game enthusiasts: "The sun," he said, "and even God Himself, looks down from heaven and remains untainted." Yet the sun shines into sewers without being soiled! If only God did not witness human sins, then perhaps we could all escape judgment. But He sees thefts, falsehoods, adulteries, frauds, idolatries, and even spectacles. Therefore, we refrain from spectacles lest we be seen by Him who sees all. {20:2} My friend, by equating the defendant with the judge, you are placing them on equal footing: the defendant is seen and judged, while the judge sees and judges. Do we perhaps indulge in frenzy outside the circus, in lewdness beyond the theater gates, in haughty behavior apart from the stadium, and in cruelty outside the amphitheater, simply because God sees beyond the seats, tiers, and stage? We are mistaken: there is no exemption from what God condemns, no permission for what is forbidden everywhere and always.

{21:1} Consistency and steadfast judgment characterize the fullness of truth and perfect morality, reverence, and obedience owed to truth. What is inherently good or evil cannot be anything else. {21:2} We maintain that all things are defined by the truth of God. Those who lack this truth form their own judgments of good and evil based on opinion and inclination, deeming good what is evil elsewhere and vice versa. Thus, the same person who hesitates to expose themselves in public will shamelessly do so in the circus, while a father who shields his daughter from foul language will take her to the theater to hear and see such things. The same person who intervenes in street fights will cheer dangerous brawls in the stadium, and one who respects natural death will cheerfully watch mangled bodies in the amphitheater. Moreover, those who claim to attend spectacles to support justice against murderers will cruelly push reluctant gladiators to commit murder, demanding liberty and rewards for savage combatants while delighting in the up-close scrutiny of those they wished dead from afar—unless, indeed, they are even more heartless.

{22:1} It's truly astounding! Look at how inconsistent people can be, blurring the lines between good and evil due to their fickle emotions and unreliable judgments. {22:2} Consider how those who manage and provide for the spectacles treat the celebrated charioteers, actors, athletes, and gladiators—people whom others idolize to the point of surrendering their souls and bodies, committing the very sins they condemn: these same individuals are both glorified for their skills and degraded and dishonored publicly. They are stripped of civil rights, barred from council chambers, speaking platforms, senatorial and equestrian ranks, and from other positions and honors. {22:3} What a paradox! They love those they punish, they disgrace those they applaud. They praise the talent while branding the talented with shame. {22:4} What kind of justice is this—condemning a person for deeds that brought them renown? It's an implicit admission that these activities are indeed harmful, given that their practitioners, at the height of their fame, are marked with disgrace.

{23:1} Since man concludes that such people should be deprived of honors and exiled to some island of infamy, how much more will divine justice punish those who follow such professions? {23:2} Will God take pleasure in the charioteer, disturber of many souls, and minister to outbursts of frenzy, flaunting his crown and dressed in bright colors like a pimp? {23:3} Will God be pleased with the man who alters his features with a razor, distorting his appearance to resemble that of Saturn or Isis, and submitting to the indignity of being slapped? {23:4} The Devil also teaches to meekly offer his cheek to be struck and makes actors taller with high shoes to contradict Christ's words. {23:5} Is this business of masks pleasing to God, who forbids making likenesses of anything, especially His own image? {23:6} He condemns all hypocrisy and feigned emotions, and His law curses the man who dresses in woman's clothes. What will be His judgment upon the pantomime trained to play the woman? {23:7} No doubt, the artist in punching will go unpunished for the marks left by boxing gloves. {23:8} I say nothing of the man who pushes another to the lion lest he seem less a murderer than the one who later cuts the same victim's throat.

{24:1} How many ways must we demonstrate that none of the activities associated with spectacles pleases God? Or, because they displease Him, are unfit for His servants? {24:2} If we prove that all these things are designed for the Devil's pleasure, sourced from his domain (since anything not of God or displeasing to Him belongs to the Devil), then we reject this pomp of the Devil in our seal of faith. {24:3} We must have no part in what we renounce, whether in action, speech, observation, or participation. If we nullify our commitment by renouncing the seal of faith, must we then seek validation from non-believers? Indeed, let them tell us if it's permissible for Christians to attend such spectacles. For renouncing them marks a crucial step in conversion to the Christian faith. {24:4} Therefore, one who removes this identifying mark openly denies his faith. What hope remains for such a person? No one defects to the enemy's camp without first discarding weapons, abandoning standards, renouncing allegiance, and committing to side with the enemy unto death.

{25:1} Will a person seated where God is absent think of God? Perhaps he finds peace in cheering for charioteers, or seeks purity in admiring actors. {25:2} In every spectacle, the greatest temptation lies not in the attire but in shared emotions, disagreements, and agreements that stir lust. {25:3} Those attending spectacles only seek to be seen. While actors perform, some may recall prophetic cries, meditate on psalms during flute melodies, or advocate for non-violence amidst athletic combat. {25:4} Yet, they might also be moved by pity as they watch bears bite or net-fighters struggle. May God spare His own from such morbid fascination! {25:5} Is it fitting to transition from God's assembly to the Devil's, from reverence to frivolity? Are the same hands lifted in prayer now applauding actors? Are lips that utter 'Amen' over the sacred now cheering gladiators? Are shouts of 'forever and ever' reserved for anyone other than God and Christ?

{26:1} Why wouldn't such individuals be susceptible to demonic influence? Consider the case of a woman who, after attending the theater, returned possessed. {26:2} During exorcism, the unclean spirit defended his actions, claiming justification for seizing a believer found within his domain. {26:3} Another woman, after watching a tragic actor, dreamt of a shroud and received a rebuke mentioning the actor by name. She died within five days. {26:4} How many more examples exist of those who, by indulging in spectacles, have strayed from the Lord? "No one can serve two masters." What communion exists between light and darkness? What does life have in common with death?

{27:1} We should detest the gatherings and assemblies of the pagans, where God's name is blasphemed, where cries to unleash lions are heard daily, where persecutions originate, and temptations run wild. {27:2} What will you do amidst that tumultuous wave of wicked applause? True, you may not face persecution there (since no one identifies you as a Christian), but consider your standing in heaven. {27:3} Do you doubt that while the Devil rages in his assembly, angels from heaven observe and record every instance of blasphemy, every listener, every participant who lends tongue and ear to the service of the Devil against God? {27:4} Shouldn't you avoid the seats of Christ's enemies, the "chair of pestilences," and the polluted air filled with sinful cries? Admittedly, there may be sweet, pleasant, harmless, and even honorable things there. But remember, poison is not mixed with bitter gall or hellebore; it lurks in well-flavored, sweet dishes. Likewise, the Devil infuses deadly poison into the most agreeable and enticing gifts of God. {27:5} Therefore, whatever you find there—whether noble, honorable, melodious, or tender—consider it as honey dripping from a poisoned cake. Don't let the sweetness of pleasure outweigh the dangers it poses.

{28:1} Let those who belong to the Devil indulge in such pleasures: the places, times, and hosts are theirs. Our banquet, our marriage feast, is yet to come. We cannot recline at their table, just as they cannot at ours. These things happen in succession. Now they rejoice while we endure affliction. {28:2} As holy Scripture says, "The world will rejoice, but you will be sorrowful." Let us mourn while the pagans rejoice, so that when their time of mourning comes, we may rejoice. If we share their joy now, we may share their sorrow then. {28:3} Christian, you are too delicate if you seek pleasure in this world. Indeed, you are entirely foolish if you mistake this for true pleasure. {28:4} The philosophers define pleasure as tranquility and peace; they find joy and diversion in it, even boast about it. But you—you yearn for arenas, theaters, dust, and stages. {28:5} Why not admit: "We cannot live without pleasure!" Yet, we should be willing to die for pleasure. Our only prayer should be to depart from the world and join the Lord. Our pleasure lies where our prayer resides.

{29:1} And if you think life should be spent in indulgence, why are you so ungrateful? God has bestowed upon you many exquisite pleasures—reconciliation with Him, the revelation of truth, acknowledgment of errors, and forgiveness for grievous sins. {29:2} What greater joy is there than the disdain of pleasure itself, the contempt for worldly gifts, true freedom, a clear conscience, a contented life, and freedom from the fear of death? {29:3} To trample the idols of the pagans, to cast out demons, to heal, to seek revelations, to live for God—these are the pleasures, the spectacles of Christians: holy, eternal, and free of charge. Here find your arena games: behold the course of the world, count the passing generations, remember the ultimate goal of consummation, strengthen the bonds of unity among local churches, wake at God's signal, rise at the trumpet call of angels, and glory in the martyr's palm. {29:4} If you delight in the literary achievements of the theater, we have our own ample literature—verses, maxims, songs, and melodies. Ours are not myths but truths, not artifice but reality. {29:5} Do you desire contests in boxing and wrestling? Here are contests of great significance aplenty. Witness impurity conquered by chastity, faithlessness defeated by faith, cruelty subdued by mercy, and audacity overshadowed by modesty. Such are our contests, and in these we earn our crowns. If you thirst for blood, you have the blood of Christ.

{30:1} Moreover, what a spectacle awaits—the second coming of the Lord, now certain, exalted, triumphant! What joy among the angels, what glory among the saints as they rise again! What a kingdom, the kingdom of the just to come! What a city, the new Jerusalem! {30:2} Yet there are more spectacles to come—the Day of Judgment with its everlasting outcomes, unexpected by pagans and mocked by them, when the ancient age of the world and all its generations will be consumed in a single blaze. {30:3} What a panorama of scenes on that day! Which sight will amaze me? Which will make me laugh? Where will I rejoice, where exult—as I see so many mighty kings, who once ascended to heaven with public acclaim, now along with Jupiter himself and their witnesses, groaning in the darkness below? Governors of provinces, who persecuted the name of the Lord, now melt in flames fiercer than those they kindled against the Christians they once scorned. {30:4} Whom else will I see? Wise philosophers ashamed before their followers, burning together with those whom they taught that the world is outside God's concern, and that souls either do not exist or will never return to their bodies. Poets trembling not before Rhadamanthus or Minos, but before Christ, whom they never expected to meet. {30:5} Then the tragic actors will be worth hearing, louder in their own tragedy; the comic actors worth watching, more agile in the fire; the charioteer worth seeing, red from his fiery wheel; the athletes worth observing, not in their gymnasiums but tossed about in flames—unless even then, I might prefer to turn an insatiable gaze upon those who vented their rage upon the Lord. {30:6} "Here is the son of the carpenter and harlot, the Sabbath-breaker, the Samaritan possessed by a demon. This is the one you bought from Judas, who was struck with reed and fist, spat upon, given gall and vinegar to drink. This is the one whom disciples secretly took away to spread the tale of His resurrection, or whom the gardener moved lest his lettuces be trampled by curious onlookers." {30:7} What magistrate, consul, quaestor, or priest, no matter how generous, could grant you the favor of witnessing and rejoicing in such sights? Yet, in a sense, these scenes are already ours through faith in the vision of the spirit. But what are those things "which eye has not seen, nor ear heard, nor have entered into the heart of man"? Delights greater, I believe, than any circus, theater, or stadium.

Tertullian on Prayer

Tertullian, a pivotal figure in early Christian theology, offers a profound exploration of prayer in his treatise "De Oratione" (On Prayer). Born in Carthage around 160 AD, Tertullian converted to Christianity in the latter part of the second century and subsequently became one of the most prolific and influential early Christian writers. His works span apologetics, theology, and moral instruction, often characterized by a rigorous and polemical style. "De Oratione," written around 198 AD, is a meticulous examination of the Lord's Prayer, reflecting Tertullian's deep concern for doctrinal purity and ethical conduct. This treatise is notable for its blend of exegetical insight and practical application, providing a comprehensive guide to the theology and practice of prayer within the Christian life. Tertullian's analysis is steeped in scriptural references and imbued with a robust Trinitarian theology, emphasizing the role of prayer in fostering a direct and personal relationship with God. His work also addresses the broader context of Christian worship and discipline, highlighting the importance of prayer in the communal and individual lives of believers. "De Oratione" is not only a theological treatise but also a pastoral manual, aiming to instruct the faithful in the proper attitude and approach to prayer. Tertullian's rigorous intellectual approach and his commitment to the moral and spiritual integrity of the Christian community are evident throughout the text, making it a seminal work in the development of Christian liturgical and devotional practices.

{1:1} Jesus Christ our Lord, the Spirit of God and the Word of God and the Reason of God—expressing the Word and possessing the Reason, infused His new disciples with a fresh approach to prayer under the New Testament. Old practices, whether abolished like circumcision, completed like the Law, fulfilled like prophecies, or perfected like faith itself, gave way to spiritual transformation through God's new grace. {1:2} This grace reveals the Spirit of God, the Word of God, and the Reason of God in Jesus Christ our Lord: the Spirit in which He prevailed, the Word through which He taught, and the Reason for which He came. {1:3} Thus, Christ's prayer incorporates three elements: the spirit giving it power, the word expressing it, and the reason for its reconciliatory effect. {1:4} John also taught prayer, but his role was preparatory for Christ, who must increase while John decreases, passing on his work and spirit to the Master. Thus, John's specific words on prayer are not recorded, as earthly teachings yielded to heavenly ones. {1:5} Christ emphasized praying in secret, requiring faith that God sees and hears all, promoting a humble approach to worship focused solely on God's omnipresence. {1:6} His subsequent teaching advises against verbose prayers, trusting that God already cares for His creation.

{2:1} The Lord's Prayer begins with an affirmation of faith and a meritorious act: "Our Father who art in heaven." This phrase not only adores God but demonstrates our faith, as believers are called "sons of God." {2:2} Jesus frequently referred to God as Father, teaching His disciples to recognize only God in heaven as their Father. {2:3} It is a blessing to know the Father, contrasting with Israel's ignorance despite being called His sons. {2:4} Addressing God as Father expresses both filial love and recognition of His authority.

{3:1} The title "God the Father" was revealed through His Son, as Moses, inquiring about God's name, learned a different one. Christ declared He came in His Father's name, manifesting it to humanity. {3:2} Praying for God's name to be hallowed does not imply He needs our wishes but signifies our reverence and acknowledgment of His holiness. {3:3} God's name inherently sanctifies and blesses all, including us who pray for His name's sanctification in ourselves and others. {3:4} By praying "Hallowed be thy name," we align with the angels' perpetual praise and fulfill our duty to glorify God.

{4:1} Adding "Thy will be done, on earth as it is in heaven" petitions for God's will to be fulfilled universally. It doesn't imply His will can be obstructed but desires its complete realization. {4:2} Whether literal or figurative, the prayer seeks alignment with God's will, emphasizing obedience to His teachings for universal salvation. {4:3} Christ exemplified God's will through His teachings and actions, urging us to follow His model in teaching, working, and enduring suffering according to God's plan. {4:4} Praying "Thy will be done" prepares us for patient endurance, as exemplified by Christ's submission to God's will even in His own suffering and death.

{5:1} The phrase "Thy kingdom come" aligns with "Thy will be done," emphasizing the arrival of God's kingdom within ourselves. While God always reigns, our hope directs us towards Him, anticipating His fulfillment. Why, then, delay this world's end when praying for God's kingdom, which promises our liberation from slavery? {5:2} Even if prayer didn't instruct us to seek His kingdom, our hearts would naturally long for its advent. The souls of martyrs cry out for justice, awaiting the ordained vengeance upon the earth at the world's end.

{6:1} The Lord's Prayer skillfully orders heavenly concerns—God's name, His will, and His kingdom—before addressing our earthly needs. Jesus' teaching emphasizes seeking God's kingdom first, trusting that our necessities will follow. {6:2} "Give us this day our daily bread" symbolizes both physical sustenance and Christ, the Bread of Life, seeking eternal life and unity with His Body.

{7:1} After addressing heavenly matters, we implore for earthly necessities, starting with forgiveness. Acknowledging our sins in prayer shows repentance, aligning with God's will for mercy over condemnation. {7:2} In Scripture, "debt" symbolizes sin, illustrating how God forgives as we forgive others. Christ's parable urges us to forgive, knowing forgiveness is reciprocal in God's eyes.

{8:1} Completing the prayer, Christ urges us to pray not to be led into temptation, seeking God's guidance against the Tempter. God tests faith, as seen with Abraham, not to tempt but to strengthen it. {8:2} Christ, tempted by the Devil, affirms the source of temptation and advises His disciples to pray against it, showing the importance of vigilance and prayer.

{9:1} The Lord's Prayer encapsulates profound teachings from prophets, evangelists, and apostles, as well as our Lord's own sermons and parables, in just a few words. It covers honoring God as Father, expressing faith, obedience to God's will, hope for His kingdom, petitioning for sustenance, seeking forgiveness, and asking for protection from temptation. {9:2} This prayer, taught by God Himself, ensures that our homage ascends to heaven as the Son's divine teaching. It aligns our prayers with His will, animated by His Spirit, making them pleasing to the Father.

{10:1} Our Lord invites us to ask and receive according to our needs, supplementing the foundational prayer with personal petitions. Yet, these requests must always align with the principles He taught, ensuring our prayers are faithful and effective.

{11:1} Before approaching God in prayer, it is essential to reconcile with others. Just as Joseph urged his brothers not to quarrel on their journey, we must settle disputes before presenting ourselves to God. {11:2} Christ emphasized that unresolved anger toward others obstructs our relationship with God. His teaching extends beyond the avoidance of murder to include forgiveness and reconciliation, fundamental to true worship.

{12:1} Prayer, directed by the Holy Spirit, requires a tranquil mind free from disturbances. The Spirit of Joy does not accommodate sadness or discord, demanding purity and peace in our approach to God.

{13:1} True prayer necessitates spiritual purity, not just physical cleanliness. Cleansing the hands symbolizes removing spiritual stains like falsehood, cruelty, and idolatry, reflecting a pure heart in communion with God.

{14:1} Unlike the symbolic washing of Israel, which never cleansed their spiritual guilt, Christians approach God boldly, confessing Christ's sacrifice as they pray.

{15:1} Critiquing vain religious practices, devoid of scriptural authority, reveals their superstitious nature. Practices like discarding cloaks during prayer lack rational basis and resemble pagan rituals, contrasting with genuine devotion.

{16:1} Some practice the odd custom of sitting down immediately after prayer ends, which seems childish and without reason. If Hermas, whose writings are titled 'The Shepherd,' sat on his bed after praying, it was merely a narrative detail, not a religious prescription. Otherwise, we'd only pray where beds are available! Sitting on chairs or benches would then violate this supposed rule, resembling pagan practices before idols, which is rightly condemned as irreverent.

{17:1} Humility and modesty enhance our prayers more than physical gestures like high-raised hands or lifted eyes. Even the publican, with bowed head and simple words, found favor over the boastful Pharisee. God listens not to loud voices but to sincere hearts, unlike the Pythian oracle's claim. Jonah's prayer from the whale's belly proves God hears silently offered prayers, negating the need for loud proclamations that only disturb neighbors.

{18:1} After communal prayers, fasting individuals often omit the kiss of peace, a sign of unity. Yet, shouldn't this affectionate gesture follow our prayers, enhancing their sincerity? Omitting it signals our fasting, though, violating the precept to conceal such practices. On Good Friday, when fasting is public, omitting the kiss of peace aligns with communal observance. Similarly, during 'station days,' attending the sacrifice prayer after communion maintains our commitment to God, as our participation in the Eucharist does not negate our duty to God's service.

{19:1} Referring to women's attire since Apostle's times, Paul and Peter urged modesty, rejecting excessive adornment and ostentatious displays of wealth. Their guidance remains relevant today, emphasizing inner virtue over outward extravagance in dress and appearance.

{20:1} Concerning attire, specifically for women, changes in customs since the time of the early Apostles have compelled me, though not a prominent figure in the Church, to address this issue—a somewhat bold endeavor, yet not entirely audacious when approached as the Apostles did. {20:2} Both Paul and Peter, inspired by the same Spirit, spoke plainly about modesty in dress. They cautioned against extravagance, the flaunting of gold, and overly elaborate hairstyles, emphasizing inner virtue over outward display in matters of adornment.

{21:1} Regarding the debate over whether virgins should wear veils, this issue persists throughout the Church. Some argue that because the Apostle specifically mentions 'women' rather than 'females,' he addresses a particular group within the female sex, not all women. They contend that if he intended to include all women, he would have used a more general term.

{22:1} Those who hold this view should consider the original meaning of 'woman' from the earliest Scriptures. From the beginning, it has denoted the female sex as a whole, not a subgroup. Even Eve, before marriage, was called 'woman,' indicating that the term encompasses virgins as well. Inspired by the same Spirit, the Apostle uses 'woman' in this broader sense, underscoring that the regulation applies universally to women, including virgins, without distinction. {22:2} The Greek language in which the Apostle wrote typically refers to 'women' rather than 'females' (y~*va;KaS rather than ~as), encompassing all females, including virgins. {22:3} His directive, 'Every woman who prays or prophesies with her head uncovered dishonors her head,' clearly extends to women of all ages and circumstances, emphasizing uniformity in the practice across the female sex. Just as he specifies norms for men, so too does he prescribe guidelines for women, including virgins, ensuring consistency in religious observance.

{23:1} Regarding the practice of kneeling during prayer, there exists variation in custom, particularly among a minority who refrain from kneeling on the Sabbath. This viewpoint is currently gaining traction in some churches. {23:2} May the Lord grant His grace so that they may either reconcile their views or hold firm to their beliefs without causing offense to others. As for our tradition, we abstain from kneeling only on the day that commemorates the Resurrection of our Lord. On this day, we also avoid any signs of anxiety or related ceremonies, including postponing business to avoid giving the Devil an opportunity. The same practice applies during the joyful celebration of Pentecost. {23:3} Who among us would hesitate to bow before God each day, especially during our first prayer as we greet the light of day? {23:4} Furthermore, during times of fasting and on station days, prayer should only be offered on bended knees and with every outward sign of humility. In these moments, we are not just praying; we are earnestly imploring and seeking reconciliation with our Lord God.

{24:1} Concerning the timing of prayer, no strict rule has been set, except that we are called to pray at all times and in all places. How can we pray everywhere if we are forbidden to pray in public? "In every place," as circumstances or necessity allow, as He said. It was not contrary to this precept when the Apostles prayed and sang to God within earshot of their guards in prison, nor was it for Paul to give thanks to God aboard ship in plain view of everyone.

{25:1} Regarding specific times, there is merit in observing certain hours for communal prayer that mark key moments of the day: Terce (the third hour), Sext (the sixth hour), and None (the ninth hour). These times are noted in Scripture for their significance. {25:2} It was at Terce that the disciples were gathered when the Holy Spirit descended upon them for the first time. {25:3} At Sext, Peter prayed after having a vision of all creatures in a sheet. {25:4} Likewise, at None, Peter and John went to the Temple and healed a paralyzed man. {25:5} Although these incidents occurred without a specific command to observe these hours, it is beneficial to establish a precedent that emphasizes regular prayer. This practice should compel us, almost like a law, to set aside our business and obligations to offer adoration at least three times a day, acknowledging our debt to the three divine Persons: Father, Son, and Holy Spirit. Daniel also adhered to this practice according to Israelite customs. Of course, this does not negate the importance of spontaneous prayers at dawn and evening. {25:6} It is fitting for the faithful to refrain from eating and bathing before saying a prayer. The nourishment and care of the spirit should take precedence over the needs of the flesh, prioritizing heavenly matters over earthly ones.

{26:1} When a fellow believer enters your home, do not let them depart without a prayer. "You have seen a brother; you have seen your Lord," as it is said. This is especially true for strangers, lest they happen to be angels. {26:2} Even after welcoming fellow believers, do not rush to offer them earthly refreshments before attending to heavenly matters. Your faith will be immediately apparent. How can you say, "Peace to this house," as the precept instructs, without exchanging the kiss of peace with those in the house?

{27:1} Some who are meticulous about prayer include an "Alleluia" and psalms in their prayers, inviting those present to respond with the concluding verses. This practice is commendable in every way, offering God a prayer that is richly adorned with praise and reverence.

{28:1} This spiritual offering supersedes the sacrifices of old. "To what purpose do you offer me the multitude of your sacrifices?" says the Lord. "I desire mercy, not sacrifice." The Gospel teaches that true worshipers worship the Father in spirit and in truth, for God is Spirit, and He seeks worshipers who are likewise spiritual. {28:2} We, the true worshipers and priests, offer prayers in the spirit, which is our spiritual sacrifice acceptable to God. This is what He desires and what He has ordained for Himself. {28:3} This prayer, offered sincerely with our whole hearts, nurtured by faith, adorned with truth, unblemished by sin, pure in chastity, crowned with love for one another, should be brought to God's altar. Accompanied by good works, sung with psalms and hymns, it will obtain from God all that we ask.

{29:1} What will God deny to prayers offered in spirit and truth, as He has commanded? The efficacy of such prayers is attested and believed. In ancient times, prayer delivered from fires, wild beasts, and starvation, but it was shaped anew by Christ. Christian prayer now operates even more powerfully, not by miraculous intervention but by transforming grace. It teaches endurance to the suffering, sensitivity to the tender-hearted, and consolation to the sorrowful. It strengthens faith to endure trials for God's name. {29:2} In the past, prayer could bring plagues, unleash enemy armies, and block beneficial rain. Now, the prayer of justice averts God's wrath, watches over against enemies, and intercedes for persecutors. Prayer has been empowered by Christ to work only for good, recalling souls from death's door, healing the weak, expelling demons, opening prison doors, releasing the innocent, forgiving sins, resisting temptations, comforting the faint-hearted, inspiring the courageous, guiding travelers, calming storms, deterring thieves, feeding the needy, advising the wealthy, lifting the fallen, supporting the upright. {29:3} Prayer is the fortress of faith, our shield and weapon against enemies who surround us. Let us never venture forth without it. Let us be vigilant day and night, guarding our general's standard beneath the protection of prayer, awaiting the trumpet call of angels. {29:4} All angels pray, every creature prays. Domestic and wild animals kneel, emerging from their stables and caves to gaze heavenward with earnest intent. Birds, upon rising at dawn, stretch their wings in a gesture resembling a cross and emit what seems like a prayer. What more need be said about the duty of prayer? Even our Lord Himself prayed, to whom be honor and power forever and ever.

Tertullian on Patience

Tertullian is known for his influential writings, including "On Patience" (De Patientia). Written in the late second or early third century during a time of persecution and doctrinal conflict, this treatise reflects his deep engagement with Christian virtues. Tertullian, a former lawyer and rhetorician, presents patience not as mere endurance but as an active, Christ-like choice amid trials. His work integrates scriptural exegesis and theological reflection, positioning patience as a divine attribute linked to God's nature and Christ's redemptive work. "On Patience" also interacts with contemporary philosophical ideas, offering a Christian reinterpretation of endurance and fortitude. This treatise is crucial for understanding early Christian ethics and spirituality, contributing to the moral and spiritual formation of believers.

{1:1} I confess to my Lord God that I have perhaps been bold, if not presumptuous, in attempting to write about patience, a virtue I am wholly inadequate to practice, being insignificant myself. Those who seek to explain and commend any virtue should first demonstrate their own practice of it, lest their words be empty compared to their actions. {1:2} Would that our embarrassment at not following our own advice could inspire improvement! Yet, some virtues, like certain vices, are so lofty that only divine grace can enable us to attain and embody them fully. {1:3} Therefore, it brings comfort to discuss that which we cannot fully embrace, much like the sick who, deprived of health, still extol its blessings. {1:4} In my own pitiful state, plagued by impatience, I yearn for the health of patience that eludes me. I plead for it, knowing well my weakness, understanding that true faith and spiritual discipline cannot thrive without it. {1:5} Patience holds such prominence in matters concerning God that no one can fulfill His commandments or perform works pleasing to Him without it. Even those who lack patience acknowledge its excellence, giving it the esteemed title of "the highest virtue." {1:6} Philosophers, esteemed for their wisdom, unanimously recognize its value despite their differing schools of thought and beliefs. They unite in esteeming patience above all, associating it with every display of wisdom and virtue. {1:7} It is noteworthy that patience motivates even worldly pursuits to acclaim and renown. Yet, is this commendable or does it diminish divine matters amidst worldly endeavors? Let those who will one day be ashamed of their earthly wisdom consider the consequences when all is revealed and judged.

{2:1} The model of patience given to us is not a human invention born of apathetic indifference, but a divine ordinance reflecting a life-giving heavenly way of life, exemplified by God Himself. {2:2} God has long bestowed the light of His sun upon both the just and the unjust, allowing even those who disregard Him to benefit from the seasons, the elements, and all creation. {2:3} His patience endures with ungrateful people who worship idols, persecute His name and His followers, and descend into moral decay day by day. Through His patience, He hopes to draw them closer to Himself.

{3:1} This divine patience seems distant and lofty. Yet, what about the patience that is openly displayed among humans on earth, within our reach? {3:2} God humbled Himself, becoming incarnate, waiting in His mother's womb, growing into manhood, and not seeking recognition. He endured reproach, was baptized by His own servant, and resisted the Tempter with His words alone. {3:3} As Lord, He taught humanity how to avoid death and make amends for affronts to patience. He did not argue or raise His voice in the streets; He did not break a bruised reed or extinguish a smoldering wick. This was prophesied and fulfilled in His Son, endowed with divine patience. {3:4} He did not force anyone to stay with Him against their will, nor did He scorn anyone's hospitality. He personally served His disciples by washing their feet. {3:5} He showed kindness to sinners and tax collectors, even withholding anger from cities that rejected Him, despite His disciples' wish for divine retribution. He healed the ungrateful and submitted to His persecutors. {3:6} He even kept in His company the one who would betray Him, refusing to denounce him firmly. Even when betrayed and led like a lamb to slaughter, He did not call for angelic assistance but instead endured patiently. {3:7} The patience of the Lord was wounded in Malchus. He condemned the use of swords forever and, by healing one He did not strike, exemplified satisfaction through forbearance, which is the essence of mercy. {3:8} Not to mention His crucifixion, for which He willingly came. Did He deserve such insults in His death? No, yet He embraced suffering with joy: spat upon, beaten, mocked, dressed in humiliation, crowned in mockery. {3:9} Marvel at His steadfast meekness: though capable of escaping notice as a man, He never displayed human impatience. Pharisees, take note—no mere man could practice such patience! {3:10} These manifestations of His patience are so profound that pagan nations reject faith because of them, while for believers, they provide a rational foundation. They demonstrate, not only through His teachings but also through His suffering, that patience is intrinsic to God's nature, the manifestation of His innate attributes.

{4:1} If we observe how all faithful servants of good character live in obedience to their master, obedience itself being the means by which they serve, then how much more should we model ourselves after our Lord? We are servants of the living God, whose authority does not come with chains or slave caps, but with the eternal consequences of salvation or punishment. {4:2} To avoid His severity or to receive His generosity, we must diligently obey in proportion to the threats of His severity and the promises of His grace. {4:3} We demand obedience not only from those legally bound to us or under our care, but even from our flocks and the wild animals provided by the Lord for our use. {4:4} Shall creatures made subject to us by God surpass us in obedience? Shouldn't we, who are subject only to the Lord, hesitate to obey Him? To do otherwise would be unjust and ungrateful, failing to repay Him from whom all blessings flow through others. {4:5} Let us not dwell further on our obedience to the Lord our God, for in recognizing God, we understand our responsibilities. However, obedience itself springs from patience: the impatient do not obey, while the patient never refuse obedience. {4:6} Who can adequately measure the patience displayed by our Lord God, the exemplar and patron of all that is good? Those who belong to God are obligated to strive wholeheartedly for every good, knowing it pertains to God. Thus, our recommendation and exhortation on patience find firm footing in this rule.

{5:1} Delving into essential aspects of faith is not tedious when it proves profitable. While verbosity can be faulted at times, it serves a purpose when it edifies. {5:2} Therefore, discussing the good necessitates examining its opposite, evil. Understanding impatience in contrast to God's patience reveals how impatience, more than anything, opposes faith. {5:3} What is conceived by God's adversary cannot support God's ways. Hostility towards God and His ways is inherent in both. God's infinite goodness contrasts sharply with the Devil's supreme evil, confirming they produce nothing for each other. {5:4} The origin of impatience is found in the Devil himself. He begrudged humanity being made in God's image, leading to deceit and envy, which sprang from impatience. {5:5} Whether impatience preceded evil or vice versa, they intertwined in the Devil, who exploited impatience to tempt humanity into sin. {5:6} This impatience led Eve to share her encounter with the Devil with Adam, ultimately causing their fall due to impatience—disobeying God's warning and falling to the Devil's deceit. {5:7} From Adam and Eve's impatience sprang all manner of sins, corrupting their descendants and leading to Cain's impatience, resulting in the first murder. {5:8} Impatience birthed wrath and other evils, spreading sin through humanity. Every sin can be traced back to impatience, the original sin in God's eyes, the root of all evil. {5:9} Israel's impatience repeatedly led to sin against God, from idolatry to rejection of prophets and even laying hands on the Lord Himself.

{6:1} Patience is intrinsic to faith, as exemplified by Abraham's faithfulness when commanded to sacrifice Isaac—an act of patience that demonstrated his trust in God. {6:2} Faith, sown through Abraham and Christ, enhances and fulfills the Law with patience, which was lacking in earlier teachings of justice. {6:3} Before Christ, retaliation and hatred prevailed under the Law. Patience was absent until Christ united faith's grace with patience, teaching to love enemies and bless persecutors, thereby reflecting the patience of our heavenly Father.

{7:1} The essence of patience is encapsulated in the fundamental principle where even lawful harm is not retaliated. As we explore the causes of impatience, other teachings will correspond accordingly. {7:2} Are you troubled by loss of possessions? Throughout the Scriptures, we are urged to disregard worldly wealth, echoing our Lord's own detachment from it. He consistently upholds the poor and condemns the rich, prioritizing indifference to wealth over sorrow for its loss. {7:3} Therefore, since our Lord did not seek wealth, we should not either. We must endure the loss of it, including theft, without regret, for even what we possess belongs ultimately to God, not to us. {7:4} The Apostle identifies the love of money as the root of all evils, encompassing not just desiring what belongs to others, but also grieving for what we consider our own, though all things truly belong to God, including ourselves. {7:5} He who mourns his loss sins against God by preferring earthly goods over heavenly ones, showing discontent with the soul received from the Lord in favor of worldly attractions. {7:6} Let us gladly relinquish earthly goods to preserve heavenly ones. A person unwilling to bear minor losses, whether from theft, violence, or their own errors, will struggle to give generously. {7:7} If we cannot endure small losses, how can we give to those in need? Without patience in loss, how can we share and give freely, making friends with righteous wealth?

{8:1} Our lives and bodies are exposed to injury in this world; shall we then be troubled by minor deprivations? Let it not be said that a servant of Christ, trained in patience through greater trials, falters at trifling matters. {8:2} When provoked to fight, recall the Lord's instruction: if struck on one cheek, turn the other. Through patience, wrongdoing grows weary; the wrongdoer suffers more from the Lord due to your meekness. {8:3} When faced with curses or quarrels, rejoice as the Lord was cursed under the Law yet remains blessed. Endure maledictions with patience to receive blessings. {8:4} If someone speaks ill of you, returning the insult only brings bitterness or hidden resentment. Retaliation contradicts our Lord's teachings, for defilement comes from words spoken, requiring accountability for every idle word. {8:5} Our Lord forbids certain actions but commands us to endure similar treatment with meekness. {8:6} Now, consider the joy found in patience. Every injury, whether verbal or physical, met with patience, loses its impact like a weapon striking a solid rock, returning to harm its sender. {8:7} By enduring without showing pain, you deny the wrongdoer their satisfaction, preserving yourself from harm and finding joy in patience.

{9:1} Even impatience over losing loved ones is not excused, though grieving is natural. The Apostle urges us not to mourn like those without hope but to believe in the resurrection through Christ. {9:2} If we believe in Christ's resurrection, we also believe in our own. Thus, there is no need for grief or impatience over death if we trust in the promise of resurrection. {9:3} Why grieve if you believe the departed is not lost forever? Patience alleviates the loneliness caused by loss, reminding us that death is but a journey's beginning. {9:4} Impatience in such matters betrays our faith and hope in Christ. Resisting His call for our departed loved ones implies pity rather than acceptance of His will. {9:5} The Apostle's desire to be with the Lord exemplifies a better prayer. Similarly, as Christians, if we begrudge others reaching their heavenly reward, we hinder our own journey toward that goal.

{10:1} Another strong motive for impatience is the desire for revenge, whether for reputation or retaliation. Yet, worldly reputation is empty, and evil is always detestable to the Lord. Seeking vengeance only perpetuates evil, escalating conflict rather than resolving it. {10:2} Revenge may seem to soothe one's pain, but in truth, it is evil opposing evil. What difference is there between the provocateur and the provoked, except the timing of their wrongdoing? Both stand guilty before the Lord, who forbids and condemns all forms of wrongdoing. {10:3} There is no hierarchy in wrongdoing; status does not justify retaliation. The command is clear: do not repay evil with evil. Like deeds deserve similar treatment. {10:4} How can we follow this command if we hate evil yet embrace revenge? What honor do we give God by taking justice into our own hands? {10:5} We, fragile vessels of clay, are offended when our servants seek revenge among themselves. We praise those who show us patience, rewarding them beyond expectation. With a just and powerful Lord, where is the risk in such conduct? {10:6} Why do we acknowledge Him as judge but deny Him as avenger? He assures us, 'Vengeance is mine; I will repay.' Have patience, and He will reward it. {10:7} When He commands, 'Judge not, lest you be judged,' isn't He asking for patience? Who refrains from judging unless willing to forgo self-defense? And who judges with the intent to forgive? To forgive is to reject the impatience of judging and leave judgment to God. {10:8} Impatience often brings regret and worsens the original offense. Impulsive actions fueled by impatience lead to violence, failure, or self-destruction. {10:9} If you react excessively, you'll be burdened; if you're too lenient, you'll be perceived as weak. Why worry about revenge when inability to endure pain limits your retaliation? Yielding and suffering injury brings no pain and no desire for revenge.

{11:1} Having outlined the primary causes of impatience, consider how to handle minor and major provocations in daily life. Satan tempts with countless minor irritations and occasional major trials. {11:2} Ignore minor annoyances for their insignificance; yield to greater challenges due to their overwhelming power. Minor injuries need no impatience, but major ones require patience as a remedy. {11:3} Endure Satan's provocations to shame his efforts to disrupt your self-control. If through imprudence or free will you bring misfortune upon yourself, patiently accept it. {11:4} If God sends adversity, show patience to Him. Rejoice in divine chastisement, for 'those whom I love, I chastise.' Blessed is the servant corrected by the Lord, not deceived by omission of His warning. {11:5} From every angle, practice patience: against your own mistakes, Satan's snares, and the Lord's admonitions. Great is the reward: happiness. {11:6} Who does the Lord bless? The patient. 'Blessed are the poor in spirit, for theirs is the kingdom of heaven.' Only the humble, who are patient, can be poor in spirit. {11:7} 'Blessed are those who mourn.' Enduring sorrow requires patience and promises comfort and joy. {11:8} 'Blessed are the meek.' Impatient people cannot be meek. Similarly, 'Blessed are the peacemakers,' children of God. Can the impatient share in peace? Only a fool would think so. {11:9} 'Rejoice and be glad when others reproach and persecute you; great is your reward in heaven.' The impatient won't rejoice in adversity unless they first learn to despise it through patience.

{12:1} Regarding the peace that pleases God: can an impatient person forgive even once, let alone 'seventy times seven'? Can they settle disputes with adversaries without first overcoming wrath, resentment, and bitterness—that is, impatience? {12:2}

How can you forgive and seek forgiveness if impatience keeps you holding onto grievances? No one in a rage against their brother can worship at the altar until reconciled through patience. {12:3} If anger persists till sunset, danger looms. Patience is indispensable daily. It governs a wholesome life and aids those who stumble in repentance. {12:4} Patience fosters repentance without making the other party an adulterer. Examples abound in Jesus' parables: the patient shepherd seeking the lost sheep and the forgiving father welcoming the prodigal son, despite the impatient older brother's anger. {12:5} Charity, the bond of faith and treasure of Christianity, is learned through patience. 'Charity is patient, kind, not envious, not proud, not self-seeking, not easily angered, enduring all things,' for it embodies patience. {12:6} Faith, hope, and charity endure, but the greatest is charity, accompanied by patience as taught by God.

{13:1} Up to now, we've discussed patience as an operation of the soul alone. But we should also pursue patience in bodily actions to please the Lord, as even the Lord Himself practiced patience in the body. The soul, as the guiding force, shares the Spirit's inspirations with the body it inhabits. {13:2} What does bodily patience entail? Primarily, it involves disciplining the flesh as a pleasing sacrifice to the Lord. It means humbly offering mourning attire, simple meals, fasting, and enduring in humility with sackcloth and ashes. {13:3} This bodily patience enhances our prayers, making them more potent, and softens God's severity, drawing forth His mercy. {13:4} Consider King Nebuchadnezzar, who, after offending the Lord, lived for seven years in degradation and filth, exiled from human society. His patient endurance of bodily discomfort not only restored his kingdom but, more importantly, reconciled him with God. {13:5} Now, consider the higher degrees of bodily patience which sanctify continence. It sustains widows in their state, seals the virgin's dedication, and elevates those who willingly choose celibacy to the kingdom of heaven. {13:6} The strength of the soul finds fulfillment in the body. In persecutions, bodily endurance engages in battle. Fleeing hardship, the body overcomes. In imprisonment, it submits to chains, wooden blocks, and bare ground. It endures dim dungeon light and the lack of worldly comforts. {13:7} When faced with trials that test one's happiness, baptismal renewal, or ascension to divine grace, nothing is more crucial than bodily endurance. If the spirit is willing but the flesh lacks patience, how can both spirit and flesh find salvation? {13:8} When the Lord acknowledges the weakness of the flesh, He shows us what's needed for strength: patience in the face of trials that threaten our faith and impose penalties. Endure stripes, fire, the cross, wild beasts, or the sword, as Prophets and Apostles did, and gain victory.

{14:1} By his endurance, Isaiah, though cut to pieces, still spoke of the Lord. Stephen, as he was stoned, prayed for his enemies' forgiveness. {14:2} Blessed is the man who, facing every attack of the Devil, displayed unwavering patience! His flocks scattered, his cattle destroyed by lightning, his children perished in a house collapse, his body afflicted with painful sores—yet, he did not waver in patience or faith in the Lord. Despite the Devil's onslaughts, he stood firm! {14:3} Instead of turning from God due to numerous misfortunes, he set an example of how to practice patience in spirit and body, enduring loss of wealth, death of loved ones, and bodily afflictions. {14:4} What a victory over the Devil God displayed through this man! What glory He revealed by raising this man's steadfastness as a banner against His enemy! Job's response to each bitter message was simply, 'Blessed be God!' He even rebuked his wife, weary of misfortune, for urging improper remedies. {14:5} God rejoiced, while the Devil was confounded, as Job, with calm composure, wiped away discharge from his ulcers and joked about the creatures crawling in his open wounds. This hero of faith triumphed over every temptation, and through patience, regained health and doubled his possessions. {14:6} If Job had desired his sons' restoration, he would have been called 'father' again. Yet, he trusted the Lord for their eventual reunion on the last day, willingly enduring their loss for the sake of his faith.

{15:1} God is the trustworthy guardian of our patience. Entrust to Him injustice suffered for justice, loss for compensation, pain for healing, and death for life. Patience grants us God as a debtor! {15:2} This isn't without reason. Patience adheres to God's commands, strengthens faith, promotes peace, sustains love, teaches humility, awaits repentance, affirms penance, disciplines the flesh, preserves the spirit, tames the tongue, restrains the hand, rejects temptations, overcomes scandals, and achieves martyrdom. {15:3} In poverty, patience brings solace; in wealth, moderation. It doesn't destroy the sick or unnecessarily prolong the healthy. For the faithful, patience is a source of joy. It attracts pagans, reconciles slaves to masters, masters to God. It beautifies women, perfects men. It's admired in children, praised in youth, esteemed in old age. At every stage of life, patience is deeply attractive. {15:4} Now, let's grasp the characteristics of patience. Its countenance is peaceful, unruffled by melancholy or anger. Its brow is clear, devoid of furrows of worry or frustration. Its relaxed eyebrows suggest joy. Its eyes reflect humility rather than gloom. {15:5} Its mouth is closed in serene silence. Its complexion mirrors tranquility and purity. It nods towards the Devil, threateningly laughing at his schemes. Its garment, white and close-fitting, remains undisturbed by the wind. {15:6} It sits calmly on its spirit's throne, gentle and mild, unruffled by storms or clouds. It's a soft breeze of clear light, akin to what Elijah saw. Where God is, patience flourishes. {15:7} When the Spirit descends, patience is its inseparable companion. If we reject patience, will the Spirit remain within us? It would likely depart, uncomfortable without its partner. Stripped of its means to endure, it cannot withstand the enemy's blows.

{16:1} This is the essence, practice, and effect of divine and true patience—Christian patience. It's not like the false and shameful patience practiced by worldly people. {16:2} The Devil attempts to mimic the Lord by teaching his own twisted form of patience. This patience subjects husbands, bought with dowries or swayed by indulgence, to their wives' dominance. It forces wives to feign affection despite irritation, aiming to seize husbands' estates as childless widows. It enslaves gluttons to their appetites, sacrificing freedom for shameful indulgence. {16:3} Such is the patience of the heathens, appropriating the noble virtue's name for ignoble ends—enduring rivals and wealthy hosts but failing to endure God. Let their patience beware, for fire awaits such endurance beneath the earth! {16:4} Let us instead embrace God's patience, the patience of Christ. Let us return to Him what He has given us. Let us, who believe in the resurrection of both flesh and spirit, offer Him the patience of both spirit and body.

Tertullian on Martyrs

Tertullian's "On Martyrs" (De Martyribus) offers a profound perspective on early Christian views of martyrdom. Written with legal precision and rhetorical flair, Tertullian portrays martyrdom as a glorious testimony of faith rather than a tragic end. He argues that martyrs, through their suffering, achieve spiritual victory, share in Christ's passion, and secure a place in heaven. Rich in New Testament references, the treatise uses vivid imagery to inspire Christians, emphasizing that martyrdom is a path to eternal glory and spiritual purification.

{1:1} Blessed martyrs, recipients of sustenance for both body and spirit from our Lady Mother Church and brethren, accept this offering from me to nourish your spirits. It's not right for the flesh to feast while the spirit starves. Care for the weak extends to the weakest. {1:2} Though I'm not one to exhort you, even seasoned gladiators are spurred not just by trainers and managers but also by spectators, whose hints often prove valuable. {1:3} First and foremost, O blessed ones, do not grieve the Holy Spirit who is with you in prison. Had He not been with you, you wouldn't be there. Ensure He remains, guiding you out to the Lord. {1:4} The prison is also the Devil's domain, his household. But you're here to trample him in his own house, having already battled him outside. Don't let him sow discord; let peace among you be his defeat. {1:5} Some, unable to find peace in the Church, seek it from imprisoned martyrs. Therefore, maintain and share peace among yourselves.

{2:1} Other burdensome attachments may have come with you to prison; relatives may have escorted you to its gates. Since then, you're separated not just from the world but its spirit and ways. Don't be troubled by this separation; the world itself is a greater prison from which you've departed rather than entered. {2:2} The world is darker, blinding hearts; it chains souls more heavily, ensnaring them. It exhales impurities—human lusts—and houses countless sinners awaiting judgment by God, not merely a proconsul. {2:3} Therefore, O blessed ones, consider yourselves transferred from prison to a place of safety. Darkness surrounds, yet you are light; chains bind, yet you are free before God. It stinks foully, yet you are sweet fragrance. Judgment awaits, yet you will judge the judges. {2:4} Those who long for worldly pleasures may find sadness. Christians, renouncing the world even outside prison, care not for its enjoyments. Consider the profit in suffering loss for greater gain. And this is only a glimpse of God's reward for martyrs. {2:5} Compare life in the world with prison; the spirit gains more here than the flesh loses. {2:6} The Church's care and brethren's charity ensure the body lacks not, while the spirit gains faith's sustenance: no idols, no pagan images, no heathen festivals, no sacrificial banquets' fumes, no torment from spectacles' noise or debauchery. You are free from sin's allure, temptation, and impure memories, and even persecution. {2:7} The prison now offers what the desert gave the Prophets. Our Lord often withdrew to solitude for prayer, away from the world. Let's call it not 'prison' but 'seclusion.' {2:8} Though the body's confined, the spirit roams free. Walk in spirit along the path to God; then, you are not in prison.

{3:1} Even for Christians, prison is unpleasant. Yet, we're called to serve in God's army from the moment we take the sacramental oath. Soldiers don't go to war laden with luxuries; they march from humble tents, toughened by toil. {3:2} Even in peace, soldiers train with toils and hardships: marching in arms, swift maneuvers, trench digging, forming shield-walls. They endure sweating toil to prepare for sudden shifts from shade to sun, silence to battle cries. {3:3} Likewise, O blessed ones, see your present hardship as mental and physical training. You're entering a noble contest where God oversees, the Holy Spirit trains—a contest for an eternal crown, angelic status, heavenly citizenship, and eternal glory. {3:4} Your Master, Jesus Christ, anointed you with His Spirit, brought you here to toughen you before the contest. Athletes undergo rigorous training to strengthen their bodies, avoiding luxury, rich food, and pleasure. They push through torturous toil, exhausted yet hopeful of victory. {3:5} We, aiming for an eternal crown, see prison as our training ground, where hardship builds strength, but softness destroys it.

{4:1} Understanding from our Lord's teachings that while the spirit is willing, the flesh is weak, let's not misconstrue His acknowledgement of the flesh's frailty. He initially emphasized the spirit's willingness to show that the flesh should submit to the spirit—strength supporting weakness. {4:2} Let the spirit reason with the flesh about their shared salvation. Instead of dwelling on the hardships of prison, focus on the impending struggle. The flesh may dread the sword, the cross, wild beasts in fury, and the worst of all punishments—death by fire. But let the spirit present the other side: many have borne these sufferings patiently, even seeking them for fame and glory. This holds true for both men and women, so that you, blessed women, too, may honor your sex. {4:3} It would take too long to recount all who, driven by their own will, ended their lives by the sword. Among women, Lucretia is well known, who, victimized, chose to gain glory for her chastity by stabbing herself in front of her family. Mucius burned his hand on the altar to enhance his reputation. {4:4} Philosophers also showed great courage: Heraclitus ended his life by covering himself in cow dung, Empedocles leapt into Mt. Etna's fires, and Peregrinus recently threw himself into a funeral pyre. Even women defied flames; Dido avoided marriage after her beloved's departure, and Hasdrubal's wife, with Carthage ablaze, chose death rather than see her husband humbled. {4:5} You might argue that fear of torture exceeds fear of death. Did the Athenian woman yield to the executioner? Privy to a conspiracy, she endured torture by a tyrant but did not betray her co-conspirators. Eventually, she bit off her own tongue and spat it at the tyrant's face, proving torment futile. {4:6} Even today, the Spartans' most revered festival is "diamastigosis," where noble youth endure whipping before their families, valuing soul's endurance over body. {4:7} If earthly glory from physical and spiritual strength is so esteemed that one disregards sword, fire, nails, beasts, and torture for human praise, then your suffering in comparison to heavenly glory and divine reward is trivial. If glass beads are prized, how much more the true pearl? Who wouldn't gladly give as much for the true as others for the false?

{5:1} I omit here an account of glory-seeking motives. Excessive ambition and a certain mental morbidity have rendered cruel contests trivial. Many from privileged classes, drawn by love of arms, become gladiators for vanity's sake, bearing scars as badges of honor. Some test themselves with fire, running in burning tunics, or face bullwhips unflinchingly. {5:2} O blessed ones, the Lord allows this in the world to encourage us now and judge us on the final day. If we shrink from suffering for truth unto salvation, what others embrace for vanity leads to perdition.

{6:1} Let's cease discussing perseverance born from excessive ambition and consider instead the common fate of humanity. If we must face such trials with fortitude, let's learn from the misfortunes befalling even unwilling victims. How many perish in fires? How many devoured by wild beasts in forests or cities after escaping cages? How many slain by robbers' swords, or subjected to crucifixion after torture and insults by enemies? {6:2} Moreover, many endure suffering for a human cause that they hesitate to endure for God. Our times attest to this truth. How often do prominent individuals meet death for or against a man, despite birth, rank, physical condition, or age seemingly protecting them?

Tertullian on Apparel of Women - I

In Tertullian on Apparel of Women - Book 1, Tertullian addresses the complexities of women's dress and personal adornment from a Christian ethical perspective. Written in the early third century CE, this text reflects Tertullian's rigorous asceticism and his belief in the moral and spiritual dangers of elaborate and ostentatious clothing. He critiques the excessive focus on hairstyles, wigs, and ornamental accessories, arguing that such preoccupations distract from spiritual salvation and proper Christian conduct. The work examines contemporary fashion trends and their impact on Christian modesty, urging women to embrace a simpler, more modest appearance in line with their spiritual commitments.

{1:1} If there existed on earth a faith as great as the reward of faith expected in heaven, none of you, beloved sisters, who have come to know the Lord and learned the truth about the condition of women, would desire an extravagant or ostentatious style of dress. Instead, you would choose to wear humble clothing and embrace modesty, as if walking around in mourning and repentance like Eve, aiming to atone for the original sin and the blame associated with it. "In pain you shall bear children, and your desire shall be for your husband, and he shall rule over you." {1:2} Do you not realize that you are all like Eve? The divine judgment on women still applies today, so the guilt remains. You are considered the gateway of the devil, the unsealer of the forbidden tree, the first to break divine law, and the one who tempted Adam, who was not strong enough to resist. Your actions led to death, and even the Son of God had to die because of it. So why would you seek to adorn yourself beyond the simple garments of skin? {1:3} Even though from the beginning of the world various peoples have engaged in activities like shearing sheep, spinning, dyeing, and embroidering, and precious materials like gold and pearls have been sought after, Eve, expelled from paradise, would not have desired these things. Thus, women should not crave or become familiar with such things if they wish to live a righteous life, as these adornments are akin to the finery of a funeral for one who is already dead.

{2:1} The origin of female ornamentation can be traced back to the fallen angels who descended to earth. These angels, condemned to death, introduced various forms of decoration to women, adding to their ignominy. They revealed hidden substances and scientific arts, including metallurgy, herbal properties, enchantments, and star interpretations, and specifically gave women the means of adornment such as jewels, gold circlets, dyed fabrics, and makeup. {2:2} The quality of these items reflects the nature of their teachers: sinners could not have provided anything conducive to integrity, nor could those driven by lust offer anything that promotes chastity or the fear of God. These gifts were not meant to elevate women but to distract them from simplicity and sincerity, ultimately making them offensive to God. If women are destined to judge these angels, it is inconsistent for them to seek after the gifts of those they are meant to judge. Women, promised the same angelic nature and dignity as men, should reject the things given by the condemned angels and maintain their purity and humility.

{3:1} I understand that some do not accept the Book of Enoch, which describes the actions of angels, because it is not included in the Jewish canon. Some might think it could not have survived the deluge that wiped out the world. However, Noah, a great-grandson of Enoch, might have preserved its teachings through oral tradition. {3:2} Even if this were not the case, the scripture could have been renewed by the Spirit after the deluge, similar to how Jewish literature was restored after the Babylonian destruction. Since Enoch's writings also mention the Lord, we should not reject anything relevant to us. Apostle Jude also references Enoch, supporting its validity.

{4:1} Assuming the origins of female adornments are not condemned by the fate of their creators and no additional blame is assigned to the angels beyond their rebellion and carnal marriages, we should evaluate the items themselves to understand their purposes. {4:2} Female attire includes both dress and ornament. "Dress" refers to what enhances a woman's appearance, while "ornament" refers to what is deemed disgraceful. The former often involves gold, silver, gems, and clothing, while the latter involves hair and skin care. The former is criticized as ambition, and the latter as prostitution. Consider what is appropriate for a handmaid of God, who is expected to embody humility and chastity.

{5:1} Gold and silver, which are highly valued for their worldly splendor, are made from earth, which is naturally more glorious. These materials are extracted through laborious processes and are transformed from earth into ornaments. However, metals like iron and brass, which are more useful in everyday life, are just as earth-born and refined. {5:2} Iron and brass are crucial for many practical functions and support gold and silver in their uses. Gold and silver are not essential for plowing fields or constructing buildings, whereas iron and brass are integral to these tasks. Thus, gold and silver's high status may be misplaced compared to their practical counterparts.

{6:1} Precious stones and pearls, which compete with gold in their grandeur, are merely stones and small particles of earth. They do not contribute to construction but only to the vanity of women. They require extensive polishing, setting, and adornment to achieve their effect. {6:2} The gems and pearls, whether from the sea or claimed to be dragon's treasure, do not add value to a Christian woman's appearance. Adorning oneself with such items might contradict the Christian goal of overcoming evil.

{7:1} The value of jewels and precious materials comes mainly from their rarity and exotic nature. In their native places, they are not as highly prized. {7:2} Some cultures even use gold to chain criminals, reflecting a disregard for its value. The nobility of gems is diminished by their casual use among other peoples. Even in Rome, where gems are not worn to show off, their value is not as significant. The excessive display of gems often contrasts with their true worth and utility.

{8:1} Similarly, the use of colors in clothing should be considered. Even the servants of those barbarians diminish the value of the colors in our garments by wearing similar ones. Their walls, for example, use simple colors to replace the elaborate Tyrian purple and violet hangings that you carefully remove and repurpose. For them, purple is less valuable than red ochre because garments cannot gain true honor from adulterated colors. If God did not create sheep with purple or sky-blue wool, it must be because He chose not to. What God did not will, we should not fashion. Thus, things not created by God, the Author of nature, are not naturally good but are attributed to the devil, the corrupter of nature. There is no rival to God other than the devil and his angels. Even if materials come from God, how they are used can be inappropriate. For instance, conchs and other elements of worldly decoration may come from God's creation, but they are misused for profane pleasures and idolatry. Christians should not embrace the excesses of worldly shows, such as races or arenas, simply because the animals and objects used are God's creations. Similarly, using materials for vanity or idolatry is inappropriate, despite their divine origin. Therefore, the use of materials for worldly glory is inconsistent with divine intention.

{9:1} Our desires should align with God's distribution, or we risk falling prey to ambition and its associated evils. Just as certain things are found in specific lands or seas and are valued or disregarded accordingly, so too do we desire what we do not have. Items that are rare or foreign are often desired simply because they are not native to us, leading to a vice of excessive desire. Even if having something is permissible, it should be within limits to prevent ambition. Ambition, driven by excessive desire for glory, is not supported by nature or truth but by a destructive passion of the mind. This vice, connected to ambition and glory, inflates the cost of items, feeding into our desire. A small object can represent a large fortune; a delicate thread can hold a great value; a slender necklace can symbolize vast wealth. Ambition's power is such that even a small body, like a woman's, can carry immense wealth, demonstrating the strength of ambition in its quest for glory.

Tertullian on Apparel of Women - II

In Tertullian on Apparel of Women - Book 2, Tertullian extends his critique of women's adornment to address broader societal and theological concerns. This continuation of his treatise delves deeper into the implications of luxurious attire and personal grooming on Christian virtue and identity. Tertullian argues that the pursuit of fashionable and extravagant dress is inconsistent with the values of humility and modesty that should characterize a Christian life. He further explores the notion that outward appearances should reflect inner spiritual truths, emphasizing the need for Christians to distinguish themselves from pagan practices. The text also touches on the social and religious contexts that influence women's choices in apparel, highlighting the need for self-restraint and spiritual integrity in personal presentation.

{1:1} Dear fellow servants and sisters in Christ, I am grateful for the privilege of addressing you on a matter of great importance—modesty, not just in its core essence but also in its outward expression. We are all temples of God, and modesty is the guardian of this sacred space, preventing anything unclean or inappropriate from entering and thus offending God. Today, I want to discuss not just modesty itself but how it should be reflected in our daily conduct, especially in our appearance. Many women, whether out of ignorance or pretense, seem to believe that modesty is only about avoiding physical sin and not about the external aspects such as dress and adornment. They often dress similarly to women from other cultures who lack true modesty, showing that their sense of modesty is incomplete and easily led astray by superficial attractions. How many are there who, even though they don't want to actively sin, still care too much about looking attractive to strangers? If we were to adhere only to the modesty seen in non-believers, it would be imperfect and vulnerable to excesses in attire. Women who fail to uphold true modesty might inadvertently blend good with evil. Therefore, you should avoid such practices and aim for a higher standard of perfection, as God commands us to be perfect just as He is perfect.

{2:1} Perfect modesty requires abstaining not only from actual sins but also from anything that might lead to sin. Trusting in our own security without being vigilant is a form of presumption, which undermines our ability to stay alert and cautious. We must maintain a constant awareness of our own vulnerability to sin and be cautious to prevent putting others in tempting situations. It is essential to walk in holiness and faith, recognizing that our own safety is not guaranteed and that we must be wary to remain secure. Presumption leads to complacency and greater risk, while fear encourages vigilance, which is crucial for our salvation. It is also important not to be a stumbling block to others, as causing another person to sin, even indirectly, is a grave offense. We must love our neighbors as ourselves and not act in ways that could lead them into temptation. Any form of physical attractiveness that invites lustful thoughts or desires should be avoided, as it contradicts the command to love others and act in their best interest.

{3:1} Even if physical beauty is not inherently dangerous, it is still unnecessary and potentially vain. Beauty serves to evoke pleasure and attraction, which is contrary to the modesty that Christians should embrace. True modesty values spiritual rather than physical attributes and should focus on inner virtues rather than outward appearances. Women should not pursue or showcase beauty for its own sake, as this goes against the Christian call to humility and simplicity. Instead, if a woman is naturally beautiful, she should not emphasize her beauty but rather minimize it to avoid drawing undue attention. This approach reflects a commitment to modesty and a focus on spiritual rather than physical glory.

{4:1} The idea that one should adorn oneself to please a husband is also misguided. A Christian wife should remember that pleasing her husband does not depend on outward beauty but on her character and faithfulness. A believing husband does not require beauty, and an unbelieving husband, influenced by worldly standards, might be suspicious or disapproving of it. Therefore, the pursuit of beauty for the sake of pleasing a husband, whether believing or not, is misguided. True contentment and approval come from living a life of modesty and faith, not from outward appearances.

{5:1} It is important to distinguish between permissible and impermissible refinements in personal appearance. While modest grooming is acceptable, excessive or artificial enhancements, such as using cosmetics or dyes, are not. Such practices are a form of altering God's creation and are influenced by the devil's temptation. Adding to or changing what God has created is a form of disrespect to His work. Christians should avoid any practices that reflect the influence of evil forces and instead embrace simplicity and natural beauty. Our appearance should reflect our commitment to modesty and avoid practices that are contrary to God's precepts.

{6:1} Some women use dyes to change the color of their hair, which reflects a desire to conform to external standards of beauty and a rejection of their natural appearance. Such actions are not only harmful to the hair but also reflect a misplaced value on superficial beauty. Changing hair color to achieve a certain look is an attempt to alter what God has created, which is a form of disobedience. Instead of striving for artificial youthfulness, Christians should embrace their natural aging process and focus on spiritual growth. The pursuit of outward beauty at the expense of spiritual integrity is a misalignment with Christian values and teachings.

{7:1} What purpose does all the effort spent on styling your hair serve in relation to salvation? Why is your hair never allowed to rest, constantly needing to be styled, loosened, shaped, or thinned? Some people go to great lengths to curl their hair, while others let it hang loose, but never in a simple manner. You also attach various forms of artificial hairpieces—sometimes like a helmet or a head covering, or a mass pulled back to the neck. The remarkable thing is that there is no visible opposition to God's commands! It has been stated that no one can increase their stature. Yet, you add to your weight by piling on rolls or decorative elements on your neck! If you feel no shame in such excess, at least feel some discomfort about the impurity; consider the possibility that you might be putting on a holy and Christian head the discarded remains of someone else's head, which could be unclean or even destined for hell. Instead, cast away all this adornment from your "free" head. It is futile to try to seem adorned and to rely on the most skilled creators of false hair. God instructs you to "be veiled," perhaps to keep some heads from being seen! And oh, that on "that day" of Christian joy, I might lift my head, even if it is beneath yours! I will see whether you rise with your make-up and dyes and all that elaborate headgear, and whether it will be women so decked out whom the angels will carry up to meet Christ in the air. If these decorations are good and of God now, they will also accompany the risen bodies and find their places then. But only flesh and spirit, pure and unblemished, will rise. Therefore, abstain from what is condemned now, so that God may see you as He will see you then.

{8:1} Certainly, as a man, I am not excluding women from these observations about personal adornment. Are there also things in men's grooming that should be avoided due to our reverence for God? If it is true, and it is, that in men, as in women, there is a natural desire to please, and if men have their own deceptive grooming practices—such as trimming their beards too sharply, plucking them, shaving around the mouth, using dyes to cover grey hair, removing body hair, applying pigments to fix each hair in place, and smoothing the rest of the body with rough powders—then once we have knowledge of God, all these things should be rejected as frivolous and contrary to modesty. Where God is, modesty is present, and sobriety supports modesty. How can we practice modesty without sobriety, and how can we ensure sobriety aids modesty if our appearance, demeanor, and general aspect are not marked by seriousness?

{9:1} Thus, in terms of clothing and other forms of self-adornment, you must also prune away excessive splendor. What is the point of showing temperance and simplicity in your face if you cover the rest of your body with luxurious and absurd decorations? It is clear how these embellishments relate to voluptuousness and undermine modesty. Without these embellishments, personal grace is rendered pointless, and with it, any inherent grace is supported by outward adornment. In times of life that are blessed with quiet and withdrawn into modesty, the splendor of dress can disturb this peace by tempting the appetites with the allure of apparel. So, sisters, avoid wearing garments that are flashy or suggestive of prostitution, and if you must appear in public due to wealth, status, or previous dignity, temper this necessity. Ensure that the enjoyment of your riches and elegance does not lead to indulgence. For humility, which our faith upholds, requires you to moderate your use of luxury and adornments, in line with the apostle's advice to use the world as if not using it, since the fashion of this world is passing away. Even those who abstain from wine and rich foods for the sake of the kingdom of God offer their humility through such abstinence. We have had enough of wealth and luxury before embracing these saving disciplines. We are living at the end of the ages, predestined by God for this final time, and thus we should be trained to chastise and transcend worldly principles, spiritually and physically.

{10:1} Was it really God who instructed the dyeing of wool with herbal juices and shellfish? Did He forget to create purple and scarlet sheep when He made the universe? Was it God who invented expensive, light garments, or the elaborate golden accessories for hair? Was He behind the painful body modifications, such as ear piercings, that resulted in the high value of such adornments? Even gold, which captivates you, was once used as chains in ancient cultures. This shows that it is not the inherent worth but the rarity of these items that determines their value. The excessive labor involved in crafting these ornaments, introduced by sinful angels who revealed such arts, increased their costliness and fueled women's desire for them. If these angels who taught these arts have been condemned by God, as Enoch tells us, how can we please God by indulging in the things associated with them?

{11:1} Christian women have no reason to appear in excessive grandeur, as they are not engaged in the public activities or worships of pagans. Public display of luxury is typically for seeking attention or glorification, but Christian life involves serious matters, such as visiting the sick, offering sacrifices, or dispensing the word of God, none of which require extravagant attire. If you are called upon by non-believers or in cases of necessity, go forth in modest dress, ensuring that you stand apart from those who are not of the faith. Your attire should reflect modesty, setting an example to others and magnifying God through your body. Avoid giving the impression that since becoming a Christian, you have become poorer or less clean. It is not according to the standards of Gentiles but according to God's standards that Christians should dress.

{12:1} It is vital to avoid causing justifiable blasphemy by dressing in a manner similar to those known for their immodesty. The increased depravity of the age has nearly equated the appearance of respectable women with that of the most dishonorable ones. The Scriptures indicate that outward adornments associated with prostitution are improper for modest women. The powerful state that sits on seven hills and many waters is described as a prostitute, decked out in purple, scarlet, gold, and precious stones. Such adornments are identified with the accursed state of prostitution. Even Thamar's use of cosmetics led Judah to mistake her for a harlot. This underscores the need for women to ensure their attire aligns with their chastity, avoiding anything that could lead to suspicion or misinterpretation.

{13:1} It is not enough for God alone to know us as chaste; we must appear so to others. This is particularly important in times of persecution, where our endurance of hardships should prepare us for potential suffering. Our appearance and behavior should reflect our faith, and we should be prepared to leave behind earthly luxuries for the sake of our hope. Love for gold, which symbolizes the sins of Israel, should be rejected. Even now, Christians should focus on enduring hardships rather than indulging in gold. As we await our transformation and the angels who will guide us, let us be adorned not with earthly cosmetics but with spiritual virtues—simplicity, modesty, and silence. Submit to your husbands, focus on home duties, and embody faithfulness. Dress in righteousness and modesty, and you will be truly adorned, pleasing God as your Lover.

Tertullian on Exhortation to Chastity

Tertullian's Exhortation to Chastity stands as a seminal text in early Christian literature, offering a profound exploration of the theological and moral dimensions of sexual purity. Written in the early third century, this work reflects Tertullian's rigorous asceticism and his belief in the superior spiritual merits of chastity over marital relations. Through a meticulous examination of scriptural injunctions and an engagement with contemporary practices and societal norms, Tertullian argues for the sanctity of single life and the intrinsic value of celibacy as a means of attaining spiritual purity and closeness to God. His treatise not only critiques the permissiveness of remarriage and sexual indulgence but also sets forth a vision of Christian discipline that prioritizes spiritual over temporal concerns. As such, the Exhortation to Chastity serves as both a doctrinal guide and a moral exhortation, contributing significantly to the early Christian discourse on ethics and spirituality.

{1:1} I am sure, brother, that after you have peacefully discussed things with your wife and are focusing on the end of your single life, you are in need of advice. While it's true that each person should consult their own faith and assess its strength in such matters, the demands of the flesh—which often oppose faith—can stir up thoughts and prompt the need for external counsel, like an advocate opposing these fleshly needs. This necessity can be managed if we focus on the will of God rather than simply His indulgence. Favor is not earned through indulgence but through prompt obedience to God's will, which aims at our sanctification. God wishes us to become like Him, to be holy as He is holy. Good sanctification can be categorized into several types, and we may be found in one of these types. The first type is virginity from birth; the second is virginity from birth or from baptism, which is either maintained in marriage through mutual agreement or persists in widowhood by choice; the third type is monogamy, where after a marriage has ended, there is a renunciation of sexual relations. The first virginity is a state of happiness, involving complete ignorance of what one might later wish to be freed from; the second virginity involves virtue, which is despising the power of something one fully understands; and the third type, not remarrying after the death of a spouse, represents the glory of virtue and moderation. Moderation means not regretting something taken away by the Lord, who controls even the smallest things like falling leaves or sparrows.

{2:1} It is not right to claim that the Lord gave and took away things merely according to His will without acknowledging that some power rests with us. If we remarry things that God has taken away, we are opposing His will. If God had willed us to remarry, He would not have taken it away in the first place. To attribute all actions to the will of God in this manner can lead to the absurd conclusion that even sins are excused, which undermines our discipline and even the concept of God. God forbids certain actions and punishes them with eternal consequences, while He commands and rewards actions that align with His will. Therefore, we have the power to choose between good and evil, as stated in the scripture. Our volition, or power of choice, is where our faith is tested. If we choose what is contrary to God's will, it originates from within us. Adam, the forefather of sin, chose to sin of his own accord, and the devil merely provided the opportunity, not the volition. Thus, the only thing truly within our power is our choice, and we must consider carefully what aligns with God's will.

{3:1} We understand manifest things, but we must examine what is meant by their manifestation. Just because something is permitted by God does not mean it is purely His will. Indulgence, which is not independent of volition, often causes permission to happen, even though it results from a constrained choice. In contrast, pure volition is seen in acts that please God where His discipline rules rather than indulgence. If God prefers certain acts over others, it follows that we should pursue those He prefers. Acts He prefers more override those He prefers less. Therefore, failing to follow what God more wills means going against His superior will and thus not deserving a reward. Even the unwillingness to seek reward can be a sin. If second marriage is permitted through God's indulgence, then it is not a pure act of His will. Instead, acts reflecting His greater will are what we should pursue. The apostle's guidance, while suggesting that marriage might be better than burning with desire, reflects his personal advice rather than divine command. His own suggestions do not override the divine preference for continence.

{4:1} The apostle's suggestion about second marriage, where he says "You are free from a wife; do not seek a wife. But if you marry, you will not sin," is based on personal advice rather than a divine command. There is a significant difference between a divine command and personal advice. The apostle himself acknowledges that he is giving personal advice rather than a command from God. In his teachings and letters, there is no divine command permitting second marriage. This supports the view that unity in marriage should be upheld as what is not permitted by God is considered forbidden. Furthermore, the apostle advises continence over marriage, suggesting that although marriage is permitted under certain circumstances, continence is more desirable. His personal advice is influenced by the Holy Spirit, and we should follow the advice that aligns with divine authority. Thus, we should adhere to the apostolic guidance that reflects divine preference rather than mere personal opinion.

{5:1} The principle of monogamy is established by the very beginning of human creation, where God created one woman from one rib of Adam, thus setting a precedent. The intention was clear that there should be one man and one woman united as one flesh, not multiple marriages. This original design signifies that marriage should be a single, unified bond. The apostle interprets the concept of "two becoming one flesh" as relating to the relationship between Christ and the Church, reinforcing the law of marriage unity. This type of union is reflected both in our physical and spiritual origins—carnal in Adam and spiritual in Christ. Thus, violating the unity of marriage is seen as deviating from both the primal and spiritual designs. The concept of multiple marriages began with Lamech, who violated this principle by marrying two women, thus deviating from the original intent of unity.

{6:1} You argue that because the blessed patriarchs had multiple wives and concubines, it might be lawful for us to marry without limit. I concede that if the old command to "be fruitful and multiply" still applies and if no new command has replaced it, then it might seem permissible. However, a new command has indeed come into effect, as stated: "The time is already winding up; it remains that those who have wives act as if they had none." By commanding chastity and restraining sexual desire, this new command has superseded the earlier directive to "grow and multiply." In the early days, God allowed a more lenient approach to marriage until the world was populated and the new discipline was ready to be established. At the end of time, however, this indulgence has been withdrawn, just as old laws have been replaced by new ones. For example, "an eye for an eye" has been surpassed by the command to "not repay evil with evil." Even under the old law, there were precedents for monogamy. For instance, Leviticus commands that "My priests shall not marry more than once." This reflects a preference for unity over multiplicity. As Christ fulfilled the law, we now have stricter rules: priests must be married only once, and violations of this rule can lead to removal from office. You might argue that this rule applies only to priests, but even laypeople are considered priests in a spiritual sense, as indicated in Scripture. Thus, if a priest is bound by certain standards, laypeople should strive to follow similar rules, particularly when it comes to second marriages. If we want to be considered for a priestly role, we should adhere to these disciplines.

{7:1} We should recognize that the old discipline had elements that anticipated the new, more perfect order. For example, the old law had provisions that limited multiple marriages, and even among the early Israelites, monogamy was a recognized ideal. The new law of Christ is more stringent, demanding a higher standard of purity and discipline. The rule requiring priests to be married only once reflects this higher standard, which is applied even more rigorously to those in religious orders. If the rule applies to priests, it is reasonable to extend similar principles to laypeople, given that priests come from among the laity.

{8:1} Even if second marriages are permissible, not all lawful things are beneficial. As the apostle says, "All things are lawful, but not all are beneficial." What is lawful may not always be good or conducive to salvation. We should aim not just for what is permitted but for what is truly beneficial. The concept of "license" often serves as a test of discipline. While the apostles were allowed to marry and support themselves through the Gospel, their example teaches us that choosing not to exercise such rights can be more spiritually advantageous. Thus, it is important to discern between what is permitted and what is truly beneficial for our spiritual growth.

{9:1} If we examine the deeper implications, second marriage can be seen as a form of fornication. When the apostle talks about married people focusing on pleasing each other, it suggests a concern with carnal desires. Since Jesus equated lustful thoughts with adultery, it follows that any marriage motivated by concupiscence is tainted by a similar issue. First marriages, too, are not immune to these concerns, as they also involve physical desires. Ideally, one should aspire to chastity and avoid even the possibility of adultery. If God has granted you the opportunity to marry once, be grateful and avoid seeking additional indulgence.

{10:1} Embrace the opportunity of widowhood as a chance to focus on spiritual growth. Without the obligations of marriage, you can devote yourself entirely to prayer and spiritual activities. Being free from the responsibilities of marriage allows you to concentrate on serving God and living a more sanctified life. The apostle recommended temporary abstinence for the sake of enhancing prayer, showing that what is beneficial for a time can be practiced more consistently for greater spiritual gain. The absence of marital obligations can lead to a deeper spiritual experience, as one's focus shifts entirely to God.

{11:1} Having multiple wives creates greater spiritual distraction. In the case of a second marriage, you face the challenge of balancing the spiritual and physical needs of two wives. You cannot disregard the first wife, whom you have a deeper spiritual connection with, having prayed for her and made offerings on her behalf. When you stand before the Lord with multiple wives, how can you reconcile this with the priesthood's call for monogamy and virginity? Will your sacrifices be accepted if you request chastity for yourself and your wives, while your life contradicts the very standard set by those in sacred orders?

{12:1} Many justify second marriages with excuses like needing support for household chores, managing a family, or ensuring financial stability. They suggest that only married men succeed in these areas, while celibates and travelers do not. However, even soldiers and travelers manage without spouses, reflecting the possibility of living a dedicated life without marriage. If you are widowed, seek a spiritual partner from among widows, rather than remarrying. Some argue that Christians need heirs, but why should a servant of God seek to prolong his life with additional offspring when the apostle is eager to be with the Lord? Children might bring burdens and concerns rather than benefits, potentially even complicating the final rites. Instead of seeking another marriage to have children, recognize that focusing on spiritual matters might be more fitting for those who have disinherited the world. Even if you remarry and have children, the potential trouble of managing a new spouse and offspring might not be worth the effort, particularly when some might resort to measures to avoid having children, which is morally questionable.

{13:1} Examples from both pagan and Christian traditions illustrate the value of monogamy and chastity. In pagan cultures, monogamy was highly esteemed; even bridesmaids were chosen from women who had only been married once. Priests and priestesses in various cultures, such as the Vestal Virgins or the priestesses of Ceres, often remained celibate or rejected marriage to honor their vows. Their dedication to chastity and the avoidance of marriage, even under religious or societal pressure, highlights the spiritual benefits of remaining single. This contrasts with Christians who sometimes fail to uphold chastity, despite its clear benefits for spiritual life. Examples from Christian history also show individuals who chose to live in chastity rather than remarrying. This greater spiritual dedication, achieved through continence, is often seen as more valuable than the act of dying for one's faith. Thus, those who wish to enter Paradise should strive to overcome the desires that contradict the purity required for entry.

Additional Corinthians

The Third Epistle to the Corinthians is an apocryphal text attributed to the Apostle Paul, often regarded as a response to heretical teachings that had infiltrated the Corinthian church. This letter, not included in the canonical New Testament, addresses key doctrinal issues such as the resurrection of the dead, the incarnation of Christ, and the creation of the world by God, in opposition to Gnostic influences that denied these fundamental Christian beliefs. The epistle is characterized by its defense of orthodox doctrine and its emphasis on the bodily resurrection, underscoring the continuity of apostolic teaching as received by Paul from the earlier apostles. Although it was not universally accepted in the early church, 3 Corinthians provides valuable insights into the theological debates of the second century.

Note: This text is also included in the Acts of Paul, a collection of early Christian writings that narrate the life and teachings of Paul, further embedding it within the context of early Christian literature and the broader struggle against heterodox interpretations of Christian doctrine.

{1:1} Stephanus and the elders, including Daphnus, Eubulus, Theophilus, and Zenon, send their eternal greetings in the Lord to Paul, their brother. {1:2} There have come to Corinth two men, Simon and Cleobius, who are leading many astray with corrupt teachings. {1:3} We urge you to examine and test their words, {1:4} for we have never heard such teachings from you or the other apostles. {1:5} We hold fast to everything we have received from you and them. {1:6} Since the Lord has shown us mercy by allowing us to hear from you again while you are still in the flesh, {1:7} if possible, we ask that you either come to us or write to us. {1:8} We believe, as it has been revealed to Theonoe, that the Lord has delivered you from the hands of the lawless one. {1:9} The things these men teach are as follows: {1:10} They claim that we should not heed the prophets, {1:11} that God is not Almighty, {1:12} that there will be no resurrection of the flesh, {1:13} that man was not created by God, {1:14} that Christ did not come in the flesh, nor was He born of Mary, {1:15} and that the world is not created by God, but by angels. {1:16} Therefore, dear brother, we earnestly ask you to make every effort to come to us, so that the church in Corinth may remain without stumbling, and so that the foolishness of these men may be exposed. Farewell always in the Lord.

{2:1} The deacons Threptus and Eutyches delivered the letter to Philippi, {2:2} and Paul received it while he was in chains because of Stratonice, the wife of Apollophanes. Yet, he momentarily forgot his chains, though he was deeply distressed, {2:3} and he cried out, saying, "It would be better for me to die and be with the Lord than to continue in the flesh and hear such things and endure the calamities of false teachings, bringing trouble upon trouble." {2:4} On top of this great affliction, I am in chains and witness these evils through which the schemes of Satan are carried out. {2:5} Therefore, in the midst of this great suffering, Paul wrote a letter in response, saying the following:

{3:1} Paul, a prisoner of Jesus Christ, sends greetings to the brothers and sisters in Corinth. {3:2} In the midst of many trials, I am not surprised that the teachings of the evil one are spreading quickly. {3:3} For my Lord Jesus Christ will soon come and will not tolerate those who distort His words. {3:4} I delivered to you from the beginning the teachings I received from the holy apostles who were always with Jesus Christ: {3:5} namely, that our Lord Jesus Christ was born of Mary, who is of the seed of David according to the flesh. The Holy Spirit was sent from heaven by the Father to her through the angel Gabriel, {3:6} so that Jesus might come into this world to redeem all flesh by His flesh and to raise us up from the dead in the flesh, as He has shown us in Himself as an example. {3:7} Because man was created by His Father, {3:8} he was sought when he was lost, so that he might be made alive by adoption. {3:9} For this reason, God Almighty, who made heaven and earth, first sent the prophets to the Jews to turn them away from their sins. {3:10} He intended to save the house of Israel, so He gave a portion of the Spirit of Christ to the prophets and sent them to the Jews first, and they proclaimed the true worship of God for a long time. {3:11} But the prince of iniquity, desiring to be God, seized them, killed them, and enslaved all flesh with evil desires, and the end of the world through judgment drew near. {3:12} But God Almighty, who is righteous, did not abandon His own creation, but had compassion on them from heaven, {3:13} and sent His Spirit into Mary in Galilee, {3:14} who believed with all her heart and received the Holy Spirit in her womb, so that Jesus might come into the world. {3:15} By the same flesh through which the wicked one brought in death, he was defeated and overcome. {3:16} By His own body, Jesus Christ saved all flesh and restored it to life, {3:17} so that He might show forth the temple of righteousness in His body. {3:18} In Him we are saved, and if we believe in Him, we are set free. {3:19} Therefore, those who reject the wisdom of God and claim that heaven and earth and all that is in them are not the work of God are not children of righteousness, but children of wrath. {3:20} They are children of wrath, for they are cursed, following the teachings of the serpent. {3:21} Flee from their doctrines and drive them out from among you, {3:22} for you are not children of disobedience, but of the beloved Church. {3:23} Therefore, the time of the resurrection has been proclaimed to all. {3:24} As for those who say there is no resurrection of the flesh, they shall indeed have no resurrection unto life, but unto judgment, {3:25} because they do not believe in Him who is risen from the dead, nor do they understand. {3:26} They do not know, O Corinthians, that the seeds of wheat or other grains, though sown bare and corrupted in the earth, rise again by the will of God with new bodies, fully clothed. {3:27} And not only does the sown body rise again, but it multiplies and prospers even more. {3:28} If we must take an example not only from seeds but from more noble bodies, {3:29} remember how Jonah, the son of Amittai, when he refused to preach to the people of Nineveh and fled, was swallowed by a sea monster. {3:30} After three days and three nights, God heard Jonah's prayer from the depths of the abyss, and not even a hair or eyelash of his was consumed. {3:31} How much more, O you of little faith, will He raise you up who have believed in Christ Jesus, just as He Himself arose. {3:32} Likewise, when a dead man was cast upon the bones of the prophet Elisha by the children of Israel, he arose, body, soul, bones, and spirit. How much more shall you, who have been cast upon the body, bones, and spirit of the Lord, arise in that day with your flesh whole, just as He arose. {3:33} Likewise, concerning the prophet Elijah, he raised up the widow's son from death. How much more shall the Lord Jesus raise you up from death at the sound of the trumpet, in the twinkling of an eye, for He has shown us an example in His own body. {3:34} If, then, you accept any other doctrine, God will be a witness against you; and let no one trouble me, {3:35} for I bear these bonds that I may gain Christ, and I bear His marks in my body so that I may attain the resurrection of the dead. {3:36} Whoever abides by the rule given by the blessed prophets and the holy gospel shall receive a reward from the Lord, and when they rise from the dead, they shall obtain eternal life. {3:37} But whoever transgresses these teachings will face the fire, along with those who follow the same path, who are without God. {3:38} They are a generation of vipers, {3:39} whom you must reject with the power of the Lord. {3:40} Peace, grace, and love shall be with you.

Martyrdom of Ignatius

The Martyrdom of Ignatius, an early Christian text, highlights the profound devotion of Ignatius of Antioch, an early bishop and martyr. Written during his journey to Rome under Emperor Trajan, the narrative includes letters Ignatius wrote to various Christian communities. These letters, filled with theological insights and pastoral advice, emphasize unity, faith, and ecclesiastical hierarchy. Ignatius's martyrdom is depicted as a voluntary sacrifice, reflecting his belief in suffering as a means of following Christ. His resolve to face execution in the Roman arena underscores his unwavering devotion. This text is crucial for understanding early Christian martyrdom and continues to inspire Christian thought and devotion.

{1:1} When Trajan recently became the emperor of Rome, Ignatius, a disciple of the apostle John and a man of apostolic character, carefully led the Church of Antioch. He had survived the severe persecutions under Domitian, guiding the church with prayer, fasting, and diligent teaching, much like a skilled pilot navigating a storm. He feared losing those who were weak or easily deceived. {1:2} Ignatius was relieved when the persecution ceased temporarily, but he felt sorrowful for himself, believing he had not yet fully attained true love for Christ or the perfect status of a disciple. He believed that martyrdom would bring him closer to the Lord. {1:3} Ignatius continued to lead the Church for a few more years, enlightening everyone with his teachings of the Scriptures. Finally, he achieved his desire for martyrdom.

{2:1} In the ninth year of his reign, Trajan, emboldened by victories over the Scythians, Dacians, and other nations, sought to compel Christians to worship idols. He threatened persecution unless they complied, forcing many faithful individuals to choose between sacrificing to idols or facing death. {2:2} Ignatius, concerned for the Church of Antioch, was brought before Trajan, who was preparing for campaigns in Armenia and Parthia. {2:3} When presented before the emperor, Trajan asked, "Who are you, wretched one, who defies our commands and leads others to do the same, causing them to perish?" Ignatius replied, "No one should call Theophorus wicked, for all evil spirits have left the servants of God. If you call me wicked for opposing these spirits, then I agree with you." {2:4} Trajan inquired, "And who is Theophorus?" Ignatius answered, "The one who has Christ within him." {2:5} Trajan retorted, "Do we not have the gods in our minds, aiding us in battles?" Ignatius replied, "You are mistaken, calling the demons of the nations gods. There is only one God, creator of all things, and one Jesus Christ, His only-begotten Son." {2:6} Trajan said, "Do you mean the one crucified under Pontius Pilate?" Ignatius answered, "Yes, the one who crucified my sin and condemned the devil's deceit." {2:7} Trajan asked, "Do you carry the crucified one within you?" Ignatius replied, "Indeed, for it is written, 'I will dwell in them and walk in them.'" {2:8} Trajan then ordered, "We command that Ignatius, who claims to carry the crucified one within him, be bound and taken to Rome to be devoured by beasts for the people's entertainment." {2:9} Upon hearing this, Ignatius rejoiced, thanking the Lord for the honor of chains and praying for the Church. He was swiftly taken away by the soldiers, eager to be a sacrifice for Christ.

{3:1} Ignatius, full of eagerness and joy for his impending martyrdom, traveled from Antioch to Seleucia, where he set sail. {3:2} After much suffering, he arrived in Smyrna and joyfully met Polycarp, the bishop of Smyrna and his former fellow disciple of St. John the Apostle. {3:3} Ignatius shared spiritual gifts with Polycarp and asked him to help fulfill his desire for martyrdom. {3:4} The churches and cities of Asia warmly received Ignatius, hoping to gain spiritual blessings from him. He especially sought the support of Polycarp to hasten his martyrdom and be united with Christ.

{4:1} Ignatius expressed his love for Christ and his eagerness for martyrdom through his letters and interactions, seeking prayers from the churches for his upcoming struggle. {4:2} He sent letters of gratitude, filled with spiritual grace, to the churches that welcomed him. {4:3} Fearing that the brotherhood's love might hinder his zeal for the Lord, Ignatius wrote to the Church of Rome, the Epistle that follows, to settle matters with the brethren there who opposed his martyrdom.

{5:1} After sending his Epistle to the Romans, Ignatius sailed from Smyrna, urged by the soldiers to hurry to Rome for the public spectacles where he would face wild beasts. {5:2} He landed at Troas, then traveled on foot through Macedonia to Epirus and finally found a ship to sail across the Adriatic Sea. {5:3} Despite wanting to disembark at Puteoli, the winds carried the ship forward, and he could only express his gratitude to the brethren there. {5:4} As they neared Rome, the soldiers grew impatient, but Ignatius remained joyful, eager to leave this world and join the Lord. {5:5} They arrived at the Roman harbor, just as the sports were ending, and the soldiers hurried to deliver Ignatius for his martyrdom.

{6:1} They departed from the place called Portus, and word of the holy martyr Ignatius spread quickly. The brethren, filled with both fear and joy, came to meet him—joyful to be in his presence, yet fearful because such a great man was facing death. {6:2} Some, in their fervent zeal, suggested they could persuade the crowd to spare him, but Ignatius, aware of this through the Spirit, asked them to remain silent. He greeted everyone warmly, urging them to show true affection and not to envy his eagerness to join the Lord. {6:3} With all the brethren kneeling beside him, Ignatius prayed to the Son of God on behalf of the Churches, asking for an end to the persecution and for mutual love among the brethren. {6:4} He was then swiftly led into the amphitheater. Following Caesar's earlier command, and as the public spectacles were concluding on a significant Roman day, Ignatius was thrown to the wild beasts. This fulfilled his desire as stated in Scripture, "The desire of the righteous is acceptable [to God]." {6:5} His remains, mostly bones, were taken to Antioch and wrapped in linen, treasured by the holy Church as a grace-filled relic from the martyr.

{7:1} These events occurred on the thirteenth day before the Kalends of January, the twentieth of December, when Sun and Senecio were consuls for the second time. We, having witnessed these events and spent the night in tears and prayer, sought assurance from the Lord about what had happened. {7:2} As we briefly fell asleep, some of us saw Ignatius in a vision, standing and embracing us, others saw him praying for us, and still others saw him sweating as if from great labor, standing by the Lord. {7:3} Rejoicing in these visions, we shared them among ourselves and praised God for the happiness of the holy martyr. {7:4} We now inform you of the day and time of these events so that we can gather to commemorate the martyrdom of this noble champion of Christ, who overcame the devil and fulfilled his course out of love for Christ. Glory and power be to the Father, with the Holy Spirit, forevermore, through Christ Jesus our Lord. Amen.

Martyrdom of Polycarp

The Martyrdom of Polycarp, dated around AD 155, is a key early Christian text detailing the arrest, trial, and execution of Polycarp, bishop of Smyrna. It vividly portrays his steadfast faith and courage during Roman persecutions, highlighting his famous declaration of unwavering devotion. The text provides insights into early Christian eschatology, ecclesiology, and martyr veneration, viewing martyrdom as a victorious testimony to faith. It also reflects on Christian liturgy and the cult of saints, emphasizing the imitation of Christ in suffering and hope in resurrection. This narrative is essential for understanding early Christian identity and responses to persecution.

The church of God in Smyrna sends greetings to the church in Philomelia and to all the communities of the holy and universal Church everywhere. May mercy, peace, and love from God the Father and our Lord Jesus Christ abound to you all.

{1:1} We write to you, brothers and sisters, about those who were martyred and about the blessed Polycarp, who brought an end to the persecution by his steadfast testimony. Nearly everything that occurred before was intended by the Lord to demonstrate to us the testimony that aligns with the gospel from above. {1:2} For he endured betrayal, just as the Lord did, so that we might follow his example—not only caring for our own concerns but also for those of our neighbors. True and steadfast love does not merely seek its own salvation but desires the salvation of all brethren as well.

{2:1} Therefore, all the testimonies that occurred according to the will of God are blessed and noble, for it is fitting that we should be diligent and acknowledge God's sovereignty over all things. {2:2} Who would not marvel at their nobility, endurance, and obedience? Even when they were beaten so severely that the inner workings of their flesh were exposed, they endured. The bystanders were moved to compassion and lamentation, while some reached such heights of nobility that they did not cry out or groan. This showed us all that in their hour of martyrdom for Christ, they departed, suffering in the flesh, yet the Lord Himself stood by them. {2:3} By embracing the grace of Christ, they scorned the tortures of this world, gaining through their endurance in a single hour deliverance from eternal punishment. The intense fires of their tormentors felt cold to them, for they kept in mind the eternal and unquenchable fire they sought to escape. With the eyes of their hearts, they looked towards the unseen blessings reserved for those who endure—blessings which no ear has heard, no eye has seen, and which have not entered into the heart of man. These were revealed to them by the Lord, transforming them from mere mortals into already angelic beings. {2:4} Likewise, those condemned to wild beasts endured dreadful punishments, lying on beds of spikes and subjected to various tortures. The tyrants hoped that relentless suffering might compel them to renounce their faith, if such a thing were possible.

{3:1} The devil devised many schemes against them, but thanks be to God, he did not overcome them all. The courageous Germanicus, renowned for his patience, strengthened their resolve, bravely facing wild beasts in combat. When the proconsul urged him to reconsider, appealing to his youth, Germanicus intentionally provoked the wild beasts, seeking a swift release from their unjust and lawless existence. {3:2} Witnessing this, the crowds marveled at the noble character of the Christians who loved and feared God, calling out, "Away with the atheists! Let Polycarp be found."

{4:1} A man named Quintus, newly arrived from Phrygia, trembled at the sight of the wild beasts. He had previously compelled himself and others to surrender voluntarily. The proconsul, with much insistence, pressured Quintus to swear oaths and offer sacrifices. Therefore, brothers, we do not commend those who surrender themselves, as the gospel does not teach such things.

{5:1} Polycarp, ever admirable, remained calm upon hearing these events initially, choosing to stay in the city. However, persuaded by the majority, he secretly withdrew and went to a villa not far from the city. There, with a few companions, he devoted himself day and night to prayer for all people and the churches worldwide, as was his custom. {5:2} While praying, three days before his capture, Polycarp fell into a trance. He saw his pillow engulfed in flames. Turning to those with him, he prophetically declared, "I must be burned alive."

{6:1} As those who pursued him continued their search, Polycarp moved to another villa. Soon after, his pursuers arrived. Failing to find him, they arrested two young men. Under torture, one of them confessed, unable to escape notice since those who betrayed him were from his own household. Eirenarchus, also known as Cleronomus, hurried to bring him to the arena, eager to fulfill his duty by making Polycarp a witness for Christ, and ensuring that his betrayers faced the same fate as Judas.

{7:1} Holding the young man with them, on the day before the Sabbath, at the hour of evening, soldiers and horsemen, armed as if going after a thief, set out. Late in the evening, they discovered him in an upper room of a certain house. Though Polycarp could have escaped to another place, he refused, saying, "May the Lord's will be done." {7:2} Upon hearing they were there, he came down and spoke with them. Those present marveled at his strength and vitality despite his advanced age, and at the effort required to apprehend him. He immediately asked for food and drink to be served to them, and requested an hour to pray undisturbed. {7:3} Allowed this, he stood and prayed, filled with the grace of God, unable to stop for two hours. Those who heard him were amazed, and many regretted coming against such a venerable man of God.

{8:1} After finishing his prayer, during which he remembered everyone he had encountered, from the least to the greatest, noble and ordinary alike, and prayed for the entire Catholic Church worldwide, the time came for his departure. They seated him on a donkey and led him into the city on the great Sabbath day. {8:2} Eirenarch Herodes and his father Nicetes met him in a chariot and invited him to join them, urging him, "What harm is there in saying, 'Caesar is Lord,' and sacrificing, to save yourself?" Initially, Polycarp remained silent, but when they persisted, he firmly replied, "I will not do what you advise." {8:3} Failing to persuade him, they hurled dreadful threats at him and forcibly pushed him out of the chariot, causing him to injure his leg. Ignoring the pain, he proceeded eagerly and zealously toward the arena, where the clamor was so loud that no one could hear anything else.

{9:1} As Polycarp entered the arena, a voice from heaven spoke to him, "Be strong and show yourself a man, O Polycarp." Though no one saw the speaker, those present among our people heard the voice. The arrival of Polycarp caused a great commotion in the arena. {9:2} When brought before the proconsul, he was asked if he was Polycarp. Upon confessing his identity, the proconsul urged him to deny his faith, saying, "Respect your age. Swear by the fortune of Caesar. Repent. Curse the Christians." Polycarp, with a solemn gaze at the lawless mob in the arena, gestured with his hand, sighed, and looked up to heaven, declaring, "Away with the Atheists!"{9:3} Pressed further by the proconsul to swear and revile Christ to gain his freedom, Polycarp responded firmly, "For eighty-six years I have served Christ, and He has never wronged me. How can I blaspheme my King who saved me?"

{10:1} When the proconsul persisted and demanded, "Swear by the fortune of Caesar," Polycarp replied firmly, "If you think I will swear by the fortune of Caesar as you suggest, and if you pretend not to know who I am, listen clearly: I am a Christian. If you wish to understand the teachings of Christianity, give me a day to speak, and listen to what I have to say." {10:2} The proconsul replied, "Convince the people." But Polycarp answered, "I consider you worthy to hear my explanation, for we are taught to give due respect, which does not harm us, to the authorities appointed by God. But those who are not worthy, I will not defend before them."

{11:1} The proconsul insisted, "I have wild beasts; I will throw you to them unless you repent." Polycarp responded firmly, "Bring them forth. For it is impossible for us to turn from good to evil. It is good to turn from wicked deeds to righteous ones." {11:2} Again, the proconsul threatened, "I will burn you with fire if you despise the wild beasts, unless you repent." Polycarp calmly replied, "You threaten me with a fire that burns briefly and then goes out. You are ignorant of the fire of the coming judgment and the eternal punishment awaiting the wicked. But why delay? Bring whatever you wish."

{12:1} As Polycarp spoke these words and more, he was filled with courage and joy, his face radiant with grace. Far from being troubled by the accusations hurled at him, he amazed the proconsul, who sent his herald into the arena once more to proclaim loudly: "Polycarp has declared himself to be a Christian." {12:2} Upon hearing this proclamation, the crowd in Smyrna, consisting of both Gentiles and Jews, erupted in uncontrollable anger and shouted loudly, "This man is the teacher of impiety, the leader of the Christians, the one who destroys our gods! He teaches many not to sacrifice or worship the gods!" With these accusations, they demanded that the Asiarch Philip release a lion against Polycarp. However, Philip refused, stating that he could not do so as the display of wild beasts had already concluded. {12:3} They then unanimously decided to call for Polycarp to be burned alive, fulfilling the vision he had seen on his pillow, where he prophetically declared, while seeing it burning, "I must be burned alive," turning to the faithful who were with him.

{13:1} These events unfolded so swiftly that they took less time than recounting them. The crowd quickly gathered logs and kindling from workshops and baths, with the Jews particularly eager to assist, as was their custom in such matters. {13:2} When the pyre was prepared, Polycarp removed his garments and untied his girdle. He attempted to remove his shoes, a gesture he had not typically done before, as each of the faithful desired to touch his body first. Even before his martyrdom, he was adorned with every virtue due to his exemplary life. {13:3} They then placed the prepared materials around him on the pyre. As they were about to nail him to it, he requested, "Let me be. The one who has granted me to endure this fire will also enable me to remain on the pyre without the need for your nails."

{14:1} They did not nail him, but bound his hands behind him. Like a prized ram chosen from a large flock for sacrifice, he prepared himself as a whole burnt offering acceptable to God. Looking up to heaven, he prayed, "O Lord God Almighty, Father of your beloved Son Jesus Christ, through whom we have received knowledge of you, God of angels and powers, of all creation, and of all the righteous who have lived before you, {14:2} I thank you for deeming me worthy of this day and hour, to share in the number of martyrs, to drink from the cup of your Christ unto eternal life, both of soul and body, in the incorruptibility of the Holy Spirit. May I be received among them today as a rich and acceptable sacrifice before you, as you have prepared and revealed beforehand, you who are the infallible and true God. {14:3} Therefore, for all these things, I praise you, bless you, and glorify you, together with the eternal and heavenly Jesus Christ, your beloved Son, with whom, to you and the Holy Spirit, be glory now and forever. Amen.

{15:1} After saying Amen and finishing his prayer, the men overseeing the fire lit it. A great flame burst forth, and those of us who witnessed it saw a remarkable sight. We were spared to witness and report to others what occurred. {15:2} The fire formed a dome-like shape, like a sail filled with wind, protecting the martyr's body all around. In the midst of the flame, his body did not burn like flesh but appeared as if baking bread or glowing like gold and silver in a furnace. We also perceived a sweet-smelling fragrance, as though from incense or some other precious perfume.

{16:1} Finally, realizing that Polycarp's body could not be consumed by the fire, these wicked men ordered the executioner to approach and thrust in a sword. When this was done, a dove and a flow of blood poured forth, extinguishing the fire. The multitude marveled at the stark contrast between the unbelievers and the chosen ones. {16:2} Among these chosen ones was the remarkable martyr Polycarp, who in our time served as an apostolic and prophetic teacher, and as bishop of the Catholic Church in Smyrna. Every word he spoke from his mouth has been fulfilled and will continue to be fulfilled.

{17:1} However, the evil one, the adversary and envier of humanity, seeing the greatness of his testimony and his blameless conduct from the beginning, how he was adorned with a crown of immortality and received an indescribable prize, plotted that not even a relic of him should be taken by us, though many desired to do so and to venerate his holy remains. {17:2} Therefore, Nicetes, the father of Herodes and brother of Alce, was bribed to influence the governor not to give Polycarp's body for burial. "Lest," they said, "they abandon the crucified Christ and begin to worship this man." These words were spoken at the instigation of the Jews, who also kept watch when we attempted to remove the body from the fire, unaware that we could never forsake Christ, who suffered for the salvation of the whole world, nor could we worship anyone else. {17:3} We worship Christ as the Son of God, but we honor the martyrs as disciples and followers of the Lord, loving them for their unparalleled devotion to their King and Teacher. May we be counted among their companions and fellow disciples.

{18:1} Therefore, seeing the conflict that had arisen among the Jews, the centurion placed Polycarp's body in the midst of the fire and burned it. {18:2} Afterwards, we gathered up his bones, more precious than jewels, and laid them in a fitting place. {18:3} There, as much as we are allowed, when we come together with joy and celebration, the Lord will enable us to commemorate the martyrs' day, honoring the memory of those who have fought the good fight and preparing ourselves for the challenges to come.

{19:1} Such were the events surrounding the blessed Polycarp, who, along with others from Philadelphia, became the twelfth martyr in Smyrna. Yet he alone is remembered universally, even among the Gentiles, not only as a distinguished teacher but also as an outstanding martyr. His witness is something we strive to emulate, for it was in accordance with the teachings of Christ. {19:2} By enduring patiently against the unjust authorities and receiving the crown of immortality, he rejoiced with the apostles and all the righteous, glorifying God the Father and blessing our Lord Jesus Christ, the Savior of our souls, the guide of our bodies, and the shepherd of the Catholic Church throughout the world.

{20:1} You have desired a more detailed account of these events, but for now, we have conveyed them briefly through our brother Marcus. Now, when you have read these things, pass on this letter to the brethren who are farther away, so that they too may glorify the Lord who selects from among his own servants. {20:2} To him who has the power to bring us all into his eternal kingdom through his grace and gift, by his only-begotten Son Jesus Christ, be glory, honor, strength, and majesty forever. Amen. Greet all the saints. Those who are with us send greetings to you, as does Evarestus who transcribed these accounts, and all his household.

{21:1} Now, the blessed Polycarp was martyred on the second day of the month Xanthicus, which is the twenty-fifth of April, on the great Sabbath, at the eighth hour. He was apprehended by Herodes during the high priesthood of Philip of Tralles, while Statius Quadratus served as proconsul. To Jesus Christ, the eternal king, may there be glory, honor, majesty, and an eternal throne from generation to generation. Amen.

{22:1} Brothers and sisters, we pray that you may walk faithfully according to the teachings of the gospel of Jesus Christ. May glory be given to God the Father and the Holy Spirit for the salvation of the chosen ones, as witnessed by the blessed Polycarp. May we follow in his footsteps in the kingdom of Jesus Christ. {22:2} These writings were transcribed by Gaius from the manuscripts of Irenaeus, who was a disciple of Polycarp and a fellow citizen of Irenaeus. I, Socrates, then made a copy in Corinth based on Gaius's copies. May grace be with all of you. {22:3} Later, I, Pionius, copied them from the aforementioned copies, diligently seeking them out after the blessed Polycarp revealed them to me through a revelation, as I will explain in what follows. I gathered these writings together when they were almost lost to time, so that the Lord Jesus Christ may gather me also with his chosen ones into his heavenly kingdom. Glory be to him together with the Father and the Holy Spirit, forever and ever. Amen.

Martyrdom of Isaiah

The Martyrdom of Isaiah is an early Christian pseudepigraphal text that forms part of the larger work known as the Ascension of Isaiah. Likely composed between the 1st and 3rd centuries CE, this text combines elements of Jewish and Christian traditions, portraying the persecution and eventual martyrdom of the prophet Isaiah under the reign of King Manasseh of Judah. The narrative reflects themes of divine revelation, apocalyptic vision, and the conflict between true prophecy and falsehood, encapsulating early Christian concerns with martyrdom and the righteousness of the faithful in the face of oppression. The Martyrdom of Isaiah is significant for its portrayal of Isaiah as a precursor to Christian martyrdom, offering a bridge between Jewish prophetic tradition and Christian theological development.

{1:1} In the twenty-sixth year of King Hezekiah's reign over Judah, he called his only son, Manasseh, into his presence. {1:2} He also summoned Isaiah, the son of Amoz, the prophet, and Josab, the son of Isaiah, to be there as well. {1:3-7} While Hezekiah was giving commands, and Josab, the son of Isaiah, stood by, Isaiah spoke to Hezekiah the king, but not only in the presence of Manasseh did he say these words: "As surely as the Lord lives, whose name has not been sent into this world, and as the Beloved of my Lord lives, and as the Spirit who speaks through me lives, all these commands and words you have given will be undone by your son Manasseh. Through him, I will suffer great torment and my body will be tortured. {1:8} Sammael Malchira will serve Manasseh and fulfill all his desires, and Manasseh will follow Beliar rather than me. {1:9} Many in Jerusalem and Judah will be led astray by him, abandoning the true faith, and Beliar will dwell in Manasseh. Through his actions, I will be sawn apart." {1:10} When Hezekiah heard these words, he wept bitterly, tore his clothes, covered his head with earth, and fell on his face. {1:11} Then Isaiah said to him, "The counsel of Sammael against Manasseh is already accomplished; nothing can stop it." {1:12} On that day, Hezekiah made up his mind to kill his son, Manasseh. {1:13} But Isaiah told Hezekiah, "The Beloved has rendered your plan ineffective, and the intention of your heart will not be fulfilled, for I have been called to this fate, and I will inherit the heritage of the Beloved."

{2:1} After Hezekiah died and Manasseh became king, he forgot the commands of his father, Hezekiah, and did not remember them. Sammael took hold of Manasseh and stayed with him. {2:2} Manasseh abandoned the service of the God of his father and instead served Satan, his angels, and his powers. {2:3} He turned away from the teachings of wisdom that had been upheld in his father Hezekiah's house, and from the service of God. Manasseh directed his heart to serve Beliar, the angel of lawlessness, who is the ruler of this world, and whose name is Matanbuchus. {2:4} Beliar took pleasure in Jerusalem because of Manasseh and strengthened him in leading Israel into apostasy and spreading lawlessness throughout Jerusalem. {2:5} Witchcraft, magic, divination, and augury increased, along with fornication, adultery, and the persecution of the righteous by Manasseh, Belchira, Tobia the Canaanite, and John of Anathoth, along with Zadok, the chief of the works. {2:6} The rest of Manasseh's deeds are recorded in the book of the Kings of Judah and Israel. {2:7} When Isaiah, the son of Amoz, saw the lawlessness being committed in Jerusalem, and the worship of Satan and his wickedness, he withdrew from Jerusalem and settled in Bethlehem of Judah. {2:8} However, there was also much lawlessness in Bethlehem, so he withdrew again and settled on a mountain in a desert place. {2:9} Micaiah the prophet, the aged Ananias, Joel, Habakkuk, Josab (Isaiah's son), and many of the faithful who believed in the ascension into heaven also withdrew and settled on the mountain with him. {2:10} They all wore garments made of hair, and they were all prophets. They had nothing with them but were naked, and they all mourned greatly because of Israel's waywardness. {2:11} They ate nothing except wild herbs that they gathered on the mountains. After cooking them, they lived on these herbs along with Isaiah the prophet. They spent two years on the mountains and hills. {2:12} After this time, while they were in the desert, there was a man in Samaria named Belchira, of the family of Zedekiah, the son of Chenaan, a false prophet who lived in Bethlehem. Hezekiah, the son of Chanani, who was the brother of Belchira's father and had been the teacher of the 400 prophets of Baal during the days of Ahab, king of Israel, {2:13} had once struck and reproved Micaiah, the son of Amada, the prophet. Micaiah had been reproved by Ahab and cast into prison. He was with Zedekiah the prophet and they were with Ahaziah, the son of Ahab, king in Samaria. {2:14} Elijah, the prophet from Tishbe in Gilead, reproved Ahaziah and Samaria, prophesying that Ahaziah would die on his sickbed and that Samaria would be handed over to Leba Nasr because he had slain the prophets of God. {2:15} When the false prophets, who were with Ahaziah, son of Ahab, and their teacher Gemarias of Mount Joel, who was the brother of Zedekiah, heard these things, they persuaded Ahaziah, the king of Akkaron, and they killed Micaiah.

{3:1} Belchira, living in Bethlehem and a follower of Manasseh, falsely prophesied in Jerusalem and gained many allies, though he was a Samaritan. {3:2} When the Assyrian king captured Samaria, taking the tribes captive, young Belchira escaped to Jerusalem during Hezekiah's reign. {3:3} Fearing Hezekiah, he did not follow his father's ways. {3:4} In Jerusalem, he spoke lawlessness. {3:5} Accused by Hezekiah's servants, he fled to Bethlehem. {3:6} Belchira accused Isaiah and the prophets of predicting Jerusalem's downfall and the captivity of Judah. {3:8} He claimed Isaiah lied, even saying he saw God, which Moses said was impossible. {3:9} He accused Isaiah of calling Jerusalem "Sodom" and its leaders "Gomorrah." {3:10} Belchira's accusations pleased Manasseh and his officials, who then seized Isaiah.

Chapter 4: Not Found

{5:1-2} They sawed Isaiah apart with a wooden saw. Belchira and the false prophets mocked and rejoiced at his suffering. {5:3} Belchira, supported by Mechembechus, mocked Isaiah as he was sawn in two. {5:4} Belchira demanded, "Say I have lied, that Manasseh's ways are good, and that my ways are good." {5:5-7} Isaiah, absorbed in a vision of the Lord, remained resolute despite the demands. {5:8} Belchira threatened to turn hearts and compel honor for Isaiah. {5:9} Isaiah replied, "Damned are you and your house. You can take nothing from me but my skin." {5:10-11} They sawed Isaiah in two. Manasseh, Belchira, the false prophets, the princes, and the people watched. {5:12-13} Before his death, Isaiah told the prophets to go to Tyre and Sidon, for this fate was his alone. {5:14} As he was sawn in two, Isaiah's lips spoke through the Holy Spirit until the end.

Epistle of Jesus Christ and King Abgarus

The Epistles of Jesus Christ and Abgarus King of Edessa are apocryphal letters exchanged between Jesus and Abgar V, king of Edessa (now southeastern Turkey). These texts, part of early Christian literature, highlight the blend of history, legend, and theology in early Christianity. Tradition holds that King Abgar, suffering from illness, wrote to Jesus seeking a cure. Jesus' response promised a disciple would come to heal him and bring salvation. This narrative, found in Eusebius of Caesarea's Ecclesiastical History, reflects early Christian missionary efforts and the gospel's spread beyond Jewish territories. The letters suggest an early recognition of Jesus' divinity and authority to perform miracles remotely. Abgar's conversion also illustrates the role of royal support in Christian expansion. Although their authenticity is debated, the epistles remain crucial for understanding early Christian evangelism, the sanctification of historical figures, and ancient religious exchanges.

{1:1} King Abgarus of Edessa sends greetings to Jesus, the good Savior who appears in Jerusalem. {1:2} I have heard about you and your miraculous healings, which are done without the use of medicines or herbs. {1:3} It is reported that you give sight to the blind, make the lame walk, cleanse lepers, cast out unclean spirits and demons, heal those with long-standing illnesses, and even raise the dead. {1:4} Upon hearing all this, I have come to believe one of two things: either you are God himself, who has come down from heaven to do these wonders, or you are the Son of God. {1:5} Because of this, I am writing to you, earnestly requesting that you take the trouble of coming here and healing me of the illness I suffer from. {1:6} I have also heard that the Jews ridicule you and are plotting against you. {1:7} My city may be small, but it is neat and more than large enough for both of us.

{2:1} Abgarus, you are blessed for believing in me without seeing me. {2:2} It is written that those who see me will not believe, so that those who have not seen may believe and have life. {2:3} I must first complete my mission and then return to the One who sent me. {2:4} After my ascension, I will send a disciple to heal you and bring life to you and all with you.

Epistle of Barnabas

The Epistle of Barnabas, dated to the late first or early second century, is a crucial early Christian text that reflects the theological and exegetical development of the time. Although traditionally attributed to Barnabas, modern scholars question its authorship. The epistle is notable for its allegorical interpretation of the Hebrew Scriptures, which it uses to argue that the new covenant in Christ supersedes the old. It critiques Jewish ritual practices and emphasizes the distinction between Christianity and Judaism, viewing Jewish laws as symbolic teachings rather than literal commands. The text also addresses eschatological themes, highlighting early Christian hopes for the end times. By reinterpreting Jewish scriptures, the Epistle of Barnabas offers insights into the early Christian effort to define its identity and relationship with Judaism.

{1:1} Greetings to all of you, sons and daughters, in the name of our Lord Jesus Christ, who loved us with peace. {1:2} I am exceedingly joyful and filled with honor to see the abundant fruits of righteousness among you. Your spirited reception of the spiritual gifts has brought me great joy, and I am hopeful for my own salvation, seeing the outpouring of the Spirit from our loving Lord among you. {1:3} Your presence and spiritual growth have amazed me, and I am convinced that since I started teaching among you, I have gained deeper understanding. The Lord has guided me in the path of righteousness, reinforcing my conviction. {1:4} Therefore, I am deeply obligated to love you more than my own soul, recognizing the profound faith, love, and hope you hold for the promised life. {1:5} Considering this, I find it rewarding to share with you some of what I have received, knowing it will enrich your faith and understanding. {1:6} Thus, I have hurriedly written to you so that you may have complete knowledge alongside your faith. {1:7} The teachings of the Lord are centered on three aspects: the hope of eternal life, its inception, and its fulfillment. {1:8} The Lord, through the prophets, has revealed to us past and present events, and has given us a glimpse into the future. {1:9} As we witness these prophecies coming to fruition, our faith should deepen, and our spirits should soar in reverence towards Him. {1:10} Therefore, not as a superior but as a fellow believer, I will share some insights that will bring you joy in your current circumstances.

{2:1} In these evil days, where Satan wields power over the world, it is crucial for us to be vigilant and deeply consider the commandments of the Lord. Fear and patience are allies of our faith, while endurance and self-control stand as our champions. When these virtues remain pure in the sight of the Lord, Wisdom, Understanding, Knowledge, and Science rejoice alongside them. {2:2} Throughout the prophets, God has made it clear that He does not require sacrifices, burnt offerings, or offerings. He says, "What is the multitude of your sacrifices to Me? I am full of burnt offerings, and I do not desire the fat of lambs or the blood of bulls and goats. When you come to appear before Me, who has required these things from your hands? Stop bringing meaningless offerings; your incense is detestable to Me, and I cannot endure your new moons and sabbaths." {2:3} Therefore, these rituals have been abolished so that the new law of our Lord Jesus Christ, which does not impose such burdens, could introduce a spiritual offering from humanity. As God further declared, "Did I command your ancestors to offer burnt offerings and sacrifices when they came out of Egypt? No, I commanded them to refrain from harboring evil in their hearts against their neighbors and not to love false oaths." {2:4} We, therefore, with understanding, should grasp the merciful intent of our Father. He speaks to us, desiring that unlike our ancestors, we seek how to approach Him rightly. For He tells us, "A sacrifice pleasing to God is a broken spirit; a heart that glorifies Him who created it is a sweet aroma to the Lord." {2:5} Therefore, brethren, let us earnestly inquire about our salvation, lest the evil one, through deceit, should deceive us and cast us away from our true life.

{3:1} Concerning these matters, God questions them again, "Why do you fast to Me on this day, expecting your voice to be heard with cries? I have not chosen this kind of fast, that a person should merely humble their soul. Even if you bow your head like a ring and wear sackcloth and ashes, I will not accept it as a true fast." {3:2} Instead, God tells us, "Here is the fast that I have chosen: not merely to humble your soul, but to loosen the chains of injustice, untie the cords of the yoke, set the oppressed free, break every yoke, share your food with the hungry, provide shelter for the homeless, clothe the naked when you see them, and not turn away from your own flesh and blood." {3:3} Then, your light will break forth like the dawn, and your healing will quickly appear; righteousness will go before you, and the glory of the Lord will be your rear guard. When you call, the Lord will answer; when you cry for help, He will say, "Here am I." If you remove the yoke of oppression, stop pointing fingers and malicious talk, and if you offer yourself to the hungry and satisfy the needs of the oppressed, then your light will rise in the darkness, and your night will become like the noonday. {3:4} Therefore, brethren, God is patient, foreseeing that the people He has prepared will believe in His Beloved with sincerity. He revealed these things beforehand so that we would not hastily accept their laws without understanding the true intent of His commandments.

{4:1} Therefore, it is imperative for us, who seek understanding about the events unfolding, to diligently investigate what can truly save us. Let us completely flee from all sinful deeds, lest they ensnare us, and let us detest the errors of this present age so that we may set our affections on the world to come. We must not allow our souls to run unrestrained with sinners and the wicked, lest we become like them. {4:2} The ultimate stumbling block is approaching, as written by Enoch: "For the Lord has shortened the times and days for this reason, that His Beloved may hasten; and He will come to His inheritance." The prophet also declares, "Ten kings will reign on the earth, and after them a little king will arise who will subdue three of the kings." {4:3} Similarly, Daniel speaks of the same, "I saw a fourth beast, dreadful and powerful, exceedingly strong; it had large iron teeth; it was devouring and breaking in pieces, and trampling the residue with its feet. It was different from all the beasts that were before it, and it had ten horns. I was considering the horns, and there was another horn, a little one, coming up among them, before whom three of the first horns were plucked out by the roots." {4:4} Therefore, understand this, my brethren. I also beseech you, as one among you and loving you individually and collectively more than my own soul, to be vigilant now and guard against falling into sin by rationalizing, "The covenant belongs to both them and us." {4:5} They ultimately lost it after Moses had received it. The Scripture says, "And Moses was fasting forty days and forty nights on Mount Sinai, and received the covenant from the Lord, tables of stone written with the finger of the Lord." But they turned aside to idols, and thus lost it. {4:6} For the Lord said to Moses, "Go down quickly; for the people whom you brought out of the land of Egypt have corrupted themselves." And Moses understood, and cast the two tablets out of his hands, and their covenant was broken, so that the covenant of the beloved Jesus might be sealed upon our hearts, in the hope that flows from believing in Him. {4:7} Now, desiring to write many things to you not as your teacher but as one who loves you, I have taken care to share with you what I myself possess, aiming for your purification. {4:8} Pay earnest attention in these last days, for the whole time of your faith in the past will not benefit you unless now, in this wicked time, we also resist impending sources of danger as becomes the children of God. {4:9} Let us flee from all vanity and hate the works of wickedness completely. Do not isolate yourself as if already fully justified; instead, come together and inquire together about what promotes your common well-being. {4:10} As Scripture says, "Woe to those who are wise in their own eyes and clever in their own sight!" Let us be spiritually-minded and strive to be a perfect temple for God. {4:11} Let us meditate on the fear of God as much as we can and keep His commandments, so that we may rejoice in His ordinances. The Lord will judge the world impartially; each will receive according to what they have done. {4:12} Beware, lest being at ease as the called ones of God, we fall asleep in our sins, allowing the wicked prince to gain power over us and thrust us away from the kingdom of the Lord. {4:13} Pay close attention, my brethren, and reflect on this: after witnessing great signs and wonders in Israel, they were eventually forsaken. Let us be cautious not to fulfill the saying, "Many are called, but few are chosen."

{5:1} The Lord endured to offer His flesh to corruption for this purpose: that through the forgiveness of sins achieved by His sacrificial blood, we might be sanctified. It is written of Him, partly concerning Israel and partly concerning us: "He was wounded for our transgressions, bruised for our iniquities; by His stripes we are healed. He was led as a sheep to the slaughter, and as a lamb before its shearer is silent." Therefore, we owe profound gratitude to the Lord, for He has revealed to us the past, granted us wisdom for the present, and not left us in ignorance of the future. {5:2} The Scripture declares, "Nets are spread out unjustly for birds," meaning that one who, knowing the path of righteousness, rushes into darkness perishes justly. Moreover, my brethren, if the Lord, being Lord of all the world, endured suffering for our souls—He to whom God said at the beginning, "Let us make man in our image, after our likeness"—consider how and why He suffered at the hands of men. {5:3} The prophets, having received grace from Him, prophesied about Him. And because it was necessary for Him to appear in the flesh, He endured in order to abolish death and reveal the resurrection. He fulfilled the promise to the fathers and prepared a new people for Himself, showing during His earthly life that He will judge mankind after raising them. {5:4} While teaching Israel with great miracles and signs, He preached the truth and loved them deeply. But when He chose His apostles to preach the Gospel, He selected sinners above all, demonstrating that He came "not to call the righteous, but sinners to repentance." {5:5} He manifested Himself as the Son of God. For had He not come in the flesh, how could men have been saved by seeing Him? Just as they cannot endure the brightness of the sun, which will eventually cease to exist, so too could they not have endured to see Him without His incarnation. {5:6} The Son of God came in the flesh to bring to completion the sins of those who had persecuted His prophets to death. For this reason, He endured. As God says, "The stroke of His flesh is from them," and "when I strike the Shepherd, the sheep of the flock will be scattered." {5:7} He willingly chose to suffer, for it was necessary for Him to suffer on the cross. As prophesied about Him, "Save my soul from the sword, fasten my flesh with nails; for assemblies of the wicked have risen against me." {5:8} And again, "Behold, I have given my back to those who strike, and my cheeks to those who pluck out the beard; I have not hidden my face from shame and spitting."

{6:1} When He had fulfilled His mission, what does He say? "Who will contend with Me? Let him confront Me. Who is he who will bring charges against Me? Let him draw near to the servant of the Lord." "Woe to you! You will all grow old like a garment, and the moth will devour you." And the prophet adds, "He is laid as a mighty stone for crushing; behold, I lay in Zion a stone, chosen, precious, a cornerstone, honored. Whoever believes in Him will not be put to shame." {6:2} Is our hope then in a mere stone? Far from it. This imagery is used because He established His flesh with power, saying, "He has made me a sure foundation." The prophet also foretold, "The stone which the builders rejected has become the chief cornerstone." And he further prophesied, "This is the day the Lord has made; let us rejoice and be glad in it." {6:3} I write to you plainly so that you may understand. I am the least esteemed among you. What does the prophet say? "The assembly of the wicked surrounded me; they encircled me like bees; they blazed like a fire among thorns, and upon my garment they cast lots." {6:4} Since His coming and suffering in the flesh were about to be revealed, the prophets foretold His sufferings. One prophet laments for Israel, saying, "Woe to their soul! They have devised an evil plan against themselves, saying, 'Let us bind the righteous man because he is inconvenient to us.'" {6:5} Moses also said to them, "Behold what the Lord God says: Enter the good land which the Lord swore to give to Abraham, Isaac, and Jacob, to inherit it—a land flowing with milk and honey." {6:6} What does Wisdom say? "Trust in Him who will be revealed to you in the flesh, that is, Jesus." For man was formed from the earth in a suffering state, as Adam was made from the face of the ground. {6:7} What does "a land flowing with milk and honey" mean? Blessed be our Lord, who has placed in us wisdom and understanding of hidden things. For the prophet says, "Who will understand the parable of the Lord except the wise and prudent, those who love Him?" {6:8} Therefore, having been renewed by the forgiveness of our sins, He has recreated us according to a new pattern, so that we may possess childlike souls, for He created us anew by His Spirit. As Scripture says about us, when God speaks to the Son, "Let us make man in our image, after our likeness, and let them have dominion over the beasts of the earth, the birds of heaven, and the fish of the sea." {6:9} And when the Lord beheld His fair creation, man, He said, "Increase and multiply, and fill the earth." These things were spoken to the Son. Again, I will show you how He has made a second creation in us in these last days. The Lord says, "Behold, I will make the last like the first." {6:10} Therefore the prophet said, "Enter into the land flowing with milk and honey, and have dominion over it." See, we have been remade, as another prophet says, "Behold, says the Lord, I will take away their stony hearts and give them hearts of flesh," because He was to appear in flesh and dwell among us. {6:11} For, my brethren, the dwelling place of our hearts is a holy temple to the Lord. For again the Lord says, "With what shall I come before the Lord, and bow myself before the high God? Shall I come before Him with burnt offerings, with calves a year old?" {6:12} He says, "I will declare to you in the assembly, 'I will praise you among my brethren.' I am led into the good land with you. What, then, do milk and honey signify? Just as an infant is kept alive first by honey, then by milk, so we, being revived and sustained by faith in the promise and the word, shall live, ruling over the earth." {6:13} He said above, "Let them increase and have dominion over the fish." Who then is able to rule over the beasts, the fish, or the birds of heaven? For we must understand that to rule implies authority, so that one commands and governs. If this does not yet exist, He has promised it to us. When? When we ourselves have been perfected to become heirs of the covenant of the Lord.

{7:1} Understand, therefore, you children of joy, that the gracious Lord has revealed everything to us so that we may know whom we should render thanksgiving and praise for all things. If the Son of God, who is the Lord of all and will judge the living and the dead, suffered to give us life through His sacrifice, then we must believe that His suffering was for our sake alone. Even when He was nailed to the cross, they offered Him vinegar mixed with gall. Consider how the priests of the people foreshadowed this. By His commandment, the Lord ordained that whoever did not observe the fast should be put to death, for He Himself was to offer the vessel of His Spirit as a sacrifice for our sins, fulfilling the type established with Isaac when he was offered on the altar. {7:2} What does the prophet say about this? "Let them eat of the goat which is offered, with fasting, for all their sins." Pay close attention: "And let only the priests eat the inner parts, unwashed with vinegar." Why so? Because to me, who will offer my flesh for the sins of my new people, you will give gall mixed with vinegar to drink. You priests eat alone, while the people fast and mourn in sackcloth and ashes. These actions were to demonstrate that His suffering was necessary for them. How did the commandment go, then? Listen carefully: "Take two good-looking goats, similar to each other, and offer them. Let the priest take one as a sin offering." {7:3} What should they do with the other goat? "Cursed," He says, "is this one." See now how this typifies Jesus. "All of you spit upon it, pierce it, and wrap its head with scarlet wool, and then send it into the wilderness." After doing all this, the one who carries the goat takes it into the desert, removes the wool, and places it on a thorny shrub called Rachia, whose fruits we eat when found in the fields. Its fruits alone are sweet. Why is this so again? Pay close attention: "One goat on the altar, the other cursed." And why do you see the cursed one crowned? Because on that day they will see Him coming with a scarlet robe from His head to His feet, and they will say, "Is this not the One we once despised, pierced, mocked, and crucified? Truly, this is the One who declared Himself to be the Son of God." {7:4} How similar He is to Him! This is why the goats had to be good-looking and identical, so that when they see Him coming, they would be amazed at the resemblance of the goat. Behold, this is the type of Jesus who was destined to suffer. But why do they place the wool amidst thorns? It is a representation of Jesus presented before the Church. They place the wool among thorns so that whoever wishes to take it must undergo much suffering, for the thorn is formidable, and thus they can obtain it only through suffering and tribulation. {7:5} Therefore, He says, "Those who desire to see Me and possess My kingdom must obtain Me through tribulation and suffering."

{8:1} What do you think this symbolizes? A command was given to Israel that men of great wickedness should offer a heifer, slay and burn it, and then boys should take the ashes and put them in vessels. They would bind purple wool around a stick along with hyssop, and sprinkle the people one by one to purify them from their sins. Consider how simply He speaks to you. The heifer represents Jesus: the sinful men offering it are those who led Him to the slaughter. But now these men are no longer guilty; they are no longer considered sinners. The boys who sprinkle the ashes represent those who proclaim to us the forgiveness of sins and the purification of the heart. Jesus gave them authority to preach the Gospel, twelve in number, corresponding to the twelve tribes of Israel. {8:2} But why are there three boys sprinkling? This corresponds to Abraham, Isaac, and Jacob, who were held in high esteem by God. And why was the wool placed on the wood? Because through the wood, symbolizing the cross, Jesus established His kingdom, so that those who believe in Him shall live forever. But why was hyssop used with the wool? Because in His kingdom, during the evil and polluted days in which we are saved, those who suffer physically are cleansed by the purifying power of hyssop. These things are clear to us for this reason, but were obscure to them because they did not heed the voice of the Lord.

{9:1} He also speaks about our ears, how He has circumcised both them and our hearts. The Lord says in the prophet, "They obeyed me when they heard with their ears." And again He says, "Those who are far off will hear and know what I have done." And, "Circumcise your hearts, says the Lord." Again He says, "Hear, O Israel, for thus says the Lord your God." And once more the Spirit of the Lord proclaims, "Whoever desires to live forever, let him hear the voice of my servant." And He says again, "Hear, O heavens, and give ear, O earth, for God has spoken." These are the proofs. And again He says, "Hear the word of the Lord, you rulers of this people." And He says again, "Hear, you children, the voice of one crying in the wilderness." Therefore, He has circumcised our ears so that we may hear His word and believe, because the physical circumcision in which they trusted has been abolished. {9:2} For He declared that circumcision is not merely of the flesh, but they transgressed because an evil angel deluded them. He says to them, "These things says the Lord your God" — here is a new commandment — "Do not sow among thorns, but circumcise yourselves to the Lord." And why does He speak thus? "Circumcise the stubbornness of your heart, and do not harden your neck." And again: "Behold, all the nations are uncircumcised in the flesh, but this people are uncircumcised in heart." But you might say, "Yes, indeed, the people are circumcised as a seal." But so are all Syrians, Arabs, and all idol priests. Are they also within the covenant bond? Yes, even the Egyptians practice circumcision. {9:3} Learn then, my children, about these things in detail. Abraham, who first instituted circumcision, looking forward in spirit to Jesus, practiced this rite, having received the mysteries of the three letters. For the Scripture says, "Abraham circumcised eighteen and three hundred men of his household." What then was the knowledge given to him in this? Learn about the eighteen first, and then the three hundred. The ten and the eight are thus denoted — Ten by I, and Eight by H. You have the initials of the name Jesus. And because the cross was to express the grace of our redemption by the letter T, he also says, "Three Hundred." He thus signifies Jesus by two letters and the cross by one. He knows this, who has implanted in us the engrafted gift of His teaching. No one has been admitted by me to a more excellent piece of knowledge than this, but I know that you are worthy.

{10:1} Why did Moses instruct, "You shall not eat the swine, nor the eagle, nor the hawk, nor the raven, nor any fish without scales?" He considered three spiritual doctrines in giving these commands. The Lord also said in Deuteronomy, "I will establish my ordinances among this people." Is there not a divine commandment against eating these things? Indeed there is, but Moses spoke with spiritual insight. He mentioned the swine to signify, "Do not associate with people who resemble swine." For when they live in luxury, they forget their Lord; but in times of need, they acknowledge Him. Similarly, the swine does not recognize its owner after it has eaten, but cries out when hungry and quiets down after being fed. "Nor shall you eat," he says, "the eagle, nor the hawk, nor the kite, nor the raven." This means, "Do not join yourself to those who do not work for their own sustenance but seize what belongs to others through wickedness. Though they may appear simple, they are always ready to exploit others." These birds, while idle, constantly plot how to devour the flesh of others, proving themselves pests through their wickedness. {10:2} "And you shall not eat the lamprey, or the polypus, or the cuttlefish." This means, "Do not resemble or join those who persist in ungodliness and face condemnation." Like these cursed fishes that lurk in the deep, not swimming like others on the surface but dwelling in the mud at the bottom. Furthermore, "You shall not eat the hare." Why? "Do not become corrupt like those who defile the innocence of children." The hare multiplies its offspring, equaling its years of life. Also, "You shall not eat the hyena." This means, "Do not be an adulterer or a corrupter, or resemble those who change their nature." The hyena changes its sex annually, being male at one time and female at another. Likewise, Moses rightly condemned the weasel, meaning, "Do not be like those who commit wickedness with their mouth due to their impurity, nor join with immoral women who engage in sinful acts with their mouths, for this animal conceives through its mouth." {10:3} Moses thus established three doctrines regarding meats with spiritual significance, but they misunderstood them in a literal sense, focused only on physical foods. However, David understood the deeper meaning and spoke similarly: "Blessed is the man who has not walked in the counsel of the ungodly," likening them to fishes that dwell in darkness in the depths; "and has not stood in the way of sinners," akin to those who profess reverence for the Lord but stray like swine; "and has not sat in the seat of scoffers," akin to birds that lie in wait for prey. Grasp firmly this spiritual knowledge. Moreover, Moses further commanded, "You shall eat every animal that is cloven-footed and ruminant." What does this mean? The ruminant animal symbolizes one who, after receiving nourishment, acknowledges the One who provides and is visibly content. Moses wisely spoke in consideration of this commandment. What, then, does it signify? That we should associate with those who fear the Lord, who meditate on His commandments in their hearts, speak and observe His judgments, and find joy in contemplating His word. {10:4} And what about being cloven-footed? It signifies that the righteous walk in this world while looking forward to the holy future ahead. See how wisely Moses legislated. But how could they understand or grasp these truths? Therefore, we, understanding His commandments rightly, interpret them as the Lord intended. For this reason, He has circumcised our ears and hearts so that we may comprehend these things fully.

{11:1} Let's delve deeper into whether the Lord intended to foreshadow baptism and the cross in the Old Testament. Concerning baptism with water, it was written about the Israelites that they did not receive the baptism leading to the forgiveness of sins, but instead sought after another. The prophet rebukes them, saying, "Be astonished, O heavens, and tremble with fear, for this people has committed two great evils: they have forsaken Me, the fountain of living waters, and dug for themselves broken cisterns. Is Zion, my holy hill, now a desolate rock? You shall be like birds that fly away when their nests are disturbed." And another prophet declares, "I will go before you and level the mountains; I will break down the gates of bronze and cut through the bars of iron. I will give you hidden treasures, so that you may know that I am the Lord." Also, "He shall dwell in a lofty cave of the strong rock." Moreover, speaking of the Son, it is said, "His water is sure; you shall see the King in His glory, and your soul shall meditate on the fear of the Lord." And in another prophecy, "The one who does these things shall be like a tree planted by streams of water, which yields its fruit in season; and its leaf does not wither, and all that he does shall prosper. But the wicked are not so; they are like chaff that the wind blows away. Therefore, the wicked will not stand in the judgment, nor sinners in the assembly of the righteous; for the Lord knows the way of the righteous, but the way of the wicked will perish." {11:2} Notice how He has depicted both water and the cross together. These words imply, "Blessed are those who, trusting in the cross, have entered the water; for they will receive their reward in due time." He continues, "I will recompense them." Now He says, "Their leaves shall not fade." This means that every word spoken in faith and love will lead to the conversion and hope of many. Another prophet adds, "And the land of Jacob will be praised above every land," signifying the vessel of His Spirit, which He will glorify. Furthermore, "And there was a river flowing on the right, and from it arose beautiful trees; and whoever eats of them will live forever." This signifies that although we descend into the water full of sins and impurities, we emerge bearing fruit in our hearts, with reverence for God and faith in Jesus in our spirits. "And whoever eats of these will live forever," meaning that whoever hears you speak and believes will have eternal life.

{12:1} Similarly, the cross of Christ is foreshadowed by another prophet who asks, "When will these things be fulfilled?" And the Lord replies, "When a tree is bent down and rises again, and when blood flows from wood." This is yet another indication concerning the cross and the crucifixion of Him who was to suffer. Moses also speaks of this when Israel was attacked by enemies. To remind them that their deliverance from death was due to their sins, the Spirit moved Moses to make a figure of the cross and of Him who would suffer upon it. Unless they put their trust in Him, they would be forever defeated. Moses thus lifted up a staff on the hill, with one weapon above another, standing higher than all the people. With his hands stretched forth, Israel prevailed. Yet when he lowered his hands, they faltered again. Why? To teach them that their salvation depended on trusting in Him alone. Another prophet declares, "All day long I have stretched forth My hands to a disobedient and contrary people." Moses also prefigures Jesus, showing it was necessary for Him to suffer and become the giver of life, though they believed Him destroyed on the cross when Israel was failing. {12:2} Since Eve's transgression through the serpent, the Lord caused every kind of serpent to bite them, showing that because of their sin, they faced death. Moses commanded, "You shall not make for yourselves a carved or molded image as your God," revealing a type of Jesus. Moses made a bronze serpent and placed it on a pole, assembling the people and instructing them that if bitten, they should look upon the serpent with hope and belief, even though it was dead, trusting it could give them life. Immediately, they were healed when they did so. Here too is a glimpse of the glory of Jesus, for all things are in Him and through Him. Moses also speaks to Joshua, prophetically naming him so the people would hear that the Father would reveal all things about His Son Jesus to Joshua. He instructed Joshua to write down that the Son of God would ultimately destroy the house of Amalek. {12:3} Jesus, revealed both in type and in the flesh, is not merely the Son of man but the Son of God. Knowing that people would claim Christ to be the son of David, fearing and understanding the error of the wicked, he declares, "The Lord said to my Lord, 'Sit at My right hand, until I make Your enemies Your footstool.'" Isaiah also prophesies, "The Lord said to Christ, my Lord, whose right hand I have held, that the nations should submit before Him, and I will break the strength of kings." See how David calls Him both Lord and the Son of God.

{13:1} Let's examine whether this people are the rightful heirs or if another precedes them, and to whom the covenant truly belongs. Consider what Scripture says about the people: Isaac prayed for his wife Rebecca because she was barren, and she conceived. Rebecca, seeking guidance from the Lord, received a profound answer: "Two nations are in your womb, and two peoples from within you shall be divided; the one people shall be stronger than the other, and the older shall serve the younger." We must grasp the identities of Isaac and Rebecca and understand the significance of God's declaration that one people would surpass the other. {13:2} In another prophecy, Jacob speaks clearly to his son Joseph, saying, "Behold, the Lord has not deprived me of your presence; bring your sons to me, that I may bless them." Joseph brought Manasseh and Ephraim, expecting Manasseh, the elder, to be blessed. Joseph positioned Manasseh at Jacob's right hand. However, Jacob, guided by spiritual insight into the future of the people, altered his actions, placing his right hand on the younger son Ephraim's head to bless him instead. Joseph objected, asking Jacob to bless Manasseh, the firstborn. But Jacob affirmed, "I know it, my son, I know it; he also shall become a people, and he also shall be great. Nevertheless, his younger brother shall be greater than he, and his offspring shall become a multitude of nations." {13:3} Thus, Jacob clearly indicated through whom the covenant and blessings would pass. If we consider Abraham's role, our understanding is further enriched. What did God say to Abraham? "Because you have believed, it is counted to you as righteousness. Behold, I have made you the father of many nations." This signifies not only those who are circumcised but also those who believe in the Lord while still uncircumcised. Thus, the true heirs of the covenant and the promise are those who follow in the footsteps of faith, regardless of their physical circumcision.

{14:1} Indeed, let us examine whether the Lord has truly given us the covenant promised to the fathers. He did give it, but the people were unworthy due to their sins. As the prophet recounts, "Moses fasted forty days and nights on Mount Sinai to receive the Lord's covenant for the people." The Lord inscribed two tablets with His own finger. Moses descended with these to deliver them to the people, but upon seeing their sin, he cast the tablets down, breaking them. Moses received the covenant, yet the people proved unworthy. {14:2} Now consider how we have received it differently. Moses, as a servant, received it, but the Lord Himself, in His suffering for us, has given us the covenant so that we might become His chosen people. He was revealed to perfect their transgressions, while we, made heirs through Him, received the testament of the Lord Jesus. His personal manifestation redeemed our hearts from darkness and the bondage of sin, establishing a covenant with us through His word. The Father ordained Him to prepare a holy people, as prophesied: "I, the Lord your God, have called you in righteousness, I will take hold of your hand and keep you. I will make you to be a covenant for the people and a light for the Gentiles, to open eyes that are blind, to free captives from prison and to release from the dungeon those who sit in darkness." {14:3} Thus, we understand our redemption. The prophet further affirms, "I have made you a light for the Gentiles, that my salvation may reach to the ends of the earth." And again, "The Spirit of the Lord is on me, because he has anointed me to proclaim good news to the poor. He has sent me to proclaim freedom for the prisoners and recovery of sight for the blind, to set the oppressed free, to proclaim the year of the Lord's favor and the day of vengeance of our God, to comfort all who mourn."

{15:1} Concerning the Sabbath, it is written in the Decalogue which the Lord spoke to Moses face to face on Mount Sinai, "Sanctify the Sabbath of the Lord with clean hands and a pure heart." And elsewhere it is said, "If my sons keep the Sabbath, then I will pour out my mercy upon them." The Sabbath is mentioned at the beginning of creation: "God made the works of His hands in six days and rested on the seventh day, sanctifying it." Understand this, my children: "He finished in six days" implies that all things will be completed in six thousand years, for a day is like a thousand years to the Lord. As He testifies, "Today will be as a thousand years." Therefore, in six days, meaning six thousand years, all things will be accomplished. "And He rested on the seventh day." This signifies that when His Son returns, He will end the age of the wicked, judge the ungodly, and renew the heavens and the earth. That will be the true rest on the seventh day. {15:2} Furthermore, He commands, "Sanctify it with pure hands and a pure heart." If anyone today claims to sanctify the day that God has sanctified without being pure in heart in all things, they are mistaken. Truly, when we, having received the promise, no longer have wickedness and all things are made new by the Lord, then we will be able to sanctify the Sabbath. We ourselves must first be sanctified. He also says, "Your new moons and your appointed feasts my soul hates." He makes it clear: Your current Sabbaths are not pleasing to Me. But the Sabbath I have established is when I bring rest to all things and initiate the eighth day, which marks the beginning of a new world. Therefore, we celebrate the eighth day with joy, the day on which Jesus rose from the dead. After revealing Himself, He ascended into heaven.

{16:1} Let me explain about the temple and how the misguided Jews, lost in error, put their trust not in God Himself but in the physical temple as if it were God's house. They worshipped Him almost like the Gentiles did, within the temple walls. But listen to how the Lord speaks when He abolishes this notion: "Heaven is My throne, and the earth is My footstool. What kind of house will you build for Me, or where is the place of My rest?" Their hope, you see, is in vain. Furthermore, He prophesies, "Behold, those who have thrown down this temple, they shall rebuild it." This has come to pass; through warfare, their enemies destroyed it, and now they, serving those enemies, will rebuild it. It was also foretold that the city, the temple, and the people of Israel would be handed over. The Scripture says, "In the last days, the Lord will deliver up the sheep of His pasture, their fold, and their tower, to destruction." This prophecy has been fulfilled just as the Lord said. {16:2} Now, let us consider if there is still a temple of God. Indeed, there is one, where He Himself declared He would establish and complete it. As it is written, "When the appointed time is completed, the temple of God shall be built in glory in the name of the Lord." Therefore, I affirm that such a temple exists. Understand how it will be constructed in the name of the Lord. Before we believed in God, our hearts were corrupt and weak, akin to a temple made by human hands. It was filled with idolatry and inhabited by demons due to our disobedience to God's will. But now, observe how it will be built in the name of the Lord, so that the temple of the Lord may be gloriously established. How does this happen? Here's how: having received forgiveness of sins and placing our trust in the name of the Lord, we have been transformed into new beings, recreated from the beginning. {16:3} Therefore, God truly dwells in us. How? Through His word of faith, His promise, His wisdom in His commandments, His doctrine. He prophesies through us, He dwells in us, He opens the doors of the temple—our mouths—previously enslaved by death, and grants us repentance, leading us into the incorruptible temple. Thus, whoever desires salvation looks not to man but to the indwelling presence of God, amazed to hear words spoken through them that they themselves never imagined saying. This is the spiritual temple built for the Lord.

{17:1} To the best of my ability and with clarity, I trust that I have covered all the matters essential for your salvation, omitting nothing that needs your attention now. If I were to write about future events, you would not comprehend, for such knowledge is veiled in parables. Therefore, these are the facts as they stand.

{18:1} Now, let's turn our attention to another type of knowledge and teaching. There exist two paths of doctrine and authority: one of light and the other of darkness. The distinction between these two paths is significant. The angels of God, who bring light, oversee one path, while the angels of Satan govern the other. God reigns as Lord forever and ever, but Satan is the prince of the time of wickedness.

{19:1} The path of light is clear and straightforward. If anyone desires to journey towards the appointed destination, they must be diligent in their actions. The knowledge given to guide us on this path is as follows: Love the Creator who made you; glorify the Redeemer who rescued you from death. Be sincere in heart and abundant in spirit. Do not associate with those who walk in the path of destruction. Detest actions that displease God; reject all forms of hypocrisy. Hold fast to the commandments of the Lord. Be humble and avoid seeking glory for yourself. Do not entertain evil intentions against your neighbor. Guard against arrogance entering your heart. Abstain from sexual immorality and corruption. Let your speech be pure and free from impurity. Show no partiality when reproving others for their wrongs. Be gentle and peaceable. Tremble at the words of truth you hear. Do not harbor ill will against your brother. Have unwavering faith in God's promises. Do not misuse the name of the Lord. Love your neighbor as yourself. Do not participate in abortion or harm children. Teach your children the fear of the Lord from their infancy. Do not covet what belongs to your neighbor; shun greed. Associate with the righteous and humble, not the arrogant. Embrace trials as opportunities for growth. Avoid deceit and hypocrisy, for they lead to destruction. Submit to the Lord and respect earthly authorities. Treat your servants with kindness and fairness. Share with others willingly, knowing God rewards generosity. Do not be quick to speak but strive for purity of soul. Be generous in giving and reluctant to take. Cherish those who share the word of the Lord with you. Remember the day of judgment continually. Seek the company of fellow believers, encourage them, and work to save souls through your actions. Give freely without complaint, trusting in God's promise of reward. Safeguard what you have been entrusted with, neither adding to it nor diminishing it. Maintain a steadfast opposition to evil. Judge with fairness. Work to reconcile those in conflict rather than fostering division. Confess your sins openly. Approach prayer with a clear conscience. This is the path of light.

{20:1} The path of darkness is twisted and filled with curses, leading to eternal death and punishment. Along this path lie the actions that destroy the soul: idolatry, arrogance, abuse of power, hypocrisy, deceit, adultery, murder, theft, pride, disobedience, malice, self-sufficiency, sorcery, greed, lack of reverence for God. Also found on this path are those who persecute the righteous, those who despise truth, those who embrace falsehood, those who do not understand the rewards of righteousness, those who do not uphold goodness, those who neglect justice for widows and orphans, those who do not fear God but pursue wickedness. They are far from meekness and patience, loving vanity and seeking personal gain, showing no pity to the needy, and not helping the oppressed. They are quick to slander, ignorant of their Creator, supporters of abortion, and destroyers of what God has made. They turn away from those in need, oppress the downtrodden, favor the wealthy, unjustly judge the poor, and in every way, they live in defiance of God's law.

{21:1} It is important, therefore, for those who have learned the Lord's commandments, as they are written, to walk in them. Those who keep these commandments will be honored in the kingdom of God, while those who choose otherwise will face destruction because of their deeds. This is why there will be a resurrection, and this is why there will be retribution. I urge you, leaders among you, to heed this counsel out of goodwill: support and show kindness to one another; do not abandon each other. The day is approaching when all things will perish along with the evil one. The Lord is near, bringing His reward. {21:2} Once again, I appeal to you: be fair judges to one another, remain faithful advisors, and rid yourselves of all hypocrisy. May God, who governs the entire world, grant you wisdom, insight, understanding, and knowledge of His judgments, along with patience. {21:3} Seek to be taught by God, diligently inquire what the Lord requires of you, and do it so that you may be secure on the day of judgment. If you remember anything good, think of me, reflecting on these matters, so that my earnest desire and vigilance may bring about some good. I implore you, requesting this as a favor. {21:4} While you are still in this life, do not neglect any of these things. Continually pursue them and fulfill every commandment, for they are worthy pursuits. That is why I have been diligent in writing to you to encourage you as best as I can. Farewell, beloved children of love and peace. May the Lord of glory and grace be with your spirit. Amen.

Epistle of Paul and Seneca

The Epistles of Paul the Apostle to Seneca, often considered apocryphal in nature, represent a fascinating intersection of early Christian thought and Stoic philosophy. These letters, purportedly exchanged between Paul of Tarsus, one of Christianity's most influential apostles, and Lucius Annaeus Seneca, a renowned Roman philosopher and statesman, encapsulate a unique dialogue between two towering figures of the first century CE. While the authenticity of these letters has been a subject of scholarly debate for centuries, their content provides a rich tapestry of theological and philosophical discourse, blending Pauline Christian doctrine with Stoic ethical precepts. The correspondence, if genuine, would signify an extraordinary cross-pollination of ideas, showcasing how Christian teachings could interface with and be understood within the framework of Greco-Roman intellectual traditions. This collection is typically analyzed within the broader context of early Christian apologetics and the Greco-Roman intellectual milieu, reflecting the attempts of early Christians to engage with and influence the dominant cultural and philosophical paradigms of their time. Moreover, the stylistic elements and rhetorical strategies employed in these letters offer insights into the methods by which early Christian thinkers sought to legitimize their beliefs to a skeptical and often hostile pagan audience. Thus, whether viewed as authentic historical documents or as literary constructs designed to advance Christian thought, this Epistle remain a significant subject of study for those interested in the intersections of early Christian theology, classical philosophy, and the sociocultural dynamics of the Roman Empire.

{1. SENECA TO PAUL, greeting} Paul, I believe you've heard about my recent conversation with Lucilius regarding the apocrypha or perhaps the secret teachings, among other topics. Some of your followers were present during our discussion. We met in the gardens of Sallust, and those individuals, unexpectedly encountering us, joined our gathering. We missed having you there and wanted you to know. Your writings have been a source of great inspiration to us. I refer specifically to the numerous letters you've written to various cities and provincial capitals, filled with profound moral teachings. These ideas, I understand, are not merely your own, but they flow through you; sometimes from you directly and at other times through your influence. They are so profound and noble that I believe it would take entire generations to fully absorb and perfect them. Wishing you good health, my brother.

{2. PAUL TO SENECA, greeting} I received your letter with joy yesterday and would have responded immediately if the messenger I intended to send to you had been available. You understand well the importance of timing and discretion in such matters—who should receive what, when, and from whom. Please understand that my delay in responding is out of respect for your esteemed position. Your kind words about my letter bring me great happiness; to earn praise from someone of your stature—a critic, a philosopher, and a teacher of emperors and many others—is truly gratifying. I wish you continued good health.

{3. SENECA TO PAUL, greeting} I have organized some writings into a volume and arranged them into proper sections. I am eager to present them to Caesar, if circumstances permit, hoping to capture his interest. Perhaps you will be present as well. If not, I will set aside another time for us to review the work together. I would not present this work without consulting you first, if it can be done safely, so that you know you are not being overlooked. Farewell, dear Paul.

{4. PAUL TO ANNAEUS SENECA, greeting} Whenever your letters are read aloud, it feels as if you are right here with us. I eagerly anticipate the day we can meet face to face. Wishing you good health.

{5. SENECA TO PAUL, greeting} We are deeply troubled by your absence. What is the reason? What keeps you away? If it is because of Lady Poppaea's displeasure over your departure from the old rituals and sects, and your conversion of others, perhaps we can reason with her to view it as a decision made with due consideration, not lightly.

{6. PAUL TO SENECA AND LUCILIUS, greeting} Regarding the topic you've written about, I must refrain from discussing it in writing, as one might outline and illustrate with pen and ink. I know among you—your households and yourselves—there are those who understand my meaning. It's important to show respect to everyone, especially as people often seize on chances to take offense. Through patience, we can overcome them at every turn, especially if they are willing to regret their actions. Farewell.

{7. ANNAEUS SENECA TO PAUL AND THEOPHILUS, greeting} I am truly pleased with the letters you sent to the Galatians, Corinthians, and Achaeans. May we live together in accordance with the divine inspiration that animates you. It is the Holy Spirit within and above you that articulates these lofty and admirable thoughts. I encourage you to pay attention to other aspects as well, ensuring that the eloquence of your style matches the majesty of your ideas. Brother, I must confess openly to you that Augustus was moved by your words. When I shared with him your discourse on virtue, he marveled how a man not formally educated could think in such ways. I explained that often the gods speak through the innocent, not those who use learning for deceit. When I recounted the tale of Vatienus the countryman, visited by Castor and Pollux in Reate, he seemed convinced. Farewell.

{8. PAUL TO SENECA, greeting} While I understand Caesar's occasional interest in extraordinary matters, I urge you not to provoke him but to counsel him. Bringing up topics contrary to his beliefs and upbringing was a serious step. Since he venerates the gods of the nations, I fail to see why you felt it necessary to inform him unless out of excessive loyalty to me. I implore you to avoid such actions in the future. We must tread carefully not to anger the empress due to your affection for me; her anger may not harm us if temporary, nor benefit us if prolonged—this seems clear. As a queen, she may not take offense; as a woman, she likely will. Farewell.

{9. SENECA TO PAUL, greeting} I understand you are less troubled by my letter concerning your correspondence with Caesar than by the nature of circumstances diverting men from sound learning and conduct—a reality confirmed by many examples. Let us proceed differently, and if any past actions have been hasty, I ask your forgiveness. I have sent you a book on eloquence. Farewell, dear Paul.

{10. SENECA TO PAUL, greeting} Whenever I write to you without placing my name after yours in the heading, I commit a serious act that goes against my principles. As I have often mentioned, I strive to adapt to different circumstances and honor the Roman custom that grants respect to the Senate, choosing to take the lower position when corresponding, rather than assert my own preferences in a disorderly or disrespectful manner. Farewell, my most devoted mentor. Written on the 27th of June; during the fourth consulship of Nero and Messala (A.D. 58).

{11. SENECA TO PAUL, greeting} Greetings, my dearest Paul. If you, such a great man, beloved in so many ways, are closely associated with me and my name—not just in title, but intimately bonded—it brings great joy to your Seneca. Since you are esteemed as the pinnacle among people, would it not please me to be so near you as to be considered a second self of yours? Do not hesitate, then, to be named first in the heading of letters, lest you think I am being tested rather than playfully engaged—especially knowing your status as a Roman citizen. I wish my rank were yours, and yours mine. Farewell, dearest Paul. Written on the 23rd of March; during the consulship of Apronianus and Capito (A.D. 59).

{12.SENECA TO PAUL, greeting} Greetings, my dear Paul. Do you think I am not saddened and grieved by the frequent unjust sufferings of your innocent people? It pains me deeply that the populace perceives you as indifferent and prone to wrongdoing, attributing every misfortune in the city to you. Let us endure this patiently and accept what fate brings until ultimate happiness ends our troubles. In past times, people endured the rule of Macedonian kings, Philip's son, and later, Darius and Dionysius, followed by our own era with Gaius Caesar wielding absolute power. The cause of the numerous fires afflicting Rome is evident. If only humble men could speak freely in this dark hour, the truth would be clear to all. Christians and Jews are commonly blamed and executed as scapegoats for these fires. The true culprits, whoever they are, hiding behind lies and reveling in destruction, will face their due punishment. Just as the best of men often sacrifice themselves for the greater good, so too will this individual face the consequences destined for him. In the span of six days, a hundred and thirty-two houses across four blocks have burned; the seventh day brought a pause. I hope you are well, brother. Written on the 28th of March; during the consulship of Frugi and Bassus (A.D. 64).

{13. SENECA TO PAUL, greeting} Greetings, Paul. Your works contain profound allegories and mysteries, reflecting the powerful intellect and talent bestowed upon you. They deserve to be adorned not merely with eloquent words, but with meticulous care. Do not fear the criticism you have mentioned before—that striving for elegance may dilute the substance and weaken its potency. Allow me to suggest that you accommodate the genius of the Latin language and enhance the beauty of your noble thoughts, so that the great gift bestowed upon you may be properly honored. Farewell. Written on the 4th of June; during the consulship of Leo and Sabinus (non-existent).

{14. PAUL TO SENECA, greeting} Seneca, I greet you. Your contemplations have unveiled insights granted to few by the divine. Therefore, I confidently sow a fertile field with an enduring seed—not material subject to decay, but the eternal word, a manifestation of God that grows and endures forever. Your wisdom has grasped this truth, recognizing that it surpasses the laws of pagans and Israelites alike. You have the potential to become a new voice, showcasing with rhetorical grace the blameless wisdom of Jesus Christ. Though persuading temporal rulers, their servants, and close associates may prove arduous, the word of God, once instilled, brings profound transformation—a new incorruptible humanity and an everlasting soul hastening towards God. Farewell, Seneca, most cherished to me.

Epistle of Paul to the Laodiceans

The Epistle of Paul the Apostle to the Laodiceans, although not present in the canonical New Testament, has garnered considerable interest and debate among scholars and theologians. This letter is thought to be referred to in Colossians 4:16, where Paul instructs the Colossians to read the epistle from Laodicea. The existence of such a letter highlights the extensive and diverse nature of early Christian correspondence and the circulation of Pauline writings. The content traditionally attributed to this epistle varies, with some manuscripts, like the Latin Vulgate, including a version that closely resembles other Pauline letters in style and theology. This non-canonical epistle reflects early Christian attempts to understand and preserve the apostolic teachings, offering insights into the theological and ecclesiastical concerns of the early church. The text emphasizes Paul's authority, apostolic mission, and pastoral care for the Christian communities, echoing themes of unity, faith, and the acknowledgment of Jesus Christ as the foundation of the church. Scholarly analysis of the epistle often delves into its historical context, linguistic style, and theological content, comparing it with the undisputed Pauline letters to discern its authenticity and doctrinal significance. The Epistle to the Laodiceans serves as a fascinating case study in the broader discourse on the formation of the New Testament canon, illustrating the dynamic and multifaceted process by which early Christian writings were transmitted, interpreted, and canonized. Despite its exclusion from the canonical New Testament, this epistle continues to be a subject of academic inquiry, contributing to our understanding of early Christian literature and the development of Christian doctrine.

{1:1} Paul, an apostle appointed not by human authority but by Jesus Christ, to the brothers and sisters in Laodicea. {1:2} Grace and peace to you from God our Father and the Lord Jesus Christ. {1:3} I give thanks to Christ in every prayer I make for you, that you continue to follow Him and persist in His work, anticipating the promise of the day of judgment. {1:4} Don't be swayed by the empty talk of some who sneak in to turn you away from the truth of the Gospel that I preach. {1:5} Now God will ensure that those who are with me will continue to advance the truth of the Gospel and accomplish goodness and the work of salvation, which is eternal life. {1:5} My imprisonment, which I endure for Christ, is known to all, and I rejoice and am glad about it. {1:7} This is for your eternal salvation, which is also achieved through your prayers and the work of the Holy Spirit, whether in life or death. {1:8} For me, living is Christ, and dying is joy. {1:9} And He will work His mercy in you so that you may have the same love and be united in mind. {1:10} Therefore, dear friends, as you have heard from me, hold firmly and work with reverence for God, and it will lead you to eternal life. {1:11} For it is God who works in you. {1:12} Do everything without hesitation or doubt. {1:13} Finally, dear friends, rejoice in Christ and be cautious of those who are greedy for money. {1:14} Make all your requests known to God openly, and stay steadfast in the mind of Christ. {1:15} Focus on what is true, noble, right, pure, and lovely. {1:16} Hold onto what you have heard and received, keeping it in your heart. {1:17} And peace will be yours. {1:18} The saints send their greetings to you. {1:19} May the grace of the Lord Jesus be with your spirit. {1:20} Make sure this letter is read to the people of Colossae, and that the letter to the Colossians is read to you.

Epistle of Ignatius to the Ephesians

The Epistle of Ignatius to the Ephesians, written by Ignatius of Antioch in the early 2nd century, is a key theological work from one of the Apostolic Fathers of the early Christian Church. Composed during Ignatius' journey to Rome for martyrdom, this letter is part of his seven epistles to various Christian communities. In this letter to the Ephesian church, Ignatius, the bishop of Antioch, emphasizes unity, obedience, and the hierarchical structure of the Church, highlighting the roles of bishops, presbyters, and deacons. He passionately defends the incarnation of Christ, countering early heresies and presenting a profound sacramental and incarnational theology. The epistle sheds light on the early Church's internal divisions and external persecutions, reflecting Ignatius' pastoral concern for his community's faith and steadfastness. Bridging the apostolic age with emerging Christian tradition, the Epistle to the Ephesians offers invaluable insights into early Christian doctrine, ecclesial identity, and communal life.

{1:1} I have come to know your esteemed reputation in God, a name you have earned through your consistent practice of righteousness, rooted in faith and love for Jesus Christ our Savior. You are devoted followers of God's love for humanity, stirring yourselves up in the spirit of Christ's sacrifice, and you have fulfilled the calling that was fitting for you. {1:2} Upon learning that I was brought bound from Syria for the sake of our common faith and hope in Christ, I hoped, through your prayers, to be allowed to face wild beasts in Rome, so that through martyrdom I might truly become a disciple of Him "who offered Himself as a sacrifice and offering to God." {1:3} You hastened to visit me upon hearing this. I welcomed your entire assembly in the name of God, facilitated by Onesimus, a man of remarkable love and your bishop in the flesh. I urge you, by Jesus Christ, to love him and strive to emulate his example. {1:4} Blessed be God, who has deemed you worthy to have such an outstanding bishop among you, reflecting your own excellence.

{2:1} Regarding our fellow servant Burrhus, who serves God as your deacon and is blessed in all things, I pray that he may continue steadfastly, both for the honor of your community and that of your esteemed bishop. {2:2} Crocus, also deserving of God's favor and your esteem, whom we have welcomed as a token of your love, has greatly refreshed me in all matters, and he has not been ashamed of my chains. May the Father of our Lord Jesus Christ also refresh him. {2:3} Likewise, I mention Onesimus, Burrhus, Euplus, and Fronto, through whom I have experienced your love. May I always find joy in you, if indeed I am deserving of it. {2:4} Therefore, it is fitting that you should glorify Jesus Christ in every way, for He has glorified you. Through united obedience, "may you be perfectly joined together in the same mind and in the same judgment, speaking the same thing concerning the same matter." {2:5} Be subject to the bishop and the presbytery, so that you may be sanctified in every respect.

{3:1} I do not command you as if I were someone of great authority. Even though I am bound for the sake of Christ, I am still growing in my journey with Jesus Christ and am not yet perfected. {3:2} At this point, I am just beginning to be a disciple, and I speak to you as fellow disciples with me. It was necessary for me to be encouraged by you in matters of faith, exhortation, patience, and endurance. {3:3} Yet, compelled by love, I cannot remain silent concerning you. Therefore, I take it upon myself to urge you first and foremost to unite in accordance with God's will. {3:4} Jesus Christ, who is our inseparable life, perfectly embodies the will of the Father. This is also true of bishops established throughout the ends of the earth—they are appointed by the will of Jesus Christ.

{4:1} Therefore, it is appropriate that you also should come together in unity according to the will of the bishop appointed by God to rule over you. Indeed, you already do this, being guided by the Spirit. {4:2} Your esteemed group of elders, who are worthy of God's approval, align perfectly with the bishop, much like strings harmonize with a harp. {4:3} Thus, united in harmony and loving concord, Jesus Christ is praised. {4:4} Each of you, as individuals, should form a choir, harmonizing in love and singing the song of God together, so that with one voice you may sing to the Father through Jesus Christ. In this way, He will hear you and recognize through your deeds that you are truly His Son's members. {4:5} Therefore, it is beneficial for you to live in blameless unity, so that you may always share communion with God. {4:6} Pursue the love of Christ, under whom Jesus Christ is the leader and guardian. As individuals, become one choir, so that in agreement and perfect unity with God, you may be in harmonious accord with God the Father and His beloved Son, Jesus Christ our Lord. {4:7} For as Jesus Himself said, "Father, may they be one as we are one." It is therefore advantageous that you, united in blameless unity with God, follow the example of Christ, of whom you are also members.

{5:1} If I have experienced such profound fellowship with your bishop in this short time—not merely on a human level, but spiritually—how much more blessed are you who are so closely united to him, as the Church is to Jesus Christ, and as Jesus Christ is to God the Father, so that all things may be in harmony! {5:2} Let no one deceive himself: if anyone is not within the altar, he is deprived of the bread of God. {5:3} For if the prayer of one or two has such power that Christ is present among them, how much greater is the prayer of the bishop and the entire Church, ascending in unity to God, and obtaining the fulfillment of all their petitions in Christ! {5:4} Therefore, anyone who separates himself and does not gather with the community where sacrifices are offered, with "the Church of the first-born whose names are written in heaven," appears gentle outwardly but is a wolf in sheep's clothing. {5:5} Beloved, be diligent to submit to the bishop, the presbyters, and the deacons. For whoever is subject to them obeys Christ who appointed them; but whoever disobeys them disobeys Christ Jesus. {5:6} And "he who does not obey the Son shall not see life, but the wrath of God remains on him." {5:7} Anyone who refuses obedience to authority is self-confident, contentious, and proud. But as Scripture says, "God opposes the proud, but gives grace to the humble," and "The proud have greatly transgressed." {5:8} The Lord also said to the priests, "He who hears you, hears Me; and he who rejects you, rejects Me; and he who rejects Me, rejects Him who sent Me."

{6:1} The more you see the bishop remain silent, the more reverence you should show him. For we should welcome anyone whom the Master of the house appoints to oversee His household, just as we would welcome the One who sent him. Therefore, it is clear that we should regard the bishop as we would regard the Lord Himself, standing as he does before the Lord. {6:2} "It is fitting for the diligent and careful man to stand before kings, and not before slothful men." {6:3} Indeed, Onesimus himself has praised your orderly conduct in God, that you all live according to the truth and no faction has taken root among you. {6:4} Moreover, you listen to none other than Jesus Christ speaking truth. {6:5} You are, as Paul wrote to you, "one body and one spirit," because you have been called to one hope through faith. {6:6} For there is one Lord, one faith, one baptism, one God and Father of all, who is above all and through all and in all. {6:7} Such are you, taught by such leaders as Paul, the bearer of Christ, and Timothy, the faithful disciple.

{7:1} Some people deceitfully carry the name of Jesus Christ while practicing unworthy deeds, which you must avoid like wild beasts. They are like ravenous dogs that bite in secret, and you must be cautious of them because they are hardly curable.

{7:2} But there is one Physician who possesses both flesh and spirit, who is both made and unmade, God existing in flesh, true life in death, born of Mary and of God, conceivable yet inconceivable—Jesus Christ our Lord. {7:3} However, there are certain individuals who carry around the name of Jesus Christ deceitfully, while practicing things that are unworthy of God and holding beliefs that oppose Christ's teaching, to their own and their followers' destruction. You must avoid them as you would avoid wild beasts. For "the righteous man who avoids them is saved forever, but the destruction of the ungodly is sudden and a cause of rejoicing." {7:4} They are like silent dogs that cannot bark, raging madly and biting secretly. Be on guard against them, for they suffer from an incurable disease. {7:5} Our Physician, however, is the only true God, the uncreated and inaccessible Lord of all, the Father who begets the only-begotten Son. Our Physician is also the Lord our God, Jesus Christ, the eternal Son and Word who existed before time began and later became a man through Mary the virgin. {7:6} "The Word became flesh." He, being incorporeal, took on a body; being impassible, He assumed a passible body; being immortal, He inhabited a mortal body; being life itself, He subjected Himself to corruption to free our souls from death and decay, to heal them, and to restore them to health when they were afflicted by ungodliness and sinful desires.

{8:1} Let no one deceive you, although indeed you are not deceived, for you are completely devoted to God. When there is no evil desire within you that could defile and trouble you, then you live in accordance with God's will and serve Christ faithfully. {8:2} Rid yourselves of anything that contaminates, you who belong to the highly esteemed Church of the Ephesians, renowned throughout the world. Those who are focused on worldly desires cannot perform spiritual deeds, just as those who are spiritual cannot engage in worldly pursuits. Faith cannot produce deeds of unbelief, nor can unbelief produce deeds of faith. {8:3} But you, filled with the Holy Spirit, do not act according to the flesh but according to the Spirit. You are complete in Christ Jesus, who is the Savior of all people, especially of those who believe. Even the actions you perform in the flesh are spiritual, for you do everything in the name of Jesus Christ.

{9:1} However, I have heard that some individuals have come among you, promoting false teachings. Yet you did not permit them to sow their divisive ideas among you. Instead, you closed your ears to their deceptive words, recognizing them as stones unsuited for the temple of God the Father, which is built up by Jesus Christ and lifted high by the Holy Spirit, with your faith as the means of ascent and your love as the path leading to God. {9:2} Therefore, both you and your fellow believers are bearers of God, bearers of the temple, bearers of Christ, carriers of holiness, adorned in every way with the teachings of Jesus Christ. I rejoice greatly that through this letter, I have had the privilege to converse and share joy with you, knowing that in your Christian lives, you cherish nothing more than God alone. {9:3} Some among you have heard the teachings of those who espouse the evil doctrines of deceitful and foreign spirits. You wisely barred their entry to spread their harmful ideas, rejecting their errors because you discerned that such deceivers do not speak the truth of Christ but their own falsehoods, as they are agents of deception. The Holy Spirit, however, speaks only the words of Christ, revealing them not from Himself but from the Lord, just as Christ Himself proclaimed the truths given to Him by the Father. {9:4} For Jesus said, "The words which you hear are not Mine but the Father's who sent Me," and of the Holy Spirit, "He will not speak on His own authority, but whatever He hears He will speak." Jesus also affirmed to the Father, "I have glorified You on the earth, I have finished the work which You have given Me to do," and concerning the Holy Spirit, "He will glorify Me, for He will take of what is Mine and declare it to you." {9:5} The spirit of deceit, however, preaches himself and speaks his own falsehoods, seeking only to please himself. He exalts himself in arrogance, deceiving with lies, flattery, and treachery, weaving together empty and discordant words. But Jesus Christ, who has established you on the firm foundation as chosen stones for God's divine building, will deliver you from his influence. {9:6} Raised up by Christ who was crucified for you, strengthened by the Holy Spirit, upheld by faith, and elevated by love from earthly concerns to heavenly heights, you walk alongside those who are pure and undefiled. For as Scripture says, "Blessed are the undefiled in the way, who walk in the law of the Lord." {9:7} This way is sure and true, namely, Jesus Christ, who declared, "I am the way, the truth, and the life." Through Him alone do we come to the Father, for "no one comes to the Father except through Me." {9:8} Therefore, blessed are you who carry God within you, who bear the Spirit, who uphold the temple of holiness, adorned in every way with the teachings of Jesus Christ, forming a royal priesthood, a holy nation, a people for God's own possession. It fills me with great joy that through this letter, I have had the privilege to communicate with "the saints who are in Ephesus, faithful in Christ Jesus." Rejoice, therefore, in your steadfastness against falsehoods and your love that is directed not towards worldly things but towards God alone.

{10:1} And pray without ceasing for others, holding onto hope that they may repent and turn to God. Just as a person who falls can rise again, so too can they attain reconciliation with God. Let your actions speak to them if no other way avails. Respond to their anger with meekness, counter their boasting with humility. In the face of their blasphemies, return prayers; steadfastly uphold faith against their errors; show gentleness in response to their cruelty. Let us never emulate their ways but instead be their brothers in genuine kindness. Let us strive to follow the example of the Lord, who endured unjust treatment, poverty, and condemnation. Thus, no seed of the devil may find root in us, and we may remain holy and sober in Jesus Christ, both in body and spirit. {10:2} Therefore, permit them to learn from you. Be the instruments of God, the mouthpieces of Christ. For the Lord declares, "If you separate the precious from the vile, you shall be as my mouth." Respond humbly to their anger; counter their blasphemies with earnest prayers. Remain steadfast in faith while they wander astray. Overcome their harshness with gentleness, their rage with meekness, for "blessed are the meek." Moses was known for his meekness above all, and David also displayed great humility. Therefore, as Paul advises, "The servant of the Lord must not strive but be gentle toward all, apt to teach, patient, instructing in meekness those who oppose themselves." {10:3} Do not seek revenge on those who harm you, for Scripture says, "Do not return evil for evil." Instead, make them your brethren through kindness. Say to those who hate you, "You are our brothers," so that the name of the Lord may be glorified. Let us imitate the Lord who, when reviled, did not retaliate; when crucified, did not protest; when suffering, did not threaten, but prayed for His enemies, "Father, forgive them, for they know not what they do." Blessed is the one who, in the face of injury, displays patience. If anyone is wronged or scorned for the sake of the Lord's name, truly they are servants of Christ. Guard against allowing any seed of the devil to take root among you, for such seeds bear bitterness and discord. Therefore, remain watchful and sober in Christ Jesus.

{11:1} The end times have arrived. Therefore, let us approach with reverence and fear the patience of God, lest we disregard the riches of His kindness and tolerance, leading to our own condemnation. Let us either fear the impending judgment or embrace the grace currently offered—one of these choices must be made. Above all, let us be found in Christ Jesus, the path to true life. Apart from Him, let nothing else entice you. It is for His sake that I carry these chains, these spiritual treasures, from Syria to Rome. Through your prayers, I hope to be perfected and to share in the sufferings of Christ, participating in His death, resurrection, and eternal life. May I attain this, that I may be counted among the Christians of Ephesus, who have remained steadfast in apostolic teaching through the power of Jesus Christ. {11:2} The last days are upon us. Therefore, let us approach with reverence and heed the patience of God, lest we despise the riches of His kindness and forbearance. Let us either fear the wrath to come or cherish the present joy found in the life that is now. Let our true and present joy be found only in Christ Jesus, that we may truly live. Never desire to be apart from Him even for a moment. For He is my hope, my boast, my enduring wealth, for whom I carry these bonds from Syria to Rome, these spiritual treasures, in which I hope to be perfected through your prayers. May I partake in the sufferings of Christ and share in His death, resurrection, and eternal life. May I attain to this, that I may be found among the Christians of Ephesus, who have always walked in fellowship with the apostles through the power of Jesus Christ, along with Paul, John, and Timothy the faithful.

{12:1} I know who I am and to whom I am writing. I am Ignatius, a man condemned to suffer, sharing the lot of those exposed to danger and condemnation. {12:2} You have received mercy and stand securely. You are the ones through whom those are passing who are martyred for the sake of God. You have been initiated into the deep truths of the Gospel alongside Paul, the holy and martyred apostle, who is most blessed. I hope to be found at his feet when I come before God, as he always mentions you in his letters concerning Christ Jesus. {12:3} I am one who has been handed over to death, the least among those who have suffered for Christ—from the time of righteous Abel to my own martyrdom. You have been initiated into the mysteries of the Gospel together with Paul, the chosen vessel of God. I pray to be found at the feet of Paul and all the saints when I meet Jesus Christ, who always remembers you in His prayers.

{13:1} Take care, then, to gather together frequently to give thanks to God and proclaim His praise. When you assemble often in the same place, you weaken the powers of Satan, and his attempts to bring about destruction are thwarted by the unity of your faith. {13:2} There is nothing more valuable than peace, which puts an end to all conflict, both in the heavenly realms and on earth. Your unity and steadfast faith undermine the plans of the enemy and frustrate the schemes of his followers. {13:3} True peace, rooted in Christ, surpasses all other blessings, bringing an end to every kind of spiritual and earthly warfare. As Scripture says, our battle is not against flesh and blood, but against the spiritual forces of evil in the heavenly realms.

{14:1} Therefore, none of the schemes of the devil will remain hidden from you, if you, like Paul, wholeheartedly possess that faith and love towards Christ which mark the beginning and the culmination of a meaningful life. The journey begins with faith and concludes with love, and these two are inseparably linked, emanating from God Himself. All other virtues necessary for a holy life flow naturally from them. {14:2} A person who professes faith should not engage in sin, and one who possesses love should not harbor hatred towards anyone. For the command to love God is inseparable from loving one's neighbor as oneself. Those who claim to follow Christ are recognized not only by their words but by their actions, for as the tree is known by its fruit, so are Christians known by their conduct.

{15:1} It is far better for a person to remain silent and be known as a Christian, than to speak profusely without living accordingly. "The kingdom of God is not just in words, but in power." True faith involves believing in the heart and confessing with the mouth—one leads to righteousness, the other to salvation. It is commendable to teach, but only if one's actions align with their words. For those who both practice and preach will be esteemed highly in the kingdom of God. {15:2} The Word of Jesus enables us to understand even His silence, urging us to live in harmony with our speech and be recognized for our integrity in silence as well. Nothing is hidden from God; even our innermost thoughts are laid bare before Him. Therefore, let us conduct ourselves as temples of God, with Him dwelling within us. Let Christ dwell in us and speak through us, as He did through Paul. Let the Holy Spirit guide us to proclaim the truths of Christ faithfully.

{16:1} My brothers and sisters, do not be deceived. Those who corrupt families will not inherit the kingdom of God. If those who corrupt earthly families face condemnation, how much more severe will be the punishment for those who distort the faith of God with wicked teachings, for which Jesus Christ Himself was crucified! Such individuals, by becoming defiled in this manner, will face eternal fire, and the same fate awaits all who heed their misleading words. {16:2} Do not be deceived, my brothers and sisters. Those who corrupt human families are condemned to death. How much more severe will be the punishment for those who attempt to corrupt the Church of Christ, for which the Lord Jesus, the only-begotten Son of God, endured the cross and submitted to death! Anyone who, having been blessed with understanding, disregards His teachings will face condemnation. "What fellowship can light have with darkness? Or what harmony does Christ have with Belial? Or what does a believer have in common with an unbeliever? Or what agreement is there between the temple of God and idols?" Likewise, what communion can truth have with falsehood? Or righteousness with unrighteousness? Or genuine doctrine with that which is false?

{17:1} The Lord allowed the ointment to be poured upon His head so that His Church might be infused with immortality. Therefore, do not allow yourselves to be tainted by the foul teachings of the ruler of this world. Do not let him ensnare you away from the life that is promised to you. Why are we not all wise, now that we have received the knowledge of God through Jesus Christ? Why do we foolishly perish without recognizing the true gift that the Lord has sent to us? {17:2} The Lord permitted the ointment to be poured upon His head so that His Church might breathe out immortality. As Scripture says, "Your name is like perfume poured out; therefore the virgins love you." Let none of us be tainted by the foul teachings of this world's ruler. Let not the holy Church of God be deceived by his cunning, as Eve was in her simplicity. Why do we, who have been endowed with reason, not act wisely? When Christ has given us the ability to discern and judge concerning God, why do we fall into ignorance? Why do we foolishly neglect to acknowledge the precious gift that we have received?

{18:1} Let my spirit be considered as nothing for the sake of the cross, which is a stumbling block to those who do not believe, but to us who believe, it is the power of God unto salvation and eternal life. Where are the wise men? Where are the debaters of this age? Where is the boasting of those who are esteemed wise in the world? For our God, Jesus Christ, was conceived in the womb of Mary by the Holy Spirit, according to God's plan, from the seed of David. He was born and baptized to sanctify the waters and fulfill all righteousness. {18:2} The cross of Christ is indeed a stumbling block to those who do not believe, but to those who believe, it is the power of God for salvation and eternal life. Where are the wise men? Where are the debaters of this age? Where is the boasting of those who are called mighty? For the Son of God, who existed before all time and established all things according to the Father's will, was conceived in the womb of Mary by the Holy Spirit, according to God's plan, from the lineage of David. As Scripture says, "Behold, the virgin shall conceive and bear a son, and they shall call His name Immanuel." He was born and baptized by John to confirm the ministry entrusted to that prophet.

{19:1} The virginity of Mary and the birth of her child, along with the death of the Lord—these three profound mysteries were hidden from the ruler of this world but have been revealed to us. A star appeared in the heavens, surpassing all others in brightness and causing great wonder among people. The sun, moon, and stars themselves seemed to join in a celestial chorus around this extraordinary star. Its light was incomparable, and its appearance stirred up questions about its origin. This phenomenon marked the beginning of a new era, ushering in the abolition of death, prepared by God Himself. {19:2} The virginity of Mary and the birth of her child, as well as the death of the Lord—these three remarkable mysteries were concealed but have now been disclosed to us. A star appeared in the sky, surpassing all others in brilliance, and its novelty astonished everyone. The rest of the stars, along with the sun and moon, formed a celestial choir around this star. It outshone them all, prompting speculation about its origin. This event caused worldly wisdom to appear foolish, magic to be seen as trivial, and all forms of wickedness to fade away. Ignorance was dispelled, and oppressive powers were overthrown as God revealed Himself in human form, initiating the restoration of eternal life. This marked the beginning of a divine plan, stirring up a tumultuous change as God set out to abolish death.

{20:1} In the next letter, if it is God's will and through your prayers, I intend to clarify further the teachings I have begun about the new life in Jesus Christ—about His faith, His love, His suffering, and His resurrection. {20:2} My dear brothers and sisters, stand firm in your faith in Jesus Christ and in His love, remembering His suffering and His triumph over death. {20:3} Come together as one body, united in the grace of God the Father and His Son Jesus Christ, who is the firstborn of all creation and yet descended from David in the flesh. {20:4} Be guided by the Holy Spirit, obeying your bishops and elders with a united purpose. {20:5} Share together in the breaking of bread, which is both a symbol of our unity and a source of spiritual nourishment, ensuring that we live in God through Jesus Christ, our Lord and Savior.

{21:1} My thoughts are with you and those you have sent to Smyrna for God's glory. It is from Smyrna that I write to you now, thanking the Lord and holding dear Polycarp just as I cherish you. {21:2} Please remember me, just as Jesus Christ remembers you, who is blessed forever. {21:3} Pray for the Church in Antioch, Syria, from where I am being taken as a prisoner to Rome. I am among the last faithful ones there, chosen to bear witness to the honor of God even in chains. {21:4} Farewell in the presence of God the Father and our Lord Jesus Christ, our shared hope, along with the Holy Spirit. Farewell and amen. May grace be with you.

Epistle of Ignatius to the Magnesians

The Epistle of Ignatius to the Magnesians is a critical piece of early Christian literature, providing deep insights into the theological and ecclesiastical development of the nascent Church. Written by Ignatius of Antioch, a prominent early Christian bishop and martyr, this letter is part of a collection known as the Ignatian Epistles, which were composed during his journey to Rome, where he anticipated his martyrdom. The Magnesians were the recipients of this letter, a Christian community located in Asia Minor, near Ephesus. The epistle emphasizes themes of unity, obedience, and the hierarchical structure of the Church, reflecting Ignatius' concerns with preserving doctrinal purity and communal harmony in the face of internal and external challenges. One of the noteworthy aspects of this letter is its focus on the role of the bishop, whom Ignatius regards as a vital figure in maintaining the integrity and unity of the Christian community. This emphasis on ecclesiastical authority is significant, as it highlights the early stages of structured church governance, which would later become a cornerstone of Christian organizational practice. Furthermore, Ignatius addresses the issue of Judaizing, urging the Magnesians to uphold the distinct identity of Christianity apart from Jewish customs and legal observances, which he viewed as obsolete in light of Christ's teachings. His writings are imbued with a sense of urgency and passionate exhortation, reflecting the perilous context of his impending martyrdom and his unwavering commitment to the faith. This epistle also offers glimpses into the liturgical practices and theological disputes of the early second century, providing valuable historical context for scholars studying the development of early Christian doctrine and community life. Overall, The Epistle to the Magnesians stands as a testament to Ignatius' theological acumen and his influential role in shaping early Christian thought and ecclesiastical structure.

{1:1} Upon learning of your commendable and well-organized devotion, I was filled with great joy. This prompted me to reach out to you, desiring to share in the faith of Jesus Christ. {1:2} As one who has been considered worthy of a revered and precious name, even in the chains I bear, I extend my blessings to the churches. I pray for a unity in both body and spirit through Jesus Christ, who is the eternal source of our life, faith, and love—qualities unmatched, especially in relation to our connection with Jesus and the Father. {1:3} It is through Him that we endure and overcome the challenges posed by the ruler of this world. By His faithfulness, we are assured that we will not face trials beyond our capacity, for He is faithful and will not allow us to be tempted beyond what we can bear.

{2:1} Because I have had the privilege of meeting with you, facilitated by your esteemed bishop Damas, and your honorable presbyters Bassus and Apollonius, as well as my fellow servant, the deacon Sotio—whose friendship I deeply value, as he submits to the bishop by the grace of God and to the presbytery under the authority of Jesus Christ—this prompts me to write to you.

{3:1} It is important not to disregard the youthfulness of your bishop, but instead, show him utmost respect, acknowledging the authority vested in him by God the Father. Even venerable elders have shown such reverence, not judging hastily based on outward appearances, but recognizing wisdom grounded in God. {3:2} Just as wisdom can manifest regardless of age—as seen in Daniel, who at twelve possessed divine insight, and Samuel, who as a child corrected an elder—youth devoted to God should not be underestimated. {3:3} Conversely, wickedness in any age is to be condemned. Remember Timothy, though young, was entrusted with great responsibility and was admonished to set an example for believers. {3:4} Therefore, it is fitting to obey your bishop without contention, for challenging such authority is not merely against a visible person but a mockery of the invisible God. Such actions are accountable to God, not merely to men.

{4:1} It is crucial not only to bear the name of Christians but to live out its reality. Mere titles do not bring blessing; true blessing comes from genuine adherence to Christ's teachings. Those who speak of having a bishop yet act independently of him will face scrutiny from the true Bishop and High Priest, Jesus Christ Himself, who will question their inconsistency: "Why do you call Me Lord, but do not obey My commands?" Such individuals, in my view, lack integrity and sincerity, appearing more as pretenders than sincere believers.

{5:1} Considering that everything comes to an end, we are confronted with two distinct destinies: life and death, each leading to its own destination. It is essential to choose wisely. Just as there are two types of currency—God's and the world's—each marked with its own distinct characteristics, so it is with people. {5:2} Those who do not believe belong to this world, while those who believe bear the likeness of God the Father through Jesus Christ, marked by love. If we are unwilling to embrace the sacrificial life of Christ, we cannot truly claim to possess His life within us. {5:3} Therefore, let us embrace life by following God's commandments and shun death, which comes from disobedience. It is evident that humanity can be divided into two categories: the genuinely devout, stamped with God's approval, and the ungodly, counterfeit and fashioned by the devil. {5:4} This is not about different human natures, but about choices—those who choose godliness reflect the image of God and belong to Him, while those who reject faith reflect the image of the devil. Let us understand that our allegiance determines our spiritual identity: the unbelieving bear the likeness of wickedness, while the believing bear the likeness of their Prince, God the Father, and Jesus Christ.

{6:1} Having witnessed your collective faith and love through the individuals mentioned, I urge you to strive for unity in all things with divine harmony. Let your bishop lead as God's representative, your presbyters as representatives of the apostolic assembly, and your beloved deacons, entrusted with the ministry of Jesus Christ who was with the Father from eternity and revealed in the end. {6:2} Therefore, imitate this divine order by honoring one another and seeing each other through the lens of Christ, not mere flesh. Continuously love one another in Jesus Christ. {6:3} Let there be no divisions among you, but rather be united under your bishop, demonstrating unity as a testament to your eternal life in Christ, and through him, your submission to God.

{7:1} Just as the Lord acted in perfect unity with the Father, not independently but in union with Him, and as the apostles likewise acted in accordance with His will, so too should you act in harmony with your bishop and presbyters. {7:2} Do not seek to justify any action on your own apart from them; instead, gather together in one place. Let there be one prayer, one supplication, one purpose, one hope, characterized by love and pure joy. {7:3} Remember, there is no one more excellent than Jesus Christ. Therefore, come together as one body into the temple of God, as if approaching one altar, to worship the one Jesus Christ, who came from the Father and is united with Him, our High Priest.

{8:1} Do not be misled by strange teachings or ancient myths that hold no value. Reject any notion that adheres strictly to Jewish laws, for it denies the grace we have received through Christ. {8:2} The greatest prophets lived in accordance with Christ Jesus and were persecuted for proclaiming His truth, empowered by His grace to convince unbelievers of the singular

God, revealed through His Son Jesus Christ. {8:3} Jesus, the eternal Word of God, is not a mere spoken word but an essential manifestation of God Himself. He pleased the Father in every way, demonstrating His divine nature and purpose.

{9:1} If those who were steeped in the traditions of old could embrace a new hope centered on Christ, forsaking the Sabbath in favor of honoring the Lord's Day—the day of His resurrection, which embodies our renewed life through Him and His death—then how can we live apart from Him? It is through this mystery of faith that we endure, striving to be recognized as disciples of Jesus Christ, our sole Master. {9:2} The prophets themselves, inspired by the Spirit, eagerly anticipated His coming as their Teacher and Saviour, affirming, "He will come and save us." {9:3} Therefore, let us abandon the Sabbath rituals of old, avoiding idleness and instead engaging in meaningful work, for as the Scriptures say, "In the sweat of thy face shalt thou eat thy bread." Let us observe the Sabbath in a spiritual manner, meditating on God's law, marveling at His creation, and abstaining from pre-prepared food and lukewarm drinks, as well as from excessive indulgence in frivolous activities. {9:4} Following the Sabbath, let every follower of Christ celebrate the Lord's Day as a festival—the day of resurrection, supreme among all days. The prophet foresaw this, proclaiming, "To the end, for the eighth day," symbolizing our new life and victory over death in Christ. {9:5} However, there are those who oppose this truth, whose desires are earthly and who distort the teachings of Christ for their own gain, indulging in pleasures and hypocrisy while denying His power. They exploit Christ's message for profit, corrupting His word and engaging in immorality and greed. May you be delivered from such influences through the mercy of God, found in our Lord Jesus Christ.

{10:1} Let us not disregard His kindness, for if He were to judge us based on our actions alone, we would not endure. Therefore, as His disciples, let us embrace the principles of Christianity. Anyone who goes by any other name is not truly of God. {10:2} So cast off the old, corrupt ways like sour leaven, and embrace the new leaven, which is Jesus Christ. Be infused with His purity, lest any among you be corrupted, for your actions will testify to your true nature. {10:3} It makes no sense to claim Christ and cling to Judaic practices. Christianity did not adopt Judaism; rather, Judaism embraced Christianity so that every believer could be united in worshiping God. {10:4} Let us live worthy of the name we have received, for those called Christians were first named so in Antioch, fulfilling the prophecy of becoming a holy people. Discard the old ways and embrace the grace of Christ. Remain steadfast in Christ, rejecting the influence of anything foreign. {10:5} It is contradictory to profess Jesus Christ with words while holding onto obsolete Judaic customs in our hearts. Where there is true Christianity, there is no place for Judaism, for in Christ, all nations and tongues are united unto God. Those once hardened in heart have become children of Abraham, God's friend, and through Christ, all who are destined for eternal life are blessed.

{11:1} These things I write to you, my beloved, not because I suspect any of you to be in such a state, but as one less than any of you, I aim to caution you beforehand against falling into the traps of empty doctrines. {11:2} Instead, may you attain full confidence in Christ, who was begotten by the Father before all ages and later born of the Virgin Mary, without the involvement of man. {11:3} He lived a holy life, healed all kinds of illnesses among the people, performed miracles, and revealed the true God, His Father, to those lost in polytheism. {11:4} He endured suffering and the cross at the hands of those who crucified Him under Pontius Pilate and Herod. He died, rose again, ascended to heaven to the One who sent Him, and now sits at His right hand. {11:5} He will return at the end of the world in the glory of His Father to judge the living and the dead, rewarding each according to their deeds. {11:6} Blessed is the one who knows and believes these truths with certainty, like you, who are lovers of God and Christ, firmly grounded in our hope, from which may none of us ever be led astray.

{12:1} May I find joy in all of you, if indeed I am worthy of it! Even though I am in chains, I do not consider myself comparable to any of you who are free. {12:2} I know that you are not arrogant, for you have Jesus Christ within you. And when I praise you, I know that you value humility, as it is written, "The righteous person is his own accuser." {12:3} Furthermore, it is said, "Declare your sins first, so that you may be justified," and also, "When you have done all that is commanded of you, say, 'We are unprofitable servants.'" For what people highly esteem is detestable in God's sight. {12:4} As the Scripture says, "God, be merciful to me, a sinner." Therefore, even great figures like Abraham and Job referred to themselves as "dust and ashes before God." David questioned, "Who am I, O Lord, that you have brought me this far?" Moses, known as the meekest of men, said to God, "I am slow of speech and tongue." {12:5} Therefore, be humble so that you may be exalted, for "whoever humbles himself will be exalted, and whoever exalts himself will be humbled."

{13:1} Study, therefore, to be firmly grounded in the teachings of the Lord and the apostles, so that everything you do may prosper in both body and spirit, in faith and love. Walk in unity with your esteemed bishop, the cohesive assembly of presbyters, and the God-honoring deacons. {13:2} Submit yourselves to the bishop and to one another, as Christ submitted to the Father, and as the apostles submitted to Christ, the Father, and the Spirit. This unity, both spiritual and physical, is essential for harmonious fellowship according to God's will.

{14:1} Knowing that you are filled with all goodness, I have given you only a brief exhortation in the love of Jesus Christ. Please remember me in your prayers, that I may draw closer to God. Also, remember the Church in Syria, of which I am unworthy to be called bishop. I greatly need your prayers and your love, so that the Church in Syria may be built up in Christ through your good order and may be considered worthy of edification.

{15:1} The Ephesians from Smyrna, where I am currently writing to you, send greetings. They are here for the glory of God, just as you are, and their presence has been a great encouragement to me. They, along with Polycarp, the bishop of Smyrna, extend their greetings to you. The other churches, in honor of Jesus Christ, also send their greetings. Farewell in harmony, to all of you who have received the inseparable Spirit through Christ Jesus, according to the will of God.

Epistle of Ignatius to the Trallians

The Epistle of Ignatius to the Trallians is one of the seven authentic letters attributed to Ignatius of Antioch, an early Christian bishop and martyr, written during his journey to Rome around AD 110-117, where he was to face execution. Addressed to the Christian community in Tralles, a city in Asia Minor, this letter is significant for its emphasis on ecclesiastical hierarchy, unity, and the proper understanding of Christ's nature. Ignatius, deeply concerned with the preservation of church order, stresses the authority of the bishop, presbyters, and deacons as essential for maintaining Christian unity and orthodoxy, particularly in the face of emerging heresies, such as Docetism, which denied the true humanity of Christ. His exhortations are rooted in a profound theological reflection on the incarnation, suffering, and resurrection of Christ, which Ignatius sees as central to salvation. The letter reflects his personal commitment to martyrdom, which he interprets as a form of imitating Christ's sacrifice, thereby encouraging the Trallians to remain steadfast in faith and obedient to their leaders. Overall, the Epistle to the Trallians offers valuable insight into early Christian thought on ecclesiology, Christology, and the importance of martyrdom, as well as the challenges faced by the second-century Church.

{1:1} I know that you possess an impeccable and sincere attitude marked by patience, not only in your current conduct but as a fundamental trait of your character, as Bishop Polybius has informed me. He came to Smyrna by the will of God the Father and the Lord Jesus Christ, empowered by the Spirit. He shared in the joy that I, imprisoned for Christ Jesus, experience, and through him, I saw your entire community. {1:2} Therefore, having received confirmation of your goodwill through him, in accordance with God's will, I rejoiced to confirm that you indeed follow Jesus Christ the Savior.

{2:1} Be subject to the bishop as you would to the Lord, for "he watches over your souls as one who will give an account." Therefore, it seems to me that you live not according to human standards but according to Jesus Christ, who died for us so that through faith in His death, you might escape eternal death. It is essential, therefore, to do nothing without the bishop's approval. {2:2} Also, be subject to the presbytery as you would to the apostles of Jesus Christ, who is our hope, in whom we hope to be found when we live faithfully. {2:3} It is also proper that the deacons, as ministers of the mysteries of Jesus Christ, should be pleasing to all in every way. They are not just servants providing food and drink but are servants of the Church of God. Therefore, they must avoid any grounds for accusation as they would avoid a blazing fire. {2:4} Let them demonstrate their worthiness in every respect.

{3:1} Similarly, honor the deacons as appointed by Jesus Christ, and respect the bishop as you would Christ Himself, who is the Son of the Father. Regard the presbyters as a council of God and an assembly of Christ's apostles. Apart from these, there is no true Church. I am confident that you share these beliefs as well. I have experienced your love firsthand, especially through your bishop, whose presence is deeply instructive and whose humility is a source of strength. Even the irreligious must surely respect him, knowing that I do not spare myself in praising him. {3:2} As you honor the deacons, remember they serve in the place of Christ Jesus, just as the bishop represents the Father of all, and the presbyters stand as the council of God and the assembly of Christ's apostles. Without these, there is no chosen Church, no gathering of the holy, no assembly of saints. I am convinced that you also hold this view. For I have received clear demonstrations of your love, especially through your bishop, whose very presence is instructive and whose humility is powerful. {3:3} Out of love for you, I refrain from writing in a more severe tone, so as not to appear harsh or lacking in compassion. Although I am imprisoned for the sake of Christ, I do not claim authority like an apostle, for I am not yet worthy. Perhaps when I am perfected, then I may be.

{4:1} I possess deep knowledge of God, yet I restrain myself from boasting, I fear that boasting might lead to my downfall. It is necessary for me to be cautious and not pay attention to those who inflate my ego. Even those who speak commendably of me can inadvertently harm me. I do desire to endure trials, but I am unsure if I am truly deserving of such challenges. This yearning, though hidden from many, fiercely overwhelms me. I recognize my need for humility, which defeats the devil, the ruler of this world. {4:2} Instead, I measure myself carefully so that I do not perish due to pride. It is better to boast in the Lord. Even if I am well-grounded in matters concerning God, I should still be cautious and not heed those who vainly inflate my ego. Those who praise me often inadvertently harm me. I do desire to face trials, yet I am uncertain if I am worthy of such tests. The envy of the wicked is not readily apparent to many, but it wages war against me. Therefore, I recognize the necessity of humility, through which the devil, the ruler of this world, is rendered powerless.

{5:1} Could I not write to you about profound and heavenly matters? But I hesitate to do so, fearing that I might harm you who are still spiritual infants. Please forgive me for this caution, lest you, unable to grasp such teachings, should be overwhelmed by them. Even though I am committed to Christ, I do not claim to fully understand heavenly things, the realms of angels, their hierarchies, both seen and unseen. Apart from these profound topics, I am still learning in many respects. There are many aspects in which I fall short of complete understanding before God. {5:2} Might I not write to you about more mysterious things? But I fear doing so, lest I should harm you who are still spiritual infants. Please forgive me in this regard, lest, unable to grasp their weighty significance, you should be overwhelmed. Even though I am committed to Christ, and understand heavenly things, the orders of angels, the various types of angelic beings and their roles, the distinctions between powers and authorities, the diversity of thrones and dominions, the majesty of the Aeons, the prominence of the cherubim and seraphim, the exalted nature of the spiritual realm, the kingdom of the Lord, and above all, the incomparable greatness of Almighty God—even though I know these things, I am not perfect, nor am I as learned as Paul or Peter. There are still many things I do not yet comprehend fully, in order not to fall short of God.

{6:1} Therefore, I urge you, not by my own authority but by the love of Jesus Christ, to consume only Christian nourishment and to abstain from any other kind of spiritual food—I mean heresy. Those who embrace heresy blend their own poison with the message of Jesus Christ, uttering things that are unworthy of belief. They are like those who mix a deadly poison into sweet wine, which someone unaware of its danger might eagerly drink, only to find it brings fatal pleasure leading to their own demise. {6:2} Therefore, I urge you, not I, but the love of Jesus Christ, "that ye all speak the same thing, and that there be no divisions among you; but that ye be perfectly joined together in the same mind and in the same judgment." For there are deceivers and empty talkers, not true Christians, but betrayers of Christ, who misuse the name of Christ deceitfully and "corrupt the word" of the Gospel. They mix their deceitful poison with persuasive speech, as if they were blending aconite with sweet wine, so that whoever drinks it, deceived by the great sweetness of the drink, may unknowingly bring about their own destruction. As an ancient proverb advises, "Let no one be called good who mixes good with evil." They speak of Christ not to preach Him, but to reject Him; they speak of the law not to uphold it, but to proclaim things contrary to it. They separate Christ from the Father and the law from Christ. They slander His birth from the Virgin, they are ashamed of His cross, they deny His suffering, and they refuse to believe in His resurrection. They depict God as an unknown entity, they claim Christ is unbegotten, and they deny the existence of the Spirit. Some say the Son is merely human, and that the Father, Son, and Holy Spirit are one person, and they attribute creation not to Christ but to some other strange power.

{7:1} Be vigilant, therefore, against such individuals, so that you do not fall into a snare that ensnares your souls. Live your life without causing offense to others, lest you become like "a trap set on a watchtower, and a net spread out." For "he who does not heal himself in his own works is akin to the brother who destroys himself." {7:2} If you discard conceit, arrogance, disdain, and haughtiness, you will have the privilege of being closely united with God, for "He is near to those who fear Him." As it is said, "Upon whom will I look, but upon the one who is humble and quiet, who trembles at my words?" Therefore, reverence your bishop as you would Christ Himself, as the blessed apostles have instructed you. {7:3} The one who serves within the altar is pure, for he is obedient to the bishop and the presbyters. But the one who acts apart from the bishop, the presbyters, and the deacons, defiles his conscience and is worse than an unbeliever. For what is the bishop but one who, above all others, possesses authority and power as much as humanly possible, striving to imitate the Christ of God? What is the presbytery but a sacred council, the advisors and co-workers of the bishop? And what are the deacons but servants who emulate the angelic powers, carrying out a pure and blameless ministry for him, just as holy Stephen did for blessed James, and Timothy and Linus did for Paul, and Anencletus and Clement did for Peter? {7:4} Therefore, anyone who refuses to obey such leaders must surely be without God, an irreverent person who despises Christ and rejects His appointments.

{8:1} I write these things to you, not because I know that such people exist among you; rather, I hope that God will never allow such reports to reach me. He who did not spare His own Son for the sake of His holy Church. But foreseeing the traps set by the evil one, I prepare you in advance through my warnings, my beloved and faithful children in Christ. I equip you to guard against the deadly influence of unruly individuals, fleeing from the corruption through the goodwill of our Lord Jesus Christ. {8:2} Therefore, clothe yourselves with humility and become imitators of His suffering and love, with which He loved us and gave Himself as a ransom to cleanse us by His blood from our former ungodliness. He bestowed life upon us when we were nearly perishing due to our own depravity. Therefore, let none of you harbor grudges against your neighbor, for our Lord says, "Forgive, and you will be forgiven." {8:3} Do not give the Gentiles any reason to slander the word and teachings of Christ because of a few foolish individuals. As the prophet spoke on behalf of God, "Woe to those by whom my name is blasphemed among the Gentiles."

{9:1} Therefore, close your ears to anyone who speaks contrary to Jesus Christ, the Son of God, who descended from David and was born of Mary. He truly assumed a human body, for "the Word became flesh," and lived on earth without sin. He ate and drank like any human being. He was genuinely persecuted under Pontius Pilate, truly crucified, and died. His death was witnessed by beings in heaven, on earth, and even under the earth. He was truly raised from the dead by His Father, just as He will raise us who believe in Him through Christ Jesus. Apart from Him, we do not possess true life. {9:2} He descended into Hades alone but arose accompanied by a multitude, fulfilling the prophecy that many bodies of the saints who had slept arose. He broke down the barrier that had separated humanity from God since the beginning of the world. After three days, the Father raised Him from the dead. He spent forty days with the apostles, then ascended to the Father and sat down at His right hand, awaiting the day when His enemies will be put under His feet. {9:3} On the day of preparation, at the third hour, Pilate pronounced the sentence. At the sixth hour, He was crucified. At the ninth hour, He breathed His last breath and was buried before sunset. He remained in the tomb through the Sabbath. At dawn on the Lord's day, He rose from the dead, fulfilling His own prophecy that He would be like Jonah in the belly of the whale for three days and nights. Thus, the day of preparation signifies His passion, the Sabbath signifies His burial, and the Lord's Day signifies His resurrection.

{10:1} However, if, as some unbelievers claim, Jesus only appeared to suffer, and did not truly take on a body or undergo real suffering, then why am I in chains? Why do I eagerly desire to face wild beasts? Would my death not then be in vain? I would be spreading falsehood about the crucifixion of the Lord. {10:2} These unbelievers are no different from those who crucified Him. But I do not put my trust in someone who only appeared to die; rather, I believe in His true suffering. For falsehood is utterly contrary to the truth. Mary truly conceived a body in which God dwelled. The Word of God was genuinely born of the Virgin, taking on a body like ours. He who forms all humans in the womb was truly in the womb Himself, forming a body from the seed of the Virgin without any human intervention. He was carried in the womb, born, nourished with milk, and ate common food and drink just like us. After living among humanity for thirty years, He was genuinely baptized by John and preached the Gospel, performing miracles. He, the Judge Himself, was falsely judged by the Jews and Pilate. He was scourged, struck, spat upon, crowned with thorns, and clothed in purple. He was condemned and truly crucified—not in appearance or deceit. He genuinely died, was buried, and rose from the dead, as He prayed to the Father, who answered and raised Him up. The Father who raised Him will also raise us up through Him, for He is the way to true life. {10:3} Therefore, flee from these godless heresies, for they are the inventions of the devil, the serpent who introduced evil and deceived Adam through Eve. These teachings deny the reality of Christ's incarnation, suffering, death, and resurrection, seeking to undermine the very foundation of our faith.

{11:1} Therefore, flee from those evil teachings that produce deadly consequences. If anyone embraces them, they face instant spiritual death. These teachings are not rooted in God the Father. If they were, they would reflect the life-giving power of Christ's cross, yielding incorruptible fruit. Through His passion, Christ calls you to be His own, as integral parts of His body. Just as a head cannot exist without its members, so God Himself, our Savior, has promised our union with Him. {11:2} Avoid also the followers of Simon, Menander, Basilides, and their misguided cohorts, who distort the truth and worship a man, denounced even by the prophet Jeremiah. Steer clear of the impure Nicolaitanes, who falsely claim legitimacy, indulging in pleasure and spreading slanderous lies. Stay away from Theodotus and Cleobulus, who bear fruit that leads to eternal death upon tasting—these are not God's creation but a cursed lineage. As the Lord declared, "Every plant that my heavenly Father has not planted will be uprooted." Had they truly been rooted in God, they would not oppose the message of the cross but instead condemn those who crucified the Lord of glory. {11:3} By denying the cross and shunning the significance of Christ's suffering, these groups cover up the sins of the Jews who opposed God and murdered the Lord. They go beyond mere persecution of prophets; they deny the very essence of Christ's mission. Instead, embrace Christ's invitation to share in His eternal life, made possible through His suffering and resurrection. For as His followers, you are joined to Him as His own body, destined for immortality.

{12:1} I send greetings to you from Smyrna, along with the congregations of God who are here with me. They have been a great source of refreshment to me, both in physical support and spiritual encouragement. As I carry my chains for the sake of Jesus Christ, I pray earnestly that I may be counted worthy to be united with God. I urge you to maintain unity among yourselves and to persist in praying together. This is fitting for each one of you, especially for the presbyters, who should support and uplift the bishop, honoring both the Father, Jesus Christ, and the apostles. {12:2} I appeal to you out of love, asking that you heed my words so that my writing does not become a testimony against you. Please also pray for me. Your love and the mercy of God are essential for me to be deemed worthy of the destiny appointed for me, and to avoid being rejected.

{13:1} The love of the Smyrnaeans and Ephesians is with you. Please pray for our Church in Syria. Remain obedient to your bishop, presbytery, and deacons, and love one another with a united heart. My spirit greets you now and in my prayers with God. Though I remain in danger, I trust that the Father, faithful in Jesus Christ, will keep us blameless. May we rejoice together in the Lord.

Epistle of Ignatius to the Romans

The Epistle of Ignatius to the Romans is a seminal text in early Christian literature, written by Ignatius of Antioch, an influential bishop and martyr of the early church. Composed around AD 107, during Ignatius' journey to Rome under Roman custody, the letter is a passionate and theologically rich plea to the Christian community in Rome. Ignatius, facing imminent martyrdom, implores the Roman Christians not to intervene on his behalf, reflecting his profound desire to emulate the passion of Christ through his own martyrdom. This epistle provides invaluable insights into the theological convictions and ecclesiastical structure of the early second-century church. Ignatius' writings emphasize the centrality of Christ's divinity, the importance of ecclesiastical unity, and the role of the bishop in maintaining doctrinal purity. The letter is also notable for its reflections on the nature of martyrdom, viewed by Ignatius as a means of attaining a deeper communion with Christ. Through his eloquent and fervent rhetoric, Ignatius seeks to inspire the Roman Christians to uphold their faith with courage and steadfastness.

{1:1} Through my prayers to God, I have been granted the privilege of seeing your esteemed faces, just as I earnestly requested. As a prisoner for Christ Jesus, I hope to greet you, if it is indeed God's will that I am deemed worthy to do so. The initial steps have been promising, and I pray for the grace to remain steadfast in my calling until the very end. I am cautious of your affection for me, fearing it may hinder my journey. While you have the power to achieve much through your love, my path to God becomes more challenging if you do not hold back from me under the guise of earthly affection.

{2:1} It is not my intention to please you as a people-pleaser, but rather to please God, as you also strive to do. I do not foresee another opportunity like this to draw closer to God, and if you remain silent now, you may miss out on participating in a noble endeavor. If you remain silent about my fate, I will belong wholly to God. But if you express your affection for my earthly existence, then I will have to continue running my race here. Therefore, I implore you not to seek to do me a greater kindness than allowing me to be offered as a sacrifice to God while the altar is ready. Gather together in love, and sing praises to the Father through Christ Jesus, acknowledging that God has deemed me, the bishop of Syria, worthy to be summoned from the east to the west, and to become a martyr for His holy cause. It is a great privilege to transition from this world to God, anticipating rising again to Him. My desire is not to please people, but to please God, as you also strive to do. This is my final opportunity to draw nearer to God; if you choose to remain silent, you will miss the chance to participate in a greater work. If you do not speak out for me, I will belong to God alone. However, if you show your affection for my earthly life, I will have to continue running my course. Therefore, I urge you not to try to do me a greater favor than to offer me as a sacrifice to God while the altar is still prepared. Gather together in love, and sing praises to the Father through Christ Jesus, acknowledging that God has judged me, the bishop of Syria, worthy to be called from the east to the west and to become a martyr for His own precious sufferings.

{3:1} You have never been envious of anyone; instead, you have instructed others. Now I hope that your actions will confirm the teachings you impart to others. Please pray on my behalf for both inner and outer strength, so that I may not only speak boldly but also act according to my words. I desire not just to be called a Christian but to truly be one. For if I am truly found to be a Christian, then I will be considered faithful when I no longer exist in this world. Remember, what is seen is temporary, but what is unseen is eternal. Our God, Jesus Christ, now glorified with the Father, is increasingly revealed in His majesty. Christianity is not merely about words but also about manifest greatness.

{4:1} I am writing to all the Churches, urging them that I am prepared to die for God willingly, unless you prevent me. I ask you not to show an untimely kindness toward me. Allow me to be consumed by the wild beasts, through whom I will attain to God. I am like the wheat of God, ground by the teeth of wild beasts, so that I may become the pure bread of Christ. Instead, urge the wild beasts on, so that they may serve as my tomb and leave nothing of my body behind. Then, when I have fallen asleep in death, I will not be a burden to anyone. Only then will I truly be a disciple of Christ, when the world no longer sees even my body. Pray to Christ on my behalf, that through these means I may be accepted as a sacrifice to God.

{5:1} From Syria to Rome, I face wild beasts, both on land and sea, day and night, bound as I am to ten soldiers who act worse even when treated kindly. Yet, their injuries only strengthen my resolve to follow Christ, though that does not justify me. I eagerly anticipate the wild beasts prepared for me; I pray they will eagerly attack me. I will not be like others whom fear has spared. If they hesitate, I will compel them. Forgive me for this, but I know what is best for me. Now, I truly begin to be a disciple, with no desire for anything visible or invisible, but only to attain Jesus Christ. Let fire and the cross, let wild beasts and every torture of the devil come upon me—only let me reach Jesus Christ.

{6:1} All the wealth and power of this world mean nothing to me. It is far better to die for Jesus Christ than to rule over all the kingdoms of the earth. "For what does it profit a man if he gains the whole world, but loses his own soul?" I earnestly seek the Lord, the Son of the true God and Father, Jesus Christ, who died and rose again for our sake. This is the ultimate gain I pursue. Brothers and sisters, forgive me: do not prevent me from attaining true life. Do not desire to keep me in a state of spiritual death. While I long to belong wholly to God, do not abandon me to the ways of the world. Allow me to reach the pure light of God's presence; only then will I truly be a person of God. Let me follow in the footsteps of my God, Jesus Christ, in His passion. If anyone truly has Christ within them, let them understand my desire and sympathize with me, knowing the constraints I face.

{7:1} The ruler of this world seeks to sway me and corrupt my devotion to God. Therefore, none of you who are [in Rome] should assist him; rather, stand with me on God's side. Do not claim allegiance to Jesus Christ while preferring the attractions of this world. Let envy find no place among you. Even if I were present to urge you, do not heed my words, but trust in what I now write to you. For though I am alive as I write this, I eagerly anticipate dying for the sake of Christ. My earthly desires have been crucified; there is no burning passion in me for anything worldly. Instead, there is a wellspring of living water within me, urging me inwardly to come to the Father. {7:2} I find no pleasure in perishable food or the pleasures of this life. My soul longs for the bread of God, the heavenly bread, which is the flesh of Jesus Christ, Son of God, who descended from David's lineage. Likewise, I yearn for the drink of God, His incorruptible love and eternal life, symbolized by His blood.

{8:1} I no longer desire to live as others do, and my wish will be fulfilled if you agree. Be willing, then, that you also may see your desires fulfilled. I appeal to you in this short letter; trust me. Jesus Christ will confirm these things to you, so that you will know I speak truthfully. He is the mouth that speaks without falsehood, through whom the Father has truly communicated. Pray for me, that I may achieve my goal. I am not writing to you according to human desires, but according to the will of God. If I suffer, it means you have wished me well; but if I am rejected, it means you have not loved me. {8:2} I no longer wish to live after the manner of men, and my desire shall be fulfilled if ye consent. "I am crucified with Christ: nevertheless I live; yet no longer I, since Christ liveth in me." I entreat you in this brief letter: do not refuse me; believe me that I love Jesus, who was delivered [to death] for my sake. "What shall I render to the Lord for all His benefits towards me ?" Now God, even the Father, and the Lord Jesus Christ, shall reveal these things to you, [so that ye shall know] that I speak truly. And do ye pray along with me, that I may attain my aim in the Holy Spirit. I have not written to you according to the flesh, but according to the will of God. If I shall suffer, ye have loved me; but if I am rejected, ye have hated me.

{9:1} Please remember in your prayers the Church in Syria, which now has the Lord as its shepherd instead of me. Jesus Christ alone will care for it, and your love for Him will also include concern for it. As for myself, I am hesitant to be counted among them; indeed, I am unworthy, being the least among them and born at an untimely moment. Yet, by God's grace, I hope to make something of myself if I attain to God. My spirit greets you, and I appreciate the love of the churches that have welcomed me in the name of Jesus Christ, not as a passing visitor. Even those churches that were distant from me in terms of physical proximity have gone ahead to support me, city by city. {9:2} Please remember in your prayers the Church in Syria, which now has for its shepherd the Lord, who says, "I am the good Shepherd." And He alone will oversee it, as well as your love towards Him. But as for me, I am ashamed to be counted one of them; for I am not worthy, as being the very last of them, and one born out of due time. But I have obtained mercy to be somebody, if I shall attain to God. My spirit salutes you, and the love of the Churches which have received me in the name of Jesus Christ, and not as a mere passerby. For even those Churches which were not near to me in the way, have brought me forward, city by city.

{10:1} I am writing these words to you from Smyrna, sent by the Ephesians, who are rightly esteemed as most blessed. Here with me is Crocus, among many others, who is dear to my heart. Regarding those who have gone ahead of me from Syria to Rome for the glory of God, I trust you are familiar with them. Please inform them that I am approaching. They are all worthy, both in the sight of God and in your estimation, and it is fitting that you support them in every way. I am concluding this letter to you on the day before the ninth of the Kalends of September (which is August 23rd). Farewell until the end, persevering in the patience that comes from Jesus Christ. Amen. {10:2} I write to you now from Smyrna, where I am accompanied by the Ephesians, who are rightly considered most fortunate. Alongside me is Crocus, whom I hold dear among many others. As for those who have gone ahead of me from Syria to Rome for God's glory, I believe you are acquainted with them. Please inform them that I am near. They are worthy of both God and your respect, and it is appropriate for you to support them in every way. I conclude this letter to you on the day before the ninth of the Kalends of September. Farewell until the end, remaining steadfast in the patience of Jesus Christ.

Epistle of Ignatius to the Philadelphians

The Epistle of Ignatius to the Philadelphians, one of the seven authentic letters attributed to Ignatius of Antioch, stands as a critical document in early Christian literature, offering profound insights into the theological and ecclesiastical concerns of the early second century. Written during Ignatius's journey to Rome, where he was to face martyrdom, the letter reflects the urgency and intensity of his pastoral care for the Christian communities. Ignatius's correspondence with the Philadelphian church underscores his commitment to ecclesiastical unity, which he deemed essential for the preservation and propagation of the faith. In his exhortation, Ignatius emphasizes the importance of obedience to the bishop, portraying the bishop as a central figure in maintaining doctrinal purity and communal harmony. This insistence on hierarchical structure is reflective of the broader Ignatian corpus, wherein the roles of bishops, presbyters, and deacons are delineated as vital to the integrity of the church. Additionally, the epistle addresses the dangers of schisms and heresies, warning against those who, by their erroneous teachings, seek to disrupt the unity of the church. Ignatius's theological reflections in this letter also touch upon the incarnation and the real presence of Christ in the Eucharist, themes that are recurrent in his other writings. The Epistle to the Philadelphians thus not only provides a window into the organizational and doctrinal priorities of early Christianity but also encapsulates the fervent spirit of a bishop who, in the face of impending death, remained steadfast in his mission to strengthen and guide the flock entrusted to his care.

{1:1} I have observed your bishop closely, and I recognize that he did not take on the responsibilities of ministry for the community out of self-promotion, through human appointment, or for the sake of vanity. Instead, he was chosen by the love of Jesus Christ and God the Father, who raised Christ from the dead. I am struck by his meekness, which is admirable, and his ability to achieve more through silence than those who speak endlessly. He adheres closely to the commandments of the Lord, much like the strings of a harp resonate in harmony. His character is blameless, reminiscent of the priest Zacharias. Thus, my soul esteems him as blessed in his devotion to God, recognizing his virtue and completeness, and understanding that his steadfastness and freedom from anger reflect the infinite gentleness of the living God. {1:2} The bishop I have seen is not one who assumed the duties of service to the community on his own or by human appointment, nor for the sake of self-glory, but out of love for Jesus Christ and God the Father, who raised Christ from the dead. His meekness impresses me, and he accomplishes much through silence rather than empty words. He adheres faithfully to the Lord's commandments and ordinances, like the strings of a harp in perfect harmony, and his integrity is akin to that of Zacharias the priest. Therefore, my soul regards him as truly blessed in his devotion to God, acknowledging his virtue and wholeness, and understanding that his steadfastness and freedom from anger reflect the boundless gentleness of the living God.

{2:1} Therefore, as children who walk in the light and truth, avoid division among yourselves and steer clear of the corrupt teachings of heretics. Instead, follow your shepherd faithfully like sheep. There are many deceptive individuals who appear credible but spread harmful doctrines that ensnare those striving towards God. However, they will find no place among you who stand united. {2:2} Therefore, as children who walk in the light and truth, avoid division among yourselves and steer clear of the corrupt teachings of heretics. Instead, follow your shepherd faithfully like sheep. There are many wolves disguised as sheep, who through deceptive pleasures, ensnare those striving towards God. However, they will find no place among you who stand united.

{3:1} Keep yourselves away from those corrupt teachings that Jesus Christ does not nurture, for they are not planted by the Father but are seeds sown by the wicked one. I write to you not because I have found division among you, but to prepare you, my dear ones, as children of God. Those who belong to Christ are united with the bishop, but those who stray and join with the accursed ones will be cut off. They do not belong to Christ's harvest but are seeds of the enemy. May you be delivered from them through the prayers of your faithful and gentle shepherd who oversees you. {3:2} Therefore, I urge you in the Lord to receive with gentleness those who repent and return to the unity of the Church. Through your kindness and patience, help them escape from the devil's trap and become worthy of Jesus Christ, securing eternal salvation in His kingdom. Brothers and sisters, do not be deceived. Anyone who follows those who cause divisions in the Church will not inherit the kingdom of God. And whoever does not stand firm against falsehood will face condemnation. It is imperative not to separate from the righteous or to associate with the ungodly. Anyone who follows strange doctrines is not aligned with Christ or a participant in His suffering, but is a destroyer of Christ's vineyard. Avoid fellowship with such individuals, even if they are your family, for as Scripture says, "Your eye shall not spare them." {3:3} Therefore, I urge you in the Lord to receive with gentleness those who repent and return to the unity of the Church. Through your kindness and patience, help them escape from the devil's trap and become worthy of Jesus Christ, securing eternal salvation in His kingdom. Brothers and sisters, do not be deceived. Anyone who follows those who cause divisions in the Church will not inherit the kingdom of God. And whoever does not stand firm against falsehood will face condemnation. It is imperative not to separate from the righteous or to associate with the ungodly. Anyone who follows strange doctrines is not aligned with Christ or a participant in His suffering, but is a destroyer of Christ's vineyard. Avoid fellowship with such individuals, even if they are your family, for as Scripture says, "Your eye shall not spare them."

{4:1} Take heed, therefore, to maintain only one Eucharist. There is one body of our Lord Jesus Christ, and one cup that shows the unity of His blood. There is one altar, just as there is one bishop, along with the presbytery and deacons, my fellow servants. Therefore, whatever you do, do it according to the will of God. {4:2} I am confident in the Lord that you will have no other mindset. Therefore, I write boldly to your love, which is worthy of God, urging you to uphold one faith, one type of preaching, and one Eucharist. For there is one body of the Lord Jesus Christ, and His blood shed for us is one. There is one loaf broken for all participants, and one cup distributed to all. There is one altar for the entire Church, and one bishop, together with the presbytery and deacons, my fellow servants. Since there is one unbegotten God, the Father, and one begotten Son, God, the Word and man, and one Spirit of truth, as well as one preaching, one faith, and one baptism, and one Church established by the holy apostles from one end of the earth to the other through the blood, sweat, and toil, it is fitting for you, as "a chosen generation, a royal priesthood, a holy nation," to perform all things in harmony in Christ. {4:3} Wives, submit yourselves to your husbands in reverence for God; and you virgins, to Christ in purity, not scorning marriage but desiring what is better, not for the reproach of wedlock but for the sake of contemplating the law. Children, obey your parents and honor them, for they are co-laborers with God in bringing you into the world. Servants, be obedient to your masters in the fear of God, that you may be freedmen of Christ. Husbands, love your wives as fellow servants of God, as your own bodies, as partners in life and co-participants in the procreation of children. Virgins, fix your gaze solely on Christ and pray to His Father, enlightened by the Spirit. May I find joy in your purity, like that of Elijah, Joshua son of Nun, Melchizedek, Elisha, Jeremiah, John the Baptist, the beloved disciple, Timothy, Titus, Evodius, and Clement, who departed in perfect chastity. {4:4} Not that I condemn the other blessed saints who entered into marriage, of whom I have just spoken. Rather, I pray that, being found worthy of God, I may be found at their feet in the kingdom, as at the feet of Abraham, Isaac, Jacob,

Joseph, Isaiah, and the other prophets, as well as Peter, Paul, and the other apostles who were married men. They entered into marriage not for selfish reasons but out of concern for the propagation of mankind. Fathers, bring up your children in the training and instruction of the Lord, teaching them the holy Scriptures and useful skills to prevent idleness. As Scripture says, "A righteous father educates his children well; his heart shall rejoice in a wise son." {4:5} Masters, be gentle with your servants, as holy Job has taught, for there is one nature and one human family. For "in Christ there is neither slave nor free." Let governors be obedient to Caesar, soldiers to their commanders, deacons to the presbyters as to high priests, and the presbyters, deacons, and clergy, together with all the people, soldiers, governors, and even Caesar himself, to the bishop. Let the bishop be obedient to Christ, just as Christ is to the Father. Thus, unity is preserved throughout. Widows should not wander about or indulge in luxuries or be gossips from house to house. Instead, let them be like Judith, known for her seriousness, and Anna, renowned for her sobriety. I do not prescribe these things as an apostle. Who am I, or what is my family, that I should claim equality with them? But as your fellow soldier, I hold the position of one who simply admonishes you.

{5:1} My brothers and sisters, my love for you has greatly expanded, and I rejoice exceedingly in you, seeking earnestly for your safety. However, it is not I alone, but the Lord Jesus working through me. Bound for His sake, I fear even more, knowing I am not yet perfect. Your prayers to God will bring me to perfection, enabling me to attain the destiny appointed to me through His mercy. I turn to the Gospel as I would to the flesh of Jesus Christ, and to the apostles as the elders of the Church. Let us honor the prophets too, for they proclaimed the Gospel, hoped in Him, and awaited His coming. By believing in Him, they were saved, united to Jesus Christ, holy men deserving of love and admiration, confirmed in the Gospel and sharing in our common hope. {5:2} My brothers and sisters, my love for you has greatly expanded, and I rejoice exceedingly in you, seeking earnestly for your safety. However, it is not I alone, but the Lord Jesus working through me. Bound for His sake, I fear even more, knowing I am not yet perfect. Your prayers to God will bring me to perfection, enabling me to attain the destiny appointed to me through His mercy. I turn to the Gospel as I would to the flesh of Jesus Christ, and to the apostles as the elders of the Church. I do also cherish the prophets, who foretold Christ and shared the same Spirit with the apostles. Just as false prophets and apostles were influenced by a deceitful spirit, the true prophets and apostles received the Holy Spirit from God through Jesus Christ—the Spirit who is good, sovereign, true, and the source of salvation. There is one God of both the Old and New Testaments, one Mediator between God and humanity, who created both intelligent and sentient beings and governs them with providence. There is also one Comforter who demonstrated His power through Moses, the prophets, and the apostles. All the saints, therefore, were saved through Christ, hoping in Him, awaiting His arrival, and obtaining salvation through Him. They were holy ones, worthy of love and admiration, confirmed in the Gospel and sharing in our common hope.

{6:1} If anyone comes to you preaching the Jewish law, do not listen to them. It is better to hear Christian doctrine even from someone who is circumcised than to entertain Judaism from someone who is not. If such individuals do not speak of Jesus Christ, they are like monuments and graves of the dead, bearing only human names. Therefore, avoid the deceitful schemes and traps of those who claim to be prophets but deny Christ as the Son of God. They are liars, following their father the devil, falsely claiming to be Jews based solely on physical circumcision. {6:2} If anyone confesses Jesus Christ as Lord but denies the God of the law and the prophets, rejecting that the Father of Christ is the Creator of heaven and earth, they have departed from the truth, akin to their father the devil, and are followers of Simon Magus rather than of the Holy Spirit. Likewise, if someone acknowledges there is one God and confesses Jesus Christ, yet considers the Lord merely a human and not the only-begotten God and Wisdom of this world, beware lest you be led astray by their cunning and weaken in your love. Remain united with an undivided heart. {6:3} I thank my God that I have a clear conscience towards you, and no one can accuse me of burdening anyone, whether in small matters or great. I desire that those among whom I have ministered would not have anything to hold against me. However, those who proclaim Christ as the Son of God and the Word made flesh, yet reduce Him to a mere soul and body, are deceivers who spread falsehoods for the ruin of people. They lack understanding and are known as Ebionites. {6:4} Likewise, those who acknowledge the truths mentioned but condemn lawful marriage and the bearing of children, or declare certain foods as unclean, have the spirit of apostasy within them. Those who confess the Father, Son, and Holy Spirit, and praise God's creation, yet regard the incarnation as mere appearance and feel ashamed of Christ's passion, have indeed denied the faith, no different from the Jews who crucified Christ. {6:5} Furthermore, anyone who affirms these truths and believes that the Word of God dwelt in a human body, being within it as the Word, just as a soul resides in a body because it was God who inhabited it—not a human soul—yet promotes unlawful unions as good and places ultimate happiness in pleasure, akin to those falsely called Nicolaitans, cannot be a lover of God or Christ. They corrupt their own flesh, devoid of the Holy Spirit and estranged from Christ. {6:6} All such individuals are like monuments and graves of the dead, bearing only the names of those who have passed. Therefore, flee from the wicked schemes and traps set by the spirit of this age, lest you be overcome and weaken in your love. Instead, be united with an undivided heart and a willing mind, of one accord and judgment, steadfast in your convictions whether in ease or danger, sorrow or joy. {6:7} I thank God, through Jesus Christ, that I have a clear conscience concerning you. No one can accuse me, privately or publicly, of burdening anyone, whether significantly or insignificantly. I pray that those among whom I have ministered will not have any grounds to testify against me.

{7:1} Though some may have tried to deceive me in worldly matters, my spirit, inspired by God, cannot be deceived. It discerns its origin and purpose, uncovering the secrets of the heart. During my time with you, I earnestly proclaimed with a loud voice: Listen to the bishop, along with the presbytery and deacons. Some suspected I spoke this because I foresaw division among you. Yet I swear by Him for whom I am imprisoned, I received no prior knowledge from anyone. It was the Spirit who revealed to me these instructions: Do nothing without the bishop; maintain your bodies as temples of God; cherish unity; shun division. Follow the example of Paul and the other apostles, just as they followed Christ. {7:2} The Spirit unequivocally declared to me: Do nothing without the bishop; regard your bodies as the sacred abodes of God; uphold unity; avoid divisions. Follow the path of Jesus Christ, just as He followed His Father.

{8:1} Therefore, I did what was necessary as someone dedicated to fostering unity among you. Where there is division, anger, and discord, God cannot dwell. To all those who repent, the Lord offers forgiveness if they sincerely return to the unity of God and communion with the bishop. I rely on the grace of Jesus Christ, who will liberate you from every bondage. I urge you, therefore, to act not out of contention, but in accordance with the teachings of Christ. {8:2} When I heard some saying, "Unless I find it in the ancient Scriptures, I will not believe the Gospel," I responded to them: "It is written." Their reply was, "That remains to be proven." But for me, Jesus Christ stands as the culmination of all antiquity. His cross, death, resurrection, and the faith centered on Him are pristine relics of ancient truth. Through your prayers, I seek justification by clinging to these sacred truths. {8:3} Therefore, I fulfilled my duty as a devoted advocate of unity. For where there is division and wrath, God does not reside. The Lord grants forgiveness to all who repent, if they turn to the unity of God and communion with the bishop. I place my trust in the grace of Jesus Christ, who will set you free from every bondage. I encourage you, therefore, to do nothing out of strife, but according to the teachings of Christ. When I heard some saying, "If it's not in the ancient Scriptures, I won't believe the Gospel," I replied, "It is written." They countered, "That remains to be proven." Yet for me, Jesus Christ embodies all that is ancient. His cross, death, resurrection, and the faith in Him are the purest testimonies of antiquity, through which I seek justification with your prayers.

{9:1} The priests and ministers of the word are indeed good, but the High Priest is better—the one entrusted with the holy of holies and the secrets of God Himself. He is the gateway to the Father, through whom Abraham, Isaac, Jacob, the prophets, the apostles, and the Church enter. All seek to achieve unity with God. However, the Gospel surpasses them all with the appearance of our Lord Jesus Christ, His suffering, and resurrection. While the beloved prophets foretold Him, the Gospel brings the perfection of immortality. All these elements are harmonious if embraced with love. {9:2} The priests and ministers of the word are good; however, the High Priest is better, to whom the holy of holies has been entrusted, and who alone has received the secrets of God. The ministries of God are good. The Holy Spirit is holy, and the Word is holy, the Son of the Father through whom He created all things and governs them all. This is the Way that leads to the Father, the Rock, the Protector, the Key, the Shepherd, the Sacrifice, the Door of knowledge, through whom Abraham, Isaac, Jacob, Moses, and all the prophets, along with the pillars of the world—the apostles—and the bride of Christ, for whose sake He shed His own blood as her dowry to redeem her, have entered. All these strive toward the unity of the one and only true God. But the Gospel possesses something superior to the former dispensation: the appearance of our Savior Jesus Christ, His suffering, and His resurrection. What the prophets foretold, saying, "Until He comes for whom it is reserved, and He shall be the expectation of the Gentiles," has been fulfilled in the Gospel, as our Lord said, "Go and make disciples of all nations, baptizing them in the name of the Father, and of the Son, and of the Holy Spirit." All these aspects—law, prophets, apostles, and all who believe through them—are good together, if we love one another.

{10:1} According to your prayers and the compassion you have in Christ Jesus, I have heard that the Church in Antioch, Syria, now enjoys peace. Therefore, as a Church of God, it would be fitting for you to appoint a representative—a bishop—to go to them on your behalf. This envoy will join them in their gatherings, glorifying the name of God. Blessed is the person in Christ Jesus who is considered worthy of such a ministry; and if you are enthusiastic about this, you will also share in the glory in Christ. If you are willing, it is entirely within your capability to do this for the sake of God. Other nearby churches have sent bishops, presbyters, and deacons for similar purposes, demonstrating that it is a feasible and commendable action.

{11:1} Now regarding Philo the deacon, a man from Cilicia known for his standing, who continues to minister to me in the word of God, along with Gaius and Agathopus, a chosen man who has faithfully accompanied me from Syria, even at the risk of his life—these individuals bear witness in your favor. I also give thanks to God for you because you have welcomed them; and the Lord will also receive you. May those who have dishonored them find forgiveness through the grace of Jesus Christ, who desires not the death of sinners but their repentance. {11:2} The brothers in Troas send their greetings to you, from where I am also writing to you through Burrhus, who was sent with me by the Ephesians and Smyrnaeans to show their regard. May the Lord Jesus Christ honor them, in whom they place their hope, in body, soul, spirit, faith, love, and harmony. Farewell in the Lord Jesus Christ, our shared hope, through the Holy Spirit.

Epistle of Ignatius to the Smyrnaeans

The Epistle of Ignatius to the Smyrnaeans is a key early Christian text by Ignatius of Antioch, written during his journey to Rome, where he expected martyrdom. The letter fiercely defends orthodox Christology, rejecting the docetist heresy, which denied the physical incarnation and suffering of Christ. Ignatius stresses the reality of Christ's birth, death, and resurrection, and advocates for ecclesiastical unity under a hierarchical structure with the bishop at its head to safeguard against doctrinal errors. He also emphasizes the Eucharist as the "medicine of immortality" and calls for adherence to the bishop, reflecting his vision of a unified and orderly Church. This epistle provides valuable insights into early Christian theology, liturgy, and communal life, highlighting Ignatius's role in shaping early Christian thought.

{1:1} I give glory to God, even Jesus Christ, who has bestowed upon you such profound wisdom. I have observed that you are firmly rooted in an unshakable faith, as if you were nailed to the cross of our Lord Jesus Christ, both in body and spirit. You are steadfast in love through the sacrificial blood of Christ, fully convinced concerning our Lord Jesus Christ: that He truly descended from the lineage of David according to the flesh, and by the will and power of God, He is the Son of God. He was born of a virgin, baptized by John to fulfill all righteousness, and indeed, under Pontius Pilate and Herod the tetrarch, He was crucified for us in His physical body. {1:2} It is through His blessed passion that we have received the fruits of redemption, establishing a lasting testament for all generations through His resurrection. This applies to all His holy and faithful followers, both Jews and Gentiles, united in His Church.

{2:1} He endured all these sufferings for our sake, so that we might be saved. His suffering was genuine, just as His resurrection was truly real. Unlike certain unbelievers who claim that His suffering was merely apparent, they themselves merely pretend to be Christians. {2:2} These unbelievers, ashamed of the human form, the cross, and death itself, argue that He only appeared to take on a body from the Virgin and suffered only in appearance. They forget the words of Scripture that affirm His incarnation and resurrection: "The Word became flesh," "Destroy this temple, and in three days I will raise it up," and "If I be lifted up from the earth, I will draw all men unto Me." {2:3} Therefore, the Word truly dwelt in flesh, fulfilling the prophecy that "Wisdom built herself a house." The Word raised His own temple on the third day after it was destroyed by those who opposed Christ. Just as the brazen serpent in the wilderness drew all who looked upon it for healing, so did Christ draw all humanity to Himself through His lifted-up sacrifice for their eternal salvation.

{3:1} I know that not only was Christ possessed of a body during His birth and crucifixion, but also after His resurrection, and I believe He still is. When He appeared to those with Peter, He said to them, "Touch Me and see; for a spirit does not have flesh and bones as you see that I have." And they touched Him, and were convinced both by His physical presence and His spirit. {3:2} This conviction empowered them to despise death and conquer it. After His resurrection, He ate and drank with them, demonstrating His physical nature, while spiritually united with the Father. {3:3} When He appeared to Thomas, He invited him to touch the wounds in His hands and side, prompting Thomas to exclaim, "My Lord and my God!" For forty days after His resurrection, He continued to eat and drink with them, confirming His bodily resurrection, before being taken up in their sight to the Father who sent Him. {3:4} Just as He ascended with His flesh, He will return in glory and power, fulfilling the Scriptures that proclaim His return in the same manner He ascended. If some claim He will return without a body at the end of the world, how then will those who pierced Him see Him, and how will they mourn? Incorporeal beings lack form and figure, unlike Christ, who possesses a glorified body, affirming His tangible and divine nature.

{4:1} I give you these instructions, beloved, confident that you share my convictions. But I warn you in advance about these savage impostors disguised as humans, from whom you should not only reject but even avoid encountering. Yet, pray for them, that perhaps they may repent, although it will be very challenging. Jesus Christ, our true life, has the power to bring about their transformation. If Christ's actions were merely superficial, then I too am superficially bound. Why else would I subject myself to death, fire, the sword, and wild beasts? Yet, whoever is close to the sword is near to God; whoever confronts wild beasts shares company with God, as long as it is in the name of Jesus Christ. I endure all these trials to suffer alongside Him, for He strengthens me inwardly. {4:2} I give you these instructions, beloved, confident that you share my convictions. But I caution you in advance about these beasts in human form, whom you must not only reject but also flee from. However, continue to pray for them, that perhaps they may come to repentance. For if the Lord only appeared in the flesh and was crucified in appearance only, then I too am bound in appearance only. Why would I subject myself to death, fire, the sword, and wild beasts? No, I endure all these hardships for Christ, not superficially, but in reality, so that I may suffer alongside Him. It is Christ Himself who strengthens me inwardly; on my own, I do not possess such strength.

{5:1} Some have ignorantly denied Him, or rather have been denied by Him, choosing falsehood over truth. These individuals have not been persuaded by the prophets, the law of Moses, or even the Gospel up to this day, nor have they understood the sufferings we have endured for our faith. They hold similar views towards us. What benefit is it if someone praises me but blasphemes my Lord, refusing to acknowledge that He truly took on human form? Anyone who denies this truth has effectively rejected Him and remains in spiritual death. I have chosen not to name such individuals, as they are unbelievers. It is far from my intention to mention them until they repent and return to a true belief in Christ's sacrifice, which is our path to resurrection.

{6:1} Let no one deceive themselves. Whether they are beings in heaven, glorious angels, rulers visible or invisible, if they do not believe in the atoning blood of Christ, they will face condemnation. "Let those who have ears to hear, listen." Let no one's position or status inflate them, for true worth lies in faith and love, which surpass all else. Consider those who oppose the grace of Christ that has come to us; they stand in defiance of God's will. They show no love, no concern for the widow, the orphan, or the oppressed—whether they are bound or free, hungry or thirsty, rich or poor, high or low. "Let those who can accept this truth, accept it." Let not wealth, position, or power puff anyone up, nor should poverty or lowly status diminish them. For what truly matters is faith in God, hope in Christ, the anticipation of the promised blessings, and love for God and our neighbors. For "You shall love the Lord your God with all your heart, and your neighbor as yourself." And Jesus said, "This is eternal life, that they know you, the only true God, and Jesus Christ whom you have sent." And He also said, "A new commandment I give to you, that you love one another. On these two commandments depend all the Law and the Prophets." Therefore, be wary of those who preach contrary doctrines, denying that the Father of Christ can be known, displaying enmity and deceit towards one another. They lack love, despise the future blessings we await, treat worldly things as if they are lasting, mock those in affliction, and laugh at those in chains.

{7:1} They abstain from partaking in the Eucharist and from prayer, because they do not acknowledge the Eucharist as the flesh of our Savior Jesus Christ, who suffered for our sins and whom the Father, in His mercy, raised from the dead. Those who speak against this gift of God bring judgment upon themselves through their disputes. It would be better for them to show reverence, so that they too might experience resurrection. Therefore, it is necessary for you to keep away from such individuals, not discussing them either privately or publicly, but instead focusing on the teachings of the prophets and especially the Gospel, where the passion of Christ is revealed to us and His resurrection is fully demonstrated. {7:2} Avoid all divisions, as they are the root of many evils. These individuals are ashamed of the cross, they ridicule the suffering of Christ, and they mock His resurrection. They are offspring of the spirit who is the originator of all evil—a spirit who deceived Adam through Eve, who led Cain to slay Abel, who opposed Job, who accused Joshua the son of Josedech, who sought to shake the faith of the apostles, who stirred the Jews against the Lord, and who presently "works in the sons of disobedience." May the Lord Jesus Christ deliver us from this evil spirit, who prayed that the apostles' faith would not fail, not because He lacked the power to sustain it Himself, but because He rejoiced in the Father's supremacy. {7:3} Therefore, it is crucial for you to keep away from such individuals, avoiding conversations with them whether in private or in public. Instead, pay attention to the teachings of the law, the prophets, and those who have proclaimed to you the message of salvation. Flee from all detestable heresies and those who cause divisions, as they are the beginning of many evils.

{8:1} Ensure that all of you follow the guidance of the bishop, just as Christ Jesus obeys the Father, and respect the presbytery as you would the apostles. Likewise, honor the deacons, for they are appointed by God. Let no one undertake any church-related matter without the bishop's approval. A proper Eucharist should only be administered by the bishop himself or by someone authorized by him. {8:2} Wherever the bishop is present, there should also be a gathering of the congregation, just as wherever Jesus Christ is present, there is the universal Church. It is not permissible to baptize or to conduct a love-feast without the bishop's consent. Whatever he approves of is also pleasing to God, ensuring that everything done is orderly and valid. {8:3} Just as in the presence of Christ, all the hosts of heaven stand ready to serve Him as the Commander of the Lord's might and the Governor of every intelligent being, so too in the church, nothing should be done without the bishop's authority. It is not lawful to baptize, offer sacrifices, or celebrate love-feasts without his approval. What he deems appropriate is also acceptable to God, ensuring the legitimacy and validity of all actions performed.

{9:1} It is reasonable that we return to sober conduct and, while we still have the chance, repent sincerely before God. Let us honor both God and the bishop. Whoever honors the bishop is honored by God, but whoever acts without the bishop's knowledge serves the devil. May grace abound in all things for you, because you are worthy. You have supported me in every way, and Jesus Christ will surely bless you. Whether you love me in my absence or my presence, may God reward you for enduring all things for His sake, leading you to attain to Him. {9:2} It is reasonable that we return to sober conduct and, while we still have the chance, repent sincerely before God. For in Hades, there is no one who can confess their sins. As it is written, "Behold the man, and his work is before him." Therefore, honor God and also honor the bishop, who bears the image of God as a ruler and of Christ as a priest. After God, honor the king as well. Among all beings, there is no one superior to God, nor anyone like Him. Similarly, in the Church, there is no one greater than the bishop, who serves as a priest to God for the salvation of the whole world. Nor is there any ruler comparable to the king, who ensures peace and order for his subjects. Those who honor the bishop will be honored by God, while those who dishonor him will be punished. Just as those who rise up against kings deserve punishment for disrupting public order, how much more severe will the punishment be for those who act without the bishop, thereby destroying the unity and order of the Church? The priesthood is the highest among human goods, and anyone who contends against it dishonors not only humanity but also God and Christ Jesus, the First-born and the High Priest by nature. Therefore, let all things be done decently and in order in Christ. Let the laity be subject to the deacons, the deacons to the presbyters, the presbyters to the bishop, and the bishop to Christ, just as Christ is subject to the Father. {9:3} As you, my brethren, have refreshed me, so will Jesus Christ refresh you. You have shown love to me both in my absence and in my presence. God will reward you for your kindness to His prisoner, even though I may not be worthy of it. Your zeal to help me is commendable, for "he who honors a prophet in the name of a prophet shall receive a prophet's reward." It is clear that those who honor a prisoner of Jesus Christ will receive the reward of the martyrs.

{10:1} You have acted commendably in welcoming Philo, Gaius, and Agathopus, who serve Christ and have followed me for God's sake. They bless the Lord on your behalf because you have refreshed them in every way. Your kindness to them will not go unnoticed. "May the Lord grant that you may find mercy from the Lord on that day!" My spirit is with you, and I appreciate your support for me and my imprisonment, which you have neither despised nor been ashamed of. Therefore, Jesus Christ, our perfect hope, will not be ashamed of you either.

{11:1} Your prayers have reached the Church in Antioch, bringing peace. As I come to you bound, I greet all there, though I consider myself unworthy to be counted among them, being the least. Yet by the will of God, I have been deemed worthy of this honor—not through any merit of my own, but by the grace of God. I pray earnestly that this grace may abound in me, enabling me through your prayers to draw closer to God. {11:2} To ensure completeness in both earthly and heavenly realms, it is fitting for your Church to select a worthy messenger. This delegate can journey to Syria to convey congratulations for their newfound peace and restored order. I suggest that someone from your community be sent with a letter, so that together they can rejoice over the tranquility that God has granted through your prayers. Let them celebrate reaching a safe harbor in Christ. {11:3} As those who strive for perfection, continue to pursue what is excellent. When you are eager to do good, know that God is ready to assist you in every way.

{12:1} The brethren in Troas send their love to you. I write to you through Burrhus, whom you sent with me, along with the Ephesians, your brethren, who have been a great source of encouragement to me. I commend Burrhus as an exemplary minister of God, deserving of grace in all things. {12:2} I greet your esteemed bishop Polycarp, your venerable presbytery, and your Christ-bearing deacons, along with all of you individually and collectively, in the name of Christ Jesus. May His flesh and blood, His passion and resurrection—both physical and spiritual—unite us with God. May grace, mercy, peace, and patience abide with you forevermore in Christ. {12:3} I also send greetings to the families of my brethren, including their wives and children, as well as those who remain virgins and the widows. Be strong in the power of the Holy Spirit. Philo, who is here with me, sends his greetings. I send my regards to the household of Tavias, praying for their steadfastness in faith and love—both in body and spirit. {12:4} I salute Alce, my beloved, along with the exceptional Daphnus, Eutecnus, and all others by name. Farewell to you all, filled with the grace of God and our Lord Jesus Christ, and enriched with the Holy Spirit and divine wisdom.

Epistle of Ignatius to the Polycarp

The Epistle of Ignatius to Polycarp, one of Ignatius of Antioch's authentic letters, offers insights into early Christian theology, ecclesiology, and pastoral care. Written around AD 107 during Ignatius's journey to martyrdom, the letter is addressed to Polycarp, bishop of Smyrna. It highlights Ignatius's high Christology, the importance of unity and church discipline, and the role of bishops in maintaining orthodoxy. Ignatius advises Polycarp on leading with diligence and courage, managing various church members, and understanding suffering as part of discipleship. This epistle sheds light on early Christian thought and church structure, reflecting the challenges faced by early leaders in preserving faith and fostering resilient communities amidst persecution.

{1:1} I rejoice greatly that I have seen firsthand how firmly your mind is anchored in God, like an immovable rock. I praise God loudly for granting me the privilege to behold your blameless face, which I pray I may always enjoy in God's presence. {1:2} I urge you, clothed with the grace of God, to continue steadfastly in your journey and to encourage others to seek salvation. Maintain your position diligently, both in body and spirit. Make every effort to preserve unity, which is of utmost importance. {1:3} Be patient with everyone, just as the Lord is patient with you. Support others with love, as you always do. Dedicate yourself to unceasing prayer. Seek further understanding beyond what you already possess. {1:4} Be vigilant and possess a spirit that is always alert. Speak to each person individually as God enables you. Bear with the weaknesses of others, as a dedicated athlete in the Christian life, just as the Lord Himself bore our infirmities and sicknesses. Remember, the greater the effort, the greater the reward.

{2:1} If you love those who are already good disciples, you deserve no special thanks for that. Instead, seek to gently tame those who are more troublesome. Not every wound heals with the same treatment. Ease intense afflictions with gentle remedies. {2:2} Be wise in your dealings, like a serpent, yet always harmless as a dove. You are both flesh and spirit, equipped to handle visible challenges with tenderness. Pray for insight into unseen challenges so that you lack nothing and abound in every spiritual gift. {2:3} The times demand your attention like a sailor needs the wind, or a storm-tossed ship seeks safe harbor, so that both you and those under your care may reach God. {2:4} Be vigilant and disciplined like an athlete of God. The prize set before you is immortality and eternal life, which you firmly believe in. May my spirit and even my bonds, which you have cherished, be of benefit to you in all things.

{3:1} Do not be troubled by those who appear credible but teach strange doctrines. Stand firm like an anvil under the hammer. It is the mark of a true champion to endure wounds and still emerge victorious. Above all, endure all things for the sake of God, so that He may also endure with us and bring us into His kingdom. {3:2} Increase your zeal continually; run your race with growing vigor. Pay close attention to the times and seasons. While you are here, strive to conquer, for here lies the racecourse and the rewards. Look for Christ, the Son of God, who existed before time began yet appeared in our midst. He was invisible by nature but took on flesh to be visible. Though impalpable and beyond touch, He became tangible for our sake. Originally impassible as God, He became capable of suffering as a man, enduring every form of suffering for our redemption.

{4:1} Do not neglect widows; be their protector and friend, following the example of the Lord. Let nothing be done without your consent, and do nothing without seeking God's approval, as you are steadfast in your faith. Ensure your gatherings are frequent; know each member by name. Treat both male and female slaves with respect, yet do not let them become arrogant. Instead, encourage them to submit willingly, honoring God, so that they may experience true freedom from Him. Do not let them desire freedom at public expense, lest they become enslaved to their own desires.

{5:1} Avoid practicing dark arts, but openly discuss them to expose their falsehood. Encourage my sisters to love the Lord and find fulfillment in their husbands both physically and spiritually. Likewise, urge my brothers in the name of Jesus Christ to love their wives as Christ loves the Church. If anyone can maintain purity in honor of the Lord's standards, let them do so without boasting. Pride leads to downfall; considering oneself greater than the bishop is a path to ruin. Both men and women who marry should seek the blessing of the bishop, ensuring their union aligns with God's will, not driven by personal desires. Let everything be done to honor God.

{6:1} Pay attention to the bishop, so that God will also pay attention to you. My soul aligns with those who submit to the bishop, the presbyters, and the deacons; may I share in their portion from God! Work together, strive together, run together, suffer together, sleep together, and awake together as stewards, associates, and servants of God. Seek to please the One under whom you serve, and from whom you will receive your reward. Let none of you be found a deserter. Let your baptism be your armor, your faith your helmet, your love your spear, and your patience your complete defense. Let your actions be your assignment, so that you may receive a worthy reward. Therefore, be patient with one another in meekness, just as God is patient with you. May I find eternal joy in you!

{7:1} Since I've heard that the Church in Antioch, Syria, is at peace through your prayers, I am encouraged and rest without anxiety in God. If it is through suffering that I may draw nearer to God, then let it be so, and may your prayers affirm me as a true disciple of Christ. Polycarp, blessed in God, it is appropriate to convene a solemn council and choose someone you deeply trust and know to be active, to serve as God's messenger. Bestow upon this person the honor of traveling to Syria, where they can magnify your steadfast love to the glory of God. A Christian is not in control of their own destiny but is always ready to serve God. This task is both God's work and yours, and when completed, it will glorify Him. I trust that, by His grace, you are prepared for every good work that serves God. Knowing your fervent love for the truth, I encourage you through this brief letter.

{8:1} Since I haven't been able to write to all the churches, having to sail suddenly from Troas to Neapolis as the emperor's will commands, I ask you, knowing God's purpose, to write to the nearby churches. Encourage them to act similarly, sending messengers if possible, or transmitting letters through those you send. This work will bring eternal glory to you, fittingly deserved. I send greetings to everyone by name, especially to Epitropus's wife and her household. I greet my beloved Attalus. I salute the one chosen to go to Syria from your midst. May grace be with him always, as with Polycarp who sends him. I pray for your eternal happiness in our God, Jesus Christ, through whom may you continue in unity and under God's protection. Greetings to Alce, my dearly beloved. Farewell in the Lord, with grace upon you.

Epistle of Polycarp to the Philippians

The Epistle of Polycarp to the Philippians is a significant document within early Christian literature, providing a unique glimpse into the theological and ecclesiastical concerns of the 2nd century church. Polycarp, the Bishop of Smyrna, was a prominent early Christian leader and a disciple of the Apostle John, making his writings particularly valuable for understanding the apostolic tradition's continuity. The epistle is traditionally dated to around 110-140 AD and was addressed to the Christian community in Philippi, a city with a notable history of early Christian activity, as evidenced by Paul's own epistle to the Philippians. Polycarp's letter is a pastoral exhortation, rich in moral instruction, and doctrinal reaffirmation, reflecting the challenges and heresies faced by the early church, such as Gnosticism and Docetism. It emphasizes virtues like faith, hope, and love, while also urging steadfastness in the face of persecution. The letter demonstrates Polycarp's deep reverence for the Pauline letters, frequently quoting and alluding to them, thus showcasing the early process of New Testament canon formation. Moreover, Polycarp's epistle provides insights into the early Christian practices of communal care, church governance, and the role of presbyters and deacons. This document not only underscores the interconnectedness of the early Christian communities but also illustrates the theological continuity and pastoral concerns that were foundational to the nascent church's identity and survival. Through his epistle, Polycarp emerges as a pivotal figure in the transmission of apostolic teaching and the defense of orthodox faith, making his letter an invaluable resource for scholars studying early Christianity's development and doctrinal evolution.

{1:1} I have found great joy in our Lord Jesus Christ because you have exemplified true love, following the example set by God. You have stood by those in chains as is fitting for saints, adorning them like crowns—the true elect of God and our Lord. {1:2} Your faith, deeply rooted and spoken of since ancient times, continues to bear fruit for our Lord Jesus Christ, who endured death for our sins but was raised by God from the grave. {1:3} Though you do not see Him now, you believe in Him and rejoice with indescribable and glorious joy. Many aspire to share in this joy, knowing that you are saved by grace through faith, not by works, but by the will of God through Jesus Christ.

{2:1} Therefore, prepare yourselves, "girding up your loins," to serve the Lord with reverence and truth. Leave behind the empty chatter and errors of the world, and instead believe in the God who raised our Lord Jesus Christ from the dead and exalted Him to His right hand, giving Him glory and authority over all in heaven and on earth. {2:2} Every spirit serves Him, for He is coming as the Judge of the living and the dead. Those who do not believe in Him will be held accountable for rejecting His sacrifice. {2:3} But just as God raised Jesus from the dead, He will also raise us up if we faithfully do His will, walk in His commandments, and love what He loves. Keep yourselves free from all unrighteousness, greed, love of money, slander, and falsehood. {2:4} Instead of repaying evil for evil, insults for insults, or curses for curses, remember the teachings of the Lord: "Do not judge, so that you may not be judged; forgive, and you will be forgiven; show mercy, so that you may receive mercy. {2:5} Whatever measure you use will be measured to you. And remember, "Blessed are the poor and those who are persecuted for righteousness' sake, for the kingdom of God belongs to them."

{3:1} Brothers and sisters, I write these things to you about righteousness not because I assume authority, but because you have asked me to do so. Neither I nor anyone else can match the wisdom of the blessed and glorified Paul. {3:2} When he was among you, he taught the word of truth with accuracy and steadfastness in the presence of the living. {3:3} Even when absent, he wrote a letter to you which, if you carefully study, will strengthen the faith given to you. This faith, accompanied by hope and preceded by love for God, Christ, and our neighbor, is the foundation of our spiritual family. {3:4} Whoever possesses these virtues inwardly has fulfilled the command of righteousness, for one who loves is far from all sin.

{4:1} "For the love of money is the root of all kinds of evil." Understanding this, and knowing that we brought nothing into the world and can take nothing out of it, let us equip ourselves with the armor of righteousness. {4:2} Let us first teach ourselves to live according to the commandments of the Lord. Then, let us instruct our wives to walk faithfully in the beliefs entrusted to them, showing love and purity towards their husbands with sincerity, and extending love equally to all with integrity and modesty. Let them raise their children to know and reverence God. {4:3} Teach the widows to live discreetly, devoted to the faith in the Lord, praying continually for everyone. They should avoid slander, gossip, false accusations, the love of money, and all forms of evil. Remember, they are dedicated to God, and He sees everything clearly, even the secrets of the heart, thoughts, and intentions.

{5:1} "Since God cannot be mocked, we must live according to His commandments and honor His glory. Deacons likewise should live blamelessly, as servants of God and Christ, not people-pleasers but faithful stewards. They must avoid slander, deceit, and greed, and instead be self-controlled, compassionate, and diligent, adhering faithfully to the truth of the Lord who served all. {5:2} By pleasing Him in this life, we anticipate our reward in the next, as He promised to raise us from the dead and share His reign with those who believe. {5:3} Similarly, young men should be blameless, especially guarding their purity and restraining themselves from all evil. They must resist worldly temptations, knowing that every indulgence opposes the spirit. Those who engage in immorality will not inherit God's kingdom. Therefore, they should heed the guidance of elders and deacons, as they would Christ Himself. {5:4} Likewise, virgins should maintain a blameless and pure conscience in their conduct."

{6:1} "Presbyters should be compassionate and merciful to everyone, bringing back those who have strayed, visiting the sick, and caring diligently for widows, orphans, and the poor. They should always act in a manner pleasing to God and humanity, avoiding anger, favoritism, and unfair judgment. They must shun greed, not hastily believing accusations against others, and refrain from harsh judgments, recognizing our shared imperfections and sins. {6:2} As we ask the Lord for forgiveness, so should we forgive others, mindful that we are accountable before our Lord and God, each of us facing judgment at the seat of Christ. Therefore, let us serve Him with reverence and fear, as commanded by the apostles who delivered the Gospel and the prophets who foretold the Lord's coming. {6:3} Let us earnestly pursue goodness, guarding against stumbling blocks, false brethren, and those who falsely claim the name of the Lord, leading astray the unsuspecting into error."

{7:1} "Anyone who denies that Jesus Christ came in the flesh is antichrist. Likewise, anyone who rejects the testimony of the cross aligns themselves with the devil. Those who twist the teachings of the Lord to suit their own desires, denying the resurrection and judgment, are deceived by Satan himself. Therefore, let us reject the emptiness of many false doctrines and return to the timeless word passed down from the beginning. {7:2} Let us be vigilant in prayer and steadfast in fasting, earnestly asking the all-seeing God in our petitions to not lead us into temptation, for as the Lord has taught, 'The spirit is willing, but the flesh is weak.'"

{8:1} "Let us continually hold fast to our hope and the assurance of our righteousness, which is found in Jesus Christ. He 'bore our sins in His own body on the tree,' and 'He committed no sin, nor was deceit found in His mouth.' He endured all things for our sake, so that through Him we might have life. {8:2} Therefore, let us follow His example of patience, and if we face suffering for His name, let us glorify Him. He has shown us the way by His own actions, and we have faith that this is true."

{9:1} "I urge you all to obey the teachings of righteousness and to practice patience, following the examples you have witnessed. Look not only to the steadfastness of blessed figures like Ignatius, Zosimus, Rufus, and others among you, but also to the endurance of Paul and the rest of the apostles. {9:2} Be assured that their efforts were not in vain; they lived with faith and integrity, and now dwell in the presence of the Lord, alongside whom they endured suffering. They did not love the fleeting pleasures of this world but instead loved Him who died for us and was raised from the dead by God for our sake."

{10.1} Therefore, stand firm in these principles and follow the Lord's example. Be steadfast and unwavering in your faith, loving the brotherhood, and maintaining unity and truth. Show the gentleness of the Lord in your interactions, and regard everyone with respect. When you have the opportunity to do good, do not delay, for "charity saves from death." Let each of you be humble and considerate, submitting to one another, and live blamelessly among those who are not believers, so that your good deeds may be recognized, and the name of the Lord may not be slandered because of you. However, woe to those who bring dishonor to the name of the Lord! Therefore, teach self-control to everyone and demonstrate it in your own conduct.

{11.1} I am deeply saddened by Valens, who once served as a presbyter among you but seems to have misunderstood his role in the Church. I urge you, therefore, to avoid greed and to live lives of purity and truthfulness. "Stay away from every kind of evil." If someone cannot control themselves in these matters, how can they instruct others? Those who cannot restrain their greed will be tainted by idolatry and judged like non-believers. We all know the judgment of the Lord, don't we? "Don't we realize that God's holy people will judge the world?" as Paul teaches. However, I have not witnessed or heard of such behavior among you, among whom the blessed Paul worked tirelessly and praised at the start of his letter. He commended you in all those churches that were the first to know the Lord, though we in Smyrna hadn't yet come to know Him. I am deeply concerned, therefore, for Valens and his wife. May the Lord grant them genuine repentance! {11:2} Approach this situation with moderation, and "don't treat them as enemies," but rather, seek to restore them as fellow members who have strayed and are suffering, so that you may save your entire community. By doing so, you will build up yourselves in faith.

{12.1} I believe you are well-versed in the Scriptures, and nothing is hidden from you, though I have not yet attained this privilege myself. The Scriptures say, "Be angry, but do not sin," and "do not let the sun go down while you are still angry." It is good if you remember these teachings, as I believe you do. May the God and Father of our Lord Jesus Christ, and Jesus Christ Himself, who is the Son of God and our eternal High Priest, strengthen you in faith, truth, meekness, gentleness, patience, endurance, tolerance, and purity. May He grant you a share among His saints, and also to us, and to all who believe in our Lord Jesus Christ and His Father, who raised Him from the dead. {12:2} Pray for all the saints, and also for kings, rulers, and authorities, and for those who persecute and oppose you, and even for those who are enemies of the gospel, so that your faithfulness may be evident to everyone, and that you may be complete in Him.

{13.1} Both you and Ignatius wrote to me about sending your letters with anyone traveling to Syria, and I will do my best to fulfill this request when the opportunity arises, whether I go myself or send someone suitable on my behalf. The letters from Ignatius that he wrote to us, along with all his other letters that we have, have been sent to you as you asked. They are included with this letter and will greatly benefit you, as they discuss matters of faith, patience, and everything that builds up our faith in the Lord. If you have any additional information about Ignatius himself or those with him, please share it with us.

{14.1} These are the things I have written to you through Crescens, whom I have recommended to you and continue to endorse. He has conducted himself honorably among us, and I believe he will do the same among you. Also, please extend respect to his sister when she visits you. Remain secure in the Lord Jesus Christ. May grace be with all of you. Amen.

Epistle of Pliny and King Trajan

The Epistle of Pliny the Younger to Emperor Trajan, and the subsequent response from Trajan, represents a crucial exchange in the early history of Christian persecution and administrative policy within the Roman Empire. Written around 112 CE, Pliny's letter seeks imperial guidance on how to handle accusations of Christianity, a religion increasingly seen as a challenge to traditional Roman religious practices and societal norms. Pliny's meticulous inquiry highlights his uncertainty about the appropriate judicial procedures and the scope of punishment for Christians, reflecting the broader ambiguity and evolving attitudes towards this nascent faith. Trajan's reply, emphasizing a pragmatic approach—punishing those who refuse to recant but pardoning those who prove their renunciation by performing traditional Roman rites—illustrates the Empire's struggle to balance legal consistency with the practicalities of governance in an era of religious and social transition.

Pliny the Younger to the Emperor Trajan:

- I regularly seek your guidance on matters where I am unsure, as no one is better suited to resolve my uncertainties or enlighten my ignorance. I have never been involved in trials of Christians before, so I am uncertain about which offenses are typically punished or investigated, and to what extent. I am particularly unsure whether there should be a distinction based on age, whether leniency should be shown for repentance, or if a person who has renounced Christianity but was once a Christian should still be punished. I am also uncertain whether the mere name "Christian" should be punished, or only the specific offenses associated with it.
- In dealing with those who were reported to me as Christians, I followed this procedure: I questioned them to determine if they were Christians, and those who confessed were interrogated a second and third time, during which I threatened them with punishment. Those who persisted in their confession were executed, as I believed that stubbornness and unyielding defiance, regardless of their beliefs, deserved punishment. There were others who exhibited the same error, but because they were Roman citizens, I ordered their cases to be sent to Rome.
- As the trials progressed, accusations spread, leading to an anonymous document listing many names. Those who denied being or having been Christians, and who complied with my demands by invoking the gods, offering incense and wine to your image, which I had brought along with statues of the gods, and cursing Christ—things that true Christians supposedly cannot be forced to do—I released. Others named in the informer's document admitted to being Christians but later denied it, claiming they had stopped practicing Christianity years ago, with some having abandoned it up to twenty-five years prior. These individuals worshipped your image and the statues of the gods, and cursed Christ.
- They explained that their only wrongdoing was meeting regularly before dawn to sing hymns to Christ as if he were a god, and binding themselves by oath to avoid committing fraud, theft, or adultery, and to return any entrusted property when asked. After these meetings, they would share a meal, which was always ordinary and harmless. They also claimed they had ceased these gatherings after my edict, which, following your orders, prohibited political associations. To uncover the truth, I tortured two female slaves who were called deaconesses, but I found only evidence of excessive superstition.
- Given the serious nature of the situation and the large number of people involved, I thought it prudent to consult you. This issue appears to be widespread, affecting not only the cities but also the villages and farms. It seems possible to address and remedy this situation. The temples, which had been nearly empty, are now being visited more frequently, established religious rites are being resumed, and sacrificial animals are being purchased in greater numbers. This suggests that many people could be reformed if given the chance for repentance.

Emperor Trajan to Pliny the Younger:

- You handled the cases of those accused of being Christians correctly. It is not possible to establish a universal rule or standard for these cases. Christians should not be actively sought out; if they are accused and found guilty, they should be punished. However, if someone denies being a Christian and proves it—by worshiping our gods, for example—then even if they were suspected before, they should be granted pardon as a sign of repentance. Additionally, accusations made anonymously should not be used in prosecutions. Such accusations set a dangerous precedent and are not in line with the principles of our time.

Epistle of Mathetes to Diognetus

The Epistle of Mathetes to Diognetus is a remarkable early Christian text, traditionally attributed to a figure known as "Mathetes," which means "disciple" in Greek, though the true authorship remains uncertain. Likely written in the late 2nd or early 3rd century, this epistle is addressed to a certain Diognetus, possibly a learned pagan or a public official curious about the nature of Christian beliefs and practices. The text is notable for its sophisticated theological discourse, apologetic tone, and eloquent defense of the Christian faith, contrasting it with both pagan polytheism and Jewish rituals. The epistle emphasizes the transformative power of Christian doctrine, the uniqueness of the Christian way of life, and the mystery of the Incarnation. It is considered one of the finest examples of early Christian apologetic literature, reflecting the intellectual and spiritual engagement of the early Church with the surrounding Greco-Roman world.

{1:1} Since I see, most excellent Diognetus, that you are deeply eager to understand the religion of the Christians, and that your questions about them are precise and thorough—asking what God they trust in, how they worship Him, why they disregard worldly things, why they do not fear death, why they pay no attention to the gods revered by the Greeks, why they reject the superstitions of the Jews, and what is the nature of the love they show one another, and what this new way of life is that has recently appeared among humanity—I gladly welcome your enthusiasm. I pray to God, Who grants both the ability to speak and the ability to hear, that He may allow me to speak in such a way that you may benefit from hearing, and that you may listen in such a way that I, as the speaker, may not be disappointed.

{2:1} So, clear your mind of all the preconceived notions that fill it, discard the habits that mislead you, and start fresh, as if you were hearing a new story for the first time, just as you admitted you needed to do. Don't just look with your eyes but also use your intellect to understand the nature and form of those beings you call and consider to be gods. {2:2} Isn't one of them made of stone, like the ground we walk on, another of bronze, no better than the utensils we use daily, another of wood, which has already started to decay, another of silver, which requires someone to guard it to prevent theft, another of iron, which is corroded by rust, and another of clay, no more beautiful than the pots used for the most disgraceful tasks? {2:3} Aren't all these materials perishable? Aren't they all crafted by fire and iron? Didn't a sculptor create one, a brass founder another, a silversmith another, and a potter yet another? Before these materials were shaped by these artisans, couldn't each of them have been made into something entirely different? Couldn't the vessels we now use, made from the same materials, be fashioned into similar objects by these craftsmen? {2:4} Could not these objects, which you now worship, be transformed again by human hands into mere vessels like any other? Are they not all deaf and blind, without soul, sense, or movement? Do they not all rot and decay? {2:5} Yet you call these things gods, you become their slaves, and you worship them, ultimately becoming just like them. {2:6} This is why you hate Christians, because they do not regard these objects as gods. {2:7} But don't you yourselves, who worship these things, despise them even more? Don't you mock and insult them, leaving the stone and clay ones unprotected, while locking up the silver and gold ones at night and placing guards over them by day to prevent theft? {2:8} As for the honors you think you offer to them, if they were capable of feeling, you would be punishing them rather than honoring them; and if they are incapable of feeling, you insult them by offering sacrifices of blood and fat. {2:9} Would any one of you willingly undergo such treatment, submitting to these rituals? No, not a single person would willingly accept such punishment, because they have the ability to feel and reason; but a stone submits because it is insensible, thus proving its lack of sensibility. {2:10} I could say much more about why Christians do not enslave themselves to such gods, but if someone finds what I've already said insufficient, I think it would be unnecessary to say more.

{3:1} Now, I suppose you are especially curious about why Christians do not practice their religion in the same way as the Jews. {3:2} The Jews, to the extent that they avoid the kind of worship described above, do well in claiming to worship one God who rules the universe and in considering Him as their Master; but in so far as they offer Him worship in similar ways to those previously mentioned, they are completely mistaken. {3:3} While the Greeks, by offering sacrifices to lifeless and deaf statues, show their foolishness, the Jews, believing they are presenting these offerings to God, as though He needed them, ought to realize that this is not true worship but rather foolishness. {3:4} For the One who made the heavens and the earth and everything within them, who provides us with all we need, does not Himself require any of the things He provides to those who mistakenly think they are giving them to Him. {3:5} Those who believe they can honor God with sacrifices of blood, fat, and burnt offerings are, in my opinion, no different from those who pay respect to lifeless idols; for while one group offers sacrifices to things incapable of receiving honor, the other offers them to a Being who needs nothing.

{4:1} But again, their concerns about which foods to eat, their obsession with the Sabbath, their vanity regarding circumcision, and the hypocrisy of their fasting and observing new moons, I believe you do not need me to tell you, are absurd and not worth serious consideration. {4:2} For when God has created things for human use, to accept some as good and reject others as useless or unnecessary, isn't this impious? {4:3} And again, to claim falsely that God forbids us to do any good thing on the Sabbath day, isn't this profane? {4:4} Furthermore, to boast about the mutilation of the flesh as a sign of being chosen by God, as if this makes them particularly beloved by Him, isn't this ridiculous? {4:5} And to watch the stars and the moon, to observe the passing months and days, and to distinguish God's arrangements and the changing seasons according to their own whims—turning some into festivals and others into times of mourning—who would consider this to be true godliness rather than foolishness? {4:6} Therefore, that Christians are right in distancing themselves from the common absurdities and errors of the Jews, as well as their excessive fussiness and pride, I believe you have already been sufficiently taught; but regarding the mystery of their own faith, do not expect to be taught by any human being.

{5:1} For Christians are not set apart from other people by their country, language, or customs. {5:2} They do not live in separate cities of their own, nor do they speak a different language, nor do they lead a strange or extraordinary life. {5:3} They do not possess any invention discovered by human intellect or study, nor do they follow any human doctrines as some do. {5:4} But while they live in Greek and barbarian cities, according to where they are placed, and follow the customs of the local people in matters of clothing, food, and the rest of life's arrangements, their way of life is remarkable and seemingly contrary to what one would expect. {5:5} They live in their own countries, but as if they are just passing through; they participate in everything as citizens, and yet they endure everything as if they are foreigners. Every foreign land is like their homeland, and every homeland is foreign to them. {5:6} They marry and have children like everyone else, but they do not discard their offspring. {5:7} They share meals together, but not their wives. {5:8} They live in the flesh, but they do not live according to the flesh. {5:9} They exist on earth, but their citizenship is in heaven. {5:10} They obey the established laws, and yet they exceed the laws in their own lives. {5:11} They love everyone, yet they are persecuted by everyone. {5:12} They are ignored, yet they are condemned; they are put to death, yet they are filled with life. {5:13} They are poor, yet they make many rich; they lack everything, yet they abound in everything. {5:14} They are dishonored, yet they are glorified in their dishonor; they are spoken ill of, yet they are vindicated. {5:15} They are cursed, yet they bless; they are insulted, yet they show respect. {5:16} They do good, yet they are punished as evildoers; when they are punished, they rejoice as if they are being given new life. {5:17} The Jews fight against them as foreigners, and the Greeks persecute them, and yet those who hate them cannot explain their hostility.

{6:1} In short, as the soul is to the body, so are Christians to the world. {6:2} The soul is spread throughout all parts of the body, and Christians are spread throughout the various cities of the world. {6:3} The soul lives within the body, yet it is not part of the body; so Christians live in the world, yet they are not of the world. {6:4} The soul, though invisible, is guarded in a visible body; so Christians are recognized as being in the world, yet their faith remains unseen. {6:5} The flesh hates the soul and wages war against it, even though it receives no harm, because the soul prevents it from indulging in pleasures; so the world hates Christians, even though they do it no harm, because they stand against its pleasures. {6:6} The soul loves the flesh that hates it, as well as its members; so Christians love those who hate them. {6:7} The soul is enclosed in the body, yet it holds the body together; so Christians are kept in the world as in a prison, yet they hold the world together. {6:8} The soul, though immortal, lives in a mortal body; so Christians dwell among perishable things while they look forward to the imperishable life in heaven. {6:9} The soul, when deprived of food and drink, becomes better; likewise, Christians, when punished, grow more and more each day. {6:10} Such is the important role God has appointed them to, a role they are not allowed to abandon.

{7:1} It is not some human discovery, as I mentioned before, that was given to them, nor do they zealously guard some earthly invention, nor have they been entrusted with the administration of human secrets. {7:2} Instead, it is truly the Almighty Creator of the Universe, the Invisible God Himself, who has placed among men the truth and holy teaching that surpasses human understanding, firmly planting it in their hearts. And He did not send a subordinate, or an angel, or a ruler, or one of those who manage earthly matters, or one of those entrusted with heavenly affairs, but He sent the very Maker and Creator of the Universe Himself, by whom He made the heavens, by whom He confined the sea within its bounds, whose orders all the elements faithfully follow, from whom the sun received its course to govern the day, whom the moon obeys, shining by night as He commands, whom the stars follow in their prescribed paths, by whom all things are ordered and set in place—the heavens and all within them, the earth and all upon it, the sea and all within its depths, fire, air, the abyss, all things in the heights and depths, and all that lies between. He sent Him. {7:3} Do you think He was sent, as some might suppose, to establish a kingdom, to instill fear and terror? {7:4} Not at all. But He was sent in gentleness and humility, just as a king might send his own son, who is also a king. He sent Him as God, He sent Him as a man to men, He sent Him as a Savior, using persuasion, not force, for force is not an attribute of God. {7:5} He sent Him to call, not to persecute; He sent Him out of love, not to pass judgment. {7:6} For He will send Him in judgment, and who will be able to endure His presence? {7:7} Do you not see them thrown to wild beasts in an attempt to make them deny the Lord, yet they remain undefeated? {7:8} Do you not see that the more they are punished, the more they multiply? {7:9} These are not the works of a man; they are the power of God; they are evidence of His presence.

{8:1} For who among men had any knowledge of what God truly was before He came? {8:2} Or do you believe the empty and foolish claims of those arrogant philosophers, some of whom said that God was fire (a destiny they themselves will share), others that He was water, and still others that He was one of the elements that God Himself created? {8:3} And yet if any of these ideas were valid, then any other created thing could equally be considered God. {8:4} But no, all this is mere quackery and deception by magicians. {8:5} No man has seen or recognized Him, but He revealed Himself. {8:6} And He revealed Himself through faith, for it is only through faith that one can see God. {8:7} For God, the Master and Creator of the Universe, who made all things and arranged them in perfect order, was found to be not only a friend to humanity but also patient and long-suffering. {8:8} And this is how He always was, and is, and will be—kind, good, impartial, and truthful, and He alone is good. {8:9} Having conceived a great and indescribable plan, He communicated it only to His Son. {8:10} As long as He kept this wise plan hidden as a mystery, He seemed to neglect us and be indifferent toward us. {8:11} But when He revealed it through His beloved Son and made known the purpose He had prepared from the beginning, He granted us all these blessings at once—participation in His benefits, and the ability to see and understand mysteries that we could never have anticipated.

{9:1} Having thus conceived everything already in His mind with His Son, He allowed us, during the previous time, to be led astray by our own disorderly desires and passions, not because He delighted in our sins, but because He was patient with us. It wasn't that He approved of the past era of wickedness, but that He was creating the present era of righteousness so that, being convicted by our past actions as unworthy of life, we might now become deserving through the goodness of God. And, having made clear our inability to enter into the kingdom of God on our own, we might now be able to do so through God's power. {9:2} When our sinfulness was fully exposed, and it was clear that punishment and death were the expected outcome, the time came that God had ordained—when He would now reveal His goodness and power. Oh, the exceeding greatness of God's kindness and love! He did not hate us, nor did He reject or hold a grudge against us. Instead, He was patient and long-suffering, and in His pity for us, He took upon Himself our sins. He gave His own Son as a ransom for us—the holy for the lawless, the innocent for the wicked, the just for the unjust, the incorruptible for the corruptible, the immortal for the mortal. {9:3} For what else but His righteousness could have covered our sins? {9:4} In whom else could we, lawless and ungodly as we were, have been justified, if not in the Son of God? {9:5} Oh, the sweet exchange, oh, the incomprehensible creation, oh, the unexpected blessings—that the sins of many should be hidden in one Righteous Man, and the righteousness of One should justify many who are sinful! {9:6} Having thus shown in the past our inability to attain life, and now revealing a Savior who can save even those who are powerless, He willed that for both reasons we should believe in His goodness and view Him as a guardian, father, teacher, counselor, healer, mind, light, honor, glory, strength, and life.

{10:1} If you also desire this faith, first seek a full understanding of the Father. {10:2} For God loved mankind, for whose sake He made the world, to whom He subjected all things on earth, to whom He gave reason and intellect, whom alone He permitted to gaze toward heaven, whom He created in His own image, to whom He sent His only begotten Son, to whom He promised the kingdom of heaven, and will give it to those who love Him. {10:3} And when you have attained this full knowledge, imagine what joy you will feel, or how deeply you will love the One who loved you first. {10:4} And in loving Him, you will become an imitator of His goodness. Do not be surprised that a man can imitate God. He can, if God wills it. {10:5} For happiness does not consist in ruling over others, or in wanting more than those who are weaker, or in possessing wealth and using power over those who are beneath you. No one can imitate God in these things, for they are not part of His greatness. {10:6} But whoever takes upon himself the burden of his neighbor, whoever desires to benefit one who is worse off in something in which he himself is superior, whoever by giving to those in need what he has received from God becomes like a god to those who receive from him—he is an imitator of God. {10:7} Then, even though you are on earth, you will see that God lives in heaven. Then you will begin to declare the mysteries of God. Then you will both love and admire those who endure suffering because they refuse to deny God. Then you will condemn the deceit and error of the world. When you perceive the true life in heaven, you will despise the apparent death on earth, and you will fear the true death, which is reserved for those who will be condemned to the eternal fire that will punish them until the end. {10:8} Then you will admire those who endure the temporary fire for righteousness' sake, and you will consider them blessed when you understand that the fire is only for a season, while the reward they gain is eternal. Their suffering is but a brief trial compared to the everlasting life and glory that awaits them in the presence of God.

{11:1} My teachings are neither strange nor filled with confusing questions; rather, as a disciple of the Apostles, I now serve as a teacher to the Gentiles, faithfully passing on the lessons that have been entrusted to me by the truth. {11:2} For who among those properly instructed and in communion with the Word does not strive to fully understand the teachings revealed openly by the Word to His disciples? These teachings were not understood by unbelievers but were plainly spoken to the disciples, who were deemed faithful and worthy by Him to receive the mysteries of the Father. {11:3} For this reason, He sent forth the Word to manifest Himself to the world. Though He was dishonored by His own people and preached by the Apostles, He was believed in by the Gentiles. {11:4} This Word, who existed from the beginning, appeared as something new yet was shown to be ancient, and remains forever young in the hearts of the saints. {11:5} He, who is eternal and today is acknowledged as the Son, enriches the Church through whom grace is revealed and multiplied among the saints. This grace bestows understanding, unveils mysteries, proclaims the seasons, delights in the faithful, and is given to those who earnestly seek it—those who remain true to the faith and do not stray from the teachings of the forefathers. {11:6} Thus, the fear inspired by the law is honored, the grace foretold by the prophets is recognized, the faith of the gospels is affirmed, the tradition of the apostles is preserved, and the joy of the Church is expressed. {11:7} If you do not grieve this grace, you will understand the teachings spoken by the Word through those whom He chooses, when and as He wills. {11:8} In all things, when we are inspired by the commanding Word to speak, even with great effort, we share this with you out of love for the truths revealed to us.

{12:1} Faced with these truths and giving them your full attention, you will come to understand how much God grants to those who love Him rightly. They become like a paradise of delight, a tree bearing all kinds of fruit and flourishing, growing within themselves, adorned with various fruits. {12:2} In this garden, both a tree of knowledge and a tree of life have been planted; yet it is not the tree of knowledge that brings death, but rather disobedience. {12:3} The scriptures clearly state how, from the beginning, God planted both a tree of knowledge and a tree of life in the midst of Paradise, revealing life through knowledge. However, because our first parents did not use this knowledge rightly, they were stripped bare by the deceit of the serpent. {12:4} For there is no true life without knowledge, nor sound knowledge without true life; therefore, the two trees are planted close to each other. {12:5} Understanding this truth and condemning the knowledge pursued apart from the life-giving commandment, the apostle declares, "Knowledge puffs up, but love builds up." {12:6} For the person who thinks they know something, but lacks the true knowledge that is attested by a life lived accordingly, is ignorant and deceived by the serpent because they have not loved life. But the one who, with reverence, acknowledges and seeks life plants with hope, anticipating the fruit to come. {12:7} Let your heart be filled with knowledge, and your life be guided by true reason, understood correctly. {12:8} If you cultivate this tree and harvest its fruit, you will continually reap the harvest that God desires—a harvest untouched by the serpent, free from deceit, where Eve is not corrupted but is instead believed to be a virgin. {12:9} Here, salvation is proclaimed, the apostles are filled with understanding, the Passover of the Lord advances, the congregations are gathered, and everything is set in order. As He instructs the saints, the Word rejoices, through whom the Father is glorified. To Him be glory forever and ever. Amen.

Epistle of Peter to Philip

The Epistle of Peter to Philip is an early Christian apocryphal text, typically associated with the Nag Hammadi library, a collection of Gnostic writings discovered in Egypt in 1945. This text, written in Coptic, offers a glimpse into the theological debates and spiritual concerns of early Christian communities, particularly those with Gnostic inclinations. The epistle is presented as a letter from the Apostle Peter to the Apostle Philip, followed by a narrative in which the apostles, led by Peter, seek divine guidance on doctrinal matters and their mission. Central themes include the struggle against cosmic powers, the nature of divine knowledge (gnosis), and the role of Jesus Christ as a spiritual redeemer who provides illumination to his followers. The text reflects a blend of orthodox Christian elements with Gnostic cosmology, emphasizing the apostolic authority and the esoteric knowledge required for salvation. Although not part of the canonical New Testament, "The Epistle of Peter to Philip" provides valuable insight into the diverse theological landscape of early Christianity.

Peter, an apostle of Jesus Christ, writes to Philip, our beloved brother and fellow apostle, along with the brethren who are with him, extending greetings. Peter informs Philip that the Lord and Savior, Jesus Christ, commanded them to gather and preach the salvation promised by Him. However, Philip had been separate from them and did not desire to join in this mission. Peter then asks if it would be agreeable for Philip to come together with them as per the Lord's command. Upon receiving the message, Philip joyfully went to Peter, who then gathered the other apostles. They went to the Mount of Olives, where they had previously gathered with Jesus. Kneeling, the apostles prayed to the Father, asking Him to hear them as He had taken pleasure in His holy child, Jesus Christ, who illuminated them in their darkness. They prayed again, calling upon Christ, the Son of life and immortality, to grant them power as their enemies sought to kill them. Suddenly, a great light appeared, illuminating the mountains, and a voice from the light, identified as Jesus Christ, assured them of His eternal presence. The apostles then asked Jesus about the deficiency of the aeons, their current state, their departure from this world, the authority of boldness, and why the powers fought against them. Jesus explained that the deficiency of the aeons originated from the disobedience and foolishness of the mother, who acted without the Father's command, leading to the rise of the Arrogant One, who sowed a part of her essence and placed powers over it, creating mortal bodies from this misrepresentation. Jesus then spoke of the pleroma, stating that He had descended into the mortal form to save the fallen seed. Though many did not recognize Him, He spoke to those who belonged to Him, giving them the authority to inherit their true fatherhood and thus transform their deficiency into pleroma. Jesus reminded them that they were detained because they belonged to Him and would become illuminators among men once they shed their corrupted selves. He then instructed them to fight against the powers by teaching salvation to the world and praying with the strength of the Father, assuring them that He would be with them forever. Thunder and lightning signaled the end of His appearance as He ascended to heaven. The apostles thanked the Lord and returned to Jerusalem, discussing the light they had witnessed and the suffering they would endure like their Lord. Peter reminded them that Jesus suffered on their behalf, and they, too, must suffer due to their human frailty. A voice confirmed that their suffering was necessary and would lead them before synagogues and governors. The apostles, filled with joy, reached Jerusalem, where they taught salvation in Jesus' name and healed many. Peter, filled with the Holy Spirit, reminded his fellow disciples of Jesus' suffering, crucifixion, and resurrection, emphasizing that while Jesus was a stranger to suffering, they suffered because of the transgression of the mother. He urged them not to obey the lawless but to follow the Lord's teachings. Afterward, the apostles, filled with the Holy Spirit, performed healings and departed to preach the gospel of Jesus. Jesus then appeared to them, blessing them with peace, joy, grace, and power, reminding them not to be afraid as He would be with them forever. The apostles then parted in four directions to spread the message of Jesus in peace.

Epistle of Ptolemy

The Epistle of Ptolemy the Gnostic, a seminal text in early Christian and Gnostic literature, presents a complex theological discourse that offers profound insights into the nature of the Law and its divine and human origins. Written by the Gnostic theologian Ptolemy, this epistle engages with contemporary debates regarding the origins and nature of Mosaic Law, addressing a dualistic interpretation that contrasts the benevolent God of the New Testament with the more malevolent deity attributed to the Old Testament by some early Christian critics. Ptolemy's treatise is distinguished by its attempt to reconcile these divergent perspectives by proposing a nuanced threefold division of the Law: divine, human, and elder traditions, each with its distinct origin and purpose. This work not only reflects the intricate theological and exegetical methods of early Gnostic thought but also engages critically with the concept of divine justice, the nature of Mosaic legislation, and its symbolic and practical implications. Through a detailed examination of scriptural references and a sophisticated hermeneutical approach, Ptolemy seeks to clarify the role of the Law within the broader framework of Christian salvation history, revealing both the limitations and the transformative potential of religious legal systems. As such, the Epistle of Ptolemy offers valuable insights into the early Christian understanding of law, justice, and divine authority, and remains a critical text for scholars exploring the intersections of Gnosticism, early Christianity, and biblical interpretation.

Dear Sister Flora,

The Law given through Moses is not well understood by many who lack a deep knowledge of either its author or its commandments. You will find the complexity of this issue clearer once you explore the diverse opinions on the matter. Some believe that the Law was given by God the Father, while others, opposing this view, insist that it was established by the Devil, whom they also claim created the world. Both views are incorrect; they contradict each other and fail to grasp the truth. It is clear that the Law was not given by the perfect God the Father, as it is secondary and imperfect, needing further completion, and contains commandments that are inconsistent with the nature of such a God. Conversely, attributing the Law to the Devil, who is unjust, is also mistaken, since the Law is fundamentally against injustice. Those who hold this view misunderstand what the Savior taught. As our Savior said, "A house divided against itself cannot stand" [Matt 12:25], and the apostle John states, "Everything was made through him, and apart from him nothing was made" [John 1:3]. This establishes that creation, and thus the Law, comes from a just God, not from one who corrupts. From this, it is evident that both groups miss the truth: the first group does not understand the God of justice, and the second does not know the Father revealed by the Savior. It remains for us, who are granted insight into both, to clarify the nature of the Law and its legislator. We will base our explanation on the Savior's words, which are the only true guide to understanding reality. Firstly, you should know that the entire Law in the Pentateuch is not from a single legislator—some commandments are from Moses, and some are from other sources. The Savior's teachings reveal this threefold division. The first part is from God alone, the second from Moses, not as God's direct legislation but based on his own perspective, and the third from the elders of the people, who introduced some laws themselves. Here is how the Savior's teachings support this division. In a discussion about divorce, the Savior said, "Because of your hard-heartedness Moses permitted a man to divorce his wife; but from the beginning it was not so. For God made this marriage, and what God has joined together, man must not separate" [Matt 19:8]. This shows that there is a divine Law against divorce, while Moses allowed it due to the people's hardness of heart. This demonstrates that Moses' law differs from God's. Moses did not create this law arbitrarily; he provided it out of necessity, knowing that the people could not adhere to God's original intention. To prevent greater injustice and potential destruction, Moses introduced a less severe law of divorce. This shows that Moses' legislation was different from God's, even if we use only one example. The Savior also pointed out that some laws are based on elder traditions. He said, "God said, 'Honor your father and your mother,' but you [elders] have declared that a gift to God nullifies the Law of God through your tradition" [Matt 15:4-9]. Isaiah also criticized this, saying, "This people honors me with their lips, but their hearts are far from me; they teach human precepts as if they were commandments from God." Therefore, it is clear that the Law is divided into three parts: the laws of Moses, the elders, and God himself. This division reveals the truth about the Law. The part of the Law from God can be further divided into three categories: first, the pure legislation not mixed with injustice, which is the Decalogue—the Ten Commandments—engraved on two tablets, which the Savior came to fulfill [Matt 5:17]. Second, the legislation mixed with injustice, such as the "eye for an eye" principle, which the Savior abolished because it was inconsistent with divine goodness. Third, the allegorical or symbolic laws, such as those related to sacrifices, circumcision, the Sabbath, fasting, Passover, and unleavened bread, which represent spiritual truths. These symbols and images were valid until the arrival of the Truth, which has now transformed their meanings. The Savior instructed us to make spiritual offerings rather than animal sacrifices, to be spiritually circumcised rather than physically, to keep a Sabbath from evil deeds, and to fast spiritually, not just physically. External fasting is still practiced as a reminder, but it should not be done out of habit or on a specific day. Similarly, Paul referred to Passover and unleavened bread as images, stating, "Christ our Passover has been sacrificed, so let us be unleavened bread, not containing leaven [evil], but being a new lump" [1 Cor 5:7]. Thus, the Law of God is divided into three parts: the pure and completed legislation, the legislation mixed with injustice, and the symbolic laws. The Savior completed the first part, abolished the second, and transformed the symbolic part into spiritual teachings. The disciples of the Savior and Paul confirm this division. They describe the part of the Law related to images as symbolic, the unjust laws as abolished, and the pure laws as holy and just [Rom 7:12; Eph 2:15]. Finally, it remains to identify the legislator of the Law. Since it was neither the perfect God nor the Devil, it must be an intermediary, the demiurge who created the universe and everything in it. This being, distinct from both the perfect God and the Devil, is just but not inherently good or evil. He is a mediator of justice and stands between the two extremes. The perfect God is good, as declared by the Savior, while the Devil represents evil and corruption. The intermediary is not purely good or evil but is just, as he mediates justice. He is inferior to the perfect God and superior to the Devil, possessing a substance that is neither wholly divine nor wholly corrupt. Do not be troubled by how these differing natures originated from a single, ungenerated, incorruptible good principle. If God permits, you will learn more about their origins and generation from the apostolic tradition we have received. I hope this brief explanation has been clear and beneficial to you, dear Flora. If you receive these teachings well, they will be valuable to you in the future.

Epistle of Pontius Pilate

The Epistle of Pontius Pilate is a purported letter addressed by Pontius Pilate, the Roman governor of Judea, to Tiberius Caesar, the Roman Emperor, regarding the trial, crucifixion, and posthumous influence of Jesus Christ. Although its authenticity remains highly contested and is generally regarded as part of the apocryphal literature surrounding the New Testament, this epistle offers a unique perspective on the events of Christ's death from the viewpoint of Roman authority. Written in the style of official correspondence, it portrays Pilate as a reluctant participant in Jesus' execution, pressured by the Jewish leaders and the public to authorize the crucifixion of a man he deemed virtuous and innocent. The document also makes reference to miraculous signs following Christ's death and acknowledges the growing influence of his disciples, framing Jesus as a figure of both historical and theological significance. While the text's historicity is dubious, it reflects early Christian efforts to situate the Passion of Christ within the context of Roman governance and to suggest the universality of Jesus' impact, even within imperial circles.

Pontius Pilate to Tiberius Caesar, the Emperor – Greetings:

Concerning Jesus Christ, whom I fully informed you about in my last report, a severe punishment has finally been carried out at the will of the people, though I was personally unwilling and apprehensive about it. In truth, no era has ever known, nor will it ever know, a man so virtuous and upright.

However, the people made an extraordinary effort to see him condemned, and all their scribes, leaders, and elders united in their decision to crucify this messenger of truth. Even their own prophets, much like the Sibyls among us, advised against this action. Yet, when he was crucified, supernatural signs appeared, which, according to the judgment of philosophers, seemed to threaten the entire world with destruction.

His disciples continue to thrive, living in a manner that reflects the teachings of their master through their behavior and self-discipline. In fact, in his name, they perform acts of great kindness and generosity. If I had not feared the potential for an uprising among the people, who were nearly in a state of frenzy, perhaps this man would still be alive today. However, feeling more obligated to maintain loyalty to your authority than following my own instincts, I did not exert my full effort to stop the execution and the shedding of innocent blood, blood that was unjustly condemned by the malice of men. As the Scriptures predict, this has only led to their own destruction.

Farewell. Written on the 5th of the Calends of April.

Epistle of Herod to Pontius Pilate

The Epistle of Herod to Pilate the Governor is a pseudepigraphical text that forms part of the apocryphal writings associated with early Christian literature. It is traditionally thought to be one of several letters exchanged between Herod Antipas, the ruler of Galilee, and Pontius Pilate, the Roman governor of Judea. Although not considered canonical or historically authentic, the letter offers insight into early Christian perceptions of the roles these figures played in the Passion narrative. In this text, Herod expresses concerns regarding the consequences of Jesus' crucifixion and reflects on the supernatural events following Christ's death. Scholars typically examine such writings to better understand how early Christian communities negotiated their beliefs concerning the interaction between Jewish and Roman authorities during the time of Jesus.

Herod to Pontius Pilate, the Governor of Jerusalem:

Greetings.

I am in great distress, and I write to you with a heavy heart, hoping that when you read these words, you will share in my grief. My beloved daughter, Herodias, was playing on a frozen pool of water when the ice suddenly broke beneath her. Her body fell into the water, and tragically, her head was severed and remained on the surface of the ice. Her mother now sits with her daughter's head resting on her lap, and our entire household is consumed by sorrow.

When I first heard of the man named Jesus, I wanted to visit you to see him in person, to hear his words, and to understand if his teachings were like those of ordinary men. But now, I am convinced that the misfortunes befalling me are a punishment for the many evils I have committed. Especially because of what I did to John the Baptist, and how I mocked Christ. I now see that I am receiving the righteous judgment I deserve, for I have spilled the blood of many innocent children. Indeed, God's judgments are just, and everyone is rewarded according to their deeds and thoughts.

Since you had the privilege of meeting this God-man, I ask that you pray for me. My son Azbonius is also at death's door, and I, too, am suffering terribly, stricken with dropsy. I am in great agony, a fitting punishment for having persecuted John, the one who introduced baptism by water. Truly, my brother, God's judgments are righteous.

On top of all this, my wife, who grieves deeply for our daughter, has lost the sight in her left eye. This affliction has come upon her because we sought to blind the Eye of righteousness. There is no peace for evildoers, as the Lord has said. And now, great tribulation is coming upon the priests and the scribes of the law, for they handed over the Just One to you. This marks the end of the world as we know it, for they have allowed the Gentiles to become heirs to the promise. The children of light are cast out because they have not obeyed the teachings concerning the Lord and his Son.

So, Pilate, prepare yourself and embrace righteousness. You and your wife should remember Jesus day and night, for the kingdom will belong to the Gentiles. We, the chosen people, mocked the Righteous One and are now paying the price for it.

If it is possible to make this request of you, Pilate, given that we once held power, I ask that you see to the proper burial of my family. It is more fitting that we be buried by you than by the priests, for as Scripture foretells, the priests themselves will soon face vengeance at the return of Jesus Christ.

Farewell to you and to your wife, Procla.

I am sending you the earrings of my daughter and my own ring, so that they may serve as a memorial of my passing. Already, my body has begun to decay, with worms emerging from it, and I know that I am facing the temporal judgment of this life. But I tremble at the thought of the judgment to come, for while this earthly judgment is temporary, the judgment of eternity is forever.

End of the Letter to Pilate the Governor.

Epistle of Pontius Pilate to Herod

The Epistle of Pilate to Herod belongs to the body of apocryphal literature circulating in the early centuries of Christianity, addressing the dramatic events surrounding the crucifixion of Jesus. In this fictional correspondence, Pilate responds to Herod, often conveying a sense of remorse or confusion regarding the political and theological implications of Jesus' death. This letter, like others in the tradition, reflects the early Christian community's attempt to engage with and reinterpret the role of Roman authority in the Passion. While the historicity of the correspondence is widely dismissed, it serves as a valuable text for understanding the narrative development of Pilate as a figure within Christian tradition, often portrayed with conflicted emotions about his involvement in the execution of Christ.

Pilate to Herod the Tetrarch:

Greetings.

Be aware that on the day you delivered Jesus to me, I washed my hands to declare my innocence. I did so because I did not want to be responsible for the death of the man who, after three days, rose from the grave. You had wanted me to participate in his crucifixion, and so I carried out your wishes. But now, I have learned from the executioners and soldiers who guarded his tomb that he has indeed risen from the dead.

I have confirmed this by further testimony. He has appeared in Galilee, in the same form, with the same voice, teaching the same doctrine, surrounded by the same disciples. He has not changed in any way, boldly proclaiming his resurrection and the promise of an eternal kingdom.

Heaven and earth rejoice at this, and my wife, Procla, has come to believe in the visions she experienced when you asked me to deliver Jesus to the people of Israel due to their hatred toward him. Upon hearing of his resurrection and appearance in Galilee, Procla took Longinus the centurion and twelve soldiers—the same who had guarded the tomb—and went to see Christ, almost as if going to witness a great spectacle. They saw him standing with his disciples.

As they stood there, amazed, Christ looked at them and asked, "What is it? Do you now believe in me?" He turned to Procla and said, "In the covenant given to the fathers, it was said that every body which has perished will live again through my death, which you have witnessed. And now, you see that I am alive, though you crucified me. I suffered greatly until I was laid in the tomb, but now, hear me and believe in my Father, God, who is within me. I have broken the cords of death and shattered the gates of Sheol, and my return will be known throughout the earth."

When Procla and the Romans heard these words, they came back to me weeping, for they too had been complicit in the wrongs done to him. This weighed heavily on me, so much so that I lay on my bed in sorrow, wearing mourning clothes. With my wife, Procla, and fifty Roman soldiers, I set out for Galilee.

On the way, I confessed to those with me that Herod was responsible for all of this, that he had conspired with me and forced me to raise my hand against this innocent man—to judge the one who judges all and to scourge the Righteous One, the Lord of the just. As we neared him, Herod, we heard a great voice from heaven, accompanied by terrifying thunder. The earth shook and released a sweet fragrance, unlike anything ever smelled even in the temple of Jerusalem. As I stood there, the Lord saw me while he was speaking with his disciples. Though I did not speak aloud, I prayed in my heart, for I knew it was he whom you had delivered to me. I understood that he was the Lord of all creation, the Creator of everything. When we saw him, all of us fell on our faces at his feet.

With a loud voice, I cried out, "I have sinned, O Lord, in that I judged you, the one who judges all in truth. Now I know you are God, the Son of God. I only saw your humanity, not your divinity. But Herod and the children of Israel forced me to do this evil against you. Have mercy on me, O God of Israel!"

My wife, in great anguish, also cried out, "God of heaven and earth, God of Israel, do not judge me according to the deeds of Pontius Pilate, or according to the will of the children of Israel, or according to the schemes of the priests. But remember my husband in your glory!"

The Lord then drew near to us and lifted up me, my wife, and the Romans. I looked at him and saw the scars of the cross on his body. He said, "What all the righteous fathers hoped for and did not see has now come to pass. In your time, the Lord of Time, the Son of Man, the Son of the Most High, has risen from the dead. He is glorified by all that he has created and established forever and ever."

(1) Justinus, a writer in the days of Augustus, Tiberius, and Gaius, wrote in his third discourse: Mary, the Galilean, who gave birth to Christ, who was crucified in Jerusalem, had not known a man. And Joseph did not abandon her, but lived in sanctity without a wife, along with his five sons from a previous marriage. Mary, too, remained without a husband.

(2) Theodorus wrote to me, Pilate the Governor: Who was the man against whom there was a complaint before you, that he was crucified by the people of Palestine? If many demanded this justly, why did you not follow through on their righteousness? And if they demanded it unjustly, how did you break the law and carry out such an unrighteous act? I responded to him: Because he performed great signs, I did not want to crucify him. But his accusers claimed he called himself a king, so I crucified him.

(3) Josephus says: King Agrippa, dressed in a robe woven with silver, watched a spectacle in the theater at Caesarea. When the people saw his garment shining, they proclaimed, "We once feared you as a man, but now you are exalted beyond the nature of mortals." Soon after, Agrippa saw an angel standing over him, and he was struck down as if unto death.

End of the Letter of Pilate to Herod.

Report of Pontius Pilate to Tiberius Caesar

The Report of Pontius Pilate, Procurator of Judaea, Sent to Rome to Tiberius Caesar is a historically significant yet debated document that purportedly details Pilate's account of the trial and crucifixion of Jesus Christ. Written as a formal communication to the Roman Emperor, Tiberius Caesar, the letter offers a first-person perspective on the events surrounding the condemnation of Jesus. Pilate, under pressure from Jewish leaders and the public, conveys his personal reluctance and sense of injustice regarding Jesus' crucifixion, emphasizing the extraordinary character of Jesus and the supernatural occurrences that followed his death. While the authenticity of the report is contested among scholars, it remains a fascinating document for its potential insights into Roman governance, early Christian history, and the political and religious tensions of 1st-century Judea.

To the most mighty, revered, and august Pilate Pontius, governor of the East:

I humbly report to your excellency, with great fear and trembling, the extraordinary events that have recently occurred, as the conclusion of these matters has shown. While I, my lord, in accordance with your command, was fulfilling my duties as governor of Jerusalem, one of the cities of the East, where the temple of the Jewish nation is located, a great multitude of the Jewish people gathered and brought before me a man named Jesus. They accused him of numerous charges, all of which were baseless, and they could not convict him of any wrongdoing.

One of their grievances against him was that he claimed the Sabbath was not their true day of rest. This man, however, performed many miraculous healings and good deeds. He made the blind see, cleansed lepers, and raised the dead. He healed paralyzed individuals who were unable to move any part of their bodies, except for their voices, and restored their ability to walk and run with just a single command. He performed another mighty miracle that even surpasses the works of our own gods: he raised a man named Lazarus, who had been dead for four days. Although Lazarus' body had begun to decay and was infested with worms, Jesus commanded him to rise with a single word. Lazarus emerged from the tomb, filled with the fragrance of life, like a bridegroom leaving the bridal chamber.

Some individuals who were tormented by demons and lived in the wilderness—eating their own flesh and dwelling with reptiles and wild beasts—he restored to sanity, allowing them to live peacefully in cities and in their own homes. With a word, he restored their minds. He cured those possessed by unclean spirits, and in one instance, he sent the demons into a herd of swine, causing the pigs to drown in the sea. He also healed a man with a withered hand, restoring him to full health.

There was also a woman who had suffered from a hemorrhage for many years, to the point that her bones were visible beneath her skin. All the physicians had abandoned her, deeming her condition incurable. One day, as Jesus passed by, she touched the fringe of his garment, and in that very moment, her body was completely healed. She ran back to her hometown of Paneas as if nothing had ever been wrong with her.

All of these things truly happened. The Jews accused Jesus of performing these miracles on the Sabbath. I myself witnessed that the miracles he performed were far greater than any of those performed by the gods we worship.

Herod, Archelaus, Philip, Annas, and Caiaphas, along with all the people, delivered him to me to be judged. They were stirring up an insurrection against me, so I ordered Jesus to be crucified.

After he was crucified, darkness covered the entire earth. The sun was completely hidden, and though it was midday, the sky appeared dark as night, and stars became visible, though they too seemed dimmed. As I believe you are aware, during this time, people around the world lit lamps from noon until evening. The moon, which was full that night, turned the color of blood and did not shine at all. Even the stars, and the constellation Orion, seemed to mourn what the Jews had done.

Then, on the first day of the week, at around the third hour of the night, the sun shone in a way it never had before, lighting up the entire sky. Majestic figures, too glorious to describe, appeared in the heavens, surrounded by countless angels. The angels cried out, "Glory to God in the highest, and on earth peace, goodwill toward men!" They proclaimed, "Come forth from Hades, you who have been held captive in the underworld." At their words, the mountains and hills shook, rocks split apart, and great chasms opened in the earth, revealing even the depths of the abyss.

Amidst this terror, witnesses reported seeing the dead rise. The Jews who saw this claimed to have seen Abraham, Isaac, Jacob, and the twelve patriarchs who had been dead for over two thousand years. They even saw Noah walking among the people. The multitude sang praises to God with loud voices, proclaiming, "The Lord our God, who has risen from the dead, has brought life to all the dead and has vanquished Hades, putting death to an end."

Throughout that entire night, the light did not fade. Many of the Jews perished, swallowed up by the chasms that opened in the earth. The bodies of those who had spoken against Jesus were never found. Of all the synagogues in Jerusalem, only one remained standing, as all those that had been against Jesus were destroyed.

In great fear and confusion, I immediately ordered all of these events to be recorded, and I now report them to your mightiness.

Report of Pontius Pilate to Augustus Caesar

The Report of Pilate the Governor, Concerning Our Lord Jesus Christ, Which Was Sent to Augustus Caesar in Rome is a pseudepigraphal text traditionally attributed to Pontius Pilate, the Roman governor who presided over the trial and crucifixion of Jesus Christ. This document, part of a larger body of early Christian apocrypha, purports to provide a firsthand account of the events surrounding Jesus' final days, his miraculous acts, and the extraordinary cosmic and supernatural occurrences that accompanied his death and resurrection. Addressed to Emperor Augustus, it reflects the early Christian effort to establish the significance of Jesus' crucifixion and its divine implications, set against a backdrop of Roman political and cultural authority. Although the historical authenticity of the report is widely disputed, it offers valuable insight into the early Christian narrative construction and the theological interpretation of Jesus' life and works as viewed through a Roman administrative lens.

In those days, when our Lord Jesus Christ was crucified under Pontius Pilate, the governor of Palestine and Phoenicia, the events here recorded took place in Jerusalem. The Jews committed these acts against the Lord. Pilate, therefore, sent an official report to Caesar in Rome, along with his personal account, writing as follows:

To the most powerful, revered, divine, and awe-inspiring Augustus Caesar, from Pilate, the governor of the Eastern Province: I have received certain information, O most excellent one, which has left me filled with fear and trembling. In this province, which I govern, there is a city called Jerusalem. The entire multitude of Jews brought before me a certain man named Jesus and made numerous accusations against him. However, they could not present consistent evidence to support their claims. The primary charge they brought against him was this: They accused Jesus of saying that the Sabbath was not to be observed as a day of rest. On that day, he performed many miraculous healings, such as giving sight to the blind, enabling the lame to walk, raising the dead, cleansing lepers, and healing paralytics who had no control over their bodies and could only speak. By his word alone, he restored their ability to move, walk, and run, removing their afflictions completely. There is another miracle he performed, which is unlike anything the gods we worship have ever done: he raised a man who had been dead for four days, solely by the power of his word. The body had already begun to decay, infested with worms and emitting the stench of death. Yet, Jesus commanded the man to rise, and immediately, as though he were a bridegroom emerging from his chamber, the man came forth from the tomb, filled with a sweet fragrance.

Moreover, even those who were strangers and possessed by demons, who lived in the wilderness, eating their own flesh and behaving like wild animals, Jesus restored to their right minds by a single word. He transformed them into rational beings, preparing them to live among people, and they became wise, powerful, and respected. He freed them from the influence of unclean spirits, which he cast into the depths of the sea. Another instance involved a man with a withered hand, but it was not just his hand—half of his body was stiff and lifeless, with no human shape or symmetry. Yet Jesus, with just a word, healed him completely, restoring his body to its full form and function. Additionally, there was a woman who had suffered from an issue of blood for many years. Her veins and arteries were depleted, and her body was lifeless, like that of a dead person. She had lost all hope of recovery, and none of the physicians could cure her. But as Jesus passed by, she mysteriously gained strength just by his shadow falling on her. She touched the hem of his garment from behind, and immediately, in that very moment, her strength was restored. She was so fully healed that she ran home to her city, Capernaum, in a journey that would normally take six days. These are the miracles that I have recently been informed about, and which Jesus performed on the Sabbath. He did even greater wonders than these, to the extent that I have witnessed more astonishing works from him than from the gods we worship.

However, Herod, Archelaus, Philip, Annas, Caiaphas, and all the Jewish leaders delivered Jesus to me. They stirred up a great commotion, demanding that I put him on trial. So, I ordered him to be crucified, after first scourging him, even though I found no valid cause for the accusations they brought against him. When he was crucified, there was darkness over the entire world, and the sun was obscured for half a day. The stars appeared, but their light was faint, and the moon turned blood red. The underworld was shaken, and even the temple—the Jews' most sacred place—seemed to vanish before their eyes. The earth split open with rolling thunder.

In the midst of this terror, the dead rose from their graves. The Jews themselves testified to seeing Abraham, Isaac, Jacob, the twelve patriarchs, Moses, and Job—men who had died centuries earlier, some over 3,500 years ago. Many others also appeared, and I, too, saw several of them with my own eyes. These risen men mourned the Jews' transgression and warned of their impending destruction for what they had done against their own law. The terror of the earthquake continued from noon until three in the afternoon. Then, as evening fell on the first day of the week, a voice was heard from heaven, and the sky became seven times brighter than on any other day. At three in the morning, the sun shone with a greater brilliance than ever before, lighting up the whole earth. It was as if lightning bolts were flashing in a storm. Men of great stature and radiant glory—an innumerable host—were seen, and their voices thundered, saying, "Jesus, who was crucified, has risen! Come forth, you who were enslaved in the depths of Hades!" The earth's chasm appeared bottomless, revealing the very foundations of the world. Those who shouted from heaven walked among the dead who had risen. And he who raised the dead, who conquered Hades itself, declared, "Tell my disciples: He goes before you into Galilee, where you will see Him."

The light did not cease shining throughout the entire night. Many of the Jews who had opposed Jesus died, swallowed up by the earth, and by the next day, most of those who had been against him were nowhere to be found. Others saw visions of men rising from the dead, men who had never before been seen. Of all the Jewish synagogues in Jerusalem, only one remained, for most had been destroyed in that great disaster.

In great fear and trembling, I have written down all that I witnessed at that time. I have included the details of what the Jews did to Jesus and sent this report to your divine excellency, my lord.

Trial and Condemnation of Pilate

The Trial and Condemnation of Pilate is another apocryphal Christian work that imagines the Roman governor's fate after the crucifixion of Jesus. In this account, Pilate is subjected to legal proceedings, either under the Roman Emperor or in a divine tribunal, for his role in condemning Christ. The trial underscores themes of justice and accountability, presenting Pilate as a figure whose condemnation mirrors his actions during the trial of Jesus. This text, often rooted in a mix of historical and legendary materials, portrays Pilate's trial as an example of how divine justice is eventually rendered upon those who contribute to Christ's death. It reflects early Christian concerns with the moral and cosmic consequences of the Passion and the ultimate triumph of divine justice over earthly authorities.

When the letters arrived in the city of Rome and were read aloud before Caesar and a large gathering, all were filled with terror. The darkness and earthquake that had affected the entire world were seen as consequences of Pilate's actions. In a fit of anger, Caesar ordered soldiers to bring Pilate to him as a prisoner.

When Pilate was brought to Rome and Caesar learned of his arrival, Caesar convened in the temple of the gods, sitting above the senate, with his army and all his authority gathered around him. He commanded that Pilate stand at the entrance. Caesar said to him, "You most impious man, when you witnessed such great signs performed by that man, how could you dare to commit such an act? By daring to do such evil, you have brought ruin to the entire world."

Pilate responded, "O King and Autocrat, I am not guilty of these things. It was the Jews who acted hastily and are to blame."
Caesar asked, "And who are these Jews?"
Pilate replied, "Herod, Archelaus, Philip, Annas, Caiaphas, and the whole multitude of the Jewish people."
Caesar asked again, "Why did you carry out their demands?"
Pilate answered, "Their nation is rebellious and refuses to submit to your authority."
Caesar said, "When they handed him over to you, you should have kept him safe and sent him to me. You should not have consented to crucify such a man, a just man who performed such great and good miracles, as you stated in your report. By those miracles, Jesus was revealed as the Christ, the King of the Jews."
When Caesar said this, and mentioned the name of Christ, all the idols of the gods around him collapsed and turned to dust where Caesar sat with the senate. All the people standing nearby were seized with fear and trembling because of the utterance of Christ's name and the fall of their gods. Terrified, everyone returned to their homes, astonished at what had happened.
Caesar ordered Pilate to be kept in custody so that he might discover the full truth about Jesus.
The next day, Caesar sat in the capitol with all the senate and again summoned Pilate for questioning. Caesar said, "Tell the truth, you most impious man, for through your wicked deed against Jesus, the downfall of the gods has been made manifest even here."
"Who was this man you crucified? His name alone has brought ruin to all the gods."
Pilate replied, "Indeed, everything I reported is true. I myself was convinced by his works that he was greater than all the gods we worship."
Caesar asked, "Why, then, did you commit such a bold and evil act against him, knowing what you did? Or were you plotting some treachery against my rule?"
Pilate answered, "I acted because of the transgression and rebellion of the lawless Jews."

Caesar, filled with anger, called a council with the senate and military leaders. He decreed the following order against the Jews: "To Licianus, Governor of the Eastern Provinces: Greetings. I have been informed of the recent audacity and lawlessness committed by the Jews of Jerusalem and the surrounding regions. They forced Pilate to crucify a certain man, Jesus, whom they called a god. As a result of their great sin, the world was darkened, and ruin came upon it. Therefore, I command you, with a force of soldiers, to go to them at once and enforce their subjugation. Scatter them across the nations, enslave them, and drive their people out of Judea. Wherever they have not yet been subdued, show the world that they are full of evil."

When this decree reached the East, Licianus, fearing Caesar's order, laid waste to the Jewish nation. He scattered those remaining in Judea, enslaving them alongside those already exiled among the Gentiles. This fulfilled Caesar's command, and Licianus sent word back to Rome of his actions to confirm that he had obeyed. Caesar then decided to have Pilate executed. He commanded a captain named Albius to behead Pilate, saying, "As he laid hands on the just man called Christ, so too shall he fall in the same manner and find no escape from justice.

When Pilate was taken to the place of execution, he prayed in silence, saying, "O Lord, do not destroy me along with the wicked Hebrews, for I would not have laid hands on You if not for the rebelliousness of the lawless Jews. They provoked me to act against You. You know that I acted in ignorance. Please do not punish me for this sin, O Lord, and do not hold the evil within me against me. Have mercy on me and on Your servant Procla, who stands with me in this hour of my death. She prophesied that You would be nailed to the cross. Do not punish her for my sin but forgive us both, and include us among Your righteous ones."

When Pilate finished his prayer, a voice came from heaven, saying, "All nations and generations of the Gentiles shall call you blessed, for under your rule the prophecies concerning Me were fulfilled. You will appear as a witness at My second coming, when I will judge the twelve tribes of Israel and those who have not confessed My name."

At that moment, the prefect beheaded Pilate, and behold, an angel of the Lord received his head. When his wife, Procla, saw the angel receive Pilate's head, she was filled with joy and immediately gave up her spirit. She was buried alongside her husband.

Death of Pilate

The Death of Pilate, Who Condemned Jesus is an apocryphal Christian text that reflects early Christian interpretations of Pilate's fate following his role in the crucifixion of Jesus Christ. According to the narrative, Pilate, the Roman governor of Judea, faces divine retribution and eventual demise as punishment for his actions in sentencing Jesus to death. This text often portrays Pilate as a conflicted figure, caught between the demands of the Jewish authorities and his own moral hesitations. Later Christian traditions, particularly in the apocrypha, have transformed Pilate's character, emphasizing his eventual recognition of Jesus' divinity and portraying his downfall as a form of divine justice. The narrative serves as a theological reflection on the consequences of failing to recognize Christ's messianic role, blending historical, legendary, and moral elements.

When Tiberius Caesar, emperor of the Romans, was suffering from a severe illness, he heard that in Jerusalem there was a certain physician named Jesus, who healed all diseases by his word alone. Unaware that the Jews and Pilate had put him to death, Caesar summoned one of his attendants, named Volusianus, and commanded him, "Go as quickly as possible across the sea and inform my servant and friend, Pilate, to send me this physician to restore my health." Volusianus, having received the emperor's orders, immediately departed and went to Pilate as instructed. Upon arriving, he told Pilate what Tiberius Caesar had commanded, saying, "Tiberius Caesar, emperor of the Romans, your lord, has heard that there is a physician in this city who heals diseases by his word alone. He urgently requests that you send this man to him to heal his illness." Pilate was greatly terrified when he heard this, knowing that he had caused Jesus to be killed out of envy. Pilate answered the messenger, saying, "This man was a criminal and drew many people to follow him. After consulting with the wise men of the city, I had him crucified."

As Volusianus was returning to his lodgings, he encountered a woman named Veronica, who had known Jesus. He said to her, "O woman, there was a physician in this city who healed the sick by his word alone. Why did the Jews kill him?" She began to weep, saying, "Alas, my lord, it was my God and my Lord whom Pilate, out of envy, delivered up, condemned, and had crucified." Grieving, Volusianus replied, "I am deeply sorry that I cannot fulfill the task my lord has sent me to do."

Veronica then said, "When my Lord was preaching, and I was sadly deprived of his presence, I wished to have his likeness painted for me, so that even in his absence, I could find comfort in his image. I was on my way to a painter with a canvas when my Lord met me and asked where I was going. When I told him the reason for my journey, he asked for the canvas, and returned it to me with the image of his holy face imprinted on it. If your lord devoutly gazes upon this likeness, he will immediately be healed."

Volusianus asked, "Can such a likeness be acquired with gold or silver?" She answered, "No, but with piety and devotion." She then offered to accompany him to Rome with the image, so Caesar could see it and be healed.

Volusianus brought Veronica to Rome, and said to Tiberius Caesar, "Jesus, whom you have long desired to see, was unjustly put to death by Pilate and the Jews. A noblewoman has brought with her a likeness of Jesus, and if you look upon it with devotion, you will be healed." Caesar ordered the path to be lined with silk cloths and the portrait presented to him. As soon as he gazed upon the image, he was immediately restored to health.

Soon after, Pontius Pilate was apprehended by Caesar's command and brought to Rome. When Caesar learned of Pilate's arrival, he was filled with great wrath. Pilate, however, wore the seamless coat of Jesus when he appeared before the emperor. As soon as Caesar saw him, his anger subsided, and he stood up and greeted Pilate, unable to speak harshly to him. The man who had seemed so terrifying in his absence now appeared gentle in his presence.

Caesar dismissed Pilate but soon became inflamed with rage again, declaring himself miserable for not having expressed his anger. He ordered Pilate to be brought back, swearing that Pilate was worthy of death and unfit to live on earth. Yet, when Pilate appeared before him again, Caesar immediately greeted him and could not speak with anger. Everyone, including Caesar himself, was astonished that while he was so enraged against Pilate in his absence, he could not rebuke him in person. Eventually, either by divine suggestion or the advice of a Christian, Caesar had Pilate stripped of Jesus' coat, and immediately, Caesar's original fury returned.

As Caesar wondered at this, he was informed that the coat belonged to the Lord Jesus. He then ordered Pilate to be imprisoned until he could consult with his advisors about what to do with him. After several days, a sentence was passed, condemning Pilate to a shameful death. When Pilate heard this, he took his own life with a dagger, thus ending his life by his own hand.

Upon hearing of Pilate's death, Caesar remarked, "Truly, he has died a most dishonorable death, sparing even himself no mercy." Pilate's body was then fastened to a large stone and thrown into the river Tiber. However, wicked and unclean spirits rejoiced over his body and caused violent storms, with lightning, thunder, and hail, filling everyone with fear. Because of this, the Romans retrieved his body from the Tiber, mocking him, and carried it to Vienne, where they threw it into the river Rhone. Vienne, at that time, was known as a cursed place, akin to Gehenna. Yet, evil spirits still caused the same disturbances there. The people of Vienne, unable to endure the harassment of the demons, removed Pilate's cursed body and sent it to be buried in the territory of Lausanne. However, even there, they were greatly troubled by similar disturbances. Eventually, they sank Pilate's body in a certain pool surrounded by mountains, where, according to some accounts, various demonic manifestations are said to still occur to this day.

Shepherd of Hermas

The Shepherd of Hermas is an early Christian text written in the first half of the 2nd century CE, which occupies a significant place in the development of early Christian thought and practice. This work, attributed to Hermas, a Roman Christian, offers a profound glimpse into the theological and moral concerns of the early church. Composed in the form of visions, parables, and commandments, the text provides an elaborate narrative framework for understanding Christian ethics, repentance, and eschatology. Its rich symbolism and allegorical content reflect the concerns of a community grappling with internal divisions and external pressures during a formative period of Christian history. As one of the major writings of the Apostolic Fathers, the Shepherd of Hermas is invaluable for scholars seeking to understand the doctrinal and disciplinary issues facing early Christians, shedding light on the evolution of Christian identity and the practical application of faith in a nascent ecclesiastical context.

{1:1} Hermas, who raised me, once sold a young maid in Rome. Many years later, I saw her again and started to care for her like a sister. Eventually, I saw her bathing in the Tiber River, reached out to her, and helped her out of the water. {1:2} When I saw her, I thought to myself how happy I would be if I had a wife like her, both in terms of beauty and character. I briefly entertained this thought, but soon after, while walking and reflecting on these ideas, I began to admire her as a creation of God, noting her nobility and beauty. {1:3} After walking a bit, I fell asleep, and a spirit carried me through a place so difficult to navigate that it was impassable, even for water. {1:4} Once past this rugged terrain, I arrived at a plain, knelt down, and began to pray to the Lord, confessing my sins. {1:5} While praying, the heavens opened, and I saw the woman I had desired greeting me from heaven, saying, "Hermas, greetings!" I responded, "Lady, what are you doing here?" She replied, "I have been brought here to accuse you of sin before the Lord." {1:6} I said, "Lady, will you accuse me?" She answered, "No, but listen to what I have to say. God, who dwells in heaven and created all things from nothing for the sake of His Holy Church, is angry with you because you have sinned against me." {1:7} I replied, "Lady, if I have sinned against you, please tell me when, where, or how I have spoken to you inappropriately or dishonestly." {1:8} "Have I not always respected you as a lady and honored you as a sister? Why then do you think these wicked things about me?" {1:9} She smiled and said, "An improper desire has arisen in your heart. Don't you think it's wrong for a righteous man to have such an evil desire?" {1:10} "Indeed, it is a serious sin for someone who is righteous. A righteous person thinks righteous thoughts, and while they do so and live uprightly, they will find favor with the Lord in all their endeavors." {1:11} "But those who harbor wicked thoughts in their hearts bring upon themselves death and captivity, especially those who love this present world, boast in their wealth, and disregard the future blessings. Their souls wander and cannot find peace." {1:12} "This is the plight of the double-minded, those who do not trust in the Lord and neglect their own lives." {1:13} "But pray to the Lord, and He will heal your sins, those of your whole household, and all His saints." {1:14} As soon as she finished speaking, the heavens closed, and I was overwhelmed with sadness and fear. I thought, "If this accusation is counted as a sin, how can I be saved?" {1:15} "How can I plead with the Lord for my many and significant sins? What words can I use to ask for His mercy?" {1:16} While I was reflecting on these thoughts, a chair made of the whitest wool, as bright as snow, was set before me. {1:17} An old woman in a brilliant garment, holding a book, came and sat alone. She greeted me, saying, "Hermas, greetings!" I, full of sorrow and tears, responded, "Greetings, Lady!" {1:18} She asked, "Why are you sad, Hermas, who are usually patient, modest, and cheerful?" I answered, "Lady, I am accused by an esteemed woman who says I have sinned against her." {1:19} "Such an accusation seems unfitting for a servant of God. But it may be that the desire of her heart has affected you. Indeed, such a thought can make the servants of God guilty of sin." {1:20} "No such vile thought should be in a servant of God, nor should one approved by the Spirit desire what is evil. Especially not you, Hermas, who restrains yourself from all wicked desires and is full of simplicity and innocence." {1:21} "Nevertheless, the Lord is not so angry with you for your own sake, but because of the wickedness in your household, which has wronged the Lord and their parents." {1:22} "And because, due to your affection for your sons, you have not corrected your household but allowed them to live wickedly, the Lord is angry with you. However, He will heal all the wrongs done in your house. Your preoccupation with secular matters has consumed you." {1:23} "But now, God's mercy has taken pity on you and your house and has greatly comforted you with glory. Just don't go astray, stay steadfast, and encourage your household." {1:24} "As a workman presents his work to whom he wishes, you must cut off great sin by teaching justice daily. Therefore, continue to admonish your sons, for the Lord knows they will repent sincerely and be written in the book of life." {1:25} When she finished speaking, she asked, "Do you want to hear me read?" I answered, "Lady, I do." {1:26} She then opened the book and read with great clarity and power, reciting words I couldn't fully remember because they were so overwhelming. {1:27} However, I retained her final words, which were few and very useful. {1:28} "Behold the mighty Lord, who by His invisible power and glorious wisdom created the world, adorned His creation with His glorious counsel, and by His strength established heaven, laid the earth upon the waters, and by this powerful virtue set up His Holy Church, which He has blessed." {1:29} "Behold, He will remove the heavens, mountains, hills, and seas; everything will be leveled for His elect so He may grant them the promise He has made, with much honor and joy, provided they keep the commandments of God with great faith." {1:30} When she finished reading, she rose from the chair, and four young men carried it to the east. {1:31} She called me over, touched my chest, and asked, "Did you enjoy my reading?" I replied, "Lady, I liked the final parts, but the earlier sections were harsh and difficult." {1:32} She said, "The final parts are for the righteous, while the earlier ones are for the rebellious and unbelievers." {1:33} As she spoke, two men appeared, lifted her on their shoulders, and took her to the east where the chair had been. {1:34} She departed cheerfully, saying to me, "Hermas, be of good cheer."

{2:1} As I was traveling to Cuma at the same time I had the previous year, I began to recall the vision I had before. Again, the spirit took me to the same place where I had been the year before. {2:2} When I arrived at the location, I knelt down and started praying to the Lord, praising His name for deeming me worthy to reveal my past sins. {2:3} After finishing my prayer, I saw the old woman from last year's vision standing in front of me, walking and reading from a book. {2:4} She asked me if I could share these teachings with the elect of God. I replied that I couldn't remember everything, but if she gave me the book, I would write it down. {2:5} She handed me the book and instructed me to return it afterward. {2:6} I took the book and went to a secluded spot in the field, where I transcribed every letter, as there were no syllables in the text. {2:7} As soon as I finished copying, the book was suddenly taken from me, but I didn't see who took it. {2:8} After fifteen days of fasting and earnestly praying to the Lord, the meaning of the writing was revealed to me. The text read: {2:9} "O Hermas! Your children have sinned against the Lord and betrayed their parents through their great wickedness. They are known as the betrayers of their parents and continue in their treachery. {2:10} They have now added lewdness to their other sins and indecent behaviors, filling up the measure of their iniquities. You rebuke your sons with these words, and also correct your wife, who will become your sister. She should learn to control her tongue, which slanders others." {2:11} "When she hears these things, she will restrain herself and find mercy. {2:12} Your sons will also be instructed after you have rebuked them with these words commanded by the Lord to be revealed to you. {2:13} They will be forgiven for their previous sins, as will all the saints who have sinned up to now, provided they repent sincerely and remove all doubts from their hearts. {2:14} For the Lord has sworn by His glory concerning His elect, that if anyone sins after this time, they will not be saved. {2:15} The repentance of the righteous has an end, and the period of repentance is complete for all saints, but there remains repentance for the heathen until the final day. {2:16} Therefore, you should instruct those who lead the church to live righteously so that they may fully receive the promise with great glory. {2:17} Stand firm, you who practice righteousness and continue to do so, so that your departure may be with the holy angels. {2:18} Blessed are those who endure the coming great trial and do not deny their faith. {2:19} For the Lord has sworn by His Son that whoever, fearing for their life, denies His Son and Him, will also be denied in the world to come. {2:20} But those who never deny Him will receive His great mercy." {2:21} "Hermas, remember not the wrongs your sons have done, nor neglect your sister, but ensure they amend their previous sins. {2:22} They will be instructed by this doctrine if you do not dwell on their past wickedness. {2:23} Remembering past evils leads to death, but forgetting them leads to eternal life. {2:24} You, Hermas, have faced many worldly troubles because of your household's offenses, as you neglected them, considering them irrelevant, while being absorbed in your significant business. {2:25} Nevertheless, you will be saved because you have not turned away from the living God. Your simplicity and unique self-restraint will preserve you if you continue in them. {2:26} Indeed, these qualities will save all who practice them, walking in innocence and simplicity. {2:27} Those who follow this path will overcome all impiety and continue until eternal life. {2:28} Blessed are all who do righteousness; they will not be consumed forever. {2:29} But you may say, 'There is a great time of affliction approaching. If you wish, deny Him again.' {2:30} The Lord is close to those who turn to Him, as written in the book of Heldam and Modal, who prophesied to the people of Israel in the wilderness. {2:31} Moreover, brethren, it was revealed to me in a dream by a very considerate young man who asked, 'What did you think of the old woman from whom you received the book? Who is she?' I answered, 'A Sybil.' {2:32} He corrected me, saying, 'She is not.' I asked, 'Who is she then, sir?' He replied, 'She is the Church of God.' {2:33} I said, 'Why does she appear old?' He responded, 'She is old because she was the first of all creation, and the world was made for her.' {2:34} After this, I had a vision in my own home: the old woman from before came to me and asked if I had delivered her book to the elders of the church. I said I had not yet done so. {2:35} She replied, 'You have done well, for I have more words to tell you. When I have finished, they will be clearly understood by the elect.' {2:36} 'You will write two books and send one to Clement and one to Grapte. Clement will send his to the foreign cities, as it is permitted for him to do, while Grapte will instruct the widows and orphans. {2:37} You will read the book in this city with the church elders.'

{3:1} The vision I had, my brothers, was this: {3:2} After I had fasted and prayed frequently to the Lord, seeking the revelation He had promised me through the old woman, she appeared to me that night and said, {3:3} "Because you have so afflicted yourself and are so eager to know everything, come to any field you choose, and at the sixth hour, I will appear to you and show you what you need to see." {3:4} I asked her, "Lady, to which part of the field should I go?" She replied, "Go wherever you like, just choose a good and private spot. Before you even mention the location, I will come there." {3:5} So, I went to the field, kept track of the time, and arrived at the place where I had planned for her to come. {3:6} There, I saw a bench set up with a linen pillow and a fine linen covering spread over it. {3:7} Seeing these arrangements and finding myself alone, I was startled, and a sense of fear overtook me. {3:8} However, regaining my composure and remembering the glory of God, I gathered my courage, fell to my knees, and began to confess my sins once again. {3:9} While I was praying, the old woman arrived with the six young men I had seen before and stood behind me, listening to my prayer and confession of sins to the Lord. {3:10} She touched me and said, "Stop praying just for your sins; also pray for righteousness, so you may have a share of it in your home." {3:11} She then lifted me from the ground, took my hand, and led me to the seat, telling the young men, "Go, and build." {3:12} As soon as they left, and we were alone, she told me, "Sit here." I responded, "Lady, let those who are older sit first." She insisted, "Sit down as I direct you." {3:13} When I tried to sit on the right side, she signaled me to sit on the left instead. {3:14} While I was pondering and feeling sorrowful that she wouldn't let me sit on the right side, she asked, "Hermas, why are you sad?" {3:15} She explained, "The right side is for those who have already attained to God and have suffered for His name's sake. There is still much for you to do before you can sit with them. {3:16} But continue in your sincerity, and you will sit with them, as will all others who do their works and endure what they have endured." {3:17} I asked, "Lady, what have they suffered?" She answered, "Wild beasts, floggings, imprisonments, and crosses for His name's sake. {3:18} For this reason, the right side of holiness belongs to them and to all who suffer for the name of God, while the left belongs to the rest. {3:19} However, gifts and promises belong to both sides, but those on the right side receive greater glory." {3:20} She added, "You desire to sit on the right side with them, but your faults are many. You will be purified from your faults, just as all who do not doubt will be cleansed from their sins." {3:21} After she said this, she was about to leave. {3:22} So, I fell at her feet and begged her for the Lord's sake to show me the vision she had promised. {3:23} She took my hand again, helped me sit on the left side, and holding up a bright wand, said, "Do you see that great thing?" I replied, "Lady, I see nothing." {3:24} She said, "Do you not see a great tower built with bright square stones, standing on the water?" {3:25} The tower was constructed on a square foundation by the six young men who had come with her. {3:26} Many thousands of other men brought stones; some drew them from the deep, others carried them from the ground, and handed them to the six young men, who then used them to build. {3:27} The stones taken from the deep were all included in the building because they were polished and fit perfectly together, with no visible gaps, making the tower look as if it were made of a single stone. {3:28} However, the stones taken from the ground were handled differently; some were rejected, while others were incorporated into the building. {3:29} The rejected stones were either cut out and thrown away or left lying around the tower, not used in the construction. {3:30} Some were rough, others had clefts, and some were white and round, unsuitable for the tower. {3:31} I saw the rejected stones being cast away from the tower, falling onto the road, but not staying on it, rolling into a desert place. {3:32} Some fell into the fire and burned; others fell near the water but couldn't roll into it, though they were eager to. {3:33} When she had shown me these things, she was about to leave, but I said, "Lady, what is the use of seeing these things if I do not understand their meaning?" {3:34} She replied, "You are very perceptive to want to understand the tower. Yes, I want to, Lady, so I can explain them to the brethren, and they may rejoice and glorify God greatly." {3:35} She said, "Many will hear these things, and some will rejoice, while others will weep. But even those who weep, if they repent, will also rejoice." {3:36} "Listen, then," she continued, "to the meaning of the parable of the tower, and do not keep asking me for revelations. {3:37} For these revelations have an end as they are fulfilled. Yet you persist in seeking more revelations, which shows your persistence." {3:38} "The tower you see being built is myself, that is, the Church, which has appeared to you now and before. So, ask about the tower, and I will reveal it to you so that you may rejoice with the saints." {3:39} I said, "Lady, since you have considered me worthy to receive the revelation of all these things, declare them to me." {3:40} She answered, "Whatever is appropriate for you to know will be revealed; just keep your heart with the Lord and do not doubt what you will see." {3:41} I asked her, "Lady, why is the tower built upon the water?" She replied, "You are very wise to inquire diligently about the building; thus, you will find the truth. {3:42} The tower is built on water because your life will be saved by water. Baptism is founded by the almighty and honorable name and supported by God's invisible power and virtue." {3:43} I answered, "These things are very admirable. But Lady, who are the six men who build?" {3:44} She said, "They are the angels of God who were first appointed, to whom the Lord has entrusted all His creatures, to frame, build, and rule over them.

Through them, the tower's construction will be completed." {3:45} I asked, "And who are the others who bring the stones?" {3:46} She replied, "They are also holy angels of the Lord, but the others are more excellent. When the tower is finished, they will all feast beside it and glorify God because the building is complete." {3:47} I asked, "I would like to know the condition of the stones and their meaning." {3:48} She answered, "Are you better than others that these things should be revealed to you? There are others before you who are better and to whom these visions should be made known. {3:49} Nevertheless, to glorify God's name, it has been and will be revealed to you for the sake of those who are doubtful and wonder if these things are true." {3:50} "Tell them that all these things are true, and nothing in them is false; they are all firm and well-established." {3:51} "Now, listen concerning the stones in the building. {3:52} The square, white stones that fit perfectly together are the apostles, bishops, doctors, and ministers who, through God's mercy, have governed, taught, and ministered holily and modestly to God's elect, both those who have died and those who remain, having always been in agreement and peace with each other." {3:53} "That is why their joints fit perfectly in the tower's construction." {3:54} "The stones drawn from the deep and put into the building, fitting with the others, are those who have suffered for the Lord's name and have died." {3:55} "And what about the other stones from the earth? I want to know what they are." {3:56} She replied, "The stones lying on the ground and not polished are those whom God has approved for walking in His law and following His commandments. {3:57} The stones brought and added to the tower are the young in faith and the faithful, who are admonished by the angels to do well, as no iniquity is found in them." {3:58} "But who are the ones rejected and left beside the tower?" {3:59} "They are those who have sinned, who have not repented, and who are not part of the Church. {3:60} They have not entered the fold of the sheep. Some are unpolished and others are cloven, or else they do not have faith. {3:61} For this reason, they have not entered the building of the tower and have been cast out." {3:62} "Those who fell into the fire and burned are those who, despite their baptism, have not been saved due to their sins." {3:63} "Those who fell near the water but could not roll into it are those who have not had faith or have not been able to live according to the law of God. {3:64} This is why they are not part of the tower's building." {3:65} "Those who rolled into the desert are those who are neither of God nor of the Church; they live in disbelief and the desert of the heart, and their faith is dry." {3:66} "You have now received a full understanding of the vision. Be content to know that all things in this vision have been accomplished by God's will."

{4:1} I had another vision, brethren, twenty days after the previous one, depicting the coming tribulation. I was walking in the field. {4:2} The path from the public road to where I was going was about ten furlongs long and rarely traveled. {4:3} As I walked alone, I prayed to the Lord to confirm the revelations He had shown me through His Holy Church, {4:4} and to grant repentance to all His servants who had sinned, so that His great and honorable name might be glorified, and because He deemed me worthy to reveal His wonders, and so I might honor and thank Him. {4:5} Suddenly, a voice answered me, "Do not doubt, Hermas." I began to wonder why I should doubt, given that I had been so firmly guided by the Lord and had seen such glorious things. {4:6} I had only walked a short distance when I saw a cloud of dust rising up to the heavens. I thought to myself, is there a herd of cattle coming that is stirring up this much dust? {4:7} The dust was about a furlong away from me, and as it grew thicker, I began to suspect something extraordinary was occurring. {4:8} The sun shone briefly, and I saw a huge beast, like a whale, with fiery locusts coming out of its mouth. The beast was about a hundred feet tall and had a head like a large earthen vessel. {4:9} I began to weep and prayed to the Lord to save me from it. Then I remembered the words I had heard: "Do not doubt, Hermas." {4:10} Therefore, putting on divine faith and recalling who had taught me these great things, I faced the beast. {4:11} The beast approached as if it could devour an entire city at once. {4:12} As I came near, the beast lay down flat on the ground and only extended its tongue, not moving until I had completely passed by. {4:13} The beast had four colors on its head: first black, then a red and bloody color, then gold, and finally white. {4:14} After I had passed it and walked about thirty feet farther, I encountered a virgin, beautifully adorned as if she had just emerged from her bridal chamber. She was dressed in white, with white shoes, a veil covering her face, and her hair shining. {4:15} I recognized her from my previous visions as representing the Church, and this made me more cheerful. She greeted me, saying, "Hello, O Man!" I responded, "Lady, hello!" {4:16} She then asked me if anything had met me. I replied, "Lady, I encountered a beast that seemed capable of devouring an entire people, but by the power of God and His mercy, I escaped it." {4:17} She said, "You escaped well because you placed your entire trust in God and opened your heart to Him, believing that you could be safe only by His great and honorable name. {4:18} This is why the Lord sent His angel, who is over the beast, named Hegrin, to stop its mouth so it would not devour you. You have avoided a great trial through your faith and because you did not doubt such a terrible beast. {4:19} Therefore, go and tell the elect of God about the great things He has done for you. You should tell them that this beast symbolizes the trial that is coming. {4:20} If you prepare yourselves, you may escape it if your heart is pure and unblemished, and if you serve God all your days without complaint. {4:21} Cast all your cares upon the Lord, and He will handle them. Believe in God, you who doubt, for He can do all things; He can both avert His wrath from you and provide you with help and security. {4:22} Woe to those who doubt, who hear these words and despise them; it would be better for them if they had never been born. {4:23} I then asked her about the four colors on the beast's head. She replied, "Again you are curious about these things." I said, "Lady, show me their meaning." {4:24} She said, "The black color represents the world you live in. The fiery and bloody color signifies that this age will be destroyed by fire and blood. {4:25} You who have escaped it are represented by the golden part. Just as gold is refined by fire, so you who live among men in this world will be tested in a similar way. {4:26} Those who are found to be pure will be refined and will endure to the end. As gold is purified and loses its dross, so you will shed all sorrow and trouble and be made pure for the building of the tower. {4:27} The white color represents the coming world, in which the elect of God will live, as they will be pure and without blemish until eternal life. {4:28} Therefore, you must not stop sharing these things with the saints. Here you have a depiction of the great tribulation that is about to come, which, if you are prepared, will not be a burden to you. Keep in mind the things I have said to you." {4:29} After she spoke these words, she departed. I did not see where she went, but suddenly I heard a noise and turned around in fear, thinking that the beast was coming after me.

Gospel of Thomas

The Gospel of Thomas, discovered in 1945 near Nag Hammadi, is a collection of 114 sayings attributed to Jesus, presenting a Gnostic perspective that diverges from the canonical gospels. Unlike the narrative gospels, it consists of brief, cryptic sayings and lacks mention of the crucifixion and resurrection. This has led to debates about its origins, with some scholars suggesting it predates the canonical texts and reflects early oral traditions, while others view it as a product of second-century Gnostic thought. The text emphasizes direct, esoteric knowledge of the divine, challenging traditional Christian doctrines and enriching our understanding of early Christian diversity and Jesus' teachings.

{1:1} Jesus said, "Whoever understands the meaning of these teachings will not experience death." {1:2} Jesus said, "Those who seek should not stop until they find. When they find, they will be troubled. When they are troubled, they will marvel and rule over all. [And after they have ruled, they will rest.]" {1:3} Jesus said, "If your leaders say to you, 'Look, the kingdom is in the sky,' then the birds will precede you. If they say, 'It is in the sea,' then the fish will precede you. Rather, the kingdom is within you and outside you. When you know yourselves, then you will be known, and you will understand that you are children of the living Father. But if you do not know yourselves, then you live in poverty, and you are that poverty." {1:4} Jesus said, "An old person will not hesitate to ask a young child of seven days about the place of life, and that person will live. For many who are first will become last, and they will become a single one." {1:5} Jesus said, "Know what is in front of your face, and what is hidden from you will be revealed. [For there is nothing hidden that will not be revealed, and there is nothing buried that will not be raised.]" {1:6} His disciples asked him and said to him, "Should we fast? How should we pray? Should we give to charity? What diet should we observe?" Jesus said, "Do not lie, and do not do what you hate, because everything is disclosed before heaven. After all, there is nothing hidden that will not be revealed, and there is nothing covered up that will remain undisclosed." {1:7} Jesus said, "Blessed is the lion that a human will eat, so that the lion becomes human. But cursed is the human that the lion will eat, and the lion will still become human." {1:8} Jesus said, "A person is like a wise fisherman who cast a net into the sea and drew it up from the sea full of small fish. Among them, the wise fisherman found a fine large fish. He threw all the small fish back into the sea and easily chose the large fish. Anyone here with two good ears should listen!" {1:9} Jesus said, "Look, the sower went out, took a handful of seeds, and scattered them. Some fell on the road, and the birds came and ate them. Others fell on rocky ground, where they did not take root in the soil and did not produce grain. Others fell among thorns, which choked the seeds, and worms ate them. But others fell on good soil and produced a good crop: they yielded sixty per measure and one hundred twenty per measure." {1:10} Jesus said, "I have set fire upon the world, and look, I am watching over it until it blazes." {1:11} Jesus said, "This heaven will pass away, and the one above it will pass away. The dead are not alive, and the living will not die. In the days when you consumed what is dead, you made it come alive. When you are in the light, what will you do? On the day when you were one, you became two. But when you become two, what will you do?" {1:12} The disciples said to Jesus, "We know that you will leave us. Who will be our leader?" Jesus said to them, "No matter where you are, go to James the Just, for whose sake heaven and earth came into being." {1:13} Jesus said to his disciples, "Compare me to something and tell me what I am like." Simon Peter said to him, "You are like a righteous messenger." Matthew said to him, "You are like a wise philosopher." Thomas said to him, "Teacher, my mouth cannot say what you are like." Jesus said, "I am not your teacher. Because you have drunk, you have become intoxicated from the bubbling spring that I have tended." And he took him, and withdrew, and spoke three sayings to him. When Thomas returned to his friends, they asked him, "What did Jesus say to you?" Thomas said to them, "If I tell you one of the sayings he spoke to me, you will pick up rocks and stone me, and fire will come from the rocks and consume you." {1:14} Jesus said to them, "If you fast, you will bring sin upon yourselves. If you pray, you will be condemned. If you give to charity, you will harm your spirits. When you enter any region and walk in the countryside, when people take you in, eat what they offer you and heal the sick among them. After all, what goes into your mouth will not defile you; rather, it is what comes out of your mouth that will defile you." {1:15} Jesus said, "When you see one who was not born of woman, fall on your faces and worship. That one is your Father." {1:16} Jesus said, "Some may think that I have come to bring peace to the world. They do not understand that I have come to bring division: fire, sword, and war. In a household of five, there will be three against two and two against three, father against son and son against father, standing alone." {1:17} Jesus said, "I will give you what no eye has seen, what no ear has heard, what no hand has touched, and what has not arisen in the human heart." {1:18} The disciples said to Jesus, "Tell us, how will our end come?" Jesus said, "Have you found the beginning, then, that you seek the end? Understand that the end will be where the beginning is. Blessed is the one who stands at the beginning; that one will know the end and will not taste death." {1:19} Jesus said, "Blessed is the one who existed before coming into being. If you become my disciples and pay attention to my teachings, even stones will serve you. There are five trees in Paradise for you; they do not change with seasons, and their leaves do not fall. Whoever knows them will not taste death." {1:20} The disciples said to Jesus, "What is Heaven's kingdom like?" He said to them, "It is like a mustard seed, the smallest of all seeds. But when it falls on prepared soil, it grows into a large plant and becomes a shelter for birds of the sky." {1:21} Mary said to Jesus, "What are your disciples like?" He said, "They are like little children living in a field that is not theirs. When the owners come, they will say, 'Give us back our field.' They will take off their clothes in front of them to return the field. Therefore, I tell you, if the owners of a house know a thief is coming, they will be on guard and not let the thief break in and steal their possessions. So be prepared against the world. Arm yourselves with great strength so that robbers cannot find a way to reach you, for the trouble you expect will come. Let there be among you one who understands. When the crop ripens, that person will come quickly with a sickle and harvest it. Anyone with ears should listen!" {1:22} Jesus saw some nursing babies. He said to his disciples, "These nursing babies are like those who enter the kingdom." They asked him, "Will we enter the kingdom as babies?" Jesus said, "When you make the two into one, and when you make the inner like the outer and the outer like the inner, and the upper like the lower, and when you make male and female into a single one, so that male is not male nor female is female, when you make eyes in place of an eye, a hand in place of a hand, a foot in place of a foot, an image in place of an image, then you will enter [the kingdom]." {1:23} Jesus said, "I will choose one from a thousand and two from ten thousand, and they will stand as a single one." {1:24} His disciples said, "Show us the place where you are, for we must seek it." He said to them, "Anyone with ears should listen! There is light within a person of light, and it shines on the whole world. If it does not shine, it is dark." {1:25} Jesus said, "Love your friends as you love your own soul. Protect them as you protect the pupil of your eye." {1:26} Jesus said, "You see the splinter in your friend's eye, but you do not see the beam in your own eye. When you remove the beam from your own eye, then you will see clearly enough to remove the splinter from your friend's eye." {1:27} "If you do not fast from the world, you will not find the kingdom. If you do not observe the sabbath as a sabbath, you will not see the Father." {1:28} Jesus said, "I stood in the midst of the world, and in flesh I appeared to them. I found them all intoxicated, and none of them thirsty. My soul mourns for the children of humanity, for they are blind in their hearts and do not see. They came into the world empty, and they seek to depart from the world empty. Yet they are intoxicated. When they sober up, they will change their ways." {1:29} Jesus said, "If the flesh came into being because of the spirit, that is a marvel. But if the spirit came into being because of the body, that is a marvel of marvels. Yet I marvel at how this great wealth has come to dwell in this poverty." {1:30} Jesus said, "Where there are three deities, they are divine. Where there are two or one, I am with that one." {1:31} Jesus said, "A prophet is not honored in his own hometown; doctors do not heal those who know them." {1:32} Jesus said, "A city built on a high hill and fortified cannot fall, nor can it be hidden." {1:33} Jesus said, "What you hear in your ear, proclaim from your rooftops. No one lights a lamp and hides it under a basket or in a hidden place. Instead, they put it on a lampstand so that all can see its light." {1:34} Jesus said, "If a blind person leads another blind person, both will fall into a hole." {1:35} Jesus said, "You cannot enter a strong person's house and take their possessions unless you tie up that strong person. Then you can plunder their house." {1:36} Jesus said, "Do not worry from morning to evening and from evening to morning about your food—what you will eat—or about your clothing—what you will wear. You are much greater than the lilies, which neither card nor spin. When you have no garment, what will you put on? Who can add to your stature? The one who clothes you will provide." {1:37} His disciples said, "When will you appear to us, and when will we see you?" Jesus said, "When you strip without shame, take your clothes, and place them under your feet like little children and trample them, then you will see the Son of the living one, and you will not be afraid." {1:38} Jesus said, "You have often desired to hear these sayings that I am speaking to you, and you have no one else from whom to hear them. There will be days when you will seek me and not find me." {1:39} Jesus said, "The Pharisees and scholars have taken the keys of knowledge and hidden them. They themselves have not entered, nor have they allowed those who want to enter to do so. Be as cunning as snakes and as innocent as doves." {1:40} Jesus said, "A grapevine that has been planted apart from the Father will be uprooted and perish, for it is not strong." {1:41} Jesus said, "Whoever possesses something will be given more, and whoever has nothing will be deprived even of the little they have." {1:42} Jesus said, "Be passersby." {1:43} His disciples said to him, "Who are you to say these things to us?" Jesus replied, "You do not understand who I am from what I say to you. You have become like the Judeans who love the tree but hate its fruit, or love the fruit but hate the tree." {1:44} Jesus said, "Whoever blasphemes against the Father will be forgiven, and whoever blasphemes against the Son will be forgiven, but whoever blasphemes against the Holy Spirit will not be forgiven, either on earth or in heaven." {1:45} Jesus said, "Grapes are not harvested from thorn bushes, nor are figs gathered from thistles, for they bear no fruit. Good people bring forth good from what they have stored up; evil people bring forth evil from the wickedness stored up in their hearts, and they speak evil. From the overflow of the heart, they produce evil." {1:46} Jesus said, "From Adam to John the Baptist, no one born of women is greater than John the Baptist, yet I say that anyone who becomes like a child will recognize the kingdom and be greater than John." {1:47} Jesus said, "You can't ride two horses or bend two bows at once. A slave cannot serve two masters, because they will honor one and offend the other. No one drinks old wine and immediately wants new wine. New wine isn't put into old wineskins, or they might burst, and old wine isn't put into new wineskins, or it might spoil. An old patch isn't sewn onto a new garment, as it would tear." {1:48} Jesus said, "If two people make peace in one house, they can tell a mountain to move from here to there, and it will move." {1:49} Jesus said, "Congratulations to those who are alone and chosen, for you will find the kingdom. You have come from it, and you will return there again." {1:50} Jesus said, "If people ask you where you come from, say, 'We come from the light, from the place where the light originated by itself, established itself, and appeared in its own image.' If they ask, 'Is it you?' say, 'We are its children, the chosen of the living Father.' If they ask, 'What is the evidence of your Father in you?' say, 'It is motion and rest.'" {1:51} His disciples asked, "When will the rest for the dead happen, and when will the new world come?" Jesus replied, "What you are looking forward to has already come, but you don't recognize it." {1:52} His disciples said, "Twenty-four prophets have spoken in Israel, and they all spoke about you." Jesus said, "You have ignored the living one in your presence and spoken only of the dead." {1:53} His disciples asked, "Is circumcision useful or not?" Jesus answered, "If it were useful, children would be born already circumcised. Instead, true circumcision is of the spirit and is beneficial in every way." {1:54} Jesus said, "Congratulations to the poor, for Heaven's kingdom belongs to you." {1:55} Jesus said, "Whoever does not hate their father and mother cannot be my disciple, and whoever does not hate their brothers and sisters and carry the cross as I do will not be worthy of me." {1:56} Jesus said, "Whoever knows the world has discovered a corpse, and whoever finds that corpse, the world is not worthy of them." {1:57} Jesus said, "The Father's kingdom is like a person who sows good seed. An enemy comes at night and sows weeds among the good seed. The person doesn't let the workers pull up the weeds, saying, 'No, you might pull up the wheat along with them.' At harvest time, the weeds will be obvious, and they will be pulled up and burned." {1:58} Jesus said, "Congratulations to the person who has worked hard and found life." {1:59} Jesus said, "Seek the living one while you live, or you might die and try to see the living one, and you will not be able to." {1:60} Jesus saw a Samaritan carrying a lamb to Judea. He said to his disciples, "That person is...," and they replied, "So that he may kill it and eat it." Jesus said, "He will not eat it while it is alive, but only after he has killed it and it has become a carcass." They said, "Otherwise, he can't do it." Jesus said, "Likewise, seek a place of rest for yourselves, or you might become a carcass and be consumed." {1:61} Jesus said, "Two people will be lying on a couch; one will die, and the other will live." Salome asked, "Who are you, stranger? You have climbed onto my couch and eaten at my table as if you belong here." Jesus replied, "I come from the wholeness of everything. I was given life by my Father." Salome said, "I am your disciple." Jesus responded, "That is why I say, if someone is whole, they will be full of light. But if they are divided, they will be full of darkness." {1:62} Jesus said, "I reveal my secrets to those who are worthy. Don't let your left hand know what your right hand is doing." {1:63} Jesus told this story: "A rich man had a lot of money. He thought, 'I will invest my money so I can sow, reap, plant, and fill my storehouses with produce, ensuring I lack nothing.' But that very night, he died. Anyone with ears should listen!" {1:64} Jesus said, "A man was preparing a dinner for guests. He sent his servant to invite them. The first guest said, 'I have merchants coming to me tonight; I cannot come.' Another said, 'I just bought a house and need to tend to it; I cannot come.' Another said, 'My friend is getting married, and I am organizing the banquet; I cannot come.' Another said, 'I bought an estate and need to collect the rent; I cannot come.' The servant reported this to his master, who then said, 'Go out and bring back anyone you find to have dinner.' Buyers and merchants will not enter my Father's places." {1:65} Jesus said, "A man owned a vineyard and rented it to farmers. He sent his servant to collect the crop, but they beat him and sent him back. The master sent another servant, who was also beaten. Then he sent his son, thinking they would respect him, but they killed him because he was the heir. Anyone with ears should listen!" {1:66} Jesus said, "Show me the stone the builders rejected; it has become the cornerstone." {1:67} Jesus said, "Those who know everything but lack self-awareness are truly lacking." {1:68} Jesus said, "Congratulations to you when you are hated and persecuted; no place will be found wherever you have been persecuted." {1:69} Jesus said, "Congratulations to those persecuted in their hearts; they have truly come to know the Father. Congratulations to those who hunger, for their need will be satisfied." {1:70} Jesus said, "If you bring forth what is within you, it will save you. If you don't, what you don't bring forth will destroy you." {1:71} Jesus said, "I will destroy this house, and no one will be able to rebuild it." {1:72} A person said to him, "Tell my brothers to divide my father's possessions with me." Jesus replied, "Who made me a divider?" Then he turned to his disciples and said, "I am not a divider, am I?" {1:73} Jesus said, "The harvest is plentiful, but the workers are few. Ask the Lord of the harvest to send out workers into his fields." {1:74} He said, "Lord, many gather around the drinking trough, but there is nothing in the well." {1:75} Jesus said, "Many stand at the door, but only those who are alone will enter the bridal chamber." {1:76} Jesus said, "The Father's kingdom is like a merchant who found a precious pearl. He sold all his goods to buy it. Similarly, seek the unfailing treasure that endures, where no moth destroys and no worm consumes." {1:77} Jesus said, "I am the light over everything. I am all things; from me, everything came forth, and to me, everything returns. Split a piece of wood, and I am there. Lift a stone, and you will find me." {1:78} Jesus said, "Why did you come to the countryside? To see a reed shaken by the wind? Or to see a person dressed in fine clothes like your rulers and powerful ones? They wear fine clothes and cannot understand truth." {1:79} A woman in the crowd said to him, "Blessed is the womb that bore you and the breasts that fed you." Jesus replied, "Blessed are those who have heard the word of the Father and truly kept it. There will come a day when you will say, 'Blessed is the womb that never bore and the breasts that never gave milk.'" {1:80} Jesus said, "Whoever knows the world has discovered the body, and whoever discovers the body, the world is not worthy of them." {1:81} Jesus said, "Let those who are wealthy rule, and let those with power give it up." {1:82} Jesus said, "Whoever is close to me is close to the fire, and whoever is far from me is far from the kingdom." {1:83} Jesus said, "Images are visible to people, but the light within them, the light of the Father, is hidden. It will be revealed, but for now, it is concealed by that light." {1:84} Jesus said, "When you see your reflection, you are happy. But when you see the images that existed before you and that do not die or become visible, you will have much to endure!" {1:85} Jesus said, "Adam came from great power and great wealth, but he was not worthy of you. If he had been worthy, he would not have tasted death." {1:86} Jesus said, "Foxes have their dens and birds have their nests, but humans have no place to lay down and rest." {1:87} Jesus said, "How unfortunate is the body that relies on another body, and how unfortunate is the soul that relies on these two." {1:88} Jesus said, "Messengers and prophets will come to you and give you what is yours. You, in turn, give them what you have and ask, 'When will they come to take what belongs to them?'" {1:89} Jesus said, "Why do you clean the outside of the cup? Don't you understand that the one who made the inside is also the one who made the outside?" {1:90} Jesus said, "Come to me, for my yoke is easy and my leadership is gentle, and you will find rest for your souls." {1:91} They asked him, "Tell us who you are so we can believe in you." He replied, "You examine the sky and the earth, but you do not recognize the one who is in your presence, nor do you know how to interpret the present moment." {1:92} Jesus said, "Seek and you will find. In the past, I did not tell you what you asked about because you were not seeking it. Now I am willing to tell you." {1:93} "Do not give what is holy to dogs, for they may throw it on the manure pile. Do not throw pearls to pigs, for they might trample them." {1:94} Jesus said, "One who seeks will find, and to one who knocks, it will be opened." {1:95} Jesus said, "If you have money, do not lend it at interest. Instead, give it to someone from whom you will not get it back." {1:96} Jesus said, "The Father's kingdom is like a woman who took some yeast, hid it in dough, and made large loaves of bread. Anyone with ears should listen!" {1:97} Jesus said, "The Father's kingdom is like a woman carrying a jar full of meal. As she walked along a distant road, the handle of the jar broke and the meal spilled behind her on the road. She did not notice it and was unaware of the problem. When she reached her house, she put the jar down and found it empty." {1:98} Jesus said, "The Father's kingdom is like a person who wanted to kill someone powerful. While still at home, he drew his sword and thrust it into the wall to see if his hand would go in. Then he killed the powerful one." {1:99} The disciples told him, "Your brothers and your mother are outside." He replied, "Those here who do what my Father wants are my brothers and my mother. They will enter my Father's kingdom." {1:100} They showed Jesus a gold coin and said, "The Roman emperor's people demand taxes from us." He replied, "Give the emperor what belongs to the emperor, give God what belongs to God, and give me what is mine." {1:101} Jesus said, "Whoever does not reject their father and mother as I do cannot be my disciple, and whoever does not love their father and mother as I do cannot be my disciple. My earthly mother gave me life, but my true mother is the one who gave me real life." {1:102} Jesus said, "Woe to the Pharisees! They are like a dog lying in a cattle trough: the dog neither eats nor lets the cattle eat." {1:103} Jesus said, "Blessed are those who know where the threats are coming from. They can prepare, gather their resources, and be ready before the danger arrives." {1:104} They said to Jesus, "Come, let us pray and fast today." Jesus replied, "What sin have I committed, or how have I been undone? When the groom leaves the bridal suite, then let people fast and pray." {1:105} Jesus said, "Whoever knows the father and the mother will be called the child of a prostitute." {1:106} Jesus said, "When you make the two into one, you will become children of Adam, and when you say, 'Mountain, move from here!' it will move." {1:107} Jesus said, "The kingdom is like a shepherd who had a hundred sheep. One of them, the largest, went astray. He left the ninety-nine and looked for the one until he found it. After much toil, he said to the sheep, 'I love you more than the ninety-nine.'" {1:108} Jesus said, "Whoever drinks from my mouth will become like me; I myself will become that person, and the hidden things will be revealed to them." {1:109} Jesus said, "The Father's kingdom is like a person who had a treasure hidden in his field but did not know it. When he died, he left it to his son. The son did not know about it either. He took over the field and sold it. The buyer went plowing, discovered the treasure, and began to lend money at interest to whomever he wished." {1:110} Jesus said, "Let one who has found the world and become wealthy renounce the world." {1:111} Jesus said, "The heavens and the earth will disappear in your presence, and whoever lives from the living one will not see death. Did not Jesus say, 'Those who have found themselves, the world is not worthy of them'?" {1:112} Jesus said, "Woe to the flesh that depends on the soul. Woe to the soul that depends on the flesh." {1:113} His disciples asked him, "When will the kingdom come?" He replied, "It will not come by watching for it. It will not be said, 'Look, here!' or 'Look, there!' The Father's kingdom is spread out upon the earth, but people do not see it." {1:114} Simon Peter said to them, "Tell Mary to leave us, because women don't deserve life." Jesus replied, "I will guide her to transform her into a male, so that she too may become a living spirit like you men. For every woman who makes herself male will enter the kingdom of Heaven."

Gospel of Philip

The Gospel of Philip, discovered in the Nag Hammadi library in 1945, is a 3rd-century Gnostic text written in Coptic and attributed to the apostle Philip. Unlike the canonical Gospels, it is a collection of sayings and theological reflections on mysticism and sacramental theology. Key themes include the bridal chamber, symbolizing the soul's union with the divine, and the belief that salvation comes through mystical knowledge rather than faith. The text provides unique insights into early Christian thought, especially on Jesus, Mary Magdalene, and the sacraments, challenging traditional views and highlighting early Christian diversity. Its symbolic language has drawn extensive scholarly attention.

{1:1} A Hebrew begets another Hebrew, known as a proselyte. Yet a proselyte cannot beget another proselyte. Some remain as they are and influence others, while others merely exist. {1:2} A slave desires freedom but not his master's estate. A son not only inherits but claims his father's legacy. {1:3} Heirs of the dead inherit death; heirs of the living inherit both life and death. The dead inherit nothing; how can the dead inherit? {1:4} Christ came to redeem, save, and ransom. He redeemed strangers, set apart his own, and willingly sacrificed from the world's beginning. {1:5} Light and darkness, life and death, right and left are inseparable brothers. The good are not inherently good, nor the evil truly evil; life is not just life, nor death mere death. All dissolve into their essence. {1:6} Names in the world mislead from truth to falsehood, even the names of God, Father, Son, Holy Spirit, life, light, resurrection, and Church. If these names were of the Aeon, they would not mislead in the world. {1:7} The Father's name given to the Son is above all; to wear the Father's name is to become Father. Those who possess this name understand but do not speak it. {1:8} Truth necessitates worldly names for teaching, as it is singular yet manifold for our learning. Powers deceive by misappropriating good names to the undeserving, binding the free to slavery. {1:9} These powers oppose man's salvation, for man's deliverance ends sacrifices to them. They offered live animals that died; they offered a dead man to God who lived. {1:10} Before Christ, no bread existed, as in Eden, abundant in nourishing trees but lacking wheat for man. {1:11} Powers erred, thinking their own might created, yet all was secretly accomplished by the Holy Spirit's will. Truth, sown since time immemorial, is seen but by a few reaped {1:12} If someone goes into water and emerges unchanged, claiming to be a Christian, they've merely borrowed the name. But those who receive the Holy Spirit receive the name as a gift—they need not repay it. This parallels the experience of a mystery. {1:13} Marriage is a profound mystery; without it, the world wouldn't exist. Human existence hinges on marriage. Consider its purity and immense power. {1:14} Unclean spirits include males and females. Males attach to female souls, and females to male souls due to past disobedience. {1:15} Without receiving either male or female spiritual power—symbolized by the bridegroom and bride—from the mirrored bridal chamber, one cannot evade these spirits. {1:16} When a solitary man is seen by wanton women, they descend upon him, defiling him. Similarly, lustful men persuade and defile solitary women. {1:17} Yet when a man and his wife are together, neither male nor female spirits can intrude. {1:18} Once someone exits the worldly realm, they cannot be detained as they were in it; they transcend desires, fears, and natural limitations. They rise above envy and possess mastery over nature. {1:19} Others claim faithfulness to avoid these unclean spirits and demons, yet only those with the Holy Spirit remain untouched. {1:20} Fear and love of the flesh are cautioned against: fear gives it power, while love entangles and paralyzes. Whether in this world, resurrection, or the "Middle" places, one must strive for spiritual ascent to rest upon shedding flesh. {1:21} Some lack desire or ability to sin; others desire but don't act, yet righteousness remains obscured for both. {1:22} An apostolic vision revealed souls in fiery torment, where lack of desire for salvation trapped them in outer darkness—a place of punishment. {1:23} Soul and spirit originate from water, fire, and light; the Son of the bridal chamber emerged from these elements. {1:24} The chrism is fire, enlightening and beautifying, distinct from formless fire. {1:25} Truth was veiled in the world through symbols and images; those who receive it must be reborn through its image. {1:26} The bridegroom and image enter the truth through the image; this is restoration. Those without it may claim the names of Father, Son, and Holy Spirit, but true acquisition is through the aromatic unction of the cross's power. {1:27} The Lord instituted baptism, chrism, Eucharist, redemption, and the bridal chamber, aiming to unite the inner and outer, below and above. {1:28} Destruction is the outer darkness, revealed by the Father who is secret, and accessed through inner contemplation. {1:29} Before Christ, souls were confined or lost, but through Christ's intervention, some were freed, others guided. {1:30} Adam and Eve's separation initiated death; Christ came to reunite them, giving life to the deceased. {1:31} Jesus' cry on the cross revealed his division, his new completeness signifying a perfected body. Flesh became true, unlike our semblance. {1:32} The bridal chamber is reserved for free individuals and virgins, not for slaves or defiled women. Through the Holy Spirit, we are reborn, anointed, and united in Christ. {1:33} Reflection and light are inseparable for self-recognition; likewise, baptism in light and water is fitting. Light symbolizes chrism. {1:34} Jerusalem's sacrificial buildings—the Holy, Holy of Holies, and Holy of the Holies—parallel baptism, redemption, and the bridal chamber. {1:35} The latter transcends all, veiled until Christ's revelation tore it asunder, allowing ascent from below. Clothed in perfect light, souls elude powers' sight, sacramentally uniting in rest. {1:36} If Eve hadn't left Adam, death wouldn't have followed. Christ came to restore their unity, where separation ceases in the bridal chamber. {1:37} Adam's soul, from breath, united with spirit; spiritual union puzzled and angered the powers, leading to their defilement of the symbolic bridal chamber. {1:38} Jesus' revelation at Jordan embodied Heaven's fullness; he reinitiated what was begotten before, anointed anew, and redeemed others. {1:39} Can mysteries be spoken? The Father united with the descending virgin; fire and light shone, creating a great bridal chamber. {1:40} Jesus' body was formed, emerging as a product of the bridal chamber's union. {1:41} Adam, born of spirit and earthly virgin, contrasts with Christ's birth from a virgin, rectifying the initial Fall. {1:42} Paradise hosts two trees: one for animals, another for humans. Adam ate from the animal tree, becoming like them. {1:43} His offspring worship animals, influenced by the tree of knowledge's fruit, increasing sin. {1:44} Had Adam eaten from the tree of life, gods would worship man, not vice versa. {1:45} A person's abilities determine their accomplishments; children are among them, reflecting the image. {1:46} In this world, slaves serve the free; in Heaven's kingdom, the bridal chamber's children serve those of marriage, united in rest and insight. {1:47} Baptism symbolizes new life in Christ, fulfilling righteousness. {1:48} Those who wait to die and rise err; resurrection must be embraced in life to receive it in death. {1:49} Joseph the carpenter planted the garden for wood, fashioning Jesus' cross. {1:50} The tree of life in Eden contrasts with the olive tree's chrism, leading to resurrection. {1:51} This world consumes and perishes; truth sustains eternal life, offered by Jesus to those who seek it. {1:52} God's garden for Adam blessed him with choices, including the tree of knowledge, leading to death. Chrism surpasses baptism, for we are called Christians from Chrism, not from baptism. It is through Chrism that Christ derives His name. The Father anointed the Son, who in turn anointed the apostles, and they anointed us. The anointed one possesses everything: resurrection, light, cross, and the Holy Spirit. These gifts were given by the Father in the bridal chamber, and the Son accepted them. The Father and Son are inseparable, embodying the Kingdom of Heaven. {1:53} The Lord spoke rightly: some enter the Kingdom laughing and leave, not remaining because they are not true Christians or regret their actions. When Christ emerged from the water, He laughed at the world, not because He scorned it but because He saw its insignificance. Those who wish to enter the Kingdom must disdain the world as trivial to find joy. The bread, cup, and oil, though significant, are surpassed by something greater. {1:54} The world came about by mistake; its creator intended it to be immortal but fell short. Only sons can achieve immortality, but they must first become sons to receive it. Those unable to receive cannot give. {1:55} The Cup of prayer contains wine and water, symbolizing the blood for which thanks are given. It is filled with the Holy Spirit and belongs to the wholly perfect. Drinking it grants the perfect man. The living water is a body; we must clothe ourselves in the living man before descending into water. {1:56} A horse begets a horse, a man a man, and a god a god. Similarly, the bridegroom and bride conceive in the bridal chamber. No Jew was born of Greek parents; likewise, Christians do not descend from Jews but belong to the chosen people of the Living God, known as the true man and Son of Man. Their place is with the sons of the bridal chamber. {1:57} In this world, union between husband and wife involves strength and weakness. In the Aeon, union takes a different form though named similarly. These names are superior and unite strength where strength excels. They are one, indivisible. {1:58} All who possess everything must first know themselves. Those who do not know cannot enjoy their possessions or detain the perfect man. Only Jesus knows their end. {1:59} The priest, holy even in body, consecrates all he touches, including the body. Jesus perfected baptism, cleansing it of death. We descend into water, not into death, to avoid being swallowed by the world's spirit. The Holy Spirit brings summer when it breathes. {1:60} He who knows truth is free and does not sin. Sinners are slaves to sin, but truth and knowledge free them. Love builds; knowledge only inflates. Love does not claim but gives all. Spiritual love is wine and fragrance, benefiting all anointed. When the anointed leave, those nearby still sense their fragrance. The Samaritan used only wine and oil to heal; love covers sin. Children resemble those loved by their mothers. Those living with the Son of God should love Him, not the world. Like joins with like: spirit with spirit, thought with thought, light with light. Human joins with human, and spirit joins with spirit. Those below cannot join those above; the horse, ass, or bull cannot love human, spirit, thought, or light. Farming requires water, earth, wind, and light. God's farming requires faith, hope, love, and knowledge. Faith roots us, hope nourishes, love grows, and knowledge ripens. Grace exists in earthborn and heavenly forms, from the highest heaven and within truth. {1:61} Blessed is he who never caused suffering; that is Jesus Christ. He burdens no one and comforts all, both great and small, believer and unbeliever. Comfort is not selective; those who do good do not inflict suffering but bear their own due to the wicked. The perfect rejoice in good; others suffer in anguish. A householder knew each thing's needs: sons, slaves, cattle, dogs, pigs, crops, and oils. He served each accordingly. Compare a disciple who understands true discipleship, discerning souls beyond appearances. Many appear human but are animal within. Discerning, the disciple provides as needed: food for the hungry, lessons for slaves, and instruction for children. {1.62} There is the Son of Man and there is the son of the Son of Man. The Son of Man is the Lord, and the son of the Son of Man is the one who created through the Son of Man. The Son of Man received from God the ability to create, and he also has the ability to beget. He who has the ability to create is a creature, and he who has the ability to beget is an offspring. One who creates cannot beget, and one who begets also has the ability to create. People say, "He who creates begets," but his so-called offspring is merely a creature. Therefore, his children are not offspring but creatures. He who creates works openly and is visible. He who begets, however, begets in private and is hidden, since he is superior to every image. {1.63} He who creates does so openly, but he who begets does so in private. No one can know when a husband and wife have intercourse except for the two of them. Marriage in the world is a mystery for those who take a wife. If there is a hidden quality to defiled marriage, how much more is undefiled marriage a true mystery! It is not carnal but pure, belonging not to desire but to will. It belongs not to darkness or night but to day and light. If a marriage is public, it becomes prostitution, and the bride acts as a harlot not only if she conceives by another man but even if she leaves her bedroom and is seen. Let her reveal herself only to the father, mother, friend of the bridegroom, and sons of the bridegroom. They are allowed to enter the bridal chamber every day. Others should long to hear her voice and enjoy her ointment, content with the crumbs that fall from the table, like dogs. Bridegrooms and brides belong to the bridal chamber. No one can see the bridegroom with the bride unless they become one. When Abraham rejoiced that he would see what he was to see, he circumcised the flesh of the foreskin, teaching us that it is appropriate to remove the flesh. {1.64} Most things in the world, as long as their inner parts are hidden, stand upright and live. If they are revealed, they die, as illustrated by the visible man: as long as a man's intestines are hidden, he lives; when his intestines are exposed and come out, he dies. The same is true of a tree: while its roots are hidden, it sprouts and grows; if its roots are exposed, the tree withers. This applies to every birth in the world, not only the visible but also the hidden. As long as the root of wickedness is hidden, it is strong; but when it is recognized, it is dissolved. When it is revealed, it perishes. That is why it is said, "Already the axe is laid at the root of the tree" (Matthew 3:10). The axe does not just cut; what is cut grows back. But the axe penetrates deeply until it uproots the root. Jesus pulled out the root of the whole place, whereas others only did so partially. As for us, each one should dig down to the root of evil within and pluck it from our hearts. It will be plucked out if we recognize it. If we are ignorant of it, it takes root and bears fruit in our hearts, mastering us and making us its slaves, forcing us to do what we do not want and preventing us from doing what we do want. It is powerful because we have not recognized it. As long as it exists, it is active. Ignorance is the mother of all evil. Ignorance leads to death, because those who come from ignorance were not, are not, and shall not be. But those in the truth will be perfect when all truth is revealed. Truth is like ignorance: while hidden, it remains with itself, but when revealed and recognized, it is praised for its strength over ignorance and error. It brings freedom. As it is said, "You will know the truth, and the truth will set you free" (John 8:32). Ignorance is slavery; knowledge is freedom. If we know the truth, we will find its fruits within us. If we are united with it, it will bring fulfillment. {1.65} Currently, we experience the manifest aspects of creation. We say, "The strong are respected, and the obscure are despised." Contrast this with the manifest aspects of truth: they are weak and despised, while the hidden aspects are strong and respected. The mysteries of truth are revealed in type and image, but the bridal chamber remains hidden. It is the Holy within the Holy. Initially, the veil concealed how God governed creation, but when the veil is torn and the contents revealed, this house will be left desolate, or rather, destroyed. However, the entire lesser divinity will flee from these places to the Holy of Holies, unable to mix with pure light and flawless fullness, but seeking shelter under the wings of the cross. This ark will be their salvation when the flood of water (?) overwhelms them. Those belonging to the order of the priesthood may enter the veil with the high priest. Therefore, the veil was not torn only at the top, which would have revealed it only to those below, but from top to bottom. Those above opened to us below, allowing us to enter the secret of truth. Truly, this is what is respected, for it is strong! We enter through humble types and forms of weakness. Compared to perfect glory, they are indeed humble. There is glory surpassing glory and power surpassing power. Thus, the perfect things have opened to us, along with the hidden truths. The Holy of Holies has been revealed, inviting us to the bridal chamber. {1.66} Wickedness, though hidden, is ineffective but remains among the seed of the Holy Spirit. They are slaves to evil. When it is revealed, the perfect light will shine, and all within it will receive the chrism. Slaves will be freed, captives ransomed. Every plant not planted by the Father will be uprooted. The separated will be united and filled. All who enter the bridal chamber will ignite the light, like marriages at night, though their fire is extinguished. This marriage, however, is perfected in perpetual daylight. If one becomes a son of the bridal chamber, they receive the light, which must be obtained in this realm to be received in the next. Those who have the light cannot be detained or tormented. Upon departing the world, they have already received truth and fullness, revealed to them in perfect day and holy light.

Secret Gospel of Mark

The Secret Gospel of Mark, often shrouded in controversy and mystery, is an apocryphal text that has intrigued scholars since its alleged discovery in the mid-20th century. This text was purportedly found by Morton Smith, a biblical scholar, in 1958 within a letter ascribed to Clement of Alexandria, which was housed in the Mar Saba Monastery near Jerusalem. The letter, commonly referred to as the Mar Saba letter, contains two excerpts of a longer version of the Gospel of Mark, which is claimed to include esoteric teachings of Jesus, reserved for a select group of followers. The authenticity of the Secret Gospel of Mark and the letter itself has been a topic of intense debate, with some scholars arguing for its legitimacy based on linguistic and historical analyses, while others dismiss it as a modern forgery, citing inconsistencies and the lack of corroborating evidence. The text's content, which includes narratives of Jesus raising a young man from the dead and a possible homoerotic undertone, adds to the controversy, as it challenges traditional Christian doctrines and raises questions about early Christian practices and beliefs. The Secret Gospel of Mark remains a focal point in the study of early Christianity, not only for its provocative content but also for the methodological and ethical questions it raises about textual discoveries and their implications for understanding the historical Jesus and the formation of Christian canon.

- **Silencing False Teachings**: You did the right thing by silencing the terrible teachings of the Carpocratians. These people are like the "wandering stars" mentioned in prophecy, who stray from the narrow path of God's commandments into a bottomless pit of sinful bodily desires. They pride themselves on their knowledge, claiming they understand "the deep things of Satan," but they don't realize they are condemning themselves to the darkness of falsehood. They boast about being free, but in reality, they have become slaves to their desires. Such people should be opposed in every way possible. Even if they say something that is true, a person who truly loves truth should not agree with them. This is because not all things that are true are the truth. We should not prefer truth that merely seems right according to human opinion over the real truth found in faith.

- **Distorted Teachings of Mark's Gospel**: Some of the things the Carpocratians say about the Gospel of Mark are outright lies, while others are only partially true but are distorted. The true things they say are mixed with falsehoods, so much so that, as the saying goes, even the salt has lost its flavor.

- **Mark's Role in Writing the Gospel**: When Mark was in Rome during Peter's stay, he wrote an account of the Lord's deeds. However, he did not reveal everything, nor did he hint at the secret teachings. Instead, he chose the things he thought would best help people grow in their faith. After Peter's martyrdom, Mark went to Alexandria, bringing with him his own notes and Peter's notes. From these, he added to his earlier work, creating a more spiritual Gospel intended for those who were further along in their faith journey. Even in this spiritual Gospel, Mark did not reveal the secret teachings of the Lord. He didn't record the deepest mysteries but added other stories, and sayings that were meant to lead believers into deeper truth. In doing so, Mark carefully prepared the text, not too cautiously but also not carelessly. When he died, he left this Gospel to the church in Alexandria, where it is still kept and is read only to those who are being initiated into the deeper mysteries of the faith.

- **Carpocrates' Corruption of the Gospel**: The evil demons, always seeking to harm humanity, influenced Carpocrates. Using deception, Carpocrates tricked a church elder in Alexandria into giving him a copy of the secret Gospel. He twisted the Gospel's teachings to fit his own corrupt, blasphemous doctrines and added lies to it. The teachings of the Carpocratians come from this corrupted version of Mark's Gospel.

- **Opposing the Carpocratians**: We must never give in to these people. When they present their corruptions, we must deny that the secret Gospel is from Mark, even under oath. As Scripture teaches, "Not all true things should be shared with everyone." That's why God's Wisdom, through Solomon, advises us to "Answer a fool according to his folly," meaning that we should keep the light of truth hidden from those who are spiritually blind. Scripture also says, "To him who has not, even what he has will be taken away," and "Let the fool walk in darkness." But we, being children of the Light, have been illuminated by the Spirit of the Lord. As Scripture says, "Where the Spirit of the Lord is, there is liberty," and "All things are pure to those who are pure."

- **Clarifying the Secret Gospel**: I will now answer the questions you've asked, using the Gospel itself to refute the falsehoods. For instance, after the phrase "And they were on the road going up to Jerusalem," and up to "After three days he will rise," the secret Gospel contains the following passage word for word: "And they came to Bethany. A woman was there whose brother had died. She approached Jesus and bowed down before him, saying, 'Son of David, have mercy on me.' But the disciples rebuked her. Jesus, however, was angered and went with her to the garden where the tomb was. A loud cry was heard from inside the tomb. Jesus went near, rolled the stone away, and entered the tomb. He stretched out his hand and raised the young man, taking him by the hand. The young man looked at Jesus, loved him, and asked to be with him. After leaving the tomb, they went to the young man's house, for he was wealthy. After six days, Jesus instructed him on what to do. That evening, the young man came to Jesus, wearing only a linen cloth over his body. He stayed with Jesus that night, and Jesus taught him about the mysteries of the Kingdom of God. Then, the next day, they crossed back over the Jordan." After this passage, the regular Gospel continues with "James and John came to him," and everything that follows. The phrases you mentioned, like "naked man with naked man" and other similar things, are not part of the Gospel.

- **Further Clarifications**: After the words, "And they came to Jericho," the secret Gospel adds: "And the sister of the young man whom Jesus loved, and his mother, and Salome were there, but Jesus did not receive them." But many of the other things you mentioned are not only false but seem to be complete fabrications.

- **True Interpretation**: The true interpretation, and the one that aligns with true philosophy...

Gospel of Bartholomew

The Gospel of Bartholomew, an enigmatic and apocryphal text, has captivated scholars and theologians alike with its intricate blend of theological reflection and narrative depth. While its precise origins remain shrouded in mystery, it is generally considered to have been composed between the 2nd and 5th centuries, possibly in the context of early Christian communities grappling with doctrinal controversies. This gospel, which survives in fragments and various references in patristic writings, is attributed to Bartholomew, one of the twelve apostles of Jesus, thereby lending it an apostolic authority that intrigued early Christians. The text is characterized by its unique exploration of post-resurrection appearances of Jesus and vivid depictions of celestial and infernal realms, themes that are less prominent in the canonical gospels. It delves into esoteric and theological inquiries, including profound discussions about the nature of the soul, the afterlife, and the cosmic battle between good and evil. Its dialogues often feature a questioning Bartholomew, who serves as a conduit for deeper spiritual revelations and insights. It also provides a rich tapestry of early Christian mysticism and apocalyptic thought, reflecting the diverse and often competing theological currents of its time. Despite its non-canonical status, the text offers invaluable insights into the beliefs, fears, and hopes of early Christians, contributing significantly to our understanding of early Christian literature and thought. Through its complex narrative and theological discourse, the Gospel of Bartholomew invites readers to ponder the mysteries of faith, the afterlife, and the divine, thus securing its place as a fascinating subject of scholarly inquiry and religious reflection.

{1:1} After the resurrection of our Lord Jesus Christ, Bartholomew approached the Lord and asked, "Lord, reveal to me the mysteries of the heavens." {1:2} Jesus responded, "If I remove the body of flesh, I will not be able to tell you." {1:3} Om. {1:4} Before the resurrection of our Lord Jesus Christ from the dead, the apostles said, "Let us ask the Lord: Lord, reveal to us the wonders." {1:5} Jesus replied, "If I remove the body of flesh, I cannot tell you." {1:6} But when he was buried and rose again, they were afraid to question him because they could not bear to look at him, seeing the fullness of his Godhead. {1:7} At that time, before Jesus Christ suffered, all the disciples gathered and asked, "Lord, show us the mystery of the heavens." {1:8} Jesus answered, "If I do not remove the body of flesh, I cannot tell you." {1:9} After he suffered and rose again, the apostles saw him but did not dare to question him, for his appearance was not the same as before but showed the fullness of power. {1:10} Bartholomew then came to the Lord and said, "Lord, I have something to ask you." {1:11} Jesus replied, "I know what you are about to say; speak, and I will answer you." {1:12} Bartholomew said, "Lord, when you were going to be crucified, I followed you from a distance and saw you on the cross. I saw angels coming down from heaven to worship you. When darkness came, {1:13} I noticed you vanished from the cross, and I heard a voice from the underworld with great wailing and gnashing of teeth. Tell me, Lord, where did you go from the cross?" {1:14} Jesus answered, "Blessed are you, Bartholomew, for you have seen this mystery. I will tell you all you ask. {1:15} When I vanished from the cross, I went down into Hades to bring up Adam and all those with him, according to the prayer of Michael the archangel." {1:16} Bartholomew asked, "Lord, what was the voice that was heard?" {1:17} Jesus said, "Hades said to Beliar, 'As I perceive, a God is coming here.' {1:18} And the angels cried to the powers, 'Lift up your gates, you rulers; lift up the eternal doors, for the King of glory is coming down.'" {1:19} Hades asked, "Who is this King of glory coming down from heaven?" {1:20} As I descended five hundred steps, Hades was troubled and said, "I hear the breath of the Most High, and I cannot endure it." {1:21} But the devil replied, "Do not submit, O Hades, but be strong, for God himself has not come down to earth." {1:22} As I descended another five hundred steps, the angels and powers cried out, "Lift up the gates, for the King of glory is coming down." Hades said, "Woe is me, for I hear the breath of God." {1:23} Beliar said to Hades, "Look carefully at who this is; it seems to be Elijah, Enoch, or one of the prophets." But Hades replied, "Not yet are six thousand years completed. Who is this, O Beliar? The number is in my hands." {1:24} The devil said, "Why do you frighten me, Hades? It is a prophet who has made himself like God; we will capture him and bring him here." Hades asked, "Which prophet is it? Is it Enoch, the scribe of righteousness? God has not allowed him to come down before the end of six thousand years. Is it Elijah, the avenger? He has not come down. What shall I do, for our end is near? The number is in my hands." {1:25} Beliar replied, "Do not be troubled; secure your gates and strengthen your bars. God does not come down to earth." {1:26} Hades answered, "These are not good words; my belly is rent, and my inward parts are in pain. It must be that God is coming here. Alas, where shall I flee from the face of the great King?" {1:27} Then I entered and scourged him, bound him with unbreakable chains, brought out all the patriarchs, and returned to the cross. {1:28} Bartholomew said, "Lord, I saw you again on the cross, and all the dead rose and worshiped you, returning to their graves. Tell me, Lord, who was the man the angels carried in their hands, who was very great in stature? {1:29} And what did you say to him that made him sigh so deeply?" {1:30} Jesus answered, "It was Adam, the first-formed, for whose sake I came down from heaven. I said to him, 'I was crucified for you and your children.' When he heard this, he groaned and said, 'So it was your good pleasure, O Lord.'" {1:31} Bartholomew asked, "Lord, I saw the angels ascending before Adam and singing praises. {1:32} But one angel, who was very great, did not ascend with them and had a fiery sword, looking only at you." {1:33} Jesus said, "Blessed are you, Bartholomew, for seeing these mysteries. This was an angel of vengeance before my Father's throne, sent to me. {1:34} He did not ascend because he wanted to destroy the world's powers. When I commanded him to ascend, a flame came from his hand, tore the temple veil in two, and served as a witness to Israel for my suffering because they crucified me." {1:35} Jesus then said to the apostles, "Wait for me here, for today a sacrifice is offered in paradise." {1:36} Bartholomew asked, "Lord, what is the sacrifice offered in paradise?" Jesus answered, "The souls of the righteous who have departed today go to paradise, and unless I am present, they cannot enter." {1:37} Bartholomew asked, "Lord, how many souls depart from the world daily?" Jesus said, "Thirty thousand." {1:38} Bartholomew asked, "Lord, when you were teaching with us, did you receive sacrifices in paradise?" Jesus answered, "Truly, I say to you, I taught with you and continually sat with my Father, receiving sacrifices in paradise every day." {1:39} Bartholomew asked, "Lord, if thirty thousand souls depart daily, how many are found righteous?" Jesus said, "Hardly fifty, my beloved." {1:40} Bartholomew asked, "How do only three enter paradise?" Jesus replied, "The fifty-three enter paradise or are laid up in Abraham's bosom, but the others go to the place of resurrection. The three are not like the fifty." {1:41} Bartholomew asked, "Lord, how many souls are born into the world daily?" Jesus answered, "One soul is born above the number of those who depart." {1:42} After saying this, Jesus gave them peace and vanished from their sight.

{2:1} The apostles were gathered with Mary in a place called Cherubim, Cheltoura, Chritir. {2:2} Bartholomew approached Peter, Andrew, and John and suggested, "Let's ask Mary, who is highly favored, how she conceived the incomprehensible, bore him who cannot be carried, and brought forth such greatness." But they hesitated to ask her. {2:3} Bartholomew then urged Peter, "You are the leader and my teacher, ask her." Peter, in turn, suggested to John, "You are a virgin and beloved, you should ask her." {2:4} While they hesitated and debated, Bartholomew approached Mary with a cheerful demeanor and said, "You who are highly favored, the tabernacle of the Most High, all the apostles ask you to tell us how you conceived the incomprehensible, bore him who cannot be carried, and brought forth such greatness." {2:5} Mary responded, "Do not ask me about this mystery. If I begin to tell you, fire will issue from my mouth and consume the world." {2:6} Despite this, they continued to ask her. Unable to refuse the apostles, she said, "Let us stand up in prayer." {2:7} The apostles stood behind Mary, but she said to Peter, "Peter, you are the chief and a great pillar; you should not stand behind us. Did not our Lord say,

'The head of the man is Christ'? Therefore, you should lead the prayer." {2:8} However, they replied, "The Lord set his tabernacle in you, and it was his pleasure that you contain him, so you should lead the prayer." {2:9} Mary said, "You are shining stars, as the prophet said, 'I lift my eyes to the hills; where does my help come from?' You are the hills, so you should pray." {2:10} The apostles insisted, "You should pray, as you are the mother of the heavenly king." {2:11} Mary responded, "God formed the sparrows in your likeness and sent them into the four corners of the world." {2:12} They replied, "He who is scarcely contained by the seven heavens was pleased to be contained in you." {2:13} Mary then stood before them, raised her hands to heaven, and began to pray, "Elphue Zarethra Charboum Nemioth Melitho Thraboutha Mephnounos Chemiath Aroura Maridon Elison Marmiadon Seption Hesaboutha Ennouna Saktinos Athoor Belelam Opheoth Abo Chrasar, O God, the exceedingly great and all-wise king of the worlds, who cannot be described, the ineffable one who established the greatness of the heavens and all things by a word, who brought order to chaos and separated the misty darkness from the light, who settled the earth and nourished it with showers of blessing: Son of the Father, you whom the seven heavens can barely contain but who were pleased to be contained in me without pain, you who are the full word of the Father in whom all things came to be, give glory to your great name and bid me to speak before your holy apostles." {2:14} When she finished the prayer, she said to the apostles, "Let us sit on the ground. Peter, sit on my right and place your left hand under my armpit. Andrew, sit on my left. John, hold my bosom. Bartholomew, brace my back and hold my shoulders, so my bones do not come apart when I begin to speak." {2:15} Once they had done this, Mary began, "When I lived in the temple of God and received food from an angel, one day an angel appeared to me, but his face was incomprehensible, and he did not have bread or a cup like the angel who came before." {2:16} Immediately, the veil of the temple was torn, and there was a great earthquake. I fell to the ground, unable to bear the sight of him. {2:17} But he raised me up, and a cloud of dew came and sprinkled me from head to toe. He wiped me with his robe. {2:18} He said to me, "Hail, highly favored one, chosen vessel, grace inexhaustible." He struck his garment on the right, and a great loaf appeared. He placed it on the altar and ate first, then gave some to me. {2:19} He struck his garment on the left, and a great cup of wine appeared. He placed it on the altar, drank first, and gave some to me. I saw the bread and the cup remain whole. {2:20} He said, "In three years, I will send my word to you, and you will conceive a son through whom all creation will be saved. Peace be with you, my beloved, and my peace will be with you continually." {2:21} After saying this, he vanished, and the temple was restored. {2:22} As Mary spoke, fire came from her mouth, and the world was on the brink of ending. But Jesus quickly appeared, laid his hand on her mouth, and said, "Do not reveal this mystery, or my whole creation will end today." The fire ceased, and the apostles feared that the Lord might be angry with them.

{3:1} Jesus went with them to Mount Mauria and sat among them. {3:2} They were too afraid to ask him questions. {3:3} Jesus said, "Ask me anything you want to learn, and I will teach you. In seven days, I will ascend to my Father and you will no longer see me in this form." {3:4} Still doubting, they asked, "Lord, show us the abyss as you promised." {3:5} Jesus replied, "It is not good for you to see the abyss, but if you desire it, come with me and see." {3:6} He led them to a place called Cherubim, the place of truth. {3:7} Jesus signaled to the angels of the West, and the earth rolled up like a scroll, revealing the abyss. {3:8} When the apostles saw it, they fell on their faces. {3:9} Jesus lifted them up and said, "Did I not tell you it is not good for you to see the abyss?" He then signaled to the angels again, and the abyss was covered up.

{4:1} And he took them and brought them again to the Mount of Olives. {4:2} Peter said to Mary, "You who are highly favored, ask the Lord to reveal to us the mysteries of heaven." {4:3} Mary replied to Peter, "O rock carved from stone, did not the Lord build his church upon you? Go, therefore, and ask him first." {4:4} Peter said again, "O tabernacle that is spread out." {4:5} Mary responded, "You are the image of Adam: was he not formed first, and then Eve? Look at the sun, which shines brightly like Adam, and the moon, which is full of clay because of Eve's transgression. God placed Adam in the east and Eve in the west, appointing the lights so that the sun should shine on Adam in the east with fiery chariots, and the moon should give light to Eve in the west with a countenance like milk. But she defied the Lord's commandment, so the moon is stained with clay and its light is not bright. Since you are the likeness of Adam, you should ask him, but in me, he was contained to restore the strength of the female." {4:6} When they reached the top of the mount, and the Master withdrew a little, Peter said to Mary, "You are the one who nullified Eve's transgression, changing it from shame to joy; it is proper, therefore, for you to ask." {4:7} When Jesus appeared again, Bartholomew said to him, "Lord, show us the adversary of men so that we may see his form, understand his works, where he comes from, and his power, since he did not even spare you but had you crucified." {4:8} Jesus looked at him and said, "You bold-hearted one! You ask for what you cannot behold." {4:9} But Bartholomew was troubled, fell at Jesus' feet, and began to speak, "O lamp that cannot be extinguished, Lord Jesus Christ, creator of the eternal light, who has given those who love you the grace that beautifies all, and has given us eternal light through your coming into the world, who has accomplished the Father's work, turned Adam's shame into mirth, and removed Eve's sorrow with a cheerful countenance by being born of a virgin. Remember not my wrongs but grant me my request." {4:10} Jesus raised him up and said, "Bartholomew, do you want to see the adversary of men? I tell you, when you behold him, not only you but all the apostles and Mary will fall on your faces as if dead." {4:11} But they all said to him, "Lord, let us see him." {4:12} And he led them down from the Mount of Olives, looked wrathfully at the angels guarding hell (Tartarus), and signaled Michael to sound the trumpet in the heavens. Michael sounded, and the earth shook as Beliar came up, held by 660 angels and bound with fiery chains. {4:13} His length was 1,600 cubits and his breadth 40 cubits, with a face like lightning and eyes full of darkness. Smoke came from his nostrils, and his mouth was like a chasm. One of his wings measured eighty cubits. {4:14} When the apostles saw him, they fell to the ground on their faces as if dead. {4:15} But Jesus approached, raised the apostles, and gave them a spirit of power, saying to Bartholomew, "Come and trample his neck, and he will tell you his work and how he deceives men." {4:16} Jesus stood afar off with the rest of the apostles. {4:17} Bartholomew was afraid but raised his voice and said, "Blessed be the name of your immortal kingdom from now and forever." Jesus then permitted him, saying, "Go and tread upon Beliar's neck." Bartholomew quickly did so, and Beliar trembled. {4:18} Bartholomew was afraid, fled, and said to Jesus, "Lord, give me a hem of your garment so I may have the courage to approach him." {4:19} But Jesus said, "You cannot take a hem of my garment, for these are not the garments I wore before I was crucified." {4:20} Bartholomew said, "Lord, I fear he may swallow me up as he did not spare your angels." {4:21} Jesus said, "Were not all things made by my word, and by my Father's will, the spirits were made subject to Solomon? Therefore, being commanded by my word, go in my name and ask him what you will." {4:22} Bartholomew made the sign of the cross, prayed to Jesus, and went behind him. Jesus said, "Draw near." As Bartholomew drew near, fire surrounded him, making his garments appear fiery. Jesus said, "As I told you, tread upon his neck and ask him his power." Bartholomew did so, pressing Beliar's face into the earth. {4:23} Bartholomew asked, "Tell me who you are and your name." Beliar replied, "Lighten my burden a little, and I will tell you who I am, my origin, my work, and my power." {4:24} Bartholomew lightened his burden and said, "Say all that you have done and do." {4:25} Beliar answered, "If you want to know my name, I was initially called Satanael, meaning 'messenger of God,' but after rejecting God's image, I was named Satanas, meaning 'angel of hell.'" {4:26} Bartholomew asked, "Reveal everything to me and hide nothing." {4:27} Beliar said, "I swear by God's glory that even if I wanted to hide something, I cannot, for he who convicts me is near. If I could, I would have destroyed you like those before you. {4:28} I was the first angel created; when God made the heavens, he took a handful of fire and formed me first, Michael second, Gabriel third, Uriel fourth, Raphael fifth, Nathanael sixth, and other angels whose names I cannot tell. {4:29} They are God's rod-bearers and smite me seven times day and night, breaking my power. These are the angels of vengeance who stand before God's throne; they were the first created. {4:30} After them, all other angels were created. In the first heaven are a hundred myriads, in the second another hundred myriads, and so on until the seventh heaven, outside of which is the first firmament, where the powers affecting men reside. {4:31} Four other angels oversee the winds: the first is Chairoum over the north, with a rod of fire to control moisture. {4:32} The second, Oertha over the north, has a torch of fire to warm his great coldness. {4:33} The third, Kerkoutha over the south, restrains his fierceness to prevent the earth from shaking. {4:34} The fourth, Naoutha over the southwest, has a rod of snow to quench the fire from his mouth, which would otherwise set the world on fire. {4:35} Another angel is over the sea, making it rough. {4:36} But the rest I will not tell you, for he who stands by forbids me." {4:37} Bartholomew asked, "How do you punish the souls of men?" {4:38} Beliar said, "Do you want me to explain the punishments for hypocrites, back-biters, jesters, idolaters, covetous, adulterers, wizards, diviners, and those who believe in us? {4:39} Bartholomew said, "Explain it briefly." {4:40} Beliar gnashed his teeth, and a wheel with a fiery sword appeared from the pit, with pipes in the sword. {4:41} Bartholomew asked, "What is this sword?" {4:42} Beliar said, "This is the sword of the gluttonous; they who sin through gluttony are sent into the first pipe, the backbiters into the second, and the hypocrites and others whom I deceive into the third." {4:43} Bartholomew asked, "Do you do these things alone?" {4:44} Satan replied, "If I could go forth by myself, I would destroy the whole world in three days, but neither I nor any of my six hundred followers go forth alone. We command other swift ministers, equipping them with hooks to catch souls with various baits like drunkenness, laughter, backbiting, hypocrisy, pleasures, fornication, and other distractions." {4:45} "I will also tell you the names of the angels: the angel of hail is Mermeoth, who holds the hail upon his head. My ministers adjure him and send him where they will. Other angels oversee snow, thunder, and lightning, and when any of us tries to go forth, these angels send fiery stones to set our limbs on fire." {4:46} Bartholomew asked, "Be silent, dragon of the pit." {4:47} Beliar said, "I will tell you more about the angels of vengeance, whose work is to smite me. The first was Jokel, who smote me sixty times daily with a fiery rod. The second was Mariok who was hidden in the northern regions and who did smite me forty times daily. The third is a fiery wheel that goes around, and whosoever it touches, he does smite. The fourth is Karkrok, a serpent who lies in the Aegean Sea, and who swims around me with his ten thousand sons. The fifth is the angel who oversees the twelve winds and holds them in his hand, releasing them one by one. The sixth is the angel who holds the sun with both hands, and when he lets go, the sun sets. The seventh is the angel of vengeance who goes around the firmament with a flaming sword and smites me. All these angels keep me from harming men as much as I wish." {4:48} Bartholomew asked, "How does man sin against God?" {4:49} Beliar replied, "When a man or woman is born, the angel of God receives them, and he sows in their hearts good works, but I sow in their hearts the works of evil. If they love evil more than good, I plant all kinds of evil in their hearts, making them sin until they die in their sins." {4:50} Bartholomew asked, "Since you do all these things, what is your power in men?" {4:51} Beliar replied, "Do you want to hear more? If a man is righteous, I cannot harm him, for the angel of righteousness keeps him. But if he strays from righteousness, then I work in him what I will. You ask how I enter a man? If he is wealthy and does not help the needy, or if he swears falsely, or if he envies his neighbor, I enter into him. If a man drinks wine and gets drunk, or if he commits fornication or swears by the head of God, I enter into him. I am the devil that enters into his heart." {4:52} Bartholomew asked, "Why do you deceive men?" {4:53} Beliar replied, "I deceive them because I envy their place, and I desire to lead them to destruction as I was led. As long as they do evil, they remain in my power."

Chapter 5: Not Found

{6:1} Bartholomew asked Jesus, "Lord, what sin is the greatest of all sins?" {6:2} Jesus replied, "Truly, I tell you, hypocrisy and backbiting are the greatest sins. The prophet said in the psalm that 'the ungodly will not stand in judgment, nor sinners in the assembly of the righteous,' nor the ungodly in the judgment of my Father. Truly, I say to you, every sin will be forgiven to every person, but the sin against the Holy Spirit will not be forgiven." {6:3} Bartholomew then asked, "What is the sin against the Holy Spirit?" {6:4} Jesus answered, "Anyone who decrees against someone who has served my holy Father has blasphemed against the Holy Spirit. For everyone who serves God worshipfully is worthy of the Holy Spirit, and whoever speaks evil against him will not be forgiven. {6:5} Woe to the one who swears by the head of God, and woe to him who swears falsely by him. For there are twelve heads of God the Most High, for he is the truth, and in him there is no lie or false oath. {6:6} Therefore, go and preach the word of truth to the whole world, and you, Bartholomew, preach this word to everyone who desires it. All who believe in it will have eternal life. {6:7} Bartholomew asked, "Lord, what is the reward for those who sin with the sins of the body?" {6:8} Jesus replied, "It is good if someone who is baptized presents their baptism blamelessly, but the pleasure of the flesh will become a lover. For a single marriage belongs to sobriety. Truly, I say to you, the one who sins after a third marriage is unworthy of God. {6:8} If lust comes upon a person, they should be the husband of one wife. Married people who are good and pay tithes will receive a hundredfold. A second marriage is lawful with the diligent performance of good works and the payment of tithes, but a third marriage is reprobated, and virginity is best. {6:9} Therefore, preach to everyone that they keep themselves from such things. I will not depart from you, and I will supply you with the Holy Spirit. {6:10} Bartholomew and the apostles worshipped Jesus and glorified God earnestly, saying, "Glory be to you, Holy Father, unquenchable Sun, incomprehensible and full of light. To you be glory, honor, and adoration, world without end. Amen."

Gospel of Nicodemus

The Gospel of Nicodemus is an apocryphal text detailing Jesus Christ's trial, crucifixion, resurrection, and descent into Hell. Though not part of the canonical New Testament, it is significant for its historical and theological insights. Traditionally dated to the fourth century, it may have earlier roots. The gospel has two main sections: the Acts of Pilate, which portrays Pontius Pilate more sympathetically and includes additional dialogues, and the Descent into Hell, which depicts Jesus liberating the righteous souls from the underworld. Influential in medieval Christianity, it offers a blend of historical and legendary elements that shaped early Christian doctrine and art.

{1:1} The chief priests and scribes assembled in council, including Annas, Caiaphas, Somne (Senes, Summas), Dothaim (Dothael, Dathaes, Datam), Gamaliel, Judas, Levi, Nepthalim, Alexander, Jairus, and other Jewish leaders, came to Pilate accusing Jesus of various offenses. They said: "We know this man is the son of Joseph the carpenter, born of Mary, and he claims to be the Son of God and a king. Moreover, he desecrates the Sabbath and seeks to destroy the law of our ancestors." Pilate asked, "What deeds does he do that would destroy the law?" The Jews replied, "We have a law that forbids healing on the Sabbath, yet this man performs miracles such as healing the lame, the bent, the withered, the blind, the paralyzed, the mute, and those possessed by demons on the Sabbath!" Pilate inquired, "By what evil deeds?" They responded, "He is a sorcerer and casts out demons by Beelzebub, the prince of demons, and they obey him." Pilate said, "This is not to cast out demons by an unclean spirit, but by the god Asclepius." {1:2} The Jews requested Pilate to have Jesus appear before him for judgment. Pilate called them and said, "How can I, a governor, judge a king?" They replied, "We are not claiming he is a king, but he claims to be one." Pilate then instructed a messenger to bring Jesus gently. The messenger went and, upon seeing Jesus, worshiped him, spread his kerchief on the ground, and said, "Lord, walk hereon and enter in, for the governor calls you." Seeing this, the Jews protested to Pilate, saying, "Why did you not summon him with a herald but with a messenger who worshiped him and made him walk on his kerchief like a king?" {1:3} Pilate called the messenger and asked why he had spread his kerchief on the ground and made Jesus walk on it. The messenger answered, "Lord governor, when you sent me to Jerusalem to Alexander, I saw Jesus riding on a donkey, and the children of the Hebrews held branches and cried out, while others spread their garments on the ground, saying, 'Save now, you who are highest: blessed is he who comes in the name of the Lord.'" {1:4} The Jews protested, "The children of the Hebrews cried out in Hebrew; how did you know it in Greek?" The messenger explained, "I asked a Jew what they cried out in Hebrew, and he translated it for me." Pilate asked, "And how did they cry out in Hebrew?" The Jews responded, "Hosanna membrone barouchamma adonai." Pilate said, "If you yourselves attest to the words the children used, where is the messenger at fault?" The Jews remained silent. Pilate instructed the messenger to bring Jesus in again in the same manner. The messenger went out and did as before, inviting Jesus to enter, and Jesus did so. {1:5} When Jesus entered, the standards and images held by the ensigns bowed and showed reverence to him. The Jews saw this and vehemently complained about the ensigns. Pilate told them, "Do not be surprised that the images bowed and showed reverence to Jesus." The Jews replied, "We saw how the ensigns made them bow and show reverence to him." Pilate then called the ensigns and asked them why they had done so. They said, "We are Greeks and serve in temples, and the images bowed and showed reverence of their own accord while we held them." {1:6} Pilate then told the rulers of the synagogue and the elders of the people, "Select strong men to hold the standards, and let us see if they bow of themselves." The elders chose twelve strong men and placed them before Pilate's judgment seat. Pilate told the messenger to take Jesus out of the judgment hall and bring him in again in the same manner. Pilate warned the men who previously held the images, "I swear by Caesar's safety that if the standards do not bow when Jesus enters, I will have your heads cut off." Pilate commanded Jesus to enter a second time. The messenger followed the previous procedure, asking Jesus to walk on his kerchief, and Jesus did so. When Jesus entered again, the standards bowed and showed reverence once more.

{2:1} When Pilate saw this, he was frightened and tried to rise from his judgment seat. Just then, his wife sent him a message saying, "Have nothing to do with this just man, for I have suffered much because of him in a dream." Pilate then gathered all the Jews and told them, "You know that my wife fears God and prefers Jewish customs. She has sent me a message saying, 'Have nothing to do with this just man; I have suffered much because of him in a dream.'" The Jews responded, "Did we not tell you he is a sorcerer? He has even sent a vision to your wife in a dream." {2:2} Pilate called Jesus and asked, "What do these people accuse you of? Do you have nothing to say?" Jesus replied, "If they did not have power, they would not have spoken at all. Everyone has power over their own words to speak good or evil; they will have to answer for it." {2:3} The Jewish elders accused Jesus, saying, "Firstly, you were born of fornication; secondly, your birth in Bethlehem led to the slaughter of children; thirdly, your parents, Joseph and Mary, fled to Egypt because they were afraid of the people." Some bystanders, devout Jews, said, "We do not believe he was born of fornication; we know Joseph was betrothed to Mary, and he was not born of fornication." Pilate told those who claimed Jesus was born of fornication, "This accusation is false, as there were espousals, as these also say. Annas and Caiaphas argued, 'The whole crowd cries out that he was born of fornication and is a sorcerer who claims to be the Son of God and a king, but we are not believed.'" {2:4} Pilate asked Annas and Caiaphas, "What are proselytes?" They answered, "They were born Greek and have now converted to Judaism." Those who testified that Jesus was not born of fornication, including Lazarus, Asterius, Antonius, Jacob, Amnes, Zenas, Samuel, Isaac, Phinees, Crispus, Agrippa, and Judas, said, "We were not born proselytes but are Jewish by birth, and we tell the truth; we were present at Joseph and Mary's espousals." Pilate called these twelve men and asked them, "Swear by Caesar's safety, is it true that Jesus was not born of fornication?" They replied, "We have a law against swearing, as it is a sin; however, if you swear by Caesar's safety that we are wrong, we will be guilty of death." Pilate asked Annas and Caiaphas, "Will you not respond to these claims?" Annas and Caiaphas said, "We are not believed, though the multitude says he was born of fornication, is a sorcerer, and claims to be the Son of God and a king." {2:5} Pilate ordered all the Jews to leave, except for the twelve who testified that Jesus was not born of fornication. He then asked Jesus to be set apart and asked the Jews, "For what reason do they want to kill him?" They answered, "They are envious because he heals on the Sabbath." Pilate responded, "Do they wish to kill him for doing good?" They confirmed, "Yes."

{3:1} Pilate was enraged and went outside the judgment hall, declaring, "I call the Sun as a witness that I find no fault in this man." The Jews retorted, "If this man were not a criminal, we would not have handed him over to you." Pilate replied, "Judge him according to your law." The Jews said, "It is not lawful for us to execute anyone." Pilate asked, "Has God forbidden you to kill, and permitted me?" {3:2} Pilate went back into the judgment hall and questioned Jesus privately, "Are you the King of the Jews?" Jesus responded, "Is this your own idea, or did others tell you about me?" Pilate answered, "I am not a Jew; your own people and chief priests have handed you over to me. What have you done?" Jesus said, "My kingdom is not of this world; if it were, my servants would fight to prevent my arrest by the Jews. But now my kingdom is not from here." Pilate asked, "So you are a king then?" Jesus answered, "You say that I am a king. For this reason, I was born, and for this I came into the world, to testify to the truth. Everyone on the side of truth listens to me." Pilate asked, "What is truth?" Jesus replied, "Truth is from heaven." Pilate asked, "Is there no truth on earth?" Jesus responded, "You see how those who speak the truth are judged by those in authority on earth."

{4:1} Pilate left Jesus in the judgment hall and went out to the Jews, saying, "I find no fault in him." The Jews responded, "This man said that he could destroy this temple and rebuild it in three days." Pilate asked, "What temple?" The Jews replied, "The one that Solomon built in forty-six years. This man says he will destroy it and rebuild it in three days." Pilate said to them, "I am innocent of the blood of this just man. You handle it yourselves." The Jews responded, "Let his blood be on us and on our children." {4:2} Pilate then privately summoned the elders, priests, and Levites and said, "Do not act this way. There is nothing deserving of death in what you have accused him of; your accusation concerns healing and breaking the Sabbath." The elders, priests, and Levites asked, "If a man blasphemes against Caesar, is he worthy of death?" Pilate said, "He is worthy of death." The Jews said to Pilate, "If a man is worthy of death for blaspheming Caesar, this man has blasphemed against God." {4:3} The governor then ordered all the Jews to leave the judgment hall and called Jesus to him, saying, "What should I do with you?" Jesus replied, "Do as it has been given to you." Pilate asked, "How has it been given?" Jesus said, "Moses and the prophets foretold my death and resurrection." The Jews, overhearing this, said to Pilate, "What more do you need to hear about this blasphemy?" Pilate said to the Jews, "If this is blasphemy, take him for his blasphemy and judge him according to your law." The Jews replied, "Our law says that if a man sins against another man, he deserves forty lashes minus one, but one who blasphemes against God should be stoned." {4:4} Pilate said to them, "Take him and avenge yourselves in whatever way you choose." The Jews said to Pilate, "We want him to be crucified." Pilate said, "He does not deserve crucifixion." {4:5} As the governor looked at the crowd of Jews standing by, he saw many weeping and said, "Not everyone wants him to die." The elder of the Jews replied, "We have all come here with the intent that he should die." Pilate asked, "Why should he die?" The Jews answered, "Because he called himself the Son of God and a king."

{5:1} Nicodemus, a Jew, approached the governor and said, "I beseech you, good lord, let me speak a few words." Pilate said, "Go ahead." Nicodemus said, "I told the elders, priests, Levites, and all the Jews in the synagogue, 'Why are you contending with this man? He performs many wonderful signs that no one else has done and no one else will do. Leave him alone and don't plot any harm against him. If the signs are from God, they will endure, but if they are from men, they will come to nothing. Moses performed many signs in Egypt as commanded by God, and there were some of Pharaoh's servants, Jannes and Jambres, who also did signs, and the Egyptians considered them gods. But because their signs were not from God, they perished along with those who believed in them. So let this man go; he is not worthy of death.'" {5:2} The Jews replied to Nicodemus, "You have become his disciple and are speaking on his behalf." Nicodemus responded, "Is the governor also his disciple, since he speaks on his behalf? Wasn't he appointed to this position by Caesar?" The Jews were enraged and gnashed their teeth at Nicodemus. Pilate asked them, "Why are you so angry with him when he has spoken the truth?" The Jews retorted, "May you receive his truth and his portion." Nicodemus replied, "Amen, amen, may I receive it as you have said."

{6:1} A Jew then came forward and asked to speak. The governor said, "If you have something to say, speak on." The Jew said, "For thirty-eight years, I suffered on a bed, and when Jesus came, many possessed and sick people were healed by him. Some faithful young men carried me with my bed to him. When Jesus saw me, he had compassion and said, 'Take up your bed and walk.' I took up my bed and walked." The Jews said to Pilate, "Ask him on which day he was healed." The healed man replied, "On the Sabbath." The Jews said, "Did we not tell you that he heals and casts out demons on the Sabbath?" {6:2} Another Jew came forward and said, "I was born blind. I heard words but never saw anyone's face. When Jesus passed by, I cried out loudly, 'Have mercy on me, Son of David.' He had pity on me, touched my eyes, and I received my sight immediately." Another Jew said, "I was bent over, and he straightened me with a word." Yet another said, "I was a leper, and he healed me with a word."

{7:1} A woman named Bernice (or Veronica) cried out from a distance, "I had a flow of blood for twelve years, and when I touched the hem of his garment, my bleeding stopped." The Jews said, "We have a law that a woman cannot give testimony."

{8:1} Others, a crowd of both men and women, cried out, "This man is a prophet, and the demons obey him." Pilate said to those who claimed that demons obeyed him, "Why were not your teachers also subject to him?" They replied, "We do not know." Others added, "He raised Lazarus from the dead after four days." The governor was frightened and said to the crowd, "Why do you want to shed innocent blood?"

{9:1} Pilate called Nicodemus and the twelve men who had testified that Jesus was not born of fornication and said to them, "What should I do, as there is unrest among the people?" They replied, "We do not know; let them deal with it." Pilate then addressed the whole crowd of Jews, "You know that it is our custom to release a prisoner at the Feast of Unleavened Bread. I have a prisoner here named Barabbas, a murderer, and also this Jesus, whom I find no fault in. Whom do you want me to release to you?" They cried out, "Barabbas." Pilate asked, "What should I do with Jesus, who is called Christ?" The Jews responded, "Let him be crucified." Some Jews added, "If you release this man, you are not a friend of Caesar's. He claims to be the Son of God and a king, so you will have him as a king instead of Caesar." {9:2} Pilate was angry and said to the Jews, "Your nation is always rebellious and resists your benefactors." The Jews asked, "Against which benefactors?" Pilate said, "According to what I've heard, your God brought you out of Egypt from hard bondage, safely through the sea as on dry land, fed you with manna and quail in the wilderness, gave you water from a rock, and gave you a law. Yet, in all these things, you provoked your God to anger, worshiped a golden calf, and sought to kill you. Moses pleaded for you, and you were not destroyed. Now you accuse me of hating the emperor." {9:3} Pilate then got up from the judgment seat and tried to leave. The Jews cried out, "We acknowledge only Caesar as our king, not Jesus. The wise men brought gifts to him as to a king, and Herod sought to kill him when he heard a king was born. Joseph and Mary fled to Egypt, and Herod killed the children born in Bethlehem." {9:4} Hearing this, Pilate was afraid. He quieted the crowd, who were still shouting, and asked, "So, this is the one Herod sought?" The Jews replied, "Yes, this is him." Pilate took water, washed his hands before the crowd, and said, "I am innocent of this man's blood. You are responsible." The Jews again shouted, "Let his blood be on us and on our children." {9:5} Pilate then ordered the veil to be drawn before the judgment seat where he sat and said to Jesus, "Your nation has accused you of being a king. Therefore, I have decided to have you scourged according to the law and then crucified. Dysmas and Gestas, the two criminals, will be crucified with you."

{10:1} Jesus went out of the judgment hall with the two criminals. When they arrived at the place, they stripped him of his clothes, wrapped him in a linen cloth, and placed a crown of thorns on his head. The two criminals were also hung up. Jesus said, "Father, forgive them, for they do not know what they are doing." The soldiers divided his clothes among themselves. {10:2} The people stood watching, and the chief priests and rulers mocked him, saying, "He saved others; let him save himself. If he is the Son of God, let him come down from the cross." The soldiers also mocked him, offering him vinegar mixed with gall and saying, "If you are the King of the Jews, save yourself." {10:3} Pilate had a sign written in Greek, Latin, and Hebrew that read, "Jesus of Nazareth, King of the Jews," and placed it above the cross. {10:4} One of the criminals named Gestas said to Jesus, "If you are the Christ, save yourself and us." But Dysmas rebuked him, saying, "Don't you fear God, since you are under the same sentence? We are justly punished, for we are receiving what our deeds deserve, but this man has done nothing wrong." He then said to Jesus, "Remember me when you come into your kingdom." Jesus replied, "Truly, I tell you, today you will be with me in paradise."

{11:1} It was about noon when darkness fell over the land until three in the afternoon, because the sun was obscured. The curtain of the temple was torn in two. Jesus called out In a loud voice, "Father, into Your hands I commend My spirit," which means, "Into Your hands I commit My spirit." After saying this, He breathed His last. When the centurion saw what had happened, he praised God, saying, "This man was righteous." The crowds who had gathered to witness the event, upon seeing what had occurred, beat their breasts and went away. {11:2} The centurion reported to the governor what had happened. When the governor and his wife heard the news, they were deeply troubled and did not eat or drink that day. Pilate then called the Jewish leaders and asked them, "Did you see what happened?" They replied, "It was just a solar eclipse, as usual." Joseph, a member of the council from Arimathea, who was also waiting for the Kingdom of God, went to Pilate and requested Jesus' body. He took it down, wrapped it in a clean linen cloth, and placed it in a new tomb where no one had yet been laid.

{12:1} When the Jews learned that Joseph had taken Jesus' body, they sought Joseph and the twelve men who had claimed that Jesus was not born of fornication, as well as Nicodemus and others who had previously testified about Jesus' good works. All of them hid themselves except Nicodemus, who was seen because he was a ruler of the Jews. Nicodemus asked them, "How did you come into the synagogue?" The Jews responded, "How did you come into the synagogue? You are allied with Him, and His share will be with you in the afterlife." Nicodemus replied, "Amen, amen." Similarly, Joseph came forward and said, "Why are you angry with me for requesting the body of Jesus? I placed it in my new tomb, wrapped in clean linen, and rolled a stone over the entrance. You did not repent after crucifying Him but even pierced Him with a spear." The Jews then seized Joseph and put him under guard until the first day of the week, telling him, "We cannot do anything against you now because the Sabbath is approaching. But know that you will not receive a proper burial; we will leave your body for the birds of the sky." Joseph replied, "This is like the boastful Goliath who reproached the living God and holy David. God said through the prophet, 'Vengeance is Mine; I will repay,' says the Lord. And now, one uncircumcised but circumcised in heart took water, washed his hands before the sun, and declared himself innocent of this just man's blood. You answered Pilate, 'His blood be on us and our children.' I fear the Lord's wrath may come upon you and your children as you have said." Hearing this, the Jews were enraged, seized Joseph, and imprisoned him in a windowless house with guards at the door, sealing it shut. {12:2} On the Sabbath, the synagogue rulers, priests, and Levites decreed that everyone should attend the synagogue on the first day of the week. Early the next morning, the crowd gathered and discussed how to execute Joseph. When the council convened and the door was opened, Joseph was nowhere to be found. The people were astonished and distressed because the seals were intact, and Caiaphas had the key. They no longer dared to lay hands on those who had defended Jesus before Pilate.

{13:1} While the people were still in the synagogue, puzzled over Joseph's disappearance, some guards who had been stationed at Jesus' tomb came and reported to the synagogue rulers, priests, and Levites. They told of a great earthquake, an angel descending from heaven, rolling away the stone from the tomb, and sitting on it. The angel's appearance was like lightning, and they were terrified, falling as if dead. They heard the angel speak to the women at the tomb, saying, "Do not be afraid; I know you are looking for Jesus who was crucified. He is not here; He has risen, just as He said. Come, see the place where He lay, and go quickly to tell His disciples that He has risen from the dead and is going to Galilee." {13:2} The Jews asked, "Which women spoke with the angel?" The guards replied, "We do not know who they were." The Jews inquired, "At what hour did this happen?" The guards answered, "At midnight." The Jews asked, "Why did you not arrest the women?" The guards said, "We were paralyzed with fear and did not see the light of day, so we could not apprehend them." The Jews declared, "As the Lord lives, we do not believe you." The guards responded, "You saw many signs in that man and did not believe; how can you believe us? Truly, you swore correctly 'as the Lord lives,' for He indeed lives." The guards also mentioned that the Jews had imprisoned Joseph, sealed the door, and found him gone upon opening it. The Jews said, "Joseph has gone to his own city." The guards added, "Jesus has also risen, as we were told by the angel, and He is in Galilee." {13:3} Hearing this, the Jews were greatly alarmed and said, "We must ensure this news does not spread and cause people to follow Jesus." They conspired and paid the soldiers a large sum of money, instructing them to say, "While we were asleep, His disciples came and stole Him away." They promised to persuade the governor if this report reached him, securing the soldiers' safety. The soldiers took the money and followed the instructions. This account was widely circulated among the people.

{14:1} A priest named Phinees, a teacher named Addas, and a Levite named Aggaeus came down from Galilee to Jerusalem. They told the synagogue rulers, priests, and Levites that they had seen Jesus with His disciples on the mountain called Mamilch. Jesus had instructed His disciples to go into all the world and preach to all creation, saying that those who believe and are baptized will be saved, but those who do not believe will be condemned. Jesus also mentioned that signs would follow believers: they would cast out demons, speak in new tongues, handle snakes, and if they drank anything deadly, it would not harm them; they would heal the sick. While Jesus was speaking to His disciples, He was taken up into heaven. {14:2} The elders, priests, and Levites asked, "Give glory to the God of Israel and confess to Him. Did you truly hear and see these things?" The men who had reported said, "As the Lord God of our fathers Abraham, Isaac, and Jacob lives, we did hear these things and saw Jesus taken up into heaven." The elders, priests, and Levites asked, "Did you come here to tell us this, or to fulfill your vows to God?" They answered, "To fulfill our vows to God." The elders and chief priests then asked, "If you came to fulfill your vows, why tell us this idle tale?" Phinees, Addas, and Aggaeus said, "If what we have spoken is a sin, we are before you. Do as you see fit." They took the book of the law, adjured them to tell no one else these words, provided them with food and drink, and sent them away with money and three companions to escort them back to Galilee. They departed in peace. {14:3} After these men left for Galilee, the chief priests, synagogue rulers, and elders gathered, lamenting with great sorrow, saying, "What is this sign that has happened in Israel?" Amlas and Caiaphas responded, "Why are you troubled and weeping? Do you not know that Jesus' disciples paid the guards to say an angel had rolled away the stone?" The priests and elders replied, "Even if His disciples stole His body, how could His soul enter His body, and how does He remain in Galilee?" They could not answer and finally concluded, "It is unlawful for us to believe the uncircumcised."

{15:1} Nicodemus stood up before the council and said, "You are right in what you say. Do you not know, O people of the Lord, about the men who came from Galilee? They fear God and are respectable men, free from greed, and they promote peace. They swore an oath saying they saw Jesus on Mount Mamilch with his disciples, teaching them everything you've heard from them, and they claimed they saw him taken up into heaven. No one questioned them about how he was taken up. Just as the scriptures teach us that Elias was taken up into heaven and Eliseus cried out loudly, Elias cast his cloak upon Eliseus, who then used it to part the Jordan River and went on to Jericho. The sons of the prophets asked Eliseus where Elias was, and he told them he had been taken up into heaven. They then suggested that a spirit might have carried him to one of the mountains, so they went to search for him but found nothing. They knew he had been taken up. Now, let us send people to all parts of Israel to see if the Christ was taken up by a spirit and cast onto one of the mountains." This suggestion pleased everyone, and they sent out a search but found no sign of Jesus. Instead, they found Joseph of Arimathaea, and no one dared to lay hands on him. {15:2} The elders, priests, and Levites were informed that Jesus could not be found, but Joseph was in Arimathaea. They rejoiced and praised the God of Israel. The rulers of the synagogue, priests, and Levites decided to consult with Joseph and wrote him a letter saying: "Peace be unto you. We know we have sinned against God and you. We have prayed to the God of Israel to allow you to come to us and your family. We are troubled because we could not find you when we opened the door. We devised evil plans against you, but the Lord protected you and made our plans ineffective. O honorable Joseph, blessed among the people." {15:3} They chose seven men who were friends of Joseph, whom he also considered friends. The rulers of the synagogue, priests, and Levites instructed these men to see if Joseph would read their letter. If he did, they hoped he would come to them; if not, they would know he was displeased. The men were sent with blessings, and they went to Joseph, greeted him respectfully, and presented the letter. Joseph read the letter, embraced it, and praised God, saying: "Blessed be the Lord God, who has redeemed Israel from shedding innocent blood. Blessed be the Lord, who sent his angel to protect me." He set a table before them, and they ate, drank, and rested there. {15:4} The next morning, Joseph prepared his donkey and traveled with the men to Jerusalem. The people welcomed him with cries of peace, and he greeted them and offered peace to everyone. Nicodemus welcomed him into his house, threw a grand feast, and invited Annas, Caiaphas, the elders, priests, and Levites. They celebrated with eating, drinking, and singing hymns before everyone went home. Joseph stayed at Nicodemus' house. {15:5} On the following day, which was the preparation day, the rulers of the synagogue, priests, and Levites came to Nicodemus' house. Nicodemus greeted them and brought them inside. The whole council was assembled, with Joseph sitting between Annas and Caiaphas. No one dared speak to him until Joseph asked why he had been called. Nicodemus explained that the revered teachers, priests, and Levites had questions for Joseph. Joseph invited them to ask their questions. Annas and Caiaphas then presented the law and required Joseph to confess the truth, just as Achar did not conceal anything when questioned by the prophet Joshua. Joseph assured them he would reveal everything. {15:6} Annas and Caiaphas expressed their concern about Joseph's actions, specifically his retrieval of Jesus' body, his wrapping it in linen, and placing it in a tomb. They had secured Joseph in a windowless house with locked doors and guards, and when they opened it on the first day of the week, they found him missing. Joseph recounted that on the preparation day, around the tenth hour, he was shut up, and during the Sabbath, his house was lifted by four corners, and a bright light appeared. He fell in fear and was touched by someone who revealed himself as Jesus, who told him not to fear and instructed him to stay in his house for forty days before going to Galilee.

{16:1} When the rulers, priests, and Levites heard Joseph's account, they were astonished and fell to the ground, fasting until the ninth hour. Nicodemus and Joseph comforted Annas, Caiaphas, and the others, encouraging them to eat and prepare for the Sabbath. They rose, prayed, and ate before returning home. {16:2} On the Sabbath, the teachers and priests debated the situation, reflecting on Jesus' life and prophecies about him. They recalled that Symeon had blessed Jesus as a light for the Gentiles and the glory of Israel and prophesied about the suffering of Mary. They sought to understand these events and sent for the three witnesses who had reported Jesus' teachings and ascension. {16:3} The three witnesses from Galilee came to Jerusalem, greeted the council, and were asked about their testimony. They affirmed that they saw Jesus taken up in a cloud from the mount Mamilch, just as they had reported. {16:4} The council questioned the witnesses separately, and their testimonies matched. They referenced the law of Moses, which stated that the truth should be confirmed by multiple witnesses. They also noted that Enoch and Moses had mysterious departures according to the law, and debated various scriptural prophecies about Jesus. {16:5} Annas and Caiaphas acknowledged the witnesses' testimonies and the scriptural references but questioned the significance of Jesus' crucifixion and resurrection. They stated that if his memorial lasted until the Jubilee, he would be a lasting figure. They warned against worshipping anything made by human hands and encouraged the people to stay faithful to the Creator. {16:6} The people agreed and sang a hymn praising the Lord, asking for healing and salvation, acknowledging that God had begun to make them his people. They concluded with a prayer for God's enduring presence and leadership, and after singing, everyone went home, glorifying God.

{17:1} Joseph then stood up and spoke to Annas, Caiaphas, and the others, saying, "It is indeed remarkable that you have heard that Jesus was seen alive after his death and ascended into heaven. However, it is even more astonishing that not only did he rise from the dead himself, but he also raised many others from their graves, who have been seen by many in Jerusalem. Remember the blessed Simeon, the high priest who held the child Jesus in his arms in the temple. Simeon had two sons, who were buried in their own tombs. Go and see their graves—they are open because they have been resurrected, and they are now in the city of Arimathaea, living in prayer. Although people hear them crying out, they do not speak to anyone. Let us go to them with honor and gentleness and ask them about the mystery of their resurrection." When they heard this, they were all pleased. Annas, Caiaphas, Nicodemus, Joseph, and Gamaliel went to Arimathaea and found the brothers kneeling in prayer. They brought them reverently to Jerusalem and took them to the synagogue. They closed the doors, brought the law of the Lord, and asked the brothers to tell them about their resurrection, invoking the God Adonai and the God of Israel. The brothers trembled and groaned but agreed to write down what they had seen and heard.

{18:1} The brothers wrote, "O Lord Jesus Christ, the life and resurrection of the dead, allow us to reveal the mysteries of your majesty that you performed after your death on the cross, as we have been commanded by your name. You instructed us not to reveal the secrets of your divine majesty, which you accomplished in hell. When we were gathered with all our ancestors in the deep and dark realm, a sudden golden light appeared, a royal purple light. All the patriarchs and prophets rejoiced, saying, 'This light is the beginning of everlasting light, which promised to send us his co-eternal light.' Esaias exclaimed, 'This is the light of the Father, the Son of God, as I prophesied: The land of Zabulon and the land of Nephthalim beyond Jordan, Galilee of the Gentiles, have seen a great light.' And now this light has come to us who sit in death." The whole multitude of saints rejoiced even more upon hearing this. {18:2} Simeon then came to us and said, "Glorify the Lord Jesus

Christ, the Son of God, for I received him in my arms in the temple when he was born. Moved by the Holy Spirit, I confessed, 'Now my eyes have seen your salvation, prepared before all people, a light to lighten the Gentiles and the glory of your people Israel.'" When they heard this, everyone rejoiced more. {18:3} Then a figure appeared, resembling someone from the wilderness. Asked about his identity, he replied, "I am John, the voice and prophet of the Most High, who came before his arrival to prepare his way and give knowledge of salvation to his people for the remission of their sins. When I saw him coming to me, I said, 'Behold the Lamb of God who takes away the sins of the world.' I baptized him in the Jordan River, saw the Holy Spirit descend upon him as a dove, and heard a voice from heaven saying, 'This is my beloved Son, in whom I am well pleased.' Now I have come to tell you that he is coming to visit us, the day spring, the Son of God, coming from on high to those of us who sit in darkness and the shadow of death."

{19:1} When Adam, the first created man, heard this, he told his son Seth, "Declare to the patriarchs and prophets all that you heard from Michael the archangel when I sent you to the gates of paradise to ask for the oil of the tree of mercy to anoint my body when I was ill." Seth approached the patriarchs and prophets and said, "When I prayed at the gates of paradise, Michael the angel of the Lord appeared to me and said, 'I am sent by the Lord. I am set over the body of man. Do not worry about the oil of mercy now, as you will only receive it in the last days, after five thousand five hundred years. Then the most beloved Son of God will come to earth to raise Adam and the dead, be baptized in Jordan, and anoint all who believe in him with the oil of mercy, giving them eternal life. He will bring Adam into paradise to the tree of mercy.'" Hearing this, all the patriarchs and prophets rejoiced greatly.

{20:1} While all the saints were rejoicing, Satan, the prince of death, spoke to Hell, saying, "Prepare to receive Jesus who boasts of being the Son of God. He is a man who fears death and says, 'My soul is sorrowful unto death.' He has been my enemy, healing many I made blind, lame, mute, leprous, and possessed. He has even raised the dead from you." Hell responded, "Who is this mighty one, if he is a man who fears death? All mighty men on earth are subjected to my power. If he is so powerful, he must be almighty in his divinity. No man can withstand his power. His claim of fearing death may be a trap for you, and woe to you for eternity." Satan replied, "Why do you doubt? I have tempted him, incited the Jews against him, and prepared a cross and nails for his crucifixion. His death is near, and he will be subject to us." Hell responded, "You said he has taken dead men from me. Others have done this through prayer to God, but not by their own power. Is this Jesus the one who restored Lazarus from death with just his command? It must be him. When I heard his command, I trembled, and all my minions were troubled. We could not hold Lazarus, and the earth released him alive. This man must be a powerful God, capable of freeing all who are imprisoned here and bringing them to eternal life."

{21:1} As Satan the prince and Hell spoke together, a voice like thunder and a spiritual cry suddenly rang out: "Lift up your heads, O gates, and be lifted up, you everlasting doors, that the King of glory may come in." When Hell heard this, it said to Satan the prince: "Depart from me and leave my realm. If you are a mighty warrior, face the King of glory yourself. What do you have to do with him?" Hell then cast Satan out of its domain. Hell told its wicked ministers: "Shut the heavy brass gates and reinforce them with iron bars. Stand firm, so we do not get taken captive ourselves." When all the saints heard this, they rebuked Hell with one voice: "Open your gates, that the King of glory may enter." David then exclaimed: "Did I not prophesy when I was alive on earth, 'Let them give thanks to the Lord for His mercies and wonders to the children of men; He has broken the gates of brass and smashed the bars of iron in pieces. He has taken them out of the way of their iniquity'?" Similarly, Esaias said: "Did I not foretell while alive on earth, 'The dead shall rise, and those in the tombs shall be resurrected; those in the earth shall rejoice, for the dew from the Lord is their healing'? And again I said, 'O death, where is your sting? O Hell, where is your victory?'" When Esaias's words were heard, all the saints said to Hell: "Open your gates; you shall now be overcome and powerless." A great voice like thunder then declared: "Lift up your heads, O gates, and be lifted up, you everlasting doors, that the King of glory may come in." When Hell heard this cry for the second time, it said, as if unsure: "Who is the King of glory?" David answered: "I know the words of this cry, for I prophesied them by the Spirit. I tell you again: The Lord strong and mighty, the Lord mighty in battle, He is the King of glory." David continued: "The Lord looked down from heaven to hear the groans of those in fetters and to deliver the children of those who have been slain. Now, O foul and stinking Hell, open your gates that the King of glory may enter." As David spoke to Hell, the Lord of majesty appeared in human form, lighting up the eternal darkness and breaking the unbreakable bonds. His everlasting power came to us who sat in deep darkness and the shadow of death.

{22:1} When Hell, death, and their wicked ministers saw this, they were struck with fear, along with their cruel officers, at the sight of such great light suddenly appearing in their own realm. They cried out: "We are overcome by you. Who are you, sent by the Lord to confound us? Who are you, who without any corruption and with your majesty untouched, condemn our power with your wrath? Who are you, so great yet so small, both humble and exalted, both a warrior and a commander, a marvelous warrior in the guise of a bondsman, and a King of glory who was slain upon the cross? You who lay dead in the tomb have come down to us alive, and at your death all creation quaked, the stars were shaken, and you have become free among the dead, routing our legions. Who are you, freeing prisoners bound by original sin and restoring them to their former liberty? Who are you, shedding divine and bright light on those blinded by their sins?" All the legions of devils, stricken with fear, cried out together in terror and confusion: "Who are you, Jesus, so mighty and bright in majesty, so pure and spotless? The world of earth, which has always been subject to us and paid tribute for our benefit, has never sent us a dead man like you, nor such a gift to Hell. Who are you that enter our domain so fearlessly, not only not fearing our torments but also trying to free all men from our bonds? Perhaps you are that Jesus, of whom Satan our prince said would gain dominion over the whole world through your death on the cross."

{23:1} Then the King of glory, in His majesty, trampled upon death, seized Satan the prince, and handed him over to Hell's power, drawing Adam into His own light. Hell, receiving Satan the prince with scorn, said: "O prince of destruction, Beelzebub, the scorn of the angels and the reproach of the righteous, why did you do this? You wanted to crucify the King of glory and promised us great spoils from His death. Like a fool, you did not know what you were doing. Behold, this Jesus drives away all the darkness of death with the brilliance of His majesty, breaks open the strong depths of the prisons, releases the prisoners, and frees those bound. All who were sighing in our torments now rejoice against us, and through their prayers, our dominions are defeated, and our realms are conquered. No nation of men fears us anymore. The dead, who were never proud, now triumph over us, and the captives, who could never be joyful, now threaten us. O prince Satan, father of all wickedness, why did you do this? You, who from the beginning until now have despaired of life and salvation—now none of their usual roars are heard, no groans sound in our ears, nor is there any sign of tears on their faces. O prince Satan, keeper of the keys of Hell, those riches you gained by the tree of transgression and the loss of paradise, you have lost by the tree of the cross, and all your joy has perished. By crucifying Christ Jesus the King of glory, you worked against yourself and against me. From now on, you will experience eternal torments and infinite pain in my keeping forever. O prince Satan, author of death and head of all pride, you should have first sought out some evil in this Jesus. Why did you unjustly crucify Him, against whom you found no fault, and bring the innocent and righteous One into our realm, losing the guilty and ungodly of the world? When Hell had spoken this to Satan the prince, the King of glory said to Hell: 'Satan the prince shall be in your power for all ages in place of Adam and his children, those who are my righteous ones.'"

{24:1} The Lord stretched out His hand and said: "Come to me, all you my saints who bear my image and likeness. You who were condemned by the tree, the devil, and death, see now that the devil and death are condemned by the tree." Immediately all the saints gathered under the Lord's hand. The Lord took Adam by the right hand and said: "Peace be unto you and all your children who are my righteous ones." Adam, falling at the Lord's knees, pleaded with tears and supplications, and said with a loud voice: "I will praise You, O Lord, for You have set me up and not allowed my enemies to triumph over me. O Lord my God, I cried to You and You healed me. Lord, You brought my soul out of hell and delivered me from those who go down to the pit. Sing praises to the Lord, all you His saints, and give thanks to Him for the remembrance of His holiness. For there is wrath in His indignation but life in His favor." All the saints of God knelt and fell at the Lord's feet, saying in unison: "You have come, O redeemer of the world; what You foretold by the law and the prophets, You have accomplished in deed. You have redeemed the living by Your cross, and by the death of the cross, You have come down to us to save us from hell and death through Your majesty. O Lord, just as You have set Your name in the heavens and made Your cross a token of redemption on earth, so, Lord, set the sign of the victory of Your cross in Hell, that death may have no more dominion." {24:2} The Lord then made the sign of the cross over Adam and all His saints, took Adam's right hand, and ascended out of Hell, with all the saints following Him. Holy David then cried out: "Sing to the Lord a new song, for He has done marvelous things. His right hand and holy arm have worked salvation for Him. The Lord has made His saving power known; He has revealed His righteousness before all nations." The whole multitude of the saints responded: "Such honor belongs to all His saints. Amen, Alleluia." Then the prophet Habacuc cried out: "You went forth for the salvation of Your people to free Your chosen ones." All the saints responded: "Blessed is He who comes in the name of the Lord. God is the Lord and has given us light. Amen, Alleluia." Similarly, the prophet Micah cried: "Who is a God like You, O Lord, taking away iniquity and removing sin? Now You withhold Your wrath, showing that You are merciful by Your own choice. You forgive all our iniquities and cast our sins into the depths of the sea, as You swore to our ancestors long ago." All the saints answered: "This is our God forever and ever; He will guide us to the end of time. Amen, Alleluia." Thus, all the prophets spoke, praising with holy words, and all the saints followed the Lord, crying out: "Amen, Alleluia."

{25:1} The Lord, holding Adam's hand, handed him over to Michael the archangel, and all the saints followed Michael. Michael brought them into the glory and grace of paradise. There they met two men, ancient figures. When asked by the saints who they were and why they were in paradise with bodies but had not been dead in Hell, one of them answered: "I am Enoch, who was taken up to heaven by the word of the Lord. This is Elias the Thesbite, who was taken up in a chariot of fire. We have not tasted death and will remain here until the coming of the Antichrist, when we will fight against him with God's signs and wonders. We will be slain in Jerusalem and then resurrected after three and a half days, taken up alive on the clouds."

{26:1} As Enoch and Elias spoke with the saints, another man appeared, bearing a cross on his shoulders. When the saints saw him, they asked, "Who are you, for your appearance is like that of a thief? And why do you carry a cross?" He replied, "You are correct; I was a thief, doing all sorts of evil on earth. The Jews crucified me alongside Jesus. I witnessed the miracles that occurred through His cross during the crucifixion, and I believed that He was the Creator and the Almighty King. I asked Him, 'Remember me, Lord, when You come into Your kingdom.' He heard my prayer and said, 'Truly, I say to you, today you will be with Me in paradise.' He then gave me the cross and instructed me to bear it and go to paradise. If the angel who guards paradise does not let me in, I should show him the cross and say, 'Jesus Christ, the Son of God who was crucified, has sent me.' When I did this, the angel opened the door, welcomed me in, and placed me at the right hand of paradise. He told me to wait a little while, for Adam and his righteous children would soon enter after Christ's ascension. Upon hearing this, all the holy patriarchs and prophets praised the Lord, the Father of eternal good, who has shown such grace to sinners and restored them to the beauty of paradise. Amen."

{27:1} These are the divine and holy mysteries that Karinus and Leucius witnessed and heard, but they were instructed by Michael the archangel not to reveal any further mysteries of God. Michael told them to go with their brethren to Jerusalem, remain in prayer, and glorify the resurrection of the Lord Jesus Christ, who raised them from the dead. They were not to speak to anyone but should stay silent until the Lord allowed them to declare His mysteries. Michael also instructed them to go across the Jordan to a fertile place where many who had risen from the dead would testify to the resurrection of Christ. They had only three days to celebrate the Lord's Passover in Jerusalem with their living relatives as a testimony of Christ's resurrection. After being baptized in the Jordan River and receiving white robes, they were taken up into the clouds and transported across the Jordan, disappearing from sight. They were told to remain in Arimathaea and continue in prayer. They were to give praise and thanksgiving to the Lord, repent, and seek His mercy. Peace be unto you from the Lord Jesus Christ, the Savior of all. Amen. After writing everything down, Karinus handed his writings to Annas, Caiaphas, and Gamaliel, while Leucius gave his to Nicodemus and Joseph. They were then transfigured, became exceedingly white, and vanished. Their writings were found identical, with not a single letter differing. Upon hearing these remarkable accounts, the Jewish synagogue members said among themselves that these things were indeed done by the Lord and blessed Him eternally. They left in great fear and confusion, each going to his own home. Joseph and Nicodemus then reported these events to the governor, and Pilate recorded all that had been said about Jesus in the public records of his judgment hall.

{28:1} After these events, Pilate went into the Jewish temple, gathered all the chief priests, teachers, scribes, and law experts, and entered the holy place of the temple. He commanded that all doors be closed and asked them to present the great Bible adorned with gold and precious stones. When the Bible was brought by four ministers, Pilate swore them by the God of their ancestors to reveal the truth. He asked if the scriptures mentioned that Jesus, whom they had crucified, was the Son of God who would come for humanity's salvation and in what year He was to come. He wanted to know if they had crucified Him in ignorance or with full knowledge. Annas and Caiaphas then ordered everyone else to leave the temple and closed all doors. They told Pilate that after crucifying Jesus, they did not know He was the Son of God but only thought He might have performed wonders by chance. They had convened a great assembly in the temple and found witnesses who claimed to have seen Jesus alive after His death, and others who said He had ascended into heaven. They also had written accounts from two witnesses whom Jesus had raised from the dead, detailing the marvelous deeds Jesus performed among the dead. Every year, they consulted this holy Bible before their assembly and had found in the first book of the Seventy that Michael the angel spoke to Seth, the third son of Adam, about Christ coming after five thousand five hundred years. They interpreted the five cubits and a half of the ark of the covenant to represent the time until Jesus's coming in the flesh. After examining all generations up to Joseph and Mary, they confirmed the period matched the prophecy. They had not disclosed this to anyone to avoid discord in their synagogues but had now revealed it to Pilate as he had sworn them by the Bible. They adjured Pilate to keep this information confidential.

{29:1} Pilate, upon hearing the statements of Annas and Caiaphas, recorded them among the acts of the Lord and Savior in the public records. He wrote a letter to King Claudius of Rome, stating: "Pontius Pilate to Claudius, greetings. Recently, I investigated a matter: the Jews, out of envy, have inflicted severe judgments upon themselves and their descendants. Despite their fathers' promises of a holy one from heaven who would be their King and born of a virgin, they rejected Him. When Jesus came, performing miracles and being called the Son of God, the chief priests, envious of Him, brought Him to me with false accusations, claiming He was a sorcerer and violated their law. I, believing their claims, had Him scourged and crucified. After His burial, guards were placed, but He rose on the third day. Despite the Jews' efforts to cover up the resurrection, the soldiers, bribed to say the body was stolen, could not keep silent and testified to His resurrection. I report this to you so you are not misled by false accounts from the Jews."

Lost Gospel of Peter

The Lost Gospel According to Peter, discovered in a grave at Akhmim, Egypt in 1886-87, is a fragmentary early Christian text likely composed in the second century CE. This brief, incomplete manuscript offers a unique narrative of Jesus' Passion and Resurrection, marked by dramatic and embellished details. It diverges significantly from canonical accounts, depicting a more supernatural portrayal of Jesus' suffering, death, and resurrection, and emphasizing themes of divine intervention and the cosmic struggle between good and evil. Notable elements include Roman soldiers witnessing the resurrection and a walking, talking cross, which have sparked extensive theological debate. Scholars are particularly interested in its Christology, portrayal of Jewish authorities, and its insights into early Christian communities, as well as its relationship to the canonical gospels and potential influence on them.

- **The Handwashing Incident**: None of the Jews, including Herod or his judges, washed their hands. When they refused, Pilate stood up. Herod then commanded that Jesus be taken away, instructing them to carry out whatever he had ordered.
- **Joseph of Arimathea's Request**: Joseph, a friend of Pilate and Jesus, came to Pilate knowing they were about to crucify Jesus. He asked Pilate for Jesus' body for burial. Pilate then contacted Herod to request the body. Herod replied that, even if no one had requested it, they intended to bury Jesus before the Sabbath began, as the law required that a body not remain exposed overnight.
- **The Mocking of Jesus**: On the day before the Feast of Unleavened Bread, they took Jesus and treated him with scorn. They dressed him in purple, placed him on a judgment seat, and mocked him as the king of Israel. They crowned him with thorns, spat on him, hit him, and scourged him, all while derisively honoring him as the Son of God.
- **The Crucifixion**: Jesus was crucified between two criminals. He remained silent, showing no sign of pain. After raising the cross, they wrote the inscription: "This is the King of Israel." They divided his clothes among themselves and cast lots for them. One of the criminals crucified alongside Jesus rebuked the others, pointing out that Jesus had done no wrong and yet suffered.
- **The Darkness and Jesus' Death**: At noon, darkness covered Judea, causing fear that the sun had set while Jesus was still alive, contrary to their law. They gave Jesus a drink mixed with gall and vinegar. As he cried out, "My power, my power, why have you forsaken me?" he died, and the temple curtain was torn in two.
- **The Earthquake and Burial**: When Jesus died, an earthquake occurred. The sun reappeared at the ninth hour. The Jews, realizing the gravity of their actions, mourned, acknowledging that judgment was near. Joseph of Arimathea took Jesus' body, washed it, and wrapped it in a linen cloth before placing it in his own tomb, known as the Garden of Joseph.
- **The Guarding of the Tomb**: The scribes, Pharisees, and elders, fearing that Jesus' disciples might steal his body and claim he had risen, asked Pilate for soldiers to guard the tomb. Pilate provided them with Petronius the centurion and soldiers, who sealed the tomb with a large stone and seven seals.
- **The Resurrection**: On the night before the Lord's Day, as the soldiers watched, there was a great voice from heaven. The heavens opened, and two men descended with great light, rolling away the stone and entering the tomb. The soldiers, terrified, woke the centurion and the elders. They saw three figures emerging from the tomb, with one carrying a cross. The heavenly voice proclaimed Jesus had preached to those who were asleep.
- **The Soldiers' Report**: The soldiers went to Pilate, distressed, and reported what they had witnessed, claiming Jesus was truly the Son of God. Pilate disclaimed responsibility, stating that the decision had been theirs. The soldiers were urged by the elders to keep silent to avoid further trouble from the Jewish people.
- **The Women at the Tomb**: On the morning of the Lord's Day, Mary Magdalene and other women went to the tomb to anoint Jesus' body but were afraid of being seen by Jews. When they arrived, they found the stone rolled away and a young man in bright clothing inside. He told them Jesus had risen and was not there. The women fled in fear.
- **Disciples' Reaction**: On the last day of the Feast of Unleavened Bread, many people returned home. The twelve disciples of Jesus were grieving and went to their homes. Simon Peter, his brother Andrew, and Levi, the son of Alphaeus, went fishing, trying to cope with the events that had occurred.

Fragments of Greek Gospel of Thomas

The Fragments of the Greek Gospel of Thomas, a pivotal piece of early Christian literature, offer significant insights into the diverse theological currents that characterized early Christianity. These fragments, primarily discovered in Oxyrhynchus, Egypt, provide critical evidence of the existence and dissemination of the Gospel of Thomas in Greek, underscoring its historical and cultural context. The Gospel of Thomas is a non-canonical text, comprising 114 sayings attributed to Jesus (these were the fragments found differently), many of which parallel those found in the canonical gospels, yet it diverges markedly in its lack of narrative structure and emphasis on secret, esoteric knowledge. Scholars date these fragments to the late second or early third century, situating them within a dynamic period of doctrinal formation and consolidation in the early Church. The Greek fragments of Thomas reveal a syncretic blend of Hellenistic and Judaic thought, reflecting the broader milieu of the Greco-Roman world where diverse religious ideas intermingled. This gospel's aphoristic style and focus on direct sayings of Jesus highlight its unique theological stance, particularly its Gnostic elements that emphasize inner enlightenment and knowledge of the divine. The discovery and analysis of these Greek fragments have fueled scholarly debate regarding the origins, authorship, and influence of the Gospel of Thomas, challenging conventional understandings of early Christian history and prompting a reevaluation of the development of Christian doctrine. The Greek fragments, thus, are not merely textual remnants but are critical to comprehending the complex interplay of religious ideas that shaped the nascent Christian tradition.

These are the hidden teachings spoken by Jesus the Living One, recorded by Judas, also known as Thomas:

- He told them, "Anyone who listens to these words will never experience death."
- Jesus said, "Persist in seeking until you find. When you find, you will marvel; marveling, you will reign; and reigning, you will rest."
- Jesus explained, "If those who lead you say, 'Look, the Kingdom is in the sky,' then the birds will precede you. If they say, 'It's underground,' the fish will lead. Instead, the Kingdom of God is within you and around you. Those who know themselves will discover it; knowing yourselves reveals you as children of the living Father. But if you remain ignorant of yourselves, you dwell in poverty, and it is this poverty that defines you."
- Jesus advised, "Let the aged not hesitate to seek wisdom from the young, for many who are first shall be last, and the last first, blending into one."
- He taught, "Recognize what is in front of you, and what is hidden will be revealed to you. Nothing concealed will remain undisclosed, nor buried forever."
- When asked about fasting, prayer, almsgiving, and diet, Jesus replied, "Do not lie or engage in what you detest, for truth exposes all. Nothing remains hidden that won't come to light."
- Jesus warned, "Unless you detach from the world, you cannot enter the Kingdom of God. Unless you sanctify the Sabbath, you will not see the Father."
- Reflecting on humanity, Jesus said, "I stood amidst them, visible in flesh, finding all inebriated and none thirsty. My heart grieved for their blindness and lack of insight."
- Jesus affirmed, "Where two are together, there is divinity, and alone, I say, 'I am with him.' Lift a stone, and there I am; split a piece of wood, and I am present."
- He remarked, "A prophet is not honored in his hometown, nor does a healer cure those who know him."
- Jesus illustrated, "A city atop a high hill, fortified, cannot fall or hide."
- He advised against worry, saying, "Do not fret from dawn to dusk about food or clothing. You are greater than the lilies, cared for by God. Trust Him for your needs."
- To his disciples' question about visibility, Jesus answered, "When you strip without shame, tread on your garments like children, then you will see the Child of the Living, without fear."

Oxyrhynchus 1224 Gospel

The Oxyrhynchus 1224 Gospel, discovered in the ancient city of Oxyrhynchus in Egypt, is a significant early Christian text dating to around the 3rd century CE. Written in Greek, this gospel fragment offers insights into the diversity of Christian writings outside the New Testament. Unearthed among the Oxyrhynchus papyri in the late 19th and early 20th centuries, P.Oxy 1224 contains unique content that does not directly correspond to known canonical or apocryphal gospels, suggesting a broader spectrum of early Christian traditions. Its discovery has sparked scholarly debate about the formation of the New Testament canon and the diversity of early Christian beliefs. Though fragmentary, the text features sayings of Jesus that differ from the canonical gospels, highlighting the fluidity of early Christian theology and narrative. This gospel enhances our understanding of early Christian communities in Egypt and the wider Mediterranean.

- I felt overwhelmed, but then Jesus appeared to me in a vision and asked, "Why are you feeling discouraged? It's not about you, but the situation you're facing."
- "You've been asked about what you've given up. What is the new teaching that they claim you're spreading, or the new baptism you're advocating? Answer and clarify."
- When the scribes, Pharisees, and priests saw Jesus eating with sinners, they were angry. But when Jesus heard their complaints, he said, "Healthy people don't need a doctor; it's the sick who do."
- "Pray for those who oppose you. Anyone who isn't against you is actually on your side. Someone who seems distant today might become close tomorrow, and in this way, you will overcome your adversaries."

Egerton Gospel

The Egerton Gospel, a fragmentary text discovered in the early 20th century, represents one of the most intriguing non-canonical gospels of early Christianity. Dating from the mid-2nd century, it provides unique insights into the diversity of early Christian thought and literature. The manuscript, composed in Greek on papyrus, was unearthed in Egypt and is named after the Egerton Collection at the British Library, where it is housed. Unlike the canonical gospels, the Egerton Gospel does not follow a continuous narrative but instead presents a series of pericopes, or separate stories, some of which parallel those found in the canonical gospels, while others are unique to this text. The fragments reveal episodes such as Jesus engaging in debates with Jewish authorities and performing miracles, highlighting a theological perspective that emphasizes Jesus' wisdom and miraculous powers. Scholars debate its origins and relationship to other gospels, particularly whether it predates or postdates the synoptic gospels. Its mixed composition suggests it may draw from multiple oral and written traditions circulating within early Christian communities. The Egerton Gospel's content and structure contribute significantly to our understanding of the complex and multi-faceted nature of early Christian writings, offering a glimpse into the diverse ways in which Jesus' life and teachings were interpreted and recorded outside the canonical framework. This gospel's existence underscores the fluid boundaries and rich textual culture of early Christianity, where numerous gospels competed for authority and authenticity before the establishment of the New Testament canon. As such, the Egerton Gospel remains a critical piece of the puzzle in reconstructing the historical and theological landscape of early Christian literature.

{1:1} And Jesus said to the lawyers, "Punish every wrongdoer and transgressor, but not me. Who judges how he does what he does?" {1:2} Turning to the rulers of the people, he said, "Search the scriptures, in which you think you have life. These are they that testify about me. Do not think that I have come to accuse you before my Father. There is one who accuses you: Moses, in whom you have hoped." {1:3} They replied, "We know that God spoke to Moses, but as for you, we do not know where you are from." {1:4} Jesus answered them, "Now your disbelief in those whom he has commended is being exposed. For if you had believed Moses, you would have believed me. For he wrote about me to your fathers." {1:5} And they picked up stones to stone him. The rulers seized him to hand him over to the crowd, but they could not do so because the time for his arrest had not yet come. The Lord himself, escaping from their grasp, withdrew from them. {1:6} And behold, a leper approached him, saying, "Teacher Jesus, while you were traveling with lepers and eating with tax collectors at the inn, I too became a leper. If you are willing, I can be cleansed." {1:7} The Lord said to him, "I am willing; be cleansed." Immediately, the leprosy left him. Jesus then said to him, "Go show yourself to the priests and offer the sacrifices for your cleansing as Moses commanded, and sin no more."

{2:1} They came to him and tested him rigorously, saying, "Teacher Jesus, we know that you have come from God, for what you do bears witness beyond all the prophets. So tell us, is it lawful to pay taxes to kings, which benefit their rule? Should we pay them or not?" {2:2} But Jesus, perceiving their intent and becoming indignant, said to them, "Why do you call me teacher with your lips but not do what I say? Isaiah rightly prophesied about you, saying, 'This people honors me with their lips, but their hearts are far from me. In vain do they worship me, teaching as doctrines the precepts of men.'" {2:3} "When a farmer encloses a small seed in the ground, making it invisible and hidden, how does its abundance become immeasurable?" As they were puzzled by this strange question, Jesus walked to the Jordan River, stood on its edge, and with his right hand, filled it with water and sprinkled it on the shore. The water made the ground moist, and it brought forth fruit before them, much to their joy.

Gospel of the Egyptians

The Gospel of the Egyptians, a text classified within the corpus of Gnostic literature, is an intriguing and complex work that offers a unique perspective on early Christian thought and esoteric traditions. This text is part of the broader Nag Hammadi Library, a collection of early Christian and Gnostic writings discovered in Egypt in 1945. Unlike the canonical Gospels, the Gospel of the Egyptians delves deeply into mystical cosmology and elaborate theological themes, reflecting the diversity of beliefs and interpretations that existed within early Christianity. It features extensive discourses on the nature of the divine, the structure of the spiritual realms, and the process of salvation, emphasizing secret knowledge (gnosis) as the path to spiritual enlightenment and liberation. The text is notable for its elaborate mythological narrative, which includes numerous figures and entities, often with complex and overlapping roles. Central to its theology is the concept of the ineffable, transcendent God, who exists beyond the material world and is distinct from the lesser divine beings involved in the creation and administration of the cosmos. The Gospel of the Egyptians also addresses themes of divine forethought and the roles of male and female principles in the spiritual hierarchy, reflecting Gnostic concerns with dualism and the reconciliation of opposites. Its rich symbolic language and metaphysical speculations provide valuable insights into the diverse religious landscape of the second and third centuries, illustrating the ways in which early Christians grappled with questions of divine nature, human existence, and ultimate salvation. The Gospel of the Egyptians remains a significant text for scholars studying the development of early Christian thought, Gnostic traditions, and the broader context of ancient religious and philosophical currents.

- After the Word spoke about the End of times, Salome asked, "How long will people keep dying?" The Scriptures talk about humans in two aspects: the physical body and the soul. It also distinguishes between those who are saved and those who are not, with sin being viewed as the death of the soul. The Lord wisely responded, "As long as women continue to give birth."
- Some people who don't follow the true Gospel often ignore the rest of what was said to Salome. She asked, "Have I done the right thing by not having children?" implying that having children might not be ideal. The Lord replied, "Eat all plants, but avoid the one that is bitter."
- When Salome asked when the things she was curious about would be revealed, the Lord answered, "When you have transcended the feeling of shame, when dualities become one, and when male and female are neither male nor female." This teaching isn't found in the four canonical Gospels but is present in the Gospel according to the Egyptians. The Second Epistle of Clement also has a similar saying: "When the two become one, and what is outside is like what is inside, and male and female are neither male nor female." This saying is also mentioned in the Apocryphal Acts.
- The Lord told Salome, "As long as women give birth, death will continue." This doesn't mean that life is bad or creation is evil, but rather to show the natural order, as birth is always followed by decay.
- The Savior told Salome that death would persist as long as women bear children, not to condemn childbirth, which is necessary for the salvation of believers.
- Some people who criticize God's creation under the guise of chastity use the words spoken to Salome. They refer to a saying thought to be in the Gospel according to the Egyptians: "The Savior said, 'I came to destroy the works of the female.'" Here, "female" is interpreted as lust, and "works" refer to birth and decay.
- The Naassenes claim that the soul is difficult to find and understand because it is constantly changing and doesn't stay in one form or emotion. These changes are described in the Gospel according to the Egyptians.
- The Sabellians are deceived by apocryphal texts, especially the Egyptian Gospel. This text includes various statements attributed to the Savior, claiming that He revealed to His disciples that the same person was Father, Son, and Holy Spirit.

Gospel of the Nazoreans

The Gospel of the Nazoreans, an enigmatic and fragmentary text, holds a significant yet mysterious place in early Christian literature. As one of the numerous texts often categorized under the broader term "Jewish-Christian Gospels," it provides a unique glimpse into the beliefs and traditions of the Nazoreans, an early Jewish-Christian sect. This gospel is primarily known through patristic citations, with early Church Fathers such as Jerome and Epiphanius referencing its contents. Jerome's Latin translation of the Gospel of Matthew and his commentary on Matthew are among the primary sources that offer fragments and insights into this elusive text. The Gospel of the Nazoreans is often considered a variant or a parallel to the canonical Gospel of Matthew, yet it contains distinct elements that reflect its Jewish-Christian origin. For instance, it is reputed to emphasize adherence to Jewish law and customs, aligning with the sect's belief in maintaining Jewish identity while recognizing Jesus as the Messiah. This gospel also showcases variant readings and unique episodes absent from the canonical texts, suggesting a diverse and rich tradition of early Christian narratives. The historical and theological significance of the Gospel of the Nazoreans lies in its testament to the plurality of early Christianities and the fluidity of gospel traditions before the establishment of the New Testament canon. The fragments that survive, though scant, offer valuable perspectives on how some early Christians navigated their dual identity within the broader Judaic tradition and the nascent Christian faith. Therefore, the study of the Gospel of the Nazoreans not only enriches our understanding of early Christian diversity but also illuminates the complex interplay between Jewish traditions and emerging Christian theology in the first few centuries of the Common Era.

- **Matthew's Use of Hebrew Texts**: The phrases "Out of Egypt have I called my son" and "For he shall be called a Nazaraean" are cited by Matthew following the Hebrew original text rather than the Septuagint.
- **John the Baptist's Baptism**: The mother of the Lord and his brethren said to him, "John the Baptist baptizes for the remission of sins; let us go and be baptized by him." But he responded, "What have I sinned that I should go and be baptized by him, unless what I have said is considered a sin of ignorance?"
- **Jerusalem in the Gospel**: The Jewish Gospel uses "to Jerusalem" rather than "into the holy city" in the account.
- **Phrase Lacking**: The phrase "without a cause" is missing in some manuscripts and in the Jewish Gospel.
- **Daily Bread in the Gospel**: In the Gospel according to the Hebrews, instead of "essential to existence," the term "mahar" is used, which means "of tomorrow," so the sense is "Our bread of tomorrow"—that is, of the future—"give us this day."
- **Casting Out of the Bosom**: The Jewish Gospel reads: "If you are in my bosom and do not do the will of my Father in heaven, I will cast you out of my bosom."
- **More Wise Than Serpents**: The Jewish Gospel states: "wise more than serpents."
- **Kingdom of Heaven Plundered**: The Jewish Gospel says: "the kingdom of heaven is plundered."
- **Thanksgiving**: The Jewish Gospel reads: "I thank thee."
- **The Withered Hand**: In the Gospel used by the Nazarenes and Ebionites, the man with the withered hand is described as a mason who pleaded, "I was a mason and earned my livelihood with my hands; I beseech you, Jesus, to restore me to health so that I may not have to beg for my bread."
- **Three Days and Nights**: The Jewish Gospel does not include the phrase "three days and nights."
- **Corban**: The Jewish Gospel states: "Corban is what you should obtain from us."
- **Missing Verses**: The passages marked with an asterisk (Matthew 16:2-3) are not found in other manuscripts or the Jewish Gospel.
- **Son of John**: The Jewish Gospel refers to "son of John" instead of "son of Barachias."
- **Forgiveness of Sins**: Jesus said, "If your brother sins and makes three reparations, receive him seven times a day." Simon, his disciple, questioned, "Seven times a day?" The Lord responded, "Yes, I say to you, until seventy times seven times. For even after they were anointed with the Holy Spirit, the prophets were found to have sinful discourse."
- **Rich Man's Challenge**: One rich man asked Jesus what good thing he must do to have eternal life. Jesus replied, "Fulfill the law and the prophets." The man said he had done so, to which Jesus responded, "Go and sell all that you possess and distribute it among the poor, then come and follow me." The rich man was displeased, and Jesus remarked, "How can you say you have fulfilled the law and the prophets when many of the brethren, sons of Abraham, are dirty and hungry, while your house is full of good things that do not reach them?" He then said to Simon, his disciple, "It is easier for a camel to go through the eye of a needle than for a rich man to enter the kingdom of heaven."
- **Son of Joiada**: In the Gospel used by the Nazarenes, "son of Joiada" is mentioned instead of "son of Barachias."
- **Threat in the Parable**: The Gospel in Hebrew characters threatens not the servant who hid the talent but the one who lived dissolutely—one who squandered his master's substance with harlots and flute-girls, one who multiplied the gain, and one who hid the talent. This suggests that the threat might refer to the first servant who feasted and drank with the drunken.
- **Peter's Denial**: The Jewish Gospel reads: "And he denied, swore, and damned himself."
- **Barabbas Interpretation**: In the Gospel according to the Hebrews, "Barabbas" is interpreted as "son of their teacher."
- **Temple Veil**: The Gospel written in Hebrew characters mentions that not the veil but the lintel of the temple collapsed.
- **Guarding the Cave**: The Jewish Gospel says: "And he delivered armed men to sit opposite the cave and guard it day and night."
- **Separations of Souls**: The Gospel in Hebrew states: "I choose for myself the most worthy: the most worthy are those whom my Father in heaven has given me."

Oxyrhynchus 840 Gospel

The Oxyrhynchus 840 Gospel, an intriguing fragmentary text discovered among the vast collection of papyri unearthed at the ancient site of Oxyrhynchus in Egypt, provides a significant yet enigmatic glimpse into early Christian literature. Dated to the third century, this gospel fragment is part of a larger corpus of writings that were uncovered in the late 19th and early 20th centuries by archaeologists Bernard Grenfell and Arthur Hunt. The manuscript, written in Greek, offers a narrative that diverges from the canonical gospels, presenting unique insights into the theological diversity and textual variations that characterized early Christianity. The fragmentary nature of the text complicates its interpretation, as scholars must piece together incomplete sentences and contextually ambiguous references. Despite these challenges, the Oxyrhynchus 840 Gospel is invaluable for understanding the heterodox traditions and the complex landscape of early Christian thought. Its content hints at alternative Christological perspectives and possibly reflects the influence of various early Christian communities or sects. The gospel's discovery in Oxyrhynchus, a prominent Hellenistic city, underscores the multicultural and religiously plural environment in which Christianity developed. This fragment, therefore, not only contributes to the corpus of apocryphal gospels but also enriches our comprehension of the dynamic and contested process of gospel formation in early Christianity. As scholars continue to analyze and debate the book, it remains a testament to the rich textual tradition and the vibrant intellectual milieu of early Christian communities.

- Earlier, before committing wrong, he would cunningly reason everything out. But be cautious not to end up suffering the same fate as they do. For not only do wrongdoers receive retribution among the living, but they also face punishment and severe torture in the afterlife.
- Taking them along, he entered the place of purification and wandered through the temple. Approaching them, a high priest of the Pharisees named Levi joined them and said to the savior, "Who allowed you to tread on this place of purification and view these holy vessels, even though you haven't bathed, nor have your disciples' feet been washed? After defiling this area of the temple, which is clean and should only be entered by someone who has bathed and changed their clothes, you dare to look upon these holy vessels."
- The savior, standing nearby with his disciples, replied, "So, being here in the temple, do you consider yourself clean?" The high priest answered, "I am clean. I bathed in the pool of David and, after descending one set of stairs and ascending another, I came back up. I put on clean white clothes and then came to look at these holy vessels."
- The savior responded, "Woe to blind people who do not see! You bathed in the waters where dogs and pigs have been cast, night and day. By washing yourselves, you scrubbed only the outer layer of skin, which even prostitutes and flute-girls use when they adorn themselves to attract men. But from within, they are filled with scorpions and all kinds of unrighteousness. However, I and my disciples, whom you say have not washed, have been cleansed in the waters of eternal life that come from the God of heaven. Woe to those who are blind to this truth. For while you focus on outward appearances and ritual cleanliness, you overlook the deeper purification of the heart and soul. True purity comes from within, from a life lived in accordance with divine principles, not merely from external rituals and appearances."

Gospel of the Nativity of Mary

The Gospel of the Nativity of Mary, an apocryphal text believed to have been composed in the early centuries of Christianity, offers a detailed narrative of the birth and early life of the Virgin Mary, mother of Jesus Christ. While not part of the canonical New Testament, this text holds significant value in Christian tradition, particularly within the context of Marian devotion and the development of Marian doctrines. The Gospel provides a backdrop to Mary's immaculate conception, her pious upbringing, and her predestined role as the mother of the Messiah. Its accounts are deeply interwoven with themes of divine intervention and prophecy, underscoring the theological belief in Mary's unique sanctity and her role in salvation history. The text begins with the story of Mary's parents, Joachim and Anne, who are depicted as righteous yet childless, enduring social stigma and personal despair until an angelic visitation announces the forthcoming birth of Mary. This narrative not only parallels the Old Testament stories of miraculous births but also establishes Mary within the lineage of the faithful, prefiguring her exceptional role in Christian theology. The Gospel of the Nativity of Mary elaborates on her early life, emphasizing her purity, devotion, and the fulfillment of Old Testament prophecies through her. The portrayal of Mary's childhood, including her presentation at the temple and her vow of virginity, reflects early Christian reverence for her and sets the stage for her acceptance of the divine will at the Annunciation. Although not universally accepted within the early Church, this Gospel significantly influenced later Christian thought, art, and liturgy, contributing to the rich tapestry of Marian lore and the development of doctrines such as the Immaculate Conception and the Assumption. The text's emphasis on Mary's holiness and her preordained role highlights the intersection of divine grace and human agency in the salvation narrative, offering insights into early Christian piety and theological reflection.

- The Blessed Virgin Mary, who came from the royal lineage of David and was born in Nazareth, was raised in the Temple of the Lord in Jerusalem. Her father was Joachim, and her mother was Anna. Joachim's family was from Galilee, specifically Nazareth, while Anna's family was from Bethlehem. They lived a righteous and blameless life before the Lord and were highly respected by others. They divided their wealth into three parts: one for the temple and its servants, another for strangers and the poor, and the third for their own needs. Despite living a chaste married life for about twenty years without children, they vowed that if they were blessed with a child, they would dedicate it to the service of the Lord. They regularly visited the temple during each of the annual festivals.
- One year, during the Festival of Dedication, Joachim traveled to Jerusalem with some men from his tribe. At that time, Issachar was the high priest. When Issachar saw Joachim with his offering among the other worshipers, he despised him and rejected his gifts. He questioned why Joachim, who had no children, dared to present offerings like those who had offspring, suggesting that Joachim's gifts were unacceptable to God because he was without children. He told Joachim that he should first have children to lift this perceived curse before coming to the Lord with his offerings. Embarrassed by this rebuke, Joachim withdrew to the shepherds' fields, avoiding his own tribe to escape further shame.
- While Joachim was in the fields, an angel of the Lord appeared to him in brilliant light. The angel reassured Joachim, telling him not to be afraid. The angel conveyed that God had heard his prayers and seen his charitable deeds. The angel explained that God, not nature, was the ultimate judge and that God sometimes closes and then miraculously opens wombs to show that births are gifts from Him, not results of human desire. The angel cited the examples of Sarah, who gave birth to Isaac at a very old age, and Rachel, who bore Joseph despite being previously barren. The angel told Joachim that Anna would give birth to a daughter named Mary, who would be dedicated to the Lord from birth, filled with the Holy Spirit, and would live in the temple. This daughter would miraculously conceive the Son of the Most High, Jesus, who would be the Savior of all nations. The angel also gave a sign: Joachim would meet Anna at the Golden Gate in Jerusalem, which would confirm the angel's message.
- The angel later appeared to Anna, telling her not to be afraid and assuring her that it was not a vision. The angel announced that she would give birth to a daughter named Mary, who would be blessed above all women. Mary would be dedicated to the Lord from a young age, living in the temple until she reached maturity. She would live a life of fasting and prayer, free from any impurity, and remain a virgin. Mary, being pure and without human intercourse, would give birth to the Savior of the world. Anna was instructed to go to Jerusalem and meet Joachim at the Golden Gate, which would be a sign that the angel's message was true.
- Following the angel's instructions, Joachim and Anna went to Jerusalem and met at the place specified by the angel. Overjoyed to see each other and confident in the divine promise, they thanked the Lord and returned home, waiting eagerly for the fulfillment of the promise. Anna later conceived and gave birth to a daughter, whom they named Mary, as instructed by the angel.
- When Mary was three years old and ready to be weaned, her parents brought her to the temple with offerings. The temple had fifteen steps leading up to it because it was built on a mountain. Her parents placed the young Mary on one of the steps, and as they changed out of their travel clothes, Mary climbed all fifteen steps by herself, without any help. This act showed her exceptional purity and was seen as a sign of her future greatness. After offering the required sacrifices and fulfilling their vow, her parents left her in the temple to be raised among other virgins and returned home.
- Mary grew up in the temple, advancing in both age and virtue. Though her parents were no longer directly involved in her life, the Lord took special care of her. She was visited by angels regularly and had divine visions, which protected her from harm and filled her with goodness. By the time she was fourteen, Mary was admired for her virtuous life, and no one could find fault with her. When the high priest announced that all virgins of marriageable age should return home to marry, Mary refused. She stated that she had been dedicated to the Lord and had vowed to remain a virgin. The high priest, unsure of how to proceed without violating Scripture or introducing a new custom, decided to seek advice from prominent people in Jerusalem and the surrounding areas. They agreed to seek God's guidance on the matter.
- The high priest consulted God through the usual method, and a voice from the oracle declared that, according to Isaiah's prophecy, a man should be chosen to whom Mary should be entrusted. The prophecy mentioned that a shoot would come from the root of Jesse, and a man filled with the Spirit of the Lord would be chosen. To determine the right person, all eligible men from David's family were to present rods at the altar. The man whose rod would produce a flower and upon which the Spirit of the Lord would rest in the form of a dove would be the chosen one.
- Among those who came, Joseph from the house of David did not bring his rod. When no sign appeared from the others, the high priest consulted God again. It was revealed that Joseph was the one chosen. When Joseph presented his rod, a dove descended and rested on it, confirming that he was the one to whom Mary should be betrothed. The customary betrothal ceremonies were completed, and Joseph returned to Bethlehem to prepare for the marriage. Mary, along with seven other virgins her age, returned to her parents' home in Galilee.

- During this time, the angel Gabriel was sent to Mary to announce the conception of the Lord and explain how it would happen. Gabriel filled the room with light and greeted Mary, saying, "Hail, Mary, full of grace! The Lord is with you; blessed are you among women and among all men born." Mary, familiar with angelic visions but puzzled by the unusual greeting, wondered about the meaning and significance of these words. Gabriel reassured her, explaining that she would conceive as a virgin by the Holy Spirit, and the child would be called Jesus. He would be great, ruling over all, and His kingdom would have no end. Mary accepted the message, acknowledging herself as the Lord's servant and agreeing to the angel's words.
- Joseph came from Judea to Galilee, intending to marry Mary after three months of their betrothal. He discovered that she was pregnant, which caused him distress because he did not want to expose her to shame or suspicion. He decided to quietly dissolve their engagement. However, an angel appeared to him in a dream, advising him not to fear or suspect Mary of wrongdoing. The angel revealed that her pregnancy was the work of the Holy Spirit and that her child would be the Savior. Following the angel's guidance, Joseph took Mary as his wife but did not have marital relations with her, maintaining her purity.
- As the ninth month of Mary's pregnancy approached, Joseph and Mary traveled to Bethlehem, Joseph's hometown, to prepare for the birth. While they were there, the time came for Mary to give birth, and she delivered her firstborn son, Jesus Christ. This event is celebrated as the birth of our Lord, who reigns eternally with the Father, the Son, and the Holy Spirit.

Protevangelium

The Book of James is also known as 'Protevangelium'. The term "Protevangelium," derived from the Greek words "protos" meaning "first" and "evangelion" meaning "good news" or "gospel," refers to the first declaration of the gospel found in the Bible. This concept is rooted in the interpretation of Genesis 3:15, where, following the fall of humanity, God pronounces a curse on the serpent and promises that the seed of the woman will crush the serpent's head. This verse has been historically viewed by Christian scholars as the initial hint of the redemptive plan for humanity, foretelling the ultimate victory of Jesus Christ over Satan and sin. The Protevangelium is thus considered a foundational prophecy, setting the stage for the messianic expectations that are fulfilled in the New Testament. It embodies the hope and anticipation of a savior who would redeem humanity from the consequences of the Fall, illustrating God's immediate provision of grace and redemption even at the moment of judgment. This early gospel message has been a cornerstone in theological discussions about the continuity of God's salvific plan from the Old Testament to the New Testament.

{1:1} In the history of the twelve tribes of Israel, there was a man named Joachim who, being very wealthy, made double offerings to the Lord, with the intention: "My wealth will benefit the entire people, and I hope to find mercy from the Lord for the forgiveness of my sins." {1:2} But during a major feast for the Lord, when the children of Israel were presenting their offerings, Reuben, the high priest, rejected Joachim's gifts, saying, "It is not lawful for you to offer your gifts because you have no children in Israel." {1:3} Distressed by this, Joachim went to review the records of the twelve tribes to see if he was the only one without children. {1:4} He discovered that all the righteous had children in Israel. {1:5} Joachim then remembered the patriarch Abraham and how, at the end of his life, God had given him a son, Isaac. He became extremely troubled and avoided his wife, {1:6} retreating into the wilderness, setting up his tent there, and fasting for forty days and forty nights. He resolved not to eat or drink until the Lord God looked upon him, dedicating his prayer as his sustenance.

{2:1} Meanwhile, his wife Anna was distressed on two counts, lamenting, "I will mourn both my widowhood and my barrenness." {2:2} As a significant feast of the Lord approached, Judith, her maid, said, "How long will you torment yourself? The feast of the Lord is here, a time when mourning is inappropriate. {2:3} Take this hood, which was made by someone who specializes in such things. It is not suitable for me, a servant, to wear it, but it suits your greater status well." {2:4} But Anna replied, "Leave me alone; I am not accustomed to such things, and besides, the Lord has humbled me greatly. {2:5} I fear that someone ill-intentioned has given you this, and you come to taint me with my sin." {2:6} Judith, her maid, responded, "What worse curse could I wish for you than the one you already bear? God has closed your womb, making you unable to be a mother in Israel." {2:7} Anna was deeply troubled by this, and dressed in her wedding garments, went out around the ninth hour to walk in her garden. {2:8} There, she saw a laurel tree, sat under it, and prayed to the Lord, saying, {2:9} "O God of my ancestors, bless me and hear my prayer as you blessed Sarah's womb and gave her a son, Isaac."

{3:1} As she gazed towards heaven, she noticed a sparrow's nest in the laurel tree. {3:2} Mourning to herself, she said, "Woe to me! Who gave me birth? And what womb bore me, that I should be so cursed before the children of Israel and mocked in the temple of my God? Woe to me! To what can I be compared? {3:3} I am not comparable even to the animals of the earth, for they are fruitful before You, O Lord! Woe to me! To what can I be compared? {3:4} I am not comparable to the brute animals, for even they are fruitful before You, O Lord! Woe to me! To what can I be compared? {3:5} I cannot be compared to the waters, for they are fruitful before You, O Lord! Woe to me! To what can I be compared? {3:6} I am not comparable to the sea waves, for they, whether calm or turbulent, with the fish in them, praise You, O Lord! Woe to me! To what can I be compared? {3:7} I am not comparable to the earth, for it produces its fruits and praises You, O Lord!"

{4:1} Then an angel of the Lord appeared to her and said, "Anna, Anna, the Lord has heard your prayer. You will conceive and give birth, and your offspring will be renowned throughout the world." {4:2} Anna replied, "As the Lord my God lives, whatever I bring forth, whether male or female, I will dedicate it to the Lord my God, and it will serve Him in holy matters all its life." {4:3} Then two angels appeared, saying to her, "Look, Joachim, your husband, is coming with his shepherds. {4:4} An angel of the Lord has also appeared to him, saying, 'The Lord God has heard your prayer; hurry and go to your wife, for Anna will conceive.'" {4:5} (Joachim went down and told his shepherds, "Bring me ten flawless she-lambs as an offering to the Lord my God. {4:6} Also bring twelve flawless calves, which will be for the priests and elders. {4:7} And bring a hundred goats, which will be for the entire people.") {4:8} Joachim came down with the shepherds, and Anna, seeing him at the gate, ran to him and embraced him, saying, "Now I know that the Lord has blessed me greatly; {4:9} for I, who was once a widow, am no longer a widow, and I, who was barren, will conceive."

{5:1} Joachim stayed at home the first day, but the next day, he brought his offerings and said, {5:2} "If the Lord is favorable to me, let the plate on the priest's forehead reveal it." {5:3} He examined the plate the priest wore and saw that no sin was found in him. {5:4} Joachim said, "Now I know that the Lord is favorable to me and has forgiven all my sins." {5:5} He left the temple justified and returned to his house. {5:6} When nine months had passed, Anna gave birth and asked the midwife, "What have I brought forth?" {5:7} The midwife replied, "A girl." {5:8} Anna said, "The Lord has greatly honored me today." She then rested in bed. {5:9} When her purification period was completed, she nursed the child and named her Mary.

{6:1} As the child grew stronger each day, when she was nine months old, her mother placed her on the ground to see if she could stand. After walking nine steps, she returned to her mother's lap. {6:2} Her mother then picked her up and said, "As the Lord my God lives, you will not walk on the earth again until I bring you to the temple of the Lord." {6:3} Consequently, she made her room a sacred space, allowing nothing impure or unusual to come near, and invited certain undefiled daughters of Israel to help her. {6:4} When the child was a year old, Joachim held a grand feast and invited the priests, scribes, elders, and all the people of Israel. {6:5} Joachim then presented the girl to the chief priests, who blessed her, saying, "May the God of our fathers bless this girl and grant her a name renowned and enduring through all generations." The people responded, "So be it. Amen." {6:6} Joachim offered her to the priests again, and they blessed her, saying, "O Most High God, look upon this girl and bless her with an everlasting blessing." {6:7} Her mother then took her, nursed her, and sang this song to the Lord: {6:8} "I will sing a new song to the Lord my God, for He has visited me and removed the reproach of my enemies. He has given me the fruit of His righteousness, so that it may be told to the children of Reuben that Anna gives suck." {6:9} She then laid the child to rest in the consecrated room and went out to serve the guests. {6:10} After the feast, the guests departed, rejoicing and praising the God of Israel.

{7:1} As the child grew, when she was two years old, Joachim said to Anna, "Let us take her to the temple of the Lord to fulfill our vow to God, lest He be angered and our offering be rejected." {7:2} Anna replied, "Let us wait until the third year, so she may recognize her father." Joachim agreed to wait. {7:3} When the child turned three, Joachim said, "Let us invite undefiled

Hebrew girls and have each carry a lamp, so that the child does not turn back and be unwilling to enter the temple of the Lord." {7:4} They did so until they arrived at the temple. The high priest received her, blessed her, and said, "Mary, the Lord God has exalted your name to all generations. Until the end of time, the Lord will reveal His redemption to the children of Israel through you." {7:5} He placed her on the third step of the altar. The Lord granted her grace, and she danced with her feet, and all the house of Israel loved her.

{8:1} Her parents left in amazement and praised God because the girl did not return to them. {8:2} Mary remained in the temple like a dove raised there, receiving her food from the hand of an angel. {8:3} When she turned twelve, the priests convened and said, "Mary is twelve years old. What shall we do with her to prevent defiling the holy place of the Lord our God?" {8:4} The priests told Zachary the high priest, "Stand at the altar of the Lord, enter the holy place, and make petitions concerning her. Do whatever the Lord reveals to you." {8:5} The high priest entered the Holy of Holies, took the breastplate of judgment, and prayed for her. {8:6} An angel of the Lord appeared to him and said, "Zachary, Zachary, go out and call together all the widowers among the people. Let each bring his rod, and the one whom the Lord shows a sign will be Mary's husband." {8:7} The criers went out throughout all Judea, and the Lord's trumpet sounded, gathering the people. {8:8} Joseph also, leaving his work, went to meet them. When they gathered, they went to the high priest, each bringing his rod. {8:9} After receiving the rods, the high priest went into the temple to pray. {8:10} When he finished praying, he took the rods, distributed them, and no miracle occurred. {8:11} The last rod was taken by Joseph, and a dove flew out of the rod and landed on Joseph's head. {8:12} The high priest said, "Joseph, you are chosen to take the Virgin of the Lord and care for her." {8:13} Joseph declined, saying, "I am an old man with children, and she is young. I fear I will seem ridiculous in Israel." {8:14} The high priest responded, "Joseph, fear the Lord your God, and remember how God dealt with Dathan, Korah, and Abiram, how the earth swallowed them up because of their rebellion. {8:15} Now, Joseph, fear God, lest similar things happen in your family." {8:16} Joseph, fearing, took Mary into his home and said to her, "Behold, I have taken you from the temple of the Lord and will now leave you in my house. I must attend to my building work. May the Lord be with you."

{9:1} A council of priests decided to make a new veil for the temple. {9:2} The high priest said, "Call seven undefiled virgins from the tribe of David." {9:3} The servants brought them to the temple, and the high priest instructed them to cast lots to determine who would spin the gold thread, blue, scarlet, fine linen, and true purple. {9:4} The high priest recognized Mary as being from the tribe of David and called her. The lot of true purple fell to her, and she went home. {9:5} From then on, Zachary the high priest became mute, and Samuel was appointed in his place until Zachary could speak again. {9:6} Mary took the true purple and spun it. {9:7} While drawing water, she heard a voice saying, "Hail, full of grace, the Lord is with you. You are blessed among women." {9:8} She looked around to find the source of the voice and, trembling, went into her house. Setting down the water pot, she took the purple and sat to work on it. {9:9} The angel of the Lord appeared to her and said, "Do not be afraid, Mary, for you have found favor with God." {9:10} She wondered about the meaning of this greeting. {9:11} The angel continued, "The Lord is with you, and you will conceive," {9:12} to which Mary replied, "How can this be? Shall I conceive by the living God and give birth like other women?" {9:13} The angel answered, "Not so, Mary. The Holy Spirit will come upon you, and the power of the Most High will overshadow you. {9:14} Therefore, the child to be born will be holy and will be called the Son of the Living God. You shall name Him Jesus, for He will save His people from their sins. {9:15} And behold, your cousin Elizabeth has also conceived a son in her old age. {9:16} This is now her sixth month, though she was called barren, for nothing is impossible with God." {9:17} Mary replied, "I am the Lord's servant; let it be to me according to your word." {9:18} After finishing her work on the purple, she took it to the high priest, who blessed her, saying, "Mary, the Lord God has exalted your name, and you will be blessed in all ages." {9:19} Mary, filled with joy, went to visit her cousin Elizabeth, and knocked on the door. {9:20} Elizabeth, hearing this, ran to open it, blessed her, and said, "Why has the mother of my Lord come to me? {9:21} For as soon as your greeting reached my ears, the baby in my womb leaped for joy and blessed you." {9:22} Mary, unaware of all the mysterious things the archangel Gabriel had told her, looked up to heaven and said, "Lord, what am I that all generations should call me blessed?" {9:23} Seeing her own growth and feeling afraid, she went home and hid herself from the children of Israel. She was sixteen years old when these events occurred.

{10:1} When the sixth month arrived, Joseph returned from his building work, finding the Virgin now visibly pregnant. {10:2} Stricken with despair, he said, "How can I face the Lord my God? What should I say about this young woman? {10:3} I received her as a Virgin from the temple of the Lord my God and have not kept her that way! Who has deceived me? {10:4} Who has committed this evil in my house and defiled the Virgin by seducing her? {10:5} Is my situation not like that of Adam? {10:6} For, in his moment of glory, the serpent came, found Eve alone, and seduced her. {10:7} In the same way, this has happened to me." {10:8} Rising from the ground, Joseph said to Mary, "O you who have been so favored by God, why have you done this? {10:9} Why have you defiled yourself, having been raised in the Holy of Holies and fed by angels?" {10:10} Mary, with tears, responded, "I am innocent and have known no man." {10:11} Joseph asked, "How then are you pregnant?" {10:12} Mary replied, "As the Lord my God lives, I do not know how this has happened." {10:13} Joseph, greatly troubled, considered what to do with her. He thought, {10:14} "If I conceal her situation, I will be found guilty under the law of the Lord; {10:15} if I reveal her to the children of Israel, I might be found guilty of betraying an innocent life, for she is pregnant by an angel. {10:16} What should I do? I will quietly dismiss her." {10:17} That night, an angel of the Lord appeared to him in a dream and said, {10:18} "Do not be afraid to take Mary as your wife, for the child she carries is from the Holy Spirit. {10:19} She will give birth to a Son, and you shall name Him Jesus, for He will save His people from their sins." {10:20} Joseph awoke, praised the God of Israel for revealing such favor, and took Mary as his wife.

{11:1} Annas the scribe came to Joseph and asked, "Why have we not seen you since your return?" {11:2} Joseph replied, "I was weary from my journey and rested on the first day." {11:3} However, Annas noticed that Mary was visibly pregnant. {11:4} Annas went to the priest and reported, "Joseph, whom you trusted so much, has committed a serious crime. He has defiled the Virgin whom he received from the temple and married her secretly, not revealing it to the people of Israel." {11:5} The priest asked, "Has Joseph really done this?" {11:6} Annas responded, "If you send any of your servants, you will find that she is with child." {11:7} The servants went and confirmed that Mary was indeed pregnant. {11:8} Consequently, both Mary and Joseph were summoned for trial. The priest said to Mary, {11:9} "Mary, what have you done? Why have you sullied yourself and forgotten your God, considering you were raised in the Holy of Holies, nourished by angels, and heard their songs? {11:10} Why have you acted this way?" {11:11} Mary, in tears, answered, "As the Lord my God lives, I am innocent before Him, for I have not known any man." {11:12} The priest then asked Joseph, "Why have you done this?" {11:13} Joseph replied, "As the Lord my God lives, I have had no dealings with her." {11:14} But the priest said, "Do not lie. Declare the truth. You have married her secretly and have not revealed it to the people of Israel, humbling yourself under God's mighty hand so your offspring might be blessed." {11:15} Joseph remained silent. {11:16} The priest then declared, "You must return the Virgin to the temple of the Lord from where you took her." {11:17} Joseph wept bitterly. The priest added, "I will make you both drink the trial water of the Lord, and thus your guilt shall be exposed." {11:18} The priest prepared the water and made Joseph drink it, then sent him to a remote place. {11:19} When Joseph returned in good health, everyone marveled that his guilt was not revealed. {11:20} The priest said, "Since the Lord has not revealed your sins, neither do I condemn you." {11:21} He sent them away. {11:22} Joseph took Mary and went home, rejoicing and praising the God of Israel.

{12:1} A decree went out from Emperor Augustus that all Jews should be registered for taxation, specifically those from Bethlehem in Judea. {12:2} Joseph said, "I will ensure that my children are registered, but what should I do with this young woman? {12:3} I am ashamed to register her as my wife, and if I register her as my daughter, everyone knows she is not my daughter. {12:4} When the time appointed by the Lord comes, He will do as He sees fit." {12:5} He saddled a donkey, placed Mary on it, and Joseph and Simon followed her, arriving near Bethlehem, about three miles away. {12:6} Joseph noticed Mary seemed sorrowful and thought, "Perhaps she is in pain because of the child within her." {12:7} But when he looked again, he saw her smiling and asked, {12:8} "Mary, why do I see both sorrow and joy on your face?" {12:9} Mary replied, "I see two people, one weeping and mourning, and the other laughing and rejoicing." {12:10} Joseph then said, "Take me down from the donkey, for the child within me is pressing to come forth." {12:11} Joseph asked, "Where shall I take you? This place is desolate." {12:12} Mary insisted, "Take me down, for the child within me is urging me strongly." {12:13} Joseph took her down and found a cave, leading her into it.

{13:1} Joseph left Mary and his sons in the cave and went to find a Hebrew midwife in Bethlehem. {13:2} As he was going, he looked up and saw the clouds astonished and the birds in mid-flight stopping. {13:3} He looked down and saw a table spread with workers sitting around it, but their hands were on the table and they did not move to eat. {13:4} Those with food in their mouths did not eat, {13:5} those lifting their hands to their heads did not lower them, {13:6} and those lifting their hands to their mouths did not put anything in, {13:7} with all their faces fixed upward. {13:8} He also saw sheep dispersed but standing still, {13:9} and a shepherd with his hand raised to strike them, but his hand remained up. {13:10} He looked at a river and saw kids with their mouths near the water, but they did not drink.

{14:1} A woman came down from the mountains and asked Joseph, "Where are you going?" {14:2} Joseph replied, "I am looking for a Hebrew midwife." {14:3} She asked, "Where is the woman about to give birth?" {14:4} Joseph answered, "In the cave; she is betrothed to me." {14:5} The midwife asked, "Is she not your wife?" {14:6} Joseph explained, "It is Mary, conceived by the Holy Spirit." {14:7} The midwife asked, "Is this true?" {14:8} Joseph said, "Come and see." {14:9} The midwife went to the cave. {14:10} A bright cloud overshadowed it, and the midwife said, "My soul is magnified, for I have seen salvation." {14:11} The cloud became a great light, too bright to bear, {14:12} until the infant appeared, suckling at Mary's breast. {14:13} The midwife exclaimed, "How glorious this day is!" {14:14} She left and met Salome. {14:15} She told Salome, "A virgin has given birth, which is against nature." {14:16} Salome replied, "I will not believe it unless I receive proof." {14:17} Salome tested Mary, {14:18} but her hand withered. {14:19} She groaned, saying, "Woe to me! My hand is withering." {14:20} Salome prayed to God for healing, {14:21} asking for mercy. {14:22} She reminded God of her charitable acts. {14:23} An angel appeared, saying, "The Lord has heard your prayer; touch the Child and be healed." {14:24} Salome, overjoyed, approached the Child, {14:25} intending to worship Him. {14:26} She touched Him and was immediately healed. {14:27} The midwife left, approved by God. {14:28} A voice instructed Salome, "Do not reveal this until the Child comes to Jerusalem." Salome also left, approved by God.

{15:1} Joseph was preparing to leave because of the chaos in Bethlehem caused by the arrival of wise men from the east. {15:2} They asked, "Where is the King of the Jews born? We have seen His star in the east and have come to worship Him." {15:3} Herod was greatly troubled when he heard this and sent messengers to the wise men and priests, asking them, {15:4} "Where is it written about Christ the King, or where should He be born?" {15:5} They told him, "In Bethlehem of Judea, for it is written: 'And you, Bethlehem, in the land of Judah, are not the least among the rulers of Judah; for out of you shall come a Ruler who will shepherd My people Israel.'" {15:6} After sending the chief priests away, Herod asked the wise men, {15:7} "What sign did you see concerning the King who is born?" {15:8} They replied, "We saw an extraordinarily large star shining among the stars, so bright that the others became invisible. We knew that a great King was born in Israel and came to worship Him." {15:9} Herod told them, "Go and search diligently for the Child, and when you find Him, let me know so that I too may come and worship Him." {15:10} The wise men departed, and the star they had seen in the east went before them, until it stood over the cave where the Child was with Mary His mother. {15:11} They presented gifts of gold, frankincense, and myrrh. {15:12} Being warned in a dream not to return to Herod, they went back to their country by another route.

{16:1} Herod, realizing that he had been deceived by the wise men and enraged, ordered the slaughter of all male children in Bethlehem aged two and under. {16:2} Mary, hearing of the decree, was fearful and took the Child, wrapping Him in swaddling clothes and laying Him in a manger because there was no room for them in the inn. {16:3} Elizabeth, hearing that her son John was also being sought, took him and went into the mountains, searching for a place to hide. {16:4} Unable to find shelter, she cried out, "O mountain of the Lord, receive the mother with her child." {16:5} As Elizabeth could not climb, the mountain split and received them. {16:6} An angel of the Lord appeared to protect them. {16:7} Herod continued to search for John, sending servants to Zechariah at the altar, demanding, "Where have you hidden your son?" {16:8} Zechariah replied, "I am a servant of God and at the altar; how should I know where my son is?" {16:9} The servants returned to Herod and reported Zechariah's response, which made him furious, and he said, "Is this son of his likely to be the King of Israel?" {16:10} Herod sent his servants back to Zechariah, saying, "Tell us where your son is, or know that your life is in my hands." {16:11} The servants went back and reported this to Zechariah. {16:12} Zechariah replied, "I am a martyr for God, and if my blood is shed, the Lord will receive my soul. {16:13} Furthermore, know that you will shed innocent blood." {16:14} Zechariah was then killed at the temple entrance and the altar, near the partition. {16:15} The people of Israel were unaware of his murder. {16:16} During the hour of blessing, the priests noticed that Zechariah did not greet them as usual. {16:17} When they waited for him and he did not come, one priest ventured into the holy place and saw congealed blood on the ground. {16:18} A voice from heaven declared, "Zechariah is murdered, and his blood will not be wiped away until the avenger comes." {16:19} Alarmed, the priest informed the others, and they all went in, seeing the blood but not the body. {16:20} The temple roofs cried out and were torn from top to bottom. {16:21} They could not find the body, only hardened blood. {16:22} They told the people about Zechariah's murder, and all the tribes of Israel mourned and lamented for him for three days. {16:23} The priests then sought a successor. {16:24} Simeon and the other priests cast lots, and the lot fell on Simeon. {16:25} He had been assured by the Holy Spirit that he would not die before seeing the Christ come in the flesh.

Arabic Gospel of the Infancy of the Saviour

The Arabic Gospel of the Infancy of the Saviour, an apocryphal text from the 5th-6th centuries CE, provides an alternative account of Jesus' early life, highlighting miracles and the Holy Family's extraordinary experiences. Its origins are unclear, with earliest manuscripts in Arabic, possibly translated from Syriac or Greek. The text includes unique stories, such as a palm tree bending to offer dates and the infant Jesus performing miracles, blending Christian themes with local traditions. Similar to other apocryphal works like the Infancy Gospel of Thomas and the Protoevangelium of James, it reflects a broad tradition of Jesus' childhood stories. Although non-canonical, it has influenced Christian art and devotion, offering insights into early Christian traditions and their interaction with Middle Eastern cultures.

In the name of the Father, the Son, and the Holy Spirit, one God.

- The book of Joseph the high priest, who lived during the time of Christ and is sometimes identified as Caiaphas, mentions that Jesus spoke while still in His cradle. He addressed Mary, His mother, saying, "I am Jesus, the Son of God, the Word (Logos), whom you have brought into the world as the Angel Gabriel announced. My Father has sent me for the salvation of the world."
- In the 309th year of the era of Alexander, Augustus issued a decree that everyone should register in their hometown. Consequently, Joseph took Mary, his wife, and traveled to Bethlehem, his ancestral city. When they reached a cave, Mary told Joseph that the time for her delivery was near and that she could not continue to the city. She suggested they use the cave. This happened at sunset. Joseph quickly went out to find a midwife. He encountered an elderly Hebrew woman from Jerusalem and asked her to come to the cave to assist Mary.
- After sunset, the elderly woman and Joseph arrived at the cave. Inside, they saw it filled with a light more radiant than lamps or candles and more brilliant than sunlight. The infant Jesus was lying in a manger, wrapped in swaddling clothes, and nursing from Mary. The old woman marveled at the light and asked Mary if she was the mother of this child. Mary confirmed this, and the old woman remarked that Mary was unlike any other woman. Mary responded that as her Son had no equal among children, so she had no equal among women. The old woman then placed her hands on the child and was instantly healed from her long-standing paralysis. She then vowed to serve the child for the rest of her life.
- Shepherds arrived and, having lit a fire and rejoicing, saw the heavenly hosts praising and celebrating God Most High. The cave seemed transformed into a heavenly temple, with both celestial and earthly voices glorifying God for the birth of Christ. The old Hebrew woman, witnessing these miracles, thanked God, saying she was grateful to have seen the birth of the Savior.
- When the time for circumcision came on the eighth day, the child was circumcised in the cave. The old Hebrew woman took the piece of skin or some say the navel-string and preserved it in a jar of old nard oil. Her son, who dealt in unguents, was instructed to keep it safe, even if offered a great sum. This jar was later bought by Mary Magdalene, who anointed Jesus' head and feet with it, wiping them with her hair.
- Ten days later, they took Jesus to Jerusalem, and on the fortieth day after His birth, they brought Him to the temple to present Him to the Lord and offer sacrifices, as prescribed by the Law of Moses. Simeon, who saw Jesus shining like a pillar of light, recognized Him as the light for all nations and the glory of Israel. He thanked God for allowing him to see the salvation prepared for all peoples. Anna, the prophetess, was also present and gave thanks to God, praising Mary.
- When Jesus was born in Bethlehem during King Herod's reign, magi from the East, following the predictions of Zoroaster, arrived in Jerusalem with gifts of gold, frankincense, and myrrh. They worshiped Jesus and presented their gifts. Mary gave them one of the swaddling bands as a token of her limited means, which they received with great honor. An angel appeared to the magi in the form of the star that had guided them and directed them back to their country.
- Upon returning home, the magi's kings and leaders questioned them about their journey and the gifts. They showed the swaddling band given by Mary. The magi celebrated and, according to their customs, burned the swaddling band in a fire. When the fire was out, the band was untouched and unburned, which they took as a sign of its truth and divine nature. They venerated it and kept it among their treasures.
- When Herod realized the magi had not returned, he consulted the priests and wise men to find out where Christ was to be born. Upon learning it was Bethlehem, he plotted to kill Jesus. An angel appeared to Joseph in a dream, instructing him to take Mary and Jesus and flee to Egypt. Joseph departed early the next morning.
- As Joseph was planning their journey, morning arrived, and he came to a large city with an idol that received offerings and worship from other Egyptian deities. A priest there, whose young son was possessed by demons, saw great agitation in the land due to the presence of the true God. The idol itself fell, and the city was thrown into turmoil. The idol declared that the true Son of God had arrived, causing fear and panic among the people and leading to the idol's fall.
- The priest's son, afflicted by his usual condition, went to the hospital where Joseph and Mary had taken refuge after others had fled. Mary had washed the clothes of Jesus and placed them on some wood. The possessed boy came, took one of the clothes, and put it on his head. The demons inside him fled in the forms of ravens and serpents from his mouth. The boy was immediately healed and began praising God and thanking Jesus for his cure. His father, seeing him restored, asked what had happened. The boy explained that when he was thrown to the ground by the demons, he went to the hospital and saw Mary with Jesus. He took one of Jesus' clothes, and the demons left him. The father rejoiced and concluded that Jesus must be the Son of the living God, especially since the idol in their land had been destroyed and all other gods had fallen.
- This fulfilled the prophecy, "Out of Egypt I called my son." Joseph and Mary, upon hearing about the fallen idol, were afraid. They worried that the Egyptians, hearing of the idol's destruction, might harm them in retaliation. They recalled how Herod had previously sought to kill Jesus, causing the slaughter of children in Bethlehem, feared a similar response from the Egyptians.
- As they traveled, they came across a group of robbers who had plundered several people and bound them. The robbers heard a noise like a great king's army with chariots and drums and, frightened, abandoned their loot. The captives freed themselves, recovered their belongings, and left. When they saw Joseph and Mary, they asked about the source of the noise. Joseph replied that the king causing the noise would come after them.
- In another city, they encountered a woman possessed by demons who had been tormented and could not bear clothing or live in a house. She would break free from chains and roam naked, causing distress to others. Mary took

pity on her, and the demons immediately departed from the woman in the form of a young man, crying out in defeat. The woman was restored to her senses, dressed, and returned to her community. Her grateful friends and family honored Mary and Joseph with great hospitality.

- The next day, after being supplied with provisions for their journey, they arrived at a town celebrating a marriage. A bride had been rendered mute by sorcery. Mary, carrying Jesus, entered the town, and upon seeing her, the mute bride reached out to Jesus, held Him, and kissed Him. Her tongue was immediately loosened, and she began to speak. The townspeople rejoiced, believing that God and His angels had visited them.

- They stayed in the town for three days, receiving great honor and living well. When they left, they arrived at another city. A woman in this city had once been attacked by a serpent, which had caused her severe torment. Upon seeing Mary and Jesus, she longed to hold the child. Mary handed Jesus to her, and the woman was instantly freed from her torment. The people praised God and the woman gave generous gifts to Mary and Joseph.

- The following day, the woman used the water from washing Jesus to wash a local girl suffering from leprosy. The girl was immediately healed. The townspeople believed Jesus and His family were divine due to these miracles. As they prepared to leave, the healed girl asked to accompany them.

- They agreed, and upon reaching a city with a prince's castle, the girl went to the prince's wife, who was mourning. The princess revealed her deep sorrow over her son's leprosy, which had led her husband to reject the child and her. The girl explained that she had been healed by Jesus and that He was with them. The princess invited them to stay, and Jesus' presence led to her son's healing. The princess held a grand banquet in honor of Joseph and Mary and sent them off with gifts and great respect.

- They continued to another city where they spent the night with a newlywed man who had been unable to consummate his marriage due to witchcraft. After their stay, he was able to fulfill his marital duties. The bridegroom insisted on hosting them with a feast.

- The next day, as they approached another city, they saw three women weeping outside a cemetery. Mary instructed the accompanying girl to inquire about their distress. The women, without answering, invited them to their home. Inside, they found the women mourning over a mule, which had once been their brother, transformed by jealousy into a mule. Despite seeking help from all possible sources, they had found no cure. They wept at their father's grave for solace.

- When the girl heard the sisters' story, she encouraged them not to lose hope, assuring them that their cure was close by. She explained that she had been cured of leprosy by using water in which Jesus had been washed. She instructed them to bring Mary to their home, reveal their secret, and plead for her help.

- The women quickly brought Mary to their home and, in tears, explained their plight. They begged her to help them because their brother had been turned into a mule by witchcraft. Mary was moved by their sorrow, took Jesus, and placed Him on the mule's back. She prayed for Jesus to restore the mule to human form. Jesus' power transformed the mule back into a young man. The man, his mother, and his sisters praised Mary and Jesus, rejoicing in their miraculous restoration.

- The sisters suggested to their mother that, since their brother was now healed and still unmarried, they should marry him to the girl who had helped them. They asked Mary for permission, which she granted. They arranged a grand wedding for the girl, and their sorrow turned into joy. The entire household celebrated with dancing and song, praising Jesus for turning their grief into happiness.

- Joseph and Mary then traveled through a desert known for being infested with robbers. To avoid danger, they decided to travel at night. They encountered two robbers, Titus and Dumachus, who were asleep along with their gang. Titus urged Dumachus to let Mary and Joseph go and offered him forty drachmas as a bribe. Mary thanked Titus and prayed for his protection. Jesus told His mother that, in thirty years, Titus and Dumachus would be crucified alongside Him, with Titus going to Paradise. Mary wished this was not the case. They then continued their journey.

- They arrived at Matarea, where Jesus caused a fountain to spring up. Mary used the water from this fountain to wash Jesus' shirt, and the sweat from Jesus produced balsam in the area.

- They then went to Memphis, where they stayed for three years. During their time there, Jesus performed many miracles that were not recorded in the infancy gospels.

- After three years, they left Egypt and returned to Judea. Although Joseph was initially afraid to return, he learned that Herod was dead and Archelaus had taken over. An angel instructed him to settle in Nazareth.

- Upon arriving in Bethlehem, they encountered many sick children suffering from eye diseases. A woman with a dying child approached Mary while she was washing Jesus. Mary told her to use the water from Jesus' washing to sprinkle on her child. The child recovered after using the water. The woman was overjoyed and thanked Mary.

- Another woman, whose child was suffering from the same disease, was advised by the healed woman's mother to use the same water. She did so, and her child was healed as well. Mary instructed her to thank God and keep the miracle a secret.

- Two women in the city, both married to the same man, had sons who were ill with fever. One woman, named Mary, took her son to Mary and offered a beautiful mantle in exchange for a small bandage. Mary agreed, and the woman made a shirt from the bandage that cured her son. The other woman's son died, leading to animosity between them. The rival woman later threw the son of Mary the mother of Cleopas into a hot oven, but he was unharmed. Mary then took him to Mary, who advised her to keep quiet about the incident for her safety. The rival woman later threw the boy into a well, but he was saved and the event was met with admiration. The rival woman eventually fell into the well herself and died as a result.

- A woman with twin sons, one of whom had died and the other was near death, brought her remaining child to Mary. Mary instructed her to place the child in Jesus' bed. The child revived upon contact with Jesus' clothes and began to eat. The mother recognized Mary's divine power and thanked her. The healed boy was later known as Bartholomew in the Gospel.

- A woman suffering from leprosy came to Mary, the mother of Jesus, asking for help. Mary asked if she wanted gold, silver, or healing from her disease. The woman wondered who could grant such healing. Mary told her to wait until she had finished washing Jesus and putting Him to bed. Once she had done so, Mary gave the woman some of the water used to wash Jesus, instructing her to pour it over herself. As soon as the woman did this, she was healed and praised God.

- After staying with Mary for three days, the woman went to a city where she saw a man who had married another chief's daughter. However, when he saw her, he noticed a leprous mark on her forehead, leading to the dissolution of the marriage. The woman, distressed, asked why they were so upset. They told her they couldn't explain their grief to anyone. She persisted, offering to help if they would reveal their issue. When she saw the leprous mark, she shared that she had once suffered from leprosy but was healed by Mary's water. She suggested they go to Bethlehem and seek out Mary for a cure. The woman agreed, and they went to Mary with gifts. Mary had compassion, gave them some of the healing water, and told them to bathe the woman with it. She was immediately healed, and everyone praised God. The chief, upon learning his wife had been healed, took her back and celebrated.

- There was also a young woman possessed by a demon that appeared as a huge dragon, draining her blood and leaving her near death. Her parents and onlookers mourned her condition. Hearing the girl's cries, a chief's daughter, who had been healed of leprosy by Mary, inquired about her. She told the girl's mother to keep her healing a secret and advised her to go to Bethlehem and seek Mary. The mother followed the advice and went to Mary, who gave her water from Jesus' washing and a cloth to use against the demon. Upon returning, when the demon appeared, the girl used the cloth, which emitted flames that drove the demon away. The girl was relieved, and everyone praised God for the miracle.
- Another woman's son was tormented by a demon, biting anyone near him, including himself. The mother, hearing about Mary and Jesus, took her son to Mary. Jesus was playing with other children when the possessed boy came up and struck Him. Jesus began to weep, and immediately the demon left the boy, who fled as if driven away by a mad dog. This boy, later known as Judas Iscariot, who would betray Jesus, struck the same side that was later pierced by a lance.
- At the age of seven, Jesus played with other boys, making clay figures of animals that moved and interacted as He commanded. The other boys, amazed, went home and told their parents, who warned them not to associate with Jesus, thinking He was a wizard.
- One day, while playing near a dyer's shop, Jesus threw all the cloths into a tub of dye, ruining them. When the dyer, Salem, discovered the damage, he angrily confronted Jesus. Jesus promised to restore the cloths to their desired colors, and He did so, which amazed the onlookers and led them to praise God.
- Joseph, a carpenter, would take Jesus along as he worked. Whenever Joseph needed to adjust something, Jesus would touch it, and it would be perfectly altered to Joseph's needs. Joseph's carpentry was greatly aided by Jesus' miraculous adjustments.
- Once, the king of Jerusalem commissioned Joseph to make a throne. After two years of work, Joseph found the throne too short by two spans. Fearing the king's anger, Joseph fasted and worried. Jesus reassured him, and together they adjusted the throne to the correct size. Those who witnessed this miracle were astonished and praised God. The throne's wood was of a prestigious variety from Solomon's time.
- Jesus was seen playing with other boys and following them. When they hid from Him, He asked some women about their whereabouts. They said they were kids in a furnace. Jesus called out to the kids, and they emerged and danced around Him. The women, astonished, praised Jesus and asked for His mercy. Jesus said He would restore the boys to their original form, and immediately, the kids turned back into boys, much to the amazement and joy of those present.
- During the month of Adar, Jesus gathered the boys together and, in a manner fitting a king, had them spread their clothes on the ground for Him to sit on. They placed a crown of flowers on His head and stood around Him like attendants. Passersby were compelled by the boys to come and pay homage to the "king" before continuing on their way.
- While this was happening, some men arrived carrying a boy who had been bitten by a serpent while collecting wood in the mountains. The boy had fallen to the ground and was unconscious. His relatives carried him to the place where Jesus was seated. The boys urged the grieving relatives to come and greet the "king," but they resisted due to their distress. Eventually, they were brought to Jesus, who asked about the boy's condition. Upon learning that he had been bitten by a serpent, Jesus told the boys to go and kill the serpent. Despite the parents' plea to leave due to their son's critical condition, the boys insisted on following Jesus. When they reached the serpent's nest, Jesus commanded the serpent to remove the poison from the boy. The serpent complied, and after Jesus cursed it, it burst apart. Jesus then healed the boy, who began to cry. Jesus told him not to weep, promising that he would become His disciple. This boy was Simon the Cananite, mentioned in the Gospel.
- On another occasion, Joseph sent his son James to gather wood, with Jesus accompanying him. While they were collecting the wood, a viper bit James's hand. Jesus approached him, blew on the wound, and James was immediately healed.
- One day, while playing with other boys on a rooftop, one of the boys fell and died instantly. The others fled, leaving Jesus alone on the roof. The boy's relatives accused Jesus of pushing their son off the roof. Jesus denied it and suggested they ask the boy himself. Standing over the dead body, Jesus called out to the boy, who then revealed that someone else had pushed him. Everyone present was amazed and praised God for this miracle.
- Mary once asked Jesus to fetch water from the well. On His way back, the pitcher broke, spilling the water. Jesus used His handkerchief to gather the water and brought it to His mother, who was astonished. She kept this event in her heart.
- Another day, Jesus and the boys were by a stream, making little fish-ponds. Jesus made twelve sparrows from clay and arranged them around the ponds. A Jew named Hanan's son, seeing this, angrily destroyed their fish-ponds, claiming they were violating the Sabbath. Jesus made the sparrows come to life and fly away. Hanan's son then kicked Jesus's fish-pond, causing the water to disappear. Jesus declared that just as the water had vanished, so would the boy's life, and the boy immediately withered away.
- On another occasion, as Jesus was walking home with Joseph, a boy ran into Him with such force that Jesus fell. Jesus told the boy that because he had knocked Him down, he would fall and not rise again. The boy fell and died immediately.
- In Jerusalem, a teacher named Zacchaeus suggested to Joseph that he should send Jesus to learn letters. Joseph agreed, and they took Jesus to the teacher. When the teacher asked Jesus to recite the alphabet, Jesus first asked for the meaning of the letter Aleph before proceeding. The teacher, frustrated, threatened to punish Jesus, but Jesus explained the meanings of the letters and their forms, revealing knowledge beyond what the teacher had ever heard. Astonished, the teacher remarked that Jesus seemed to have been born before Noah and said that Jesus was more learned than all the teachers. Mary was told her son needed no further instruction.
- They then took Jesus to another more learned teacher. When this teacher demanded that Jesus recite Aleph, Jesus asked for the meaning of the letter first. The teacher, infuriated, struck Jesus, and his hand withered and he died. Joseph then told Mary that they would no longer allow Jesus to leave the house since anyone who opposed Him suffered dire consequences.

- When Jesus turned twelve, He went to Jerusalem for the feast. After the feast, His family returned home, but Jesus stayed behind in the temple, discussing various subjects with the teachers and elders. He asked them about the Messiah, pointing out inconsistencies in their answers. The teachers were amazed at His understanding & knowledge, which went beyond their own.
- A philosopher skilled in astronomy asked Jesus if He had studied the subject. Jesus explained the spheres, heavenly bodies, their movements, and other complex astronomical concepts.
- Another philosopher, an expert in natural science, inquired if Jesus had studied medicine. Jesus explained various aspects of physics, metaphysics, and medicine, including the functions of the body, its organs, and the soul's effects. The philosopher was so impressed that he declared he would become Jesus's disciple.
- After three days of searching, Mary and Joseph found Jesus in the temple. Mary asked why He had treated them so, as they had been anxiously searching for Him. Jesus replied that He needed to be in His Father's house. Mary and Joseph did not fully understand His words, but the teachers praised Mary for having such a son. Jesus returned to Nazareth and obeyed His parents. Mary kept all these events in her heart, and Jesus grew in wisdom and favor with God and man.
- From that time on, Jesus began to keep His miracles and divine secrets hidden and focused on studying the law until He turned thirty. At that point, His Father publicly declared Him at the Jordan River, with a voice from heaven saying, "This is my beloved Son, in whom I am well pleased," while the Holy Spirit appeared as a dove.
- We adore and offer our prayers to this Son, who has given us life and brought us from our mothers' wombs. He took on human form to redeem us and embrace us with eternal compassion, showing us His mercy and generosity. To Him be glory, power, and dominion forever. Amen.

Infancy Gospel of Thomas

The Infancy Gospel of Thomas is a unique and enigmatic text from early Christian literature, often classified among the New Testament apocrypha. Dating from the second century, it explores Jesus' childhood, an aspect largely omitted from the canonical gospels, offering stories of his miraculous yet sometimes precocious behavior. Unlike the adult-focused narratives of the canonical gospels, this text portrays Jesus as both divine and human, with a strong awareness of his divine origin. However, its depiction of a young, at times vengeful Jesus contrasts with the compassionate figure in the canonical accounts. The purpose and origins of the gospel remain debated, with some scholars viewing it as a theological exploration of Jesus' divinity from childhood, while others see it as a collection of popular tales. Surviving in Greek, Latin, Syriac, and other languages, the Infancy Gospel of Thomas reflects early Christian thought, the development of Christology, and cultural ideas about childhood and divinity.

{1:1} I, Thomas the Israelite, share these accounts with you, dear brethren, especially those of you among the Gentiles, to reveal the miraculous works done by our Lord Jesus Christ in His childhood, as He grew up in our land. These events, which took place in His early years, began as follows:

{2:1} When Jesus was about five years old, He was playing near a stream. As He played, He gathered the flowing waters into small pools with His words alone, and made them clean. {2:2} Then, using soft clay, He formed twelve sparrows. It was the Sabbath when He did this, and other children were playing nearby as well. {2:3} A certain Jew, seeing Jesus playing on the Sabbath, immediately ran to inform Joseph, saying, "Your child is down by the stream, shaping clay into twelve little birds. He is violating the Sabbath!" {2:4} Joseph hurried to the scene and scolded Jesus, saying, "Why are you doing this on the Sabbath, a day when it is not lawful to work?" But Jesus, in response, clapped His hands and told the sparrows to fly. At His command, the sparrows flew away, chirping. {2:5} The Jews who witnessed this were astonished, and they quickly went to tell the elders about what they had seen Jesus do.

{3:1} Also present was the son of Annas, the scribe, standing there with Joseph. He took a willow branch and disturbed the water Jesus had gathered into pools. {3:2} Seeing this, Jesus became angry and said to him, "You wicked and senseless person! What harm did the water or pools cause you? Now, just as this water is scattered, so too will you be dried up like a tree, without leaves, roots, or fruit." {3:3} Immediately, the boy's body withered completely. Jesus left the scene and returned to Joseph's house. The boy's parents, seeing their son withered, mourned for him and went to Joseph, accusing him, saying, "Your child has caused this terrible thing to happen!"

{4:1} A little while later, as Jesus was walking through the village, another boy ran and bumped into Him. Jesus, feeling provoked, said to him, "You will not finish your journey." {4:2} Instantly, the boy collapsed and died. People who saw what happened said, "Where did this child come from, that every word He speaks becomes reality?" The parents of the dead child went to Joseph and said, "You cannot live in this village with us if your son continues to act this way. Teach Him to bless instead of curse, for He is killing our children."

{5:1} Joseph took Jesus aside and scolded Him, saying, "Why do You do such things? People are suffering, and now they hate and persecute us." But Jesus replied, "I know these words are not yours, but because you have spoken them, I will remain silent for now. However, they will face the consequences of their actions." {5:2} Immediately, the people who had accused Him were struck blind. Those who witnessed these events were filled with fear and confusion. They said that every word Jesus spoke, whether good or bad, became a miraculous deed. {5:3} Upon seeing this, Joseph grabbed Jesus by the ear and twisted it in anger. Jesus, now angry, said to him, "It is enough for you to seek and not find. You have acted foolishly. Do you not know that I am yours? Do not vex me any further."

{6:1} A teacher named Zacchaeus was nearby and overheard part of what Jesus had said to Joseph. He was astonished that such a young child could speak so profoundly. {6:2} After a few days, Zacchaeus approached Joseph and said, "Your child is wise beyond His years and seems to have a great understanding. Allow me to teach Him letters and all manner of knowledge, so that He may grow in wisdom and learn to respect the elders as fathers and grandfathers, and love those of His own age." {6:3} Zacchaeus then began to teach Jesus, starting with the alphabet, from Alpha to Omega. But Jesus looked at him and said, "How can you teach the Beta when you do not even understand the Alpha? You hypocrite! First, if you truly know it, explain the Alpha to me, and then I will believe that you understand the Beta." Jesus began to challenge Zacchaeus with questions about the first letter, and the teacher was unable to respond. {6:4} In the presence of many people, Jesus said to Zacchaeus, "Listen, teacher, and learn the meaning of the first letter. Understand its significance, how it is composed of lines and a central mark that you can see. It divides and unites, it rises and stands firm. It contains three signs, balanced and equal in form." And He continued to explain to Zacchaeus the rules of the Alpha.

{7:1} When Zacchaeus the teacher heard the many profound allegories about the first letter that the young child spoke, he was utterly bewildered by Jesus' great understanding and said to those present, "Woe to me, for I am a miserable man! I am completely confounded. I have brought shame upon myself by attempting to teach this child. {7:2} Please, my brother Joseph, take him away, for I cannot endure his intense gaze. I am unable to explain even a single word in his presence. This child is not of this world. He must be one who can control even fire. Perhaps He was born before the world was created. What womb could have carried Him? What mother could have nurtured Him? I am at a loss. Woe is me, my friend! He has shaken my understanding to its core. I am a thrice-wretched man who sought a student, only to find myself with a master. {7:3} I think of the shame I feel, for I, an old man, have been bested by a mere child. I feel as though I might faint or even die because of Him. I cannot even bear to look Him in the face. When others say that I have been overcome by a child, what explanation can I give? How can I speak about the meanings of the first letter that He explained to me? I know nothing, my friends. I know neither the beginning nor the end of it—or Him. {7:4} Therefore, my brother Joseph, I beg you to take Him back to your home. He is far greater than I am able to understand—whether He is a god, an angel, or something else, I do not know."

{8:1} As the Jews continued to counsel Zacchaeus, the young child laughed joyfully and said, "Let those who were once barren bear fruit, and let those who were blind in heart now see. I have come from above to bring judgment upon them and to call them to things that are heavenly, just as He who sent Me has commanded for your sake." {8:2} When the young child finished speaking, all those who had been cursed by Him were immediately healed. From that point on, no one dared to provoke Him, for they feared being cursed and maimed.

{9:1} Some days later, Jesus was playing with other children in the upper level of a house, when one of the children fell from the roof and died. The other children, seeing this, fled, leaving Jesus alone. {9:2} The parents of the dead child came and accused Jesus of pushing him from the roof. (But Jesus said, "I did not push him.") Still, they continued to revile Him. {9:3} Then Jesus jumped down from the roof and stood beside the body of the dead child. He called out with a loud voice, saying, "Zeno" (for that was the child's name), "arise and tell me, did I push you down?" Immediately, Zeno rose and said, "No, Lord, You did not push me down, but You have lifted me up." Those who saw this were astonished. The parents of the child glorified God for the miracle that had occurred, and they worshipped Jesus.

{10:1} A few days later, a young man nearby was splitting wood, and the axe slipped and struck his foot, cutting it deeply and causing him to lose a great amount of blood. He was on the verge of death. {10:2} When a crowd gathered around him, Jesus, the young child, forced His way through the people and reached the wounded man. He took hold of the young man's foot, and immediately, the injury was healed. Jesus said to him, "Arise now, and continue splitting the wood. And remember Me." The people, witnessing this, were filled with awe and worshipped the young child, saying, "Truly, the Spirit of God dwells in this young child."

{11:1} When Jesus was six years old, His mother sent Him to fetch water from the well, giving Him a pitcher to carry it. But in the crowded street, He accidentally bumped into someone, and the pitcher broke. {11:2} Jesus then spread out the cloak He was wearing, filled it with water, and carried it back to His mother. When Mary saw what had happened, she kissed Him and pondered the mysteries she had witnessed Him perform, keeping them close to her heart.

{12:1} Once, during the time of sowing, the young child Jesus went out with His father to sow wheat in their land. As His father sowed the seed, the young Jesus also sowed a single grain of wheat. {12:2} When it was time to harvest, He reaped it, threshed it, and made one hundred measures from it. He then called all the poor people of the village to the threshing floor and gave them the wheat. Joseph took what remained. Jesus was eight years old when He performed this miracle.

{13:1} At that time, Jesus' father Joseph was a carpenter who made plows and yokes. A rich man came to him, requesting a bed to be made. However, one of the beams, specifically the shifting beam, was too short, and Joseph didn't know what to do. {13:2} Jesus said to His father, "Lay the two pieces of wood down and make them even at the end next to you." Joseph followed His instruction. Then Jesus stood at the other end, took hold of the shorter beam, and stretched it until it was the same length as the other. Joseph was amazed by this and embraced the young child, kissing Him, and saying, "I am blessed that God has given me this child."

{14:1} Seeing Jesus' wisdom even at a young age, Joseph decided it was time for Him to learn letters. He brought Him to a teacher who planned to teach Him Greek first, then Hebrew. The teacher, aware of Jesus' abilities, was afraid but wrote down the alphabet. Jesus studied it without responding. {14:2} Jesus then asked the teacher to explain the power of Alpha before He would discuss Beta. Angered, the teacher struck Jesus, who cursed him, causing the teacher to faint. {14:3} Jesus returned home, and a distressed Joseph told Mary, "Do not let Him leave the house, as anyone who angers Him seems to die."

{15:1} After some time, another teacher, who was a close friend of Joseph, said, "Bring the child to me. Perhaps I can teach Him the letters by being gentle with Him." Joseph replied, "If you are not afraid, my brother, then take Him." The man took Jesus with fear and concern, but the child gladly followed him. {15:2} Entering the school with confidence, Jesus saw a book on the lectern. Instead of reading the letters in the book, He opened His mouth and, inspired by the Holy Spirit, began teaching the law to those present. A large crowd gathered, amazed at the beauty and wisdom of His teaching, and how such profound words could come from one so young. {15:3} When Joseph heard about it, he feared the teacher had fallen ill. But the teacher said, "Brother, I accepted this child as my student, but He is full of grace and wisdom. Please, take Him back home." {15:4} Hearing this, Jesus smiled and said, "Because you have spoken well and testified truly, the teacher who was struck will also be healed." Immediately, the teacher was healed, and Joseph took Jesus back home.

{16:1} One day, Joseph sent his son James to gather firewood and bring it home. The young child Jesus followed him. As James was collecting wood, a viper bit his hand. {16:2} James was in great pain and on the verge of death, but Jesus approached, breathed on the bite, and immediately the pain ceased. The viper burst apart, and James was healed instantly, continuing his work as though nothing had happened.

{17:1} After these events, a child in the neighborhood fell ill and died. His mother was overcome with grief and wept bitterly. Jesus heard about the mourning and quickly went to the house. He found the child dead and touched his chest, saying, "Child, I say to you, do not die but live and be with your mother." Instantly, the child opened his eyes and laughed. {17:2} Jesus told the mother, "Take him and give him milk, and remember me." The crowd that had gathered was amazed and said, "Surely this child is a god or an angel of God, for everything He says becomes reality." Then Jesus left and continued playing with the other children.

{18:1} Some time later, there was a construction project in progress, and a commotion arose. Jesus went to see what had happened and found a man who had died. Taking the man's hand, Jesus said, "Man, I say to you, rise and finish your work." Immediately, the man stood up and worshipped Him. {18:2} The crowd, seeing this, was astonished and said, "This young child is surely from heaven, for He has saved many from death and possesses the power to save all His life long."

{19:1} When Jesus was twelve years old, His parents went to Jerusalem for the Passover feast, as was their custom. After the feast, they set out to return home, but Jesus stayed behind in Jerusalem, though His parents believed He was with their traveling group. {19:2} After traveling for a day, they realized He was missing and began searching for Him among their relatives. When they could not find Him, they became worried and returned to Jerusalem to search for Him. On the third day, they found Him in the temple, sitting among the teachers, listening to them and asking questions. {19:3} All who heard Him were amazed at His understanding and wisdom, for He silenced the elders and teachers with His explanations of the law and the parables of the prophets. His mother, Mary, approached Him and said, "Child, why have You treated us this way? We have been searching for You anxiously." Jesus replied, "Why were you searching for me? Didn't you know I must be in My Father's house?" {19:4} The scribes and Pharisees then asked Mary, "Are You the mother of this child?" She answered, "I am." They said, "Blessed are You among women, for God has truly blessed the fruit of Your womb. We have never seen such wisdom and glory before." {19:5} Jesus then returned with His parents and was obedient to them, and His mother kept all these things in her heart. Jesus continued to grow in wisdom, stature, and favor with God and men. To Him be glory forever & ever.

Gospel of Pseudo-Matthew

The Gospel of Pseudo-Matthew, also known as the Infancy Gospel of Matthew, is an apocryphal text expanding the canonical narratives of Jesus' early life. Composed between the 6th and 8th centuries and falsely attributed to the Apostle Matthew, this text fills gaps left by the canonical gospels, focusing on Jesus' childhood and Mary's life. It draws from earlier texts like the Protoevangelium of James and other infancy gospels, adding unique episodes such as the flight into Egypt and miracles by the infant Jesus. This text significantly influenced medieval Christian piety, iconography, and theological views of the Holy Family. Though not part of the official canon, it was widely read in some Christian communities, offering insights into early Christian thought, the veneration of Mary, and the interplay between canonical and non-canonical writings.

- In Jerusalem, there was a man named Joachim from the tribe of Judah, a shepherd who lived with integrity and devotion to the Lord. He managed his flock with care and divided everything he had into three parts: one for orphans, widows, strangers, and the poor; another for those who worshipped God; and the last for himself and his household. Joachim's generous practices led to his herds multiplying, making him unmatched among the people of Israel. He began this practice at fifteen and married Anna, a daughter of the tribe of Judah and the family of David, when he was twenty. Despite their twenty years of marriage, they had no children.
- During a festival, Joachim went to the temple to offer his gifts, but the priest Ruben told him he could not participate in the sacrifices because he had no children, implying God's disfavor. Ashamed, Joachim left the temple and went to his flocks, staying away from his home and wife Anna for five months. Anna, distressed by her husband's absence and their childlessness, prayed fervently, lamenting to God about her barrenness and the loss of her husband. While praying, she saw a sparrow's nest and mourned that even creatures had offspring while she remained childless. An angel appeared to Anna, assuring her that she would bear a daughter who would be revered by all generations. Overwhelmed by fear and awe, Anna fell into a state of trembling and prayer, eventually collapsing into her bed.
- At the same time, Joachim was visited by a young man on the mountains while tending his flocks. The man, an angel, told Joachim to return to his wife because she was pregnant with a daughter. The angel explained that Anna's child would be blessed beyond all holy women, and Joachim should thank God for this blessing. Joachim, grateful, offered a lamb in sacrifice, and the angel explained that his offering was acceptable. The angel and the smoke from the offering ascended to heaven. Joachim then prayed deeply until evening, and his servants, thinking he was dead, came to him. He told them about his vision, and they urged him to reunite with Anna. Joachim, encouraged by a subsequent dream where the angel reaffirmed his message, set out to return to his wife.
- After a month-long journey, Joachim and his flocks were near home when Anna was told by an angel to meet Joachim at the Golden Gate. Anna, excited, hurried to the gate, and upon seeing Joachim, ran to him and expressed her joy, thanking God for their reunion and the blessing of a child. They rejoiced together, and their neighbors celebrated the news.
- When Anna's pregnancy reached full term, she gave birth to a daughter named Mary. After weaning Mary by her third year, Joachim and Anna took her to the temple to offer sacrifices and dedicated her to the service of God. Mary, even as a small child, made her way up the temple steps without looking back or seeking her parents, astonishing everyone present.
- Filled with the Holy Spirit, Anna proclaimed that God had visited His people with a holy blessing, turning their enemies' hearts and bringing joy to Israel. She celebrated that her long-held prayers had been answered, bringing joy and lasting happiness.
- Mary, admired by all the people of Israel, was exceptional even as a child. At just three years old, she walked with a mature step, spoke flawlessly, and devoted herself to praising God. Her devotion and appearance were so striking that it was difficult for anyone to look directly at her. She spent her days in constant prayer and wool work, performing tasks with skill that surpassed even that of older women. Her daily schedule involved prayer from morning until the third hour, weaving from the third to the ninth hour, and more prayer from the ninth hour onward. She only stopped praying when the angel of the Lord appeared to her with food. Mary became increasingly perfect in her spiritual practice, never showing anger or speaking ill. Her speech was always graceful, reflecting the presence of God. She was vigilant not to sin with her words or actions, maintaining constant prayer and studying the law of God.
- Abiathar the priest tried to secure Mary as a wife for his son by offering numerous gifts to the high priests. Mary rejected these offers, stating that she could not marry because she valued her virginity, which she believed was dear to God. She cited examples like Abel and Elijah, who received special blessings because they maintained their purity.
- At fourteen, when the Pharisees declared that no girl of that age should remain in the temple, they decided to hold a gathering. Abiathar the high priest addressed the people, explaining that although many virgins had been in the temple, Mary alone had chosen to remain a virgin for God. A lottery was conducted to determine who would take Mary into their care, with the lot falling on the tribe of Judah. Each eligible man was to bring his rod to the high priest. When the rods were placed in the holy of holies, none showed the sign. Eventually, Joseph's rod, which had been overlooked, was found to have a dove emerge from it, signifying that he was chosen to take Mary.
- Despite his initial reluctance due to his old age and his own children, Joseph was persuaded to accept Mary. He requested that some of Mary's companions, including Rebecca, Sephora, Susanna, Abigea, and Cael, be given to her for support. They were assigned tasks related to their gifts of silk and other fine materials, with Mary receiving the purple cloth for the temple veil. The virgins initially mocked her as "queen of virgins," but the angel of the Lord confirmed this as a true prophecy, leading them to apologize and ask for her forgiveness.
- On the second day, while Mary was drawing water, the angel of the Lord told her she was blessed because she would bear the Lord. On the third day, as she worked with purple dye, the angel Gabriel appeared to her, greeting her as "full of grace" and telling her that she would conceive a child who would reign forever.
- When Joseph returned from his work as a carpenter, he found Mary pregnant. Distressed, he considered hiding or fleeing because he believed Mary had been unfaithful. The virgins who lived with Mary testified to her continued virginity and divine favor, but Joseph doubted their claims.
- That night, an angel reassured Joseph in a dream, explaining that Mary's pregnancy was a result of the Holy Spirit and that the child would be named Jesus, who would save people from their sins. Joseph awoke relieved and resolved to accept Mary, acknowledging his earlier doubts as a sin.

- Despite the reassurance, rumors spread that Mary was unfaithful, leading to her being brought before the high priest and priests. They reproached Joseph for "defiling" Mary, who had been cared for by angels. Joseph swore he had not touched Mary. Abiathar, the high priest, proposed the trial by ordeal, where both Joseph and Mary would drink the "water of bitterness" to reveal any sin.
- Mary drank the water and walked around the altar seven times without any sign of guilt. The people were amazed at her purity, while conflicting opinions arose among them. Mary publicly declared her devotion to God and her vow of virginity, asserting that she had remained untainted. The people, moved by her steadfastness, began to embrace and honor her, celebrating her purity. Mary was then joyfully returned to her home with admiration and support from all.
- Some time after, an enrolment was ordered by Caesar Augustus, requiring everyone to register in their hometown. This was done by Cyrenius, the governor of Syria. Joseph and Mary had to register in Bethlehem because they were from the tribe of Judah and the house of David.
- As Joseph and Mary traveled to Bethlehem, Mary saw a vision of two groups of people: one weeping and one rejoicing. Joseph dismissed her words as unnecessary, but an angel appeared and explained that the Jews were weeping because they had strayed from God, while the Gentiles were rejoicing because they were being brought closer to God as promised to Abraham, Isaac, and Jacob. The angel then instructed Joseph to stop and helped Mary find a place to give birth.
- Mary gave birth in a dark cave that suddenly became filled with light, as if it were the brightest part of the day. Angels surrounded the newborn Jesus, who stood upright and was adored by the angels with the hymn: "Glory to God in the highest, and on earth peace to men of good will."
- Joseph had gone to find midwives, Zelomi and Salome. He returned to find Mary with the baby. Zelomi entered and was amazed to find Mary had given birth without pain or bloodshed. Salome, wanting to verify, touched Mary but her hand withered in pain. She cried out to God, asking for mercy for her unbelief. An angel then told her to touch the child, and she was healed instantly. She went out, proclaiming the miracle and many believed because of her testimony.
- Shepherds also reported seeing angels singing a hymn at midnight, announcing the birth of the Savior who would bring salvation to Israel.
- A great star, larger than any seen before, shone over the cave from evening until morning. The prophets in Jerusalem said this star marked the birth of Christ, who would fulfill the promise to all nations.
- On the third day after Jesus' birth, Mary and Joseph moved into a stable where they placed the child in a stall. The ox and the donkey adored Him, fulfilling the prophecy that "the ox knows its owner and the donkey its master's crib."
- After staying in the stable for three days, they went to Bethlehem and spent the seventh day there. On the eighth day, they circumcised Jesus and named Him as instructed by the angel.
- Following Mary's purification period, Joseph and Mary took Jesus to the temple. They offered two turtle-doves or two young pigeons, as was customary. Simeon, a righteous and devout man who had been promised he would not die before seeing Christ, recognized Jesus as the Savior and praised God. He declared that he could now die in peace having seen God's salvation. Anna, a prophetess who had been a widow for 84 years, also praised Jesus, proclaiming Him as the redeemer of the world.
- After about two years, Magi from the east arrived in Jerusalem, seeking the newborn king. They had seen His star and came to worship Him. King Herod was troubled and consulted the Jewish scholars who informed him that the Messiah was to be born in Bethlehem. Herod instructed the Magi to find the child and report back, but they were warned in a dream not to return to Herod. They departed by another route.
- Enraged by the Magi's avoidance, Herod ordered the massacre of all male children under two years old in Bethlehem and its vicinity. Joseph, warned by an angel, fled with Mary and Jesus to Egypt via the desert.
- While traveling, Mary and Joseph rested in a cave. Mary was holding the baby Jesus in her arms. There were also three boys with Joseph and a girl with Mary. Suddenly, dragons emerged from the cave, frightening the children. Jesus got down and stood in front of the dragons, who then worshipped Him and retreated. Jesus told His parents not to be afraid and assured them that all creatures are under His command.
- Lions and panthers also showed reverence to Jesus and guided Mary and Joseph through the desert. They led the way and bowed their heads in submission. Initially, Mary was frightened by the wild animals, but Jesus comforted her, explaining that they came to serve them, not to harm them. The lions behaved peacefully among the other animals and did not attack any of them. This fulfilled the prophecy that predators would live peacefully with their prey.
- On the third day of their journey, Mary, exhausted by the desert heat, asked Joseph to stop under a palm tree for some rest. She wished for some of its fruit, but Joseph was concerned about their lack of water. Jesus then spoke to the palm tree, asking it to lower its branches and provide fruit for them. The tree complied and bent down, allowing them to gather the fruit. Jesus also instructed the tree to spring forth water from its roots. The palm tree obeyed, and a clear, cool spring emerged, satisfying everyone's thirst.
- The next day, as they prepared to leave, Jesus blessed the palm tree, saying that one of its branches would be taken to paradise by angels and that it would symbolize victory in contests. An angel took a branch of the tree to heaven, and Mary and Joseph were astonished. Jesus reassured them that this tree would be a symbol of blessings in paradise and they were filled with joy.
- During their journey, Joseph suggested traveling by the sea to rest in coastal cities. Jesus promised to shorten their journey, making a trip that would take thirty days cover in one day. As they spoke, they soon saw the mountains and cities of Egypt.
- They arrived in Hermopolis and entered a city called Sotinen, where they did not know anyone to ask for lodging. They went into a temple known as the Capitol of Egypt, which housed 355 idols that received daily offerings. The priests managed the sacrifices according to the gods' honor.
- When Mary and Jesus entered the temple, all the idols fell prostrate and were shattered, revealing their worthlessness. This fulfilled Isaiah's prophecy that God would come to Egypt and disrupt the work of its idols.
- The governor of the city, Affrodosius, heard about the incident and went to the temple with his army. The priests initially feared he came to punish those responsible for the idols' downfall. However, upon seeing the idols fallen and Mary holding Jesus, Affrodosius worshipped Jesus and declared that the idols' prostration proved Jesus' superiority. He warned his people to honor Jesus to avoid destruction like Pharaoh's. The people of the city then came to believe in Jesus Christ.
- Soon after, an angel instructed Joseph to return to Judah, as those who sought to harm Jesus were dead.

- After returning from Egypt and as He was approaching His fourth year, Jesus was playing with other children near the Jordan River on a Sabbath. He created seven clay pools with channels for water to flow in and out. One envious child, who was considered wicked, blocked the channels and destroyed the pools. Jesus then condemned the child and immediately, the boy died. The parents of the deceased child accused Jesus, causing Mary and Joseph to come to Him in response to the uproar. Joseph privately asked Mary to address Jesus and ask why He had incited such anger. Mary asked Jesus why the child had to die. Jesus explained that the boy deserved death for destroying His work. To ease Mary's distress, Jesus revived the boy with a touch and restored the pools.
- Later, Jesus made twelve clay sparrows on the Sabbath, and a Jew criticized Joseph for allowing Jesus to work on the Sabbath. When Joseph reprimanded him, Jesus commanded the clay sparrows to fly, and they did. This miracle astonished the witnesses, with some praising and others criticizing Jesus. The news of His miracles spread among the twelve tribes of Israel.
- Another child, the son of Annas, a temple priest, destroyed the dams Jesus had made and blocked the aqueduct. Jesus cursed the boy, causing him to wither and die instantly. Joseph and Mary, fearful of the commotion, took Jesus home. On their way, another boy tried to harm Jesus but fell and died after Jesus foretold his fate. The boy's parents demanded that Jesus be removed from the town, urging Joseph to teach Jesus to bless rather than curse. Joseph then admonished Jesus, expressing concern over the growing hostility and blame they were receiving. Jesus responded that only the righteous are affected by curses and that His words were meant for those who do evil.
- The schoolmaster Zachyas criticized Joseph and Mary for not sending Jesus to learn from him. Zachyas suggested that Jesus should be taught human knowledge and reverence. Joseph agreed if Zachyas could teach Jesus, but Jesus responded that He was beyond their teachings. He challenged Zachyas to explain the letters of the alphabet, revealing his profound knowledge and causing amazement among those present. Zachyas, overwhelmed, admitted his inability to understand Jesus and fled, acknowledging that Jesus might be more than human—perhaps a divine being.
- Zachyas proposed to Joseph and Mary that Jesus be taught by master Levi. When they agreed, Jesus remained silent when Levi instructed Him. Levi, angry, struck Jesus on the head. Jesus then told Levi that He could teach him more than he could teach Jesus and criticized Levi's lack of understanding. Levi, astonished by Jesus's deep knowledge, declared that Jesus was beyond ordinary human comprehension. Levi admitted his own inadequacy and decided to leave town, unable to grasp Jesus's wisdom. Jesus then declared that all who were suffering from diseases would be healed, which happened immediately. The crowd, amazed, remained silent and did not challenge Jesus further.
- After these events, Joseph and Mary returned to Nazareth with Jesus, where He lived with them. One day, while Jesus was playing with other children on a rooftop, one of the children pushed another off the roof, causing the child to fall and die. The child's parents, who hadn't witnessed the incident, blamed Jesus for the boy's death. When Mary and Joseph hurried to Jesus, Mary asked Him if He had pushed the boy. Jesus then went down to where the dead boy was, called him by name, and the boy responded. Jesus clarified that He had not pushed him. The boy's parents were amazed and honored Jesus for this miracle. Joseph, Mary, and Jesus then left for Jericho.
- At six years old, Jesus was sent by His mother to fetch water from a well. After drawing water, one of the children struck His pitcher, breaking it. Jesus then spread out His cloak, gathered the water in it, and carried it home. Mary was astonished and kept these events in her heart.
- On another occasion, Jesus took some wheat from His mother's barn, sowed it in the field, and it grew abundantly. When it was harvest time, He reaped the wheat and gathered three measures, which He distributed to His friends.
- When Jesus was eight years old, He went from Jericho to the Jordan River. Near the river was a cave where a lioness had given birth. Despite the danger, Jesus entered the cave, and the lions came to Him, showing respect and affection. Jesus sat calmly, and the lions and their cubs played around Him. Observing this, people were amazed that the animals treated Jesus with reverence. Jesus then addressed the people, pointing out that even animals recognized and honored Him, while humans did not.
- Jesus then crossed the Jordan River with the lions, and the river miraculously parted to allow them through. He instructed the lions to cause no harm and to return to their place. The lions left peacefully, and Jesus went back to His mother.
- Joseph, a carpenter, was asked to make a six-cubit long couch. His servant mistakenly cut the wood pieces unevenly. Jesus, seeing Joseph's dilemma, suggested they align the pieces end to end and adjust them. Jesus then miraculously made the shorter piece the same length as the longer one, allowing Joseph to complete the couch.
- Joseph and Mary were asked again to send Jesus to school to learn letters. They complied and brought Him to a teacher. When the teacher ordered Jesus to say "Alpha," Jesus responded by asking about "Betha" first. Angered, the teacher struck Jesus and immediately fell dead. Jesus then went home, and Joseph, worried about the potential danger to Jesus, expressed his fears to Mary. She reassured him that God would protect Jesus.
- The people requested a third time that Jesus be sent to school. Joseph and Mary, despite knowing Jesus learned from God, took Him to another teacher. Jesus took the book from the teacher and began to teach in a divine manner. His profound knowledge and teaching astonished everyone, causing the teacher to fall down and worship Him. The people were amazed, and Joseph feared for the teacher's life but was reassured by the teacher's acknowledgment of Jesus as a master.
- After these events, Joseph, Mary, and Jesus moved to Capernaum due to opposition. In Capernaum, there was a wealthy man named Joseph who had died. Jesus instructed his namesake to place a handkerchief on the dead man's face and say, "Christ heal thee." The dead man revived and asked about Jesus.
- Joseph, Mary, and Jesus then went to Bethlehem. Joseph sent His son James to gather vegetables for a meal, and Jesus followed him. While James was in the garden, he was bitten by a viper and cried out in pain. Jesus healed him by blowing on his hand, which cured him and killed the serpent. Joseph and Mary, alerted by James's cry, arrived to find the serpent dead and James healed.
- During a feast, Jesus sanctified and blessed the meal. None of the guests, including Joseph's children and their relatives, would eat or drink until Jesus had first done so. They observed Jesus closely and honored Him for His holiness. His presence was marked by divine light, and He was revered and adored by all. Amen, amen.

Gospel of Truth

The Gospel of Truth is a seminal text within early Christian literature, dating back to the 2nd century CE, and is attributed to Valentinus, a prominent Gnostic teacher. Discovered among the Nag Hammadi library in 1945, this text provides profound insight into Gnostic theology and Christology. The Gospel of Truth is not a narrative gospel like the canonical ones but rather a theological treatise that elaborates on the nature of truth, the divine, and the human condition. Central to its message is the concept of ignorance as a fundamental flaw in humanity, which can only be remedied through the knowledge (gnosis) of the divine. The text employs rich, symbolic language and metaphors, portraying the universe as emanating from the divine fullness (Pleroma) and depicting Christ as the embodiment of divine wisdom sent to rectify the ignorance and suffering of humanity. It integrates a deep mystical understanding of Jesus' role, focusing on his revelation of hidden truths rather than his historical deeds. The Gospel of Truth's interpretation of salvation is intrinsically linked to self-knowledge and the internal discovery of one's divine origin. This work's esoteric nature and philosophical depth reflect the Gnostic view of a complex, layered reality, contrasting sharply with the more straightforward narratives of the New Testament gospels. By exploring themes of error, enlightenment, and divine harmony, it provides a unique perspective on early Christian thought, emphasizing the transformative power of divine knowledge and the ultimate reunion of the soul with its divine source.

The Gospel of Truth brings joy to those who have received from the Father of Truth the gift of knowing Him through the power of the Logos. The Logos came from the Pleroma and is in the mind and thought of the Father. He is called "the Savior" because He has come to redeem those who do not yet know the Father. The Gospel reveals hope because it is the discovery sought by those who search for Him, as the All sought the source from which it came. The All was within the Father, the boundless and incomprehensible One, who surpasses all thought. This ignorance of the Father caused fear and terror. Fear became dense and obscured everything, making it impossible to see. As a result, error became powerful. But error worked in vain, as it did not understand the truth. It was preparing a distorted version of truth in terms of power and beauty. This did not humble the boundless and incomprehensible One. Fear, ignorance, and falsehood were nothing compared to the established truth, which remains unchanging, undisturbed, and perfectly beautiful. Therefore, do not take error too seriously. Since error had no foundation, it was lost in confusion about the Father, creating works and illusions to deceive and capture those in between. The forgetfulness brought by error was never revealed or illuminated beside the Father. Forgetfulness did not exist within the Father, though it existed because of Him. What exists in the Father is knowledge, which was revealed to destroy forgetfulness and help people come to know Him. As soon as people come to know the Father, forgetfulness will cease.

The Gospel reveals the one whom people seek, Jesus the Christ, who enlightened those in darkness caused by forgetfulness. He gave them a path, which is the truth He taught. Error was angered by Him, leading to His persecution and suffering. He was nailed to a cross, but His death became the source of joy for those who discovered the truth. Jesus found people within Himself, and they found Him within themselves. He is the boundless and incomprehensible One, the perfect Father who created everything. The Father retained their perfection within Himself, giving it as a way for them to return to Him and to gain unique knowledge of perfection. The Father was not jealous; even if the Aeon had received their perfection, it would not have matched the Father's perfection. The Father desired that they know and love Him, as the All lacked only the knowledge of the Father. Jesus came as a guide, teaching quietly and leisurely. He spoke the Word as a teacher in a school setting. The so-called wise men came to test Him but were proven to be empty-headed. They hated Him because they were not truly wise. Then came the little children, those who had the knowledge of the Father. As they grew strong, they learned about the Father's nature. They came to know and be known, bringing glory to the Father. In their hearts, the living book of the Living was manifested—a book written in the Father's thought and mind from before the creation of the world.

This book could not be taken by anyone until it appeared with Jesus. The compassionate and faithful Jesus was patient in His suffering until He took the book, knowing His death would bring life to many. Just as a will remains hidden until it is opened, so the true nature of the All was hidden until the Father was revealed. Jesus appeared, took the book as His own, and was nailed to the cross, which bore the Father's decree. Such profound teaching! Though He is eternal life, Jesus humbled Himself to death. He shed His perishable garments and clothed Himself in incorruptibility. Entering into the realm of fear, He passed before those burdened by forgetfulness, being both knowledge and perfection. He proclaimed the things in the Father's heart, becoming wisdom for those who received instruction. The living, who are inscribed in the book of the living, learn for themselves from the Father, turning back to Him. Since the All's perfection is in the Father, it is necessary for everything to ascend to Him. Those who have knowledge receive what belongs to them and draw it to themselves. Ignorance is a significant deficiency, as it lacks what is needed for perfection. Since the All's perfection is in the Father, everything must ascend to Him, and each one must obtain their rightful place. The Father first registered and prepared these things to be given to those who came from Him. Those known by the Father from the beginning are called last so that those who have knowledge are the ones whose names the Father has called. If a person's name has not been spoken, they remain ignorant. How can someone hear if their name has not been called? Those who remain ignorant until the end are creatures of forgetfulness and will perish with it. If this were not true, why do these individuals lack a name or sound? Therefore, those who have knowledge are from above. If called, they hear, respond, turn toward the caller, ascend, and know their call. They do the will of the caller, seeking to please Him and finding rest. They receive a certain name. Those who gain knowledge understand where they came from and where they are going, like someone who has awakened from drunkenness and restored their true self. He has turned many away from error. He went ahead of them to their original places, from which they had departed due to their ignorance of the depth of the One who encompasses all things, while nothing surrounds Him. It is indeed remarkable that they were within the Father without knowing Him and were able to leave on their own, as they could neither contain nor comprehend the One in whom they were, since His will had not yet been revealed. He disclosed it as knowledge, which all its manifestations agree upon. This knowledge is embodied in the living book that He finally revealed to the Aeons as His letters, showing them that these are not just arbitrary letters or symbols without meaning. Instead, they are letters that convey the truth. They are pronounced only when truly understood. Each letter represents a perfect truth, akin to a perfect book, as they are written by the hand of unity. The Father wrote them for the Aeons so they could come to know Him through His letters.

As wisdom mediates through the Logos and His teachings, His knowledge has been made manifest. His honor crowns this knowledge, His joy aligns with it, and His glory exalts it. It has revealed His image and secured His rest. His love took physical form around it, and His trust embraced it. Thus, the Logos of the Father extends into the All, being the fruit of His heart and the expression of His will. It sustains the All, chooses it, and also takes its form, purifying it and leading it back to the Father and the Mother, Jesus of supreme sweetness. The Father opens His embrace, which is the Holy Spirit, revealing His hidden self—His Son—so that through the Father's compassion, the Aeons may come to know Him, end their exhausting search, and find rest in Him. After completing what was lacking, He discarded the form, which is the world, that which served the form. Where there is envy and strife, there is incompleteness; where there is unity, there is completeness. Since this incompleteness arose from not knowing the Father, knowing the Father will end incompleteness from that moment on. Just as ignorance fades with knowledge and darkness with light, so incompleteness is removed by completeness. Hence, the form will cease to manifest and will merge into unity. Currently, their works are scattered, but unity will eventually make all things complete. Through unity, each will understand itself and will purify itself of diversity, consuming matter like fire consumes darkness and life overcomes death.

If these transformations have happened to each of us, it is fitting to reflect on the All so that the realm may be holy and unified. Like people moving from an old neighborhood, if they have some defective items, they usually discard them. The householder does not suffer loss but rejoices because the broken items are replaced with perfect ones. This judgment comes from above, wielding a two-edged sword that cuts both ways. When the Logos appeared, it was not just a sound but took on form, causing great disruption among things. Some were emptied, others filled; some were provided for, others removed; some were purified, others broken. All spaces were shaken and disturbed, lacking composure and stability. Error was thrown into confusion, not knowing what to do. It was distressed, lamenting, and disoriented because it knew nothing. When knowledge, which abolishes error, approached with all its manifestations, error was rendered empty, as it contained nothing. Truth appeared, and all its manifestations recognized it. They greeted the Father with complete power, uniting them with Him. Each one loves truth because truth represents the Father's voice. His tongue is the Holy Spirit, who connects Him to truth and binds Him to the Father's voice when He receives the Holy Spirit.

This is the manifestation of the Father and His revelation to His Aeons. He unveiled His hidden self and explained it. Who else exists if not the Father Himself? All spaces are His emanations. They understood they came from Him, like children from a perfect father. They knew they had not yet received form or a name, which the Father produces. If they receive form based on His knowledge, they are truly in Him but still do not know Him. The Father is perfect and knows every space within Him. If He wishes, He reveals anyone He desires by giving them form and a name. Those who do not yet exist are not nothing; they are in Him who will desire their existence in due time. He knows what He will create before anything is revealed, while the unmanifested fruit knows nothing and is not yet anything. Each space, from its part, is in the Father and comes from the existent One who created it from the nonexistent. [...] Those who do not exist at all will never exist. So, what should he think? "I am like the shadows and phantoms of the night." When morning comes, he realizes that the fear he experienced was illusory. In the same way, they were ignorant of the Father; He was the one they did not see. Fear, confusion, lack of confidence, and division caused many illusions, like troubled dreams. They might flee to a place or lack strength, engage in conflict, or suffer injuries. Sometimes, it feels like others are trying to harm them, even though there is no one pursuing them, or they might harm others, stained by their blood. Until those who experience these confusions wake up, they see that the dreams were nothing. Thus, those who cast off ignorance like sheep do not see it as real, renouncing it as a dream, and they recognize the knowledge of the Father as the true dawn. Each person acts as if asleep in ignorance and awakens to understand, and blessed is the one who awakens and opens the eyes of the blind. And the Spirit came swiftly to Him when it raised Him up. Offering its hand to the one lying prone, it set him firmly on his feet, as he had not yet stood. It provided the means to understand the knowledge of the Father and the revelation of His Son. When they saw and heard it, they were allowed to taste, smell, and grasp the beloved Son.

He appeared, revealing the Father, the boundless One. He inspired them with thoughts in alignment with His will. Many received the light and turned towards Him, but material people were alien to Him and did not recognize Him. He came in flesh-like form, with nothing obstructing Him because it was incorruptible and unrestricted. He spoke new things, revealing what was in the Father's heart, proclaiming the faultless word. Light spoke through Him, and His voice brought forth life. He gave them thought, understanding, mercy, salvation, and the Spirit of strength from the limitless Father and sweetness. He ended punishments and scourges, which had led many astray in error and chains. He destroyed these with great knowledge, becoming the path for the lost, knowledge for the ignorant, a discovery for seekers, and support for the fearful. He purified those who were defiled.

He is the shepherd who left behind the ninety-nine sheep that were not lost and went to find the one that was. He rejoiced when He found it. Ninety-nine represents the left hand, which holds it. When He finds the one, the whole number is transferred to the right hand. Thus, when there is one lacking, the right hand draws in what is missing from the left, completing it to one hundred. This number signifies the Father. He worked even on the Sabbath to rescue the sheep that had fallen into a pit. He saved its life, bringing it out to demonstrate what the Sabbath truly is to those who understand fully. It is a day when salvation should not be idle, speaking of the eternal day with no night and the sun that never sets. Thus, say in your heart that you are this perfect day and that within you dwells the unending light. Speak about the truth to those who are searching for it and share knowledge with those who have sinned in their ignorance. Support those who are struggling and offer help to the sick. Feed the hungry and comfort those who are troubled. Encourage those who are asleep to awaken and become aware. You are the understanding that inspires. If the strong follow this path, they become even stronger. Focus on your own inner growth and do not be concerned with what you have left behind or dismissed. Do not revisit old mistakes or become corrupted by them. Do not be a place for negativity, as you have already overcome it. Do not reinforce your remaining weaknesses, as this is not constructive. The lawless person harms himself more than the law does. Lawless actions are driven by a lack of discipline, whereas righteous actions are done for the benefit of others. Therefore, act according to the will of the Father, for you are part of him. The Father is kind, and his will is good. He knows what belongs to you, so you can find rest in him. One recognizes the Father's children by their fruits, and the scent of the Father's presence reveals that you come from his grace. The Father loves this fragrance, which manifests everywhere, and when it mixes with matter, it enhances the light. The Spirit, with its sense of smell, draws in this fragrance, which it recognizes as coming from the Father. It returns it to its origin, like cold water soaking into soft soil. Eventually, it becomes warm, as cold aromas signify separation. Thus, God came to end division and bring the warmth of love and unity, so that division may not return, but the unity of the Perfect Thought may prevail.

This is the message of the Gospel about the discovery of the Pleroma for those waiting for salvation from above. When their hope aligns with the light, which has no shadow, the Pleroma will come. The deficiency of matter is not a result of the Father's limitless nature, but no one can predict how the incorruptible One will come. The Father's depth grows, and error has no place in him. The turning back or repentance is a return to wholeness. The incorruptible One brings rest to those who have erred, offering forgiveness as the light fills the deficiency. Like a physician hurrying to heal the sick, the Pleroma fills the deficiency, bringing grace to those lacking it. The presence of grace diminishes in its absence, but the Pleroma fills what is lacking and restores grace. The Pleroma, as the embodiment of truth and light, shines forth from the Father's unchanging nature. Those who have been troubled speak of Christ to find healing and anointing. The anointing represents the Father's mercy, and those anointed are perfect. After an anointing, the vessel may be empty, but the perfect Father fills it again. He knows his creations because he planted them in his Paradise, which is his place of rest.

This is the perfection of the Father's thought and the expression of his will. The Logos, who emerged first from the depth of the Father's mind, caused creation to manifest. This Logos, representing the Father's will, is the source of all knowledge and action. Everything happens according to the Father's will, which is incomprehensible. His will is his mark, known only to him, and everything occurs at his appointed time. The end of all things is the recognition of the hidden Father, from whom everything originates and to whom all will return. The Father's name is the Son, given by the Father himself. The name of the Father is revealed through the Son, who embodies it. The Son, who received his name from the Father, represents the perfect and authoritative name. The name is invisible and unique, understood only by the Father. He alone can name himself and his Son, and this name represents the Father's absolute goodness and perfection. Those who are blessed rest in this perfection and do not experience envy, moaning, or death. They find rest and refreshment in the Father's presence, embodying truth and living in the eternal light. They are complete and united with the Father, experiencing perfect harmony and joy. The blessed place is where one finds true rest and where nothing is lacking. The Father's love is evident among those who embody his name and live in eternal life. They reflect the Father's light and joy, which is rooted in his heart and Pleroma. The Father, being good, loves his children who are perfect and worthy of his name. These are the children whom he loves and cares for.

Lost Sayings Gospel Q

The Lost Sayings Gospel Q, often referred to simply as "Q," is a hypothetical textual source for the canonical Gospels of Matthew and Luke. Its name derives from the German word "Quelle," meaning "source." Q is posited to have existed as a collection of Jesus' sayings and teachings, which both Matthew and Luke drew upon independently of each other. This hypothetical document, not directly attested in any extant manuscript, is reconstructed through scholarly analysis of common material found in Matthew and Luke but absent in Mark's Gospel. The Q source is considered a significant element in the Synoptic Problem, a scholarly endeavor to understand the literary relationship among the Synoptic Gospels. The existence of Q is inferred based on the two-source hypothesis, which asserts that Matthew and Luke utilized both Mark's Gospel and a sayings source. This hypothetical document is believed to have originated in the early Christian communities of the first century CE, reflecting an oral tradition that prioritized the wisdom and parables of Jesus over narrative accounts. The content of Q is primarily composed of aphorisms, parables, and moral teachings, emphasizing themes such as the Kingdom of God, ethical conduct, and eschatological urgency. The scholarly reconstruction of Q offers insights into the earliest strata of Jesus' teachings, providing a glimpse into the theological and ethical concerns of the early Christian movement.

The actual Q document has never been found; its existence is inferred from the patterns of similarities and differences in the Synoptic Gospels. The hypothetical reconstruction of Q is based on the double tradition material found in Matthew and Luke, but not in Mark. Here's a detailed reconstruction of the content believed to be in the reconstructed Q source:

Preaching of John the Baptist (Matthew 3:7-10 / Luke 3:7-9)
- "You brood of vipers! Who warned you to flee from the coming wrath? Produce fruit in keeping with repentance. And do not think you can say to yourselves, 'We have Abraham as our father.' For I tell you that out of these stones God can raise up children for Abraham. The ax is already at the root of the trees, and every tree that does not produce good fruit will be cut down and thrown into the fire."

Baptism by John (Matthew 3:11-12 / Luke 3:16-17)
- "I baptize you with water for repentance. But after me comes one who is more powerful than I, whose sandals I am not worthy to carry. He will baptize you with the Holy Spirit and fire. His winnowing fork is in his hand, and he will clear his threshing floor, gathering his wheat into the barn and burning up the chaff with unquenchable fire."

Temptations of Jesus (Matthew 4:1-11 / Luke 4:1-13)
- Three temptations by the devil:
  - Turn stones into bread.
  - Throw yourself from the temple pinnacle.
  - Worship Satan to receive all the kingdoms of the world.

Beatitudes and Woes (Matthew 5:3-12 / Luke 6:20-23)
- "Blessed are the poor in spirit, for theirs is the kingdom of heaven. Blessed are those who mourn, for they will be comforted. Blessed are the meek, for they will inherit the earth. Blessed are those who hunger and thirst for righteousness, for they will be filled. Blessed are the merciful, for they will be shown mercy. Blessed are the pure in heart, for they will see God. Blessed are the peacemakers, for they will be called children of God. Blessed are those who are persecuted because of righteousness, for theirs is the kingdom of heaven."

Love for Enemies (Matthew 5:38-48 / Luke 6:27-36)
- "You have heard that it was said, 'Eye for eye, and tooth for tooth.' But I tell you, do not resist an evil person. If anyone slaps you on the right cheek, turn to them the other cheek also. And if anyone wants to sue you and take your shirt, hand over your coat as well. If anyone forces you to go one mile, go with them two miles. Give to the one who asks you, and do not turn away from the one who wants to borrow from you."

Judging Others (Matthew 7:1-5 / Luke 6:37-42)
- "Do not judge, or you too will be judged. For in the same way you judge others, you will be judged, and with the measure you use, it will be measured to you. Why do you look at the speck of sawdust in your brother's eye and pay no attention to the plank in your own eye? How can you say to your brother, 'Let me take the speck out of your eye,' when all the time there is a plank in your own eye? You hypocrite, first take the plank out of your own eye, and then you will see clearly to remove the speck from your brother's eye."

The Lord's Prayer (Matthew 6:9-13 / Luke 11:2-4)
- "Our Father in heaven, hallowed be your name, your kingdom come, your will be done, on earth as it is in heaven. Give us today our daily bread. And forgive us our debts, as we also have forgiven our debtors. And lead us not into temptation, but deliver us from the evil one."

Parable of the Wise and Foolish Builders (Matthew 7:24-27 / Luke 6:47-49)
- "Therefore everyone who hears these words of mine and puts them into practice is like a wise man who built his house on the rock. The rain came down, the streams rose, and the winds blew and beat against that house; yet it did not fall, because it had its foundation on the rock. But everyone who hears these words of mine and does not put them into practice is like a foolish man who built his house on sand. The rain came down, the streams rose, and the winds blew and beat against that house, and it fell with a great crash."

Parable of the Lost Sheep (Matthew 18:12-14 / Luke 15:3-7)
- "If a man owns a hundred sheep, and one of them wanders away, will he not leave the ninety-nine on the hills and go to look for the one that wandered off? And if he finds it, truly I tell you, he is happier about that one sheep than about the ninety-nine that did not wander off. In the same way, your Father in heaven is not willing that any of these little ones should perish."

Instructions for Mission (Matthew 10:1-16 / Luke 10:1-12)
- "Do not take a purse or bag or sandals; and do not greet anyone on the road. When you enter a house, first say, 'Peace to this house.' If someone who promotes peace is there, your peace will rest on them; if not, it will return to

you. Stay there, eating and drinking whatever they give you, for the worker deserves his wages. Do not move around from house to house."

Acknowledgment of Jesus before Men (Matthew 10:26-33 / Luke 12:2-9)
- "What I tell you in the dark, speak in the daylight; what is whispered in your ear, proclaim from the roofs. Do not be afraid of those who kill the body but cannot kill the soul. Rather, be afraid of the One who can destroy both soul and body in hell. Are not two sparrows sold for a penny? Yet not one of them will fall to the ground outside your Father's care."

Do Not Fear (Matthew 10:26-31 / Luke 12:2-7)
- "So do not be afraid; you are worth more than many sparrows."

Unforgivable Sin (Matthew 12:31-32 / Luke 12:10)
- "And so I tell you, every kind of sin and slander can be forgiven, but blasphemy against the Spirit will not be forgiven."

Parable of the Rich Fool (Matthew 6:19-21 / Luke 12:16-21)
- "And he told them this parable: 'The ground of a certain rich man yielded an abundant harvest. He thought to himself, "What shall I do? I have no place to store my crops." Then he said, "This is what I'll do. I will tear down my barns and build bigger ones, and there I will store my surplus grain. And I'll say to myself, 'You have plenty of grain laid up for many years. Take life easy; eat, drink and be merry.' But God said to him, "You fool! This very night your life will be demanded from you. Then who will get what you have prepared for yourself?"

Anxiety and Trust in God (Matthew 6:25-34 / Luke 12:22-31)
- "Therefore I tell you, do not worry about your life, what you will eat or drink; or about your body, what you will wear. Is not life more than food, and the body more than clothes? Look at the birds of the air; they do not sow or reap or store away in barns, and yet your heavenly Father feeds them."

Coming Persecutions (Matthew 10:17-25 / Luke 12:11-12)
- "But when they arrest you, do not worry about what to say or how to say it. At that time you will be given what to say, for it will not be you speaking, but the Spirit of your Father speaking through you."

Conditions of Discipleship (Matthew 10:37-39 / Luke 14:25-27)
- "Anyone who loves their father or mother more than me is not worthy of me; anyone who loves their son or daughter more than me is not worthy of me. Whoever does not take up their cross and follow me is not worthy of me. Whoever finds their life will lose it, and whoever loses their life for my sake will find it."

Cost of Discipleship (Matthew 8:19-22 / Luke 9:57-60)
- "Another disciple said to him, 'Lord, first let me go and bury my father.' But Jesus told him, 'Follow me, and let the dead bury their own dead.'"

On Divorce (Matthew 5:31-32 / Luke 16:18)
- "It has been said, 'Anyone who divorces his wife must give her a certificate of divorce.' But I tell you that anyone who divorces his wife, except for sexual immorality, makes her the victim of adultery, and anyone who marries a divorced woman commits adultery."

Woes to the Pharisees (Matthew 23:1-36 / Luke 11:37-54)
- "Woe to you, teachers of the law and Pharisees, you hypocrites! You give a tenth of your spices—mint, dill and cumin. But you have neglected the more important matters of the law—justice, mercy and faithfulness. You should have practiced the latter, without neglecting the former. You blind guides! You strain out a gnat but swallow a camel."

This is a detailed reconstruction of the Q source based on scholarly consensus, though variations exist among scholars.

Passion of the Scillitan Martyrs

The Passion of the Scillitan Martyrs, a pivotal document from the early Christian era, offers a profound glimpse into the trials faced by early Christians under Roman persecution. Dating from the late 2nd century CE, this account details the trial and execution of a group of North African Christians, including Speratus, Nartzalus, and others, who were condemned for their steadfast refusal to renounce their faith. The text not only reflects the intense conflict between emerging Christian communities and the Roman state but also serves as a testament to the resilience of early Christians in the face of severe adversity. By examining the interrogations and responses recorded in this document, scholars gain insight into the nature of early Christian identity, the legal and societal pressures they encountered, and the development of martyrdom as a powerful expression of religious conviction. This document highlights the intersection of faith and imperial authority, illustrating the unwavering commitment of the martyrs to their beliefs despite the threat of death. As one of the earliest surviving Christian martyr texts, it provides invaluable context for understanding the theological and historical foundations of Christian martyrdom and its role in shaping early Christian identity.

- **Date and Location**: On July 17th, at Carthage, during the consulship of Praesens and Claudianus, the following individuals were in the judgment hall: Speratus, Nartzalus, Cittinus, Donata, Secunda, and Vestia.
- **Proconsul Saturninus**: Saturninus, the proconsul, addressed the group, suggesting they could gain the Emperor's favor if they renounced their beliefs and returned to traditional Roman practices.
- **Speratus's Response**: Speratus responded by stating that they had never acted wrongly, spoken ill, or caused trouble. Instead, they had responded to mistreatment with gratitude, adhering to their own beliefs.
- **Saturninus's Argument**: Saturninus countered that he too was religious, following the simple Roman rites and swearing by the genius of the Emperor, and expected them to do the same.
- **Speratus's Refusal**: Speratus replied that he did not recognize the authority of the worldly empire but served God, who cannot be seen by human eyes. He affirmed that he had committed no crime and paid taxes for anything purchased, as he served the ultimate King of kings.
- **Proconsul's Command**: Saturninus instructed the others to abandon their beliefs.
- **Others' Reactions**:
  - **Cittinus**: Declared that they feared only their Lord God in heaven.
  - **Donata**: Mentioned honoring Caesar but fearing God.
  - **Vestia**: Simply declared, "I am a Christian."
  - **Secunda**: Stated, "What I am, that I wish to be."
- **Speratus's Stand**: When asked if he would renounce his Christianity, Speratus affirmed, "I am a Christian," and the others agreed with him.
- **Consideration Time**: Saturninus offered them thirty days to reconsider their stance.
- **Speratus's Persistence**: Speratus reiterated that in a matter as clear as this, no reconsideration was necessary.
- **Confession of Beliefs**: Asked about their possessions, Speratus mentioned they had books and letters from Paul, a righteous man.
- **Final Decree**: Saturninus read out the decree: Since Speratus, Nartzalus, Cittinus, Donata, Vestia, Secunda, and others had persistently refused to abandon their Christian faith despite being offered a chance to return to Roman customs, they were sentenced to death by execution.
- **Martyrdom**:
  - **Speratus**: Expressed gratitude to God.
  - **Nartzalus**: Rejoiced, declaring they were martyrs in heaven and thanked God.
- **Execution Announcement**: Saturninus ordered the herald to declare that Speratus, Nartzalus, Cittinus, Veturius, Felix, Aquilinus, Laetantius, Januaria, Generosa, Vestia, Donata, and Secunda were to be executed.
- **Final Words**: All of them collectively said, "Thanks be to God," and were martyred. They are said to reign with the Father, the Son, and the Holy Spirit forever. Amen.

Dialogue of the Savior

The Dialogue of the Savior is a significant Gnostic text discovered in the Nag Hammadi library, a collection of early Christian and Gnostic writings unearthed in Egypt in 1945. This dialogue-based scripture presents a series of conversations between Jesus and his disciples, notably including figures like Matthew, Mary, and Judas. The text is structured as a catechetical dialogue, where Jesus imparts esoteric knowledge and wisdom, addressing profound theological and philosophical questions. Central themes include the nature of salvation, the soul's journey, and the mystical union with the divine. "The Dialogue of the Savior" reflects the distinctive features of Gnostic thought, emphasizing direct, personal spiritual knowledge (gnosis) over orthodox doctrine. The text is particularly valuable for its insight into early Christian diversity and the complex interplay between emerging orthodoxies and heterodox beliefs. Its fragmentary state, however, poses challenges for interpretation, leaving some aspects of its teachings open to scholarly debate. Nonetheless, The Dialogue of the Savior remains a crucial resource for understanding the spiritual landscape of early Christianity and the diverse expressions of belief that characterized the period.

The Savior said to his disciples, "The time has come for us to stop our work and rest. For those who rest will find eternal rest. I tell you, always be above time, and do not be afraid of it. Anger can be terrifying and can lead to more anger. Yet, because you have accepted these teachings with reverence, they have appointed leaders, though they produced no results. But when I came, I opened the path and taught them about the journey they will undertake—the chosen and solitary ones, who have known the Father, believed the truth, and praised Him. When you offer praise, do it like this: 'Hear us, Father, as you heard your only-begotten Son, received Him, and gave Him rest from all troubles. You are the power whose armor is light, living and active. You are the wisdom and serenity of the solitary. Hear us as you heard your chosen ones. Through your sacrifice, they will enter; through their good deeds, they have saved their souls from blindness, so they may exist eternally. Amen.'

I will teach you something. When the time of dissolution comes, the first power of darkness will approach you. Do not be afraid or panic. But when you see a single staff, understand the work and the leaders that come upon you. Fear is indeed powerful. If you fear what is to come, it will overwhelm you. There is no one among them who will show you mercy. Instead, focus on the truth you have mastered, for it will lead you to a place without rulers or tyrants. When you reach this place, you will see those who understand and know the true reasoning power. They will tell you about the place of truth. But as you know the truth, you will find joy. Make sure your souls are prepared so that they are not overwhelmed by darkness. The crossing place is daunting. Yet, with a single-minded focus, you will pass through. Its depth is great and its height enormous, but with your focused mind and fire of spirit, you will overcome all powers. Remember, you are the essence of the truth. Do not forget the Son of Man and what you have learned.

Matthew asked, "How should we prepare?"
The Savior replied, "The things within you will remain. You will be sustained by them."

Judas asked, "Lord, where will the souls of the righteous and the innocent go? What happens to their spirits?"
The Lord answered, "They will be received. These souls do not die or perish because they have recognized their true companions and the one who would receive them. The truth seeks out the wise and the righteous."

The Savior continued, "The lamp of the body is the mind. As long as your inner self is in order, your body will shine with light. But if your heart is dark, the light you expect will not come. I have spoken, and I will continue to speak my word."

His disciples asked, "Lord, who seeks, and who reveals the truth?"
The Lord responded, "The one who seeks is also the one who reveals."

Matthew asked, "Lord, when I speak and act, who listens and who observes?"
The Lord replied, "The speaker is also the listener, and the one who sees is the one who reveals."

Mary asked, "Lord, why do I bear my body while I weep, and why does my body laugh?"
The Lord said, "The body weeps due to its deeds and remains in the mind while it laughs. If one does not overcome darkness, he will not be able to see the light. I tell you that light is hidden within darkness, and those who cannot see the light will be misled by falsehood. You will give thanks and exist forever. The powers above and below will be amazed at you. In that place, there will be weeping and gnashing of teeth over the end of all things."

Judas asked, "Tell us, Lord, what existed before heaven and earth?"
The Lord replied, "There was darkness and water, with the Spirit over the water. Seek within yourself for the power and mystery of the Spirit, for from this comes all understanding. Wickedness and the mind are connected. The Spirit will reveal the truth to you."

Matthew asked, "Lord, where is the truth established, and where does the true mind exist?"
The Lord said, "The fire of the Spirit created both. Therefore, the true mind was established within this. If someone raises his soul high, he will be exalted."

Matthew asked, "Lord, who takes on this task?"
The Lord replied, "The one who is stronger than you, who follows the path and the works of your heart. Just as your heart determines your actions, so too will it provide the means to overcome the powers above and below. Let him who has power renounce it and repent, and let him who seeks find joy."

Judas said, "I see that all things exist like signs. Why did they happen this way?"
The Lord answered, "When the Father created the cosmos, He separated the water from it. His Word came forth and inhabited many places. It was higher than the path that surrounds the earth and the collected waters outside. The waters were encircled by a great fire. When things separated from within, the Father looked at the cosmos and said, 'Go, and produce from yourself, so that there may always be abundance.' The cosmos then produced fountains of milk, honey, oil, wine, fruits, sweet flavors, and good roots, ensuring it would remain fruitful through generations. Above all, it stood in beauty and light, ruling over all aeons. It was taken from the fire and scattered above and below. Everything that depends on these works is governed by them. And all things are dependent on this."

Upon hearing this, Judas bowed down, praised the Lord, and gave thanks.

Mary asked her brethren, "Where will these teachings be placed in the heart of the Son?"
The Lord replied, "Only someone who has a place in their heart for them can understand and hold them. They must come forth and enter, so they do not hold back from this imperfect world."

Matthew said, "Lord, I want to see the place of life, where there is no wickedness, but only pure light!"
The Lord said, "Brother Matthew, you cannot see it while you still have a physical body."

Matthew replied, "Even if I cannot see it, let me know of it!"
The Lord said, "Anyone who understands themselves has seen it in all they do and has come to know it through their goodness."

Judas asked, "Tell me, Lord, how it is that the earth shakes and moves."
The Lord picked up a stone and asked, "What am I holding?"
Judas replied, "It is a stone."
The Lord said, "That which supports the earth also supports the heavens. A Word from the Greatness sustains both. The earth does not move; if it did, it would fall. But it remains still so that the First Word might not fail. The cosmos was established and filled with the breath of the Greatness. The things that do not move are a lesson to all humanity. You are from that place. In the hearts of those who speak joyfully and truthfully, you exist. Even if it comes forth in the body of the Father among humans and is not received, it will return to its place. Whoever does not understand the work of perfection knows nothing. If one does not experience darkness, they will not see the light. If one does not understand fire's origin, they will burn in it. If one does not understand water, how can they be baptized in it? If one does not grasp the nature of wind, they will be blown away. If one does not understand the body they bear, they will perish with it. And if someone does not know the Son, they will not know the Father. Those who do not understand the root of all things will find them hidden. They are no stranger to wickedness. Those who do not know their origin will not understand their end and are not apart from this world."

Then He took Judas, Matthew, and Mary to the edge of heaven and earth. He placed His hand upon them, and they hoped to reach it. Judas looked up and saw a very high place and the abyss below. He said to Matthew, "Brother, who can ascend to such heights or descend to the abyss? It is a terrifying place!" At that moment, a Word descended. As it stood there, Judas saw how it had come down. He asked, "Why have you come down?"

The Son of Man greeted them and said, "A seed from a power was missing and went down to the abyss. The Greatness remembered it and sent the Word to retrieve it. It brought it back into His presence so that the First Word might not fail."

The disciples were amazed by what they had heard and accepted it with faith. They concluded that it is useless to consider wickedness.
Then the Savior said to His disciples, "Did I not tell you that the good will be taken up to the light like a visible voice and a flash of lightning?"

All His disciples praised Him, saying, "Lord, before You appeared here, who offered You praise? All praise comes from You. Or who will bless You? All blessings derive from You."

As they stood there, Jesus saw two spirits bringing a single soul with them in a great flash of lightning. A Word came forth from the Son of Man, saying, "Give them their garment!" And the small one became like the big one. They were given the same status as those who received them, and they recognized each other. Then the disciples, whom he had taught, inquired about this.

Mary asked, "Why do we see evil coming from them from the very beginning and how they influence each other?"
The Lord responded, "When you see them become immense, they will be greater. But when you see the Eternal Existent, that is the true vision."

They all asked him, "Tell us more about it!"
He replied, "How do you wish to see it? Through a temporary vision or an eternal vision?" He continued, "Strive to save what can follow you, seek it out, and speak from within it, so that as you seek it, everything might be in harmony with you. For I tell you truly, the living God dwells in you and in Him."

Judas said, "I truly want to understand." The Lord replied, "The living God dwells within the entire creation, even amidst the deficiencies."

Judas asked, "Who does this apply to?"
The Lord answered, "To all the works which are the remainder of creation, it is they which you are to understand."
Judas commented, "The governors are above us, so they will rule over us!"
The Lord said, "It is you who will rule over them! But when you rid yourselves of jealousy, you will be clothed in light and enter the bridal chamber."

Judas inquired, "How will our garments be given to us?"
The Lord explained, "There are those who will provide for you, and others who will receive you. They will give you your garments. Who can reach the place that is the reward? But the garments of life are given to man because he knows the path by which he will leave. Even I find it difficult to reach it!"
Mary said, "In relation to 'the wickedness of each day,' 'the laborer is worthy of his food,' and 'the disciple resembles his teacher,' I understand these fully."

The disciples asked, "What is the fullness, and what is the deficiency?"
He said, "You come from the fullness and dwell in the place where there is deficiency. And behold, His light has poured down upon me!"

Matthew asked, "Tell me, Lord, how the dead die and how the living live."
The Lord answered, "You have asked about something that no eye has seen nor have I heard it except from you. When what invigorates a man is removed, he is called 'dead.' When what is alive leaves what is dead, what is alive will be called upon."
Judas asked, "Why do they die and live for the sake of truth?"
The Lord said, "Whatever is born of truth does not die. Whatever is born of woman dies."

Mary asked, "Lord, why have I come to this place to either profit or forfeit?"
The Lord replied, "You clarify the abundance of the revealer!"

Mary said, "Is there a place that is lacking truth?"
The Lord said, "The place where I am not!"
Mary responded, "Lord, you are awe-inspiring and wonderful, and you make those who do not know you feel inadequate."

Matthew asked, "Why do we not rest immediately?"
The Lord replied, "When you lay down your burdens!"
Matthew continued, "How does the small join with the big?"
The Lord said, "When you abandon the works that cannot follow you, then you will rest."

Mary said, "I want to understand all things as they truly are!"
The Lord replied, "He who seeks life will find it, for this is their wealth. The wealth of this cosmos is fleeting, and its gold and silver are misleading."

His disciples asked, "What should we do to ensure our work is perfect?"
The Lord said, "Be prepared for everything. Blessed is the person who has found victory in the contest, who neither kills nor is killed but emerges victorious."

Judas asked, "What is the beginning of the path?"
He said, "Love and goodness. If these qualities existed among the rulers, wickedness would never have come into being."

Matthew said, "Lord, you have spoken about the end of everything without concern."
The Lord said, "You have understood and accepted all that I have said. If you have understood them, they are yours. If not, then they are not yours."

They asked him, "What is the place to which we are going?" The Lord replied, "Stand in the place you can reach!"
Mary said, "Everything established thus is visible." The Lord said, "I have told you that it is the one who can see who reveals."

The twelve disciples asked, "Teacher, how can we achieve serenity? Teach us."
The Lord said, "Everything I have taught you will guide you in everything."
Mary said, "There is one saying I will speak to the Lord regarding the mystery of truth: In this, we have taken our stand, and to the cosmic, we are transparent."

Judas asked Matthew, "We want to understand the kind of garments we will wear when we leave the decaying flesh."
The Lord said, "The governors and the administrators have garments that are temporary and do not last. But you, as children of truth, should not clothe yourselves with these transient garments. Rather, I tell you that you will be blessed when you strip yourselves of these, for it is no great thing to be outside."

Mary asked, "What about the mustard seed? Is it something from heaven or from earth?"
The Lord said, "When the Father established the cosmos, He left much over from the Mother of the All. Therefore, He speaks and acts."

Judas asked, "You have told us this from the mind of truth. How should we pray?"
The Lord said, "Pray in a place where there is no woman."
Matthew interpreted, "Pray in a place where there is no woman means 'Destroy the works of womanhood,' not because there is another manner of birth but because they will cease giving birth."

Mary said, "They will never be obliterated." The Lord said, "Who knows if they will not dissolve?"

Judas said to Matthew, "The works of womanhood will dissolve, and the governors will... Thus, we will be prepared for them."
The Lord said, "Correct. For do they see you? Do they see those who receive you? Now behold! A true Word is coming forth from the Father to the abyss, in silence with a flash of lightning, giving birth. Do they see it or overpower it? But you are even more aware of the path, which belongs to the Father and the Son, because they are both a single entity. You will follow the path you know. Even if the governors become immense, they will not be able to reach it. But listen—I tell you it is difficult even for me to reach it!"

Mary asked the Lord, "When the works dissolve, what happens to the work?"
The Lord said, "Yes. For you know that if I dissolve something, it will go to its place."

Judas asked, "How is the spirit apparent?" The Lord responded, "How is the sword apparent?"
Judas then asked, "How is the light apparent?" The Lord said, "It is apparent in its essence forever."

Judas asked, "Who forgives the works of whom? The works that have affected the cosmos—who forgives them?" The Lord said, "It is the one who understands the works who is able to do the will of the Father. For you, strive to rid yourselves of anger and jealousy, and to strip yourselves of your faults, so that you may become clean and free from error. Those who do this will live forever. I tell you that it is essential to guide your spirits and souls correctly, avoiding all forms of error and maintaining a pure understanding of the truth."

Preaching of Peter

The Preaching of Peter, also known as the Kerygma Petrou, is an ancient Christian text that occupies a significant position in early Christian literature, representing one of the earliest attempts to articulate a systematic presentation of Christian beliefs and practices attributed to the Apostle Peter. Though the original text is lost, its content is partially reconstructed through references and quotations in the works of early Church Fathers such as Clement of Alexandria, Origen, and Eusebius of Caesarea. The document is believed to have been composed in the second century, likely in Alexandria, a hub of theological and philosophical activity during this period. The Preaching of Peter provides invaluable insights into the formative stages of Christian theology, reflecting a blend of Jewish monotheistic tradition and Hellenistic philosophical thought. It emphasizes the life, teachings, death, and resurrection of Jesus Christ, underscoring His role as the promised Messiah and the fulfillment of Old Testament prophecies. The text also addresses issues of ethics, eschatology, and the nature of the Church, illustrating early Christian attempts to define their identity in a pluralistic religious landscape. The Kerygma Petrou is notable for its apologetic tone, aiming to defend the Christian faith against both Jewish and pagan criticisms while also appealing to converts from diverse cultural backgrounds. Its theological depth and rhetorical style indicate a well-educated author familiar with contemporary philosophical discourse, suggesting that early Christian evangelism involved a sophisticated engagement with the intellectual currents of the time. Despite its fragmentary preservation, the Preaching of Peter remains a key subject of scholarly research, providing insights into the early Christian proclamation and doctrinal development.

- Peter, in his preaching, explains that the most respected Greek philosophers do not know God directly, but only indirectly. He says, "Understand that there is one God who created everything and has control over its end. He is invisible, yet sees everything; He is uncontainable, yet contains all; He needs nothing, yet everything needs Him. He is incomprehensible, eternal, incorruptible, uncreated, and made everything through His powerful Word, which is the Son."
- Peter continues, "Worship this God, but not in the way the Greeks do. Although we and the Greeks worship the same God, they do so with incomplete knowledge because they don't know about the Son. Peter does not instruct to worship the God of the Greeks but to do so in a new way. The Greeks worship objects they have created, forgetting their true purpose. They sacrifice animals and food, showing ingratitude to God and denying His existence through these practices."
- Peter further explains, "Do not worship God as the Jews do either. They think they know God, but they serve angels and celestial bodies. If the moon is not visible, they do not properly observe their holy days. Instead, follow the holy and righteous ways we teach, and worship God through Christ in a new manner. The Lord said, 'I make a new covenant with you, not like the one with your ancestors at Mount Horeb.' As Christians, we worship God in a new way, distinct from both the Greeks and Jews."
- Clement adds that Peter references Paul, who mentions the Sibyl and Hystaspes. Clement also notes that Peter says, "If any person from Israel repents and believes in God through my name, their sins will be forgiven. After twelve years, go out into the world so that no one can claim they never heard the message."
- In the following chapter, Peter says, "I chose you twelve as my disciples because you were worthy and faithful. I sent you to preach the Gospel to all nations so that people would know there is one God and believe in me. Those who hear and believe will be saved, and those who do not believe will have no excuse."
- He continues, "All reasonable souls who did not have clear knowledge of God before will have their sins forgiven if they acted in ignorance."
- Peter, in his preaching, says, "We studied the books of the prophets and found references to Jesus Christ. They spoke of His coming, His death, His suffering, and His resurrection. Our belief in God is based on what was written about Him."
- Peter also states that the prophecies came through Divine guidance: "We know that God commanded them, and we base our teachings on Scripture alone."
- The mention of various animals and objects in the context of worship suggests that the Egyptian origins and use of Peter's Preaching are noted. It was considered an orthodox text and was regarded as genuine by Origen. Early Christian apologists like Aristides likely used it.
- A Syriac version of Peter's Preaching in Rome has different content: Peter talks about Jesus' life, death, the apostles' calling, and warns against idolatry and Simon Magus. It also covers Peter's role as bishop, his martyrdom, and other events.
- The Clementine Recognitions mention books of Peter's Preachings, but these are largely speculative. There may be fragments of a 'Teaching of Peter,' which could be another name for the Preaching.
- Origen's *First Principles* mention the Doctrine of Peter, where the Savior says, "I am not a bodiless spirit." This book is not recognized by the church.
- Gregory of Nazianzus cites Peter: "A soul in trouble is close to God."
- John of Damascus quotes Peter: "Wretched that I am, I forgot that God sees the mind and hears the voice of the soul."
- From the Teaching of Peter: "Blessed is the person who shows mercy to many. Imitate God, be generous, for God has given everything to all. The rich should help those in need, following God's fairness."
- Oecumenius on James quotes Peter: "One builds up, another tears down, and they gain nothing but their labor."

Basilides

The "Book of Basilides" is a significant text associated with the early Christian Gnostic thinker Basilides, who flourished in Alexandria during the first half of the 2nd century CE. Basilides' teachings and writings, although largely lost to history, are primarily known through the critiques and references of early Church Fathers, such as Irenaeus, Clement of Alexandria, and Hippolytus of Rome. Basilides developed a complex cosmology and theology that diverged sharply from orthodox Christianity, positing a sophisticated system of emanations from an unknowable God, and the existence of numerous divine beings or Aeons. Basilides' cosmology was centered on the notion of a primal, ineffable Father from whom emanated a series of lesser divine beings. These emanations ultimately led to the creation of the material world, which Basilides viewed as flawed and governed by inferior deities, or Archons. His system also incorporated a doctrine of salvation through esoteric knowledge (gnosis), which he believed could liberate the divine spark within humans from the confines of the material world. The surviving fragments of Basilides' writings, such as those cited by Hippolytus in "Refutation of All Heresies," reveal a distinctive reinterpretation of biblical narratives and an emphasis on secret teachings purportedly derived from the apostle Matthias. Despite the fragmentary nature of the textual evidence, the "Book of Basilides" provides critical insights into the diversity of early Christian thought and the rich tapestry of beliefs that characterized early Gnosticism.

- In the beginning, there was nothing—no thing that exists, no matter, substance, emptiness of substance, simplicity, or any state of being or non-being that humanity has ever named. There was no possibility of composition, no concept or perception that could be grasped or understood. When I use the term "was," it's not to imply existence, but to convey the idea of absolute nothingness. There was no man, angel, or God; nothing within the scope of human perception or conception could be found or imagined.
- In Basilides' "Commentaries," he discusses the idea that those undergoing suffering, seen as martyrs, likely have committed sins unbeknownst to them, leading to their current ordeal. He suggests that divine providence arranges for them to face accusations that are unrelated to their actual sins, sparing them from being condemned for crimes like adultery or murder. Instead, their suffering is attributed to their innate disposition towards Christianity. Basilides argues that even if someone suffers without having committed any known sins — a rare occurrence — this suffering isn't a result of malicious intent. He compares it to the natural suffering of a newborn, who is innocent of deliberate wrongdoing but still experiences pain. This perspective underscores his belief that suffering serves a purpose in spiritual purification rather than being punitive in nature.
- Further in his commentary, Basilides elaborates on the concept by likening a newborn baby to a person who has not committed any actual sins but harbors the potential for sin within. When such an individual experiences suffering, Basilides argues, it serves a beneficial purpose, akin to the learning gained from unpleasant experiences. Similarly, if a grown adult has refrained from sinful deeds yet undergoes suffering, it is because of the inherent capacity for sinfulness within them, not due to any actual transgression they have committed. Therefore, the absence of outward sin cannot absolve them of the internal inclination towards sin. Basilides draws parallels, stating that someone intending to commit adultery or murder is already morally accountable, even if they do not carry out the actions. If he witnesses a person who is deemed sinless suffering without having committed any wrongdoing, Basilides contends that this suffering arises from an internal predisposition towards sin, rather than divine punishment. He underscores the complexity of providence, avoiding the attribution of evil to divine justice, and continues to discuss the nature of the Lord in human terms.
- However, let's suppose you disregard all these points and attempt to challenge me by citing specific cases, saying, "Surely so-and-so must have sinned, since he suffered!" If you allow me, I would argue that suffering does not necessarily indicate sin; it could be likened to the suffering of a newborn baby. But if you insist on pressing the argument, I would assert that every human being is fallible; only God is perfectly righteous. As someone once remarked, no one is entirely free from impurity. Basilides, however, posits that the soul may have sinned in a previous life and is now undergoing punishment in the present one. Souls deemed excellent are honored with martyrdom as their punishment, while others undergo different forms of purification appropriate to their circumstances.
- We understand that a fundamental aspect of what is commonly considered to be God's will includes loving all beings unconditionally. Another part of this will entails desiring nothing selfishly but instead aligning with divine purpose. Lastly, God's will also involves harboring no hatred towards any creation, emphasizing compassion and forgiveness as essential virtues.
- Certainly, the Apostle Paul declared, "Once, I was alive apart from the law," [Romans 7:9] referring to a time before entering this current existence. He meant that in a previous state, he inhabited a body not bound by human laws—a body akin to that of a domestic animal or a bird.

Epiphanes on Righteousness

Epiphanes, an early Christian philosopher and theologian, has left a significant yet often overlooked mark on the discourse of early Christian thought. His treatise on righteousness, commonly referred to as "On Righteousness," offers a profound exploration of ethical and moral principles as understood within the nascent Christian tradition. While not as widely studied as other early Church Fathers, Epiphanes' contributions provide critical insights into the development of Christian ethical teachings and the integration of Hellenistic philosophical concepts into Christian doctrine. In "On Righteousness," Epiphanes engages with the concept of δικαιοσύνη (dikaiosynē), commonly translated as righteousness or justice, a central tenet in both Greco-Roman philosophical traditions and Judeo-Christian teachings. His work reflects an attempt to reconcile the moral philosophies of Plato and Aristotle with the ethical imperatives found in the Hebrew Scriptures and the emerging Christian canon.

- God's righteousness is a form of sharing that ensures equality. In the expansive heavens that encompass the earth, there is no distinction among people; the night displays all stars equally, and the sun, which brings daylight and is considered the father of light, shines equally on everyone. Regardless of one's status—rich or poor, common person or leader, uneducated or educated, male or female, free or enslaved—everyone receives the same amount of sunlight. This fairness extends to animals as well, with the sun shining equally on them too. God's justice ensures that no one receives more than their fair share of light, preventing anyone from taking more than their neighbor.
- The sun provides nourishment for all living beings equally. There is no difference in the way food grows for different animals or plants; all species receive the same amount of sustenance. This abundance is not governed by human laws but is a natural gift from God.
- Birth, like other aspects of existence, is not governed by written laws but is a natural process where all beings have an inherent equality. God, the Creator, has granted everyone the same basic rights, such as sight, without distinguishing between male and female or between different kinds of beings. Human laws, by creating distinctions, undermine the universal equality established by divine justice.
- Laws introduced the concepts of personal property, which have disrupted the original intention of shared resources. God designed the earth, money, and marriage to be shared among all. The natural world, including plants like vines and crops, was meant to be enjoyed communally. However, human laws and notions of private ownership have led to theft and inequality. Originally, everything was meant to be common property, including human relationships. The concept of exclusive possession, particularly in marriage, contradicts this universal sharing.
- The commandment "You shall not desire" may seem ironic given that God instilled in humans a strong desire for procreation, a drive that laws and customs cannot easily suppress. The prohibition against coveting your neighbor's possessions, especially their spouse, highlights the contradiction between the divine intention for common ownership and human laws that enforce private possession.

Marcion

The Book of Marcion, or the Marcionite Bible, is a key yet controversial text in early Christian studies. Compiled by Marcion of Sinope in the second century, it contrasts with the proto-orthodox canon. Influenced by Pauline epistles and critical of the Hebrew Scriptures, Marcion created a Christian canon that excluded the Old Testament and emphasized a dualistic theology, viewing the God of the Hebrew Bible as a lesser deity than the benevolent God of the New Testament. His views led to excommunication and theological debates. The Book of Marcion, featuring an edited Luke's Gospel and ten Pauline epistles, offers insights into the New Testament's formation, early Christian diversity, and the dynamics of heresy and orthodoxy. Despite being condemned, Marcion's work played a role in shaping the New Testament canon.

{1:1} In the fifteenth year of Tiberius Caesar's reign, when Pontius Pilate was governor of Judea, Jesus taught in the synagogue in Capernaum on the Sabbath, impressing everyone with his authority. {1:2} A man possessed by an unclean spirit cried out, "What do you want with us, Jesus of Nazareth? I know you are the Holy One of God!" Jesus commanded the spirit to leave, and it did, leaving the crowd amazed. {1:3} News of Jesus spread. After leaving the synagogue, Jesus healed Simon Peter's mother-in-law of a fever. She immediately got up and served them. {1:4} Jesus went to Nazareth and taught in the synagogue. The people were astonished but asked him to perform miracles like in Capernaum. {1:5} Jesus responded, "No prophet is accepted in his hometown," giving examples from Elijah and Elisha. {1:6} The crowd became enraged and tried to throw him off a hill, but Jesus passed through them and left. {1:7} At sunset, Jesus healed many and cast out demons, who recognized him as the Son of God, but he silenced them. {1:8} The next day, Jesus went to a solitary place, but the crowds found him. He said, "I must proclaim the good news of the kingdom of God to other towns," and continued preaching throughout Galilee.

{2:1} One day, as a large crowd pressed in to hear the word of God, Jesus stood by the shore of Lake Gennesaret. {2:2} He saw two boats at the water's edge, left there by the fishermen who were washing their nets. {2:3} Jesus got into one of the boats, which belonged to Simon, and asked him to push out a little from the shore. Then he sat down and taught the people from the boat. {2:4} When he had finished speaking, he said to Simon, "Put out into deep water, and let down the nets for a catch." {2:5} Simon answered, "Master, we've worked hard all night and haven't caught anything. But because you say so, I will let down the nets." {2:6} When they had done so, they caught such a large number of fish that their nets began to break. {2:7} They signaled their partners in the other boat to come and help them, and they came and filled both boats so full that they began to sink. {2:8} When Simon Peter saw this, he fell at Jesus' knees and said, "Go away from me, Lord; I am a sinful man!" {2:9} For he and all his companions were astonished at the catch of fish they had taken, {2:10} and so were James and John, the sons of Zebedee, Simon's partners. Then Jesus said to Simon, "Don't be afraid; from now on you will fish for people." {2:11} So they pulled their boats up on shore, left everything and followed him. {2:12} While Jesus was in one of the towns, a man came along who was covered with leprosy. When he saw Jesus, he fell with his face to the ground and begged him, "Lord, if you are willing, you can make me clean." {2:13} Jesus reached out his hand and touched the man. "I am willing," he said. "Be clean!" And immediately the leprosy left him. {2:14} Then Jesus ordered him, "Don't tell anyone, but go, show yourself to the priest and offer the sacrifices that Moses commanded for your cleansing, as a testimony to them." {2:15} Yet the news about him spread all the more, so that crowds of people came to hear him and to be healed of their sicknesses. {2:16} But Jesus often withdrew to lonely places and prayed. {2:17} One day Jesus was teaching, and Pharisees and teachers of the law were sitting there. They had come from every village of Galilee and from Judea and Jerusalem. And the power of the Lord was with Jesus to heal the sick. {2:18} Some men came carrying a paralyzed man on a mat and tried to take him into the house to lay him before Jesus. {2:19} When they could not find a way to do this because of the crowd, they went up on the roof and lowered him on his mat through the tiles into the middle of the crowd, right in front of Jesus. {2:20} When Jesus saw their faith, he said, "Friend, your sins are forgiven." {2:21} The Pharisees and the teachers of the law began thinking to themselves, "Who is this fellow who speaks blasphemy? Who can forgive sins but God alone?" {2:22} Jesus knew what they were thinking and asked, "Why are you thinking these things in your hearts? {2:23} Which is easier: to say, 'Your sins are forgiven,' or to say, 'Get up and walk'? {2:24} But I want you to know that the Son of Man has authority on earth to forgive sins." So he said to the paralyzed man, "I tell you, get up, take your mat and go home." {2:25} Immediately he stood up in front of them, took what he had been lying on and went home praising God. {2:26} Everyone was amazed and gave praise to God. They were filled with awe and said, "We have seen remarkable things today." {2:27} After this, Jesus went out and saw a tax collector named Levi sitting at his tax booth. "Follow me," Jesus said to him, {2:28} and Levi got up, left everything and followed him. {2:29} Then Levi held a great banquet for Jesus at his house, and a large crowd of tax collectors and others were eating with them. {2:30} But the Pharisees and the teachers of the law who belonged to their sect complained to his disciples, "Why do you eat and drink with tax collectors and sinners?" {2:31} Jesus answered them, "It is not the healthy who need a doctor, but the sick. {2:32} I have not come to call the righteous, but sinners to repentance." {2:33} They said to him, "John's disciples often fast and pray, and so do the disciples of the Pharisees, but yours go on eating and drinking." {2:34} Jesus answered, "Can you make the friends of the bridegroom fast while he is with them? {2:35} But the time will come when the bridegroom will be taken from them; in those days they will fast." {2:36} He told them this parable: "No one tears a piece out of a new garment to patch an old one. Otherwise, they will have torn the new garment, and the patch from the new will not match the old. {2:37} And no one pours new wine into old wineskins. Otherwise, the new wine will burst the skins; the wine will run out and the wineskins will be ruined. {2:38} No, new wine must be poured into new wineskins. {2:39} And no one after drinking old wine wants the new, for they say, 'The old is better.'"

{3:1} On another Sabbath day, Jesus was walking through the grainfields. His disciples were hungry and began to pick some heads of grain, rub them in their hands, and eat the kernels. {3:2} Some of the Pharisees asked, "Why are you doing what is unlawful on the Sabbath?" {3:3} Jesus answered them, "Have you never read what David did when he and his companions were hungry? {3:4} He entered the house of God, and taking the consecrated bread, he ate what is lawful only for priests to eat. And he also gave some to his companions." {3:5} Then Jesus said to them, "The Son of Man is Lord of the Sabbath." {3:6} On another Sabbath he went into the synagogue and was teaching, and a man was there whose right hand was shriveled. {3:7} The Pharisees and the teachers of the law were looking for a reason to accuse Jesus, so they watched him closely to see if he would heal on the Sabbath. {3:8} But Jesus knew what they were thinking and said to the man with the shriveled hand, "Get up and stand in front of everyone." So he got up and stood there. {3:9} Then Jesus said to them, "I ask you, which is lawful on the Sabbath: to do good or to do evil, to save life or to destroy it?" {3:10} He looked around at them all, and then said to the man, "Stretch out your hand." He did so, and his hand was completely restored. {3:11} But the Pharisees and the teachers of the law were furious and began to discuss with one another what they might do to Jesus. {3:12} One of those days Jesus went out to a mountainside to pray, and spent the night praying to God. {3:13} When morning came, he called his disciples to him and chose twelve of them, whom he also designated apostles: {3:14} Simon (whom he named Peter), his brother Andrew, James, John, Philip, Bartholomew, {3:15} Matthew, Thomas, James son of Alphaeus, Simon who was called the Zealot, {3:16} Judas son of James, and Judas Iscariot, who became a traitor. {3:17} He went down with them and stood on a level place. A large crowd of his disciples was there and a great number of people from all over Judea, from Jerusalem, and from the coastal region around Tyre and Sidon, {3:18} who had come to hear him and to be healed of their diseases. Those troubled by impure spirits were cured, {3:19} and the people all tried to touch him, because power was coming from him and healing them all. {3:20} Looking at his disciples, he said: "Blessed are you who are poor, for yours is the kingdom of God. {3:21} Blessed are you who hunger now, for you will be satisfied. Blessed are you who weep now, for you will laugh. {3:22} Blessed are you when people hate you, when they exclude you and insult you and reject your name as evil, because of the Son of Man. {3:23} Rejoice in that day and leap for joy, because great is your reward in heaven. For that is how their ancestors treated the prophets. {3:24} But woe to you who are rich, for you have already received your comfort. {3:25} Woe to you who are well fed now, for you will go hungry. Woe to you who laugh now, for you will mourn and weep. {3:26} Woe to you when everyone speaks well of you, for that is how their ancestors treated the false prophets. {3:27} But to you who are listening I say: Love your enemies, do good to those who hate you, {3:28} bless those who curse you, pray for those who mistreat you. {3:29} If someone slaps you on one cheek, turn to them the other also. If someone takes your coat, do not withhold your shirt from them. {3:30} Give to everyone who asks you, and if anyone takes what belongs to you, do not demand it back. {3:31} Do to others as you would have them do to you. {3:32} If you love those who love you, what credit is that to you? Even sinners love those who love them. {3:33} And if you do good to those who are good to you, what credit is that to you? Even sinners do that. {3:34} And if you lend to those from whom you expect repayment, what credit is that to you? Even sinners lend to sinners, expecting to be repaid in full. {3:35} But love your enemies, do good to them, and lend to them without expecting to get anything back. Then your reward will be great, and you will be children of the Most High, because he is kind to the ungrateful and wicked. {3:36} Be merciful, just as your Father is merciful. {3:37} Do not judge, and you will not be judged. Do not condemn, and you will not be condemned. Forgive, and you will be forgiven. {3:38} Give, and it will be given to you. A good measure, pressed down, shaken together and running over, will be poured into your lap. For with the measure you use, it will be measured to you." {3:39} He also told them this parable: "Can the blind lead the blind? Will they not both fall into a pit? {3:40} The student is not above the teacher, but everyone who is fully trained will be like their teacher. {3:41} Why do you look at the speck of sawdust in your brother's eye and pay no attention to the plank in your own eye? {3:42} How can you say to your brother, 'Brother, let me take the speck out of your eye,' when you yourself fail to see the plank in your own eye? You hypocrite, first take the plank out of your eye, and then you will see clearly to remove the speck from your brother's eye. {3:43} A good tree does not bear bad fruit, nor does a bad tree bear good fruit. {3:44} Each tree is recognized by its own fruit. People do not pick figs from thornbushes, or grapes from briers. {3:45} A good man brings good things out of the good stored up in his heart, and an evil man brings evil things out of the evil stored up in his heart. For the mouth speaks what the heart is full of. {3:46} Why do you call me, 'Lord, Lord,' and do not do what I say? {3:47} As for everyone who comes to me and hears my words and puts them into practice, I will show you what they are like. {3:48} They are like a man building a house, who dug down deep and laid the foundation on rock. When a flood came, the torrent struck that house but could not shake it, because it was well built. {3:49} But the one who hears my words and does not put them into practice is like a man who built a house on the ground without a foundation. The moment the torrent struck that house, it collapsed and its destruction was complete."

{4:1} After finishing his teachings among the people, Jesus entered Capernaum. {4:2} A centurion there had a servant whom he valued highly, and who was ill and close to death. {4:3} When the centurion heard about Jesus, he sent some Jewish elders to him, asking him to come and heal his servant. {4:4} They came to Jesus and pleaded earnestly with him, "This man deserves to have you do this, because he loves our nation and has built our synagogue." {4:5} So Jesus went with them. He was not far from the house when the centurion sent friends to say to him: "Lord, don't trouble yourself, for I do not deserve to have you come under my roof. {4:6} That is why I did not even consider myself worthy to come to you. But say the word, and my servant will be healed. {4:7} For I myself am a man under authority, with soldiers under me. I tell this one, 'Go,' and he goes; and that one, 'Come,' and he comes. I say to my servant, 'Do this,' and he does it." {4:8} When Jesus heard this, he was amazed at him, and turning to the crowd following him, he said, "I tell you, I have not found such great faith even in Israel." {4:9} Then the men who had been sent returned to the house and found the servant well. {4:10} The next day Jesus was going to a town called Nain, and his disciples and a large crowd were going along with him. {4:11} As he approached the town gate, a dead person was being carried out—the only son of his mother, and she was a widow. And a large crowd from the town was with her. {4:12} When the Lord saw her, his heart went out to her and he said, "Don't cry." {4:13} Then he went up and touched the bier they were carrying him on, and the bearers stood still. He said, "Young man, I say to you, get up!" {4:14} The dead man sat up and began to talk, and Jesus gave him back to his mother. {4:15} They were all filled with awe and praised God. "A great prophet has appeared among us," they said. "God has come to help his people." {4:16} This news about Jesus spread throughout Judea and the surrounding country. {4:17} John's disciples told him about all these things. Calling two of them, {4:18} he sent them to the Lord to ask, "Are you the one who is to come, or should we expect someone else?" {4:19} When the men came to Jesus, they said, "John the Baptist sent us to you to ask, 'Are you the one who is to come, or should we expect someone else?'" {4:20} At that very time Jesus cured many who had diseases, sicknesses and evil spirits, and gave sight to many who were blind. {4:21} So he replied to the messengers, "Go back and report to John what you have seen and heard: The blind receive sight, the lame walk, those who have leprosy are cleansed, the deaf hear, the dead are raised, and the good news is proclaimed to the poor. {4:22} Blessed is anyone who does not stumble on account of me." {4:23} After John's messengers left, Jesus began to speak to the crowd about John: "What did you go out into the wilderness to see? A reed swayed by the wind? {4:24} If not, what did you go out to see? A man dressed in fine clothes? No, those who wear expensive clothes and indulge in luxury are in palaces. {4:25} But what did you go out to see? A prophet? Yes, I tell you, and more than a prophet. {4:26} This is the one about whom it is written: 'I will send my messenger ahead of you, who will prepare your way before you.' {4:27} I tell you, among those born of women there is no one greater than John; yet the one who is least in the kingdom of God is greater than he." {4:28} All the people, even the tax collectors, when they heard Jesus' words, acknowledged that God's way was right, because they had been baptized by John. {4:29} But the Pharisees and the experts in the law rejected God's purpose for themselves, because they had not been baptized by John. {4:30} Jesus went on to say, "To what, then, can I compare the people of this generation? What are they like? {4:31} They are like children sitting in the marketplace and calling out to each other: 'We played the pipe for you, and you did not dance; we sang a dirge, and you did not cry.' {4:32} For John the Baptist came neither eating bread nor drinking wine, and you say, 'He has a demon.' {4:33} The Son of Man came eating and drinking, and you say, 'Here is a glutton and a drunkard, a friend of tax collectors and sinners.' {4:34} But wisdom is proved right by all her children." {4:35} One of the Pharisees invited Jesus to have dinner with him, so he went to the Pharisee's house and reclined at the table. {4:36} When a woman who had lived a sinful life in that town learned that Jesus was eating at the Pharisee's house, she brought an alabaster jar of perfume, {4:37} and as she stood behind him at his feet weeping, she began to wet his feet with her tears. Then she wiped them with her hair, kissed them and poured perfume on them. {4:38} When the Pharisee who had invited him saw this, he said to himself, "If this man were a prophet, he would know who is touching him and what kind of woman she is—that she is a sinner." {4:39} Jesus answered him, "Simon, I have something to tell you." "Tell me, teacher," he said. {4:40} "Two people owed money to a certain moneylender. One owed him five hundred denarii, and the other fifty. {4:41} Neither of them had the money to pay him back, so he forgave the debts of both. Now which of them will love him more?" {4:42} Simon replied, "I suppose the one who had the bigger debt forgiven." "You have judged correctly," Jesus said. {4:43} Then he turned toward the woman and said to Simon, "Do you see this woman? I came into your house. You did not give me any water for my feet, but she wet my feet with her tears and wiped them with her hair. {4:44} You did not give me a kiss, but this woman, from the time I entered, has not stopped kissing my feet. {4:45} You did not put oil on my head, but she has poured perfume on my feet. {4:46} Therefore, I tell you, her many sins have been forgiven—as her great love has shown. But whoever has been forgiven little loves little." {4:47} Then Jesus said to her, "Your sins are forgiven." {4:48} The other guests began to say among themselves, "Who is this who even forgives sins?" {4:49} Jesus said to the woman, "Your faith has saved you; go in peace."

{5:1} Afterward, Jesus traveled from city to city and village to village, proclaiming the good news of the kingdom of God. The Twelve were with him, {5:2} and also some women who had been healed of evil spirits and illnesses: Mary called Magdalene, from whom seven demons had been expelled, {5:3} Joanna the wife of Chuza, the manager of Herod's household, Susanna, and many others. These women were helping to support them out of their own means. {5:4} While a large crowd was gathering and people were coming to Jesus from town after town, he told this parable: {5:5} "A farmer went out to sow his seed. As he was scattering the seed, some fell along the path; it was trampled on, and the birds ate it up. {5:6} Some fell on rocky ground, and when it came up, the plants withered because they had no moisture. {5:7} Other seed fell among thorns, which grew up with it and choked the plants. {5:8} Still other seed fell on good soil. It came up and yielded a crop, a hundred times more than was sown." When he said this, he called out, "Whoever has ears to hear, let them hear." {5:9} His disciples asked him what this parable meant. {5:10} He said, "The knowledge of the secrets of the kingdom of God has been given to you, but to others I speak in parables, so that, 'though seeing, they may not see; though hearing, they may not understand.' {5:11} "This is the meaning of the parable: The seed is the word of God. {5:12} Those along the path are the ones who hear, and then the devil comes and takes away the word from their hearts, so that they may not believe and be saved. {5:13} Those on the rocky ground are the ones who receive the word with joy when they hear it, but they have no root. They believe for a while, but in the time of testing they fall away. {5:14} The seed that fell among thorns stands for those who hear, but as they go on their way they are choked by life's worries, riches and pleasures, and they do not mature. {5:15} But the seed on good soil stands for those with a noble and good heart, who hear the word, retain it, and by persevering produce a crop. {5:16} "No one lights a lamp and hides it in a clay jar or puts it under a bed. Instead, they put it on a stand, so that those who come in can see the light. {5:17} For there is nothing hidden that will not be disclosed, and nothing concealed that will not be known or brought out into the open. {5:18} Therefore consider carefully how you listen. Whoever has will be given more; whoever does not have, even what they think they have will be taken from them." {5:19} Now Jesus' mother and brothers came to see him, but they were not able to get near him because of the crowd. {5:20} Someone told him, "Your mother and brothers are standing outside, wanting to see you." {5:21} He replied, "My mother and brothers are those who hear God's word and put it into practice." {5:22} One day Jesus said to his disciples, "Let us go over to the other side of the lake." So they got into a boat and set out. {5:23} As they sailed, he fell asleep. A squall came down on the lake, so that the boat was being swamped, and they were in great danger. {5:24} The disciples went and woke him, saying, "Master, Master, we're going to drown!" He got up and rebuked the wind and the raging waters; the storm subsided, and all was calm. {5:25} "Where is your faith?" he asked his disciples. In fear and amazement they asked one another, "Who is this? He commands even the winds and the water, and they obey him." {5:26} They sailed to the region of the Gerasenes, which is across the lake from Galilee. {5:27} When Jesus stepped ashore, he was met by a demon-possessed man from the town. For a long time this man had not worn clothes or lived in a house, but had lived in the tombs. {5:28} When he saw Jesus, he cried out and fell at his feet, shouting at the top of his voice, "What do you want with me, Jesus, Son of the Most High God? I beg you, don't torture me!" {5:29} For Jesus had commanded the impure spirit to come out of the man. Many times it had seized him, and though he was chained hand and foot and kept under guard, he had broken his chains and had been driven by the demon into solitary places. {5:30} Jesus asked him, "What is your name?" "Legion," he replied, because many demons had gone into him. {5:31} And they begged Jesus repeatedly not to order them to go into the Abyss. {5:32} A large herd of pigs was feeding there on the hillside. The demons begged Jesus to let them go into the pigs, and he gave them permission. {5:33} When the demons came out of the man, they went into the pigs, and the herd rushed down the steep bank into the lake and was drowned. {5:34} When those tending the pigs saw what had happened, they ran off and reported this in the town and countryside, {5:35} and the people went out to see what had happened. When they came to Jesus, they found the man from whom the demons had gone out, sitting at Jesus' feet, dressed and in his right mind; and they were afraid. {5:36} Those who had seen it told the people how the demon-possessed man had been cured. {5:37} Then all the people of the region of the Gerasenes asked Jesus to leave them, because they were overcome with fear. So he got into the boat and left. {5:38} The man from whom the demons had gone out begged to go with him, but Jesus sent him away, saying, {5:39} "Return home and tell how much God has done for you." So the man went away and told all over town how much Jesus had done for him. {5:40} Now when Jesus returned, a crowd welcomed him, for they were all expecting him. {5:41} Then a man named Jairus, a synagogue leader, came and fell at Jesus' feet, pleading with him to come to his house {5:42} because his only daughter, a girl of about twelve, was dying. As Jesus was on his way, the crowds almost crushed him. {5:43} And a woman was there who had been subject to bleeding for twelve years, but no one could heal her. {5:44} She came up behind him and touched the edge of his cloak, and immediately her bleeding stopped. {5:45} "Who touched me?" Jesus asked. When they all denied it, Peter said, "Master, the people are crowding and pressing against you." {5:46} But Jesus said, "Someone touched me; I know that power has gone out from me." {5:47} Then the woman, seeing that she could not go unnoticed, came trembling and fell at his feet. In the presence of all the people, she told why she had touched him and how she had been instantly healed. {5:48} Then he said to her, "Daughter, your faith has healed you. Go in peace." {5:49} While Jesus was still speaking, someone came from the house of Jairus, the synagogue leader. "Your daughter is dead," he said. "Don't bother the teacher anymore." {5:50} Hearing this, Jesus said to Jairus, "Don't be afraid; just believe, and she will be healed." {5:51} When he arrived at the house of Jairus, he did not let anyone go in with him except Peter, John and James, and the child's father and mother. {5:52} Meanwhile, all the people were wailing and mourning for her. "Stop wailing," Jesus said. "She is not dead but asleep." {5:53} They laughed at him, knowing that she was dead. {5:54} But he took her by the hand and said, "My child, get up!" {5:55} Her spirit returned, and at once she stood up. Then Jesus told them to give her something to eat. {5:56} Her parents were astonished, but he ordered them not to tell anyone what had happened.

Acts of Peter and the Twelve Apostles

The Acts of Peter and the Twelve Apostles is a fascinating apocryphal text that forms part of the broader corpus of early Christian literature, providing a unique window into the diverse theological and narrative traditions that emerged in the first few centuries of the Common Era. This text, preserved in Coptic as part of the Nag Hammadi library discovered in Egypt in 1945, offers rich insights into early Christian mysticism and the development of Gnostic thought. Unlike the canonical Acts of the Apostles in the New Testament, which focuses on the spread of Christianity through the missionary journeys of Peter and Paul, the Acts of Peter and the Twelve Apostles presents a distinct narrative that emphasizes mystical and esoteric themes. The text is notable for its allegorical style and symbolic content, which reflect the Gnostic worldview and its emphasis on hidden knowledge (gnosis) as the path to spiritual enlightenment and salvation. It portrays the apostles, led by Peter, as spiritual guides who embark on a mystical journey, encountering and overcoming various spiritual obstacles through divine wisdom and power. This narrative not only serves to edify its readers about the importance of spiritual insight and the perils of ignorance but also underscores the central Gnostic tenet that true knowledge is revealed through divine revelation rather than through conventional religious practice. The Acts of Peter and the Twelve Apostles thus represents an important artifact of early Christian diversity, illustrating the rich tapestry of beliefs and practices that characterized the nascent Christian movement and highlighting the complex interplay between orthodoxy and heresy in the formation of Christian doctrine and identity.

- **Purpose and Journey**:
  - We, the apostles, set out to fulfill our ministry as appointed by the Lord. We sailed out of the body of the church with our hearts united and made a covenant with each other.
  - At the right time, which we believed was sent by the Lord, we found a ship ready to depart. The sailors welcomed us warmly, as was meant to be. We sailed for a day and a night until the wind carried us to a small city in the sea.
- **Arrival in the City**:
  - I, Peter, asked the locals on the dock for the name of the city. They told me it was called "Habitation," which means "Foundation of Endurance."
  - A man at the dock, who was elegantly dressed and carried a book and staff, was calling out "Pearls! Pearls!" His appearance and manner made me think he was a local.
- **Meeting the Man with Pearls**:
  - I approached him, addressing him as "My brother and my friend." He responded affirmatively and inquired about my needs. I asked him for lodging for myself and the other apostles since we were strangers.
  - He said he was also a stranger and then continued calling out for pearls. The wealthy citizens, hearing him, ignored him as he had nothing to sell visibly. The poor, however, were interested and asked to see the pearls, hoping to view them even if they couldn't afford them.
- **The Man's Invitation**:
  - The man, still calling for pearls, invited the poor to come to his city to see the pearls and receive them for free. The poor were delighted by this offer.
- **Peter's Inquiry and Response**:
  - I asked the man, who introduced himself as Lithargoel (meaning "light, gazelle-like stone"), about the hardships of the road to his city. He explained that the road was fraught with dangers and required forsaking worldly possessions and fasting daily to traverse safely.
- **Encouragement and Revelation**:
  - I sighed at the thought of such hardships, hoping for strength from Jesus. Lithargoel, understanding my concern, reassured me that Jesus, whom I knew and believed in, could provide strength.
  - Lithargoel's city was named "Nine Gates," and he emphasized that the tenth gate is symbolic of the head or chief.
- **Exploration of the City**:
  - As I prepared to call my companions, I saw that the city was surrounded by high walls. I spoke with an elderly resident who confirmed the city's name and explained its significance as a place of endurance and faith.
- **Journey and Encounter with Lithargoel**:
  - We set out for Lithargoel's city, forsaking worldly possessions as advised. We managed to avoid all dangers and finally arrived. We rested and discussed our journey.
  - Lithargoel, now appearing as a healer with a disciple carrying medical supplies, approached us. Peter recognized him as Jesus, who revealed his true identity after testing our knowledge of him.
- **Instructions and Mission**:
  - Jesus instructed us to return to Habitation, continue enduring, and teach in His name. He gave us the medical supplies to heal the sick in the city and advised us to avoid the wealthy who had shown disdain, focusing instead on the poor.
  - Jesus explained that His teachings and wisdom surpass material wealth and emphasized that healing the body would lead people to believe in the spiritual healing He offers.
- **Final Command**:
  - Jesus instructed us to use the medicines to heal the bodies in Habitation and to teach the poor, promising to provide for them eventually.
  - He warned against partiality towards the rich and stressed the importance of uprightness and integrity in our ministry.
- **Conclusion**:
  - We bowed down in reverence and worshipped Jesus. He blessed us, gave us peace, and departed. Amen.

Didache

The Didache, also known as "The Teaching of the Twelve Apostles," is an early Christian text that serves as a critical witness to the practices and beliefs of the nascent Christian community. Likely composed in the late first or early second century, this document is an invaluable source for understanding the liturgical, ethical, and ecclesiastical norms of early Christianity. The Didache is structured as a manual for Christian living, divided into sections that include instructions on morality, rituals such as baptism and the Eucharist, and guidelines for church organization and leadership. Its moral teachings are heavily influenced by Jewish ethical traditions, reflecting the early Christians' roots in Judaism. The text's emphasis on the "Two Ways"—the Way of Life and the Way of Death—highlights its didactic nature, aiming to instruct converts in the basics of Christian ethics and conduct. Moreover, the Didache provides one of the earliest known descriptions of Christian liturgical practices, offering insights into the forms of worship and community organization that predate the more formalized church structures of the later centuries. The document's pragmatic approach to church leadership, advocating for itinerant prophets and teachers while also recognizing the roles of bishops and deacons, reveals a community in transition, balancing charismatic leadership with emerging institutional structures. As such, the Didache is crucial for studying early Christianity, bridging the apostolic age and early church hierarchy, and providing insight into the earliest Christian practices.

{1:1} There are two paths, one of life and one of death, and they are vastly different. The path of life is this: First, love the God who created you; second, love your neighbor as yourself, and do not do to others what you would not want done to you. Here's the teaching: Bless those who curse you, pray for your enemies, and fast for those who persecute you. What reward is there if you only love those who love you? Even Gentiles do that. Instead, love those who hate you, and you won't have enemies. Avoid worldly desires and lusts. If someone strikes your right cheek, offer the other also; strive for perfection. If someone compels you to go one mile, go two. If someone takes your cloak, give them your coat too. Don't demand back what is taken from you, for you cannot. Give to whoever asks, and don't ask for it back, for the Father desires generosity from all. Blessed is the one who gives as commanded, for they are blameless. Woe to those who receive without need, for they will be accountable. They will be scrutinized in confinement for their deeds and will not escape until they repay every debt. Regarding this, it is said, hold your alms until you know whom to give them to.

{2:1} The second commandment of the Teaching is this: Do not commit murder, adultery, pederasty, fornication, theft, sorcery, witchcraft, abortion, or infanticide. Do not covet your neighbor's belongings, swear falsely, speak evil, or hold grudges. Do not be deceitful or speak with a double tongue, for deceit leads to death. Let your words be truthful and backed by action. Do not be greedy, rapacious, hypocritical, or arrogant. Do not conspire against your neighbor. Love all people, rebuke some, pray for others, and love some more than your own life.

{3:1} My child, flee from every form of evil and its appearance. Do not be quick to anger, for it leads to violence. Avoid jealousy, quarreling, and hot temper, for they breed violence. Avoid lust, for it leads to sexual immorality. Do not engage in obscene talk or haughty behavior, for they lead to adultery. Stay away from divination and fortune-telling, for they lead to idolatry. Do not be enchanted by astrology or purifiers, for they foster idolatry. Do not lie, for lies lead to theft. Avoid greed and vanity, for they lead to stealing. Do not grumble, for it leads to blasphemy. Do not be stubborn or evil-minded, for they lead to blasphemy. Instead, be humble, for the meek will inherit the earth. Be patient, compassionate, sincere, gentle, and kind. Always be in awe of the teachings you have received. Do not boast or be overly confident. Associate your soul with the just and humble, not the proud. Accept whatever comes your way as good, knowing that everything happens with God's will.

{4:1} My child, remember day and night those who speak God's word to you, and honor them as you honor the Lord. Wherever the authority of the Lord is proclaimed, there the Lord is present. Seek out the company of the saints daily so you may find peace in their teachings. Avoid discord; instead, reconcile those who argue. Judge fairly and impartially when correcting wrongs. Do not be hesitant in giving or withdrawing support. If you have something, use it to atone for your sins. Be generous without complaint, for you will find a generous reward. Do not turn away from those in need; share everything with your brothers and sisters, not claiming anything as exclusively yours. If you partake in eternal things, how much more should you share in earthly possessions? Teach your children the fear of God from their youth. Do not impose embittered commands on your servants who also hope in God, lest they lose reverence for the true God who judges the heart, not appearances. Bondservants, obey your masters as you would obey God, with humility and respect. Abhor hypocrisy and anything displeasing to the Lord. Never forsake the Lord's commandments; hold fast to what you have received, neither adding nor subtracting from them. Confess your sins in church and do not pray with a guilty conscience. This is the way of life.

{5:1} The path of death, on the other hand, is cursed and evil: it includes murder, adultery, lust, fornication, theft, idolatry, sorcery, witchcraft, rape, false testimony, hypocrisy, deceit, arrogance, depravity, self-will, greed, obscene speech, jealousy, pride, boasting, persecution of the righteous, hatred of truth, love of falsehood, ignorance of righteousness, lack of good judgment, preference for evil, neglect of good, love of vanity, pursuit of revenge, lack of compassion for the poor, neglect of the afflicted, ignorance of the Creator, murder of children, destruction of God's creation, neglect of the needy, oppression of the distressed, favoritism toward the wealthy, unjust treatment of the poor, and outright sinfulness. Children, turn away from all these evils.

{6:1} Guard against anyone leading you away from this teaching, for it comes from God. If you can bear the full weight of the Lord's teachings, you will be perfect; if not, do your best. Concerning food, eat what you can, but be extremely cautious about food sacrificed to idols, as it honors false gods.

{7:1} Regarding baptism, baptize as follows: After teaching all these things, baptize in the name of the Father, the Son, and the Holy Spirit, using living water. If living water is unavailable, use other water; if cold water is not possible, use warm water. If none of these is available, pour water three times over the head in the name of the Father, Son, and Holy Spirit. Before baptism, the baptizer, the baptized, and anyone else able should fast. Instruct the baptized to fast one or two days beforehand.

{8:1} Concerning fasting, do not imitate the hypocrites who fast on Mondays and Thursdays. Instead, fast on Wednesdays and Fridays. Do not pray like hypocrites, but as the Lord commanded in His Gospel, saying: "Our Father in heaven, may Your name be honored. May Your kingdom come soon. May Your will be done here on earth, just as it is in heaven. Give us today the food we need, and forgive us our sins, as we have forgiven those who sin against us. And don't let us yield to temptation, but rescue us from the evil one." Pray this prayer three times each day.

{9:1} Concerning the Eucharist, give thanks in this manner: First, concerning the cup: "We thank You, Father, for the holy vine of Your servant David, which You have made known to us through Your servant Jesus. To You be the glory forever." And concerning the broken bread: "We thank You, Father, for the life and knowledge You have revealed to us through Your servant Jesus. To You be the glory forever. Just as this broken bread was scattered over the hills and then was gathered together and became one, so let Your Church be gathered together from the ends of the earth into Your kingdom. For Yours is the glory and the power through Jesus Christ forever." Let no one partake of your Eucharist unless they have been baptized in the name of the Lord, for the Lord has said, "Do not give what is holy to dogs."

{10:1} After you have received communion, offer thanks in this manner: "We thank you, holy Father, for your holy name which you have caused to dwell in our hearts, and for the knowledge, faith, and immortality which you have revealed to us through Jesus your servant. To you be the glory forever. Almighty Master, you created all things for your name's sake, and you gave food and drink to humanity for enjoyment, that they might give thanks to you. But to us, you have freely given spiritual food and drink and eternal life through your servant. Above all, we thank you for your power; to you be the glory forever. Remember, Lord, your Church, deliver it from all evil, perfect it in your love, and gather it from the four winds, sanctified for your kingdom which you have prepared for it. For yours is the power and the glory forever. Let grace come, and may this world pass away. Hosanna to the God of David! If anyone is holy, let him come; if anyone is not, let him repent. Maranatha. Amen." Allow the prophets to offer thanksgiving as much as they desire.

{11:1} Regarding teachers, apostles, and prophets, receive whoever comes to you teaching these truths previously stated. But if a teacher turns and teaches another doctrine that undermines this teaching, do not listen to him. However, if he teaches to promote righteousness and knowledge of the Lord, accept him as you would the Lord. Concerning apostles and prophets, follow the Gospel's decree: Receive every apostle who comes to you as you would the Lord, but let him stay only one day, or two days if necessary. If he stays three days, he is a false prophet. When the apostle leaves, let him take nothing except bread to eat. If he asks for money, he is a false prophet. Do not judge or test every prophet who speaks in the Spirit, for every sin will be forgiven except this one. Not every spirit-speaking person is a prophet; they are recognized by their actions according to the Lord's ways. Thus, you can discern false prophets from true ones. Any prophet who orders a meal in the Spirit but does not eat it is a false prophet. A prophet who teaches truth but does not practice it is a false prophet. A true prophet who works for the Church's mystery in the world but does not teach others to do the same will not be judged among you; God will judge him. If someone speaks in the Spirit, asking for money or anything else, do not listen. But if he asks for giving to those in need, let no one judge him.

{12:1} Receive everyone who comes in the name of the Lord, and test and get to know them afterward, for you will discern clearly. If a traveler comes, help them as much as you can, but they should not stay with you more than two or three days if necessary. If they want to stay and they are a craftsman, let them work and eat. If they have no trade, ensure they do not live idle as a Christian. If they refuse to work, they are exploiting Christ's name. Be vigilant to avoid such people.

{13:1} Every true prophet who wishes to live among you deserves support, as does a true teacher, for they are your spiritual guides. Therefore, do not disregard them, for they are worthy, along with the prophets and teachers. Correct one another not in anger but in peace, as instructed in the Gospel. If anyone wrongs another, do not speak to or hear from them until they repent. Perform your prayers, alms, and all your deeds according to the Gospel of our Lord.

{14:1} Gather together every Lord's day, break bread, and give thanks after confessing your sins, ensuring your offering remains pure. Do not allow anyone at odds with another to join you until they are reconciled, lest your offering be defiled. For the Lord said: "Offer to me in every place and time a pure sacrifice, for I am a great King, and my name is revered among the nations."

{15:1} Choose for yourselves bishops and deacons who are worthy of the Lord, humble, not fond of money, truthful, and proven, for they serve you as prophets and teachers. Therefore, honor them, along with the prophets and teachers. Admonish each other not in anger but in peace, as prescribed by the Gospel. If anyone wrongs another, let no one speak to or hear from them until they repent. But perform your prayers, almsgiving, and all your actions as you have them in the Gospel of our Lord.

{16:1} Be vigilant for your own sake. Keep your lamps burning and your loins girded; be prepared, for you do not know when our Lord will come. Gather often, seeking what is suitable for your souls; for your faith will not profit you fully unless perfected in the last days. In the end times, false prophets and corrupters will multiply, turning sheep into wolves, love into hate. Lawlessness will increase, leading to hatred, persecution, and betrayal among people. Then the world deceiver will appear as the Son of God, performing signs and wonders, seizing control of the earth, committing unprecedented wickedness. Human creation will be tested by fire, causing many to stumble and perish, but those who endure in faith will be saved from the curse. Signs of truth will appear: first, a spreading in heaven, then the sound of a trumpet, and thirdly, the resurrection of the dead—not all, but as it is written: "The Lord will come, and all his saints with him." Then the world will witness the Lord coming on the clouds of heaven.

Prayer of Thanksgiving

The Prayer of Thanksgiving, an ancient Gnostic text discovered among the Nag Hammadi library, offers a profound insight into early Christian mysticism and theology. This prayer is notable for its intricate blend of Christian and Hellenistic thought, reflecting the syncretistic nature of Gnostic spirituality. It is traditionally attributed to the community known as the Sethians, who were prominent among the Gnostic sects. The text is characterized by its rich, poetic language and its focus on the theme of divine illumination. It presents a vision of the divine as an all-encompassing light, emphasizing the intimate connection between the believer and the divine source. The prayer opens with a thanksgiving for the knowledge and wisdom imparted by the divine, which is seen as the true path to salvation. This knowledge, or gnosis, is not merely intellectual but experiential, transforming the believer's understanding of reality and their place within it. The Prayer of Thanksgiving also includes elements of ritual, suggesting that it may have been used in liturgical settings, perhaps as part of initiation ceremonies or other communal rites. The text's emphasis on gratitude and enlightenment reflects broader Gnostic themes of transcendence and the quest for spiritual awakening.

This is the prayer that they spoke:

{1:1} We thank You! Every soul and heart is uplifted to You, revered with the name 'God' and honored with the name 'Father,' for You bestow fatherly kindness, affection, and love to everyone and everything. You provide us with sweet and clear teachings, granting us mind, speech, and knowledge: mind, so that we can understand You; speech, so that we can express You; and knowledge, so that we can truly know You. We rejoice because Your knowledge has illuminated us. We rejoice because You have revealed Yourself to us. We rejoice because, even while we are in the body, You have made us divine through Your knowledge. {1:2} The ultimate thanksgiving of someone who reaches You is simply to know You. We have known You, the intellectual light. We have known You, the life of all life. We have known You, the source of every creature. We have known You, the source carrying the nature of the Father. We have known You, the eternal essence of the begetting Father. Thus, we have worshiped Your goodness. Our only request is to remain steadfast in knowledge. Our only desire for protection is that we do not falter in this life. {1:3} After saying these things in their prayer, they embraced each other and went to share their sacred meal, which is free of blood.

Sinodos

The Ethiopian Bible, central to Ethiopian Orthodox Christianity, includes unique texts such as the Book of Sinodos. This significant ecclesiastical document offers insights into the liturgical, doctrinal, and administrative aspects of the Ethiopian Orthodox Tewahedo Church. Known also as the Synodicon, it compiles canonical decrees, ecclesiastical laws, and theological expositions attributed to early church fathers and synodal decisions. The Sinodos guides clergy and laity in sacramental procedures, ethical conduct, and church hierarchy. Reflecting ancient traditions and the church's apostolic foundation through St. Matthew, the Sinodos is a profound reflection of the Ethiopian Church's identity, preserving its theological heritage and distinct practices. It underscores the church's historical autonomy and unique Christian tradition, shaped by Ethiopia's geographical isolation and cultural continuity. The Sinodos offers scholars valuable insights into the interplay of faith, culture, and governance in one of the world's oldest Christian communities, highlighting its enduring legacy and contribution to global Christianity.

{1:1} And it came to pass, that the Church set forth guidelines for the ordination of bishops, priests, and deacons. {1:2} Let the candidate for the office of bishop be of good repute, not given to drunkenness, nor a lover of money. {1:3} He must be well-versed in the Holy Scriptures and able to teach sound doctrine. {1:4} A priest shall be ordained after he has been tested and found blameless, being a man of prayer and integrity. {1:5} Deacons shall be chosen from among those who have served faithfully, demonstrating humility and a willingness to assist the priest in all duties.

{2:1} Let the clergy conduct themselves with piety and holiness, being examples to the flock in word and deed. {2:2} They shall abstain from idle talk, and avoid quarrels and disputes. {2:3} A bishop must visit the faithful regularly, offering counsel and spiritual guidance. {2:4} Priests shall perform the sacraments with reverence, ensuring that the liturgy is conducted according to the traditions of the Church. {2:5} Deacons shall assist in the distribution of the Eucharist, and in the care of the poor and needy.

{3:1} Baptism shall be administered in the name of the Father, and of the Son, and of the Holy Spirit, using water as the outward sign of inward grace. {3:2} The Eucharist, being the true Body and Blood of Christ, shall be celebrated with unleavened bread and wine. {3:3} Confession shall be heard by a priest, who shall offer absolution in the name of Christ. {3:4} Marriage shall be solemnized in the presence of the congregation, with vows exchanged before God and witnesses. {3:5} Anointing of the sick shall be performed with oil, invoking the healing power of the Holy Spirit.

{4:1} The faithful shall observe fasting as a means of spiritual discipline, abstaining from meat and dairy on appointed days. {4:2} Wednesdays and Fridays shall be days of fasting, in remembrance of the betrayal and crucifixion of our Lord. {4:3} During Lent, the faithful shall engage in more rigorous fasting and increased prayer, preparing for the celebration of the Resurrection. {4:4} Prayer shall be offered daily, with morning and evening prayers being a duty of every Christian. {4:5} Let the clergy lead the congregation in prayers, hymns, and psalms, fostering a spirit of devotion.

{5:1} Let any member of the clergy found guilty of grievous sin be brought before the bishop for judgment. {5:2} A process of repentance and reconciliation shall be established for the restoration of those who have fallen. {5:3} Heresy and schism shall be addressed with firmness, ensuring the purity of doctrine and unity of the Church. {5:4} Disputes among the faithful shall be resolved through mediation and the application of biblical principles. {5:5} The administration of the church's temporal goods shall be conducted with honesty and transparency.

{6:1} The laity shall support the clergy in their ministry, offering prayers, tithes, and alms. {6:2} They shall participate in the sacraments and the liturgical life of the Church. {6:3} Every member of the Church is called to live a life of holiness, bearing witness to the Gospel in word and deed. {6:4} The laity shall educate their children in the faith, ensuring they are instructed in the Scriptures and the traditions of the Church. {6:5} Let the faithful care for one another, showing hospitality and acts of charity, thereby fulfilling the law of Christ.

{7:1} The liturgy shall be conducted with reverence and order, following the ancient traditions handed down by the fathers. {7:2} Hymns and psalms shall be sung, lifting the hearts of the faithful to God. {7:3} Incense shall be used as a symbol of the prayers of the saints rising to heaven. {7:4} The reading of the Scriptures shall be central to the worship service, with the homily providing instruction and exhortation. {7:5} The celebration of the Eucharist shall be the high point of the liturgy, a sacred communion with the Lord.

{8:1} The Church shall observe the feasts of the Lord with joy and reverence, commemorating the great events of salvation history. {8:2} The Feast of the Nativity shall be celebrated on the 25th of December, in honor of the birth of our Lord Jesus Christ. {8:3} The Feast of the Resurrection shall be celebrated on the first Sunday after the first full moon following the vernal equinox, commemorating the resurrection of Christ from the dead. {8:4} The faithful shall also observe the feasts of the saints, remembering their holy lives and seeking their intercession. {8:5} The Church shall follow a liturgical calendar, marking the seasons of Advent, Lent, Easter, and Pentecost.

{9:1} The Church shall be a beacon of charity, caring for the poor, the orphaned, and the widowed. {9:2} Alms shall be collected regularly and distributed to those in need, as an expression of Christ's love. {9:3} The faithful shall be encouraged to engage in acts of mercy, visiting the sick, comforting the afflicted, and supporting the downtrodden. {9:4} Let the Church advocate for justice and peace, standing against oppression and violence. {9:5} The Church shall work to promote education and the well-being of all members of society.

{10:1} Those called to the monastic life shall dedicate themselves to prayer, work, and the study of the Scriptures. {10:2} Monks and nuns shall live in communities, following the rule of their order and seeking to grow in holiness. {10:3} The monastic community shall be a place of hospitality, welcoming pilgrims and offering spiritual guidance. {10:4} Monasteries shall be self-sustaining, engaging in agriculture, crafts, and other works. {10:5} The abbot or abbess shall lead the community with wisdom and compassion, ensuring the well-being of all members.

{11:1} The Church shall establish schools and centers of learning, providing education in the faith and other subjects. {11:2} Catechesis shall be offered to all ages, ensuring that the faithful are well-grounded in the doctrines and traditions of the Church. {11:3} Clergy and teachers shall be well-trained and equipped to instruct others in the faith. {11:4} The Scriptures shall be studied diligently, with the aim of understanding and living out their teachings. {11:5} Let the faithful be encouraged to grow in knowledge and wisdom, seeking to live lives that glorify God.

{12:1} The Church shall be committed to the Great Commission, spreading the Gospel to all nations. {12:2} Missionaries shall be sent out, supported by the prayers and resources of the Church. {12:3} Let the Church engage in evangelistic efforts, using every means available to proclaim the Good News of Jesus Christ. {12:4} New believers shall be welcomed into the community, baptized, and instructed in the faith. {12:5} The Church shall work to establish new congregations, nurturing them to maturity in Christ.

{13:1} The Church shall manage its financial resources with integrity and transparency. {13:2} Tithes and offerings shall be collected and used for the work of the ministry, the support of clergy, and the care of the needy. {13:3} A financial committee shall be established to oversee the proper allocation and use of funds. {13:4} Regular financial reports shall be presented to the congregation, ensuring accountability {13:5} The faithful are encouraged to give generously, recognizing that all gifts come from God.

{14:1} The Church shall maintain its properties and assets with diligence, ensuring they are used for the glory of God. {14:2} All church properties shall be held in trust, managed by appointed stewards. {14:3} Any sale or purchase of church property shall be approved by the governing body of the church. {14:4} Church buildings shall be kept in good repair, providing a suitable place for worship and ministry. {14:5} The use of church facilities for non-religious purposes shall be governed by clear policies, ensuring they align with the mission of the Church.

{15:1} The clergy shall provide pastoral care to all members of the congregation, offering spiritual guidance and support. {15:2} Counseling shall be available to those facing personal, familial, or spiritual challenges, with confidentiality and compassion. {15:3} Training in pastoral care shall be provided to clergy and lay leaders, equipping them to minister effectively. {15:4} Let the Church establish support groups for various needs, fostering a community of healing and growth. {15:5} The clergy shall visit the sick and the homebound, offering the sacraments and words of comfort.

{16:1} The Church shall seek to maintain unity and fellowship with other branches of the Christian faith. {16:2} Let there be regular communication and cooperation with neighboring churches and denominations. {16:3} The Church shall participate in ecumenical councils and initiatives, working towards the common good. {16:4} Differences in doctrine and practice shall be addressed with humility and respect, seeking mutual understanding. {16:5} Joint efforts in mission, charity, and education shall be pursued, reflecting the unity of the body of Christ.

{17:1} The Church shall ensure the safety and protection of all its members, particularly children and vulnerable adults. {17:2} Policies and procedures shall be in place to prevent abuse, and to respond swiftly and justly to any allegations. {17:3} Training in safeguarding shall be mandatory for all clergy and volunteers. {17:4} A dedicated team shall oversee the implementation and monitoring of safeguarding measures. {17:5} Let the Church work with civil authorities as necessary, ensuring that justice and protection are upheld.

{18:1} The Church shall keep accurate records of all its activities, including baptisms, marriages, and funerals. {18:2} Membership records shall be maintained, providing a clear account of the congregation. {18:3} Financial records shall be meticulously kept, ensuring accountability and transparency. {18:4} Historical documents and archives shall be preserved, maintaining the heritage and memory of the Church. {18:5} Let all records be securely stored and accessible to those with legitimate need.

{19:1} The Church shall use various media to communicate the Gospel and the teachings of the Church. {19:2} A communications team shall be established to manage the church's online presence, publications, and outreach. {19:3} Social media shall be used responsibly, promoting the values and mission of the Church. {19:4} Publications such as newsletters, bulletins, and magazines shall be produced to inform and edify the congregation. {19:5} The Church shall engage with the wider community through media, being a voice of hope and truth.

{20:1} The Church shall provide mechanisms for resolving disputes among its members, promoting peace and unity. {20:2} Mediation and arbitration shall be offered as means of resolving conflicts, in accordance with biblical principles. {20:3} A reconciliation committee shall be established to facilitate healing and restoration. {20:4} Disciplinary actions shall be carried out with fairness and a spirit of redemption. {20:5} Let forgiveness and reconciliation be pursued diligently, reflecting the love and grace of Christ.

{21:1} The Church shall promote the use of liturgical arts and music in worship, enhancing the beauty and reverence of the liturgy. {21:2} Choirs and music ministries shall be established, with members trained in the traditions and practices of sacred music. {21:3} Art and iconography shall be used to inspire and educate the faithful, in accordance with the traditions of the Church. {21:4} Liturgical vestments and sacred vessels shall be crafted and maintained with care, reflecting the sanctity of worship. {21:5} The Church shall encourage the development of new works of liturgical art and music, fostering creativity and devotion.

{22:1} The Church shall recognize the responsibility to care for God's creation, promoting environmental stewardship. {22:2} Initiatives to reduce waste, conserve resources, and protect natural habitats shall be supported. {22:3} Educational programs on environmental issues shall be provided, encouraging sustainable practices. {22:4} The Church shall advocate for policies and actions that protect the environment and promote justice for all living beings. {22:5} Let the faithful be reminded of the biblical call to be stewards of the earth, acting with reverence and respect for all of creation. Amen.

Nicene Creed

The Nicene Creed, a seminal statement of Christian orthodoxy, emerged from the theological crucible of the early fourth century, shaped by the intricate interplay of doctrinal disputes and imperial politics. Formulated at the First Council of Nicaea in 325 AD, convened by Emperor Constantine, the Creed was primarily crafted to address the Arian controversy, which questioned the divinity of Jesus Christ. This ecumenical council, attended by bishops from across the Roman Empire, sought to establish a unified Christian doctrine to preserve the unity of the burgeoning church and the stability of the empire. The Nicene Creed's articulation of the consubstantiality (homoousios) of the Son with the Father was a direct repudiation of Arianism, affirming that Jesus Christ is "begotten, not made, being of one substance with the Father." This assertion was pivotal in establishing the foundational tenet of the Trinity, emphasizing the co-equal and co-eternal nature of the Father, Son, and Holy Spirit. Over time, the Creed underwent further refinement, notably at the First Council of Constantinople in 381 AD, to address additional theological challenges and heresies, resulting in the Niceno-Constantinopolitan Creed. This creed not only solidified the theological bedrock of mainstream Christianity but also became a central liturgical element, recited in various Christian traditions. Its enduring significance lies in its role as a touchstone of orthodox belief, encapsulating the core doctrines of the faith in a concise and universally recognized formula.

Belief in God	I believe in one God, the Father Almighty, the Creator of heaven and earth, and of everything visible and invisible.
Belief in Jesus Christ	And I believe in one Lord Jesus Christ, the only Son of God, begotten of the Father before all time; God from God, Light from Light, true God from true God; begotten, not made, of one substance with the Father, through whom all things were made.
Incarnation and Mission	Who, for our salvation, came down from heaven, became incarnate by the Holy Spirit from the Virgin Mary, and was made man; He was crucified for us under Pontius Pilate; He suffered and was buried; on the third day He rose again, as the Scriptures said; He ascended into heaven, and sits at the right hand of the Father; He will come again with glory to judge the living and the dead; His kingdom will have no end.
Belief in the Holy Spirit	And I believe in the Holy Spirit, the Lord and Giver of Life; who proceeds from the Father [and the Son]; who, with the Father and the Son, is worshipped and glorified; who spoke through the prophets.
Belief in the Church and the Resurrection	And I believe in one holy, catholic, and apostolic Church. I acknowledge one baptism for the forgiveness of sins; and I look forward to the resurrection of the dead and the life of the world to come. Amen.

Traditions of Matthias

The Traditions of Matthias, associated with the Apostle Matthias who replaced Judas Iscariot, is a significant but often overlooked early Christian text. Although the original manuscript is lost, early Church Fathers like Clement of Alexandria and Origen referenced it, highlighting its importance. Likely composed in the late first or early second century, it reflects early Christian diversity and offers mystical and esoteric teachings attributed to Jesus, distinct from the canonical Gospels. The text also addressed ecclesiastical authority and community organization, providing insight into the varied theological interpretations of the time and the development of early Christian thought.

- The first step towards understanding deeper truths is to marvel at things, as Plato states in the Theatetus and Matthias emphasizes in the Traditions, urging us to "Marvel at what is present."
- Matthias also taught this principle: "To combat and subdue the flesh without yielding to its undisciplined pleasures, thereby strengthening the soul through faith and knowledge."
- Zaccheus, also known as Matthias, the chief tax collector, when he heard that the Lord valued him enough to be with him, declared, "Look, I give half of my possessions to the poor, and if I have extorted money from anyone, I repay it fourfold." At this, the Savior remarked, "When the Son of Man came today, he found what was lost."
- Matthias the apostle reportedly said in the Traditions, "If the neighbor of an elect person sins, the elect person also bears responsibility. For if the elect had lived according to the word, their neighbor would have been inspired by their life and refrained from sinning."

Epistula Apostolorum

The Epistula Apostolorum, or Letter of the Apostles, is an early Christian text discovered in an Ethiopian manuscript in 1895. It blends apocalyptic literature, epistolary narrative, and catechetical dialogue, reflecting the second-century efforts to define Christian beliefs. Attributed pseudonymously to the apostles to lend authority, the text features a dialogue between the risen Christ and his apostles, addressing theological issues like Christ's resurrection, his return, and scriptural prophecies. Emphasizing apostolic authority, the Epistula Apostolorum situates itself in the context of early Christian efforts to consolidate orthodoxy and ecclesiastical structure. Its eschatological themes highlight the tension between the Church's present experience and anticipated divine fulfillment. Although not part of the New Testament canon, the text offers valuable insights into early Christian thought and the development of foundational doctrines, showcasing the rich diversity of early Christian literature.

{1:1} This is the book that Jesus Christ revealed to his disciples, the book meant for all people. It is written against Simon and Cerinthus, false apostles who deceive and lead people to ruin. This book is written so that you may remain steadfast and not be troubled, holding fast to the Gospel as you have heard it. We have recorded it for the whole world, remembering it as we heard it. We commend you, our sons and daughters, with joy in the grace of God, in the name of God the Father, the Lord of the world, and Jesus Christ. May grace be multiplied upon you.

{2:1} We, John, Thomas, Peter, Andrew, James, Philip, Bartholomew, Matthew, Nathanael, Judas Zelotes, and Cephas, write to the churches in the east, west, north, and south, to declare and share what we have witnessed concerning our Lord Jesus Christ. We write as we have seen, heard, and touched Him after He rose from the dead, revealing to us mighty, wonderful, and true things.

{3:1} We know that our Lord and Redeemer Jesus Christ is the Son of God, sent by God, the Lord of the whole world, the Creator of all. He is called by all names, exalted above all powers, Lord of lords, King of kings, Ruler of rulers, seated above the cherubim and seraphim at the right hand of the Father's throne. By His word, He made the heavens, formed the earth, and set the boundaries of the sea. He created the deep springs and fountains, established day and night, the sun and moon, and the stars in the sky. He separated light from darkness, called forth the underworld, and ordained the rain, snow, hail, and seasons. He makes the earth quake and establishes it again. He created man in His own image and spoke through the fathers and prophets. The apostles preached Him, and the disciples touched Him. We believe in God, the Lord, the Son of God, the Word made flesh, who took a body from Mary, the holy virgin, conceived by the Holy Spirit, not by fleshly desire but by God's will. He was born in Bethlehem, wrapped in swaddling clothes, grew up, reached maturity, and we witnessed it all.

{4:1} Our Lord Jesus Christ, sent by Joseph and Mary, was taught, and when asked to say "Alpha," He replied, "Tell me first what Beta is." This event is true and verified.

{5:1} There was a wedding in Cana of Galilee, where He was invited with His mother and brothers, and He turned water into wine. He raised the dead, made the lame walk, healed a man with a withered hand, and cured a woman with a twelve-year issue of blood who touched His garment. When we marveled at the miracle, He asked, "Who touched me?" We said, "Lord, the crowd is pressing against you." He replied, "I feel power has gone out from me." The woman confessed, and He told her, "Your faith has made you whole." He made the deaf hear, the blind see, cast out unclean spirits, and cleansed lepers. A man possessed by a legion of spirits cried out, and Jesus rebuked the spirit, sending it into swine, which then drowned. {5:2} He walked on the sea, calmed the winds and waves. When we had no money, He told us to catch a fish, and inside, we found a coin for the tax collector. When we had only five loaves and two fish, He fed five thousand men, plus women and children, with twelve baskets of leftovers. We wondered about the loaves, symbolizing our faith in the Almighty Father, Jesus Christ our Redeemer, the Holy Spirit the Comforter, the holy church, and the forgiveness of sins.

{6:1} Our Lord and Savior revealed and taught us these things so that you might share in His grace, our ministry, and our thanksgiving. Reflect on eternal life. Be steadfast and unwavering in your knowledge and faith in Jesus Christ, and He will have mercy on you and save you eternally.

{7:1} Cerinthus and Simon roam the world, but they are enemies of our Lord Jesus Christ. They distort the truth and faith in Jesus Christ. Stay away from them, for they bring death, corruption, and destruction, and judgment will come upon them.

{8:1} We did not hesitate to write to you about the testimony of Christ our Savior, what He did as we followed Him, and how He enlightened our understanding.

{9:1} We testify that the Lord, who was crucified by Pontius Pilate and Archelaus between two thieves, was buried in a place called Golgotha. Three women, Mary, the relative of Martha, and Mary Magdalene, went to the tomb with ointments to anoint His body, weeping over what had happened. When they arrived, they found the stone rolled away and the entrance open.

{10:1} As they mourned, the Lord appeared to them and asked, "Why do you weep? I am the one you seek. Let one of you go to your brethren and say, 'Come, the Master is risen from the dead.'" Martha told us, but we did not believe her. She returned to the Lord and said, "None of them believed me." He said, "Let another go and tell them." Mary told us again, and we still did not believe her, and she also returned to the Lord.

{11:1} Then the Lord said to Mary and her sisters, "Let us go to them." He found us inside and called us out, but we thought it was a ghost and did not believe it was the Lord. He said, "Do not be afraid. I am your Master, the one you, Peter, denied three times. Will you deny me again?" We approached Him, still doubting. He said, "Why do you doubt and disbelieve? I am the one who spoke of my flesh, death, and resurrection. To prove it, Peter, touch the nail prints in my hands, and Thomas, put your finger in the spear wound in my side. Andrew, look at my feet and see if they touch the ground, for a ghost leaves no footprints."

{12:1} We touched Him to see if He was truly risen in the flesh. We fell on our faces, confessing our unbelief. The Lord then said, "Rise, and I will reveal what is above the heavens and in the heavens, and your rest in the kingdom of heaven. My Father has given me the power to bring you there, along with all who believe in me."

{13:1} What He revealed to us is this: When I was about to come from the Father, I passed through the heavens and put on the wisdom and power of the Father. I passed by the archangels and angels in their forms, as if I were one of them, among the principalities and powers. They thought I was one of them because of the wisdom given to me by my Father. The chief angels, Michael, Gabriel, Uriel, and Raphael, followed me to the fifth heaven, thinking I was one of them. On that day, I adorned the archangels with a wonderful voice so they would go to the altar of the Father and serve until I returned to Him. I became all things to all beings to fulfill the glory of the Father who sent me and return to Him.

{14:1} You know that the angel Gabriel brought the message to Mary. We answered, "Yes, Lord." He replied, "Remember that I told you I became an angel among the angels and all things to all people? On that day, I took the form of Gabriel, appeared to Mary, and spoke with her. She accepted me in her heart and believed, and I entered her body, becoming flesh. I was my own messenger in the form of an angel, for this was necessary. Afterward, I returned to my Father."

{15:1} "Remember my death. When Passover comes, one of you will be imprisoned for my name's sake, and he will grieve because he cannot celebrate Passover with you. I will send my power as the angel Gabriel, the prison doors will open, and he will join you until the cock crows. After celebrating, he will be imprisoned again until he can preach my teachings." {15:2} We asked, "Lord, must we take the cup and drink again?" He replied, "Yes, until I come again with those who have been martyred for my sake."

{16:1} We asked, "Lord, how will you come? In what form?" He answered, "I will come like the rising sun, shining seven times brighter. The clouds will bear me, and the sign of the cross will go before me. I will come to judge the living and the dead."

{17:1} We asked, "When will this happen?" He said, "When a hundred and twenty years are fulfilled, between Pentecost and the Feast of Unleavened Bread, my Father will come." {17:2} We asked, "You say you will come, but also that the one who sent you will come. How is this?" He said, "I am in the Father, and the Father is in me. Just as I have been here, I have also been with Him. I am wholly in the Father, and the Father is in me because of our shared form, power, fullness, light, and voice. I am the Word, made complete in Him."

{18:1} After He was crucified, died, and rose again, fulfilling His work in the flesh, He said, "You will see the fulfillment of all things after redemption. You will see me ascend to my Father. Now, I give you a new commandment: Love one another and obey one another so that peace may always be among you. Love your enemies and do to no one what you would not want done to you."

{19:1} "Preach and teach those who believe in me about the kingdom of heaven and how my Father has given me the power to bring His children near. Preach so they may have faith and bring others to heaven." {19:2} We said, "Lord, you can accomplish this, but how can we?" He replied, "Preach as I command, for I will be with you. It is my pleasure to be with you, so you may inherit the kingdom of heaven. You will be my brothers and friends, and so will those who believe through you. Great joy is prepared for you, joy that even the angels desire to see but cannot behold. We asked, "Lord, what is this joy?" {19:3} He answered, "You will see a light brighter than any light, a perfect light. The Son will be perfected through the Father, who brings about death and resurrection. You will see me ascend to my Father in heaven. Now, I give you a new commandment: Love one another, and let peace rule among you. Love your enemies and do unto others as you would have them do unto you." {19:4} We said, "Lord, you have given us salvation and life by revealing this hope. He said, "Be courageous and rest in me. Your rest will be in a place without eating, drinking, or sorrow, where you will be received in the everlastingness of my Father. Just as I am in Him, you will be in me." {19:5} We asked, "In what form? As angels or in the flesh?" He answered, "I put on your flesh, was born, crucified, and rose again through my Father in heaven to fulfill David's prophecy about my death and resurrection: 'Lord, they have increased who fight against me; many rise up against me. Many say to my soul, 'There is no help for him in God.' But You, O Lord, are my defender, my glory, and the lifter of my head. I cried to the Lord with my voice, and He heard me from His holy hill. I lay down and slept; I awoke, for the Lord sustained me. I will not be afraid of ten thousand people who have set themselves against me. Arise, O Lord; save me, O my God. For You have struck all my enemies on the cheekbone; You have broken the teeth of the ungodly. Salvation belongs to the Lord. Your blessing is upon Your people.'" {19:6} "If all the words spoken by the prophets have been fulfilled in me, how much more will what I say to you come to pass, so that the one who sent me may be glorified by you and those who believe in me?"

{20:1} After He spoke to us, we said, "You have shown mercy and saved us, revealing all things. May we ask you something if you permit?" He replied, "I know you listen and are pleased to hear me. Regarding what you desire, I will speak good words to you."

{21:1} "Truly, just as my Father raised me from the dead, so shall you also rise and be taken to the highest heaven, the place prepared for you. I will fulfill all grace, even though I am unbegotten yet born of mankind, without flesh yet having borne flesh. I came so that you might rise from the dead in your flesh, in a second birth, with a body that will not decay, along with all who hope and believe in Him who sent me. This is my Father's will, that I give you and those who please me the hope of the kingdom." {21:2} We said, "Great is what you allow us to hope for and tell us." He asked, "Do you believe that everything I tell you will come to pass?" We answered, "Yes, Lord." He continued, "Truly, I have obtained all power from my Father to bring light to those in darkness, to turn corruption into incorruption, to bring life to the dead, and to free those in bondage. What is impossible with men is possible with the Father. I am the hope for the hopeless, the helper of the helpless, the wealth of the poor, the health of the sick, and the resurrection of the dead."

{22:1} We asked, "Lord, is it true that the flesh will be judged with the soul and spirit, and that one part will rest in heaven while the other is punished forever?" He replied, "How long will you inquire and doubt?"

{23:1} We said, "Lord, we need to inquire because you commanded us to preach. We need to learn from you to be effective preachers so that those we teach may believe in you. Therefore, we must inquire."

{24:1} He answered, "Truly, the resurrection of the flesh will happen with the soul and spirit. We asked, "Lord, is it possible for what is dissolved to become whole again? We ask not in unbelief but with faith." He was upset and said, "O you of little faith, how long will you question? Tell me what you will, and I will tell you without reluctance. Just keep my commandments, do what I bid, and turn not away from anyone, so I will not turn away from you. Serve without fear or favoritism, and my Father will rejoice over you."

{25:1} We said, "Lord, we are ashamed to burden you with questions." He answered, "I know you question me in faith and with your whole heart; this brings me joy. Truly, I rejoice, and my Father in me rejoices because you question me. Your persistence gives you life." We were glad and said, "Lord, you give us life and mercy in all things. Will you now answer what we ask?" He said, "Is it the flesh or the spirit that passes away?" We answered, "The flesh passes away." He replied, "What has fallen shall rise again, what was lost shall be found, and what was weak shall recover, so that the glory of my Father may be revealed. As He has done to me, so will I do to all who believe in me."

{26:1} "Truly, I say to you, the flesh shall rise, and the soul will live, so they may be judged for what they have done, whether good or evil. This will allow the faithful who kept my Father's commandments to be chosen, and judgment will be strict. My Father told me: 'On judgment day, do not show favor to the rich or pity the poor. Judge each person according to their sins and deliver them to eternal torment. But to my beloved who followed my Father's commandments, I will give eternal life in the kingdom of heaven, where they will see what He has given me. He gave me the authority to do as I will and to grant what I have promised.'"

{27:1} "I went to the place of Lazarus to preach to the righteous and prophets, so they could rise from the rest below to the place above. I gave them the water of life, forgiveness, and salvation, just as I have done for you and those who believe in me. But if anyone believes in me yet does not follow my commandments, even if they confess my name, they gain nothing and run in vain. Such people will face perdition and destruction for despising my commandments."

{28:1} "I have redeemed you, children of light, from all evil and the rulers' authority, and everyone who believes in me through your message. I will give them what I promised you, so they may be freed from the prison and fetters of the rulers. We responded, 'Lord, you have given us the rest of life and joy through wonders, confirming our faith. Will you now preach the same to us, as you did to the righteous and prophets?' He replied, 'Truly, all who believe in me and in Him who sent me will be taken to heaven, to the place my Father prepared for the elect. I will give you the chosen kingdom, in rest and everlasting life.'"

{29:1} "But those who disobey my commandments and teach false doctrines, perverting Scripture for their own glory and leading believers astray, will receive everlasting punishment. We asked, 'Lord, will there be teachings different from what you have told us?' He said, 'It must be so, to reveal the good and evil, and judgment will be upon those who do such things, according to their deeds, and they will be delivered to death.'" {29:2} "We said, 'Lord, we are blessed to see and hear you declaring these things, witnessing the great wonders you have done.' He replied, 'Yes, but more blessed are those who have not seen and yet believed, for they shall be called children of the kingdom, perfect among the perfect, and I will be their life in my Father's kingdom.'"

{30:1} "We asked, 'Lord, how will people believe that you will leave us, as you say there will come a day and hour when you ascend to your Father?' He answered, 'Go and preach to the twelve tribes, and to the heathen, across all the land of Israel from east to west, and from south to north. Many will believe in me, the Son of God.' We asked, 'Lord, who will believe us or listen to us? How can we perform the signs and wonders you have done?' He said, 'Go and preach the mercy of my Father. What He did through me, I will do through you, for I am in you. I will give you my peace and the power of my spirit so you may prophesy to them for eternal life. I will also give others my power, so they may teach the remaining peoples.'"

{31:1} "A man named Saul, who will be called Paul, will meet you. He is a Jew, circumcised according to the law, and he will hear my voice from heaven with fear and trembling. His eyes will be blinded, and by your hands and the sign of the cross, they will be healed. Do for him what I have done for you. Deliver my word to him, and he will open his eyes and praise the Lord, my Father in heaven. He will gain power among the people and will preach and instruct, leading many to glory and redemption. But later, people will be angry with him and hand him over to his enemies. He will testify before kings and, in the end, will turn to me, even though he once persecuted me. He will preach and teach, staying with the elect as a chosen vessel and an unbreakable wall. The last of the last will become a preacher to the Gentiles, perfected by my Father's will. As the prophets spoke of me in Scripture, it will be fulfilled."

{32:1} "He told us, 'You will also be guides to them. Tell them all that I have said to you and written about me, that I am the word of the Father and the Father is in me. You should be to this man as you ought to be, instructing him and reminding him of what is spoken of me in the Scriptures and fulfilled, so he can become the salvation of the Gentiles.' We asked, 'Lord, do we and they have the same expectation of inheritance?' He answered, 'Are the fingers of a hand alike, or the ears of corn in a field, or do all fruit trees bear the same fruit? Each bears fruit according to its nature.' We said, 'Lord, will you speak to us in parables again?' He replied, 'Do not lament. Truly, you are my brethren and companions in the kingdom of heaven with my Father, for this is His good pleasure. Truly, I say to you, I will give the same expectation to those you teach and who believe in me.'"

{33:1} "We asked again, 'When will we meet this man, and when will you depart to your Father and our God and Lord?' He answered, 'This man will come from the land of Cilicia to Damascus of Syria to uproot the church you must establish there. I speak through you, and he will come quickly, becoming strong in faith, fulfilling the prophecy: 'Out of Syria, I will call together a new Jerusalem, and I will subdue Zion to myself, making it a child of my Father and my bride.' I will turn him back so he does not accomplish his evil desire, and my Father's praise will be perfected in him. After I return to my Father, I will speak to him from heaven, and all things I have told you about him will be accomplished.'"

{34:1} "We said to him, 'Lord, you have revealed great things to us and given us rest and grace. After your resurrection, you revealed all things so we might be saved. But you said there would be wonders and strange signs in heaven and on earth before the end of the world. How will we recognize them?' He answered, 'I will teach you. Not only what will happen to you but also to those you teach and who believe, as well as those who hear that man and believe in me. These things will happen in those years and days.' We asked, 'Lord, what will happen?' He said, 'Believers and non-believers will hear a trumpet in heaven, see a vision of great stars visible in the day, wonderful sights in heaven reaching down to earth; stars falling like fire, and a great hail of fire. The sun and moon will fight each other, there will be continuous thunder and lightning, earthquakes, cities falling, and people perishing. There will be a continuous drought, terrible pestilence, and great mortality, so the dead will lack burial. Brothers and sisters will be buried together, and kin will show no favor to each other. The pestilence will be full of hatred, pain, and envy, with men taking from one and giving to another. It will get worse than before. Those who did not listen to my commandments will suffer greatly.'"

{35:1} "My Father will be angry at the wickedness of men, for their many transgressions and the abomination of their uncleanness weigh heavily on them. We asked, 'What about those who trust in you?' He answered, 'You are slow of heart; how long will you take to understand? Truly, as the prophet David spoke of me and my people, so it will be for those who believe in me. But deceivers and enemies of righteousness will face the fulfillment of David's prophecy: 'Their feet are swift to shed blood, their tongues utter slander, adders' poison is under their lips. I see you associating with thieves and adulterers, speaking against your brother and putting stumbling blocks before your own mother's son. Do you think I will be like you? Look how the prophet of God spoke of all things to be fulfilled as he said before.'"

{36:1} "We asked him, 'Lord, won't the nations say, "Where is their God?"' He replied, 'The elect will be known because they will endure such afflictions and come forth. We asked, 'Will their departure from the world be due to a painful pestilence?' He answered, 'No, but if they suffer such affliction, it will test their faith and whether they remember my words and follow my commandments. They will rise, and their expectation will be short, so that the one who sent me will be glorified, and I with him. He sent me to tell you these things, so you can share them with Israel and the Gentiles, so they may hear, be redeemed, believe in me, and escape destruction. Those who escape death will be held in torment, like a thief in prison.' We asked, 'Lord, will believers be treated like unbelievers and punished after escaping the pestilence?' He said, 'If believers act like sinners, it is as if they did not believe.' We asked again, 'Lord, do those who suffer this fate have no life?' He answered, 'Those who fulfill the praise of my Father will remain in His resting place.'"

{37:1} "We asked, 'Lord, what will happen after this?' He replied, 'In those days, wars will break out, and the four corners of the earth will be in turmoil, fighting against each other. There will be clouds, darkness, famine, and persecution of those who believe in me and the elect. Doubt, strife, and transgressions will arise. Many will believe in my name but follow evil and spread false doctrine. People will follow them, seeking riches and being subject to pride, lust for drink, and bribery, with respect for persons among them.'"

{38:1} "But those who desire to see the face of God and do not respect the rich sinners, nor are ashamed before those who lead them astray, but rebuke them, will be crowned by the Father. Those who rebuke their neighbors will also be saved, for they are children of wisdom and faith. However, if they do not become children of wisdom, those who hate and persecute their brother and show no favor will be despised and rejected by God. Those who walk in truth and the knowledge of faith, and love me, enduring insults, will be praised for their poverty and endurance. Though they are despised and stripped naked, they will have the blessedness of heaven and be with me forever. But woe to those who walk in pride and boasting, for their end is perdition.'"

{39:1} "We asked him, 'Lord, is it your intention to leave us for these things to come upon them?' He responded, 'How will the judgment be, whether righteous or unrighteous?' We said, 'Lord, in that day, will they not say, "You have not distinguished between righteousness and unrighteousness, between light and darkness, good and evil?"' He said, 'I will answer them: To Adam was given the power to choose; he chose the light and cast away the darkness. Therefore, everyone has the power to believe in the light, which is life, sent by the Father. Those who believe and do the works of light will live in it. But those who claim to belong to the light and do the works of darkness have no defense and cannot look upon the Son of God, who I am. I will say to them: As you sought, so you found; as you asked, so you received. Do you condemn me, O man? Why did you depart from and deny me? Have not all men the power to live and die? Those who keep my commandments will be children of the light, of the Father in me. But because of those who corrupt my words, I came down from heaven. I am the word made flesh, I suffered and taught, saying: The heavy laden shall be saved, and those who go astray will be lost forever. They will be chastised and tormented in their flesh and soul.'"

{40:1} "We said to him, 'Lord, we are truly sorrowful for their sake.' He replied, 'You do well, for the righteous are sorry for the sinners and pray for them, making intercession to my Father.' We asked, 'Lord, is there no one who makes intercession for them?' He said, 'Yes, and I will listen to the prayer of the righteous on their behalf.' When he had said this, we told him, 'Lord, you have taught us all things, shown us mercy, and saved us, so we might preach to those worthy of salvation and obtain a reward with you.'"

{41:1} "He told us, 'Go and preach. You will be laborers, fathers, and ministers.' We asked, 'Lord, are you the one who will preach through us?' He answered, 'Are you not all fathers or all masters?' We reminded him, 'Lord, you told us not to call anyone on earth our father, for we have one Father in heaven and one Master. Why do you now say we will be fathers, servants, and masters?' He replied, 'You have spoken correctly. Whoever hears you and believes in me will receive the light of the seal and baptism through me. You will be fathers, servants, and masters.'"

{42:1} "We asked, 'Lord, how can each of us be all three?' He explained, 'You will be called fathers because you reveal the kingdom of heaven with a praiseworthy heart and love. You will be called servants because you administer the baptism of life and remission of sins through me. You will be called masters because you give the word without hesitation and admonish those who turn away. You are not afraid of their riches or ashamed before them, but you keep my Father's commandments. You will have a great reward in heaven, and they will have forgiveness and everlasting life in the kingdom of heaven.' We said, 'Lord, even if we had ten thousand tongues, we could not thank you enough for these promises.' He replied, 'Just do what I say, as I have done.'"

{43:1} "He continued, 'You will be like the wise virgins who watched and did not sleep, entering the bridechamber with the lord. The foolish virgins could not watch and fell asleep. We asked, 'Lord, who are the wise and foolish?' He said, 'The wise are Faith, Love, Grace, Peace, and Hope. They will guide those who believe in me and the one who sent me. I am the Lord and the bridegroom, and they have entered the bridegroom's house and rejoice with me. The foolish, when they awoke, knocked on the door, but it was shut. They wept and lamented because no one opened the door.' We asked, 'Lord, did their wise sisters inside not open the door or plead with the bridegroom?' He replied, 'They could not obtain favor for them yet.' We asked, 'Lord, when will they enter for their sisters' sake?' He said, 'Those shut out will remain shut out.' We asked, 'Lord, who are the foolish?' He replied, 'They are Knowledge, Understanding, Obedience, Patience, and Compassion. They believed and confessed me but did not fulfill my commandments. Because of their slumber, they will remain outside the kingdom, and the wolves will devour them.'"

{44:1} "We said, 'Lord, you have revealed everything to us.' He replied, 'Do you understand these words?' We said, 'Yes, Lord. By five will people enter your kingdom, and by five will people be shut out. The wise will be with you, rejoicing, but they will also be sorrowful for their sisters who slumbered. All ten are daughters of God, the Father.' We asked, 'Lord, will you show favor to them for their sisters' sake?' He replied, 'It is not mine to give, but His who sent me.'"

{45:1} "He told us, 'Be upright, preach rightly, and teach. Do not fear any man, especially the rich, for they do not follow my commandments but boast in their riches.' We asked, 'Lord, is it only the rich?' He replied, 'If someone who is not rich gives to the poor and needy, they are called a benefactor.'"

{46:1} "He continued, 'If someone falls into sin, their neighbor should correct them because of the good they have done. If the sinner repents, they will be saved, and the neighbor who corrected them will receive a reward and live forever. If a needy person sees their benefactor sinning and does not correct them, they will be judged severely. If a blind man leads a blind man, both fall into a ditch. Those who respect persons for their sake will be like the blind. As the prophet said, woe to those who respect persons and justify the ungodly for reward. Their God is their belly, and judgment will be their portion. On that day, I will neither respect the rich nor pity the poor.'"

{47:1} "If someone falls into sin, their neighbor should correct them because of the good they have done. If the sinner repents, they will be saved, and the neighbor who corrected them will be rewarded and live forever. If a needy person sees their benefactor sinning and does not correct them, they will be judged severely. If a blind man leads a blind man, both will fall into a ditch. Those who show favoritism will be like the blind. As the prophet said, 'Woe to those who justify the ungodly for a reward, whose God is their belly.' They will face judgment. On that day, I will neither show respect to the rich nor pity the poor."

{48:1} "If you see a sinner, admonish them privately. If they listen, you have gained a brother. If they do not, take one or two others and instruct them. If they still do not listen, treat them as a heathen or a tax collector."

{49:1} "If you hear something against your brother, do not believe it. Do not slander or take pleasure in hearing slander. As it is written, 'Do not let your ears receive anything against your brother.' If you see something wrong, correct, rebuke, and convert him."

{50:1} "We asked, 'Lord, you have taught us well, but among the believers, will there be doubt, division, jealousy, confusion, hatred, and envy? You said they would find fault with each other, respect sinners, and hate those who rebuke them.' He answered, 'How else will the judgment come, where the wheat is gathered and the chaff is burned?' Those who hate such things, love me, and rebuke those who do not follow my commandments will be hated, persecuted, despised, and mocked. People will spread lies about them and band together against those who love me. Yet, those who rebuke them will be trying to save them. The rebukers will be hated, shunned, and despised by those who need correction. But those who endure this will be like martyrs with the Father, for they have strived for righteousness, not corruption.'"

{51:1} "We asked, 'Lord, will this happen among us?' He replied, 'Fear not; it will happen to only a few.' We asked, 'How will it happen?' He said, 'Another doctrine will arise, causing confusion. People will seek their own advancement and teach an unprofitable doctrine, leading believers away from my commandments and cutting them off from eternal life. Woe to those who falsify my word and commandments, leading others away from the doctrine of life. They will face everlasting judgment together with their followers.'"

{52:1} "When he finished speaking, he told us, 'On the third day at the third hour, the one who sent me will come, and I will depart with him.' As he spoke, there was thunder, lightning, and an earthquake. The heavens parted, and a bright cloud lifted him up. We heard the voices of many angels rejoicing and singing praises, saying, 'Gather us, O Priest, into the light of majesty.' As they approached the firmament, we heard his voice saying, 'Depart in peace.'"

Pre-Markan Passion Narrative

The Pre-Markan Passion Narrative, often referred to in scholarly literature, is a hypothesized source believed to predate the Gospel of Mark. This source is thought to have significantly influenced the Passion narratives found in the Synoptic Gospels—Matthew, Mark, and Luke. The narrative likely originated within the early Christian communities and circulated orally or in written form before being incorporated into the canonical Gospels. Scholars suggest that this early account of Jesus' suffering, crucifixion, and death provided a foundational framework for the later Gospel writers. The Pre-Markan Passion Narrative is posited to contain specific elements that exhibit a more primitive theological understanding and stylistic features compared to the more developed theological reflections found in the canonical Gospels. Critical analysis of the Synoptic texts, particularly Mark's account, reveals structural and thematic consistencies that suggest reliance on this earlier source. These include details of Jesus' arrest, trial, crucifixion, and burial, with particular emphasis on his suffering and fulfillment of Old Testament prophecies. The exploration of this hypothesized narrative offers valuable insights into the early Christian community's beliefs, the process of Gospel formation, and the historical Jesus. It underscores the significance of the Passion events in early Christian theology and the role of oral tradition in shaping the New Testament texts. By examining the textual and thematic traces of the Pre-Markan Passion Narrative, scholars can better understand the evolution of the Gospel traditions and the early Christian portrayal of Jesus' final days.

- **14:32** They went to a place called Gethsemane, and Jesus said to his disciples, "Sit here while I pray."
- **14:33** He took Peter, James, and John with him and began to be deeply distressed and troubled.
- **14:34** He said to them, "My soul is overwhelmed with sorrow to the point of death. Stay here and keep watch."
- **14:35** Going a little farther, he fell to the ground and prayed that, if possible, the hour might pass from him.
- **14:36** He said, "Abba, Father, everything is possible for you. Take this cup from me. Yet not what I will, but what you will."
- **14:37** Returning, he found them sleeping. He said to Peter, "Simon, are you asleep? Couldn't you keep watch for one hour?"
- **14:38** "Watch and pray so that you will not fall into temptation. The spirit is willing, but the flesh is weak."
- **14:39** Once more he went away and prayed the same thing.
- **14:40** When he came back, he found them sleeping again, for their eyes were heavy, and they did not know what to say to him.
- **14:41** Returning the third time, he said to them, "Are you still sleeping and resting? Enough! The hour has come. Look, the Son of Man is delivered into the hands of sinners."
- **14:42** "Rise, let us go. Here comes my betrayer."
- **14:43** Just as he was speaking, Judas, one of the Twelve, arrived. With him was a crowd armed with swords and clubs, sent by the chief priests, the teachers of the law, and the elders.
- **14:44** Now the betrayer had arranged a signal with them: "The one I kiss is the man; arrest him and lead him away under guard."
- **14:45** Going at once to Jesus, Judas said, "Rabbi!" and kissed him.
- **14:46** The men seized Jesus and arrested him.
- **14:47** Then one of those standing near drew his sword and struck the servant of the high priest, cutting off his ear.
- **14:48** "Am I leading a rebellion," Jesus said, "that you have come out with swords and clubs to capture me?"
- **14:49** "Every day I was with you, teaching in the temple courts, and you did not arrest me. But the Scriptures must be fulfilled."
- **14:50** Then everyone deserted him and fled.
- **14:51** A young man, wearing nothing but a linen cloth, was following Jesus. When the crowd seized him,
- **14:52** he fled naked, leaving his linen cloth behind.
- **14:53** They took Jesus to the high priest, and all the chief priests, elders, and teachers of the law came together.
- **14:54** Peter followed him at a distance, right into the courtyard of the high priest. There he sat with the guards and warmed himself at the fire.
- **14:55** The chief priests and the whole Sanhedrin were looking for evidence against Jesus so that they could put him to death, but they did not find any.
- **14:56** Many testified falsely against him, but their statements did not agree.
- **14:57** Then some stood up and gave this false testimony against him:
- **14:58** "We heard him say, 'I will destroy this temple made with human hands and in three days will build another, not made with hands.'"
- **14:59** Yet even then their testimony did not agree.
- **14:60** Then the high priest stood up before them and asked Jesus, "Aren't you going to answer? What is this testimony that these men are bringing against you?"
- **14:61** But Jesus remained silent and gave no answer. Again the high priest asked him, "Are you the Messiah, the Son of the Blessed One?"
- **14:62** "I am," said Jesus. "And you will see the Son of Man sitting at the right hand of the Mighty One and coming on the clouds of heaven."
- **14:63** The high priest tore his clothes. "Why do we need any more witnesses?" he asked.
- **14:64** "You have heard the blasphemy. What do you think?" They all condemned him as worthy of death.
- **14:65** Then some began to spit at him; they blindfolded him, struck him with their fists, and said, "Prophesy!" And the guards took him and beat him.
- **14:66** While Peter was below in the courtyard, one of the servant girls of the high priest came by.
- **14:67** When she saw Peter warming himself, she looked closely at him and said, "You also were with that Nazarene Jesus."
- **14:68** But he denied it. "I don't know or understand what you're talking about," he said, and he went out into the entryway.
- **14:69** When the servant girl saw him there, she said again to those standing around, "This fellow is one of them."
- **14:70** Again he denied it. After a little while, those standing near said to Peter, "Surely you are one of them, for you are a Galilean."
- **14:71** He began to call down curses, and he swore to them, "I don't know this man you're talking about."
- **14:72** Immediately the cock crowed the second time. Then Peter remembered the word Jesus had spoken to him: "Before the cock crows twice, you will disown me three times." And he broke down and wept.
- **15:1** Very early in the morning, the chief priests with the elders, teachers of the law, and the whole Sanhedrin made their plans. So they bound Jesus, led him away, and handed him over to Pilate.

- **15:2** "Are you the king of the Jews?" asked Pilate. "You have said so," Jesus replied.
- **15:3** The chief priests accused him of many things.
- **15:4** So again Pilate asked him, "Aren't you going to answer? See how many things they are accusing you of!"
- **15:5** But Jesus still made no reply, and Pilate was amazed.
- **15:6** Now it was the custom at the festival to release a prisoner whom the people requested.
- **15:7** A man called Barabbas was in prison with the insurrectionists who had committed murder during the uprising.
- **15:8** The crowd came up and asked Pilate to do for them what he usually did.
- **15:9** "Do you want me to release to you the king of the Jews?" asked Pilate,
- **15:10** knowing it was out of self-interest that the chief priests had handed Jesus over to him.
- **15:11** But the chief priests stirred up the crowd to have Pilate release Barabbas instead.
- **15:12** "What shall I do, then, with the one you call the king of the Jews?" Pilate asked them.
- **15:13** "Crucify him!" they shouted.
- **15:14** "Why? What crime has he committed?" asked Pilate. But they shouted all the louder, "Crucify him!"
- **15:15** Wanting to satisfy the crowd, Pilate released Barabbas to them. He had Jesus flogged, and handed him over to be crucified.
- **15:16** The soldiers led Jesus away into the palace (that is the Praetorium) and called together the whole company of soldiers.
- **15:17** They put a purple robe on him, then twisted together a crown of thorns and set it on him.
- **15:18** And they began to call out to him, "Hail, King of the Jews!"
- **15:19** Again and again they struck him on the head with a staff and spit on him. Falling on their knees, they paid homage to him.
- **15:20** And when they had mocked him, they took off the purple robe and put his own clothes on him. Then they led him out to crucify him.
- **15:21** A certain man from Cyrene, Simon, the father of Alexander and Rufus, was passing by on his way in from the country, and they forced him to carry the cross.
- **15:22** They brought Jesus to the place called Golgotha (which means "The Place of the Skull").
- **15:23** Then they offered him wine mixed with myrrh, but he did not take it.
- **15:24** And they crucified him. Dividing up his clothes, they cast lots to see what each would get.
- **15:25** It was nine in the morning when they crucified him.
- **15:26** The written notice of the charge against him read: THE KING OF THE JEWS.
- **15:27** They crucified two rebels with him, one on his right and one on his left.
- **15:29** Those who passed by hurled insults at him, shaking their heads and saying, "So! You who are going to destroy the temple and build it in three days,
- **15:30** come down from the cross and save yourself!"
- **15:31** In the same way the chief priests and the teachers of the law mocked him among themselves. "He saved others," they said, "but he can't save himself!
- **15:32** Let this Messiah, this king of Israel, come down now from the cross, that we may see and believe." Those crucified with him also heaped insults on him.
- **15:33** At noon, darkness came over the whole land until three in the afternoon.
- **15:34** And at three in the afternoon Jesus cried out in a loud voice, "Eloi, Eloi, lema sabachthani?" (which means "My God, my God, why have you forsaken me?").
- **15:35** When some of those standing near heard this, they said, "Listen, he's calling Elijah."
- **15:36** Someone ran, filled a sponge with wine vinegar, put it on a staff, and offered it to Jesus to drink. "Now leave him alone. Let's see if Elijah comes to take him down," he said.
- **15:37** With a loud cry, Jesus breathed his last.
- **15:38** The curtain of the temple was torn in two from top to bottom.
- **15:39** And when the centurion, who stood there in front of Jesus, heard his cry and saw how he died, he said, "Surely this man was the Son of God!"
- **15:40** Some women were watching from a distance. Among them were Mary Magdalene, Mary the mother of James the younger and of Joses, and Salome.
- **15:41** In Galilee, these women had followed him and cared for his needs. Many other women who had come up with him to Jerusalem were also there.
- **15:42** It was Preparation Day (that is, the day before the Sabbath). So as evening approached,
- **15:43** Joseph of Arimathea, a prominent member of the Council, who was himself waiting for the kingdom of God, went boldly to Pilate and asked for Jesus' body.
- **15:44** Pilate was surprised to hear that he was already dead. Summoning the centurion, he asked him if Jesus had already died.
- **15:45** When he learned from the centurion that it was so, he gave the body to Joseph.
- **15:46** So Joseph bought some linen cloth, took down the body, wrapped it in the linen, and placed it in a tomb cut out of rock. Then he rolled a stone against the entrance of the tomb.
- **15:47** Mary Magdalene and Mary the mother of Joses saw where he was laid.

Athanasian Creed

The Athanasian Creed, also known as the Quicunque Vult, stands as a significant doctrinal statement within the Christian tradition, particularly revered in Western Christianity. Originating in the early centuries of the Church, this creed is traditionally attributed to Athanasius of Alexandria, a staunch defender of Nicene orthodoxy and a pivotal figure in early Christian theological development. However, modern scholarship largely discredits this attribution, suggesting instead that the creed was composed in the Latin West around the 5th or 6th century. The Athanasian Creed is distinguished by its detailed exposition of Trinitarian doctrine and Christology, emphasizing the co-equality and co-eternity of the Father, Son, and Holy Spirit, while also affirming the full divinity and full humanity of Jesus Christ. Its uncompromising tone underscores the necessity of holding these beliefs for salvation, reflecting the theological and ecclesiastical concerns of its time, particularly against Arianism and other Christological heresies. The creed's precise and elaborate formulations reflect the broader patristic tradition's efforts to articulate the mystery of the Trinity and the incarnation in response to various doctrinal controversies. Despite its historical and theological importance, the Athanasian Creed is not as widely recited in contemporary liturgical practice as the Nicene or Apostles' Creeds, yet it remains a crucial text for understanding the development of Christian doctrinal orthodoxy and the Church's response to early heretical challenges.

{1:1} Anyone who wants to be saved must first hold the Catholic faith. {1:2} Unless everyone keeps this faith whole and undefiled, they will undoubtedly be lost forever. {1:3} The Catholic faith is this: We worship one God in Trinity and Trinity in Unity. {1:4} We must not confuse the persons or divide the substance. {1:5} The Father is one person, the Son is another, and the Holy Spirit is another. {1:6} Yet the divinity of the Father, Son, and Holy Spirit is one, their glory is equal, and their majesty is coeternal. {1:7} What the Father is, the Son is, and the Holy Spirit is. {1:8} The Father is uncreated, the Son is uncreated, and the Holy Spirit is uncreated. {1:9} The Father is incomprehensible, the Son is incomprehensible, and the Holy Spirit is incomprehensible. {1:10} The Father is eternal, the Son is eternal, and the Holy Spirit is eternal. {1:11} Yet there are not three eternals but one eternal. {1:12} Similarly, there are not three uncreated beings or three incomprehensible beings, but one uncreated and one incomprehensible. {1:13} The Father is almighty, the Son is almighty, and the Holy Spirit is almighty. {1:14} Yet there are not three almighties, but one almighty. {1:15} The Father is God, the Son is God, and the Holy Spirit is God; {1:16} yet there are not three Gods, but one God. {1:17} Similarly, the Father is Lord, the Son is Lord, and the Holy Spirit is Lord; {1:18} and yet there are not three Lords, but one Lord. {1:19} As we are compelled by Christian truth to acknowledge each Person as God and Lord; {1:20} so by Catholic doctrine, we must not say there are three Gods or three Lords. {1:21} The Father is not made, nor created, nor begotten. {1:22} The Son is from the Father alone; not made or created, but begotten. {1:23} The Holy Spirit is from the Father and the Son; neither made, created, nor begotten, but proceeding. {1:24} Thus, there is one Father, not three Fathers; one Son, not three Sons; one Holy Spirit, not three Holy Spirits. {1:25} In this Trinity, none is before or after another; none is greater or less than another. {1:26} But all three persons are coeternal and coequal. {1:27} Therefore, in all things, the Unity in Trinity and the Trinity in Unity is to be worshipped. {1:28} Therefore, anyone who wishes to be saved must think of the Trinity in this way. {1:29} It is also necessary for eternal salvation to rightly believe in the incarnation of our Lord Jesus Christ. {1:30} The correct faith is that we believe and confess that our Lord Jesus Christ, the Son of God, is both God and man. {1:31} God by the substance of the Father, begotten before the worlds; and man by the substance of His mother, born in the world. {1:32} Perfect God and perfect man, with a reasonable soul and human flesh. {1:33} Equal to the Father in His divinity, and inferior to the Father in His humanity. {1:34} Although He is both God and man, He is not two Christs but one Christ. {1:35} One, not by changing divinity into flesh, but by taking on humanity into God. {1:36} One altogether, not by mixing substances, but by the unity of His person. {1:37} Just as the reasonable soul and flesh make one man, so God and man make one Christ. {1:38} He suffered for our salvation, descended into hell, rose again from the dead on the third day; {1:39} He ascended into heaven, and sits at the right hand of God the Father Almighty; {1:40} from there He will come to judge the living and the dead. {1:41} At His coming, all people will rise with their bodies; {1:42} and they will give an account of their works. {1:43} Those who have done good will enter eternal life, and those who have done evil will enter everlasting fire. {1:44} This is the Catholic faith; unless a person believes it faithfully, they cannot be saved.

Avenging of the Saviour

The Avenging of the Saviour, also known as "Vindicta Salvatoris," is an intriguing piece of medieval Christian apocryphal literature. This text, which emerged in the context of the burgeoning Christendom of late antiquity or the early Middle Ages, reflects the cultural and theological concerns of its time. The narrative centers on the retributive justice exacted by the Roman Emperor Tiberius and the Apostle Peter against the perpetrators of Christ's crucifixion, namely the Jewish authorities and the people of Jerusalem. This work is imbued with a palpable sense of divine retribution and serves as a theological assertion of Christ's enduring power and the ultimate victory of Christianity over its adversaries. The story weaves together historical figures, such as Tiberius and Pilate, with legendary embellishments, creating a dramatic tableau that underscores the inevitability of divine justice. The text is part of a broader tradition of apocryphal writings that sought to fill in the gaps left by canonical Gospels, offering readers imaginative expansions on the life and aftermath of Jesus Christ. It is significant for its reflection of the polemical attitudes of early Christians toward Judaism and its role in shaping medieval Christian thought. Furthermore, "The Avenging of the Saviour" provides valuable insights into the ways early Christian communities interpreted and reimagined their sacred history, blending it with contemporary socio-political narratives to reinforce their religious convictions and identity. This apocryphal account, though not part of the canonical scriptures, provides valuable insight into the devotional and doctrinal concerns of its time, making it significant for scholars of early Christian literature and theology.

- In the days of Emperor Tiberius Caesar, when Herod was tetrarch, Christ was delivered by the Jews to Pontius Pilate and revealed to Tiberius.
- During this time, Titus was a prince under Tiberius in the region of Equitania, in a city called Burgidalla in Libya. Titus had a severe sore in his right nostril due to a cancer, which disfigured his face up to his eye. A man from Judea, named Nathan, the son of Nahum, an Ishmaelite, traveled extensively across the lands and seas. Nathan was sent from Judea to Emperor Tiberius in Rome with a treaty. Tiberius was ill, suffering from ulcers and nine kinds of leprosy. Nathan's journey was diverted by a strong north wind, bringing him to a harbor in Libya. Titus, recognizing the ship from Judea, was curious and summoned the captain, who introduced himself as Nathan, sent by Pontius Pilate in Judea to deliver a treaty to Tiberius but blown off course by the wind.
- Titus, desperate for a cure for his disfigurement, asked Nathan if he knew of any remedies. Nathan responded that he knew nothing of such cures but mentioned a prophet named Emmanuel from Jerusalem, who had performed numerous miracles, including turning water into wine, cleansing lepers, healing the blind and paralyzed, casting out demons, and raising the dead. This prophet, after being crucified and buried, rose again on the third day, descended to Hades to free the patriarchs and prophets, appeared to his disciples, and ascended to heaven.
- Upon hearing this, Titus lamented that Emperor Tiberius, afflicted with ulcers and leprosy, had allowed such an injustice in his kingdom without bringing this healer to them. As he spoke, Titus' wound miraculously healed, and many other sick people in the vicinity were also cured. Titus, in gratitude and belief, declared his intention to travel to the land of Jesus' birth to avenge His death and asked to be baptized. Nathan baptized Titus in the name of the Father, Son, and Holy Spirit.
- Titus then sent for Vespasian, who brought five thousand soldiers to join him. They set sail to Jerusalem, besieging and destroying the city. Fear and famine struck the Jewish kings, leading Archelaus to take his own life. The soldiers, seeing no hope, decided to kill themselves rather than be defeated by the Romans.
- The remaining Jews, unable to bury their dead, surrendered to Titus and Vespasian, acknowledging their guilt in condemning Christ. Titus and Vespasian executed many Jews, sold others, and divided the spoils among themselves. They then searched for and found Veronica, who had a portrait of Jesus. Pilate was imprisoned, and Velosianus was sent to Rome with the portrait to seek a disciple of Jesus who could heal Tiberius.
- Velosianus sailed for over a year, eventually arriving in Jerusalem and learning of Jesus' miracles and resurrection from Joseph of Arimathea, Nicodemus, and Veronica. He rebuked Pilate for his role in Jesus' death and took the portrait of Jesus back to Rome. Tiberius, upon seeing the portrait, was healed of his leprosy and other ailments, as were many others present. Tiberius, now a believer, was baptized by Nathan and praised God for his healing and salvation.
- Tiberius vowed to follow Christ faithfully and thanked God for delivering him from sin and illness. He expressed his commitment to the faith and prayed for protection and eternal life, ending his reign with gratitude and devotion to God Almighty. Amen.

Glossary

The glossary section contains definitions and meanings for a wide range of Christian terms organized alphabetically from A to Z. Each term is explained in detail to provide a clear understanding of its meaning and usage.

A

Apostle: One of the original 12 disciples chosen by Jesus to follow Him and spread His teachings. The term can also refer to other significant early Christian missionaries like Paul.
Ascension: The event where Jesus was taken up to heaven 40 days after His resurrection, as described in the New Testament.

B

Baptism: A Christian sacrament of initiation and purification, typically involving the immersion in or sprinkling with water, symbolizing the washing away of sin and entry into the Christian community.
Beatitudes: A series of blessings pronounced by Jesus in the Sermon on the Mount, found in the Gospel of Matthew (Matthew 5:3-12).
Bible: The holy scriptures of Christianity, consisting of the Old Testament and the New Testament.

C

Christ: The title given to Jesus, meaning "the Anointed One." It is derived from the Greek word "Christos" and is equivalent to the Hebrew term "Messiah."
Christian: A follower of Jesus Christ and adherent of Christianity.
Church: The community of Christian believers worldwide. It can also refer to a local congregation or the building where Christians gather for worship.
Communion: Also known as the Eucharist or the Lord's Supper, it is a sacrament commemorating the Last Supper of Jesus with His disciples, involving the eating of bread and drinking of wine (or grape juice).

D

Disciple: A follower or student of a teacher. In Christianity, it commonly refers to the followers of Jesus, especially the original twelve.

E

Epistle: A letter or written communication, particularly those found in the New Testament, such as the letters written by Paul to various Christian communities.
Evangelism: The act of preaching or spreading the Christian gospel.

F

Faith: Trust or belief in God and the doctrines of Christianity, often without empirical evidence.
Fellowship: The companionship and mutual support among Christians, often expressed in community worship, study, and activities.

G

Gospel: The "good news" of Jesus Christ's life, death, and resurrection. It also refers to the first four books of the New Testament (Matthew, Mark, Luke, and John) that recount Jesus' life and teachings.
Grace: The free and unmerited favor of God, as manifested in the salvation of sinners and the bestowal of blessings.

H

Holy Spirit: The third person of the Trinity, who is believed to dwell in and empower believers.
Holy Trinity: The Christian doctrine that God exists as three persons (Father, Son, and Holy Spirit) in one divine essence.

I

Incarnation: The belief that God became flesh in the person of Jesus Christ.

J

Justification: The act by which God declares a sinner righteous through their faith in Jesus Christ.

K

Kingdom of God: The reign of God, both in the hearts of believers and in the eventual establishment of God's will on earth as it is in heaven.

L

Liturgy: The customary public worship performed by a religious group, particularly by Christians in their churches.

M

Messiah: The promised deliverer of the Jewish nation prophesied in the Hebrew Bible. Christians believe Jesus is the Messiah.

Missionary: A person sent to spread the Christian faith in foreign lands.

N

New Testament: The second part of the Christian Bible, detailing the life and teachings of Jesus and the early Christian church.

O

Old Testament: The first part of the Christian Bible, corresponding to the Hebrew Bible, containing the religious writings of ancient Israel.

Ordinance: A religious ritual whose intent is to demonstrate an adherent's faith. In Christianity, this often refers to baptism and communion.

P

Parable: A simple story used by Jesus to illustrate a moral or spiritual lesson.

Pentecost: The event when the Holy Spirit descended upon the apostles, empowering them to preach the gospel. It is celebrated 50 days after Easter.

Prophet: A person regarded as an inspired teacher or proclaimer of the will of God.

R

Redemption: The action of saving or being saved from sin, error, or evil through Jesus Christ.

Resurrection: The belief that Jesus rose from the dead on the third day after His crucifixion, conquering death and sin.

S

Sacrament: A religious ceremony or act considered to have sacred significance and impart divine grace, such as baptism and communion.

Salvation: Deliverance from sin and its consequences, believed by Christians to be brought about by faith in Christ.

Scripture: The sacred writings of Christianity contained in the Bible.

T

Theology: The study of the nature of God and religious beliefs.

Trinity: The doctrine that God exists as three persons but is one being.

V

Virgin Birth: The belief that Jesus was conceived by the Holy Spirit and born of the Virgin Mary.

W

Worship: Acts of devotion and praise to God, often involving prayer, singing, and reading of scripture.

X

Xenoglossy: The phenomenon where a person speaks or writes in a language they have not learned. In Christian contexts, it is sometimes associated with the gift of tongues.

Christ (Greek: Χριστός, Christos): Although "X" isn't directly used for a word, it is often a shorthand symbol for "Christ," derived from the Greek letter Chi (X).

Y

Yahweh: The personal name of God in the Hebrew Bible, often rendered as "LORD" in English translations. It is considered the most sacred name of God in Judaism and Christianity.

Yeshua: The Hebrew name for Jesus, meaning "salvation."

Z

Zealot: Originally, a member of a Jewish political movement in the first century that sought to overthrow Roman rule. In Christian contexts, it can refer to someone with fervent devotion to their faith.

Zion: A term that can refer to the hill in Jerusalem where the Temple was built, the city of Jerusalem itself, or, symbolically, the heavenly city or the kingdom of God.

Thank You For Reading

A Holy Thank You!

I am deeply grateful that you have chosen to read "The Most Complete Apocrypha" with 150 books. Your interest and dedication to exploring these sacred texts are truly appreciated. As it is written in Proverbs 2:6, "For the Lord gives wisdom; from his mouth come knowledge and understanding." May your journey through these writings be filled with divine wisdom and insight.

I kindly ask you to consider sharing your thoughts and leaving a positive review. Your words can help spread the knowledge and spiritual insights contained within these pages to others who are on a similar quest for understanding. As Jesus said in Matthew 5:14-16, "You are the light of the world. A town built on a hill cannot be hidden. Neither do people light a lamp and put it under a bowl. Instead, they put it on its stand, and it gives light to everyone in the house." Your review can be that light, guiding others to the treasures within this book.

With the grace and guidance of God, we aspire to compile an even more extensive collection of 200 apocryphal books in the future. Stay connected with us through our newsletter for updates and announcements. Together, we can continue this journey of discovery and spiritual growth, trusting in the promise of Philippians 4:13, "I can do all this through him who gives me strength."

To further aid your journey, we are offering free resources such as modern English translations of the Ethiopian Bible and the Geneva Bible. Simply scan the QR code below to access these invaluable materials. As it says in 2 Timothy 3:16-17, "All Scripture is God-breathed and is useful for teaching, rebuking, correcting and training in righteousness, so that the servant of God may be thoroughly equipped for every good work." These resources are provided to equip you further in your studies.

Thank you once again for your support. I invite you to explore other books authored by me, each crafted with the same dedication to spiritual growth and enlightenment. May God's peace be with you as you continue your journey.

May God bless you abundantly.